Fundamentals of Investments

Valuation and Management

The McGraw-Hill/Irwin Series in Finance, Insurance, and Real Estate

Stephen A. Ross
Franco Modigliani Professor of Finance and Economics
Sloan School of Management
Massachusetts Institute of Technology
Consulting Editor

Financial Management

Benninga and Sarig
Corporate Finance: A Valuation Approach

Block and Hirt
Foundations of Financial Management
Eleventh Edition

Brealey and Myers
Principles of Corporate Finance
Seventh Edition

Brealey, Myers, and Marcus
Fundamentals of Corporate Finance
Fourth Edition

Brooks
FinGame Online 4.0

Bruner
Case Studies in Finance: Managing for Corporate Value Creation
Fourth Edition

Chew
The New Corporate Finance: Where Theory Meets Practice
Third Edition

Chew and Gillan
Corporate Governance at the Crossroads: A Book of Readings

DeMello
Cases in Finance

Grinblatt and Titman
Financial Markets and Corporate Strategy
Second Edition

Helfert
Techniques of Financial Analysis: A Guide to Value Creation
Eleventh Edition

Higgins
Analysis for Financial Management
Seventh Edition

Kester, Ruback, and Tufano
Case Problems in Finance
Twelfth Edition

Ross, Westerfield, and Jaffe
Corporate Finance
Seventh Edition

Ross, Westerfield, and Jordan
Essentials of Corporate Finance
Fourth Edition

Ross, Westerfield, and Jordan
Fundamentals of Corporate Finance
Sixth Edition

Smith
The Modern Theory of Corporate Finance
Second Edition

White
Financial Analysis with an Electronic Calculator
Fifth Edition

Investments

Bodie, Kane, and Marcus
Essentials of Investments
Fifth Edition

Bodie, Kane, and Marcus
Investments
Sixth Edition

Cohen, Zinbarg, and Zeikel
Investment Analysis and Portfolio Management
Fifth Edition

Corrado and Jordan
Fundamentals of Investments: Valuation and Management
Third Edition

Farrell
Portfolio Management: Theory and Applications
Second Edition

Hirt and Block
Fundamentals of Investment Management
Seventh Edition

Financial Institutions and Markets

Cornett and Saunders
Fundamentals of Financial Institutions Management

Rose and Hudgins
Commercial Bank Management
Sixth Edition

Rose
Money and Capital Markets: Financial Institutions and Instruments in a Global Marketplace
Eighth Edition

Santomero and Babbel
Financial Markets, Instruments, and Institutions
Second Edition

Saunders and Cornett
Financial Institutions Management: A Risk Management Approach
Fourth Edition

Saunders and Cornett
Financial Markets and Institutions: A Modern Perspective
Second Edition

International Finance

Beim and Calomiris
Emerging Financial Markets

Eun and Resnick
International Financial Management
Third Edition

Levich
International Financial Markets: Prices and Policies
Second Edition

Real Estate

Brueggeman and Fisher
Real Estate Finance and Investments
Twelfth Edition

Corgel, Ling, and Smith
Real Estate Perspectives: An Introduction to Real Estate
Fourth Edition

Ling and Archer
Real Estate Principles: A Value Approach

Financial Planning and Insurance

Allen, Melone, Rosenbloom, and Mahoney
Pension Planning: Pension, Profit-Sharing, and Other Deferred Compensation Plans
Ninth Edition

Crawford
Life and Health Insurance Law
Eighth Edition (LOMA)

Harrington and Niehaus
Risk Management and Insurance
Second Edition

Hirsch
Casualty Claim Practice
Sixth Edition

Kapoor, Dlabay, and Hughes
Personal Finance
Seventh Edition

Williams, Smith, and Young
Risk Management and Insurance
Eighth Edition

Fundamentals of Investments

Valuation and Management

Third Edition

Charles J. Corrado
University of Technology—Sydney

Bradford D. Jordan
University of Kentucky

Boston   Burr Ridge, IL   Dubuque, IA   Madison, WI   New York   San Francisco   St. Louis
Bangkok   Bogotá   Caracas   Kuala Lumpur   Lisbon   London   Madrid   Mexico City
Milan   Montreal   New Delhi   Santiago   Seoul   Singapore   Sydney   Taipei   Toronto

FUNDAMENTALS OF INVESTMENTS: VALUATION AND MANAGEMENT

Published by McGraw-Hill/Irwin, a business unit of the McGraw-Hill Companies, Inc., 1221 Avenue of the Americas, New York, NY, 10020. Copyright © 2005, 2002, 2000 by The McGraw-Hill Companies, Inc. All rights reserved. No part of this publication may be reproduced or distributed in any form or by any means, or stored in a database or retrieval system, without the prior written consent of The McGraw-Hill Companies, Inc., including, but not limited to, in any network or other electronic storage or transmission, or broadcast for distance learning. Some ancillaries, including electronic and print components, may not be available to customers outside the United States.

This book is printed on acid-free paper.

domestic   1 2 3 4 5 6 7 8 9 0 DOW/DOW 0 9 8 7 6 5 4
international 1 2 3 4 5 6 7 8 9 0 DOW/DOW 0 9 8 7 6 5 4

ISBN   0-07-282919-2

Publisher: *Stephen M. Patterson*
Sponsoring editor: *Michele Janicek*
Developmental editor: *Jennifer V. Rizzi*
Executive marketing manager: *Rhonda Seelinger*
Lead producer, Media technology: *Kai Chiang*
Project manager: *Harvey Yep*
Senior production supervisor: *Sesha Bolisetty*
Lead designer: *Pam Verros*
Senior supplement producer: *Rose M. Range*
Senior digital content specialist: *Brian Nacik*
Cover design: *Pam Verros*
Interior design: *Pam Verros*
Typeface: *10/12 Times Roman*
Compositor: *GAC Indianapolis*
Printer: *R. R. Donnelley*

Library of Congress Cataloging-in-Publication Data

Corrado, Charles J.
   Fundamentals of investments : valuation and management / Charles J. Corrado, Bradford
D. Jordan.—3rd ed.
      p. cm.
   Includes index.
   ISBN 0-07-282919-2 (alk. paper) — ISBN 0-07-111108-5 (international : alk. paper)
   1. Investments. I. Jordan, Bradford D. II. Title.
HG4521.C66 2005
332.6—dc22   2003066539

INTERNATIONAL EDITION ISBN 0-07-111108-5
Copyright © 2005. Exclusive rights by The McGraw-Hill Companies, Inc., for manufacture
and export. This book cannot be re-exported from the country to which it is sold by McGraw-Hill.
The International Edition is not available in North America.

www.mhhe.com

To my parents, Charles and Clotilda, who sacrificed for my benefit; I miss them dearly.

CJC

To my late father, S. Kelly Jordan, Sr., a great stock picker.

BDJ

About the Authors

Charles J. Corrado

University of Technology—Sydney

Charles J. Corrado is Professor of Finance at the University of Technology—Sydney in Australia. He has taught in the area of investments throughout his academic career at the undergraduate, graduate, and doctoral levels. Professor Corrado has published numerous research articles on topics related to fixed-income securities, financial derivatives, international finance, and statistical methods in financial markets research.

Bradford D. Jordan

Gatton College of Business and Economics, University of Kentucky

Bradford D. Jordan is Professor of Finance and holder of the Richard W. and Janis H. Furst Endowed Chair in Finance at the University of Kentucky. He has a long-standing interest in both applied and theoretical issues in investments, and he has extensive experience teaching all levels of investments. Professor Jordan has published numerous research articles on issues such as valuation of fixed-income securities, tax effects in investments analysis, the behavior of security prices, IPO valuation, and pricing of exotic options. He is co-author of *Fundamentals of Corporate Finance, Sixth Edition*, and *Essentials of Corporate Finance, Fourth Edition*, two of the most widely used finance textbooks in the world.

Preface

So why *did* we write this book?

As we toiled away, we asked ourselves this question many times, and the answer was always the same: *Our students made us*.

Traditionally, investments textbooks tend to fall into one of two camps. The first type has a greater focus on portfolio management and covers a significant amount of portfolio theory. The second type is more concerned with security analysis and generally contains fairly detailed coverage of fundamental analysis as a tool for equity valuation. Today, most texts try to cover all the bases by including some chapters drawn from one camp and some from another.

The result of trying to cover everything is either a very long book or one that forces the instructor to bounce back and forth between chapters. The result is frequently a noticeable lack of consistency in treatment. Different chapters have completely different approaches: Some are computational, some are theoretical, and some are descriptive. Some do macroeconomic forecasting, some do mean-variance portfolio theory and beta estimation, and some do financial statements analysis. Options and futures are often essentially tacked on the back to round out this disconnected assortment.

The goal of these books is different from the goal of our students. Our students told us they come into an investments course wanting to learn how to make investment decisions. As time went by, we found ourselves supplying more and more supplemental materials to the texts we were using and constantly varying chapter sequences while chasing this elusive goal. We finally came to realize that the financial world had changed tremendously, and investments textbooks had fallen far behind in content and relevance.

What we really wanted, and what our students really needed, was a book that would do several key things:

- Focus on the students as investment managers by giving them information they can act on instead of concentrating on theories and research without the proper context.
- Offer strong, consistent pedagogy, including a balanced, unified treatment of the main types of financial investments as mirrored in the investment world.
- Organize topics in a way that would make them easy to apply—whether to a portfolio simulation or to real life—and support these topics with hands-on activities.

We made these three goals the guiding principles in writing this book. The next several sections explain our approach to each and why we think they are so important.

Who Is This Book For?

This book is aimed at introductory investments classes with students who have relatively little familiarity with investments. A typical student may have taken a principles of finance class and had some exposure to stocks and bonds, but not much beyond the basics. The introductory investments class is often a required course for finance majors, but students from other areas often take it as an elective. One fact of which we are acutely aware is that this may be the only investments class many students will ever take.

We intentionally wrote this book in a relaxed, informal style that engages the student and treats him or her as an active participant rather than a passive information absorber. We think the world of investments is exciting and fascinating, and we hope to share our considerable enthusiasm for investing with the student. We appeal to intuition and basic principles whenever possible because we have found that this approach effectively promotes understanding. We also make extensive use of examples throughout, drawing on "real world" material and familiar companies wherever appropriate.

By design, the text is not encyclopedic. As the table of contents indicates, we have a total of 19 chapters. Chapter length is about 30–40 pages, so the text is aimed at a single-term course; most of the book can be covered in a typical quarter or semester.

Aiming the book at a one-semester course necessarily means some picking and choosing, both with regard to topics and depth of coverage. Throughout, we strike a balance by introducing and covering the essentials while leaving some of the detail to follow-up courses in security analysis, portfolio management, and options and futures.

How Does the Third Edition of This Book Expand upon the Goals Described Above?

Based on user feedback, we have made numerous improvements and refinements in the third edition *of Fundamentals of Investments: Valuation and Management*. We updated every chapter to reflect current market practice and conditions, and we significantly expanded and improved the end-of-chapter material. Also, in a notable change, we moved the material on portfolio theory and performance analysis from Chapters 17–19 to Chapters 11–13. This placement corresponds more closely to the sequencing preferred by many of our users.

To give some examples of new content:

- Chapter 1 now contains a discussion of long-run expected returns and Blume's formula. We also discuss the calculation and interpretation of arithmetic versus geometric returns.

- Chapter 2 now has explicit formulas for critical stock prices in margin purchases and short sales and an expanded, though still concise, discussion of taxes and investment accounts.

- Chapter 4 contains a new section covering hedge funds.

- Chapter 5 has a new discussion of stop orders and an expanded discussion of stock market indexes.

- Chapter 6 now illustrates the calculation of arithmetic and geometric average dividend growth rates.

- Chapter 10 discusses bond accrued interest and the difference between clean and dirty prices.

- Chapter 13 contains expanded analysis of Sharpe optimal portfolios.

- Chapter 15 briefly considers employee stock options and also now covers the VIX and VIXN volatility indexes.

- Chapter 16 covers the new (in the U.S.) single-stock futures contracts and their trading.

- Chapter 17 covers the important new TRACE bond price reporting engine.

For the third edition, we significantly expanded and improved the end-of-chapter material. We added new problems throughout, and we increased the number of CFA questions. We created a new series of questions that test understanding of concepts with no calculations involved. We also added three completely new features. First, we now offer a block of questions called *What's on the Web?* These questions give students assignments to perform based on information they retrieve from various websites. Second, we added *Standard & Poor's* Problems. These problems require the use of the educational version of Market Insight, which provides access to S&P's well-known Compustat database, and they provide instructors with an easy way to incorporate current, real-world data. Finally, in selected chapters, we have created spreadsheet assignments, which ask students to create certain types of spreadsheets to solve problems.

We continue to emphasize the use of the Web in investments analysis, and we integrate Web-based content in several ways. First, wherever appropriate, we provide a commented link in the margin. These links send readers to selected, particularly relevant websites. Second, our *Work the Web* feature, expanded and completely updated for this edition, appears in most chapters. These boxed readings use screen shots to show students how to access, use, and interpret various types of key financial and market data. Finally, as previously noted, new end-of-chapter problems rely on data retrieved from the Web.

We continue to provide *Spreadsheet Analysis* exhibits, which we have enhanced for this edition. These exhibits illustrate directly how to use spreadsheets to do certain types of important problems, including such computationally intensive tasks as calculating Macauley duration, finding Black-Scholes-Merton option prices, and determining optimal portfolios based on Sharpe ratios. We also continue to provide, where relevant, readings from *The Wall Street Journal*, which have been thoroughly updated for this edition. Finally, we have expanded our *Stock-Trak* portfolio simulation exercises and improved our illustrations of certain types of trades.

How Is This Book Relevant to the Student?

Fundamental changes in the investments universe drive our attention to relevance. The first major change is that individuals are being asked to make investment decisions for their own portfolios more often than ever before. There is, thankfully, a growing recognition that traditional "savings account" approaches to investing are decidedly inferior. At the same time, the use of employer-sponsored "investment accounts" has expanded enormously. The second major change is that the investments universe has exploded with an ever-increasing number of investment vehicles available to individual investors. As a result, investors must choose from an array of products, many of which are very complex, and they must strive to choose wisely as well.

Beyond this, students are more interested in subjects that affect them directly (aren't we all). By taking the point of view of the student as an investor, we are better able to illustrate and emphasize the relevance and importance of the material.

Our approach is evident in the table of contents. Our first chapter is motivational; we have found that this material effectively "hooks" students and even motivates a semester-long discourse on risk and return. Our second chapter answers the student's next natural question: "How do I get started investing and how do I buy and sell securities?" The third chapter surveys the different types of investments available. After only three chapters, very early in the term, students have learned something about the risks and rewards from investing, how to get started investing, and what investment choices are available.

We close the first part of the text with a detailed examination of mutual funds. Without a doubt, mutual funds have become the most popular investment vehicles for individual investors. There are now more mutual funds than there are stocks on the NYSE! Given the size and enormous growth in the mutual fund industry, this material is important for investors. Even so, investments texts typically cover mutual funds in a cursory way, often banishing the material to a back chapter under the obscure (and obsolete) heading of "investment companies." Our early placement lets students quickly explore a topic they have heard a lot about and are typically very interested in.

How Does This Book Allow Students to Apply the Investments Knowledge They Learn?

After studying this text, students will have the basic knowledge needed to move forward and actually act on what they have learned. We have developed two features to encourage making decisions as an investment manager. Learning to make good investment decisions comes with experience, while experience (regrettably) comes from making bad investment decisions. As much as possible, we press our students to get those bad decisions out of their systems before they start managing real money!

Not surprisingly, most students don't know how to get started buying and selling securities. We have learned that providing some structure, especially with a portfolio simulation, greatly enhances the experience. Therefore, we first have a series of *Get Real!* boxes. These boxes (at the end of each chapter) usually describe actual trades for students to explore. The intention is to show students how to gain real experience with the principles and instruments covered in the chapter. The second feature is a series of *Stock-Trak* exercises that take students through specific trading situations using *Stock-Trak Portfolio Simulations*.

Because we feel that portfolio simulations are so valuable, we have taken steps to assist instructors who, like us, plan to integrate portfolio simulations into their courses. Beyond the features mentioned above, we have organized the text so that the essential material needed before participating in a simulation is covered at the front of the book. Most notably, with every book, we have included a *free* subscription to *Stock-Trak Portfolio Simulations*. *Stock-Trak* is the leading provider of investment simulation services to the academic community; providing it free represents a significant cost savings to students. To our knowledge, ours is the first (and only) investments text to directly offer a full-featured online brokerage account simulation with the book at no incremental cost.

How Does This Book Maintain a Consistent, Unified Treatment?

In most investments texts, depth of treatment and presentation vary dramatically from instrument to instrument, stranding the student without an overall framework for understanding the many types of investments. We stress early on that there are essentially only four basic types of financial investments—stocks, bonds, options, and futures. In parts 2 through 6, our simple goal is to take a closer look at each of these instruments. We take a unified approach to each by answering these basic questions:

1. What are the essential features of the instrument?
2. What are the possible rewards?
3. What are the risks?
4. What are the basic determinants of investment value?

5. For whom is the investment appropriate and under what circumstances?

6. How is the instrument bought and sold, and how does the market for the instrument operate?

By covering investment instruments in this way, we teach the students which questions to ask when looking at any potential investment.

Unlike other introductory investments texts, we devote several chapters beyond the basics to the different types of fixed-income investments. Students are often surprised to learn that the fixed-income markets are so much bigger than the equity markets and that money management opportunities are much more common in the fixed-income arena. Possibly the best way to see this is to look at recent CFA exams and materials and note the extensive coverage of fixed-income topics. We have placed these chapters toward the back of the text because we recognize not everyone will want to cover all this material. We have also separated the subject into several shorter chapters to make it more digestible for students and to allow instructors more control over what is covered.

Acknowledgments

We have received extensive feedback from reviewers at each step along the way, and we are very grateful to the following dedicated scholars and teachers for their time and expertise:

Charles Appeadu, University of Wisconsin–Madison

Felix Ayadi, Fayetteville State University

Scott Barnhart, Clemson University

Scott Beyer, University of Wisconsin–Parkside

Howard W. Bohnen, St. Cloud State University

Paul Bolster, Northeastern University

Joe Brocato, Tarleton State University

John Paul Broussard, Rutgers, The State University of New Jersey

Jorge Omar R. Brusa, University of Arkansas

Johnny Chan, University of Dayton

Carl R. Chen, University of Dayton

Ji Chen, University of Colorado

Ronald Christner, Loyola University–New Orleans

Patricia Clarke, Simmons College

John Clinebell, University of Northern Colorado

Michael C. Ehrhardt, University of Tennessee–Knoxville

William Elliott, Oklahoma State University

Christos Giannikos, Bernard M. Baruch College

Ann Hackert, Idaho State University

Yvette Harman, Miami University of Ohio

Nozar Hashemzadeh, Radford University

Gay B. Hatfield, University of Mississippi

Thomas M. Krueger, University of Wisconsin–La Crosse

William Lepley, University of Wisconsin–Green Bay

Steven Lifland, High Point University

David Louton, Bryant College

David Loy, Illinois State University

Jeff Manzi, Ohio University

Linda Martin, Arizona State University

Stuart Michelson, University of Central Florida

Edward Miller, University of New Orleans

Lalatendu Misra, University of Texas–San Antonio

Deborah Murphy, University of Tennessee–Knoxville

M. J. Murray, Winona State University

Samuel H. Penkar, University of Houston

Percy S. Poon, University of Nevada, Las Vegas

John Romps, St. Anselm College

Lisa Schwartz, Wingate University

David Stewart, Winston-Salem State University

Richard W. Taylor, Arkansas State University

Jim Tipton, Baylor University

Howard Van Auken, Iowa State University

Joe Walker, University of Alabama–Birmingham

John Wingender, Creighton University

We'd like to thank Thomas W. Miller, Jr., St. Louis University, for developing the Instructor's Manual and PowerPoint presentation for this text, and Joe Smolira, Belmont University, for developing the Test Bank and the self-study questions.

The following doctoral students did outstanding work on this text: Steve Dolvin, Clay McDaniel, and Denver Travis; to them fell the unenviable task of technical proofreading, and, in particular, careful checking of each calculation throughout the text and supplements.

We are deeply grateful to the select group of professionals who served as our development team on this edition: Michele Janicek, Sponsoring Editor; Jen Rizzi, Development Editor; Rhonda Seelinger, Executive Marketing Manager; Harvey Yep, Project Manager; Pam Verros, Designer; and Sesha Bolisetty, Production Supervisor.

Charles J. Corrado

Bradford D. Jordan

Supplements

We have developed a number of supplements for both teaching and learning to accompany this text:

For Instructors

Instructor's Resource CD-ROM
ISBN 0-07-287794-4

The Instructor's Resource CD-ROM contains the following assets:

Instructor's Manual, *prepared by Thomas W. Miller, Jr.,*
St. Louis University
Developed to clearly outline the chapter material as well as provide extra teaching support, the first section of the Instructor's Manual includes an annotated outline of each chapter with suggested websites, references to PowerPoint slides, teaching tips, additional examples, and current events references. The second section contains complete worked-out solutions for the end-of-chapter questions and problems, prepared by Joe Smolira, Belmont University.

Test Bank, *prepared by Joe Smolira*, Belmont University
With almost 1,500 questions, this Test Bank, in Microsoft Word, provides a variety of question formats (true-false, multiple-choice, fill-in-the-blank, and problems) and levels of difficulty to meet any instructor's testing needs.

Computerized Test Bank
Available in Windows format, this software provides you with the Test Bank in electronic form. The keyword search option lets you browse through the question bank for problems containing a specific word or phrase. Password protection is available for saved tests or for the entire database. Questions can be added, modified, or deleted.

PowerPoint Presentation, *prepared by Thomas W. Miller, Jr.,*
St. Louis University
More than 300 full-color slides of images and tables from the text, lecture outlines, and additional examples and data are available with this product.

Videos
ISBN 0-07-287796-0

McGraw-Hill/Irwin produced a new series of finance videos that are 10-minute case studies on topics such as Financial Markets, Stocks, Bonds, Portfolio Management, Derivatives, and Going Public.

For Students

Student CD-ROM

The Student CD-ROM is packaged free with each new book purchased and contains the following assets:

Self-Study Software, *prepared by Joe Smolira*, Belmont University
This tutorial program provides students with questions written specifically for this text. Students can choose one chapter or a number of chapters, and the program will select random questions to be answered.

Links to:
- The book's Online Learning Center (OLC)
- Investments Online
- Finance Around the World
- Select videoclips on key investment topics

Stock-Trak Portfolio Stimulation

Give your students investment management experience! McGraw-Hill/Irwin has partnered with *Stock-Trak* and is providing a **free** subscription to the *Stock-Trak Portfolio Simulation* for one semester with the purchase of every new copy of *Fundamentals of Investments: Valuation and Management, Third Edition* by Corrado and Jordan. *Stock-Trak* gives students $500,000 and allows them to trade stocks, options, futures, bonds, mutual funds, and international stocks—no other simulation offers all these types of securities! Over 600 professors have used this service, and around 30,000 college students each semester participate. Instructors receive reports every week. All trades are done on the Web at www.stocktrak.com/cj. See this site for more information.

Ready Notes
ISBN 0-07-295641-0

Ready Notes provides a reduced copy of every PowerPoint slide as an inexpensive, but valuable, note-taking system. Ask your McGraw-Hill/Irwin representative about packaging options.

Online Resources

Online Learning Center (OLC) with PowerWeb
www.mhhe.com/cj3e

This website follows the text chapter-by-chapter with digital supplementary content specific to this book. The Instructor's Manual and PowerPoint Presentation are available to the instructor in the password-protected Instructor's Center. As students read the book, they can go online to the Student Center to take self-grading quizzes, review material, and work through interactive exercises. Included with new copies of this book is an insert card that includes a password for access to Premium Content, including PowerWeb for Investments. Thanks to embedded PowerWeb content, students can get quicker access to real-world news and essays that pertain to the discipline they are studying. OLCs can be delivered in multiple ways—through the textbook website, through PageOut, or within a course management system (i.e., Blackboard, WebCT, TopClass, and eCollege).

Investments Online
As part of this OLC, instructors and students will also have access to Investments Online, found on the opening page of the textbook website. Investments Online is an exclusive Web tool from McGraw-Hill/Irwin. For each of 18 key investments topics, students complete challenging exercises and discussion questions that draw on recent articles, company reports, government data, and other Web-based resources. For instructors, there are also password-protected teaching notes to assist with classroom integration of the material.

Pedagogical Features

From your feedback, we have included many pedagogical features in this text that will be valuable learning tools for your students. This walkthrough highlights some of the most important elements.

Chapter Openers

These one-paragraph introductions for each chapter present facts and misconceptions that may surprise you. An explanation is more fully developed in the chapter.

Chapter 12

Return, Risk, and the Security Market Line

"To be alive at all involves some risk."

–Harold MacMillan

An important insight of modern financial theory is that some investment risks yield an expected reward, while other risks do not. Essentially, risks that can be eliminated by diversification do not yield an expected reward, and risks that cannot be eliminated by diversification do yield an expected reward. Thus, financial markets are somewhat fussy regarding what risks are rewarded and what risks are not. ■

Chapter 1 presented some important lessons from capital market history. The most noteworthy, perhaps, is that there is a reward, on average, for bearing risk. We called this reward a *risk premium*. The second lesson is that this risk premium is positively correlated with an investment's risk.

In this chapter, we return to an examination of the reward for bearing risk. Specifically, we have two tasks to accomplish. First, we have to define risk more precisely and then discuss how to measure it. Second, once we have a better understanding of just what we mean by "risk," we will go on to quantify the relation between risk and return in financial markets.

When we examine the risks associated with individual assets, we find there are two types of risk: systematic and unsystematic. This distinction is crucial because, as we will see, systematic risk affects almost all assets in the economy, at least to some

Key Terms

Key terms are indicated in bold and defined in the margin. The running glossary in the margin helps students quickly review the basic terminology for the chapter.

Web Addresses

Websites are called out in the margins, along with a notation of how they relate to the chapter material.

Why Diversification Works

Why diversification reduces portfolio risk as measured by the portfolio standard deviation is important and worth exploring in some detail. The key concept is **correlation**, which is the extent to which the returns on two assets move together. If the returns on two assets tend to move up and down together, we say they are *positively* correlated. If they tend to move in opposite directions, we say they are *negatively* correlated. If there is no particular relationship between the two assets, we say they are *uncorrelated*.

The *correlation coefficient*, which we use to measure correlation, ranges from -1 to $+1$, and we will denote the correlation between the returns on two assets, say A and B, as $\text{Corr}(R_A, R_B)$. The Greek letter ρ (rho) is often used to designate correlation as well. A correlation of $+1$ indicates that the two assets have a *perfect* positive correlation. For example, suppose that whatever return Asset A realizes, either up or down, Asset B does the same thing by exactly twice as much. In this case, they are perfectly correlated because the movement on one is completely predictable from the movement on the other. Notice, however, that perfect correlation does not necessarily mean they move by the same amount.

A zero correlation means that the two assets are uncorrelated. If we know that one asset is up, then we have no idea what the other one is likely to do; there simply is no relation between them. Perfect negative correlation [$\text{Corr}(R_A, R_B) = -1$] indicates that they always move in opposite directions. Figure 11.2 illustrates the three benchmark cases of perfect positive, perfect negative, and zero correlation.

correlation The tendency of the returns on two assets to move together.

Measure portfolio diversification using Instant X-ray at www.morningstar.com

---

Check This!

Every major section in each chapter ends with questions for review. This feature helps students test their understanding of the material before moving on to the next section.

Check This

12.2a	What are the two basic types of risk?
12.2b	What is the distinction between the two types of risk?

Investment Updates

These boxed readings, reprinted from various business press sources, provide additional real-world events and examples to illustrate the material in the chapter. Some articles are from the past two years to highlight very recent events, and others present events of more historical significance.

INVESTMENT UPDATES   Credit Markets

Greenspan Remarks Lift Long-Dated Treasurys

Longer-dated Treasurys bounced back Wednesday after Federal Reserve Chairman Alan Greenspan's congressional testimony on the economy.

At midday, the benchmark 10-year Treasury was up 5/32, or $1.5625 for each $1,000 invested, to 102 13/32. Its yield fell to 3.338%. The 30-year bond jumped 1 point to 117 9/32, yielding 4.302%. Meanwhile, the two-year note slipped 3/32 to 100 19/32, yielding 1.310%, and the five-year issue shed 2/32 to 101 15/32, yielding 2.307%.

Treasury prices slipped after the opening bell as traders awaited Mr. Greenspan's testimony before the Joint Economic Committee of Congress. Prices fell further in typical knee-jerk fashion as he began speaking.

The initial reaction in the Treasury market was "very whippy," said Paul Calvetti, head of Treasury-securities trading at Deutsche Bank in New York. "It looks like somebody is using it as an opportunity to sell," and "the headlines were bullish for the market, but the actual text is not so bullish."

However, some buying emerged as the market digested the Fed chief's remarks and after he reminded the market that the central bank can buy Treasurys to combat falling inflation. That sent the price of 30-year bond up sharply.

"There is an underlying bid in the market, driven by demand for long-dated securities," said John Spinello, fixed-income strategist at Merrill Lynch in New York.

Mr. Greenspan reiterated concerns about falling inflation, which has buoyed longer-dated Treasury prices since the Fed's statement from its May 6 meeting, when policy makers highlighted the risk of deflation.

However, Drew Matus, economist at Lehman Brothers in New York, noted that Mr. Greenspan "chose to phrase his concerns in terms of falling inflation" and didn't explicitly refer to disinflation. "This shift in language may suggest that Greenspan was unhappy with the market's focus on potential deflation," Mr. Matus said.

During the question-and-answer part of his testimony Wednesday, Mr. Greenspan said "we at the Federal Reserve recognize that deflation is a possibility," although not a likely one.

Renewed buying of the long bond contributed to a flatter yield curve. The spread between the two-year note's yield and that of the long bond flattened to around three percentage points from Tuesday's close of 3.10 percentage points. The spread between the two-year and 10-year yields had also narrowed to 2.04 percentage points from its prior session close around 2.11 percentage points.

The weakness of the front end was a function of Mr. Greenspan failing to signal that a rate cut is imminent,

Work the Web

Various actual screenshots are showcased throughout the text to illustrate how to access specific features of selected websites.

WORK THE WEB

Suppose you want to find the beta for a company like Amazon.com. One way is to work the Web. We went to money.cnn.com, entered the ticker symbol AMZN for Amazon, and followed the "Profile" link. This is the result:

Key Ratios & Statistics

Price & Volume		Valuation Ratios	
Recent Price $	46.32	Price/Earnings (TTM)	NM
52 Week High $	46.95	Price/Sales (TTM)	4.07
52 Week Low $	14.24	Price/Book (MRQ)	NM
Avg Daily Vol (Mil)	9.06	Price/Cash Flow (TTM)	NM
Beta	2.55	**Per Share Data**	
Share Related Items		Earnings (TTM) $	-0.22
Mkt. Cap. (Mil) $	18,388.48	Sales (TTM) $	11.38
Shares Out (Mil)	396.99	Book Value (MRQ) $	-3.14
Float (Mil)	275.90	Cash Flow (TTM) $	0.00
Dividend Information		Cash (MRQ) $	2.49
Yield %	NA	**Mgmt Effectiveness**	
Annual Dividend	0.00	Return on Equity (TTM)	NM
Payout Ratio (TTM) %	0.00	Return on Assets (TTM)	-5.12
Financial Strength		Return on Investment (TTM)	-9.74
Quick Ratio (MRQ)	1.29	**Profitability**	
Current Ratio (MRQ)	1.63	Gross Margin (TTM) %	24.55
LT Debt/Equity (MRQ)	NM	Operating Margin (TTM) %	3.18
Total Debt/Equity (MRQ)	NM	Profit Margin (TTM) %	-1.89

Mil = Millions MRQ = Most Recent Quarter TTM = Trailing Twelve Months
Asterisk (*) Indicates numbers are derived from Earnings Announcements
Pricing and volume data as of 08/29/2003

The reported beta for Amazon.com is 2.55, which means that Amazon has about 2.5 times the systematic risk of a typical stock. Notice that Amazon's ROA is −5.12 percent and its profit margin is −1.89 percent. ROE is not even reported. Why? If you calculate the ROE using the earnings per share and the book value per share, you will find that ROE is almost 7 percent, which is not particularly impressive. In fact, the only reason ROE is even positive is that Amazon has a negative book value. Oddly, in such a case, the more the company loses, the higher the ROE becomes! In all, Amazon appears to be a good candidate for a high beta.

Spreadsheet Analysis

Self-contained spreadsheet examples show students how to set up spreadsheets to solve problems—a vital part of every business student's education.

SPREADSHEET ANALYSIS

	A	B	C	D	E	F	G	H
1								
2			**Treasury Bill Price and Yield Calculations**					
3								
4	A Treasury bill traded on March 14, 2004 pays $100 on June 1, 2004. Assuming a							
5	discount rate of 6 percent, what are its price and bond equivalent yield?							
6	Hint: Use the Excel function TBILLPRICE and TBILLEQ.							
7								
8		$98.6833	= TBILLPRICE("3/14/04","6/1/04",0.06)					
9								
10		6.164%	= TBILLEQ("3/14/04","6/1/04",0.06)					
11								
12								
13	A credit card charges a nominal annual interest rate of 15 percent. With interest							
14	charged monthly, what is the effective annual rate (EAR) on this credit card?							
15	Hint: Use the Excel function EFFECT.							
16								
17		16.075%	= EFFECT(0.15,12)					
18								
19								
20								

Numbered Examples

Separate numbered and titled examples are integrated throughout the chapters. Each example illustrates an intuitive or mathematical application in a step-by-step format. There is enough detail in the explanations so the student doesn't have to look elsewhere for additional information.

MORE UNEQUAL PROBABILITIES

EXAMPLE 11.3

Suppose we had the following projections on three stocks:

State of Economy	Probability of State of Economy	Returns		
		Stock A	Stock B	Stock C
Boom	.50	10%	15%	20%
Bust	.50	8	4	0

We want to calculate portfolio expected returns in two cases. First, what would be the expected return on a portfolio with equal amounts invested in each of the three stocks? Second, what would be the expected return if half of the portfolio were in A, with the remainder equally divided between B and C?

From our earlier discussion, the expected returns on the individual stocks are

$$E(R_A) = 9.0\% \qquad E(R_B) = 9.5\% \qquad E(R_C) = 10.0\%$$

(Check these for practice.) If a portfolio has equal investments in each asset, the portfolio weights are all the same. Such a portfolio is said to be *equally weighted*. Since there are three stocks in this case, the weights are all equal to 1/3. The portfolio expected return is thus

$$E(R_P) = 1/3 \times 9.0\% + 1/3 \times 9.5\% + 1/3 \times 10.0\% = 9.5\%$$

In the second case, check that the portfolio expected return is 9.375%.

Numbered Equations

Key equations are highlighted and numbered sequentially in each chapter for easy reference.

Bank Discount Rate Quotes

bank discount basis A method for quoting interest rates on money market instruments.

Interest rates for some key money market securities, including Treasury bills and banker's acceptances, are quoted on a **bank discount basis**, or simply discount basis. An interest rate quoted on a discount basis is often called a discount yield. If we are given an interest rate quoted on a bank discount basis for a particular money market instrument, then we calculate the price of that instrument as follows:

$$\text{Current price} = \text{Face value} \times \left(1 - \frac{\text{Days to maturity}}{360} \times \text{Discount yield}\right)$$

(9.1)

The term "discount yield" here simply refers to the quoted interest rate. It should not be confused with the Federal Reserve's discount rate discussed earlier.

To give an example, suppose a banker's acceptance has a face value of $1 million that will be paid in 90 days. If the interest rate, quoted on a discount basis, is 5 percent, what is the current price of the acceptance?

As the following calculation shows, a discount yield of 5 percent and maturity of 90 days gives a current price of $987,500.

$$\$987,500 = \$1,000,000 \times \left(1 - \frac{90}{360} \times .05\right)$$

The difference between the face value of $1 million and the price of $987,500 is $12,500 and is called the "discount." This discount is the interest earned over the 90-day period until the acceptance matures.

Standard & Poor's Educational Version of Market Insight
McGraw-Hill/Irwin and the Institutional Market Services division of Standard
& Poor's are pleased to announce an exclusive partnership that offers instructors and students **free** access to the educational version of Standard & Poor's
Market Insight with each new textbook. The Educational Version of Market
Insight is a rich online resource that provides six years of fundamental financial
data for more than 370 companies in the database. S&P-specific problems
can be found at the end of almost all chapters in this text. For more details,
please see the bound-in card inside the front cover of this text, or visit
www.mhhe.com/edumarketinsight.

Finance Around the World
Located on the homepage of the textbook's website, this product is a McGraw-
Hill/Irwin outstanding global financial resource, providing real-time links for
researching and exploring investments and corporate finance online, country
by country.

Brief Contents

Contents

 **PART FOUR**   Portfolio Management 361

Contents

Appendixes

A Brief History of Risk and Return

"If you want to make money, go where the money is."

–Joseph Kennedy

Who wants to be a millionaire? Actually, anyone can retire as a millionaire. How? Consider this: Suppose you, at the age of 25, begin saving $3,000 per year. Forty years later, you retire at age 65. How much will you have? The answer might surprise you. If you earn 10 percent per year, you will have about $1.3 million. Are these numbers realistic? Based on the history of financial markets, the answer appears to be yes. For example, over the last 77 years, the widely-followed Standard and Poor's index of large-company common stocks has actually yielded about 12 percent per year. ■

The study of investments could begin in many places. After thinking it over, we decided that a brief history lesson is in order, so we start our discussion of risk and return by looking back at what has happened to investors in U.S. financial markets since 1925. In 1931, for example, the stock market lost 43 percent of its value. Just two years later, the market reversed itself and gained 54 percent. In more recent times, the stock market lost about 25 percent of its value on October 19, 1987, alone, and it gained almost 40 percent in 1995. Very recently, following nine years of consecutive gains, the stock market lost value in three straight years, 2000 through 2002. What lessons, if any, should investors learn from such shifts in the stock market? We explore the last seven decades of market history to find out.

Our primary goal in this chapter is to see what financial market history can tell us about risk and return. One of the most important things to get out of this discussion is a perspective on the numbers. What is a high return? What is a low return? More generally, what returns should we expect from financial assets such as stocks and bonds, and what are the risks from such investments? Beyond this, we hope that by studying what *did* happen in the past, we will at least gain some insight into what *can* happen in the future.

The history of risk and return is made day by day in global financial markets. The Internet is an excellent source of information on financial markets. Visit our website (at www.mhhe.com/cj3e) for suggestions on where to find information on recent financial market events. We will suggest other sites later in the chapter.

Not everyone agrees on the value of studying history. On the one hand, there is philosopher George Santayana's famous comment, "Those who do not remember the past are condemned to repeat it." On the other hand, there is industrialist Henry Ford's equally famous comment, "History is more or less bunk." These extremes aside, perhaps everyone would agree with Mark Twain, who observed, with remarkable foresight (and poor grammar), that "October. This is one of the peculiarly dangerous months to speculate in stocks in. The others are July, January, September, April, November, May, March, June, December, August, and February."

Two key observations emerge from a study of financial market history. First, there is a reward for bearing risk, and, at least on average, that reward has been substantial. That's the good news. The bad news is that greater rewards are accompanied by greater risks. The fact that risk and return go together is probably the single most important fact to understand about investments, and it is a point to which we will return many times.

1.1 Returns

We wish to discuss historical returns on different types of financial assets. First, we need to know how to compute the return from an investment. We will consider buying shares of stock in this section, but the basic calculations are the same for any investment.

Dollar Returns

If you buy an asset of any type, your gain (or loss) from that investment is called the *return* on your investment. This return will usually have two components. First, you may receive some cash directly while you own the investment. Second, the value of the asset you purchase may change. In this case, you have a capital gain or capital loss on your investment.[1]

To illustrate, suppose you purchased 100 shares of stock in Harley-Davidson on January 1. At that time, Harley was selling for $37 per share, so your 100 shares cost you $3,700. At the end of the year, you want to see how you did with your investment.

The first thing to consider is that over the year, a company may pay cash dividends to its shareholders. As a stockholder in Harley, you are a part owner of the company, and you are entitled to a portion of any money distributed. So if Harley chooses to pay a dividend, you will receive some cash for every share you own.

---

[1]As a practical matter, what is and what is not a capital gain (or loss) is determined by the Internal Revenue Service. Even so, as is commonly done, we use these terms to refer to a change in value.

In addition to the dividend, the other part of your return is the capital gain or loss on the stock. This part arises from changes in the value of your investment. For example, consider these cash flows:

	Case 1	Case 2
Ending Stock Price	**$40.33**	**$34.78**
January 1 value	$3,700	$3,700
December 31 value	4,033	3,478
Dividend income	185	185
Capital gain or loss	333	−222

Our favorite investments website is Finance Yahoo! at finance.yahoo.com Visit this site and look around!

At the beginning of the year, on January 1, the stock is selling for $37 per share, and, as we calculated above, your total outlay for 100 shares is $3,700. Over the year, Harley pays dividends of $1.85 per share. By the end of the year, then, you received dividend income of

$$\text{Dividend income} = \$1.85 \times 100 = \$185$$

As in Case 1, suppose that as of December 31, Harley was selling for $40.33, meaning that the value of your stock increased by $3.33 per share. Your 100 shares are now worth $4,033, so you have a capital gain of

$$\text{Capital gain} = (\$40.33 - \$37) \times 100 = \$333$$

On the other hand, if the price had dropped to, say, $34.78 (Case 2), you would have a capital loss of

$$\text{Capital loss} = (\$34.78 - \$37) \times 100 = -\$222$$

Notice that a capital loss is the same thing as a negative capital gain.

The **total dollar return** on your investment is the sum of the dividend and the capital gain (or loss):

$$\text{Total dollar return} = \text{Dividend income} + \text{Capital gain (or loss)}$$

In our first example here, the total dollar return is thus given by

$$\text{Total dollar return} = \$185 + \$333 = \$518$$

total dollar return
The return on an investment measured in dollars that accounts for all cash flows and capital gains or losses.

Overall, between the dividends you received and the increase in the price of the stock, the value of your investment increased from $3,700 to $3,700 + $518 = $4,218.

A common misconception often arises in this context. Suppose you hold on to your Harley-Davidson stock and don't sell it at the end of the year. Should you still consider the capital gain as part of your return? Isn't this only a "paper" gain and not really a cash gain if you don't sell it?

The answer to the first question is a strong yes, and the answer to the second is an equally strong no. The capital gain is every bit as much a part of your return as the dividend, and you should certainly count it as part of your return. The fact that you decide to keep the stock and don't sell (you don't "realize" the gain) is irrelevant because you could have converted it to cash if you had wanted to. Whether you choose to do so is up to you.

After all, if you insist on converting your gain to cash, you could always sell the stock and immediately reinvest by buying the stock back. There is no difference between doing this and just not selling (assuming, of course, that there are no transaction costs or tax consequences from selling the stock). Again, the point is that whether you actually cash out and buy pizzas (or whatever) or continue to hold the investment doesn't affect the return you actually earn.

Percentage Returns

It is usually more convenient to summarize information about returns in percentage terms than in dollar terms, because that way your return doesn't depend on how much you actually invested. With percentage returns the question we want to answer is: How much do we get *for each dollar* we invest?

To answer this question, let P_t be the price of the stock at the beginning of the year and let D_{t+1} be the dividend paid on the stock during the year. The following cash flows are the same as those shown earlier, except that we have now expressed everything on a per-share basis:

	Case 1	Case 2
Ending Stock Price	$40.33	$34.78
January 1 value	$37.00	$37.00
December 31 value	40.33	34.78
Dividend income	1.85	1.85
Capital gain or loss	3.33	−2.22

In our example, the price at the beginning of the year was $37 per share and the dividend paid during the year on each share was $1.85. If we express this dividend as a percentage of the beginning stock price, the result is the **dividend yield**:

dividend yield The annual stock dividend as a percentage of the initial stock price.

$$\text{Dividend yield} = D_{t+1} / P_t \tag{1.1}$$
$$= \$1.85 / \$37 = .05 = 5\%$$

This says that for each dollar we invested we received 5 cents in dividends.

The second component of our percentage return is the **capital gains yield**. This yield is calculated as the change in the price during the year (the capital gain) divided by the beginning price. With the $40.33 ending price, we get:

capital gains yield The change in stock price as a percentage of the initial stock price.

$$\text{Capital gains yield} = (P_{t+1} - P_t) / P_t \tag{1.2}$$
$$= (\$40.33 - \$37) / \$37$$
$$= \$3.33 / \$37 = .09 = 9\%$$

This 9 percent yield means that for each dollar invested we got 9 cents in capital gains.

Putting it all together, per dollar invested, we get 5 cents in dividends and 9 cents in capital gains for a total of 14 cents. Our **total percent return** is 14 cents on the dollar, or 14 percent. When a return is expressed on a percentage basis, we often refer to it as the *rate of return*, or just "return," on the investment. Notice that if we combine the formulas for the dividend yield and capital gains yield, we get a single formula for the total percentage return:

total percent return The return on an investment measured as a percentage that accounts for all cash flows and capital gains or losses.

$$\text{Percentage return} = \text{Dividend yield} + \text{Capital gains yield} \tag{1.3}$$
$$= D_{t+1} / P_t + (P_{t+1} - P_t) / P_t$$
$$= (D_{t+1} + P_{t+1} - P_t) / P_t$$

To look up information on common stocks using the Web, you need to know the "ticker" symbol for the ones you are interested in. You can look up ticker symbols in many places, including one of our favorite sites, finance.yahoo.com. Here we have looked up (using the "Symbol Lookup" link) and entered ticker symbols for some well-known "tech" stocks:

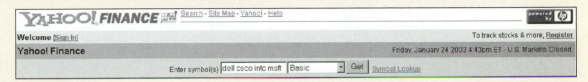

Once we hit "Get Quotes," this is what we got:

Views: Basic [edit] - DayWatch - Performance - Real-time Mkt - Detailed - [Create New View]

Symbol	Last Trade		Change		Volume	Related Information
DELL	4:00pm	24.38	-0.83	-3.29%	21,352,392	Chart, Messages, Profile, **more...**
CSCO	4:00pm	13.86	-0.73	-5.00%	67,850,176	Chart, Messages, Profile, **more...**
INTC	4:00pm	15.85	-0.82	-4.92%	59,831,376	Chart, Messages, Profile, **more...**
MSFT	4:00pm	49.85	-2.43	-4.65%	51,085,204	Chart, Messages, Profile, **more...**

As you can see, we get the price for each stock, along with information about the change in price and volume (the number of shares traded). There are a lot of links for you to hit and learn more, so have at it!

To check our calculations, notice that we invested $3,700 and ended up with $4,218. By what percentage did our $3,700 increase? As we saw, we picked up $4,218 − $3,700 = $518. This is an increase of $518 / $3,700, or 14 percent.

CALCULATING PERCENTAGE RETURNS

EXAMPLE 1.1

Suppose you buy some stock for $25 per share. After one year, the price is $35 per share. During the year, you received a $2 dividend per share. What is the dividend yield? The capital gains yield? The percentage return? If your total investment was $1,000, how much do you have at the end of the year?

Your $2 dividend per share works out to a dividend yield of

Dividend yield $= D_{t+1} / P_t$

$= \$2 / \$25$

$= 8\%$

(continued)

The per-share capital gain is $10, so the capital gains yield is

Capital gains yield $= (P_{t+1} - P_t) / P_t$

$= (\$35 - \$25) / \$25$

$= \$10 / \$25$

$= 40\%$

The total percentage return is thus 8% + 40% = 48%.

If you had invested $1,000, you would have $1,480 at the end of the year. To check this, note that your $1,000 would have bought you $1,000 / $25 = 40 shares. Your 40 shares would then have paid you a total of 40 × $2 = $80 in cash dividends. Your $10 per share gain would give you a total capital gain of $10 × 40 = $400. Add these together and you get $480, which is a 48 percent total return on your $1,000 investment.

Now that you know how to calculate returns on a hypothetical stock, you should begin looking at real stocks. The nearby *Work the Web* box describes how to get going. Meanwhile, in the next several sections, we will take a look at the returns that some common types of investments have earned over the last 77 years.

Check This

1.1a What are the two parts of total return?

1.1b Why are unrealized capital gains or losses included in the calculation of returns?

1.1c What is the difference between a dollar return and a percentage return? Why are percentage returns usually more convenient?

1.2   The Historical Record

We now examine year-to-year historical rates of return on five important categories of financial investments. These returns can be interpreted as what you would have earned if you had invested in portfolios of the following asset categories:

Annual historical financial market data can be downloaded for free at www.globalfindata. com

1. Large-company stocks. The large-company stock portfolio is based on the Standard and Poor's (S&P's) 500 index, which contains 500 of the largest companies (in terms of total market value of outstanding stock) in the United States.

2. Small-company stocks. This is a portfolio composed of stock of smaller companies, where "small" corresponds to the smallest 20 percent of the companies listed on the New York Stock Exchange, again as measured by market value of outstanding stock.

3. Long-term corporate bonds. This is a portfolio of high-quality bonds with 20 years to maturity.

4. Long-term U.S. government bonds. This is a portfolio of U.S. government bonds with 20 years to maturity.

5. U.S. Treasury bills. This is a portfolio of Treasury bills (T-bills for short) with a three-month maturity.

If you are not entirely certain what these investments are, don't be overly concerned. We will have much more to say about each in later chapters. For now, just take it as given that these are some of the things that you could have put your money into in years gone by. In addition to the year-to-year returns on these financial instruments, the year-to-year percentage changes in the Consumer Price Index (CPI) are also computed. The CPI is a standard measure of consumer goods price inflation.

Here is a bit of market jargon for you. A company's *total market capitalization* (or market "cap" for short) is equal to its stock price multiplied by the number of shares of stock. In other words, it's the total value of the company's stock. Large companies are often called "large-cap" stocks, and small companies are called "small-cap" stocks. We'll use these terms frequently.

A First Look

Before examining the different portfolio returns, we first take a look at the "big picture." Figure 1.1 shows what happened to $1 invested in these different portfolios at the beginning of 1926 and held over the 77-year period ending in 2002 (for clarity, the long-term corporate bonds are omitted). To fit all the information on a single graph, some modification in scaling is used. As is commonly done with financial time series, the vertical axis is scaled so that equal distances measure equal percentage (as opposed to dollar) changes in value. Thus, the distance between $10 and $100 is the same as that between $100 and $1,000, since both distances represent the same 900 percent increases.

Looking at Figure 1.1, we see that the small-company investment did the best overall. Every dollar invested grew to a remarkable $6,816.41 over the 77 years. The larger common stock portfolio did less well; a dollar invested in it grew to $1,775.34.

At the other end, the T-bill portfolio grew to only $17.48. This is even less impressive when we consider the inflation over this period. As illustrated, the increase in the price level was such that $10.09 is needed just to replace the original $1.

Given the historical record, why would anybody buy anything other than small-company stocks? If you look closely at Figure 1.1, you will probably see the answer—risk. The T-bill portfolio and the long-term government bond portfolio grew more slowly than did the stock portfolios, but they also grew much more steadily. The small stocks ended up on top, but, as you can see, they grew quite erratically at times. For example, the small stocks were the worst performers for about the first 10 years and had a smaller return than long-term government bonds for almost 15 years.

A Longer Range Look

The data available on the stock returns before 1925 are not comprehensive, but it is nonetheless possible to trace reasonably accurate returns in U.S. financial markets as far back as 1802. Figure 1.2 shows the values, in 2001, of $1 invested in stocks, long-term bonds, short-term bills, and gold. The CPI is also included for reference.

FIGURE 1.1

A $1 Investment in Different Types of Portfolios: 1926–2002
(Year-end 1925 = $1)

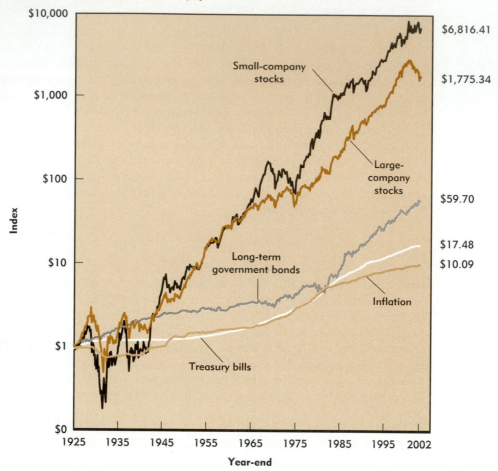

Inspecting Figure 1.2, we see that $1 invested in stocks grew to an astounding $8.80 million over this 200-year period. During this time, the returns from investing in stocks dwarf those earned on other investments. Notice also in Figure 1.2 that, after two centuries, gold has managed to keep up with inflation, but that is about it.

What we see thus far is that there has been a powerful financial incentive for long-term investing. The real moral of the story is this: Get an early start!

A Closer Look

To illustrate the variability of the different investments, Figures 1.3 through 1.6 plot the year-to-year percentage returns in the form of vertical bars drawn from the horizontal axis. The height of a bar tells us the return for the particular year. For

FIGURE 1.2   **Financial Market History**

Total return indexes (1801–2001)

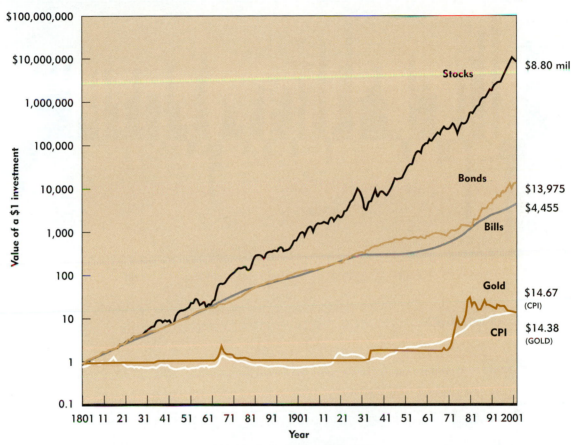

Source: Jeremy J. Siegel, *Stocks for the Long Run,* 3rd ed. (New York: McGraw-Hill, 2003).

example, looking at the long-term government bonds (Figure 1.5), we see that the largest historical return (40.35 percent) occurred in 1982. This was a good year for bonds. In comparing these charts, notice the differences in the vertical axis scales. With these differences in mind, you can see how predictably the Treasury bills (bottom of Figure 1.5) behaved compared to the small stocks (Figure 1.4).

The returns shown in these bar graphs are sometimes very large. Looking at the graphs, we see, for example, that the largest single-year return was a remarkable 143 percent for the small-cap stocks in 1933. In the same year, the large-company stocks returned "only" 53 percent. In contrast, the largest Treasury bill return was 15 percent, in 1981. For future reference, the actual year-to-year returns for the S&P 500, long-term government bonds, Treasury bills, and the CPI are shown in Table 1.1 on pages 13 and 14.

FIGURE 1.3   Year-to-Year Total Returns on Large-Company Stocks: 1926–2002

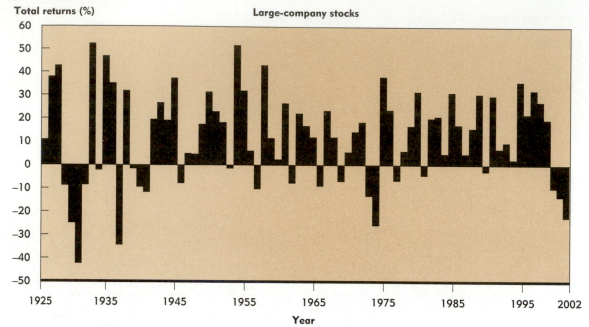

Source: *Stocks, Bonds, Bills, and Inflation Yearbook*™, Ibbotson Associates, Inc., Chicago (annually updates work by Roger G. Ibbotson and Rex A. Sinquefield). All rights reserved.

FIGURE 1.4   Year-to-Year Total Returns on Small-Company Stocks: 1926–2002

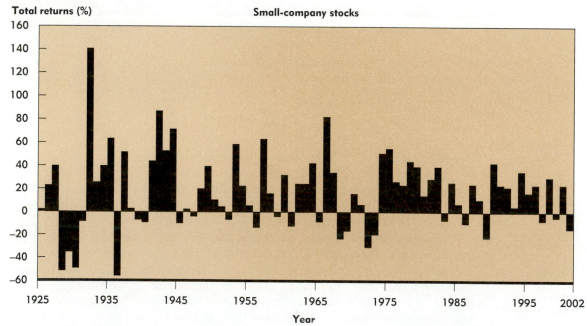

Source: *Stocks, Bonds, Bills, and Inflation Yearbook*™, Ibbotson Associates, Inc., Chicago (annually updates work by Roger G. Ibbotson and Rex A. Sinquefield). All rights reserved.

FIGURE 1.5   **Year-to-Year Total Returns on Bonds and Bills: 1926–2002**

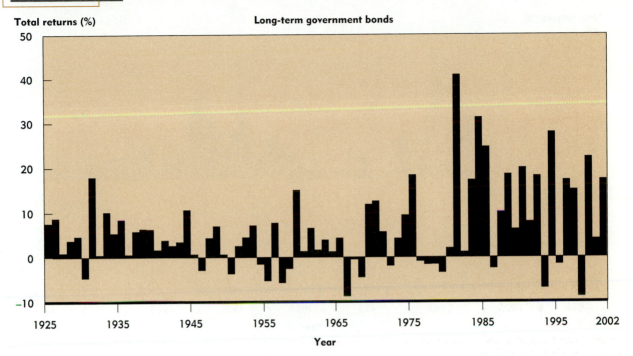

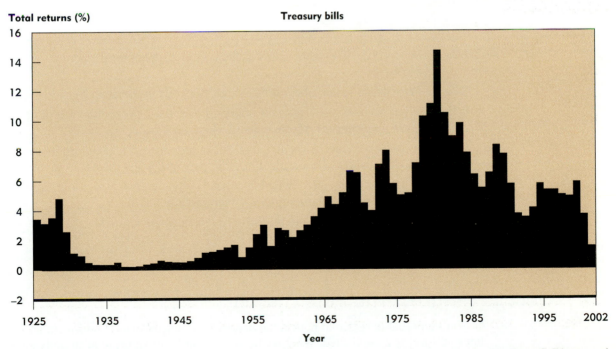

| FIGURE 1.6 | Year-to-Year Inflation: 1926–2002 |

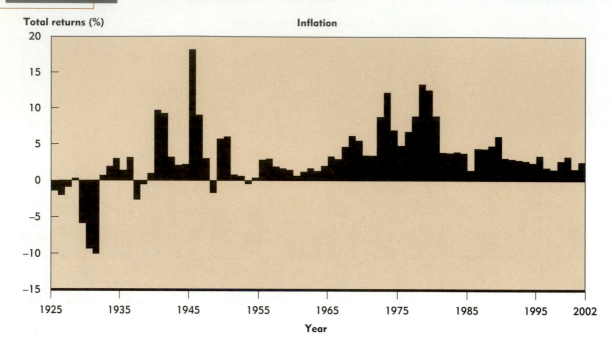

Source: *Stocks, Bonds, Bills, and Inflation Yearbook*™, Ibbotson Associates, Inc., Chicago (annually updates work by Roger G. Ibbotson and Rex A. Sinquefield).

✓ **Check This**

1.2a With 20-20 hindsight, what was the best investment for the period 1926–35?

1.2b Why doesn't everyone just buy small stocks as investments?

1.2c What was the smallest return observed over the 77 years for each of these investments? Approximately when did it occur?

1.2d About how many times did large stocks (common stocks) return more than 30 percent? How many times did they return less than −20 percent?

1.2e What was the longest "winning streak" (years without a negative return) for large stocks? For long-term government bonds?

1.2f How often did the T-bill portfolio have a negative return?

1.3 Average Returns: The First Lesson

As you've probably begun to notice, the history of financial market returns in an undigested form is complicated. What we need are simple measures to accurately summarize and describe all these numbers. Accordingly, we discuss how to go about condensing detailed numerical data. We start by calculating average returns.

TABLE 1.1	Year-to-Year Total Returns: 1926–2002			
Year	Large-Company Stocks	Long-Term Government Bonds	U.S. Treasury Bills	Consumer Price Index
1926	13.75%	5.69%	3.30%	−1.12%
1927	35.70	6.58	3.15	−2.26
1928	45.08	1.15	4.05	−1.16
1929	−8.80	4.39	4.47	0.58
1930	−25.13	4.47	2.27	−6.40
1931	−43.60	−2.15	1.15	−9.32
1932	−8.75	8.51	0.88	−10.27
1933	52.95	1.92	0.52	0.76
1934	−2.31	7.59	0.27	1.52
1935	46.79	4.20	0.17	2.99
1936	32.49	5.13	0.17	1.45
1937	−35.45	1.44	0.27	2.86
1938	31.63	4.21	0.06	−2.78
1939	−1.43	3.84	0.04	0.00
1940	−10.36	5.70	0.04	0.71
1941	−12.02	0.47	0.14	9.93
1942	20.75	1.80	0.34	9.03
1943	25.38	2.01	0.38	2.96
1944	19.49	2.27	0.38	2.30
1945	36.21	5.29	0.38	2.25
1946	−8.42	0.54	0.38	18.13
1947	5.05	−1.02	0.62	8.84
1948	4.99	2.66	1.06	2.99
1949	17.81	4.58	1.12	−2.07
1950	30.05	−0.98	1.22	5.93
1951	23.79	−0.20	1.56	6.00
1952	18.39	2.43	1.75	0.75
1953	−1.07	2.28	1.87	0.75
1954	52.23	3.08	0.93	−0.74
1955	31.62	−0.73	1.80	0.37
1956	6.91	−1.72	2.66	2.99
1957	−10.50	6.82	3.28	2.90
1958	43.57	−1.72	1.71	1.76
1959	12.01	−2.02	3.48	1.73
1960	0.47	11.21	2.81	1.36
1961	26.84	2.20	2.40	0.67
1962	−8.75	5.72	2.82	1.33
1963	22.70	1.79	3.23	1.64
1964	16.43	3.71	3.62	0.97
1965	12.38	0.93	4.06	1.92
1966	−10.06	5.12	4.94	3.46
1967	23.98	−2.86	4.39	3.04
1968	11.03	2.25	5.49	4.72
1969	−8.43	−5.63	6.90	6.20

(continued)

TABLE 1.1		Year-to-Year Total Returns: 1926–2002 *(concluded)*		
Year	Large-Company Stocks	Long-Term Government Bonds	U.S. Treasury Bills	Consumer Price Index
1970	3.94%	18.92%	6.50%	5.57%
1971	14.30	11.24	4.36	3.27
1972	18.99	2.39	4.23	3.41
1973	−14.69	3.30	7.29	8.71
1974	−26.47	4.00	7.99	12.34
1975	37.23	5.52	5.87	6.94
1976	23.93	15.56	5.07	4.86
1977	−7.16	0.38	5.45	6.70
1978	6.57	−1.26	7.64	9.02
1979	18.61	1.26	10.56	13.29
1980	32.50	−2.48	12.10	12.52
1981	−4.92	4.04	14.60	8.92
1982	21.55	44.28	10.94	3.83
1983	22.56	1.29	8.99	3.79
1984	6.27	15.29	9.90	3.95
1985	31.73	32.27	7.71	3.80
1986	18.67	22.39	6.09	1.10
1987	5.25	−3.03	5.88	4.43
1988	16.61	6.84	6.94	4.42
1989	31.69	18.54	8.44	4.65
1990	−3.10	7.74	7.69	6.11
1991	30.46	19.36	5.43	3.06
1992	7.62	7.34	3.48	2.90
1993	10.08	13.06	3.03	2.75
1994	1.32	−7.32	4.39	2.67
1995	37.58	25.94	5.61	2.54
1996	22.96	0.13	5.14	3.32
1997	33.36	12.02	5.19	1.70
1998	28.58	14.45	4.86	1.61
1999	21.04	−7.51	4.80	2.68
2000	−9.10	17.22	5.98	3.39
2001	−11.89	5.51	3.33	1.55
2002	−22.10	15.15	1.61	2.72

Source: Author calculations based on data obtained from *Global Financial Data.*

Calculating Average Returns

The obvious way to calculate average returns on the different investments in Figures 1.3 to 1.6 is to simply add up the yearly returns and divide by 77. The result is the historical average of the individual values. For example, if you add the returns for large common stocks for the 77 years, you will get about 939.4 percent. The average annual return is thus 939.4 / 77 = 12.2%. You can interpret this 12.2 percent just like any

TABLE 1.2	Average Annual Returns: 1926–2002		
Investment	Average Return	Maximum	Minimum
Large stocks	12.2%	53.99%	−43.34%
Small stocks	16.9	142.87	−58.01
Long-term corporate bonds	6.2	43.79	−8.09
Long-term government bonds	5.8	40.35	−9.19
U.S. Treasury bills	3.8	14.71	−0.02
Inflation	3.1	13.31	−10.30

Source: *Stocks, Bonds, Bills, and Inflation Yearbook™*, Ibbotson Associates, Inc., Chicago (annually updates work by Roger G. Ibbotson and Rex A. Sinquefield). All rights reserved.

other average. If you picked a year at random from the 77-year history and you had to guess the return in that year, the best guess is 12.2 percent.

Average Returns: The Historical Record

Table 1.2 shows the average returns for the investments we have discussed. These averages don't reflect the impact of inflation. Notice that over this 77-year period the average inflation rate was 3.1 percent per year while the average return on U.S. Treasury bills was 3.8 percent per year. Thus, the average return on Treasury bills exceeded the average rate of inflation by only .70 percent per year. At the other extreme, the return on large-cap common stocks exceeded the rate of inflation by a whopping $12.2\% - 3.1\% = 9.1\%$!

Our analysis thus far has covered market history going back to 1925. You might be wondering about the more recent past. The nearby *Investment Updates* box provides more detail on the stock market's ups and downs since 1970.

Risk Premiums

Now that we have computed some average returns, it seems logical to see how they compare with each other. Based on our discussion above, one such comparison involves government-issued securities. These are free of much of the variability we see in, for example, the stock market.

The government borrows money by issuing debt securities, which come in different forms. The ones we focus on here are Treasury bills. Because these instruments have a very short investment life and because the government can always raise taxes or print money to pay its bills, at least in the short run, there is essentially no risk associated with buying them. Thus, we call the rate of return on such debt the **risk-free rate**, and we will use it as a kind of investing benchmark.

risk-free rate The rate of return on a riskless investment.

A particularly interesting comparison involves the virtually risk-free return on T-bills and the risky return on common stocks. The difference between these two returns can be interpreted as a measure of the **risk premium** on the average risky asset (assuming that the stock of a large U.S. corporation has about average risk compared to all risky assets). We call this the risk premium because it is the additional return we earn by moving from a risk-free investment to a typical risky one, and we interpret it as a reward for bearing risk.

risk premium The extra return on a risky asset over the risk-free rate; the reward for bearing risk.

After 30 Years of Investing, Market Has No Sure Thing

The stock market exists to enrich investors, while utterly humiliating them. With great regularity, I receive e-mails from readers who are convinced that you should own only blue-chip companies, or only high-dividend stocks, or only technology companies. And all I can think about is the market's litany of once-sure things. It happens again and again. Hot stocks turn cold. Highflying stock funds crash and burn. Time-tested stock-picking strategies suddenly falter. To understand just how capricious the market can be, consider results from the past three decades.

As the Decades Turn

Take a look at the accompanying table (Swings and Roundabouts), which shows returns calculated by Baltimore's T. Rowe Price Associates using data from Chicago's Ibbotson Associates. In particular, focus on the performance of large, small and foreign stocks in each of the past three decades. I think of these as the three key stock-market sectors.

As you will see, large-company stocks—which are so beloved after their dazzling gains in the 1990s—didn't fare quite so well in the prior two decades. They ranked second behind foreign stocks in the 1980s and they lagged behind both small and foreign stocks in the 1970s. Similarly, small stocks ranked first in the 1970s, second in the 1990s and third in the 1980s. Meanwhile, foreign stocks were first in the 1980s, second in the 1970s and third in the 1990s.

In other words, none of the sectors consistently ranked as the top performer and all had periods of dreadful performance. Moreover, if you look at results for the 30 years through December 2001, there isn't a huge difference between the average annual returns for large, small and foreign stocks. Of course, if you were really clever, you would figure out which sector was going to be the decade's top performer, and then invest everything in that sector. But I am not smart enough to

make that sort of market call, and I don't think anybody else is, either.

Gerald Perritt, a money manager in Largo, Fla., and editor of the Mutual Fund Letter, a monthly newsletter, says he has lately met many investors who got themselves into financial trouble. All have one thing in common: They failed to diversify and instead made big investment bets that turned sour. "Diversification is good," Mr. Perritt says. "But if it's so good, why don't more people practice it? Return is the most visible element in the investing process. The least visible is risk. People see the return they miss by diversifying. We don't think about what will happen if a big bet goes in the wrong direction."

My hunch is that the current decade will be a lackluster one for blue-chip shares. Large-company stocks have been dazzling performers over the past two decades, and now they are burdened by lofty share price-to-earnings multiples and boast only skimpy dividend yields. Indeed, I suspect foreign and small stocks will prove to be the market's new darlings. But I am unwilling to invest based on such hunches. So what should an investor do? Owning a little bit of everything has worked well in the past, and it still seems like a mighty fine strategy to me.

Glancing at the performance of narrower market sectors strengthens the case for humility. In the past two years, three of the market's best-performing segments have been gold, bargain-priced "value" stocks and real-estate investment trusts, or REITs. Meanwhile, "growth" stocks, including once-sparkling technology shares, have been crushed. But look at the accompanying table to see results from earlier decades. Unfortunately, data aren't available for all time periods. Still, there are enough results to see how unpredictable market returns can be. Sure, value stocks were strong performers in 2000 and 2001. But they lagged behind growth stocks in the 1990s. True, REITs have generated great

(continued)

The First Lesson

From the data in Table 1.2, we can calculate risk premiums for the five different categories of investments. The results are shown in Table 1.3. Notice that the risk premium on T-bills is shown as zero in the table because they are our riskless benchmark. Looking at Table 1.3, we see that the average risk premium earned by the large-cap common stock portfolio is $12.2\% - 3.8\% = 8.4\%$. This is a significant reward. The fact that it

Swings and Roundabouts

All market sectors enjoy periods of dazzling gains. But none performs well all the time.

	Bear Markets		Long-Run Annual Performance			
	1973–74	**2000–01**	**1970s**	**1980s**	**1990s**	**30 Years***
Large-company stocks	−42.6%	−29.3%	5.9%	17.6%	18.2%	12.2%
Small-company stocks	−43.2	−19.4	11.5	15.8	15.1	14.9
Foreign markets	−35.2	−36.6	10.1	22.8	7.3	11.2
Growth stocks	NA	−42.2	NA	16.3	20.6	NA
Value stocks	NA	−13.4	NA	18.3	15.4	NA
Real-estate trusts	−52.6	35.2	NA	12.5	8.1	9.4
Intermediate bonds	4.9	19.4	7.0	11.9	7.2	8.5
Treasury bills	13.5	7.9	6.3	8.9	4.9	6.7
Gold	133.1	5.9	30.7	−2.5	−3.1	6.4

*Through December 31, 2001.

Note: All returns are annualized, except for the two bear markets, for which cumulative performance is shown.

NA: Not available.

results recently. But they didn't do much better than intermediate-term government bonds in the 1990s. And gold? You have to go back to the 1970s to find a decent decade for the yellow metal.

When the Bear Growls

To get a handle on down-market performance, I had T. Rowe Price calculate returns for the two most-searing bear markets of recent decades, the 1973–74 debacle and the 2000–01 tech wreck. In both stock-market declines, gold, bonds and Treasury bills posted gains, even as other sectors were crushed. Clearly, if you want a little bear-market protection, these are good assets to own.

But how did different stock-market sectors fare? Consider the 1973–74 crash. The two hardest-hit sectors were REITs and small-company stocks. If you were worried about a bear market and you had taken your cues from the 1973–74 crash, you would have avoided both sectors. Yet REITs, the hardest-hit sector in the 1973–74 crash, were the biggest winners in the recent bear market. Small-company stocks, meanwhile, didn't perform quite so impressively in the 2000–01 market decline. Nonetheless, they lost far less money than large-company stocks.

As the data make clear, there aren't many sure things in investing. But that doesn't mean you can't make good money over time. If you simply build a well-diversified portfolio and hang on for the long haul, history suggests you will be handsomely rewarded. "Here's a 30-year period that includes two grueling bear markets and one awful decade, the 1970s," notes Steven Norwitz, a T. Rowe Price vice president. "But if you invested through the whole period, you got pretty attractive returns."

Source: Jonathan Clements, *The Wall Street Journal*, April 28, 2002. © 2002 Dow Jones & Company, Inc. All Rights Reserved Worldwide.

exists historically is an important observation, and it is the basis for our first lesson: Risky assets, on average, earn a risk premium. Put another way, there is a reward, on average, for bearing risk.

Why is this so? Why, for example, is the risk premium for stocks so much larger than the risk premium for bonds? More generally, what determines the relative sizes of the risk premiums for the different assets? These questions speak to the heart of the modern theory of investments, and we will discuss the issues involved many times in

TABLE 1.3	Average Annual Returns and Risk Premiums: 1926–2002	
Investment	Average Return	Risk Premium
Large stocks	12.2%	8.4%
Small stocks	16.9	13.1
Long-term corporate bonds	6.2	2.4
Long-term government bonds	5.8	2.0
U.S. Treasury bills	3.8	0.0

Source: *Stocks, Bonds, Bills, and Inflation Yearbook*™, Ibbotson Associates, Inc., Chicago (annually updates work by Roger G. Ibbotson and Rex A. Sinquefield). All rights reserved.

the chapters ahead. For now, part of the answer can be found by looking at the historical variability of returns of these different investments. So, to get started, we now turn our attention to measuring variability in returns.

Check This

1.3a   What is a risk premium?

1.3b   What was the historical risk premium on common stocks? On U.S. Treasury bonds?

1.3c   What is the first lesson from financial market history?

1.4   Return Variability: The Second Lesson

We have already seen that year-to-year returns on common stocks tend to be more volatile than returns on, say, long-term government bonds. We now discuss how to measure this variability so we can begin examining the important subject of risk.

Frequency Distributions and Variability

To get started, we can draw a *frequency distribution* for large-company stock returns like the one in Figure 1.7. What we have done here is to count the number of times that an annual return on the large-company stock portfolio falls within each 10 percent range. For example, in Figure 1.7, the height of 12 for the bar within the interval 20 percent to 30 percent means that 12 of the 77 annual returns are in that range. Notice also that most of the returns are in the −10 to 40 percent range. In three cases, the large-company stock portfolio's return fell within a particular range 13 times in 77 years.

What we need to do now is to actually measure the spread in these returns. We know, for example, that the return on the S&P 500 index of common stocks in a typical year was 12.2 percent. We now want to know by how much the actual return differs from this average in a typical year. In other words, we need a measure of returns volatility. The **variance** and its square root, the **standard deviation**, are the most commonly used measures of volatility. We briefly review how to calculate these next. If you've already studied basic statistics, you should notice that we are simply calculating an ordinary sample variance and standard deviation, just as you may have done many times before.

variance A common measure of volatility.

standard deviation The square root of the variance.

FIGURE 1.7

Frequency Distribution of Returns on Common Stocks: 1926–2002

Return (%)

Source: *Stocks, Bonds, Bills, and Inflation Yearbook*™, Ibbotson Associates, Inc., Chicago (annually updates work by Roger G. Ibbotson and Rex A. Sinquefield).

The Historical Variance and Standard Deviation

Variance measures the average squared difference between the actual returns and the average return. The bigger this number is, the more the actual returns tend to differ from the average return. To illustrate how we calculate historical variance, suppose a particular investment had returns of 10 percent, 12 percent, 3 percent, and −9 percent over the last four years. The average return is $(10\% + 12\% + 3\% - 9\%) / 4 = 4\%$.

Notice that the return is never actually equal to 4 percent. Instead, the first return deviates from the average by $10\% - 4\% = 6\%$, the second return deviates from the average by $12\% - 4\% = 8\%$, and so on. To compute the variance, we square each of these deviations, add them up, and divide the result by the number of returns less one, or three in this case.[2] These calculations are summarized immediately below.

For an easy-to-read review of basic statistics, see www.robertniles. com/stats/

$$
\begin{aligned}
(10 - 4)^2 &= 36 \\
(12 - 4)^2 &= 64 \\
(3 - 4)^2 &= 1 \\
(-9 - 4)^2 &= \underline{169} \\
&\ 270 \quad \rightarrow \quad \rightarrow \quad 270 / 3 = 90
\end{aligned}
$$

[2]The reason for dividing by $N - 1$ rather than simply N is based on statistical sampling theory, which is beyond the scope of this book. Just remember that to calculate a variance about a sample average divide the sum of squared deviations from the average by $N - 1$.

To recap, we first calculate the differences between actual returns and their average by subtracting out 4 percent. Second, we square each difference. Third, we sum all squared deviations to get 270. Finally, we divide the sum of the squared deviations by $4 - 1 = 3$.

By these calculations we get $Var(R)$ or σ^2 (read this as "sigma squared"), which is the variance of the return:

$$Var(R) = \sigma^2 = 270 / (4 - 1) = 90$$

The standard deviation is the square root of the variance. So, if $SD(R)$ or σ stands for the standard deviation of return:

$$SD(R) = \sigma = \sqrt{90} = 9.487\%$$

The square root of the variance is used because the variance is measured in "squared" percentages and is hard to interpret. The standard deviation is an ordinary percentage, which here is 9.487 percent.

In general, if we have N historical returns, where N is some number, we can write the historical variance as:

$$Var(R) = [(R_1 - \bar{R})^2 + [(R_2 - \bar{R})^2 + \cdots + (R_N - \bar{R})^2]/(N - 1) \qquad (1.4)$$

This formula tells us to do just what we did above: Take each of the N individual returns $(R_1, R_2, \ldots, R_N)$ and subtract the average return, $\bar{R}$; then square the results, and add them all up; finally, divide this total by the number of returns less one $(N - 1)$. The standard deviation is always the square root of $Var(R)$.

CALCULATING THE VARIANCE AND STANDARD DEVIATION

EXAMPLE 1.2

Calculate return averages, variances, and standard deviations for S&P 500 large-cap stocks and Treasury bonds (T-bonds) using data for the first five years in Table 1.1, 1926–1930.

First, calculate return averages as follows:

S&P 500 Large-Company Stocks	T-Bonds
13.75	5.69
35.70	6.58
45.08	1.15
−8.80	4.39
−25.13	4.47
60.60	22.8
Average return: 60.60 / 5 = 12.12	22.8 / 5 = 4.46

Using the averages above, calculate the squared deviations from the average returns and sum the squared deviations as follows:

S&P 500 Large-Company Stocks	T-Bonds
$(13.75 - 12.12)^2 = 2.66$	$(5.69 - 4.46)^2 = 1.53$
$(35.70 - 12.12)^2 = 556.02$	$(6.58 - 4.46)^2 = 4.51$
$(45.08 - 12.12)^2 = 1{,}086.36$	$(1.15 - 4.46)^2 = 10.93$
$(-8.80 - 12.12)^2 = 437.65$	$(4.39 - 4.46)^2 = 0.00$
$(-25.13 - 12.12)^2 = 1{,}387.56$	$(4.47 - 4.46)^2 = 0.00$
3,470.24	16.97

(continued)

Calculate return variances by dividing the sums of squared deviations by four, the number of returns less one.

S&P 500: 3,470.24 / 4 = 867.56   **T-bonds: 16.97 / 4 = 4.24**

Standard deviations are then calculated as the square root of the variance:

S&P 500: $\sqrt{867.56}$ **= 29.45**   **T-bonds:** $\sqrt{4.24}$ **= 2.06**

Notice that the large-company stock portfolio had a volatility almost 10 times greater than the T-bond portfolio, which is not unusual during periods of market turbulence.

The Historical Record

Figure 1.8 summarizes much of our discussion of capital market history so far. It displays average returns, standard deviations, and frequency distributions of annual returns on a common scale. In Figure 1.8, notice, for example, that the standard deviation for the small-stock portfolio (33.2 percent per year) is more than 10 times larger than the T-bill portfolio's standard deviation (3.2 percent per year). We will return to these figures momentarily.

normal distribution
A symmetric, bell-shaped frequency distribution that is completely defined by its average and standard deviation.

Normal Distribution

For many different random events in nature, a particular frequency distribution, the **normal distribution** (or *bell curve*), is useful for describing the probability of ending

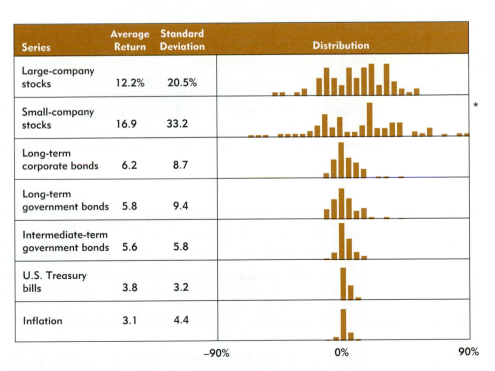

FIGURE 1.8

Historical Returns, Standard Deviations, and Frequency Distributions: 1926–2002

Source: *Stocks, Bonds, Bills, and Inflation Yearbook*™, Ibbotson Associates, Inc., Chicago (annually updates work by Roger G. Ibbotson and Rex A. Sinquefield). All rights reserved.

Series	Average Return	Standard Deviation	Distribution
Large-company stocks	12.2%	20.5%	
Small-company stocks	16.9	33.2	*
Long-term corporate bonds	6.2	8.7	
Long-term government bonds	5.8	9.4	
Intermediate-term government bonds	5.6	5.8	
U.S. Treasury bills	3.8	3.2	
Inflation	3.1	4.4	

−90%   0%   90%

*The 1933 small-company stock total return was 142.9 percent.

FIGURE 1.9

The Normal Distribution: Ilustrated Returns Based on the Historical Return and Standard Deviation for a Portfolio of Large Common Stocks

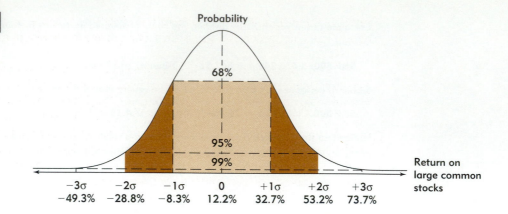

up in a given range. For example, the idea behind "grading on a curve" comes from the fact that exam scores often resemble a bell curve.

Figure 1.9 illustrates a normal distribution and its distinctive bell shape. As you can see, this distribution has a much cleaner appearance than the actual return distributions illustrated in Figure 1.7. Even so, like the normal distribution, the actual distributions do appear to be at least roughly mound shaped and symmetric. When this is true, the normal distribution is often a very good approximation.

Also, keep in mind that the distributions in Figure 1.8 are based on only 77 yearly observations, while Figure 1.9 is, in principle, based on an infinite number. So, if we had been able to observe returns for, say, 1,000 years, we might have filled in a lot of the irregularities and ended up with a much smoother picture. For our purposes, it is enough to observe that the returns are at least roughly normally distributed.

The usefulness of the normal distribution stems from the fact that it is completely described by the average and the standard deviation. If you have these two numbers, then there is nothing else to know. For example, with a normal distribution, the probability that we end up within one standard deviation of the average is about ⅔. The probability that we end up within two standard deviations is about 95 percent. Finally, the probability of being more than three standard deviations away from the average is less than 1 percent. These ranges and the probabilities are illustrated in Figure 1.9.

To see why this is useful, recall from Figure 1.8 that the standard deviation of returns on the large common stocks is 20.5 percent. The average return is 12.2 percent. So, assuming that the frequency distribution is at least approximately normal, the probability that the return in a given year is in the range of −8.3 percent to 32.7 percent (12.2 percent plus or minus one standard deviation, 20.5 percent) is about ⅔. This range is illustrated in Figure 1.9. In other words, there is about one chance in three that the return will be *outside* this range. This literally tells you that, if you buy stocks in large companies, you should expect to be outside this range in one year out of every three. This reinforces our earlier observations about stock market volatility. However, there is only a 5 percent chance (approximately) that we would end up outside the range of −28.8 percent to 53.2 percent (12.2 percent plus or minus 2 × 20.5%). These points are also illustrated in Figure 1.9.

The Second Lesson

Our observations concerning the year-to-year variability in returns are the basis for our second lesson from capital market history. On average, bearing risk is handsomely rewarded, but, in a given year, there is a significant chance of a dramatic change in value. Thus, our second lesson is this: The greater the potential reward, the greater is the risk.

Thus far in this chapter, we have emphasized the year-to-year variability in returns. We should note that even day-to-day movements can exhibit considerable volatility. For example, not long ago, on September 17, 2001, the Dow Jones Industrial Average (DJIA) plummeted 684.81 points, or 7.13 percent. By historical standards, it was a bad day for the 30 stocks that comprise the DJIA (as well as for a majority of stocks in the market). Still, while the drop was the largest one-day decrease in the DJIA ever in terms of points, it actually wasn't quite in the top 12 largest one-day percentage decreases in history, as illustrated in the following table:

Top 12 One-Day Percentage Declines in the Dow-Jones Industrial Average			
December 12, 1914	−24.4%	August 12, 1932	−8.4%
October 19, 1987	−22.6	March 14, 1907	−8.3
October 28, 1929	−12.8	October 26, 1987	−8.0
October 29, 1929	−11.7	July 21, 1933	−7.8
November 6, 1929	− 9.9	October 18, 1937	−7.7
December 18, 1899	− 8.7	February 1, 1917	−7.2

Source: *Dow Jones.*

This discussion highlights the importance of looking at returns in terms of percentages rather than dollar amounts or index points. For example, prior to 2001, the biggest one-day loss in terms of points was on April 14, 2000, when the DJIA declined by 618 points. The second worst was the 554-point drop of October 27, 1987. By contrast, the 5.57-point drop in the DJIA on December 18, 1899, marked the fifth worst day in the history of the index, but a 5.6-point loss in the DJIA in today's market would hardly be noticed. This is precisely why we relied on percentage returns when we examined market history in this chapter.[3]

INVESTING IN GROWTH STOCKS

EXAMPLE 1.3

As a practical matter, the phrase *growth stock* is frequently a euphemism for small-company stock. Are such investments suitable for "widows and orphans"? Before answering, you should consider historical volatility. For example, from the historical record, what is the approximate probability that you will actually lose 16 percent or more of your money in a single year if you buy stocks from a group of such companies?

The historical average return on a small-company stock portfolio is about 17 percent, with an annual standard deviation of about 33 percent. From our rule of thumb, there is about a ⅓ probability that you will experience a return outside the range −16 percent to 50 percent (17% ± 33%).   *(continued)*

---

[3]By the way, as you may have noticed, what's kind of weird is that 6 of the 12 worst days in the history of the DJIA occurred in October, including the top 3. We have no clue as to why. Furthermore, looking back at the Mark Twain quote near the beginning of the chapter, how do you suppose he knew? Sounds like a case for the X-Files.

The odds of being above or below this range are about equal. There is thus about a ⅙ chance (half of ⅓) that you will lose more than 16 percent. So you should expect this to happen once in every six years, on average. Such investments can thus be *very* volatile, and they are not well-suited for those who cannot afford to bear the risk.

Now that you know how to calculate and, more importantly, interpret average returns and standard deviations, the nearby *Spreadsheet Analysis* box shows how to do the calculations using Excel, which can really speed up things when we have a lot of data.

Check This

1.4a	In words, how do we calculate a variance? A standard deviation?
1.4b	What is the first lesson from financial market history? The second lesson?

SPREADSHEET ANALYSIS

Using a Spreadsheet to Calculate Average Returns and Volatilities

Here is an Excel spreadsheet summarizing the formulas and analysis needed to calculate average returns and standard deviations using the 1990s as an example:

	A	B	C	D	E	F	G	H
1								
2		**Using a spreadsheet to calculate average returns and standard deviations**						
3								
4	Looking back in the chapter, the data suggest that the 1990s were one							
5	of the best decades for stock market investors. We will find out just how good by							
6	calculating the average returns and standard deviations for this period. Here are the							
7	year-by-year returns on the large company S&P 500 index:							
8								
9		*Year*	*Return(%)*	*Year*	*Return(%)*			
10		1990	−3.10	1995	37.58			
11		1991	30.46	1996	22.96			
12		1992	7.62	1997	33.36			
13		1993	10.08	1998	28.58			
14		1994	1.32	1999	21.04			
15								
16		Average return (%):		18.99				
17		Standard deviation (%):		14.16				
18								
19	The formulas we used to do the calculations are just =AVERAGE(C10:C14;E10:E14)							
20	and =STDEV(C10:C14;E10:E14). Notice that the average return in the 1990s was 18.99							
21	percent per year, which is larger than the long-run average of 12 percent. At the same							
22	time, the standard deviation, 14.16 percent, was smaller than the 20 percent long-run value.							

1.5 More on Average Returns

Thus far in this chapter, we have looked closely at simple average returns. But there is another way of computing an average return. The fact that average returns are calculated two different ways leads to some confusion, so our goal in this section is to explain the two approaches and also the circumstances under which each is appropriate.

Arithmetic versus Geometric Averages

Let's start with a simple example. Suppose you buy a particular stock for $100. Unfortunately, the first year you own it, it falls to $50. The second year you own it, it rises back to $100, leaving you where you started (no dividends were paid).

What was your average return on this investment? Common sense seems to say that your average return must be exactly zero since you started with $100 and ended with $100. But if we calculate the returns year-by-year, we see that you lost 50 percent the first year (you lost half of your money). The second year, you made 100 percent (you doubled your money). Your average return over the two years was thus $(-50\% + 100\%)/2 = 25\%$!

geometric average return The average compound return earned per year over a multiyear period.

So which is correct, 0 percent or 25 percent? The answer is that both are correct; they just answer different questions. The 0 percent is called the **geometric average return**. The 25 percent is called the **arithmetic average return**. The geometric average return answers the question *"What was your average compound return per year over a particular period?"* The arithmetic average return answers the question *"What was your return in an average year over a particular period?"*

arithmetic average return The return earned in an average year over a multiyear period.

Notice that, in previous sections, the average returns we calculated were all arithmetic averages, so we already know how to calculate them. What we need to do now is (1) learn how to calculate geometric averages and (2) learn the circumstances under which one average is more meaningful than the other.

Calculating Geometric Average Returns

First, to illustrate how we calculate a geometric average return, suppose a particular investment had annual returns of 10 percent, 12 percent, 3 percent, and −9 percent over the last four years. The geometric average return over this four-year period is calculated as $(1.10 \times 1.12 \times 1.03 \times .91)^{1/4} - 1 = 3.66\%$. In contrast, the average arithmetic return we have been calculating is $(.10 + .12 + .03 - .09)/4 = 4.0\%$.

In general, if we have N years of returns, the geometric average return over these N years is calculated using this formula:

$$\text{Geometric average return} = [(1 + R_1) \times (1 + R_2) \times \cdots \times (1 + R_N)]^{1/N} - 1$$

(1.5)

This formula tells us that four steps are required:

1. Take each of the N annual returns $R_1, R_2, \ldots, R_N$ and add a one to each (after converting them to decimals!).
2. Multiply all the numbers from step 1 together.
3. Take the result from step 2 and raise it to the power of $1/N$.
4. Finally, subtract one from the result of step 3. The result is the geometric average return.

CALCULATING THE GEOMETRIC AVERAGE RETURN

EXAMPLE 1.4

Calculate the geometric average return for S&P 500 large-cap stocks for the first five years in Table 1.1, 1926–1930.

First, convert percentages to decimal returns, add one, and then calculate their product.

S&P 500 Returns	Product
13.75	1.1375
35.70	× 1.3570
45.08	× 1.4508
−8.80	× 0.9120
−25.13	× 0.7487
	1.5291

Notice that the number 1.5291 is what our investment is worth after five years if we started with a one dollar investment. The geometric average return is then calculated as

Geometric average return = $1.5291^{1/5} - 1 = 0.0887$, or 8.87%

Thus the geometric average return is about 8.87 percent in this example. In contrast, in Example 1.2, the average arithmetic return was calculated as 12.12 percent. Here is a tip: If you are using a financial calculator, you can put $1 in as the present value, $1.5291 as the future value, and 5 as the number of periods. Then, solve for the unknown rate. You should get the same answer we did.

One thing you may have noticed in our examples thus far is that the geometric average returns seem to be smaller. It turns out that this will always be true (as long as the returns are not all identical, in which case the two "averages" would be the same). To illustrate, Table 1.4 shows the arithmetic averages and standard deviations from Figure 1.8, along with the geometric average returns.

As shown in Table 1.4, the geometric averages are all smaller, but the magnitude of the difference varies quite a bit. The reason is that the difference is greater for more volatile investments. In fact, there is useful approximation. Assuming all the numbers are expressed in decimals (as opposed to percentages), the geometric average return is approximately equal to the arithmetic average return minus half the variance. For

TABLE 1.4	Geometric versus Arithmetic Average Returns: 1926–2002		
Series	Geometric Mean	Arithmetic Mean	Standard Deviation
Large-company stocks	10.2%	12.2%	20.5%
Small-company stocks	12.1	16.9	33.2
Long-term corporate bonds	5.9	6.2	8.7
Long-term government bonds	5.5	5.8	9.4
Intermediate-term government bonds	5.4	5.6	5.8
U.S. Treasury bills	3.8	3.8	3.2
Inflation	3.0	3.1	4.4

example, looking at the large-company stocks, the arithmetic average is .122 and the standard deviation is .205, implying that the variance is .042025. The approximate geometric average is thus .122 − .04025/2 = .1019, which is quite close to the actual value.

MORE GEOMETRIC AVERAGES

EXAMPLE 1.5

Take a look back at Figure 1.1. There, we showed the value of a $1 investment after 77 years. Use the value for the large-company stock investment to check the geometric average in Table 1.4.

In Figure 1.1, the large-company investment grew to $1,775.34 over 77 years. The geometric average return is thus

Geometric average return = $1{,}775.34^{1/77} - 1$ = .1020, or 10.2%

This 10.2% is the value shown in Table 1.4. For practice, check some of the other numbers in Table 1.4 the same way.

Arithmetic Average Return or Geometric Average Return?

When we look at historical returns, the difference between the geometric and arithmetic average returns isn't too hard to understand. To put it slightly differently, the geometric average tells you what you actually earned per year on average, compounded annually. The arithmetic average tells you what you earned in a typical year. You should use whichever one answers the question you want answered.

A somewhat trickier question concerns forecasting the future, and there's a lot of confusion about this point among analysts and financial planners. The problem is this. If we have *estimates* of both the arithmetic and geometric average returns, then the arithmetic average is probably too high for longer periods and the geometric average is probably too low for shorter periods.

The good news is that there is a simple way of combining the two averages, which we will call *Blume's formula*.[4] Suppose we calculated geometric and arithmetic return averages from N years of data and we wish to use these averages to form a T-year average return forecast, $R(T)$, where T is less than N. Here's how we do it:

$$R(T) = \frac{T-1}{N-1} \times Geometric\ average + \frac{N-T}{N-1} \times Arithmetic\ average$$

For example, suppose that, from 25 years of annual returns data, we calculate an arithmetic average return of 12 percent and a geometric average return of 9 percent. From these averages, we wish to make 1-year, 5-year, and 10-year average return forecasts. These three average return forecasts are calculated as follows:

---

[4]This elegant result is due to Marshal Blume. ("Unbiased Estimates of Long-Run Expected Rates of Return," *Journal of the American Statistical Association,* September 1974, pp. 634–638).

$$R(1) = \frac{1-1}{24} \times 9\% + \frac{25-1}{24} \times 12\% = 12\%$$

$$R(5) = \frac{5-1}{24} \times 9\% + \frac{25-5}{24} \times 12\% = 11.5\%$$

$$R(10) = \frac{10-1}{24} \times 9\% + \frac{25-10}{24} \times 12\% = 10.875\%$$

Thus, we see that 1-year, 5-year, and 10-year forecasts are 12 percent, 11.5 percent, and 10.875 percent, respectively.

FORECASTING AVERAGE RETURNS

EXAMPLE 1.6

Over the 77-year period 1926–2002, the geometric average return for the S&P 500 index was 10.2 percent and the arithmetic average return was 12.2 percent. Calculate average return forecasts for 1, 5, 10, and 25 years into the future.

In this case, we would use Blume's formula with values of $T = 1, 5, 10,$ and 25 and $N = 77$:

$$R(T) = \frac{T-1}{76} \times 10.2\% + \frac{77-T}{76} \times 12.2\%$$

T	R(T)
1	12.2%
5	12.1
10	12.0
25	11.6
77	10.2

Notice that short-term forecasts are closer to the arithmetic average return and long-term forecasts are closer to the geometric average return.

This concludes our discussion of geometric versus arithmetic averages. One last note: In the future, when we say "average return," we mean arithmetic average unless we explicitly say otherwise.

Check This

1.5a   Over a five-year period, an investment in a broad market index yielded annual returns of 10, 16, −5, −8, and 7 percent. What were the arithmetic and geometric average annual returns for this index?

1.5b   Over a 25-year period, an investment in a broad market index yielded an arithmetic average return of 4 percent and a geometric average return of 3.6 percent. Using Blume's formula, what would be the 5-year and 10-year average return forecasts?

1.6   Risk and Return

In previous sections we explored financial market history to see what we could learn about risk and return. In this section we summarize our findings and then conclude our discussion by looking ahead at the subjects we will be examining in later chapters.

The Risk-Return Trade-Off

Figure 1.10 is a way of putting together our findings on risk and return. What it shows is that there is a risk-return trade-off. At one extreme, if we are unwilling to bear any risk at all, but we are willing to forgo the use of our money for a while, then we can earn the risk-free rate. Because the risk-free rate represents compensation for just waiting, it is often called the *time value of money*.

If we are willing to bear risk, then we can expect to earn a risk premium, at least on average. Further, the more risk we are willing to bear, the greater is the risk premium. Investment advisers like to say that an investment has a "wait" component and a "worry" component. In our figure, the time value of money is the compensation for waiting, and the risk premium is the compensation for worrying.

There are two important caveats to this discussion. First, risky investments do not *always* pay more than risk-free investments. Indeed, that's precisely what makes them risky. In other words, there is a risk premium *on average*, but, over any particular time interval, there is no guarantee. Second, we've intentionally been a little imprecise about what we mean exactly by risk. As we will discuss in the chapters ahead, not all risks are compensated. Some risks are cheaply and easily avoidable, and there is no expected reward for bearing them. It is only those risks that cannot be easily avoided that are compensated (on average).

FIGURE 1.10   **Risk-Return Trade-Off**

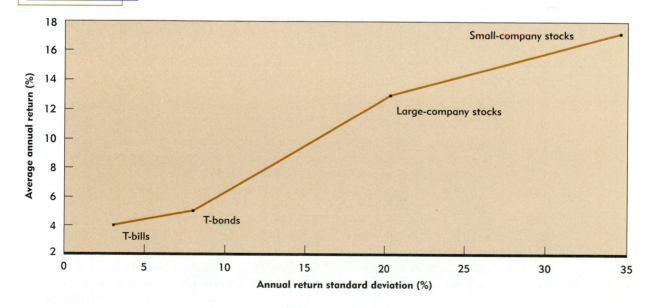

A Look Ahead

In the remainder of this text, we focus exclusively on financial assets. An advantage of this approach is that it is limited to four major types: stocks, bonds, options, and futures, in the order that we cover them. This means that we won't be discussing collectibles such as classic automobiles, baseball cards, coins, fine art, or stamps. We also won't be discussing real estate or precious metals such as gold and platinum. It's not that these are unimportant; rather, they are very specialized. So, instead of treating them superficially, we leave a discussion of them for another day (and another book).

As we've indicated, to understand the potential reward from an investment, it is critical to first understand the risk involved. There is an old saying that goes like this: It's easy to make a small fortune investing in _____ (put your favorite investment here)—just start with a large fortune! The moral is that the key to successful investing is to make informed, intelligent decisions about risk. For this reason, we are going to pay particular attention to the things that determine the value of the different assets we discuss and the nature of the associated risks.

One common characteristic that these assets have is that they are bought and sold around the clock and around the world in vast quantities. The way they are traded can be very different, however. We think it is important and interesting to understand exactly what happens when you buy or sell one of these assets, so we will be discussing the different trading mechanisms and the way the different markets function. We will also describe actual buying and selling at various points along the way to show you the steps involved and the results of placing buy and sell orders and having them executed.

1.7   Summary and Conclusions

This chapter explores financial market history. Such a history lesson is useful because it tells us what to expect in the way of returns from risky assets. We summarized our study of market history with two key lessons:

1. Risky assets, on average, earn a risk premium. There is a reward for bearing risk.

2. The greater the potential reward from a risky investment, the greater is the risk.

When we put these two lessons together, we concluded that there is a risk-return trade-off: The only way to earn a higher return is to take on greater risk.

Get Real

This chapter took you through some basic, but important, investment-related calculations. We then walked through the modern history of risk and return. How should you, as an investor or investment manager, put this information to work?

The answer is that you now have a rational, objective basis for thinking about what you stand to make from investing in some important broad asset classes. For the stock market as a whole, as measured by the performance of large-company stocks, you know that you might realistically expect to make 12 percent or so per year on average.

Equally important, you know that you won't make 12 percent in any one year; instead, you'll make more or less. You know that the standard deviation is about 20 percent per year, and you should know what that means in terms of risk. In particular, you

(continued)

need to understand that in one year out of every six, you should expect to lose more than 8 percent (12 percent minus one standard deviation), so this will be a relatively common event. The good news is that in one year out of six, you can realistically expect to earn more than 32 percent (12 percent plus one standard deviation).

The other important, practical thing to understand from this chapter is that a strategy of investing in very low risk assets (such as T-bills) has historically barely kept up with inflation. This might be sufficient for some investors, but if your goal is to do better than that, then you will have to bear some amount of risk to achieve it.

Key Terms

total dollar return 3
dividend yield 4
capital gains yield 4
total percent return 4
risk-free rate 15
risk premium 15

variance 18
standard deviation 18
normal distribution 21
geometric average return 25
arithmetic average return 25

Chapter Review Problems and Self-Test

1. **Calculating Returns**   You bought 400 shares of Metallica Heavy Metal, Inc., at $30 per share. Over the year, you received $.75 per share in dividends. If the stock sold for $33 at the end of the year, what was your dollar return? Your percentage return?

2. **Calculating Returns and Variability**   Using the following returns, calculate the arithmetic average returns, the variances, the standard deviations, and the geometric returns for the following stocks:

Year	Michele, Inc.	Janicek Co.
1	12%	5%
2	−4	−15
3	0	10
4	20	38
5	2	17

3. **Forecasting Returns**   Over a 30-year period an asset had an arithmetic return of 12.8 percent and a geometric return of 10.7 percent. Using Blume's formula, what is your best estimate of the future annual returns over the next 5 years? 10 years? 20 years?

Answers to Self-Test Problems

1. Your dollar return is just your gain or loss in dollars. Here, we receive $.75 in dividends on each of our 400 shares, for a total of $300. In addition, each share rose from $30 to $33, so we make $3 × 400 shares = $1,200. Our total dollar return is thus $300 + $1,200 = $1,500.

   Our percentage return (or just "return" for short) is equal to the $1,500 we made divided by our initial outlay of $30 × 400 shares = $12,000; so $1,500/12,000 = .125 = 12.5%. Equivalently, we could have just noted that each share paid a $.75 dividend and each

www.mhhe.com/cj3e

share gained $3, so the total dollar gain per share was $3.75. As a percentage of the cost of one share ($30), we get $3.75 / 30 = .125 = 12.5\%$.

2. First, calculate arithmetic averages as follows:

Michele, Inc.	Janicek Co.
12%	5%
−4	−15
0	10
20	38
2	17
30%	55%
Average return: 30 / 5 = 6%	55 / 5 = 11%

Using the arithmetic averages above, calculate the squared deviations from the arithmetic average returns and sum the squared deviations as follows:

Michele, Inc.	Janicek Co.
$(12 - 6)^2 = 36$	$(5 - 11)^2 = 36$
$(-4 - 6)^2 = 100$	$(-15 - 11)^2 = 676$
$(0 - 6)^2 = 36$	$(10 - 11)^2 = 1$
$(20 - 6)^2 = 196$	$(38 - 11)^2 = 729$
$(2 - 6)^2 = 16$	$(17 - 11)^2 = 36$
384	1,478

Calculate return variances by dividing the sums of squared deviations by four, which is the number of returns less one.

$$\text{Michele: } 384 / 4 = 96 \qquad \text{Janicek: } 1{,}478 / 4 = 369.5$$

Standard deviations are then calculated as the square root of the variance.

$$\text{Michele: } \sqrt{96} = 9.8\% \qquad \text{Janicek: } \sqrt{369.5} = 19.22\%$$

Geometric returns are then calculated as:

$$\text{Michele: } [(1 + .12)(1 - .04)(1 + .00)(1 + .20)(1 + .02)]^{1/5} - 1 = 5.65\%$$
$$\text{Janicek: } [(1 + .05)(1 - .15)(1 + .10)(1 + .38)(1 + .17)]^{1/5} - 1 = 9.65\%$$

3. To find the best forecast, we apply Blume's formula as follows:

$$R(5) = \frac{5 - 1}{29} \times 10.7\% + \frac{30 - 5}{29} \times 12.8\% = 12.51\%$$

$$R(10) = \frac{10 - 1}{29} \times 10.7\% + \frac{30 - 10}{29} \times 12.8\% = 12.15\%$$

$$R(20) = \frac{20 - 1}{29} \times 10.7\% + \frac{30 - 20}{29} \times 12.8\% = 11.42\%$$

www.mhhe.com/cj3e

Test Your Investment Quotient

1. **Prices and Returns**   You plan to buy a common stock and hold it for one year. You expect to receive both $1.50 from dividends and $26 from the sale of the stock at the end of the year. If you wanted to earn a 15 percent rate of return, what is the maximum price you would pay for the stock today?

   a. $22.61
   b. $23.91
   c. $24.50
   d. $27.50

2. **Returns**   A portfolio of non-dividend-paying stocks earned a geometric mean return of 5 percent between January 1, 1994, and December 31, 2000. The arithmetic mean return for the same period was 6 percent. If the market value of the portfolio at the beginning of 1995 was $100,000, the market value of the portfolio at the end of 2000 was *closest* to:

   a. $135,000
   b. $140,710
   c. $142,000
   d. $150,363

3. **Standard Deviation**   Which of the following statements about standard deviation is true? Standard devision

   a. Is the square of the variance.
   b. Can be a positive or negative number.
   c. Is denominated in the same units as the original data.
   d. Is the arithmetic mean of the squared deviations from the mean.

4. **Normal Distribution**   An investment strategy has an expected return of 12 percent and a standard deviation of 10 percent. If the investment returns are normally distributed, the probability of earning a return less than 2 percent is closest to:

   a. 10 percent
   b. 16 percent
   c. 32 percent
   d. 34 percent

5. **Normal Distribution**   What are the mean and standard deviation of a standard normal distribution?

	Mean	Standard Deviation
a.	0	0
b.	0	1
c.	1	0
d.	1	1

6. **Normal Distribution**   Given a data series that is normally distributed with a mean of 100 and a standard deviation of 10, about 95 percent of the numbers in the series will fall within which of the following ranges?

   a. 60 to 140
   b. 70 to 130
   c. 80 to 120
   d. 90 to 110

7. **Asset Types**   Stocks, bonds, options, and futures are the four major types of

   a. Debt
   b. Real assets
   c. Equity
   d. Financial assets

8. **Investment Returns**   Suppose the value of an investment doubles in a one-year period. In this case, the rate of return on this investment over that one-year period is what amount?

   a. 100 percent even if the gain is not actually realized.
   b. 200 percent even if the gain is not actually realized.
   c. 100 percent only if the gain is actually realized.
   d. 200 percent only if the gain is actually realized.

9. **Historical Returns**   Which of the following asset categories has an annual returns history most closely linked to historical annual rates of inflation?

   a. U.S. Treasury bills
   b. Corporate bonds
   c. Large-company stocks
   d. Small-company stocks

10. **Historical Returns**   Based on the annual returns history since 1926, which asset category, on average, has yielded the highest risk premium?

    a. U.S. government bonds
    b. Corporate bonds
    c. Large-company stocks
    d. Small-company stocks

11. **Stat 101**   Over a four-year period, an investment in Outa'Synch common stock yields returns of -10, 40, 0, and 20. What is the arithmetic return over this period?

    a. 5 percent
    b. 7.5 percent
    c. 10 percent
    d. 12.5 percent

12. **Stat 101**   You calculate an average historical return of 20 percent and a standard deviation of return of 10 percent for an investment in Stonehenge Construction Co. You believe these values well represent the future distribution of returns. Assuming that returns are normally distributed, what is the probability that Stonehenge Construction will yield a negative return?

    a. 17 percent
    b. 33 percent
    c. 5 percent
    d. 2.5 percent

13. **Stat 101**   Which of the following statements about a normal distribution is incorrect?

    a. A normal distribution is symmetrically centered on its mean.
    b. The probability of being within one standard deviation from the mean is about 68 percent.
    c. The probability of being within two standard deviations from the mean is about 95 percent.
    d. The probability of a negative value is always one-half.

14. **Normal Distribution**   Based on a normal distribution with a mean of 500 and a standard deviation of 150, the z-value for an observation of 200 is closest to:

    a. -2.00
    b. -1.75
    c. 1.75
    d. 2.00

15. **Normal Distribution**   A normal distribution would least likely be described as:

    a. Asymptotic.
    b. A discreet probability distribution.

    c. A symmetrical or bell-shaped distribution.

    d. A curve that theoretically extends from negative infinity to positive infinity.

Concept Questions

1. **Risk versus Return** Based on the historical record, rank the following investments in increasing order of risk. Rank the investments in increasing order of average returns. What do you conclude about the relationship between the risk of an investment and the return you expect to earn on it?

   a. Large stocks
   b. Treasury bills
   c. Long-term government bonds
   d. Small stocks

2. **Return Calculations** A particular stock had a return last year of 4 percent. However, you look at the stock price and notice that it actually didn't change at all last year. How is this possible?

3. **Returns Distributions** What is the probability that the return on small stocks will be less than −100 percent in a single year (think about it)? What are the implications for the distribution of returns?

4. **Arithmetic versus Geometric Returns** What is the difference between arithmetic and geometric returns? Suppose you have invested in a stock for the last 10 years. Which number is more important to you, the arithmetic or geometric return?

5. **Blume's Formula** What is Blume's formula? When would you want to use it in practice?

6. **Inflation and Returns** Look at Table 1.1 and Figures 1.5 and 1.6. When were T-bill rates at their highest? Why do you think they were so high during this period?

7. **Inflation and Returns** The returns we have examined are not adjusted for inflation. What do you suppose would happen to our estimated risk premiums if we did account for inflation?

8. **Taxes and Returns** The returns we have examined are not adjusted for taxes. What do you suppose would happen to our estimated returns and risk premiums if we did account for taxes? What would happen to our volatility measures?

9. **Taxes and Treasury Bills** As a practical matter, most of the return you earn from investing in Treasury bills is taxed right away as ordinary income. Thus, if you are in a 40 percent tax bracket and you earn 5 percent on a Treasury bill, your aftertax return is only $.05 \times (1 - .40) = .03$, or 3 percent. In other words, 40 percent of your return goes to pay taxes, leaving you with just 3 percent. Once you consider inflation and taxes, how does the long-term return from Treasury bills look?

10. **The Long Run** Given your answer to the last question and the discussion in the chapter, why would any rational person do anything other than load up on 100 percent small stocks?

Questions and Problems

Core Questions

1. **Calculating Returns** Suppose you bought 100 shares of stock at an initial price of $65 per share. The stock paid a dividend of $1.70 per share during the following year, and the share price at the end of the year was $73. Compute your total dollar return on this investment. Does your answer change if you keep the stock instead of selling it? Why or why not?

2. **Calculating Yields** In the previous problem, what is the capital gains yield? The dividend yield? What is the total rate of return on the investment?

3. **Calculating Returns**   Rework Problems 1 and 2 assuming that you buy 750 shares of the stock and the ending share price is $56.25.

4. **Historical Returns**   What is the historical rate of return on each of the following investments? What is the historical risk premium on these investments?

   a. Long-term government bonds
   b. Treasury bills
   c. Large stocks
   d. Small stocks

5. **Calculating Average Returns**   The rate of return on Jurassic Jalopies, Inc., stock over the last five years was 18 percent, 28 percent, −22 percent, 6 percent, and 9 percent. Over the same period, the return on Stonehenge Construction Company's stock was 4 percent, 10 percent, −3 percent, 8 percent, and 6 percent. What was the arithmetic average return on each stock over this period?

6. **Calculating Returns and Variability**   Using the following returns, calculate the arithmetic average returns, the variances, and the standard deviations for stocks A and B.

Year	A	B
1	16%	38%
2	5	−5
3	−10	−10
4	32	21
5	11	17

7. **Return Calculations**   A particular stock has a dividend yield of 3.2 percent. Last year, the stock price fell from $60 to $53. What was the return for the year?

8. **Geometric Returns**   A stock has had returns of 18 percent, −6 percent, 9 percent, 25 percent, and 12 percent over the last five years. What is the geometric return for the stock?

9. **Arithmetic and Geometric Returns**   A stock has had returns of 34 percent, 3 percent, 11 percent, −2 percent, −24 percent, and 27 percent over the last six years. What are the arithmetic and geometric returns for the stock?

Intermediate Questions

10. **Returns and the Bell Curve**   An investment has an expected return of 11 percent per year with a standard deviation of 22 percent. Assuming that the returns on this investment are at least roughly normally distributed, how frequently do you expect to earn between −11 percent and +33 percent? How often do you expect to earn less than −11 percent?

11. **Returns and the Bell Curve**   An investment has an expected return of 6 percent per year with a standard deviation of 3 percent. Assuming that the returns on this investment are at least roughly normally distributed, how frequently do you expect to lose money?

12. **Using Returns Distributions**   Based on the historical record, if you invest in long-term U.S. Treasury bonds, what is the approximate probability that your return will be less than −3.6 percent in a given year? What range of returns would you expect to see 95 percent of the time? 99 percent of the time?

13. **Using Returns Distributions**   Based on the historical record, what is the approximate probability that an investment in small stocks will double in value in a single year? How about triple in a single year?

14. **Risk Premiums**   Refer to Table 1.1 for large-stock and T-bill returns for the period 1973–1977:

    a. Calculate the observed risk premium in each year for the common stocks.

   b. Calculate the average returns and the average risk premium over this period.

   c. Calculate the standard deviation of returns and the standard deviation of the risk premium.

   d. Is it possible that the observed risk premium can be negative? Explain how this can happen and what it means.

15. **Geometric Return**   Your grandfather invested $1,000 in a stock 45 years ago. Currently the value of his account is $285,000. What is his geometric return over this period?

16. **Forecasting Returns**   You have found an asset with a 13.1 percent arithmetic average return and a 10.2 percent geometric return. Your observation period is 40 years. What is your best estimate of the return of the asset over the next 5 years? 10 years? 20 years?

17. **Geometric Averages**   Look back to Figure 1.1 and find the value of $1 invested in each asset class over this 77-year period. Calculate the geometric return for small-company stocks, long-term government bonds, Treasury bills, and inflation.

18. **Arithmetic and Geometric Returns**   A stock has returns of 38 percent, 24 percent, 18 percent, −15 percent, and 2 percent. What are the arithmetic and geometric returns?

19. **Arithmetic and Geometric Returns**   A stock has had the following year-end prices and dividends:

Year	Price	Dividend
0	$41.07	$ –
1	48.20	0.55
2	56.10	0.60
3	50.96	0.63
4	55.03	0.72
5	68.29	0.81

   What are the arithmetic and geometric returns for the stock?

20. **Arithmetic versus Geometric Returns**   You are given the returns for the following three stocks:

Year	Stock A	Stock B	Stock C
1	10%	7%	−10%
2	10	14	28
3	10	9	19
4	10	8	2
5	10	12	11

   Calculate the arithmetic return, geometric return, and standard deviation for each stock. Do you notice anything about the relationship between an asset's arithmetic return, standard deviation, and geometric return? Do you think this relationship will always hold?

Spreadsheet Problems

21. **Return and Standard Deviation**   The 1980s was a good decade for investors in S&P 500 stocks. To find out how good, construct a spreadsheet that calculates the arithmetic average return, variance, and standard deviation for the S&P 500 returns during the 1980s using spreadsheet functions.

www.mhhe.com/cj3e

STANDARD
&POOR'S

S&P Problems

www.mhhe.com/edumarketinsight

1. **Industry Comparison**   On the Market Insight Home Page, follow the "Industry" link to go to the industry home page. The drop down menu allows you to select different industries. Answer the following questions for these industries: Air Freight & Logistics, Apparel Retail, Department Stores, Electric Utilities, Home Improvement Retail, Investment Banking & Brokerage, and Regional Banks.

    a. How many companies are in each industry?
    b. What are the total sales in each industry?
    c. Do the industries with the largest total sales have the most companies in the industry? What does this tell you about competition in the various industries?

2. **Calculating Returns**   Download the historical stock prices for Boeing (BA) under the "Mthly. Adj. Prices" link. Use the closing stock prices to calculate the monthly return each month for the last twelve months. Do your calculations match the return calculations given in the file? Why or why not? Now calculate the dividends paid each month.

3. **Calculating Standard Deviation**   Download the historical stock prices for Canon (CAJ) under the "Mthly. Adj. Prices" link. Using the monthly returns in the file, calculate the monthly standard deviation of Canon stock for the past twelve months.

What's on the Web?

1. **Ticker Symbols**   Go to finance.yahoo.com and look up the ticker symbols for the following companies: 3M Company, International Business Machines, Dell Computer, Advanced Micro Devices, American Standard Company, and Bed, Bath & Beyond.

2. **Average Return and Standard Deviation**   Go to finance.yahoo.com and enter the ticker symbol for your favorite stock. Now, look for the historical prices and find the monthly closing stock price for the last six years. Calculate the annual arithmetic average return, the standard deviation, and the geometric return for this period.

3. **Stock Performance**   What are the best-performing stocks over the past year? Go to finance.yahoo.com and select the "Stock Screener" link. You will see a "Performance" category and a pull-down menu labeled "1 Yr Stock Perf." Select "Up more than 200%" and "Find Stocks." How many stocks have increased more than 200 percent over the past year? Now go back and select "Down more than 90%." How many stocks have dropped more than 90 percent in value over the past year?

Stock-Trak®
Portfolio Simulations

Portfolio Trading Simulations with Stock-Trak

Stock-Trak provides an effective, low-cost way to learn the basics of securities trading on the Internet. With a Stock-Trak account, you can trade stocks, bonds, options, and futures through the Stock-Trak website (www.mhhe.com/cj3e). Stock-Trak trading is conducted in much the same way as you would trade through your own brokerage account with a broker that supports trading on the Internet. With the Stock-Trak Portfolio Trading Simulation you gain valuable experience trading securities at actual market prices. However, you can't lose real money since Stock-Trak is a simulation.

This textbook contains several sections intended to provide specialized instructions on trading securities through Stock-Trak. We recommend that you start by reading the section *"Trading Common Stocks with Stock-Trak"* at the end of Chapter 2. This section will bring you up to speed on the mechanics of trading common stocks on the Internet. Similar Stock-Trak sections are dispersed throughout the textbook. For example, the section *"Trading Stock Options with Stock-Trak"* at the end of Chapter 14 explains how ticker symbols for stock options must be constructed before submitting an order to trade stock options on the Internet through Stock-Trak. Similarly, the section *"Trading Futures Contracts with Stock-Trak"* at the end of Chapter 16 discusses the intricacies of submitting orders to trade futures contracts. These sections are designed to supplement instructions provided by Stock-Trak in its brochure and on the Stock-Trak website. Remember, you can't lose real money with Stock-Trak, so feel free to experiment!

Stock-Trak Exercises

1. Log on to the Stock-Trak website through www.mhhe.com/cj3e.

2. While logged on to the Stock-Trak website, review the most current rules and regulations pertaining to Stock-Trak accounts.

3. Explore some of the Internet links to stock market research tools provided by Stock-Trak.

4. Look up stock ticker symbols for these companies: American Express, Delta Air Lines, ExxonMobil, Liz Claiborne, McDonald's, Procter & Gamble, and Xerox.

5. Some companies have ticker symbols with only a single letter, for example, the letters A, B, C, D, E, F, G, K, L, N, O, Q, R, S, T, V, X, Y, and Z are one-letter tickers. What are these companies' names?

6. Can you guess what the company names are for the ticker symbols AAPL, BUD, DIS, FDX, LZB, PEP, PILL, PZZA, REV, SBUX, TOY, and YUM?

www.mhhe.com/cj3e

Chapter 2

Buying and Selling Securities

"Don't gamble! Take all your savings and buy some good stock and hold it till it goes up. If it don't go up, don't buy it."

–Will Rogers

You might wish to try Will Rogers's well-known stock market advice, but first you must know the basics of securities trading. Fortunately, trading is a relatively simple task, as attested to by the billions of shares of stocks that trade among investors on a typical day. Essentially, you begin the process by opening a trading account with a brokerage firm and then submitting trading orders. But you should know about some important details beforehand. ■

We hope reading about the history of risk and return in our previous chapter generated some interest in investing on your own. To help you get started, this chapter covers the basics of the investing process. We begin by describing how you go about buying and selling securities such as stocks and bonds. We then outline some of the most important considerations and constraints to keep in mind as you get more involved in the investing process.

2.1   Getting Started

Suppose you have some money that you want to invest. One way to get started is to open an account with a securities broker, such as A.G. Edwards or Merrill Lynch. Such accounts are often called *brokerage* or *trading accounts*. Opening a trading account is straightforward and really much like opening a bank account. You will be asked to supply some basic information about yourself and sign an agreement (often simply called a customer's agreement) that spells out your rights and obligations and those of your broker. You then give your broker a check and instructions on how you want the money invested.

To illustrate, suppose that instead of going to Disneyland, you would rather own part of it. You therefore open an account with $10,000. You instruct your broker to purchase 100 shares of Walt Disney stock and to retain any remaining funds in your account. Your broker will locate a seller and purchase the stock on your behalf. Say shares of stock in Walt Disney Corporation are selling for about $60 per share, so your 100 shares will cost $6,000. In addition, for providing this service, your broker will charge you a commission. How much depends on a number of things, including the type of broker and the size of your order, but on this order, $50 wouldn't be an unusual commission charge. After paying for the stock and paying the commission, you would have $3,950 left in your account. Your broker will hold your stock for you or deliver the shares to you, whichever you wish. At a later date, you can sell your stock by instructing your broker to do so. You would receive the proceeds from the sale, less another commission charge. You can always add money to your account and purchase additional securities, and you can withdraw money from your account or even close it altogether.

In broad terms, this basic explanation is really all there is to it. As we begin to discuss in the next section, however, there is a range of services available to you, and there are important considerations that you need to take into account before you actually begin investing.

Choosing a Broker

The first step in opening an account is choosing a broker. Brokers are traditionally divided into three groups: full-service brokers, discount brokers, and deep-discount brokers. Table 2.1 lists well-known brokers in each category. What distinguishes the three groups is the level of service they provide and the resulting commissions they charge.

With a deep-discount broker, essentially the only services provided are account maintenance and order execution—that is, buying and selling. You generally deal with a deep-discount broker over the telephone or, increasingly, using a Web browser (see the next section on online brokers for a discussion).

At the other extreme, a full-service broker will provide investment advice regarding the types of securities and investment strategies that might be appropriate for you to consider (or avoid). The larger brokerage firms do extensive research on individual companies and securities and maintain lists of recommended (and not recommended) securities. They maintain offices throughout the country, so, depending on where you live, you can actually stop in and speak to the person assigned to your account. A full-service broker will even manage your account for you if you wish.

Discount brokers fall somewhere between the two cases we have discussed so far, offering more investment counseling than the deep-discounters and lower commissions

TABLE 2.1	Brokerage Firms and Representative Commissions		
	Commissions ($20 share price)*		
Examples	100 Shares	500 Shares	1,000 Shares
Full-Service Brokers			
A.G. Edwards	$70	$240	$400
Merrill Lynch			
Discount Brokers			
Charles Schwab	$55	$110	$180
Fidelity Brokerage			
Deep-Discount Brokers			
Olde Discount	$50	$ 85	$110
Quick & Reilly			

*These commissions are approximate and representative only. They do not necessarily correspond to actual rates charged by firms listed in this table. Only "market" orders are considered.

than the full-service brokers. Which type of broker should you choose? It depends on how much advice and service you need or want. If you are the do-it-yourself type, then you may seek out the lower commissions. If you are not, then a full-service broker might be more suitable. Often investors begin with a full-service broker, then, as they gain experience and confidence, move on to a discount broker.

We should note that the brokerage industry is very competitive, and differences between broker types seem to be blurring. Full-service brokers frequently discount commissions to attract new customers (particularly those with large accounts), and you should not hesitate to ask about commission rates. Similarly, discount brokers have begun to offer securities research and extensive account management services. Basic brokerage services have become almost commodity-like, and, more and more, brokerage firms are competing by offering financial services such as retirement planning, credit cards, and check-writing privileges, to name a few.

Online Brokers

The most important recent change in the brokerage industry is the rapid growth of online brokers, also known as e-brokers or cyberbrokers. With an online broker, you place buy and sell orders over the Internet using a Web browser. If you are currently participating in a portfolio simulation such as Stock-Trak, then you already have a very good idea of how an online account looks and feels.

Before 1995, online accounts essentially did not exist; by 2000, many millions of investors were buying and selling securities online. The industry is growing so rapidly that it is difficult to even count the number of online brokers. By 2000, the number was at least 100, but the final tally will probably be much larger.

Online investing has fundamentally changed the discount and deep-discount brokerage industry by slashing costs dramatically. In a typical online trade, no human intervention is needed by the broker as the entire process is handled electronically, so operating costs are held to a minimum. As costs have fallen, so have commissions. Even for relatively large trades, online brokers typically charge less than $20 per trade. For budget-minded investors and active stock traders, the attraction is clear.

TABLE 2.2	Top-Rated Full-Service and Discount Brokerages
Broker	**Internet Address**
Full-Service Brokers	
1. Salomon Smith Barney	www.smithbarney.com
2. Merrill Lynch Online	www.ml.com
3. UBS PaineWebber	financialservices.ubs.com
4. Morgan Stanley	www.morganstanley.com
5. Wells Fargo Investments	www.wellsfargo.com
6. Prudential Financial	www.prudential.com
7. DB Alex Brown	www.alexbrown.db.com
8. McDonald Investments	www.key.com
9. Piper Jaffray	www.piperjaffray.com
10. Legg Mason	www.leggmason.com
Discount Brokers	
1. Charles Schwab	www.schwab.com
2. Fidelity Investments	www.fidelity.com
3. E*Trade	www.etrade.com
4. Harrisdirect	www.harrisdirect.com
5. TD Waterhouse	www.waterhouse.com
6. Ameritrade	www.ameritrade.com
7. Quick & Reilly	www.quickandreilly.com
8. Scottrade	www.scottrade.com
9. Cititrade	www.mycititrade.com
10. American Express Brokerage	www.americanexpress.com
11. Muriel Siebert	www.murielsiebert.com
12. T. Rowe Price Brokerage	www.troweprice.com
13. JB Oxford	www.jboxford.com
14. Firstrade	www.firstrade.com
15. Vanguard	www.vanguard.com
16. Netvest	www.netvest.com
17. Brown	www.brownco3.com
18. Bank One	www.bankone.com

Which online broker is the best? See ratings at www.gomez.com

Competition among online brokers is fierce. Some take a no-frills approach, offering only basic services and very low commission rates. Others, particularly the larger ones, charge a little more but offer a variety of services, including research and various banking services such as check-writing privileges, credit cards, debit cards, and even mortgages. As technology continues to improve and investors become more comfortable using it, online brokerages will almost surely become the dominant form because of their enormous convenience—and the low commission rates.

When online brokers first appeared they were generally just discount and deep-discount brokers. Today, however, even full-service brokers offer extensive online services. Table 2.2 lists the top 10 full-service brokers and top 18 discount brokers based on online performance ratings carried out by Gomez Internet Quality Management.

Remember, however, that the online brokerage business continues to evolve, so these ratings are likely to change frequently.

Security Investors Protection Corporation

As you are probably aware, when you deposit money in a bank, your account is normally protected (up to $100,000) by the Federal Deposit Insurance Corporation, or FDIC, which is an agency of the U.S. government. However, brokerage firms, even though they are often called investment banks, cannot offer FDIC coverage. Most brokerage firms do belong to the **Security Investors Protection Corporation**, or **SIPC**, which was created in 1970. The SIPC insures your account for up to $500,000 in cash and securities, with a $100,000 cash maximum. Some brokers carry additional insurance beyond SIPC minimums. Unlike the FDIC, the SIPC is not a government agency; it is a private insurance fund supported by the securities industry. However, by government regulations, almost all brokerage firms operating in the United States are required to be members of the SIPC.

There is a very important difference between SIPC coverage and FDIC coverage. Up to the maximum coverage, the value of whatever you deposit in a bank is fully guaranteed by the FDIC; you will not lose a cent under any circumstances with FDIC coverage. In contrast, the SIPC insures only that you will receive whatever cash and securities were held for you by your broker in the event of fraud or other failure. The value of any securities, however, is not guaranteed. In other words, you can lose everything in an SIPC-covered account if the value of your securities falls to zero.

Broker–Customer Relations

There are several other important things to keep in mind when dealing with a broker. First, any advice you receive is *not* guaranteed. Far from it—buy and sell recommendations carry the explicit warning that you rely on them at your own risk. Your broker does have a duty to exercise reasonable care in formulating recommendations and not recommend anything grossly unsuitable, but that is essentially the extent of it.

Second, your broker works as your agent and has a legal duty to act in your best interest; however, brokerage firms are in the business of generating brokerage commissions. This fact will probably be spelled out in the account agreement that you sign. There is, therefore, the potential for a conflict of interest. On rare occasions, a broker is accused of "churning" an account, which refers to extensive trading for the sole purpose of generating commissions. In general, you are responsible for checking your account statements and notifying your broker in the event of any problems, and you should certainly do so.

Finally, in the unlikely event of a significant problem, your account agreement will probably specify very clearly that you must waive your right to sue and/or seek a jury trial. Instead, you agree that any disputes will be settled by arbitration and that arbitration is final and binding. Arbitration is not a legal proceeding, and the rules are much less formal. In essence, a panel is appointed by a self-regulatory body of the securities industry to review the case. The panel will be composed of a small number of individuals who are knowledgeable about the securities industry, but a majority of them will not be associated with the industry. The panel makes a finding, and, absent extraordinary circumstances, its findings cannot be appealed. The panel does not have to disclose factual findings or legal reasoning.

Security Investors Protection Corporation (SIPC) Insurance fund covering investors' brokerage accounts with member firms.

To learn more about dispute resolution, visit www.nasd.com

Check This

2.1a	What are the differences between full-service and deep-discount brokers?
2.1b	What is the SIPC? How does SIPC coverage differ from FDIC coverage?

2.2 Brokerage Accounts

The account agreement that you sign has a number of important provisions and details specifying the types of trades that can be made and who can make them. Another important concern is whether the broker will extend credit and the terms under which credit will be extended. We discuss these issues next.

Cash Accounts

cash account A brokerage account in which all transactions are made on a strictly cash basis.

A **cash account** is the simplest arrangement. Securities can be purchased to the extent that sufficient cash is available in the account. If additional purchases are desired, then the needed funds must be promptly supplied.

Margin Accounts

margin account A brokerage account in which, subject to limits, securities can be bought and sold on credit.

call money rate The interest rate brokers pay to borrow bank funds for lending to customer margin accounts.

With a **margin account**, you can, subject to limits, purchase securities on credit using money loaned to you by your broker. Such a purchase is called a *margin purchase*. The interest rate you pay on the money you borrow is based on the broker's **call money rate**, which is, loosely, the rate the broker pays to borrow the money. You pay some amount over the call money rate, called the *spread;* the exact spread depends on your broker and the size of the loan. Suppose the call money rate has been hovering around 7 percent. If a brokerage firm charges a 2.5 percent spread above this rate on loan amounts under $10,000, then you would pay a total of about 9.5 percent. However, this is usually reduced for larger loan amounts. For example, the spread may decline to .75 percent for amounts over $100,000.

There are several important concepts and rules involved in a margin purchase. For concreteness, we focus on stocks in our discussion. The specific margin rules for other investments can be quite different, but the principles and terminology are usually similar.

margin The portion of the value of an investment that is *not* borrowed.

In general, when you purchase securities on credit, some of the money is yours and the rest is borrowed. The amount that is yours is called the **margin**. Margin is usually expressed as a percentage. For example, if you take $7,000 of your own money and borrow an additional $3,000 from your broker, your total investment will be $10,000. Of this $10,000, $7,000 is yours, so the margin is $7,000 / $10,000 = .70, or 70 percent.

It is useful to create an account balance sheet when thinking about margin purchases (and some other issues we'll get to in just a moment). To illustrate, suppose you open a margin account with $5,000. You tell your broker to buy 100 shares of Microsoft. Microsoft is selling for $80 per share, so the total cost will be $8,000. Since you have only $5,000 in the account, you borrow the remaining $3,000. Immediately following the purchase, your account balance sheet would look like this:

Assets		Liabilities and Account Equity	
100 shares of Microsoft	$8,000	Margin loan	$3,000
		Account equity	5,000
Total	$8,000	Total	$8,000

On the left-hand side of this balance sheet we list the account assets, which, in this case, consist of the $8,000 in Microsoft stock you purchased. On the right-hand side we first list the $3,000 loan you took out to partially pay for the stock; this is a liability because, at some point, the loan must be repaid. The difference between the value of the assets held in the account and the loan amount is $5,000. This amount is your *account equity*, that is, the net value of your investment. Notice that your margin is equal to the account equity divided by the value of the stock owned and held in the account: $5,000 / $8,000 = .625, or 62.5 percent.

THE ACCOUNT BALANCE SHEET

EXAMPLE 2.1

You want to buy 1,000 shares of Wal-Mart at a price of $24 per share. You put up $18,000 and borrow the rest. What does your account balance sheet look like? What is your margin?

The 1,000 shares of Wal-Mart cost $24,000. You supply $18,000, so you must borrow $6,000. The account balance sheet looks like this:

Assets		Liabilities and Account Equity	
1,000 shares of Wal-Mart	$24,000	Margin loan	$ 6,000
		Account equity	18,000
Total	$24,000	Total	$24,000

Your margin is the account equity divided by the value of the stock owned:

Margin = $18,000 / $24,000

= .75 = 75 percent

initial margin The minimum margin that must be supplied on a securities purchase.

Initial Margin When you first purchase securities on credit, there is a minimum margin that you must supply. This percentage is called the **initial margin**. The minimum percentage (for stock purchases) is set by the Federal Reserve (the "Fed"), but the exchanges and individual brokerage firms may require higher amounts.

The Fed's power to set initial margin requirements was established in the Securities Exchange Act of 1934. In subsequent years, initial margin requirements ranged from a low of 45 percent to a high of 100 percent. Since 1974, the minimum has been 50 percent (for stock purchases). In other words, if you have $10,000 in cash that is not borrowed, you can borrow up to an additional $10,000, but no more.

We emphasize that these initial margin requirements apply to stocks. In contrast, for the most part, there is little initial margin requirement for government bonds. On the other hand, margin is not allowed at all on certain other types of securities.

CALCULATING INITIAL MARGIN

EXAMPLE 2.2

Suppose you have $6,000 in cash in a trading account with a 50 percent initial margin requirement. What is the largest order you can place (ignoring commissions)? If the initial margin were 60 percent, how would your answer change?

When the initial margin is 50 percent, you must supply half of the total, so $12,000 is the largest order you could place. When the initial margin is 60 percent, your $6,000 must equal 60 percent of the total. In other words, it must be the case that

$$\$6,000 = 0.60 \times \text{Total order}$$

$$\text{Total order} = \$6,000 \,/\, .60$$

$$= \$10,000$$

As this example illustrates, the higher the initial margin required, the less you can borrow.

maintenance margin
The minimum margin that must be present at all times in a margin account.

Maintenance Margin In addition to the initial margin requirement set by the Fed, brokerage firms and exchanges generally have a **maintenance margin** requirement. For example, the New York Stock Exchange (NYSE) requires a minimum of 25 percent maintenance margin. This amount is the minimum margin required at all times after the purchase.

The maintenance margin set by your broker is sometimes called the "house" margin requirement. The level is established by your broker, who may vary it depending on what you are buying. For low-priced and very volatile stocks, the house margin can be as high as 100 percent, meaning no margin at all.

margin call A demand for more funds that occurs when the margin in an account drops below the maintenance margin.

A typical maintenance margin would be 30 percent. If your margin falls below 30 percent, then you may be subject to a **margin call**, which is a demand by your broker to add to your account, pay off part of the loan, or sell enough securities to bring your margin back up to an acceptable level. If you do not or cannot comply, your securities may be sold. The loan will be repaid out of the proceeds, and any remaining amounts will be credited to your account.

To illustrate, suppose your account has a 50 percent initial margin requirement and a 30 percent maintenance margin. A particular stock is selling for $50 per share. You have $20,000, and you want to buy as much of this stock as you possibly can. With a 50 percent initial margin, you buy up to $40,000 worth, or 800 shares. The account balance sheet looks like this:

Assets		Liabilities and Account Equity	
800 shares @$50/share	$40,000	Margin loan	$20,000
		Account equity	20,000
Total	$40,000	Total	$40,000

Unfortunately, right after you buy it, the company reveals that it has been artificially inflating earnings for the last three years (this is not good), and the share price falls to $35 per share. What does the account balance sheet look like when this happens? Are you subject to a margin call?

To create the new account balance sheet, we recalculate the total value of the stock. The margin loan stays the same, so the account equity is adjusted as needed:

Assets		Liabilities and Account Equity	
800 shares @$35/share	$28,000	Margin loan	$20,000
		Account equity	8,000
Total	$28,000	Total	$28,000

As shown, the total value of your "position" (i.e., the stock you hold) falls to $28,000, a $12,000 loss. You still owe $20,000 to your broker, so your account equity is $28,000 − $20,000 = $8,000. Your margin is therefore $8,000 / $28,000 = .286, or 28.6 percent. You are below the 30 percent minimum, so you are undermargined and subject to a margin call.

The Effects of Margin Margin is a form of *financial leverage*. Any time you borrow money to make an investment, the impact is to magnify both your gains and losses, hence the use of the term "leverage." The easiest way to see this is through an example. Imagine that you have $30,000 in an account with a 60 percent initial margin. You now know that you can borrow up to an additional $20,000 and buy $50,000 worth of stock (why?). The call money rate is 5.50 percent; you must pay this rate plus a .50 percent spread. Suppose you buy 1,000 shares of IBM at $50 per share. One year later, IBM is selling for $60 per share. Assuming the call money rate does not change and ignoring dividends, what is your return on this investment?

At the end of the year, your 1,000 shares are worth $60,000. You owe 6 percent interest on the $20,000 you borrowed, or $1,200. If you pay off the loan with interest, you will have $60,000 − $21,200 = $38,800. You started with $30,000 and ended with $38,800, so your net gain is $8,800. In percentage terms, your return was $8,800/ $30,000 = .2933, or 29.33 percent.

How would you have done without the financial leverage created from the margin purchase? In this case, you would have invested just $30,000. At $50 per share, you would have purchased 600 shares. At the end of the year, your 600 shares would be worth $60 apiece, or $36,000 total. Your dollar profit is $6,000, so your percentage return would be $6,000 / $30,000 = .20, or 20 percent. If we compare this to the 29.33 percent that you made above, it's clear that you did substantially better by leveraging.

The downside is that you would do much worse if IBM's stock price fell (or didn't rise very much). For example, if IBM had fallen to $40 a share, you would have lost (check these calculations for practice) $11,200, or 37.33 percent on your margin investment, compared to $6,000, or 20 percent on the unmargined investment. This example illustrates how leveraging an investment through a margin account can cut both ways.

A MARGINAL INVESTMENT?

EXAMPLE 2.3

A year ago, you bought 300 shares of Ford at $55 per share. You put up the 60 percent initial margin. The call money rate plus the spread you paid was 8 percent. What is your return if the price today is $50? Compare this to the return you would have earned if you had not invested on margin.

(continued)

Your total investment was 300 shares at $55 per share, or $16,500. You supplied 60 percent, or $9,900, and you borrowed the remaining $6,600. At the end of the year, you owe $6,600 plus 8 percent interest, or $7,128. If the stock sells for $50, then your position is worth 300 × $50 = $15,000. Deducting the $7,128 leaves $7,872 for you. Since you originally invested $9,900, your dollar loss is $9,900 − $7,872 = $2,028. Your percentage return is −$2,028/$9,900 = −20.48 percent.

If you had not leveraged your investment, you would have purchased $9,900/$55 = 180 shares. These would have been worth 180 × $50 = $9,000. You therefore would have lost $900; your percentage return would have been −$900/$9,900 = −9.09 percent, compared to the −20.48 percent that you lost on your leveraged position.

HOW LOW CAN IT GO?

EXAMPLE 2.4

In our previous example (Example 2.3), suppose the maintenance margin was 40 percent. At what price per share would you have been subject to a margin call?

To answer, let P^* be the critical price. You own 300 shares, so, at that price, your stock is worth $300 \times P^*$. You borrowed $6,600, so your account equity is equal to the value of your stock less the $6,600 you owe, or $300 \times P^* - \$6,600$. We can summarize this information as follows:

$$\text{Amount borrowed} = \$6,600$$
$$\text{Value of stock} = 300 \times P^*$$
$$\text{Account equity} = 300 \times P^* - \$6,600$$

From our preceding discussion, your percentage margin is your dollar margin (or account equity) divided by the value of the stock:

$$\text{Margin} = \frac{\text{Account equity}}{\text{Value of stock}}$$

$$= \frac{300 \times P^* - \$6,600}{300 \times P^*}$$

To find the critical price, we will set this margin to the maintenance margin and solve for P^*:

$$\text{Maintenance margin} = \frac{\text{Number of shares} \times P^* - \text{Amount borrowed}}{\text{Number of shares} \times P^*}$$

Solving for P^* yields

$$P^* = \frac{\text{Amount borrowed / Number of shares}}{1 - \text{Maintenance margin}}$$

Finally, setting the maintenance margin equal to 40 percent, we obtain this critical price for P^*:

$$P^* = \frac{\$6,600 / 300}{1 - .40}$$

$$= \frac{\$6,600}{180} = \$36.67$$

At any price below $36.67, your margin will be less than 40 percent, and you will be subject to a margin call, so this is the lowest possible price that could be reached before that occurs.

As Example 2.4 shows, you can calculate the critical price (the lowest price before you get a margin call) as follows:

$$P^* = \frac{\text{Amount borrowed / Number of shares}}{1 - \text{Maintenance margin}} \qquad (2.1)$$

For example, suppose you had a margin loan of $40,000, which you used to purchase, in part, 1,000 shares. The maintenance margin is 37.5 percent. What's the critical stock price, and how do you interpret it?

See if you don't agree that the critical stock price, P^*, is $40/.625 = $64. The interpretation is straightforward: If the stock price falls below $64, you're subject to a margin call.

A Note on Annualizing Returns

In Chapter 1, we talked about the need to compute percentage returns, but, so far, we've only considered annual returns. Of course, the actual length of time you own an investment will almost never be exactly a year. To compare investments, however, we will usually need to express returns on a per-year or "annualized" basis, so we need to do a little bit more work.

For example, suppose you bought 200 shares of Cisco at a price of $80 per share. In three months, you sell your stock for $85. You didn't receive any dividends. What is your return for the three months? What is your annualized return?

In this case, we say that your *holding period*, which is the length of time you own the stock, is three months. From our discussion in Chapter 1, with a zero dividend, you know that the percentage return can be calculated as:

Percentage return = $(P_{t+1} - P_t) / P_t$ = ($85 - $80)/$80 = .0625 = 6.25%

This 6.25 percent is your return for the three-month holding period, but what does this return amount to on a per-year basis? To find out, we need to convert this to an annualized return, meaning a return expressed on a per-year basis. Such a return is often called an **effective annual return**, or EAR for short. The general formula is this:

effective annual return (EAR) The return on an investment expressed on a per-year, or "annualized," basis.

$$1 + EAR = (1 + \text{holding period percentage return})^m \qquad (2.2)$$

where m is the number of holding periods in a year.

In our example, the holding period percentage return is 6.25 percent, or .0625. The holding period is three months, so there are four (12 months/3 months) periods in a year. The annualized return, or *EAR*, is thus:

$$\begin{aligned}1 + EAR &= (1 + \text{holding period percentage return})^m \\ &= (1 + .0625)^4 \\ &= 1.2744\end{aligned}$$

So, your annualized return is 27.44 percent.

A "QWEST" FOR RETURNS

EXAMPLE 2.5

Suppose you buy some stock in Qwest (no, that's not a typo, that's how the company spells it) at a price of $60 per share. Four months later, you sell it for $63. No dividend is paid. What is your annualized return on this investment?

(continued)

For the four-month holding period, your return is:

Percentage return $= (P_{t+1} - P_t) / P_t = (\$63 - \$60)/\$60 = .05 = 5\%$

There are three four-month periods in a year, so the annualized return is:

$$1 + EAR = (1 + \text{holding period percentage return})^m$$
$$= (1 + .05)^3$$
$$= 1.1576$$

Subtracting the one, we get an annualized return of .1576, or 15.76 percent.

MORE ANNUALIZED RETURNS

EXAMPLE 2.6

Suppose you buy some stock in America Online at a price of $80 per share. Three *years* later, you sell it for $100. No dividends were paid. What is your annualized return on this investment?

The situation here is a bit different because your holding period is now longer than a year, but the calculation is basically the same. For the three-year holding period, your return is:

Percentage return $= (P_{t+1} - P_t) / P_t = (\$100 - \$80)/\$80 = .25 = 25\%$

How many three-year holding periods are there in a single year? The answer is one-third, so *m* in this case is 1/3. The annualized return is:

$$1 + EAR = (1 + \text{holding period percentage return})^m$$
$$= (1 + .25)^{1/3}$$
$$= 1.0772$$

Subtracting the one, we get an annualized return of .0772, or 7.72 percent.

Things get a little more complicated when we consider holding periods different from a year on a margin purchase. For example, suppose the call money rate is 9 percent, and you pay a spread of 2 percent over that. You buy 1,000 shares of Costco at $40 per share, but you only put up half the money. In three months, Costco is selling for $42 per share, and you close out your position. What is your annualized return assuming no dividends are paid?

In this case, you invested $40,000, half of which, $20,000, is borrowed. How much do you have to repay in three months? Here we have to adjust for the fact that the interest rate is 11 percent per year, but you only borrowed the money for three months. In this case, the amount you repay is equal to:

Amount repaid = Amount borrowed $\times$ $(1 + \text{interest rate year})^t$

where *t* is the fraction of a year. In our case, *t* would be 3 months/12 months, or .25. So, plugging in our numbers, we get:

$$\text{Amount repaid} = \text{Amount borrowed} \times (1 + \text{interest rate per year})^t$$
$$= \$20,000 \times (1 + .11)^{.25}$$
$$= \$20,000 \times 1.02643$$
$$= \$20,528.67$$

So, when you sell your stock, you get $42,000, of which $20,528.67 is used to pay off the loan, leaving you with $21,471.33. You invested $20,000, so your dollar gain is $1,471.33, and your percentage return for your three-month holding period is $1,471.33/$20,000 = .0736, or 7.36 percent.

Finally, we have to convert this 7.36 percent to an annualized return. There are four three-month periods in a year, so:

$$1 + EAR = (1 + \text{holding period percentage return})^m$$
$$= (1 + .0736)^4$$
$$= 1.3285$$

So, your annualized return is 32.85 percent.

Hypothecation and Street Name Registration

As part of your margin account agreement, you must agree to various conditions. We discuss two of the most important next.

Hypothecation Any securities you purchase in your margin account will be held by your broker as collateral against the loan made to you. This practice protects the broker because the securities can be sold by the broker if the customer is unwilling or unable to meet a margin call. Putting securities up as collateral against a loan is called **hypothecation**. In fact, a margin agreement is sometimes called a hypothecation agreement. In addition, to borrow the money that it loans to you, your broker will often *re*-hypothecate your securities, meaning that your broker will pledge them as collateral with its lender, normally a bank.

hypothecation
Pledging securities as collateral against a loan.

street name An arrangement under which a broker is the registered owner of a security.

Street Name Registration Securities in a margin account are normally held in **street name**. This means that the brokerage firm is actually the registered owner. If this were not the case, the brokerage firm could not legally sell the securities should a customer refuse to meet a margin call or otherwise fail to live up to the terms of the margin agreement. With this arrangement, the brokerage firm is the "owner of record," but the account holder is the "beneficial owner."

When a security is held in street name, anything mailed to the security owner, such as an annual report or a dividend check, goes to the brokerage firm. The brokerage firm then passes these on to the account holder. Street name ownership is actually a great convenience to the owner. In fact, because it is usually a free service, even customers with cash accounts generally choose street name ownership. Some of the benefits are:

1. Since the broker holds the security, there is no danger of theft or other loss of the security. This is important because a stolen or lost security cannot be easily or cheaply replaced.

2. Any dividends or interest payments are automatically credited, and they are often credited more quickly (and conveniently) than they would be if the owner received the check in the mail.

3. The broker provides regular account statements showing the value of securities held in the account and any payments received. Also, for tax purposes, the broker will provide all the needed information on a single form at the end of the year, greatly reducing the owner's record-keeping requirements.

Other Account Issues

If you do not wish to manage your account yourself, you can set up an *advisory account*. In this case, you pay someone else to make buy and sell decisions on your behalf. You are responsible for paying any commissions or other costs, as well as a management fee.

In a relatively recent innovation, brokerage firms have begun to offer *wrap accounts*. In such an account, you choose a money manager or set of money managers from a group offered by the brokerage firm. All of the costs, commissions, and expenses associated with your account are "wrapped" into a single fee that you pay, hence the name. If you simply authorize your broker to trade for you, then there is no management fee, but you are still responsible for any commissions. This arrangement is termed a *discretionary account*.

Most of the large brokerage firms offer accounts that provide for complete money management, including check-writing privileges, credit cards, and margin loans, especially for larger investors. Such accounts are generally called *asset management accounts*. The terms of these accounts differ from broker to broker, and the services provided frequently change in response to competition.

Finally, if you want to buy and sell a broad variety of individual securities, then a brokerage account is almost a requirement. It is true that some companies and other entities (such as the U.S. government) do sell directly to the public, at least at certain times and subject to various restrictions, so you can buy securities directly in some cases. In fact, you could buy and sell through the want ads in your local paper if you were so inclined, but given the modest commissions charged by deep-discount brokers, this hardly seems worth the trouble.

However, you should be aware that if you do not wish to actively buy and sell securities, but you do want to own stocks, bonds, or other financial assets, there is an alternative to a brokerage account: a *mutual fund*. Mutual funds are a means of combining or pooling the funds of a large group of investors. The buy and sell decisions for the resulting pool are then made by a fund manager, who is compensated for the service. Mutual funds have become so important that we will devote an entire chapter to them (Chapter 4) rather than give them short shrift here.

Check This

2.2a	What is the difference between a cash and margin account?
2.2b	What is the effect of a margin purchase on gains and losses?
2.2c	What is a margin call?

2.3 Short Sales

An investor who buys and owns shares of stock is said to be *long* in the stock or to have a *long position*. An investor with a long position will make money if the price of the stock increases and lose money if it goes down. In other words, a long investor hopes that the price will increase.

Now consider a different situation. Suppose you thought, for some reason, that the stock in a particular company was likely to *decrease* in value. You obviously wouldn't want to buy any of it. If you already owned some, you might choose to sell it.

short sale A sale in which the seller does not actually own the security that is sold.

Beyond this, you might decide to engage in a **short sale**. In a short sale, you actually sell a security that you do not own. This is referred to as *shorting* the stock. After the short sale, the investor is said to have a *short position* in the security.

Financial assets of all kinds are sold short, not just shares of stock, and the terms "long" and "short" are universal. However, the mechanics of a short sale differ quite a bit across security types. Even so, regardless of how the short sale is executed, the essence is the same. An investor with a long position benefits from price increases, and, as we will see, an investor with a short position benefits from price decreases. For the sake of illustration, we focus here on shorting shares of stock. Procedures for shorting other types of securities are discussed in later chapters.

Basics of a Short Sale

How can you sell stock you don't own? It is easier than you might think: You borrow the shares of stock from your broker and then you sell them. At some future date, you will buy the same number of shares that you originally borrowed and return them, thereby eliminating the short position. Eliminating the short position is often called *covering the position* or, less commonly, *curing the short*.

You might wonder where your broker will get the stock to loan you. Normally, it will simply come from other margin accounts. Often, when you open a margin account, you are asked to sign a loan-consent agreement, which gives your broker the right to loan shares held in the account. If shares you own are loaned out, you still receive any dividends or other distributions and you can sell the stock if you wish. In other words, the fact that some of your stock may have been loaned out is of little or no consequence as far as you are concerned.

An investor with a short position will profit if the security declines in value. For example, assume that you short 1,000 shares of Liz Claiborne at a price of $10 per share. You receive $10,000 from the sale (more on this in a moment). A month later, the stock is selling for $6 per share. You buy 1,000 shares for $6,000 and return the stock to your broker, thereby covering your position. Because you received $10,000 from the sale and it cost you only $6,000 to cover, you made $4,000.

Conventional Wall Street wisdom states that the way to make money is to "buy low, sell high." With a short sale, we hope to do exactly that, just in opposite order—sell high, buy low. If a short sale strikes you as a little confusing, it might help to think about the everyday use of the terms. Whenever we say that we are "running short" on something, we mean we don't have enough of it. Similarly, when someone says "don't sell me short" they mean don't bet on them not to succeed.

THE LONG AND SHORT OF IT

EXAMPLE 2.7

Suppose you short 2,000 shares of Lucent at $35 per share. Six months later you cover your short. If Lucent is selling for $30 per share at that time, did you make money or lose money? How much? What if you covered at $40?

If you shorted at $35 per share and covered at $30, you originally sold 2,000 shares at $35 and later bought them back at $30, so you made $5 per share, or $10,000. If you covered at $40, you lost $10,000.

Short Sales: Some Details

When you short a stock, you must borrow it from your broker, so there are various requirements you must fulfill. First, there is an initial margin and a maintenance margin. Second, after you sell the borrowed stock, the proceeds from the sale are credited to your account, but you cannot use them. They are, in effect, frozen until you return the stock. Finally, if there are any dividends paid on the stock while you have a short position, you must pay them.

To illustrate, we will again create an account balance sheet. Suppose you want to short 100 shares of Sears when the price is $30 per share. This means you will borrow shares of stock worth a total of $30 \times 100 = \$3,000$. Your broker has a 50 percent initial margin and a 40 percent maintenance margin on short sales.

An important thing to keep in mind with a margin purchase of securities is that margin is calculated as the value of your account equity relative to the value of the securities purchased. With a short sale, margin is calculated as the value of your account equity relative to the value of the securities sold short. Thus, in both cases margin is equal to equity value divided by security value.

In our example here, the initial value of the securities sold short is $3,000 and the initial margin is 50 percent, at a minimum, so you must deposit half of $3,000, or $1,500, in your account. With this in mind, after the short sale, your account balance sheet is as follows:

Assets		Liabilities and Account Equity	
Proceeds from sale	$3,000	Short position	$3,000
Initial margin deposit	1,500	Account equity	1,500
Total	$4,500	Total	$4,500

As shown, there are four items on the account balance sheet:

1. *Proceeds from sale.* This is the $3,000 you received when you sold the stock. This amount will remain in your account until you cover your position. Note that you will not earn interest on this amount—it will just sit there as far as you are concerned.

2. *Margin deposit.* This is the 50 percent margin that you had to post. This amount will not change unless there is a margin call. Depending on the circumstances and your particular account agreement, you may earn interest on the initial margin deposit.

3. *Short position.* Because you must eventually buy back the stock and return it, you have a liability. The current cost of eliminating that liability is $3,000.

4. *Account equity.* As always, the account equity is the difference between the total account value ($4,500) and the total liabilities ($3,000).

We now examine two scenarios: (1) the stock price falls to $20 per share, and (2) the stock price rises to $40 per share.

If the stock price falls to $20 per share, then you are still liable for 100 shares, but the cost of those shares is now just $2,000. Your account balance sheet becomes:

There are many sites devoted to the fine art of short selling. Try www.bearmarket central.com

Bumpy Market Reminds Investors to Assess Their Risk Tolerance

Do-It-You...
Courage o...

Risk

For many
peared fr
1990s, sto
down, mo
buying op
again.

But th
woken in
volatile t
ing an in

Did y
when it
for your
when th
and Apri
the mar

Thes
fact th
haven't
instead
riskless,

The
wealth
erage i
Shiller,
author
In the
think c

Unf
what
manag
tireme
phistic
year s
profile

Th
duty
tione
and
tradi
nanc
due
they

It
struc
with
best

60

(*concluded*)

A Sell and take the immediate $2,000 loss (a 100% chance of loss).

B Hold on to it with a 50% chance of recouping the $2,000 and a 50% chance of losing an additional $2,000.

C No preference.

6 Assume that you have recently invested $10,000 in a stock and that the value of this stock has dropped 15% in value in one week. You can discover no reason for this decline, and the broader market has not dipped accordingly. Which of the following actions would you be most likely to take? (Circle one answer only.)

A Buy more.

B Sell all your holdings in the fund immediately and put the money into a less volatile investment.

C Sell half of your holdings in the fund immediately and put the money elsewhere.

D Wait for the price to recover and then sell all your holdings in the fund.

E Do nothing (occasional dips in price are to be expected).

Scoring

1 – A. 15; B. 0; C. 7

FOR EACH QUESTION:
2a) – A. 0; B. 1; C. 2
2b) through 2e)
   A. 2; B. 1; C. 0

FOR EACH QUESTION:
2f) through 2h)
   A. 0; B. 1; C. 2

FOR EACH QUESTION:
3a) through 3c)
   Yes. 5; No. 0

4 – A. 10; B. 0
5 – A. 0; B. 10; C. 10
6 – A. 15; B. 0; C. 5; D. 0;
   E. 10

7 – A. 10; B. 0
8 – A. 20; B. 15; C. 10;
   D. 5; E. 0

---

7 The following charts show quarterly performance of two equity mutual funds over the past two years. Which do you prefer to invest in?

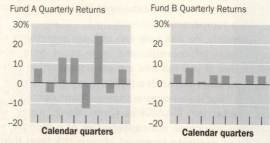

Fund A Quarterly Returns   Fund B Quarterly Returns

Calendar quarters   Calendar quarters

8 As an investor in stock and bond markets, how would you rate your degree of experience relative to other individual investors? (Please circle one.)

A Extremely experienced
B More than average experience
C Average experience
D Less than average experience
E Little or no experience

Source: Investment Technologies Inc.

Score In Points	Suitable Investments*
0–11	Avoid risk! Open a money-market account—or buy a bigger mattress.
12–33	Gentlemen (and ladies) prefer bonds, and are most at home with high-grade corporate and government bonds of an intermediate duration.
34–55	You're still a bond buyer. But you're willing to live a bit closer to the edge with interest-only U.S. Treasury STRIPS.
56–77	Mix it up. Convertible bonds and stocks are to your liking. But safer utilities and large blue chips are as risky as you go. Real-estate investment trusts fit too.
78–99	Stock up on stocks. At the low end, you're comfortable with larger value stocks; at the high end, riskier midcap and growth stocks work.
100+	Viva Las Vegas, baby! Place your bets on 'Net stocks and new-tech issues. Risks are high, but so are the payoffs.

*Suitable investments are based upon an analysis of the volatility of 75 various bond and stock indices, and apply to investment horizons of between 10 and 15 years.

broad principles
ment savings ac
mous, and, as a
limited. There a
it is important to

In terms of ta
counts. With the
vest the aftertax
you take the mon
not taxed, a big
tirement Account

With the seco
if you invest it.
sponsored retiren
you retire, you ov
types of accounts
taxes later, or vic

Special Circumst

everyone will hav
ple, many compar
dollar-for-dollar b
double your mone
sion any other inv
probably be taken
zon considerations

A list of possibl
attempt to produce
pendents and their
for dependents wil
companies whose p
able, and some inv
nally, some investo
on their investing,
least ethically *shou*
interest.

Strategies an

In formulating an i
dressed are investm
lection. We discuss

Investment Manag

make is whether you
it. At the one extrem
and sell decisions yo
a managed account,

Often investors pa
fessional managers.

How risk-averse are
you? Take a test at
moneycentral.
msn.com
Look for "Prepare to
Invest" under
"Investing Insight."

stock, you can lose *much more* than $10,000 because the stock price can keep rising without any particular limit. In fact, as our previous chapter showed, stock prices do tend to rise, at least on average. With this in mind, potential short sellers should remember the following classic bit of Wall Street wisdom: "He that sells what isn't his'n, must buy it back or go to prison!"[1]

Check This

2.3a   What is a short sale?

2.3b   Why might an investor choose to short a stock?

2.3c   What is the maximum possible loss on a short sale? Explain.

2.4   Investor Objectives, Constraints, and Strategies

Different investors will have very different investment objectives and strategies. For example, some will be very active, buying and selling frequently; others will be relatively inactive, buying and holding for long periods of time. Some will be willing to bear substantial risk in seeking out returns; for others, safety is a primary concern. In this section, we describe, in general terms, some strategies that are commonly pursued and their relationship to investor constraints and objectives.

In thinking about investor objectives, the most fundamental question is: Why invest at all? For the most part, the only sensible answer is that we invest today to have more tomorrow. In other words, investment is simply deferred consumption; instead of spending today, we choose to wait because we wish to have (or need to have) more to spend later. There is no difference, really, between investing and saving.

Given that we invest now to have more later, the particular investment strategy chosen will depend on, among other things, willingness to bear risk, the time horizon, and taxes. We discuss these and other issues next.

Risk and Return

Probably the most fundamental decision that an investor must make concerns the amount of risk that she is willing to bear. Most investors are *risk-averse*, meaning that, all other things the same, they dislike risk and want to expose themselves to the minimum risk level possible. However, as our previous chapter indicated, larger returns are generally associated with larger risks, so there is a trade-off. In formulating investment objectives, the individual must therefore balance return objectives with risk tolerance.

Attitudes toward risk are strictly personal preferences, and individuals with very similar economic circumstances can have very different degrees of risk aversion. For this reason, the first thing that must be assessed in evaluating the suitability of an investment strategy is risk tolerance. Unfortunately, this is not an easy thing to do. Most individuals have a difficult time articulating in any precise way their attitude toward risk (what's yours?). One reason is that risk is not a simple concept; it is not easily defined or measured. Nevertheless, the nearby *Investment Updates* box contains an article from *The Wall Street Journal* about risk tolerance that has a short quiz that might help you assess your attitude toward risk. When you take the quiz, remember there are

---

[1] Of course, the same is true for "she that sells what isn't hers'n"; it just doesn't rhyme as well.

no right or wrong
of the article.

Investor Con...

In addition to attitu...
by various constrai...
next.

Resources Probabl...
can most easily rela...
vest at all! Beyond...
explicitly or effectiv...
must normally have...

What is the minir...
and there is no preci...
can be made for as li...
or less. However, sin...
and other costs asso...
actively trading on h...

Horizon The investr...
ample, individuals fr...
pending on your age,...
a house in the near fu...

The reason horizo...
stocks outperformed t...
over which they did n...
stocks are probably n...
riskiness of an invest...
needed.

Liquidity For some in...
quickly. In such cases...
high degree of liquidit...
cession. Such an asset...

Notice that liquidit...
quickly and easily if th...
with which an asset ca...
assets are clearly much...
to imagine buying an a...
on this "round-trip" tra...

Taxes Different types...
the return on an investr...
taxes are a vital conside...
ment strategies with fav...
investors will focus mor...

In addition, the way...
status. The tax laws and...

---

2. **Short Sales** Suppose that in the previous problem you shorted 10,000 shares instead of buying. The initial margin is 60 percent. What does the account balance sheet look like following the short?

3. **Margin Calls** You purchased 500 shares of stock at a price of $56 per share on 50 percent margin. If the maintenance margin is 30 percent, what is the critical stock price?

Answers to Self-Test Problems

1. The 10,000 shares of Intel cost $300,000. You supply $200,000, so you must borrow $100,000. The account balance sheet looks like this:

Assets		Liabilities and Account Equity	
10,000 shares of Intel	$300,000	Margin loan	$100,000
		Account equity	200,000
Total	$300,000	Total	$300,000

Your margin is the account equity divided by the value of the stock owned:

$$\text{Margin} = \$200,000 / \$300,000$$
$$= .666 \ldots$$
$$= 67\%$$

2. Following the short, your account is as follows:

Assets		Liabilities and Account Equity	
Proceeds from sale	$300,000	Short position	$300,000
Initial margin deposit	180,000	Account equity	180,000
Total	$480,000	Total	$480,000

Notice that you shorted $300,000 worth of stock, so, with a 60 percent margin requirement, you deposited $180,000.

3. The lowest price the stock can drop before you receive a margin call is:

$$P^* = \frac{\text{Amount borrowed / Number of shares}}{1 - \text{Maintenance margin}}$$

You borrowed $500 \times \$56 \times .50 = \$14,000$. Therefore:

$$P^* = \frac{\$14,000 / 500}{1 - .30} = \$40.00$$

You will receive a margin call if the stock drops below $40.00.

Test Your Investment Quotient

CFA® PROBLEMS

1. **Investment Objectives** An individual investor's investment objectives should be expressed in terms of:

a. Risk and return.
b. Capital market expectations.

Con

1. M
2. S
3. M
4.

5.

6.

7.

8

Core Questions

c. Liquidity needs and time horizon.
d. Tax factors and legal and regulatory constraints.

2. **Asset Allocation**   Which of the following best reflects the importance of the asset allo- cation decision to the investment process? The asset allocation decision:
   a. Helps the investor decide on realistic investment goals.
   b. Identifies the specific securities to include in a portfolio.
   c. Determines most of the portfolio's returns and volatility over time.
   d. Creates a standard by which to establish an appropriate investment horizon.

3. **Leverage**   You deposit $100,000 cash in a brokerage account and purchase $200,000 of stocks on margin by borrowing $100,000 from your broker. Later, the value of your stock holdings falls to $150,000, whereupon you get nervous and close your account. What is the percentage return on your investment (ignore interest paid)?
   a. 0 percent
   b. −25 percent
   c. −50 percent
   d. −75 percent

4. **Leverage**   You deposit $100,000 cash in a brokerage account and short sell $200,000 of stocks. Later, the value of the stocks held short rises to $250,000, whereupon you get ner- vous and close your account. What is the percentage return on your investment?
   a. 0 percent
   b. −25 percent
   c. −50 percent
   d. −75 percent

5. **Account Margin**   You deposit $100,000 cash in a brokerage account and purchase $200,000 of stocks on margin by borrowing $100,000 from your broker. Later, the value of your stock holdings falls to $175,000. What is your account margin in dollars?
   a. $50,000
   b. $75,000
   c. $100,000
   d. $150,000

6. **Account Margin**   You deposit $100,000 cash in a brokerage account and purchase $200,000 of stocks on margin by borrowing $100,000 from your broker. Later, the value of your stock holdings falls to $150,000. What is your account margin in percent?
   a. 25 percent
   b. 33 percent
   c. 50 percent
   d. 75 percent

7. **Account Margin**   You deposit $100,000 cash in a brokerage account and short sell $200,000 of stocks on margin. Later, the value of the stocks held short rises to $225,000. What is your account margin in dollars?
   a. $50,000
   b. $75,000
   c. $100,000
   d. $150,000

8. **Account Margin**   You deposit $100,000 cash in a brokerage account and short sell $200,000 of stocks on margin. Later, the value of the stocks held short rises to $250,000. What is your account margin in percent?
   a. 20 percent
   b. 25 percent

c. 33

d. 50

9. **Marg**

$200

main

stoc

a. $

b. $

c.

d.

10. **M**

$2

th

s

11.

8. **Margin Calls on Short Sales**   The stock of Lockman Industries is trading at $92. You feel the stock price will decline, so you short 700 shares at an initial margin of 50 percent. If the maintenance margin is 30 percent, at what share price will you receive a margin call?

9. **Margin Calls on Short Sales**   You short sold 1,000 shares of stock at a price of $45 and an initial margin of 60 percent. If the maintenance margin is 40 percent, at what share price will you receive a margin call? What is your account equity at this stock price?

10. **Taxes and Returns**   You purchase a stock at the beginning of the year at a price of $63. At the end of the year the stock pays a dividend of $1.20 and you sell the stock for $71. What is your return for the year? Now suppose that dividends are taxed at your marginal tax rate of 31 percent and long-term capital gains (over 11 months) are taxed at 20 percent. What is your aftertax return for the year?

11. **Calculating Margin**   Using the information in Problem 1, construct your equity account balance sheet at the time of your purchase. What does your balance sheet look like if the share price rises to $90? What if it falls to $65 per share? What is your margin in both cases?

12. **Calculating Margin**   You've just opened a margin account with $10,000 at your local brokerage firm. You instruct your broker to purchase 400 shares of Smolira Golf stock, which currently sells for $43 per share. What is your initial margin? Construct the equity account balance sheet for this position.

13. **Margin Call**   Suppose you purchase 300 shares of stock at $80 per share with an initial cash investment of $15,000. If your broker requires a 30 percent maintenance margin, at what share price will you be subject to a margin call? If you want to keep your position open despite the stock price plunge, what alternatives do you have?

14. **Margin and Leverage**   In the previous problem, suppose the call money rate is 5 percent and you are charged a 1.5 percent premium over this rate. Calculate your return on investment for each of the following share prices one year later. What would your rate of return be in each case if you purchased $15,000 of stock with no margin? Ignore dividends.

   a. $96
   b. $80
   c. $64

15. **Margin and Leverage**   Suppose the call money rate is 8 percent, and you pay a spread of 2 percent over that. You buy 1,000 shares at $40 per share with an initial margin of 50 percent. One year later, the stock is selling for $57 per share, and you close out your position. What is your return assuming no dividends are paid?

16. **Margin and Leverage**   Suppose the call money rate is 6 percent, and you pay a spread of 2.5 percent over that. You buy 1,000 shares of stock at $40 per share. You put up $25,000. One year later, the stock is selling for $45 per share, and you close out your position. What is your return assuming a dividend of $1 per share is paid?

17. **Margin Interest**   Suppose you take out a margin loan for $120,000. The rate you pay is a 9 percent effective rate. If you repay the loan in six months, how much interest will you pay?

18. **Margin Interest**   Suppose you take out a margin loan for $80,000. You pay a 7 percent effective rate. If you repay the loan in two months, how much interest will you pay?

19. **Annualized Returns**   Suppose you hold a particular investment for 9 months. You calculate that your holding-period return is 14 percent. What is your annualized return?

20. **Annualized Returns**   In the previous question, suppose your holding period was 7 months instead of 9. What is your annualized return? What do you conclude in general about the length of your holding period and your annualized return?

21. **Annualized Returns**   Suppose you buy stock at a price of $50 per share. Four months later, you sell it for $43. You also received a dividend of $.40 per share. What is your annualized return on this investment?

22. **Calculating Returns**   Looking back at Problem 12, suppose the call money rate is 6 percent and your broker charges you a spread of 1.25 percent over this rate. You hold the stock for six months and sell at a price of $48 per share. The company paid a dividend of $.75 per share the day before you sold your stock. What is your total dollar return from this investment? What is your effective annual rate of return?

23. **Short Sales**   You believe that Gonas, Inc., stock is going to fall and you've decided to sell 3,000 shares short. If the current share price is $80, construct the equity account balance sheet for this trade. Assume the initial margin is 100 percent.

24. **Short Sales**   Repeat the previous problem assuming you short the 3,000 shares on 75 percent margin.

25. **Calculating Short Sale Returns**   You just sold short 1,500 shares of Wetscope, Inc., a fledgling software firm, at $50 per share. You cover your short when the price hits $36 per share one year later. If the company paid $.80 per share in dividends over this period, what is your rate of return on the investment? Assume an initial margin of 50 percent.

26. **Short Sales**   You believe the stock in Taylor Co. is going to fall, so you short 2,000 shares at a price of $85. The initial margin is 50 percent. Construct the equity balance sheet for the original trade. Now construct an equity balance sheet for a stock price of $75 and a stock price of $95. What is your margin at each of these stock prices? What is your effective annual return if you cover your short position at each of these prices in four months?

STANDARD &POOR'S

S&P Problems

www.mhhe.com/edumarketinsight

1. **Margin**   Download the historical stock prices for Tootsie Roll Industries (TR) under the "Mthly. Adj. Prices" link. Assume you purchased 400 shares of Tootsie Roll stock at the closing price six months ago. The initial margin requirement is 50 percent and the maintenance margin is 30 percent. Show the account balance sheet based on monthly closing prices for the last five months. At what stock price will you receive a margin call? Are any margin deposits required over this period? What is your return on this investment?

2. **Short Sales**   Download the historical stock prices for Ford (F) under the "Mthly. Adj. Prices" link. Assume you short sold 200 shares of Ford stock at the closing price six months ago. The initial margin requirement is 50 percent and the maintenance margin is 30 percent. Show the account balance sheet based on monthly closing prices for the last five months. At what stock price will you receive a margin call? Are any margin deposits required over this period? What is your return on this investment?

What's on the Web

1. **Risk Tolerance**   As we discussed in the chapter, risk tolerance is based on an individual's personality and investment goals. There are numerous risk tolerance questionnaires on the Web. One, provided by Merrill Lynch, is located at individual.ml.com. Go to the website, locate the questionnaire and take the quiz. How conservative or aggressive are you?

2. **Short Interest**   You can find the number of short sales on a particular stock at <u>finance.yahoo.com</u>. Go to the site and find the number of shares short sold for ExxonMobil (XOM) under the "Profile" link. How many shares are sold short in the current month? What about the previous month? What do the "Percent of Float" and "Short Ratio" mean?

3. **Broker Call Money Rate**   What is the current broker call money rate? To find out, go to <u>www.money-rates.com</u> and look up "Key Interest Rates."

4. **Margin Purchases**   Suppose you have a margin account with TDWaterhouse. You purchase 1,000 shares of IBM stock on 50 percent margin at today's price. Go to <u>finance.yahoo.com</u> to find your purchase price. Ignoring transaction costs, how much will you borrow? Next, go to <u>www.money-rates.com</u> to find the current broker call money rate. Finally, go to <u>www.tdwaterhouse.com</u> to find out how much above the current broker call money rate you will pay. Hint: Do a search for "margin rates" on this site. If you keep your investment for one year, how much will you pay in interest assuming the margin rate stays the same? What does the stock price have to be in one year for you to break even on your investment?

Stock-Trak®
Portfolio Simulations

Trading Common Stocks with Stock-Trak

Stock-Trak allows you to trade common stocks in much the same way you would with an individual brokerage account that supported trading on the Internet. This includes buying, selling, and selling short common stocks trading on the major markets—NYSE, AMEX (the American Stock Exchange), and Nasdaq. There are a few restrictions, however. For example, Stock-Trak restricts trading to common stocks trading at a price of $5.00 or more per share. Thus, many small-company stocks cannot be traded. Stock-Trak also requires that all stock trades be in multiples of 25 shares. You should consult the most recent Stock-Trak rules at the website (<u>www.mhhe.com/cj3e</u>) for other possible restrictions that might apply.

There are four basic types of stock trades:

1. Buy to open or increase a long position.
2. Sell to close or reduce a long position.
3. Short sell to open or increase a short position.
4. Buy to cover or reduce a short position.

When buying a stock, you take a long position with the hope that the stock price will increase. By selling stock you are closing all or part of a long position. Selling short refers to selling stock shares that you don't own with the hope that you can later buy them back at a lower price. Buying stock shares back to close all or part of a short position is called covering a short position. We will discuss these four types of orders in the sequence of transactions described immediately below.

Suppose you want to buy 1,000 shares of Texas Instruments and short sell 800 shares of Citigroup. These stocks trade on the NYSE under the ticker symbols TXN and C, respectively. Your orders would look like this:

What type of trade will this be?	Number of shares (example: 500)	Ticker Symbol (all capital letters):
Buy to open or increase a long position Sell to close or reduce a long position Sell short Cover a short position	1000	TXN

What type of trade will this be?	Number of shares (example: 500)	Ticker Symbol (all capital letters):
Buy to open or increase a long position Sell to close or reduce a long position **Sell short** Cover a short position	800	C

After execution, you would have a 1,000-share long position in Texas Instruments (TXN) and an 800-share short position in Citigroup (C).

Now, suppose you later want to reduce your long position in TXN to 600 shares and increase your short position in C to 1,200 shares. The necessary orders would look like this:

What type of trade will this be?	Number of shares (example: 500)	Ticker Symbol (all capital letters):
Buy to open or increase a long position **Sell to close or reduce a long position** Sell short Cover a short position	400	TXN

What type of trade will this be?	Number of shares (example: 500)	Ticker Symbol (all capital letters):
Buy to open or increase a long position Sell to close or reduce a long position **Sell short** Cover a short position	400	C

After execution, you would have a 600-share long position in TXN and a 1,200-share short position in C.

To close out your long and short positions completely, you would submit these orders:

What type of trade will this be?	Number of shares (example: 500)	Ticker Symbol (all capital letters):
Buy to open or increase a long position **Sell to close or reduce a long position** Sell short Cover a short position	600	TXN

What type of trade will this be?	Number of shares (example: 500)	Ticker Symbol (all capital letters):
Buy to open or increase a long position Sell to close or reduce a long position Sell short **Cover a short position**	1200	C

After execution, you will have closed out both positions completely. Your Stock-Trak account will then reflect any gains or losses on these transactions, including commission costs.

We should note here that Stock-Trak (and most brokerage accounts) has a restriction on margin purchases. For example, after reading the chapter, you have decided to purchase a stock on margin. Stock-Trak will not permit a margin purchase as long as you have cash in your account. In other words, in your Stock-Trak account, you cannot purchase on margin until you have the initial $500,000 fully invested. Any purchases above this amount will be margin purchases.

www.mhhe.com/cj3e

Stock-Trak Exercises

1. **Stock Transactions**   You have decided to purchase 1,000 shares of Caterpillar and short 600 shares of SBC Communications. Complete these transactions on Stock-Trak.

2. **Stock Transactions**   The next day, you decide that you want only 600 shares of Caterpillar and want to short 200 more shares of SBC Communications. Complete the necessary transactions.

3. **Stock Transactions**   You have now decided to close your long position in Caterpillar and close out your short position in SBC Communications. Complete the necessary transactions. What is your total dollar gain or loss on these transactions?

Chapter 3

Security Types

"An investment operation is one which upon thorough analysis promises safety of principal and an adequate return. Operations not meeting these requirements are speculative."

–Benjamin Graham

You invest $5,000 in Yahoo! common stock and just months later sell the shares for $7,500, realizing a 50 percent return. Not bad! At the same time, your neighbor invests $5,000 in Yahoo! stock options, which are worth $25,000 at expiration—a 400 percent return. Yahoo! Alternatively your Yahoo! shares fall in value to $2,500, and you realize a 50 percent loss. Too bad! But at the same time your neighbor's Yahoo! stock options are now worthless. Clearly there is a big difference between stock shares and stock options. Security type matters. ■

Our goal in this chapter is to introduce you to some of the different types of securities that are routinely bought and sold in financial markets around the world. As we mentioned in Chapter 1, we will be focusing on financial assets such as bonds, stocks, options, and futures in this book, so these are the securities we briefly describe here. The securities we discuss are covered in much greater detail in the chapters ahead, so we touch on only some of their most essential features in this chapter.

For each of the securities we examine, we ask three questions. First, what is its basic nature and what are its distinguishing characteristics? Second, what are the potential gains and losses from owning it? Third, how are its prices quoted in the financial press?

Low-Key Preferred Stock Could Ease Low-Yield Blues

Bruce Miller is on a hunt for higher yields. And the financial planner from Vancouver, Wash., has found his quarry in a place few individual investors ever venture—preferred stocks. With interest rates on traditional havens such as bonds and certificates of deposit tumbling seemingly toward zero, scores of preferred stocks currently offer dividend yields of between 7% and 10%. These aren't junk-bond-caliber investments. Investors can get those yields on the highly rated securities of stable companies generating plenty of cash to cover the dividend—Bank of New York Co., Bear Stearns Cos. and Equity Office Properties Trust among them. "You never hear about these stocks in the popular media, but there really are some good opportunities for yield right now in preferreds," says Mr. Miller, who has as much as 25% of his clients' income portfolios in a variety of high-yielding preferred issues. "These things are just ignored."

There are some reasons why. Preferred stock is an unusual investment that behaves like debt yet is actually equity. And though preferred stock acts like debt, when it comes to liquidation proceedings, preferred shareholders are in line behind bondholders. Preferred shares are held primarily by institutional investors, not individuals. Indeed, the market value of preferred shares on the New York Stock Exchange, where most preferred shares trade, amounts to just $56.7 billion, a sliver of the $10.9 trillion market value of NYSE-listed stocks.

The result is that searching out even the most basic information—such as which companies have preferred shares outstanding—is a chore. While research on common stocks is abundant and readily available through a variety of channels, "preferreds don't get much attention," and few organizations provide any research, says Jim Moss, managing director of North American banks for Fitch Inc., a ratings agency. Adding to the challenges of preferred stock is that there are a variety of permutations—cumulative, noncumulative, redeemable and even convertible—which, because it's tied to the performance of the underlying stock, can be as complicated to understand as a derivative investment.

There are other caveats. Preferred shares often trade so infrequently that some issues go for days without seeing any action. That means they aren't appropriate investments for people who may need to quickly liquidate their holdings. What's more, if you're going to invest in preferred issues, you need to understand credit risk—the chief consideration on which issues to avoid. More on that later.

Investors seeking high yields don't have a lot of safe alternatives these days. Real-estate investment trusts, or REITs, which are required by law to pay out nearly all their earnings in dividends, already have had a nice run-up in their share prices. Although the average REIT still

(continued)

by the ticker symbol, which is a unique shorthand symbol assigned to each company. The Johnson & Johnson ticker symbol is JNJ.

Following the ticker symbol is the dividend, labeled "DIV," and the dividend yield, labeled "YLD %." Like most dividend-paying companies, Johnson & Johnson pays dividends on a quarterly basis; the dividend number reported here, $.82, is actually four times the most recent quarterly dividend. The dividend yield is this annualized dividend divided by the closing price (discussed just below). Next, the price-earnings ratio, or "PE," is reported. This ratio, as the name suggests, is equal to the price per share divided by earnings per share. Earnings per share is calculated as the sum of earnings per share over the last four quarters. We will discuss dividends, dividend yields, and price-earnings ratios in detail in Chapter 6.

The next piece of information, "VOL 100S," is the trading volume for the day, measured in hundreds. Stocks are usually traded in multiples of 100 called "round lots." Anything that is not a multiple of 100 is called an "odd lot." On this particular day, then, 76,603 round lots, or about 8 million shares, were traded.

The column labeled "CLOSE" is the closing price, meaning the last price at which a trade occurred before regular trading hours ended at 4:00 P.M. EST. Finally, the "NET

yields 7%, there is growing concern that share prices of REITs will slip next year if the economy goes into deep recession. In other industries, high dividends that seem alluring can be an indication of a troubled stock. Consider Ford Motor Co., which last week sliced its dividend in half because of a cash squeeze in its auto operations. Overnight, holders of Ford stock saw their payout decline to 3.33% from 6.67%. By contrast, the dividend on preferred stock is much more secure from earnings malaise. For one, the payout is fixed, and the dividend has to be paid before those on the common shares. Moreover, most preferred dividends are cumulative, meaning that if they are cut or suspended they must be repaid in full before common shareholders see another cent. Dividend suspensions, though they have happened, are nonetheless a rare event, according to credit-ratings concerns.

Preferred stocks aren't for everybody. Investors seeking capital appreciation probably should avoid them. Because the dividends are fixed, and because preferred shares don't move based on a company's earnings growth, there's typically very little stock-price movement. Preferreds usually move "maybe within 10% of either side of the issue's par value," says Todd Lebor, an equities analyst at Morningstar, the Chicago market-research firm, which doesn't issue opinions on preferred stocks. But if you are solely interested in yield, then there are some interesting buys these days in the world of preferred stock.

Most tend to be concentrated in financial services, utilities and REITs, with a few industrial and telecom names thrown in as well. Several financially robust foreign banks, such as Royal Bank of Scotland, also offer safe, high-yielding preferred shares listed in the U.S.

Finding information on preferred stock isn't easy. "It's a bit like a treasure hunt at times," says Mr. Miller, who runs B&L Financial Advisors, a fee-only planning firm. He frequently taps numerous sources of data to build a picture of the preferred issue in which he's interested. QuantumOnline.com, a financial-services site, provides one of the most comprehensive lists of available preferred shares. Yahoo Inc.'s financial website, meanwhile, offers up the dividend, current yield and payment date. The Securities and Exchange Commission's Edgar site offers access to a company's financial filings, where you can read up on the preferred shares they have issued, as well as find the numbers needed to track coverage ratios, along with a company's general financial health. To ferret out credit ratings, head to Moodys.com, the website of Moody's, or Fitch.com. Both provide free of charge their ratings on each security of the companies they track.

Source: Jeff D. Opdyke. *The Wall Street Journal*, October 15, 2002. © 2001 Dow Jones & Company, Inc. All Rights Reserved Worldwide.

CHG" is the change in the closing price from the previous trading day. So, on this particular day, Johnson & Johnson closed at $55, down $1.36 from the day before.

The information contained in *The Wall Street Journal* can be obtained online in many places, of course. The nearby *Work the Web* box describes one way. You can also get preferred stock quotes in *The Wall Street Journal*. They appear in a separate section with a relatively simple format.

Stock price information is also available all day long on television and on the Web. Our nearby *Investment Updates* box explains how to interpret a very common site on television, the on-air ticker. As explained there, once you understand the display, you can actually create your own ticker to track the investments that interest you the most.

Check This

3.3a   What are the two types of equity securities?

3.3b   Why is preferred stock sometimes classified as a fixed-income security?

The Tale of the Tape

The on-air "ticker tape" is a familiar site on television, particularly on financially oriented shows and networks. The most widely watched such channel is CNBC. All day long, at the bottom of the screen, two rows of information scroll by.

The display is called a "ticker tape" because, at one time, it was printed on a thin strip of paper by a "ticker" machine (so named because of the sound it made while printing). In fact, the reason for ticker symbols in the first place was to make information quicker and easier to print. Perhaps you have seen old film footage of a "ticker tape parade" in New York. The paper that rains down on the celebrities and dignitaries is ticker tape.

Ticker machines date to an era before television (if you can imagine such a thing). The first one was introduced in 1867 and was later improved by none other than Thomas Edison. To learn more, visit the website www.stocktickercompany.com.

A typical stock quote on CNBC's ticker looks like this:

This quote tells us that a trade in Dell Computer has just occurred and then provides details about the trade. As indicated, the first thing is the ticker symbol, which we discussed at the end of Chapter 2. Next, we have the size of the trade (the "Volume") and the price, in this case 2,500 shares at $36.25 per share. The downward pointing "Change Direction" arrow indicates that this price is down compared to yesterday's closing price. The "Change Amount" tells us by how much, $5.25 in this case. The quote would actually be in red, also indicating that the stock was trading lower. Quotes in green are up for the day, while quotes in white are unchanged.

The upper band shows trading on the New York Stock Exchange, and the lower band shows trading on the Nasdaq Stock Market. We discuss these exchanges in detail in Chapter 5. A lot of other information (too much, in fact, for us to cover here) in addition to stock quotes will periodically scroll by. To learn more, visit moneycentral.msn.com/investor and link to CNBC TV. As you will see, you can create your own ticker for display on your computer screen just by following the directions given. A personalized ticker allows you to track just the things that interest you the most.

3.4 Derivatives

primary asset
Security originally sold by a business or government to raise money.

derivative asset A financial asset that is derived from an existing traded asset rather than issued by a business or government to raise capital. More generally, any financial asset that is not a primary asset.

There is a clear distinction between real assets, which are essentially tangible items, and financial assets, which are pieces of paper describing legal claims. Financial assets can be further subdivided into primary and derivative assets. A **primary asset** (sometimes called a *primitive asset*) is a security that was originally sold by a business or government to raise money, and a primary asset represents a claim on the assets of the issuer. Thus, stocks and bonds are primary financial assets.

In contrast, as the name suggests, a **derivative asset** is a financial asset that is derived from an existing primary asset rather than issued by a business or government to raise capital. As we will see, derivative assets usually represent claims either on other financial assets, such as shares of stock or even other derivative assets, or on the future price of a real asset such as gold. Beyond this, it is difficult to give a general definition of the term "derivative asset" because there are so many different types, and new ones are created almost every day. On the most basic level, however, any financial asset that is not a primary asset is a derivative asset.

To give a simple example of a derivative asset, imagine that you and a friend buy 1,000 shares of a dividend-paying stock, perhaps the Johnson & Johnson stock we discussed. You each put up half the money, and you agree to sell your stock in one year.

WORK THE WEB

Throughout this chapter, we have looked at information from *The Wall Street Journal*. One problem is that prices reported in the financial press are always from the previous day. Before you trade, you'll want more up-to-date pricing, particularly in fast-moving markets. Using an Internet server, such as Yahoo!, let's do this. Here, as in Chapter 1, we have entered a ticker symbol ("Dell" for Dell Computer), but now we have selected "Detailed" in the dropdown box:

Here is what we get:

Most of the information here is self-explanatory. The abbreviation "Mkt Cap" is short for "market capitalization" which is the total value of all outstanding shares. Notice, on this particular day, Dell was up .71 percent, compared to the $23.86 ("Prev Cls") that you would see in *The Wall Street Journal*. We'll discuss other unfamiliar terms, such as "Bid" and "Ask," a little later in the book. For now, a good exercise is to select a detailed quote yourself and find out what information is in the links below the stock quote.

Furthermore, the two of you agree that you will get all the dividends paid while your friend gets all the gains or absorbs all the losses on the 1,000 shares.

This simple arrangement takes a primary asset, shares of Johnson & Johnson stock, and creates two derivative assets, the dividend-only shares that you hold and the no-dividend shares held by your friend. Derivative assets such as these actually exist, and there are many variations on this basic theme.

of $100,000 in face value of T-bonds, you make $20 \times \$5,000 = \$100,000$, so your profit is a tidy $100,000. Of course, if the price had decreased by five dollars, you would have lost $100,000 on your 20-contract position.

FUTURE SHOCK

EXAMPLE 3.3

Suppose you purchase five March T-bond contracts at a settle price of 110-09. How much will you pay today? Suppose in one month you close your position and the March futures price at that time is 105-08. Did you make or lose money? How much?

When you purchase the five contracts, you pay nothing today because the transaction is for March. However, you have agreed to pay 110-09 per $100 par value. If, when you close your position in a month, the futures price is 105-08, you have a loss of $110\text{-}09 - 105\text{-}08 = 5\frac{1}{32}$ per $100 par value, or $5\frac{1}{32} \times 1,000 = \$5,031.25$ per contract. Your total loss is thus $\$5,031.25 \times 5$ contracts, or $25,156.25 in all (ouch!).

Check This

3.4a   What is a futures contract?

3.4b   What are the general types of futures contracts?

3.4c   Explain how you make or lose money on a futures contract.

3.5   Option Contracts

option contract An agreement that gives the owner the right, but not the obligation, to buy or sell a specific asset at a specified price for a set period of time.

An **option contract** is an agreement that gives the owner the right, but not the obligation, to buy or sell (depending on the type of option) a specific asset at a specific price for a specific period of time. The most familiar options are stock options. These are options to buy or sell shares of stock, and they are the focus of our discussion here. Options are a very flexible investment tool, and a great deal is known about them. We present some of the most important concepts here; our detailed coverage begins in Chapter 14.

Option Terminology

call option An option that gives the owner the right, but not the obligation, to buy an asset.

put option An option that gives the owner the right, but not the obligation, to sell an asset.

Options come in two flavors, calls and puts. The owner of a **call option** has the right, but not the obligation, to *buy* an underlying asset at a fixed price for a specified time. The owner of a **put option** has the right, but not the obligation, to *sell* an underlying asset at a fixed price for a specified time.

Options occur frequently in everyday life. Suppose, for example, that you are interested in buying a used car. You and the seller agree that the price will be $3,000. You give the seller $100 to hold the car for one week, meaning that you have one week to come up with the $3,000 purchase price, or else you lose your $100.

This agreement is a call option. You paid the seller $100 for the right, but not the obligation, to buy the car for $3,000. If you change your mind because, for example, you find a better deal elsewhere, you can just walk away. You'll lose your $100, but

short) are seen as they appear in *The Wall Street Journal*. Looking at Figure 3.3, we see these are quotes for delivery of T-bonds with a total par, or face, value of $100,000.

WORK THE WEB

Throughout this chapter, we have looked at information from *The Wall Street Journal.* One problem is that prices reported in the financial press are always from the previous day. Before you trade, you'll want more up-to-date pricing, particularly in fast-moving markets. Using an Internet server, such as Yahoo!, let's do this. Here, as in Chapter 1, we have entered a ticker symbol ("Dell" for Dell Computer), but now we have selected "Detailed" in the dropdown box:

Here is what we get:

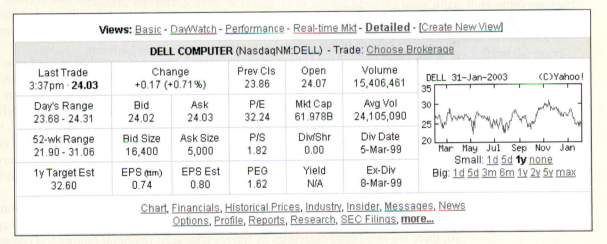

Most of the information here is self-explanatory. The abbreviation "Mkt Cap" is short for "market capitalization" which is the total value of all outstanding shares. Notice, on this particular day, Dell was up .71 percent, compared to the $23.86 ("Prev Cls") that you would see in *The Wall Street Journal.* We'll discuss other unfamiliar terms, such as "Bid" and "Ask," a little later in the book. For now, a good exercise is to select a detailed quote yourself and find out what information is in the links below the stock quote.

Furthermore, the two of you agree that you will get all the dividends paid while your friend gets all the gains or absorbs all the losses on the 1,000 shares.

This simple arrangement takes a primary asset, shares of Johnson & Johnson stock, and creates two derivative assets, the dividend-only shares that you hold and the no-dividend shares held by your friend. Derivative assets such as these actually exist, and there are many variations on this basic theme.

of $100,000 in face value of T-bonds, you make 20 × $5,000 = $100,000, so your profit is a tidy $100,000. Of course, if the price had decreased by five dollars, you would have lost $100,000 on your 20-contract position.

FUTURE SHOCK

EXAMPLE 3.3

Suppose you purchase five March T-bond contracts at a settle price of 110-09. How much will you pay today? Suppose in one month you close your position and the March futures price at that time is 105-08. Did you make or lose money? How much?

When you purchase the five contracts, you pay nothing today because the transaction is for March. However, you have agreed to pay 110-09 per $100 par value. If, when you close your position in a month, the futures price is 105-08, you have a loss of 110-09 − 105-08 = 5½ per $100 par value, or 5½ × 1,000 = $5,031.25 per contract. Your total loss is thus $5,031.25 × 5 contracts, or $25,156.25 in all (ouch!).

Check This

3.4a	What is a futures contract?
3.4b	What are the general types of futures contracts?
3.4c	Explain how you make or lose money on a futures contract.

3.5 Option Contracts

option contract An agreement that gives the owner the right, but not the obligation, to buy or sell a specific asset at a specified price for a set period of time.

An **option contract** is an agreement that gives the owner the right, but not the obligation, to buy or sell (depending on the type of option) a specific asset at a specific price for a specific period of time. The most familiar options are stock options. These are options to buy or sell shares of stock, and they are the focus of our discussion here. Options are a very flexible investment tool, and a great deal is known about them. We present some of the most important concepts here; our detailed coverage begins in Chapter 14.

Option Terminology

call option An option that gives the owner the right, but not the obligation, to buy an asset.

put option An option that gives the owner the right, but not the obligation, to sell an asset.

Options come in two flavors, calls and puts. The owner of a **call option** has the right, but not the obligation, to *buy* an underlying asset at a fixed price for a specified time. The owner of a **put option** has the right, but not the obligation, to *sell* an underlying asset at a fixed price for a specified time.

Options occur frequently in everyday life. Suppose, for example, that you are interested in buying a used car. You and the seller agree that the price will be $3,000. You give the seller $100 to hold the car for one week, meaning that you have one week to come up with the $3,000 purchase price, or else you lose your $100.

This agreement is a call option. You paid the seller $100 for the right, but not the obligation, to buy the car for $3,000. If you change your mind because, for example, you find a better deal elsewhere, you can just walk away. You'll lose your $100, but that is the price you paid for the right, but not the obligation, to buy. The price you pay to purchase an option, the $100 in this example, is called the **option premium**.

option premium The price you pay to buy an option.

A few other definitions will be useful. First, the specified price at which the underlying asset can be bought or sold with an option contract is called the **strike price**, the *striking price*, or the *exercise price*. Using an option to buy or sell an asset is called *exercising* the option. The last day on which an option can be exercised is the day before the *expiration date* on the option contract. Finally, an *American option* can be exercised anytime up to and including the expiration date, whereas a *European option* can be exercised only on the expiration date.

strike price The price specified in an option contract at which the underlying asset can be bought (for a call option) or sold (for a put option). Also called the striking price or exercise price.

Options versus Futures

Our discussion thus far illustrates the two crucial differences between an option contract and a futures contract. The first is that the purchaser of a futures contract is *obligated* to buy the underlying asset at the specified price (and the seller of a futures contract is obligated to sell). The owner of a call option is not obligated to buy, however, unless she wishes to do so; she has the right, but not the obligation.

The second important difference is that when you buy a futures contract, you pay no money (and you receive none if you sell). However, if you buy an option contract, you pay the premium; if you sell an option contract, you receive the premium.

Option Price Quotes

Like futures contracts, most option contracts are standardized. One call option contract, for example, gives the owner the right to buy 100 shares (one round lot) of stock. Similarly, one put option contract gives the owner the right to sell 100 shares.

To learn more about options visit the Learning Center at www.cboe.com

Figure 3.4 presents *Wall Street Journal* quotes for call and put options on common stock in several companies, including Amazon. The company identifier, "Amazon," appears in the first column. Just below this identifier is the number $22.27. This is simply the most recent closing price on Amazon's common stock.

The second column in Figure 3.4 lists some available strike prices. Only the most actively traded options are shown. The third column lists expiration months. So, for example, the Amazon options listing has strike prices ranging from $20 to $25, and expiration months of January and July.

FIGURE 3.4

Options Trading

Source: Reprinted from *The Wall Street Journal*, January 16, 2003, with permission via Copyright Clearance Center, Inc. © 2003 Dow Jones and Company. All Rights Reserved Worldwide.

LISTED OPTIONS QUOTATIONS

THURSDAY, JANUARY 16, 2003

OPTION/STRIKE		EXP	-CALL- VOL	-CALL- LAST	-PUT- VOL	-PUT- LAST
AOL TW	12.50	Jan	1553	2.80	...	...
15.24	15	Jan	2878	0.35	1009	0.10
15.24	15	Feb	4295	0.95	795	0.75
15.24	17.50	Apr	19558	0.60	53	2.65
AT&T	27.50	Jul	...	...	3250	3
27.46	30	Jul	4055	1.60	2	4.50
AdvAuto	55	Mar	1100	0.50	...	...
A M D	7.50	Jan	3416	0.25	609	0.40
Amazon	20	Jan	1095	2.25	262	0.05
22.27	22.50	Jan	1917	0.25	554	0.50
22.27	25	Jul	2221	2.65	2020	5.40
AmbacF	55	Feb	...	...	1510	1.70
Flextrn	7.50	Feb	53	1.60	1077	0.35
8.70	10	Jan	1911	0.05	85	1.30
FordM	10	Jan	1338	0.35	1283	0.05
10.30	10	Feb	534	0.70	1341	0.50
10.30	10	Jun	144	1.45	2539	1.35
ForstL	55	Jan	1079	0.85	191	1.10
Gap	17.50	Jun	5110	1.10	...	...
Genentc	35	Jan	268	1.05	1046	0.75
Gen El	25	Jan	4369	0.55	9097	0.25
25.19	25	Feb	1505	1.20	1287	0.95
25.19	25	Mar	193	1.55	3183	1.45
25.19	25	Jun	986	2.35	1042	2.05

The fourth and fifth columns give trading volume and premium information about call options. Referring to the first line, the Jan 20 options, we see that 1,095 call option contracts were traded and the last (closing) price was $2.25 per share. Because each contract actually involves 100 shares, the price per contract is $2.25 × 100 = $225. Finally, the last two columns give the same information for put options.

Suppose you wanted the right to buy 500 shares of Amazon for $25 sometime between now and July. What would you buy? Based on the information in Figure 3.4, how much would you have to pay?

You want the right to buy, so you want to purchase call options. Since each contract is for 100 shares, and you want the right to buy 500 shares, you need five contracts. The contract you want would be described as the Amazon July 25 call option. From Figure 3.4, the option premium for the contract with a $25 strike and a July expiration is $2.65, so one contract would cost $2.65 × 100 = $265. The cost for five contracts would therefore be 5 × $265 = $1,325.

PUT OPTIONS

EXAMPLE 3.4

Suppose you want the right to sell 200 shares of Amazon between now and July at a price of $25. In light of the information in Figure 3.4, what contract should you buy? How much will it cost you?

You want the right to sell stock at a fixed price, so you want to buy put options. Specifically, you want to buy two July 25 put contracts. In Figure 3.4, the premium for this contract is given as $5.40. Recalling that this is the premium per share, one contract will cost you $540; so two contracts would be $1,080.

Gains and Losses on Option Contracts

As with futures contracts, option contracts have the potential for large gains and losses. To examine this, let's consider our previous example in which you paid $1,325 for five Amazon July 25 call contracts. Suppose you hold on to your contracts until July rolls around, and they are just about to expire. What are your gains (or losses) if Amazon is selling for $55 per share? $15 per share?

If Amazon is selling for $55 per share, you will profit handsomely. You have the right to buy 500 shares at a price of $25 per share. Since the stock is worth $55, your options are worth $30 per share, or $15,000 in all. So you invested $1,325 and ended up with more than 10 times that in just about three months. Not bad.

If the stock ends up at $15 per share, however, the result is not so pretty. You have the right to buy the stock for $25 when it is selling for $15, so your call options expire worthless. You lose the entire $1,325 you originally invested. In fact, if the stock price is anything less than $25, you lose it all.

MORE ON PUTS

EXAMPLE 3.5

In Example 3.4, you bought two Amazon July 25 put contracts for $1,080. Suppose that July arrives, and Amazon is selling for $5 per share. How did you do? What's the break-even stock price, that is, the price at which you just make enough to cover your $1,080 cost?

Your put contracts give you the right to sell 200 shares of Amazon at a price of $25 per share. If the stock is worth only $5 per share, your put options are worth $20 per share, or $4,000 in all. To

(continued)

determine the break-even stock price, notice that you paid $5.40 per share for the option, so this is what you must make per share to break even. The break-even stock price is thus $25 − $5.40 = $19.60.

Investing in Stocks versus Options

To get a better idea of the potential gains and losses from investing in stocks compared to investing in options, let's suppose you have $10,000 to invest. You're looking at Macron Technology, which is currently selling for $50 per share. You also notice that a call option with a $50 strike price and three months to maturity is available. The premium is $4. Macron pays no dividends.

You're considering investing all $10,000 either in the stock or in the call options. What is your return from these two investments, if, in three months, Macron is selling for $55 per share? What about $45 per share?

First, if you buy the stock, your $10,000 will purchase two round lots, meaning 200 shares. A call contract costs $400 (why?), so you can buy 25 of them. Notice that your 25 contracts give you the right to buy 2,500 shares at $50 per share.

If, in three months, Macron is selling for $55, your stock will be worth 200 shares × $55 = $11,000. Your dollar gain will be $11,000 less the $10,000 you invested, or $1,000. Since you invested $10,000, your return for the three-month period is $1,000/$10,000 = 10%. If Macron is going for $45 per share, then you lose $1,000, and your return is −10 percent.

At the $55 price, your call options are worth $55 − $50 = $5 each, but now you control 2,500 shares, so your options are worth 2,500 shares × $5 = $12,500 total. You invested $10,000, so your dollar return is $12,500 − $10,000 = $2,500, and your percentage return is $2,500/$10,000 = 25%, compared to 10 percent on the stock investment. However, if Macron is selling for $45 when your options mature, then you lose everything, and your return is −100 percent.

PUT RETURNS

EXAMPLE 3.6

In our example for Macron Technology, suppose a put option is also available with a premium of $2.50. Calculate your percentage return for the three-month holding period if the stock price declines to $47 per share. What is your annualized return?

One put contract costs $250, so you can buy 40 of them. Notice that your 40 contracts give you the right to *sell* 4,000 shares at $50 per share.

If, in three months, Macron is selling for $47, your put options are worth $50 − $47 = $3 each. You control 4,000 shares, so your options are worth 4,000 shares × $3 = $12,000 total. You invested $10,000, so your dollar return is $12,000 − $10,000 = $2,000, and your percentage return is $2,000/$10,000 = 20%.

To annualize your return, we need to compute the effective annual return, recognizing that there are 4 three-month periods in a year:

$$1 + EAR = 1.20^4$$
$$= 2.0736$$
$$EAR = 1.0736 = 107.36\%$$

Your annualized return is thus about 107 percent.

Check This

3.5a	What is a call option? A put option?
3.5b	If you buy a call option, what do you hope will happen to the underlying stock? What if you buy a put option?
3.5c	What are the two key differences between a futures contract and an option contract?

3.6 Summary and Conclusions

This chapter examines the basic types of financial assets. It discusses three broad classes: interest-bearing assets, equities, and derivative assets. Each of these major groups can be further subdivided. Interest-bearing assets include money market instruments and fixed-income securities. The two major equity types are common stock and preferred stock. The two most important types of derivative assets are options and futures.

For each of the major types of financial assets, we cover three topics. We first describe the basic nature of the asset with an emphasis on what the owner of the asset is entitled to receive. We then illustrate how prices are quoted in the financial press, and we show how to interpret information presented in *The Wall Street Journal*. Finally, we indicate, in fairly broad terms, the potential gains and losses from buying and selling each type of asset.

Get Real

This chapter covered the basics of the four main types of financial assets: stocks, bonds, options, and futures. In addition to discussing basic features, we alerted you to some of the risks associated with these instruments. We particularly stressed the large potential gains and losses possible with derivative assets. How should you, as an investor or investment manager, put this information to work?

Following up on our previous chapter, you need to execute each of the possible transaction types suggested by this chapter in a simulated brokerage account. Your goal is to experience some of the large gains (and losses) to understand them on a personal level. Try to do at least the following:

1. Buy a corporate or government bond.
2. Buy put and call option contracts.
3. Sell put and call option contracts.
4. Buy agriculture, natural resource, and financial futures contracts.
5. Sell agriculture, natural resource, and financial futures contracts.

In each case, once you have created the position, be sure to monitor it regularly by checking prices, trading activity, and relevant news using *The Wall Street Journal* or an online information service to understand why it changes in value.

One thing you will discover if you execute these trades is that some of these investments carry relatively low risk and some relatively high risk. Which are which? Under

(continued)

what circumstances is each of these investments appropriate? We will have more to say about these investments later, but you'll get a lot more out of our discussion (and have some fun stories to tell) if you already have some personal experience. As always, it's better to become educated about these things with play money before you commit real money.

Key Terms

money market instruments 80
fixed-income securities 81
primary asset 88
derivative asset 88
futures contract 90

option contract 92
call option 92
put option 92
option premium 93
strike price 93

Chapter Review Problems and Self-Test

1. **Corporate Bond Quotes**   In Figure 3.1, locate the AT&T bond that matures in the year 2029. What is the coupon rate on this issue? Suppose you purchase $100,000 in face value. How much will this cost? Assuming semiannual payments, what will you receive in coupon payments? Verify the reported current yield.

2. **Call Options**   In Figure 3.4, locate the AOL TW February 15 call option. If you buy 10 contracts, how much will you pay? Suppose that in February, just as the option is about to expire, AOL TW is selling for $20 per share. What are your options worth? What is your net profit?

Answers to Self-Test Problems

1. Based on Figure 3.1, the AT&T issue that matures in 2029 (shown as 29) has a 6.5 percent coupon rate. The price, as a percentage of face value, is 87.88, or 87.88 percent. If you buy $100,000 in face value, you would thus pay $87,880. You will receive 6.5 percent of $100,000, or $6,500, in coupon payments every year, paid in two $3,250 semiannual installments. Finally, the current yield is the coupon rate divided by the price, or 6.5/87.88 = 7.4 percent, the number shown.

2. From Figure 3.4, the February 15 call premium is .95, or $.95. Because one contract involves 100 shares, the cost of a contract is $95, and 10 contacts would cost $950. In February, if AOL TW is selling for $20, then you have the right to buy 10 contracts × 100 shares = 1,000 shares at $20. Your contracts are thus worth $20 − $15 = $5 per share, or $5,000 total. Since they cost you $950, your net profit is $4,050.

Test Your Investment Quotient

1. **Money Market Securities**   Which of the following is not a common characteristic of money market securities?

   a. Sold on a discount basis.
   b. Mature in less than one year.
   c. Most important risk is default risk.
   d. All of the above are characteristics.

2. **Money Market Securities**   Which of the following money market securities is the most liquid?

   a. U.S. Treasury bills.
   b. Bank certificates of deposit.
   c. Corporate money market debt.
   d. Municipality money market debt.

3. **Options**   A European option can be exercised

   a. Only after American options.
   b. Anytime up to and including the expiration date.
   c. Only on the day before the expiration date.
   d. Only on a European exchange.

4. **Fixed-Income Securities**   Your friend told you she just received her semiannual coupon payment on a U.S. Treasury note with a $100,000 face value that pays a 6 percent annual coupon. How much money did she receive from this coupon payment?

   a. $3,000
   b. $6,000
   c. $30,000
   d. $60,000

5. **Common Stock**   A corporation with common stock issued to the public pays dividends

   a. At the discretion of management, who are elected by the shareholders.
   b. At the discretion of shareholders, since they own the corporation.
   c. At the discretion of the company's board of directors, who are elected by shareholders.
   d. At the discretion of the company's board of directors, who are appointed by management.

6. **Futures Contracts**   You buy (go long) five copper futures contracts at 100 cents per pound, where the contract size is 25,000 pounds. At contract maturity, copper is selling for 102 cents per pound. What is your profit (+) or loss (−) on the transaction?

   a. −$2,500
   b. +$2,500
   c. −$25,000
   d. +$25,000

7. **Futures Contracts**   You sell (go short) 10 gold futures contracts at $400 per ounce, where the contract size is 100 ounces. At contract maturity, gold is selling for $410 per ounce. What is your profit (+) or loss (−) on the transaction?

   a. −$1,000
   b. +$1,000
   c. −$10,000
   d. +$10,000

8. **Option Contracts**   You buy 100 CJC call option contracts with a strike price of 95 at a quoted price of $1. At option expiration, CJC sells for $97. What is your net profit on the transaction?

   a. $2,000
   b. $5,000
   c. $10,000
   d. $20,000

9. **Option Contracts**   You buy 100 CJC put option contracts with a strike price of 92 at a quoted price of $8. At option expiration, CJC sells for $83.80. What is your net profit on the transaction?

   a. $200

b. $1,000

c. $2,000

d. $10,000

10. **Short Sales**   Which of the following statements about short selling is true?

a. A short position may be hedged by writing call options.

b. A short position may be hedged by purchasing put options.

c. Short sellers may be subject to margin calls if the stock price increases.

d. Stocks that pay large dividends should be sold short before the ex-dividend date and bought afterward to take advantage of the large price declines in a short time period.

Concept Questions

1. **Money Market Instruments**   What are the distinguishing features of a money market instrument?

2. **Preferred Stock**   Why is preferred stock "preferred"?

3. *WSJ* **Stock Quotes**   What is the PE ratio reported for stocks in *The Wall Street Journal?* In particular, how is it computed?

4. **Yields**   The current yield on a bond is very similar to what number reported for common and preferred stocks?

5. **Volume Quotations**   Explain how volume is quoted for stocks, corporate bonds, futures, and options.

6. **Futures Contracts**   Changes in what price lead to gains and/or losses in futures contracts?

7. **Futures Contracts**   What is the open interest on a futures contract? What do you think will usually happen to open interest as maturity approaches?

8. **Futures versus Options**   What is the difference between a futures contract and an option contract? Do the buyer of a futures contract and the buyer of an option contract have the same rights? What about the seller?

9. **Asset Types**   What is the distinction between a real asset and a financial asset? What are the two basic types of financial assets, and what does each represent?

10. **Puts versus Calls**   Suppose a share of stock is selling for $100. A put and a call are offered, both with $100 strike prices and nine months to maturity. Intuitively, which do you think is more valuable?

Questions and Problems

Core Questions

1. **Stock Quotations**   You found the following stock quote for DRK Enterprises, Inc., at your favorite website. What was the closing price for this stock yesterday? How many round lots of stock were traded yesterday?

| YTD | 52 Weeks | | | | | Yld | | Vol | | Net |
% Chg	Hi	Lo	Stock	Sym	Div	%	PE	100s	Last	Chg
−8.1	65	28.25	DRK	DRK	1.40	4.20	12	8153	??	0.43

2. **Stock Quotations**   In the previous problem, assume the company has 25 million shares of stock outstanding. What was net income for the most recent four quarters?

www.mhhe.com/cj3e

3. **Dividend Yields**   The following stock quote for Ehrhardt-Daves Corporation (EDC) appeared on an online quote server:

| YTD | 52 Week | | Stock | Sym | Div | Yld | PE | Vol | Close | Net |
% Chg	Hi	Lo				%		100s		Chg
10.2	84.30	52.05	EDC	EDC	??	4	16	295	81.05	−0.25

What was the last quarterly dividend paid by EDC?

4. **Earnings per Share**   In the previous problem, what is the earnings per share (EPS) for the company?

5. **Bonds**   You buy $500,000 in face value of bonds that mature in 10 years and carry a 7.5 percent coupon rate. If the coupon payments are made semiannually, how much will you receive on the next coupon payment date? How much will you receive when the bonds mature?

6. **Futures Profits**   The contract size for platinum futures is 50 troy ounces. Suppose you need 800 troy ounces of platinum and the current futures price is $750 per ounce. How many contracts do you need to purchase? How much will you pay for your platinum? What is your dollar profit if platinum sells for $785 a troy ounce when the futures contract expires? What if the price is $730 at expiration?

7. **Option Profits**   You purchase 10 call option contracts with a strike price of $55 and a premium of $3. If the stock price at expiration is $62.21, what is your dollar profit? What if the stock price is $53.90?

8. **Stock Quotations**   You found the following stock quote for Gigantus Corporation in today's newspaper. What was the stock selling for on January 1?

| YTD | 52 Week | | Stock | Sym | Div | Yld | PE | Vol | Close | Net |
% Chg	Hi	Lo				%		100s		Chg
+16.5	94.02	73.20	Gigantus	GIG	1.75	1.9	34	12690	93.60	+1.25

9. **Bond Quotations**   Suppose the following bond quote for ISU Corporation appears in the financial pages of today's newspaper. If this bond has a face value of $1,000, what closing price appeared in yesterday's newspaper?

Bonds	Cur Yld	Vol	Close	Net Chg
ISU 6¾15	7.4	10	??	−.32

10. **Bond Quotations**   In the previous problem, in what year does the bond mature? If you currently own 25 of these bonds, how much money will you receive on the next coupon payment date?

Intermediate Questions

11. **Futures Quotations**   The following quotations for cotton futures trading on the New York Cotton Exchange appear in today's newspaper. How many of the March contracts are currently open? How many of these contracts should you sell if you wish to deliver 400,000 pounds of cotton in March? If you actually make delivery, how much will you receive? Assume you locked in the settle price.

COTTON (CTN)—50,000 LBS.; CENTS PER LB.							
					Lifetime		Open
	Open	High	Low	Settle	Chg	High	Low	Int
Mar	49.20	49.45	48.65	48.72	−.39	55.25	36.20	45,070
May	53.15	53.35	52.60	52.69	−.36	55.50	38.70	16,187
July	54.30	54.40	53.80	53.80	−.40	56.00	39.50	6,068
Dec	54.60	54.60	54.40	54.40	−.65	55.85	43.80	4,081

Est vol 4,814; vol Fri 5,356; open int 73,040, −11.

12. **Futures Quotations** In the previous problem, approximately how many cotton futures contracts of all maturities were traded yesterday? The day before yesterday?

13. **Using Futures Quotations** In Problem 11, suppose you buy 15 of the December cotton futures contracts. One month from now, the futures price of this contract is 63.21, and you close out your position. Calculate your dollar profit on this investment.

14. **Options Quotations** Suppose the following stock options quotations for GNR, Inc., appear in today's financial pages. What was the closing share price of the underlying stock? If you wanted to purchase the right to sell 1,500 shares of GNR stock in January at a strike price of $50 per share, how much would this cost you?

Option/Strike		Exp.	Call		Put	
			Vol.	Last	Vol.	Last
GNR	40	Dec	3	6.50	1	0.05
45.87	45	Dec	21	1.20	16	0.50
45.87	45	Jan	42	2.25	67	1.40
45.87	50	Dec	85	0.10	89	3.50
45.87	50	Jan	8	0.35	124	3.80
45.87	50	Feb	160	0.75	193	4.40
45.87	50	Dec	35	0.10	68	8.50
45.87	55	Jan	28	0.10	19	9.20
45.87	55	Feb	9	0.10	4	9.40
45.87	60	Feb	2	0.05	7	13.50

15. **Options Quotations** In the previous problem, which put contract sells for the lowest price? Which one sells for the highest price? Explain why these respective options trade at such extreme prices.

16. **Using Options Quotations** In Problem 14, suppose GNR stock sells for $42 per share immediately prior to your options' expiration. What is the rate of return on your investment? What is your rate of return if the stock sells for $56 per share (think about it)? Assume your holding period for this investment is exactly three months.

17. **Options versus Stock** You've located the following option quote for Eric-Cartman, Inc. (ECI):

Option/Strike		Exp.	Call		Put	
			Vol.	Last	Vol.	Last
ECI	10	Sep	29	5.50	...	...
20.25	15	Sep	333	7	69	1
20.25	25	Dec	5	2	...	...
20.25	30	Sep	76	2	188	8.75
20.25	35	Oct	89	0.50	...	...

Three of the premiums shown can't possibly be correct. Which three? Why?

18. **Annualized Returns**   Suppose you have $20,000 to invest. You're considering Miller-Moore Equine Enterprises (MMEE), which is currently selling for $25 per share. You also notice that a call option with a $25 strike price and six months to maturity is available. The premium is $2.50. MMEE pays no dividends. What is your annualized return from these two investments if, in six months, MMEE is selling for $31 per share? What about $22 per share?

19. **Annualized Returns**   In the previous question, suppose a dividend of $.50 per share is paid. Comment on how the returns would be affected.

20. **Option Returns**   In Problem 18, suppose a put option with a $25 strike is also available with a premium of $2. Calculate your percentage return for the six-month holding period if the stock price declines to $21.50 per share.

What's on the Web?

1. **Option Prices**   You want to find the option prices for ConAgra Foods (CAG). Go to finance.yahoo.com, get a stock quote, and follow the "Options" link. What is the option premium and strike price for the highest and lowest strike price options that are nearest to expiring? What are the option premium and strike price for the highest and lowest strike price options expiring next month?

2. **Futures Quotes**   Go to www.cbot.com and find the contract specifications for corn futures. What is the size of the corn futures contract? On the CBOT website, find the settle price for the corn futures contract that will expire the soonest. If you go long 10 contracts, how much will the corn cost at the current price?

3. **LEAPS**   Go to www.cboe.com, highlight the "Products" tab, then follow the "LEAPS" link. What are LEAPS? What are the two types of LEAPS? What are the benefits of equity LEAPS? What are the benefits of index LEAPS?

4. **FLEX Options**   Go to www.cboe.com, highlight the "Institutional" tab, then follow the "FLEX Options" link. What is a FLEX option? When do FLEX options expire? What is the minimum size of a FLEX option?

Stock-Trak®
Portfolio Simulation

Trading Corporate Bonds with Stock-Trak

You can trade a limited number of corporate bond issues with Stock-Trak. Currently Stock-Trak lists about 30 different bond issues. These are bonds that trade in sufficient volume for Stock-Trak to obtain accurate prices. The list may change from time to time, so you should consult the list available on the bond purchase screen on the Stock-Trak website. You do not need a ticker symbol for the bond as Stock-Trak lists the bonds by issuer name, coupon, and maturity. Here are three corporate bonds listed on Stock-Trak:

AT&T 8.125 2022

Dow Chemical 6.85 2013

IBM 6.45 2007

As in standard practice, corporate bonds on Stock-Trak trade in $1,000 face values.

To find the current market price of the bond you are interested in, go to the quote link on Stock-Trak and follow the corporate bond link. This connects you to www.bondpage.com, an online trading site for corporate bonds. You can follow the links here to find current prices on the bond you are interested in. Your actual purchase price will be slightly higher than the quoted price, because you have to pay the interest that has accrued since the last coupon payment. We will discuss this in more detail in a later chapter. Suppose you want to buy 10 of the IBM 6.45 2007 bonds. Your order would look like this:

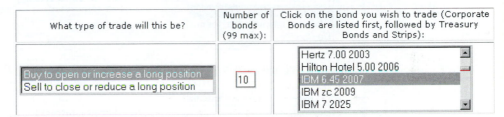

After execution, you would have a long position in 10 of these IBM bonds. To sell the bonds, your transaction would look like this:

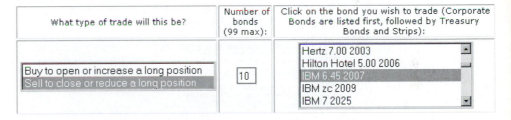

Trading Options with Stock-Trak

You can trade any call or put option on Stock-Trak that currently trades in the market. With options, you need to enter the ticker symbol. The ticker symbol for a stock is not necessarily the ticker symbol for stock options, especially with companies listed on Nasdaq. We will discuss how an option ticker symbol is constructed later. For now, you can find the ticker symbol on a quote screen. On the option purchase screen, simply follow the link "Stock-Trak option ticker symbol look-up." This takes you to a stock quote service. Here, you enter the stock ticker symbol and follow the "Option" link. Find the option you would like to trade, whether a call or a put, the strike price, and the expiration month. When you find the option, remember the ticker symbol. For instance, the quote service lists Microsoft February calls with a strike price of $55 as MSQBK. The ticker symbol for options trading on Stock-Trak is the option ticker symbol, with the last two letters separated by a hyphen. So these options on Stock-Trak would be MSQ-BK.

There are four basic options transactions:

1. Buy to open or increase a long position.

2. Sell to close or reduce a long position.

3. Write an option to create a short position.

4. Buy to close an option previously written.

The important idea to remember is to close your position properly. If you buy an option, writing an option will net out your position, but Stock-Trak will give you a long position and a short

www.mhhe.com/cj3e

position in the option. You must "Sell to close a position" to properly offset your long position. If you want to buy 20 of the Microsoft options, your transaction would look like this:

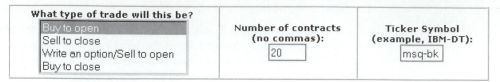

To sell options to offset your position, your transaction would look like this:

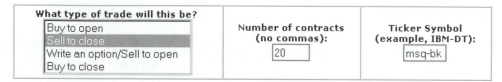

To write 20 call option contracts, your transaction would look like:

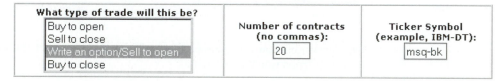

And to close out your short position, you would:

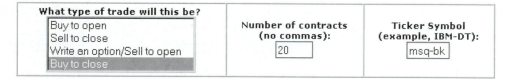

Trading Commodity Futures with Stock-Trak

Commodity futures are futures contracts on a physical asset such as corn, wheat, hogs, gold, palladium, crude oil, and natural gas. In addition to commodity futures, you can also trade financial futures such as index futures, interest rate futures, and currency futures on Stock-Trak. We will discuss financial futures later and concentrate on commodity futures for now. There are several things we need to discuss regarding commodity futures trading on Stock-Trak. First, you do not need the ticker symbol for the futures contract. Stock-Trak lists the commodity and expiration of the contract on the purchase screen. Second, when you buy a futures contract, you do not put up the entire contract value, but simply put up margin. Margin on futures is similar to margin on a stock. To find the amount you must put up in initial margin on a futures contract, click on the margin requirement link on the purchase page. This will give you the initial margin for each contract. To find the contract size, go to www.cbot.com or look in *The Wall Street Journal*. You will need this information to calculate your gain or loss at any point in time. There are four basic transaction types for futures contracts:

1. Buy to open, go long, or increase a long position.
2. Sell to close or reduce a long position.
3. Short to open a position.
4. Buy to close a previously short position.

As with options, you must pair your buy and sell orders correctly to close out your position. If you want to buy five futures contracts on corn in December 2003, your trade would look like this:

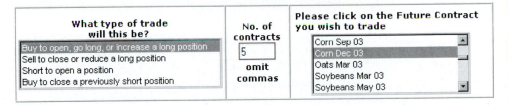

To close this position, you would:

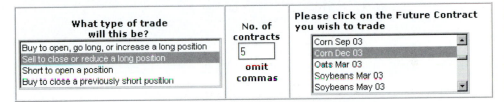

If you think the price of corn will decline and want to sell 10 futures contracts, your transaction is:

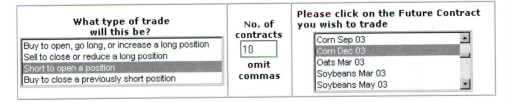

And to close out this short position:

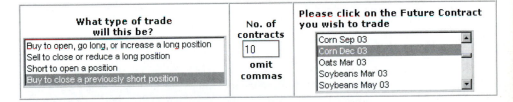

Remember, trades on Stock-Trak are not real money, so don't feel too bad if you lose money on these transactions. The idea is to learn from your mistakes.

Stock-Trak Exercises

1. **Corporate Bonds**   You decide to buy 10 corporate bonds. Go to Stock-Trak and find the list of available bonds. Before you purchase the bonds, get a price quote. Now go back and buy the bonds. Three days later you decide to sell your bonds. Make the necessary transactions. What is your dollar return for this transaction?

2. **Option Purchase**   Find a stock you think will increase in value, and buy 20 call option contracts. Now find a stock you think will decrease in value and buy 20 put contracts. One week later, close out each position. What was your dollar return on each transaction?

www.mhhe.com/cj3e

3. **Option Writing**   Find a stock you do not think will increase in value and write 10 call option contracts. Write 10 put option contracts on a stock you think will increase in value. What is the most you can make from each of these transactions? When you close your positions, calculate your dollar return.

4. **Commodity Futures**   Find the list of commodity futures available through Stock-Trak. Pick your favorite commodity and purchase five contracts. How much is the initial margin for each contract? After several days, close your position and calculate your dollar return.

5. **Commodity Futures**   Now choose a different commodity that you think will decrease in value over the next several days and short three futures contracts. How much is the initial margin for these contracts? After several days, close your position and calculate your dollar return.

Chapter 4

Mutual Funds

"And the trouble is, if you don't risk anything, you risk even more."

—Erica Jong

With only $2,000 to invest, you can easily own shares in Microsoft, GM, McDonald's, IBM, Coke, and many more stocks through a mutual fund. Or, you can invest in a portfolio of government bonds or other investments. Indeed, there are many thousands of different mutual funds available to investors. In fact, there are about as many mutual funds as there are different stocks traded on the Nasdaq and the New York Stock Exchange combined. There are funds for aggressive investors, conservative investors, short-term investors, and long-term investors. There are bond funds, stock funds, international funds, and you-name-it funds. Is there a right fund for you? This chapter will help you find out. ∎

As we discussed in an earlier chapter, if you do not wish to actively buy and sell individual securities on your own, you can invest in stocks, bonds, or other financial assets through a *mutual fund*. Mutual funds are simply a means of combining or pooling the funds of a large group of investors. The buy and sell decisions for the resulting pool are then made by a fund manager, who is compensated for the service provided.

Since mutual funds provide indirect access to financial markets for individual investors, they are a form of financial intermediary. In fact, mutual funds are now the largest type of intermediary in the United States, followed by commercial banks and life insurance companies.

Mutual funds have become so important that we devote this entire chapter to them. The number of funds and the different fund types available have grown tremendously in recent years. As of the end of 2001, an estimated 93 million Americans in 55 million households owned mutual funds, up from just 5 million households in 1980. Investors contributed $505 billion to mutual funds in 2001, and, by the end of the year, mutual fund assets totaled $7 *trillion*.

One of the reasons for the proliferation of mutual funds and fund types is that mutual funds have become, on a very basic level, consumer products. They are created and marketed to the public in ways that are intended to promote buyer appeal. As every business student knows, product differentiation is a basic marketing tactic, and in recent years mutual funds have become increasingly adept at practicing this common marketing technique.

In fact, if you are not already a mutual fund investor, it is very likely that you will be in the near future. The reason has to do with a fundamental change in the way businesses of all types provide retirement benefits for employees. It used to be that most large employers offered so-called defined benefit pensions. With such a plan, when you retire, your employer pays you a pension typically based on years of service and salary. The key is that the pension benefit you receive is based on a predefined formula, hence the name.

Defined benefit plans are rapidly being replaced by "defined contribution" plans. With a defined contribution plan, your employer will contribute money each pay period to a retirement account on your behalf, but you have to select where the funds go. With this arrangement, the benefit you ultimately receive depends entirely on how your investments do; your employer only makes contributions. Most commonly, you must choose from a group of mutual funds for your investments, so it is very important that you understand the different types of mutual funds, as well as their risks and returns.

4.1 Investment Companies and Fund Types

investment company A business that specializes in pooling funds from individual investors and investing them.

At the most basic level, a company that pools funds obtained from individual investors and invests them is called an **investment company**. In other words, an investment company is a business that specializes in managing financial assets for individual investors. All mutual funds are, in fact, investment companies. As we will see, however, not all investment companies are mutual funds.

In the sections that follow, we will be discussing various aspects of mutual funds and related entities. Figure 4.1 is a big-picture overview of some of the different types of funds and how they are classified. It will serve as a guide for the next several sections. We will define the various terms that appear as we go along.

Open-End versus Closed-End Funds

open-end fund An investment company that stands ready to buy and sell shares at any time.

As Figure 4.1 shows, there are two fundamental types of investment companies, *open-end funds* and *closed-end funds*. The difference is very important. Whenever you invest in a mutual fund, you do so by buying shares in the fund. However, how shares are bought and sold depends on which type of fund you are considering.

With an **open-end fund**, the fund itself will sell new shares to anyone wishing to buy and will redeem (i.e., buy back) shares from anyone wishing to sell. When an

FIGURE 4.1   **Fund Types**

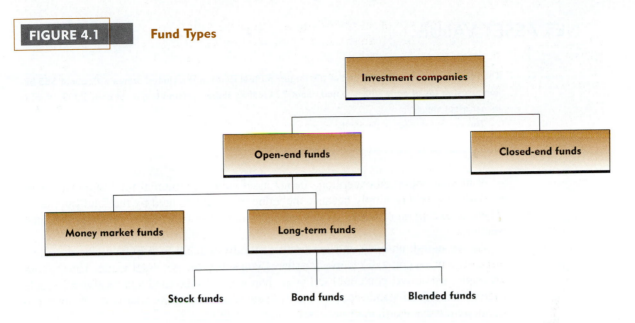

investor wishes to buy open-end fund shares, the fund simply issues them and then invests the money received. When someone wishes to sell open-end fund shares, the fund sells some of its assets and uses the cash to redeem the shares. As a result, with an open-end fund, the number of shares outstanding fluctuates through time.

closed-end fund An investment company with a fixed number of shares that are bought and sold only in the open stock market.

With a **closed-end fund**, the number of shares is fixed and never changes. If you want to buy shares, you must buy them from another investor. Similarly, if you wish to sell shares that you own, you must sell them to another investor.

Thus, the key difference between an open-end fund and a closed-end fund is that, with a closed-end fund, the fund itself does not buy or sell shares. In fact, as we discuss below, shares in closed-end funds are listed on stock exchanges just like ordinary shares of stock, where their shares are bought and sold in the same way. Open-end funds are more popular among individual investors than closed-end funds.

Strictly speaking, the term "mutual fund" actually refers only to an open-end investment company. Thus the phrase "closed-end fund" is a bit of an oxymoron, kind of like jumbo shrimp, and the phrase "open-end mutual fund" is a redundancy, an unnecessary repetition, or restatement. Nonetheless, particularly in recent years, the term "investment company" has all but disappeared from common use, and investment companies are now generically called mutual funds. We will stick with this common terminology whenever it won't lead to confusion.

Net Asset Value

net asset value The value of assets less liabilities held by a mutual fund, divided by the number of shares outstanding. Abbreviated NAV.

A mutual fund's **net asset value** is an important consideration. Net asset value is calculated by taking the total value of the assets held by the fund less any liabilities and then dividing by the number of outstanding shares. For example, suppose a mutual fund has $105 million in assets and $5 million in liabilities based on current market values and a total of 5 million shares outstanding. Based on the value of net assets held by the fund, $100 million, each share has a value of $100 million/5 million = $20. This $20 is the fund's net asset value, often abbreviated as NAV.

NET ASSET VALUE

EXAMPLE 4.1

The Fidelity Magellan Fund is one of the largest mutual funds in the United States with about $55 billion invested (as of early 2003). It had about 724 million shares outstanding as of early 2003. What is its net asset value?

The net asset value is simply the asset value per share, or $55 billion/724 million = $76.

With one important exception, the net asset value of a mutual fund will change essentially every day simply because the value of the assets held by the fund fluctuates. The one exception concerns money market mutual funds, which we discuss in a later section.

As we noted, an open-end fund will generally redeem or buy back shares at any time. The price you will receive for shares you sell is the net asset value. Thus, in our example just above, you could sell your shares back to the fund and receive $20 each. Because the fund stands ready to redeem shares at any time, shares in an open-end fund are always worth their net asset value.

In contrast, because the shares of closed-end funds are bought and sold in the stock markets, their share prices at any point in time may or may not be equal to their net asset values. We examine this issue in more detail in a later section.

Check This

4.1a   What is an investment company?

4.1b   What is the difference between an open-end fund and a closed-end fund?

4.2   Mutual Fund Operations

In this section, we discuss some essentials of mutual fund operations. We focus on how mutual funds are created, marketed, regulated, and taxed. Our discussion here deals primarily with open-end funds, but much of it applies to closed-end funds as well. Further details on closed-end funds are provided in a later section.

Mutual Fund Organization and Creation

A mutual fund is simply a corporation. Like a corporation, a mutual fund is owned by its shareholders. The shareholders elect a board of directors; the board of directors is responsible for hiring a manager to oversee the fund's operations. Although mutual funds often belong to a larger "family" of funds, every fund is a separate company owned by its shareholders.

Most mutual funds are created by investment advisory firms, which are businesses that specialize in managing mutual funds. Investment advisory firms are also called mutual fund companies. Increasingly, such firms have additional operations such as discount brokerages and other financial services.

There are hundreds of investment advisory firms in the United States. The largest, and probably best known, is Fidelity Investments, with 150 mutual funds, $800+ billion

All the major fund families have websites. Try, e.g., www.vanguard.com

in assets under management, and 19 million customers. Dreyfus, Franklin, and Vanguard are some other well-known examples. Many brokerage firms, such as Merrill Lynch and Charles Schwab, also have large investment advisory operations.

Investment advisory firms create mutual funds simply because they wish to manage them to earn fees. A typical management fee might be .75 percent of the total assets in the fund per year. A fund with $200 million in assets would not be especially large but could nonetheless generate management fees of about $1.5 million per year. Thus, there is a significant economic incentive to create funds and attract investors to them.

For example, a company like Fidelity might one day decide that there is a demand for a fund that buys stock in companies that grow and process citrus fruits. Fidelity could form a mutual fund that specializes in such companies and call it something like the Fidelity Lemon Fund.[1] A fund manager would be appointed, and shares in the fund would be offered to the public. As shares are sold, the money received is invested. If the fund is a success, a large amount of money will be attracted and Fidelity would benefit from the fees it earns. If the fund is not a success, the board can vote to liquidate it and return shareholders' money or merge it with another fund.

As our hypothetical example illustrates, an investment advisory firm such as Fidelity can (and often will) create new funds from time to time. Through time, this process leads to a family of funds all managed by the same advisory firm. Each fund in the family will have its own fund manager, but the advisory firm will generally handle the record keeping, marketing, and much of the research that underlies the fund's investment decisions.

In principle, the directors of a mutual fund in a particular family, acting on behalf of the fund shareholders, could vote to fire the investment advisory firm and hire a different one. As a practical matter, this rarely, if ever, occurs. At least part of the reason is that the directors are originally appointed by the fund's founder, and they are routinely reelected. Unhappy shareholders generally "vote with their feet"—that is, sell their shares and invest elsewhere.

Taxation of Investment Companies

As long as an investment company meets certain rules set by the Internal Revenue Service, it is treated as a "regulated investment company" for tax purposes. This is important because a regulated investment company does not pay taxes on its investment income. Instead, the fund passes through all realized investment income to fund shareholders, who then pay taxes on these distributions as though they owned the securities directly. Essentially, the fund simply acts as a conduit, funneling gains and losses to fund owners.

To qualify as a regulated investment company, the fund must follow three basic rules. The first rule is that it must in fact be an investment company holding almost all of its assets as investments in stocks, bonds, and other securities. The second rule limits the fund to using no more than 5 percent of its assets when acquiring a particular security. This is a diversification rule. The third rule is that the fund must pass through all realized investment income to fund shareholders.

The Fund Prospectus and Annual Report

Mutual funds are required by law to produce a document known as a *prospectus*. The prospectus must be supplied to any investor wishing to purchase shares. Mutual funds

---

[1]Fidelity would probably come up with a better name.

must also provide an annual report to their shareholders. The annual report and the prospectus, which are sometimes combined, contain financial statements along with specific information concerning the fund's expenses, gains and losses, holdings, objectives, and management. We discuss many of these items in the next few sections.

Check This

4.2a	How do mutual funds usually get started?
4.2b	How are mutual funds taxed?

4.3 Mutual Fund Costs and Fees

All mutual funds have various expenses that are paid by the fund's shareholders. These expenses can vary considerably from fund to fund, however, and one of the most important considerations in evaluating a fund is its expense structure. All else the same, lower expenses are preferred, of course, but, as we discuss, matters are not quite that cut-and-dried.

Types of Expenses and Fees

There are basically four types of expenses or fees associated with buying and owning mutual fund shares:

1. Sales charges or "loads."
2. 12b-1 fees.
3. Management fees.
4. Trading costs.

We discuss each of these in turn.

front-end load A sales charge levied on purchases of shares in some mutual funds.

Sales Charges Many mutual funds charge a fee whenever shares are purchased. These fees are generally called **front-end loads**. Funds that charge loads are called *load funds*. Funds that have no such charges are called *no-load funds*.

When you purchase shares in a load fund, you pay a price in excess of the net asset value, called the *offering price*. The difference between the offering price and the net asset value is the *load*. Shares in no-load funds are sold at net asset value.

Front-end loads can range as high as 8.5 percent, but 5 percent or so would be more typical. Some funds, with front-end loads in the 2 percent to 3 percent range, are described as *low-load funds*.

Front-end loads are expressed as a percentage of the offering price, not the net asset value. For example, suppose a load fund has an offering price of $100 and a net asset value of $98. The front-end load is $2, which, as a percentage of the $100 offering price, is $2/$100 = 2 percent. The way front-end loads are calculated understates the load slightly. In our example here, you are paying $100 for something worth only $98, so the load is really $2/$98 = 2.04 percent.

FRONT-END LOADS

EXAMPLE 4.2

On a particular day, according to *The Wall Street Journal*, the Common Sense Growth fund had a net asset value of $13.91. The offering price was $15.20. Is this a load fund? What is the front-end load?

Since the offering price, which is the price you must pay to purchase shares, exceeds the net asset value, this is definitely a load fund. The load can be calculated by taking the difference between the offering price and the net asset value, $1.29, and dividing by the $15.20 offering price. The result is a hefty front-end load of 8.5 percent.

Some funds have "back-end" loads, which are charges levied on redemptions. These loads are often called *contingent deferred sales charges* and abbreviated CDSC. The CDSC usually declines through time. It might start out at 6 percent for shares held less than one year, then drop to 3 percent for shares held for two years, and disappear altogether on shares held for three or more years.

12b-1 fees Named for SEC Rule 12b-1, which allows funds to spend up to 1 percent of fund assets annually to cover distribution and marketing costs.

12b-1 Fees So-called **12b-1 fees** are named for the Securities and Exchange Commission (SEC) rule that permits them. Mutual funds are allowed to use a portion of the fund's assets to cover distribution and marketing costs. Funds that market directly to the public may use 12b-1 fees to pay for advertising and direct mailing costs. Funds that rely on brokers and other sales force personnel often use 12b-1 fees to provide compensation for their services. The total amount of these fees could be .75 percent to 1.0 percent of the fund's assets per year.

Frequently, 12b-1 fees are used in conjunction with a CDSC. Such funds will often have no front-end load, but they effectively make it up through these other costs. Such funds may look like no-load funds, but they are really disguised load funds. Mutual funds with no front-end or back-end loads and no or minimal 12b-1 fees are often called "pure" no-load funds to distinguish them from the "not-so-pure" funds that may have no loads but still charge hefty 12b-1 fees.

Management Fees We briefly discussed management fees in an earlier section. Fees are usually based first on the size of the fund. Beyond this, there is often an incentive provision that increases the fee if the fund outperforms some benchmark, often the S&P 500 (this index is discussed in Chapter 1). Management fees generally range from .25 percent to 1.0 percent of total fund assets every year.

turnover A measure of how much trading a fund does, calculated as the lesser of total purchases or sales during a year divided by average daily assets.

Trading Costs Mutual funds have brokerage expenses from trading just like individuals do. As a result, mutual funds that do a lot of trading will have relatively high trading costs.

Trading costs can be difficult to get a handle on because they are not reported directly. However, in the prospectus, funds are required to report something known as **turnover**. A fund's turnover is a measure of how much trading a fund does. It is calculated as the lesser of a fund's total purchases or sales during a year, divided by average daily assets.[2]

---

[2]Purchases and sales for a fund are usually different because of purchases and redemptions of fund shares by shareholders. For example, if a fund is growing, purchases will exceed sales.

TURNOVER

EXAMPLE 4.3

Suppose a fund had average daily assets of $50 million during 2001. It bought $80 million worth of stock and sold $70 million during the year. What is its turnover?

The lesser of purchases or sales is $70 million, and average daily assets are $50 million. Turnover is thus $70/$50 = 1.4 times.

A fund with a turnover of 1.0 has, in effect, sold off its entire portfolio and replaced it once during the year. Similarly, a turnover of .50 indicates that, loosely speaking, the fund replaced half of its holdings during the year. All else the same, a higher turnover indicates more frequent trading and higher trading costs.

Expense Reporting

Mutual funds are required to report expenses in a fairly standardized way in the prospectus. The exact format varies, but the information reported is generally the same. There are three parts to an expense statement. Figure 4.2 shows this information as it was reported for the Fidelity Low-Priced Stock Fund.

To see a fund that really discloses information, try www.ipsfunds.com Check out the "plain language" risk disclosure!

The first part of the statement shows shareholder transaction expenses, which are generally loads and deferred sales charges. As indicated, for this fund, there is a 3 percent front-end load on shares purchased, but none on dividends received that are reinvested in the fund (it's common for mutual fund shareholders to simply reinvest any dividends received from the fund). The next item shows that there is no CDSC. The fourth item, labeled "redemption fee," refers to a back-end load that is applied under certain circumstances.

The second part of the statement, "Annual fund operating expenses," includes the management and 12b-1 fees. This fund's management fee was .75 percent of assets. There was no 12b-1 fee. The other expenses include things like legal, accounting, and reporting costs along with director fees. At .24 percent of assets, these costs are not trivial. The sum of these three items is the fund's total operating expense expressed as a percentage of assets, .99 percent in this case. To put this in perspective, this fund has about $15 billion in assets, so operating costs were about $150 million, of which about $112.5 million was paid for the fund manager.

The third part of the expense report gives a hypothetical example showing the total expense you would incur over time per $10,000 invested. The example is strictly hypothetical, however, and is only a rough guide. As shown here, your costs would amount to $1,477 after 10 years per $10,000 invested, assuming a return of 5 percent per year. This third part of the expense statement is not all that useful, really. What matters for this fund is that expenses appear to run about .99 percent per year, so that is what you pay in addition to loads.

One thing to watch out for is that funds may have 12b-1 plans but may choose not to spend anything in a particular year. Similarly, the fund manager can choose to rebate some of the management fee in a particular year (especially if the fund has done poorly). These actions create a low expense figure for a given year, but this does not mean that expenses won't be higher in the future.

FIGURE 4.2

Mutual Fund
Expenses

Fidelity®
Low-Priced Stock
Fund

Prospectus

Fee Table

The following table describes the fees and expenses that are incurred when you buy, hold, or sell shares of the fund.

The annual fund operating expenses provided below for the fund do not reflect the effect of any reduction of certain expenses during the period.

Shareholder fees (paid by the investor directly)

Maximum sales charge (load) on purchases (as a % of offering price)[A]	3.00%
Sales charge (load) on reinvested distributions	None
Deferred sales charge (load) on redemptions	None
Redemption fee on shares held less than 90 days (as a % of amount redeemed)[B]	1.50%

[A] *Lower sales charges may be available for fund balances over $250,000.*

[B] *A redemption fee may be charged when you sell your shares or if your fund balance falls below the balance minimum for any reason, including solely due to declines in the fund's net asset value per share (NAV).*

Annual fund operating expenses (paid from fund assets)

Management fee	0.75%
Distribution and/or Service (12b-1) fees	None
Other expenses	0.24%
Total annual fund operating expenses	**0.99%**

A portion of the brokerage commissions that the fund pays is used to reduce the fund's expenses. In addition, through arrangements with the fund's custodian and transfer agent, credits realized as a result of uninvested cash balances are used to reduce custodian and transfer agent expenses. Including these reductions, the total fund operating expenses, would have been 0.97%.

This **example** helps you compare the cost of investing in the fund with the cost of investing in other mutual funds.

Let's say, hypothetically, that the fund's annual return is 5% and that your shareholder fees and the fund's annual operating expenses are exactly as described in the fee table. This example illustrates the effect of fees and expenses, but is not meant to suggest actual or expected fees and expenses or returns, all of which may vary. For every $10,000 you invested, here's how much you would pay in total expenses if you sell all of your shares at the end of each time period indicated:

1 year	$ 398
3 years	$ 606
5 years	$ 831
10 years	$ 1,477

Why Pay Loads and Fees?

Given that pure no-load funds exist, you might wonder why anyone would buy load funds or funds with substantial CDSC or 12b-1 fees. It is becoming increasingly difficult to give a good answer to this question. At one time, there simply weren't many no-load funds, and those that existed weren't widely known. Today, there are many good no-load funds, and competition among funds is forcing many funds to lower or do away with loads and other fees.

Having said this, there are basically two reasons that you might want to consider a load fund or a fund with above-average fees. First, you may simply want a fund run by a particular manager. A good example of this is the Fidelity Magellan Fund we mentioned earlier. For many years, it was run by Peter Lynch, who is widely regarded as one of the most successful managers in the history of the business. The Magellan Fund was (and is) a load fund, leaving you no choice but to pay the load to obtain Lynch's expertise.

The other reason to consider paying a load is that you want a specialized type of fund. For example, you might be interested in investing in a fund that invests only in a particular foreign country, such as Brazil. We'll discuss such specialty funds in a later section, but for now we note that there is little competition among specialty funds, and, as a result, loads and fees tend to be higher.

Check This

4.3a	What is the difference between a load fund and a no-load fund?	
4.3b	What are 12b-1 fees?	

4.4   Short-Term Funds

Mutual funds are usually divided into two major groups, short-term funds and long-term funds. Short-term funds are collectively known as *money market mutual funds.* Long-term funds essentially include everything that is not a money market fund. We discuss long-term funds in our next section; here we focus on money market funds.

Money Market Mutual Funds

money market mutual fund A mutual fund specializing in money market instruments.

As the name suggests, **money market mutual funds**, or MMMFs, specialize in money market instruments. As we described in Chapter 3, these are short-term debt obligations issued by governments and corporations. Money market funds were introduced in the early 1970s and have grown tremendously. By 2003, about 1,000 money market funds managed more than $2.3 trillion in assets. All money market funds are open-end funds.

Most money market funds invest in high-quality, low-risk instruments with maturities of less than 90 days. As a result, they have relatively little risk. However, some buy riskier assets or have longer maturities than others, so they do not all carry equally low risk. For example, some buy only very short-term U.S. government securities and are therefore essentially risk-free. Others buy mostly securities issued by corporations which entail some risk. We discuss the different types of money market instruments and their relative risks in Chapter 9.

Visit www.mfea.com for info on thousands of funds, including MMMFs.

Money Market Fund Accounting A unique feature of money market funds is that their net asset values are always $1 per share. This is purely an accounting gimmick, however. A money market fund simply sets the number of shares equal to the fund's assets. In other words, if the fund has $100 million in assets, then it has 100 million shares. As the fund earns interest on its investments, the fund owners are simply given more shares.

The reason money market mutual funds always maintain a $1 net asset value is to make them resemble bank accounts. As long as a money market fund invests in very safe, interest-bearing, short-maturity assets, its net asset value will not drop below $1 per share. However, there is no guarantee that this will not happen, and the term "breaking the buck" is used to describe dropping below $1 in net asset value. This is a very rare occurrence, but, in 1994, several large money market funds experienced substantial losses because they purchased relatively risky derivative assets and broke the buck, so it definitely can happen.

Taxes and Money Market Funds Money market funds are either taxable or tax-exempt. Taxable funds are more common; of the $2.3 trillion in total money market fund assets in 2003, taxable funds accounted for about 87 percent. As the name suggests, the difference in the two fund types lies in their tax treatment. As a general rule, interest earned on state and local government (or "municipal") securities is exempt from federal income tax. Nontaxable money market funds therefore buy only these types of tax-exempt securities.

Some tax-exempt funds go even further. Interest paid by one state is often subject to state taxes in another. Some tax-exempt funds therefore buy only securities issued by a single state. For residents of that state, the interest earned is free of both federal and state taxes. For beleaguered New York City residents, there are even "triple-tax-free" funds that invest only in New York City obligations, thereby allowing residents to escape federal, state, and local income taxes on the interest received.

Because of their favorable tax treatment, tax-exempt money market instruments have much lower interest rates, or *yields*.[3] For example, in mid-2003, taxable money funds offered about 1.2 percent interest, whereas tax-exempt funds offered only .9 percent interest. Which is better depends on your individual tax bracket. If you're in a 40 percent bracket, then the taxable fund is paying only $.012 \times (1 - .40) = .0072$, or .72 percent, on an aftertax basis, so you're better off with the tax-exempt fund.

TAXES AND MONEY MARKET FUND YIELDS

EXAMPLE 4.4

In our discussion just above, suppose you were in a 20 percent tax bracket. Which type of fund is more attractive?

On an aftertax basis, the taxable fund is offering $.012 \times (1 - .20) = .0096$, or .96 percent, so the taxable fund is more attractive.

---

[3]We discuss how yields on money market instruments are calculated in Chapter 9.

Money Market Deposit Accounts

Most banks offer what are called "money market" deposit accounts, or MMDAs, which are much like money market mutual funds. For example, both money market funds and money market deposit accounts generally have limited check-writing privileges.

There is a very important distinction between such a bank-offered money market account and a money market fund, however. A bank money market account is a bank deposit and offers FDIC protection, whereas a money market fund does not. A money market fund will generally offer SIPC protection, but this is not a perfect substitute. Confusingly, some banks offer both money market accounts and, through a separate, affiliated entity, money market funds.

Check This

4.4a	What is a money market mutual fund? What are the two types?
4.4b	How do money market mutual funds maintain a constant net asset value?

4.5   Long-Term Funds

There are many different types of long-term funds. Historically, mutual funds were classified as stock, bond, or income funds. As a part of the rapid growth in mutual funds, however, it is becoming increasingly difficult to place all funds into these three categories. Also, providers of mutual fund information do not use the same classification schemes.

Mutual funds have different goals, and a fund's objective is the major determinant of the fund type. All mutual funds must state the fund's objective in the prospectus. For example, the Fidelity Independence Fund states:

> The fund's objective is capital appreciation. Normally, the fund's strategy is to invest primarily in common stocks of domestic and foreign issuers. The fund strategy may result in the realization of capital gains without considering the tax consequences to shareholders. Fidelity Management & Research Company (FMR) is not constrained by any particular investment style and may invest in "growth" stocks, "value" stocks, or both, at any given time.

Thus, this fund invests in different types of stocks with the goal of capital appreciation. This is clearly a stock fund, and it might further be classified as a "capital appreciation" fund or "aggressive growth" fund, depending on whose classification scheme is used.

Mutual fund objectives are an important consideration; unfortunately, the truth is they frequently are too vague to provide useful information. For example, a very common objective reads like this: "The Big Bucks Fund seeks capital appreciation, income, and capital preservation." Translation: The fund seeks to (1) increase the value of its shares, (2) generate income for its shareholders, and (3) not lose money. Well, don't we all! More to the point, funds with very similar-sounding objectives can have very different portfolios and, consequently, very different risks. As a result, it is a mistake to look only at a fund's stated objective: Actual portfolio holdings speak louder than prospectus promises.

One of the best mutual fund sites is www.morningstar. com

Stock Funds

Stock funds exist in great variety. We consider nine separate general types and some subtypes. We also consider some new varieties that don't fit in any category.

Capital Appreciation versus Income The first four types of stock funds trade off capital appreciation and dividend income.

1. *Capital appreciation.* As in our example just above, these funds seek maximum capital appreciation. They generally invest in companies that have, in the opinion of the fund manager, the best prospects for share price appreciation without regard to dividends, company size, or, for some funds, country. Often this means investing in unproven companies or perceived out-of-favor companies.

2. *Growth.* These funds also seek capital appreciation, but they tend to invest in larger, more established companies. Such funds may be somewhat less volatile as a result. Dividends are not an important consideration.

3. *Growth and income.* Capital appreciation is still the main goal, but at least part of the focus is on dividend-paying companies.

4. *Equity income.* These funds focus almost exclusively on stocks with relatively high dividend yields, thereby maximizing the current income on the portfolio.

Among these four fund types, the greater the emphasis on growth, the greater the risk, at least as a general matter. Again, however, these are only rough classifications. Equity income funds, for example, frequently invest heavily in public utility stocks; such stocks had heavy losses in the first part of the 1990s.

Company Size–Based Funds These next two fund types focus on companies in a particular size range.

1. *Small company.* As the name suggests, these funds focus on stocks in small companies, where "small" refers to the total market value of the stock. Such funds are often called "small-cap" funds, where "cap" is short for total market value or capitalization. In Chapter 1, we saw that small stocks have traditionally performed very well, at least over the long run, hence the demand for funds that specialize in such stocks. With small-company mutual funds, what constitutes small is variable, ranging from perhaps $10 million up to $1 billion or so in total market value, and some funds specialize in smaller companies than others. Since most small companies don't pay dividends, these funds necessarily emphasize capital appreciation.

2. *Midcap.* These funds usually specialize in stocks that are too small to be in the S&P 500 index but too large to be considered small stocks.

International Funds The next two fund groups invest internationally. Research has shown that diversifying internationally can significantly improve the risk-return trade-off for investors, and international funds have been among the most rapidly growing. However, that growth slowed sharply in the late 1990s.

1. *Global.* These funds have substantial international holdings but also maintain significant investments in U.S. stocks.

2. *International.* These funds are like global funds, except they focus on non-U.S. equities.

Among international funds, some specialize in specific regions of the world, such as Europe, the Pacific Rim, or South America. Others specialize in individual countries. Today, there is at least one mutual fund specializing in essentially every country in the world that has a stock market, however small.

International funds that specialize in countries with small or recently established stock markets are often called *emerging markets funds*. Almost all single-country funds, and especially emerging markets funds, are not well-diversified and have historically been extremely volatile.

Many funds that are not classified as international funds may actually have substantial overseas investments, so this is one thing to watch out for. It is not unusual for a fund to call itself a "growth" fund and actually invest heavily outside the United States.

Sector Funds   Sector funds specialize in specific sectors of the economy and often focus on particular industries or particular commodities. There are far too many different types to list here. There are funds that only buy software companies, and funds that only buy hardware companies. There are funds that specialize in natural gas producers, oil producers, and precious metals producers. In fact, essentially every major industry in the U.S. economy is covered by at least one fund.

One thing to notice about sector funds is that, like single-country funds, they are obviously not well-diversified. Every year, many of the best performing mutual funds (in terms of total return) are sector funds simply because whatever sector of the economy is hottest will generally have the largest stock price increases. Funds specializing in that sector will do well. In the same vein, and for the same reason, the worst performing funds are also almost always some type of sector fund. When it comes to mutual funds, past performance is almost always an unreliable guide to future performance; nowhere is this more true than with sector funds.

Other Fund Types and Issues   Three other types of stock funds that don't fit easily into one of the above categories bear discussing: *index funds*, so-called *social conscience funds*, and *tax-managed funds*.

1. *Index funds.* Index funds simply hold the stocks that make up a particular index in the same relative proportions as the index. The most important index funds are S&P 500 funds, which are intended to track the performance of the S&P 500, the large stock index we discussed in Chapter 1. By their nature, index funds are passively managed, meaning that the fund manager trades only as necessary to match the index. Such funds are appealing in part because they are generally characterized by low turnover and low operating expenses. Another reason index funds have grown rapidly is that there is considerable debate over whether mutual fund managers can consistently beat the averages. If they can't, the argument runs, why pay loads and management fees when it's cheaper just to buy the averages by indexing? See our nearby *Investment Updates* box for more.

2. *Social conscience funds.* These funds are a relatively new creation. They invest only in companies whose products, policies, or politics are viewed as socially desirable. The specific social objectives range from environmental issues to

To learn more about "social conscience" funds, visit www.socialinvest.org and www.domini.com

On Wall Street, there's no such thing as free advice. But a conversation with Vanguard Group Chairman Jack Brennan comes pretty darn close. All too often, what you get from Wall Street are dubious investment tips packaged as enduring wisdom. Brokerage firms push you to trade stocks. Financial planners think you need professional hand-holding. Money managers hold out the prospect of market-beating returns. These folks are, to use one of my favorite phrases, "talking their book." They may want to make money for their investors. But they also want to make money for themselves, and those two goals are constantly clashing. The 46-year-old Mr. Brennan also talks his book, promoting the index funds that Vanguard specializes in and touting the importance of low costs, a hallmark of Vanguard's 109 mutual funds. But Mr. Brennan's advice is less suspect, because Vanguard serves just one master: its fund shareholders. In a unique arrangement, these fund investors own the Malvern, Pa., company, which rewards its owners by operating its funds at the lowest possible cost.

Result? Here's some of the garbage you hear on Wall Street and, for refreshing contrast, Mr. Brennan's perspective:

"Investors are idiots." Wall Streeters constantly decry the foolishness of ordinary investors. But are investors really so stupid? Wall Street certainly hopes so, because that means investors need the expensive counseling that brokers and financial planners provide. "They make it sound like the average investor is day trading and swinging from value to growth and buying Internet funds," says Mr. Brennan, who became Vanguard's chief executive in 1996, succeeding the even-more-fiery John Bogle.

Mr. Brennan argues that, while a minority of investors may behave foolishly, most aren't nearly so trigger-happy. For proof, he notes that 75% of investors in Vanguard-managed 401(k) plans didn't make any trades in either of the past two years. "The average investor stood pat during the frenzy of the run-up and stood pat as the market retreated," Mr. Brennan says. "A decade ago, I don't think the reaction would have been the same. Investors have become better able to make money." In fact, Mr. Brennan seems to relish the recent market turmoil. He notes that, while the Nasdaq Composite Index took a beating, broader market indexes didn't fall nearly as much. "People have learned a ton" from the market decline, he says. "The interesting thing is, it's not been an expensive lesson."

"Buy and hold doesn't work." Do you need to change tack with every shift in the investment wind? Wall Street seems to think so. As analysts change their opinions on stocks, strategists revise their market outlook and newsletter writers offer fresh fund recommendations, some investors inevitably are spurred to action. This activity is wonderful for Wall Street, which profits from the resulting commissions and trading spreads. But investors don't fare nearly so well. "The quickest way to make a small fortune is to start with a big one and trade a lot," Mr. Brennan quips. The trading culture of the late 1990s was fostered by brokerage firms, especially discount brokers, which used rock-bottom commission rates to lure investors out of funds and into individual stocks. But along the way, risk got forgotten. Mr. Brennan points out that, over the past three calendar years, 60% of individual stocks posted losses, while just 6% of diversified U.S. stock funds were underwater. "The idea that 20 stocks offer diversification just isn't valid," he says.

"You can beat the market." This is Wall Street's most self-serving myth. The harder investors try to outperform the market average, the more they incur in investment costs. Those hefty costs are good for Wall Street, but bad for investors, because it makes it even more unlikely they will beat the market. So why not give up on costly efforts to beat the market and instead buy low-cost market-tracking index funds? Not surprisingly, the idea is an anathema to many on Wall Street. At every turn, detractors seem to find new arguments for steering folks away from index funds.

Many, for instance, predicted that index funds would fare poorly during a market plunge. But Mr. Brennan points out that in the recent decline, index funds outperformed the average for actively managed stock funds in seven of the nine U.S. stock-fund style categories tracked by Chicago fund researchers Morningstar Inc. "Clearly, indexing has passed the test with flying colors," Mr. Brennan says. "There's this myth that the average manager is going to go to cash at the right time. It didn't happen."

Many are predicting lower returns in the years ahead, which means investment costs will snag a bigger portion of investors' returns. As a result, Mr. Brennan believes costs will figure more prominently in investors' decisions. I am not so optimistic, but I sure hope he isn't right. "A high-cost investment program isn't going to just hurt you," Mr. Brennan says. "It'll kill you. The impact of cost is finally going to take hold."

Source: Jonathan Clements, *The Wall Street Journal*, May 29, 2001.

personnel policies. The Parnassus Fund is a well-known example, avoiding the alcoholic beverage, tobacco, gambling, weapons, and nuclear power industries. Of course, consensus on what is socially desirable or responsible is hard to find. In fact, there are so-called sin funds (and sector funds) that specialize in these very industries!

3. *Tax-managed funds.* Taxable mutual funds are generally managed without regard for the tax liabilities of fund owners. Fund managers focus on (and are frequently rewarded based on) total pretax returns. However, recent research has shown that some fairly simple strategies can greatly improve the aftertax returns to shareholders and that focusing just on pretax returns is not a good idea for taxable investors. Tax-managed funds try to hold down turnover to minimize realized capital gains, and they try to match realized gains with realized losses. Such strategies work particularly well for index funds. For example, the Schwab 1000 Fund is a fund that tracks the Russell 1000 Index, a widely followed 1,000-stock index. However, the fund will deviate from strictly following the index to a certain extent to avoid realizing taxable gains, and, as a result, the fund holds turnover to a minimum. Fund shareholders have largely escaped taxes as a result. We predict funds promoting such strategies will become increasingly common as investors become more aware of the tax consequences of fund ownership.

Is vice nice? Visit www.vicefund.com to find out.

Taxable and Municipal Bond Funds

Most bond funds invest in domestic corporate and government securities, although some invest in foreign government and non-U.S. corporate bonds as well. As we will see, there are a relatively small number of bond fund types.

There are basically five characteristics that distinguish bond funds:

1. Maturity range. Different funds hold bonds of different maturities, ranging from quite short (2 years) to quite long (25–30 years).

2. Credit quality. Some bonds are much safer than others in terms of the possibility of default. United States government bonds have no default risk, while so-called junk bonds have significant default risk.

3. Taxability. Municipal bond funds buy only bonds that are free from federal income tax. Taxable funds buy only taxable issues.

4. Type of bond. Some funds specialize in particular types of fixed-income instruments such as mortgages.

5. Country. Most bond funds buy only domestic issues, but some buy foreign company and government issues.

Short-Term and Intermediate-Term Funds As the names suggest, these two fund types focus on bonds in a specific maturity range. Short-term maturities are generally considered to be less than five years. Intermediate-term would be less than 10 years. There are both taxable and municipal bond funds with these maturity targets.

One thing to be careful of with these types of funds is that the credit quality of the issues can vary from fund to fund. One fund could hold very risky intermediate-term bonds, while another might hold only U.S. government issues with similar maturities.

General Funds For both taxable and municipal bonds, this category is kind of a catch-all. Funds in this category simply don't specialize in any particular way. Our warning just above concerning varied credit quality applies here. Maturities can differ substantially as well.

High-Yield Funds High-yield municipal and taxable funds specialize in low-credit quality issues. Such issues have higher yields because of their greater risks. As a result, high-yield bond funds can be quite volatile.

Mortgage Funds A number of funds specialize in so-called mortgage-backed securities such as GNMA (Government National Mortgage Association, referred to as "Ginnie Mae") issues. We discuss this important type of security in detail in Chapter 13. There are no municipal mortgage-backed securities (yet), so these are all taxable bond funds.

World Funds A relatively limited number of taxable funds invest worldwide. Some specialize in only government issues; others buy a variety of non-U.S. issues. These are all taxable funds.

Insured Funds This is a type of municipal bond fund. Municipal bond issuers frequently purchase insurance that guarantees the bond's payments will be made. Such bonds have very little possibility of default, so some funds specialize in them.

Single-State Municipal Funds Earlier we discussed how some money market funds specialize in issues from a single state. The same is true for some bond funds. Such funds are especially important in large states such as California and other high-tax states. Confusingly, this classification refers only to long-term funds. Short and intermediate single-state funds are classified with other maturity-based municipal funds.

Stock and Bond Funds

This last major fund group includes a variety of funds. The only common feature is that these funds don't invest exclusively in either stocks or bonds. For this reason, they are often called "blended" or "hybrid" funds. We discuss a few of the main types.

Balanced Funds Balanced funds maintain a relatively fixed split between stocks and bonds. They emphasize relatively safe, high-quality investments. Such funds provide a kind of "one-stop" shopping for fund investors, particularly smaller investors, because they diversify into both stocks and bonds.

Asset Allocation Funds Two types of funds carry this label. The first is an extended version of a balanced fund. Such a fund holds relatively fixed proportional investments in stocks, bonds, money market instruments, and perhaps real estate or some other investment class. The target proportions may be updated or modified periodically.

The other type of asset allocation fund is often called a *flexible portfolio fund*. Here, the fund manager may hold up to 100 percent in stocks, bonds, or money market instruments, depending on her views about the likely performance of these investments. These funds essentially try to time the market, guessing which general type of investment will do well (or least poorly) over the months ahead.

Convertible Funds Some bonds are convertible, meaning they can be swapped for a fixed number of shares of stock at the option of the bondholder. Some mutual funds specialize in these bonds.

Income Funds An income fund emphasizes generating dividend and coupon income on its investments, so it would hold a variety of dividend-paying common, as well as preferred, stocks and bonds of various maturities.

Mutual Fund Objectives: Recent Developments

As we mentioned earlier, a mutual fund's stated objective may not be all that informative. In recent years, there has been a trend toward classifying a mutual fund's objective based on its actual holdings. For example, Figure 4.3 illustrates the classifications used by *The Wall Street Journal*.

A key thing to notice in Figure 4.3 is that most general-purpose funds (as opposed to specialized types such as sector funds) are classified based on the market "cap" of the stocks they hold (small, midsize, or large) and also on whether the fund tends to invest in either "growth" or "value" stocks (or both). We will discuss growth versus value stocks in a later chapter; for now, it is enough to know that "growth" stocks are those considered more likely to grow rapidly. "Value" stocks are those that look to be relatively undervalued and thus may be attractive for that reason. Notice that, in this

FIGURE 4.3   **Mutual Fund Objectives**

MUTUAL-FUND OBJECTIVES
Categories compiled by The Wall Street Journal, based on classifications by Lipper Inc.

STOCK FUNDS

Emerging Markets (EM): Funds that invest in emerging-market equity securities, where the "emerging market" is defined by a country's GNP per capita and other economic measures.
Equity Income (EI): Funds that seek high current income and growth of income through investment in equities.
European Region (EU): Funds that invest in markets or operations concentrated in the European region.
Global Stock (GL): Funds that invest in securities traded outside of the U.S. and may own U.S. securities as well.
Gold Oriented (AU): Funds that invest in gold mines, gold-oriented mining finance houses, gold coins or bullion.
Health/Biotech (HB): Funds that invest in companies related to health care, medicine and biotechnology.
International Stock (IL) (non-U.S.): Canadian; International; International Small Cap.
Latin American (LT): Funds that invest in markets or operations concentrated in the Latin American region.
Large-Cap Growth (LG): Funds that invest in large companies with long-term earnings that are expected to grow significantly faster than the earnings of stocks in major indexes. Funds normally have above-average price-to-earnings ratios, price-to-book ratios and three-year earnings growth.
Large-Cap Core (LC): Funds that invest in large companies, with wide latitude in the type of shares they buy. On average, the price-to-earnings ratios, price-to-book ratios, and three-year earnings growth are in line with those of the U.S. diversified large-cap funds' universe average.
Large-Cap Value (LV): Funds that invest in large companies that are considered undervalued relative to major stock indexes based on price-to-earnings ratios, price-to-book ratios or other factors.
Midcap Growth (MG): Funds that invest in midsize companies with long-term earnings that are expected to grow significantly faster than the earnings of stocks in major indexes. Funds normally have above-average price-to-earnings ratios, price-to-book ratios and three-year earnings growth.
Midcap Core (MC): Funds that invest in midsize companies, with wide latitude in the type of shares they buy. On average, the price-to-earnings ratios, price-to-book ratios, and three-year earnings growth are in line with those of the U.S. diversified midcap funds' universe average.
Midcap Value (MV): Funds that invest in midsize companies that are considered undervalued relative to major stock indexes based on price-to-earnings ratios, price-to-book ratios or other factors.
Multicap Growth (XG): Funds that invest in companies of various sizes, with long-term earnings that are expected to grow significantly faster than the earnings of stocks in major indexes. Funds normally have above-average price-to-earnings ratios, price-to-book ratios, and three-year earnings growth.
Multicap Core (XC): Funds that invest in companies of various sizes with average price-to-earnings ratios, price-to-book ratios and earnings growth.
Multicap Value (XV): Funds that invest in companies of various size, normally those that are considered undervalued relative to major stock indexes based on price-to-earnings ratios, price-to-book ratios or other factors.
Natural Resources (NR): Funds that invest in natural-resource stocks.
Pacific Region (PR): Funds that invest in China Region; Japan; Pacific Ex-Japan; Pacific Region.
Science & Technology (TK): Funds that invest in science and technology stocks. Includes Telecommunication funds.
Sector (SE): Funds that invest in financial services; real estate; specialty & miscellaneous.

S&P 500 Index (SP): Funds that are passively managed, and are designed to replicate the performance of the Standard & Poor's 500-stock Index on a reinvested basis.
Small-Cap Growth (SG): Funds that invest in small companies with long-term earnings that are expected to grow significantly faster than the earnings of stocks in major indexes. Funds normally have above-average price-to-earnings ratios, price-to-book ratios, and three-year earnings growth.
Small-Cap Core (SC): Funds that invest in small companies, with wide latitude in the type of shares they buy. On average, the price-to-earnings ratios, price-to-book ratios, and three-year earnings growth are in line with those of the U.S. diversified small-cap funds' universe average.
Small-Cap Value (SV): Funds that invest in small companies that are considered undervalued relative to major stock indexes based on price-to-earnings ratios, price-to-book ratios or other factors.
Specialty Equity (SQ): Funds that invest in all market capitalization ranges, with no restrictions for any one range. May have strategies that are distinctly different from other diversified stock funds.
Utility (UT): Funds that invest in utility stocks.

TAXABLE BOND FUNDS

Short-Term Bond (SB): Ultra-short Obligation; Short Investment Grade Debt; Short-Intermediate Investment Grade Debt.
Short-Term U.S. (SU): Short U.S. Treasury; Short U.S. Government; Short-Intermediate U.S. Government debt.
Intermediate Bond (IB): Funds that invest in investment-grade debt issues (rated in the top four grades) with dollar-weighted average maturities of five to 10 years.
Intermediate U.S. (IG): Intermediate U.S. Government; Intermediate U.S. Treasury.
Long-Term Bond (AB): Funds that invest in corporate and government debt issues in the top grades.
Long-Term U.S. (LU): General U.S. Government; General U.S. Treasury; Target Maturity.
General U.S. Taxable (GT): Funds that invest in general bonds.
High-Yield Taxable (HC): Funds that aim for high current yields from fixed-income securities and tend to invest in lower-grade debt.
Mortgage (MT): Adjustable Rate Mortgage; GNMA; U.S. Mortgage.
World Bond (WB): Emerging Markets Debt; Global |Income; International Income; Short World Multi-Market Income.

MUNICIPAL DEBT FUNDS

Short-Term Muni (SM): California Short-Intermediate Muni Debt; Other States Short-Intermediate Muni Debt; Short-Intermediate Muni Debt; Short Muni Debt.
Intermediate Muni (IM): Intermediate-term Muni Debt including single states.
General Muni (GM): Funds investing in muni-debt issues in the top four credit ratings.
Single-State Municipal (SS): Funds that invest in debt of individual states.
High-Yield Municipal (HM): Funds that invest in lower rated muni debt.
Insured Muni (NM): California Insured Muni Debt; Florida Insured Muni Debt; Insured Muni Debt; New York Insured Muni Debt.

STOCK & BOND FUNDS

Balanced (BL): Primary objective is to conserve principal, by maintaining a balanced portfolio of both stocks and bonds.
Stock/Bond Blend (MP): Multipurpose funds such as Balanced Target Maturity; Convertible Securities; Flexible Income; Flexible Portfolio; Global Flexible and Income funds, that invest in both stocks and bonds.

WORK THE WEB

As we discussed in the chapter, there are thousands of mutual funds, so how do you pick one? One answer is to visit one of the many mutual fund sites on the Web and use a fund selector. Most of the websites we mention in the chapter have one. Here is an example of how they are used. We went to www.morningstar.com and clicked on the "Fund Selector." We then indicated that we were interested in a domestic stock fund that invests in large capitalization growth stocks with relatively low expenses and several other features. Out of a database of over 15,000 funds, here is what we got:

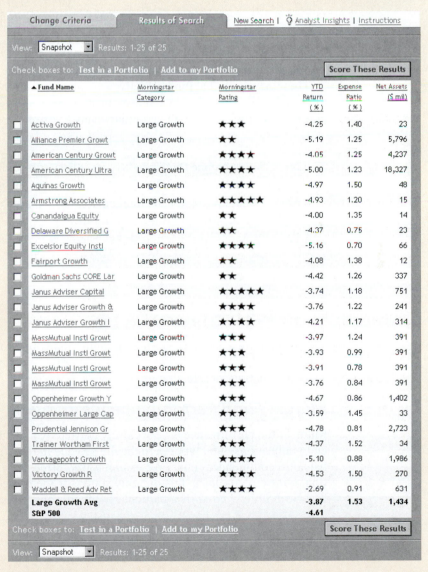

Fund Name	Morningstar Category	Morningstar Rating	YTD Return (%)	Expense Ratio (%)	Net Assets ($ mil)
Activa Growth	Large Growth	★★★	-4.25	1.40	23
Alliance Premier Growt	Large Growth	★★	-5.19	1.25	5,796
American Century Growt	Large Growth	★★★★	-4.05	1.25	4,237
American Century Ultra	Large Growth	★★★★	-5.00	1.23	18,327
Aquinas Growth	Large Growth	★★★★	-4.97	1.50	48
Armstrong Associates	Large Growth	★★★★★	-4.93	1.20	15
Canandaigua Equity	Large Growth	★★	-4.00	1.35	14
Delaware Diversified G	Large Growth	★★	-4.37	0.75	23
Excelsior Equity Instl	Large Growth	★★★★	-5.16	0.70	66
Fairport Growth	Large Growth	★★	-4.08	1.38	12
Goldman Sachs CORE Lar	Large Growth	★★	-4.42	1.26	337
Janus Adviser Capital	Large Growth	★★★★★	-3.74	1.18	751
Janus Adviser Growth &	Large Growth	★★★★	-3.76	1.22	241
Janus Adviser Growth I	Large Growth	★★★★	-4.21	1.17	314
MassMutual Instl Growt	Large Growth	★★★	-3.97	1.24	391
MassMutual Instl Growt	Large Growth	★★★	-3.93	0.99	391
MassMutual Instl Growt	Large Growth	★★★	-3.91	0.78	391
MassMutual Instl Growt	Large Growth	★★★	-3.76	0.84	391
Oppenheimer Growth Y	Large Growth	★★★	-4.67	0.86	1,402
Oppenheimer Large Cap	Large Growth	★★★	-3.59	1.45	33
Prudential Jennison Gr	Large Growth	★★★	-4.78	0.81	2,723
Trainer Wortham First	Large Growth	★★★	-4.37	1.52	34
Vantagepoint Growth	Large Growth	★★★★	-5.10	0.88	1,986
Victory Growth R	Large Growth	★★★★	-4.53	1.50	270
Waddell & Reed Adv Ret	Large Growth	★★★★	-2.69	0.91	631
Large Growth Avg			**-3.87**	**1.53**	**1,434**
S&P 500			**-4.61**		

This search narrowed things down in a hurry! Now we have a list of 25 funds. Clicking on the name of a fund takes you to the Morningstar website on the fund where you can learn more about the fund.

scheme, *all* stocks are "growth," "value," or a blend of the two, a classic example of the Lake Wobegon effect.[4]

The mutual fund "style" box is an increasingly common sight. A style box is a way of visually representing a fund's investment focus by placing the fund into one of nine boxes like this:

Style

	Value	Blend	Growth
Large			
Medium			
Small			

Size

As shown, this particular fund focuses on large-cap, value stocks.

These newer mutual fund objectives are also useful for screening mutual funds. As our nearby *Work the Web* box shows, many websites have mutual fund selectors that allow you to find funds with particular characteristics.

Check This

4.5a   What are the three major types of long-term funds? Give several examples of each and describe their investment policies.

4.5b   What do single-state municipal funds, single-country stock funds, and sector stock funds have in common?

4.5c   What are the distinguishing characteristics of a bond fund?

4.6   Mutual Fund Performance

We close our discussion of open-end mutual funds by looking at some of the performance information reported in the financial press. We then discuss the usefulness of such information for selecting mutual funds.

Mutual Fund Performance Information

Mutual fund performance is very closely tracked by a number of organizations. Financial publications of all types periodically provide mutual fund data, and many provide lists of recommended funds. We examine *Wall Street Journal* information in this section, but by no means is this the only source or the most comprehensive.[5] However, *The Wall Street Journal* is a particularly timely source because it reports mutual fund

---

[4]Lake Wobegon is a mystical place in Minnesota made famous by Garrison Keillor where "the men are strong, the women are beautiful, and all the children are above average." See www.phc.mpr.org for more.
[5]For more detailed information, publications from companies such as Morningstar, Weisenberger, and Value Line are often available in the library or online. Of course, a mutual fund's prospectus and annual report contain a great deal of information as well.

Mutual-Fund Yardsticks

Mutual-Fund Yardsticks: How Fund Categories Stack Up

All data are as of Jan. 29 and are preliminary. Fund-category abbreviations used in performance tables appear in parentheses after category name.

INVESTMENT OBJECTIVE	JANUARY	12 MONTHS	3 YEARS*	5 YEARS*	10 YEARS*
DIVERSIFIED STOCK and STOCK/BOND FUNDS					
Large-Cap Core (LC)	-1.76%	-21.65%	-14.12%	-2.57%	+7.17%
Large-Cap Growth (LG)	-0.82	-25.69	-21.58	-3.88	+5.61
Large-Cap Value (LV)	-1.98	-18.18	- 5.81	-1.49	+7.87
Midcap Core (MC)	-2.00	-17.33	- 4.47	+2.78	+8.88
Midcap Growth (MG)	-0.69	-25.17	-19.83	-1.81	+5.67
Midcap Value (MV)	-2.23	-13.73	+ 3.27	+3.24	+9.21
Small-Cap Core (SC)	-2.34	-17.96	- 0.46	+1.65	+7.44
Small-Cap Growth (SG)	-1.78	-27.63	-18.46	-2.55	+5.20
Small-Cap Value (SV)	-2.71	-12.19	+ 7.36	+3.22	+9.74
Multicap Core (XC)	-1.52	-20.30	-11.41	-0.96	+7.70
Multicap Growth (XG)	+0.00	-25.95	-22.76	-2.36	+6.59
Multicap Value (XV)	-1.70	-16.93	- 2.16	+0.93	+9.22
Equity Income (EI)	-2.48	-15.70	- 3.95	-0.56	+7.94
S&P 500 Funds (SP)	-1.72	-20.67	-13.32	-1.73	+8.66
Specialty Divers. Stock (SQ)	-0.70	+7.34	+ 7.60	-0.32	+1.23
Balanced (BL)	-1.16	-10.72	- 4.17	+0.94	+6.90
Stock/Bond Blend (MP)	-0.86	-8.45	- 4.60	+1.26	+7.03
Avg. U.S. Stock Fund [1]	-1.55	-20.71	-10.97	-1.06	+7.29
SECTOR STOCK FUNDS					
Science & Technology (TK)	+2.57%	-38.89%	-36.13%	-3.62%	+ 8.03%
Health/Biotechnology (HB)	-0.09	-23.76	- 2.76	+4.78	+11.28
Utility (UT)	-2.77	-20.81	-13.64	-2.54	+ 4.88
Natural Resources (NR)	-2.89	- 3.56	+ 3.42	+2.66	+ 8.55
Sector (SE)	-2.55	- 5.37	+ 6.75	+2.38	+ 9.86
Real Estate	-3.21	+ 1.35	+11.43	+2.51	+ 8.10
Financial Services	-1.70	- 9.68	+ 5.73	+3.22	+12.10

INVESTMENT OBJECTIVE	JANUARY	12 MONTHS	3 YEARS*	5 YEARS*	10 YEARS*
WORLD STOCK FUNDS					
Global (GL)	-2.71%	-18.57%	-14.75%	-1.645	+5.64%
International (IL)	-4.29	-16.70	-17.89	-3.37	+4.27
European Region (EU)	-5.34	-18.32	-16.03	-3.10	+6.47
Emerging Markets (EM)	-1.20	- 9.52	-13.97	-3.00	-0.20
Latin American (LT)	-5.25	-23.14	-13.77	-6.74	+0.49
Pacific Region (PR)	-0.78	-12.04	-18.99	-1.37	-0.65
Gold Oriented (AU)	+1.57	+51.21	+21.92	+7.72	+3.89
TAXABLE BOND FUNDS					
Short-Term (SB)	+0.01%	+ 4.53%	+ 6.69%	+5.52%	+5.55%
Long-Term (AB)	-0.01	+ 7.02	+ 8.17	+5.55	+6.69
Intermediate Bond (IB)	-0.11	+ 7.10	+ 8.60	+6.14	+6.49
Intermediate U.S. (IG)	-0.30	+ 8.96	+ 9.26	+6.49	+6.18
Short-Term U.S. (SU)	-0.14	+ 5.78	+ 7.24	+5.73	+5.58
Long-Term U.S. (LU)	-0.54	+ 8.88	+ 9.55	+6.34	+6.73
General U.S. Taxable (GT)	+0.06	+ 5.53	+ 6.65	+4.73	+6.48
High-Yield Taxable (HC)	+1.85	- 0.77	- 2.30	-1.36	+4.52
Mortgage (MT)	+0.07	+ 6.95	+ 8.55	+6.20	+6.15
World Bond (WB)	+1.82	+14.21	+ 8.33	+5.09	+6.24
Avg. Taxable Bond Fund [2]	+0.30	+ 5.45	+ 6.14	+4.67	+6.01
MUNICIPAL BOND FUNDS					
Short-Term Muni (SM)	+0.02%	+ 4.43%	+ 5.37%	+4.16%	+4.49%
Intermediate Muni (IM)	-0.49	+ 6.26	+ 7.09	+4.67	+5.28
General Muni (GM)	-0.60	+ 6.18	+ 7.68	+4.32	+5.58
Single State Muni (SS)	-0.54	+ 6.14	+ 7.65	+4.50	+5.60
High-Yield Muni (HM)	-0.43	+ 4.34	+ 5.48	+2.89	+5.26
Insured Muni (NM)	-0.73	+ 6.56	+ 8.10	+4.64	+5.78

year-to-date returns on a daily basis, and it provides a summary of average investment performance by fund category on a regular basis. The information we consider here applies only to open-end funds.

Figure 4.4 reproduces "Mutual-Fund Yardsticks," a feature appearing in the *Journal* each month. This table compares the recent investment performance of the major fund categories, including equity funds, bond funds, and balanced stock and bond funds.

Figure 4.5 is a small section of the mutual fund price quotations reported in *The Wall Street Journal* each month. All of the funds listed in Figure 4.5 belong to the very large family of funds managed by Fidelity Investments. The Blue Chip Growth Fund (abbreviated BluCh) is highlighted. The first piece of information given is the net asset value, NAV, for the fund. Following the fund name is the fund objective based on

NAV$ 1/31	FUND NAME	INV OBJ	JAN	TOTAL RETURN & RANK 1 YR	3 YR	5 YR	10 YR	MAX INIT CHRG	EXP RAT
	Fidelity Invest								
13.67	A Mgr	MP	−0.9	−8.6 C	−3.0 C	3.2 B	8.1 B	0.00	0.73
11.13	AggrGr r	XG	−0.5	−37.3 E	−39.1 E	−8.0 E	3.6 E	0.00	0.97
10.32	AggrInt	IL	−3.8	−12.5 A	−16.7 B	−1.5 B	NS ..	0.00	1.16
6.95	AMgrAggr	MP	0.3	−32.0 E	−13.2 E	NS ..	NS ..	0.00	0.89
11.78	AMgrGr	MP	−1.6	−14.7 D	−7.2 D	0.2 D	7.7 B	0.00	0.81
10.91	AMgrIn	MP	0.5	−0.1 A	2.2 A	3.9 A	6.7 D	0.00	0.64
13.11	Balanc	BL	−1.4	−9.4 B	−0.2 A	4.7 A	8.1 B	0.00	0.69
31.07	BluCh	LC	−2.7	−26.3 D	−17.4 D	−2.3 C	8.8 A	0.00	0.76
16.15	CapAp	XC	−0.2	−20.5 B	−14.5 D	0.7 B	8.9 B	0.00	0.94
10.87	ChinaReg	PR	0.1	−13.4 C	−12.8 B	4.3 A	NS ..	3.00	1.32
6.51	CpInc r	HC	4.3	4.3 A	−3.5 D	0.7 B	6.2 A	0.00	0.81
37.42	Contra	XG	−3.1	−11.9 A	−9.6 A	3.3 A	10.8 A	3.00	0.96
8.51	ContraII	LC	−1.8	−17.2 A	−10.7 A	NS ..	NS ..	3.00	1.11
16.55	CnvSc	MP	1.3	−10.6 C	−2.3 B	9.0 A	10.7 A	0.00	0.81
9.47	DestI	LC	−2.9	−24.3 C	−18.8 E	−8.2 E	5.9 D	8.24	0.40
9.01	DestII	LC	−1.6	−16.5 A	−12.0 B	0.8 A	10.8 A	8.24	0.60
17.60	DisEq	LC	−2.1	−19.8 A	−11.5 A	−0.3 A	8.4 B	0.00	0.85
21.67	DivGth	LC	−2.9	−21.6 B	−4.2 A	3.7 A	NS ..	0.00	0.98
16.74	DivIntl	IL	−2.4	−8.5 A	−9.1 A	3.2 A	10.1 A	0.00	1.21
7.16	EmrMkt r	EM	−0.7	−11.0 C	−15.3 D	−4.1 C	−3.5 E	3.00	1.54
38.31	Eq Inc	EI	−3.4	−19.0 C	−4.7 C	0.0 C	9.3 B	0.00	0.69
16.73	EQII	EI	−3.8	−18.5 C	−5.6 D	0.7 B	9.0 B	0.00	0.67
17.49	Europ r	EU	−4.5	−26.9 E	−17.5 C	−5.6 D	6.8 C	0.00	1.06
13.51	ErCapAp r	EU	−2.3	−14.7 B	−10.5 A	−0.4 B	NS ..	0.00	1.26
190.19	Exch	LC	−2.4	−17.8 A	−9.2 A	−1.3 B	8.9 A	0.00	0.63
13.45	Export	XC	−2.2	−19.9 B	−4.5 A	6.7 A	NS ..	0.00	0.89
21.55	Fidel	LC	−3.2	−23.6 C	−14.7 C	−0.7 B	9.2 A	0.00	0.59
15.93	Fifty	XV	−0.7	−1.5 A	−5.0 D	7.0 A	NS ..	0.00	1.12
17.63	FournOne	XV	−2.3	−16.5 B	−10.8 E	NS ..	NS ..	0.00	0.08
11.24	GNMA	MT	0.3	7.8 B	9.3 B	6.7 A	6.6 B	0.00	0.60
10.42	GovtInc	LU	−0.3	9.8 B	10.0 B	6.8 B	6.8 B	0.00	0.69
34.45	GroCo	XG	−2.7	−32.4 D	−24.2 C	0.5 B	8.3 B	0.00	0.98
29.58	GroInc	LC	−2.4	−19.2 A	−9.4 A	−0.2 A	9.7 A	0.00	0.69
7.42	GroIncII	LC	−2.2	−17.8 A	−9.7 A	NS ..	NS ..	0.00	0.90
7.76	HighInc r	HC	2.7	4.2 A	−4.7 D	−1.1 C	6.4 A	0.00	0.76
12.90	Indepndnc	XC	−1.3	−18.7 A	−14.2 D	3.5 A	8.9 B	0.00	0.97
10.69	InProBnd	IG	0.7	NS ..	NS ..	NS ..	NS ..	0.00	NA
10.71	IntBd	SB	0.1	8.6 A	9.4 A	6.9 A	6.7 A	0.00	0.63
10.32	IntGov	SU	−0.3	9.2 A	9.5 A	6.9 A	6.6 A	0.00	0.59
16.27	IntGr	IL	−3.3	−10.0 A	−13.4 B	0.7 A	6.3 B	0.00	1.14
7.56	InvGB	IB	0.1	8.8 B	9.7 B	6.8 B	7.0 B	0.00	0.66
8.07	Japan r	PR	−4.3	−1.6 A	−26.2 E	−0.5 B	1.1 B	3.00	1.42
6.38	JpnSmCo r	PR	−0.9	3.6 A	−25.4 E	9.8 A	NS ..	3.00	1.21
10.83	LargeCap	LC	−2.9	−24.5 C	−18.4 E	−1.4 B	NS ..	0.00	0.91
8.97	LatinAm r	LT	−3.9	−24.5 E	−14.1 C	−9.0 E	NS ..	3.00	1.41
24.59	LowP r	MV	−2.3	−9.8 A	12.4 A	7.8 B	13.7 A	3.00	1.02
76.78	MagIn	LC	−2.8	−23.4 C	−14.5 C	−0.5 B	8.6 B	3.00	0.89
15.99	MidCap	MC	−1.7	−27.3 E	−6.9 D	5.8 B	NS ..	0.00	0.94
11.25	MtgSec	MT	0.2	8.2 A	9.6 A	6.9 A	7.4 A	0.00	0.66
11.50	NewMkt r	WB	2.1	12.8 C	12.3 A	8.3 A	NS ..	0.00	1.00
21.24	NewMill	XG	−4.1	−23.8 A	−14.7 A	9.9 A	16.0 A	3.00	1.01
23.01	OTC	XG	−3.8	−26.9 B	−24.6 C	−0.6 B	6.9 C	0.00	1.14
21.23	Ovrse	IL	−3.5	−18.2 D	−18.7 C	−4.6 C	4.4 C	0.00	1.18
12.41	PcBas r	PR	−2.7	−7.6 B	−20.7 C	1.1 B	3.0 A	3.00	1.48
15.46	Puritn	BL	−2.1	−9.4 B	−0.6 A	2.7 B	9.0 A	0.00	0.64
17.88	RealE	SE	−2.8	3.1 A	14.2 A	3.9 B	9.1 D	0.00	0.84
8.98	STBF	SB	0.2	6.5 B	7.5 B	6.1 B	5.5 C	0.00	0.58
11.60	SmallCap r	SC	−2.0	−18.9 C	−0.6 C	NS ..	NS ..	0.00	1.12
13.08	SmCapInd	SC	−1.7	−21.6 D	−3.1 D	−1.3 D	NS ..	0.00	0.86
9.72	SE Asia r	PR	0.6	−14.5 D	−15.7 B	2.8 A	NS ..	3.00	1.55
9.51	StratInc	GT	1.6	10.7 A	7.7 A	NS ..	NS ..	0.00	0.94
16.13	StkSlc	LC	−2.7	−22.2 B	−13.1 B	−2.4 C	7.3 C	0.00	0.67
9.55	TarTime03	LU	0.3	4.3 E	7.6 E	5.7 D	NS ..	0.00	0.69
37.71	Trend	LC	−2.4	−21.4 A	−13.2 B	−1.9 C	4.3 E	0.00	0.78
11.22	USBI	IB	0.1	9.6 A	10.1 A	7.2 A	7.3 A	0.00	0.32
9.44	Utility	UT	−2.7	−24.3 E	−22.0 E	−4.9 D	5.0 C	0.00	0.94
44.88	Value	MV	−3.3	−12.5 B	5.2 B	3.0 C	10.4 B	0.00	0.81
11.53	Wrldw	GL	−2.9	−19.7 C	−10.6 B	−1.3 C	6.3 C	0.00	1.12

the categories shown in Figure 4.3. As its name suggests, the Blue Chip Fund has a large cap focus.[6]

After the fund objective comes a series of performance measures. The first number is the return for the month just ended. So, in this case, the Blue Chip Fund was down 2.7 percent for the month. Next, we have returns for the previous 1, 3, 5, and 10 years. The returns for the periods longer than a year are annualized. Thus, the Blue Chip Fund

---

[6]A blue chip stock is a well-established, profitable, very-well regarded company. A good example might be GE. The term "blue chip" refers to the game of poker, in which chips are used for betting. The blue chips are the most valuable.

averaged 8.8 percent per year over the previous 10 years. An "NS" for a performance number just means that the fund did not exist at the start of the period.

A letter grade is assigned to each of the 1-, 3-, 5-, and 10-year returns. A grade of "A" means that the fund's return is in the top 20 percent of all funds in the same category. A grade of "B" means the next 20 percent, and so on. Notice that the grades are strictly relative, so mutual funds, in effect, are graded on the curve!

Finally, the last two columns report the maximum front-end load ("MAX INIT CHRG") and the fund's annual expenses ("EXP RAT"). The expense figure includes management fees, 12b-1 fees, and any other fees. Many of the funds in Figure 4.5, such as the Aggressive Growth Fund ("AggGr"), have a small letter after the name, indicating a footnote. These footnotes generally alert you to back-end loads and similar charges; a small "r," for example, indicates a redemption charge, which is similar to a back-end load.

How Useful Are Fund Performance Ratings?

If you look at the performance ratings reported in Figure 4.5, you might wonder why anyone would buy a fund in a category other than those with the highest returns. Well, the lessons learned in Chapter 1 suggest the answer that these historical returns do not consider the riskiness of the various fund categories. For example, if the market has done well, the best ranked funds may simply be the riskiest funds, since the riskiest funds normally perform the best in a rising market. In a market downturn, however, these best ranked funds are most likely to become the worst ranked funds, since the riskiest funds normally perform the worst in a falling market.

These problems with performance measures deal with the evaluation of historical performance. However, there is an even more fundamental criterion. Ultimately, we don't care about historical performance; we care about *future* performance. Whether historical performance is useful in predicting future performance is the subject of ongoing debate. However, one thing we can say is that some of the poorest-performing funds are those with very high costs. These costs act as a constant drag on performance, and such funds tend to have persistently poorer returns than otherwise similar funds. The accompanying *Investment Update* box provides some case studies of poor performance, including the famous Steadman funds, better known on Wall Street as the "deadman" funds.

Check This	**4.6a**	Which mutual fund in Figure 4.5 had the best year-to-date return? The worst?
	4.6b	What are some of the problems with comparing historical performance numbers?

4.7   Closed-End Funds, Exchange Traded Funds, and Hedge Funds

It is probably fitting that we close our mutual fund chapter with a discussion of closed-end funds and exchange traded funds. As we will see, such funds have some unusual aspects.

Longtime Losers: Some Funds Have Spent Much of Their Lives on the Down Side

You've seen those charts in mutual-fund ads, showing how $10,000 invested at a fund's launch would have multiplied into a mountain of money over time.

Well, here is a group of charts you aren't likely to see: At some Wobegon funds, that hypothetical initial investment has declined in value—sometimes by half and even more. While these funds usually have had their moments in the sun, they have spent much more time in performance darkness to produce overall negative results since their launches.

The fund with the longest money-losing longevity? It is Ameritor Industry Fund, founded way back in 1959 and still in business today despite a cumulative loss of 42.90%, according to fund tracker Lipper Inc. The tiny fund was previously known as Steadman American Industry Fund and is a member of a fund family that for many years was known for poor performance and large annual expenses.

Runners-up in this mostly bad-from-birth competition: U.S. Global Investors Gold Shares Fund, launched in 1970, followed by other precious metals funds introduced in the early 1980s. U.S. Global Gold has delivered a negative 87.8% return since inception, according to Lipper, meaning that an initial $10,000 stake now would be down to $1,220.

A look at long-longevity losers serves as a cautionary tale about some individual funds investors may want to avoid. But more than that, it is a reminder of fund fads and once-popular strategies that didn't pan out for many investors.

Back in the 1980s, for instance, many financial advisers routinely suggested that investors park a small percentage of their assets in gold bullion or mining-stock funds as a hedge against runaway inflation or other financial crises. "That was the nonthinking advice. It was everywhere," recalls Roy Weitz, publisher of the Fundalarm.com website.

Such advice is rare today, after years of far-from-golden results. These days, Mr. Weitz says, investing in gold "seems more like a philosophy than an investment."

Another once-hot category with plenty of since-inception losers: emerging-markets funds, which buy stocks in the developing nations of Asia and Latin America. Such funds multiplied most dramatically in 1994—only to be clobbered by the Mexican peso crisis in December of that year and the Asian financial crisis that unfolded in 1997 and 1998. Numerous emerging-markets funds that appeared in 1994 and 1995 are still in the red since inception even after a huge 1999 when the average emerging-markets fund gained more than 70%, according to Lipper.

In hindsight, there is a warning for investors about rushing into a suddenly hot sector. Most of the emerging-markets funds appeared only after one of the category's best years, 1993. "Funds can come out at precisely the wrong time," at the tail end of a period of strong results, notes Edward Rosenbaum, director of research at Lipper, a unit of Reuters Group PLC. It can take months to get a new fund up and running, he explains, and by then the hot performance that spurred the fund's creation may have cooled.

Another type of fund showing up on the longest-losers list: bear-market funds that are positioned to shield investors from—or perhaps profit from—declining stock prices. One of the granddaddies of this category is Gabelli Comstock Capital Value Fund, down a cumulative 18% from its start in 1985.

A far younger bear-market fund has posted the absolute steepest-since-inception negative return, according to Lipper: ProFunds UltraShort OTC Fund has declined 96.39% since its June 1998 launch, meaning that an initial $10,000 now would be worth only $361. Of course, that is not a big surprise given the fund's mandate: it aims to move in the opposite direction as the Nasdaq 100 index, and with twice the magnitude. Over the past few years, the tech-heavy Nasdaq 100 has been one of the hottest market measures around.

To be sure, there are few investors who hold any fund continuously from inception. And a negative return since inception doesn't mean a fund is fatally flawed, or that it hasn't proved profitable for some investors. For instance, in market swoons including the 1987 crash, the Gabelli Comstock fund "has done what it is designed to do, which is to make money," says Henry Van der Ebb, head of a group of "nonmarket-correlated" funds at Gabelli Funds, Rye, N.Y. Bearish funds also starred for a while this past spring, when stock-market barometers tumbled.

(continued)

Still, a long negative record racked up by a fund should give investors pause. In the case of bear-market funds, for instance, it is a reminder that, historically, stocks have gone up more often than down. Bear-market funds will certainly have periods of strong performance, says Scott Wells, a financial adviser in Coral Gables, Fla. But, he adds, "I don't think people are going to be able to time the market" and get in and out of those funds at the right times.

All told, Lipper counts 491 individual stock funds or stock-fund share classes with negative returns since their inception—6.5% of a total of 7,598 vehicles for which the data firm has since-inception results. (Many funds have multiple share classes that differ in their sales commissions and annual expenses.) Not surprisingly, many of the funds are far smaller than they were years ago.

Because relatively few diversified U.S. stock funds are on the list, it is interesting to look at the ones that are. After Ameritor Industry, the oldest such funds with negative results are Frontier Equity Fund, down a cumulative 58.73% from its April 1992 start, and Apex Mid Cap Growth Fund, down 9.79% from its December 1992 start. One of the best-known managers on the list is Donald Yacktman, whose Yacktman Focused Fund is down 16.09% since its launch in April 1997.

How do such losing funds manage to hold on to investors? A 1997 page one story in *The Wall Street Journal* profiled investors who held shares in various Steadman funds for decades, despite their dismal record. Some investors were driven by inertia or an unwillingness to part with fund shares received as a gift for a special occasion. In other cases, the shares had been forgotten and ended up on state unclaimed-property lists.

Today at Ameritor Financial Corp. in Washington, new company President Jerome Kinney, son-in-law of the deceased Charles Steadman, says he and his wife, Carole, are working to turn things around for the three small Ameritor funds. Last month Ameritor hired portfolio manager Paul Dietrich, who also is manager of Dominion Insight Growth Fund. Moving to less-expensive offices is one of the steps Mr. Kinney says he has taken to trim "horrendous" expenses.

Over the years, Frontier Equity, which invests in volatile stocks of tiny companies, has tended to careen between the top and the bottom of fund-performance charts. Manager James Fay says the fund's biggest problem has been its "terrible" expenses, recently around 14% of assets a year. The fund has under $1 million in assets, like Ameritor Industry, so fixed costs take a big bite out of investors' returns.

Suresh Bhirud, manager of Apex Mid Cap, didn't return phone calls yesterday.

At Yacktman Focused, Mr. Yacktman says he continues to be enthusiastic about big holdings, including tobacco giant Philip Morris Co. "We'll have other periods where we will look like rocket scientists, I'm sure," he says, adding, "But, hey, right now we look like dummies."

Dubious Distinction: The Longest Losing Records

Among stock funds with negative returns since inception, these have been in business the longest.

Fund	Cumulative from Inception*	Assets (in mils)	Date First Offered
Ameritor Industry	−42.9%	$ 0.7	12/01/59
U.S. Global: Gold Shares	−87.8	25.8	06/05/70
U.S. Global: Resources**	−13.38	13.6	08/03/83
Invesco Gold	−69.31	80.2	02/07/84
USAA Gold Fund	−41.91	76.2	08/15/84
Lexington Silver	−50.54	18.6	08/30/84
Gabelli Comstock Cap. Value	−18.15	36.7	10/10/85
U.S. Global: World Gold	−24.01	57.1	11/29/85

*Return through July 19.

**Originally a gold fund.

Source: Lipper.

CLOSED-END FUNDS

Friday, January 31, 2003

STOCK (SYM)	EXCH	NAV	CLOSE	NET CHG	VOL 100s	PREM /DISC	DIV	52 WK MKT RET
World Equity Funds								
♣AbrdnAusEq IAF	A	7	6.20	−0.07	162	−11.4	.17	10.2
AsiaPacFd APB	N	9.94	9.18	−0.07	161	−7.6		−2.8
AsiaTigers GRR	N	7.65	6.90	−0.01	1	−9.8		−10.6
♣BrazilFd BZF	N	13.09	11.18	0.43	1152	−14.6	.27	−22.2
BrazilEqty BZL	N	3.60	3.34	−0.01	320	−7.2	.03	−20.6
Cdn Genl Inv CGI y	T	12.41	8.55	NA	NA	−31.1	NA	−4.5
Cdn Wrld Fd Ltd CWF cy	T	3.58	2.70	NA	NA	−24.6	NA	−13.1
CntlEurFd CEE	N	16.44	14.19	−0.02	69	−13.7		10.6
ChileFd CH	N	8.17	7.39	0.02	177	−9.5	.09	−12.5
ChinaFund CHN	N	17.32	15.27	−0.08	229	−11.8	.21	16.0
Economic Inv Tr EVT cy	T	59.68	38.86	NA	NA	−34.9	NA	−12.8
EmergMktTele ETF	N	6.66	5.50	0.00	127	−17.4		−23.2
♣EuropeFd EF	N	7.77	6.96	−0.04	525	−10.4	.84	−23.8
EuroWtFd EWF c	N	2.53	2.18	0.03	153	−13.8	.03	−42.4
FstIsrael ISL	N	9.38	7.48	−0.02	1	−20.3	.17	−25.7
FstPhilpnFd FPF	N		2.30	0.01	104	NA		−30.3
FraGrthFd FRF	N	6.41	5.51	−0.04	37	−14.0		−21.9
GermanyFd GER	N	5.08	4.45	0.10	116	−12.4	.01	−37.7
♣GtChina GCH	N	10.52	9.25	0.04	110	−12.1	.04	−0.9
HerzfldCarib CUBA	O	3.35	3.09	0.02	16	−7.8	.08	−18.8
IndiaFd IFN	N	12.29	10.53	−0.10	555	−14.3	.09	7.5
IndiaGrFd IGF d	N	10.11	9.82	−0.08	63	−2.9		18.1
Indonesia IF	O	1.95	1.95	NA	NA	0.0	NA	7.1
Italy Fd ITA	N	6.68	6.47	0.04	47	−3.1	.18	4.6
♣JapanEquity JEQ c	N	4.51	4.40	0.03	101	−2.4		−3.0
JapanSmlCap JOF	N	5.80	6.56	0.01	617	13.1		21.4
JF China JFC	N	8.30	7.30	0.10	11	−12.0		9.7
♣JF India JFI c	N	8.65	8.05	0.10	7	−6.9		4.0
KoreaEqty KEF	N	4.05	3.53	−0.01	2	−12.8		−2.7
♣KoreaFd KF	N	16.01	13.23	0.18	601	−17.4	.85	−4.5
LatAmEq LAQ	N	11.40	9.40	0.10	248	−17.5	.21	−24.7
LatAmDiscv LDF	N	9.01	7.45	0.10	203	−17.3	.16	−22.2
MalaysaFd MF	N	4.71	3.99	0.04	30	−15.3	.15	−4.6
MexEqIncoFd MXE	N	8.09	7.34	0.14	81	−9.3		−28.2
♣MexicoFd MXF	N	12.57	10.96	0.03	220	−12.8	1.79	−27.3
MSAsia APF	N	8.40	7.16	−0.10	213	−14.8	.01	−7.8
MS EstEur RNE	N	20.11	17.42	0.17	23	−13.4	.58	2.5
MS EmMktFd MSF	N	10.03	8.55	−0.04	197	−14.8	.01	−8.0
MSIndia IIF	N	11.83	9.75	−0.16	969	−17.6	j	4.6
NewGrmnyFd GF	N	4.66	3.72	0.02	270	−20.2		−37.6
NewIrelandFd IRL	N	11.70	9.27	0.02	27	−20.8		−11.7
ROC TwnFd ROC	N		4.03	0.00	325	NA		−17.4
♣ScddrNwAsia SAF	N	9.44	8	−0.10	122	−15.3		−6.9
♣SingaporeFd SGF c	N	5.90	4.90	−0.02	27	−16.9	.01	−14.9
SoAfricaFd SOA	N	12.23	10.30	−0.05	19	−15.8	.28	17.7
SpainFd SNF	N	6.35	6.63	−0.07	27	4.4	.71	−9.9
♣SwissHelvFd SWZ	N	11.49	9.62	−0.08	178	−16.3	.63	−2.9
TaiwanFd TWN	N	11.23	9.31	−0.06	69	−17.1		−24.0
TemplChinaFd TCH cl	N	11.39	10.65	−0.08	227	−6.5	.20	27.8
TempltnDrgn TDF	N	10.18	9.45	0.18	417	−7.2	.17	26.6
TemplMktFd EMF	N	8.56	8.35	−0.06	196	−2.5	.15	−5.7
TempltnRusEEur fd TRF cl	N	21.03	19.01	−0.09	50	−9.6	.10	2.3
♣Thai Capital TF c	N	4.57	3.70	NA	NA	−19.0	NA	NA
ThaiFd TTF	N	4.28	4.27	0.01	557	−0.2	.05	−1.7
Third Canadian THD cy	T	17.93	14.50	NA	NA	−19.1	NA	3.4
TurkishFd TKF	N	4.72	4.25	0.06	294	−10.0		−33.5
United Corps Ltd UNC cy	T	50.87	33.37	NA	NA	−34.4	NA	−3.3
ZSevenFd ZSEV	O	3.89	3.35		NA	−13.9		−21.1

Closed-End Funds Performance Information

As we described earlier, the major difference between a closed-end fund and an open-end fund is that closed-end funds don't buy and sell shares. Instead, there is a fixed number of shares in the fund, and these shares are bought and sold on the open market. About 450 closed-end funds have their shares traded on U.S. stock exchanges, which is far fewer than the roughly 7,000 long-term, open-end mutual funds available to investors.

Figure 4.6 shows some quotes for a particular type of closed-end fund, "World Equity Funds." As the name suggests, these funds generally invest outside the United States, and they are a relatively common type (single-state municipal funds are the most common). The entry for the single-country Korea Fund is highlighted.

Examining the entry for the Korea Fund, the first entry after the name and ticker symbol is the exchange where the shares are traded (N is NYSE, O is Nasdaq, A is

American, T is Toronto). Next, we have the NAV, followed by the closing price, the change in the closing price, and the trading volume in round lots. For the Korea Fund, notice that the closing price per share ($13.23) is less than the NAV ($16.01). On a percentage basis, the difference is ($13.23 − $16.01) / $16.01 = −17.4 percent, which is the next number reported. We will say more about this discount in a moment. Finally, there is information about the fund's dividend and its return performance over the previous 52 weeks.

The Closed-End Fund Discount Mystery

Wall Street has many unsolved puzzles, and one of the most famous and enduring has to do with prices of shares in closed-end funds. As we noted earlier, shares in closed-end funds trade in the marketplace. Furthermore, as the Korea Fund shows, share prices can differ from net asset values. In fact, most closed-end funds sell at a discount relative to their net asset values, and the discount is sometimes substantial.

For example, suppose a closed-end fund owns $100 million worth of stock. It has 10 million shares outstanding, so the NAV is clearly $10. It would not be at all unusual, however, for the share price to be only $9, indicating a 10 percent discount. What is puzzling about this discount is that you can apparently buy $10 worth of stock for only $9!

To make matters even more perplexing, the typical discount fluctuates over time. Sometimes the discount is very wide; at other times, it almost disappears. Despite a great deal of research, the closed-end fund discount phenomenon remains largely unexplained.

Because of the discount available on closed-end funds, it is often argued that funds with the largest discounts are attractive investments. The problem with this argument is that it assumes that the discount will narrow or disappear. Unfortunately, this may or may not happen; the discount might get even wider.

Sometimes, certain closed-end funds sell at a premium, implying that investors are willing to pay more than the NAV for shares. This case is not quite as perplexing; however, after all, investors in load funds do the same thing. The reasons we discussed for paying loads might apply to these cases.

One last comment on closed-end funds seems appropriate. When a closed-end fund is first created, its shares are offered for sale to the public. For example, a closed-end fund might raise $50 million by selling 5 million shares to the public at $10 per share (the original offer price is almost always $10), which is the fund's NAV.

If you pay $10, then you are very likely to shortly discover two unpleasant facts. First, the fund promoter will be paid, say, 7 percent of the proceeds right off the top, or about $3.5 million (this will be disclosed in the prospectus). This fee will come out of the fund, leaving a total value of $46.5 million and a NAV of $9.30. Further, as we have seen, the shares will probably trade at a discount relative to NAV in the market, so you would lose another piece of your investment almost immediately. In short, newly offered closed-end funds are generally very poor investments.

Exchange Traded Funds

Exchange traded funds, or ETFs, are a relatively recent innovation. Although they have been around since 1993, they really began to grow in the late 1990s. As of 2003, there were over 100 traded ETFs. Basically, an ETF is an index fund, and, when you buy an ETF, you are buying the particular basket of stocks in the index. For example, the best known ETF is a "Standard and Poor's Depositary Receipt," or SPDR (pronounced "spider"), which is simply the S&P 500 index.

What makes an ETF different from an index fund is that, as the name suggests, an ETF actually trades like a closed-end fund. ETFs can be bought and sold during the day, and they can be sold short. They generally have very low expenses, lower even than index funds, but you must pay a commission when you buy and sell shares.

The fact that ETFs trade like shares in closed-end funds raises the possibility that they too could sell at a discount to their net asset values, but this probably won't happen. The reason is a little complicated, but, in essence, the fund will buy and sell directly like an open-end fund, but there is usually a minimum size of, say, 50,000 shares. Furthermore, an ETF will redeem shares in kind, meaning that if you sell a block of 50,000 shares to the fund, you actually receive the underlying stock instead of cash. So, if an ETF were to sell for a discount, big investors would buy up shares, redeem them in exchange for stock, and then sell the stock, thereby capturing the discount.

Which is better, an ETF or a more traditional index fund? It's hard to say. For an index like the S&P 500, it probably doesn't make much difference. However, one place where ETFs seem to have an edge is with some of the more specialized indexes. For example, ETFs provide a very cheap way of purchasing non-U.S. indexes. Similarly, there are ETFs that track industry indexes for which few ordinary index funds are available.

Hedge Funds

Hedge funds are a special type of investment company. They are like mutual funds in that a fund manager invests a pool of money obtained from investors. However, unlike mutual funds, hedge funds are not required to register with the Securities and Exchange Commission (SEC). They are only lightly regulated and are generally free to pursue almost any investment style they wish. In contrast, as we have discussed, mutual funds are regulated and are relatively limited in their permitted investment strategies. For example, mutual funds are usually not allowed to do things like sell short or use large degrees of leverage.

Hedge funds are also not required to maintain any particular degree of diversification or liquidity. They don't have to redeem shares on demand, and they have little in the way of disclosure requirements. The reason that hedge funds avoid many of the restrictions placed on mutual funds is that they only accept "financially sophisticated" investors, and they do not offer their securities for sale to the public. A financially sophisticated investor is, as a practical matter, usually either an institution or a high net worth (i.e., rich) individual. Some types of hedge funds are limited to no more than 100 investors.

Hedge fund fees Hedge funds typically have a special fee structure, where, in addition to a general management fee of one to two percent of fund assets, the manager is paid a special performance fee. This special performance fee is often in the range from 20 to 40 percent of profits realized by the fund's investment strategy. A modest fee structure might be one that charges an annual management fee of one percent of the fund's assets plus twenty percent of any profits realized; however, more elaborate fee structures are common.

Hedge fund styles Worldwide there are thousands of hedge funds, and the number keeps growing. Big hedge funds may require a minimum investment of $1 million or

For more on ETFs, visit www.morningstar.com

hedge fund An unregistered investment company not accessible by the general public and significantly less regulated than a mutual fund.

Extensive information about hedge funds is available on the Internet. Try Hedge World www.hedgeworld.com and Hedge Fund Center www.hedgefundcenter.com

more. Small hedge funds may only require a minimum investment of $50,000 or less. Whether large or small, each fund develops its own investment style or niche.

For example, a hedge fund may focus on a particular sector, like technology, or a particular global region, like Asia or Eastern Europe. Alternatively, a hedge fund may pursue a particular investment strategy, like the "market neutral strategy" in which the fund maintains a portfolio approximately equally split between long and short positions. By being long in some securities and short in others, the portfolio is hedged against market risk and hence the term "market neutral." Incidentally, this is often thought to be the source of the term "hedge fund," originally referring to funds that were hedged against market risk. Today, however, the term hedge fund refers to any unregistered fund pursuing any type of investment style.

Starting your own hedge fund Ever dreamed about becoming an investment portfolio manager? You can by starting your own hedge fund. It may be easier than you think. A hedge fund is typically structured as a limited partnership in which the manager is a general partner and the investors are limited partners. Rather than stumble through the legal details, we simply advise that you will need the services of a lawyer familiar with investment companies, but the bottom line is that it's not difficult to do. Actually, the hardest part about setting up your own hedge fund is finding willing investors. Essentially, you need to find well-to-do individuals who have faith in your investment ideas. Getting a grade of "A" from your investments course could be a helpful step.

Information about starting your own hedge fund is available at Turn Key Hedge Funds www.turnkeyhedge funds.com

Check This

4.7a	What is a closed-end fund and how does it differ from a mutual fund?
4.7b	What is meant by the Net Asset Value (NAV) of a closed-end fund?
4.7c	What is a hedge fund? What are the important differences between a hedge fund and a mutual fund?
4.7d	What is a market neutral investment strategy? Why is this strategy available to hedge funds but not to mutual funds?

4.8 Summary and Conclusions

We have covered many aspects of mutual fund investing in this chapter. We have seen that there are thousands of mutual funds and dozens of types. A few of the more important distinctions we made can be summarized as follows:

1. Some funds are open-end and some are closed-end. Open-end funds stand ready to buy or sell shares. Closed-end funds do not; instead, their shares trade on the stock exchanges.

2. Some open-end funds have front-end loads, meaning that there is a fee tacked on to the fund's net asset value when you buy. Other funds are no-load. Various costs and fees exist, including back-end loads and 12b-1 fees.

3. Funds have very different objectives and, as a result, very different risk and return potentials. Furthermore, funds with similar-sounding objectives can, in fact, be quite different. It is important to consider a fund's actual holdings and investment policies, not just read its stated objective.

4. Mutual fund information is widely available, but performance information should be used with caution. The best performing funds are often the ones with the greatest risks or the ones that just happened to be in the right investment at the right time.

Get Real

This chapter covered the essentials of mutual funds. How should you, as an investor or investment manager, put this information to work?

The first thing to do is to start looking at mutual fund prospectuses. These are written to be accessible to novice investors (or, at least, they are *supposed* to be written that way). The best way to begin exploring is to visit websites. Almost any large mutual fund company will have extensive online information available. Links to some of the better known families are available at our web page. It is important to look at different funds within a given family and also to look across families. Compare growth funds to growth funds, for example. This adventure will give you some of the real-life background you need to select the types of funds most suitable for you or someone else.

Once you have examined prospectuses on different funds, it's time to invest. Beginning with your simulated account, pick a few funds, invest, and observe the outcomes. Open-end mutual funds are probably the place most of you will begin investing real dollars. An initial purchase can be made with a relatively small amount, perhaps $500, and subsequent purchases can be made in amounts of as little as $100 or less.

Most important of all, as we discussed to start the chapter, most employers now provide employees with retirement plans. The way these work is that, typically, your employer will make a contribution to a mutual fund you select (often from a fairly limited set). Your employer may even match, or more than match, a contribution you make. Such plans may be the only retirement benefit offered, but they can be an extraordinary opportunity for those who take full advantage of them by getting the largest possible match and then investing in a suitable fund. It's an important choice, so the more knowledge you have regarding mutual funds, the better your outcome is likely to be.

Key Terms

Chapter Review Problems and Self-Test

1. **Front-End Loads**   The Madura HiGro Fund has a net asset value of $50 per share. It charges a 3 percent load. How much will you pay for 100 shares?

2. **Turnover**   The Starks Income Fund's average daily total assets were $100 million for the year just completed. Its stock purchases for the year were $20 million, while its sales were $12.5 million. What was its turnover?

Answers to Self-Test Problems

1. You will pay 100 times the offering price. Since the load is computed as a percentage of the offering price, we can compute the offering price as follows:

$$\text{Net asset value} = (1 - \text{Front-end load}) \times \text{Offering price}$$

In other words, the NAV is 97 percent of the offering price. Since the NAV is \$50, the offering price is \$50/.97 = \$51.55. You will pay \$5,155 in all, of which \$155 is a load.

2. Turnover is the lesser of purchases or sales divided by average daily assets. In this case, sales are smaller at \$12.5, so turnover is \$12.5/\$100 = .125 times.

Test Your Investment Quotient

1. **Investment Companies** Which of the following statements typically does not characterize the structure of an investment company?
   a. An investment company adopts a corporate form of organization.
   b. An investment company invests a pool of funds belonging to many investors in a portfolio of individual investments.
   c. An investment company receives an annual management fee ranging from 3 to 5 percent of the total value of the fund.
   d. The board of directors of an investment company hires a separate investment management company to manage the portfolio of securities and handle other administrative duties.

2. **Expense Statement** Which of the following is *not* part of the expense statement?
   a. Shareholder transactions expenses
   b. Shareholder demographic profile
   c. Annual operating expenses
   d. A hypothetical example of expenses

3. **Mutual Fund Investing** Which of the following is the least likely advantage of mutual fund investing?
   a. Diversification
   b. Professional management
   c. Convenience
   d. Mutual fund returns are normally higher than market average returns

4. **Open-End Funds** An open-end mutual fund is owned by which of the following?
   a. An investment company
   b. An investment advisory firm
   c. A "family of funds" mutual fund company
   d. Its shareholders

5. **Closed-End Funds** Which of the following is most true of a closed-end investment company?
   a. The fund's share price is usually greater than net asset value.
   b. The fund's share price is set equal to net asset value.
   c. Fund shares outstanding vary with purchases and redemptions by shareholders.
   d. Fund shares outstanding are fixed at the issue date.

6. **Closed-End Funds** A closed-end fund is owned by which of the following?
   a. An investment company
   b. An investment advisory firm
   c. A "family of funds" mutual fund company
   d. Its shareholders

7. **Investment Advisory Firms**   Which of the following is not true about the typical relationship between a mutual fund and an investment advisory firm? The investment advisory firm

   a. Owns the mutual fund.
   b. Manages the mutual fund's assets.
   c. Manages shareholder purchase and redemption operations.
   d. Receives a management fee for services rendered.

8. **Fund Types**   Which mutual fund type is most likely to own stocks paying the highest dividend yields?

   a. Capital appreciation fund
   b. Equity income fund
   c. Growth and income fund
   d. Growth fund

9. **Fund Types**   Which mutual fund type is most likely to own stocks paying the lowest dividend yields?

   a. Capital appreciation fund
   b. Equity income fund
   c. Growth and income fund
   d. Growth fund

10. **Fund Types**   Which mutual fund type will most likely incur the greatest tax liability for its investors?

   a. Index fund
   b. Municipal bond fund
   c. Income fund
   d. Growth fund

11. **Fund Types**   Which mutual fund type will most likely incur the smallest tax liability for its investors?

   a. Index fund
   b. Municipal bond fund
   c. Income fund
   d. Growth fund

12. **Fund Types**   Which mutual fund type will most likely incur the greatest overall risk levels for its investors?

   a. Large-cap index fund
   b. Insured municipal bond fund
   c. Money market mutual fund
   d. Small-cap growth fund

13. **Mutual Fund Fees**   Which of the following mutual fund fees is assessed on an annual basis?

   a. 12b-1 fees
   b. Front-end load
   c. Back-end load
   d. Contingent deferred sales charge (CDSC)

14. **Mutual Fund Fees**   Which of the following mutual fund fees will most likely be the biggest expense for a long-term fund investor?

   a. 12b-1 fees
   b. Front-end load
   c. Back-end load
   d. Contingent deferred sales charge (CDSC)

15. **Mutual Fund Fees**   Which of the following mutual fund fees and expenses is the most difficult for investors to assess?

   a. Sales charges or "loads"
   b. 12b-1 fees
   c. Management fees
   d. Trading costs

Concept Questions

1. **Fund Ownership**   Who actually owns a mutual fund? Who runs it?

2. **Loads**   Given that no-load funds are widely available, why would a rational investor pay a front-end load? More generally, why don't fund investors always seek out funds with the lowest loads, management fees, and other fees?

3. **Money Market Funds**   Is it true that the NAV of a money market mutual fund never changes? How is this possible?

4. **Money Market Deposit Accounts**   What is the difference between a money market deposit account and a money market mutual fund? Which is riskier?

5. **Fund Goals**   What is a capital appreciation fund? An equity income fund? Which is likely to be riskier? Why?

6. **Front-End Loads**   You are interested in investing in a mutual fund that charges a front-end load of 5 percent. If the length of your investment is one year, would you invest in this fund? Suppose the length of your investment is 20 years? How are the length of your investment and front-end loads related?

7. **Open versus Closed-End Funds**   An open-end mutual fund typically keeps a percentage, often around 5 percent, of its assets in cash or liquid money market assets. How does this affect the fund's return in a year in which the market increases in value? How about during a bad year? Closed-end funds do not typically hold cash. What is it about the structure of open-end and closed-end funds that would influence this difference?

8. **12b-1 Fees**   What are 12b-1 fees? What expenses are 12b-1 fees intended to cover? Many closed-end mutual funds charge a 12b-1 fee. Does this make sense to you? Why or why not?

9. **Open versus Closed-End Funds**   If you were concerned about the liquidity of mutual funds shares that you held, would you rather hold shares in a closed-end fund or an open-end fund? Why?

10. **Performance**   Refer to Figure 4.5. Look at the 10-year performance for the funds listed. Why do you suppose there are so few poor performers? Hint: Think about the hit TV show *Survivor*.

Questions and Problems

Core Questions

1. **Net Asset Value**   The World Income Appreciation Fund has current assets with a market value of $3.5 billion and has 110 million shares outstanding. What is the net asset value (NAV) for this mutual fund?

2. **Front-End Loads**   Suppose the mutual fund in the previous problem has a current market price quotation of $33.67. Is this a load fund? If so, calculate the front-end load.

3. **Calculating NAV**   The Tiki Growth and Equity Fund is a "low-load" fund. The current offer price quotation for this mutual fund is $40.30, and the front-end load is 2.0 percent.

What is the NAV? If there are 12.5 million shares outstanding, what is the current market value of assets owned by the Tiki fund?

4. **Money Market Funds**   The Johnson Liquid Assets Money Market Mutual Fund has a NAV of $1 per share. During the year, the assets held by this fund appreciated by 4.3 percent. If you had invested $25,000 in this fund at the start of the year, how many shares would you own at the end of the year? What will the NAV of this fund be at the end of the year? Why?

5. **NAV**   An open-end mutual fund has the following stocks:

Stock	Shares	Stock Price
A	3,000	$42
B	8,000	27
C	5,500	38
D	9,200	35

If there are 50,000 shares of the market fund, what is the NAV?

6. **NAV**   Suppose the fund in the previous problem has liabilities of $75,000. What is the NAV of the fund now?

7. **Front-End Load**   In the previous problem, assume the fund is sold with a 5 percent front-end load. What is the offering price of the fund?

8. **Turnover**   A mutual fund sold $80 million of assets during the year and purchased $90 million in assets. If the average daily assets of the fund was $130 million, what was the fund turnover?

9. **Closed-End Funds**   A closed-end fund has total assets of $300 million and liabilities of $1.5 million. Currently, 20 million shares are outstanding. What is the NAV of the fund? If the shares currently sell for $12.85, what is the premium or discount on the fund?

10. **Mutual Fund Returns**   You invested $10,000 in a mutual fund at the beginning of the year when the NAV was $34.85. At the end of the year the fund paid $.64 in short-term distributions and $1.15 in long-term distributions. If the NAV of the fund at the end of the year was $37.97, what was your return for the year?

Intermediate Questions

11. **Calculating Turnover**   A sector fund specializing in commercial bank stocks had average daily assets of $1.6 billion in 2004. This fund sold $800 million worth of stock during the year, and its turnover ratio was .48. How much stock did this mutual fund purchase during the year?

12. **Calculating Fees**   In the previous problem, suppose the annual operating expense ratio for the mutual fund in 2004 is 1.25 percent, and the management fee is .85 percent. How much money did the fund's management earn during 2004? If the fund doesn't charge any 12b-1 fees, how much were miscellaneous and administrative expenses during the year?

13. **Calculating Fees**   You purchased 2,000 shares in the New Pacific Growth Fund on January 2, 2004, at an offering price of $30.50 per share. The front-end load for this fund is 6 percent, and the back-end load for redemptions within one year is 3 percent. The underlying assets in this mutual fund appreciate (including reinvested dividends) by 12 percent during 2004, and you sell back your shares at the end of the year. If the operating expense ratio for the New Pacific Fund is 1.35 percent, what is your total return from this investment? What do you conclude about the impact of fees in evaluating mutual fund performance?

14. **Calculating Fees**   Suppose in the previous problem that the mutual fund has no front-end load or back-end load. Further suppose that the operating expense ratio for the fund is .85 percent. What is your return on investment now?

Refer to Figure 4.5 to answer Questions 15–18.

15. **Fund Objectives**   Locate the OTC Portfolio Fund. What is its objective? What is its one-year return? How does this compare to other mutual funds with the same objective?

16. **Fund Loads**   Of the funds listed, what is the highest load?

17. **Fund Costs**   Of the funds listed, what types have the lowest costs? The highest?

18. **Purchase Prices**   Locate the Emerging Markets Fund. If you buy 1,000 shares, what would you pay?

19. **Front-End Loads and Returns**   You are considering an investment in a mutual fund with a 5 percent front-end load. Assuming the fund return is 11 percent per year, what is your return in 1 year? 2 years? 5 years? 10 years? 20 years? 50 years? Graph and explain your answers.

20. **Expenses and Returns**   The Bruin Stock Fund sells Class A shares that have a front-end load of 5 percent, a 12b-1 fee of .30 percent, and other fees of .66 percent. There are also Class B shares with a 5 percent CDSC that declines 1 percent per year, a 12b-1 fee of 1.00 percent, and other fees of .66 percent. If the portfolio return is 10 percent per year and you plan to sell after the third year, should you invest in Class A or Class B shares? What if your investment horizon is 20 years?

21. **Expenses and Returns**   You are going to invest in a stock mutual fund with a 4 percent front-end load and a 1.25 percent expense ratio. You also can invest in a money market mutual fund with a 6 percent return and an expense ratio of .20 percent. If you plan to keep your investment for two years, what annual return must the stock mutual fund earn to exceed an investment in the money market fund? What if your investment horizon is 10 years?

22. **Taxes and MMMFs**   Suppose you're evaluating three alternative MMMF investments. The first fund buys a diversified portfolio of municipal securities from across the country and yields 3.0 percent. The second fund buys only taxable, short-term commercial paper and yields 4.5 percent. The third fund specializes in the municipal debt from the state of New Jersey and yields 2.8 percent. If you are a New Jersey resident, your federal tax bracket is 35 percent, and your state tax bracket is 8 percent, which of these three MMMFs offers you the highest aftertax yield?

23. **Taxes and MMMFs**   In the previous problem, which MMMF offers you the highest yield if you are a resident of Texas, which has no state income tax?

24. **Closed-End Funds**   The Argentina Fund has $312 million in assets and sells at a 13.5 percent discount to NAV. If the quoted share price for this closed-end fund is $10.50, how many shares are outstanding? If you purchase 1,000 shares of this fund, what will the total shares outstanding be now?

25. **Closed-End Fund Discounts**   Suppose you purchase 5,000 shares of a closed-end mutual fund at its initial public offering; the offer price is $20 per share. The offering prospectus discloses that the fund promoter gets an 8 percent fee from the offering. If this fund sells at a 12 percent discount to NAV the day after the initial public offering, what is the value of your investment?

What's on the Web?

1. **Bond Funds**   One of the best Internet sites for information on mutual funds is www.morningstar.com. Go to the website and find the ticker symbol for the Harbor Bond Fund. Find all of the following information on the website for this fund: loads, expense ratio, top five holdings, bond quality ratings, the fund's rank in its category for the last seven years, and the Morningstar rating. Next, find out how the Morningstar star ranking system works.

2. **Stock Funds** Go to www.morningstar.com and find the ticker symbol for a domestic stock fund. Enter the ticker symbol and find the following information for the fund: manager and manager start date, year-to-date return, three-year return, five-year return, front-end or back-end loads, actual and maximum 12b-l fees, management fees, expense ratio, the top 25 holdings, and the fund address and phone number.

3. **Morningstar Fund Selector** Find the Mutual Fund Selector on the Morningstar website. How many funds fit the following criteria: domestic stock fund, minimum initial purchase equal to or less than $500, expense ratio less than or equal to category average, and turnover less than 75 percent?

4. **ETFs** Go to www.amex.com. Once there, find out the advantages Amex lists for individuals buying ETFs. Now, find out how many ETFs AMEX lists. How many ETFs are international? What are Diamonds, Spyders, and Cubes (QQQ)? What do each of these three invest in?

Stock-Trak®
Portfolio Simulation

Trading Mutual Funds and ETFs with Stock-Trak

Stock-Trak allows you to trade mutual funds and ETFs as simply as it allows you to trade common stocks. There are restrictions: You cannot use margin to buy mutual fund shares and fund shares cannot be sold short. You should consult the most recent rules at the Stock-Trak website (www.stocktrak.com) for other restrictions that might apply.

To trade mutual funds with Stock-Trak, you must know the ticker symbol of the fund whose shares you wish to buy or sell. Unfortunately, you cannot find ticker symbols in *The Wall Street Journal*. Mutual fund symbols can be conveniently obtained through many quote servers on the Internet, such as finance.yahoo.com. To find even more information on mutual funds, the Morningstar website (www.morningstar.com) is one of the best. You simply type the name of the mutual fund into the look-up box and submit it to the server. After you have the ticker symbol for the fund of interest, you can use it just like a stock ticker. On the Morningstar website, you can also find detailed information such as the asset allocation, loads, 12b-1 fees, the largest holdings of the fund, and more.

Mutual fund tickers normally have five letters, where the last letter is an X. For example, FMAGX is the ticker for the Fidelity Magellan Fund, VFINX is the ticker for the Vanguard Index Trust 500 Fund, and SNXFX is the ticker for the Schwab 1000 Equity Fund.

When buying mutual fund shares, you are taking a long position, hoping the fund's share price will increase. Suppose you want to invest $10,000 in Scudder Dreman Small Cap Value A shares, which has the ticker symbol KDSAX. You would place the following order:

What type of trade will this be?	$ amount to invest ($500 increments). Enter **99999**, to sell your entire position.	Ticker Symbol (all CAPS):
Buy to open or increase a long position Sell to close or reduce a long position	10000	KDSAX

Later, suppose you wanted to sell $4,000 in KDSAX shares. You would submit this order:

What type of trade will this be?	$ amount to invest ($500 increments). Enter **99999**, to sell your entire position.	Ticker Symbol (all CAPS):
Buy to open or increase a long position Sell to close or reduce a long position	4000	KDSAX

Since you are selling dollar amounts, not shares, and the mutual fund may have paid a dividend that was reinvested, you should enter 99999 in the dollar amount for the sell order to sell your entire position in the mutual fund.

With ETFs, unlike mutual funds, margin can be used, and short selling is allowed. To trade ETFs, you must look up the ticker. As of 2003, all available ETFs are listed on the American Stock Exchange, so an easy way to get an ETF ticker (and learn more about ETFs) is to go to www.amex.com.

Stock-Trak Exercises

1. **Mutual Fund Purchases**   Find a bond fund on Morningstar that interests you and invest $25,000 in the fund.

2. **Stock Fund Purchases**   Find a stock fund on Morningstar that interests you and invest $20,000 in the fund.

3. **Stock Transactions**   You have decided to reduce your position in the bond fund by $10,000 and sell all of the stock fund. Complete the necessary transactions.

4. **ETFs**   Go to www.amex.com and find the list of available ETFs. Pick an ETF you think will decline in value and short 200 shares. Cover your short in a week and calculate your return.

5. **ETFs**   Go to www.amex.com and find the list of available ETFs. Pick an ETF you think will increase in value and buy 200 shares. Sell the ETF in two weeks and calculate your return.

www.mhhe.com/cj3e

The Stock Market

"One of the funny things about the stock market is that every time one man buys, another sells, and both think they are astute."

–William Feather

"If you don't know who you are, the stock market is an expensive place to find out."

–Adam Smith
(pseud. for George J. W. Goodman)

On May 17, 1792, a group of commodity brokers met and signed the now famous Buttonwood Tree Agreement, thereby establishing the forerunner of what soon became the New York Stock Exchange. Today, the NYSE is the world's largest and best known stock market. On a typical day, the NYSE executes buy and sell transactions in well over a billion shares. Established in 1971, and now famous as an arena for "tech" stock investing, the Nasdaq daily executes trades for a similar number of stock shares. Together, the NYSE and Nasdaq account for the vast majority of stock trading in the United States. ■

With this chapter, we begin in earnest our study of stock markets. This chapter presents a "big picture" overview of how a stock market works and how to read and understand stock market information reported in the financial press.

5.1 The Primary and Secondary Stock Markets

primary market The market in which new securities are originally sold to investors.

The stock market consists of a **primary market** and a **secondary market**. In the primary, or new-issue market, shares of stock are first brought to the market and sold to investors. In the secondary market, existing shares are traded among investors.

In the primary market, companies issue new securities to raise money. In the secondary market, investors are constantly appraising the values of companies by buying and selling shares previously issued by these companies. We next discuss the operation of the primary market for common stocks, and then we turn our attention to the secondary market for stocks.

secondary market The market in which previously issued securities trade among investors.

The Primary Market for Common Stock

initial public offering (IPO) An initial public offering occurs when a company offers stock for sale to the public for the first time.

The primary market for common stock is how new securities are first brought to market. It is best known as the market for **initial public offerings (IPOs)**. An IPO occurs when a company offers stock for sale to the public for the first time. Typically, the company is small and growing, and it needs to raise capital for further expansion.

To illustrate how an IPO occurs, suppose that several years ago you started a software company. Your company was initially set up as a privately held corporation with 100,000 shares of stock, all sold for one dollar per share. The reason your company is privately held is that shares were not offered for sale to the general public. Instead, you bought 50,000 shares for yourself and sold the remaining 50,000 shares to a few supportive friends and relatives.

investment banking firm A firm specializing in arranging financing for companies.

Fortunately, your company has prospered beyond all expectations. However, company growth is now hampered by a lack of capital. At an informal stockholders' meeting, it is agreed to take the company public. Not really knowing how to do this, you consult your accountant, who recommends an **investment banking firm**. An investment banking firm, among other things, specializes in arranging financing for companies by finding investors to buy newly issued securities.

underwrite To assume the risk of buying newly issued securities from a company and reselling them to investors.

After lengthy negotiations, including an examination of your company's current financial condition and plans for future growth, your investment banker suggests an issue of 4 million shares of common stock. Two million shares will be distributed to the original stockholders (you and your original investors) in exchange for their old shares. These 2 million shares distributed to the original stockholders ensure that effective control of the corporation will remain in their hands.

fixed commitment Underwriting arrangement in which the investment banker guarantees the firm a fixed amount for its securities.

After much haggling, your investment banker agrees to **underwrite** the stock issue by purchasing the other 2 million shares from your company for $10 per share. The net effect of this transaction is that you have sold half the company to the underwriter for $20 million. The proceeds from the sale will allow your company to construct its own headquarters building and double its staff of programmers and sales consultants.

best effort Arrangement in which the investment banker does not guarantee the firm a fixed amount for its securities.

Your investment banker will not keep the 2 million shares but instead will resell them in the primary market. She thinks the stock can probably be sold for $12 per share in an IPO. The difference between the $12 the underwriter sells the stock for and the $10 per share you received is called the *underwriter spread* and is a basic part of the underwriter's compensation.

This agreement, under which the underwriter pays the firm a fixed amount, is called a **fixed commitment**. With a fixed (or firm) commitment, the underwriter assumes the risk that investors cannot be persuaded to buy the stock at a price above $10 per share. The other major type of arrangement, called a **best effort**, is just that. Here, the investment banker devotes a best effort to sell as many shares of the issue as possible at

For more on IPOs, check out IPO Central at www.hoovers.com

the stated fixed offering price. Strictly speaking, a best-effort arrangement is therefore *not* underwritten, but the phrase "best-effort underwriting" is often used nonetheless. Fixed commitment is, by far, the more common type.

As is common with an IPO, some restrictions are imposed on you as part of the underwriting contract. Most important, you and the other original stockholders agree not to sell any of your personal stockholdings for six months after the underwriting. This ties most of your wealth to the company's success and makes selling the stock to investors a more credible undertaking by the underwriter. Essentially, investors are assured that you will be working hard to expand the company and increase its earnings.

After the underwriting terms are decided, much of your time will be devoted to the mechanics of the offering. In particular, before shares can be sold to the public, the issue must obtain an approved registration with the **Securities and Exchange Commission (SEC)**. The SEC is the federal regulatory agency charged with regulating U.S. securities markets.

SEC regulations governing IPOs are especially strict. To gain SEC approval, you must prepare a **prospectus**, normally with the help of outside accounting, auditing, and legal experts. The prospectus contains a detailed account of your company's financial position, its operations, and investment plans for the future. Once the prospectus is prepared, it is submitted to the SEC for approval. The SEC makes no judgment about the quality of your company or the value of your stock. Instead, it only checks to make sure that various rules regarding full disclosure and other issues have been satisfied.

While awaiting SEC approval, your investment banker will circulate a preliminary prospectus among investors to generate interest in the stock offering. This document is commonly called a **red herring** because the cover page is stamped in red ink, indicating that final approval for the stock issue has not yet been obtained. The preliminary prospectus is essentially complete except for the final offering price and a few other pieces of information. These are not set because market conditions might change while SEC approval is being sought. Upon obtaining SEC approval, the prospectus will be updated and completed, and your underwriter can begin selling your company's shares to investors.

To publicize an offering, the underwriter will usually place announcements in newspapers and other outlets. Because of their appearance, these announcements are known as *tombstones*, and they are a familiar sight in the financial press. A sample tombstone as it appeared in *The Wall Street Journal* is shown in Figure 5.1.

As Figure 5.1 shows, a typical tombstone states the name of the company, some information about the stock issue being sold, and the underwriters for the issue. All but very small issues generally involve more than one underwriter, and the names of the participating underwriters are usually listed at the bottom of the tombstone. Those listed first are the "lead" underwriters, who are primarily responsible for managing the issue process.

Initial public stock offerings vary in size a great deal. The 2 million share issue for your hypothetical software company discussed above is a fairly small issue. The largest public offering in the United States as of 2003 was AT&T Wireless, a subsidiary of AT&T. The new shares were offered at $29.50 per share to create a $70 billion public offering.

The Secondary Market for Common Stock

In the secondary market for common stock, investors buy and sell shares with other investors. If you think of the primary market as the new-car showroom at an automotive

Securities and Exchange Commission (SEC) Federal regulatory agency charged with enforcing U.S. securities laws and regulations.

prospectus Document prepared as part of a security offering detailing a company's financial position, its operations, and investment plans for the future.

red herring A preliminary prospectus not yet approved by the SEC.

FIGURE 5.1   **IPO Tombstone**

This announcement is neither an offer to sell nor a solicitation of an offer to buy any of these Securities. The offer is made only by the Prospectus.

3,450,000 Shares

Class A Common Stock

Price $69 a Share

Copies of the Prospectus may be obtained in any State from only such of the undersigned as may legally offer these Securities in compliance with the securities laws of such State.

MORGAN STANLEY DEAN WITTER

BT ALEX.BROWN
Incorporated

CREDIT SUISSE FIRST BOSTON

HAMBRECHT & QUIST

MERRILL LYNCH & CO.

dealer, where cars are first sold to the public, then the secondary market is just the used-car lot.

Secondary market stock trading among investors is directed through three channels. An investor may trade:

1. Directly with other investors.
2. Indirectly through a broker who arranges transactions for others.
3. Directly with a dealer who buys and sells securities from inventory.

As we discussed in Chapter 2, for individual investors, almost all common stock transactions are made through a broker. However, large institutional investors, such as pension funds and mutual funds, trade through both brokers and dealers, and also trade directly with other institutional investors.

Dealers and Brokers

dealer A trader who buys and sells securities from inventory.

broker An intermediary who arranges security transactions among investors.

bid price The price a dealer is willing to pay.

ask price The price at which a dealer is willing to sell. Also called the *offer* or *offering* price.

spread The difference between the bid and ask prices.

Since most securities transactions involve dealers and brokers, it is important that you understand exactly what these terms mean. A **dealer** maintains an inventory and stands ready to buy and sell at any time. By contrast, a **broker** brings buyers and sellers together but does not maintain an inventory. Thus, when we speak of used-car dealers and real estate brokers, we recognize that the used-car dealer maintains an inventory, whereas the real estate broker normally does not.

In the securities markets, a dealer stands ready to buy securities from investors wishing to sell them and sell securities to investors wishing to buy them. An important part of the dealer function involves maintaining an inventory to accommodate temporary buy and sell order imbalances. The price a dealer is willing to pay is called the **bid price**. The price at which a dealer will sell is called the **ask price** (sometimes called the offer or offering price). The difference between the bid and ask prices is called the **spread**.

A dealer attempts to profit by selling securities at a higher price than the average price paid for them. Of course, this is a goal for all investors, but the distinguishing characteristic of securities dealers is that they hold securities in inventory only until the first opportunity to resell them. Essentially, trading from inventory is their business.

Dealers exist in all areas of the economy, of course, not just in the stock markets. For example, your local university bookstore is both a primary and secondary market textbook dealer. If you buy a new book, then this is a primary market transaction. If you buy a used book, this is a secondary market transaction, and you pay the store's ask price. If you sell the book back, you receive the store's bid price, often half the ask price. The bookstore's spread is the difference between the bid and ask prices.

In contrast, a securities broker arranges transactions between investors, matching investors wishing to buy securities with investors wishing to sell securities. Brokers may match investors with other investors, investors with dealers, and sometimes even dealers with dealers. The distinctive characteristic of securities brokers is that they do not buy or sell securities for their own account. Facilitating trades by others is their business.

Most common stock trading is directed through an organized stock exchange or a trading network. Whether a stock exchange or a trading network, the goal is to match investors wishing to buy stocks with investors wishing to sell stocks. The largest, most active organized stock exchange in the United States is the New York Stock Exchange (NYSE). Second and third in size are the Chicago Stock Exchange (CHX) and the American Stock Exchange (AMEX), respectively. These are followed by four regional exchanges: the Boston Stock Exchange (BSE), the Cincinnati Stock Exchange (CSE) (which is actually located in Chicago!), the Pacific Stock Exchange (PSE) in Los Angeles, and the Philadelphia Stock Exchange (PHLX). The major competitor to the organized stock exchanges is the vast trading network known as Nasdaq. In 1998, Nasdaq and the AMEX merged to form a single company, but the two organizations retained their original features. We next discuss the organization of the NYSE, and then we turn to a discussion of Nasdaq.

Check This

5.1a   Is an IPO a primary or secondary market transaction?

5.1b   Which is bigger, the bid price or the ask price? Why?

5.1c   What is the difference between a securities broker and a securities dealer?

5.2   The New York Stock Exchange

The New York Stock Exchange (NYSE, pronounced "Ny-see"), popularly known as the Big Board, celebrated its bicentennial in 1992. It has occupied its current building on Wall Street since the turn of the century, and today it is a not-for-profit New York State corporation. You may be surprised to read that a stock exchange could be a not-for-profit corporation. Actually, this is not unusual since a stock exchange is owned by its members and exists only to provide facilities for exchange members to conduct business. In this capacity, the NYSE operates as a cooperative on a not-for-profit basis. However, NYSE members conducting business on the exchange generally represent securities firms and brokerage companies that all most definitely operate on a for-profit basis.

NYSE Membership

NYSE member The owner of a seat on the NYSE.

The NYSE has 1,366 exchange **members**, who are said to own "seats" on the exchange. Technically, a seat is the personal property of the individual purchasing it. Typically, however, the individual who is the registered owner of a seat is an employee of a securities firm such as Merrill Lynch. The securities firm has actually paid for the seat and is effectively the owner. The firm is said to be a member organization (or member firm), and some member organizations own numerous seats on the exchange in this way.

Exchange seat owners can buy and sell securities on the exchange floor without paying commissions. For this and other reasons, exchange seats are valuable assets and are regularly bought and sold. Interestingly, prior to 1986, the highest seat price paid was $625,000 just before the 1929 market crash. Since then, the lowest seat price paid was $55,000 in 1977. As it turns out, that was a very good price for the buyer. In 2003, seats were going for about $2 million, down from a record $2.65 million paid in 1999.

In addition to paying the price of a seat, a prospective NYSE member must be sponsored by two current members and possess a clean record with regard to security laws violations or felony convictions of any kind. However, it is not necessary to actually own a seat to trade commission-free on the exchange floor, since seats can be leased. Leasing is common, and about half of all NYSE seats are leased. Even if you only wish

For up-to-date info on the NYSE, hit www.nyse.com

to lease a seat on the exchange, you must pass the same close scrutiny as someone wishing to buy a seat.

Exchange members elect 24 members of a 27-member board of directors. The three additional board members—the chairman of the board, the executive vice chairman, and the president—are *ex officio* members selected by the Board. "*Ex officio*" means that they are members of the board of directors by virtue of their positions as appointed professional managers of the exchange. While the board sets exchange policy, actual management is performed by a professional staff. Technically, NYSE members collectively own the exchange, but the NYSE is organized to insulate professional staff from undue pressure from exchange members.

Types of Members

commission brokers
Agents who execute customer orders to buy and sell stock transmitted to the exchange floor. Typically, they are employees of NYSE member firms.

The largest number of NYSE members are registered as **commission brokers**. The business of a commission broker is to execute customer orders to buy and sell stocks. A commission broker's primary responsibility to customers is to get the best possible prices for their orders. Their number varies, but over 500 NYSE members are commission brokers.

NYSE commission brokers typically are employees of brokerage companies that are NYSE member firms. Member firms operating as brokerage companies accept customer orders to buy and sell securities and relay these orders to their commission brokers for execution. Member firm activities represent the most vital functions of the NYSE, simply because their business is the original reason the exchange exists.

specialist NYSE member acting as a dealer on the exchange floor. Often called a *market maker*.

Second in number of NYSE members are **specialists**, so named because each acts as an assigned dealer for a small set of securities. With a few exceptions, each security listed for trading on the NYSE is assigned to a single specialist. Specialists are also called *market makers* because they are obligated to maintain a fair and orderly market for the securities assigned to them.

As market makers, specialists post bid prices and ask prices for securities assigned to them. The bid price is the price at which a specialist is obligated to buy a security from a seller, and an ask price is the price at which a specialist is obligated to sell a security to a buyer. As we have discussed elsewhere, the difference between the bid price and the ask price is called the bid-ask spread, or simply the spread.

Specialists make a market by standing ready to buy at bid prices and sell at ask prices when there is a temporary disparity between the flow of buy and sell orders for a security. In this capacity, they act as dealers for their own accounts. In so doing, they provide liquidity to the market. Their function is vital, since the work of commission brokers would be quite difficult without the specialists. As we discuss in the next section, specialists also act as brokers.

Almost 500 NYSE members are specialists. These specialists work for one of ten (as of 2003) specialist firms, and over half of all NYSE trading is concentrated in stocks managed by the three largest specialist firms. These three largest specialist firms and the number of stocks for which they act as specialists as of 2003 are shown immediately below.

Specialist Firm	Number of Stocks
LaBranche & Co.	587
Spear, Leeds & Kellogg Specialists	575
Fleet Specialist	434

floor brokers NYSE members who execute orders for commission brokers on a fee basis. Sometimes called *two-dollar brokers*.

Third in number of exchange members are **floor brokers**. Floor brokers are often used by commission brokers when they are too busy to handle certain orders themselves. Instead, they will delegate some orders to floor brokers for execution. Floor brokers are sometimes called two-dollar brokers, a name earned at a time when the standard fee for their service was only two dollars. Today the fee is variable, and certainly higher than two dollars. Floor brokers do well when stock trading volume is high, but with low volume they may be inactive for lengthy periods.

SuperDOT system Electronic NYSE system allowing orders to be transmitted directly to specialists for immediate execution.

In recent years, floor brokers have become less important on the exchange floor because of the efficient **SuperDOT system** (the "DOT" stands for designated order turnaround), which allows orders to be transmitted electronically directly to the specialist. SuperDOT trading now accounts for a substantial percentage of all trading on the NYSE, particularly on small orders.

floor traders NYSE members who trade for their own accounts, trying to anticipate and profit from temporary price fluctuations.

Finally, a small number of NYSE members are **floor traders**, who independently trade for their own accounts. Floor traders try to anticipate temporary price fluctuations and profit from them by buying low and selling high. In recent decades, the number of floor traders has declined substantially, suggesting that it has become increasingly difficult to profit from short-term trading on the exchange floor.

NYSE-Listed Stocks

A company is said to be "listed" on the NYSE if its stock is traded there. In 2003, stocks from about 2,800 companies were listed on the "Big Board," as the NYSE is sometimes called, with a market value of about $15 trillion. This total includes many large companies so well known that we easily recognize them by their initials—for example, IBM, AT&T, GE, and GM. This total also includes many companies that are not so readily recognized. For example, relatively few would instantly recognize AEP as American Electric Power, but AEX might be recognized as American Express.

U.S. companies that wish to have their stock listed for trading on the Big Board must apply for the privilege. If the application is approved, the company must pay an initial listing fee. In 2003, this fee was $36,800, plus a per-share charge that ranged from $14,750 per million shares for the first 2 million shares, to $1,900 for each million shares above 300 million. In addition to an initial listing fee, the NYSE assesses an annual listing fee. In 2003, the annual listing fee was $930 per million (subject to a $35,000 minimum fee).

The NYSE has minimum requirements for companies wishing to apply for listing on the Big Board. Although the requirements might change from time to time, some example minimum requirements in effect in 2003 included:

1. The company's total number of shareholders must be at least 2,200, and stock trading in the previous six months must have been at least 100,000 shares a month on average.
2. At least 1.1 million stock shares must be held in public hands.
3. Publicly held shares must have at least $100 million in market value ($60 million for IPOs).
4. The company must have annual earnings of $2.5 million before taxes in the most recent year and $2 million pretax earnings in each of the preceding two years.

In practice, most companies with stock listed on the NYSE easily exceed these minimum listing requirements.

Check This

5.2a   What are the four types of members of the New York Stock Exchange?

5.2b   Which NYSE member type is the most numerous? Which type is the second most numerous?

5.3   Operation of the New York Stock Exchange

Now that we have a basic idea of how the NYSE is organized and who the major players are, we turn to the question of how trading actually takes place. Fundamentally, the business of the NYSE is to attract and process *order flow*—the flow of customer orders to buy and sell stocks. Customers of the NYSE are the millions of individual investors and tens of thousands of institutional investors who place their orders to buy and sell NYSE-listed stock shares with member-firm brokers.

The NYSE has been quite successful in attracting order flow. In 2003, the average stock trading volume on the NYSE was well over 1 billion shares per day. About one-third of all NYSE stock trading volume is attributable to individual investors, and almost half is derived from institutional investors. The remainder represents NYSE-member trading, which is largely attributed to specialists acting as market makers.

NYSE Floor Activity

Quite likely you have seen film footage of the NYSE trading floor on television, or you may have visited the NYSE and viewed exchange floor activity from the gallery (it's worth the trip). Either way, you saw a big room, about the size of a small basketball gym. This big room is called "the big room." There are several other, smaller rooms that you normally don't see. One is called "the garage" because that is what it was before it was taken over for securities trading, and the other is called the "blue room" because, well, the room is painted blue.

On the floor of the exchange are a number of stations, each with a roughly figure-eight shape. These stations have multiple counters with numerous computer terminal screens above and on the sides. People operate behind and in front of the counters in relatively stationary positions.

Other people move around on the exchange floor, frequently returning to the many telephone booths positioned along the exchange walls. In all, you may have been reminded of worker ants moving around an ant colony. It is natural to wonder: What are all those people doing down there (and why are so many wearing funny-looking coats)?

specialist's post Fixed place on the exchange floor where the specialist operates.

As an overview of exchange floor activity, here is a quick look at what goes on. Each of the counters at the figure-eight shaped stations is a **specialist's post**. Specialists normally operate in front of their posts to monitor and manage trading in the stocks assigned to them. Clerical employees working for the specialists operate behind the counters. Moving from the many telephone booths out to the exchange floor and back again are swarms of commission brokers, receiving relayed customer orders, walking out to specialist posts where the orders can be executed, and returning to confirm order executions and receive new customer orders.

To better understand activity on the NYSE trading floor, imagine yourself as a commission broker. Your phone clerk has just handed you an order to sell 3,000 shares of

market order A
customer order to buy
or sell securities
marked for immediate
execution at the
current market price.

KO (the ticker symbol for Coca-Cola common stock) for a customer of the broker-age company that employs you. The order is a **market order**, meaning that the customer wants to sell the stock at the best possible price as soon as possible. You immediately walk (running violates exchange rules) to the specialist's post where KO stock is traded.

Upon approaching the specialist's post where KO is traded, you check the terminal screen for information on the current market price for KO stock. The screen reveals that the last executed trade for KO was at 70.63 and that the specialist is bidding 70.50 per share. You could immediately sell to the specialist at 70.50, but that would be too easy.

Instead, as the customer's representative, you are obligated to get the best possible price. It is your job to "work" the order, and your job depends on providing satisfactory order execution service. So you look around for another broker who represents a customer who wants to buy KO stock. Luckily, you quickly find another broker at the specialist's post with a market order to buy 3,000 shares of KO. Noticing that the specialist is asking 70.75 per share, you both agree to execute your orders with each other at a price of 70.63. This price, about halfway between the specialist's bid and ask prices, saves each of your customers approximately $.13 $\times$ 3,000 = $390 compared to the specialist's prices.

In a trade of this type, in which one commission broker buys from another, the specialist acts only as a broker assisting in matching buy orders and sell orders. On an actively traded stock, there can be many commission brokers buying and selling. In such cases, trading is said to occur "in the crowd." Thus, the specialist functions as a broker as long as there are buyers and sellers available. The specialist steps in as a dealer only when necessary to fill an order that would otherwise go unfilled.

In reality, not all orders are executed so easily. For example, suppose you are unable to quickly find another broker with an order to buy 3,000 shares of KO. Since you have a market order, you may have no choice but to sell to the specialist at the bid price of 70.50. In this case, the need to execute an order quickly takes priority, and the specialist provides the necessary liquidity to allow immediate order execution.

In this situation, the specialist is often able to help commission brokers by agreeing to "stop" the stock. By stopping stock for a sell order, the specialist agrees to try to help you get a better price while also guaranteeing a minimum price. For your sell order, the specialist might guarantee a minimum price of 70.50 but try to get a better price, say, 70.63. So agreed, you leave the order with the specialist. If the next offer to buy KO is at a price of 70.63, the specialist will fill your order at that price. But if no better offer appears forthcoming, the specialist will execute the order at the guaranteed price of 70.50—if necessary, from the specialist's own inventory.

Stopping stock is also a goodwill gesture. The NYSE places great emphasis on the quality of performance by specialists, which is evaluated regularly through surveys of commission brokers' satisfaction. Specialists are expected to assist brokers in getting the best prices for customer orders, to provide liquidity to the market, and to maintain an orderly market for all securities assigned to them. Stopping stock helps accomplish these objectives.

Note an important caveat concerning this discussion of NYSE floor operations. If you think about it, there's no way that the NYSE could trade more than a billion shares a day using this system. It's just not physically possible. What actually happens is that over 99 percent of orders are processed electronically using the SuperDOT. Based on volume of orders submitted, however, that number drops to about 75 percent. The implication is that larger orders are handled by commission brokers, but smaller orders are not.

Special Order Types

limit order Customer order to buy or sell securities with a specified "limit" price. The order can be executed only at the limit price or better.

Many orders are transmitted to the NYSE floor as **limit orders**. A limit order is an order to buy or sell stock, where the customer specifies a maximum price he is willing to pay in the case of a buy order, or a minimum price he will accept in the case of a sell order. For example, suppose that as a NYSE commission broker, you receive a limit order to sell 3,000 shares of KO stock at 70.75. This means that the customer is not willing to accept any price below 70.75 per share, even if it means missing the trade.

One strategy for handling limit orders is to hold the order and frequently check for potential buyers at the specialist post for KO stock. However, this is unnecessary because you can leave a limit order with the specialist. As a service to brokers, NYSE specialists display unfilled limit orders on the terminal screens at their posts for all approaching brokers to see. If another broker wants to buy KO at 70.75, the specialist will execute the sale for you. This service saves considerable time and energy for busy commission brokers. Indeed, monitoring and executing unfilled limit orders is a very important function of the NYSE specialist.

stop order Customer order to buy or sell securities when a preset "stop" price is reached.

A **stop order** may appear similar to a limit order, but there is an important difference. With a stop order, the customer specifies a "stop" price. This stop price serves as a trigger point. No trade can occur until the stock price reaches this stop price. When the stock price reaches the stop price, the stop order is immediately converted into a market order. Since the order is now a market order, the customer may get a price that is better or worse than the stop price. Thus, the stop price only serves as a trigger point for conversion into a market order. Unlike a limit price, the stop price places no limit on the price at which a trade can occur. Once converted to a market order, the trade is executed just like any other market order.

The most common type of stop order is a *stop-sell* order, which is an order to sell shares if the stock price falls to a specified stop price below the current stock price. This type of order is generally called a *stop-loss* because it is usually intended to limit losses on a long position. The other type is a *stop-buy* order, which is an order to buy shares if the price rises to a specified stop price above the current stock price. Stop-buy orders are often placed in conjunction with short sales, again as means of limiting losses.

Placing stop-loss orders is frequently touted as a smart trading strategy, but there are a couple of issues we should mention. For concreteness, suppose you buy 1,000 shares of GoGo Corp. at $20. You simultaneously place a stop-sell order at $15. Thus you seem to have limited your potential loss to $5 per share.

Unfortunately, after the market closes, a rumor circulates that GoGo has uncovered a significant accounting fraud. The next morning, the stock opens at $8, meaning the first trade occurs at $8 per share. Because this price is below your $15 stop price, a market order to sell your stock will be placed and executed, and you'll lose much more than $5 per share. What you discover is that your stop-loss guarantees only that a market order to sell will be placed as soon as the stock trades at $15 *or below*.

Adding insult to injury, after your stock is sold, a creditable announcement is made indicating that the rumor is false. GoGo shares promptly bounce back to $20, but you were sold out at a big loss. Thus, a second danger in blindly using stop-loss orders is that volatile conditions can lead to an unfavorable stop sale. Table 5.1 summarizes the characteristics of limit and stop orders.

TABLE 5.1	Stock Market Order Types	
Order Type	**Buy**	**Sell**
Market order	Buy at best price available for immediate execution.	Sell at best price available for immediate execution.
Limit order	Buy at best price available, but not more than the preset limit price. Forgo purchase if limit is not met.	Sell at best price available, but not less than the preset limit price. Forgo sale if limit is not met.
Stop order	Convert to a market order to buy when the stock price crosses the stop price from below.	Convert to a market order to sell when the stock price crosses the stop price from above. Also known as a "stop-loss."
Stop-limit order	Convert to a limit order to buy when the stock price crosses the stop price from below.	Convert to a limit order to sell when the stock price crosses the stop price from above.

A limit price can be attached to a stop order to create a *stop-limit order*. This is different from a simple stop order in that once the stock price reaches the preset stop price the order is converted into a limit order. By contrast, a simple stop order is converted into a market order. At this point, the limit order is just like any other limit order. Notice that with a stop-limit order you must specify two prices, the stop and the limit. The two prices can be the same, or they can be different. In our GoGo Corp. example, you could place a stop-limit sell order at $15 stop, $12 limit. This order converts to a limit order to sell at $12 or better if the price ever hits $15 or below. Thus you will never sell below $12. Of course, you may never sell at all unless your limit price is reached! Our nearby *Work the Web* box shows how these orders are entered in an actual online brokerage account.

Another type of order that requires special attention is the *short-sale order*. As explained in Chapter 2, a short sale involves borrowing stock shares and then selling the borrowed shares in the hope of buying them back later at a lower price. Short-sale loans are normally arranged through the customer's broker. New York Stock Exchange rules require that when shares are sold as part of a short-sale transaction, the order must be marked as a short-sale transaction when it is transmitted to the NYSE floor.

NYSE uptick rule
Rule for short sales requiring that before a short sale can be executed, the last price change must be an uptick.

Sell orders marked as short sales are subject to the **NYSE uptick rule**. According to the NYSE uptick rule, a short sale can be executed only if the last price change was an uptick. For example, suppose the last two trades were executed at 55.50 and then 55.63. The last price change was an uptick of .13, and a short sale can be executed at a price of 55.63 or higher. Alternatively, suppose the last two trades were executed at 55.50 and 55.25, where the last price change was a downtick of .25. In this case, a short sale can be executed only at a price higher than 55.25.

The NYSE enacted the uptick rule to make it more difficult for speculators to drive down a stock's price by repeated short sales. Interestingly, the uptick rule is a NYSE rule only and does not necessarily apply to short-sale transactions executed elsewhere. Since many NYSE-listed stocks are now traded elsewhere, the uptick rule is less of a constraint than it once was. The Nasdaq has a similar rule.

Finally, colored coats are worn by many of the people on the floor of the exchange. The color of the coat indicates the person's job or position. Clerks, runners, visitors, exchange officials, and so on, wear particular colors to identify themselves. Also, since things can get a little hectic on a busy day with the result that good clothing may not last long, the cheap coats offer some protection. Nevertheless, many specialists and floor brokers wear a good business suit every day simply out of habit and pride.

To illustrate how important it is to get order types straight, we've captured the actual trading screen from one of the largest online brokers, Ameritrade. Looking at the screen below, the stock entered is HD, which is the home improvement retailer Home Depot. The order being placed is a limit order to buy 100 shares at $21.25. The limit order is good for the day only. We've requested that the order be filled "all or none," meaning we don't want less than the full 100 shares.

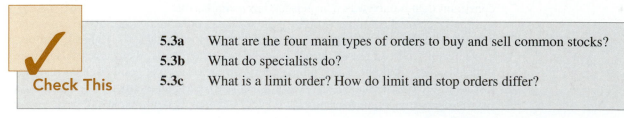

Clicking on the "Preview Order" button allows you to double-check your order before you submit it for transaction. Here is our preview screen:

Please review the following before placing this order:

You have requested an order to:
BUY 100 shares of **HD**, Home Depot
at **LIMIT** of **21.25 DAY** , **AON**, on Account **77**

Current Quote

Symbol	Bid	Ask	Last	Change	B/A Size	Last Trade	Exchange
HD			21.31	-0.32		02-07-2003 16:01:00	NYSE

Place Order   Do NOT Place Order

After checking to ensure we have entered everything correctly, we just hit the "Place Order" button to submit our order.

✔ **Check This**

5.3a   What are the four main types of orders to buy and sell common stocks?

5.3b   What do specialists do?

5.3c   What is a limit order? How do limit and stop orders differ?

5.4   Nasdaq

In terms of total dollar volume of trading, the second largest stock market in the United States is Nasdaq (say "Naz-dak"). In fact, in terms of companies listed and, on most days recently, number of shares traded, Nasdaq is bigger than the NYSE. The somewhat odd name is derived from the acronym NASDAQ, which stands for National Association of Securities Dealers Automated Quotations system. But Nasdaq is now a name in its own right and the all-capitals acronym should no longer be used.

Nasdaq Operations

Nasdaq's website is www.nasdaq.com Click on "About Nasdaq."

Introduced in 1971, the Nasdaq market is a computer network of securities dealers who disseminate timely security price quotes to Nasdaq subscribers. These dealers act as market makers for securities listed on Nasdaq. As market makers, Nasdaq dealers post bid and ask prices at which they accept sell and buy orders, respectively. With each price quote, they also post the number of stock shares that they obligate themselves to trade at their quoted prices.

Like NYSE specialists, Nasdaq market makers trade on an inventory basis, using their inventory as a buffer to absorb buy and sell order imbalances. Unlike the NYSE specialist system, Nasdaq features multiple market makers for actively traded stocks. Thus, there are two key differences between the NYSE and Nasdaq:

1. Nasdaq is a computer network and has no physical location where trading takes place.
2. Nasdaq has a multiple market maker system rather than a specialist system.

over-the-counter (OTC) market
Securities market in which trading is almost exclusively done through dealers who buy and sell for their own inventories.

Traditionally, a securities market largely characterized by dealers who buy and sell securities for their own inventories is called an **over-the-counter (OTC) market**. Consequently, Nasdaq is often referred to as an OTC market. However, in their efforts to promote a distinct image, Nasdaq officials prefer that the term OTC not be used when referring to the Nasdaq market. Nevertheless, old habits die hard, and many people still refer to Nasdaq as an OTC market.

By the year 2003, the Nasdaq had grown to the point that it was, by many measures, bigger than the NYSE. For example, in 2001, some 471 billion shares were traded on the Nasdaq versus 308 billion on the NYSE. In dollars, however, based on the total value of listed securities, the NYSE was still a good deal bigger, $15 trillion versus $3 trillion.

The Nasdaq is actually made up of two separate markets, the Nasdaq National Market (NNM) and the Nasdaq SmallCap Market. As the market for Nasdaq's larger and more actively traded securities, the Nasdaq National Market lists about 4,000 securities, including some of the best-known companies in the world. The Nasdaq SmallCap Market is for small companies and lists about 1,000 individual securities. As you might guess, an important difference in the two markets is that the National Market has more stringent listing requirements. Of course, as SmallCap companies become more established, they may move up to the National Market.

Nasdaq Participants

As we mentioned previously, the Nasdaq has historically been a dealer market, characterized by competing market makers. In 2003, there were about 500 such market

WORK THE WEB

You can actually watch trading take place on the Web by visiting one of the biggest ECNs, Island (www. island.com). Island is unusual in that the "order book," meaning the list of buy and sell orders, is public in real time.

As shown, we have captured a sample of orders for Cisco Systems. On the left-hand side are buy orders. On the right-hand side are sell orders. All orders are limit orders, and both the limit price and quantity are shown. The inside quotes (the highest bid, or buy, and the lowest ask, or sell, prices) in this market are those at the top, so we sometimes hear the expression "top of the book" quotes.

If you visit the site, you can see trading take place as limit orders are entered and executed. Notice that on this particular day, by 4:15 P.M., Island had traded more than 6 million shares of Cisco. At that time, the inside quotes were 62 shares bid at $13.20 and 4,950 shares offered at $13.23. Also, even though trading on the major exchanges had stopped for the day, you could still trade stocks on Island.

refresh | island home | disclaimer | help

CSCO

GET STOCK
CSCO go
Symbol Search

LAST MATCH		TODAY'S ACTIVITY	
Price	13.2300	Orders	61,177
Time	16:15:03.769	Volume	6,019,832

BUY ORDERS		SELL ORDERS	
SHARES	PRICE	SHARES	PRICE
62	13.2000	4,950	13.2300
62	13.2000	1,010	13.2490
990	13.1900	400	13.2500
11,800	13.1900	300	13.2600
600	13.1700	1,000	13.2800
1,000	13.1600	5,000	13.2900
5,000	13.1600	200	13.3000
2,000	13.1500	6,000	13.3500
10,000	13.1500	3,000	13.3600
900	13.1500	1,500	13.4600
1,000	13.1300	1,640	13.4800
50	13.0800	2,000	13.4900
140	13.0500	1,500	13.5000
1,700	13.0500	1,000	13.5000
2,000	13.0500	5,000	13.5300
(221 more)		(419 more)	

makers, which amounts to about 15 or so per stock. The biggest market makers cover thousands of stocks.

In a very important development, in the late 1990s, the Nasdaq system was opened to so-called **electronic communications networks (ECNs)**. ECNs are basically websites that allow investors to trade directly with one another. Our nearby *Work the Web* box describes one of the biggest ECNs, Island (www.island.com), and contains important information about ECN "order books." Be sure to read it. In 2003, about 10 ECNs were integrated into the Nasdaq, including Archipelago and Instinet, which are two of the better known.

Investor buy and sell orders placed on ECNs are transmitted to the Nasdaq and displayed along with market maker bid and ask prices. As a result, the ECNs open up the Nasdaq by essentially allowing individual investors to enter orders, not just market makers. As a result, the ECNs act to increase liquidity and competition.

If you check prices on the Web for both Nasdaq- and NYSE-listed stocks, you'll notice an interesting difference. For Nasdaq stocks, you can actually see the bid and

electronic communications network (ECN) A website that allows investors to trade directly with each other.

inside quotes Highest bid quotes and the lowest ask quotes offered by dealers for a security.

ask prices as well as recent transactions information. The bid and ask prices for the Nasdaq listings you see represent **inside quotes**, that is, the highest bid and the lowest ask prices. For a relatively small fee (or possibly even free from your broker), you can even have access to "Level II" quotes, which show all of the posted bid and ask prices and, frequently, the identity of the market maker. Of course, NYSE specialists post bid and ask prices as well, they are just not disclosed to the general public (they may be available by subscription at a cost substantially higher than that for Level II Nasdaq quotes).

The success of the Nasdaq National Market as a competitor to NYSE and other organized exchanges can be judged by its ability to attract stock listings by companies that traditionally might have chosen to be listed on the NYSE. Such well-known companies as Microsoft, Apple Computer, Intel, Dell, Yahoo!, and Starbucks list their securities on Nasdaq.

Check This

5.4a   How does Nasdaq differ from the NYSE?

5.4b   What are the different levels of access to the Nasdaq network?

5.5   NYSE and Nasdaq Competitors

third market Off-exchange market for securities listed on an organized exchange.

The NYSE and Nasdaq face strong competition in the market for order execution services from securities trading firms operating in the **third market**. The phrase "third market" refers to trading in exchange-listed securities that occurs off the exchange on which the security is listed. For example, a substantial volume of NYSE-listed stock trading is executed through independent securities trading firms.

One well-known example of third-market trading is the securities trading firm of Bernard L. Madoff Investment Securities. Independent trading firms like Madoff Securities lure a large volume of trades away from the New York Stock Exchange by paying a small commission, say, a half-cent per share, to brokerage firms that direct customer orders to them for execution. This practice is called "paying for order flow" and is controversial. Nevertheless, the SEC permits it.

fourth market Market for exchange-listed securities in which investors trade directly with other investors, usually through a computer network.

Nasdaq and NYSE also face substantial competition from the **fourth market**. The term "fourth market" refers to direct trading of exchange-listed securities among investors. A good example of fourth-market trading activity is Instinet, an ECN (and one of the oldest) that facilitates trading among its subscribers, particularly after-hours trading. However, as we discussed in our previous section, these fourth-market ECNs are increasingly becoming integrated into the Nasdaq system.

The third and fourth markets are not the only NYSE and Nasdaq competitors. Regional exchanges also attract substantial trading volume away from NYSE and Nasdaq. For example, thousands of stocks are dually listed on NYSE and either on Nasdaq or on at least one regional exchange.

Check This

5.5a   What is the third market for securities?

5.5b   What is the fourth market for securities?

5.6 Stock Market Information

Many newspapers publish current price information for a selection of stocks. In the United States, the newspaper best known for reporting stock price information is *The Wall Street Journal*. Investors interested in an overview of stock market activity refer to daily summaries. Among other things, these summaries contain information regarding several stock market indexes. Immediately below, we describe the most important stock market indexes.

The Dow Jones Industrial Average

The most widely followed barometer of day-to-day stock market activity is the Dow Jones Industrial Average (DJIA), often called the "Dow" for short. The DJIA is an index of the stock prices of 30 large companies representative of American industry. There are two more specialized Dow Jones averages, a utilities average and a transportation average. We will focus on the industrial average. Figure 5.2 reproduces a chart of the DJIA from "The Dow Jones Averages" column, which is published every day in *The Wall Street Journal*.

Figure 5.2 shows daily high, low, and closing prices for the DJIA from August 2002 through February 2003. As indicated in the upper right-hand portion, the vertical bars in the chart indicate the range of index high and low values on each trading day. The tick mark on the right side of each day's bar marks the closing value of the index on that day. We therefore see that, based on closing prices, the Dow reached a high of about 9,000 in late August and then fell to about 7,100 in early October, for a substantial decrease. (This was a scary time to be in the market!) Later the market recovered to about 8,000 by February.

Figure 5.2 also contains a box that discusses the implications of a stock split by Microsoft. We will discuss this aspect of the index a little later.

For more on the Dow, visit averages.dowjones.com Look for "About the Averages."

FIGURE 5.2

Dow Jones Industrial Average

Source: *The Wall Street Journal,* February 20, 2003. Reprinted by permission of Dow Jones & Company, Inc. via Copyright Clearance Center, Inc. © 2003 Dow Jones & Company, Inc. All Rights Reserved Worldwide.

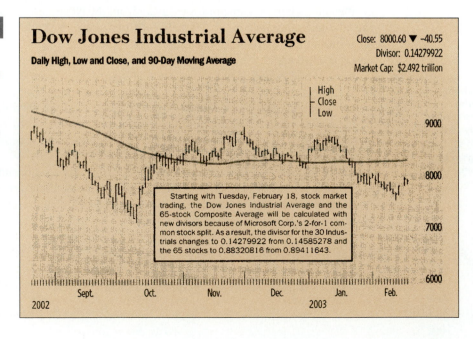

What are the Russell indexes? Visit www.russell.com to find out.

Major Stock Indexes

Dow Jones Averages	HIGH	LOW	CLOSE	NET CHG	% CHG	HIGH	LOW	% CHG	YTD % CHG
30 Industrials	8043.11	7935.27	8000.60	−40.55	−0.50	10635.25	7286.27	−19.52	−4.09
20 Transportations	2142.33	2097.15	2105.39	−35.26	−1.65	3049.96	2013.02	−21.94	−8.86
15 Utilities	199.16	195.54	196.77	− 1.52	−0.77	310.75	167.57	−28.49	−8.56
65 Composite	2249.58	2215.64	2230.66	−18.80	−0.84	3093.84	2033.44	−21.86	−6.08
Dow Jones Indexes									
US Total Market	197.74	194.92	196.30	− 1.42	−0.72	271.69	179.60	−22.74	−4.01
US Large-Cap	187.58	184.85	186.30	− 1.26	−0.67	261.25	172.31	−24.14	−3.89
US Mid-Cap	219.31	216.45	217.61	− 1.67	−0.76	291.12	192.15	−19.20	−3.94
US Small-Cap	236.22	232.75	233.75	− 2.43	−1.03	320.03	209.81	−18.86	−5.36
US Growth	762.76	750.71	757.27	− 5.29	−0.69	1140.25	687.99	−29.18	−2.34
US Value	1033.34	1019.01	1025.57	− 7.78	−0.75	1352.27	938.11	−18.17	−5.08
Global Titans 50	145.03	142.55	143.44	− 1.38	−0.95	198.86	134.76	−22.52	−5.12
Asian Titans 50	81.30	80.49	80.80	+ 0.30	+0.37	107.20	78.92	− 9.44	−2.07
DJ STOXX 50	2273.06	2209.31	2209.76	−67.82	−2.98	3707.12	2145.49	−35.53	−8.21
Nasdaq Stock Market									
Composite	1344.59	1322.12	1334.32	−12.22	−0.91	1929.67	1114.11	−24.85	−0.09
Nasdaq 100	1014.64	994.25	1005.88	− 9.03	−0.89	1555.11	804.64	−28.57	+2.19
Biotech	483.99	478.46	481.76	+ 0.35	+0.07	825.34	403.98	−37.22	−3.04
Computer	640.76	627.09	634.93	− 5.59	−0.87	976.12	505.26	−29.11	+1.98
Telecommunications	114.41	111.76	113.14	− 1.99	−1.73	195.62	81.43	−31.44	+4.00
Standard & Poor's Indexes									
500 Index	851.17	839.03	845.13	− 6.04	−0.71	1170.29	776.76	−23.03	−3.94
MidCap 400	407.87	402.06	404.06	− 3.81	−0.93	550.38	372.88	−18.86	−5.99
SmallCap 600	185.62	182.98	183.64	− 1.98	−1.07	257.81	170.73	−19.08	−6.60
SuperComp 1500	187.41	184.70	186.03	− 1.38	−0.74	256.74	171.10	−22.58	−4.19
New York Stock Exchange									
Composite	4805.73	4739.86	4763.45	−42.28	−0.88	6445.01	4452.49	−20.85	−4.73
Industrials	559.94	552.94	556.16	− 3.58	−0.64	763.43	532.91	−22.38	−4.76
Finance	490.85	485.97	489.04	− 1.79	−0.36	622.09	437.72	−13.88	−4.20
Others									
Russell 2000	364.53	358.92	360.28	− 4.25	−1.17	522.95	327.04	−22.89	−5.95
Wilshire 5000	8051.71	7942.13	7995.72	−55.99	−0.70	10953.64	7342.84	−22.01	−4.16
Value Line	249.15	245.29	246.45	− 2.70	−1.08	382.26	219.50	−29.37	−6.64
Amex Composite	817.20	812.06	813.72	− 1.80	−0.22	962.69	771.87	− 3.93	−1.29

Although the Dow is the most familiar stock market index, there are a number of other widely followed indexes. In fact, as we begin to discuss next, the Dow is not the most representative index by any means, and the way it is computed presents various problems that can make it difficult to interpret.

Stock Market Indexes

The "Dow Jones Averages" column is informative, but a serious market watcher may be interested in more detail regarding recent stock market activity. A more comprehensive view of stock market trading is contained in Figure 5.3, which is also published daily in *The Wall Street Journal*.

The excerpt we examine here, "Major Stock Indexes," reports information about a variety of stock market indexes in addition to the Dow Jones averages. Of the non–Dow Jones indexes shown, by far the best known and most widely followed is the Standard and Poor's Index of 500 stocks, commonly abbreviated as the S&P 500, or often just the S&P. We have seen this index before. In Chapter 1, we used it as a benchmark to track the performance of large common stocks for the last seven decades.

If you were to scrutinize the various indexes in Figure 5.3, you would quickly find that there are essentially four differences between them: (1) the market covered; (2) the types of stocks included; (3) how many stocks are included; and (4) how the index is calculated.

The first three of these differences are straightforward. Some indexes listed in Figure 5.3, such as the Dow Jones Utilities, focus on specific industries. Others, such as the Nasdaq Composite, focus on particular markets. Some have a small number of stocks; others, such as the Wilshire 5000 (which actually has about 5,700!), have a huge number.

How stock market indexes are computed is not quite so straightforward, but it is important to understand. There are two major types of stock market index: price-weighted and value-weighted. With a **price-weighted index**, stocks are held in the index in proportion to their share prices. With a **value-weighted index**, stocks are held in proportion to their total company market values.

The best way to understand the difference between price and value weighting is to consider an example. To keep things relatively simple, we suppose that there are only two companies in the entire market. We have the following information about their shares outstanding, share prices, and total market values:

price-weighted index
Stock market index in which stocks are held in proportion to their share price.

value-weighted index
Stock market index in which stocks are held in proportion to their total company market value.

	Shares Outstanding	Price per Share		Total Market Value	
		Beginning of Year	End of Year	Beginning of Year	End of Year
Company A	50 million	$10	$14	$500 million	$700 million
Company B	1 million	$50	$40	$ 50 million	$ 40 million

As shown, Company A has a lower share price but many more shares outstanding. Ignoring dividends, notice that Company A's stock price rose by 40 percent ($10 to $14) while Company B's stock price fell by 20 percent ($50 to $40).

The question we want to answer here is simply: How did the market do for the year? There are several ways we could answer this question. We could first focus on what happened to the average share price. The average share price was ($10 + $50)/2 = $30 at the beginning of the year, and ($14 + $40)/2 = $27 at the end, so the average share price fell. If we take the average share price as our index, then our index fell from 30 to 27, for a change of −3 points. Since the index began at 30, this is a −3/30 = −10% decrease. We might therefore say that the market was "off" by 10 percent.

This is an example of a price-weighted index. Because Company B's stock price is five times bigger than Company A's, it carries five times as much weight in the index. This explains why the index was down even though Company A's stock gained 40 percent whereas Company B's stock only lost 20 percent. The Dow Jones indexes are price weighted.

Alternatively, instead of focusing on the price of a typical share, we could look at what happened to the total value of a typical company. Here we notice that the average total value, in millions, rose from ($500 + $50)/2 = $275 to ($700 + $40)/2 = $370. If we take average total company value as our index, then our index rose from 275 to 370, a 35 percent *increase*.

This is an example of a value-weighted index. The influence a company has in this case depends on its overall change in total market value, not just its stock price change. Because Company A has a much larger total value, it carries a much larger weight in

Take a look at the "value" and "growth" indexes at www.barra.com

the index. With the exception of the Dow Jones indexes, most of the other indexes in Figure 5.3, including the Standard & Poor's, are value weighted.

Now we have a problem. One index tells us the market was down by 10 percent, while the other tells us it was up by 35 percent. Which one is correct? The answer seems fairly obvious. The total value of the market as a whole grew from $550 million to $740 million, so the market as a whole increased in value. Put differently, investors as a whole owned stock worth $550 million at the beginning of the year and $740 million at the end of the year. So, on the whole, stock market investors earned 35 percent, even though the average share price went down.

This example shows that a price-weighted index can be misleading as an indicator of total market value. The basic flaw in a price-weighted index is that the effect a company has on the index depends on the price of a single share. However, the price of a single share is only part of the story. Unless the number of shares is also considered, the true impact on the overall market isn't known, and a distorted picture can emerge.

CAUTION: INDEXES UNDER CONSTRUCTION

EXAMPLE 5.1

Suppose there are only two stocks in the market and the following information is given:

	Shares Outstanding	Price per Share Beginning of Year	Price per Share End of Year
Quark Co.	10 million	$10	$11
Bashir, Inc.	20 million	$20	$25

Construct price- and value-weighted indexes and calculate the percentage changes in each.

The average share price rose from $15 to $18, or $3, so the price-weighted index would be up by $3/15 = 20$ percent. Average total market value, in millions, rose from $250 to $305, so the value-weighted index rose by $55/250 = 22$ percent.

More on Price-Weighted Indexes

Earlier we indicated that the Dow Jones averages are price weighted. Given this, you may wonder why the Dow Jones Industrial Average has such a high value when the stock prices used to calculate the average are much smaller. To answer this question, we must explain one last detail about price-weighted indexes.

The extra detail concerns the effects of stock splits on price-weighted indexes. For example, in a 2-for-1 stock split, all current shareholders receive two new shares in exchange for each old share that they own. However, the total value of the company does not change because it is still the same company after the stock split. There are just twice as many shares, each worth half as much.

A stock split has no effect on a value-weighted index since the total value of the company does not change. But it can have a dramatic effect on a price-weighted index. To see this, consider what happens to the price-weighted and value-weighted indexes we created above when Company B enacts a 2-for-1 stock split. Based on beginning prices, with a 2-for-1 split, Company B's shares fall to $25. The price-weighted index falls to $(10 + 25)/2 = 17.50$ from 30, even though nothing really happened.

For a price-weighted index, the problem of stock splits can be addressed by adjusting the divisor each time a split occurs. Once again, an example is the best way to illustrate. In the case stated just above, suppose we wanted the index value to stay at 30 even though B's price per share fell to $25 as a result of the split. The only way to accomplish this is to add together the new stock prices and divide by something less than 2.

This new number is called the *index divisor*, and it is adjusted as needed to remove the effect of stock splits. To find the new divisor in our case, the stock prices are $25 and $10, and we want the index to equal 30. We solve for the new divisor, d, as follows:

$$\text{Index level} = \frac{\text{Sum of stock prices}}{\text{Divisor}}$$

$$30 = \frac{25 + 10}{d}$$

$$d = \frac{35}{30} = 1.16666\ldots$$

The new divisor is thus approximately 1.17.

Adjusting the divisor takes care of the problem in one sense, but it creates another problem. Since we are no longer dividing the sum of the share prices by the number of companies in the index, we can no longer interpret the change in the index as the change in price of an average share.

ADJUSTING THE DIVISOR

EXAMPLE 5.2

Take a look back at Example 5.1. Suppose that Bashir splits 5-for-1. Based on beginning information, what is the new divisor?

Following a 5-for-1 split, Bashir's share price will fall from $20 to $4. With no adjustment to the divisor, the price-weighted index would drop from 15 to $(10 + 4)/2 = 7$. To keep the index at its old level of 15, we need to solve for a new divisor such that $(10 + 4)/d = 15$. In this case, the new divisor would be $14/15 = .93333\ldots$, illustrating that the divisor can drop below 1.0.

The Dow Jones Divisors

The method we described of adjusting the divisor on a price-weighted index for stock splits is the method used to adjust the Dow Jones averages. Through time, with repeated adjustments for stock splits, the divisor becomes smaller and smaller. As Figure 5.2 shows, as of February 20, 2003, the divisor was a nice, round .14279922. Since there are 30 stocks in the index, the divisor on the DJIA would be 30 if it were never adjusted, so it has declined substantially. The other Dow Jones averages have similarly odd values.

Given its shortcomings, you might wonder why the financial press continues to report the Dow Jones averages. The reason is tradition; the Dow Jones averages have been around for more than 100 years, and each new generation of investors becomes accustomed to its quirks.

More on Index Formation: Base-Year Values

We next discuss one or two more details about indexes. First, to ease interpretation, the starting value of an index is usually set equal to some simple base number, like 100 or 1,000. For example, if you were to create a value-weighted index for the NYSE, the actual value of the index would be very large and cumbersome, so adjusting it makes sense.

To illustrate, suppose we have a value-weighted index with a starting value of 1.4 million. If we want the starting value to be 100, we just divide the starting value, and every subsequent value, by 1.4 million and then multiply by 100. So, if the next value of the index is 1.6 million, the "reindexed" value would be 1.6 million/1.4 million $\times$ 100 = 114.29, which is easily interpreted as a 14.29 percent increase over a base of 100.

REINDEXING

EXAMPLE 5.3

You've calculated values for an index over a four-year period as follows:

Year 1:   1,687 million

Year 2:   1,789 million

Year 3:   1,800 million

Year 4:   1,700 million

Suppose you wanted the index to start at 1,000. What would the reindexed values be?

To reindex these numbers, we need to (1) divide each of them by the starting value, 1,687 million, and then (2) multiply each by 1,000. Thus, we have:

Year 1:   1,687 million/1,687 million $\times$ 1,000 = 1,000.00

Year 2:   1,789 million/1,687 million $\times$ 1,000 = 1,060.46

Year 3:   1,800 million/1,687 million $\times$ 1,000 = 1,066.98

Year 4:   1,700 million/1,687 million $\times$ 1,000 = 1,007.71

Finally, an important consideration in looking at indexes is whether dividends are included. Most indexes don't include them. As a result, the change in an index measures only the capital gain (or loss) component of your return. When you're trying to evaluate how a particular type of stock market investment has done over time, dividends have to be included to get an accurate picture.

So which index is the best? The most popular alternative to the DJIA is the value-weighted S&P 500. You might further wonder, however, why this popular index limits itself to 500 stocks. The answer is timeliness and accuracy. Almost all stocks in the S&P 500 index trade every day, and therefore accurate daily updates of market prices are available each day. Stocks that do not trade every day can cause **index staleness**. Index staleness occurs when an index does not reflect all current price information because some of the stocks in the index have not traded recently. Also, as a practical matter, the largest 500 companies account for a very large portion of the value of the overall stock market.

index staleness
Condition that occurs when an index does not reflect all current price information because some of the stocks in the index have not traded recently.

Check This

5.6a   What is the difference between price- and value-weighting in the construction of stock market indexes? Give an example of a well-known index of each type.

5.6b   Which is better, price or value weighting? Why?

5.6c   Which stock market index is likely to contain the greater degree of index staleness, the S&P 500 or the Wilshire 5000 index?

5.7   Summary and Conclusions

This chapter introduced you to stock markets. We discussed who owns stocks, how the stock exchanges operate, and how stock market indexes are constructed and interpreted. Along the way we saw that:

1. Individual investors, directly or through mutual funds, own over half of all traded stocks. The rest are owned mostly by financial institutions such as pension funds and insurance companies.

2. The stock market is composed of a primary market, where stock shares are first sold, and a secondary market, where investors trade shares among themselves. In the primary market, companies raise money for investment projects. Investment bankers specialize in arranging financing for companies in the primary market. Investment bankers often act as underwriters, buying newly issued stock from the company and then reselling the stock to the public. The primary market is best known as the market for initial public offerings (IPOs).

3. In the secondary market, investors trade securities with other investors. Secondary market transactions are directed through three channels: directly with other investors, indirectly through a broker, or directly with a dealer. We saw that a broker matches buyers and sellers; a dealer buys and sells out of inventory.

4. Most common stock trading is directed through an organized stock exchange or through a trading network. The largest organized stock exchange in the United States is the New York Stock Exchange (NYSE). Popularly known as the Big Board, NYSE is owned by its members. There are four major types of NYSE members: commission brokers, specialists, floor brokers, and floor traders. We discussed the role of each in the functioning of the exchange.

5. The second largest stock market in the United States is Nasdaq. Nasdaq is a computer network of securities dealers and electronic communications networks (ECNs).

6. The NYSE and Nasdaq face strong competition from securities trading firms operating in the third and fourth markets. The third market refers to off-exchange trading of exchange-listed securities by securities firms. The fourth market refers to direct trading among investors. The regional stock exchanges also attract substantial trading volume away from NYSE and Nasdaq.

7. The most widely followed barometer of day-to-day stock market activity is the Dow Jones Industrial Average (DJIA). The DJIA is an index of the stock prices

of 30 large companies representative of American industry. Other indexes are also common. Among these, the best known is the Standard & Poor's Index of 500 stocks, abbreviated as the S&P 500. We described how these indexes are computed, with particular attention to some of the problems encountered.

Get Real

This chapter covered the operations and organization of the major stock markets. It also covered some of the most important order types and the construction of stock market indexes. How should you, as an investor or investment manager, put this information to work?

First, as in some previous chapters, you need to submit as many as possible of the different order types suggested by this chapter in a simulated brokerage account (note that not all simulated brokerage accounts allow all trade types). Your goal is to gain experience with the different order types and what they mean and accomplish for you as an investor or investment manager.

In each case, once you have placed the order, be sure to monitor the price of the stock in question to see if any of your orders should be executed. When an order is executed, compare the result to the stop or limit price to see how you did.

The second thing to do is to start observing the different indexes and learning how they are computed, what's in them, and what they are intended to cover. For example, the Nasdaq 100 is made up of the largest Nasdaq stocks. Is this index broadly representative of big stocks in general? Of Nasdaq stocks in general? Why is the Russell 2000 index widely followed (note that it *doesn't* contain 2,000 big stocks)? Visit www.russell.com to learn more.

Key Terms

primary market 145
secondary market 145
initial public offering (IPO) 145
investment banking firm 145
underwrite 145
fixed commitment 145
best effort 145
Securities and Exchange Commission
   (SEC) 146
prospectus 146
red herring 146
dealer 148
broker 148
bid price 148
ask price 148
spread 148
NYSE member 149
commission broker 150

specialist 150
floor brokers 151
SuperDOT system 151
floor traders 151
specialist's post 152
market order 153
limit order 154
stop order 154
NYSE uptick rule 155
over-the-counter (OTC) market 157
electronic communications
   network (ECN) 158
inside quotes 159
third market 159
fourth market 159
price-weighted index 162
value-weighted index 162
index staleness 165

www.mhhe.com/cj3e

Chapter Review Problems and Self-Test

1. **Index Construction**   Suppose there are only two stocks in the market and the following information is given:

	Shares Outstanding	Price per Share	
		Beginning of Year	End of Year
Ally Co.	100 million	$ 60	$ 66
McBeal, Inc.	400 million	$120	$100

Construct price- and value-weighted indexes and calculate the percentage changes in each.

2. **Stock Splits**   In the previous problem, suppose that McBeal splits 3-for-1. Based on beginning information, what is the new divisor?

Answers to Self-Test Problems

1. The average share price at the beginning of the year is ($60 + 120)/2 = $90. At the end of the year, the average price is $83. Thus, the average price declined by $7 from $90, a percentage drop of −$7/$90 = −7.78%. Total market cap at the beginning of the year is $60 × 100 + $120 × 400 = $54 billion. It falls to $46.6 billion, a decline of $7.4 billion. The percentage decline is −$7.4 billion/$54 billion = −13.7%, or almost twice as much as the price-weighted index.

2. Following a 3-for-1 split, McBeal's share price falls from $120 to $40. To keep the price-weighted index at its old level of 90, we need a new divisor such that (60 + 40)/d = 90. In this case, the new divisor would be 100/90 = 1.1111.

Test Your Investment Quotient

1. **Stop-Loss Order**   If you place a stop-loss order to sell 100 shares of stock at $55 when the current price is $62, how much will you receive for each share if the price drops to $52?

   a. $50
   b. $55
   c. $54.87
   d. Cannot tell from the information given.

2. **Uptick Rule**   You wish to sell short 100 shares of XYZ Corporation stock. If the last two transactions were $34.12 followed by $34.25, you can short on the next transaction only at a price of

   a. $34.12 or higher.
   b. $34.25 or higher.
   c. $34.25 or lower.
   d. $34.12 or lower.

3. **Uptick Rule**   Which of the following is false regarding the NYSE uptick rule?

   a. The rule does not apply to short sales executed on other exchanges.
   b. The NYSE enacted the rule to make it more difficult for speculators to drive down a stock's price by repeated short sales.
   c. The rule has become less of a constraint than it once was.
   d. The rule applies when shorting a stock or when covering a short.

4. **Value-Weighted Index**   An analyst gathered the following data about stocks J, K, and L, which together form a value-weighted index:

	December 31, Year 1		December 31, Year 2	
Stock	Price	Shares Outstanding	Price	Shares Outstanding
J	$40	10,000	$50	10,000
K	$30	6,000	$20	12,000*
L	$50	9,000	$40	9,000

*2-for-1 stock split.

The ending value-weighted index (base index = 100) is closest to:

a. 92.31
b. 93.64
c. 106.80
d. 108.33

5. **Dow Jones Index**   The divisor for the Dow Jones Industrial Average (DJIA) is most likely to decrease when a stock in the DJIA

a. Has a stock split.
b. Has a reverse split.
c. Pays a cash dividend.
d. Is removed and replaced.

6. **New York Stock Exchange**   Which of the following activities are *not* conducted by specialists on the NYSE?

a. Acting as dealers for their own accounts.
b. Monitoring compliance with margin requirements.
c. Providing liquidity to the market.
d. Monitoring and executing unfilled limit orders.

7. **Stock Markets**   What is a securities market characterized by dealers who buy and sell securities for their own inventories called?

a. A primary market.
b. A secondary market.
c. An over-the-counter market.
d. An institutional market.

8. **Stock Markets**   What is the over-the-counter market for exchange-listed securities called?

a. Third market
b. Fourth market
c. After-market
d. Block market

9. **Stock Indexes**   If the market prices of each of the 30 stocks in the Dow Jones Industrial Average all change by the same percentage amount during a given day, which stock will have the greatest impact on the DJIA?

a. The one whose stock trades at the highest dollar price per share.
b. The one whose total equity has the highest market value.
c. The one having the greatest amount of equity in its capital structure.
d. The one having the lowest volatility.

www.mhhe.com/cj3e

10. **Stock Indexes**   In calculating the Standard & Poor's stock price indexes, how are adjustments for stock splits made?

   a. By adjusting the divisor.
   b. Automatically, due to the manner in which the index is calculated.
   c. By adjusting the numerator.
   d. Quarterly, on the last trading day of each quarter.

11. **Stock Indexes**   Which of the following indexes includes the largest number of actively traded stocks?

   a. The Nasdaq Composite Index.
   b. The NYSE Composite Index.
   c. The Wilshire 5000 Index.
   d. The Value Line Composite Index.

12. **New York Stock Exchange**   The largest number of NYSE members are registered as:

   a. Stockholders
   b. Commission brokers
   c. Specialists
   d. Floor traders

13. **New York Stock Exchange**   The second largest number of NYSE members are registered as:

   a. Stockholders
   b. Commission brokers
   c. Specialists
   d. Floor traders

14. **Stock Trading**   An institutional investor wishing to sell a very large block of stock, say, 10,000 shares or more, is most likely to get the best price in which market?

   a. The primary market
   b. The secondary market
   c. The third market
   d. The fourth market

15. **Stock Indexes**   Which one of the following statements regarding the Dow Jones Industrial Average is false?

   a. The DJIA contains 30 well-known large-company stocks.
   b. The DJIA is affected equally by dollar changes in low- and high-priced stocks.
   c. The DJIA is affected equally by percentage changes in low- and high-priced stocks.
   d. The DJIA divisor must be adjusted for stock splits.

Concept Questions

1. **Primary and Secondary Markets**   If you were to visit your local Chevrolet retailer, there is both a primary and a secondary market in action. Explain. Is the Chevy retailer a dealer or a broker?

2. **Specialists**   On the NYSE, does a specialist act as a dealer or a broker? Or both?

3. **Market and Limit Orders**   What is the difference between a market order and a limit order? What is the potential downside to each type of order?

4. **Stop That!**   What is a stop-loss order? Why might it be used? Is it sure to stop a loss?

5. **Order Types**   Suppose Microsoft is currently trading at $100. You want to buy it if it reaches $120. What type of order should you submit?

6. **Order Types**   Suppose Dell is currently trading at $65. You think that if it reaches $70, it will continue to climb, so you want to buy it if and when it gets there. Should you submit a limit order to buy at $70?

7. **Nasdaq Quotes**   With regard to the Nasdaq, what are inside quotes?

8. **Index Composition**   There are basically four factors that differentiate stock market indexes. What are they? Comment on each.

9. **Index Composition**   Is it necessarily true that, all else the same, an index with more stocks is better? What is the issue here?

10. **Upticks**   What is the uptick rule? Where does it apply? Why does it exist?

Questions and Problems

Core Questions

1. **Price-Weighted Divisor**   Able, Baker, and Charlie are the only three stocks in an index. The stocks sell for $30, $148, and $89, respectively. If Baker undergoes a 2-for-1 stock split, what is the new divisor for the price-weighted index?

2. **Price-Weighted Divisor**   In the previous problem, assume that Baker undergoes a 3-for-1 stock split. What is the new divisor now?

3. **Order Books**   You find the following order book on a particular stock. The last trade on the stock was at $81.03.

Buy Orders		Sell Orders	
Shares	**Price**	**Shares**	**Price**
350	$81.01	100	$81.04
100	81.00	600	81.05
900	80.98	1,000	81.07
75	80.96	700	81.08
		900	81.10

a. If you place a market buy order for 100 shares, at what price will it be filled?
b. If you place a market sell order for 100 shares, at what price will it be filled?
c. Suppose you place a market order to buy 400 shares. At what price will it be filled?

4. **Price-Weighted Index**   You are given the following information concerning two stocks that make up an index. What is the price-weighted return for the index?

	Shares Outstanding	Price per Share	
		Beginning of Year	**End of Year**
Kirk, Inc.	35,000	$95	$102
Picard Co.	65,000	54	63

5. **Value-Weighted Index**   Calculate the index return for the information in the previous problem using a value-weighted index.

6. **Reindexing**   In Problem 5, assume that you want to reindex with the index value at the beginning of the year equal to 100. What is the index level at the end of the year?

7. **Index Level**   In Problem 5, assume the value-weighted index level was 408.16 at the beginning of the year. What is the index level at the end of the year?

8. **Reindexing**   You have calculated the following values for an index over a five-year period:

Year 1: 5,897 million

Year 2: 6,194 million

Year 3: 6,598 million

Year 4: 6,084 million

Year 5: 6,722 million

Suppose you wanted the index to start at 500. What would the reindexed values be?

Intermediate Questions

9. **Price-Weighted Divisor**   Look back at Problem 1. Assume that Able undergoes a 1-for-3 reverse stock split. What is the new divisor?

10. **DJIA**   On February 6, 2003, the DJIA closed at 7,929.30. The divisor at that time was .14585278. Suppose the next day the prices for 29 of the stocks remained unchanged and one stock increased $5.00. What would the DJIA level be the next day?

11. **DJIA**   In February 2003, MMM was one of the highest priced stocks in the DJIA and Disney was one of the lowest. The closing price for MMM on February 6, 2003, was $123.14 and the closing price for Disney was $17.00. Suppose the next day the other 29 stock prices remained unchanged and MMM increased 5 percent. What would the new DJIA level be? Now assume Disney increased by 5 percent and find the new DJIA level.

12. **DJIA**   Looking back at the previous problems, what would the new index level be if all stocks on the DJIA increased by $1.00 per share on February 7, 2003?

13. **Price-Weighted Divisor**   You construct a price-weighted index of 40 stocks. At the beginning of the day the index is 2,432.54. During the day, 39 stock prices remain the same, and one stock price increases $5.00. At the end of the day, your index value is 2,439.87. What is the divisor on your index?

14. **Price-Weighted Indexes**   Suppose the following three defense stocks are to be combined into a stock index in January 2001 (perhaps a portfolio manager believes these stocks are an appropriate benchmark for his or her performance):

	Shares (millions)	Price		
		1/1/01	1/1/02	1/1/03
Douglas McDonnell	450	$65	$70	$68
Dynamics General	500	30	48	41
International Rockwell	400	50	61	53

a. Calculate the initial value of the index if a price-weighting scheme is used.
b. What is the rate of return on this index for the year ending December 31, 2002? For the year ending December 31, 2003?

15. **Price-Weighted Indexes**   In the previous problem, suppose that Douglas McDonnell shareholders approve a 5-for-1 stock split on January 1, 2002. What is the new divisor for the index? Calculate the rate of return on the index for the year ending December 31, 2002, if Douglas McDonnell's share price on January 1, 2003, is $13.60 per share.

16. **Value-Weighted Indexes**   Repeat Problem 14 if a value-weighted index is used. Assume the index is scaled by a factor of 10 million; that is, if the average firm's market value is $5 billion, the index would be quoted as 500.

17. **Value-Weighted Indexes**   In the previous problem, will your answers change if Douglas McDonnell stock splits? Why or why not?

18. **Equally-Weighted Indexes**   In addition to price-weighted and value-weighted indexes, an equally-weighted index is one in which the index value is computed from the average rate of return of the stocks comprising the index. Equally-weighted indexes are frequently used by financial researchers to measure portfolio performance.

    a. Using the information in Problem 14, compute the rate of return on an equally-weighted index of the three defense stocks for the year ending December 31, 2001.

    b. If the index value is set to 100 on January 1, 2001, what will the index value be on January 1, 2003? What is the rate of return on the index for 2002?

19. **Equally-Weighted versus Value-Weighted Indexes**   Historically there have been periods where a value-weighted index has a higher return than an equally-weighted index and other periods where the opposite has occurred. Why do you suppose this would happen? Hint: Look back to Chapter 1.

20. **Geometric Indexes**   Another type of index is the geometric index. The calculation of a geometric index is similar to the calculation of a geometric return:

$$1 + R_G = [(1 + R_1)(1 + R_2) \ldots (1 + R_N)]^{1/N}$$

    The difference in the geometric index construction is the returns used are the returns for the different stocks in the index for a particular period, such as a day or year. Construct the geometric index returns for Problem 14 over each of the two years. Assume the beginning index level is 100.

21. **Geometric Indexes**   We have seen the importance of geometric returns through time. A geometric index is across different stocks at a particular point in time, such as a day. Constructing a portfolio that exactly replicates a geometric index is thus impossible. Given this, why would you want to use a geometric index? In other words, what does a geometric index measure? Now consider the Value Line Arithmetic Index (VLA), which is equally-weighted, and the Value Line Geometric Index (VLG). On February 1, 1988, both indexes were set to a value of 210.75. As of the close of the market on February 10, 2003, the VLA was at 973.81 and the VLG was at 245.92. Why would you expect to see such a disparity in the two index levels?

22. **Interpreting Index Values**   Suppose you want to replicate the performance of several stock indexes, some of which are price-weighted, others value-weighted, and still others equally-weighted. Describe the investment strategy you need for each of the index types. Are any of the three strategies passive, in that no portfolio rebalancing need be performed to perfectly replicate the index (assuming no stock splits or cash distributions)? Which of the three strategies do you think is most often followed by small investors? Which strategy is the most difficult to implement?

STANDARD &POOR'S

S&P Problems

www.mhhe.com/edumarketinsight

1. **Index Construction**   You have decided that you want a stock market index that tracks publishing companies. The three constituent companies you have decided to use are McGraw-Hill Companies (MHP), Dow Jones & Company (DJ), and Value Line Inc. (VALU). For each company, download the monthly stock prices. Under the "Financial Hlts" link you can find the number of shares outstanding. Construct a price-weighted and a value-weighted index for the publishing industry for the last six months. Use a beginning index value of 100 where appropriate. What are the monthly returns for each index?

What's on the Web?

1. **Specialists**   Go to www.nyse.com and find the discussion of NYSE members. What are the five essential functions of the specialist according to the website?

2. **DJIA**   As you have seen, in a price-weighted index, a stock with a higher price has a higher weight in the index return. To find out the weight of the stocks in the DJIA, go to www.djindexes.com. Which stock in the DJIA has the highest weight? The lowest weight?

3. **DJIA**   You want to find the current divisor for the DJIA. Go to www.djindexes.com and look up the current divisor.

4. **S&P 500**   To find out the most recent changes in the S&P 500, go to www2.standardandpoors.com. Once at the website, find the 10 most recent additions and deletions to the stocks in the index.

5. **Nikkei 225**   The Nikkei 225 Index is a highly followed index that measures the performance of the Japanese stock market. Go to www.nni.nikkei.co.jp and find out if the Nikkei 225 is a price-weighted or value-weighted index. What is the divisor for this index? When was the latest reconstitution of the index? Which stocks were added? Which stocks were deleted?

Stock-Trak®
Portfolio Simulations

Stock Market Day Trading with Stock-Trak

The Internet has given rise to a new breed of stock market investors—day traders. Day traders buy and sell common stocks within a day and typically close out their positions before the end of the day to avoid carrying a stock position overnight. The most popular trading strategy among day traders is "momentum trading," whereby the day trader tries to identify stocks that have started moving up and will continue to move up through the day. Once a stock is identified, the day trader buys the stock and tracks its progress through the day. Some time later—perhaps a few minutes, perhaps a few hours—the day trader sells the stock to close out the position before the end of trading that day.

How do you identify stocks with sustainable momentum? Day traders often use sophisticated computer programs to assist their decision processes, but they must ultimately depend on instincts. While most day traders have a difficult time recouping their trading expenses, there are often spectacular successes to inspire the would-be trader. The beauty of a Stock-Trak account is that you can try your hand at day trading without risking your own capital.

To try your hand at day trading using your Stock-Trak account, simultaneously log on to an Internet stock quote server and the Stock-Trak website in the morning, ideally about an hour or two after NYSE trading has started. Note that Web browsers support several different sessions at one time and many stock quote servers also provide stock price charts. Next, identify several stocks that are up since the opening of trading that day. Most stock quote servers report intraday stock price statistics, including high and low prices along with an opening price and change in price. Pick two or three stocks and submit an order to Stock-Trak to buy these stocks. Stock-Trak will return a trade confirmation indicating the trade prices for your order. Print the trade confirmation so you don't forget your trade prices. Later in the day, log on to Stock-Trak to close out your position and calculate your profits and losses. Remember, a real day trader will not hold a position overnight. It's easier to sleep that way.

Stock-Trak Exercise

1. If it's a rainy day and you're bored, log on to Stock-Trak and a stock quote server and stay logged on for several hours. Indulge yourself with frequent buying and selling based on your instincts. Try to set a pace of executing at least five or six trades an hour. Be careful—day trading can be addictive and you might forget to go to your investments class.

Chapter 6

Common Stock Valuation

"Ignore the stock market, ignore the economy and buy a business you understand."

–Warren Buffett

"Prediction is difficult, especially about the future."

–Niels Bohr[1]

Common stock valuation is one of the most challenging tasks in financial analysis. A fundamental assertion of finance holds that the value of an asset is based on the present value of its future cash flows. Accordingly, common stock valuation attempts the difficult task of predicting the future. Consider that the dividend yield for a typical large-company stock might be about 2 percent. This implies that the present value of dividends to be paid over the next 10 years constitutes only a portion of the current stock price. Thus, much of the value of a typical stock is derived from dividends to be paid more than 10 years away! ■

In this chapter, we examine several methods commonly used by financial analysts to assess the economic value of common stocks. These methods are grouped into two categories: dividend discount models and price ratio models. After studying these models, we provide an analysis of a real company to illustrate the use of the methods discussed in this chapter.

---

[1]This quote has also been attributed to Yogi Berra, Samuel Goldwyn, and Mark Twain.

6.1 Security Analysis: Be Careful Out There

It may seem odd that we start our discussion with an admonition to be careful, but in this case, we think it is a good idea. The methods we discuss in this chapter are examples of those used by many investors and security analysts to assist in making buy and sell decisions for individual stocks. The basic idea is to identify both "undervalued" or "cheap" stocks to buy and "overvalued" or "rich" stocks to sell. In practice, however, many stocks that look cheap may in fact be correctly priced for reasons not immediately apparent to the analyst. Indeed, the hallmark of a good analyst is a cautious attitude and a willingness to probe further and deeper before committing to a final investment recommendation.

The type of security analysis we describe in this chapter falls under the heading of **fundamental analysis**. Numbers such as a company's earnings per share, cash flow, book equity value, and sales are often called *fundamentals* because they describe, on a basic level, a specific firm's operations and profits (or lack of profits).

Fundamental analysis represents the examination of these and other accounting statement–based company data used to assess the value of a company's stock. Information regarding such things as management quality, products, and product markets is often examined as well.

Our cautionary note is based on the skepticism these techniques should engender, at least when applied simplistically. As our later chapter on market efficiency explains, there is good reason to believe that too-simple techniques that rely on widely available information are not likely to yield systematically superior investment results. In fact, they could lead to unnecessarily risky investment decisions. This is especially true for ordinary investors (like most of us) who do not have timely access to the information that a professional security analyst working for a major securities firm would possess.

As a result, our goal here is not to teach you how to "pick" stocks with a promise that you will become rich. Certainly, one chapter in an investments text is not likely to be sufficient to acquire that level of investment savvy. Instead, an appreciation of the techniques in this chapter is important simply because buy and sell recommendations made by securities firms are frequently couched in the terms we introduce here. Much of the discussion of individual companies in the financial press relies on these concepts as well, so some background is necessary just to interpret commonly presented investment information. In essence, you must learn both the lingo and the concepts of security analysis.

fundamental analysis
Examination of a firm's accounting statements and other financial and economic information to assess the economic value of a company's stock.

Visit the New York Society of Security Analysts website at
www.nyssa.org

Check This

6.1a What is fundamental analysis?

6.1b What is a "rich" stock? What is a "cheap" stock?

6.1c Why does valuing a stock necessarily involve predicting the future?

6.2 The Dividend Discount Model

A fundamental principle of finance holds that the economic value of a security is properly measured by the sum of its future cash flows, where the cash flows are adjusted for risk and the time value of money. For example, suppose a risky security will pay either \$100 or \$200 with equal probability one year from today. The expected future payoff is \$150 = (\$100 + \$200) / 2, and the security's value today is the \$150 expected future value discounted for a one-year waiting period.

If the appropriate discount rate for this security is, say, 5 percent, then the present value of the expected future cash flow is \$150 / 1.05 = \$142.86. If instead the appropriate discount rate is 15 percent, then the present value is \$150 / 1.15 = \$130.43. As this example illustrates, the choice of a discount rate can have a substantial impact on an assessment of security value.

dividend discount model (DDM)
Method of estimating the value of a share of stock as the present value of all expected future dividend payments.

A popular model used to value common stock is the **dividend discount model**, or **DDM**. The dividend discount model values a share of stock as the sum of all expected future dividend payments, where the dividends are adjusted for risk and the time value of money.

For example, suppose a company pays a dividend at the end of each year. Let $D(t)$ denote a dividend to be paid t years from now, and let $V(0)$ represent the present value of the future dividend stream. Also, let k denote the appropriate risk-adjusted discount rate. Using the dividend discount model, the present value of a share of this company's stock is measured as this sum of discounted future dividends:

$$V(0) = \frac{D(1)}{(1 + k)} + \frac{D(2)}{(1 + k)^2} + \frac{D(3)}{(1 + k)^3} + \cdots + \frac{D(T)}{(1 + k)^T} \qquad (6.1)$$

This expression for present value assumes that the last dividend is paid T years from now, where the value of T depends on the specific valuation problem considered. Thus, if $T = 3$ years and $D(1) = D(2) = D(3) = \$100$, the present value, $V(0)$, is stated as

$$V(0) = \frac{\$100}{(1 + k)} + \frac{\$100}{(1 + k)^2} + \frac{\$100}{(1 + k)^3}$$

Check out the American Association of Individual Investors website at www.aaii.com

If the discount rate is $k = 10$ percent, then a quick calculation yields $V(0) = \$248.69$, so the stock price should be about \$250 per share.

USING THE DIVIDEND DISCOUNT MODEL

EXAMPLE 6.1

Suppose again that a stock pays three annual dividends of \$100 per year and the discount rate is $k = 15$ percent. In this case, what is the present value $V(0)$ of the stock?

With a 15 percent discount rate, we have

$$V(0) = \frac{\$100}{(1.15)} + \frac{\$100}{(1.15)^2} + \frac{\$100}{(1.15)^3}$$

Check that the answer is $V(0) = \$228.32$.

MORE DIVIDEND DISCOUNT MODEL

EXAMPLE 6.2

Suppose instead that the stock pays three annual dividends of \$10, \$20, and \$30 in years 1, 2, and 3, respectively, and the discount rate is $k = 10$ percent. What is the present value $V(0)$ of the stock?

(continued)

In this case, we have

$$V(0) = \frac{\$10}{(1.10)} + \frac{\$20}{(1.10)^2} + \frac{\$30}{(1.10)^3}$$

Check that the answer is $V(0) = \$48.16$.

Constant Dividend Growth Rate Model

constant growth rate model A version of the dividend discount model that assumes a constant dividend growth rate.

For many applications, the dividend discount model is simplified substantially by assuming that dividends will grow at a constant growth rate. This is called a **constant growth rate model**. Letting a constant growth rate be denoted by g, then successive annual dividends are stated as $D(t + 1) = D(t)(1 + g)$.

For example, suppose the next dividend is $D(1) = \$100$, and the dividend growth rate is $g = 10$ percent. This growth rate yields a second annual dividend of $D(2) = \$100 \times 1.10 = \$110$ and a third annual dividend of $D(3) = \$100 \times 1.10 \times 1.10 = \$100 \times (1.10)^2 = \$121$. If the discount rate is $k = 12$ percent, the present value of these three sequential dividend payments is the sum of their separate present values:

$$V(0) = \frac{\$100}{(1.12)} + \frac{\$110}{(1.12)^2} + \frac{\$121}{(1.12)^3}$$
$$= \$263.10$$

If the number of dividends to be paid is large, calculating the present value of each dividend separately is tedious and possibly prone to error. Fortunately, if the growth rate is constant, some simplified expressions are available to handle certain special cases. For example, suppose a stock will pay annual dividends over the next T years and these dividends will grow at a constant growth rate g and be discounted at the rate k. The current dividend is $D(0)$, the next dividend is $D(1) = D(0)(1 + g)$, the following dividend is $D(2) = D(1)(1 + g) = D(0)(1 + g)^2$, and so forth. The present value of the next T dividends, that is, $D(1)$ through $D(T)$, can be calculated using this relatively simple formula:

$$V(0) = \frac{D(0)(1 + g)}{k - g}\left[1 - \left(\frac{1 + g}{1 + k}\right)^T\right] \qquad g \neq k \qquad (6.2)$$

Notice that this expression requires that the growth rate and the discount rate not be equal to each other, that is, $k \neq g$, since this requires division by zero. Actually, when the growth rate is equal to the discount rate, that is, $k = g$, the effects of growth and discounting cancel exactly, and the present value $V(0)$ is simply the number of payments T times the current dividend $D(0)$:

$$V(0) = T \times D(0) \qquad g = k$$

As a numerical illustration of the constant growth rate model, suppose that the growth rate is $g = 8$ percent, the discount rate is $k = 10$ percent, the number of future annual dividends is $T = 20$ years, and the current dividend is $D(0) = \$10$. In this case, a present value calculation yields this amount:

$$V(0) = \frac{\$10(1.08)}{.10 - .08}\left[1 - \left(\frac{1.08}{1.10}\right)^{20}\right]$$
$$= \$165.88$$

EXAMPLE 6.3

Suppose that the dividend growth rate is 10 percent, the discount rate is 8 percent, there are 20 years of dividends to be paid, and the current dividend is $10. What is the value of the stock based on the constant growth model?

Plugging in the relevant numbers, we have

$$V(0) = \frac{\$10(1.10)}{.08 - .10}\left[1 - \left(\frac{1.10}{1.08}\right)^{20}\right]$$
$$= \$243.86$$

Thus the price should be $V(0) = \$243.86$.

Constant Perpetual Growth

A particularly simple form of the dividend discount model occurs in the case where a firm will pay dividends that grow at the constant rate g forever. This case is called the **constant perpetual growth model**. In the constant perpetual growth model, present values are calculated using this relatively simple formula:

$$V(0) = \frac{D(0)(1 + g)}{k - g} \qquad g < k \tag{6.3}$$

constant perpetual growth model A version of the dividend discount model in which dividends grow forever at a constant rate, and the growth rate is strictly less than the discount rate.

Since $D(0)(1 + g) = D(1)$, we could also write the constant perpetual growth model as

$$V(0) = \frac{D(1)}{k - g} \qquad g < k \tag{6.4}$$

Either way, we have a very simple, and very widely used, expression for the value of a share of stock based on future dividend payments.

Notice that the constant perpetual growth model requires that the growth rate be strictly less than the discount rate, that is, $g < k$. It looks like the share value would be negative if this were not true. Actually, the formula is simply not valid in this case. The reason is that a perpetual dividend growth rate greater than a discount rate implies an *infinite* value because the present value of the dividends keeps getting bigger and bigger. Since no security can have infinite value, the requirement that $g < k$ simply makes good economic sense.

To illustrate the constant perpetual growth model, suppose that the growth rate is $g = 4$ percent, the discount rate is $k = 9$ percent, and the current dividend is $D(0) = \$10$. In this case, a simple calculation yields

$$V(0) = \frac{\$10(1.04)}{.09 - .04} = \$208$$

USING THE CONSTANT PERPETUAL GROWTH MODEL

EXAMPLE 6.4

Suppose dividends for a particular company are projected to grow at 5 percent forever. If the discount rate is 15 percent and the current dividend is $10, what is the value of the stock?

(continued)

$$V(0) = \frac{\$10(1.05)}{.15 - .05} = \$105$$

As shown, the stock should sell for $105.

Applications of the Constant Perpetual Growth Model

Visit the AEP and DTE websites at
www.aep.com
www.dteenergy.com

In practice, the simplicity of the constant perpetual growth model makes it the most popular dividend discount model. Certainly, the model satisfies Einstein's famous dictum: "Simplify as much as possible, but no more." However, experienced financial analysts are keenly aware that the constant perpetual growth model can be usefully applied only to companies with a history of relatively stable earnings and dividend growth expected to continue into the distant future.

A standard example of an industry for which the constant perpetual growth model can often be usefully applied is the electric utility industry. Consider American Electric Power, which is traded on the New York Stock Exchange under the ticker symbol AEP. In mid-2003, AEP's annual dividend was $1.40; thus we set $D(0) = \$1.40$.

To use the constant perpetual growth model, we also need a discount rate and a growth rate. An old quick and dirty rule of thumb for a risk-adjusted discount rate for electric utility companies is the yield to maturity on 20-year maturity U.S. Treasury bonds, plus 2 percent. At the time this example was written, the yield on 20-year maturity T-bonds was about 4.5 percent. Adding 2 percent, we get a discount rate of $k = 6.5$ percent.

In 2003, AEP had not increased its dividend in more than 10 years. However, a future growth rate of zero percent for AEP might be unduly pessimistic, since earnings growth in the electric utilities industry was projected to be about 2 percent per year. Thus, a rate of, say, 1.5 percent might be more realistic as an estimate of future growth for AEP.

Putting it all together, we have $k = 6.5$ percent, $g = 1.5$ percent, and $D(0) = \$1.40$. Using these numbers, we obtain this estimate for the value of a share of AEP stock:

$$V(0) = \frac{\$1.40(1.015)}{.065 - .015} = \$28.42$$

This estimate is relatively close to the mid-2003 AEP stock price of $25.88, possibly suggesting that AEP stock was fairly valued.

We emphasize the word "possibly" here because we made several assumptions in the process of coming up with this estimate. A change in any of these assumptions could easily lead us to a different conclusion. We will return to this point several times in future discussions.

VALUING DETROIT ED

EXAMPLE 6.5

In 2002, the utility company Detroit Edison (DTE) paid a $2.06 dividend. Using $D(0) = \$2.06$, $k = 6.5$ percent, and an industry average growth rate of $g = 2$ percent, calculate a present value estimate for DTE. Compare this with the late-2002 DTE stock price of $45.81.

(continued)

Plugging in the relevant numbers, we immediately have:

$$V(0) = \frac{\$2.06(1.02)}{.065 - .02} = \$46.69$$

We see that our estimated price is a little higher than the $45.81 stock price.

Historical Growth Rates

In the constant growth model, a company's historical average dividend growth rate is frequently taken as an estimate of future dividend growth. Sometimes historical growth rates are provided in published information about the company. Other times it is necessary to calculate a historical growth rate yourself. There are two ways to do this: (1) using a **geometric average dividend growth rate** or (2) using an **arithmetic average dividend growth rate**. Both methods are relatively easy to implement, as we will now illustrate.

To illustrate the difference between a geometric average and an arithmetic average of historical dividend growth, suppose that the Kwik Kiwi Company paid the following dividends at the end of each of the years indicated immediately below.

2003:	$2.20	2000:	$1.75
2002:	2.00	1999:	1.70
2001:	1.80	1998:	1.50

We begin with a geometric average growth rate because it is the easiest to calculate. Notice that five years elapsed between the $1.50 dividend paid at the end of 1998 and the $2.20 dividend paid at the end of 2003. A geometric average growth rate is equivalent to a constant rate of growth over the five-year period that would grow the dividend from $1.50 to $2.20. That is, it is the growth rate that solves this growth equation:

$$\$2.20 = \$1.50(1 + g)^5$$

$$g = \left(\frac{\$2.20}{\$1.50}\right)^{1/5} - 1 = .08$$

Thus, in this case, the five-year geometric average dividend growth rate is 8 percent. Notice that this calculation is similar to our calculation of the geometric average return in Chapter 1.

In general, if $D(0)$ is the earliest dividend and $D(N)$ is the latest dividend to be used, to calculate a geometric average dividend growth rate over N years, the general equation used is:

$$g = \left[\frac{D(N)}{D(0)}\right]^{1/N} - 1 \qquad (6.5)$$

In the above example, $D(0) = \$1.50$, $D(N) = \$2.20$, and $N = 5$, which yields $g = 8\%$.

An arithmetic average growth rate takes a little more effort to calculate, since it requires that we first calculate each year's dividend growth rate separately and then calculate an arithmetic average of these annual growth rates. For our Kwik Kiwi example, the arithmetic average of five years of dividend growth is calculated as follows:

geometric average dividend growth rate
A dividend growth rate based on a geometric average of historical dividends.

arithmetic average dividend growth rate
A dividend growth rate based on an arithmetic average of historical dividends.

Year	Dividend	Yearly Growth Rates
2003	$2.20	10.00% = (2.20 − 2.00)/2.00
2002	2.00	11.11% = (2.00 − 1.80)/1.80
2001	1.80	2.86% = (1.80 − 1.75)/1.75
2000	1.75	2.94% = (1.75 − 1.70)/1.70
1999	1.70	13.33% = (1.70 − 1.50)/1.50
1998	1.50	
		40.24/5 = 8.05%

Summing the five yearly growth rates yields 40.24, and dividing by five yields an arithmetic average growth rate of 40.24/5 = 8.05%. Notice that this arithmetic average growth rate is close to the geometric average growth rate of 8.0 percent that we first calculated. This is usually the case for dividend growth rates, but not always. A large difference means that the dividend grew erratically, which makes the use of the constant growth formula a little questionable in the first place.

ERRATIC DIVIDEND GROWTH

EXAMPLE 6.6

To illustrate how the geometric average and the arithmetic average of historical dividend growth can differ, consider the following dividends paid by the Kwerky Kiwi Company:

2003: $2.20   2000: $2.00

2002:   2.00   1999:   1.50

2001:   1.80   1998:   1.50

For Kwerky Kiwi, the arithmetic average of five years of dividend growth is calculated as follows:

Year	Dividend	Yearly Growth Rates
2003	$2.20	10.00% = (2.20 − 2.00)/2.00
2002	2.00	11.11% = (2.00 − 1.80)/1.80
2001	1.80	−10.00% = (1.80 − 2.00)/2.00
2000	2.00	33.33% = (2.00 − 1.50)/1.50
1999	1.50	0.00% = (1.50 − 1.50)/1.50
1998	1.50	
		44.44/5 = 8.89%

In this case, summing the five yearly growth rates yields 44.44, and dividing by five yields an arithmetic average growth rate of 44.44/5 = 8.89%. Notice that this arithmetic average growth rate is somewhat larger than the geometric average growth rate of 8.0 percent.

As this example shows, sometimes the arithmetic and geometric growth rate averages can yield rather different results. In practice, most analysts prefer to use a geometric average when calculating an average historical dividend growth rate. In any case, a historical average growth rate may or may not be a reasonable estimate of future dividend growth. Many analysts adjust their estimates to reflect other information available to them, for example, whether the growth rate appears to be sustainable.

The Sustainable Growth Rate

As we have seen, when using the constant perpetual growth model, it is necessary to come up with an estimate of g, the growth rate in dividends. In our previous discussions, we described two ways to do this: (1) using the company's historical average growth rate or (2) using an industry median or average growth rate. We now describe a third way, known as the **sustainable growth rate**, which involves using a company's earnings to estimate g.

As we have discussed, a limitation of the constant perpetual growth model is that it should be applied only to companies with stable dividend and earnings growth. Essentially, a company's earnings can be paid out as dividends to its stockholders or kept as **retained earnings** within the firm to finance future growth. The proportion of earnings paid to stockholders as dividends is called the **payout ratio**. The proportion of earnings retained for reinvestment is called the **retention ratio**.

If we let D stand for dividends and EPS stand for earnings per share, then the payout ratio is simply D/EPS. Since anything not paid out is retained, the retention ratio is just one minus the payout ratio. For example, if a company's current dividend is \$4 per share, and its earnings per share are currently \$10, then the payout ratio is \$4 / \$10 = .40, or 40 percent, and the retention ratio is $1 - .40 = .60$, or 60 percent.

A firm's sustainable growth rate is equal to its return on equity (ROE) times its retention ratio.[2]

$$\text{Sustainable growth rate} = \text{ROE} \times \text{Retention ratio}$$
$$= \text{ROE} \times (1 - \text{Payout ratio}) \quad (6.6)$$

Return on equity is commonly computed using an accounting-based performance measure and is calculated as a firm's net income divided by stockholders' equity:

$$\text{Return on equity (ROE)} = \text{Net Income / Equity} \quad (6.7)$$

> **sustainable growth rate** A dividend growth rate that can be sustained by a company's earnings.
>
> **retained earnings** Earnings retained within the firm to finance growth.
>
> **payout ratio** Proportion of earnings paid out as dividends.
>
> **retention ratio** Proportion of earnings retained for reinvestment.

CALCULATING SUSTAINABLE GROWTH

EXAMPLE 6.7

In 2003, American Electric Power (AEP) had a return on equity of ROE = 10 percent, projected earnings per share of EPS = \$2.20, and a per-share dividend of $D(0)$ = \$1.40. What was AEP's retention rate? Its sustainable growth rate?

AEP's dividend payout was \$1.40/\$2.20 = .636, or 63.6 percent. Its retention ratio was thus $1 - .636 = .364$, or 36.4 percent. Finally, AEP's sustainable growth rate was $10\% \times .364 = 3.64\%$.

---

[2]Strictly speaking, this formula is correct only if ROE is calculated using beginning-of-period stockholders' equity. If ending figures are used, then the precise formula is ROE × Retention ratio / [1 − (ROE × Retention ratio)]. However, the error from not using the precise formula is usually small, so most analysts do not bother with it.

VALUING AMERICAN ELECTRIC POWER (AEP)

EXAMPLE 6.8

Using AEP's sustainable growth rate of 3.64 percent (see Example 6.7) as an estimate of perpetual dividend growth and its current dividend of $1.40, what is the value of AEP's stock assuming a discount rate of 6.5 percent?

If we plug the various numbers into the perpetual growth model, we obtain a value of $V(0) = $1.40(1.0364)/(.065 − .0364) = 50.73. This is much higher than AEP's late-2002 stock price of $27.74, suggesting that AEP stock was significantly undervalued. In fact, AEP's share price fell from over $46 in May 2002 to as low as $18 in October 2002 based on news of declining operations. The stock subsequently rose to $30 before falling to $20 again. Thus, at the time of our analysis, there was much uncertainty regarding the future for AEP. Such severe uncertainty is not captured well in dividend growth analysis.

VALUING DETROIT EDISON (DTE)

EXAMPLE 6.9

In 2002, DTE had a return on equity of ROE = 11.5 percent, earnings per share of EPS = $3.85, and a per-share dividend of $D(0) = 2.06. Assuming a 6.5 percent discount rate, what is the value of DTE's stock?

DTE's payout ratio was $2.06/$3.85 = .535, or 53.5 percent. Thus, DTE's retention ratio was 1 − .535 = .465, or 46.5 percent. DTE's sustainable growth rate was thus 11.5% × .465 = 5.35%. Finally, using the constant growth model, we obtain a value of $2.06(1.0535)/(.065 − .0535) = 188.71. This value is obviously far too high, as in late 2002 DTE's share price was just $45.81. The problem lies with the sustainable growth rate of 5.35 percent calculated here. This is far too high for a utility company. Using the utility industry average growth rate of 2 percent yields a much more realistic value.

As illustrated by Example 6.9, a common problem with sustainable growth rates is that they are sensitive to year-to-year fluctuations in earnings. As a result, security analysts routinely adjust sustainable growth rate estimates to smooth out the effects of earnings variations. Unfortunately, there is no universally standard method to adjust a sustainable growth rate, and analysts depend a great deal on personal experience and their own subjective judgment. Our nearby *Work the Web* box contains more information on analyst-estimated growth rates.

Check This

6.2a   Compare the dividend discount model, the constant growth model, and the constant perpetual growth model. How are they alike? How do they differ?

6.2b   What is a geometric average growth rate? How is it calculated?

6.2c   What is a sustainable growth rate? How is it calculated?

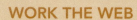

WORK THE WEB

We discussed use of the sustainable growth formula to estimate a company's growth rate; however, the formula is not foolproof. Changes in the variables of the model can have a dramatic effect on growth rates. One of the most important tasks of an equity analyst is estimating future growth rates. These estimates entail a detailed analysis of the company. One place to find earnings and sales growth rates on the Web is Yahoo! Finance at finance.yahoo.com. Here, we pulled up a quote for Coca-Cola (KO) and followed the "Research" link. Below you will see an abbreviated look at the results.

Consensus Estimates	This Qtr. (Mar 03)	Next Qtr (Jun 03)	This Year (Dec 03)	Next Year (Dec 04)
Earnings Estimates				
Avg Estimate	0.38	0.54	1.84	2.03
# of Analysts	11	8	18	11
Low Estimate	0.36	0.52	1.80	1.99
High Estimate	0.41	0.56	1.93	2.13
Year Ago EPS	0.34	0.49	1.66	1.84
Revenue Estimates				
Avg Estimate	$4.5B	$5.8B	$20.6B	$22.0B
# of Analysts	1	1	9	5
Low Estimate	$4.5B	$5.8B	$20.1B	$21.7B
High Estimate	$4.5B	$5.8B	$21.1B	$22.6B
Year Ago Sales	$4.1B	$5.4B	N/A	$20.6B
Sales Growth	11.5%	8.5%	N/A	6.9%

As shown, analysts expect revenue (sales) of $20.6 billion in 2003, growing to $22.0 billion in 2004, an increase of 6.8 percent. We also have the following table comparing Coca-Cola to some benchmarks:

Earnings Growth	Coca-Cola Co.	Industry	Sector	S&P 500
This Quarter Est.	11.8%	11.1%	4.1%	6.3%
Next Quarter Est.	10.2%	12.6%	8.4%	14.3%
This Year Est.	10.8%	11.8%	8.9%	16.6%
Next Year Est.	10.3%	11.2%	10.4%	15.0%
Past 5 Years	5.4%	N/A	N/A	N/A
Next 5 Years Est.	11.0%	11.27%	10.55%	11.59%
Price/Earnings (ttm)	22.1	19.31	15.38	15.75
PEG Ratio	2.01	1.71	1.46	1.36

As you can see, the estimated earnings future growth for KO is slightly lower than the industry and S&P 500 estimates, but slightly higher than the sector growth rate. Here is an assignment for you: What is the PEG ratio? Locate a financial glossary on the Web (there are lots of them) to find out.

6.3   The Two-Stage Dividend Growth Model

two-stage dividend growth model
Dividend model that assumes a firm will temporarily grow at a rate different from its long-term growth rate.

In the previous section, we examined dividend discount models based on a single growth rate. You may have already thought that a single growth rate is often unrealistic, since companies experience temporary periods of unusually high or low growth, with growth eventually converging to an industry average or an economywide average. In such cases as these, financial analysts frequently use a **two-stage dividend growth model**.

A two-stage dividend growth model assumes that a firm will initially grow at a rate g_1 during a first stage of growth lasting T years and thereafter grow at a rate g_2 during a perpetual second stage of growth. The present value formula for the two-stage dividend growth model is stated as follows:

$$V(0) = \frac{D(0)(1 + g_1)}{k - g_1}\left[1 - \left(\frac{1 + g_1}{1 + k}\right)^T\right] + \left(\frac{1 + g_1}{1 + k}\right)^T \frac{D(0)(1 + g_2)}{k - g_2} \quad (6.8)$$

At first glance, this expression looks a little complicated. However, it simplifies if we look at its two distinct parts individually. The first term on the right-hand side measures the present value of the first T dividends and is the same expression we used earlier for the constant growth model. The second term then measures the present value of all subsequent dividends.

Using the formula is mostly a matter of "plug and chug" with a calculator. For example, suppose a firm has a current dividend of $2, and dividends are expected to grow at the rate $g_1 = 20$ percent for $T = 5$ years, and thereafter grow at the rate $g_2 = 5$ percent. With a discount rate of $k = 12$ percent, the present value $V(0)$ is calculated as

$$V(0) = \frac{\$2(1.20)}{.12 - .20}\left[1 - \left(\frac{1.20}{1.12}\right)^5\right] + \left(\frac{1.20}{1.12}\right)^5 \frac{\$2(1.05)}{.12 - .05}$$
$$= \$12.36 + \$42.36$$
$$= \$54.72$$

In this calculation, the total present value of $54.72 is the sum of a $12.36 present value for the first five dividends plus a $42.36 present value for all subsequent dividends.

USING THE TWO-STAGE MODEL

EXAMPLE 6.10

Suppose a firm has a current dividend of $D(0) = \$5$, which is expected to "shrink" at the rate $g_1 = -10$ percent for $T = 5$ years and thereafter grow at the rate $g_2 = 4$ percent. With a discount rate of $k = 10$ percent, what is the value of the stock?

Using the two-stage model, present value, $V(0)$, is calculated as

$$V(0) = \frac{\$5(.90)}{.10 - (-.10)}\left[1 - \left(\frac{.90}{1.10}\right)^5\right] + \left(\frac{.90}{1.10}\right)^5 \frac{\$5(1.04)}{.10 - .04}$$
$$= \$14.25 + \$31.78$$
$$= \$46.03$$

The total present value of $46.03 is the sum of a $14.25 present value of the first five dividends plus a $31.78 present value of all subsequent dividends.

The two-stage growth formula requires that the second-stage growth rate be strictly less than the discount rate, that is, $g_2 < k$. However, the first-stage growth rate g_1 can be greater, smaller, or equal to the discount rate. In the special case where the first-stage growth rate is equal to the discount rate, that is, $g_1 = k$, the two-stage formula reduces to this form:

$$V(0) = D(0) \times T + \frac{D(0)(1 + g_2)}{k - g_2}$$

You may notice with satisfaction that this two-stage formula is much simpler than the general two-stage formula. However, a first-stage growth rate is rarely exactly equal to a risk-adjusted discount rate, so this simplified formula sees little use.

VALUING AMERICAN EXPRESS (AXP)

EXAMPLE 6.11

American Express is a large financial services company whose shares trade on the New York Stock Exchange under the ticker symbol AXP. In 2002, AXP paid a $.32 dividend, and analysts were forecasting a five-year growth rate of 11.5 percent. Assuming a future industry average growth rate of 11 percent thereafter and a 12 percent discount rate, what value would we place on AXP?

Plugging all the relevant numbers into a two-stage present value calculation yields

$$V(0) = \frac{\$.32 \times 1.115}{.12 - .115}\left[1 - \left(\frac{1.115}{1.12}\right)^5\right] + \left(\frac{1.115}{1.12}\right)^5 \frac{\$.32 \times 1.11}{.12 - .11}$$

$$= \$1.58 + \$34.73$$

$$= \$36.31$$

This present value estimate is slightly lower than AXP's then current stock price of $38.54.

HAVE A PEPSI? (PEP)

EXAMPLE 6.12

PepsiCo shares trade on the New York Stock Exchange under the ticker symbol PEP. In 2002, analysts forecasted a five-year growth rate of 10 percent when the then current dividend was $.60. Suppose Pepsi grows at 10 percent for five years and then at 6 percent thereafter. Assuming an 8 percent discount rate, what value would we place on PEP?

Once again, we round up all the relevant numbers and plug them in to get

$$V(0) = \frac{\$.60 \times 1.10}{.08 - .10}\left[1 - \left(\frac{1.10}{1.08}\right)^5\right] + \left(\frac{1.10}{1.08}\right)^5 \frac{\$.60 \times 1.06}{.08 - .06}$$

$$= \$3.17 + \$34.86$$

$$= \$38.03$$

This present value estimate is lower than Pepsi's then current stock price of $40.51, suggesting that Pepsi might be a little overvalued or, more likely, that our growth rate or discount rate estimates are a bit off.

Visit AXP and PEP websites at www.americanexpress.com and www.pepsico.com

The last case we consider is nonconstant growth in the first stage. As a simple example of nonconstant growth, consider the case of a company that is currently not paying dividends. You predict that, in five years, the company will pay a dividend for the first time. The dividend will be $.50 per share. You expect that this dividend will then grow at a rate of 10 percent per year indefinitely. The required return on companies such as this one is 20 percent. What is the price of the stock today?

To see what the stock is worth today, we first find out what it will be worth once dividends are paid. We can then calculate the present value of that future price to get today's price. The first dividend will be paid in five years, and the dividend will grow steadily from then on. Using the dividend growth model, we can say that the price in four years will be:

$$
\begin{aligned}
V(4) &= D(4) \times (1 + g)/(k - g) \\
&= D(5)/(k - g) \\
&= \$.50/(.20 - .10) \\
&= \$5
\end{aligned}
$$

If the stock will be worth $5 in four years, then we can get the current value by discounting this price back four years at 20 percent:

$$
V(0) = \$5/1.20^4 = \$5/2.0736 = \$2.41
$$

The stock is therefore worth $2.41 today.

The problem of nonconstant growth is only slightly more complicated if the dividends are not zero for the first several years. For example, suppose that you have come up with the following dividend forecasts for the next three years:

Year	Expected Dividend
1	$1.00
2	2.00
3	2.50

After the third year, the dividend will grow at a constant rate of 5 percent per year. The required return is 10 percent. What is the value of the stock today?

In dealing with nonconstant growth, a time line can be very helpful. Figure 6.1 illustrates one for this problem. The important thing to notice is when constant growth starts. As we've shown, for this problem, constant growth starts at Time 3. This means that we can use our constant growth model to determine the stock price at Time 3, $V(3)$. By far the most common mistake in this situation is to incorrectly identify the start of the constant growth phase and, as a result, calculate the future stock price at the wrong time.

FIGURE 6.1

Time Line

As always, the value of the stock is the present value of all future dividends. To calculate this present value, we first have to compute the present value of the stock price three years down the road, just as we did before. We then have to add in the present value of the dividends that will be paid between now and then. So, the price in three years is

$$V(3) = D(3) \times (1 + g)/(k - g)$$
$$= \$2.50 \times 1.05/(.10 - .05)$$
$$= \$52.50$$

We can now calculate the total value of the stock as the present value of the first three dividends plus the present value of the price at Time 3, $V(3)$.

$$V(0) = \frac{D(1)}{(1 + k)^1} + \frac{D(2)}{(1 + k)^2} + \frac{D(3)}{(1 + k)^3} + \frac{V(3)}{(1 + k)^3}$$

$$= \frac{\$1}{1.10} + \frac{2}{1.10^2} + \frac{2.50}{1.10^3} + \frac{52.50}{1.10^3}$$

$$= \$.91 + 1.65 + 1.88 + 39.44$$

$$= \$43.88$$

The value of the stock today is thus \$43.88.

"SUPERNORMAL" GROWTH

EXAMPLE 6.13

Chain Reaction, Inc., has been growing at a phenomenal rate of 30 percent per year because of its rapid expansion and explosive sales. You believe that this growth rate will last for three more years and that the rate will then drop to 10 percent per year. If the growth rate then remains at 10 percent indefinitely, what is the total value of the stock? Total dividends just paid were \$5 million, and the required return is 20 percent.

Chain Reaction's situation is an example of supernormal growth. It is unlikely that a 30 percent growth rate can be sustained for any extended length of time. To value the equity in this company, we first need to calculate the total dividends over the supernormal growth period:

Year	Total Dividends (in millions)
1	$5.00 \times 1.3 = \$ 6.500$
2	$6.50 \times 1.3 = \ 8.450$
3	$8.45 \times 1.3 = \ 10.985$

The price at Time 3 can be calculated as

$$V(3) = D(3) \times (1 + g)/(k - g)$$

where g is the long-run growth rate. So we have

$$V(3) = \$10.985 \times 1.10/(.20 - .10) = \$120.835$$

(continued)

To determine the value today, we need the present value of this amount plus the present value of the total dividends:

$$V(0) = \frac{D(1)}{(1+k)^1} + \frac{D(2)}{(1+k)^2} + \frac{D(3)}{(1+k)^3} + \frac{V(3)}{(1+k)^3}$$

$$= \frac{\$6.50}{1.20} + \frac{8.45}{1.20^2} + \frac{10.985}{1.20^3} + \frac{120.835}{1.20^3}$$

$$= \$5.42 + 5.87 + 6.36 + 69.93$$

$$= \$87.58$$

The total value of the stock today is thus $87.58 million. If there were, for example, 20 million shares, then the stock would be worth $87.58/20 = $4.38 per share.

Discount Rates for Dividend Discount Models

You may wonder where the discount rates used in the preceding examples come from. The answer is that they come from the *capital asset pricing model* (CAPM). Although a detailed discussion of the CAPM is deferred to a later chapter, we can point out here that, based on the CAPM, the discount rate for a stock can be estimated using this formula:

Discount rate = U.S. T-bill rate + (Stock beta × Stock market risk premium)

(6.9)

The components of this formula, as we use it here, are defined as follows:

U.S. T-bill rate:	Return on 90-day U.S. T-bills
Stock beta:	Risk relative to an average stock
Stock market risk premium:	Risk premium for an average stock

The basic intuition for this approach can be traced back to Chapter 1. There we saw that the return we expect to earn on a risky asset had two parts, a "wait" component and a "worry" component. We labeled the wait component as the *time value of money*, and we noted that it can be measured as the return we earn from an essentially riskless investment. Here we use the return on a 90-day Treasury bill as the riskless return.

We called the worry component the *risk premium*, and we noted that the greater the risk, the greater the risk premium. Depending on the exact period studied, the risk premium for the market as a whole over the past 75 or so years has averaged about 9.0 percent. This 9.0 percent can be interpreted as the risk premium for bearing an average amount of stock market risk, and we use it as the stock market risk premium.

beta Measure of a stock's risk relative to the stock market average.

Finally, when we look at a particular stock, we recognize that it may be more or less risky than an average stock. A stock's **beta** is a measure of a single stock's risk relative to an average stock, and we discuss beta at length in a later chapter. For now, it suffices to know that the market average beta is 1.0. A beta of 1.5 indicates that a stock has 50 percent more risk than the average stock, so its risk premium is 50 percent higher. A beta of .50 indicates that a stock is 50 percent less risky than average and has a smaller risk premium.

When this chapter was written, the T-bill rate was 6 percent. Taking it as given for now, a stock beta of .8 yields an estimated discount rate of 6% + (.8 × 9%) = 13.2%.

Similarly, a stock beta of 1.2 yields the discount rate 6% + (1.2 × 9%) = 16.8%. For the remainder of this chapter, we use discount rates calculated according to this CAPM formula.

Observations on Dividend Discount Models

We have examined three dividend discount models: the constant perpetual growth model, the two-stage dividend growth model, and the nonconstant growth model. Each model has advantages and disadvantages. Certainly, the main advantage of the constant perpetual growth model is that it is simple to compute. However, it has several disadvantages: (1) it is not usable for firms not paying dividends, (2) it is not usable when a growth rate is greater than a discount rate, (3) it is sensitive to the choice of growth rate and discount rate, (4) discount rates and growth rates may be difficult to estimate accurately, and (5) constant perpetual growth is often an unrealistic assumption.

The two-stage dividend growth model offers several improvements: (1) it is more realistic, since it accounts for low, high, or zero growth in the first stage, followed by constant long-term growth in the second stage, and (2) it is usable when a first-stage growth rate is greater than a discount rate. However, the two-stage model is also sensitive to the choice of discount rate and growth rates, and it is not useful for companies that don't pay dividends. The nonconstant growth model is more flexible in this regard, but it still remains sensitive to the discount and growth rates assumed.

Financial analysts readily acknowledge the limitations of dividend discount models. Consequently, they also turn to other valuation methods to expand their analyses. In the next section, we discuss some popular stock valuation methods based on price ratios.

Check This

6.3a   What are the three parts of a CAPM-determined discount rate?

6.3b   Under what circumstances is a two-stage dividend discount model appropriate?

6.4   Price Ratio Analysis

Price ratios are widely used by financial analysts, more so even than dividend discount models. Of course, all valuation methods try to accomplish the same thing, which is to appraise the economic value of a company's stock. However, analysts readily agree that no single method can adequately handle this task on all occasions. In this section, we therefore examine several of the most popular price ratio methods and provide examples of their use in financial analysis.

Price-Earnings Ratios

price-earnings (P/E) ratio Current stock price divided by annual earnings per share (EPS).

earnings yield Inverse of the P/E ratio: earnings per share divided by price per share (E/P).

The most popular price ratio used to assess the value of common stock is a company's **price-earnings ratio**, abbreviated as **P/E ratio**. In fact, as we saw in Chapter 3, P/E ratios are reported in the financial press every day. As we discussed, a price-earnings ratio is calculated as the ratio of a firm's current stock price divided by its annual earnings per share (EPS).

The inverse of a P/E ratio is called an **earnings yield**, and it is measured as earnings per share divided by a current stock price (E/P). Clearly, an earnings yield and a price-earnings ratio are simply two ways to measure the same thing. In practice, earnings yields are less commonly stated and used than P/E ratios.

Since most companies report earnings each quarter, annual earnings per share can be calculated either as the most recent quarterly earnings per share times four or as the sum of the last four quarterly earnings per share figures. Most analysts prefer the first method of multiplying the latest quarterly earnings per share value times four. However, some published data sources, including *The Wall Street Journal*, report annual earnings per share as the sum of the last four quarters' figures. The difference is usually small, but it can sometimes be a source of confusion.

Financial analysts often refer to high-P/E stocks as **growth stocks**. To see why, notice that a P/E ratio is measured as a *current* stock price over *current* earnings per share. Now, consider two companies with the same current earnings per share, where one company is a high-growth company and the other is a low-growth company. Which company do you think should have a higher stock price, the high-growth company or the low-growth company?

This question is a no-brainer. All else equal, we would be surprised if the high-growth company did not have a higher stock price, and therefore a higher P/E ratio. In general, companies with higher expected earnings growth will have higher P/E ratios, which is why high-P/E stocks are often referred to as growth stocks.

To give an example, Starbucks Corporation is a specialty coffee retailer with a history of aggressive sales growth. Its stock trades on the Nasdaq under the ticker symbol SBUX. In early 2003, SBUX stock traded at $21.98 per share with earnings per share of EPS = $.57, and therefore had a P/E ratio of $21.98/$.57 = 38.6. This value was well above that of a typical stock in the S&P 500 (of which SBUX was a member). SBUX has never paid dividends and instead reinvests all earnings. So far this strategy has been successful as earnings grew by an average rate of 33 percent over the preceding five years.

The reasons high-P/E stocks are called growth stocks seems obvious enough; however, in a seeming defiance of logic, low-P/E stocks are often referred to as **value stocks**. The reason is that low-P/E stocks are often viewed as "cheap" relative to *current* earnings. (Notice again the emphasis on "current.") This suggests that these stocks may represent good investment values, and hence the term value stocks.

In early 2003, the well-known retailer Sears was an S&P 500 stock trading at a price of $23.24. With earnings per share of EPS = $4.96, the P/E ratio was $23.24/$4.96 = 4.7. This was a fraction of a typical P/E ratio for S&P 500 stocks. Because of its low P/E ratio, Sears might be considered a value stock.

Having said all this, we want to emphasize that the terms "growth stock" and "value stock" are mostly just commonly used labels. Of course, only time will tell whether a high-P/E stock turns out to actually be a high-growth stock, or whether a low-P/E stock is really a good value. The nearby *Investment Updates* box contains additional discussion of P/E ratios.

Price-Cash Flow Ratios

Instead of price-earnings (P/E) ratios, many analysts prefer to look at price-cash flow (P/CF) ratios. A **price-cash flow (P/CF) ratio** is measured as a company's current stock price divided by its current annual cash flow per share. Like earnings, cash flow is normally reported quarterly and most analysts multiply the last quarterly cash flow figure by four to obtain annual cash flow. Again, like earnings, many published data sources report annual cash flow as a sum of the latest four quarterly cash flows.

There are a variety of definitions of **cash flow**. In this context, the most common measure is simply calculated as net income plus depreciation, so this is the one we use here. In the next chapter, we examine in detail how cash flow is calculated in a firm's

growth stocks A term often used to describe high-P/E stocks.

Visit the Starbucks and Sears websites at www.starbucks.com and www.sears.com

value stocks A term often used to describe low-P/E stocks.

price-cash flow (P/CF) ratio Current stock price divided by current cash flow per share.

cash flow In the context of the price-cash flow ratio, usually taken to be net income plus depreciation.

Small Stocks May Offer Investors Huge Returns

Let others fret about the recession. Smart investors should focus on the recovery. Nobody knows when the economy and the stock market will revive. But when the turn comes, history's lesson is clear: Small stocks, and especially small, growth companies, are likely to be huge winners. With that in mind, now could be a great time to start spooning money into some small-stock mutual funds. But make no mistake: This strategy isn't for the faint of heart.

"Coming off market bottoms and coming out of recessions, small stocks historically lead," says John Laporte, manager of the $4 billion-in-assets T. Rowe Price New Horizons Fund. "That's the good news. The bad news is, in down markets and going into recessions, small caps typically underperform." So far, however, the bad news hasn't been all that bad. "Going into this recession, small stocks have done inexplicably well," says David Booth, co-chairman of Dimensional Fund Advisors in Santa Monica, Calif.

Indeed, after being scorned for much of the late 1990s, small stocks have outpaced larger companies over the past 2½ years. Small-company "growth" stocks dazzled in the year running up to the March 2000 market peak. Since then, the big winners in the small-cap sector have been bargain-priced "value" stocks. But even after that relatively strong performance, small stocks still look cheap. Consider some numbers from

Leuthold Group in Minneapolis, which keeps tabs on the share price/earnings multiple for 3,000 stocks.

To measure the valuation put on large companies, Leuthold calculates a P/E that is weighted by each company's stock-market capitalization. That produces an earnings multiple of 28.3, based on the past year's operating earnings. But Leuthold also keeps tabs on the valuation of small and midsize companies by looking at the P/E for the median, or typical, stock in its 3,000-stock universe. That generates a P/E of just 14.8. Because of their greater risk, smaller stocks typically trade at lower earnings multiples. But historically, the P/E discount has averaged 18% less, far less than today's 48% haircut.

"Everything is in place for small caps to be the better performers once the recovery starts," argues Andrew Engel, a senior research analyst at Leuthold. "And they should hold up better until then, because they're so much cheaper." In the 12 months following each of the last eight recessions, small stocks have outperformed large companies, according to Baltimore's T. Rowe Price Associates. But investors shouldn't wait for signs of economic recovery before buying small companies. The fact is, the spurt of outperformance usually starts before the recession ends.

(continued)

---

financial statements. Cash flow is usually reported in a firm's financial statements and labeled as cash flow from operations (or operating cash flow).

The difference between earnings and cash flow is often confusing, largely because of the way that standard accounting practice defines net income. Essentially, net income is measured as revenues minus expenses. Obviously, this is logical. However, not all expenses are actually cash expenses. The most important exception is depreciation.

When a firm acquires a long-lived asset such as a new factory facility, standard accounting practice does not deduct the cost of the factory all at once, even though it is actually paid for all at once. Instead, the cost is deducted over time. These deductions do not represent actual cash payments, however. The actual cash payment occurred when the factory was purchased. At this point you may be a little confused about why the difference is important, but hang in there for a few more paragraphs.

Most analysts agree that in examining a company's financial performance, cash flow can be more informative than net income. To see why, consider the hypothetical example of two identical companies: Twiddle-Dee Co. and Twiddle-Dum Co. Suppose that both companies have the same constant revenues and expenses in each year over a three-year period. These constant revenues and cash expenses (excluding depreciation) yield the same constant annual cash flows, and they are stated as follows:

"Stocks generally start to rally halfway through the recession," says Steven DeSanctis, director of small-cap research at Prudential Securities. "And in that second half, small beats large by almost five percentage points. In the next couple of months, you should position your portfolio to take advantage of the recovery." Even if small stocks don't outperform in the year ahead, they still deserve a place in your portfolio, both for the added diversification and also for the potentially higher long-run return. According to Chicago's Ibbotson Associates, over the past 75 years, small stocks have clocked average annual gains of 12.4%, handily ahead of the 11% a year notched by the Standard & Poor's 500-stock index.

That higher return seems to be a reward for taking on the extra risk involved in buying smaller stocks. "It's not just an American thing," Mr. Booth says. "Everywhere you look around the world, you see this size effect going on." The superior performance of U.S. small stocks is built on some long stretches of dazzling results. Two of the most dazzling winning streaks followed severe economic downturns. In the five years following the 1932 stock-market trough, small stocks outpaced larger companies by 18 percentage points a year, calculates Ibbotson. Meanwhile, in the five years after the 1974 market bottom, small stocks beat large companies by 21.8 percentage points annually.

Will we get the same sort of sparkling performance coming out of the current recession? For small-stock aficionados, that's the big hope. The No-Load Fund Analyst, a newsletter in Orinda, Calif., typically allocates 15% of its model stock portfolio to smaller U.S. companies. But right now, Steve Savage, the newsletter's editor, favors a 19% weighting. "We increased our weighting to small caps in September," Mr. Savage says. "Small caps still offer a valuation advantage. They consistently outperform coming out of a recession. And this time, they've also outperformed on the downside."

Mr. Savage recommends small and midcap funds such as ABN Amro/Veredus Aggressive Growth, Artisan Mid Cap and Rainier Small/Mid Cap. But because there is still so much uncertainty, investors might want to take it slowly with these funds, building up positions over the next three to six months. "There are some compelling reasons to think small caps will do better," Mr. Savage says. "But if there's another terrorist attack or if the recession lasts longer than expected, the danger is that people won't want to own small stocks because they're more illiquid. If the market gets hit again, my fear is that small caps could really underperform."

Source: Jonathan Clements, *The Wall Street Journal*, October 2, 2001. © 2001 Dow Jones & Company, Inc. All Rights Reserved Worldwide.

	Twiddle-Dee	Twiddle-Dum
Revenues	$5,000	$5,000
Cash expenses	− 3,000	− 3,000
Cash flow	$2,000	$2,000

Thus, both companies have the same $2,000 cash flow in each of the three years of this hypothetical example.

Next, suppose that both companies incur total depreciation of $3,000 spread out over the three-year period. Standard accounting practice sometimes allows a manager to choose among several depreciation schedules. Twiddle-Dee Co. chooses straight-line depreciation, and Twiddle-Dum Co. chooses accelerated depreciation. These two depreciation schedules are tabulated below:

	Twiddle-Dee	Twiddle-Dum
Year 1	$1,000	$1,500
Year 2	1,000	1,000
Year 3	1,000	500
Total	$3,000	$3,000

Note that total depreciation over the three-year period is the same for both companies. However, Twiddle-Dee Co. has the same $1,000 depreciation in each year, while Twiddle-Dum Co. has accelerated depreciation of $1,500 in the first year, $1,000 in the second year, and $500 depreciation in the third year.

Now, let's look at the resulting annual cash flows and net income figures for the two companies, recalling that in each year, Cash flow = Net income + Depreciation:

	Twiddle-Dee		Twiddle-Dum	
	Cash Flow	Net Income	Cash Flow	Net Income
Year 1	$2,000	$1,000	$2,000	$ 500
Year 2	2,000	1,000	2,000	1,000
Year 3	2,000	1,000	2,000	1,500
Total	$6,000	$3,000	$6,000	$3,000

Note that Twiddle-Dum Co.'s net income is lower in the first year and higher in the third year than Twiddle-Dee Co.'s net income. This is purely a result of Twiddle-Dum Co.'s accelerated depreciation schedule, and has nothing to do with Twiddle-Dum Co.'s actual profitability. However, an inexperienced analyst observing Twiddle-Dum Co.'s rapidly rising annual earnings figures might incorrectly label Twiddle-Dum as a growth company. An experienced analyst would observe that there was no cash flow growth to support this naive conclusion.

Financial analysts typically use both price-earnings ratios and price-cash flow ratios. They point out that when a company's earnings per share is not significantly larger than its cash flow per share (CFPS), this is a signal, at least potentially, of good-quality earnings. The term "quality" means that the accounting earnings mostly reflect actual cash flow, not just accounting numbers. When earnings are bigger than cash flow, this may be a signal of poor quality earnings.

Going back to some of our earlier examples, Starbucks Corporation had cash flow per share of CFPS = $1.28, yielding a P/CF ratio of $21.98/$1.28 = 17.2. Notice that this cash flow per share was almost double earnings per share, an indication of high quality earnings. Sears had cash flow per share of CFPS = $2.01, yielding a P/CF ratio of $23.24/$2.01 = 11.6. Sears's cash flow was less than half its earnings, possibly suggesting poor quality earnings.

Price-Sales Ratios

price-sales (P/S) ratio
Current stock price divided by annual sales per share.

An alternative view of a company's performance is provided by its **price-sales (P/S) ratio**. A price-sales ratio is calculated as the current price of a company's stock divided by its current annual sales revenue per share. A price-sales ratio focuses on a company's ability to generate sales growth. Essentially, a high P/S ratio would suggest high sales growth, while a low P/S ratio might indicate sluggish sales growth.

For example, Starbucks Corporation had sales per share of $8.73 to yield a price-sales ratio of P/S = 2.5. Sears had sales per share of $131.30 for a price-sales ratio of P/S = .18. Notice the large variation in price-sales ratios for these two companies. A major reason for this difference is the types of businesses these companies represent. But analysts also generally recognize that price-sales ratios are not as informative as ratios based on earnings and cash flow.

Price-Book Ratios

price-book (P/B) ratio
Market value of a company's common stock divided by its book (or accounting) value of equity.

A very basic price ratio for a company is its **price-book (P/B) ratio**, sometimes called the market-book ratio. A price-book ratio is measured as the market value of a company's outstanding common stock divided by its book value of equity.

Price-book ratios are appealing because book values represent, in principle, historical cost. The stock price is an indicator of current value, so a price-book ratio simply measures what the equity is worth today relative to what it cost. A ratio bigger than 1.0 indicates that the firm has been successful in creating value for its stockholders. A ratio smaller than 1.0 indicates that the company is actually worth less than it cost.

This interpretation of the price-book ratio seems simple enough, but the truth is that because of varied and changing accounting standards, book values are difficult to interpret. For this and other reasons, price-book ratios may not have as much information value as they once did.

Applications of Price Ratio Analysis

Check out the Intel website at
www.intel.com

Price-earnings ratios, price-cash flow ratios, and price-sales ratios are commonly used to calculate estimates of expected future stock prices. This is done by multiplying a historical average price ratio by an expected future value for the price-ratio denominator variable. For example, Table 6.1 summarizes such a price ratio analysis for Intel Corporation (INTC) based on late-2002 information.

In Table 6.1, the current value row contains values for earnings per share, cash flow per share, and sales per share. The five-year average ratio row contains five-year average P/E, P/CF, and P/S ratios, and the growth rate row contains five-year projected growth rates for EPS, CFPS, and SPS.

The expected price row contains expected stock prices one year hence. The basic idea is this. Since Intel has had an average P/E ratio of 38.72, we will assume that Intel's stock price will be 38.72 times its earnings one year from now. To estimate Intel's earnings one year from now, we note that Intel's earnings are projected to grow at a rate of 5.50 percent per year. If earnings continue to grow at this rate, then next year's earnings will be equal to this year's earnings multiplied by 1.055. Putting it all together, we have

$$
\begin{aligned}
\text{Expected price} &= \text{Historical P/E ratio} \times \text{Projected EPS} \\
&= \text{Historical P/E ratio} \times \text{Current EPS} \times \\
&\quad (1 + \text{Projected EPS growth rate}) \\
&= 38.72 \times 0.48 \times 1.055 \\
&= \$19.61
\end{aligned}
$$

TABLE 6.1	Price Ratio Analysis for Intel Corporation (INTC) Early 2003 Stock Price: $15.05		
	Earnings (P/E)	**Cash Flow (P/CF)**	**Sales (P/S)**
Current value per share	$.48	$1.20	$4.00
Five-year average price ratio	38.72	21.55	7.50
Growth rate	5.50%	6.50%	5.5%
Expected stock price	$19.61	$27.54	$31.63

TABLE 6.2	Price Ratio Analysis for Disney Corporation (DIS) Early 2003 Stock Price: $16.35		
	Earnings (P/E)	Cash Flow (P/CF)	Sales (P/S)
Current value per share	$.55	$1.10	$9.91
Five-year average price ratio	38.14	19.59	2.53
Growth rate	5.50%	4.00%	4.5%
Expected stock price	$22.13	$22.41	$26.20

The same procedure is used to calculate an expected price based on cash flow per share.

$$\text{Expected price} = \text{Historical P/CF ratio} \times \text{Projected CFPS}$$
$$= \text{Historical P/CF ratio} \times \text{Current CFPS} \times (1 + \text{Projected CFPS growth rate})$$
$$= 21.55 \times 1.20 \times 1.065$$
$$= \$27.54$$

Finally, an expected price based on sales per share is calculated as

$$\text{Expected price} = \text{Historical P/S ratio} \times \text{Projected SPS}$$
$$= \text{Historical P/S ratio} \times \text{Current SPS} \times (1 + \text{Projected SPS growth rate})$$
$$= 7.50 \times 4.00 \times 1.055$$
$$= \$31.65$$

Notice that each price ratio method yields a different expected price, sometimes with rather large differences. For example, the projected Intel share price based on price-sales ratios is much larger than that based on price-earnings ratios.

GOING TO DISNEYLAND

EXAMPLE 6.14

See Mickey's
website at
www.disney.go.com

Table 6.2 contains information about Walt Disney Corporation. Calculate expected share prices using each of the three price ratio approaches we have discussed.

Using the P/E approach, we come up with the following estimate of the price of Walt Disney stock in one year:

Expected price = Historical P/E ratio × Current EPS × (1 + Projected EPS growth rate)
$$= 38.14 \times 0.55 \times 1.055$$
$$= \$22.13$$

Check that the price-cash flow and price-sales approaches give estimates of $22.42 and $26.20, respectively.

Check This

6.4a Why are high-P/E stocks sometimes called growth stocks?

6.4b Why might an analyst prefer a price-cash flow ratio to a price-earnings ratio?

Flaws in Market Gauges

Even before last week's impressive rally, the stock market was outrageously expensive. At least that's what some key market yardsticks show.

But hold on to your sell orders. Many investment experts reckon the fault lies not with the market, but with the measuring sticks. In particular, these experts see serious shortcomings in three popular stock-market gauges: the price-to-book value ratio, dividend yield, and the price-to-earnings multiple.

The three standard measures "are all flawed in some way," says Frazier Evans, senior economist at Colonial Group, the Boston mutual-fund company. "You have to look under the surface. I'd say that the market is not as expensive as it looks."

Dwindling Dividends

Consider, for instance, the market's dividend yield. The companies in the Standard & Poor's 500-stock index are paying annual dividends amounting to 2.8% of their current stock prices. That's well below the historical average dividend yield of 4.7% and not far above the all-time low of 2.64%, which was hit in 1987, just before that year's stock-market crash.

A danger signal? Maybe not. The reason is that corporations seem to be paying out far less of their earnings as dividends these days. Instead, companies are using profits to expand their businesses and buy their own shares—actions designed to boost stock prices.

The shift should please most investors. Because dividend income is taxed more heavily than capital gains, shareholders benefit more if returns come in the form of higher stock prices, rather than big dividends.

The dividend-yield gauge also is being thrown out of whack by other factors, says Arnold Kaufman, editor of Standard & Poor's Outlook, a weekly newsletter. For instance, "dividends are being held down by the special problems of large dividend-paying industry groups, such as telephones, utilities, and drugs," he says.

Effect on Book Value

At first blush, the market's price-to-book value also suggests shares are richly priced. Bargain hunters often look for stocks that are trading below book value, which is the difference between a company's assets and its liabilities expressed on a per-share basis.

But these days, precious few stocks trade below book value. Indeed, Mr. Kaufman figures stocks on average are trading at more than three times book value, compared with just 1.2 times book in the late 1970s.

But once again, the measuring gauge may be faulty. Book value has been distorted by share repurchases, special charges due to corporate restructurings, and the adoption of a new accounting rule concerning retiree health benefits. "Price-to-book value has lost a lot of its usefulness," Mr. Kaufman concludes.

What about price-to-earnings multiples? Right now, the market is trading at about 15 times expected 1995 earnings, a tad above the historical average. "There are fewer problems with P/E ratios than with the other two measures," says Kathleen Crowley, a senior vice president with Chicago's Stratford Advisory Group.

Even so, earnings multiples also can mislead. In recent years, reported earnings have been depressed by special charges. In addition, experts say the market's earnings multiple shouldn't be viewed in isolation, but instead should be considered in the context of items like interest rates and inflation.

6.5 An Analysis of the McGraw-Hill Company

Stock market investors have available to them many sources of information about the financial performance of companies with publicly traded stock shares. Indeed, the sheer volume of information available can often be overwhelming. For this reason, several sources publish reference summaries for individual companies.

One well-known example is the *Value Line Investment Survey*, a published reference with frequent updates. *Value Line* provides what many investors consider to be the best one-page company summaries available. Current updates to the *Value Line Investment Survey* are available at most stock brokerage offices and many public

Visit the McGraw-Hill website at
www.mcgraw-hill.com

libraries. Figure 6.2 presents a one-page summary for the McGraw-Hill Corporation published by *Value Line* in late 2000. We will make frequent reference to information found in the *Value Line* summary in the discussion of McGraw-Hill.

As shown in the title bar of Figure 6.2, McGraw-Hill stock trades on the New York Stock Exchange (NYSE) under the ticker symbol MHP. When this survey went to press in February 2003, McGraw-Hill's stock price was $54.49, with a P/E ratio of 17.7. *Value Line* calculates a P/E ratio as the most recent stock price divided by the latest six months' earnings per share plus earnings per share estimated for the next six months. McGraw-Hill's relative P/E ratio of 1.20 is obtained by dividing its current P/E by the median P/E ratio of all stocks under review by *Value Line*. The dividend yield of 2 percent is calculated by dividing estimated dividends for the coming year by the current stock price.

At this point, as you look over *Value Line*'s summary in Figure 6.2, you realize that *Value Line* has packed a considerable amount of information onto a single page. We acknowledge the efficiency of the *Value Line* one-page surveys by not trying to cover all items on the entire page. Most items are well-explained in Figure 6.3, which contains a complete sample page (see p. 202). However, some items in Figure 6.2 may differ from those in Figure 6.3 reflecting changes made by *Value Line*. In the following discussion, we refer only to information needed to illustrate the analytic methods discussed previously in this chapter.

Our first task is to estimate a discount rate for McGraw-Hill. *Value Line* reports a beta of .80 for McGraw-Hill. Using a then current Treasury bill rate of 1 percent and a historical stock market risk premium of 9 percent, we obtain a discount rate estimate for McGraw-Hill using the CAPM of $1\% + .80 \times 9\% = 8.2\%$.

Our next task is to calculate a sustainable growth rate. *Value Line* reports projected 2003 earnings per share of $3.20 and dividends per share of $1.08. *Value Line* also reports a return on equity of ROE = 26 percent (reported as "Return on Shr. Equity"), implying a retention ratio of $1 - \$1.08/\$3.20 = 66.25\%$. Putting these together yields a sustainable growth rate of $.6625 \times 26\% = 17.23\%$, which is a relatively large value.

Finally, with a discount rate and sustainable growth rate we can calculate a present value for McGraw-Hill stock. Using a constant perpetual growth model with the 2002 dividend of $D(0) = \$1.02$, a discount rate of $k = 8.2$ percent, and a growth rate of 17.23 percent, we calculate this present value of expected future dividends for McGraw-Hill stock:

$$V(0) = \frac{\$1.02 \times 1.1723}{.082 - .1723}$$
$$= -\$13.24$$

Whoops! This growth rate is greater than the discount rate, so we cannot use the constant growth model.

In reality, a sustainable growth rate of almost 18 percent is probably impossible. *Value Line* reports that the actual dividend growth rate over the previous 10 years was 5.5 percent (from the box labeled "Annual Rates"). If we use this rate to value the stock, we get a stock price of $39.86 (check this for practice), which is substantially less than the current price.

Value Line also reports annual growth rates for sales, cash flow, earnings, dividends, and book value in the box labeled "Annual Rates." These include historical 5-year and 10-year growth rates, along with expected growth rates for the next 3–5 years provided by *Value Line* analysts. As we have seen, these growth rates could also be used as a basis for present value calculations, and different answers would result.

Check out Value-Line's website at www.valueline.com

FIGURE 6.2 — *Value Line* Analysis Chart

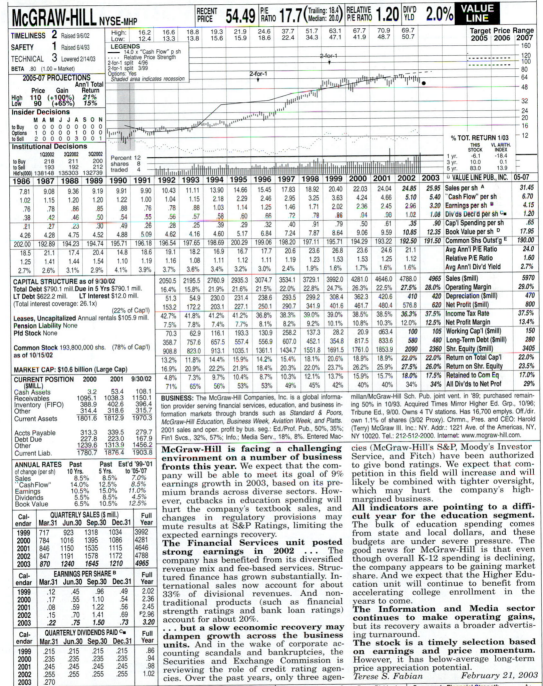

FIGURE 6.3   *Value Line* Analysis Chart

Getting the Most from the Value Line Page

The LEGENDS box contains the "Cash Flow" multiple as well as the amounts and dates of recent stock splits and dividends. Also shows if options are traded on the stock.

Monthly price ranges of the stock—plotted on a ratio (logarithmic) grid to show percentage changes in true proportion.

The "Cash Flow" line—a graphic presentation of cash flow per share, multiplied by a number selected so that the line correlates with a stock's monthly price range.

P/E ratio—the stock's recent price divided by the latest six months' earnings per share plus earnings estimated for the next six months.

Trailing P/E —the recent price divided by the sum of earnings per share during the past 12 months.

Median P/E —the mean of the four middle values of the average annual price-earnings ratios over the past ten years.

Relative P/E ratio—the stock's P/E divided by the median P/E for all stocks under Value Line review.

Dividend yield—cash dividends estimated to be declared in the next 12 months divided by the recent price.

Here is the core of Value Line's advice—the rank for Timeliness; the rank for Safety; the Technical rank. And next to each is normally the date each last changed. Beta shows the stock's sensitivity to fluctuations in the market as a whole.

Projected stock price returns to 2003-05, both absolute (gain/loss without dividends) and total (annual, including dividends).

The record of insider decisions—decisions by officers and directors to buy or sell as reported to the SEC.

The number of large institutions —including banks, insurance companies, mutual funds—buying or selling during the past three quarters and the total number of shares owned.

The capital structure as of recent date showing the percentage of capital in long-term debt and shareholders' equity. Also, Market Capitalization.

Current position—current assets and current liabilities, the components of working capital.

Annual rates of change (on a per-share basis). Actual past, estimated future.

Sales and earnings are shown for each quarter, with earnings on a per share basis.

Quarterly dividends paid are actual payments. The total of dividends paid in four quarters may not equal the figure shown in the annual series on dividends declared. (Sometimes a dividend declared at the end of the year will be paid in the first quarter of the following year).

Footnotes explain a number of things, such as the way earnings are reported, and the net effect of nonrecurring items.

The stock's highest and lowest prices of the year.

The 3- to 5-year Target Price Range, estimated. These are the same ranges shown numerically in the "2003-05 Projections" box on the left side of the price chart.

The % Total Return shows price appreciation (plus dividends) of the stock for the past 1, 3, and 5 years and also for the stock market, as measured by the Value Line Arithmetic Index.

The number of shares traded monthly as a percentage of the total outstanding.

Statistical array that reveals significant long-term trends. Note that the statistics for the current and future years are estimated. The estimates are revised when necessary in the weekly *Summary & Index.*

A condensed summary of the business, significant shareholders (holding over 5%) and the company's address, telephone number, and Internet address.

Analyst's Commentary is a 350-word report on recent developments and prospects, issued once every three months on a preset schedule.

The date of delivery to the subscribers. *The Investment Survey* is mailed on a schedule that aims for delivery to every subscriber on Friday.

Value Line's Indexes of Financial Strength, Price Stability, Price Growth Persistence, and Earnings Predictability.

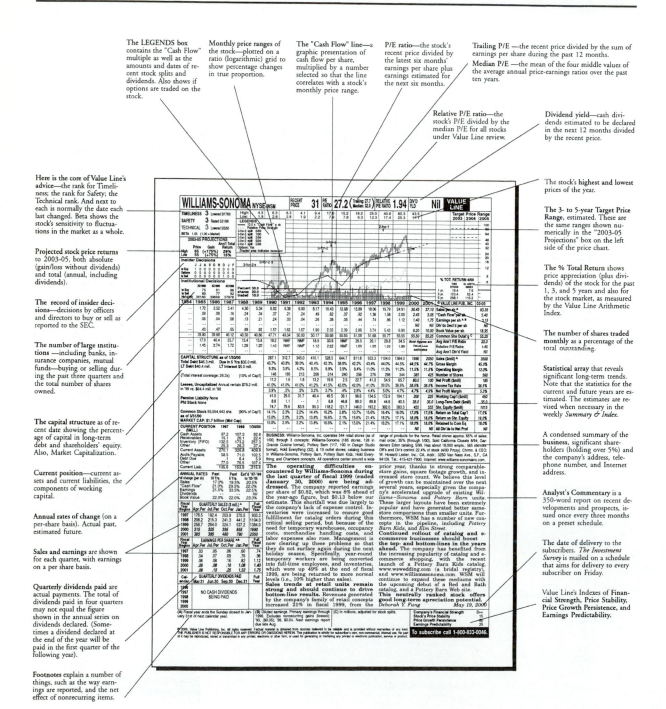

Source: *Value Line,* "How to Invest in Common Stocks: A Guide to Using the Value Line Investment Survey," 2003.

TABLE 6.3	Price Ratio Calculations for McGraw-Hill Company (MHP)					
	1998	**1999**	**2000**	**2001**	**2002**	**Average**
EPS	1.71	2.02	2.36	2.45	2.96	2.3
P/E	23.6	26.8	23.6	24.6	21.1	23.94
CFPS	3.25	3.63	4.24	4.66	5.10	4.18
P/CFPS	12.42	14.91	13.14	12.93	12.25	13.13
SPS	18.92	20.40	22.03	24.04	24.85	22.05
P/SPS	2.13	2.65	2.53	2.51	2.51	2.47

TABLE 6.4	Price Ratio Analysis for McGraw-Hill (MHP) Mid-2003 Stock Price: $54.49		
	Earnings (P/E)	**Cash Flow (P/CF)**	**Sales (P/S)**
Current value per share	$2.96	$5.10	$24.85
Five-year average price ratio	23.94	13.13	2.47
Growth rate	11.0%	8.5%	7.0%
Expected stock price	$78.66	$72.65	$65.68

We next turn to a price ratio analysis for McGraw-Hill. We will estimate expected future stock prices using five-year average price ratios that we will calculate along with expected growth rates supplied by *Value Line* analysts. The *Value Line* survey page reports annual average price-earnings ratios, but does not report average price-cash flow ratios or average price-sales ratios. In this case, a quick way to calculate an average P/CF ratio is to multiply an average P/E ratio by the ratio of earnings per share over cash flow per share: P/CF = P/E × EPS / CFPS.

For example, McGraw-Hill's 2001 average P/E was 24.6, EPS was $2.45, CFPS was $4.66, and SPS was $24.04. Thus, a quick calculation of McGraw-Hill's 2001 average P/CF ratio is 24.6 × 2.45/4.66 = 12.93. Similarly, the 2001 average P/S ratio is 24.6 × 2.45/24.04 = 2.51. Average price ratio calculations for P/CF and P/S ratios for the years 1998 through 2002 are provided in Table 6.3, along with five-year averages for each price ratio. Be sure that you understand where all the numbers come from.

The five-year average price ratios calculated in Table 6.3 are used in the price ratio analysis in Table 6.4. The expected growth rates for earnings, cash flow, and sales provided by *Value Line* analysts (from the "Annual Rates" box) are used to calculate expected stock prices for McGraw-Hill one year hence. For reference, the three formulas used to calculate expected prices are restated here:

$$\text{Expected price} = \text{P/E ratio} \times \text{EPS} \times (1 + \text{EPS growth rate})$$
$$\text{Expected price} = \text{P/CF ratio} \times \text{CFPS} \times (1 + \text{CFPS growth rate})$$
$$\text{Expected price} = \text{P/S ratio} \times \text{SPS} \times (1 + \text{SPS growth rate})$$

We can now summarize our analysis by listing the stock prices obtained by the methods described in this chapter along with the model used to derive them:

Dividend discount model (sustainable growth):	Not defined
Dividend discount model (historical growth):	$39.86
Price-earnings model:	$78.66
Price-cash flow model:	$72.65
Price-sales model:	$65.68

The price ratio methods suggest that in early 2003 McGraw-Hill's stock might be undervalued at a market price of $54.49. However, only time will tell if this is so. Perhaps the market has not accounted for future sales growth for this textbook, which is published by McGraw-Hill.

In contrast, our dividend discount analysis suggests that the stock might be overvalued. Why are we getting such different answers from the two approaches? One reason derives from the fact that part of our five-year base period used in the ratio analysis corresponds to a time of very high stock market valuations, implying relatively large values for our various ratios. However, valuations subsequently declined dramatically. Notice, for example, that the P/E ratio at the time of the *Value Line* report was 17.7 compared to our five-year average of 23.94. With our dividend discount model, the answer turns out to be very sensitive to the dividend growth rate. For example, if we use 6.5 percent instead of 5.5, we get a stock price of $63.90. In sum, for a variety of reasons, McGraw-Hill is difficult to value with confidence at this time.

Check This

> **6.5a** Locate *Value Line*'s projected growth rate in dividends. How does it compare to the sustainable growth rate we estimated? The historical growth rates? Revalue the stock using the constant perpetual dividend model and this growth rate.
>
> **6.5b** Assume that the sustainable growth rate we calculated is the growth rate for the next five years only and that dividends will grow thereafter at the rate projected by *Value Line* analysts. Using these growth rates, revalue the stock using the two-stage dividend growth model.

6.6 Summary and Conclusions

In this chapter, we examined several methods of fundamental analysis used by financial analysts to value common stocks. These methods belong to two categories: dividend discount models and price ratio models. We saw that:

1. Dividend discount models value common stock as the sum of all expected future dividend payments, where the dividends are adjusted for risk and the time value of money.

2. The dividend discount model is often simplified by assuming that dividends will grow at a constant growth rate. A particularly simple form of the dividend discount model is the case in which dividends grow at a constant perpetual growth rate. The simplicity of the constant perpetual growth model makes it the most popular dividend discount model. However, it should be applied only to companies with stable earnings and dividend growth.

3. Dividend models require an estimate of future growth. We described the sustainable growth rate, which is measured as a firm's return on equity times its retention ratio, and illustrated its use.

4. Companies often experience temporary periods of unusually high or low growth, where growth eventually converges to an industry average. In such cases, analysts frequently use a two-stage dividend growth model.

5. Price ratios are widely used by financial analysts. The most popular price ratio is a company's price-earnings ratio. A P/E ratio is calculated as the ratio of a firm's stock price divided by its earnings per share (EPS).

6. Financial analysts often refer to high-P/E stocks as growth stocks and low-P/E stocks as value stocks. In general, companies with high expected earnings growth will have high P/E ratios, which is why high-P/E stocks are referred to as growth stocks. Low-P/E stocks are referred to as value stocks because they are viewed as cheap relative to current earnings.

7. Instead of price-earnings ratios, many analysts prefer to look at price-cash flow (P/CF) ratios. A price-cash flow ratio is measured as a company's stock price divided by its cash flow per share. Most analysts agree that cash flow can provide more information than net income about a company's financial performance.

8. An alternative view of a company's performance is provided by its price-sales (P/S) ratio. A price-sales ratio is calculated as the price of a company's stock divided by its annual sales revenue per share. A price-sales ratio focuses on a company's ability to generate sales growth. A high P/S ratio suggests high sales growth, while a low P/S ratio suggests low sales growth.

9. A basic price ratio for a company is its price-book (P/B) ratio. A price-book ratio is measured as the market value of a company's outstanding common stock divided by its book value of equity. A high P/B ratio suggests that a company is potentially expensive, while a low P/B value suggests that a company may be cheap.

10. A common procedure using price-earnings ratios, price-cash flow ratios, and price-sales ratios is to calculate estimates of expected future stock prices. However, each price ratio method yields a different expected future stock price. Since each method uses different information, each makes a different prediction.

Get Real

This chapter introduced you to some of the basics of common stock valuation and fundamental analysis. It focused on two important tools used by stock analysts in the real world to assess whether a particular stock is "rich" or "cheap": dividend discount models and price ratio analysis. How should you, as an investor or investment manager, put this information to use?

The answer is that you need to pick some stocks and get to work! As we discussed in the chapter, experience and judgment are needed to use these models, and the only way to obtain these is through practice. Try to identify a few stocks that look cheap and buy them in a simulated brokerage account such as Stock-Trak. At the same time, find a few that look rich and short them. Start studying P/E ratios. Scan *The Wall Street Journal* (or a similar source of market information) and look at the range of P/Es. What's a low P/E? What's a high one? Do they really correspond to what you would call growth and value stocks?

The Internet is a copious source for information on valuing companies. Try, for example, Stock Sheet (www.stocksheet.com), Wall Street Research (www.wsrn.com), Hoovers Online (www.hoovers.com), and Zacks (www.zacks.com). Don't forget to check out the Motley Fool (www.fool.com).

(continued)

Several trade associations have informative websites that can be helpful. For individual investors there is the American Association of Individual Investors (www.aaii.com) and for professional security analysts there is the New York Society of Security Analysts (www.nyssa.org). The Association for Investment Management and Research (www.aimr.com) provides a financial analyst's certification that is highly respected among security analysts.

Key Terms

fundamental analysis 177
dividend discount model (DDM) 178
constant growth rate model 179
constant perpetual growth model 180
geometric average dividend
    growth rate 182
arithmetic average dividend
    growth rate 182
sustainable growth rate 184
retained earnings 184
payout ratio 184

retention ratio 184
two-stage dividend growth model 187
beta 191
price-earnings (P/E) ratio 192
earnings yield 192
growth stocks 193
value stocks 193
price-cash flow (P/CF) ratio 193
cash flow 193
price-sales (P/S) ratio 196
price-book (P/B) ratio 197

Chapter Review Problems and Self-Test

1. **The Perpetual Growth Model** Suppose dividends for Tony's Pizza company are projected to grow at 6 percent forever. If the discount rate is 16 percent and the current dividend is $2, what is the value of the stock?

2. **The Two-Stage Growth Model** Suppose the Titanic Ice Cube Co.'s dividend grows at a 20 percent rate for the next three years. Thereafter, it grows at a 12 percent rate. What value would we place on Titanic assuming a 15 percent discount rate? Titanic's most recent dividend was $3.

3. **Price Ratio Analysis** The table below contains some information about the Jordan Air Co. Provide expected share prices using each of the three price ratio approaches we have discussed.

PRICE RATIO ANALYSIS FOR JORDAN AIR	CURRENT STOCK PRICE: $40	
	Earnings (P/E)	Cash Flow (P/CF)	Sales (P/S)
Current value per share	$2.00	$6.00	$30.00
Five-year average price ratio	25	7	1.5
Growth rate	10%	16%	14%

Answers to Self-Test Problems

1. Plugging the relevant numbers into the constant perpetual growth formula results in

$$V(0) = \frac{\$2(1.06)}{.16 - .06} = \$21.20$$

As shown, the stock should sell for $21.20.

2. Plugging all the relevant numbers into the two-stage formula gets us

$$V(0) = \frac{\$3(1.20)}{.15 - .20}\left[1 - \left(\frac{1.20}{1.15}\right)^3\right] + \left(\frac{1.20}{1.15}\right)^3 \frac{\$3(1.12)}{.15 - .12}$$

$$= \$9.81 + \$127.25$$

$$= \$137.06$$

Thus, the stock should go for about $137.

3. Using the P/E approach, we come up with the following estimate of the price of Jordan Air in one year:

$$\text{Estimated price} = \text{Average P/E} \times \text{Current EPS} \times (1 + \text{Growth rate})$$

$$= 25 \times \$2 \times 1.10$$

$$= \$55$$

Using the P/CF approach, we get:

$$\text{Estimated price} = \text{Average P/CF} \times \text{Current CFPS} \times (1 + \text{Growth rate})$$

$$= 7 \times \$6 \times 1.16$$

$$= \$48.72$$

Finally, using the P/S approach, we get:

$$\text{Estimated price} = \text{Average P/S} \times \text{Current SPS} \times (1 + \text{Growth rate})$$

$$= 1.5 \times \$30 \times 1.14$$

$$= \$51.30$$

Test Your Investment Quotient

1. **Sustainable Growth**   A company has a return on equity of ROE = 20 percent, and from earnings per share of EPS = $5, it pays a $2 dividend. What is the company's sustainable growth rate?

   a. 8 percent
   b. 10 percent
   c. 12 percent
   d. 20 percent

2. **Sustainable Growth**   If the return on equity for a firm is 15 percent and the retention ratio is 40 percent, the sustainable growth rate of earnings and dividends is which of the following?

   a. 6 percent
   b. 9 percent
   c. 15 percent
   d. 40 percent

3. **Dividend Discount Model**   A common stock pays an annual dividend per share of $2.10. The risk-free rate is 7 percent and the risk premium for this stock is 4 percent. If the annual dividend is expected to remain at $2.10, the value of the stock is closest to:

   a. $19.09
   b. $30.00
   c. $52.50
   d. $70.00

4. **Dividend Discount Model**   Suppose a security pays a current dividend of $5 and all future dividends will grow at a rate of 8 percent per year forever. Assuming the appropriate discount rate is 12 percent, what is the value of this security?

   a. $135
   b. $270
   c. $13.50
   d. $1,350

5. **Dividend Discount Model**   The constant-growth dividend discount model will not produce a finite value if the dividend growth rate is which of the following?

   a. Above its historical average.
   b. Above the required rate of return.
   c. Below its historical average.
   d. Below the required rate of return.

6. **Dividend Discount Model**   In applying the constant-growth dividend discount model, a stock's intrinsic value will do which of the following when the required rate of return is lowered?

   a. Decrease.
   b. Increase.
   c. Remain unchanged.
   d. Decrease or increase, depending on other factors.

7. **Dividend Discount Model**   The constant-growth dividend discount model would typically be most appropriate for valuing the stock of which of the following?

   a. New venture expected to retain all earnings for several years.
   b. Rapidly growing company.
   c. Moderate growth, mature company.
   d. Company with valuable assets not yet generating profits.

8. **Dividend Discount Model**   A stock has a required return of 15 percent, a constant growth rate of 10 percent, and a dividend payout ratio of 50 percent. What should the stock's P/E ratio be?

   a. 3.0
   b. 4.5
   c. 9.0
   d. 11.0

9. **Dividend Discount Model**   Which of the following assumptions does the constant growth dividend discount model require?

   I. Dividends grow at a constant rate.
   II. The dividend growth rate continues indefinitely.
   III. The required rate of return is less than the dividend growth rate.

   a. I only
   b. III only
   c. I and II only
   d. I, II, and III

10. **CAPM Discount Rate**   If the U.S. Treasury bill rate is 5 percent and the stock market risk premium is 8 percent, then the CAPM discount rate for a security with a beta of 1.25 is

   a. 12 percent
   b. 13 percent
   c. 14.25 percent
   d. 15 percent

11. **CAPM Discount Rate** If the U.S. Treasury bill rate is 5 percent and the stock market risk premium is 8 percent, then the CAPM discount rate for a security with a beta of .75 is

   a. 6 percent
   b. 8 percent
   c. 11 percent
   d. 13 percent

12. **Dividend Discount Model** A stock will not pay dividends until three years from now. The dividend then will be $2.00 per share, the dividend payout ratio will be 40 percent, and return on equity will be 15 percent. If the required rate of return is 12 percent, which of the following is closest to the value of the stock?

   a. $27
   b. $33
   c. $53
   d. $67

13. **Dividend Discount Model** Assume that at the end of the next year, Company A will pay a $2.00 dividend per share, an increase from the current dividend of $1.50 per share. After that, the dividend is expected to increase at a constant rate of 5 percent. If you require a 12 percent return on the stock, what is the value of the stock?

   a. $28.57
   b. $28.79
   c. $30.00
   d. $31.78

14. **Dividend Discount Model** A share of stock will pay a dividend of $1.00 one year from now, with dividend growth of 5 percent thereafter. In the context of a dividend discount model, the stock is correctly priced at $10 today. According to the constant dividend growth model, if the required return is 15 percent, what should the value of the stock be two years from now?

   a. $11.03
   b. $12.10
   c. $13.23
   d. $14.40

15. **Cash Flow** Which of the following implies the highest quality earnings?

   a. Cash flow less than earnings.
   b. Cash flow greater than depreciation.
   c. Cash flow less than earnings minus depreciation.
   d. Cash flow greater than earnings.

16. **Price Ratios** Two similar companies have the same price-sales and price-earnings ratios. However, company A has a lower price-cash flow ratio than company B. This most likely indicates that

   a. A has lower quality earnings than B.
   b. A has lower quality cash flow than B.
   c. A uses straight-line depreciation, while B uses accelerated depreciation.
   d. A uses accelerated depreciation, while B uses straight-line depreciation.

17. **Price Ratios** Two similar companies acquire substantial new production facilities, which they both will depreciate over a 10-year period. However, Company A uses accelerated depreciation while Company B uses straight-line depreciation. In the first year that the assets are depreciated, which of the following is most likely to occur?

   a. A's P/CF ratio will be higher than B's.
   b. A's P/CF ratio will be lower than B's.

www.mhhe.com/cj3e

c. A's P/E ratio will be higher than B's.
d. A's P/E ratio will be lower than B's.

18. **Price Ratios**   An analyst estimates the earnings per share and price-to-earnings ratio for a stock market series to be $43.50 and 26 times, respectively. The dividend payout ratio for the series is 65 percent. The value of the stock market series is closest to

   a. 396
   b. 735
   c. 1131
   d. 1866

19. **P/E Ratio**   An analyst gathered the following information about a stock market index:

Required rate of return:	16%
Expected dividend payout ratio:	30%
Expected return on equity investment:	20%

The expected price-earnings (P/E) ratio of the index is closest to

   a. 3.5
   b. 7.0
   c. 15.0
   d. 35.00

20. **P/E Ratio**   A company's return on equity is greater than its required return on equity. The earnings multiplier (P/E) for that company's stock is most likely to be positively related to the

   a. Risk-free rate.
   b. Market risk premium.
   c. Earnings retention ratio.
   d. Stock's capital asset pricing model beta.

Concept Questions

1. **Dividend Discount Model**   What is the basic principle behind dividend discount models?

2. **P/E Ratios**   Why do growth stocks tend to have higher P/E ratios than value stocks?

3. **Earnings Yields**   What is the earnings yield on a stock?

4. **Cash Flow**   In computing the price-cash flow ratio, how is cash flow per share usually measured?

5. **Stock Valuation**   Why does the value of a share of stock depend on dividends?

6. **Stock Valuation**   A substantial percentage of the companies listed on the NYSE and the Nasdaq don't pay dividends, but investors are nonetheless willing to buy shares in them. How is this possible given your answer to the previous question?

7. **Dividends**   Referring to the previous two questions, under what circumstances might a company choose not to pay dividends?

8. **Constant Perpetual Growth Model**   Under what two assumptions can we use the constant perpetual growth model presented in the chapter to determine the value of a share of stock? Comment on the reasonableness of these assumptions.

9. **Dividend Growth Models**   Based on the dividend growth models presented in the chapter, what are the two components of the total return of a share of stock? Which do you think is typically larger?

10. **Constant Perpetual Growth Model**   In the context of the constant perpetual growth model, is it true that the growth rate in dividends and the growth rate in the price of the stock are identical?

Questions and Problems

1. **Dividend Valuation** CJ Industries will pay a regular dividend of $4.00 per share for each of the next four years. At the end of the four years, the company will also pay out a $40 per share liquidating dividend, and the company will cease operations. If the discount rate is 11 percent, what is the current value of the company's stock?

2. **Dividend Valuation** In the previous problem, suppose the current share price is $50. If all other information remains the same, what must the liquidating dividend be?

3. **Dividend Discount Model** Trust Bankers just paid an annual dividend of $3 per share. The expected dividend growth rate is 6 percent, the discount rate is 12 percent, and the dividends will last for 5 more years. What is the value of the stock? What if the dividends last for 10 more years? 30 years? 100 years?

4. **Dividend Discount Model** Apple Grove, Inc., will pay dividends for the next 10 years. The expected dividend growth rate for this firm is 8 percent, the discount rate is 16 percent, and the stock currently sells for $30 per share. How much must the most recent dividend payment have been?

5. **Dividend Growth Model** Suppose that Kojak, Inc., just paid a dividend of $3.50 per share. The company will continue to pay dividends for the next 25 years, and then go out of business. If the discount rate is 11 percent per year, what is the value of the stock for a dividend growth rate of 20 percent? 12 percent? 6 percent? 0 percent? −5 percent?

6. **Perpetual Dividend Growth** A company just paid a dividend of $3.00. If the dividends will grow at 5.5 percent per year and you require a return of 11.8 percent, what is the most you should be willing to pay for the stock?

7. **Perpetual Dividend Growth** Atlantis Seafood Company stock currently sells for $80 per share. The company is expected to pay a dividend of $4.10 per share next year, and analysts project that dividends should increase at 4 percent per year for the indefinite future. What must the relevant discount rate be for Atlantis stock?

8. **Perpetual Dividend Growth** Xytex Products just paid a dividend of $1.80 per share, and the stock currently sells for $30. If the discount rate is 13 percent, what is the dividend growth rate?

9. **Perpetual Dividend Growth** Star Light & Power increases its dividend 5 percent per year every year. This utility is valued using a discount rate of 9 percent, and the stock currently sells for $80 per share. If you buy a share of stock today and hold on to it for at least three years, what do you expect the value of your dividend check to be three years from today?

10. **Sustainable Growth** Johnson Products earned $8.60 per share last year and paid a $3.20 per share dividend. If ROE was 20 percent, what is the sustainable growth rate?

11. **Sustainable Growth** Caterwallar stock has a sustainable growth rate of 6 percent, ROE of 19 percent, and dividends per share of $2.20. If the P/E ratio is 21, what is the value of a share of stock?

12. **Two-Stage Dividend Growth Model** Underwood Industries just paid a dividend of $2.16 per share. The dividends are expected to grow at a 25 percent rate for the next eight years and then level off to a 7 percent growth rate indefinitely. If the required return is 14 percent, what is the value of the stock today?

13. **Two-Stage Dividend Growth Model** The dividend for Weaver, Inc., is expected to grow at 19 percent for the next 12 years before leveling off at a 6 percent rate indefinitely. If the firm just paid a dividend of $1.34 and you require a return of 12 percent on the stock, what is the most you should pay per share?

14. **Multiple Growth Rates** Netscrape Communications does not currently pay a dividend. You expect the company to begin paying a $4 per share dividend in 10 years, and you

expect dividends to grow perpetually at 8 percent per year thereafter. If the discount rate is 15 percent, how much is the stock currently worth?

15. **Multiple Growth Rates**   PerfectlySoft Corp. is experiencing rapid growth. Dividends are expected to grow at 30 percent per year during the next three years, 20 percent over the following year, and then 6 percent per year thereafter indefinitely. The required return on this stock is 14 percent, and the stock currently sells for $56.20 per share. What is the projected dividend for the coming year?

16. **Multiple Growth Rates**   Callaway Corporation is expected to pay the following dividends over the next four years: $14.00, $10.00, $5.00, $2.00. Afterwards, the company pledges to maintain a constant 7 percent growth rate in dividends forever. If the required return on the stock is 15 percent, what is the current share price?

17. **Multiple Required Returns**   My Money, Inc., just paid a dividend of $3.00 per share on its stock. The growth rate in dividends is expected to be a constant 6.5 percent per year indefinitely. Investors require a 20 percent return on the stock for the first three years, then a 15 percent return for the next three years, and then a 10 percent return thereafter. What is the current share price for My Money?

18. **Price Ratio Analysis**   Given the information below for Cuchia Corporation, compute the expected share price at the end of 2004 using price ratio analysis.

Year:	1998	1999	2000	2001	2002	2003
Price	$38.00	$46.00	$55.00	$61.00	$68.00	$72.00
EPS	2.55	2.70	2.80	2.90	3.40	3.75
CFPS	6.00	7.20	7.60	7.71	7.83	8.20
SPS	53.00	57.50	59.25	64.75	69.00	74.05

19. **Dividend Growth Analysis**   In the previous problem, suppose the dividends per share over the same period were $.77, $.82, $.89, $.94, $1.01, and $1.09, respectively. Compute the expected share price for 2004 using the perpetual growth method. Assume the market risk premium is 8.5 percent, Treasury bills yield 5 percent, and the projected beta of the firm is .90.

20. **Price Ratio Analysis for Internet Companies**   Given the information below for HooYah! Corporation, compute the expected share price at the end of 2004 using price ratio analysis.

Year:	1998	1999	2000	2001	2002	2003
Price	$52.00	$244.00	$480.00	$620.00	$85.00	$ 6.00
EPS	−5.00	−2.30	−0.80	0.05	0.03	0.12
CFPS	−9.00	−5.20	−3.20	−1.05	0.01	0.10
SPS	10.00	14.00	16.00	15.25	16.10	16.05

21. **Price Ratio Analysis for Internet Companies**   Given the information below for StartUp.Com, compute the expected share price at the end of 2004 using price ratio analysis.

Year:	1998	1999	2000	2001	2002	2003
Price			N/A	$89.25	$26.00	$ 4.10
EPS			N/A	−13.20	−11.65	−10.20
CFPS			N/A	−15.65	−14.20	−13.85
SPS			N/A	4.80	9.10	21.05

22. **Price Ratio Analysis for Internet Companies**   Given the information below for Rock-n-Roll.Com, compute the expected share price at the end of 2004 using price ratio analysis.

Year:	1998	1999	2000	2001	2002	2003
Price	$280.00	$320.00	$140.00	$68.00	$28.00	$12.00
EPS	−14.00	−11.80	−6.25	1.05	1.30	−4.10
CFPS	−18.00	−12.10	−5.00	0.10	1.20	−4.90
SPS	21.00	28.75	32.10	34.50	37.20	23.25

23. **Price Ratio Analysis**   The current price of Parador Industries stock is $60 per share. Current earnings per share are $4.50, the earnings growth rate is 10 percent, and Parador does not pay a dividend. The expected return on Parador stock is 15 percent. What one-year ahead P/E ratio is consistent with Parador's expected return and earnings growth rate?

24. **Price Ratio Analysis**   The current price of Parador Industries stock is $60 per share. Current sales per share are $23, the sales growth rate is 12 percent, and Parador does not pay a dividend. The expected return on Parador stock is 15 percent. What one-year ahead P/S ratio is consistent with Parador's expected return and sales growth rate?

Use the following information for Problems 25–28.

Oxford Industries (OXM) is a leading clothing manufacturer. Its major brands include Lanier Clothes, Lands' End, Tommy Hilfiger shirts and golf apparel, Slates, Geoffrey Beene, and Oscar De La Renta. Below you will find selected information from the February 2003 *Value Line* report on Oxford Industries. The beta reported in *Value Line* was .80, and the risk-free rate was 1.06 percent. Assume a market risk premium of 9 percent.

OXFORD INDS. NYSE-OXM	RECENT PRICE **23.09**	P/E RATIO **10.3** (Trailing: 11.1 / Median: 11.0)	RELATIVE P/E RATIO **0.68**	DIV'D YLD **3.6%**

1998	1999	2000	2001	2002	2003	VALUE LINE PUB., INC.
87.78	108.73	109.73	109.71	90.12		Sales per sh A
3.71	4.45	4.29	3.32	2.59		"Cash Flow" per sh
2.75	3.11	3.02	2.05	1.40		Earnings per sh B
.80	.82	.84	.84	.84		Div'ds Decl'd per sh C
1.00	.89	.77	.59	.20		Cap'l Spending per sh
18.11	19.46	21.48	22.81	23.31		Book Value per sh
8.82	7.93	7.65	7.41	7.52		Common Shs Outst'g D
11.6	9.2	6.9	9.0	17.3		Avg Ann'l P/E Ratio
.60	.52	.45	.46	.87		Relative P/E Ratio
2.5%	2.9%	4.0%	4.6%	3.5%		Avg Ann'l Div'd Yield
774.5	862.4	839.5	812.5	677.3		Sales ($mill) A
6.7%	6.6%	6.1%	4.8%	3.9%		Operating Margin
8.1	8.9	9.4	9.2	8.9		Depreciation ($mill) E
24.6	26.4	23.4	15.3	10.6		Net Profit ($mill)
39.0%	39.0%	38.0%	38.0%	38.8%		Income Tax Rate
3.2%	3.1%	2.8%	1.9%	1.6%		Net Profit Margin
169.5	154.7	163.0	130.3	144.9		Working Cap'l ($mill)
41.4	40.7	40.5	.4	.1		Long-Term Debt ($mill)
159.8	154.4	164.3	168.9	175.2		Shr. Equity ($mill)
12.8%	14.2%	12.1%	9.8%	6.1%		Return on Total Cap'l
15.4%	17.1%	14.3%	9.1%	6.0%		Return on Shr. Equity

The high and low share price each year were:

	1998	1999	2000	2001	2002
High	$37.70	$29.80	$22.50	$26.10	$30.30
Low	22.50	19.00	13.80	15.30	19.50

25. **Constant Perpetual Growth Model**   What is the sustainable growth rate and required return for Oxford Industries in 2002? Using these values, calculate the 2002 share price of Oxford Industries stock.

26. **Price Ratios**   Using the P/E, P/CF, and P/S ratios, estimate the 2002 share price for Oxford Industries.

27. **Stock Valuation**   Given your answers in the previous two problems, do you feel Oxford Industries is overvalued or undervalued at its current price? What price do you feel the stock should sell?

28. **Growth Rates**   As we mentioned, Oxford Industries manufactures clothes for Lands' End. Soon after the end of Oxford's fiscal year, Sears purchased Lands' End and started to put clothing with the Lands' End label in its department stores. Does this information affect your analysis? How would it affect your estimate of the stock price?

CFA®
PROBLEMS

The following questions are from the 2000 Level II CFA® Exam. Use this information to answer Problems 29–34.

The management of Telluride, an international diversified conglomerate based in the United States, believes the recent strong performance of its wholly owned medical supply subsidiary, Sundanci, has gone unnoticed. In order to realize Sundanci's full value, Telluride has announced that it will divest Sundanci in a tax-free spinoff.

   Sue Carroll, CFA, is the Director of Research at Kesson and Associates. In developing an investment recommendation for Sundanci, Carroll has directed her analysts to determine a valuation of Sundanci using various disciplines. To assist her analysts, Carroll has gathered the information shown below.

Sundanci Actual 1999 and 2000 Financial Statements for Fiscal Years Ending May 31 ($ in millions except per-share data)		
Income Statement	**1999**	**2000**
Revenue	$474	$598
Depreciation	20	23
Other operating expenses	368	460
Income before taxes	86	115
Taxes	26	35
Net income	60	80
Dividends	18	24
Earnings per share	$0.714	$0.952
Dividend per share	$0.214	$0.286
Common shares outstanding	84.0	84.0
Balance sheet		
Current assets	$201	$326
Net property, plant and equipment	474	489
Total assets	675	815
		(continued)

Current liabilities	57	141
Long-term debt	0	0
Total liabilities	57	141
Shareholder equity	618	674
Total liabilities and equity	675	815
Capital expenditures	34	38
Selected Financial Information		
Required rate of return on equity	14%	
Growth rate of industry	13%	
Industry P/E ratio	26	

29. **Sustainable Growth Rate**   Calculate the ROE for 2000. What is the sustainable growth rate?

30. **Sustainable Growth Rate**   Carroll learns that Sundanci's Board of Directors is considering the following policy changes that will affect Sundanci's sustainable growth rate:

    Director A proposes an increase in the quarterly dividend to $.15 per share. This would increase the annual dividend to $.60.

    Director B proposes a two-for-one stock split.

    Would each of these changes increase, decrease, or not affect Sundanci's sustainable growth rate, given that the other factors remain unchanged? Identify which component of the sustainable growth rate model, if any, is affected by each proposal.

31. **Two-State Dividend Growth Model**   Helen Morgan, CFA, has been asked by Carroll to determine the potential valuation for Sundanci using the dividend discount model. Morgan anticipates that Sundanci's earnings and dividends will grow at 32 percent for two years and 13 percent thereafter. Calculate the current value of a share of Sundanci stock using the two-stage dividend discount model.

32. **P/E Ratio Valuation**   Christie Johnson, CFA, has been assigned by Carroll to analyze Sundanci using the constant dividend growth price-earnings ratio model. Johnson assumes that Sundanci's earnings and dividends will grow at a constant rate of 13 percent. Note: The constant dividend growth price-earnings ratio using next year's earnings is P/E ratio = Payout ratio/$(k - g)$. Calculate the P/E ratio based on the information given and Johnson's assumptions.

33. **P/E Ratio**   Identify, within the context of the constant dividend growth model, how each of the following factors will affect the P/E ratio of Sundanci. In other words, will each of the following factors increase, decrease, or possibly increase or decrease the P/E ratio? Assume all other factors remain constant.

    a. The beta of Sundanci increases substantially.
    b. The estimated growth rate of Sundanci's earnings and dividends increases.
    c. The dividend payout ratio of Sundanci increases.
    d. The market risk premium increases.

34. **Payout Ratio and P/E**   Explain why an increase in the dividend payout ratio may not have the effect that the constant dividend growth P/E model suggests.

STANDARD & POOR'S

S&P Problems

www.mhhe.com/edumarketinsight

1. **Constant Perpetual Growth Model**   Locate the information for Emerson Electric Co. (EMR). If you follow the "Financial Hlts" link you will find the current stock price, most recent dividend, and the five-year growth rate for dividends. Assuming the five-year dividend growth rate is equal to the perpetual growth rate, what is the implied required return for Emerson shareholders? Does this number make sense?

2. **Sustainable Growth**   What is the sustainable growth rate for Bob Evans Farms (BOBE)? Under "Excel Analytics" you will find a link for annual ratios. This report shows return on equity and the payout ratio. Calculate the sustainable growth rate for Bob Evans Farms each year for the past five years. Is the sustainable growth rate the same every year? Why or why not?

3. **Price Ratio Analysis**   Locate the information for Walgreen (WAG). All of the information used in this problem is found under "Excel Analytics." Use the "Mthly. Adj. Prices" link and find the year-end stock price for Walgreen for all available years. Next, find the earnings per share for the last five years using EPS Basic from Operations. Locate the balance sheet for each of the past five years and record the Common Equity and Common Shares Outstanding. Use the Annual Cash Flow Statement to find the Net Cash Flow from Operating Activities. Divide both common equity and cash flow by the shares outstanding each year to find the annual book value per share and cash flow per share. Record these numbers. Calculate the price-earnings ratio, price-cash flow ratio, and price-book value ratio for each year. Using this information, compute the expected share price for Walgreen at the end of the next year using price ratio analysis.

What's on the Web?

1. **Sustainable Growth Rate**   You can find the home page for Caterpillar, Inc., at www.caterpillar.com. Go to this page and find the most recent annual report for Caterpillar. Calculate the sustainable growth rate for each of the past two years. Are these values the same? Why or why not?

2. **Sustainable Growth Rate**   Go to finance.yahoo.com and get the information for Hewlett-Packard. Under the "Research" link you should find analysts' estimates for Hewlett-Packard's growth rate over the next five years. How does this compare to the industry, sector, and S&P 500 growth rates? Now find the EPS and dividends per share for Hewlett-Packard and calculate the sustainable growth rate. How does your number compare to analysts' estimates for the company? Why might these estimates differ?

3. **Perpetual Dividend Growth Model**   Go to finance.yahoo.com and find the following information for IBM: the beta, the most recent annual dividend, and analysts' estimated growth rate. Next, find the three-month Treasury bill yield on finance.yahoo.com. Assuming the market risk premium is 9 percent, what is the required return for IBM? What is the value of IBM stock using the perpetual dividend growth model? Does IBM appear overpriced, underpriced, or correctly priced? Why might this analysis be inappropriate, or at least misleading?

www.mhhe.com/cj3e

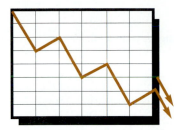

Stock-Trak®
Portfolio Simulations

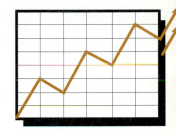

Dogs of the Dow Stock Trading with Stock-Trak

A popular investment strategy that many investment advisors recommend to their clients is the so-called dogs of the Dow strategy. Under this strategy, an investor ranks the 30 stocks in the Dow Jones Industrials average according to their dividend yields. The investor then buys the 10 Dow stocks with the highest dividend yields. Six months or a year later, the 10 stocks in the DJIA with the highest dividend yields are again identified and the investor switches funds into these stocks. The "Dow dogs" strategy became popular in the 1990s after beating the 30-stock Dow average by 6 percent per year over a 25-year period. For recent information on the performance of the dogs-of-the-Dow strategy, visit the Dogs-of-the-Dow website (www.dogsofthedow.com). To find more extensive information about this investment strategy, enter "Dogs of the Dow" into your favorite Internet search engine.

If you would like to try the dogs of the Dow strategy with your Stock-Trak account, obtain the names of the 30 stocks in the DJIA from *The Wall Street Journal*. Next, find these stocks in *The Wall Street Journal* stock price listings and record their dividend yields. Identify the 10 Dow stocks with the highest dividend yields and, just for fun, also record the 10 Dow stocks with the lowest dividend yields. You might try investing all your Stock-Trak funds in the high-dividend Dow stocks following a pure dogs of the Dow strategy. Alternatively, you can invest half of your funds in the low-dividend Dow stocks and the other half in the high-dividend Dow stocks and then compare which dividend strategy performs the best.

Value Versus Growth Stock Trading with Stock-Trak

Portfolio managers often pursue investment strategies based on either value stocks or growth stocks. With Stock-Trak you can try out these strategies yourself. Looking through *The Wall Street Journal* stock price listings, identify several low-P/E stocks and several high-P/E stocks. Try to find P/E ratios below 10 for the low-P/E stocks and P/E ratios greater than 40 for the high-P/E stocks. Use the low-P/E stocks to form a *value* portfolio and the high-P/E stocks to form a *growth* portfolio.

Using your Stock-Trak account, you can try several strategies based on your value and growth portfolios. You can invest all your Stock-Trak funds in the value portfolio or you can invest all your funds in the growth portfolio. Alternatively, you can invest half of your funds in each of the value and growth portfolios and compare which strategy performs the best. Extensive information about value and growth investing can be found on the Internet. Try entering "value versus growth" or "growth versus value" into your favorite Internet search engine. Other useful search phrases are "value investing" and "growth investing."

Stock-Trak Exercises

1. In a more sophisticated version of the dogs of the Dow strategy, you buy the high-dividend Dow stocks and short sell the low-dividend Dow stocks. This strategy requires a little more effort, but the results might be a little more interesting.

2. The "Leveraged Dogs Fund" allocates 75 percent of its portfolio to the dogs of the Dow strategy and holds the remaining 25 percent in U.S. Treasury securities. You can trade shares in this fund with Stock-Trak using the ticker symbol HDOGX for this fund. For more information on this fund, visit the Hennessy Funds website (www.hennessy-funds.com).

3. The S&P 500 index of large-company stocks, S&P 400 index of midsize company stocks, and S&P 600 index of small-company stocks have each been split into growth index shares and value index shares. Index shares are portfolios of stocks that trade like individual stocks and can be traded with Stock-Trak using their individual ticker symbols. Some suggested index shares and their ticker symbols are:

   S&P 500/Barra Large-Cap Value Index Shares (IVE)
   S&P 500/Barra Large-Cap Growth Index Shares (IVW)
   S&P 400/Barra Mid-Cap Growth Index Shares (IJK)
   S&P 400/Barra Mid-Cap Value Index Shares (IJJ)
   S&P 600/Barra Small-Cap Growth Index Shares (IJT)
   S&P 600/Barra Small-Cap Value Index Shares (IJS)

   For more information on index shares, visit the I-Shares website (www.ishares.com).

4. The Vanguard family of funds has several value and growth funds that you can trade through Stock-Trak. Some suggested funds and their ticker symbols are:

   Vanguard U.S. Value Fund (VUVLX)
   Vanguard U.S. Growth Equity Fund (VGEQX)
   Vanguard International Value Fund (VTRIX)
   Vanguard International Growth Fund (VWIGX)

   For more information on these funds, visit the Vanguard Funds website (www.vanguard.com).

Chapter 7

Earnings and Cash Flow Analysis

"Because that's where the money is."

–Willy Sutton

Of course, Willy Sutton was referring to banks in his famous response to a reporter's query of why he robbed them. But the same answer might be elicited from a security analyst explaining why so much attention is paid to analyzing cash flow. Cash flow is a company's lifeblood, and, for a healthy company, the primary source of cash flow is earnings. Little wonder that security analysts are obsessed with both. Their goal is to accurately predict future earnings and cash flow. An analyst who predicts well has a head start in assessing which stocks will do well and which stocks will do poorly. ■

In the previous chapter, we examined some important concepts of stock analysis and valuation. Here we probe deeper into the topic of common stock valuation through an analysis of earnings and cash flow. In particular, we focus on earnings and cash flow forecasting. This chapter will acquaint you with financial accounting concepts necessary to understand basic financial statements and perform earnings and cash flow analysis using these financial statements. You may not become an expert analyst—this requires experience. But you will have a grasp of the fundamentals, which is a good start.

Unfortunately, most investors have difficulty reading financial statements and instead rely on various secondary sources of financial information. Of course, this is good for those involved with publishing secondary financial information. Bear in mind, however, that no one is paid well just for reading such sources of financial information. By reading this chapter, you take an important step toward becoming financial statement literate, and an extra course in financial accounting is also helpful. But ultimately you learn to read financial statements by reading financial statements! Like a good game of golf or tennis, financial statement reading skills require practice. If you have an aptitude for it, financial statement analysis is a skill worth mastering. Good analysts are paid well, but good analysis is expected in return. Maybe you, too, can become one of the few, the proud—a financial analyst.

7.1 Sources of Financial Information

Good financial analysis begins with good financial information. An excellent primary source of financial information about any company is its annual report to stockholders. Most companies expend considerable resources preparing and distributing annual reports. In addition to their stockholders, companies also make annual reports available to anyone requesting a copy. A convenient way to request copies of annual reports from several companies simultaneously is to use the annual reports service provided by *The Wall Street Journal.* If you open the *Journal* to its daily stock price reports, you will see a shamrock symbol (♣) next to entries for many individual stocks. The shamrock indicates that the company will send annual reports to readers who request them through *The Wall Street Journal.* Requests can be submitted by telephone or by fax.

The Internet is a convenient source of financial information about many companies. For example, the New York Stock Exchange website (www.nyse.com) provides a directory of websites for companies whose stock trades on the exchange. The content of company websites varies greatly, but many provide recent quarterly or annual financial reports.

In addition to company annual reports, a wealth of primary financial information is available to investors through the Securities and Exchange Commission. The SEC requires corporations with publicly traded securities to prepare and submit financial statements on a regular basis. When received, these documents are made available for immediate public access through the SEC's Electronic Data Gathering and Retrieval (EDGAR) archives. The **EDGAR** archives are accessible free of charge through the Internet (www.sec.gov) and are an excellent source of timely financial information.

The most important EDGAR document is the annual **10K** report, often simply called the "10K." Companies are required to submit an EDGAR-compatible 10K file to the SEC at the end of each fiscal year. They are also required to file quarterly updates, called 10Qs. The **10Q** is a mini-10K filed each quarter, except when the 10K is filed. Every 10K and 10Q report contains three important financial statements: a balance sheet, an income statement, and a cash flow statement. You must be familiar with these three financial statements to analyze company earnings and cash flow.

The Securities and Exchange Commission's **Regulation FD (Fair Disclosure)** stipulates that when a company discloses material nonpublic information to security analysts and stockholders who may well trade on the basis of the information, it must also make a simultaneous disclosure of that information to the general public. Most companies satisfy Regulation FD by distributing important announcements via e-mail

Review Regulation FD at the SEC website www.sec.gov

EDGAR Electronic archive of company filings with the SEC.

10K Annual company report filed with the SEC.

10Q Quarterly updates of 10K reports filed with the SEC.

Regulation FD (Fair Disclosure) Requires companies making a public disclosure of material nonpublic information to do so fairly without preferential recipients.

alerts. To receive these e-mail alerts automatically, you need only register for the service at the company's website. You can usually find the registration page in the investor relations section of the company's website.

7.2 Financial Statements

balance sheet
Accounting statement that provides a snapshot view of a company's assets and liabilities on a particular date.

income statement
Summary statement of a firm's revenues and expenses over a specific accounting period, usually a quarter or a year.

cash flow statement
Analysis of a firm's sources and uses of cash over the accounting period, summarizing operating, investing, and financing cash flows.

Financial statements reveal the hard facts about a company's operating and financial performance. This is why the SEC requires timely dissemination of financial statements to the public. It's also why security analysts spend considerable time poring over a firm's financial statements before making an investment recommendation. A firm's balance sheet, income statement, and cash flow statement are essential reading for security analysts. Each of these interrelated statements offers a distinct perspective. The **balance sheet** provides a snapshot view of a company's assets and liabilities on a particular date. The **income statement** measures operating performance over an accounting period, usually a quarter or a year, and summarizes company revenues and expenses. The **cash flow statement** reports how cash was generated and where it was used over the accounting period. Understanding the format and contents of these three financial statements is a prerequisite for understanding earnings and cash flow analysis.

We begin by considering the basic structure and general format of financial statements through a descriptive analysis of the balance sheet, income statement, and cash flow statement of a hypothetical intergalactic company—the Borg Corporation.

The Balance Sheet

Look at the Research/Tools section at www.street.com

Table 7.1 presents year-end 2535 and 2536 balance sheets for Borg Corporation. The format of these balance sheets is typical of that contained in company annual reports distributed to stockholders and 10K filings with the SEC. Get used to the accounting practice of specifying subtraction with parentheses and calculating subtotals while moving down a column of numbers. For example, Borg's 2536 fixed assets section is reproduced below, with the left numerical column following standard accounting notation and the right numerical column following standard arithmetic notation:

Fixed Assets	Accounting Style	Numeric Style
Plant facilities	$35,000	$35,000
Production equipment	20,000	+20,000
Administrative facilities	15,000	+15,000
Patents	10,000	+10,000
Accumulated depreciation	(20,000)	−20,000
Total fixed assets	$60,000	$60,000

Common to both numerical columns, an underline indicates that the numbers listed above should be summed. However, accounting notation omits the plus "+" sign and subtraction is indicated by parentheses "( )" instead of the more familiar minus "−" sign. Referring to Table 7.1, notice that total fixed assets is a subtotal used to calculate total assets, which is indicated by a double underline. With these conventions in mind, let us look over these sample balance sheets and try to become familiar with their format and contents.

TABLE 7.1	Borg Corporation Balance Sheets, 2536 and 2535	
	Year 2536	**Year 2535**
Current assets		
Cash	$ 2,000	$ 1,356
Accounts receivable	1,200	1,200
Prepaid expenses	500	500
Materials and supplies	300	300
Inventory	6,000	6,000
Total current assets	$ 10,000	$ 9,356
Fixed assets		
Plant facilities	$ 35,000	$35,000
Production equipment	20,000	20,000
Administrative facilities	15,000	15,000
Patents	10,000	10,000
Accumulated depreciation	(20,000)	(17,000)
Total fixed assets	$60,000	$63,000
Investments		
Cardassian Mining		
7% Preferred stock	$ 10,000	$10,000
Klingon Enterprises		
Common stock	10,000	
Goodwill	5,000	
Total investments	$ 25,000	$10,000
Other assets	5,000	5,000
Total assets	$100,000	$87,356
Current liabilities		
Short-term debt	$ 10,000	$10,000
Accounts payable	2,000	2,000
Leasing obligations	3,000	3,000
Total current liabilities	$ 15,000	$15,000
Long-term debt	$ 30,000	$20,000
Other liabilities	5,000	5,000
Total liabilities	$ 50,000	$40,000
Stockholder equity		
Paid-in capital	$ 10,000	$10,000
Retained earnings	40,000	37,356
Total stockholder equity	$ 50,000	$47,356
Total liabilities and equity	$100,000	$87,356
Shares outstanding	2,000	2,000
Year-end stock price	$40	$36

asset Anything a company owns that has value.

The Borg Corporation balance sheet has four major **asset** categories: current assets, fixed assets, investments, and other assets. Current assets are cash or items that will be converted to cash or be used within a year. For example, inventory will be sold, accounts receivable will be collected, and materials and supplies will be used within a year. Cash is, of course, the quintessential current asset. Fixed assets have an expected life longer than one year and are used in normal business operations. Fixed assets may be tangible or intangible. Property, plant, and equipment are the most common tangible fixed assets. Rights, patents, and licenses are common intangible assets. Except for land, all fixed assets normally depreciate in value over time. Investments include various securities held for investment purposes. Goodwill measures the premium paid over market value to acquire an asset. For example, a company may pay $50 per share for stock with a market price of $40 per share when acquiring a very large block of stock. Other assets includes miscellaneous items not readily fitting into any of the other asset categories. The sum of these four categories of assets is the firm's total assets.

liability A firm's financial obligation.

The Borg balance sheet has three major **liability** categories: current liabilities, long-term debt, and other liabilities. Current liabilities normally require payment or other action within a one-year period. These include accounts payable and accrued taxes. Long-term debt includes notes, bonds, or other loans with a maturity longer than one year. Other liabilities include miscellaneous items not belonging to any other liability category.

equity An ownership interest in the company.

Stockholder **equity** is the difference between total assets and total liabilities. It includes paid-in capital, which is the amount received by the company from issuing common stock, and retained earnings, which represent accumulated income not paid out as dividends but instead used to finance company growth.

A fundamental accounting identity for balance sheets states that assets are equal to liabilities plus equity:

$$\text{Assets} = \text{Liabilities} + \text{Equity} \qquad (7.1)$$

This identity implies that the balance sheet always "balances" because the left side is always equal in value to the right side. If an imbalance occurs when a balance sheet is created, then an accounting error has been made and needs to be corrected.

Financial analysts often find it useful to condense a balance sheet down to its principal categories. This has the desirable effect of simplifying further analysis while still revealing the basic structure of the company's assets and liabilities. How much a balance sheet can be condensed and still be useful is a subjective judgment of the analyst. When making this decision, recall Albert Einstein's famous dictum: "Simplify as much as possible, but no more."

Table 7.2 is a condensed version of Borg's 2536 balance sheet that still preserves its basic structure. Notice that the current assets rows are reduced to two components, cash and operating assets. We separate cash from operating assets for a good reason.

TABLE 7.2	Borg Corporation Condensed 2536 Balance Sheet		
Cash	$ 2,000	Current liabilities	$ 15,000
Operating assets	8,000	Long-term debt	30,000
Fixed assets	60,000	Other liabilities	5,000
Investments	25,000		
Other assets	5,000	Stockholder equity	50,000
Total assets	$100,000	Total liabilities and equity	$100,000

Later, we show that the net cash increase from the cash flow statement is used to adjust cash on the balance sheet. This adjustment is more clearly illustrated by first separating current assets into cash and operating assets.

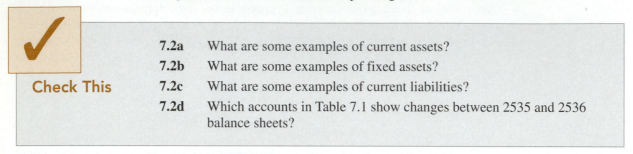

Check This		
	7.2a	What are some examples of current assets?
	7.2b	What are some examples of fixed assets?
	7.2c	What are some examples of current liabilities?
	7.2d	Which accounts in Table 7.1 show changes between 2535 and 2536 balance sheets?

The Income Statement

Table 7.3 is a condensed income statement for Borg Corporation. The left column follows standard accounting notation, and the right column follows familiar arithmetic notation. Of course, the right column would not appear in an actual financial statement and is included here for convenience only. This income statement reports revenues and expenses for the corporation over a one-year accounting period. Examine it carefully and be sure you are familiar with its top-down structure.

The income statement begins with net sales, from which cost of goods sold (COGS) is subtracted to yield gross profit. Cost of goods sold represents direct costs of production and sales, that is, costs that vary directly with the level of production and sales. Next, operating expenses are subtracted from gross profit to yield operating **income**. Operating expenses are indirect costs of administration and marketing; that is, costs that do not vary directly with production and sales.

income The difference between a company's revenues and expenses, used to pay dividends to stockholders or kept as retained earnings within the company to finance future growth.

TABLE 7.3	Borg Corporation Condensed Income Statement	
Net sales	$90,000	$90,000
Cost of goods sold	(70,000)	−70,000
Gross profit	$20,000	$20,000
Operating expenses	(13,000)	−13,000
Operating income	$ 7,000	$ 7,000
Investment income	700	+700
Interest expense	(2,000)	−2,000
Pretax income	$ 5,700	$ 5,700
Income taxes[a]	(2,056)	−2,056
Net income	$ 3,644	$ 3,644
Dividends	(1,000)	−1,000
Retained earnings	$ 2,644	$ 2,644

[a]A tax rate of 40 percent is applied to the total of operating income less interest expense plus the taxable 20 percent portion of preferred stock dividends (recorded as investment income): $7,000 − $2000 + 20% × $700 = $5,140 and 40% × $5,140 = $2,056.

In addition to operating income from its own business operations, Borg Corporation has investment income from preferred stock dividends. Adding this investment income and then subtracting interest expense on debt yields pretax income. Finally, subtracting income taxes from pretax income yields net income. Net income is often referred to as the "bottom line" because it is normally the last line of the income statement. In this example, however, we have added dividends and retained earnings information, items that often appear in a separate financial statement. To avoid a separate statement, we show here that Borg Corporation paid dividends during the year. The sum of dividends and retained earnings is equal to net income:

$$\text{Net income} = \text{Dividends} + \text{Retained earnings} \qquad (7.2)$$

The footnote to Table 7.3 explains that only 20 percent of preferred stock dividends are taxable. This feature of the federal tax code allows a company to exclude 80 percent of dividends received from another company from federal income tax.[1] In this case, Borg receives $700 in dividends from Cardassian Mining and pays taxes on only $140 (20 percent) of this amount. Assuming a 40 percent tax rate, the actual tax amount is $56 = 40\% \times \$140$.

Check This

7.2e	What is cost of goods sold (COGS)?
7.2f	What is the difference between gross profit and operating income?
7.2g	What is the difference between net income and pretax income?
7.2h	What is meant by retained earnings?

The Cash Flow Statement

cash flow Income realized in cash form.

noncash items Income and expense items not realized in cash form.

operating cash flow Cash generated by a firm's normal business operations.

investment cash flow Cash flow resulting from purchases and sales of fixed assets and investments.

The cash flow statement reports where a company generated cash and where cash was used over a specific accounting period. The cash flow statement assigns all cash flows to one of three categories: operating cash flows, investment cash flows, or financing cash flows.

Table 7.4 is a condensed cash flow statement for Borg Corporation. (This is the last appearance of both accounting and arithmetic notation.) The cash flow statement begins with net income, which is the principal accounting measure of earnings for a corporation. However, net income and **cash flow** are not the same and often deviate greatly from each other. A primary reason why income differs from cash flow is that income contains **noncash items**. For example, depreciation is a noncash expense that must be added to net income when calculating cash flow. Adjusting net income for noncash items yields **operating cash flow**.

Operating cash flow is the first of three cash flow categories reported in the cash flow statement. The second and third categories are investment cash flow and financing cash flow. **Investment cash flow** (or "investing" cash flow) includes any

[1] Actually, the exclusion is either 70 or 80 percent depending on how much of another company's stock is held.

TABLE 7.4	Borg Corporation Condensed Cash Flow Statement			
Net income		$ 3,644		$ 3,644
Depreciation		3,000		+3,000
Operating cash flow		$ 6,644		$ 6,644
Investment cash flow[a]		(15,000)		−15,000
Financing cash flow[b]		9,000		+9,000
Net cash increase		$ 644		$ 644

[a]December 2536 purchase of 50 percent interest in Klingon Enterprises for $15,000 (including $5,000 goodwill).

[b]Issue of $10,000 par value 8 percent coupon bonds, less a $1,000 dividend payout.

purchases or sales of fixed assets and investments. For example, Borg's purchase of Klingon Enterprises common stock reported in footnote "a" is an investment cash flow. **Financing cash flow** includes any funds raised by an issuance of securities or expended by a repurchase of outstanding securities. In this example, Borg's $10,000 debt issue and $1,000 dividend payout reported in footnote "b" are examples of financing cash flows.

financing cash flow
Cash flow originating from the issuance or repurchase of securities and the payment of dividends.

Standard accounting practice specifies that dividend payments to stockholders are financing cash flows, whereas interest payments to bondholders are operating cash flows. One reason is that dividend payments are discretionary, while interest payments are mandatory. Also, interest payments are tax-deductible expenses, but dividend payouts are not tax deductible. In any case, interest payments are cash expenses reported on the income statement. Since they are cash expenses, they do not appear in the cash flow statement to reconcile the difference between income and cash flow.

The sum of operating cash flow, investment cash flow, and financing cash flow yields the net change in the firm's cash. This change is the "bottom line" of the cash flow statement and reveals how much cash flowed into or out of the company's cash account during an accounting period.

Check This

7.2i	What is the difference between net income and operating cash flow?
7.2j	What are some noncash items used to calculate operating cash flow?
7.2k	What is the difference between an investment cash flow and a financing cash flow?
7.2l	What is meant by net increase in cash?
7.2m	Can you explain why a cash item like interest expense does not appear on the cash flow statement?

Performance Ratios and Price Ratios

Annual reports and 10Ks normally contain various items of supplemental information about the company. For example, certain profitability ratios may be reported to assist interpretation of the company's operating efficiency. For Borg Corporation, some standard profitability ratios for 2536 are calculated as follows.

Ratio	Formula	Calculation
Gross margin	$\dfrac{\text{Gross profit}}{\text{Net sales}}$	$\dfrac{\$20,000}{\$90,000} = 22.22\%$
Operating margin	$\dfrac{\text{Operating income}}{\text{Net sales}}$	$\dfrac{\$7,000}{\$90,000} = 7.78\%$
Return on assets (ROA)	$\dfrac{\text{Net income}}{\text{Total assets}}$	$\dfrac{\$3,644}{\$100,000} = 3.64\%$
Return on equity (ROE)	$\dfrac{\text{Net income}}{\text{Stockholder equity}}$	$\dfrac{\$3,644}{\$50,000} = 7.29\%$

return on assets (ROA) Net income stated as a percentage of total assets.

return on equity (ROE) Net income stated as a percentage of stockholder equity.

Notice that **return on assets (ROA)** and **return on equity (ROE)** are calculated using current year-end values for total assets and stockholder equity. It could be argued that prior-year values should be used for these calculations. However, the use of current year-end values is more common.

Annual reports and 10Ks may also report per-share calculations of book value, earnings, and operating cash flow, respectively. Per-share calculations require the number of common stock shares outstanding. Borg's balance sheet reports 2,000 shares of common stock outstanding. Thus, for Borg Corporation, these per-share values are calculated as follows:

Check out the security analysis sections at www.uoutperform.com

Ratio	Formula	Calculation
Book value per share (BVPS)	$\dfrac{\text{Stockholder equity}}{\text{Shares outstanding}}$	$\dfrac{\$50,000}{2,000} = \$25$
Earnings per share (EPS)	$\dfrac{\text{Net income}}{\text{Shares outstanding}}$	$\dfrac{\$3,644}{2,000} = \$1.82$
Cash flow per share (CFPS)	$\dfrac{\text{Operating cash flow}}{\text{Shares outstanding}}$	$\dfrac{\$6,644}{2,000} = \$3.32$

Notice that cash flow per share (CFPS) is calculated using operating cash flow—*not* the bottom line on the cash flow statement! Most of the time when you hear the term "cash flow," it refers to operating cash flow.

Recall that in the previous chapter, we made extensive use of price ratios to analyze stock values. Using per-share values calculated immediately above, and Borg's year-end stock price of $40 per share, we get the following (rounded) price ratios:

Ratio	Formula	Calculation
Price-book (P/B)	$\dfrac{\text{Stock price}}{\text{BVPS}}$	$\dfrac{\$40}{\$25} = 1.6$
Price-earnings (P/E)	$\dfrac{\text{Stock price}}{\text{EPS}}$	$\dfrac{\$40}{\$1.82} = 22$
Price-cash flow (P/CF)	$\dfrac{\text{Stock price}}{\text{CFPS}}$	$\dfrac{\$40}{\$3.32} = 12$

WORK THE WEB

One of the more common uses of financial ratios is stock screening. Stock screening is the process of selecting stocks based on specific criteria. A popular method used by the legendary investor Warren Buffett, among others, is searching for value stocks that have high growth potential. A value stock has relatively low price ratios. However, low price ratios can also be an indication of low future growth potential, so we also want to determine if these stocks have future growth possibilities. We went to www.valueline.com and used the stock screener we found there. We searched for companies with low price ratios and high estimated future growth. Here is what we found:

Value Line Stock Screener - Result Table	Click here to edit display options					
Results: 1 - 8 out of 8 stock(s) « Previous 1 - 8 ▼ Next » Export Results Print-Friendly						
Company (Ticker)	PE Trailing 12 Mo	Price to Book Value	Price/Sales Ratio	Total Return 10-Year	Cash Flow Growth 10-Year	EPS Growth 10-Year
(1) Aviall, Inc. (AVL)	10.03	0.88	0.22	-	-	-
(2) Centex Corp. (CTX)	8.80	1.32	0.55	16.71	20.00	21.00
(3) Enesco Group (ENC)	17.24	0.80	0.44	-9.26	-13.50	-19.00
(4) Fedders Corp. (FJC)	16.21	1.22	0.25	-	-	-
(5) Hancock Fabrics (HKF)	13.65	1.72	0.63	7.19	-4.00	-5.50
(6) Hovnanian Enterpr. 'A' (HOV)	9.90	1.49	0.59	13.85	50.50	-
(7) Sunrise Asst. Living (SRZ)	9.82	1.23	1.07	-	-	-
(8) Thor Inds. (THO)	14.23	1.98	0.69	17.15	21.00	23.00

Examining the stocks we uncovered, Centex Corporation, Hovnanian Enterprises, and Thor Industries appear to be classic value stocks since they have low price ratios and high estimated future growth. These three companies have also had excellent returns over the past 10 years.

Using stock screening as an investment tool is not really this simple. What we have done here is narrowed the universe of stocks to a few stocks that meet our criteria. It is now up to us to further examine the companies to determine if they are actually good investments. In other words, stock screening is not the end of the investment process—it simply narrows the field.

We use these price ratios later when assessing the potential impact of a sales campaign on Borg Corporation's future stock price. Our nearby *Work the Web* box shows another use for price ratios.

Check This

7.2n	What is the difference between gross margin and operating margin?
7.2o	What is the difference between return on assets and return on equity?
7.2p	What is the difference between earnings per share and cash flow per share?
7.2q	How is cash flow per share calculated?

7.3 Financial Statement Forecasting

In December 2536, Borg publicly announced the completed acquisition of a 50 percent financial interest in Ferengi Traders. However, half the acquired shares do not carry voting rights, so the acquisition is treated as a simple investment on the balance sheet. The stated purpose of the acquisition was to expand sales outlets. Complementing the acquisition, Borg also announces plans for a marketing campaign to increase next year's net sales to a targeted $120,000.

pro forma financial statements
Statements prepared using certain assumptions about future income, cash flow, and other items. Pro forma literally means according to prescribed form.

As a Borg analyst, you must examine the potential impact of these actions. You immediately contact Borg management to inquire about the details of the acquisition and the marketing campaign. Armed with this additional information, you decide to construct **pro forma financial statements** for Borg Corporation for the year 2537. You also decide to formulate your analysis by considering two scenarios: an optimistic sales scenario and a pessimistic sales scenario. Under the optimistic scenario, the marketing campaign is successful and targeted net sales of $120,000 are realized with an assumed cost of goods sold of $90,000. Under the pessimistic scenario, only $100,000 of net sales are realized with a cost of goods sold of $80,000. Operating expenses will be $17,000 under both scenarios, reflecting the costs of the marketing campaign. The appropriate sequence for your analysis is to construct pro forma income statements, then pro forma cash flow statements, followed by pro forma balance sheets.

The Pro Forma Income Statement

Table 7.5 contains side-by-side pro forma income statements for Borg Corporation corresponding to optimistic and pessimistic sales scenarios in the coming year. These

TABLE 7.5	Borg Corporation Pro Forma Income Statements	
	Optimistic	**Pessimistic**
Net sales	$120,000	$100,000
Cost of goods sold	(90,000)	(80,000)
Gross profit	$ 30,000	$ 20,000
Operating expenses	(17,000)	(17,000)
Operating income	$ 13,000	$ 3,000
Investment income[a]	2,200	700
Interest expense[b]	(2,800)	(2,800)
Pretax income	$ 12,400	$ 900
Income taxes[c]	(4,136)	(136)
Net income	$ 8,264	$ 764
Dividends[d]	$ 1,000	$ 1,000
Retained earnings	$ 7,264	$ (236)

[a]Preferred stock dividends of $700 plus $1,500 noncash investment income from Ferengi Traders under optimistic sales results and $0 under pessimistic sales results, i.e., $700 + $1,500 = $2,200.

[b]Prior-year interest expense of $2,000 plus payment of 8 percent coupons on the December 2536 debt issue of $10,000, i.e. $2,000 + 8% × $10,000 = $2,800.

[c]Tax rate of 40% applied to the sum of operating income less interest expense plus the 20 percent taxable portion of preferred stock dividends, i.e., ($13,000 − $2,800 + 20% × $700) × 40% = $4,136.

[d]Assumes no change in dividends from prior year.

Visit the
Education Center at
www.sec.gov

begin with the assumed net sales and cost of goods sold values for both scenarios. They then proceed with the standard top-down calculations of income where several calculation methods and additional assumptions are explained in footnotes. The optimistic sales scenario produces a net income of $8,264, of which $1,000 is paid as dividends and $7,264 is kept as retained earnings. Under the pessimistic sales scenario net income is only $764, with $1,000 of dividends and −$236 of retained earnings.

Footnote "a" explains that investment income is $2,200 under optimistic sales and $700 under pessimistic sales. This reflects constant preferred stock dividends of $700 and assumed noncash investment income from Ferengi Traders of $1,500 under optimistic sales and $0 under pessimistic sales. The difference in scenario investment incomes stems from the fact that Ferengi is involved with the sales campaign.

Footnote "c" explains that taxes are paid on operating income less interest expense plus the taxable portion of preferred stock dividends. Notice that Borg's noncash investment income from Ferengi Traders is not taxed because Ferengi paid no dividends. In this situation, Borg records the value of its investment in Ferengi as its share of Ferengi's stockholder equity value. Thus, when Ferengi adds retained earnings to its equity value, Borg records its share of the addition as noncash income and changes the balance sheet value of its investment in Ferengi accordingly. The next step of your analysis is construction of pro forma cash flow statements.

Check This

7.3a	Create a pro forma income statement for Borg Corporation corresponding to pessimistic sales results assuming noncash investment losses of $1,000.

The Pro Forma Cash Flow Statement

Table 7.6 contains side-by-side pro forma cash flow statements for Borg Corporation under optimistic and pessimistic sales scenarios. Under the optimistic sales scenario

TABLE 7.6	Borg Corporation Pro Forma Cash Flow Statements	
	Optimistic	**Pessimistic**
Net income	$ 8,264	$ 764
Depreciation/amortization[a]	3,200	3,200
Increase in operating assets[b]	(2,000)	(3,000)
Noncash investment income	(1,500)	0
Operating cash flow	$ 7,964	$ 964
Investment cash flow[c]	$ 0	$ 0
Financing cash flow[d]	$ (1,000)	$ (1,000)
Net cash increase	$ 6,964	$ (36)

[a]Assumes the same $3,000 depreciation as in the prior year and annual goodwill amortization of $200 based on a 25-year amortization schedule.
[b]Assumes an increase in operating assets of $2,000 under optimistic sales and $3,000 under pessimistic sales.
[c]Assumes no new investments.
[d]Assumes no change in dividend payouts.

the net cash increase is $6,964; under the pessimistic scenario the net cash change is −$36. The net cash increase is applied to adjust the cash account on the pro forma balance sheet. This adjustment is now more convenient since you separated cash from operating assets in Borg's condensed balance sheet.

Footnote "a" explains that goodwill amortization is $200 per year based on a 25-year amortization schedule. This amortization is applied to the $5,000 of goodwill on Borg's prior-year balance sheet associated with its purchase of a 50 percent stake in Ferengi Traders. Footnote "b" explains that operating assets are assumed to increase by $2,000 under optimistic sales and $3,000 under pessimistic sales. These increases are realistic since a sales campaign will surely require additional inventory. The increase is bigger under pessimistic sales because more inventory goes unsold. Your next step is to create the pro forma balance sheet for Borg Corporation.

Check This

7.3b Create a pro forma cash flow statement for Borg Corporation under pessimistic sales results assuming noncash investment losses of $1,000.

The Pro Forma Balance Sheet

Table 7.7 contains side-by-side pro forma balance sheets for Borg Corporation as they might result from optimistic and pessimistic sales scenarios. This balance sheet is

TABLE 7.7	Borg Corporation Pro Forma Balance Sheets		
		Optimistic	**Pessimistic**
Cash[a]		$ 8,964	$ 1,964
Operating assets[b]		10,000	11,000
Fixed assets[c]		57,000	57,000
Investments[d]		26,300	24,800
Other assets		5,000	5,000
Total assets		$107,264	$99,764
Current liabilities		$ 15,000	$15,000
Long-term debt		30,000	30,000
Other liabilities		5,000	5,000
Stockholder equity[e]		57,264	49,764
Total liabilities and equity		$107,264	$99,764

[a]Prior-year cash of $2,000 plus $6,964 (optimistic) and −$36 (pessimistic) net cash increase from the pro forma cash flow statement.
[b]Prior-year operating assets of $8,000 plus an additional $2,000 under optimistic sales and $3,000 under pessimistic sales.
[c]Prior-year fixed assets of $60,000 less the assumed $3,000 depreciation.
[d]Prior-year investments of $25,000 plus noncash investment income of $1,500 under optimistic sales only less $200 goodwill amortization.
[e]Prior-year equity of $50,000 plus $7,264 (optimistic) and −$236 (pessimistic) retained earnings from the pro forma income statement.

created by starting with the prior-year condensed balance sheet and then making the following adjustments consistent with the pro forma income statements and cash flow statements:

1. Cash of $2,000 is adjusted by a net cash increase of $6,964 under the optimistic sales scenario and −$36 under the pessimistic sales scenario.

2. Operating assets of $8,000 are increased by $2,000 under the optimistic sales scenario and increased by $3,000 under the pessimistic sales scenario.

3. Fixed assets of $60,000 are adjusted by depreciation of $3,000, which is the same under both sales scenarios.

4. Investments of $25,000 are increased by the assumed noncash investment income from Ferengi Traders of $1,500 under optimistic sales and $0 under pessimistic sales, less $200 of goodwill amortization. As noted earlier, the difference by scenario is based on the fact that Ferengi is involved with the sales campaign.

5. Equity of $50,000 is adjusted for retained earnings of $7,264 under optimistic sales and −$236 under pessimistic sales.

All other accounts remain unchanged, which is a simplifying assumption made to focus attention on the immediate impact of the sales campaign.

7.3c   Create a pro forma balance sheet for Borg under a pessimistic sales scenario assuming noncash investment losses of $1,000.

Check This

Projected Profitability and Price Ratios

In addition to preparing pro forma financial statements, you also decide to calculate projected profitability ratios and per-share values under optimistic and pessimistic sales scenarios. These are reported immediately below and compared with their original year-end values.

	Original	Optimistic	Pessimistic
Gross margin	22.22%	25%	20%
Operating margin	7.78%	10.83%	3%
Return on assets (ROA)	3.64%	7.70%	.77%
Return on equity (ROE)	7.29%	14.43%	1.54%
Book value per share (BVPS)	$25	$28.63	$24.88
Earnings per share (EPS)	$1.82	$4.13	$.38
Cash flow per share (CFPS)	$3.32	$3.98	$.48

One common method of analysis is to calculate projected stock prices under optimistic and pessimistic sales scenarios using prior-period price ratios and projected per-share values from pro forma financial statements. Similar procedures were performed in the previous chapter using prior-period average price ratios and per-share values based on growth rate projections. For Borg Corporation, you decide to take your previously calculated year-end 2536 price ratios and multiply each ratio by its corresponding pro forma per-share value. The results of these projected stock price calculations (rounded) are shown immediately below.

	Projected Stock Prices	
	Optimistic	**Pessimistic**
BVPS $\times$ P/B	$45.81	$39.81
EPS $\times$ P/E	$90.86	$ 8.36
CFPS $\times$ P/CF	$47.76	$ 5.76

These projected stock prices reflect widely varying degrees of sensitivity to optimistic and pessimistic sales scenario outcomes. For example, projected prices based on EPS and CFPS are especially sensitive to which scenario is realized. On the other hand, projected stock prices based on BVPS are far less sensitive to scenario realization.

Which projected stock price is correct? Well, it clearly depends on which sales scenario is realized and which price ratio the financial markets will actually use to value Borg Corporation's stock. This is where experience and breadth of knowledge count immensely. Of course, no one can make perfectly accurate predictions, but the analyst's job is to expertly assess the situation and make an investment recommendation supported by reasonable facts and investigation. But some analysts are better than others. Like professional baseball players, professional stock analysts with better batting averages can do very well financially.

7.4   Adolph Coors Company Case Study

After carefully reading the analysis of Borg Corporation, you should have a reasonably clear picture of how earnings and cash flow analyses might proceed using pro forma financial statements. To further illustrate the use of pro forma financial statements in earnings and cash flow analysis, this section presents an analysis based on the 2002 financial statements for Adolph Coors Company. Using data for a real company provides a real challenge.

This section begins with a review of Coors 2002 financial statements. We then proceed to analyze the effects on earnings and cash flow that might result from product sales either rising or falling by 10 percent. The analysis is similar to that for Borg Corporation, but there are a few important differences. Note that amounts shown are in thousands of dollars (except earnings per share).

Adolph Coors 2002 condensed balance sheet is shown in Table 7.8. This balance sheet shows that at year-end 2002 Coors had $4.297 billion of total assets and $981.9 million of shareholder equity. In Table 7.9, the Adolph Coors 2002 condensed income statement, the bottom line reveals that Coors earned $161.7 million in net income from $3,776 million in net sales. From these values, we calculate Adolph Coors's return on assets as 3.76 percent and return on equity as 16.46 percent. Also, with 36.16 million shares outstanding, Coors realized 2002 earnings per share of $4.47. Finally, based on Coors 2002 year-end stock price of $61.25, we obtain a price-book ratio of 2.26 and a price-earnings ratio of 13.70.

The operating cash flow section of Adolph Coors condensed 2002 cash flow statement (Table 7.10) shows that in 2002 deferred taxes decreased and losses were realized on property sales. The investing cash flow section reveals large net purchases of

Visit Coors website at www.coors.com

TABLE 7.8	Adolph Coors Company 2002 Balance Sheet ($ in 000)	
Cash	$ 59,167	
Operating assets	994,729	
Property, plant, equipment	1,380,239	
Goodwill	727,069	
Other assets	1,136,207	
Total assets	$4,297,411	
Current liabilities	$1,147,891	
Long-term debt	1,383,392	
Other liabilities	784,277	
Total liabilities	$3,315,560	
Paid-in capital & other	$ (105,114)	
Retained earnings	1,086,965	
Total shareholder equity	$ 981,851	
Total liabilities and equity	$4,297,411	

TABLE 7.9	Adolph Coors Company 2002 Income Statement ($ in 000)	
Net sales	$3,776,322	
Cost of goods sold	(2,414,530)	
Gross profit	$1,361,792	
Operating expenses	(1,063,507)	
Operating income	$ 298,285	
Other income	(41,685)	
Pretax income	$ 256,600	
Income tax	(94,947)	
Net income	$ 161,653	
Earnings per share	$4.47	
Shares outstanding (000)	36,164	

properties. The financing cash flow section shows that cash was raised by issuing long-term debt. The bottom line of the cash flow statement is that Coors realized a 2002 operating cash flow of $258.5 million, with cash flow per share of $7.15 and a price-cash flow ratio of 8.57.

We now move on to what-if analyses of earnings and cash flow. Specifically, what might happen to earnings and cash flow if product sales increased or decreased by 10 percent? To perform this analysis, we proceed through the same sequence of operations as before. That is, we first create a pro forma income statement, then a pro forma cash flow statement, and finally a pro forma balance sheet.

TABLE 7.10	Adolph Coors Company 2002 Cash Flow Statement ($ in 000)
Net income	$ 161,653
Depreciation and amortization	230,299
Earnings in joint ventures	(54,958)
Loss on sale of properties	(9,816)
Change in deferred taxes	(2,819)
Changes in operating assets	(447,367)
Changes in current liabilities	630,346
Other operating cash flows	(248,793)
Operating cash flow	$ 258,545
Net additions to properties	$(1,836,892)
Changes in other assets	252,554
Investing cash flow	$(1,584,338)
Issuance/redemption of long-term debt	$ 2,391,934
Payment on debt and lease obligations	(1,379,718)
Issuance/purchase of stock	15,645
Dividends paid	(29,669)
Other financing	293,476
Financing cash flow	$ 1,291,668
Net cash increase	$ (34,125)

Pro forma income statements corresponding to a 10 percent increase and a 10 percent decrease in net sales and cost of goods sold for Coors are shown in Table 7.11. For convenience, italics indicate times for which constant 2002 values are used. The ± 10 percent changes in net sales and cost of goods sold cause gross profit to increase and decrease by 10 percent also. However, since operating expenses are assumed to be a constant 2002 value across the two sales scenarios, operating income varies considerably. By assuming the same average tax rate as in 2002, we obtain net income values across both sales scenarios. Then, letting 2002 dividends continue unchanged, we get very different pro forma retained earnings values. These retained earnings values from the pro forma income statement will be used to adjust cumulative retained earnings on the pro forma balance sheet. But first we take these pro forma net income values as starting points to create pro forma cash flow statements.

Pro forma cash flow statements for Coors appear in Table 7.12, where italics indicate that constant 2002 values are used. These statements begin with pro forma net income values, to which we add back constant 2002 depreciation and amortization expenses and also adjust for constant 2002 changes in operating assets and current liabilities. This yields operating cash flows across both sales scenarios. Since our intention is to isolate the impacts of changes in net sales, we set investment cash flow equal to zero in both sales scenarios. Similarly, for financing cash flows, we set the change in long-term debt to zero. Then, summing operating, investment, and financing cash flows yields net cash increases for the two sales scenarios. Now, we move on to the pro forma balance sheets.

To create Coors pro forma balance sheets as in Table 7.13, the first two steps are:

1. Adjust retained earnings on the balance sheet with retained earnings from the income statement.

TABLE 7.11	Adolph Coors Company Pro Forma 2003 Income Statements ($ in 000, except earnings per share)	
Sales Growth (%)	+10%	−10%
Net sales	$4,153,954	$3,398,690
Cost of goods sold[a]	(2,655,983)	(2,173,077)
Gross profit	$1,497,971	$1,225,613
*Operating expenses**	(1,063,507)	(1,063,507)
Operating income	$ 434,464	$ 162,106
Other income	(41,685)	(41,685)
Pretax income	$ 392,779	$ 120,421
Income tax[b]	(145,368)	(44,568)
Net income	$ 247,412	$ 75,853
Dividends	$ 29,669	$ 29,669
Retained earnings	$ 217,743	$ 46,184
Earnings per share	$6.84	$2.10
Shares outstanding	36,164	36,164

[a]Assumes a constant 2002 gross margin, which implies that cost of goods sold changes by the same ±10% as net sales.

[b]Assumes a constant 2002 average tax rate of 37.01 percent.

*Italics indicate items with constant 2002 values.

TABLE 7.12	Adolph Coors Company Pro Forma 2003 Cash Flow Statements ($ in 000)	
Sales Growth (%)	+10%	−10%
Net income	$247,412	$ 75,853
*Depreciation/amortization**	230,299	230,299
Changes in operating assets	(447,367)	(447,367)
Changes in current liabilities	630,346	630,346
Other operating cash flows	(248,793)	(248,793)
Operating cash flow	$411,897	$240,338
Investing cash flow[a]	0	0
Financing cash flow[b]	(29,669)	(29,669)
Net cash increase	$382,228	$210,669

[a]Assumes zero investment cash flows.

[b]Assumes a zero change in shares outstanding, long-term debt, and other financing, but constant 2002 dividends of $29,669.

*Italics indicate items with constant 2002 values.

2. Adjust cash on the balance sheet with net cash increase from the cash flow statement.

Since retained earnings and the net cash increase are not equal, at this point the balance sheets will not balance. However, all items making up the difference between retained earnings and the net cash increase appear on the cash flow statement. Therefore, all

TABLE 7.13	Adolph Coors Company Pro Forma 2003 Balance Sheet ($ in 000)	
Sales Growth (%)	+10%	−10%
Cash	$ 441,395	$ 269,836
Operating assets[a]	1,690,889	1,690,889
Property, plant, equipment[b]	1,222,647	1,222,647
Goodwill	654,362	654,362
Other assets*	1,136,207	1,136,207
Total assets	$5,145,500	$4,973,941
Current liabilities[c]	$1,778,237	$1,778,237
Long-term debt	1,383,392	1,383,392
Other liabilities	784,277	784,277
Total liabilities	$3,945,906	$3,945,906
Paid-in capital	$ (105,114)	$ (105,114)
Retained earnings	1,304,708	1,133,149
Total shareholder equity	$1,199,549	$1,028,035
Total liabilities and equity	$5,145,500	$4,973,941

[a]2002 Operating assets of $994,729 plus an increase of $447,367 + 248,793 = $696,160.

[b]Depreciation and amortization of $230,299 is allocated as $72,707 of amortization (10 percent of 2002 goodwill) and $157,592 of depreciation.

[c]2002 Current liabilities of $1,147,891 plus $630,346.

*Italics indicate items with constant 2002 values.

subsequent adjustments will come from the cash flow statement. In this example, two adjustments are needed.

First, property, plant, and equipment and goodwill accounts must be adjusted to reflect depreciation and amortization. For realistic detail, notice that constant 2002 depreciation and amortization of $230,299 is allocated in 2003 as $72,707 of amortization (10 percent of 2002 goodwill) and $157,592 of depreciation as follows.

2002 Property, plant, and equipment	$1,380,239
2003 Depreciation	(157,592)
2003 Property, plant, and equipment	$1,222,647
2002 Goodwill	$ 727,069
2003 Amortization	(72,707)
2003 Goodwill	$ 654,362

Since depreciation and amortization are part of the difference between retained earnings and net cash flow, these adjustments move the balance sheet closer to balancing. Second, the operating assets line is increased by $696,160 and current liabilities increased by $630,346. This brings the balance sheet to a complete balance.

To complete the analysis of Adolph Coors, projected profitability ratios and per-share values under increased and decreased sales scenarios are reported immediately below and compared with their original year-end 2002 values.

Scenario	Original	+10 Percent	−10 Percent
Gross margin	36.06%	36.06%	36.06%
Operating margin	7.90%	10.46%	4.77%
Return on assets (ROA)	3.76%	4.81%	1.53%
Return on equity (ROE)	16.46%	20.62%	7.38%
Book value per share (BVPS)	$27.15	$33.17	$28.43
Earnings per share (EPS)	$4.47	$6.84	$2.10
Cash flow per share (CFPS)	$7.15	$11.39	$6.65

For Adolph Coors Company, taking year-end 2002 price ratios and multiplying each ratio by its corresponding projected 2003 per-share value results in the following projected stock price calculations (subject to minor rounding errors):

Scenario	Projected Stock Prices	
	+10 Percent	−10 Percent
BVPS × P/B	$74.83	$64.13
EPS × P/E	$93.74	$28.74
CFPS × P/CF	$97.58	$56.94

These projected stock prices reflect widely varying degrees of sensitivity to sales scenario outcomes. Earnings per share and cash flow per share are especially sensitive to which scenario is realized, while book value per share is less sensitive to scenario realization.

7.5   Summary and Conclusions

This chapter focuses on earnings and cash flow analysis using financial statement information. Several important aspects of financial statements and their use were covered. These are summarized as follows:

1. A primary source of financial information is a company's annual report. In addition, the annual 10K report and the quarterly 10Q updates filed with the SEC are available from the EDGAR archives.

2. Three financial statements are essential reading for securities analysts: the balance sheet, the income statement, and the cash flow statement.

3. The balance sheet has three sections: assets, which are used to generate earnings; liabilities, which are financial obligations; and equity, representing ownership claims. A fundamental accounting identity for balance sheets states that assets are equal to liabilities plus equity:

$$Assets = Liabilities + Equity$$

4. The balance sheet has four major asset categories: current assets, fixed assets, investments, and other assets.

5. The balance sheet has three major liability categories: current liabilities, long-term debt, and other liabilities.

6. The income statement reports revenues and expenses. Income is used to pay dividends or retained to finance future growth. Net income is the "bottom line" for a company.

7. The cash flow statement reports how cash was generated and where it was used. The cash flow statement assigns all cash flows to one of three categories: operating cash flow, investment cash flow, or financing cash flow. The sum of operating cash flow, investment cash flow, and financing cash flow yields the net cash increase.

8. Profitability ratios based on financial statement information are often reported to assist interpretation of a company's operating efficiency. Some standard profitability ratios are calculated as follows:

$$\text{Gross margin} = \frac{\text{Gross profit}}{\text{Net sales}}$$

$$\text{Operating margin} = \frac{\text{Operating income}}{\text{Net sales}}$$

$$\text{Return on assets (ROA)} = \frac{\text{Net income}}{\text{Total assets}}$$

$$\text{Return on equity (ROE)} = \frac{\text{Net income}}{\text{Stockholder equity}}$$

9. Annual reports and 10Ks may also report per-share calculations of book value, earnings, and operating cash flow, respectively. These per-share values are calculated as follows:

$$\text{Book value per share (BVPS)} = \frac{\text{Stockholder equity}}{\text{Shares outstanding}}$$

$$\text{Earnings per share (EPS)} = \frac{\text{Net income}}{\text{Shares outstanding}}$$

$$\text{Cash flow per share (CFPS)} = \frac{\text{Operating cash flow}}{\text{Shares outstanding}}$$

Dividing the common stock price by the preceding per-share values, we get the following price ratios:

$$\text{Price-book ratio (P/B)} = \frac{\text{Stock price}}{\text{BVPS}}$$

$$\text{Price-earnings ratio (P/E)} = \frac{\text{Stock price}}{\text{EPS}}$$

$$\text{Price-cash flow ratio (P/CF)} = \frac{\text{Stock price}}{\text{CFPS}}$$

10. One common method of analysis is to calculate projected stock prices using prior-period price ratios and projected per-share values from pro forma financial statements. These projected stock prices are calculated as follows:

$$\text{BVPS} \times \text{P/B} = \text{Projected price based on pro forma book value}$$

$$\text{EPS} \times \text{P/E} = \text{Projected price based on pro forma earnings}$$

$$\text{CFPS} \times \text{P/CF} = \text{Projected price based on pro forma cash flow}$$

Get Real

This chapter builds on the preceding chapter by going deeper into earnings and cash flow concepts, which are two of the most important tools of fundamental analysis. It focuses on using financial statement information to develop pro forma numbers to use in stock valuation. How should you, as an investor or investment manager, get started putting this information to work? The answer is you need to get your fingers dirty! Dig into the financial statements of a few companies and develop your own pro forma financial statements.

Excellent sources for financial statement information are the SEC Edgar database (www.sec.gov) and Free EDGAR (www.freeedgar.com). Other useful online sources are Report Gallery (www.reportgallery.com), Annual Report Service (www.annualreport-service.com), and Free Annual Reports (www.prars.com). Other useful Internet sites for company analysis are Global Reports (www.global-reports.com) and Corporate Information (www.corporateinformation.com).

A good place to start is to download the most recent financial reports for Coors from SEC Edgar (www.sec.gov) or the Coors company website (www.coors.com). Then try your hand at developing pro forma financial statements for Coors similar to the ones developed in this chapter.

A next step is to pick a company you are interested in and examine its financial statements. As you read a company's financial statements, an important exercise is to try to understand what each number really represents. Why is it there? Is it a cash or market value? Or is it just an accounting number (like depreciation)? Once you are familiar with a company's current financial statements, try to develop pro forma statements for various sales scenarios as was done in this chapter. You really can learn a lot by doing this.

Key Terms

EDGAR 220
10K 220
10Q 220
Regulation FD 220
balance sheet 221
income statement 221
cash flow statement 221
asset 222
liability 223
equity 223

income 224
cash flow 225
noncash items 225
operating cash flow 225
investment cash flow 225
financing cash flow 226
return on assets (ROA) 227
return on equity (ROE) 227
pro forma financial statements 229

Chapter Review Problems and Self-Test

1. **Margin Calculations** Use the following income statement for Paul Bunyan Lumber Co. to calculate gross and operating margins.

**Paul Bunyan Lumber
2003 Income Statement**

Net sales	$8,000
Cost of goods sold	(6,400)
Gross profit	$1,600
Operating expenses	(400)
Operating income	$1,200
Other income	80
Net interest expense	(120)
Pretax income	$1,160
Income tax	464
Net income	$ 696
Earnings per share	$3.48
Recent share price	$76.56

2. **Return Calculations**   Use the following balance sheet for Paul Bunyan Lumber Co. along with the income statement in the previous question to calculate return on assets and return on equity.

**Paul Bunyan Lumber
2003 Balance Sheet**

Cash and cash equivalents	$ 400
Operating assets	400
Property, plant, and equipment	3,160
Other assets	216
Total assets	$4,176
Current liabilities	$ 720
Long-term debt	612
Other liabilities	60
Total liabilities	$1,392
Paid-in capital	$ 600
Retained earnings	2,184
Total shareholder equity	$2,784
Total liabilities and equity	$4,176

3. **Pro Forma Income Statements**   Prepare a pro forma income statement for Paul Bunyan Lumber Co. assuming a 5 percent increase in sales. Based only on the pro forma income statement, what is the projected stock price? (*Hint:* What is the price-earnings ratio?)

Answers to Self-Test Problems

1. Gross margin is $1,600/$8,000 = 20%
   Operating margin is $1,200/$8,000 = 15%

www.mhhe.com/cj3e

2. Return on assets is $696/$4,176 = 16.67%
   Return on equity is $696/$2,784 = 25%

3. With 5 percent sales growth, sales will rise to $8,400 from $8,000. The pro forma income statement follows. A constant gross margin is assumed, implying that cost of goods sold will also rise by 5 percent. A constant tax rate of 40 percent is used. Items in italics are carried over unchanged.

Paul Bunyan Lumber Pro Forma 2004 Income Statement	
Net sales	$8,400
Cost of goods sold	(6,720)
Gross profit	$1,680
Operating expenses	(400)
Operating income	$1,280
Other income	80
Net interest expense	(120)
Pretax income	$1,240
Income tax	496
Net income	$744
Earnings per share	$3.72

To get a projected stock price, notice that the price-earnings ratio was $76.56/$3.48 = 22. Using this ratio as a benchmark, the pro forma earnings of $3.72 imply a stock price of 22 × $3.72 = $81.84.

Test Your Investment Quotient

CFA® PROBLEMS

1. **Balance Sheet Assets**   White Company assets as of December 31, 1999:

Cash and cash equivalents	$ 150
Operating assets	$1,190
Property, plant, and equipment	$1,460
Total assets	$2,800

White Co. experienced the following events in 2000:

Old equipment that cost $120 and that was fully depreciated was scrapped

Depreciation expense was $125

Cash payments for new equipment were $200

Based on the information above, what was White Co.'s net amount of property, plant, and equipment at the end of 2000?

a. $1,415
b. $1,535

   c. $1,655
   d. $1,660

2. **Cash Flow**   Cash flow per share is calculated as

   a. Net cash flow/Shares outstanding.
   b. Operating cash flow/Shares outstanding.
   c. Investing cash flow/Shares outstanding.
   d. Financing cash flow/Shares outstanding.

3. **Cash Flow**   Which of the following is not an adjustment to net income used to obtain operating cash flow?

   a. Changes in operating assets
   b. Changes in current liabilities
   c. Loss on sale of assets
   d. Dividends paid

4. **Cash Flow**   The difference between net income and operating cash flow is at least partially accounted for by which of the following items?

   a. Retained earnings
   b. Cash and cash equivalents
   c. Depreciation
   d. Dividends paid

5. **Financial Ratios**   Which of the following profitability ratios is incorrect?

   a. Gross margin = Gross profit/Cost of goods sold
   b. Operating margin = Operating income/Net sales
   c. Return on assets = Net income/Total assets
   d. Return on equity = Net income/Stockholder equity

6. **Financial Ratios**   Which of the following per-share ratios is incorrect?

   a. Book value per share = Total assets/Shares outstanding
   b. Earnings per share = Net income/Shares outstanding
   c. Cash flow per share = Operating cash flow/Shares outstanding
   d. Dividends per share = Dividends paid/Shares outstanding

7. **Stock Repurchase**   A company repurchase of common stock outstanding has which of the following effects on the balance sheet?

   a. An increase in shares outstanding
   b. An increase in stockholder equity
   c. A decrease in paid-in capital
   d. A positive investment cash flow

8. **Dividend Payment**   A dividend payment has which of the following effects on the balance sheet?

   a. An increase in shares outstanding
   b. A decrease in stockholder equity
   c. A decrease in paid-in capital
   d. An increase in retained earnings

9. **Stock Split**   A 2-for-1 stock split has which of the following effects on the balance sheet?

   a. An increase in shares outstanding
   b. A decrease in stockholder equity
   c. A decrease in paid-in capital
   d. An increase in retained earnings

www.mhhe.com/cj3e

Use the following raw data to answer the next four questions:

Net income:	$16
Depreciation/amortization:	$4
Repurchase of outstanding common stock:	$10
Issuance of new debt:	$18
Sale of property:	$12
Purchase of equipment:	$14
Dividend payments:	$4

10. **Cash Flow Analysis**   Operating cash flow is
   a. $20
   b. $16
   c. $12
   d. $30

11. **Cash Flow Analysis**   Investing cash flow is
   a. $2
   b. $(2)
   c. $12
   d. $(12)

12. **Cash Flow Analysis**   Financing cash flow is
   a. $8
   b. $(8)
   c. $4
   d. $(4)

13. **Cash Flow Analysis**   Net cash increase is
   a. $18
   b. $20
   c. $22
   d. $24

Use the following financial data to answer the next three questions:

Cash payments for interest:	$(12)
Retirement of common stock:	$(32)
Cash payments to merchandise suppliers:	$(85)
Purchase of land:	$(8)
Sale of equipment:	$30
Payments of dividends:	$(37)
Cash payment for salaries:	$(35)
Cash collection from customers:	$260
Purchase of equipment:	$(40)

14. **Cash Flow Analysis**   Cash flows from operating activities are
   a. $91
   b. $128
   c. $140
   d. $175

15. **Cash Flow Analysis**   Cash flows from investing activities are
   a. $(67)
   b. $(48)

    c. $(18)
    d. $(10)

16. **Cash Flow Analysis**   Cash flows from financing activities are

    a. $(81)
    b. $(69)
    c. $(49)
    d. $(37)

17. **Cash Flow Analysis**   A firm has net sales of $3,000, cash expenses (including taxes) of $1,400, and depreciation of $500. If accounts receivable increase over the period by $400, cash flow from operations equals

    a. $1,200
    b. $1,600
    c. $1,700
    d. $2,100

18. **Cash Flow Analysis**   A firm using straight-line depreciation reports gross investment in fixed assets of $80 million, accumulated depreciation of $45 million, and annual depreciation expense of $5 million. The approximate average age of fixed assets is

    a. 7 years
    b. 9 years
    c. 15 years
    d. 16 years

19. **Preferred Dividends**   What proportion of preferred stock dividends received by a corporation is normally exempt from federal income taxation?

    a. 25–35 percent
    b. 50–60 percent
    c. 70–80 percent
    d. 90–100 percent

20. **Price Ratios**   All else the same, which of the following ratios is unaffected by an increase in depreciation?

    a. Price-earnings (P/E)
    b. Price-book (P/B)
    c. Price-cash flow (P/CF)
    d. Price-sales (P/S)

Concept Questions

1. **10K and 10Q**   What are the 10K and 10Q reports? Who are they filed by? What do they contain? Who are they filed with? What is the easiest way to retrieve one?

2. **Financial Statements**   In very broad terms, what is the difference between an income statement and a balance sheet?

3. **Current Events**   What makes current assets and liabilities "current"? Are operating assets "current"?

4. **Income and EPS**   What is the relationship between net income and earnings per share (EPS)?

5. **Noncash Items**   Why do we say depreciation is a "noncash item"?

6. **Cash Flow**   What are the three sections on a standard cash flow statement?

7. **Operating Cash Flow**   In the context of the standard cash flow statement, what is operating cash flow?

8. **Pro Forma**   What is a pro forma financial statement?

9. **Retained Earnings**   What is the difference between the "retained earnings" number on the income statement and the balance sheet?

10. **Gross!**   What is the difference between gross margin and operating margin? What do they tell us? Generally speaking, are larger or smaller values better?

11. **More Gross**   Which is larger, gross margin or operating margin? Can either be negative? Can both?

12. **Dividends and Taxes**   Are dividends paid a tax-deductible expense to the paying company? Suppose a company receives dividends from another. How are these taxed?

13. **Cash Flow**   The bottom line on a standard cash flow statement is calculated how? What exactly does it represent?

14. **Retained Earnings**   Take a look at the balance sheet for Coors (Table 7.8). On it, retained earnings are about $982 million. How do you interpret this amount? Does it mean that Coors has $982 million in cash available to spend?

15. **Price Ratios**   Peninsular Research has a client who has inquired about the valuation method best suited for comparison of companies in an industry that has the following characteristics:

Principal competitors within the industry are located in the United States, France, Japan, and Brazil.

The industry is currently operating at a cyclical low, with many firms reporting losses.

The industry is subject to rapid technological change.

John Jones, CFA, recommends that the client consider the price-earnings ratio, price-book value ratio, and price-sales ratio. Determine which one of the three valuation ratios is most appropriate for comparing companies in this industry. Support your answer with two reasons that make that ratio superior to either of the other two ratios.

Questions and Problems

Core Questions

1. **Income Statements**   Given the following information for Smashville, Inc., construct an income statement for the year:

Cost of goods sold:	$118,000
Investment income:	$1,500
Net sales:	$195,000
Operating expense:	$41,000
Interest expense:	$4,200
Dividends:	$4,000
Tax rate:	35%

What are retained earnings for the year?

2. **Balance Sheets**   Given the following information for Smashville, Inc., construct a balance sheet:

Current liabilities:	$24,000
Cash:	$28,000
Long-term debt:	$91,000
Other assets:	$18,000

Fixed assets:	$105,000
Other liabilities:	$7,000
Investments:	$23,000
Operating assets:	$62,000

3. **Performance Ratios**   Given the information in the previous two problems calculate the gross margin, the operating margin, return on assets, and return on equity for Smashville, Inc.

4. **Per-share Ratios**   During the year, Smashville, Inc., had 12,000 shares of stock outstanding and depreciation expense of $13,000. Calculate the book value per share, earnings per share, and cash flow per share.

5. **Price Ratios**   At the end of the year, Smashville stock sold for $48 per share. Calculate the price-book ratio, price-earnings ratio, and the price-cash flow ratio.

6. **Price Ratios**   You are given the following information concerning a company and its forecasts for next year:

	Optimistic	Pessimistic
BVPS	$17.20	$16.35
EPS	1.86	1.53
CFPS	4.10	3.61

You also find the following ratios for the company: price-book = 3.1, price-earnings = 22.5, and price-cash flow = 11.5. What is the projected stock price under the optimistic and pessimistic scenarios?

7. **Operating Cash Flow**   Weston Corporation had earnings per share of $1.82, depreciation expense of $280,000, and 180,000 shares outstanding. What was the operating cash flow per share? If the share price was $26, what was the price-cash flow ratio?

8. **Earnings per Share**   Alphonse Inc. has a return on equity of 25 percent, 20,000 shares of stock outstanding, and a net income of $50,000. What are earnings per share?

9. **Addition to Retained Earnings**   Oranges Co. has net income of $125,000 and 30,000 shares of stock. If the company pays a dividend of $1.75, what are the additions to retained earnings?

10. **Cash Flow Statement**   Given the following information for Hetrich, Inc., calculate the operating cash flow, investment cash flow, financing cash flow, and net cash flow:

Net income:	$100
Depreciation:	40
Issuance of new stock:	10
Repurchase of debt:	20
Sale of property:	15
Purchase of equipment:	45
Dividend payments:	5
Interest payments:	35

Intermediate Questions

Use the following financial statement information to answer the next five questions. Amounts are in thousands of dollars (except number of shares and price per share):

Kiwi Fruit Company Balance Sheet

Cash and cash equivalents	$ 300
Operating assets	500
Property, plant, and equipment	2,100
Other assets	80
Total assets	$2,980
Current liabilities	$ 400
Long-term debt	1,200
Other liabilities	100
Total liabilities	$1,700
Paid-in capital	$ 300
Retained earnings	980
Total shareholder equity	$1,280
Total liabilities and equity	$2,980

Kiwi Fruit Company Income Statement

Net sales	$6,000
Cost of goods sold	(4,700)
Gross profit	$1,300
Operating expenses	(625)
Operating income	$ 675
Other income	140
Net interest expense	(200)
Pretax income	$ 615
Income tax	(210)
Net income	$ 405
Earnings per share	$1.01
Shares outstanding	400,000
Recent price	$18

Kiwi Fruit Company Cash Flow Statement

Net income	$ 405
Depreciation and amortization	205
Changes in operating assets	(135)
Changes in current liabilities	(110)
Operating cash flow	$ 365
Net additions to properties	$ 405
Changes in other assets	(130)
Investing cash flow	$ 275
Issuance/redemption of long-term debt	$(250)
Dividends paid	(120)
Financing cash flow	$(370)
Net cash increase	$ 270

11. **Calculating Margins**   Calculate the gross and operating margins for Kiwi Fruit.

12. **Calculating Profitability Measures**   Calculate ROA and ROE for Kiwi Fruit and interpret these ratios.

13. **Calculating Per-Share Measures**   Calculate the price-book, price-earnings, and price-cash flow ratios for Kiwi Fruit.

14. **Pro Forma Financial Statements**   Following the examples in the chapter, prepare a pro forma income statement, balance sheet, and cash flow statement for Kiwi Fruit assuming a 10 percent increase in sales.

15. **Projected Share Prices**   Based on the previous two questions, what is the projected stock price assuming a 10 percent increase in sales?

STANDARD & POOR'S

S&P Problems

www.mhhe.com/edumarketinsight

1. **Company Performance**   Under the "S&P Stock Reports" for American Eagle Outfitters (AOES), download the Stock Report and Industry Outlook. What is the outlook for the industry? What is the outlook for the company? What are the factors mentioned in the Stock Report that affect the future outlook for American Eagle Outfitters?

2. **Cash Flow Statement**   Under the "Excel Analytics" link, download the Cash Flow Statement for Barnes & Noble (BKS). Using the most recent cash flow statement, explain the various cash flows for Barnes & Noble. Make sure you note whether each item is an inflow or an outflow.

3. **Cash Flow Statement**   Look up the information for Apple Computer (APPL). Under "Excel Analytics," you will find the annual income statements, balance sheets, and cash flow statements. Although we covered the basics of the cash flow statement in this chapter, you can see that Apple's cash flow statement is much more detailed. For the most recent year, use the income statement and balance sheets to reproduce the cash flow statement provided. Confirm the numbers provided on the cash flow statement where possible.

What's On the Web?

1. **Ratio Analysis**   Go to www.multexinvestor.com and enter the ticker symbol PFE for Pfizer. Look under the "Ratio Comparison" link to find ratios for Pfizer, the industry, the sector, and the S&P 500. Discuss Pfizer's performance using the following ratios: gross margin, operating margin, return on assets, return on equity, book value per share, earnings per share, cash flow per share, price-book, price-earnings, and price-cash flow.

2. **Ratio Calculation**   Under the Investor Center at Du Pont's website (www.dupont.com) you will find financial statements for the company. Using the most recent 10K form, calculate the following ratios for Du Pont over the three years reported: gross margin, operating margin, return on assets, return on equity, book value per share, earnings per share, cash flow per share, price-book, price-earnings, and price-cash flow. How have these ratios changed over this period?

3. **Cash Flow Statement**   You can find financial statements for 3M in the company's Annual Report located in the Investor Relations section of the company's website, www.mmm.com. Locate the Statement of Cash Flows in the Annual Report. How have the items changed over the years? Explain 3M's most recent cash flow statement in words.

Chapter 8

Stock Price Behavior and Market Efficiency

"If you see a bandwagon, it's too late."

–Sir James Goldsmith

"Don't try to buy at the bottom and sell at the top. It can't be done except by liars."

–Bernard Baruch

Our discussion of investments in this chapter ranges from the most controversial issues, to the most intriguing, to the most baffling. We begin with bull markets, bear markets, and market psychology. We then move into the question of whether you, or indeed anyone, can consistently "beat the market." Finally, we close the chapter by describing market phenomena that sound more like carnival side shows, such as "the amazing January effect." ■

8.1   Technical Analysis

technical analysis
Techniques for predicting market direction based on (1) historical price and volume behavior and (2) investor sentiment.

In our previous two chapters, we discussed fundamental analysis. We saw that fundamental analysis focuses mostly on company financial information. There is a completely different, and controversial, approach to stock market analysis called **technical analysis**. Technical analysis boils down to an attempt to predict the direction of future stock price movements based on two major types of information: (1) historical price and volume behavior and (2) investor sentiment.

Technical analysis techniques are centuries old, and their number is enormous. Many, many books on the subject have been written. For this reason, we only touch on the subject and introduce some of its key ideas in the next few sections. Although we focus on the use of technical analysis in the stock market, you should be aware that it is very widely used in the commodity markets, and most comments or discussion here apply to those markets as well.

As you probably know, investors with a positive outlook on the market are often called "bulls," and a rising market is called a bull market. Pessimistic investors are called "bears," and a falling market is called a bear market (just remember that bear markets are hard to bear). Technical analysts essentially search for bullish or bearish signals, meaning positive or negative indicators about stock prices or market direction.

Dow Theory

Dow theory Method for predicting market direction that relies on the Dow Industrial and the Dow Transportation averages.

Dow theory is a method of analyzing and interpreting stock market movements that dates back to the turn of the twentieth century. The theory is named after Charles Dow, a cofounder of the Dow Jones Company and an editor of the Dow Jones–owned newspaper, *The Wall Street Journal.*

The essence of Dow theory is that there are, at all times, three forces at work in the stock market: (1) a primary direction or trend, (2) a secondary reaction or trend, and (3) daily fluctuations. According to the theory, the primary direction is either bullish (up) or bearish (down), and it reflects the long-run direction of the market.

However, the market can, for limited periods of time, depart from its primary direction. These departures are called secondary reactions or trends and may last for several weeks or months. These are eliminated by *corrections*, which are reversions back to the primary direction. Daily fluctuations are essentially noise and are of no real importance.

Learn more about Dow theory at www.dowtheory.com and www.thedowtheory. com

The basic purpose of the Dow theory is to signal changes in the primary direction. To do this, two stock market averages, the Dow Jones Industrial Average (DJIA) and the Dow Jones Transportation Average (DJTA), are monitored. If one of these departs from the primary trend, the movement is viewed as secondary. However, if a departure in one is followed by a departure in the other, then this is viewed as a *confirmation* that the primary trend has changed. The Dow theory was, at one time, very well known and widely followed. It is less popular today, but its basic principles underlie more contemporary approaches to technical analysis.

Support and Resistance Levels

support level Price or level below which a stock or the market as a whole is unlikely to fall.

resistance level Price or level above which a stock or the market as a whole is unlikely to rise.

A key concept in technical analysis is the identification of support and resistance levels. A **support level** is a price or level below which a stock or the market as a whole is unlikely to fall. A **resistance level** is a price or level above which a stock or the market as a whole is unlikely to rise.

The idea behind these levels is straightforward. As a stock's price (or the market as a whole) falls, it reaches a point where investors increasingly believe that it can fall no further—the point at which it "bottoms out." Essentially, buying by bargain-hungry investors ("bottom feeders") picks up at that point, thereby "supporting" the price. A resistance level is the same thing in the opposite direction. As a stock (or the market) rises, it eventually "tops out" and investor selling picks up. This selling is often referred to as "profit taking."

Resistance and support areas are usually viewed as psychological barriers. As the DJIA approaches levels with three zeroes, such as 10,000, talk of "psychologically important" barriers picks up in the financial press. A "breakout" occurs when a stock (or the market) passes through either a support or a resistance level. A breakout is usually interpreted to mean that the price or level will continue in that direction. As this discussion illustrates, there is much colorful language used under the heading of technical analysis. We will see many more examples just ahead.

Technical Indicators

Technical analysts rely on a variety of so-called technical indicators to forecast the direction of the market. Every day, *The Wall Street Journal* publishes a variety of such indicators. An excerpt of the "Diaries" section (from wsj.com) appears in Figure 8.1.

Much, but not all, of the information presented is self-explanatory. The first item listed in Figure 8.1 is the number of "issues traded." This number fluctuates because, on any given day, there may be no trading in certain issues. In the following lines, we see the number of price "advances," the number of price "declines," and the number of "unchanged" prices. Also listed are the number of stock prices reaching "new highs" and "new lows."

One popular technical indicator is called the "advance/decline line." This line shows, for some period, the cumulative difference between advancing issues and declining issues. For example, suppose we had the following information for a particular trading week:

Learn more about technical analysis at www.stockcharts.com Select "Chart School."

	Advance / Decline Line Calculation			
Weekday	**Issues Advancing**	**Issues Declining**	**Difference**	**Cumulative**
Monday	1,015	1,200	−185	−185
Tuesday	900	1,312	−412	−597
Wednesday	1,100	1,108	−8	−605
Thursday	1,250	1,000	+250	−355
Friday	1,100	1,080	+20	−335

In the table just above, notice how we take the difference between the number of issues advancing and declining on each day and then cumulate the difference through time. For example, on Monday, 185 more issues declined than advanced. On Tuesday, 412 more issues declined than advanced. Over the two days, the cumulative advance/decline is thus $-185 + -412 = -597$.

This cumulative advance/decline, once plotted, is the advance/decline line. A downward sloping advance/decline line would be considered a bearish signal, but an upward slope is a positive sign. The advance/decline line is often used to measure market "breadth." If the market is going up, for example, then technical analysts view it as a

FIGURE 8.1

Market Diaries

Source: *The Wall Street Journal,* February 21, 2003. Reprinted by permission of Dow Jones, Inc., via Copyright Clearance Center, Inc. © 2003 Dow Jones & Company, Inc. All Rights Reserved Worldwide.

Closing Stock Market Diaries
Friday, February 21, 2003

For Market Close of February 21, 2003

NYSE Market Diary	Latest Close	Previous Close	Week 02-21
Issues Traded	3404	3410	3527
Advancing Issues	2269	1498	2354
Declining Issues	963	1734	1086
Unchanged Issues	172	178	87
New Highs	58	26	105
New Lows	60	60	139
Advancing volume	980,704,600	384,700,630	2,697,393,550
Declining volume	375,892,500	754,540,570	2,033,976,510
Volume Traded	1,369,652,810	1,171,128,530	4,801,944,970
Closing Tick	+582	+165	
Closing Arms (trin)	0.90	1.69	
Block Trades	21,403	18,500	72,906
NASDAQ Market Diary	**Latest Close**	**Previous Close**	**Week 02-21**
Issues Traded	3398	3428	3742
Advancing Issues	1972	1569	2240
Declining Issues	1156	1545	1367
Unchanged Issues	270	314	135
New Highs	44	40	144
New Lows	57	62	194
Advancing volume	859,582,686	632,104,266	2,982,039,950
Declining volume	434,146,642	661,464,252	2,058,633,753
Volume Traded	1,316,318,965	1,320,412,974	5,120,358,479
BlockTrades	0	10,969	31,825
Amex Market Diary	**Latest Close**	**Previous Close**	**Week 02-21**
IssuesTraded	852	833	993
Advancing Issues	442	359	565
Declining Issues	304	352	350
Unchanged Issues	106	122	78
New Highs	9	9	19
New Lows	18	16	44
Advancing volume	45,610,610	12,761,540	112,788,200
Declining volume	6,991,320	28,332,400	79,213,420
Volume Traded	54,495,530	44,675,840	200,013,200
BlockTrades	0	922	3,117

Closing Tick = The net difference of the number of stocks closing higher than their previous trade from those closing lower; NYSE trading only.

Closing Arms = A comparison of the number of advancing and declining issues with the volume of shares rising and falling. Generally, an Arms of less than 1.00 indicates buying demand; above 1.00 indicates selling pressure.

Advancing, Declining, and Volume Traded and Block Trades reflect volume and trades on the NYSE or Amex exchanges only, not composite numbers.

good sign if the advance is widespread as measured by advancing versus declining issues, rather than being concentrated in a small number of issues.

The next few lines in Figure 8.1 deal with trading volume. These lines represent trading volume for advancing issues, declining issues, and unchanged issues, respectively. For a technical analyst, heavy advancing volume is generally viewed as a bullish signal of buyer interest. This is particularly true if more issues are up than down and if there are a lot of new highs to go along.

The last three numbers are also of interest to technicians. The first, labeled "Closing Tick," is the difference between the number of shares that closed on an uptick and those that closed on a downtick. From our discussion of the NYSE short sale rule in Chapter 5, you know that an uptick occurs when the last price change was positive; a downtick is just the reverse. The tick gives an indication of where the market was heading as it closed.

The entry labeled "Closing Arms (trin)" is the ratio of average trading volume in declining issues to average trading volume in advancing issues. It is calculated as follows:

$$\text{Arms} = \frac{\text{Declining volume/Declines}}{\text{Advancing volume/Advances}} \qquad (8.1)$$

The ratio is named after its inventor, Richard Arms; it is often called the "trin," which is an acronym for "tr(ading) in(dex)." Notice that the numerator (the top part) in this ratio is just the average volume for issues that declined on the day. The denominator (the bottom part) is average volume in advancing issues. Values greater than 1.0 are considered bearish because the indication is that declining shares had heavier volume. Using the numbers from Figure 8.1 for Friday, we can calculate this value as follows:

$$\text{Arms} = \frac{375,892,500/963}{980,704,600/2,269} = \frac{390,335}{432,219} = .90$$

which is the value shown. A caveat: Some sources reverse the numerator and denominator in this ratio.

The final piece of information in Figure 8.1, "Block Trades," refers to trades in excess of 10,000 shares. At one time, such trades were taken to be indicators of buying or selling by large institutional investors. However, today such trades are routine, and it is difficult to see how this information is particularly useful.

Charting

Technical analysts rely heavily on charts showing recent market activity in terms of either prices or, less commonly, volume. In fact, technical analysis is sometimes called "charting," and technical analysts are often called "chartists." There are many types of charts, but the basic idea is that by studying charts of past market prices (or other information), the chartist identifies particular patterns that signal the direction of a stock or the market as a whole.

We will briefly describe four charting techniques—relative strength charts, moving average charts, hi-lo-close and candlestick charts, and point-and-figure charts—just to give you an idea of some common types.

Relative Strength Charts

relative strength A measure of the performance of one investment relative to another.

Relative strength charts illustrate the performance of one company, industry, or market relative to another. If you look back at the *Value Line* exhibit in Chapter 6, you will see a plot labeled "relative strength." Very commonly, such plots are created to analyze how a stock has done relative to its industry or the market as a whole.

To illustrate how such plots are constructed, suppose that on some particular day, we invest equal amounts, say $100, in both Ford and GM (the amount does not matter;

what matters is that the original investment is the same for both). On every subsequent day, we take the ratio of the value of our Ford investment to the value of our GM investment, and we plot it. A ratio bigger than 1.0 indicates that, on a relative basis, Ford has outperformed GM, and vice versa. Thus, a value of 1.20 indicates that Ford has done 20 percent better than GM over the period studied. Notice that if both stocks are down, a ratio bigger than 1.0 indicates that Ford is down by less than GM.

RELATIVE STRENGTH

EXAMPLE 8.1

Consider the following series of monthly stock prices for two hypothetical companies:

Month	Stock A	Stock B
1	$25	$50
2	24	48
3	22	45
4	22	40
5	20	39
6	19	38

On a relative basis, how has stock A done compared to stock B?

To answer, suppose we had purchased four shares of A and two shares of B for an investment of $100 in each. We can calculate the value of our investment in each month and then take the ratio of A to B as follows:

	Investment Value		
Month	Stock A (4 shares)	Stock B (2 shares)	Relative Strength
1	$100	$100	1.00
2	96	96	1.00
3	88	90	0.98
4	88	80	1.10
5	80	78	1.03
6	76	76	1.00

What we see is that over the first four months both stocks were down, but A outperformed B by 10 percent. However, after six months the two had done equally well (or equally poorly).

Moving Average Charts

moving average An average daily price or index level, calculated using a fixed number of previous days' prices or levels, updated each day.

Technical analysts frequently study **moving average** charts. Such charts are used in an attempt to identify short- and long-term trends, often along the lines suggested by Dow theory. The way we construct a 30-day moving average stock price, for example, is to take the prices from the previous 30 trading days and average them. We do this for every day, so that the average "moves" in the sense that each day we update the average by dropping the oldest day and adding the most recent day. Such an average has the effect of smoothing out day-to-day fluctuations.

Charts are easy to draw online. Two of the best sites are stockcharts.com and www.bigcharts.com. Here is an example from finance.yahoo.com:

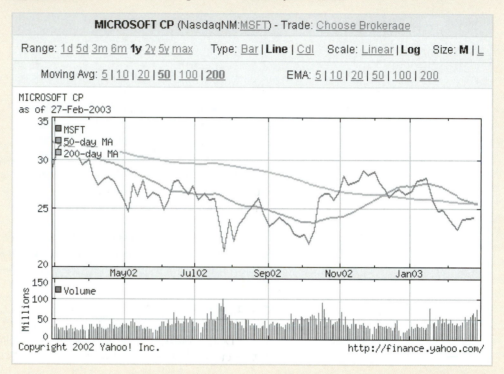

As illustrated, we have drawn a moving average chart for Microsoft. The jagged line tracks Microsoft's daily stock price over the past year. The two smoother lines are the 50-day and 200-day moving averages. Notice the 50-day average crosses the 200-day average in December from below. Such a crossing is sometimes interpreted as a signal to buy. This signal worked briefly (and for a small gain) before the stock price dropped and the 50-day average crossed the 200-day average from above, a potential sell signal. The sell signal, unfortunately, came too late. This illustrates an important point about moving averages: They do smooth out price fluctuations, but they lag behind any recent changes.

For example, it is common to compare 50-day moving averages to 200-day moving averages. The 200-day average might be thought of as indicative of the long-run trend, while the 50-day average would be the short-run trend. If the 200-day average was rising while the 50-day average was falling, the indication might be that price declines are expected in the short term, but the long-term outlook is favorable. Alternatively, the indication might be that there is a danger of a change in the long-term trend. Our nearby *Work the Web* box gives an example.

A MOVING EXPERIENCE

EXAMPLE 8.2

Using the stock prices in Example 8.1, construct three-month moving averages for both stocks.

In the table that follows, we repeat the stock prices and then provide the requested moving averages. Notice that the first two months do not have a moving average figure. Why?

Month	Stock Prices Stock A	Stock B	Moving Averages Stock A	Stock B
1	$25	$50		
2	24	48		
3	22	45	$23.67	$47.67
4	22	40	22.67	44.33
5	20	39	21.33	41.33
6	19	38	20.33	??.??

To give an example of these calculations, to get the month 5 average for stock A, we take the three most recent prices—$20, $22, and $22—and average them: $(20 + 22 + 22) / 3 = 21.33$. Supply the missing number. (*Hint:* its square root is about 6.245!)

Hi-Lo-Close and Candlestick Charts

hi-lo-close chart Plot of high, low, and closing prices.

A **hi-lo-close chart** is a bar chart showing, for each day, the high price, the low price, and the closing price. We have already seen such a chart in Chapter 5, where these values were plotted for the Dow Jones Industrial Averages. Technical analysts study such charts, looking for particular patterns. We describe some patterns in a section just below.

candlestick chart Plot of high, low, open, and closing prices that shows whether the closing price was above or below the opening price.

Candlestick charts have been used in Japan to chart rice prices for several centuries, but they have only recently become popular in the United States.[1] A **candlestick chart** is an extended version of a hi-lo-close chart that provides a compact way of plotting the high, low, open, and closing prices through time while also showing whether the opening price was above or below the closing price. The name stems from the fact that the resulting figure looks like a candlestick with a wick at both ends. Most spreadsheet packages for personal computers can automatically generate both hi-lo-close and candlestick charts. Candlestick charts are sometimes called hi-lo-close-open charts, abbreviated HLCO.

Figure 8.2 illustrates the basics of candlestick charting. As shown, the body of the candlestick is defined by the opening and closing prices. If the closing price is higher than the opening, the body is clear or white; otherwise, it is black. Extending above and below the body are the upper and lower shadows, which are defined by the high and low prices for the day.

To a candlestick chartist, the length of the body, the length of the shadows, and the color of the candle are all important. Plots of candlesticks are used to foretell future

---

[1]This discussion relies, in part, on Chapter 6 of *The Handbook of Technical Analysis,* Darrell R. Jobman, ed. (Chicago: Probus Publishing, 1995).

According to
Forbes and *Barron's*,
the number one
website on technical
analysis is
www.prophet.net

FIGURE 8.2

**Candlestick
Making**

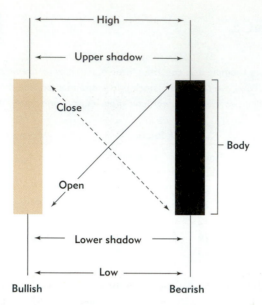

The longer the body, the more bullish
or bearish the implication may be.

market or stock price movements. For example, a series of white candles is a bullish signal; a series of black candles is a bearish signal.

CANDLESTICKS

EXAMPLE 8.3

On December 22, 2000, the DJIA opened at 10,487.29 and closed at 10,635.56. The high and low were 10,640.87 and 10,475.35. Describe the candlestick that would be created with these data.

The body of the candle would be white because the closing price is above the open. It would be $10,635.56 - 10,487.29 = 148.27$ points in height. The upper shadow would be short since the high price for the day is $10,640.87 - 10,635.56 = 5.31$ points above the body. The lower shadow would extend $10,487.29 - 10,475.35 = 11.94$ points below the body.

Certain patterns, some with quite exotic-sounding names, are especially meaningful to the candlestick chartist. We consider just a very few examples in Figure 8.3. The leftmost candlesticks in Figure 8.3 show a "dark cloud cover." Here a white candle with a long body is followed by a long-bodied black candle. When this occurs during a general uptrend, the possibility of a slowing or reversal in the uptrend is suggested. The middle candlesticks in Figure 8.3 show a "bearish engulfing pattern." Here the market opened higher than the previous day's close, but closed lower than the previous day's open. In the context of an uptrend, this would be considered a bearish indicator. Finally, the rightmost candles in Figure 8.3 show a "harami" (Japanese for "pregnant") pattern. The body of the second day's candle lies inside that of the first day's. To a candlestick chartist, the harami signals market uncertainty and the possibility of a change in trend.

FIGURE 8.3

Candlestick Formations

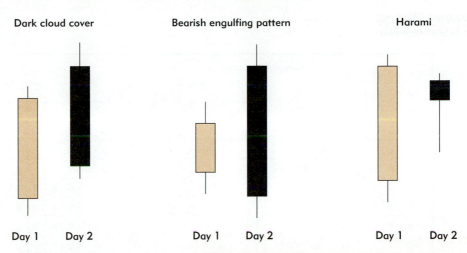

Dark cloud cover

Bearish engulfing pattern

Harami

Day 1 Day 2

Day 1 Day 2

Day 1 Day 2

TABLE 8.1		Stock Price Information			
Date	Price	Date	Price	Date	Price
July 2	$50	July 13	$55	July 25	$55
July 3	51	July 16	56	July 26	56 X
July 5	52 X	July 17	54 O	July 27	58 X
July 6	51	July 18	54	July 30	60 X
July 9	54 X	July 19	54	July 31	54 O
July 10	54	July 20	53	August 1	55
July 11	56 X	July 23	52 O	August 2	52 O
July 12	55	July 24	54 X	August 3	50 O

TABLE 8.2	Point-and-Figure Chart			
60			X	
58			X	
56	X		X	
54	X	O	X	O
52	X	O		O
50				O

Point-and-Figure Charts

point-and-figure chart
Technical analysis chart showing only major price moves and their direction.

Point-and-figure charts are a way of showing only major price moves and their direction. Because minor, or "sideways," moves are ignored, some chartists feel that point-and-figure charts provide a better indication of important trends. This type of charting is much easier to illustrate than explain, so Table 8.1 contains 24 days of stock prices that we will use to construct the point-and-figure chart in Table 8.2.

To build a point-and-figure chart, we have to decide what constitutes a "major" move. We will use $2 here, but the size is up to the user. In Table 8.1, the stock price starts at $50. We take no action until it moves up or down by at least $2. Here, it moves to $52 on July 5, and, as shown in the table, we mark an upmove with an "X."

| FIGURE 8.4 | **Point-and-Figure Chart** |

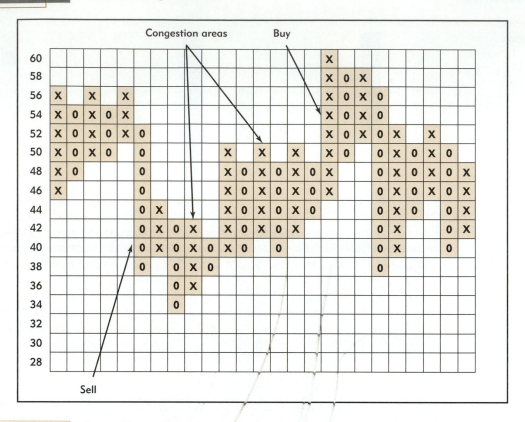

In looking at Table 8.2, notice that we put an "X" in the first column at $52. We take no further action until the stock price moves up or down by another $2. When it hits $54, and then $56, we mark these prices with an X in Table 8.1, and we put X's in the first column of Table 8.2 in the boxes corresponding to $54 and $56.

After we reach $56, the next $2 move is down to $54. We mark this with an "O" in Table 8.1. Because the price has moved in a new direction, we start a new column in Table 8.2, marking an O in the second column at $54. From here, we just keep on going, marking every $2 move as an X or an O, depending on its direction, and then coding it in Table 8.2. A new column starts every time there is a change in direction.

As shown in the more detailed point-and-figure chart in Figure 8.4, buy and sell signals are created when new highs (buy) or new lows (sell) are reached. A lateral series of price reversals, indicating periods of indecisiveness in the market, is called a *congestion area*.

Chart Formations

Once a chart is drawn, technical analysts examine it for various formations or pattern types in an attempt to predict stock price or market direction. There are many such formations, and we cover only one example here. Figure 8.5 shows a stylized example of one particularly well-known formation, the head-and-shoulders. Although it sounds like a dandruff shampoo, it is, in the eyes of the technical analyst, a decisively bearish indicator. When the stock price "pierces the neckline" after the right shoulder is finished, it's time to sell, or so a technical analyst would suggest.

All of the charts we discuss can be drawn online at stockcharts.com Select "Tools & Charts."

Jeff Sagarin has a good point-and-figure chart. See www.kiva.net/ ~jsagarin

FIGURE 8.5

Head-and-Shoulders Formation

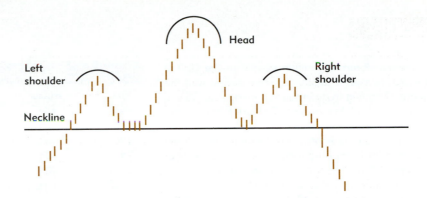

The head-and-shoulders formation in Figure 8.5 is quite clear, but real data rarely produce such a neat picture. In reality, whether a particular pattern is present or not seems to be mostly in the eye of the chartist. Technical analysts agree that chart interpretation is more a subjective art than an objective science. This subjectivity is one reason that technical analysis is viewed by many with skepticism. We will discuss some additional problems with technical analysis shortly.

There is one other thing to note under the heading of predicting market direction. Although we are not trained technical analysts, we are able to predict the direction of the stock market with about 70 percent accuracy. Don't be impressed; we just say "up" every time. (The market indeed goes up about 70 percent of the time.)

Other Technical Indicators

We close our discussion of technical analysis by describing a few additional technical indicators. The "odd-lot" indicator looks at whether odd-lot purchases (purchases of fewer than 100 shares) are up or down. One argument is that odd-lot purchases represent the activities of smaller, unsophisticated investors, so when they start buying, it's time to sell. This is a good example of a "contrarian" indicator. In contrast, some argue that since short selling is a fairly sophisticated tactic, increases in short selling are a negative signal.

Some indicators can seem a little silly. For example, there is the "hemline" indicator. The claim here is that hemlines tend to rise in good times, so rising hemlines indicate a rising market. One of the most famous (or fatuous, depending on how you look at it) indicators is the Super Bowl indicator, which forecasts the direction of the market based on whether the National Football Conference or the American Football Conference wins. A win by the National Football Conference is bullish. This probably strikes you as absurd, so you might be surprised to learn that for the period 1967–1988, this indicator forecast the direction of the stock market with more than 90 percent accuracy! A nearby *Investment Updates* box has more on this indicator.

See a head-and-shoulders pattern at www.chartpatterns.com

Another good site on technical analysis is www.stockta.com

Check This

8.1a	What is technical analysis?
8.1b	What is the difference between a hi-lo-close chart and a point-and-figure chart?
8.1c	What does a candlestick chart show?

The Super Guide to Investing

Every January, about 90 million people in the United States watch television for a prediction of how well the stock market is going to do in the upcoming year. So you missed it this year? Maybe not. The predictor we are talking about is the Super Bowl!

The Super Bowl indicator has become one of the more famous (or infamous) predictors of stock market performance. Here's how it works. In the 1960s, the original National Football League (NFL) and the upstart American Football League (AFL) were fighting for dominance. Eventually, the two leagues merged into what is now the National Football League. The Super Bowl indicator says that if a team from the original AFL wins the Super Bowl, the market will post a negative return for the year, and, if a team from the original NFL wins, the market will post a gain for the year.

So, how has the Super Bowl predicator performed? Take a took at the numbers in the table shown in the next column that we obtained from cnn.com.

For the first 31 Super Bowls, the indicator was correct 28 out of 31 times! The Miami Dolphins are perhaps the best market predictor. When Miami won the Super Bowl in 1973, the market proceeded to drop by 14.7 percent. The next year was an even better indicator. The Dolphins beat the Minnesota Vikings, and the S&P 500 lost 26.5 percent, the worst one-year performance in its history. When the Dolphins lost the Super Bowl in 1972, 1983, and 1985, the S&P 500 posted double-digit gains in each of those years.

So you are not ready to bet the ranch on the Super Bowl indicator? It's probably a good thing since the Super Bowl indicator was dead wrong in 1998, 1999, and 2000. The performance in 2001 is not as clear. The Baltimore Ravens won the Super Bowl that year, and the market lost 7.6 percent. The Ravens are the descendants of the original Cleveland Browns, a member of the original NFL. In this case, the Super Bowl indicator was incorrect. However, purists (especially in Cleveland) argue that since the Browns have been revived, the Ravens cannot be considered a member of the original NFL.

So you want more indicators? How about the hemline indicator, also known as the "bull markets and bare knees" indicator. Through much of the 19th century, long skirts dominated women's fashion, and the stock market experienced many bear markets. In the 1920s, flappers revealed their knees and the stock market boomed. Even the stock market crash of October 1987 was predicted by hemlines. During the 1980s, miniskirts flourished, but by October 1987, a fashion shift had women wearing longer skirts.

Super Bowl Indicator			
Year	Winner		Dow
1967	NFL	Packers	13.2%
1968	NFL	Packers	4.1
1969	AFL	Jets	−17.9
1970	AFL	Chiefs	4.6
1971	NFL	Colts	5.8
1972	NFL	Cowboys	12.7
1973	AFL	Dolphins	−19.9
1974	AFL	Dolphins	−38.1
1975	NFL	Steelers	27.7
1976	NFL	Steelers	15.2
1977	AFL	Raiders	−20.9
1978	NFL	Cowboys	−3.2
1979	NFL	Steelers	4.0
1980	NFL	Steelers	13.0
1981	AFL	Raiders	−10.2
1982	NFL	49ers	16.4
1983	NFL	Redskins	16.9
1984	AFL	Raiders	−3.9
1985	NFL	49ers	21.7
1986	NFL	Bears	18.4
1987	NFL	Giants	2.2
1988	NFL	Redskins	10.6
1989	NFL	49ers	21.2
1990	NFL	49ers	−4.5
1991	NFL	Giants	16.9
1992	NFL	Redskins	4.0
1993	NFL	Cowboys	12.1
1994	NFL	Cowboys	2.1
1995	NFL	49ers	25.1
1996	NFL	Cowboys	20.6
1997	NFL	Packers	18.5
1998	AFL	Broncos	13.9
1999	AFL	Broncos	20.1
2000	NFL	Rams	−6.6
2001	NFL	Ravens	−7.6

There is even a new trading rule for day traders, called Mendleson's To The Moon Predictor. Alan Mendelson, the money reporter for KCAL-TV, has documented the tendency of the Dow to rise on the day of a manned space launch.

These are just three trading rules. There are lots of others. How seriously should you take them? That's up to you, but our advice is to keep in mind that life is full of odd coincidences. Just because a bizarre stock market predictor seems to have worked well in the past doesn't mean it's going to work in the future.

8.2 Market Efficiency

market efficiency
Relation between stock prices and information available to investors indicating whether it is possible to "beat the market"; if a market is efficient, it is not possible, except by luck.

Now we come to what is probably the most controversial and intriguing issue in investments, **market efficiency**. The debate regarding market efficiency has raged for several decades now, and it shows little sign of abating. The central issue is simple enough: Can you, or can anyone, consistently "beat the market"?

We will give a little more precise definition below, but, in essence, if the answer to this question is "no," then the market is said to be efficient. The **efficient markets hypothesis (EMH)** asserts that, as a practical matter, the organized financial markets, particularly the NYSE, are efficient. This is the core controversy.

efficient markets hypothesis (EMH) As a practical matter, the major financial markets reflect all relevant information at a given time.

In the sections that follow, we discuss the issues surrounding the EMH. We focus on the stock markets because that is where the debate (and the research) has concentrated. However, the same principles and arguments would exist in any of the organized financial markets.

What Does "Beat the Market" Mean?

Good question. As we discussed in Chapter 1 and elsewhere, there is a risk-return trade-off. On average at least, we expect riskier investments to have larger returns than less risky investments. So the fact that an investment appears to have a high or low return doesn't tell us much. We need to know if the return was high or low relative to the risk involved.

excess return A return in excess of that earned by other investments having the same risk.

Instead, to determine if an investment is superior, we need to compare **excess returns**. The excess return on an investment is the difference between what that investment earned and what other investments with the same risk earned. A positive excess return means that an investment has outperformed other investments of the same risk. Thus *consistently earning a positive excess return* is what we mean by "beating the market."

Forms of Market Efficiency

Now that we have a little more precise notion of what it means to beat the market, we can be a little more precise about market efficiency. A market is efficient *with respect to some particular information* if that information is not useful in earning a positive excess return. Notice the emphasis we place on "with respect to some particular information."

For example, it seems unlikely that knowledge of Shaquille O'Neal's low free-throw shooting percentage would be of any use in beating the market. If so, we would say that the market is efficient with respect to the information in O'Neal's free throw percentage. On the other hand, if you have prior knowledge concerning impending takeover offers, you could most definitely use that information to earn a positive excess return. Thus, the market is not efficient with regard to this information. We hasten to add that such information is probably "insider" information, and insider trading is illegal (in the United States, at least). Using it might well earn you a jail cell and a stiff financial penalty.

Thus, the question of whether a market is efficient is meaningful only relative to some type of information. Put differently, if you are asked whether a particular market is efficient, you should always reply, "With respect to what information?" Three general types of information are particularly interesting in this context, and it is traditional to define three forms of market efficiency: weak, semistrong, and strong.

weak-form efficient market A market in which past prices and volume figures are of no use in beating the market.

A **weak-form efficient market** is one in which the information reflected in past prices and volume figures is of no value in beating the market. You probably realize immediately what is controversial about this. If past prices and volume are of no use, then technical analysis is of no use whatsoever. You might as well read tea leaves as stock price charts if the market is weak-form efficient.

semistrong-form efficient market A market in which publicly available information is of no use in beating the market.

In a **semistrong-form efficient market**, publicly available information of any and all kinds is of no use in beating the market. If a market is semistrong-form efficient, then the fundamental analysis techniques we described in our previous chapter are useless. Also, notice that past prices and volume data are publicly available information, so if a market is semistrong-form efficient, it is also weak-form efficient.

The implications of semistrong-form efficiency are, at a minimum, semistaggering. What it literally means is that nothing in the library, for example, is of any value in earning a positive excess return. How about a firm's financial statements? Useless. Information in the financial press? Worthless. This book? Sad to say, if the market is semistrong-form efficient, there is nothing in this book that will be of any use in beating the market. You can probably imagine that this form of market efficiency is hotly disputed.

strong-form efficient market A market in which information of any kind, public or private, is of no use in beating the market.

Finally, in a **strong-form efficient market** no information of any kind, public or private, is useful in beating the market. Notice that if a market is strong-form efficient, it is necessarily weak- and semistrong-form efficient as well. Ignoring the issue of legality, it is clear that nonpublic inside information of many types would enable you to earn essentially unlimited returns, so this case is not particularly interesting. Instead the debate focuses on the first two forms.

Why Would a Market Be Efficient?

The driving force toward market efficiency is simply competition and the profit motive. Investors constantly try to identify superior performing investments. Using the most advanced information processing tools available, investors and security analysts constantly appraise stock values, buying those that look even slightly undervalued and selling those that look even slightly overvalued. This constant appraisal and buying and selling activity, and the research that backs it all up, act to ensure that prices never differ much from their efficient market price.

To give you an idea of how strong the incentive is to identify superior investments, consider a large mutual fund such as the Fidelity Magellan Fund. As we mentioned in Chapter 4, this is one of the largest equity funds in the United States, with over $100 billion under management (as of early 2001). Suppose Fidelity was able through its research to improve the performance of this fund by 20 basis points (recall that a basis point is 1 percent of 1 percent, i.e., .0001) for one year only. How much would this one-time 20-basis point improvement be worth?

The answer is .002 × $100 billion, or $200 million. Thus, Fidelity would be willing to spend up to $200 million to boost the performance of this one fund by as little as 1/5 of 1 percent for a single year only. As this example shows, even relatively small performance enhancements are worth tremendous amounts of money and, thereby, create the incentive to unearth relevant information and use it.

Because of this incentive, the fundamental characteristic of an efficient market is that prices are correct in the sense that they fully reflect relevant information. If and when new information comes to light, prices may change, and they may change by a lot. It just depends on the new information. However, in an efficient market, right here, right now, price is a consensus opinion of value, where that consensus is based on the information and intellect of hundreds of thousands, or even millions, of investors around the world.

Are Financial Markets Efficient?

Financial markets are the most extensively documented of all human endeavors. Mountains of financial market data are collected and reported every day. These data, and stock market data in particular, have been analyzed and reanalyzed and then reanalyzed some more to address market efficiency.

You would think that with all this analysis going on, we would know whether markets are efficient, but we really don't. Instead, what we seem to have, at least in the minds of many researchers, is a growing realization that beyond a point, we just can't tell.

For example, it is not difficult to program a computer to test trading strategies that are based solely on historic prices and volume figures. Many such strategies have been tested, and the bulk of the evidence indicates that such strategies are not useful as a realistic matter. The implication is that technical analysis does not work.

However, a technical analyst would protest that a computer program is just a beginning. The technical analyst would say that other, nonquantifiable information and analysis are also needed. This is the subjective element we discussed earlier, and, since it cannot even be articulated, it cannot be programmed in a computer to test, so the debate goes on.

More generally, there are four basic reasons why market efficiency is so difficult to test:

1. The risk-adjustment problem.
2. The relevant information problem.
3. The dumb luck problem.
4. The data snooping problem.

We will briefly discuss each in turn.

The first issue, the risk adjustment problem, is the most straightforward to understand. Earlier, we noted that beating the market means consistently earning a positive excess return. To determine whether an investment has a positive excess return, we have to adjust for its risk. As we will discuss in a later chapter, the truth is that we are not even certain exactly what we mean by risk, much less how to precisely measure it and adjust for it. Thus, what appears to be a positive excess return may just be the result of a faulty risk adjustment procedure.

The second issue, the relevant information problem, is even more troublesome. Remember that market efficiency is meaningful only relative to some particular information. As we look back in time and try to assess whether some particular behavior was inefficient, we have to recognize that we cannot possibly know all the information that may have been underlying that behavior.

For example, suppose we see that 10 years ago the price of a stock shot up by 100 percent over a short period of time and then subsequently collapsed (it happens). We dig through all the historical information we can find, but we can find no reason for this behavior. What can we conclude? Nothing, really. For all we know, a rumor existed of a takeover that never materialized, and, relative to this information, the price behavior was perfectly efficient.

In general, there is no way to tell whether we have all the relevant information. Without *all* the relevant information, we cannot tell if some observed price behavior is

Is astrology useful in beating the market? Some people think so. (We don't.) Visit www.afund.com for more.

inefficient. Put differently, any price behavior, no matter how bizarre, could probably be efficient, and therefore explainable, with respect to *some* information.

The third problem has to do with evaluating investors and money managers. *The Wall Street Journal* article reproduced in the nearby *Investment Updates* box gives some information on the track record of Warren Buffett and other investment superstars. One type of evidence frequently cited to prove that markets can be beaten is the enviable track record of certain legendary investors. For example, in 2003, Warren Buffett was the second wealthiest person in the United States; he made his $35 billion fortune primarily from shrewd stock market investing over many years.

The argument presented in the *Investment Updates* box is that, since at least some investors seem to be able to beat the market, it must be the case that there are inefficiencies. Is this correct? Maybe yes, maybe no. You may be familiar with the following expression: "If you put 1,000 monkeys in front of 1,000 typewriters for 1,000 years, one of them will produce an entire Shakespeare play." It is equally true that if you put thousands of monkeys to work picking stocks for a portfolio, you would find that some monkeys appear to be amazingly talented and rack up extraordinary gains. As you surely recognize, however, this is just caused by random chance.

Now we don't mean to be insulting by comparing monkeys to money managers (some of our best friends are monkeys), but it is true that if we track the performance of thousands of money managers over some period of time, some managers will accumulate remarkable track records and a lot of publicity. Are they good or are they lucky? If we could track them for many decades, we might be able to tell, but for the most part, money managers are not around long enough for us to accumulate enough data.

Our final problem has to do with what is known as "data snooping." Instead of monkeys at typewriters, think now of 1,000 untenured assistant professors of finance with 1,000 computers all studying the same data, looking for inefficiencies. Apparent patterns will surely be found.

In fact, researchers *have* discovered extremely simple patterns that, at least historically, have been quite successful and very hard to explain (we discuss some of these in the next section). These discoveries raise another problem: ghosts in the data. If we look long enough and hard enough at any data, we are bound to find some apparent patterns by sheer chance (such as the Super Bowl indicator we discussed earlier), but are they real? Only time will tell.

Notwithstanding the four problems we have discussed, based on the last 20 to 30 years of scientific research, three generalities about market efficiency seem in order. First, short-term stock price and market movements appear to be very difficult, or even impossible, to predict with any accuracy, at least with any objective method of which we are aware. Second, the market reacts quickly and sharply to new information, and the vast majority of studies of the impact of new information find little or no evidence that the market underreacts or overreacts to new information in a way that can be profitably exploited. Third, if the stock market can be beaten, the way to do it is at least not *obvious,* so the implication is that the market is not grossly inefficient.

Some Implications of Market Efficiency

To the extent that you think a market is efficient, there are some important investment implications. Going back to Chapter 2, we saw that the investment process can be viewed as having two parts: asset allocation and security selection. Even if all markets are efficient, asset allocation is still important because the way you divide your money

Is Warren Buffett the greatest investor of all time? That question can never be settled, any more than baseball fans can settle the question of whether Babe Ruth was greater than Hank Aaron. But a good case can be made for Mr. Buffett.

The table lists a few of the most successful investors in history. A couple of them—George Soros and Peter Lynch—show higher compound average annual returns than Mr. Buffett's. But that doesn't truly settle the debate.

Mr. Lynch, for example, compiled a sparkling 29% annual return as manager of the Fidelity Magellan Fund. At first blush, that seems to top Mr. Buffett's 27% annual return. However, during the 13-year stretch when Mr. Lynch was burning up the track, Mr. Buffett did even better: up 39% a year, according to Morningstar, Inc.

Mr. Soros, manager of Quantum Fund, also has a higher annual return than Mr. Buffett. But Mr. Buffett has maintained his performance for a longer time. Also, notes Edward Macheski, a money manager in Chatham, N.Y., Mr. Buffett racked up his king-sized returns without much use of leverage, or debt, to magnify investment results. Hedge funds, such as those run by Mr. Soros, Michael Steinhardt, and Julian Robertson, often use heavy leverage.

The Buffett record shown in the table is a composite. From 1957 to 1969, his main investment vehicle was Buffett Partnership Ltd. In 1965, the partnership acquired a controlling interest in Berkshire, which became Mr. Buffett's main vehicle in 1970.

Source: John R. Dorfman, *The Wall Street Journal*, August 18, 1995. Reprinted by permission of Dow Jones, Inc., via Copyright Clearance Center, Inc. © 1995 Dow Jones & Company, Inc. All Rights Reserved Worldwide.

A Pantheon of Great Investors Financial professionals consider these people among the greatest investors of all time. Even in this select group, Warren Buffett stands out.

Name	Main Affiliation	Estimated Returns*	Comments
Warren Buffett	Berkshire Hathaway	Up 27% a year since 1957	Wants to invest in "wonderful businesses." Favorite holding period: forever.
Benjamin Graham	Graham-Newman	Up 17% a year, 1929–1956	Considered the father of value investing. Liked stocks that are cheap relative to earnings or book value.
John Maynard Keynes	National Mutual Life Assurance Society (Britain)	Up most years during treacherous 1930s markets	Famous economist was also an avid and serious investor. Posted big losses but even bigger gains.
Peter Lynch	Fidelity Magellan Fund	Up 29% a year, May 1977–May 1990	Bought dozens of stocks in industries he favored. Workaholic until his surprise "retirement."
Julian Robertson	Tiger Fund	Up 27% a year since September 1980	Names hedge funds after big cats—"Tiger," "Puma," "Jaguar." Big player in Latin America, Japan, etc.
George Soros	Quantum Fund	Up 34% a year since 1969	Huge bets on international currencies and bonds; uses major leverage.
Michael Steinhardt	Steinhardt Partners	Up 21% a year since 1968	Hunch player, bold trader in both U.S. and foreign markets.
John Templeton	Templeton Growth Fund	Up 18% a year, November 1954–March 1987	Bargain hunter worldwide; a pioneer of international investing.

*Estimated compound annual returns, after fees. With certain funds, publicly available results for foreign clients are used to approximate results for U.S. clients.
Source: Morningstar Inc.; U.S. Offshore Funds Directory; "Benjamin Graham on Value Investing" by Jane Lowe, *Wall Street Journal* research.

between the various types of investments will strongly influence your overall risk-return relation.

However, if markets are efficient, then security selection is less important, and you do not have to worry too much about overpaying or underpaying for any particular security. In fact, if markets are efficient, you would probably be better off just buying a large basket of stocks and following a passive investment strategy. Your main goal would be to hold your costs to a minimum while maintaining a broadly diversified portfolio. We discussed index funds, which exist for just this purpose, in Chapter 4.

In broader terms, if markets are efficient, then little role exists for professional money managers. You should not pay load fees to buy mutual fund shares, and you should shop for low management fees. You should not work with full-service brokers, and so on. From the standpoint of an investor, it's a commodity-type market.

If markets are efficient, there is one other thing that you should not do: You should not try to time the market. Recall that market timing amounts to moving money in and out of the market based on your expectations of future market direction. All you accomplish with an efficient market is to guarantee that you will, on average, underperform the market.

In fact, market efficiency aside, market timing is hard to recommend. Historically, most of the gains earned in the stock market have tended to occur over relatively short periods of time. If you miss even a single one of these short market runups, you will likely never catch up. Put differently, successful market timing requires phenomenal accuracy to be of any benefit, and anything less than that will, based on the historic record, result in underperforming the market.

8.2a	What does it mean to "beat the market"?	
8.2b	What are the forms of market efficiency?	
8.2c	Why is market efficiency difficult to evaluate?	

Check This

8.3 Stock Price Behavior and Market Efficiency

This section concludes our discussion of market efficiency. We first discuss some aspects of stock price behavior that are both baffling and hard to reconcile with market efficiency. We then examine the track records of investment professionals and find results that are both baffling and hard to reconcile with anything *other* than market efficiency.

The Day-of-the-Week Effect

In the stock market, which day of the week has, on average, the biggest return? The question might strike you as a little ridiculous; after all, what would make one day different from any other on average? On further reflection, though, you might realize that one day is different: Monday.

When we calculate a daily return for the stock market, we take the percentage change in closing prices from one trading day to the next. For every day except Monday this is a 24-hour period. However, since the markets are closed on the weekends, the average return on Monday is based on the percentage change from Friday's close

TABLE 8.3	Average Daily S&P 500 Returns by Day of the Week, Dividends Included				
Weekday:	Monday	Tuesday	Wednesday	Thursday	Friday
Average return:	−.053%	.048%	.084%	.028%	.062%

Source: Author calculations.

day-of-the-week effect The tendency for Monday to have a negative average return.

to Monday's close, a 72-hour period. Thus, the average Monday return would be computed over a three-day period, not just a one-day period. We therefore conclude that Monday should have the highest average return; in fact, Monday's average return should be three times as large.

Given this reasoning, it may come as a surprise to you to learn that Monday has the *lowest* average return! In fact, Monday is the only day with a *negative* average return. This is the **day-of-the-week effect**. Table 8.3 shows the average return by day of the week for the S&P 500 for the period July 1962 through December 2001.

The negative return on Monday is quite significant, both in a statistical sense and in an economic sense. This day-of-the-week effect does not appear to be a fluke; it exists in other markets, such as the bond market, and it exists in stock markets outside the United States. It has eluded explanation since it was first carefully documented in the early 1980s, and it continues to do so as this is written.

Critics of the EMH point to this strange behavior as evidence of market inefficiency. The problem with this criticism is that while the behavior is odd, how it can be used to earn a positive excess return is not clear, so whether it points to inefficiency is hard to say.

The Amazing January Effect

We saw in Chapter 1 that small common stocks have significantly outdistanced large common stocks over the last seven decades. Beginning in the early 1980s, researchers reported that the difference was too large even to be explained by differences in risk. In other words, small stocks appeared to earn positive excess returns.

January effect Tendency for small stocks to have large returns in January.

Further research found that, in fact, a substantial percentage of the return on small stocks has historically occurred early in the month of January, particularly in the few days surrounding the turn of the year. Even closer research documents that this peculiar phenomenon is more pronounced for stocks that have experienced significant declines in value, or "losers."

Thus, we have the famous "small-stock-in-January-especially-around-the-turn-of-the-year-for-losers effect," or SSIJEATTOTYFLE for short. For obvious reasons, this phenomenon is usually just dubbed the **January effect**. To give you an idea of how big this effect is, we have first plotted average returns by month going back to 1925 for the S&P 500 in Figure 8.6A. As shown, the average return per month has been just under 1 percent.

In Figure 8.6A, there is nothing remarkable about January; the largest average monthly return occurred in July; the lowest in September. From a statistical standpoint, there is nothing too exceptional about these large stock returns. After all, some month has to be highest, and some month has to be the lowest.

Figure 8.6B, however, shows average returns by month for small stocks (notice the difference in vertical axis scaling between Figures 8.6A and 8.6B). The month of January definitely jumps out. Over the 76 years covered, small stocks have gained, on

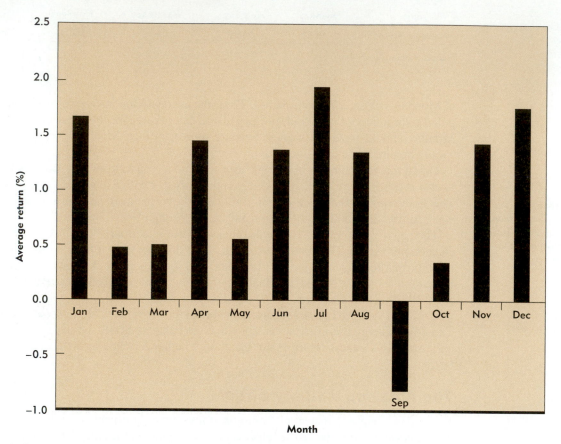

FIGURE 8.6A   S&P 500 Average Monthly Returns: 1925–2001
(dividends included)

Source: Author calculations.

average, almost 7 percent in the month of January alone! Comparing Figures 8.6A and
8.6B, we see that outside the month of January, and, to a smaller extent, February,
small stocks have not done especially well relative to the S&P 500.

The January effect appears to exist in most major markets around the world, so it's
not unique to the United States (it's actually more pronounced in some other markets).
It also exists in some markets other than the stock markets. Critics of market efficiency
point to enormous gains to be had from simply investing in January and ask: How can
an efficient market have such unusual behavior? Why don't investors take advantage
of this opportunity and thereby drive it out of existence?

Unlike the day-of-the-week effect, the January effect is at least partially understood.
There are two factors that are thought to be important. The first is tax-loss selling. Investors have a strong tax incentive to sell stocks that have gone down in value to realize the loss for tax purposes. This leads to a pattern of selling near the end of the year
and buying after the turn of the year. In large stocks, this activity wouldn't have much
effect, but in the smaller stocks it could. Or so the argument runs.

The tax-loss selling argument is plausible. One study, for example, examined
whether the January effect existed in the United States before there was an income tax

FIGURE 8.6B   Small Stocks' Average Monthly Returns: 1925–2001 (dividends included)

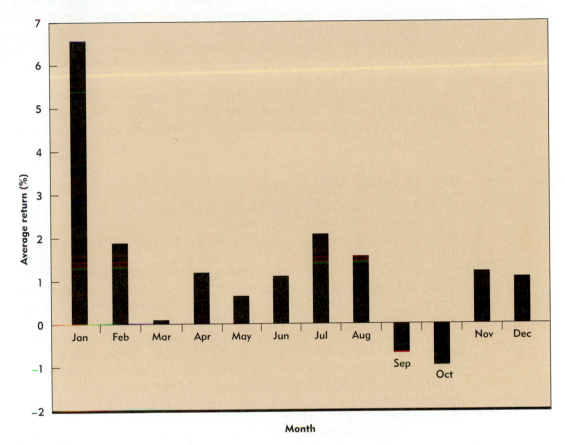

Source: Author calculations.

(yes, Virginia, there was such a time) and found no January effect. However, the January effect has been found in other countries that didn't (or don't) have calendar tax years or didn't (or don't) have capital gains taxes. However, foreign investors in those markets (such as U.S. investors) did (or do). So, debate continues about the tax-loss selling explanation.

The second factor has to do with institutional investors. The argument here has several pieces, but the gist of it is that these large investors compensate portfolio managers based on their performance over the calendar year. Portfolio managers therefore pile into small stocks at the beginning of the year because of their growth potential, bidding up prices. Over the course of the year, they shed the stocks that do poorly because they don't want to be seen as having a bunch of "losers" in their portfolios (this is called "window dressing"). Also, because performance is typically measured relative to the S&P 500, portfolio managers who begin to lag because of losses in small stocks have an incentive to move into the S&P to make sure they don't end up too far behind. Managers who are well ahead late in the year have an incentive to move into the S&P to preserve their leads (this is called "bonus lock-in").

A lot more could be said about the January effect, but we will leave it here. In evaluating this oddity, keep in mind that, unlike the day-of-the-week effect, the January effect does not even exist for the market as a whole, so, in "big-picture" terms, it is not all that important. Also, it doesn't happen every year, so attempts to exploit it will occasionally result in substantial losses.

The day-of-the-week and January effects are examples of calendar effects. There are others. For example, there is a general "turn-of-the-month" effect: stock market returns are highest around the turn of every month. There are noncalendar anomalies as well. For example, the market does worse on cloudy days than sunny days. Rather than continuing with a laundry list of anomalies, however much fun they might provide, we will instead turn to what was arguably the most spectacular event in market history—the Crash of 1987.

The October 1987 Crash

Once, when we spoke of "Black Monday" and "the Crash," we meant October 29, 1929. On that day alone, the market lost about 13 percent of its value on heavy trading of 16.4 million shares. As the DJIA fell some 38 points to 260, investors lost over $10 billion.

Then along came October 19, 1987, which we *now* call Black Monday. It was indeed a dark and stormy day on Wall Street; the market lost over 20 percent of its value on a record volume of 600 million shares traded. The Dow plummeted 500 points to 1,700, leaving investors with about $500 billion in losses that day. To put this decline in perspective, before October 1987, the Dow had never fallen by more than 100 points, and more than 300 million shares had never traded on a single day.[2]

What happened? It's not exactly ancient history, but, here again, debate rages (you're probably getting tired of hearing that). One faction says that irrational investors had bid up stock prices to ridiculous levels until Black Monday, when the bubble popped, leading to panic selling as investors headed for the exits.

The other faction says that before October 19, markets were volatile, volume was heavy, and some ominous signs about the economy were filtering in. On October 14–16, the market fell by over 10 percent, the largest three-day drop since May 1940 when German troops broke through French lines near the start of World War II. To top it all off, market values had risen sharply because of a dramatic increase in takeover activity, but Congress was in session (meaning that nobody's money was safe) and was actively considering antitakeover legislation.

Another factor is that beginning a few years before the crash, large investors had developed techniques known as *program trading* for very rapidly selling enormous quantities of stock following a market decline. These techniques were still largely untested because the market had been strong for years. However, on Friday, October 16, the Dow fell by 108 points on heavy volume. When the market opened on Monday, sell orders came pouring in at a pace never before seen. In fact, these program trades were (and are) blamed for much of what happened.

About the only thing we know for certain about the crash is that the exchanges suffered a meltdown. The NYSE simply could not handle the volume. Posting of prices was delayed by hours, so investors had no idea what their positions were worth. The specialists couldn't handle the order flow, and some specialists actually began selling.

---

[2]We thank Jay R. Ritter of the University of Florida for supplying us with some of this information.

Nasdaq basically went off-line as it became impossible to get through to market makers. It has been alleged that many quit answering the phone.

On the two days following the crash, prices *rose* by about 14 percent, one of the biggest short-term gains ever. Prices remained volatile for some time, but, as antitakeover talk died down, the market recovered.

As a result of the crash, changes have occurred. Upgrades have made it possible to handle much heavier trading volume, for example. One of the most interesting changes was the introduction of the **NYSE circuit breakers**. Different circuit breakers are triggered if the DJIA drops by 10, 20, or 30 percent. These 10, 20, and 30 percent decline levels, respectively, in the DJIA will result in the following actions:

NYSE circuit breakers
Rules that kick in to slow or stop trading when the DJIA declines by more than a preset amount in a trading session.

1. A 10 percent drop in the DJIA will halt trading for one hour if the decline occurs before 2 P.M.; for 30 minutes if before 2:30 P.M.; and have no effect between 2:30 and 4 P.M.

2. A 20 percent drop will halt trading for two hours if the decline occurs before 1 P.M.; for one hour if before 2 P.M.; and for the remainder of the day if between 2 and 4 P.M.

3. A 30 percent drop will halt trading for the remainder of the day regardless of when the decline occurs.

These specific circuit breaker trigger levels were implemented in October 1998. Because circuit breakers are designed to slow a market decline, they are often called "speed bumps." Naturally, how well they work is a matter of debate.

One of the most remarkable things about the crash is how little impact it seems to have had. If you look back to Chapter 1, you'll see that the market was actually up slightly in 1987. The postcrash period was one of the better times to be in the market, and the crash increasingly looks like a blip in one of the greatest bull markets U.S. investors have ever seen. One thing seems clearly true: October is the cruelest month for market investors. Indeed, two years after the crash, on October 13, 1989, a mini-crash occurred as the Dow fell 190 points in the afternoon following the collapse of a proposed buyout of United Airlines.

Performance of Professional Money Managers

By now you're probably wondering how anyone could think that markets are efficient. Before you make up your mind, there's one last "anomaly" that we need to tell you about. It has to do with the performance of professional money managers, a subject we touched on briefly in Chapter 4.

Starting with managers as a group, Figure 8.7 shows, for 1963 through mid-1998, the percentage of general equity mutual funds (GEFs) that were outperformed by the S&P 500 index. As shown, out of 36 years, the *index* won 22 times.

Figure 8.7 raises a difficult question for security analysts and other investment professionals. If markets are inefficient, and tools like fundamental analysis are valuable, why don't mutual fund managers do better? Why can't they even beat the averages? Why do they actually *lag* the averages?

The performance of professional money managers is especially troublesome when we consider the enormous resources at their disposal and the substantial survivor bias that exists. The survivor bias comes into being because managers and funds that do especially poorly disappear. If it were possible to beat the market, then this Darwinian process of elimination should lead to a situation in which the survivors, as a group, are capable of doing it.

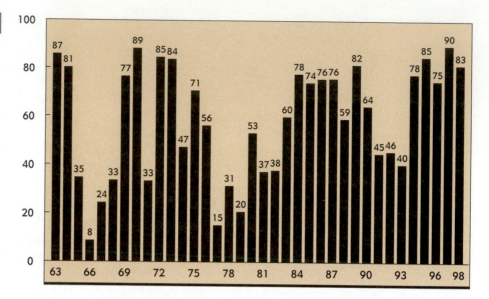

FIGURE 8.7

**Equity Funds vs.
S&P 500**

Source: John C. Bogle,
*Common Sense on
Mutual Funds* (New
York: John Wiley & Sons,
1999).

It is sometimes thought that while professional managers as a group tend to lag the market indexes, some managers are consistently better. There is evidence indicating that some managers are better than other managers, but even this evidence is fairly weak, particularly for recent years. There is little evidence of consistent ability by anyone to beat the averages.

To give an example, we briefly discussed the usefulness of mutual fund rankings in Chapter 4. The most widely read investment magazine, *Forbes*, publishes extensive mutual fund information. Every year since 1975, *Forbes* has produced a short "honor role" of mutual funds. These are funds judged by *Forbes* as the overall top performers in up and down markets. How useful is this advice?

To answer, suppose that you, as an investor, had followed *Forbes*'s advice from 1975 to 1990 and purchased the honor role funds every year. How would you have done? Over the 16-year period 1975–1990, you would have earned an average annual return of 13.38 percent. Not bad, but if you had purchased the S&P 500 instead, you would have earned 14.86 percent! Furthermore, in the second half of the 16 years, the *Forbes* funds earned an average of 10.46 percent while the S&P averaged 16.43 percent.[3] Finally, the 13.38 percent earned by the *Forbes* honor role does *not* include load fees, so your actual return would have been worse.

Check This

> **8.3a**   What are the day-of-the-week and January effects?
>
> **8.3b**   Why is the performance of professional money managers puzzling?

---

[3]The figures are from Table VIII in Burton G. Malkiel, "Returns from Investing in Mutual Funds 1971–1991," *Journal of Finance* 50, June 1995.

8.4   Summary and Conclusions

In this chapter, we examined technical analysis, market efficiency, and stock price behavior. We saw that:

1. Technical analysts rely on past price and volume figures to predict the future. They use various indicators and rely heavily on the interpretation of different types of charts.

2. Beating the market means consistently earning a positive excess return. A positive excess return is a return above that earned by investments of the same risk.

3. If it is not possible to beat the market using a particular type of information, we say that the market is efficient with respect to that information.

4. If markets are weak-form efficient, past price and volume figures are of no use in earning a positive excess return, implying that technical analysis would be of little or no value. If markets are semistrong-form efficient, no public information is of use in earning a positive excess return, implying that fundamental analysis would be of no value. Strong-form efficiency implies that no information, public or private, would be of any use.

5. Market efficiency is difficult to test. We examined four reasons: (1) the risk-adjustment problem, (2) the relevant information problem, (3) the dumb luck problem, and (4) the data snooping problem.

6. Stock prices have exhibited peculiar, difficult to explain, behavior. We discussed the day-of-the-week effect, the January effect, and the Crash of 1987 as examples.

7. Despite their tremendous resources, experience, opportunities, and incentives, and despite the patterns and other oddities that have existed historically in the stock market, professional money managers have been unable to consistently beat the market. This is true both for professionals as a group and for individuals. This one fact, more than anything else, seems to suggest that markets are generally rather efficient.

Get Real

This chapter covered technical analysis and market efficiency. In it, we raised a significant question. Can you, or indeed anyone, consistently beat the market? In other words, is the market efficient? This is a question that every investor needs to think about because it has direct, practical implications for investing and portfolio management.

If you think the market is relatively efficient, then your investment strategy should focus on minimizing costs and taxes. Asset allocation is your primary concern, and you will still need to establish the risk level you are comfortable with. But beyond this, you should be a buy-and-hold investor, transacting only when absolutely necessary. Investments such as low-cost, low-turnover mutual funds make a lot of sense. Tools for analyzing the market, particularly the tools of technical analysis, are irrelevant at best. Thus, in some ways, the appropriate investment strategy is kind of boring, but it's the one that will pay off over the long haul in an efficient market.

(continued)

In contrast, if you think the market is not particularly efficient, then you've got to be a security picker. You also have to decide what tools—technical analysis, fundamental analysis, or both—will be the ones you use. This is also true if you are in the money management business; you have to decide which specific stocks or bonds to hold.

In the end, the only way to find out if you've got what it takes to beat the market is to try, and the best way to try is with a simulated brokerage account such as Stock-Trak. Be honest with yourself: You think you can beat the market; most novice investors do. Some change their minds and some don't. As to which tools to use, try some technical analysis and see if it works for you. If it does, great. If not, well, there are other tools at your disposal.

Key Terms

technical analysis 251
Dow theory 251
support level 251
resistance level 251
relative strength 254
moving average 255
hi-lo-close chart 257
candlestick chart 257
point-and-figure chart 259

market efficiency 263
efficient markets hypothesis (EMH) 263
excess return 263
weak-form efficient market 264
semistrong-form efficient market 264
strong-form efficient market 264
day-of-the-week effect 269
January effect 269
NYSE circuit breaker 273

Chapter Review Problems and Self-Test

1. **It's All Relative**   Consider the following series of monthly stock prices for two companies:

Week	Phat Co	GRRL Power
1	$10	$80
2	12	82
3	16	80
4	15	84
5	14	85
6	12	88

On a relative basis, how has Phat done compared to GRRL Power?

2. **Moving Averages**   Using the prices from the previous problem, calculate the three-month moving average prices for both companies.

Answers to Self-Test Problems

1. Suppose we had purchased eight shares of Phat and one share of GRRL Power. We can calculate the value of our investment in each month and then take the ratio of Phat to GRRL Power as follows:

| | Investment Value | | |
Week	Phat Co. (8 shares)	GRRL Power (1 share)	Relative Strength
1	$ 80	$80	1.00
2	96	82	1.17
3	128	80	1.60
4	120	84	1.43
5	112	85	1.32
6	96	88	1.09

Phat Co. has significantly outperformed GRRL Power over much of this period; however, after six weeks, the margin has fallen to about 9 percent from as high as 60 percent.

2. The moving averages must be calculated relative to the share price; also note that results can't be computed for the first two weeks because of insufficient data.

Week	Phat Co.	Phat Co. Moving Average	GRRL Power	GRRL Power Moving Average
1	$10	—	$80	—
2	12	—	82	—
3	16	$12.67	80	$80.67
4	15	14.33	84	82.00
5	14	15.00	85	83.00
6	12	13.67	88	85.67

Test Your Investment Quotient

CFA® PROBLEMS

1. **Technical Analysis**   Which of the following is a basic assumption of technical analysis in contrast to fundamental analysis?
   a. Financial statements provide information crucial in valuing a stock.
   b. A stock's market price will approach its intrinsic value over time.
   c. Aggregate supply and demand for goods and services are key determinants of stock value.
   d. Security prices move in patterns, which repeat over long periods.

CFA® PROBLEMS

2. **Efficient Markets Hypothesis**   A market anomaly refers to
   a. An exogenous shock to the market that is sharp but not persistent.
   b. A price or volume event that is inconsistent with historical price or volume trends.
   c. A trading or pricing structure that interferes with efficient buying or selling of securities.
   d. Price behavior that differs from the behavior predicted by the efficient markets hypothesis.

www.mhhe.com/cj3e

3. **Efficient Markets Hypothesis**   Which of the following assumptions does not imply an informationally efficient market?

   a. Security prices adjust rapidly to reflect new information.
   b. The timing of one news announcement is independent of other news announcements.
   c. The risk-free rate exists, and investors can borrow and lend unlimited amounts at the risk-free rate.
   d. Many profit-maximizing participants, each acting independently of the others, analyze and value securities.

4. **Technical Analysis**   Which of the following is least likely to be of interest to a technical analyst?

   a. A 15-day moving average of trading volume.
   b. A relative strength analysis of stock price momentum.
   c. Company earnings and cash flow growth.
   d. A daily history of the ratio of advancing issues over declining issues.

5. **Dow Theory**   Dow theory asserts that there are three forces at work in the stock market at any time. Which of the following is not one of these Dow theory forces?

   a. Daily price fluctuations
   b. A secondary reaction or trend
   c. A primary direction or trend
   d. Reversals or overreactions

6. **Technical Indicators**   The advance/decline line is typically used to

   a. Measure psychological barriers.
   b. Measure market breadth.
   c. Assess bull market sentiment.
   d. Assess bear market sentiment.

7. **Technical Indicators**   The Closing Arms (trin) ratio is the ratio of

   a. Average trading volume in declining issues to advancing issues.
   b. Average trading volume in NYSE issues to Nasdaq issues.
   c. The number of advancing issues to the number of declining issues.
   d. The number of declining issues to the number of advancing issues.

8. **Technical Indicators**   Resistance and support areas for a stock market index are viewed as technical indicators of

   a. Economic barriers
   b. Psychological barriers
   c. Circuit breakers
   d. Holding patterns

9. **Technical Charts**   Which of the following pieces of information cannot be observed in a daily candlestick chart covering a several-month period?

   a. Daily high and low prices.
   b. Weekly high and low prices.
   c. Daily opening and closing prices.
   d. Daily opening and closing trading volume.

10. **Technical Charts**   Which of the following pieces of information cannot be observed in a point-and-figure chart covering a several-month period?

   a. Amount of time elapsed during a major price trend.
   b. Number of major price upmoves.
   c. Number of major price downmoves.
   d. Number of major price moves forming a trend.

11. **Efficient Markets Hypothesis**   After lengthy trial and error, you discover a trading system that would have doubled the value of your investment every six months if applied

over the last three years. Which of the following problems makes it difficult to conclude that this is an example of market inefficiency?

    a. Risk-adjustment problem
    b. Relevant information problem
    c. Dumb luck problem
    d. Data snooping problem

12. **Efficient Markets Hypothesis** In discussions of financial market efficiency, which of the following is not one of the stylized forms of market efficiency?

    a. Strong form
    b. Semistrong form
    c. Weak form
    d. Economic form

13. **Beating the Market** Which of the following is not considered a problem when evaluating the ability of a trading system to "beat the market"?

    a. Risk-adjustment problem
    b. Relevant information problem
    c. Data measurement problem
    d. Data snooping problem

14. **Calendar Anomalies** Which month of the year, on average, has had the highest stock market returns as measured by a small-stock portfolio?

    a. January
    b. March
    c. June
    d. December

15. **Circuit Breakers** Which of the following intraday changes in the Dow Jones Industrial Average (DJIA) will trigger a circuit breaker halting NYSE trading for one hour?

    a. 10 percent drop before 2 P.M.
    b. 10 percent drop after 2 P.M.
    c. 10 percent rise before 2 P.M.
    d. 10 percent rise after 2 P.M.

Concept Questions

1. **Dow Theory** In the context of Dow theory, what are the three forces at work at all times? Which is the most important?

2. **Technical Analysis** To a technical analyst, what are support and resistance areas?

3. **Dow Theory** In the context of Dow theory, what are corrections and confirmations?

4. **Bad Breadth?** On a particular day, the stock market as a whole is up; however, losers outnumber gainers by 2,000 to 1,600. What might a technical analyst conclude?

5. **A Call to Arms** How is the Arms ratio computed? What is it designed to capture?

6. **January** With regard to the January effect, what is the role that institutional investors are thought to play?

7. **Bad Timing?** A key concern in technical analysis such as the Dow theory is to identify turning points in market direction and thereby time the market. What are the implications of market efficiency for market timing?

8. **Point-and-Figure Plots** Point-and-figure plots differ from high-low-close and candlestick charts in one important way. What is it? Why might a point-and-figure chart be more informative?

9. **Efficient Markets**   A stock market analyst is able to identify mispriced stocks by comparing the average price for the last 10 days to the average price for the last 60 days. If this is true, what do you know about the market?

10. **Efficient Markets**   Critically evaluate the following statement: "Playing the stock market is like gambling. Such speculative investing has no social value, other than the pleasure people get from this form of gambling."

11. **Misconceptions about Efficient Markets**   There are several celebrated investors and stock pickers who have recorded huge returns on their investments over the past two decades. Is the success of these particular investors an invalidation of an efficient stock market? Explain.

12. **Interpreting Efficient Markets**   For each of the following scenarios, discuss whether profit opportunities exist from trading in the stock of the firm under the conditions that (1) the market is not weak-form efficient, (2) the market is weak-form but not semistrong-form efficient, (3) the market is semistrong-form but not strong-form efficient, and (4) the market is strong-form efficient.

   a. The stock price has risen steadily each day for the past 30 days.
   b. The financial statements for a company were released three days ago, and you believe you've uncovered some anomalies in the company's inventory and cost control reporting techniques that are understating the firm's true liquidity strength.
   c. You observe that the senior management of a company has been buying a lot of the company's stock on the open market over the past week.
   d. Your next-door neighbor, who happens to be a computer analyst at the local steel plant, casually mentions that a German steel conglomerate hinted yesterday that it might try to acquire the local firm in a hostile takeover.

13. **Dow Theory**   Why do you think the industrial and transportation averages are the two that underlie Dow theory?

14. **Performance of the Pros**   In the mid- to late-1990s, the performance of the pros was unusually poor—on the order of 90 percent of all equity mutual funds underperformed a passively managed index fund. How does this bear on the issue of market efficiency?

15. **Efficient Markets**   In the early 1900s, companies did not compile annual reports. Even if you owned stock in a particular company, you were unlikely to be allowed to see the balance sheet and income statement for the company. Assuming the market is semistrong-form efficient, what does this say about market efficiency then compared to now?

Questions and Problems

Core Questions

1. **Advance/Decline Lines**   Use the data below to construct the advance/decline line for the stock market. Volume figures are in thousands of shares.

	Advancing	Adv. Vol.	Declining	Dec. Vol.
Monday	1,150	205,000	840	92,000
Tuesday	1,410	263,000	685	61,000
Wednesday	810	84,000	1,210	218,000
Thursday	780	68,000	1,360	256,000
Friday	1,050	174,000	920	168,000

2. **Calculating Arms Ratio**   Using the data in the previous problem, construct the Arms ratio on each of the five trading days.

3. **Relative Strength Trends**   The table below shows end-of-month stock prices for Coca-Cola and Pepsi over a six-month period. Construct the relative strength indicator over this period for Coca-Cola stock relative to Pepsi.

Month	Coca-Cola	Pepsi
1	$48	$37
2	46	44
3	45	42
4	44	42
5	40	41
6	39	38

4. **Moving Average Indicators**   Using the data in the previous problem, calculate the three-month moving average for Coca-Cola and Pepsi stock.

5. **Candlesticks**   Suppose that on a particular day the S&P 500 opened at 818.68, closed at 817.37, and the high and low for the day were 821.25 and 806.29, respectively. Describe how you would construct a candlestick plot for these data. Construct the candlestick chart for this day.

Use the following information on the DJIA to answer the next two questions:

Date	Open	High	Low	Close
24-Feb-03	8017.34	8017.34	7828.06	7858.24
25-Feb-03	7856.42	7931.14	7700.53	7909.50
26-Feb-03	7907.39	7944.93	7767.62	7806.98

6. **Hi-Lo-Close Chart**   Construct a hi-lo-close chart for the DJIA.

7. **Candlestick Chart**   Construct a candlestick chart for the DJIA.

8. **Moving Average**   Suppose you are given the following information on the S&P 500:

Date	Close
13-Feb-03	817.37
14-Feb-03	834.89
18-Feb-03	851.17
19-Feb-03	845.13
20-Feb-03	837.10
21-Feb-03	848.17
24-Feb-03	832.58
25-Feb-03	838.57
26-Feb-03	827.55
27-Feb-03	837.28

Calculate the three-day moving average for the S&P 500. Why would you want to know the moving average for an index? If the close on February 28, 2003, was above the three-day moving average, would it be a buy or sell signal?

www.mhhe.com/cj3e

9. **Support and Resistance Levels**   Below you will see a stock price chart for American Express from finance.yahoo.com. Do you see any resistance or support levels? What do support and resistance levels mean for the stock price?

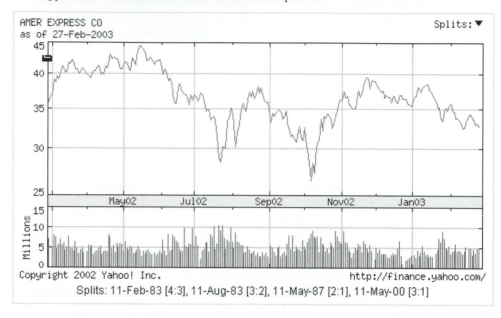

Intermediate Questions

10. **Point-and-Figure Plots**   Daily closing prices for U.S. Surgical, Inc., are shown below for a six-week period. If you consider a major move to be $4, construct the point-and-figure chart for U.S. Surgical stock over this time period.

Week	M	T	W	R	F
1	120	119	117	113	108
2	105	99	90	93	94
3	96	96	93	88	83
4	87	93	90	84	87
5	85	93	103	105	105
6	108	105	102	103	109

Use the following information to answer the next three questions. Below you will find the Hi, Lo, Open, and Close for Dell Computer stock for two weeks in February 2003 (February 17 was a holiday).

Date	Open	High	Low	Close
10-Feb-03	$23.27	$23.31	$22.59	$22.86
11-Feb-03	23.24	23.70	23.04	23.24
12-Feb-03	23.25	23.54	22.93	22.94
13-Feb-03	23.03	23.35	22.82	23.25
14-Feb-03	24.55	25.79	24.50	25.77
18-Feb-03	25.73	26.50	25.51	26.49
19-Feb-03	26.20	26.39	25.73	26.11
20-Feb-03	26.15	26.50	26.13	26.34
21-Feb-03	26.45	27.00	26.16	26.84

11. **Hi-Lo-Close Chart**   Construct a hi-lo-close chart for Dell.

12. **Candlestick Chart**   Construct a candlestick chart for Dell.

13. **Moving Average**   Construct the five-day moving average for Dell based on the closing price.

14. **Put-Call Ratio**   Another technical indicator is the put-call ratio. The put-call ratio is the number of put options traded divided by the number of call options traded. The put-call ratio can be constructed on the market or an individual stock. Below you will find the number of puts and calls traded over a four-week period for all stocks:

Week	Puts	Calls
1	783,158	809,562
2	521,753	454,678
3	521,075	495,373
4	544,410	487,199

How would you interpret the put-call ratio? Calculate the put-call ratio for each week. From this analysis, does it appear the market is expected to be upward trending or downward trending?

15. **Investor Sentiment**   A technical analysis tool that is sometimes used to predict market movements is an investor sentiment index. AAII, the American Association of Individual Investors, publishes an investor sentiment index based on a survey of its members. Below you will find the percentage of investors who were bullish, bearish, or neutral during a four-week period.

Week	Bullish	Bearish	Neutral
1	37	25	38
2	52	14	34
3	29	35	36
4	43	26	21

What is the investor sentiment index intended to capture? How might it be useful in technical analysis?

STANDARD
&POOR'S

S&P Problems

www.mhhe.com/edumarketinsight

1. **Advance/Decline Indicators**   Choose any company. Follow the "Charting by Prophet™" link, then click the "+" by "Technical Indicators," and finally the "+" by "Market Studies." Under this link, examine the Advance/Decline Line, the Advance/Decline Ratio, and the Advancing/Declining Issues. What are these indicators supposed to measure? In examining these market indicators, predict the future movement of the market. Follow the market for the next several weeks on your favorite financial website to determine if your prediction was correct.

2. **Relative Strength**   Enter the ticker symbol INTC for Intel and follow the "Charting by Prophet™" link, then click the "+" by "Technical Indicators," and finally the "+" by "Lower Studies II." Prophet will construct a relative strength line for any stock compared to the S&P 500 Index. Click on "Relative Strength." How has Intel performed compared to the S&P 500 over the past three years? The past two years? The past year?

3. **Moving Average**   Enter the ticker symbol INTC for Intel and follow the "Charting by Prophet™" link, then click the "+" by "Technical Indicators," and finally the "+" by "Moving Averages." Prophet shows the moving average price for a stock for the past 15 days. Examine the price chart with a 15-day moving average over the past year. Look at every time the stock price broke the moving average over this period, and note whether the chart predicted an upswing or a downswing. How many times did the stock cross the moving average line? How many times did the crossing point predict the stock price correctly if you examine the time between when the stock crossed the moving average line and the stock price two weeks later? One week later? One month later?

4. **Candlestick Charts**   Enter the ticker symbol INTC for Intel and follow the "Charting by Prophet™" link. Use the pull-down menus at the top to draw a candlestick chart for the past three months. Use a sheet of paper to cover the candlestick chart and uncover the chart one day at a time. Examining the candlestick chart by this process, try to use the candlesticks to predict Intel's stock price movements. Note how many times you are successful and how many times you are unsuccessful.

What's on the Web?

1. **Bollinger Bands**   What is a Bollinger Band? Go to www.chartsmart.com and look under the Investor Learning Center to find out. How are Bollinger Bands constructed? How do you use Bollinger Bands in technical analysis? Now go to finance.yahoo.com and enter your favorite stock. There is a technical analysis section under the chart option. Use this site to construct the Bollinger Band for your stock. What does this chart tell you?

2. **Elliott Wave Theory**   Elliott Wave Theory is a popular technical trading rule. Go to www.borsanaliz.com/eng to find out what it is. Describe the theory in your own words.

3. **Triangles**   Go to www.borsanaliz.com/eng. How many different types of triangles are listed on the site? What does each type of triangle mean to a technical analyst?

4. **Market Volume**   An important tool for most technical traders is market volume. Go to www.marketvolume.com. Look on the site to find the reasons market volume is considered important.

Stock-Trak®
Portfolio Simulations

Beating the Market with Stock-Trak

A personal Stock-Trak account provides an excellent opportunity for you to try your favorite strategy to beat the market without putting your personal funds at risk. The material in this chapter suggests several strategies. For example, Charles Dow originally intended Dow theory as a method to analyze movements of the overall stock market. However, the basic tenets of Dow theory can also be usefully applied to individual stocks. Essentially, this involves distinguishing genuine price trends from background noise. Since your investment horizon with a Stock-Trak account is probably no longer than a few months, you will want to identify secondary trends expected to last from only a few weeks to a few months. Beginning with about a dozen stock price charts, cull out three or four with the most distinguishable short-term price trends. If a stock has an upward price trend, you should buy that stock. If a stock has a downward price trend, then you should short sell it.

In examining price charts for various stocks, you will observe many other types of patterns. Support and resistance levels are examples of simple, yet intriguing patterns. Suppose you discover a stock price bumping up against a resistance ceiling, and you conclude that a breakout appears imminent. Then, you should buy the stock.

There are many other patterns that you might look for. Indeed, technical analysis is based largely on the detection of patterns that might repeat themselves in the near future. Remember, however, that technical analysis is part science and part art. You can learn the science by reading books, but you can absorb the art only through experience. If there is some special strategy that you want to experiment with, do it risk-free with your Stock-Trak account. No matter what happens, you will probably learn something useful from the experience.

To find stocks with distinct trends, support or resistance levels, or other technical trading tools, you will need to peruse a number of stock price charts. Fortunately, many websites provide free stock price charts. Three of the best and most accessible are finance.yahoo.com, stockcharts.com, and www.bigcharts.com. If you want more sites, enter "Technical Analysis" in a search engine. We did and found over 3.5 million results. To complete the Stock-Trak exercises below you will need to spend time on the Internet to find appropriate stocks.

Stock-Trak Exercises

1. Identify a stock whose 50-day moving average recently crossed the 200-day moving average from below and another stock whose 50-day moving average crossed the 200-day moving average from above. Buy the first stock and short sell the second stock. This strategy captures the trend in stock prices while maintaining a market-neutral portfolio.

2. Identify two stocks with upward price trends and two stocks with downward price trends. Buy the first two stocks and short sell the second two stocks. This strategy focuses on identifying price trends while reducing the risk of an overall market movement that might simultaneously affect all four stocks in your portfolio.

3. Identify two stocks bumping up against a resistance ceiling and another two stocks bumping down against a support floor. Buy the first two stocks and short sell the second two stocks. This strategy focuses on capturing price breakouts while maintaining a market-neutral portfolio.

Chapter 9

Interest Rates

"Remember that time is money."

–Benjamin Franklin

Benjamin Franklin stated a fundamental truth of commerce when he sagely advised young tradesmen that time is money. In finance, we call this the time value of money. But how much time corresponds to how much money? Interest constitutes a rental payment for money, and an interest rate tells us how much money for how much time. But there are many interest rates, each corresponding to a particular money market. Interest rates state money prices in each of these markets. ■

This chapter is the first dealing specifically with interest-bearing assets. As we discussed in Chapter 3, there are two basic types of interest-bearing assets, money market instruments and fixed-income securities. For both types of assets, interest rates are a key determinant of asset values. Furthermore, since there are trillions of dollars in interest-bearing assets outstanding, interest rates play a pivotal role in financial markets and the economy.

Because interest rates are one of the most closely watched financial market indicators, we devote this entire chapter to them. We first discuss the many different interest rates that are commonly reported in the financial press, along with some of the different ways interest rates are calculated and quoted. We then go on to describe the basic determinants and separable components of interest rates.

9.1 Interest Rate History and Money Market Rates

Recall from Chapter 3 that money market instruments are debt obligations that have a maturity of less than one year at the time they are originally issued. Each business day, *The Wall Street Journal* publishes a list of current interest rates for several categories of money market securities in its "Money Rates" report. We will discuss each of these interest rates and the securities they represent immediately below. First, however, we take a quick look at the history of interest rates.

Interest Rate History

In Chapter 1, we saw how looking back at the history of returns on various types of investments gave us a useful perspective on rates of return. Similar insights are available from interest rate history. For example, in mid-2003, short-term interest rates were about 1 percent and long-term rates were about 4.5 percent. We might ask, "Are these rates unusually high or low?" To find out, we examine Figure 9.1, which graphically illustrates 200 years of interest rates in the United States.

Two interest rates are plotted in Figure 9.1, one for bills and one for bonds. Both rates are based on U.S. Treasury securities, or close substitutes. We discuss bills and bonds in detail in this chapter and the next chapter. For now, it is enough to know that bills are short term and bonds are long term, so what is plotted in Figure 9.1 are short- and long-term interest rates.

FIGURE 9.1 **Interest Rate History (U.S. Interest Rates, 1800–2001)**

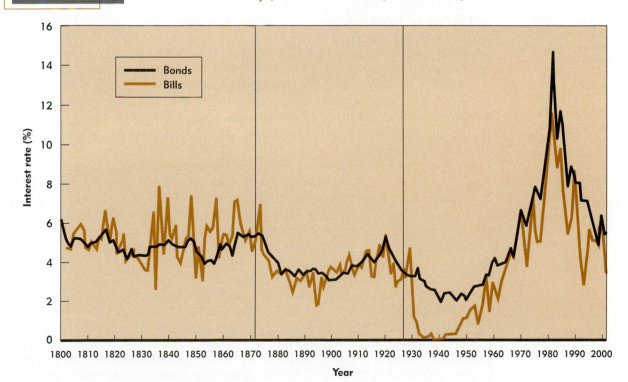

Source: Adapted from Jeremy J. Siegel, *Stocks for the Long Run,* 3rd ed., © McGraw-Hill, 2002.

Probably the most striking feature in Figure 9.1 is the fact that the highest interest rates in U.S. history occurred in the not-too-distant past. Rates began rising sharply in the 1970s, and then peaked at extraordinary levels in the early 1980s. They have generally declined since then. The other striking aspect of U.S. interest rate history is the very low short-term interest rates that prevailed from the 1930s to the 1960s. This was the result, in large part, of deliberate actions by the Federal Reserve Board to keep short-term rates low—a policy that ultimately proved unsustainable and even disastrous. Much was learned by the experience, however, and now the Fed is more concerned with controlling inflation.

With long-term rates around 4.5 percent as this chapter was written, many market observers have commented that these interest rate levels are extraordinarily low. Based on the history of interest rates illustrated in Figure 9.1, however, 4.5 percent may be low relative to the last 30 years, but it is not at all low compared to rates during the 170-year period from 1800 to 1970. Indeed, long-term rates would have to fall well below 4 percent to be considered low by historical standards.

Money Market Rates

prime rate The basic interest rate on short-term loans that the largest commercial banks charge to their most creditworthy corporate customers.

bellwether rate Interest rate that serves as a leader or as a leading indicator of future trends, e.g., interest rates as a bellwether of inflation.

Federal funds rate Interest rate that banks charge each other for overnight loans of $1 million or more.

discount rate The interest rate that the Fed offers to commercial banks for overnight reserve loans.

For the latest on money market rates visit www.money-rates.com

Figure 9.2 reproduces a *Wall Street Journal* "Money Rates" report of interest rates for the most important money market instruments. A commonly quoted interest rate is the **prime rate**. The prime rate is a key short-term interest rate since it is the basis for interest rates that large commercial banks charge on short-term loans (rates are quoted as prime plus or minus a spread). The prime rate is well known as a **bellwether rate** of bank lending to business. Besides a prime rate for the United States, the "Money Rates" report also lists foreign prime rates for Canada, the European Central Bank, Japan, Switzerland, and Great Britain.

The **Federal funds rate** (or just "Fed funds") is a fundamental interest rate for commercial bank activity. The Fed funds rate is the interest rate that banks charge each other for overnight loans of $1 million or more. This interbank rate is set by continuous bidding among banks, where banks wishing to lend funds quote "offer rates" (rates at which they are willing to lend), and banks wishing to borrow funds quote "bid rates" (rates they are willing to pay). Notice that four different rates are stated: *high* is the highest rate offered and *low* is the lowest rate bid during a day's trading; *near closing bid* is a bid rate to borrow and *near closing offered* is an offered rate to lend near the end of the day's trading.

The Federal Reserve's **discount rate** is another pivotal interest rate for commercial banks. The discount rate is the interest rate that the Fed offers to commercial banks for overnight reserve loans. You might recall from your Money and Banking class that banks are required to maintain reserves equal to some fraction of their deposit liabilities. When a bank cannot supply sufficient reserves from internal sources, it must borrow reserves from other banks through the Federal funds market. Therefore, the Fed discount rate and the Fed funds rate are usually closely linked.

The Federal Reserve Bank is the central bank of the United States. It is charged with the responsibility of managing interest rates and the money supply to control inflation and promote stable economic growth. The discount rate is a basic tool of monetary policy for the Federal Reserve Bank. An announced change in the discount rate is often interpreted as a signal of the Federal Reserve's intentions regarding future monetary policy. For example, by increasing the discount rate, the Federal Reserve may be signaling that it intends to pursue a tight-money policy, most likely to control budding inflationary pressures. Similarly, by decreasing the discount rate, the Federal Reserve

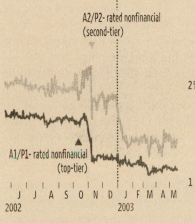

Money Rates

Monday, May 19, 2003

The key U. S. and foreign annual interest rates below are a guide to general levels but don't always represent actual transactions.

Commercial Paper

Yields paid by corporations for short-term financing, typically for daily operation

A2/P2- rated nonfinancial (second-tier)

2%

A1/P1- rated nonfinancial (top-tier)

1

J J A S O N D J F M A M

2002   2003

Source: Federal Reserve

Prime Rate: 4.25% (effective 11/07/02).
Discount Rate: 2.25% (effective 01/09/03).
Federal Funds: 1.281% high, 1.250% low, 1.219 near closing bid, 1.250% offered. Effective rate: 1.26%. Source: Prebon Yamane (USA) Inc. Federal-funds target rate: 1.250% (effective 11/06/02).
Call Money: 3.00% (effective 11/07/02).
Commercial Paper: Placed directly by General Electric Capital Corp.: 1.24% 30 to 35 days; 1.05% 36 to 50 days; 1.22% 51 to 69 days; 1.20% 70 to 100 days; 1.17% 101 to 127 days; 1.05% 128 to 140 days; 1.15% 141 to 155 days; 1.13% 156 to 270 days.
Euro Commercial Paper: Placed directly by General Electric Capital Corp.: 2.47% 30 days; 2.37% two months; 2.32%

three months; 2.27% four months; 2.24% five months; 2.21% six months.
Dealer Commercial Paper: High-grade unsecured notes sold through dealers by major corporations: 1.19% 30 days; 1.18% 60 days; 1.17% 90 days.
Certificates of Deposit: 1.26% one month; 1.20% three months; 1.16% six months.
Bankers Acceptances: 1.25% 30 days; 1.23% 60 days; 1.20% 90 days; 1.18% 120 days; 1.16% 150 days; 1.14% 180 days. Source: Prebon Yamane (USA) Inc.
Eurodollars: 1.25% - 1.27% one month; 1.22% - 1.25% two months; 1.21% - 1.24% three months; 1.16% - 1.20% four months; 1.15% - 1.19% five months; 1.13% - 1.16% six months. Source: Prebon Yamane (USA) Inc.
London Interbank Offered Rates (Libor): 1.3175% one month; 1.27875% three months; 1.20625% six months; 1.18875% one year. Effective rate for contracts entered into two days from date appearing at top of this column.
Euro Libor: 2.54438% one month; 2.38250% three months; 2.26563% six months; 2.20688% one year. Effective rate for contracts entered into two days from date appearing at top of this column.
Euro Interbank Offered Rates (Euribor): 2.546% one month; 2.381% three months; 2.265% six months; 2.207% one year. Source: Reuters.
Foreign Prime Rates: Canada 5.00%; European Central Bank 2.50%; Japan 1.375%; Switzerland 2.25%; Britain 3.75%.
Treasury Bills: Results of the Monday, May 19, 2003, auction of short-term U.S. government bills, sold at a discount from face value in units of $1,000 to $1 million: 1.000% 13 weeks; 1.070% 26 weeks. Tuesday, May 13, 2003 auction: 1.000% 4 weeks.
Overnight Repurchase Rate: 1.23%. Source: Garban Intercapital.
Freddie Mac: Posted yields on 30-year mortgage commitments. Delivery within 30 days 4.85%, 60 days 4.94%, standard conventional fixed-rate mortgages: 3.625%, 2% rate capped one-year adjustable rate mortgages.
Fannie Mae: Posted yields on 30 year mortgage commitments (priced at par) for delivery within 30 days 4.89%, 60 days 4.97%, standard conventional fixed-rate mortgages; 3.00%, 6/2 rate capped one-year adjustable rate mortgages. Constant Maturity Debt Index: 1.157% three months; 1.130% six months; 1.141% one year.
Merrill Lynch Ready Assets Trust: 0.81%.
Consumer Price Index: April, 183.8, up 2.2% from a year ago. Bureau of Labor Statistics.

---

may be signaling an intent to pursue a loose-money policy to stimulate economic activity. Of course, many times a discount rate change is simply a case of the Federal Reserve catching up to financial market conditions rather than leading them. Indeed, the Federal Reserve often acts like the lead goose, who, upon looking back and seeing the flock heading in another direction, quickly flies over to resume its position as "leader" of the flock.

The next interest rate reported is the **call money rate**, or simply the call rate. "Call money" refers to loans from banks to security brokerage firms, and the call rate is the interest rate that brokerage firms pay on call money loans. As we discussed in Chapter 2, brokers use funds raised through call money loans to make margin loans to customers to finance leveraged stock and bond purchases. The call money rate is the basic rate that brokers use to set interest rates on customer call money loans. Brokers typically charge their customers the call money rate plus a premium, where the broker and the customer may negotiate the premium. For example, a broker may charge a

call money rate The interest rate brokerage firms pay for call money loans, which are bank loans to brokerage firms. This rate is used as the basis for customer rates on margin loans.

customer the basic call money rate plus 1 percent for a margin loan to purchase common stock.

Commercial paper is short-term, unsecured debt issued by the largest corporations. The commercial paper market is dominated by financial corporations, such as banks and insurance companies, or financial subsidiaries of large corporations. As shown in Figure 9.2, a leading commercial paper rate is the rate that General Electric Capital Corporation (the finance arm of General Electric) pays on short-term debt issues. This commercial paper rate is a benchmark for this market because General Electric Capital is one of the largest single issuers of commercial paper. Most other corporations issuing commercial paper will pay a slightly higher interest rate than this benchmark rate. Commercial paper is a popular investment vehicle for portfolio managers and corporate treasurers with excess funds on hand that they wish to invest on a short-term basis. "Euro" commercial paper refers to commercial paper denominated in euros rather than dollars.

Certificates of deposit, or **CDs**, represent large-denomination deposits of $100,000 or more at commercial banks for a specified term. The interest rate paid on CDs usually varies according to the term of the deposit. For example, a one-year CD may pay a higher interest rate than a six-month CD, which in turn may pay a higher interest rate than a three-month CD.

Large-denomination certificates of deposit are generally negotiable instruments, meaning that they can be bought and sold among investors. Consequently, they are often called negotiable certificates of deposit, or negotiable CDs. Negotiable CDs can be bought and sold through a broker. The large-denomination CDs described here should not be confused with the small-denomination CDs that banks offer retail customers. These small-denomination CDs are simply bank time deposits. They normally pay a lower interest rate than large-denomination CDs and are not negotiable instruments.

A **banker's acceptance** is essentially a postdated check upon which a commercial bank has guaranteed payment. Banker's acceptances are normally used to finance international trade transactions. For example, as an importer, you wish to purchase computer components from a company in Singapore and pay for the goods three months after delivery, so you write a postdated check. You and the exporter agree, however, that once the goods are shipped, your bank will guarantee payment on the date specified on the check.

After your goods are shipped, the exporter presents the relevant documentation, and, if all is in order, your bank stamps the word *ACCEPTED* on your check. At this point your bank has created an acceptance, which means it has promised to pay the acceptance's face value (the amount of the check) at maturity (the date on the check). The exporter can then hold on to the acceptance or sell it in the money market. The banker's acceptance rate published in "Money Rates" is the interest rate for acceptances issued by the largest commercial banks.

Eurodollars are certificates of deposit denominated in U.S. dollars at commercial banks in London. Eurodollar rates are interest rates paid for large-denomination deposits. Eurodollar CDs are negotiable and are traded in a large, very active Eurodollar money market. The "Money Rates" report lists Eurodollar rates for various maturities obtained from transactions occurring late in the day.

The **London Interbank Offered Rate (LIBOR)** is the interest rate offered by London commercial banks for dollar deposits from other banks. The LIBOR rate is perhaps the most frequently cited rate used to represent the London money market. Bank lending rates are often stated as LIBOR plus a premium, where the premium is

commercial paper Short-term, unsecured debt issued by the largest corporations.

Visit General Motors Acceptance at www.gmacfs.com Visit General Electric Capital at www.gecapital.com

certificate of deposit (CD) Large-denomination deposits of $100,000 or more at commercial banks for a specified term.

banker's acceptance A postdated check on which a bank has guaranteed payment; commonly used to finance international trade transactions.

Eurodollars Certificates of deposit denominated in U.S. dollars at commercial banks in London.

London Interbank Offered Rate (LIBOR) Interest rate that international banks charge one another for overnight Eurodollar loans.

negotiated between the bank and its customer. For example, a corporation may be quoted a loan rate from a London bank at LIBOR plus 2 percent. Euro LIBOR refers to deposits denominated in euros rather than eurodollars. Euribor is the rate in "euroland" rather than London.

U.S. Treasury bill (T-bill) A short-term U.S. government debt instrument issued by the U.S. Treasury.

U.S. Treasury bills, or just **T-bills**, represent short-term U.S. government debt issues through the U.S. Treasury. The Treasury bill market is the largest market for short-term debt securities in the world. As such, the Treasury bill market leads all other credit markets in determining the general level of short-term interest rates. "Money Rates" reports Treasury bill interest rates set during the most recent weekly Treasury bill auction. Interest rates determined at each Treasury bill auction are closely watched by professional money managers throughout the world. The overnight repurchase, or "repo," rate is essentially the rate charged on overnight loans that are collateralized by U.S. Treasury securities.

The Federal Home Loan Mortgage Corporation (FHLMC), commonly called "Freddie Mac," and the Federal National Mortgage Association (FNMA), commonly called "Fannie Mae," are government-sponsored agencies that purchase large blocks of home mortgages and combine them into mortgage pools, where each pool may represent several tens of millions of dollars of home mortgages. We will discuss mortgage pools in depth in Chapter 19. The interest rates reported in "Money Rates" are an indicator of rates on newly created home mortgages. Since home mortgages are long-term obligations, these are not actually money market rates. However, with several trillion dollars of mortgages outstanding, the mortgage market has a considerable influence on money market activity.

The Merrill Lynch Ready Assets Trust is a money market fund for customer accounts with the brokerage firm of Merrill Lynch. Recall from Chapter 4 that money market funds are mutual funds that invest in money market instruments. The interest rate reported in the "Money Rates" report is an average of interest rates paid on fund accounts over the previous month.

For more on LIBOR, visit www.bba.org.uk

Check This

9.1a Which money market interest rates are most important to commercial banks?

9.1b Which money market interest rates are most important to nonbank corporations?

9.2 Money Market Prices and Rates

pure discount security An interest-bearing asset that makes a single payment of face value at maturity with no payments before maturity.

Money market securities typically make a single payment of face value at maturity and make no payments before maturity. Such securities are called **pure discount securities** because they sell at a discount relative to their face value. In this section, we discuss the relationship between the price of a money market instrument and the interest rate quoted on it.

One of the things you will notice in this section is that there are several different ways market participants quote interest rates. This presents a problem when we wish to compare rates on different investments. But before we can do this, we must put them on a common footing.

After going through the various interest rate conventions and conversions needed to compare them, you might wonder why everybody doesn't just agree to compute interest rates and prices in some uniform way. Well perhaps they should, but they definitely do not. As a result, we must review some of the various procedures actually used in money markets. We hope you come to recognize that the calculations are neither mysterious nor even especially difficult, although they are rooted in centuries-old procedures and may sometimes be tedious. However, given the billions of dollars of securities traded every day based on these numbers, it is important to understand them.

One other thing to notice is that the word "yield" appears frequently. For now, you can take it as given that the yield on an interest-bearing asset is simply a measure of the interest rate being offered by the asset. We will discuss the topic of yields in greater detail in the next chapter.

Bond yields and many interest rates are quoted as a percentage with two decimal places, such as 11.82 percent. With this quote, the smallest possible change would be .01 percent, or .0001. This amount, which is 1 percent of 1 percent, is called a **basis point**. So, if our 11.82 percent rose to 11.94 percent, we would say rates rose by $94 - 82 = 12$ basis points. The quantity to the left of the decimal point (the "11") is called the "handle." Traders frequently omit the handle when quoting or discussing rates since, presumably, anyone actively trading would know it.

basis point With regard to interest rates or bond yields, one basis point is 1 percent of 1 percent.

Bank Discount Rate Quotes

Interest rates for some key money market securities, including Treasury bills and banker's acceptances, are quoted on a **bank discount basis**, or simply discount basis. An interest rate quoted on a discount basis is often called a discount yield. If we are given an interest rate quoted on a bank discount basis for a particular money market instrument, then we calculate the price of that instrument as follows:

bank discount basis A method for quoting interest rates on money market instruments.

$$\text{Current price} = \text{Face value} \times \left(1 - \frac{\text{Days to maturity}}{360} \times \text{Discount yield}\right)$$

(9.1)

The term "discount yield" here simply refers to the quoted interest rate. It should not be confused with the Federal Reserve's discount rate discussed earlier.

To give an example, suppose a banker's acceptance has a face value of $1 million that will be paid in 90 days. If the interest rate, quoted on a discount basis, is 5 percent, what is the current price of the acceptance?

As the following calculation shows, a discount yield of 5 percent and maturity of 90 days gives a current price of $987,500.

$$\$987,500 = \$1,000,000 \times \left(1 - \frac{90}{360} \times .05\right)$$

The difference between the face value of $1 million and the price of $987,500 is $12,500 and is called the "discount." This discount is the interest earned over the 90-day period until the acceptance matures.

Notice that the formula used to calculate the acceptance price assumes a 360-day business year. This practice dates back to a time when calculations were performed manually. Assuming a 360-day business year, with exactly four 90-day quarters rather than a true 365-day calendar year, made manual discount calculations simpler and less subject to error. Consequently, if $1 million is discounted over a full calendar year of

365 days using a bank discount yield of 5 percent and an assumed 360-day business year, the resulting price of $949,305.56 is calculated as follows:

$$\$949,305.56 = \$1,000,000 \times \left(1 - \frac{365}{360} \times .05\right)$$

MONEY MARKET PRICES

EXAMPLE 9.1

The rate on a particular money market instrument, quoted on a discount basis, is 6 percent. The instrument has a face value of $100,000 and will mature in 71 days. What is its price? What if it had 51 days to maturity?

Using the bank discount basis formula, we have

$$\text{Current price} = \text{Face value} \times \left(1 - \frac{\textbf{Days to maturity}}{360} \times \text{Discount yield}\right)$$

$$\$98,816.67 = \$100,000 \times \left(1 - \frac{71}{360} \times .06\right)$$

Check for yourself that the price in the second case of a 51-day maturity is $99,150.

Treasury Bill Quotes

The Wall Street Journal reports current interest rates on U.S. Treasury bills each business day. Figure 9.3 reproduces a "Treasury Bills" interest rate report. The maturity of each bill issue is stated in month-day-year format, followed by the number of days remaining until the bill matures. The two columns following the days to maturity give the bid and asked discounts for each bill issue. The bid discount is used by Treasury bill dealers to state what they are willing to pay for a Treasury bill, and the asked discount is used to state what price a dealer will accept to sell a Treasury bill. The next column shows the change in the asked discount from the previous day.

For example, consider a bill issue with 154 days to maturity, with a bid discount rate of 5.06 percent and an asked discount rate of 5.04 percent. For a $1 million face value Treasury bill, the corresponding bid and asked prices can be calculated by using the discounts shown along with our bank discount basis pricing formula. For example, the bid price would be

$$\text{Bid price} = \$978,354.44 = \$1,000,000 \times \left(1 - \frac{154}{360} \times .0506\right)$$

Check that the ask price would be $978,440.00.

For price and yield data on U.S. Treasury securities visit www.govpx.com

T-BILL PRICES

EXAMPLE 9.2

Suppose you wanted to buy a T-bill with 80 days to maturity and a face value of $5,000,000. How much would you have to pay if the asked discount is 5.49 percent?

(continued)

Since you are buying, you must pay the asked price. To calculate the asked price, we use the asked discount in the bank discount basis formula:

$$\text{Asked price} = \$4{,}939{,}000 = \$5{,}000{,}000 \times \left(1 - \frac{80}{360} \times .0549\right)$$

Calculate a bid price for this T-bill assuming a bid discount of 5.54 percent. Notice that the asked price is higher than the bid price even though the asked discount is lower than the bid discount. The reason is that a bigger discount produces a lower price.

Treasury bill prices may be calculated using a built-in spreadsheet function. An example of how to use an Excel™ spreadsheet to calculate a Treasury bill price is shown in the nearby *Spreadsheet Analysis* box.

The last column in Figure 9.3 lists the asked yield ("ASK YLD") for each Treasury bill issue. It is important to realize that the asked yield is *not* quoted on a discount basis. Instead, it is a "bond equivalent yield." Unlike a discount rate, a bond equivalent yield assumes a 365-day calendar year. Bond equivalent yields are principally used to compare yields on Treasury bills with yields on other money market instruments as well as Treasury bonds and other bonds (we discuss these long-term yields in the next chapter).

Bank Discount Yields versus Bond Equivalent Yields

A bank discount yield is converted to a bond equivalent yield using the following formula:

$$\text{Bond equivalent yield} = \frac{365 \times \text{Discount yield}}{360 - \text{Days to maturity} \times \text{Discount yield}} \quad (9.2)$$

This conversion formula is correct for maturities of six months or less. Calculation of bond equivalent yields for maturities greater than six months is a little more compli-

---

FIGURE 9.3

U.S. Treasury Bills

Source: *The Wall Street Journal,* March 20, 2003. Reprinted by permission of Dow Jones, Inc. via Copyright Clearance Center, Inc., © 2003 Dow Jones and Company, Inc. All Rights Reserved Worldwide.

Treasury Bills

MATURITY	DAYS TO MAT	BID	ASKED	CHG	ASK YLD
May 22 03	2	1.10	1.09	0.04	1.11
May 29 03	9	1.01	1.00	0.02	1.01
Jun 05 03	16	0.98	0.97	0.01	0.98
Jun 12 03	23	0.99	0.98	0.03	0.99
Jun 19 03	30	1.04	1.03	0.07	1.05
Jun 26 03	37	1.00	0.99	0.03	1.00
Jul 03 03	44	1.01	1.00	...	1.02
Jul 10 03	51	1.01	1.00	...	1.02
Jul 17 03	58	1.01	1.00	...	1.02
Jul 24 03	65	1.01	1.00	0.02	1.02
Jul 31 03	72	1.01	1.00	0.01	1.02
Aug 07 03	79	1.00	0.99	...	1.01
Aug 14 03	86	1.03	1.02	...	1.04
Aug 21 03	93	1.03	1.02	...	1.04
Aug 28 03	100	1.03	1.02	-0.02	1.04
Sep 04 03	107	1.03	1.02	-0.01	1.04
Sep 11 03	114	1.03	1.02	-0.01	1.04
Sep 18 03	121	1.04	1.03	...	1.05
Sep 25 03	128	1.04	1.03	...	1.05
Oct 02 03	135	1.04	1.03	-0.01	1.05
Oct 09 03	142	1.04	1.03	-0.01	1.05
Oct 16 03	149	1.03	1.02	-0.01	1.04
Oct 23 03	156	1.03	1.02	-0.01	1.04
Oct 30 03	163	1.04	1.03	...	1.05
Nov 06 03	170	1.04	1.03	...	1.05
Nov 13 03	177	1.04	1.03	-0.01	1.05

SPREADSHEET ANALYSIS

	A	B	C	D	E	F	G	H
1								
2			Treasury Bill Price and Yield Calculations					
3								
4	A Treasury bill traded on March 14, 2004, pays $100 on June 1, 2004. Assuming a							
5	discount rate of 6 percent, what are its price and bond equivalent yield?							
6	Hint: Use the Excel function TBILLPRICE and TBILLEQ.							
7								
8		$98.6833	= TBILLPRICE("3/14/04","6/1/04",0.06)					
9								
10		6.164%	= TBILLEQ("3/14/04","6/1/04",0.06)					
11								
12								
13	A credit card charges a nominal annual interest rate of 15 percent. With interest							
14	charged monthly, what is the effective annual rate (EAR) on this credit card?							
15	Hint: Use the Excel function EFFECT.							
16								
17		16.075%	= EFFECT(0.15,12)					
18								
19								
20								

cated, and we will not discuss it here, particularly since T-bills with maturities greater than six months are no longer sold.

For example, suppose the asked discount rate on a T-bill with 170 days to maturity is 3.22 percent. What is the bond equivalent yield? Plugging into the conversion formula, a 3.22 percent discount is converted into a bond equivalent yield as follows:

$$3.315\% = \frac{365 \times .0322}{360 - 170 \times .0322}$$

The bond equivalent yield is thus 3.315 percent.

BOND EQUIVALENT YIELDS

EXAMPLE 9.3

Suppose a T-bill has 45 days to maturity and an asked discount of 5 percent. What is the bond equivalent yield?

Using the bond equivalent yield conversion formulas, we have

$$5.101\% = \frac{365 \times .05}{360 - 45 \times .05}$$

(continued)

The bond equivalent yield is thus 5.101 percent.

Bond equivalent yields may be calculated using a built-in spreadsheet function. An example of how to use an Excel™ spreadsheet to calculate a bond equivalent yield is shown in the nearby *Spreadsheet Analysis* box.

One common cause of confusion about bond equivalent yield calculations is the way that leap years are handled. The rule is that we must use 366 days if February 29 occurs within the next 12 months. For example, 2008 will be a leap year. So, beginning on March 1, 2007, we must use 366 days in Equation 9.2. Then beginning on March 1, 2008, we must revert back to using 365 days.

BACK TO THE FUTURE: LEAP YEAR BOND EQUIVALENT YIELDS

EXAMPLE 9.4

Calculate the asked yield (bond equivalent yield) for a T-bill price quoted in December 2007 with 119 days to maturity and an asked discount of 5.41 percent.

Since the 12-month period following the date of the price quote includes February 29, we must use 366 days. Plugging this into the conversion formula, we get:

$$5.60\% = \frac{366 \times .0541}{360 - 119 \times .0541}$$

This 5.60 percent is the ask yield stated as a bond equivalent yield.

We can calculate a Treasury bill asked price using the asked yield, which is a bond equivalent yield, as follows:

$$\text{Bill price} = \frac{\text{Face value}}{1 + \text{Bond equivalent yield} \times \text{Days to maturity}/365} \quad (9.3)$$

For example, just above we calculated the 3.315 percent bond equivalent yield on a T-bill with 170 days to maturity and a 3.22 percent asked discount rate. If we calculate its price using this bond equivalent yield, we get

$$\$984,795 = \frac{\$1,000,000}{1 + .03315 \times 170/365}$$

Check that, ignoring a small rounding error, you get the same price using the bank discount formula.

Bond Equivalent Yields, APRs, and EARs

Money market rates not quoted on a discount basis are generally quoted on a "simple" interest basis. Simple interest rates are calculated just like the annual percentage rate (APR) on a consumer loan. So, for the most part, money market rates are either bank discount rates or APRs. For example, CD rates are APRs.

In fact, the bond equivalent yield on a T-bill with less than six months to maturity is also an APR. As a result, like any APR, it understates the true interest rate, which is usually called the *effective annual rate*, or EAR. In the context of the money market, EARs are sometimes referred to as effective annual yields, effective yields, or annualized yields. Whatever it is called, to find out what a T-bill, or any other money market instrument, is *really* going to pay you, yet another conversion is needed. We will get to the needed conversion in a moment.

First, however, recall that an APR is equal to the interest rate per period multiplied by the number of periods in a year. For example, if the rate on a car loan is 1 percent per month, then the APR is $1\% \times 12 = 12\%$. In general, if we let m be the number of periods in a year, an APR is converted to an EAR as follows:

$$1 + EAR = \left(1 + \frac{APR}{m}\right)^m \qquad (9.4)$$

For example, on our 12 percent APR car loan, the EAR can be determined by

$$
\begin{aligned}
1 + EAR &= \left(1 + \frac{.12}{12}\right)^{12} \\
&= 1.01^{12} \\
&= 1.126825 \\
EAR &= 12.6825\%
\end{aligned}
$$

Thus, the rate on the car loan is really 12.6825 percent per year.

APRS AND EARS

EXAMPLE 9.5

A typical credit card may quote an APR of 18 percent. On closer inspection, you will find that the rate is actually 1.5 percent per month. What annual interest rate are you *really* paying on such a credit card?

With 12 periods in a year, an APR of 18 percent is converted to an EAR as follows:

$$
\begin{aligned}
1 + EAR &= \left(1 + \frac{.18}{12}\right)^{12} \\
&= 1.015^{12} \\
&= 1.1956 \\
EAR &= 19.56\%
\end{aligned}
$$

Thus, the rate on this credit card is really 19.56 percent per year.

Effective annual rates may be calculated using a built-in spreadsheet function. An example of how to use an Excel™ spreadsheet to calculate an effective annual rate is shown in a previous *Spreadsheet Analysis* box.

Now, to see that the bond equivalent yield on a T-bill is just an APR, we can first calculate the price on the bill we considered earlier (3.22 percent asked discount, 170 days to maturity). Using the bank discount formula, the asked price, for $1 million in face value, is

$$\text{Asked price} = \$984,794 = 1,000,000 \times \left(1 - \frac{170}{360} \times .0322\right)$$

The discount is $15,206. Thus, on this 170-day investment, you earn $15,206 in interest on an investment of $984,794. On a percentage basis, you earned

$$1.544\% = \frac{\$15,206}{\$984,794}$$

In a 365-day year, there are 365/170 = 2.147 periods of 170-day length. So if we multiply what you earned over the 170-day period by the number of 170-day periods in a year, we get

$$3.315\% = 2.147 \times 1.544\%$$

This is precisely the bond equivalent yield we calculated earlier.

Finally, for this T-bill we can calculate the EAR using this 3.315 percent:

$$1 + EAR = \left(1 + \frac{.03315}{2.147}\right)^{2.147}$$
$$= 1.03344$$
$$EAR = 3.344\%$$

In the end, we have three different rates for this simple T-bill. The last one, the EAR, finally tells us what we really want to know: What are we actually going to earn?

DISCOUNTS, APRS, AND EARS

EXAMPLE 9.6

A money market instrument with 60 days to maturity has a quoted ask price of 99, meaning $99 per $100 face value. What are the banker's discount yield, the bond equivalent yield, and the effective annual return?

First, to get the discount yield, we have to use the bank discount formula and solve for the discount yield:

$$\$99 = \$100 \times \left(1 - \frac{60}{360} \times \text{Discount yield}\right)$$

With a little algebra, we see that the discount yield is 6 percent.

We convert this to a bond equivalent yield as follows:

$$6.145\% = \frac{365 \times .06}{360 - 60 \times .06}$$

The bond equivalent yield is thus 6.145 percent.

Finally, to get the EAR, note that there are 6.0833 sixty-day periods in a year, so

$$1 + EAR = \left(1 + \frac{.06145}{6.0833}\right)^{6.0833}$$
$$= 1.06305$$
$$EAR = 6.305\%$$

This example illustrates the general result that the discount rate is lower than the bond equivalent yield, which in turn is less than the EAR.

Check This

9.2a	What are the three different types of interest rate quotes that are important for money market instruments?
9.2b	How are T-bill rates quoted? How are CD rates quoted?
9.2c	Of the three different types of interest rate quotes, which is the largest? Which is the smallest? Which is the most relevant?

9.3 Rates and Yields on Fixed-Income Securities

For more information on fixed-income securities visit www.bondmarkets.com

Thus far we have focused on short-term interest rates, where "short-term" means one year or less. Of course, these are not the only interest rates we are interested in, so we now begin to discuss longer-term rates by looking at fixed-income securities. To keep this discussion to a manageable length, we defer the details of how some longer-term rates are computed to Chapter 10.

Fixed-income securities include long-term debt contracts from a wide variety of issuers. The largest single category of fixed-income securities is debt issued by the U.S. government. The second largest category of fixed-income securities is mortgage debt issued to finance real estate purchases. The two other large categories of fixed-income securities are debt issued by corporations and debt issued by municipal governments. Each of these categories represents several trillion dollars of outstanding debt. Corporate bonds are covered in detail in Chapter 17, and municipal government bonds are covered in Chapter 18.

For the latest U.S. Treasury rates, check www.bloomberg.com

Because of its sheer size, the leading world market for debt securities is the market for U.S. Treasury securities. Interest rates for U.S. Treasury debt are closely watched throughout the world, and daily reports can be found in most major newspapers. *The Wall Street Journal* provides a daily summary of activity in the U.S. Treasury market in its "Credit Markets" column, as seen in the nearby *Investment Updates* box.

The Treasury Yield Curve

Treasury yield curve
A graph of Treasury yields plotted against maturities.

Every day, *The Wall Street Journal* contains a graphical display of a current **Treasury yield curve**, which is a plot of Treasury yields against maturities. Yields are measured along the vertical axis, and maturities are measured along the horizontal axis. The light gray line represents the most current yield curve, while the background lines represent recent yield curves. Thus, the "Treasury Yield Curve" box illustrates both where Treasury interest rates are now and where they were recently.

Check out the "living yield curve" at www.smartmoney.com/bonds

The Treasury yield curve is fundamental to bond market analysis because it represents the interest rates that financial markets are charging to the world's largest debtor with the world's highest credit rating—the U.S. government. In essence, the Treasury yield curve represents interest rates for default-free lending across the maturity spectrum. As such, almost all other domestic interest rates are determined with respect to U.S. Treasury interest rates. Our nearby *Work the Web* box shows how to get yield curves online.

Greenspan Remarks Lift Long-Dated Treasurys

Longer-dated Treasurys bounced back Wednesday after Federal Reserve Chairman Alan Greenspan's congressional testimony on the economy.

At midday, the benchmark 10-year Treasury was up 5/32, or $1.5625 for each $1,000 invested, to 102 13/32. Its yield fell to 3.338%. The 30-year bond jumped 1 point to 117 9/32, yielding 4.302%. Meanwhile, the two-year note slipped 3/32 to 100 19/32, yielding 1.310%, and the five-year issue shed 2/32 to 101 15/32, yielding 2.307%.

Treasury prices slipped after the opening bell as traders awaited Mr. Greenspan's testimony before the Joint Economic Committee of Congress. Prices fell further in typical knee-jerk fashion as he began speaking.

The initial reaction in the Treasury market was "very whippy," said Paul Calvetti, head of Treasury-securities trading at Deutsche Bank in New York. "It looks like somebody is using it as an opportunity to sell," and "the headlines were bullish for the market, but the actual text is not so bullish."

However, some buying emerged as the market digested the Fed chief's remarks and after he reminded the market that the central bank can buy Treasurys to combat falling inflation. That sent the price of 30-year bond up sharply.

"There is an underlying bid in the market, driven by demand for long-dated securities," said John Spinello, fixed-income strategist at Merrill Lynch in New York.

Mr. Greenspan reiterated concerns about falling inflation, which has buoyed longer-dated Treasury prices since the Fed's statement from its May 6 meeting, when policy makers highlighted the risk of deflation.

However, Drew Matus, economist at Lehman Brothers in New York, noted that Mr. Greenspan "chose to phrase his concerns in terms of falling inflation" and didn't explicitly refer to disinflation. "This shift in language may suggest that Greenspan was unhappy with the market's focus on potential deflation," Mr. Matus said.

During the question-and-answer part of his testimony Wednesday, Mr. Greenspan said "we at the Federal Reserve recognize that deflation is a possibility," although not a likely one.

Renewed buying of the long bond contributed to a flatter yield curve. The spread between the two-year note's yield and that of the long bond flattened to around three percentage points from Tuesday's close of 3.10 percentage points. The spread between the two-year and 10-year yields had also narrowed to 2.04 percentage points from its prior session close around 2.11 percentage points.

The weakness of the front end was a function of Mr. Greenspan failing to signal that a rate cut is imminent,

(continued)

Rates on Other Fixed-Income Investments

The "Yield Comparisons" table beside the Treasury yield curve in the *Investment Updates* box gives interest rates based on bond market indexes constructed by the securities firm Merrill Lynch. Current interest rates and the highest and lowest interest rates over the previous 52-week period are reported for a number of bond indexes. These bond market indexes provide yield information on many different types of bonds. Since we will be discussing these in much more detail in several subsequent chapters, we touch on them only briefly here.

The first two indexes represent U.S. Treasury securities with 1- to 10-year maturities and 10- to 30-year maturities. The next two indexes represent U.S. government agency debt with 1- to 10-year maturities and debt with more than 10 years to maturity. A variety of government agencies borrow money in financial markets. The Tennessee Valley Authority (TVA) is an example.

In recent years, U.S. government agencies have issued debt with maturities as long as 50 years. U.S. government agency debt does not carry the same credit guarantee as U.S. Treasury debt, and therefore interest rates on agency debt reflect a premium over interest rates on Treasury debt. Also, agency securities are often subject to state taxes, whereas Treasury securities are not.

Visit these mortgage security websites:
www.fanniemae.com
www.ginniemae.gov
www.freddiemac.com

Treasury Yield Curve

Yield to maturity of current bills, notes and bonds.

1 Year Ago ▶

1 Month Ago ▶

◀ Yesterday

| month(s) years | maturity |
| 1 3 6 2 5 10 30 |

Source: Reuters

analysts said. "He took some of the bloom off market expectations pricing in an another ease," Mr. Spinello said.

Source: Michael MacKenzie, *The Wall Street Journal*, May 21, 2003. Reprinted by permission of Dow Jones, Inc., via Copyright Clearance Center, Inc. © 2003 Dow Jones & Company, Inc. All Rights Reserved Worldwide. Joy Shaw of Dow Jones Newswires contributed to this article.

Yield Comparisons

Based on Merrill Lynch Bond Indexes, priced as of midafternoon Eastern time.

	5/19	5/16	52-WEEK HIGH	52-WEEK LOW
Corp. Govt. Master	3.08%	3.11%	5.20%	3.08%
Treasury				
1-10 yr	1.80	1.83	3.72	1.80
10+ yr	4.16	4.15	5.69	4.15
Agencies				
1-10 yr	2.00	2.04	4.17	2.00
10+ yr	4.50	4.50	6.21	4.50
Corporate				
1-10 yr High Quality	2.78	2.83	5.02	2.78
Medium Quality	3.77	3.80	6.48	3.77
10+ yr High Quality	5.06	5.12	6.96	5.06
Medium Quality	5.75	5.73	7.91	5.73
Yankee bonds (1)	3.55	3.56	5.91	3.55
Current-coupon mortgages (2)				
GNMA 6.50% (3)	4.06	4.08	6.31	3.70
FNMA 6.50%	4.33	4.38	6.28	4.33
FHLMC 6.50%	4.36	4.41	6.31	4.36
High-yield corporates	9.17	9.15	13.96	9.14
Tax-Exempt Bonds				
7-12 yr G.O. (AA)	3.11	3.12	4.31	3.11
12-22 yr G.O. (AA)	4.01	4.01	5.19	4.01
22+ yr revenue (A)	4.52	4.52	5.35	4.52

Note: High quality rated AAA-AA; medium quality A-BBB/Baa; high yield, BB/Ba-C.
(1) Dollar-denominated, SEC-registered bonds of foreign issuers sold in the U.S. (2) Reflects the 52-week high and low of mortgage-backed securities indexes rather than the individual securities shown. (3) Government guaranteed.

The next four indexes represent debt issued by domestic corporations according to their maturity and credit rating. Notice that corporate debt with a high credit quality pays a higher interest rate than U.S. government agency debt, which in turn pays a higher interest rate than U.S. Treasury debt. As expected, medium credit quality corporate debt pays a higher interest rate than high credit quality corporate debt.

"Yankee bonds" are issued by foreign corporations for sale in the United States. These bonds are denominated in U.S. dollars so investors do not have to worry that changing foreign exchange rates will affect debt values.

As we noted previously, the Federal Home Loan Mortgage Corporation (FHLMC), or Freddie Mac, and the Federal National Mortgage Association (FNMA), or Fannie Mae, are government-sponsored agencies that repackage home mortgages into mortgage pools, where each pool represents several tens of millions of dollars of home mortgages. A third agency, the Government National Mortgage Association (GNMA), better known as "Ginnie Mae," is also an active mortgage repackager. The interest rates reported for these agencies correspond to indexes constructed from many mortgage pools.

"High-yield corporates" refers to corporate bonds with above-average default risk. These bonds are usually avoided by conservative investors, but they may be attractive

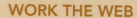

WORK THE WEB

What does the current Treasury yield curve look like? You can find the answer on the Web many different places. We went to www.bloomberg.com, and here is what we found:

U.S. Treasuries
Fri, 07 Mar 2003, 2:41pm EST

Bills		Mat Date	Previous Price/Yield	Current Price/Yield	Yld Chg	Prc Chg
3month		6/05/03	1.14(1.16)	1.09(1.11)	-0.05	-5
6month		9/04/03	1.13(1.16)	1.08(1.10)	-0.05	-5

Notes/ Bonds	Coupon	Mat Date	Previous Price/Yield	Current Price/Yield	Yld Chg	Prc Chg
2year	1.500	2/28/05	100-03(1.45)	100-07+(1.38)	-0.07	+0-04+
5year	3.000	2/15/08	101-27(2.60)	102-04(2.54)	-0.06	+0-09
10year	3.875	2/15/13	101-26(3.66)	102-05+(3.61)	-0.04	+0-11+
30year	5.375	2/15/31	110-15+(4.70)	111-00+(4.67)	-0.03	+0-17

As you can see, Bloomberg shows you the yield curve for today and yesterday. On this particular day, the yield curve shifted downward, as can be seen from the decrease in the yield (or increase in price) for each maturity. This yield curve might be considered a fairly typical, upward-sloping yield curve. The short-term rates are slightly over 1 percent, although the six-month rate is slightly lower than the three-month rate. For maturities greater than six months, the yield increases with maturity. Here's a question for you: Notice the date of this yield curve is March 7, 2003. The 2-, 5-, and 10-year maturity notes are dated 2, 5, and 10 years from this date. However the 30-year maturity is actually only 28 years. Why would the 28-year maturity Treasury bond be used for the 30-year interest rate?

to investors who understand and are willing to accept the risks involved. Because of their much higher credit risk, the interest rates for these bonds are significantly higher than those for even medium-quality corporate bonds.

"Tax-exempts" are bonds issued by municipal governments. Coupon interest payments on most municipal bonds are exempt from federal income taxes, and they are often exempt from state income taxes as well. The tax-exempt interest rates reported in the "Yield Comparisons" table are based on indexes for high-quality municipal bonds corresponding to 10-year maturity and 20-year maturity general obligation bonds (GOs) and 30-year maturity revenue bonds.

General obligation bonds are secured by the general taxing power of the issuing municipality. Revenue bonds are secured by revenues generated from specific projects, for example, toll roads, airports, or user fees for services. As shown, because of their tax-exempt status, interest rates on high-quality municipal bonds are lower than interest rates on comparable U.S. Treasury securities.

Check This

9.3a	What is the yield curve? Why is it important?
9.3b	Why are corporate bond yields higher than Treasury bond yields?
9.3c	Why are municipal bond yields lower than Treasury bond yields?
9.3d	What are Yankee bonds?

9.4 The Term Structure of Interest Rates

term structure of interest rates
Relationship between time to maturity and interest rates for default-free, pure discount instruments.

The yield curve tells us the relationship between Treasury bond yields and time to maturity. The **term structure of interest rates** (or just "term structure") is a similar, but not identical, relationship. Recall that a pure discount instrument has a single payment of face value at maturity with no other payments until then. Treasury bonds are *not* pure discount instruments because they pay coupons every six months. Pure discount instruments with more than a year to maturity are often called "zero coupon bonds," or just "zeroes," because they are, in effect, bonds with a zero coupon rate.

The term structure of interest rates is the relationship between time to maturity and interest rates for default-free, pure discount instruments. So, the difference between the yield curve and the term structure is that the yield curve is based on coupon bonds, whereas the term structure is based on pure discount instruments. The term structure is sometimes called the "zero coupon yield curve" to distinguish it from the Treasury yield curve.

Treasury STRIPS

U.S. Treasury STRIPS
Pure discount securities created by stripping coupons and principal payments of Treasury notes and bonds. Stands for Separate Trading of Registered Interest and Principal of Securities.

Until about 1987, the term structure of interest rates was not directly observable simply because default-free, pure discount instruments with maturities greater than one year did not exist or reliable data on them were not available. Today, however, the term structure of interest rates can be easily seen by examining yields on **U.S. Treasury STRIPS**.

STRIPS are pure discount instruments created by "stripping" the coupons and principal payments of U.S. Treasury notes and bonds into separate parts and then selling the parts separately. The term STRIPS stands for Separate Trading of Registered Interest and Principal of Securities. For example, a Treasury note with 10 years to maturity will make 20 semiannual coupon payments during its life and will also make a principal payment at maturity. This note can therefore be stripped into 21 separate parts, and each part can be bought and sold separately. The Treasury originally allowed notes and bonds with 10 years or more to maturity (at the time they are issued) to be stripped. Today, any note or bond is strippable.

Figure 9.4 is a sample "U.S. Treasury STRIPS" daily report of individual STRIPS prices and yields as it appeared in *The Wall Street Journal.* Only maturities of 10 years or less are reported, but longer maturities exist. The first column of Figure 9.4 gives the maturity of each STRIPS listed. The second column reports whether the STRIPS were created from a coupon payment or a principal payment. There are three possible symbols in column 2: *ci* stands for coupon interest, *np* stands for note principal, and *bp* stands for bond principal. The next two columns contain bid and asked prices for each STRIPS. As always, the bid price is a quote of what dealers were willing to pay to buy the STRIPS, and the asked price is a quote of what dealers were willing to accept to sell the STRIPS.

STRIPS prices are stated as a price per $100 of face value. For example, consider a coupon interest STRIPS with an asked price quote of 74:08. This means that the price per $100 face value is $74.25, since the 08 to the right of the colon in the stated price 74:08 stands for thirty-seconds of a dollar. Thus 74:08 stands for $74\frac{8}{32}$. The next-to-the-last column in Figure 9.4 reports the change in the asked price quote from the previous

Read more about STRIPS at www.publicdebt. treas.gov

FIGURE 9.4

Treasury STRIPS

Source: *The Wall Street Journal,* May 20, 2003. Reprinted by permission of Dow Jones and Company, Inc., via Copyright Clearance Center, Inc. © 2003 Dow Jones and Company, Inc. All Rights Reserved Worldwide.

U.S. Treasury Strips

MATURITY	TYPE	BID	ASKED	CHG	ASK YLD
Jul 03	ci	99:27	99:27	...	1.06
Aug 03	ci	99:24	99:24	...	1.00
Aug 03	np	99:24	99:24	...	1.00
Oct 03	ci	99:20	99:20	...	0.92
Nov 03	ci	99:17	99:18	...	0.94
Nov 03	np	99:15	99:16	...	1.06
Jan 04	ci	99:10	99:11	...	1.03
Feb 04	ci	99:07	99:07	...	1.07
Feb 04	np	99:06	99:07	...	1.07
Apr 04	ci	98:30	98:31	...	1.17
May 04	ci	98:26	98:27	...	1.20
May 04	np	98:30	98:30	...	1.08
Jul 04	ci	98:29	98:30	2	0.94
Aug 04	ci	98:25	98:26	2	0.98
Aug 04	np	98:22	98:22	2	1.06
Nov 04	ci	98:10	98:11	2	1.14
Nov 04	bp	98:10	98:11	2	1.13
Nov 04	np	98:09	98:10	2	1.15
Jan 05	ci	98:19	98:20	5	0.85
Feb 05	ci	97:30	97:31	4	1.18
Feb 05	np	97:29	97:30	3	1.21
Apr 05	ci	97:16	97:18	...	1.31
May 05	ci	97:11	97:12	3	1.34
May 05	bp	97:15	97:16	3	1.27
May 05	np	97:14	97:15	3	1.29
May 05	np	97:13	97:14	3	1.32
Jul 05	ci	97:22	97:23	4	1.07
Aug 05	ci	96:28	96:29	4	1.40
Aug 05	bp	96:28	96:29	4	1.40
Aug 05	np	96:30	97:00	4	1.37
Oct 05	ci	96:21	96:23	...	1.40
Nov 05	ci	96:15	96:17	4	1.43
Nov 05	np	96:11	96:13	4	1.48
Nov 05	np	96:13	96:14	4	1.46
Jan 06	ci	96:24	96:26	4	1.23
Feb 06	ci	95:25	95:26	4	1.56
Feb 06	bp	95:27	95:28	4	1.54
Feb 06	np	95:28	95:30	4	1.52
Apr 06	ci	95:11	95:13	...	1.63
May 06	ci	95:04	95:06	4	1.66
May 06	np	95:02	95:04	4	1.68
Jul 06	ci	95:22	95:24	5	1.38
Jul 06	np	94:19	94:21	5	1.75
Aug 06	ci	94:18	94:20	5	1.72
Oct 06	np	93:29	93:31	...	1.84
Oct 06	ci	93:29	93:31	...	1.83
Nov 06	ci	93:22	93:24	5	1.87
Nov 06	np	93:22	93:24	5	1.87

MATURITY	TYPE	BID	ASKED	CHG	ASK YLD
Feb 07	ci	92:24	92:26	5	2.01
Feb 07	np	92:28	92:30	3	1.97
May 07	ci	91:28	91:30	5	2.12
May 07	np	92:01	92:04	5	2.07
Aug 07	np	91:08	91:10	5	2.16
Aug 07	ci	91:09	91:11	5	2.15
Aug 07	np	91:05	91:07	5	2.18
Nov 07	ci	91:03	91:05	5	2.07
Nov 07	np	90:13	90:15	6	2.24
Feb 08	ci	89:17	89:20	6	2.33
Feb 08	np	89:17	89:19	6	2.33
May 08	ci	88:15	88:18	6	2.45
May 08	np	88:15	88:18	4	2.45
Aug 08	ci	88:01	88:04	6	2.43
Nov 08	ci	87:00	87:03	6	2.54
Nov 08	np	86:19	86:22	5	2.62
Feb 09	ci	85:15	85:18	2	2.73
May 09	ci	84:11	84:15	2	2.84
May 09	np	84:27	84:31	4	2.74
Aug 09	ci	83:23	83:27	2	2.85
Aug 09	np	83:19	83:22	4	2.88
Nov 09	ci	83:09	83:13	2	2.82
Nov 09	bp	81:08	81:11	2	3.21
Feb 10	ci	81:00	81:03	2	3.13
Feb 10	np	81:14	81:18	2	3.05
May 10	ci	80:00	80:04	2	3.20
Aug 10	ci	79:10	79:13	2	3.21
Aug 10	np	79:19	79:22	2	3.16
Nov 10	ci	78:21	78:25	2	3.21
Feb 11	ci	76:31	77:03	2	3.39
Feb 11	np	77:26	77:30	2	3.25
May 11	ci	75:31	76:03	2	3.45
Aug 11	ci	75:07	75:11	1	3.46
Aug 11	np	75:28	75:31	2	3.36
Nov 11	ci	74:11	74:15	1	3.51
Feb 12	ci	73:10	73:14	2	3.57
Feb 12	np	74:02	74:06	2	3.44
May 12	ci	72:07	72:11	2	3.63
Aug 12	ci	71:15	71:19	2	3.65
Aug 12	np	72:14	72:18	2	3.50
Nov 12	ci	70:18	70:22	2	3.69
Nov 12	np	71:19	71:23	2	3.54
Feb 13	ci	69:19	69:24	2	3.74
May 13	ci	68:19	68:24	2	3.79
Aug 13	ci	67:20	67:24	2	3.84
Nov 13	ci	66:22	66:27	2	3.88

day. Price changes are also rated in thirty-seconds of a dollar. Thus a 1 means + 1/32 of a dollar, or + 3.125 cents per $100 face value (a decrease would have a negative sign).

Why are STRIPS prices quoted in thirty-seconds? Nobody really knows. That's the way they have been quoted historically, and the tradition continues. Why don't traders go to decimal quotes? They probably will someday, but don't hold your breath.

The last column in Figure 9.4 lists asked yields, which are yields on the STRIPS based on their asked price quotes. Notice that there is a different asked yield, or interest rate, for each maturity. This tells us that interest rates determined in financial markets generally differ according to the maturity of a security.

Yields for U.S. Treasury STRIPS

An asked yield for a U.S. Treasury STRIPS is an APR (APRs were discussed earlier in this chapter). It is calculated as two times the true semiannual rate. Calculation of the yield on a STRIPS is a standard time value of money calculation. The price today of the STRIPS is the *present value*; the face value received at maturity is the *future value*. As you probably know, the relationship between present values and futures values is

$$\text{Present value} = \frac{\text{Future value}}{(1 + r)^N}$$

In this equation, r is the rate per period and N is the number of periods. Notice that a period is not necessarily one year long.[1] For Treasury STRIPS, the number of periods is two times the number of years to maturity, here denoted by $2M$, and the interest rate is the "yield to maturity" (YTM) divided by 2:

$$\textbf{STRIPS price} = \frac{\textbf{Face value}}{\textbf{(1 + YTM/2)}^{\textbf{2M}}} \qquad (9.5)$$

Consider a STRIPS with an asked price of 42:23, a reported yield of 6.40, and 13.5 years to maturity. The actual semiannual rate is 6.40%/2 = 3.20%. Also, 13.5 years to maturity converts to 2 × 13.5, or 27, semiannual periods. To check that the reported price is correct given the reported yield, we plug in future value, rate per period, and number of periods:

$$\text{STRIPS price} = \frac{\$100}{(1 + .032)^{27}}$$

$$42.72 = 42{:}23$$

The price shown is rounded to the nearest thirty-second.

If we need to go the other way and calculate the asked yield on a STRIPS given its price, we can rearrange the basic present value equation to solve it for r:

$$r = \left(\frac{\text{Future value}}{\text{Present value}}\right)^{\frac{1}{N}} - 1$$

For STRIPS, $N = 2M$ is the number of semiannual periods, and $r = YTM/2$ is the semiannual interest rate, so the formula is:

$$\textbf{YTM} = \textbf{2} \times \left[\left(\frac{\textbf{Face value}}{\textbf{STRIPS price}}\right)^{\frac{1}{2M}} - \textbf{1}\right] \qquad (9.6)$$

---

[1] Any financial calculator can perform these calculations, but we will work them the hard way for the benefit of those who don't have financial calculators.

Consider a STRIPS maturing in six years with an asked price of 73:01. Its yield to maturity of 5.3072 percent as calculated immediately below becomes 5.31 percent after rounding to two decimal places.

$$5.3072\% = 2 \times \left[\left(\frac{100}{73.03125} \right)^{\frac{1}{12}} - 1 \right]$$

As another example, consider a STRIPS maturing in 20 years with an asked price of 26:06. As calculated immediately below, its yield to maturity of 6.8129 percent becomes 6.81 percent after rounding to two decimal places.

$$6.8129\% = 2 \times \left[\left(\frac{100}{26.1875} \right)^{\frac{1}{40}} - 1 \right]$$

Check This

9.4a   What is the yield to maturity (YTM) on a STRIPS maturing in five years if its asked price quote is 77:24?

9.4b   What is the YTM of a STRIPS maturing in 15 years if its asked price quote is 38:26?

9.4c   What is the YTM of a STRIPS maturing in 25 years if its asked price quote is 18:21?

9.5   Nominal versus Real Interest Rates

nominal interest rates
Interest rates as they are normally observed and quoted, with no adjustment for inflation.

There is a fundamental distinction between *nominal* and *real* interest rates. **Nominal interest rates** are interest rates as we ordinarily observe them, for example, as they are reported in *The Wall Street Journal*. Thus, all the money market rates we discussed earlier in this chapter and the STRIPS yields we discussed just above are nominal rates.

Real Interest Rates

real interest rates
Interest rates adjusted for the effect of inflation, calculated as the nominal rate less the rate of inflation.

Real interest rates are nominal rates adjusted for the effects of price inflation. To obtain a real interest rate, simply subtract an inflation rate from a nominal interest rate:

Real interest rate = Nominal interest rate − Inflation rate   (9.7)

The real interest rate is so-called because it measures the real change in the purchasing power of an investment. For example, if the nominal interest rate for a one-year certificate of deposit is 7 percent, then a one-year deposit of $100,000 will grow to $107,000. But if the inflation rate over the same year is 4 percent, you would need $104,000 after one year passes to buy what cost $100,000 today. Thus, the real increase in purchasing power for your investment is only $3,000, and, therefore, the real interest rate is only 3 percent.

Figure 9.5 displays real interest rates based on annual rates of return on U.S. Treasury bills and inflation rates over the 50-year period 1950 through 2000. As shown in Figure 9.5, following a negative spike at the beginning of the Korean War in 1950, real interest rates for Treasury bills were generally positive until the Organization of

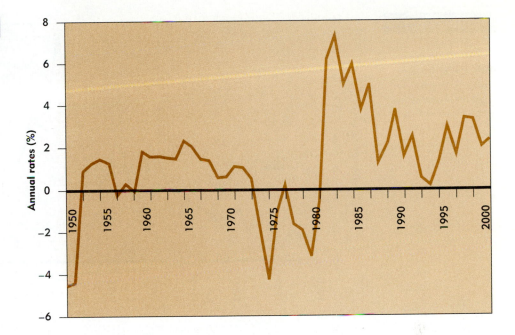

FIGURE 9.5

Real T-Bill Rates

Source: Federal Reserve Board of Governors and Global Financial Data.

Petroleum-Exporting Countries' (OPEC) oil embargo in 1973. After this, real rates were generally negative until the Federal Reserve Board initiated a tight-money policy to fight an inflationary spiral in the late 1970s. The tight-money policy caused the 1980s to begin with historically high real interest rates. Throughout the 1980s, real Treasury bill rates were falling as inflation subsided. During this 50-year period the average real Treasury bill interest rate was slightly less than 1 percent.

The Fisher Hypothesis

The relationship between nominal interest rates and the rate of inflation is often couched in terms of the *Fisher hypothesis*, which is named for the famous economist Irving Fisher, who formally proposed it in 1930. The **Fisher hypothesis** simply asserts that the general level of nominal interest rates follows the general level of inflation.

According to the Fisher hypothesis, interest rates are on average higher than the rate of inflation. Therefore, it logically follows that short-term interest rates reflect current inflation, while long-term interest rates reflect investor expectations of future inflation. Figure 9.6 graphs nominal interest rates and inflation rates used to create Figure 9.5. Notice that when inflation rates were high, Treasury bill returns tended to be high also, as predicted by the Fisher hypothesis.

Fisher hypothesis
Assertion that the general level of nominal interest rates follows the general level of inflation.

Check This

9.5a   What is the difference between a nominal interest rate and a real interest rate?

9.5b   What does the Fisher hypothesis assert?

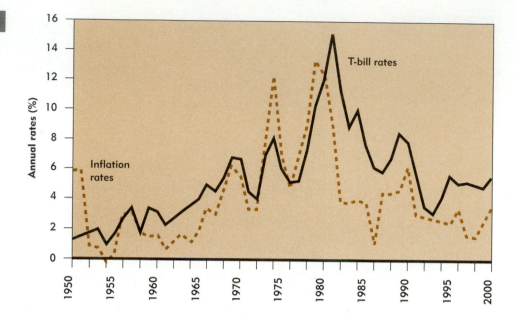

FIGURE 9.6

Inflation Rates and T-Bill Rates

Source: Federal Reserve Board of Governors and Global Financial Data.

9.6   Traditional Theories of the Term Structure

Yield curves have been studied by financial economists for well over a century. During this period a number of different theories have been proposed to explain why yield curves may be upward sloping at one point in time and then downward sloping or flat at another point in time. We discuss three of the most popular traditional theories of the term structure in this section. We then present a modern perspective on the term structure in the following section.

Expectations Theory

expectations theory
The term structure of interest rates is a reflection of financial market beliefs regarding future interest rates.

According to the **expectations theory** of the term structure of interest rates, the shape of a yield curve expresses financial market expectations regarding future interest rates. Essentially, an upward-sloping yield curve predicts an increase in interest rates, and a downward-sloping yield curve predicts a decrease in interest rates. A flat yield curve expresses the sentiment that interest rates are not expected to change in the near future.

Expectations and Forward Rates The basic principles of the expectations theory can be explained with a two-period example. Let r_1 stand for the current market interest rate on a one-year investment, and let r_2 be the current market interest rate on a two-year investment. Also, let $r_{1,1}$ be the market interest rate on a one-year investment that will be available in one year. Of course, this rate is not known today.

For a two-year investment, you have two strategies available. First, you can invest for two years at the rate r_2. In this case, \$1 invested today will become $\$(1 + r_2)^2$ in two years. For example, if $r_2 = 10$ percent, you would have $\$1 \times (1.10)^2 = \$1.21$ in two years for every dollar you invest.

Alternatively, you can invest for one year at the rate r_1, and, at the end of one year, you can reinvest the proceeds at the rate $r_{1,1}$. In this case, \$1 invested today will become $\$(1 + r_1)(1 + r_{1,1})$ in two years. For example, suppose $r_1 = 10$ percent and, after a year passes, it turns out that $r_{1,1} = 8$ percent. Then you would end up with $\$1 \times 1.10 \times 1.08 = \$1.19$. Alternatively, suppose that after a year passes it turns out that $r_{1,1} = 12$ percent; then you would have $\$1 \times 1.10 \times 1.12 = \$1.232$. Notice that this second strategy entails some uncertainty since the next year's interest rate, $r_{1,1}$, is not known when you originally select your investment strategy.

The expectations theory of the term structure of interest rates asserts that, on average, the two-year investment proceeds, $\$(1 + r_2)^2$ and $\$(1 + r_1)(1 + r_{1,1})$, will be equal. In fact, we can obtain what is known as the implied **forward rate**, $f_{1,1}$, by setting the two total proceeds equal to each other:

forward rate An expected future interest rate implied by current interest rates.

$$(1 + r_2)^2 = (1 + r_1)(1 + f_{1,1})$$

Solving for the forward rate, $f_{1,1}$, we see that

$$f_{1,1} = \frac{(1 + r_2)^2}{1 + r_1} - 1$$

Notice that this forward interest rate is simply a future interest rate implied by current interest rates.

According to expectations theory, the forward rate $f_{1,1}$ is an accurate predictor of the rate $r_{1,1}$ to be realized one year in the future. Thus, if $r_2 = 10$ percent and $r_1 = 8$ percent, then $f_{1,1} = 12$ percent, approximately, which predicts that the one-year interest rate will increase from its current value of 10 percent to 12 percent. Alternatively, if $r_2 = 10$ percent and $r_1 = 12$ percent, then $f_{1,1} = 8$ percent, approximately, which predicts that the one-year interest rate will decrease from its current value of 10 percent to 8 percent.

In general, if $r_2 > r_1$, such that the term structure is upward sloping, then expectations theory predicts an interest rate increase. Similarly, if $r_2 < r_1$, indicating a downward-sloping term structure, then expectations theory predicts an interest rate decrease. Thus, the slope of the term structure points in the predicted direction of future interest rate changes.

LOOKING FORWARD

EXAMPLE 9.7

Suppose the yield on a two-year STRIPS is 7 percent and the yield on a one-year STRIPS is 6 percent. Based on the expectations theory, what will the yield on a one-year STRIPS be one year from now?

According to the expectations theory, the implied forward rate is an accurate predictor of what the interest rate will be. Thus, solving for the forward rate, we have

$$(1 + r_2)^2 = (1 + r_1)(1 + f_{1,1})$$
$$(1 + .07)^2 = (1 + .06)(1 + f_{1,1})$$

and the forward rate is

$$f_{1,1} = \frac{1.07^2}{1.06} - 1 = 8.00943\%$$

Based on the expectations theory, the rate next year will be about 8 percent. Notice that this is higher than the current rate, as we would predict since the term structure is upward sloping.

Expectations Theory and the Fisher Hypothesis The expectations theory is closely related to the Fisher hypothesis we discussed earlier. The relationship between the expectations theory of interest rates and the Fisher hypothesis is stated as follows. If expected future inflation is higher than current inflation, then we are likely to see an upward-sloping term structure where long-term interest rates are higher than short-term interest rates. Similarly, if future inflation is expected to be lower than its current level, we would then be likely to see a downward-sloping term structure where long rates are lower than short rates.

In other words, taken together, the expectations theory and the Fisher hypothesis assert that an upward-sloping term structure tells us that the market expects that nominal interest rates and inflation are likely to be higher in the future.

Maturity Preference Theory

Another traditional theory of the term structure asserts that lenders prefer to lend short-term to avoid tying up funds for long periods of time. In other words, they have a preference for shorter maturities. At the same time, borrowers prefer to borrow long-term to lock in secure financing for long periods of time.

maturity preference theory Long-term interest rates contain a maturity premium necessary to induce lenders into making longer-term loans.

According to the **maturity preference theory**, then, borrowers have to pay a higher rate to borrow long-term rather than short-term to essentially bribe lenders into loaning funds for longer maturities. The extra interest is called a *maturity premium*.[2]

The Fisher hypothesis, maturity preference theory, and expectations theory can coexist without problem. For example, suppose the shape of a yield curve is basically determined by expected future interest rates according to expectations theory. But where do expected future interest rates come from? According to the Fisher hypothesis, expectations regarding future interest rates are based on expected future rates of inflation. Thus, expectations theory and the Fisher hypothesis mesh quite nicely.

Furthermore, a basic yield curve determined by inflationary expectations could also accommodate maturity preference theory. All we need to do is add a maturity premium to longer term interest rates. In this view, long-term, default-free interest rates have three components: a real rate, an anticipated future inflation rate, and a maturity premium.

Market Segmentation Theory

market segmentation theory Debt markets are segmented by maturity, with the result that interest rates for various maturities are determined separately in each segment.

An alternative theory of the term structure of interest rates is the **market segmentation theory**, which asserts that debt markets are segmented according to the various maturities of debt instruments available for investment. By this theory, each maturity represents a separate, distinct market. For example, one group of lenders and borrowers may prefer to lend and borrow using securities with a maturity of 10 years, while another group may prefer to lend and borrow using securities with a maturity of 5 years. Segmentation theory simply states that interest rates corresponding to each

[2]Traditionally, maturity preference theory has been known as "liquidity" preference theory and the maturity premium was termed a "liquidity" premium. However, as we discussed in Chapter 2, the term "liquidity" is universally used to indicate the relative ease with which an asset can be sold. Also, the term "liquidity premium" now has a different meaning. To avoid confusion and to make this theory more consistent with modern views of liquidity, interest rates, and the term structure, we have adopted the more descriptive name of maturity premium.

maturity are determined separately by supply and demand conditions in each market segment.

Another theory of the term structure, known as the *preferred habitat theory*, is essentially a compromise between market segmentation and maturity preference. In the preferred habitat theory, as in the market segmentation theory, different investors have different preferred maturities. The difference is that they can be induced to move to less preferred maturities by a higher interest rate. In the maturity preference theory, the preferred habitat is always toward shorter maturities rather than longer maturities.

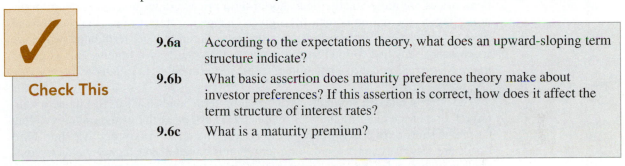

Check This

9.6a According to the expectations theory, what does an upward-sloping term structure indicate?

9.6b What basic assertion does maturity preference theory make about investor preferences? If this assertion is correct, how does it affect the term structure of interest rates?

9.6c What is a maturity premium?

9.7 Determinants of Nominal Interest Rates: A Modern Perspective

Our understanding of the term structure of interest rates has increased significantly in the last few decades. Also, the evolution of fixed-income markets has shown us that, at least to some extent, traditional theories discussed in our previous section may be inadequate to explain the term structure. We discuss some problems with these theories next and then move on to a modern perspective.

Problems with Traditional Theories

To illustrate some problems with traditional theories, we could examine the behavior of the term structure in the last two decades. What we would find is that the term structure is almost always upward sloping. But contrary to the expectations hypothesis, interest rates have not always risen. Furthermore, as we saw with STRIPS term structure, it is often the case that the term structure turns down at very long maturities. According to the expectations hypothesis, market participants apparently expect rates to rise for 20 or so years and then decline. This seems to be stretching things a bit.

In terms of maturity preference, the world's biggest borrower, the U.S. government, borrows much more heavily short term than long term. Furthermore, many of the biggest buyers of fixed-income securities, such as pension funds, have a strong preference for *long* maturities. It is hard to square these facts with the behavioral assumptions underlying the maturity preference theory.

Finally, in terms of market segmentation, the U.S. government borrows at all maturities. Many institutional investors, such as mutual funds, are more than willing to move among maturities to obtain more favorable rates. At the same time, there are bond trading operations that do nothing other than buy and sell various maturity issues to exploit even very small perceived premiums. In short, in the modern fixed-income market, market segmentation does not seem to be a powerful force.

Modern Term Structure Theory

Going back to Chapter 1, we saw that long-term government bonds had higher returns, on average, than short-term T-bills. They had substantially more risk as well. In other words, there appears to be a risk-return trade-off for default-free bonds as well, and long-term bonds appear to have a risk premium.

Notice that this risk premium doesn't result from the possibility of default since it exists on default-free U.S. government debt. Instead, it exists because longer-term bond prices are more volatile than shorter-term prices. As we discuss in detail in the next chapter, the reason is that, for a given change in interest rates, long-term bond prices change more than short-term bonds. Put differently, long-term bond prices are much more sensitive to interest rate changes than short-term bonds. This is called *interest rate risk,* and the risk premium on longer-term bonds is called the *interest rate risk premium.*

The interest rate risk premium carried by long-term bonds leads us to a modern reinterpretation of the maturity preference hypothesis. All other things the same, investors do prefer short-term bonds to long-term bonds. The reason is simply that short-term bonds are less risky. As a result, long-term bonds have to offer higher yields to compensate investors for the extra interest rate risk.

Putting it together, the modern view of the term structure suggests that nominal interest rates on default-free securities can be stated as follows:

$$NI = RI + IP + RP \tag{9.8}$$

where: NI = Nominal interest rate
RI = Real interest rate
IP = Inflation premium
RP = Interest rate risk premium

In this decomposition, the real rate of interest is assumed to be the same for all securities, and, on average, the real interest rate is positive, as predicted by the Fisher hypothesis.

As we discussed above, the inflation premium (IP) reflects investor expectations of future price inflation. The inflation premium may be different for securities with different maturities because expected inflation may be different over different future horizons. For example, the expected average rate of inflation over the next two years may be different from the expected average rate of inflation over the next five years.

In addition to the real rate and the inflation premium, nominal rates reflect an interest rate risk premium (RP) which increases with the maturity of the security being considered. As a result, if interest rates are expected to remain constant through time, the term structure would have a positive slope. This is consistent with maturity preference theory. Indeed, for zero coupon bonds the interest rate risk premium and the maturity premium are the same thing.

The separate effects of the inflation premium and the interest rate risk premium are difficult to distinguish. For example, the yields for U.S. Treasury STRIPS in Figure 9.4 reveal a substantial yield premium for long-maturity STRIPS over short-term STRIPS. This yield premium for long-maturity STRIPS reflects the combined effects of the inflation premium and the risk premium. However, it is unclear how much of the total premium is caused by an inflation premium and how much is caused by a risk premium.

Liquidity and Default Risk

Thus far we have examined the components of interest rates on default-free, highly liquid securities such as Treasury STRIPS. We now expand our coverage to securities that are less liquid, not default-free, or both, to present a more detailed decomposition of nominal interest rates. When we are finished, what we will see is that nominal interest rates for individual securities can be decomposed into five basic components as follows:

$$NI = RI + IP + RP + LP + DP \tag{9.9}$$

where: NI = Nominal interest rate
   RI = Real interest rate
   IP = Inflation premium
   RP = Interest rate risk premium
   LP = Liquidity premium
   DP = Default premium

We have already discussed the first three components of the nominal interest rate. We now consider the two new ones on our list, the default and liquidity premiums.

The *liquidity premium* (LP) is a reflection of the fact that two otherwise identical securities may have very different degrees of liquidity. All else the same, the one with less liquidity would have to offer a higher yield as compensation.

The fifth, and final, component of a nominal interest rate is a *default premium* (DP). Investors demand a default premium to assume the risk of holding a security that might default on its promised payments. Naturally, the greater is the risk of default for a particular bond issue, the larger is the default premium required by investors. The topic of default risk is discussed in detail for corporate bonds in Chapter 17 and municipal bonds in Chapter 18.

In addition to the five basic components we have discussed, there is one more important determinant of nominal interest rates, namely, tax status. As we briefly discussed in an earlier chapter, municipal bonds are not taxed at the federal level, but all other bonds are (including Treasury bonds). All else the same, taxable bonds must pay higher rates than nontaxable bonds. As a result, the rate on a high-quality municipal issue will normally be less than the rate on a Treasury issue, even though the Treasury is more liquid and has no default risk.

9.8 Summary and Conclusions

The time value of money is arguably the most important principle of finance. Interest rates are a convenient way to measure and state the time value of money. Furthermore, understanding interest rates is essential for understanding money market and fixed-income securities. In this chapter, we covered a number of topics relating to interest rates, including:

1. Important short-term money market rates include the prime rate, the Federal funds rate, and the Federal Reserve's discount rate. The prime rate is a bellwether of bank lending to business, while the Federal funds rate and the Federal Reserve's discount rate are indicators of the availability of money and credit within the banking system.

2. A Treasury yield curve graphs the relationship between yields on U.S. Treasury securities and their maturities. The Treasury yield curve is fundamental to bond market analysis because it represents the interest rates that financial markets are charging to the world's largest debtor with the world's highest credit rating—the U.S. government.

3. The term structure of interest rates is the fundamental relationship between time to maturity and interest rates for default-free, pure discount instruments such as U.S. Treasury STRIPS.

4. A number of different theories—including the expectations theory, the maturity preference theory, and the market segmentation theory—have been proposed to explain why the term structure of interest rates and yield curves may be upward sloping at one point in time and then downward sloping or flat at another time. In a modern view of the term structure, yields on default-free, pure discount bonds are determined by the real rate of interest, expectations of future inflation, and an interest rate risk premium.

5. Interest rates have five basic components: the real rate, an inflation premium, an interest rate risk premium, a liquidity premium, and a default premium. U.S. Treasury securities are free of default risk and are very liquid, so the last two components are absent from such instruments. For other issues, however, these components are very important. Tax status is also an important determinant.

Get Real

This chapter covered the essentials of interest rates. How should you, as an investor or investment manager, put this information to work?

The best thing to do is to buy a variety of instruments discussed in this chapter. STRIPS, in particular, are an important investment vehicle both for institutional and individual investors. To gain some practical experience with the risks and rewards from STRIPS investing, you should invest equal dollar amounts in several different STRIPS with different maturities. Pick short-term (a few years), intermediate-term (10 or so years), and long-term (25 years or longer), for example. Once you make these investments, monitor their yields and prices.

A good place to start with a study of interest rates is to visit some federal government websites. Try the U.S. Treasury (www.ustreas.gov), the Bureau of Public Debt (www.publicdebt.treas.gov), the Federal Reserve Board of Governors (www. federalreserve.gov), and the New York (www.ny.frb.org) and St. Louis (www.stls.frb.org) Federal Reserve banks. For the latest money market rates see Money Rates (www.money-rates.com), and for bank lending rates check out Banx (www.banx.com) or Bankrate (www.bankrate.com). Price and yield data for U.S. Treasury securities can be found at GovPX (www.govpx.com).

Key Terms

prime rate 288
bellwether rate 288

Federal funds rate 288
discount rate 288

Chapter Review Problems and Self-Test

1. **Money Market Prices**   The rate on a particular money market instrument, quoted on a discount basis, is 5 percent. The instrument has a face value of $100,000 and will mature in 40 days. What is its price?

2. **Bond Equivalent Yields**   Suppose a T-bill has 75 days to maturity and an asked discount of 4 percent. What is the bond equivalent yield?

Answers to Self-Test Problems

1. Using the bank discount basis formula, we have

$$\text{Current price} = \text{Face value} \times \left(1 - \frac{\text{Days to maturity}}{360} \times \text{Discount yield} \right)$$

$$\$99{,}444.44 = \$100{,}000 \times \left(1 - \frac{40}{360} \times .05 \right)$$

You would pay $99,444.44.

2. Using the bond equivalent yield conversion formula, we have

$$4.09\% = \frac{365 \times .04}{360 - 75 \times .04}$$

The bond equivalent yield is thus 4.09 percent.

Test Your Investment Quotient

1. **Interest Rates**   Which of the following interest rates is a bellwether (leading indicator) rate of bank lending to business?

    a. Unsecured business loan rate.
    b. Prime rate.
    c. Commercial paper rate.
    d. Banker's acceptance rate.

2. **Interest Rates**   Among the following interest rates, which is normally the highest rate?

    a. Commercial paper rate.
    b. U.S. Treasury bill rate.
    c. Federal funds rate.
    d. Federal Reserve discount rate.

3. **T-Bill Yields**   A U.S. Treasury bill with 180 days to maturity has a discount yield of 5 percent and a face value of $100,000. What is its current price?

   a. $97,500
   b. $95,000
   c. $92,500
   d. $90,000

4. **T-Bill Yields**   A U.S. Treasury bill with 90 days to maturity has a price of $95,000. What is its discount yield?

   a. 5 percent
   b. 10 percent
   c. 15 percent
   d. 20 percent

5. **T-bill Yields**   A 30-day U.S. Treasury bill is selling at a 12 percent yield on a discount basis. Which of the following is the approximate bond equivalent yield?

   a. 6.0 percent
   b. 11.7 percent
   c. 12.0 percent
   d. 12.3 percent

6. **Effective Annual Rates**   A credit card company states an annual percentage rate (APR) of 12 percent, which is actually a rate of 1 percent per month. What is the EAR?

   a. 12 percent
   b. 12.68 percent
   c. 13.08 percent
   d. 13.76 percent

7. **STRIPS Yields**   A U.S. Treasury STRIPS maturing in 10 years has a current price of $502.57 for $1,000 of face value. What is the yield to maturity of this STRIPS?

   a. 7.0 percent
   b. 7.12 percent
   c. 8.0 percent
   d. 8.12 percent

8. **STRIPS Yields**   A U.S. Treasury STRIPS with $1,000 face value maturing in 5 years has a yield to maturity of 7 percent. What is the current price of this STRIPS?

   a. $930
   b. $712.99
   c. $708.92
   d. $650

9. **Bond Yields**   An analyst finds that the semiannual interest rate that equates the present value of the bond's cash flow to its current market price is 3.85 percent. Consider the following possible alternatives:
   I. The bond equivalent yield on this security is 7.70 percent.
   II. The effective annual yield on the bond is 7.85 percent.
   III. The bond's yield-to-maturity is 7.70 percent.
   IV. The bond's horizon return is 8.35 percent.
   Which of these alternatives are true?

   a. I and II only
   b. II, III, and IV only
   c. I, II, and III only
   d. III only

10. Forward Rates   An analyst gathered the following spot rates:

Time (years)	Annual Spot Rate
1	15.0%
2	12.5
3	10.0
4	7.5

The one-year forward rate two years from now is closest to

a. −4.91 percent
b. 5.17 percent
c. 10.05 percent
d. 7.5 percent

11. Zeroes   If an investor's required return is 12 percent, the value of a 10-year maturity zero coupon bond with a maturity value of $1,000 is closest to:

a. $312
b. $688
c. $1,000
d. $1,312

12. Fisher Hypothesis   The Fisher hypothesis essentially asserts which of the following?

a. Nominal interest rates follow inflation.
b. Real interest rates follow inflation.
c. Inflation follows real interest rates.
d. Inflation follows nominal interest rates.

13. Term Structure Theory   Which one of the following statements about the term structure of interest rates is true?

a. The expectations hypothesis indicates a flat yield curve if anticipated future short-term rates exceed current short-term rates.
b. The expectations hypothesis contends that the long-term rate is equal to the anticipated short-term rate.
c. The liquidity premium theory indicates that, all else being equal, longer maturities will have lower yields.
d. The market segmentation theory contends that borrowers and lenders prefer particular segments of the yield curve.

14. Term Structure Theory   Which one of the following is not an explanation of the relationship between a bond's interest rate and its term to maturity?

a. Default (credit) risk hypothesis
b. Expectations hypothesis
c. Liquidity preference hypothesis
d. Segmentation hypothesis

15. Term Structure Theory Which theory explains the shape of the yield curve by considering the relative demands for various maturities?

a. Relative strength theory
b. Segmentation theory
c. Unbiased expectations theory
d. Liquidity premium theory

www.mhhe.com/cj3e

16. **Term Structure Theory** The concepts of spot and forward rates are most closely associated with which one of the following explanations of the term structure of interest rates?

    a. Expectations hypothesis
    b. Liquidity premium theory
    c. Preferred habitat hypothesis
    d. Segmented market theory

17. **Forward Rates** The current one-year interest rate is 6 percent and the current two-year interest rate is 7 percent. What is the implied forward rate for next year's one-year rate?

    a. 9 percent
    b. 8 percent
    c. 7 percent
    d. 6 percent

18. **Forward Rates** The current one-year interest rate is 7 percent and the current two-year interest rate is 6 percent. What is the implied forward rate for next year's one-year rate?

    a. 7 percent
    b. 6 percent
    c. 5 percent
    d. 4 percent

19. **Forward Rates** The 6-month Treasury bill spot rate is 4 percent, and the 1-year Treasury bill spot rate is 5 percent. The implied 6-month forward rate 6 months from now is which of the following?

    a. 3.0 percent
    b. 4.5 percent
    c. 5.5 percent
    d. 5.9 percent

20. **Forward Rates** An analyst gathers the following information:

Years to Maturity	Spot Rate
1	5.00%
2	6.00
3	6.50

Based on the data above, the one-year implied forward rate two years from now is *closest* to:

    a. 6.25 percent
    b. 7.01 percent
    c. 7.26 percent
    d. 7.51 percent

Concept Questions

1. **Interest Rate History** Based on the history of interest rates, what is the range of short-term rates that has occurred in the United States? The range of long-term rates? What is a typical value for each?

2. **Discount Securities** What are pure discount securities? Give two examples.

3. **Fed Funds versus the Discount Rate** Compare and contrast the Fed funds rate and the discount rate. Which do you think is more volatile? Which market do you think is more active? Why?

4. **Commercial Paper** Compare and contrast commercial paper and Treasury bills. Which would typically offer a higher interest rate? Why?

5. **LIBOR** What is LIBOR? Why is it important?

6. **Bank Discount Rates** Why do you suppose rates on some money market instruments are quoted on a bank discount basis? (*Hint:* Why use a 360-day year?)

7. **STRIPS** With regard to STRIPS, what do "ci," "np," and "bp" represent?

8. **Nominal and Real Rates** When we observe interest rates in the financial press, do we see nominal or real rates? Which are more relevant to investors?

9. **Munis versus Treasuries** Which would have a higher yield, a municipal bond or a Treasury bond of the same maturity?

10. **Term Structure** Discuss how each of the following theories for the term structure of interest rates could account for a downward-sloping term structure of interest rates:

    a. Pure expectations
    b. Liquidity preference
    c. Market segmentation

CFA® PROBLEMS

Questions and Problems

Core Questions

1. **STRIPS** What is the price of a Treasury STRIPS with a face value of $100 that matures in six years and has a yield to maturity of 5.2 percent?

2. **STRIPS** A Treasury STRIPS matures in 9.5 years and has a yield to maturity of 6.8 percent. If the par value is $100,000, what is the price of the STRIPS? What is the quoted price?

3. **STRIPS** A Treasury STRIPS is quoted at 75:28 and has seven years until maturity. What is the yield to maturity?

4. **STRIPS** What is the yield to maturity on a Treasury STRIPS with 10 years to maturity and a quoted price of 50:12?

5. **Fisher Effect** A stock had a return of 13.4 percent last year. If the inflation rate was 3.9 percent, what was the approximate real return?

6. **Fisher Effect** Your investments increased in value by 10.1 percent last year but your purchasing power increased by only 6.2 percent. What was the inflation rate?

7. **Treasury Bill Prices** What is the price of a U.S. Treasury bill with 110 days to maturity quoted at a discount yield of 4.80 percent? Assume a $1 million face value.

8. **Treasury Bill Prices** In the previous problem, what is the bond-equivalent yield?

9. **Treasury Bill Prices** How much would you pay for a U.S. Treasury bill with 43 days to maturity quoted at a discount yield of 2.05 percent? Assume a $1 million face value.

10. **Treasury Bill Prices** In the previous problem, what is the bond-equivalent yield?

Intermediate Questions

11. **Treasury Bills** A Treasury bill with 80 days to maturity is quoted at 99:07. What is the bank discount yield, the bond equivalent yield, and the effective annual return?

12. **Treasury Bills** A Treasury bill purchased in December 2007 has 34 days until maturity and a bank discount yield of 4.24 percent. What is the price of the bill as a percentage of face value? What is the bond equivalent yield?

13. **Money Market Prices** The treasurer of a large corporation wants to invest $20 million in excess short-term cash in a particular money market investment. The prospectus quotes the instrument at a true yield of 6.20 percent; that is, the EAR for this investment is 6.20 percent. However, the treasurer wants to know the money market yield on this instrument to make it comparable to the T-bills and CDs she has already bought. If the

term of the instrument is 140 days, what are the bond-equivalent and discount yields on this investment?

Use the following information to answer the next six questions:
    U.S. Treasury STRIPS, close of business February 15, 2004:

Maturity	Price	Maturity	Price
Feb05	96:05	Feb08	82:01
Feb06	91:31	Feb09	75:03
Feb07	86:18	Feb10	70:09

14. **Zero Coupon Bonds**   Calculate the quoted yield for each of the six STRIPS given in the table above. Does the market expect interest rates to go up or down in the future?

15. **Zero Coupon Bonds**   What is the yield of the two-year STRIPS expressed as an EAR?

16. **Forward Interest Rates**   According to the pure expectations theory of interest rates, how much do you expect to pay for a one-year STRIPS on February 15, 2005? What is the corresponding implied forward rate? How does your answer compare to the current yield on a one-year STRIPS? What does this tell you about the relationship between implied forward rates, the shape of the zero-coupon yield curve, and market expectations about future spot interest rates?

17. **Forward Interest Rates**   According to the pure expectations theory of interest rates, how much do you expect to pay for a five-year STRIPS on February 15, 2005? How much do you expect to pay for a two-year STRIPS on February 15, 2007?

18. **Forward Interest Rates**   This problem is a little harder. Suppose the term structure is set according to pure expectations and the maturity preference theory. To be specific, investors require no compensation for holding investments with a maturity of one year, but they demand a premium of .30 percent for holding investments with a maturity of two years. Given this information, how much would you pay for a one-year STRIPS on February 15, 2005? What is the corresponding implied forward rate? Compare your answer to the solutions you found in Problem 16. What does this tell you about the effect of a maturity premium on implied forward rates?

19. **Bond Price Changes**   Suppose the (quoted) yield on each of the six STRIPS increases by .25 percent. Calculate the percentage change in price for the one-year, three-year, and six-year STRIPS. Which one has the largest price change? Now suppose that the quoted price on each STRIPS decreases by 16/32. Calculate the percentage change in (quoted) yield for the one-year, three-year, and six-year STRIPS. Which one has the largest yield change? What do your answers tell you about the relationship between prices, yields, and maturity for discount bonds?

20. **Inflation and Returns**   You observe that the current interest rate on short-term U.S. Treasury bills is 8.15 percent. You also read in the newspaper that the GDP deflator, which is a common macroeconomic indicator used by market analysts to gauge the inflation rate, currently implies that inflation is 3.5 percent. Given this information, what is the approximate real rate of interest on short-term Treasury bills? Is it likely that your answer would change if you used some alternative measure for the inflation rate, such as the CPI? What does this tell you about the observability and accuracy of real interest rates compared to nominal interest rates?

21. **Forward Interest Rates**   Consider the following spot interest rates for maturities of one, two, three, and four years.

$$r_1 = 4.5\% \qquad r_2 = 5.4\% \qquad r_3 = 4.8\% \qquad r_4 = 5.9\%$$

What are the following forward rates, where $f_{1,k}$ refers to a forward rate for the period beginning in one year and extending for k years?

$$f_{1,1} =; f_{1,2} =; f_{1,3} =$$

Hint: Use the equation $(1 + r_1)(1 + f_{1,k})^k = (1 + r_{k+1})^{k+1}$ to solve for $f_{1,k}$.

22. **Forward Interest Rates**   Based on the spot interest rates in the previous question, what are the following forward rates, where $f_{k,1}$ refers to a forward rate beginning in k years and extending for 1 year?

$$f_{2,1} =; f_{3,1} =$$

Hint: Use the equation $(1 + r_k)^k(1 + f_{k,1}) = (1 + r_{k+1})^{k+1}$ to solve for $f_{k,1}$.

23. **Expected Inflation Rates**   Based on the spot rates in Question 21, and assuming a constant real interest rate of 2 percent, what are the expected inflation rates for the next four years?

    Hint: Use the Fisher hypothesis and the unbiased expectations theory.

Spreadsheet Problems

24. **Treasury Bills**   A Treasury bill that settles on May 13, 2004, pays $100,000 on July 1, 2004. Assuming a discount rate of 5.30 percent, what is the price and bond equivalent yield?

25. **Effective Annual Rate**   You have a car loan with a nominal rate of 7.8 percent. With interest charged monthly, what is the effective annual rate (EAR) on this loan?

What's on the Web?

1. **Yield Curve**   What is the shape of the Treasury yield curve today? Go to www.bloomberg.com and find out. Is the yield curve upward sloping or downward sloping? According to the expectations theory, are interest rates in the future expected to be higher or lower than they are today?

2. **STRIPS**   Go to www.publicdebt.treas.gov and follow the "Treasury Securities at a Glance" link to find information on Treasury STRIPS. Answer the following questions: Which Treasury securities are eligible to be stripped? What are minimum par amounts for stripping? How do I buy STRIPS? Why do investors hold STRIPS?

3. **STRIPS**   Go to www.bondsonline.com and find the quotes for STRIPS that are offered for sale on the site. How many STRIPS are offered for sale? What is the lowest and highest yield to maturity? Are there STRIPS with the same maturity that have different prices? How could this happen?

Stock-Trak®
Portfolio Simulations

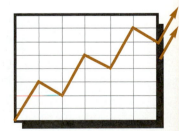

Trading Interest Rates with Stock-Trak

Your Stock-Trak account allows you to trade on changes in interest rates by buying and selling securities whose values depend on interest rates. U.S. Treasury STRIPS are the simplest instruments used to trade interest rates, since specific STRIPS are available for trading short-term, intermediate-term, and long-term interest rates. Stock-Trak supports trading in about a dozen different STRIPS issues. A current list of STRIPS available for Stock-Trak trading is found on our website in the Stock-Trak Section (www.mhhe.com/cj3e).

Suppose you believe that long-term interest rates will fall over the next few weeks. This will cause long-term maturity STRIPS prices to rise, so the appropriate trading strategy is to buy long-maturity STRIPS now and sell them later, after they rise in value. For example, you wish to buy 50 STRIPS maturing in 2023. Stock-Trak does not require a ticker symbol to trade STRIPS. You would enter the following order:

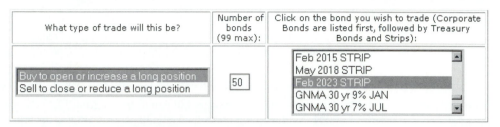

Each STRIPS has a face value of $1,000 and a current price that depends on its yield to maturity. For example, a STRIPS maturing in 20 years with a 6 percent yield has a price of $306.56. A decrease in the yield of 50 basis points to 5.50 percent will increase the price to $337.85. This represents a trading profit of $31.29 for each STRIPS you bought. Thus, if you bought 50 STRIPS, your total profit would be $1,564.50.

Several websites provide current interest rates. For the latest money market rates see Money Rates (www.money-rates.com), and, for bank lending rates, check out Banx (www.banx.com) or Bankrate (www.bankrate.com). Price and yield data for U.S. Treasury securities can be found at GovPX (www.govpx.com).

Stock-Trak Exercises

1. Read several "Credit Markets" sections in *The Wall Street Journal* and look at the interest rate discussions on various websites. Attempt to deduce which direction interest rates will move. You must purchase at least 50 STRIPS contracts, but the maturity of the contract is up to you. With your interest rate prediction, buy the appropriate short-term or long-term STRIPS contract. Also, write down the price of the STRIPS contract that you would be least likely to purchase assuming your interest rate forecast is correct. After three weeks, close out your position and assess your success in forecasting interest rates. How would you have performed if you had purchased the other STRIPS?

2. To try more advanced interest rate trading strategies, you will need to master the basics of trading futures contracts on interest rate–sensitive securities. If your interest is piqued, then peer ahead to the end of Chapter 16 for a discussion of trading interest rate futures contracts with Stock-Trak.

Chapter 10

Bond Prices and Yields

"More money has been lost reaching for yield than at the point of a gun."
–Raymond Devoe

Interest rates go up and bond prices go down. But which bonds go down the most and which go down the least? Interest rates go down and bond prices go up. But which bonds go up the most and which go up the least? For bond portfolio managers, these are important questions about interest rate risk. For anyone managing a bond portfolio, an understanding of interest rate risk rests on an understanding of the relationship between bond prices and yields. ■

In the preceding chapter on interest rates, we introduced the subject of bond yields. As we promised there, we now return to this subject and discuss bond prices and yields in some detail. We first describe how bond yields are determined and how they are interpreted. We then go on to examine what happens to bond prices as yields change. Finally, once we have a good understanding of the relation between bond prices and yields, we examine some of the fundamental tools of bond risk analysis used by fixed-income portfolio managers.

10.1 Bond Basics

A bond essentially is a security that offers the investor a series of fixed interest payments during its life, along with a fixed payment of principal when it matures. So long as the bond issuer does not default, the schedule of payments does not change. When originally issued, bonds normally have maturities ranging from 2 years to 30 years, but bonds with maturities of 50 or 100 years also exist. Bonds issued with maturities of less than 10 years are usually called notes. A very small number of bond issues have no stated maturity, and these are referred to as perpetuities or consols.

Straight Bonds

The most common type of bond is the so-called straight bond. By definition, a straight bond is an IOU that obligates the issuer to pay the bondholder a fixed sum of money at the bond's maturity along with constant, periodic interest payments during the life of the bond. The fixed sum paid at maturity is referred to as bond principal, par value, stated value, or face value. The periodic interest payments are called coupons. Perhaps the best example of straight bonds are U.S. Treasury bonds issued by the federal government to finance the national debt. However, business corporations and municipal governments also routinely issue debt in the form of straight bonds.

In addition to a straight bond component, many bonds have additional special features. These features are sometimes designed to enhance a bond's appeal to investors. For example, convertible bonds have a conversion feature that grants bondholders the right to convert their bonds into shares of common stock of the issuing corporation. As another example, "putable" bonds have a put feature that grants bondholders the right to sell their bonds back to the issuer at a special put price.

These and other special features are attached to many bond issues, but we defer discussion of special bond features until later chapters. For now, it is only important to know that when a bond is issued with one or more special features, strictly speaking, it is no longer a straight bond. However, bonds with attached special features will normally have a straight bond component, namely, the periodic coupon payments and fixed principal payment at maturity. For this reason, straight bonds are important as the basic unit of bond analysis.

The prototypical example of a straight bond pays a series of constant semiannual coupons, along with a face value of $1,000 payable at maturity. This example is used in this chapter because it is common and realistic. For example, most corporate bonds are sold with a face value of $1,000 per bond, and most bonds (in the United States at least) pay constant semiannual coupons.

Coupon Rate and Current Yield

A familiarity with bond yield measures is important for understanding the financial characteristics of bonds. As we briefly discussed in Chapter 3, two basic yield measures for a bond are its coupon rate and current yield.

A bond's **coupon rate** is defined as its annual coupon amount divided by its par value, or, in other words, its annual coupon expressed as a percentage of face value:

$$\text{Coupon rate} = \frac{\text{Annual coupon}}{\text{Par value}} \qquad (10.1)$$

For example, suppose a $1,000 par value bond pays semiannual coupons of $40. The annual coupon is then $80, and, stated as a percentage of par value, the bond's coupon

coupon rate A bond's annual coupon divided by its par value. Also called *coupon yield* or *nominal yield*.

Check out the bonds section at www.bondmarkets.com

rate is $80/$1,000 = 8%. A coupon rate is often referred to as the *coupon yield* or the *nominal yield*. Notice that the word "nominal" here has nothing to do with inflation.

A bond's **current yield** is its annual coupon payment divided by its current market price:

current yield A bond's annual coupon divided by its market price.

$$\text{Current yield} = \frac{\text{Annual coupon}}{\text{Bond price}} \qquad (10.2)$$

For example, suppose a $1,000 par value bond paying an $80 annual coupon has a price of $1,032.25. The current yield is $80/$1,032.25 = 7.75%. Similarly, a price of $969.75 implies a current yield of $80/$969.75 = 8.25%. Notice that whenever there is a change in the bond's price, the coupon rate remains constant. However, a bond's current yield is inversely related to its price, and it changes whenever the bond's price changes.

Check This

10.1a   What is a straight bond?

10.1b   What is a bond's coupon rate? Its current yield?

10.2 Straight Bond Prices and Yield to Maturity

yield to maturity (YTM) The discount rate that equates a bond's price with the present value of its future cash flows. Also called *promised yield* or just *yield*.

The single most important yield measure for a bond is its **yield to maturity**, commonly abbreviated as **YTM**. By definition, a bond's yield to maturity is the discount rate that equates the bond's price with the computed present value of its future cash flows. A bond's yield to maturity is sometimes called its *promised yield*, but, more commonly, the yield to maturity of a bond is simply referred to as its *yield*. In general, if the term "yield" is being used with no qualification, it means yield to maturity.

Straight Bond Prices

For straight bonds, the following standard formula is used to calculate a bond's price given its yield:

$$\text{Bond price} = \frac{C/2}{YTM/2}\left[1 - \frac{1}{(1 + YTM/2)^{2M}}\right] + \frac{FV}{(1 + YTM/2)^{2M}}$$

This formula can be simplified just a bit as follows:

$$= \frac{C}{YTM}\left[1 - \frac{1}{(1 + YTM/2)^{2M}}\right] + \frac{FV}{(1 + YTM/2)^{2M}} \qquad (10.3)$$

where: C = Annual coupon, the sum of two semiannual coupons
FV = Face value
M = Maturity in years
YTM = Yield to maturity

In this formula, the coupon used is the annual coupon, which is the sum of the two semiannual coupons. As discussed in our previous chapter for U.S. Treasury STRIPS, the yield on a bond is an annual percentage rate (APR), calculated as twice the true semiannual yield. As a result, the yield on a bond somewhat understates its effective annual rate (EAR).

The straight bond pricing formula has two separate components. The first component is the present value of all the coupon payments. Since the coupons are fixed and paid on a regular basis, you may recognize that they form an ordinary annuity, and the first piece of the bond pricing formula is a standard calculation for the present value of an annuity. The other component represents the present value of the principal payment at maturity, and it is a standard calculation for the present value of a single lump sum.

Calculating bond prices is mostly "plug and chug" with a calculator. In fact, a good financial calculator or spreadsheet should have this formula built into it. In any case, we will work through a few examples the long way just to illustrate the calculations.

Suppose a bond has a $1,000 face value, 20 years to maturity, an 8 percent coupon rate, and a yield of 9 percent. What's the price? Using the straight bond pricing formula, the price of this bond is calculated as follows:

1. Present value of semiannual coupons:

$$\frac{\$80}{.09}\left[1 - \frac{1}{(1.045)^{40}}\right] = \$736.06337$$

2. Present value of $1,000 principal:

$$\frac{\$1,000}{(1.045)^{40}} = \$171.92871$$

The price of the bond is the sum of the present values of coupons and principal:

$$\text{Bond price} = \$736.06 + \$171.93 = \$907.99$$

So, this bond sells for $907.99.

CALCULATING STRAIGHT BOND PRICES

EXAMPLE 10.1

Suppose a bond has 20 years to maturity and a coupon rate of 8 percent. The bond's yield to maturity is 7 percent. What's the price?

In this case, the coupon rate is 8 percent and the face value is $1,000, so the annual coupon is $80. The bond's price is calculated as follows:

1. Present value of semiannual coupons:

$$\frac{\$80}{0.07}\left[1 - \frac{1}{(1.035)^{40}}\right] = \$854.20289$$

2. Present value of $1,000 principal:

$$\frac{\$1,000}{(1.035)^{40}} = \$252.57247$$

The bond's price is the sum of coupon and principal present values:

Bond price = $854.20 + $252.57 = $1,106.77

This bond sells for $1,106.77.

Straight bond prices may be calculated using a built-in spreadsheet function. An example of how to use an Excel™ spreadsheet to calculate a bond price is shown in the nearby *Spreadsheet Analysis* box.

SPREADSHEET ANALYSIS

	A	B	C	D	E	F	G	H
1								
2				Calculating the Price of a Coupon Bond				
3								
4	A Treasury bond traded on March 30, 2004 matures in 20 years on March 30, 2024.							
5	Assuming an 8 percent coupon rate and a 7 percent yield to maturity, what is the							
6	price of this bond?							
7	Hint: Use the Excel function PRICE.							
8								
9		$110.6775	= PRICE("3/30/2004","3/30/2024",0.08,0.07,100,2,3)					
10								
11	For a bond with $1,000 face value, multiply the price by 10 to get $1,106.78.							
12								
13	This function uses the following arguments:							
14								
15		=PRICE("Now","Maturity", Coupon,Yield,100,2,3)						
16								
17	The 100 indicates redemption value as a percent of face value.							
18	The 2 indicates semi-annual coupons.							
19	The 3 specifies an actual day count with 365 days per year.							
20								
21								
22								
23								

Premium and Discount Bonds

Bonds are commonly distinguished according to whether they are selling at par value or at a discount or premium relative to par value. These three relative price descriptions—premium, discount, and par bonds—are defined as follows:

1. **Premium bonds:** Bonds with a price greater than par value are said to be selling at a premium. The yield to maturity of a premium bond is less than its coupon rate.

2. **Discount bonds:** Bonds with a price less than par value are said to be selling at a discount. The yield to maturity of a discount bond is greater than its coupon rate.

3. **Par bonds:** Bonds with a price equal to par value are said to be selling at par. The yield to maturity of a par bond is equal to its coupon rate.

The important thing to notice is that whether a bond sells at a premium or discount depends on the relation between its coupon rate and its yield. If the coupon rate exceeds the yield, the bond will sell at a premium. If the coupon is less than the yield, the bond will sell at a discount.

PREMIUM AND DISCOUNT BONDS

EXAMPLE 10.2

Consider two bonds, both with eight years to maturity and a 7 percent coupon. One bond has a yield to maturity of 5 percent while the other has a yield to maturity of 9 percent. Which of these bonds is selling at a premium and which is selling at a discount? Verify your answer by calculating each bond's price.

For the bond with a 9 percent yield to maturity, the coupon rate of 7 percent is less than the yield, indicating a discount bond. The bond's price is calculated as follows:

$$\frac{\$70}{.09}\left[1 - \frac{1}{(1.045)^{16}}\right] + \frac{\$1,000}{(1.045)^{16}} = \$877.66$$

For the bond with a 5 percent yield to maturity, the coupon rate of 7 percent is greater than the yield, indicating a premium bond. The bond's price is calculated as follows:

$$\frac{\$70}{.05}\left[1 - \frac{1}{(1.025)^{16}}\right] + \frac{\$1,000}{(1.025)^{16}} = \$1,130.55$$

The relationship between bond prices and bond maturities for premium and discount bonds is graphically illustrated in Figure 10.1 for bonds with an 8 percent coupon rate. The vertical axis measures bond prices, and the horizontal axis measures bond maturities.

Figure 10.1 also describes the paths of premium and discount bond prices as their maturities shorten with the passage of time, assuming no changes in yield to maturity. As shown, the time paths of premium and discount bond prices follow smooth curves. Over time, the price of a premium bond declines and the price of a discount bond rises. At maturity, the price of each bond converges to its par value.

FIGURE 10.1   **Premium, Par, and Discount Bond Prices**

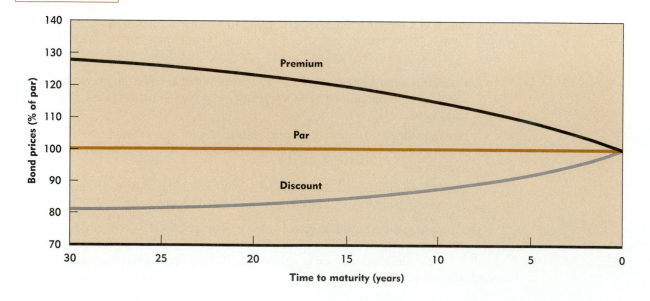

Figure 10.1 illustrates the general result that, for discount bonds, holding the coupon rate and yield to maturity constant, the longer the term to maturity of the bond the greater is the discount from par value. For premium bonds, holding the coupon rate and yield to maturity constant, the longer the term to maturity of the bond the greater is the premium over par value.

PREMIUM BONDS

EXAMPLE 10.3

Consider two bonds, both with a 9 percent coupon rate and the same yield to maturity of 7 percent, but with different maturities of 5 and 10 years. Which has the higher price? Verify your answer by calculating the prices.

First, since both bonds have a 9 percent coupon and a 7 percent yield, both bonds sell at a premium. Based on what we know, the one with the longer maturity will have a higher price. We can check these conclusions by calculating the prices as follows:

5-year maturity premium bond price:

$$\frac{\$90}{.07}\left[1 - \frac{1}{(1.035)^{10}}\right] + \frac{\$1,000}{(1.035)^{10}} = \$1,083.17$$

10-year maturity premium bond price:

$$\frac{\$90}{.07}\left[1 - \frac{1}{(1.035)^{20}}\right] + \frac{\$1,000}{(1.035)^{20}} = \$1,142.12$$

Notice that the longer maturity premium bond has a higher price, as we predicted.

DISCOUNT BONDS

EXAMPLE 10.4

Now consider two bonds, both with a 9 percent coupon rate and the same yield to maturity of 11 percent, but with different maturities of 5 and 10 years. Which has the higher price? Verify your answer by calculating the prices.

These are both discount bonds. (Why?) The one with the shorter maturity will have a higher price. To check, the prices can be calculated as follows:

5-year maturity discount bond price:

$$\frac{\$90}{.11}\left[1 - \frac{1}{(1.055)^{10}}\right] + \frac{\$1,000}{(1.055)^{10}} = \$924.62$$

10-year maturity discount bond price:

$$\frac{\$90}{.11}\left[1 - \frac{1}{(1.055)^{20}}\right] + \frac{\$1,000}{(1.055)^{20}} = \$880.50$$

In this case, the shorter maturity discount bond has the higher price.

Relationships among Yield Measures

We have discussed three different bond rates or yields in this chapter—the coupon rate, the current yield, and the yield to maturity. We've seen the relationship between coupon rates and yields for discount and premium bonds. We can extend this to include current yields by simply noting that the current yield is always between the coupon rate and the yield to maturity (unless the bond is selling at par, in which case all three are equal).

Putting together our observations about yield measures, we have the following:

Premium bonds:	Coupon rate > Current yield > Yield to maturity
Discount bonds:	Coupon rate < Current yield < Yield to maturity
Par value bonds:	Coupon rate = Current yield = Yield to maturity

Thus, when a premium bond and a discount bond both have the same yield to maturity, the premium bond has a higher current yield than the discount bond. However, as shown in Figure 10.1, the advantage of a high current yield for a premium bond is offset by the fact that the price of a premium bond must ultimately fall to its face value when the bond matures. Similarly, the disadvantage of a low current yield for a discount bond is offset by the fact that the price of a discount bond must ultimately rise to its face value at maturity. For these reasons, current yield is not a reliable guide to what an actual yield will be.

If you wish to get current price and yield information for Treasury note and bond issues, try the Internet. The nearby *Work the Web* box displays a typical search query and the search results from a popular website.

A Note on Bond Price Quotes

clean price The price of a bond net of accrued interest; this is the price that is typically quoted.

dirty price The price of a bond including accrued interest, also known as the *full* or *invoice price*. This is the price the buyer actually pays.

If you buy a bond between coupon payment dates, the price you pay will usually be more than the price you are quoted. The reason is that standard convention in the bond market is to quote prices net of "accrued interest," meaning that accrued interest is deducted to arrive at the quoted price. This quoted price is called the **clean price**. The price you actually pay, however, includes the accrued interest. This price is the **dirty price**, also known as the "full" or "invoice" price.

An example is the easiest way to understand these issues. Suppose you buy a bond with a 12 percent annual coupon, payable semiannually. You actually pay $1,080 for this bond, so $1,080 is the dirty, or invoice, price. Further, on the day you buy it, the next coupon is due in four months, so you are between coupon dates. Notice that the next coupon will be $60.

The accrued interest on a bond is calculated by taking the fraction of the coupon period that has passed, in this case two months out of six, and multiplying this fraction by the next coupon, $60. So, the accrued interest in this example is $2/6 \times \$60 = \$20$. The bond's quoted price (i.e., its clean price) would be $1,080 - $20 = $1,060.[1]

---

[1]The way accrued interest is calculated actually depends on the type of bond being quoted, for example, Treasury or corporate. The difference has to do with exactly how the fractional coupon period is calculated. In our example just above, we implicitly treated the months as having exactly the same length (i.e., 30 days each, 360 days in a year), which is consistent with the way corporate bonds are quoted. In contrast, for Treasury bonds, actual day counts are used. If you look back at our *Spreadsheet Analysis* exhibit, you'll see that we had to specify this treatment to value our Treasury bond.

WORK THE WEB

Current information on Treasury bond prices and yields is available using the search tool at Bonds Online (www.bondsonline.com). An example query definition and the search results are shown below.

Treasury *Query Definition*

Ranges

	Minimum	Maximum
Maturity	2013	2016
Coupon		
Yield		
Price		
Call Prot		

Express Search

Issue:
CUSIP:

Display Properties

Sort: Maturity
Number Of Bonds To Display: 100
Find Offerings Since: (Eastern)

Run Query

Find Bonds   Clear

Bonds Found: 11   Bonds Displayed: 1 through 11

Size	Min	Issue	Coupon	Maturity	Yield	Price
3000		T-NOTE	3.875	02-15-2013	4.003	98.961
1000		T-BOND	12.000	08-15-2013C	6.236	143.632
1000		T-BOND	13.250	05-15-2014C	6.378	154.222
1000		T-BOND	12.500	08-15-2014C	6.172	151.260
1000		T-BOND	11.750	11-15-2014C	5.945	148.284
1000		T-BOND	11.250	02-15-2015	4.277	164.518
1000		T-BOND	10.625	08-15-2015	4.346	159.712
1000		T-BOND	9.875	11-15-2015	4.397	152.718
1000		T-BOND	9.250	02-15-2016	4.447	146.772
1000		T-BOND	7.250	05-15-2016	4.520	126.832
1000		T-BOND	7.500	11-15-2016	4.570	129.510

Notice that four of the bonds have a much higher yield to maturity than the rest. The reason is these four bonds are callable, denoted by the "C" after the maturity date. We will have more to say about callable bonds in a later chapter.

Keep in mind that clean prices and accrued interest are purely a quoting convention. The price that matters to you is the invoice price, because that is what you will actually pay for the bond. The only thing that's important about accrued interest on a bond is that it may impact the taxes you owe on the first coupon you receive.

Check This

10.2a	A straight bond's price has two components. What are they?
10.2b	What do you call a bond that sells for more than its face value?
10.2c	What is the relationship between a bond's price and its term to maturity when the bond's coupon rate is equal to its yield to maturity?
10.2d	Does current yield more strongly overstate yield to maturity for long-maturity or short-maturity premium bonds?

10.3 More on Yields

In the previous section, we focused on finding a straight bond's price given its yield. In this section, we reverse direction to find a bond's yield given its price. We then discuss the relationship among the various yield measures we have seen. We finish the section with some additional yield calculations.

Calculating Yields

To calculate a bond's yield given its price, we use the same straight bond formula used previously. The only way to find the yield is by trial and error. Financial calculators and spreadsheets do it this way at very high speed.

To illustrate, suppose we have a 6 percent bond with 10 years to maturity. Its price is 90, meaning 90 percent of face value. Assuming a $1,000 face value, the price is $900 and the coupon is $60 per year. What's the yield?

To find out, all we can do is try different yields until we come across the one that produces a price of $900. However, we can speed things up quite a bit by making an educated guess using what we know about bond prices and yields. We know the yield on this bond is greater than its 6 percent coupon rate because it is a discount bond. So let's first try 8 percent in the straight bond pricing formula:

$$\frac{\$60}{.08}\left[1 - \frac{1}{(1.04)^{20}}\right] + \frac{\$1,000}{(1.04)^{20}} = \$864.10$$

The price with an 8 percent yield is $864.10, which is somewhat less than the $900 price, but not too far off.

To finish, we need to ask whether the 8 percent we used was too high or too low. We know that the higher the yield, the lower is the price, thus 8 percent is a little too high. So let's try 7.5 percent:

$$\frac{\$60}{.075}\left[1 - \frac{1}{(1.0375)^{20}}\right] + \frac{\$1,000}{(1.0375)^{20}} = \$895.78$$

Now we're very close. We're still a little too high on the yield (since the price is a little low). If you try 7.4 percent, you'll see that the resulting price is $902.29, so the yield is between 7.4 and 7.5 percent (it's actually 7.435 percent).

SPREADSHEET ANALYSIS

	A	B	C	D	E	F	G	H
1								
2			**Calculating the Yield to Maturity of a Coupon Bond**					
3								
4	A Treasury bond traded on March 30, 2004, matures in 8 years on March 30, 2012.							
5	Assuming an 8 percent coupon rate and a price of 110, what is this bond's yield							
6	to maturity?							
7	Hint: Use the Excel function YIELD.							
8								
9		6.3843%	= YIELD("3/30/2004","3/30/2012",0.08,110,100,2,3)					
10								
11	This function uses the following arguments:							
12								
13			= YIELD("Now","Maturity",Coupon,Price,100,2,3)					
14								
15	Price is entered as a percent of face value.							
16	The 100 indicates redemption value as a percent of face value.							
17	The 2 indicates semi-annual coupons.							
18	The 3 specifies an actual day count with 365 days per year.							
19								
20								

CALCULATING YTM

EXAMPLE 10.5

Suppose a bond has eight years to maturity, a price of 110, and a coupon rate of 8 percent. What is its yield?

This is a premium bond, so its yield is less than the 8 percent coupon. If we try 6 percent, we get (check this) $1,125.61. The yield is therefore a little bigger than 6 percent. If we try 6.5 percent, we get (check this) $1,092.43, so the answer is slightly less than 6.5 percent. Check that 6.4 percent is almost exact (the exact yield is 6.3843 percent).

Yields to maturity may be calculated using a built-in spreadsheet function. An example of how to use an Excel™ spreadsheet to calculate a yield to maturity is shown in the nearby *Spreadsheet Analysis* box.

Yield to Call

callable bond A bond is callable if the issuer can buy it back before it matures.

call price The price the issuer of a callable bond must pay to buy it back.

The discussion in this chapter so far has assumed that a bond will have an actual maturity equal to its originally stated maturity. However, this is not always so since most bonds are **callable bonds**. When a bond issue is callable, the issuer can buy back outstanding bonds before the bonds mature. In exchange, bondholders receive a special **call price**, which is often equal to face value, although it may be slightly higher. When a call price is equal to face value, the bond is said to be *callable at par*.

Bonds are called at the convenience of the issuer, and a call usually occurs after a fall in market interest rates allows issuers to refinance outstanding debt with new bonds paying lower coupons. However, an issuer's call privilege is often restricted so

call protection period
The period during which a callable bond cannot be called. Also called a *call deferment period.*

that outstanding bonds cannot be called until the end of a specified **call protection period**, also termed a *call deferment period*. As a typical example, a bond issued with a 20-year maturity may be sold to investors subject to the restriction that it is callable anytime after an initial five-year call protection period.

If a bond is callable, its yield to maturity may no longer be a useful number. Instead, the **yield to call**, commonly abbreviated **YTC**, may be more meaningful. Yield to call is a yield measure that assumes a bond issue will be called at its earliest possible call date.

yield to call (YTC)
Measure of return that assumes a bond will be redeemed at the earliest call date.

We calculate a bond's yield to call using the straight bond pricing formula we have been using with two changes. First, instead of time to maturity, we use time to the first possible call date. Second, instead of face value, we use the call price. The resulting formula is thus:

$$\text{Callable bond price} = \frac{C}{YTC}\left[1 - \frac{1}{(1 + YTC/2)^{2T}}\right] + \frac{CP}{(1 + YTC/2)^{2T}} \quad (10.4)$$

where: C = Constant annual coupon
CP = Call price of the bond
T = Time in years until earliest possible call date
YTC = Yield to call assuming semiannual coupons

Calculating a yield to call requires the same trial-and-error procedure as calculating a yield to maturity. Most financial calculators will either handle the calculation directly or can be tricked into it by just changing the face value to the call price and the time to maturity to time to call.

To give a trial-and-error example, suppose a 20-year bond has a coupon of 8 percent, a price of 98, and is callable in 10 years. The call price is 105. What are its yield to maturity and yield to call?

Based on our earlier discussion, we know the yield to maturity is slightly bigger than the coupon rate. (Why?) After some calculation, we find it to be 8.2 percent.

To find the bond's yield to call, we pretend it has a face value of 105 instead of 100 ($1,050 versus $1,000) and will mature in 10 years. With these two changes, the procedure is exactly the same. We can try 8.5 percent, for example:

$$\frac{\$80}{.085}\left[1 - \frac{1}{(1.0425)^{20}}\right] + \frac{\$1,050}{(1.0425)^{20}} = \$988.51$$

Since this $988.51 is a little too high, the yield to call is slightly bigger than 8.5 percent. If we try 8.6, we find that the price is $981.83, so the yield to call is about 8.6 percent (it's 8.6276 percent).

A natural question comes up in this context. Which is bigger, the yield to maturity or the yield to call? The answer depends on the call price. However, if the bond is callable at par (as many are), then, for a premium bond, the yield to maturity is greater. For a discount bond, the reverse is true.

YIELD TO CALL

EXAMPLE 10.6

An 8.5 percent coupon bond maturing in 15 years is callable at 105 in 5 years. If the price is 100, which is bigger, the yield to call or the yield to maturity?

(continued)

SPREADSHEET ANALYSIS

	A	B	C	D	E	F	G	H
1								
2				**Calculating Yield to Call**				
3								
4	A bond traded on March 30, 2004 matures in 15 years on March 30, 2019 and may							
5	be called anytime after March 30, 2009 at a call price of 105. The bond pays an							
6	8.5 percent coupon and currently trades at par. What are the yield to maturity							
7	and yield to call for this bond?							
8								
9	Yield to maturity is based on the 2019 maturity and the current price of 100.							
10								
11		8.500%		= YIELD("3/30/2004","3/30/2019",0.085,100,100,2,3)				
12								
13	Yield to call is based on the 2009 call date and the call price of 105.							
14								
15		9.308%		= YIELD("3/30/2004","3/30/2009",0.085,100,105,2,3)				
16								
17								

Since this is a par bond callable at a premium, the yield to call is bigger. We can verify this by calculating both yields. Check that the yield to maturity is 8.50 percent, whereas the yield to call is 9.308 percent.

Yields to call may be calculated using a built-in spreadsheet function. An example of how to use an Excel™ spreadsheet to calculate a yield to call is shown in the nearby *Spreadsheet Analysis* box.

Check This

10.3a What does it mean for a bond to be callable?

10.3b What is the difference between yield to maturity and yield to call?

10.3c Yield to call is calculated just like yield to maturity except for two changes. What are the changes?

10.4 Interest Rate Risk and Malkiel's Theorems

interest rate risk The possibility that changes in interest rates will result in losses in a bond's value.

Bond yields are essentially interest rates, and, like interest rates, they fluctuate through time. When interest rates change, bond prices change. This is called **interest rate risk**. The term "interest rate risk" refers to the possibility of losses on a bond from changes in interest rates.

Promised Yield and Realized Yield

realized yield The yield actually earned or "realized" on a bond.

The terms *yield to maturity* and *promised yield* both seem to imply that the yield originally stated when a bond is purchased is what you will actually earn if you hold the bond until it matures. Actually, this is not generally correct. The return or yield you actually earn on a bond is called the **realized yield**, and an originally stated yield to maturity is almost never exactly equal to the realized yield.

The reason a realized yield will almost always differ from a promised yield is that interest rates fluctuate, causing bond prices to rise or fall. One consequence is that if a bond is sold before maturity, its price may be higher or lower than originally anticipated, and, as a result, the actually realized yield will be different from the promised yield.

Another important reason why realized yields generally differ from promised yields relates to the bond's coupons. We will get to this in the next section. For now, you should know that, for the most part, a bond's realized yield will equal its promised yield only if its yield doesn't change at all over the life of the bond, an unlikely event.

Interest Rate Risk and Maturity

While changing interest rates systematically affect all bond prices, it is important to realize that the impact of changing interest rates is not the same for all bonds. Some bonds are more sensitive to interest rate changes than others. To illustrate, Figure 10.2 shows how two bonds with different maturities can have different price sensitivities to changes in bond yields.

In Figure 10.2, bond prices are measured on the vertical axis, and bond yields are measured on the horizontal axis. Both bonds have the same 8 percent coupon rate, but one bond has a 5-year maturity while the other bond has a 20-year maturity. Both bonds display the inverse relationship between bond prices and bond yields. Since both bonds have the same 8 percent coupon rate, and both sell for par, their yields are 8 percent.

FIGURE 10.2   **Bond Prices and Yields**

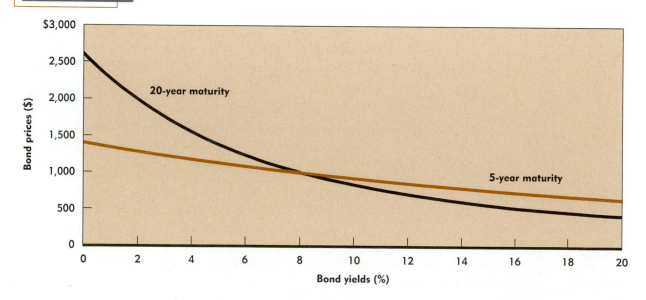

However, when bond yields are greater than 8 percent, the 20-year maturity bond has a lower price than the 5-year maturity bond. In contrast, when bond yields are less than 8 percent, the 20-year maturity bond has a higher price than the 5-year maturity bond. Essentially, falling yields cause both bond prices to rise, but the longer maturity bond experiences a larger price increase than the shorter maturity bond. Similarly, rising yields cause both bond prices to fall, but the price of the longer maturity bond falls by more than the price of the shorter maturity bond.

Malkiel's Theorems

The effect illustrated in Figure 10.2, along with some other important relationships among bond prices, maturities, coupon rates, and yields, is succinctly described by Burton Malkiel's five bond price theorems.[2] These five theorems are:

1. Bond prices and bond yields move in opposite directions. As a bond's yield increases, its price decreases. Conversely, as a bond's yield decreases, its price increases.

2. For a given change in a bond's yield to maturity, the longer the term to maturity of the bond, the greater will be the magnitude of the change in the bond's price.

3. For a given change in a bond's yield to maturity, the size of the change in the bond's price increases at a diminishing rate as the bond's term to maturity lengthens.

4. For a given change in a bond's yield to maturity, the absolute magnitude of the resulting change in the bond's price is inversely related to the bond's coupon rate.

5. For a given absolute change in a bond's yield to maturity, the magnitude of the price increase caused by a decrease in yield is greater than the price decrease caused by an increase in yield.

The first, second, and fourth of these theorems are the simplest and most important. The first one says that bond prices and yields move in opposite directions. The second one says that longer-term bonds are more sensitive to changes in yields than shorter-term bonds. The fourth one says that lower coupon bonds are more sensitive to changes in yields than higher coupon bonds.

The third theorem says that a bond's sensitivity to interest rate changes increases as its maturity grows, but at a diminishing rate. In other words, a 10-year bond is much more sensitive to changes in yield than a 1-year bond. However, a 30-year bond is only slightly more sensitive than a 20-year bond. Finally, the fifth theorem says essentially that the loss you would suffer from, say, a 1 percent increase in yields is less than the gain you would enjoy from a 1 percent decrease in yields.

Table 10.1 illustrates the first three of these theorems by providing prices for 8 percent coupon bonds with maturities of 5, 10, and 20 years and yields to maturity of 7 percent and 9 percent. Be sure to check these for practice. As the first theorem says, bond prices are lower when yields are higher (9 percent versus 7 percent). As the second theorem indicates, the differences in bond prices between yields of 7 percent and 9 percent are greater for bonds with a longer term to maturity. However, as the third theorem states, the effect increases at a diminishing rate as the maturity lengthens. To

---

[2]Burton C. Malkiel, "Expectations, Bond Prices, and the Term Structure of Interest Rates," *Quarterly Journal of Economics,* May 1962, pp. 197–218.

Bond-Market Diversification Is an Option for "Chickens"

Don't put all your eggs in one basket, especially if you're a little chicken. In the past year, tech-stock-crazed stock jockeys got a vicious lesson in the virtues of diversification. But spreading bets widely is also a smart strategy for antsy investors with big bond portfolios.

True, that might not be apparent from looking at recent results. Investors tend to favor high-quality U.S. corporate and government bond funds, and these funds performed admirably during the past 12 months, often gaining 9% or 10%. Meanwhile, more-exotic bond funds fared less well. High-yield, or junk-bond, funds sank an average 5.4%, and foreign-bond funds eked out a gain of just 0.9%, calculates Chicago fund researcher Morningstar Inc.

But the virtues of bond-market diversification are clear if you look at longer-term performance. In the 15 years through year-end 2000, intermediate-term U.S. government bonds gained an average 8.1% a year, according to Chicago's Ibbotson Associates. The journey wasn't always smooth, with intermediate bonds losing money in two years, 1994 and 1999. Over the same stretch, junk bonds had an even rougher time, suffering three calendar-year losses, while foreign bonds got slapped with four losing years. Still, if you had combined an 80% stake in intermediate governments with 10% positions in junk and foreign bonds, you would have been pleasantly surprised.

That three-sector portfolio, like intermediate-term government bonds, lost money in 1994 and 1999, but its losses were smaller, calculates Baltimore's T. Rowe Price Associates. The reason: While the three sectors each had their rough moments, those moments didn't always coincide, and thus the diversification tended to smooth out performance. Moreover, despite the reduced volatility, the portfolio had a slightly higher return, gaining 8.4% a year. "Investors don't perceive the need to diversify with bonds," says T. Rowe Price Vice President Steven Norwitz. "But, in fact, diversification may be more worthwhile in the bond area. The correlation between high-quality bonds and junk bonds tends to be lower than the correlation between different sectors of the U.S. stock market."

The correlation between U.S. and foreign bonds is also low. Much of this comes from currency swings, and thus you will likely get more diversification benefit from funds such as American Century International Bond Fund and T. Rowe Price International Bond Fund, which rarely or never hedge. But Chris Cordaro, a financial planner in Chatham, N.J., prefers funds that limit their currency exposure, such as Payden Global Fixed Income Fund. "If you leave your foreign bonds unhedged, you get greater diversification benefit, but you also get

(continued)

TABLE 10.1	Bond Prices and Yields		
	Time to Maturity		
Yields	5 Years	10 Years	20 Years
7%	$1,041.58	$1,071.06	$1,106.78
9%	960.44	934.96	907.99
Price difference	$ 81.14	$ 136.10	$ 198.79

see this, notice that $136.10 is 67.7 percent larger than $81.14, while $198.79 is only 46.1 percent larger than $136.10.

To illustrate the last two theorems, we present prices for 20-year maturity bonds with coupon rates and yields to maturity of 6 percent, 8 percent, and 10 percent (again, calculate these for practice) in Table 10.2. To illustrate the fourth theorem, compare the loss on the 6 percent and the 8 percent bonds as yields move from 8 percent to 10 percent. The 6 percent bond loses ($656.82 − $802.07)/$802.07 = −18.1%. The 8 percent bond loses ($828.41 − $1,000)/$1,000 = −17.2%, showing that the bond with greater volatility in the individual fund," he says. "People view bonds as a safety net. From a behavioral standpoint, you're probably better off with a hedged fund, because you'll be happier and stick with it for longer."

As you build your diversified bond portfolio, also consider adding some inflation-indexed Treasury bonds, which will provide protection against rapidly rising consumer prices. Such inflation can be devastating to traditional bonds. Rising consumer prices eat away at the spending power of the interest kicked off by these bonds. Additionally, accelerating inflation drives up interest rates, depressing bond values. But in that situation, inflation-indexed Treasury bonds should fare well. With these bonds, which were first sold by the Treasury in 1997, you get a fixed interest payment, which is currently above 3%. But in addition, the bonds' principal value is stepped up each year along with inflation. Thus, today's buyer can be confident of clocking an annual pretax return equal to more than three percentage points a year above inflation. Find inflation-indexed Treasury bonds intriguing? Also check out the government's Series I savings bonds. For further information on both types of bond, visit www.publicdebt.treas.gov.

Savings bonds may seem like the stodgiest of investments. But the Series I bonds could be a great addition to your portfolio. Like inflation-indexed Treasurys, these bonds provide a guaranteed return above inflation. Cur-

rently, Series I bonds pay three percentage points a year more than inflation. That is slightly less than the real yield on inflation-Indexed Treasurys. Moreover, if you hold I bonds for less than five years, you have to pay a penalty equal to three months' earnings. Still, I bonds have a few key advantages. The interest grows tax-deferred until the bonds are sold. By contrast, with inflation-indexed Treasury bonds, you have to pay taxes each year on both the interest you receive and the step-up in value as a result of inflation.

The I bonds also offer an attractive interest-rate play, says William Reichenstein, an investments professor at Baylor University in Waco, Texas. He suggests buying the I bonds today, even though they yield less than inflation-indexed Treasurys, and then holding them for five years, to get beyond the penalty period. If, at that juncture, inflation-indexed Treasurys offer a much higher yield, you could swap into those bonds. But "if five years from now the real interest rate on [inflation-indexed Treasurys] is less than that 3%, you have the option to continue with the I bonds for up to 25 more years," Mr. Reichenstein says. "To me, that's a valuable option."

Source: Jonathan Clements, *The Wall Street Journal*, July 24, 2001. © 2001 Dow Jones & Company, Inc. All Rights Reserved Worldwide.

TABLE 10.2	Twenty-Year Bond Prices and Yields		
	Coupon Rates		
Yields	**6 Percent**	**8 Percent**	**10 Percent**
6%	$1,000.00	$1,231.15	$1,462.30
8%	802.07	1,000.00	1,197.93
10%	656.82	828.41	1,000.00

the lower coupon is more sensitive to a change in yields. You can (and should) verify that the same is true for a yield increase.

Finally, to illustrate the fifth theorem, take a look at the 8 percent coupon bond in Table 10.2. As yields decrease by 2 percent from 8 percent to 6 percent, its price climbs by $231.15. As yields rise by 2 percent, the bond's price falls by $171.59.

As we have discussed, bond maturity is an important factor determining the sensitivity of a bond's price to changes in interest rates. However, bond maturity is an incomplete measure of bond price sensitivity to yield changes. For example, we have seen that a bond's coupon rate is also important. An improved measure of interest rate risk for bonds that accounts both for differences in maturity and differences in coupon rates is our next subject. A nearby *Investment Updates* box discusses some recent real-world gains and losses from bond investing.

Check This

10.4a True or false: A bond price's sensitivity to interest rate changes increases at an increasing rate as maturity lengthens.

10.4b Which is more sensitive to an interest rate shift: a low-coupon bond or a high-coupon bond?

10.5 Duration

duration A widely used measure of a bond's sensitivity to changes in bond yields.

To account for differences in interest rate risk across bonds with different coupon rates and maturities, the concept of **duration** is widely applied. As we will explore in some detail, duration measures a bond's sensitivity to interest rate changes. The idea behind duration was first presented by Frederick Macaulay in an early study of U.S. financial markets.[3] Today, duration is a very widely used measure of a bond's price sensitivity to changes in bond yields.

Macaulay Duration

There are several duration measures. The original version is called *Macaulay duration*. The usefulness of Macaulay duration stems from the fact that it satisfies the following approximate relationship between percentage changes in bond prices and changes in bond yields:

$$\text{Percentage change in bond price} \approx -\text{ Duration} \times \frac{\text{Change in YTM}}{(1 + \text{YTM}/2)} \quad (10.5)$$

As a consequence, two bonds with the same duration, but not necessarily the same maturity, have approximately the same price sensitivity to a change in bond yields. This approximation is quite accurate for relatively small changes in yields, but it becomes less accurate when large changes are considered.

To see how we use this result, suppose a bond has a Macaulay duration of six years, and its yield decreases from 10 percent to 9.5 percent. The resulting percentage change in the price of the bond is calculated as follows:

$$-6 \times \frac{.095 - .10}{1.05} = 2.86\%$$

Thus, the bond's price rises by 2.86 percent in response to a yield decrease of 50 basis points.

---

[3]Frederick Macaulay, *Some Theoretical Problems Suggested by the Movements of Interest Rates, Bond Yields, and Stock Prices in the United States since 1856* (New York: National Bureau of Economic Research, 1938).

MACAULAY DURATION

EXAMPLE 10.7

A bond has a Macaulay duration of 11 years, and its yield increases from 8 percent to 8.5 percent. What will happen to the price of the bond?

The resulting percentage change in the price of the bond can be calculated as follows:

$$-11 \times \frac{.085 - .08}{1.04} = -5.29\%$$

The bond's price declines by approximately 5.29 percent in response to a 50 basis point increase in yields.

Modified Duration

Some analysts prefer to use a variation of Macaulay duration called *modified duration*. The relationship between Macaulay duration and modified duration for bonds paying semiannual coupons is simply:

$$\text{Modified duration} = \frac{\text{Macaulay duration}}{(1 + YTM/2)} \quad (10.6)$$

As a result, based on modified duration, the approximate relationship between percentage changes in bond prices and changes in bond yields is just:

$$\text{Percentage change in bond price} \approx - \text{Modified duration} \times \text{Change in } YTM \quad (10.7)$$

In other words, to calculate the percentage change in the bond's price, we just multiply the modified duration by the change in yields.

MODIFIED DURATION

EXAMPLE 10.8

A bond has a Macaulay duration of 8.5 years and a yield to maturity of 9 percent. What is its modified duration?

The bond's modified duration is calculated as follows:

$$\frac{8.5}{1.045} = 8.134$$

Notice that we divided the yield by 2 to get the semiannual yield.

MODIFIED DURATION

EXAMPLE 10.9

A bond has a modified duration of seven years. Suppose its yield increases from 8 percent to 8.5 percent. What happens to its price?

(continued)

We can very easily determine the resulting percentage change in the price of the bond using its modified duration:

$$-7 \times (.085 - .08) = -3.5\%$$

The bond's price declines by about 3.5 percent.

Calculating Macaulay Duration

Macaulay duration is often described as a bond's *effective maturity*. For this reason, duration values are conventionally stated in years. The first fundamental principle for calculating the duration of a bond concerns the duration of a zero coupon bond. Specifically, the duration of a zero coupon bond is equal to its maturity. Thus, on a pure discount instrument, such as the U.S. Treasury STRIPS we discussed in Chapter 9, no calculation is necessary to come up with Macaulay duration.

The second fundamental principle for calculating duration concerns the duration of a coupon bond with multiple cash flows. The duration of a coupon bond is a weighted average of individual maturities of all the bond's separate cash flows. The weights attached to the maturity of each cash flow are proportionate to the present values of each cash flow.

A sample duration calculation for a bond with three years until maturity is illustrated in Table 10.3. The bond sells at par value. It has an 8 percent coupon rate and an 8 percent yield to maturity.

As shown in Table 10.3, calculating a bond's duration can be laborious—especially if the bond has a large number of separate cash flows. Fortunately, relatively simple formulas are available for many of the important cases. For example, if a bond is selling for par value, its duration can be calculated easily using the following formula:

$$\text{Par value bond duration} = \frac{(1 + YTM/2)}{YTM}\left[1 - \frac{1}{(1 + YTM/2)^{2M}}\right] \quad (10.8)$$

where: M = Bond maturity in years

YTM = Yield to maturity assuming semiannual coupons

For example, using $YTM = 8\%$ and $M = 3$ years we obtain the same duration value (2.7259 years) computed in Table 10.3.

TABLE 10.3	Calculating Bond Duration			
Years	Cash Flow	Discount Factor	Present Value	Years × Present Value ÷ Bond Price
0.5	$ 40	.96154	$ 38.4615	.0192 years
1	40	.92456	36.9822	.0370
1.5	40	.88900	35.5599	.0533
2	40	.85480	34.1922	.0684
2.5	40	.82193	32.8771	.0822
3	1,040	.79031	821.9271	2.4658
			$1,000.00	2.7259 years
			Bond Price	Bond Duration

DURATION FOR A PAR VALUE BOND

EXAMPLE 10.10

Suppose a par value bond has a 6 percent coupon and 10 years to maturity. What is its duration?

Since the bond sells for par, its yield is equal to its coupon rate, 6 percent. Plugging this into the par value bond duration formula, we have:

$$\text{Par value bond duration} = \frac{(1 + .06/2)}{.06}\left[1 - \frac{1}{(1 + .06/2)^{20}}\right]$$

After a little work on a calculator, we find that the duration is 7.66 years.

The par value bond duration formula (Equation 10.8) is useful for calculating the duration of a bond that is actually selling at par value. Unfortunately, the general formula for bonds not necessarily selling at par value is somewhat more complicated. The general duration formula for a bond paying constant semiannual coupons is:

$$\text{Duration} = \frac{1 + YTM/2}{YTM} - \frac{(1 + YTM/2) + M(CPR - YTM)}{YTM + CPR[(1 + YTM/2)^{2M} - 1]} \quad (10.9)$$

where: CPR = Constant annual coupon rate
M = Bond maturity in years
YTM = Yield to maturity assuming semiannual coupons

Although somewhat tedious for manual calculations, this formula is used in many computer programs that calculate bond durations. Some popular personal computer spreadsheet packages also have a built-in function to perform this calculation.

DURATION FOR A DISCOUNT BOND

EXAMPLE 10.11

A bond has a yield to maturity of 7 percent. It matures in 12 years. Its coupon rate is 6 percent. What is its modified duration?

We first must calculate the Macaulay duration using the unpleasant-looking formula just above. We finish by converting the Macaulay duration to modified duration. Plugging into the duration formula, we have:

$$\text{Duration} = \frac{1 + .07/2}{.07} - \frac{(1 + .07/2) + 12(.06 - .07)}{.07 + .06[(1 + .07/2)^{24} - 1]}$$

$$= \frac{1.035}{.07} - \frac{1.035 + 12(-.01)}{.07 + .06(1.035^{24} - 1)}$$

After a little button pushing, we find that the duration is 8.56 years. Finally, converting to modified duration, we find that the modified duration is equal to 8.56/1.035 = 8.27 years.

Bond durations may be calculated using a built-in spreadsheet function. An example of how to use an Excel™ spreadsheet to calculate a Macaulay duration and modified duration are shown in the nearby *Spreadsheet Analysis* box.

SPREADSHEET ANALYSIS

	A	B	C	D	E	F	G	H
1								
2			**Calculating Macaulay and Modified Durations**					
3								
4	A Treasury bond traded on March 30, 2004, matures in 12 years on March 30, 2016.							
5	Assuming a 6 percent coupon rate and a 7 percent yield to maturity, what are the							
6	Macaulay and Modified durations of this bond?							
7	Hint: Use the Excel functions DURATION and MDURATION.							
8								
9		8.561	= DURATION("3/30/2004","3/30/2016",0.06,0.07,2,3)					
10								
11		8.272	= MDURATION("3/30/2004","3/30/2016",0.06,0.07,2,3)					
12								
13	These functions use the following arguments convention:							
14								
15			= DURATION("Now","Maturity",Coupon,Yield,2,3)					
16								
17	The 2 indicates semi-annual coupons.							
18	The 3 specifies an actual day count with 365 days per year.							
19								
20								

Properties of Duration

Macaulay duration has a number of important properties. For straight bonds, the basic properties of Macaulay duration can be summarized as follows:

1. All else the same, the longer a bond's maturity, the longer is its duration.
2. All else the same, a bond's duration increases at a decreasing rate as maturity lengthens.
3. All else the same, the higher a bond's coupon, the shorter is its duration.
4. All else the same, a higher yield to maturity implies a shorter duration, and a lower yield to maturity implies a longer duration.

As we saw earlier, a zero coupon bond has a duration equal to its maturity. The duration on a bond with coupons is always less than its maturity. Because of the second principle, durations much longer than 10 or 15 years are rarely seen. There is an exception to some of these principles that involves very long maturity bonds selling at a very steep discount. This exception rarely occurs in practice, so these principles are generally correct.

A graphical illustration of the relationship between duration and maturity is presented in Figure 10.3, where duration is measured on the vertical axis and maturity is measured on the horizontal axis. In Figure 10.3, the yield to maturity for all bonds is 10 percent. Bonds with coupon rates of 0 percent, 5 percent, 10 percent, and 15 percent are presented. As the figure shows, the duration of a zero coupon bond rises step for

FIGURE 10.3   **Bond Duration and Maturity**

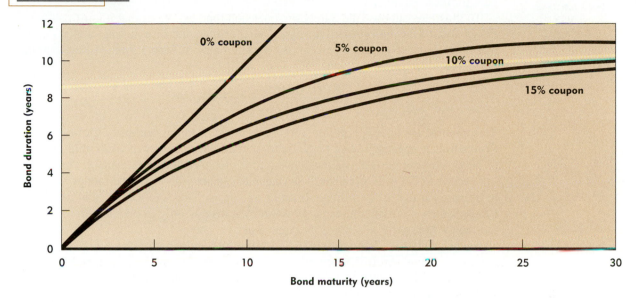

step with maturity. For the coupon bonds, however, the duration initially moves closely with maturity, as our first duration principle suggests, but, consistent with the second principle, the lines begin to flatten out after four or five years. Also, consistent with our third principle, the lower coupon bonds have higher durations.

Check This

10.5a What does duration measure?

10.5b What is the duration of a zero coupon bond?

10.5c What happens to a bond's duration as its maturity grows?

10.6 Dedicated Portfolios and Reinvestment Risk

Duration has another property that makes it a vital tool in bond portfolio management. To explore this subject, we first need to introduce two important concepts, dedicated portfolios and reinvestment risk.

Dedicated Portfolios

dedicated portfolio A bond portfolio created to prepare for a future cash outlay.

Bond portfolios are often created for the purpose of preparing for a future liability payment or other cash outlay. A portfolio formed for such a specific purpose is called a **dedicated portfolio**. When the future liability payment of a dedicated portfolio is due on a known date, that date is commonly called the portfolio's *target date*.

Pension funds provide a good example of dedicated portfolio management. A pension fund normally knows years in advance the amount of benefit payments it must

For a practical view of bond portfolio management visit www.jamesbaker.com

make to its beneficiaries. The fund then purchases bonds in the amount needed to prepare for these payments.

To illustrate, suppose the Safety First pension fund estimates that it must pay benefits of about $100 million in five years. Using semiannual discounting, and assuming that bonds currently yield 8 percent, the present value of Safety First's future liability is calculated as follows:

$$\frac{\$100,000,000}{(1.04)^{10}} \approx \$67,556,417$$

This amount, about $67.5 million, represents the investment necessary for Safety First to construct a dedicated bond portfolio to fund a future liability of $100 million.

Next, suppose the Safety First pension fund creates a dedicated portfolio by investing exactly $67.5 million in bonds selling at par value with a coupon rate of 8 percent to prepare for the $100 million payout in five years. The Safety First fund decides to follow a maturity matching strategy whereby it invests only in bonds with maturities that match the portfolio's five-year target date.

Since Safety First is investing $67.5 million in bonds that pay an 8 percent annual coupon, the fund receives $5.4 million in coupons each year, along with $67.5 million of principal at the bonds' five-year maturity. As the coupons come in, Safety First reinvests them. If all coupons are reinvested at an 8 percent yield, the fund's portfolio will grow to about $99.916 million on its target date. This is the future value of $67.5 million compounded at 4 percent semiannually for five years:

$$\$67.5 \text{ million} \times (1.04)^{10} \approx \$100 \text{ million}$$

This amount is also equal to the future value of all coupons reinvested at 8 percent, plus the $67.5 million of bond principal received at maturity. To see this, we calculate the future value of the coupons (using the standard formula for the future value of an annuity) and then add the $67.5 million:

$$\frac{\$5.4 \text{ million}}{.08} [(1.04)^{10} - 1] + \$67.5 \text{ million} \approx \$100 \text{ million}$$

Thus, as long as the annual coupons are reinvested at 8 percent, Safety First's bond fund will grow to the amount needed.

Reinvestment Risk

As we have seen, the bond investment strategy of the Safety First pension fund will be successful if all coupons received during the life of the investment can be reinvested at a constant 8 percent yield. However, in reality, yields at which coupons can be reinvested are uncertain, and a target date surplus or shortfall is therefore likely to occur.

The uncertainty about future or target date portfolio value that results from the need to reinvest bond coupons at yields that cannot be predicted in advance is called **reinvestment rate risk**. Thus, the uncertain portfolio value on the target date represents reinvestment risk. In general, more distant target dates entail greater uncertainty and reinvestment risk.

To examine the impact of reinvestment risk, we continue with the example of the Safety First pension fund's dedicated bond portfolio. We will consider two cases, one in which all bond coupons are reinvested at a higher 9 percent yield, and one in which all coupons are reinvested at a lower 7 percent yield. In this case, the payment of the fixed $67.5 million principal plus the future value of the 10 semiannual coupons

reinvestment rate risk
The uncertainty about future or target date portfolio value that results from the need to reinvest bond coupons at yields not known in advance.

compounded at an uncertain rate, either 9 percent or 7 percent, comprises the total five-year target date portfolio value.

For 9 percent and 7 percent yields, these target date portfolio values are calculated as follows:

$$\frac{\$5.4 \text{ million}}{.09}[(1.045)^{10} - 1] + \$67.5 \text{ million} = \$100.678 \text{ million}$$

and

$$\frac{\$5.4 \text{ million}}{.07}[(1.035)^{10} - 1] + \$67.5 \text{ million} = \$99.175 \text{ million}$$

As shown, a target date portfolio value of $100.678 million is realized through a 9 percent reinvestment rate, and a value of $99.175 million is realized by a 7 percent reinvestment rate. The difference between these two amounts, about $1.5 million, represents reinvestment risk.

As this example illustrates, a maturity matching strategy for a dedicated bond portfolio entails substantial reinvestment risk. Indeed, this example understates a pension fund's total reinvestment risk since it considers only a single target date. In reality, pension funds have a series of target dates, and a shortfall at one target date typically coincides with shortfalls at other target dates as well.

A simple solution for reinvestment risk is to purchase zero coupon bonds that pay a fixed principal at a maturity chosen to match a dedicated portfolio's target date. Since there are no coupons to reinvest, there is no reinvestment risk! However, a zero coupon bond strategy has its drawbacks. As a practical matter, U.S. Treasury STRIPS are the only zero coupon bonds issued in sufficient quantity to even begin to satisfy the dedicated portfolio needs of pension funds, insurance companies, and other institutional investors. However, U.S. Treasury securities have lower yields than even the highest quality corporate bonds. A yield difference of only .25 percent between Treasury securities and corporate bonds can make a substantial difference in the initial cost of a dedicated bond portfolio.

For example, suppose that Treasury STRIPS have a yield of 7.75 percent. Using semiannual compounding, the present value of these zero coupon bonds providing a principal payment of $100 million at a five-year maturity is calculated as follows:

$$\frac{\$100 \text{ million}}{(1.03875)^{10}} \approx \$68.374 \text{ million}$$

This cost of $68.374 million based on a 7.75 percent yield is significantly higher than the previously stated cost of $67.556 million based on an 8 percent yield. From the perspective of the Safety First pension fund, this represents a hefty premium to pay to eliminate reinvestment risk. Fortunately, as we discuss in the next section, other methods are available at lower cost.

Check This

10.6a   What is a dedicated portfolio?

10.6b   What is reinvestment rate risk?

10.7 Immunization

immunization
Constructing a portfolio to minimize the uncertainty surrounding its target date value.

Constructing a dedicated portfolio to minimize the uncertainty in its target date value is called **immunization**. In this section, we show how duration can be used to immunize a bond portfolio against reinvestment risk.

Price Risk versus Reinvestment Rate Risk

To understand how immunization is accomplished, suppose you own a bond with eight years to maturity. However, your target date is actually just six years from now. If interest rates rise, are you happy or unhappy?

price risk The risk that bond prices will decrease, which arises in dedicated portfolios when the target date value of a bond or bond portfolio is not known with certainty.

Your initial reaction is probably "unhappy" because you know that as interest rates rise, bond values fall. However, things are not so simple. Clearly, if interest rates rise, then, in six years, your bond will be worth less than it would have been at a lower rate. This is called **price risk**. However, it is also true that you will be able to reinvest the coupons you receive at a higher interest rate. As a result, your reinvested coupons will be worth more. In fact, the net effect of an interest rate increase might be to make you *better* off.

As our simple example illustrates, for a dedicated portfolio, interest rate changes have two effects. Interest rate increases act to decrease bond prices (price risk) but increase the future value of reinvested coupons (reinvestment rate risk). In the other direction, interest rate decreases act to increase bond values but decrease the future value of reinvested coupons. The key observation is that these two effects—price risk and reinvestment rate risk—tend to offset each other.

You might wonder if it is possible to engineer a portfolio in which these two effects offset each other more or less precisely. As we illustrate next, the answer is most definitely yes.

Immunization by Duration Matching

The key to immunizing a dedicated portfolio is to match its duration to its target date. If this is done, then the impacts of price and reinvestment rate risk will almost exactly offset, and interest rate changes will have a minimal impact on the target date value of the portfolio. In fact, immunization is often simply referred to as duration matching.

To see how a duration matching strategy can be applied to reduce target date uncertainty, suppose the Safety First pension fund initially purchases $67.5 million of par value bonds paying 8 percent coupons with a maturity of 6.2 years. From the par value duration formula we discussed earlier, a maturity of 6.2 years corresponds to a duration of 5 years. Thus, the duration of Safety First's dedicated bond portfolio is now matched to its five-year portfolio target date.

Suppose that immediately after the bonds are purchased, a one-time shock causes bond yields to either jump up to 10 percent or jump down to 6 percent. As a result, all coupons are reinvested at either a 10 percent yield or a 6 percent yield, depending on which way rates jump.

This example is illustrated in Figure 10.4, where the left vertical axis measures initial bond portfolio values, and the right vertical axis measures bond portfolio values realized by holding the portfolio until the bonds mature in 6.2 years. The horizontal axis measures the passage of time from initial investment to bond maturity. The positively sloped lines plot bond portfolio values through time for bond yields that have jumped to either 10 percent or 6 percent immediately after the initial investment of

Bond Price and Reinvestment Rate Risk

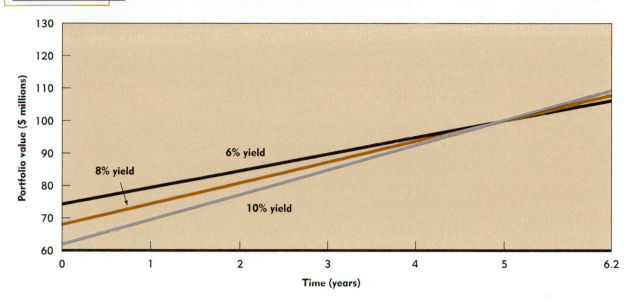

$67.5 million in par value 8 percent coupon bonds. This example assumes that after their initial jump, bond yields remain unchanged.

As shown in Figure 10.4, the initial jump in yields causes the value of Safety First's bond portfolio to jump in the opposite direction. If yields increase, bond prices fall, but coupons are reinvested at a higher interest rate, thereby leading to a higher portfolio value at maturity. In contrast, if yields decrease, bond prices rise, but a lower reinvestment rate reduces the value of the portfolio at maturity.

However, what is remarkable is that regardless of whether yields rise or fall, there is almost no difference in Safety First's portfolio value at the duration-matched five-year target date. Thus, the immunization strategy of matching the duration of Safety First's dedicated portfolio to its portfolio target date has almost entirely eliminated reinvestment risk.

Dynamic Immunization

The example of the Safety First pension fund immunizing a dedicated bond portfolio by a duration matching strategy assumed that the bond portfolio was subject to a single yield shock. In reality, bond yields change constantly. Therefore, successful immunization requires that a dedicated portfolio be rebalanced frequently to maintain a portfolio duration equal to the portfolio's target date.

For example, by purchasing bonds with a maturity of 6.2 years, the Safety First pension fund had matched the duration of the dedicated portfolio to the fund's 5-year target date. One year later, however, the target date is four years away, and bonds with a duration of four years are required to maintain a duration matching strategy. Assuming interest rates haven't changed, the par value duration formula shows that a maturity of 4.7 years corresponds to a duration of 4 years. Thus, to maintain a duration-matched target date, the Safety First fund must sell its originally purchased bonds now with a maturity of 5.2 years and replace them with bonds having a maturity of 4.7 years.

dynamic immunization
Periodic rebalancing of a dedicated bond portfolio to maintain a duration that matches the target maturity date.

The strategy of periodically rebalancing a dedicated bond portfolio to maintain a portfolio duration matched to a specific target date is called **dynamic immunization**. The advantage of dynamic immunization is that reinvestment risk caused by continually changing bond yields is greatly reduced. The drawback of dynamic immunization is that each portfolio rebalancing incurs management and transaction costs. Therefore, portfolios should not be rebalanced too frequently. In practice, rebalancing on an intermittent basis, say, each quarter, is a reasonable compromise between the costs of rebalancing and the benefits of dynamic immunization.

Check This

10.7a   What are the two effects on the target date value of a dedicated portfolio of a shift in yields? Explain why they tend to offset.

10.7b   How can a dedicated portfolio be immunized against shifts in yields?

10.7c   Why is rebalancing necessary to maintain immunization?

10.8 Summary and Conclusions

This chapter covers the basics of bonds, bond yields, duration, and immunization. In this chapter we saw that:

1. Bonds are commonly distinguished according to whether they are selling at par value or at a discount or premium relative to par value. Bonds with a price greater than par value are said to be selling at a premium; bonds with a price less than par value are said to be selling at a discount.

2. There are three different yield measures: coupon yield or rate, current yield, and yield to maturity. Each is calculated using a specific equation, and which is the biggest or smallest depends on whether the bond is selling at a discount or premium.

3. Important relationships among bond prices, maturities, coupon rates, and yields are described by Malkiel's five bond price theorems.

4. A stated yield to maturity is almost never equal to an actually realized yield because yields are subject to bond price risk and coupon reinvestment rate risk. Bond price risk is the risk that a bond sold before maturity must be sold at a price different from the price predicted by an originally stated yield to maturity. Coupon reinvestment risk is the risk that bond coupons must be reinvested at yields different from an originally stated yield to maturity.

5. To account for differences in interest rate risk across bonds with different coupon rates and maturities, the concept of duration is widely applied. Duration is a direct measure of a bond's price sensitivity to changes in bond yields.

6. Bond portfolios are often created for the purpose of preparing for a future liability payment. Portfolios formed for such a specific purpose are called dedicated portfolios. When the future liability payment of a dedicated portfolio is due on a known date, that date is called the portfolio's target date.

7. Minimizing the uncertainty of the value of a dedicated portfolio's future target date value is called immunization. A strategy of matching a bond portfolio's duration to the target maturity date accomplishes this goal.

Get Real

This chapter covered bond basics. How should you, as an investor or investment manager, put this information to work?

Now that you've been exposed to basic facts about bonds, their prices, and their yields, you might try applying the various principles we have discussed. Do this by buying some bonds and then observing the behavior of their prices and yields. Buying Treasury bonds is the best place to start.

With a simulated brokerage account (such as Stock-Trak), buy two Treasury bonds with the same maturity but different coupons. This will let you see the impact of coupon rates on price volatility. Similarly, buy two bonds with very different maturities but similar coupon rates. You'll see firsthand how maturity determines the risk of a bond.

While you're at it, calculate the durations of the bonds you buy. As their yields fluctuate, check that the percentage change in price is very close to what your calculated duration suggests it should be.

To learn more about bond prices and yields, visit some interesting websites such as Bonds Online (www.bondsonline.com), Investing in Bonds (www.investinginbonds.com), and James Baker & Assoc. (www.jamesbaker.com).

Key Terms

coupon rate 324
current yield 325
yield to maturity (YTM) 325
clean price 330
dirty price 330
callable bond 333
call price 333
call protection period 334
yield to call (YTC) 334

interest rate risk 335
realized yield 336
duration 340
dedicated portfolio 345
reinvestment rate risk 346
immunization 348
price risk 348
dynamic immunization 350

Chapter Review Problems and Self-Test

1. **Straight Bond Prices** Suppose a bond has 10 years to maturity and a coupon rate of 6 percent. The bond's yield to maturity is 8 percent. What's the price?

2. **Premium Bonds** Suppose we have two bonds, both with a 6 percent coupon rate and the same yield to maturity of 4 percent, but with different maturities of 5 and 15 years. Which has the higher price? Verify your answer by calculating the prices.

3. **Macaulay Duration** A bond has a Macaulay duration of nine years, and its yield increases from 6 percent to 6.25 percent. What will happen to the price of the bond?

Answers to Self-Test Problems

1. Here, the coupon rate is 6 percent and the face value is $1,000, so the annual coupon is $60. The bond's price is calculated as follows:

Present value of semiannual coupons:

$$\frac{\$60}{.08}\left[1 - \frac{1}{(1.04)^{20}}\right] = \$407.70979$$

Present value of $1,000 principal:

$$\frac{\$1,000}{(1.04)^{20}} = \$456.38695$$

The bond's price is the sum of coupon and principal present values:

$$\text{Bond price} = \$407.71 + \$456.39 = \$864.10$$

2. Because both bonds have a 6 percent coupon and a 4 percent yield, both bonds sell at a premium, and the one with the longer maturity will have a higher price. We can verify these conclusions by calculating the prices as follows:

5-year maturity premium bond price:

$$\frac{\$60}{.04}\left[1 - \frac{1}{(1.02)^{10}}\right] + \frac{\$1,000}{(1.02)^{10}} = \$1,089.83$$

15-year maturity premium bond price:

$$\frac{\$60}{.04}\left[1 - \frac{1}{(1.02)^{30}}\right] + \frac{\$1,000}{(1.02)^{30}} = \$1,223.96$$

Notice that the longer maturity premium bond has a higher price, just as we thought.

3. The resulting percentage change in the price of the bond can be calculated as follows:

$$-9 \times \frac{.0625 - .06}{1.03} = -2.18\%$$

The bond's price declines by approximately 2.18 percent in response to a 25 basis point increase in yields.

Test Your Investment Quotient

1. **Yield to Maturity**   The yield to maturity on a bond is
    a. Below the coupon rate when the bond sells at a discount and above the coupon rate when the bond sells at a premium.
    b. The interest rate that makes the present value of the payments equal to the bond price.
    c. Based on the assumption that all future payments received are reinvested at the coupon rate.
    d. Based on the assumption that all future payments received are reinvested at future market rates.

2. **Bond Yields**   In which one of the following cases is the bond selling at a discount?
    a. Coupon rate is greater than current yield, which is greater than yield to maturity.
    b. Coupon rate, current yield, and yield to maturity are all the same.
    c. Coupon rate is less than current yield, which is less than yield to maturity.
    d. Coupon rate is less than current yield, which is greater than yield to maturity.

3. **Bond Yields**   When are yield to maturity and current yield on a bond equal?
    a. When market interest rates begin to level off.
    b. If the bond sells at a price in excess of its par value.
    c. When the expected holding period is greater than one year.
    d. If the coupon and market interest rate are equal.

4. **Bond Yields** Which of the following states the correct relationship among yield measures for discount bonds?

   a. Coupon rate < Current yield < Yield to maturity
   b. Current yield < Coupon rate < Yield to maturity
   c. Coupon rate < Yield to maturity < Current yield
   d. Yield to maturity < Coupon rate < Current yield

5. **Bond Yields** Which of the following states the correct relationship among yield measures for premium bonds?

   a. Coupon rate > Current yield > Yield to maturity
   b. Current yield > Coupon rate > Yield to maturity
   c. Coupon rate > Yield to maturity > Current yield
   d. Yield to maturity > Coupon rate > Current yield

6. **Bond Prices** Consider a five-year bond with a 10 percent coupon that is presently trading at a yield to maturity of 8 percent. If market interest rates do not change, one year from now the price of this bond

   a. Will be higher
   b. Will be lower
   c. Will be the same
   d. Cannot be determined

7. **Bond Prices** Using semiannual compounding, what would the price of a 15-year, zero coupon bond that has a par value of $1,000 and a required return of 8 percent be?

   a. $308
   b. $315
   c. $464
   d. $555

8. **Bond Prices** If an investor's required return is 12 percent, the value of a 10-year maturity zero coupon bond with a maturity value of $1,000 is *closest* to

   a. $312
   b. $688
   c. $1,000
   d. $1,312

9. **Duration** Another term for bond duration is

   a. Actual maturity
   b. Effective maturity
   c. Calculated maturity
   d. Near-term maturity

10. **Duration** Which of the following is not a property of duration?

   a. A longer maturity generally yields a longer duration.
   b. Duration generally increases at a decreasing rate as maturity lengthens.
   c. A bigger coupon generally yields a longer duration.
   d. A higher yield to maturity generally yields a shorter duration.

11. **Duration** Which statement is true for the Macaulay duration of a zero coupon bond?

   a. It is equal to the bond's maturity in years.
   b. It is equal to one-half the bond's maturity in years.
   c. It is equal to the bond's maturity in years divided by its yield to maturity.
   d. It cannot be calculated because of the lack of coupons.

12. **Duration** Which of the following states the correct relationship between Macaulay duration and modified duration?

   a. Modified duration = Macaulay duration/$(1 + YTM/2)$
   b. Modified duration = Macaulay duration $\times$ $(1 + YTM/2)$

c. Modified duration = Macaulay duration/*YTM*
d. Modified duration = Macaulay duration × *YTM*

13. **Duration**   Which one of the following bonds has the shortest duration?

  a. Zero coupon, 10-year maturity.
  b. Zero coupon, 13-year maturity.
  c. 8 percent coupon, 10-year maturity.
  d. 8 percent coupon, 13-year maturity.

14. **Duration**   Identify the bond that has the longest duration (no calculations necessary).

  a. 20-year maturity with an 8 percent coupon.
  b. 20-year maturity with a 12 percent coupon.
  c. 15-year maturity with a 0 percent coupon.
  d. 10-year maturity with a 15 percent coupon.

15. **Duration**   Which bond has the longest duration?

  a. 8-year maturity, 6 percent coupon.
  b. 8-year maturity, 11 percent coupon.
  c. 15-year maturity, 6 percent coupon.
  d. 15-year maturity, 11 percent coupon.

16. **Duration**   The duration of a bond normally increases with an increase in

  a. Term to maturity
  b. Yield to maturity
  c. Coupon rate
  d. All of the above

17. **Duration**   When interest rates decline, what happens to the duration of a 30-year bond selling at a premium?

  a. It increases.
  b. It decreases.
  c. It remains the same.
  d. It increases at first, then declines.

18. **Duration**   An 8 percent, 20-year corporate bond is priced to yield 9 percent. The Macaulay duration for this bond is 8.85 years. Given this information, how many years is the bond's modified duration?

  a. 8.12
  b. 8.47
  c. 8.51
  d. 9.25

19. **Using Duration**   A 9-year bond has a yield to maturity of 10 percent and a modified duration of 6.54 years. If the market yield changes by 50 basis points, what is the change in the bond's price?

  a. 3.27 percent
  b. 3.66 percent
  c. 6.54 percent
  d. 7.21 percent

20. **Using Duration**   A 6 percent coupon bond paying interest semiannually has a modified duration of 10 years, sells for $800, and is priced at a yield to maturity (YTM) of 8 percent. If the YTM increases to 9 percent, the predicted change in price, using the duration concept, is which of the following amounts?

  a. $76.56
  b. $76.92
  c. $77.67
  d. $80.00

21. **Immunization**   Which of the following strategies is most likely to yield the best interest rate risk immunization results for a bond portfolio?

    a. Maturity matching.
    b. Duration matching.
    c. Buy and hold.
    d. Investing in interest rate-sensitive stocks.

22. **Immunization**   Consider two dedicated bond portfolios both with the same 10-year target dates. One is managed using a buy-and-hold strategy with reinvested coupons. The other is managed using a dynamic immunization strategy. The buy-and-hold portfolio is most likely to outperform the immunized portfolio under what kind of interest rate environment?

    a. Steadily rising interest rates.
    b. Steadily falling interest rates.
    c. Constant interest rates.
    d. Performance will be the same under any environment.

23. **Bond Yields**   A zero coupon bond paying $100 at maturity 10 years from now has a current price of $50. Its yield to maturity is *closest* to which of the following?

    a. 5 percent
    b. 6 percent
    c. 7 percent
    d. 8 percent

24. **Bond Price**   A newly issued 10-year option-free bond is valued at par on June 1, 2000. The bond has an annual coupon of 8.0 percent. On June 1, 2003, the bond has a yield to maturity of 7.1 percent. The first coupon is reinvested at 8.0 percent and the second coupon is reinvested at 7.0 percent. The price of the bond on June 1, 2003, is closest to

    a. 100.0 percent of par
    b. 102.5 percent of par
    c. 104.8 percent of par
    d. 105.4 percent of par

25. **Interest Rate Risk**   The interest rate risk of a noncallable bond is most likely to be positively related to the

    a. Risk-free rate
    b. Bond's coupon rate
    c. Bond's time to maturity
    d. Bond's yield to maturity

Concept Questions

1. **Bond Prices**   What are premium, discount, and par bonds?

2. **Bond Features**   In the United States, what is the normal face value for corporate and U.S. government bonds? How are coupons calculated? How often are coupons paid?

3. **Coupon Rates and Current Yields**   What are the coupon rate and current yield on a bond? What happens to these if a bond's price rises?

4. **Interest Rate Risk**   What is interest rate risk? What are the roles of a bond's coupon and maturity in determining its level of interest rate risk?

5. **Bond Yields**   For a premium bond, which is greater, the coupon rate or the yield to maturity? Why? For a discount bond? Why?

6. **Bond Yields**   What is the difference between a bond's promised yield and its realized yield? Which is more relevant? When we calculate a bond's yield to maturity, which of these are we calculating?

X

X

X

X

X

X

X

X

X

X

X

X

X

X

X

X

X

X

X

7. **Interpreting Bond Yields** Is the yield to maturity (YTM) on a bond the same thing as the required return? Is YTM the same thing as the coupon rate? Suppose that today a 10 percent coupon bond sells at par. Two years from now, the required return on the same bond is 8 percent. What is the coupon rate on the bond now? The YTM?

8. **Interpreting Bond Yields** Suppose you buy a 9 percent coupon, 15-year bond today when it's first issued. If interest rates suddenly rise to 15 percent, what happens to the value of your bond? Why?

9. **Bond Prices versus Yields** (a) What is the relationship between the price of a bond and its YTM? (b) Explain why some bonds sell at a premium to par value, and other bonds sell at a discount. What do you know about the relationship between the coupon rate and the YTM for premium bonds? What about discount bonds? For bonds selling at par value? (c) What is the relationship between the current yield and YTM for premium bonds? For discount bonds? For bonds selling at par value?

10. **Yield to Call** For callable bonds, the financial press generally reports either the yield to maturity or the yield to call. Often yield to call is reported for premium bonds, and yield to maturity is reported for discount bonds. What is the reasoning behind this convention?

Questions and Problems

Core Questions

1. **Bond Prices** CIR Inc. has 8 percent coupon bonds on the market that have 10 years left to maturity. If the YTM on these bonds is 7 percent, what is the current bond price?

2. **Bond Yields** Trincor Company bonds have a coupon rate of 9.5 percent, 21 years to maturity, and a current price of $1,289. What is the YTM? The current yield?

3. **Bond Prices** A bond has a coupon rate of 8.5 percent and 18 years until maturity. If the yield to maturity is 6.7 percent, what is the price of the bond?

4. **Bond Prices** A bond with 25 years until maturity has a coupon rate of 7 percent and a yield to maturity of 9 percent. What is the price of the bond?

5. **Yield to Maturity** A bond sells for $864.50 and has a coupon rate of 6 percent. If the bond has 16 years until maturity, what is the yield to maturity of the bond?

6. **Yield to Maturity** A bond with a maturity of 23 years sells for $1,132. If the coupon rate is 6 percent, what is the yield to maturity of the bond?

7. **Yield to Maturity** Fatima Industries has a bond outstanding that sells for $1,080. The bond has coupon rate of 7.5 percent and six years until maturity. What is the yield to maturity of the bond?

8. **Yield to Maturity** Sealord Fisheries issues zero coupon bonds on the market at a price of $150 per bond. Each bond has a face value of $1,000 payable at maturity in 20 years. What is the yield to maturity for these bonds?

9. **Yield to Call** Sealord Fisheries zero coupon bonds referred to above are callable in 10 years at a call price of $500. Using semiannual compounding, what is the yield to call for these bonds?

10. **Yield to Call** If instead the Sealord Fisheries zero coupon bonds referred to above are callable in 10 years at a call price of $475, what is their yield to call?

Intermediate Questions

11. **Coupon Rates** Dunbar Corporation has bonds on the market with 11.5 years to maturity, a YTM of 7.5 percent, and a current price of $1,084. What must the coupon rate be on Dunbar's bonds?

12. **Bond Prices** Corrado's Pizzeria issued 10-year bonds *one year ago* at a coupon rate of 10.25 percent. If the YTM on these bonds is 9.26 percent, what is the current bond price?

13. **Bond Yields** Soprano's Spaghetti Factory issued 12-year bonds *two years ago* at a coupon rate of 3.5 percent. If these bonds currently sell for 65 percent of par value, what is the YTM?

www.mhhe.com/cj3e

14. **Bond Price Movements**   A zero coupon bond with a 9 percent YTM has 15 years to maturity. Two years later, the price of the bond remains the same. What's going on here?

15. **Realized Yield**   For the bond referred to in the previous question, what would be the realized yield if it were held to maturity?

16. **Bond Price Movements**   Bond X is a premium bond with an 8 percent coupon, a YTM of 6 percent, and 15 years to maturity. Bond Y is a discount bond with an 8 percent coupon, a YTM of 10 percent, and also 15 years to maturity. If interest rates remain unchanged, what do you expect the price of these bonds to be 1 year from now? In 5 years? In 10 years? In 14 years? In 15 years? What's going on here?

17. **Interest Rate Risk**   Both bond A and bond B have 7 percent coupons and are priced at par value. Bond A has 2 years to maturity, while bond B has 15 years to maturity. If interest rates suddenly rise by 2 percent, what is the percentage change in price of bond A? Of bond B? If rates were to suddenly fall by 2 percent instead, what would the percentage change in price of bond A be now? Of bond B? Illustrate your answers by graphing bond prices versus YTM. What does this problem tell you about the interest rate risk of longer term bonds?

18. **Interest Rate Risk**   Bond J is a 4 percent coupon bond. Bond K is a 10 percent coupon bond. Both bonds have 10 years to maturity and have a YTM of 7 percent. If interest rates suddenly rise by 2 percent, what is the percentage price change of these bonds? What if rates suddenly fall by 2 percent instead? What does this problem tell you about the interest rate risk of lower-coupon bonds?

19. **Finding the Bond Maturity**   ABC Co. has 8 percent coupon bonds with a YTM of 6.90 percent. The current yield on these bonds is 7.21 percent. How many years do these bonds have left until they mature?

20. **Finding the Bond Maturity**   You've just found a 10 percent coupon bond on the market that sells for par value. What is the maturity on this bond?

21. **Realized Yields**   Suppose you buy an 11 percent coupon bond today for $1,100. The bond has 15 years to maturity. What rate of return do you expect to earn on your investment? Two years from now, the YTM on your bond has increased by 2 percent, and you decide to sell. What price will your bond sell for? What is the realized yield on your investment? Compare this yield to the YTM when you first bought the bond. Why are they different? Assume interest payments are reinvested at the original YTM.

22. **Yield to Call**   XYZ Company has a 10 percent callable bond outstanding on the market with 15 years to maturity, call protection for the next 5 years, and a call premium of $80. What is the yield to call (YTC) for this bond if the current price is 118 percent of par value?

23. **Calculating Duration**   What is the Macaulay duration of a 6 percent coupon bond with eight years to maturity and a current price of $1,084.50? What is the modified duration?

24. **Using Duration**   In the previous problem, suppose the yield on the bond suddenly increases by 2 percent. Use duration to estimate the new price of the bond. Compare your answer to the new bond price calculated from the usual bond pricing formula. What do your results tell you about the accuracy of duration?

25. **Calculating Duration**   A bond with a coupon rate of 7 percent sells at a yield to maturity of 8 percent. If the bond matures in 13 years, what is the Macaulay duration of the bond? What is the modified duration?

26. **Calculating Duration**   Assume the bond in the previous problem has a yield to maturity of 6 percent. What is the Macaulay duration now? What does this tell you about the relationship between duration and yield to maturity?

27. **Calculating Duration**   You find a bond with 20 years until maturity that has a coupon rate of 8 percent and a yield to maturity of 6 percent. What is the Macaulay duration? The modified duration?

28. **Using Duration**   Suppose the yield to maturity on the bond in the previous problem increases by .25 percent. What is the new price of the bond using duration? What is the new price of the bond using the bond pricing formula? What if the yield to maturity increases by 1 percent? By 2 percent? By 5 percent? What does this tell you about using duration to estimate bond price changes for large interest rate changes?

29. **Using Duration**   Noah Kramer, a fixed-income portfolio manager based in the country of Sevista, is considering the purchase of Sevista government bonds. Sevista currently has government bonds evenly distributed among 5-, 10-, and 25-year maturities. Noah decides to evaluate two strategies for investing in Sevista bonds. The following table shows the details of the two strategies.

Strategy	5-Year Maturity Modified Duration = 4.83	15-Year Maturity Modified Duration = 14.35	25-Year Maturity Modified Duration = 23.81
I	$5 million	$0	$5 million
II	$0	$10 million	$0

The market value of the bonds purchased will be $10 million and the target modified duration is 15 years. Before choosing one of the two bond investment strategies, Kramer wants to study how the market value of the bonds will change if an instantaneous interest rate shift occurs immediately after his investment. The details of the interest rate shift are shown below.

Interest Rate Maturity (years)	Interest Rate Change (basis points)
5	Down 75
15	Up 25
25	Up 50

Calculate, for this instantaneous interest rate shift, the percentage change in the market value of the bonds that will occur under each investment strategy.

30. **Bootstrapping**   One method of obtaining an estimate of the term structure of interest rates is called bootstrapping. Suppose you have a one-year zero coupon bond with a rate of r_1 and a two-year bond with an annual coupon payment of C. To bootstrap the two-year rate, you can set up the following equation for the price (P) of the coupon bond:

$$P = \frac{C_1}{1 + r_1} + \frac{C_2 + \text{Par value}}{(1 + r_2)^2}$$

Since you can observe all of the variables except r_2, the spot rate for two years, you can solve for this interest rate. Suppose there is a zero coupon bond with one year to maturity that sells for $945 and a two-year bond with an 8 percent coupon paid annually that sells for $1,032. What is the interest rate for two years? Suppose a bond with three years until maturity and a 9 percent annual coupon sells for $1,081. What is the interest rate for three years?

31. **Bootstrapping**   You find that the one-, two-, three-, and four-year interest rates are 5.50 percent, 6.25 percent, 6.80 percent, and 7.30 percent. What is the yield to maturity of a four-year bond with a coupon rate of 8 percent? *Hint:* Use the bootstrapping technique in the previous problem to find the price of the bond.

Spreadsheet Problems

32. **Yield to Maturity**   A Treasury bond traded on August 8, 2004, matures on February 15, 2009. The coupon rate is 6.4 percent and the quoted price is 108:24. What is the bond's yield to maturity? Use an actual day count with 365 days per year.

33. **Bond Yields**   A bond traded on December 15, 2004, matures on July 1, 2028, and may be called at any time after July 1, 2013, at a price of 105. The coupon rate on the bond is 7.4 percent and the yield to maturity is 6.7 percent. What is the yield to maturity and yield to call on this bond? Use an actual day count with 365 days per year.

34. **Duration**   A Treasury bond traded on October 18, 2004, matures on March 30, 2015. The coupon rate is 7.2 percent and the bond has a 5.1 yield to maturity. What are the Macaulay duration and modified duration?

What's on the Web?

1. **Bond Markets**   Go to www.bondsonline.com and follow "The Outlook: Today's Market" link. What is the outlook for the bond market today? What are the major news items today that are expected to influence the bond market?

2. **Government Bonds**   Go to www.bloomberg.com and look up the yields for U.S. government bonds. You should also find a listing for foreign government bonds. Are the yields on all government bonds the same? Why or why not?

3. **Bond Quotes and Yields**   Go to www.bondsonline.com and find all available Treasury STRIPS quotes. Print these quotes. Now try to find a Treasury bond that has the same maturity as one of the Treasury STRIPS you found. Do these two bonds have the same yield to maturity? Why or why not?

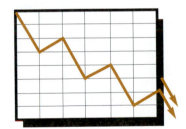

Stock-Trak®
Portfolio Simulations

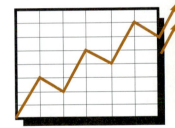

Using Duration when Trading Interest Rates with Stock-Trak

Duration is an effective measure of interest rate risk and can be usefully applied to strategies for trading interest rates. In the preceding chapter, we recommended using U.S. Treasury STRIPS as a vehicle for trading interest rates with Stock-Trak. In this chapter, we pointed out that the duration of a STRIPS is equal to its maturity and therefore requires no special calculations. This implies this simple relationship between STRIPS price changes and STRIPS yield changes:

$$\text{Percentage change in STRIPS price} \approx -\text{STRIPS maturity} \times \frac{\text{Change in } YTM}{(1 + YTM/2)}$$

Suppose you are holding 20-year STRIPS with a yield of 6 percent and believe that the yield on these STRIPS could fall by 50 basis points over the next few weeks. If this occurs, it will cause 20-year STRIPS prices to rise by about 9.7 percent. But if instead the yield rose by 50 basis points, it would cause 20-year STRIPS prices to fall by about 9.7 percent.

Stock-Trak Exercises

1. Buy a STRIPS security and record its price, maturity, and yield. After a week or two, calculate the percentage change in price and change in yield for your STRIPS. Plug in the original yield, change in yield, and maturity into the right-hand side of the above equation

to compute the predicted percentage change in the STRIPS price. How closely does this predicted percentage change in the STRIPS price compare with the actual percentage change in the STRIPS price?

2. We have seen in this chapter how a bond's duration affects its price. You have to make a bond investment of $50,000. Stock-Trak has numerous corporate bonds with different maturities and coupon rates as well as Treasury STRIPS. Research the current interest rate environment and make a prediction about where interest rates will move. Using this estimate, buy $50,000 in bonds. Make sure your decision of which bonds to purchase is consistent with your interest rate prediction. Now find the bonds that will perform the worst if you are correct. Do not buy these bonds, but write down the price. Calculate the duration of each of these bonds. Two weeks later, look at the prices of the bonds you purchased and the bonds you did not purchase. Was your decision correct? How closely does the price change estimated with duration compare with the actual price change of the bonds?

Chapter 11

Diversification and Asset Allocation

"Out of this nettle, danger,

We pluck this flower, safety."

–Shakespeare, *Henry IV*

Intuitively, we all know that diversification is important for managing investment risk. But how exactly does diversification work, and how can we be sure we have an efficiently diversified portfolio? Insightful answers can be gleaned from the modern theory of diversification and asset allocation. ■

In this chapter, we examine the role of diversification and asset allocation in investing. Most of us have a strong sense that diversification is important. After all, "Don't put all your eggs in one basket" is a bit of folk wisdom that seems to have stood the test of time quite well. Even so, the importance of diversification has not always been well understood. For example, noted author and market analyst Mark Twain recommended: "Put all your eggs in the one basket and—WATCH THAT BASKET!" This chapter shows why this was probably not Twain's best piece of advice.[1]

As we will see, diversification has a profound effect on portfolio risk and return. The role and impact of diversification were first formally explained in the early 1950s by financial pioneer Harry Markowitz, who shared the 1986 Nobel Prize in Economics

---

[1]This quote has been attributed to both Mark Twain (*The Tragedy of Pudd'nhead Wilson,* 1894) and Andrew Carnegie (*How to Succeed in Life,* 1903).

for his insights. The primary goal of this chapter is to explain and explore the implications of Markowitz's remarkable discovery.

11.1 Expected Returns and Variances

In Chapter 1, we discussed how to calculate average returns and variances using historical data. We now begin to discuss how to analyze returns and variances when the information we have concerns future possible returns and their probabilities.

Expected Returns

We start with a straightforward case. Consider a period of time such as a year. We have two stocks, say, Netcap and Jmart. Netcap is expected to have a return of 25 percent in the coming year; Jmart is expected to have a return of 20 percent during the same period.

In a situation such as this, if all investors agreed on these expected return values, why would anyone want to hold Jmart? After all, why invest in one stock when the expectation is that another will do better? Clearly, the answer must depend on the different risks of the two investments. The return on Netcap, although it is *expected* to be 25 percent, could turn out to be significantly higher or lower. Similarly, Jmart's *realized* return could be significantly higher or lower than expected.

For example, suppose the economy booms. In this case, we think Netcap will have a 70 percent return. But if the economy tanks and enters a recession, we think the return will be −20 percent. In this case, we say that there are *two states of the economy*, which means that there are two possible outcomes. This scenario is oversimplified, of course, but it allows us to illustrate some key ideas without a lot of computational complexity.

Suppose we think boom and recession are equally likely to happen, that is, a 50–50 chance of each outcome. Table 11.1 illustrates the basic information we have described and some additional information about Jmart. Notice that Jmart earns 30 percent if there is a recession and 10 percent if there is a boom.

Obviously, if you buy one of these stocks, say, Jmart, what you earn in any particular year depends on what the economy does during that year. Suppose these probabilities stay the same through time. If you hold Jmart for a number of years, you'll earn 30 percent about half the time and 10 percent the other half. In this case, we say your **expected return** on Jmart, $E(R_J)$, is 20 percent:

$$E(R_J) = .50 \times 30\% + .50 \times 10\% = 20\%$$

In other words, you should expect to earn 20 percent from this stock, on average.

expected return
Average return on a risky asset expected in the future.

Find expected returns at www.411stocks.com

TABLE 11.1	States of the Economy and Stock Returns		
State of Economy	Probability of State of Economy	Netcap	Jmart
Recession	.50	−20%	30%
Boom	.50	70	10
	1.00		

TABLE 11.2	Calculating Expected Returns					
		Netcap		Jmart	
(1)	(2)	(3)	(4)	(5)	(6)
State of Economy	Probability of State of Economy	Return if State Occurs	Product (2) × (3)	Return if State Occurs	Product (2) × (5)
Recession	.50	−20%	−.10	30%	.15
Boom	.50	70	.35	10	.05
	1.00		$E(R_N) = 25\%$		$E(R_J) = 20\%$

For Netcap, the probabilities are the same, but the possible returns are different. Here we lose 20 percent half the time, and we gain 70 percent the other half. The expected return on Netcap, $E(R_N)$, is thus 25 percent:

$$E(R_N) = .50 \times -20\% + .50 \times 70\% = 25\%$$

Table 11.2 illustrates these calculations.

In Chapter 1, we defined a risk premium as the difference between the returns on a risky investment and a risk-free investment, and we calculated the historical risk premiums on some different investments. Using our projected returns, we can calculate the *projected* or *expected risk premium* as the difference between the expected return on a risky investment and the certain return on a risk-free investment.

For example, suppose risk-free investments are currently offering 8 percent. We will say that the risk-free rate, which we label R_f, is 8 percent. Given this, what is the projected risk premium on Jmart? On Netcap? Since the expected return on Jmart, $E(R_J)$, is 20 percent, the projected risk premium is

$$\text{Risk premium} = \text{Expected return} - \text{Risk-free rate} \qquad (11.1)$$
$$= E(R_J) - R_f$$
$$= 20\% - 8\%$$
$$= 12\%$$

Similarly, the risk premium on Netcap is $25\% - 8\% = 17\%$.

In general, the expected return on a security or other asset is simply equal to the sum of the possible returns multiplied by their probabilities. So, if we have 100 possible returns, we would multiply each one by its probability and then add up the results. The sum would be the expected return. The risk premium would then be the difference between this expected return and the risk-free rate.

UNEQUAL PROBABILITIES

EXAMPLE 11.1

Look again at Tables 11.1 and 11.2. Suppose you thought a boom would occur 20 percent of the time instead of 50 percent. What are the expected returns on Netcap and Jmart in this case? If the risk-free rate is 10 percent, what are the risk premiums?

The first thing to notice is that a recession must occur 80 percent of the time $(1 - .20 = .80)$ since there are only two possibilities. With this in mind, Jmart has a 30 percent return in 80 percent of the

(continued)

TABLE 11.3		Calculating Expected Returns				
		Netcap		Jmart		
(1)	(2)	(3)	(4)	(5)	(6)
State of Economy	Probability of State of Economy	Return if State Occurs	Product (2) × (3)	Return if State Occurs	Product (2) × (5)
Recession	.80	−20%	−.16	30%	.24
Boom	.20	70	.14	10	.02
	1.00		$E(R_N) = -.02 = -2\%$		$E(R_J) = .26 = 26\%$

years and a 10 percent return in 20 percent of the years. To calculate the expected return, we just multiply the possibilities by the probabilities and add up the results:

$$E(R_J) = .80 \times 30\% + .20 \times 10\% = 26\%$$

Table 11.3 summarizes the calculations for both stocks. Notice that the expected return on Netcap is −2 percent.

The risk premium for Jmart is 26% − 10% = 16% in this case. The risk premium for Netcap is negative: −2% − 10% = −12%. This is a little unusual, but, as we will see, it's not impossible.

Calculating the Variance

To calculate the variances of the returns on our two stocks, we first determine the squared deviations from the expected return. We then multiply each possible squared deviation by its probability. Next we add these up, and the result is the variance.

To illustrate, one of our stocks above, Jmart, has an expected return of 20 percent. In a given year, the return will actually be either 30 percent or 10 percent. The possible deviations are thus 30% − 20% = 10% or 10% − 20% = −10%. In this case, the variance is

$$\text{Variance} = \sigma^2 = .50 \times (10\%)^2 + .50 \times (-10\%)^2 = .01$$

The standard deviation is the square root of this:

$$\text{Standard deviation} = \sigma = \sqrt{.01} = .10 = 10\%$$

Table 11.4 summarizes these calculations and the expected return for both stocks. Notice that Netcap has a much larger variance. Netcap has the higher return, but Jmart has less risk. You could get a 70 percent return on your investment in Netcap, but you could also lose 20 percent. Notice that an investment in Jmart will always pay at least 10 percent.

TABLE 11.4	Expected Returns and Variances		
		Netcap	Jmart
Expected return, $E(R)$		25%	20%
Variance, σ^2		.2025	.0100
Standard deviation, σ		45%	10%

Which of these stocks should you buy? We can't really say; it depends on your personal preferences regarding risk and return. We can be reasonably sure, however, that some investors would prefer one and some would prefer the other.

You've probably noticed that the way we calculated expected returns and variances here is somewhat different from the way we did it in Chapter 1 (and, probably, different from the way you learned it in "sadistics"). The reason is that we were examining historical returns in Chapter 1, so we estimated the average return and the variance based on some actual events. Here, we have projected *future* returns and their associated probabilities, so this is the information with which we must work.

MORE UNEQUAL PROBABILITIES

EXAMPLE 11.2

Going back to Table 11.3 in Example 11.1, what are the variances on our two stocks once we have unequal probabilities? What are the standard deviations?

We can summarize the needed calculations as follows:

(1) State of Economy	(2) Probability of State of Economy	(3) Return Deviation from Expected Return	(4) Squared Return Deviation	(5) Product (2) × (4)
Netcap				
Recession	.80	$-.20 - (-.02) = -.18$	.0324	.02592
Boom	.20	$.70 - (-.02) = .72$	.5184	.10368
				$\sigma_N^2 = .12960$
Jmart				
Recession	.80	$.30 - .26 = .04$	.0016	.00128
Boom	.20	$.10 - .26 = -.16$	.0256	.00512
				$\sigma_J^2 = .00640$

Based on these calculations, the standard deviation for Netcap is $\sigma_N = \sqrt{.1296} = 36\%$. The standard deviation for Jmart is much smaller, $\sigma_J = \sqrt{.0064}$, or 8 percent.

Check This

11.1a How do we calculate the expected return on a security?

11.1b In words, how do we calculate the variance of an expected return?

11.2 Portfolios

portfolio Group of assets such as stocks and bonds held by an investor.

Thus far in this chapter, we have concentrated on individual assets considered separately. However, most investors actually hold a **portfolio** of assets. All we mean by this is that investors tend to own more than just a single stock, bond, or other asset. Given that this is so, portfolio return and portfolio risk are of obvious relevance. Accordingly, we now discuss portfolio expected returns and variances.

Portfolio Weights

portfolio weight
Percentage of a portfolio's total value invested in a particular asset.

There are many equivalent ways of describing a portfolio. The most convenient approach is to list the percentages of the total portfolio's value that are invested in each portfolio asset. We call these percentages the **portfolio weights**.

For example, if we have $50 in one asset and $150 in another, then our total portfolio is worth $200. The percentage of our portfolio in the first asset is $50/$200 = .25. The percentage of our portfolio in the second asset is $150/$200 = .75. Notice that the weights sum up to 1.00 since all of our money is invested somewhere.[2]

Portfolio Expected Returns

Let's go back to Netcap and Jmart. You put half your money in each. The portfolio weights are obviously .50 and .50. What is the pattern of returns on this portfolio? The expected return?

To answer these questions, suppose the economy actually enters a recession. In this case, half your money (the half in Netcap) loses 20 percent. The other half (the half in Jmart) gains 30 percent. Your portfolio return, R_P, in a recession will thus be

$$R_P = .50 \times -20\% + .50 \times 30\% = 5\%$$

Table 11.5 summarizes the remaining calculations. Notice that when a boom occurs, your portfolio would return 40 percent:

$$R_P = .50 \times 70\% + .50 \times 10\% = 40\%$$

As indicated in Table 11.5, the expected return on your portfolio, $E(R_P)$, is 22.5 percent.

We can save ourselves some work by calculating the expected return more directly. Given these portfolio weights, we could have reasoned that we expect half our money to earn 25 percent (the half in Netcap) and half of our money to earn 20 percent (the half in Jmart). Our portfolio expected return is thus

$$\begin{aligned} E(R_P) &= .50 \times E(R_N) + .50 \times E(R_J) \\ &= .50 \times 25\% + .50 \times 20\% \\ &= 22.5\% \end{aligned}$$

This is the same portfolio return that we calculated in Table 11.5.

This method of calculating the expected return on a portfolio works no matter how many assets there are in the portfolio. Suppose we had n assets in our portfolio, where

TABLE 11.5	Expected Portfolio Return		
(1) State of Economy	(2) Probability of State of Economy	(3) Portfolio Return if State Occurs	(4) Product (2) × (3)
Recession	.50	.50 × −20% + .50 × 30% = 5%	.025
Boom	.50	.50 × 70% + .50 × 10% = 40%	.200
		$E(R_P)$ = .225 = 22.5%	

[2]Some of it could be in cash, of course, but we would then just consider cash to be another of the portfolio assets.

n is any number at all. If we let x_i stand for the percentage of our money in Asset i, then the expected return is

$$E(R_P) = x_1 \times E(R_1) + x_2 \times E(R_2) + \cdots + x_n \times E(R_n) \qquad (11.2)$$

This says that the expected return on a portfolio is a straightforward combination of the expected returns on the assets in that portfolio. This seems somewhat obvious, but, as we will examine next, the obvious approach is not always the right one.

MORE UNEQUAL PROBABILITIES

EXAMPLE 11.3

Suppose we had the following projections on three stocks:

State of Economy	Probability of State of Economy	Returns Stock A	Stock B	Stock C
Boom	.50	10%	15%	20%
Bust	.50	8	4	0

We want to calculate portfolio expected returns in two cases. First, what would be the expected return on a portfolio with equal amounts invested in each of the three stocks? Second, what would be the expected return if half of the portfolio were in A, with the remainder equally divided between B and C?

From our earlier discussion, the expected returns on the individual stocks are

$$E(R_A) = 9.0\% \qquad E(R_B) = 9.5\% \qquad E(R_C) = 10.0\%$$

(Check these for practice.) If a portfolio has equal investments in each asset, the portfolio weights are all the same. Such a portfolio is said to be *equally weighted*. Since there are three stocks in this case, the weights are all equal to 1/3. The portfolio expected return is thus

$$E(R_P) = 1/3 \times 9.0\% + 1/3 \times 9.5\% + 1/3 \times 10.0\% = 9.5\%$$

In the second case, check that the portfolio expected return is 9.375%.

Portfolio Variance

From the preceding discussion, the expected return on a portfolio that contains equal investments in Netcap and Jmart is 22.5 percent. What is the standard deviation of return on this portfolio? Simple intuition might suggest that half of our money has a standard deviation of 45 percent, and the other half has a standard deviation of 10 percent. So the portfolio's standard deviation might be calculated as follows:

$$\sigma_P = .50 \times 45\% + .50 \times 10\% = 27.5\%$$

Unfortunately, this approach is *completely incorrect!*

Let's see what the standard deviation really is. Table 11.6 summarizes the relevant calculations. As we see, the portfolio's variance is about .031, and its standard deviation is less than we thought—it's only 17.5 percent. What is illustrated here is that the variance on a portfolio is *not* generally a simple combination of the variances of the assets in the portfolio.

We can illustrate this point a little more dramatically by considering a slightly different set of portfolio weights. Suppose we put 2/11 (about 18 percent) in Netcap and

TABLE 11.6	Calculating Portfolio Variance			
(1) State of Economy	(2) Probability of State of Economy	(3) Portfolio Returns if State Occurs	(4) Squared Deviation from Expected Return	(5) Product (2) × (4)
Recession	.50	5%	$(.05 - .225)^2 = .030625$	.0153125
Boom	.50	40	$(.40 - .225)^2 = .030625$	.0153125
			$\sigma_P^2 = .030625$	
			$\sigma_P = \sqrt{.030625} = 17.5\%$	

the other 9/11 (about 82 percent) in Jmart. If a recession occurs, this portfolio will have a return of

$$R_P = 2/11 \times -20\% + 9/11 \times 30\% = 20.91\%$$

If a boom occurs, this portfolio will have a return of

$$R_P = 2/11 \times 70\% + 9/11 \times 10\% = 20.91\%$$

Notice that the return is the same no matter what happens. No further calculation is needed: This portfolio has a *zero* variance and no risk!

This is a nice bit of financial alchemy. We take two quite risky assets and, by mixing them just right, we create a riskless portfolio. It seems very clear that combining assets into portfolios can substantially alter the risks faced by an investor. This is a crucial observation, and we will begin to explore its implications in the next section.[3]

PORTFOLIO VARIANCE AND STANDARD DEVIATIONS

EXAMPLE 11.4

In Example 11.3, what are the standard deviations of the two portfolios?

To answer, we first have to calculate the portfolio returns in the two states. We will work with the second portfolio, which has 50 percent in Stock A and 25 percent in each of stocks B and C. The relevant calculations are summarized as follows:

State of Economy	Probability of State of Economy	Returns			
		Stock A	Stock B	Stock C	Portfolio
Boom	.50	10%	15%	20%	13.75%
Bust	.50	8	4	0	5.00

The portfolio return when the economy booms is calculated as

$$R_P = .50 \times 10\% + .25 \times 15\% + .25 \times 20\% = 13.75\%$$

(continued)

---

[3]Earlier, we had a risk-free rate of 8 percent. Now we have, in effect, a 20.91 percent risk-free rate. If this situation actually existed, there would be a very profitable opportunity! In reality, we expect that all riskless investments would have the same return.

The return when the economy goes bust is calculated the same way. Check that it's 5 percent and also check that the expected return on the portfolio is 9.375 percent. The variance is thus

$$\sigma_P^2 = .50 \times (.1375 - .09375)^2 + .50 \times (.05 - .09375)^2 = .0019141$$

The standard deviation is thus about 4.375 percent. For our equally weighted portfolio, redo these calculations and check that the standard deviation is about 5.5 percent.

Check This

11.2a	What is a portfolio weight?
11.2b	How do we calculate the variance of an expected return?

11.3 Diversification and Portfolio Risk

Our discussion to this point has focused on some hypothetical securities. We've seen that portfolio risks can, in principle, be quite different from the risks of the assets that make up the portfolio. We now look more closely at the risk of an individual asset versus the risk of a portfolio of many different assets. As we did in Chapter 1, we will examine some stock market history to get an idea of what happens with actual investments in U.S. capital markets.

The Effect of Diversification: Another Lesson from Market History

In Chapter 1, we saw that the standard deviation of the annual return on a portfolio of large common stocks was about 20 percent per year. Does this mean that the standard deviation of the annual return on a typical stock in that group is about 20 percent? As you might suspect by now, the answer is no. This is an extremely important observation.

To examine the relationship between portfolio size and portfolio risk, Table 11.7 on page 372 illustrates typical average annual standard deviations for equally weighted portfolios that contain different numbers of randomly selected NYSE securities.

In column 2 of Table 11.7, we see that the standard deviation for a "portfolio" of one security is just under 50 percent per year at 49.24 percent. What this means is that if you randomly select a single NYSE stock and put all your money into it, your standard deviation of return would typically have been about 50 percent per year. Obviously, such a strategy has significant risk! If you were to randomly select two NYSE securities and put half your money in each, your average annual standard deviation would have been about 37 percent.

The important thing to notice in Table 11.7 is that the standard deviation declines as the number of securities is increased. By the time we have 100 randomly chosen stocks (and 1 percent invested in each), the portfolio's volatility has declined by 60 percent, from 50 percent per year to 20 percent per year. With 500 securities, the standard deviation is 19.27 percent per year, similar to the 20 percent per year we saw in Chapter 1 for large common stocks. The small difference exists because the portfolio securities, portfolio weights, and the time periods covered are not identical. The nearby *Investment Updates* box offers further historical perspective on the need for diversification.

Why a Broad Mix Helps in Long Term

Stock-market diversification is sold as a short-term sedative for antsy investors. But it's also your best bet for ensuring decent long-run returns. In recent columns, I've written a lot about diversification. There's a good reason for that: If this bear market has anything to teach us, it is the value of spreading your stock-market bets widely. Over the past year, the hardest-hit investors have been those who pooh-poohed diversification and loaded up on technology stocks, only to see their portfolios decimated by Nasdaq's implosion. Clearly, these folks would have fared far better with a broader array of stocks. But diversification is more than just a defense against short-run market gyrations. To understand why, consider the performance of large, small and foreign stocks over the past 30 years.

At first blush, the results seem to encourage investors to shun diversification and instead stick with the big blue-chip stocks they know and love. After all, over the 30 years, large, small and foreign stocks generated almost exactly the same average annual total return. According to Chicago researchers Ibbotson Associates, Standard & Poor's 500-stock index of large-company stocks was up an average 13.2% a year, smaller U.S. companies gained 14.7% and Morgan Stanley's Europe, Australasia and Far East index climbed 13.1%. In other words, if all you owned was a smattering of blue-chip stocks, you should have done just fine over the past 30 years.

But the raw data don't tell the whole story. Here's why:

Tenacity Tested: Suppose that in 1970 you settled on a portfolio consisting exclusively of large U.S. stocks. Would you have hung onto that portfolio through the entire 30 years? I doubt it. For starters, you had to sit tight through the unnerving stock-market declines of 1973–74, 1976–78, 1980–82, 1987 and 1990. That would have been tough with an all-stock portfolio. But even if you had an unflinching determination to stick with stocks, you would have been constantly second-guessing your commitment to blue-chip companies. For instance, in the 1970s, you would have been tempted to swap into small companies and foreign shares, both of which outpaced U.S. large-company stocks. In the 1980s, foreign markets again outstripped U.S. large companies. Indeed, it was only in the 1990s that these blue-chip stocks reigned supreme.

Out of Time: Planning on sticking with U.S. large-company stocks for the next three decades? Circumstances may intervene. Maybe you will be forced to liquidate your stock portfolio early because you get divorced, lose your job or get hit with hefty medical bills. Alternatively, maybe your time horizon isn't quite as long as you imagine. For instance, you might be looking at a 30-year retirement. But if you are living off your portfolio, you will probably have to sell many of your stocks before the 30 years are up.

In that case, you will definitely want to be globally diversified, because that will provide vital portfolio protection over this shorter period. For proof, check out the accompanying table. It takes the past 30 years, picks out the roughest 5, 10, 15 and 20-year stretches for large-company stocks and then shows how other investments fared.

"In each of these bad periods, small stocks and international stocks did better," notes William Reichenstein, an investments professor at Baylor University. "There's a lot to be said for a portfolio that includes a little bit of everything."

(continued)

The Principle of Diversification

Figure 11.1 illustrates the point we've been discussing. What we have plotted is the standard deviation of the return versus the number of stocks in the portfolio. Notice in Figure 11.1 that the benefit in terms of risk reduction from adding securities drops off as we add more and more. By the time we have 10 securities, most of the diversification effect is already realized, and by the time we get to 30 or so, there is very little remaining benefit. In other words, the benefit of further diversification increases at a decreasing rate, so the "law of diminishing returns" applies here as it does in so many other places.

On Target: Diversification won't just limit your losses during rough markets. When it's combined with regular rebalancing, it can also boost returns. When you rebalance, you set targets for what percentage of your portfolio is in different investments. Then, every so often, you re-jigger your portfolio to get back to these targets. If you invest in two market sectors, "a rebalanced portfolio may actually do better than the two assets on their own, because rebalancing forces you to buy low and sell high," says William Bernstein, an investment adviser in North Bend, Ore., and author of "The Intelligent Asset Allocator." "Rebalancing is the only form of market timing that works."

Suppose you held a portfolio that was one-third large stocks, one-third small stocks and one-third foreign stocks. At the end of each year, you rebalanced to get back to these portfolio targets. Result? According to Ibbotson, over the past 30 years, your portfolio would have gained 14.2% a year before taxes and trading costs, compared with 13.7% if you had never rebalanced. You are most likely to get this performance bonus when you rebalance among different stock-market sectors, which should have roughly comparable long-run returns. But sometimes, you can also bolster returns by rebalancing between stocks and bonds. Consider, for instance, the 10 years through December 1981. Over that stretch, large stocks struggled, climbing just 6.5% a year, but they still outpaced intermediate government bonds, which returned 5.8%. But an annually rebalanced mix of 50% stocks and 50% bonds did even better, gaining 6.6% a year, Mr. Reichenstein calculates.

Source: Jonathan Clements, *The Wall Street Journal*, April 3, 2001.
© 2001 Dow Jones & Company, Inc. All Rights Reserved Worldwide.

Hiding Places How various investments fared during the roughest patches for large-company stocks over the past 30 years.

| | Worst | | | | 30 Years |
	5 Years*	10 Years*	15 Years*	20 Years*	(through Dec. 2000)
Large companies	−0.2%	+6.5%	+9.9%	+11.2%	+13.2%
Small companies	+10.8	+17.3	+16.2	+13.3	+14.7
Foreign stocks	+2.6	+10.6	+15.6	+15.4	+13.1
Intermediate bonds	+6.4	+5.8	+9.2	+9.1	+8.5
Inflation	+7.9	+8.6	+6.9	+6.3	+5.0

Note: The results shown are annual averages and include reinvested dividends.

*Through year-end 1977, 1981, 1987, and 1990, respectively.

Source: Ibbotson Associates.

principle of diversification
Spreading an investment across a number of assets will eliminate some, but not all, of the risk.

Figure 11.1 illustrates two key points. First, some of the riskiness associated with individual assets can be eliminated by forming portfolios. The process of spreading an investment across assets (and thereby forming a portfolio) is called *diversification*. The **principle of diversification** tells us that spreading an investment across many assets will eliminate some of the risk. Not surprisingly, risks that can be eliminated by diversification are called "diversifiable" risks.

The second point is equally important. There is a minimum level of risk that cannot be eliminated by simply diversifying. This minimum level is labeled "nondiversifiable risk" in Figure 11.1. Taken together, these two points are another important lesson

TABLE 11.7	Portfolio Standard Deviations	
(1) Number of Stocks in Portfolio	**(2)** Average Standard Deviation of Annual Portfolio Returns	**(3)** Ratio of Portfolio Standard Deviation to Standard Deviation of a Single Stock
1	49.24%	1.00
2	37.36	.76
4	29.69	.60
6	26.64	.54
8	24.98	.51
10	23.93	.49
20	21.68	.44
30	20.87	.42
40	20.46	.42
50	20.20	.41
100	19.69	.40
200	19.42	.39
300	19.34	.39
400	19.29	.39
500	19.27	.39
1,000	19.21	.39

Source: These figures are from Table 1 in Meir Statman, "How Many Stocks Make a Diversified Portfolio?" *Journal of Financial and Quantitative Analysis* 22 (September 1987), pp. 353–64. They were derived from E. J. Elton and M. J. Gruber, "Risk Reduction and Portfolio Size: An Analytic Solution," *Journal of Business* 50 (October 1977), pp. 415–37.

FIGURE 11.1   **Portfolio Diversification**

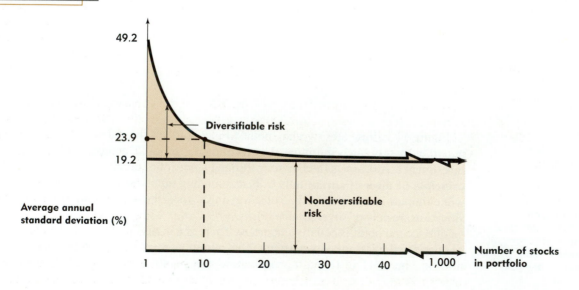

from financial market history: Diversification reduces risk, but only up to a point. Put another way, some risk is diversifiable and some is not.

Check This

11.3a What happens to the standard deviation of return for a portfolio if we increase the number of securities in the portfolio?

11.3b What is the principle of diversification?

11.4 Correlation and Diversification

We've seen that diversification is important. What we haven't discussed is how to get the most out of diversification. For example, in our previous section, we investigated what happens if we simply spread our money evenly across randomly chosen stocks. We saw that significant risk reduction resulted from this strategy, but you might wonder whether even larger gains could be achieved by a more sophisticated approach. As we begin to examine that question here, the answer is yes.

Why Diversification Works

correlation The tendency of the returns on two assets to move together.

Why diversification reduces portfolio risk as measured by the portfolio standard deviation is important and worth exploring in some detail. The key concept is **correlation**, which is the extent to which the returns on two assets move together. If the returns on two assets tend to move up and down together, we say they are *positively* correlated. If they tend to move in opposite directions, we say they are *negatively* correlated. If there is no particular relationship between the two assets, we say they are *uncorrelated*.

The *correlation coefficient*, which we use to measure correlation, ranges from -1 to $+1$, and we will denote the correlation between the returns on two assets, say A and B, as $\text{Corr}(R_A, R_B)$. The Greek letter ρ (rho) is often used to designate correlation as well. A correlation of $+1$ indicates that the two assets have a *perfect* positive correlation. For example, suppose that whatever return Asset A realizes, either up or down, Asset B does the same thing by exactly twice as much. In this case, they are perfectly correlated because the movement on one is completely predictable from the movement on the other. Notice, however, that perfect correlation does not necessarily mean they move by the same amount.

Measure portfolio diversification using Instant X-ray at www.morningstar. com

A zero correlation means that the two assets are uncorrelated. If we know that one asset is up, then we have no idea what the other one is likely to do; there simply is no relation between them. Perfect negative correlation [$\text{Corr}(R_A, R_B) = -1$] indicates that they always move in opposite directions. Figure 11.2 illustrates the three benchmark cases of perfect positive, perfect negative, and zero correlation.

Diversification works because security returns are generally not perfectly correlated. We will be more precise about the impact of correlation on portfolio risk in just a moment. For now, it is useful to simply think about combining two assets into a portfolio. If the two assets are highly correlated (the correlation is near $+1$), then they have a strong tendency to move up and down together. As a result, they offer limited diversification benefit. For example, two stocks from the same industry, say, General Motors and Ford, will tend to be relatively highly correlated since the companies are in

FIGURE 11.2   Correlations

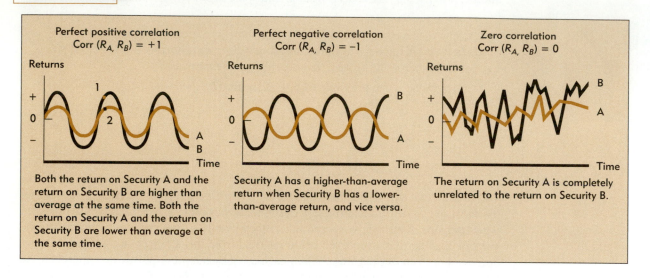

Perfect positive correlation
Corr (R_A, R_B) = +1

Returns

Both the return on Security A and the return on Security B are higher than average at the same time. Both the return on Security A and the return on Security B are lower than average at the same time.

Perfect negative correlation
Corr (R_A, R_B) = −1

Returns

Security A has a higher-than-average return when Security B has a lower-than-average return, and vice versa.

Zero correlation
Corr (R_A, R_B) = 0

Returns

The return on Security A is completely unrelated to the return on Security B.

essentially the same business, and a portfolio of two such stocks is not likely to be very diversified.

In contrast, if the two assets are negatively correlated, then they tend to move in opposite directions; whenever one zigs, the other tends to zag. In such a case, there will be substantial diversification benefit because variation in the return on one asset tends to be offset by variation in the opposite direction from the other. In fact, if two assets have a perfect negative correlation [Corr(R_A, R_B) = −1], then it is possible to combine them such that all risk is eliminated. Looking back at our example involving Jmart and Netcap in which we were able to eliminate all of the risk, what we now see is that they must be perfectly negatively correlated.

To further illustrate the impact of diversification on portfolio risk, suppose we observed the actual annual returns on two stocks, A and B, for the years 1999–2003. We summarize these returns in Table 11.8. In addition to actual returns on stocks A and B, we also calculated the returns on an equally weighted portfolio of A and B in Table 11.8. We label this portfolio as AB. In 1999, for example, Stock A returned 10 percent and Stock B returned 15 percent. Since Portfolio AB is half invested in each, its return for the year was

$$1/2 \times 10\% + 1/2 \times 15\% = 12.5\%$$

TABLE 11.8   Annual Returns on Stocks A and B

Year	Stock A	Stock B	Portfolio AB
1999	10%	15%	12.5%
2000	30	−10	10
2001	−10	25	7.5
2002	5	20	12.5
2003	10	15	12.5
Average returns	9	13	11
Standard deviations	14.3	13.5	2.2

The returns for the other years are calculated similarly.

At the bottom of Table 11.8, we calculated the average returns and standard deviations on the two stocks and the equally weighted portfolio. These averages and standard deviations are calculated just as they were in Chapter 1 (check a couple just to refresh your memory). The impact of diversification is apparent. The two stocks have standard deviations in the 13 percent to 14 percent per year range, but the portfolio's volatility is only 2.2 percent. In fact, if we compare the portfolio to Stock B, it has a higher return (11 percent vs. 9 percent) and much less risk.

Figure 11.3 illustrates in more detail what is occurring with our example. Here we have three bar graphs showing the year-by-year returns on Stocks A and B and Portfolio AB. Examining the graphs, we see that in 2000, for example, Stock A earned 30 percent while Stock B lost 10 percent. The following year, Stock B earned 25 percent while A lost 10 percent. These ups and downs tend to cancel out in our portfolio, however, with the result that there is much less variation in return from year to year. In other words, the correlation between the returns on stocks A and B is relatively low.

Calculating the correlation between stocks A and B is not difficult, but it would require us to digress a bit. Instead, we will explain the needed calculation in the next chapter, where we build on the principles developed here.

Calculating Portfolio Risk

We've seen that correlation is an important determinant of portfolio risk. To further pursue this issue, we need to know how to calculate portfolio variances directly. For a portfolio of two assets, A and B, the variance of the return on the portfolio, σ_P^2, is given by Equation 11.3:

$$\sigma_P^2 = x_A^2 \sigma_A^2 + x_B^2 \sigma_B^2 + 2x_A x_B \sigma_A \sigma_B \text{Corr}(R_A, R_B) \qquad (11.3)$$

In this equation, x_A and x_B are the percentages invested in assets A and B. Notice that $x_A + x_B = 1$. (Why?)

| FIGURE 11.3 | Impact of Diversification |

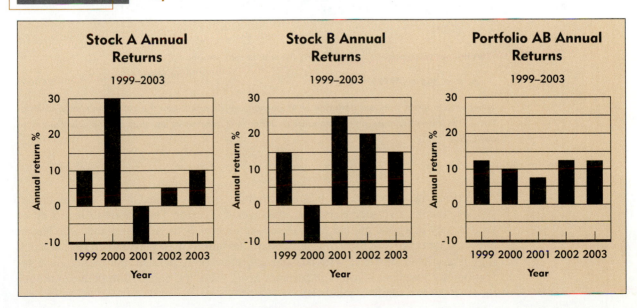

Equation 11.3 looks a little involved, but its use is straightforward. For example, suppose Stock A has a standard deviation of 40 percent per year and Stock B has a standard deviation of 60 percent per year. The correlation between them is .15. If you put half your money in each, what is your portfolio standard deviation?

To answer, we just plug the numbers into Equation 11.3. Note that x_A and x_B are each equal to .50, while σ_A and σ_B are .40 and .60, respectively. Taking $\text{Corr}(R_A, R_B) = .15$, we have

$$\sigma_P^2 = .50^2 \times .40^2 + .50^2 \times .60^2 + 2 \times .50 \times .50 \times .40 \times .60 \times .15$$
$$= .25 \times .16 + .25 \times .36 + .018$$
$$= .148$$

Thus, the portfolio variance is .148. As always, variances are not easy to interpret since they are based on squared returns, so we calculate the standard deviation by taking the square root:

$$\sigma_P = \sqrt{.148} = .3847 = 38.47\%$$

Once again, we see the impact of diversification. This portfolio has a standard deviation of 38.47 percent, which is less than either of the standard deviations on the two assets that are in the portfolio.

PORTFOLIO VARIANCE AND STANDARD DEVIATION

EXAMPLE 11.5

In the example we just examined, Stock A has a standard deviation of 40 percent per year and Stock B has a standard deviation of 60 percent per year. Suppose now that the correlation between them is .35. Also suppose you put one-fourth of your money in Stock A. What is your portfolio standard deviation?

If you put 1/4 (or .25) in Stock A, you must have 3/4 (or .75) in Stock B, so $x_A = .25$ and $x_B = .75$. Making use of our portfolio variance equation (11.3), we have

$$\sigma_P^2 = .25^2 \times .40^2 + .75^2 \times .60^2 + 2 \times .25 \times .75 \times .40 \times .60 \times .35$$
$$= .0625 \times .16 + .5625 \times .36 + .0315$$
$$= .244$$

Thus the portfolio variance is .244. Taking the square root, we get

$$\sigma_P = \sqrt{.244} = .49396 \approx 49\%$$

This portfolio has a standard deviation of 49 percent, which is between the individual standard deviations. This shows that a portfolio's standard deviation isn't necessarily less than the individual standard deviations.

To illustrate why correlation is an important, practical, real-world consideration, suppose that as a very conservative, risk-averse investor, you decide to invest all of your money in a bond mutual fund. Based on your analysis, you think this fund has an expected return of 6 percent with a standard deviation of 10 percent per year. A stock fund is available, however, with an expected return of 12 percent, but the standard deviation of 15 percent is too high for your taste. Also, the correlation between the returns on the two funds is about .10.

TABLE 11.9		Risk and Return with Stocks and Bonds	
Portfolio Weights			
Stocks	Bonds	Expected Return	Standard Deviation
1.00	.00	12.00%	15.00%
.95	.05	11.70	14.31
.90	.10	11.40	13.64
.85	.15	11.10	12.99
.80	.20	10.80	12.36
.75	.25	10.50	11.77
.70	.30	10.20	11.20
.65	.35	9.90	10.68
.60	.40	9.60	10.21
.55	.45	9.30	9.78
.50	.50	9.00	9.42
.45	.55	8.70	9.12
.40	.60	8.40	8.90
.35	.65	8.10	8.75
.30	.70	7.80	8.69
.25	.75	7.50	8.71
.20	.80	7.20	8.82
.15	.85	6.90	9.01
.10	.90	6.60	9.27
.05	.95	6.30	9.60
.00	1.00	6.00	10.00

Is the decision to invest 100 percent in the bond fund a wise one, even for a very risk-averse investor? The answer is no; in fact, it is a bad decision for any investor. To see why, Table 11.9 shows expected returns and standard deviations available from different combinations of the two mutual funds. In constructing the table, we begin with 100 percent in the stock fund and work our way down to 100 percent in the bond fund by reducing the percentage in the stock fund in increments of .05. These calculations are all done just like our examples just above; you should check some (or all) of them for practice.

Beginning on the first row in Table 11.9, we have 100 percent in the stock fund, so our expected return is 12 percent, and our standard deviation is 15 percent. As we begin to move out of the stock fund and into the bond fund, we are not surprised to see both the expected return and the standard deviation decline. However, what might be surprising to you is the fact that the standard deviation falls only so far and then begins to rise again. In other words, beyond a point, adding more of the lower risk bond fund actually *increases* your risk!

The best way to see what is going on is to plot the various combinations of expected returns and standard deviations calculated in Table 11.9 as we do in Figure 11.4. We simply placed the standard deviations from Table 11.9 on the horizontal axis and the corresponding expected returns on the vertical axis.

Examining the plot in Figure 11.4, we see that the various combinations of risk and return available all fall on a smooth curve (in fact, for the geometrically inclined, it's a hyperbola). This curve is called an **investment opportunity set** because it shows the

investment opportunity set
Collection of possible risk–return combinations available from portfolios of individual assets.

FIGURE 11.4

Risk and Return with Stocks and Bonds

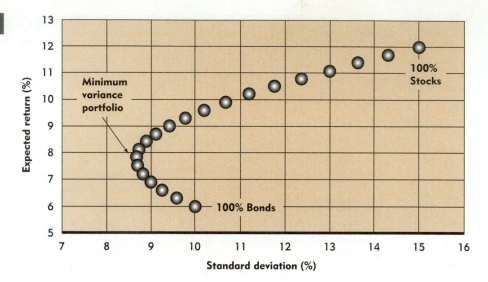

Review modern portfolio theory at www.moneychimp.com

possible combinations of risk and return available from portfolios of these two assets. One important thing to notice is that, as we have shown, there is a portfolio that has the smallest standard deviation (or variance—same thing) of all. It is labeled "minimum variance portfolio" in Figure 11.4. What are (approximately) its expected return and standard deviation?

Now we see clearly why a 100 percent bonds strategy is a poor one. With a 10 percent standard deviation, the bond fund offers an expected return of 6 percent. However, Table 11.9 shows us that a combination of about 60 percent stocks and 40 percent bonds has almost the same standard deviation, but a return of about 9.6 percent. Comparing 9.6 percent to 6 percent, we see that this portfolio has a return that is fully 60 percent greater ($6\% \times 1.6 = 9.6\%$) with the same risk. Our conclusion? Asset allocation matters.

Going back to Figure 11.4, notice that any portfolio that plots below the minimum variance portfolio is a poor choice because, no matter which one you pick, there is another portfolio with the same risk and a much better return. In the jargon of finance, we say that these undesirable portfolios are *dominated* and/or *inefficient*. Either way, we mean that given their level of risk, the expected return is inadequate compared to some other portfolio of equivalent risk. A portfolio that offers the highest return for its level of risk is said to be an **efficient portfolio**. In Figure 11.4, the minimum variance portfolio and all portfolios that plot above it are therefore efficient.

efficient portfolio A portfolio that offers the highest return for its level of risk.

MORE PORTFOLIO VARIANCE AND STANDARD DEVIATION

EXAMPLE 11.6

Looking at Table 11.9, suppose you put 57.627 percent in the stock fund. What is your expected return? Your standard deviation? How does this compare with the bond fund?

If you put 57.627 percent in stocks, you must have 42.373 percent in bonds, so $x_A = .57627$ and $x_B = .42373$. Making use of our portfolio variance equation (11.3), we have

$$\sigma_P^2 = .57627^2 \times .15^2 + .42373^2 \times .10^2 + 2 \times .57627 \times .42373 \times .15 \times .10 \times .10$$
$$= .332 \times .0225 + .180 \times .01 + .0007325$$
$$= .01$$

(continued)

Thus, the portfolio variance is .01, so the standard deviation is .1, or 10 percent. Check that the expected return is 9.46 percent. Compared to the bond fund, the standard deviation is now identical, but the expected return is almost 350 basis points higher.

More on Correlation and the Risk-Return Trade-Off

Given the expected returns and standard deviations on the two assets, the shape of the investment opportunity set in Figure 11.4 depends on the correlation. The lower the correlation, the more bowed to the left the investment opportunity set will be. To illustrate, Figure 11.5 shows the investment opportunity for correlations of -1, 0, and $+1$ for two stocks, A and B. Notice that Stock A has an expected return of 12 percent and a standard deviation of 15 percent, while Stock B has an expected return of 6 percent and a standard deviation of 10 percent. These are the same expected returns and standard deviations we used to build Figure 11.4, and the calculations are all done the same way; just the correlations are different. Notice also that we use the symbol ρ to stand for the correlation coefficient.

In Figure 11.5, when the correlation is $+1$, the investment opportunity set is a straight line connecting the two stocks, so, as expected, there is little or no diversification benefit. As the correlation declines to zero, the bend to the left becomes pronounced. For correlations between $+1$ and zero, there would simply be a less pronounced bend.

Finally, as the correlation becomes negative, the bend becomes quite pronounced, and the investment opportunity set actually becomes two straight-line segments when the correlation hits -1. Notice that the minimum variance portfolio has a *zero* variance in this case.

It is sometimes desirable to be able to calculate the percentage investments needed to create the minimum variance portfolio. We will just state the result here, but a problem at the end of the chapter asks you to show that the weight on Asset A in the minimum variance portfolio, x_A^*, is

$$x_A^* = \frac{\sigma_B^2 - \sigma_A\sigma_B\text{Corr}(R_A,R_B)}{\sigma_A^2 + \sigma_B^2 - 2\sigma_A\sigma_B\text{Corr}(R_A,R_B)} \tag{11.4}$$

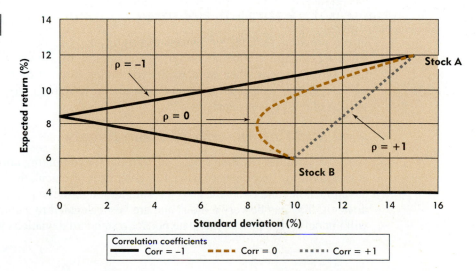

FIGURE 11.5

Risk and Return with Two Assets

In Equation 11.4, we will take Asset A to be the one with the larger standard deviation. If the standard deviations happened to be the same, then Asset A could be either.

FINDING THE MINIMUM VARIANCE PORTFOLIO

EXAMPLE 11.7

Looking back at Table 11.9, what combination of the stock fund and the bond fund has the lowest possible standard deviation? What is the minimum possible standard deviation?

Recalling that the standard deviations for the stock fund and bond fund were .15 and .10, respectively, and noting that the correlation was .1, we have

$$x_A^* = \frac{.10^2 - .15 \times .10 \times .10}{.15^2 + .10^2 - 2 \times .15 \times .10 \times .10}$$

$$= .288136$$

$$\approx 28.8\%$$

Thus, the minimum variance portfolio has 28.8 percent in stocks and the balance, 71.2 percent, in bonds. Plugging these into our formula for portfolio variance, we have

$$\sigma_P^2 = .288^2 \times .15^2 + .712^2 \times .10^2 + 2 \times .288 \times .712 \times .15 \times .10 \times .10$$

$$= .007551$$

The standard deviation is the square root of .007551, about 8.7 percent. Notice that this is where the minimum occurs in Figure 11.5.

Check This

11.4a Fundamentally, why does diversification work?

11.4b If two stocks have positive correlation, what does this mean?

11.4c What is an efficient portfolio?

11.5 The Markowitz Efficient Frontier

In the previous section, we looked closely at the risk-return possibilities available when we consider combining two risky assets. Now we are left with an obvious question: What happens when we consider combining three or more risky assets? As we will see, at least on a conceptual level, the answer turns out to be a straightforward extension of our previous analysis.

Risk and Return with Multiple Assets

When we consider multiple assets, the formula for computing portfolio standard deviation becomes cumbersome; indeed, a great deal of calculation is required once we have much beyond two assets. As a result, although the required calculations are not difficult, they can be very tedious and are best relegated to a computer. We therefore will not delve into how to calculate portfolio standard deviations when there are many assets.

FIGURE 11.6

Markowitz Efficient Portfolio

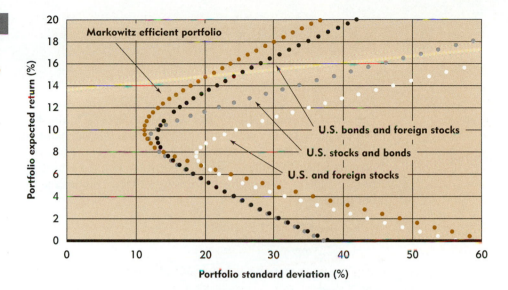

Figure 11.6 shows the result of calculating the expected returns and portfolio standard deviations when there are three assets. To illustrate the importance of asset allocation, we calculated expected returns and standard deviations from portfolios composed of three key investment types: U.S. stocks, foreign (non-U.S.) stocks, and U.S. bonds. These asset classes are not highly correlated in general; we assume a zero correlation in all cases. The expected returns and standard deviations are as follows:

	Expected Returns	Standard Deviations
Foreign stocks	18%	35%
U.S. stocks	12	22
U.S. bonds	8	14

Markowitz efficient frontier The set of portfolios with the maximum return for a given standard deviation.

In Figure 11.6, each point plotted is a possible risk-return combination. Comparing the result with our two-asset case in Figure 11.4, we see that now not only do some assets plot below the minimum variance portfolio on a smooth curve, but we have portfolios plotting inside as well. Only combinations that plot on the upper left-hand boundary are efficient; all the rest are inefficient. This upper left-hand boundary is called the **Markowitz efficient frontier**, and it represents the set of portfolios with the maximum return for a given standard deviation.

Once again, Figure 11.6 makes it clear that asset allocation matters. For example, a portfolio of 100 percent U.S. stocks is highly inefficient. For the same standard deviation, there is a portfolio with an expected return almost 400 basis points, or 4 percent, higher. Or, for the same expected return, there is a portfolio with about half as much risk! Our nearby *Work the Web* box shows you how an efficient frontier can be created online.

Check out the online journal at www.efficientfrontier.com

The analysis in this section can be extended to any number of assets or asset classes. In principle, it is possible to compute efficient frontiers using thousands of assets. As a practical matter, however, this analysis is most widely used with a relatively small

WORK THE WEB

Several websites allow you to perform a Markowitz-type analysis. Here is an example from www.finportfolio.com. This portfolio has four stocks, Citigroup (C), General Electric (GE), Intel (INTC), and Wal-Mart (WMT). It also has two mutual funds, the AIM Aggressive Growth Fund (AAGFX) and the Vanguard Total International Stock Index Fund (VGTSX). The column labeled "Current" shows our current portfolio. The column labeled "Optimal" shows a portfolio with the same risk but with a much better return. The graph shows the Markowitz efficient frontier and illustrates how inefficient our portfolio is.

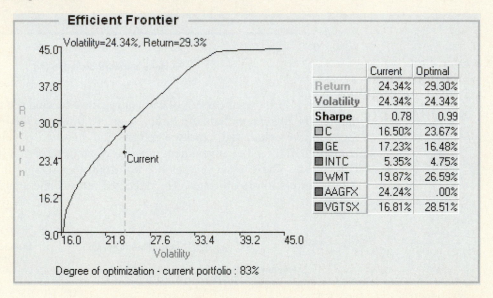

The reason our portfolio is 83 percent optimized is that the return of 24.34 percent is 83 percent of the potential return of 29.30 percent. The entry labeled "Sharpe" is a common measure of the risk-return trade-off. We will discuss it in a later chapter.

number of asset classes. For example, most investment banks maintain so-called model portfolios. These are simply recommended asset allocation strategies typically involving three to six asset categories.

A primary reason that the Markowitz analysis is not usually extended to large collections of individual assets has to do with data requirements. The inputs into the analysis are (1) expected returns on all assets; (2) standard deviations on all assets; and (3) correlations between every pair of assets. Moreover, these inputs have to be measured with some precision, or we just end up with a garbage-in, garbage-out (GIGO) system.

Suppose we just look at 2,000 NYSE stocks. We need 2,000 expected returns and standard deviations. This is already a problem since returns on individual stocks cannot be predicted with precision at all. To make matters worse, however, we need to know the correlation between every *pair* of stocks. With 2,000 stocks, there are 2,000 × 1,999 / 2 = 1,999,000, or almost 2 million unique pairs![4] Also, as with expected returns, correlations between individual stocks are very difficult to predict accurately. We will return to this issue in our next chapter, where we show that there may be an extremely elegant way around the problem.

Check This

11.5a	What is the Markowitz efficient frontier?
11.5b	Why is Markowitz portfolio analysis most commonly used to make asset allocation decisions?

11.6 Summary and Conclusions

In this chapter, we covered the basics of diversification and portfolio risk and return. From this material we saw that:

1. A portfolio's expected return is a simple weighted combination of the expected returns on the assets in the portfolio, but the standard deviation on a portfolio is not.

2. Diversification is a very important consideration. The principle of diversification tells us that spreading an investment across many assets can reduce some, but not all, of the risk. Based on U.S. stock market history, for example, about 60 percent of the risk associated with owning individual stocks can be eliminated by naive diversification.

3. Diversification works because asset returns are not perfectly correlated. All else the same, the lower the correlation, the greater is the gain from diversification.

4. When we consider the possible combinations of risk and return available from portfolios of assets, we find that some are inefficient (or dominated), meaning that they offer too little return for their risk.

5. Finally, for any group of assets, there is a set that is efficient. That set is known as the Markowitz efficient frontier.

The most important thing to carry away from this chapter is an understanding of diversification and why it works. Once you understand this, then the importance of asset allocation follows immediately. Our story is not complete, however, because we have not considered one important asset class: riskless assets. This will be the first task in our next chapter.

---

[4]With 2,000 stocks, there are $2,000^2 = 4,000,000$ possible pairs. Of these, 2,000 involve pairing a stock with itself. Further, we recognize that the correlation between A and B is the same as the correlation between B and A, so we only need to actually calculate half of the remaining 3,998,000 correlations.

Get Real

This chapter explained diversification, a very important consideration for real-world investors and money managers. The chapter also explored the famous Markowitz efficient portfolio concept, which shows how (and why) asset allocation affects portfolio risk and return.

Building a diversified portfolio is not a trivial task. Of course, as we discussed many chapters ago, mutual funds provide one way for investors to build diversified portfolios, but there are some significant caveats concerning mutual funds as a diversification tool. First of all, investors sometimes assume a fund is diversified simply because it holds a relatively large number of stocks. However, with the exception of some index funds, most mutual funds will reflect a particular style of investing, either explicitly, as stated in the fund's objective, or implicitly, as favored by the fund manager. For example, in the mid- to late-1990s, stocks as a whole did very well, but mutual funds that concentrated on smaller stocks generally did not do well at all.

It is tempting to buy a number of mutual funds to ensure broad diversification, but even this may not work. Within a given fund family, the same manager may actually be responsible for multiple funds. In addition, managers within a large fund family frequently have similar views about the market and individual companies.

Thinking just about stocks for the moment, what does an investor need to consider to build a well-diversified portfolio? At a minimum, such a portfolio probably needs to be diversified across industries, with no undue concentrations in particular sectors of the economy; it needs to be diversified by company size (small, midcap, and large), and it needs to be diversified across "growth" (i.e., high-P/E) and "value" (low-P/E) stocks. Perhaps the most controversial diversification issue concerns international diversification. The correlation between international stock exchanges is surprisingly low, suggesting large benefits from diversifying globally.

Perhaps the most disconcerting fact about diversification is that it leads to the following paradox: A well-diversified portfolio will always be invested in something that does not do well! Put differently, such a portfolio will almost always have both winners and losers. In many ways, that's the whole idea. Even so, it requires a lot of financial discipline to stay diversified when some portion of your portfolio seems to be doing poorly. The payoff is that, over the long run, a well-diversified portfolio should provide much steadier returns and be much less prone to abrupt changes in value.

Key Terms

expected return 362
portfolio 365
portfolio weight 366
principle of diversification 371

correlation 373
investment opportunity set 377
efficient portfolio 378
Markowitz efficient frontier 381

Chapter Review Problems and Self-Test

Use the following table of states of the economy and stock returns to answer the review problems:

State of Economy	Probability of State of Economy	Security Returns if State Occurs	
		Roten	Bradley
Bust	.40	−10%	30%
Boom	.60	40	10
	1.00		

1. **Expected Returns**   Calculate the expected returns for Roten and Bradley.
2. **Standard Deviations**   Calculate the standard deviations for Roten and Bradley.
3. **Portfolio Expected Returns**   Calculate the expected return on a portfolio of 50 percent Roten and 50 percent Bradley.
4. **Portfolio Volatility**   Calculate the volatility of a portfolio of 50 percent Roten and 50 percent Bradley.

Answers to Self-Test Problems

1. We calculate the expected return as follows:

		Roten		Bradley	
(1)	(2)	(3)	(4)	(5)	(6)
State of Economy	Probability of State of Economy	Return if State Occurs	Product (2) × (3)	Return if State Occurs	Product (2) × (5)
Bust	.40	−10%	−.04	30%	.12
Boom	.60	40	.24	10	.06
			$E(R) = 20\%$		$E(R) = 18\%$

2. We calculate the standard deviation as follows:

(1)	(2)	(3)	(4)	(5)
State of Economy	Probability of State of Economy	Return Deviation from Expected Return	Squared Return Deviation	Product (2) × (4)
Roten				
Bust	.40	−.30	.09	.036
Boom	.60	.20	.04	.024
				$\sigma^2 = .06$
Bradley				
Bust	.40	.12	.0144	.00576
Boom	.60	−.08	.0064	.00384
				$\sigma^2 = .0096$

Taking square roots, the standard deviations are 24.495 percent and 9.798 percent.

3. We calculate the expected return on a portfolio of 50 percent Roten and 50 percent Bradley as follows:

www.mhhe.com/cj3e

(1)	(2)	(3)	(4)
State of Economy	Probability of State of Economy	Portfolio Return if State Occurs	Product (2) × (3)
Bust	.40	10%	.04
Boom	.60	25	.15
			$E(R_P) =$ 19%

4. We calculate the volatility of a portfolio of 50 percent Roten and 50 percent Bradley as follows:

(1)	(2)	(3)	(4)	(5)
State of Economy	Probability of State of Economy	Portfolio Return if State Occurs	Squared Deviation from Expected Return	Product (2) × (4)
Bust	.40	.10	.0081	.00324
Boom	.60	.25	.0036	.00216
				$\sigma_P^2 =$ .0054
				$\sigma_P =$ 7.3485%

Test Your Investment Quotient

1. **Diversification** Netcap has an expected return of 25 percent and Jmart has an expected return of 20 percent. What is the likely investment decision for a risk-averse investor?

   a. Invest all funds in Netcap.
   b. Invest all funds in Jmart.
   c. Do not invest any funds in Netcap and Jmart.
   d. Invest funds partly in Netcap and partly in Jmart.

2. **Return Standard Deviation** Netcap experiences returns of 5 percent or 45 percent, each with an equal probability. What is the return standard deviation for Netcap?

   a. 30 percent
   b. 25 percent
   c. 20 percent
   d. 10 percent

3. **Return Standard Deviation** Jmart experiences returns of 0 percent, 25 percent, or 50 percent, each with a one-third probability. What is the approximate return standard deviation for Jmart?

   a. 30 percent
   b. 25 percent
   c. 20 percent
   d. 10 percent

4. **Expected Return** An analyst estimates that a stock has the following return probabilities and returns depending on the state of the economy:

State of Economy	Probability	Return
Good	.1	15%
Normal	.6	13
Poor	.3	7

What is the expected return of the stock?

   a. 7.8 percent
   b. 11.4 percent
   c. 11.7 percent
   d. 13.0 percent

5. Risk Aversion   Which of the following statements best reflects the importance of the asset allocation decision to the investment process? The asset allocation decision

   a. Helps the investor decide on realistic investment goals.
   b. Identifies the specific securities to include in a portfolio.
   c. Determines most of the portfolio's returns and volatility over time.
   d. Creates a standard by which to establish the appropriate investment time horizon.

6. Efficient Frontier   The Markowitz efficient frontier is best described as the set of portfolios that has

   a. The minimum risk for every level of return.
   b. Proportionally equal units of risk and return.
   c. The maximum excess rate of return for every given level of risk.
   d. The highest return for each level of beta used on the capital asset pricing model.

7. Diversification   An investor is considering adding another investment to a portfolio. To achieve the maximum diversification benefits, the investor should add an investment that has a correlation coefficient with the existing portfolio closest to

   a. −1.0
   b. −.5
   c. .0
   d. +1.0

8. Risk Premium   Netcap has an expected return of 25 percent, Jmart has an expected return of 20 percent, and the risk-free rate is 5 percent. You invest half your funds in Netcap and the other half in Jmart. What is the risk premium for your portfolio?

   a. 20 percent
   b. 17.5 percent
   c. 15 percent
   d. 12.5 percent

9. Return Standard Deviation   Both Netcap and Jmart have the same return standard deviation of 20 percent, and Netcap and Jmart returns have zero correlation. You invest half your funds in Netcap and the other half in Jmart. What is the return standard deviation for your portfolio?

   a. 20 percent
   b. 14.14 percent
   c. 10 percent
   d. 0 percent

10. Return Standard Deviation   Both Netcap and Jmart have the same return standard deviation of 20 percent, and Netcap and Jmart returns have a correlation of +1. You invest half your funds in Netcap and the other half in Jmart. What is the return standard deviation for your portfolio?

   a. 20 percent
   b. 14.14 percent
   c. 10 percent
   d. 0 percent

11. Return Standard Deviation   Both Netcap and Jmart have the same return standard deviation of 20 percent, and Netcap and Jmart returns have a correlation of −1. You invest half your funds in Netcap and the other half in Jmart. What is the return standard deviation for your portfolio?

CFA® PROBLEMS

www.mhhe.com/cj3e

    a. 20 percent
    b. 14.14 percent
    c. 10 percent
    d. 0 percent

12. **Minimum Variance Portfolio** Both Netcap and Jmart have the same return standard deviation of 20 percent, and Netcap and Jmart returns have zero correlation. What is the minimum attainable return variance for a portfolio of Netcap and Jmart?

    a. 20 percent
    b. 14.14 percent
    c. 10 percent
    d. 0 percent

13. **Minimum Variance Portfolio** Both Netcap and Jmart have the same return standard deviation of 20 percent, and Netcap and Jmart returns have a correlation of -1. What is the minimum attainable return variance for a portfolio of Netcap and Jmart?

    a. 20 percent
    b. 14.14 percent
    c. 10 percent
    d. 0 percent

14. **Minimum Variance Portfolio** Stocks A, B, and C each have the same expected return and standard deviation. The following shows the correlations between returns on these stocks:

	Stock A	Stock B	Stock C
Stock A	+1.0		
Stock B	+0.9	+1.0	
Stock C	+0.1	−0.4	+1.0

Given these correlations, which of the following portfolios constructed from these stocks would have the lowest risk?

    a. One equally invested in stocks A and B.
    b. One equally invested in stocks A and C.
    c. One equally invested in stocks B and C.
    d. One totally invested in stock C.

15. **Markowitz Efficient Frontier** Which of the following portfolios cannot lie on the efficient frontier as described by Markowitz?

	Portfolio	Expected Return	Standard Deviation
a.	W	9%	21%
b.	X	5	7
c.	Y	15	36
d.	Z	12	15

Concept Questions

1. **Diversification and Market History** Based on market history, what is the average annual standard deviation of return for a single, randomly chosen stock? What is the average annual standard deviation for an equally weighted portfolio of many stocks?

2. **Interpreting Correlations** If the returns on two stocks are highly correlated, what does this mean? If they have no correlation? If they are negatively correlated?

3. **Efficient Portfolios**   What is an efficient portfolio?

4. **Expected Returns**   True or false: If two stocks have the same expected return of 12 percent, then any portfolio of the two stocks will also have an expected return of 12 percent.

5. **Portfolio Volatility**   True or false: If two stocks have the same standard deviation of 45 percent, then any portfolio of the two stocks will also have a standard deviation of 45 percent.

6. **Diversification**   You are an investment adviser and a client makes the following statement: I do not want a diversified portfolio since I will never get the highest possible return. How do you respond to your client?

7. **Investment Opportunity Set**   You have a portfolio created from two assets. As you add more of the lower risk asset to your portfolio, the risk of your portfolio increases. What do you know about your current portfolio?

8. **Minimum Variance Portfolio**   Why is the minimum variance portfolio important in regard to the Markowitz efficient frontier?

9. **Markowitz Efficient Frontier**   True or false: It is impossible for a single asset to lie on the Markowitz efficient frontier.

10. **Portfolio Variance**   Suppose two assets have zero correlation and the same standard deviation. What is true about the minimum variance portfolio?

Questions and Problems

Core Questions

1. **Expected Returns**   Use the following information on states of the economy and stock returns to calculate the expected return for Dingaling Telephone:

State of Economy	Probability of State of Economy	Security Return if State Occurs
Recession	.20	−10%
Normal	.60	20
Boom	.20	30
	1.00	

2. **Standard Deviations**   Using the information in the previous question, calculate the standard deviation of return.

3. **Expected Returns and Deviations**   Repeat Questions 1 and 2 assuming that all three states are equally likely.

Use the following information on states of the economy and stock returns to answer Questions 4–7:

State of Economy	Probability of State of Economy	Security Returns if State Occurs	
		Roll	Ross
Bust	.40	−10%	40%
Boom	.60	50	10
	1.00		

4. **Expected Returns**   Calculate the expected returns for Roll and Ross by filling in the following:

		Roll		Ross	
(1)	**(2)**	**(3)**	**(4)**	**(5)**	**(6)**
State of Economy	**Probability of State of Economy**	**Return if State Occurs**	**Product (2) × (3)**	**Return if State Occurs**	**Product (2) × (5)**
Bust					
Boom					

5. **Standard Deviations**   Calculate the standard deviations for Roll and Ross by filling in the following:

(1)	**(2)**	**(3)**	**(4)**	**(5)**
State of Economy	**Probability of State of Economy**	**Return Deviation from Expected Return**	**Squared Return Deviation**	**Product (2) × (4)**
Roll				
Bust				
Boom				
Ross				
Bust				
Boom				

6. **Portfolio Expected Returns**   Calculate the expected return on a portfolio of 40 percent Roll and 60 percent Ross by filling in the following:

(1)	**(2)**	**(3)**	**(4)**
State of Economy	**Probability of State of Economy**	**Portfolio Return if State Occurs**	**Product (2) × (3)**
Bust			
Boom			

7. **Portfolio Volatility**   Calculate the volatility of a portfolio of 70 percent Roll and 30 percent Ross by filling in the following:

(1)	**(2)**	**(3)**	**(4)**	**(5)**
State of Economy	**Probability of State of Economy**	**Portfolio Return if State Occurs**	**Squared Deviation from Expected Return**	**Product (2) × (4)**
Bust				
Boom				
$\sigma_P^2 =$				
$\sigma_P =$				

8. **Calculating Returns and Standard Deviations**   Based on the following information, calculate the expected return and standard deviation for the two stocks.

State of Economy	Probability of State of Economy	Rate of Return if State Occurs	
		Stock A	Stock B
Recession	.20	.06	−.20
Normal	.60	.07	.13
Boom	.20	.11	.33

9. **Returns and Standard Deviations**   Consider the following information:

State of Economy	Probability of State of Economy	Rate of Return if State Occurs		
		Stock A	Stock B	Stock C
Boom	.20	.30	.45	.33
Good	.40	.12	.10	.15
Poor	.30	.01	−.15	−.05
Bust	.10	−.06	−.30	−.09

    a. Your portfolio is invested 30 percent each in A and C, and 40 percent in B. What is the expected return of the portfolio?
    b. What is the variance of this portfolio? The standard deviation?

10. **Portfolio Returns and Volatilities**   Fill in the missing information in the following table. Assume that Portfolio AB is 60 percent invested in Stock A.

Year	Annual Returns		Portfolio AB
	Stock A	Stock B	
1999	18%	50%	
2000	40	−30	
2001	−15	45	
2002	20	2	
2003	4	20	
Average returns			
Standard deviations			

Intermediate Questions

11. **Portfolio Returns and Volatilities**   Given the following information, calculate the expected return and standard deviation for a portfolio that has 30 percent invested in Stock A, 40 percent in Stock B, and the balance in Stock C.

State of Economy	Probability of State of Economy	Returns		
		Stock A	Stock B	Stock C
Boom	.70	15%	18%	20%
Bust	.30	10	0	−10

12. **Portfolio Variance**   Use the following information to calculate the expected return and standard deviation of a portfolio that is 40 percent invested in 3 Doors, Inc., and 60 percent invested in Down Co.:

	3 Doors, Inc.	Down Co.
Expected return, $E(R)$	19%	11%
Standard deviation, σ	65	45
Correlation	.20	

13. **More Portfolio Variance**   In the previous question, what is the standard deviation if the correlation is $+1$? 0? -1? As the correlation declines from $+1$ to -1 here, what do you see happening to portfolio volatility? Why?

14. **Minimum Variance Portfolio**   In Problem 12, what are the expected return and standard deviation on the minimum variance portfolio?

15. **Asset Allocation**   Fill in the missing information assuming a correlation of $-.20$.

Portfolio Weights		Expected	Standard
Stocks	Bonds	Return	Deviation
1.00		13%	22%
.80			
.60			
.40			
.20			
.00		6%	9%

16. **Minimum Variance Portfolio**   Consider two stocks, Stock D with an expected return of 17 percent and a standard deviation of 54 percent and Stock I, an international company, with an expected return of 15 percent and a standard deviation of 78 percent. The correlation between the two stocks is $-.40$. What is the weight of each stock in the minimum variance portfolio?

17. **Minimum Variance Portfolio**   What are the expected return and standard deviation of the minimum variance portfolio in the previous problem?

18. **Minimum Variance Portfolio**   You have a portfolio consisting of 70 percent Asset K and the remainder in Asset L. Asset K has an expected return of 17 percent and a standard deviation of 34 percent. Asset L has an expected return of 6 percent and a standard deviation of 9 percent. The correlation between the assets is .08. What are the expected return and standard deviation of the minimum variance portfolio?

19. **Minimum Variance Portfolio**   The stock of Bruin, Inc., has an expected return of 18 percent and a standard deviation of 48 percent. The stock of Wildcat Co. has an expected return of 15 percent and a standard deviation of 54 percent. The correlation between the two stocks is .25. Is it possible for there to be a minimum variance portfolio since the highest-return stock has the lowest standard deviation? If so, calculate the expected return and standard deviation of the minimum variance portfolio. Graph the investment opportunity set for these two stocks.

20. **Portfolio Variance**   You have a three-stock portfolio. Stock A has an expected return of 14 percent and a standard deviation of 53 percent, Stock B has an expected return of 16 percent and a standard deviation of 67 percent, and Stock C has an expected return of 13 percent and a standard deviation of 48 percent. The correlation between Stocks A and B is

.30, between Stocks A and C is .20, and between Stocks B and C is .05. Your portfolio consists of 30 percent Stock A, 50 percent Stock B, and 20 percent Stock C. Calculate the expected return and standard deviation of your portfolio. The formula for calculating the variance of a three-stock portfolio is

$$\sigma_P^2 = x_A^2\sigma_A^2 + x_B^2\sigma_B^2 + x_C^2\sigma_C^2 + 2x_Ax_B\sigma_A\sigma_B\text{Corr}(R_A,R_B)$$
$$+ 2x_Ax_C\sigma_A\sigma_C\text{Corr}(R_A,R_C) + 2x_Bx_C\sigma_B\sigma_C\text{Corr}(R_B,R_C)$$

21. **Minimum Variance Portfolio**   You are going to invest in Asset J and Asset S. Asset J has an expected return of 16 percent and a standard deviation of 58 percent. Asset S has an expected return of 8 percent and a standard deviation of 15 percent. The correlation between the two assets is .30. What are the standard deviation and expected return of the minimum variance portfolio? What is going on here?

22. **Portfolio Variance**   Suppose two assets have perfect positive correlation. Show that the standard deviation on a portfolio of the two assets is simply

$$\sigma_P = x_A \times \sigma_A + x_B \times \sigma_B$$

(*Hint*: Look at the expression for the variance of a two-asset portfolio. If the correlation is +1, the expression is a perfect square.)

23. **Portfolio Variance**   Suppose two assets have perfect negative correlation. Show that the standard deviation on a portfolio of the two assets is simply

$$\sigma_P = \pm (x_A \times \sigma_A - x_B \times \sigma_B)$$

(*Hint*: See previous problem.)

24. **Portfolio Variance**   Using the result in Problem 23, show that whenever two assets have perfect negative correlation it is possible to find a portfolio with a zero standard deviation. What are the portfolio weights? (*Hint*: Let x be the percentage in the first asset and $(1 - x)$ be the percentage in the second. Set the standard deviation to zero and solve for x.)

25. **Portfolio Variance**   Derive our expression in the chapter for the portfolio weight in the minimum variance portfolio. (Danger! Calculus required!) (*Hint*: Let x be the percentage in the first asset and $(1 - x)$ the percentage in the second. Take the derivative with respect to x, and set it to zero. Solve for x.)

Chapter 12

Return, Risk, and the Security Market Line

"To be alive at all involves some risk."

–Harold MacMillan

An important insight of modern financial theory is that some investment risks yield an expected reward, while other risks do not. Essentially, risks that can be eliminated by diversification do not yield an expected reward, and risks that cannot be eliminated by diversification do yield an expected reward. Thus, financial markets are somewhat fussy regarding what risks are rewarded and what risks are not. ■

Chapter 1 presented some important lessons from capital market history. The most noteworthy, perhaps, is that there is a reward, on average, for bearing risk. We called this reward a *risk premium*. The second lesson is that this risk premium is positively correlated with an investment's risk.

In this chapter, we return to an examination of the reward for bearing risk. Specifically, we have two tasks to accomplish. First, we have to define risk more precisely and then discuss how to measure it. Second, once we have a better understanding of just what we mean by "risk," we will go on to quantify the relation between risk and return in financial markets.

When we examine the risks associated with individual assets, we find there are two types of risk: systematic and unsystematic. This distinction is crucial because, as we will see, systematic risk affects almost all assets in the economy, at least to some degree, whereas unsystematic risk affects at most only a small number of assets. This observation allows us to say a great deal about the risks and returns on individual assets. In particular, it is the basis for a famous relationship between risk and return called the *security market line*, or SML. To develop the SML, we introduce the equally famous beta coefficient, one of the centerpieces of modern finance. Beta and the SML are key concepts because they supply us with at least part of the answer to the question of how to go about determining the expected return on a risky investment.

12.1 Announcements, Surprises, and Expected Returns

In our previous chapter, we discussed how to construct portfolios and evaluate their returns. We now begin to describe more carefully the risks and returns associated with individual securities. Thus far, we have measured volatility by looking at the difference between the actual return on an asset or portfolio, R, and the expected return, $E(R)$. We now look at why those deviations exist.

Expected and Unexpected Returns

To begin, consider the return on the stock of a hypothetical company called Flyers. What will determine this stock's return in, say, the coming year?

The return on any stock traded in a financial market is composed of two parts. First, the normal, or expected, return from the stock is the part of the return that investors predict or expect. This return depends on the information investors have about the stock, and it is based on the market's understanding today of the important factors that will influence the stock in the coming year.

The second part of the return on the stock is the uncertain, or risky, part. This is the portion that comes from unexpected information revealed during the year. A list of all possible sources of such information would be endless, but here are a few basic examples:

News about Flyers's product research.

Government figures released on gross domestic product.

The results from the latest arms control talks.

The news that Flyers's sales figures are higher than expected.

A sudden, unexpected drop in interest rates.

Based on this discussion, one way to express the return on Flyers stock in the coming year would be

$$\text{Total return} - \text{Expected return} = \text{Unexpected return} \qquad (12.1)$$

or

$$R - E(R) = U$$

where R stands for the actual total return in the year, $E(R)$ stands for the expected part of the return, and U stands for the unexpected part of the return. What this says is that the actual return, R, differs from the expected return, $E(R)$, because of surprises that occur during the year. In any given year, the unexpected return will be positive or negative, but, through time, the average value of U will be zero. This simply means that, on average, the actual return equals the expected return.

Announcements and News

We need to be careful when we talk about the effect of news items on stock returns. For example, suppose Flyers's business is such that the company prospers when gross domestic product (GDP) grows at a relatively high rate and suffers when GDP is relatively stagnant. In this case, in deciding what return to expect this year from owning stock in Flyers, investors either implicitly or explicitly must think about what GDP is likely to be for the coming year.

When the government actually announces GDP figures for the year, what will happen to the value of Flyers stock? Obviously, the answer depends on what figure is released. More to the point, however, the impact depends on how much of that figure actually represents new information.

Visit the earnings calendar at www.individualinvestor. com

At the beginning of the year, market participants will have some idea or forecast of what the yearly GDP figure will be. To the extent that shareholders have predicted GDP, that prediction will already be factored into the expected part of the return on the stock, $E(R)$. On the other hand, if the announced GDP is a surprise, then the effect will be part of U, the unanticipated portion of the return.

As an example, suppose shareholders in the market had forecast that the GDP increase this year would be .5 percent. If the actual announcement this year is exactly .5 percent, the same as the forecast, then the shareholders don't really learn anything, and the announcement isn't news. There will be no impact on the stock price as a result. This is like receiving redundant confirmation about something that you suspected all along; it reveals nothing new.

To give a more concrete example, Nabisco once announced it was taking a massive $300 million charge against earnings for the second quarter in a sweeping restructuring plan. The company also announced plans to cut its workforce sharply by 7.8 percent, eliminate some package sizes and small brands, and relocate some of its operations. This all seems like bad news, but the stock price didn't even budge. Why? Because it was already fully expected that Nabisco would take such actions, and the stock price already reflected the bad news.

A common way of saying that an announcement isn't news is to say that the market has already discounted the announcement. The use of the word "discount" here is different from the use of the term in computing present values, but the spirit is the same. When we discount a dollar to be received in the future, we say it is worth less to us today because of the time value of money. When an announcement or a news item is discounted into a stock price, we say that its impact is already a part of the stock price because the market already knew about it.

Going back to Flyers, suppose the government announces that the actual GDP increase during the year has been 1.5 percent. Now shareholders have learned something, namely, that the increase is 1 percentage point higher than they had forecast. This difference between the actual result and the forecast, 1 percentage point in this example, is sometimes called the *innovation* or the *surprise*.

This distinction explains why what seems to be bad news can actually be good news. For example, Gymboree, a retailer of children's apparel, had a 3 percent decline in same-store sales for a particular month, yet its stock price shot up 13 percent on the news. In the retail business, same-store sales, which are sales by existing stores in operation at least a year, are a crucial barometer, so why was this decline good news? The reason was that analysts had been expecting significantly sharper declines, so the situation was not as bad as previously thought.

A key fact to keep in mind about news and price changes is that news about the future is what matters. For example, America Online (AOL) once announced third-quarter earnings that exceeded Wall Street's expectations. That seems like good news, but America Online's stock price promptly dropped 10 percent. The reason was that America Online also announced a new discount subscriber plan, which analysts took as an indication that future revenues would be growing more slowly. Similarly, shortly thereafter, Microsoft reported a 50 percent jump in profits, exceeding projections. That seems like *really* good news, but Microsoft's stock price proceeded to decline sharply. Why? Because Microsoft warned that its phenomenal growth could not be sustained indefinitely, so its 50 percent increase in current earnings was not such a good predictor of future earnings growth.

To summarize, an announcement can be broken into two parts, the anticipated, or expected, part plus the surprise, or innovation:

See recent earnings surprises at earnings.nasdaq.com

$$\text{Announcement} = \text{Expected part} + \text{Surprise} \qquad (12.2)$$

The expected part of any announcement is the part of the information that the market uses to form the expectation, $E(R)$, of the return on the stock. The surprise is the news that influences the unanticipated return on the stock, U.

Our discussion of market efficiency in Chapter 8 bears on this discussion. We are assuming that relevant information known today is already reflected in the expected return. This is identical to saying that the current price reflects relevant publicly available information. We are thus implicitly assuming that markets are at least reasonably efficient in the semistrong-form sense. Henceforth, when we speak of news, we will mean the surprise part of an announcement and not the portion that the market had expected and therefore already discounted.

IN THE NEWS

EXAMPLE 12.1

Suppose Intel were to announce that earnings for the quarter just ending were up by 40 percent relative to a year ago. Do you expect that the stock price would rise or fall on the announcement?

The answer is that you can't really tell. Suppose the market was expecting a 60 percent increase. In this case, the 40 percent increase would be a negative surprise, and we would expect the stock price to fall. On the other hand, if the market was expecting only a 20 percent increase, there would be a positive surprise, and we would expect the stock to rise on the news.

Check This

12.1a What are the two basic parts of a return on common stock?

12.1b Under what conditions will an announcement have no effect on common stock prices?

12.2 Risk: Systematic and Unsystematic

It is important to distinguish between expected and unexpected returns because the unanticipated part of the return, that portion resulting from surprises, is the significant risk of any investment. After all, if we always receive exactly what we expect, then the investment is perfectly predictable and, by definition, risk-free. In other words, the risk of owning an asset comes from surprises—unanticipated events.

There are important differences, though, among various sources of risk. Look back at our previous list of news stories. Some of these stories are directed specifically at Flyers, and some are more general. Which of the news items are of specific importance to Flyers?

Announcements about interest rates or GDP are clearly important for nearly all companies, whereas the news about Flyers's president, its research, or its sales is of specific interest to Flyers investors only. We distinguish between these two types of events, because, as we will see, they have very different implications.

Systematic and Unsystematic Risk

systematic risk Risk that influences a large number of assets. Also called *market risk*.

The first type of surprise, the one that affects most assets, we label **systematic risk**. A systematic risk is one that influences a large number of assets, each to a greater or lesser extent. Because systematic risks have marketwide effects, they are sometimes called *market risks*.

unsystematic risk Risk that influences a single company or a small group of companies. Also called *unique* or *asset-specific risk*.

The second type of surprise we call **unsystematic risk**. An unsystematic risk is one that affects a single asset, or possibly a small group of assets. Because these risks are unique to individual companies or assets, they are sometimes called *unique* or *asset-specific risks*. We use these terms interchangeably.

As we have seen, uncertainties about general economic conditions, such as GDP, interest rates, or inflation, are examples of systematic risks. These conditions affect nearly all companies to some degree. An unanticipated increase, or surprise, in inflation, for example, affects wages and the costs of supplies that companies buy; it affects the value of the assets that companies own; and it affects the prices at which companies sell their products. Forces such as these, to which all companies are susceptible, are the essence of systematic risk.

In contrast, the announcement of an oil strike by a particular company will primarily affect that company and, perhaps, a few others (such as primary competitors and suppliers). It is unlikely to have much of an effect on the world oil market, however, or on the affairs of companies not in the oil business, so this is an unsystematic event.

Systematic and Unsystematic Components of Return

Analyze risk at
www.portfolioscience.com

The distinction between a systematic risk and an unsystematic risk is never really as exact as we would like it to be. Even the most narrow and peculiar bit of news about a company ripples through the economy. This is true because every enterprise, no matter how tiny, is a part of the economy. It's like the tale of a kingdom that was lost because one horse lost a shoe. This is mostly hairsplitting, however. Some risks are clearly much more general than others.

The distinction between the two types of risk allows us to break down the surprise portion, U, of the return on the Flyers stock into two parts. Earlier, we had the actual return broken down into its expected and surprise components: $R - E(R) = U$. We now recognize that the total surprise component for Flyers, U, has a systematic and an unsystematic component, so

$$R - E(R) = \text{Systematic portion} + \text{Unsystematic portion} \qquad (12.3)$$

Because it is traditional, we will use the Greek letter epsilon, ϵ, to stand for the unsystematic portion. Because systematic risks are often called "market" risks, we use the letter m to stand for the systematic part of the surprise. With these symbols, we can rewrite the formula for the total return:

$$R - E(R) = U = m + \epsilon \qquad (12.4)$$

The important thing about the way we have broken down the total surprise, U, is that the unsystematic portion, ϵ, is unique to Flyers. For this reason, it is unrelated to the unsystematic portion of return on most other assets. To see why this is important, we need to return to the subject of portfolio risk.

SYSTEMATIC VERSUS UNSYSTEMATIC EVENTS

EXAMPLE 12.2

Suppose Intel were to unexpectedly announce that its latest computer chip contains a significant flaw in its floating point unit that left it unable to handle numbers bigger than a couple of gigatrillion (meaning that, among other things, the chip cannot calculate Intel's quarterly profits). Is this a systematic or unsystematic event?

Obviously, this event is for the most part unsystematic. However, it would also benefit Intel's competitors to some degree and, at least potentially, harm some users of Intel products such as personal computer makers. Thus, as with most unsystematic events, there is some spillover, but the effect is mostly confined to a relatively small number of companies.

Check This

    12.2a What are the two basic types of risk?

    12.2b What is the distinction between the two types of risk?

12.3 Diversification, Systematic Risk, and Unsystematic Risk

In the previous chapter, we introduced the principle of diversification. What we saw was that some of the risk associated with individual assets can be diversified away and some cannot. We are left with an obvious question: Why is this so? It turns out that the answer hinges on the distinction between systematic and unsystematic risk.

Diversification and Unsystematic Risk

By definition, an unsystematic risk is one that is particular to a single asset or, at most, a small group of assets. For example, if the asset under consideration is stock in a single company, such things as successful new products and innovative cost savings will tend to increase the value of the stock. Unanticipated lawsuits, industrial accidents, strikes, and similar events will tend to decrease future cash flows and thereby reduce share values.

Here is the important observation: If we hold only a single stock, then the value of our investment will fluctuate because of company-specific events. If we hold a large portfolio, on the other hand, some of the stocks in the portfolio will go up in value because of positive company-specific events, and some will go down in value because of negative events. The net effect on the overall value of the portfolio will be relatively small, however, because these effects will tend to cancel each other out.

Now we see why some of the variability associated with individual assets is eliminated by diversification. When we combine assets into portfolios, the unique, or unsystematic, events—both positive and negative—tend to "wash out" once we have more than just a few assets. This is an important point that bears repeating:

> **Unsystematic risk is essentially eliminated by diversification, so a portfolio with many assets has almost no unsystematic risk.**

In fact, the terms *diversifiable risk* and *unsystematic risk* are often used interchangeably.

Diversification and Systematic Risk

We've seen that unsystematic risk can be eliminated by diversification. What about systematic risk? Can it also be eliminated by diversification? The answer is no because, by definition, a systematic risk affects almost all assets. As a result, no matter how many assets we put into a portfolio, systematic risk doesn't go away. Thus, for obvious reasons, the terms *systematic risk* and *nondiversifiable risk* are used interchangeably.

Because we have introduced so many different terms, it is useful to summarize our discussion before moving on. What we have seen is that the total risk of an investment can be written as

$$\text{Total risk} = \text{Systematic risk} + \text{Unsystematic risk} \qquad (12.5)$$

Systematic risk is also called *nondiversifiable risk* or *market risk*. Unsystematic risk is also called *diversifiable risk*, *unique risk*, or *asset-specific risk*. Most important, for a well-diversified portfolio, unsystematic risk is negligible. For such a portfolio, essentially all risk is systematic.

12.3a	Why is some risk diversifiable? Why is some risk not diversifiable?
12.3b	Why can't systematic risk be diversified away?

Check This

12.4 Systematic Risk and Beta

We now begin to address another question: What determines the size of the risk premium on a risky asset? Put another way, why do some assets have a larger risk premium than other assets? The answer, as we discuss next, is also based on the distinction between systematic and unsystematic risk.

The Systematic Risk Principle

Thus far, we've seen that the total risk associated with an asset can be decomposed into two components: systematic and unsystematic risk. We have also seen that unsystematic risk can be essentially eliminated by diversification. The systematic risk present in an asset, on the other hand, cannot be eliminated by diversification.

systematic risk principle The reward for bearing risk depends only on the systematic risk of an investment.

Based on our study of capital market history in Chapter 1, we know that there is a reward, on average, for bearing risk. However, we now need to be more precise about what we mean by risk. The **systematic risk principle** states that the reward for bearing risk depends only on the systematic risk of an investment.

The underlying rationale for this principle is straightforward: Because unsystematic risk can be eliminated at virtually no cost (by diversifying), there is no reward for bearing it. In other words, the market does not reward risks that are borne unnecessarily.

The systematic risk principle has a remarkable and very important implication:

The expected return on an asset depends only on its systematic risk.

There is an obvious corollary to this principle: No matter how much total risk an asset has, only the systematic portion is relevant in determining the expected return (and the risk premium) on that asset.

Measuring Systematic Risk

beta coefficient (β)
Measure of the relative systematic risk of an asset. Assets with betas larger (smaller) than 1 have more (less) systematic risk than average.

Because systematic risk is the crucial determinant of an asset's expected return, we need some way of measuring the level of systematic risk for different investments. The specific measure we will use is called the **beta coefficient**, designated by the Greek letter β. A beta coefficient, or just beta for short, tells us how much systematic risk a particular asset has relative to an average asset. By definition, an average asset has a beta of 1.0 relative to itself. An asset with a beta of .50, therefore, has half as much systematic risk as an average asset. Likewise, an asset with a beta of 2.0 has twice as much systematic risk.

Table 12.1 presents the estimated beta coefficients for the stocks of some well-known companies. (This particular source rounds numbers to the nearest .05.) The range of betas in Table 12.1 is typical for stocks of large U.S. corporations. Betas outside this range occur, but they are less common.

The important thing to remember is that the expected return, and thus the risk premium, on an asset depends only on its systematic risk. Because assets with larger betas have greater systematic risks, they will have greater expected returns. Thus, from Table 12.1, an investor who buys stock in Exxon, with a beta of .65, should expect to earn less, on average, than an investor who buys stock in General Motors, with a beta of about 1.15.

Find betas at valuation.ibbotson.com and www.money.com

One cautionary note is in order: Not all betas are created equal. For example, in Table 12.1, the source used, *Value Line*, reports a beta for Harley-Davidson of 1.65. At the same time, however, another widely used source, *S&P Stock Reports*, puts Harley-Davidson's beta at 1.13, substantially smaller. The difference results from the different procedures used to come up with beta coefficients. We will have more to say on this subject when we explain how betas are calculated in a later section. Our nearby *Work the Web* box shows one way to get betas online.

TABLE 12.1	Beta Coefficients	
	Company	**Beta β**
	Exxon	.65
	AT&T	.90
	IBM	.95
	Wal-Mart	1.10
	General Motors	1.15
	Microsoft	1.30
	Harley-Davidson	1.65
	America Online	2.40

Source: *Value Line* Investment Survey.

WORK THE WEB

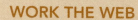

Suppose you want to find the beta for a company like Amazon.com. One way is to work the Web. We went to money.cnn.com, entered the ticker symbol AMZN for Amazon, and followed the "Profile" link. This is the result:

Key Ratios & Statistics

Price & Volume		Valuation Ratios	
Recent Price $	46.32	Price/Earnings (TTM)	NM
52 Week High $	46.95	Price/Sales (TTM)	4.07
52 Week Low $	14.24	Price/Book (MRQ)	NM
Avg Daily Vol (Mil)	9.06	Price/Cash Flow (TTM)	NM
Beta	2.55	**Per Share Data**	
Share Related Items		Earnings (TTM) $	-0.22
Mkt. Cap. (Mil) $	18,388.48	Sales (TTM) $	11.38
Shares Out (Mil)	396.99	Book Value (MRQ) $	-3.14
Float (Mil)	275.90	Cash Flow (TTM) $	0.00
Dividend Information		Cash (MRQ) $	2.49
Yield %	NA	**Mgmt Effectiveness**	
Annual Dividend	0.00	Return on Equity (TTM)	NM
Payout Ratio (TTM) %	0.00	Return on Assets (TTM)	-5.12
Financial Strength		Return on Investment (TTM)	-9.74
Quick Ratio (MRQ)	1.29	**Profitability**	
Current Ratio (MRQ)	1.63	Gross Margin (TTM) %	24.55
LT Debt/Equity (MRQ)	NM	Operating Margin (TTM) %	3.18
Total Debt/Equity (MRQ)	NM	Profit Margin (TTM) %	-1.89

Mil = Millions   MRQ = Most Recent Quarter   TTM = Trailing Twelve Months
Asterisk (*) Indicates numbers are derived from Earnings Announcements
Pricing and volume data as of 08/29/2003

The reported beta for Amazon.com is 2.55, which means that Amazon has about 2.5 times the systematic risk of a typical stock. Notice that Amazon's ROA is −5.12 percent and its profit margin is −1.89 percent. ROE is not even reported. Why? If you calculate the ROE using the earnings per share and the book value per share, you will find that ROE is almost 7 percent, which is not particularly impressive. In fact, the only reason ROE is even positive is that Amazon has a negative book value. Oddly, in such a case, the more the company loses, the higher the ROE becomes! In all, Amazon appears to be a good candidate for a high beta.

TOTAL RISK VERSUS BETA

EXAMPLE 12.3

Consider the following information on two securities. Which has greater total risk? Which has greater systematic risk? Greater unsystematic risk? Which asset will have a higher risk premium?

	Standard Deviation	Beta
Security A	40%	.50
Security B	20	1.50

From our discussion in this section, Security A has greater total risk, but it has substantially less systematic risk. Because total risk is the sum of systematic and unsystematic risk. Security A must have greater unsystematic risk. Finally, from the systematic risk principle, Security B will have a higher risk premium and a greater expected return, despite the fact that it has less total risk.

Portfolio Betas

Earlier, we saw that the riskiness of a portfolio has no simple relation to the risks of the assets in the portfolio. By contrast, a portfolio beta can be calculated just like a portfolio expected return. For example, looking again at Table 12.1, suppose you put half of your money in AT&T and half in General Motors. What would the beta of this combination be? Because AT&T has a beta of .90 and General Motors has a beta of 1.15, the portfolio's beta, β_p, would be

$$\beta_p = .50 \times \beta_{AT\&T} + .50 \times \beta_{GM}$$
$$= .50 \times .90 + .50 \times 1.15$$
$$= 1.025$$

In general, if we had a large number of assets in a portfolio, we would multiply each asset's beta by its portfolio weight and then add the results to get the portfolio's beta.

PORTFOLIO BETAS

EXAMPLE 12.4

Suppose we have the following information:

Security	Amount Invested	Expected Return	Beta
Stock A	$1,000	8%	.80
Stock B	2,000	12	.95
Stock C	3,000	15	1.10
Stock D	4,000	18	1.40

What is the expected return on this portfolio? What is the beta of this portfolio? Does this portfolio have more or less systematic risk than an average asset?

(continued)

To answer, we first have to calculate the portfolio weights. Notice that the total amount invested is $10,000. Of this, $1,000/$10,000 = 10% is invested in Stock A. Similarly, 20 percent is invested in Stock B, 30 percent is invested in Stock C, and 40 percent is invested in Stock D. The expected return, $E(R_p)$, is thus

$$E(R_p) = .10 \times E(R_A) + .20 \times E(R_B) + .30 \times E(R_C) + .40 \times E(R_D)$$
$$= .10 \times 8\% + .20 \times 12\% + .30 \times 15\% + .40 \times 18\%$$
$$= 14.9\%$$

Similarly, the portfolio beta, β_p, is

$$\beta_p = .10 \times \beta_A + .20 \times \beta_B + .30 \times \beta_C + .40 \times \beta_D$$
$$= .10 \times .80 + .20 \times .95 + .30 \times 1.10 + .40 \times 1.40$$
$$= 1.16$$

This portfolio thus has an expected return of 14.9 percent and a beta of 1.16. Because the beta is larger than 1, this portfolio has greater systematic risk than an average asset.

Check This

12.4a   What is the systematic risk principle?

12.4b   What does a beta coefficient measure?

12.4c   How do you calculate a portfolio beta?

12.4d   True or false: The expected return on a risky asset depends on that asset's total risk. Explain.

12.5 The Security Market Line

We're now in a position to see how risk is rewarded in the marketplace. To begin, suppose that Asset A has an expected return of $E(R_A) = 20\%$ and a beta of $\beta_A = 1.6$. Further suppose that the risk-free rate is $R_f = 8\%$. Notice that a risk-free asset, by definition, has no systematic risk (or unsystematic risk), so a risk-free asset has a beta of zero.

Beta and the Risk Premium

Consider a portfolio made up of Asset A and a risk-free asset. We can calculate some different possible portfolio expected returns and betas by varying the percentages invested in these two assets. For example, if 25 percent of the portfolio is invested in Asset A, then the expected return is

$$E(R_p) = .25 \times E(R_A) + (1 - .25) \times R_f$$
$$= .25 \times 20\% + .75 \times 8\%$$
$$= 11\%$$

Similarly, the beta on the portfolio, β_p, would be

$$\beta_p = .25 \times \beta_A + (1 - .25) \times 0$$
$$= .25 \times 1.6$$
$$= .40$$

For more information on risk management visit
www.fenews.com

Notice that, because the weights have to add up to 1, the percentage invested in the risk-free asset is equal to 1 minus the percentage invested in Asset A.

One thing that you might wonder about is whether it is possible for the percentage invested in Asset A to exceed 100 percent. The answer is yes. This can happen if the investor borrows at the risk-free rate and invests the proceeds in stocks. For example, suppose an investor has $100 and borrows an additional $50 at 8 percent, the risk-free rate. The total investment in Asset A would be $150, or 150 percent of the investor's wealth. The expected return in this case would be

$$E(R_p) = 1.50 \times E(R_A) + (1 - 1.50) \times R_f$$
$$= 1.50 \times 20\% - .50 \times 8\%$$
$$= 26\%$$

The beta on the portfolio would be

$$\beta_p = 1.50 \times \beta_A + (1 - 1.50) \times 0$$
$$= 1.50 \times 1.6$$
$$= 2.4$$

We can calculate some other possibilities, as follows:

Percentage of Portfolio in Asset A	Portfolio Expected Return	Portfolio Beta
0%	8%	.0
25	11	.4
50	14	.8
75	17	1.2
100	20	1.6
125	23	2.0
150	26	2.4

In Figure 12.1A, these portfolio expected returns are plotted against portfolio betas. Notice that all the combinations fall on a straight line.

The Reward-to-Risk Ratio

What is the slope of the straight line in Figure 12.1A? As always, the slope of a straight line is equal to the rise over the run. In this case, as we move out of the risk-free asset into Asset A, the beta increases from zero to 1.6 (a run of 1.6). At the same time, the expected return goes from 8 percent to 20 percent, a rise of 12 percent. The slope of the line is thus 12% / 1.6 = 7.5%.

Notice that the slope of our line is just the risk premium on Asset A, $E(R_A) - R_f$ divided by Asset A's beta, β_A:

$$\text{Slope} = \frac{E(R_A) - R_f}{\beta_A}$$
$$= \frac{20\% - 8\%}{1.6}$$
$$= 7.50\%$$

What this tells us is that Asset A offers a *reward-to-risk* ratio of 7.5 percent.[1] In other words, Asset A has a risk premium of 7.50 percent per "unit" of systematic risk.

---

[1]This ratio is sometimes called the *Treynor index*, after one of its originators.

FIGURE 12.1

**Betas and
Portfolio Returns**

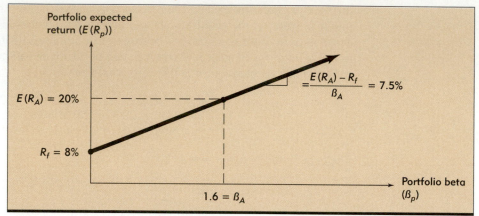

A. Portfolio expected returns and betas for Asset A

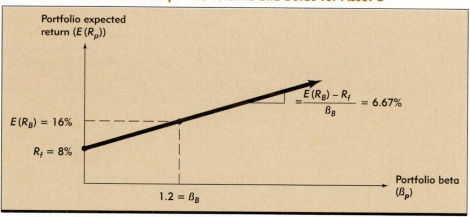

B. Portfolio expected returns and betas for Asset B

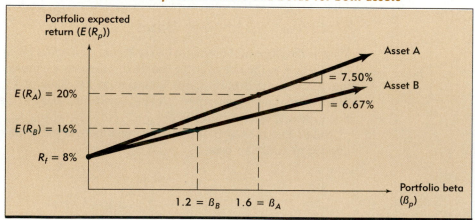

C. Portfolio expected returns and betas for both assets

The Basic Argument

Now suppose we consider a second asset, Asset B. This asset has a beta of 1.2 and an expected return of 16 percent. Which investment is better, Asset A or Asset B? You might think that we really cannot say—some investors might prefer A; some investors might prefer B. Actually, however, we can say: A is better because, as we will demonstrate, B offers inadequate compensation for its level of systematic risk, at least relative to A.

To begin, we calculate different combinations of expected returns and betas for portfolios of Asset B and a risk-free asset, just as we did for Asset A. For example, if we put 25 percent in Asset B and the remaining 75 percent in the risk-free asset, the portfolio's expected return will be

$$E(R_p) = .25 \times E(R_B) + (1 - .25) \times R_f$$
$$= .25 \times 16\% + .75 \times 8\%$$
$$= 10\%$$

Similarly, the beta on the portfolio, β_p, would be

$$\beta_p = .25 \times \beta_B + (1 - .25) \times 0$$
$$= .25 \times 1.2$$
$$= .30$$

Some other possibilities are as follows:

Percentage of Portfolio in Asset B	Portfolio Expected Return	Portfolio Beta
0%	8%	.0
25	10	.3
50	12	.6
75	14	.9
100	16	1.2
125	18	1.5
150	20	1.8

When we plot these combinations of portfolio expected returns and portfolio betas in Figure 12.1B, we get a straight line, just as we did for Asset A.

The key thing to notice is that when we compare the results for Assets A and B, as in Figure 12.1C, the line describing the combinations of expected returns and betas for Asset A is higher than the one for Asset B. What this tells us is that for any given level of systematic risk (as measured by beta), some combination of Asset A and the risk-free asset always offers a larger return. This is why we were able to state that Asset A is a better investment than Asset B.

Another way of seeing that Asset A offers a superior return for its level of risk is to note that the slope of our line for Asset B is

$$\text{Slope} = \frac{E(R_B) - R_f}{\beta_B}$$
$$= \frac{16\% - 8\%}{1.2}$$
$$= 6.67\%$$

Thus, Asset B has a reward-to-risk ratio of 6.67 percent, which is less than the 7.5 percent offered by Asset A.

The Fundamental Result

The situation we have described for Assets A and B could not persist in a well-organized, active market because investors would be attracted to Asset A and away from Asset B. As a result, Asset A's price would rise and Asset B's price would fall. Because prices and expected returns move in opposite directions, A's expected return would decline and B's would rise.

This buying and selling would continue until the two assets plotted on exactly the same line, which means they would offer the same reward for bearing risk. In other words, in an active, competitive market, we must have the situation that

$$\frac{E(R_A) - R_f}{\beta_A} = \frac{E(R_B) - R_f}{\beta_B} \tag{12.6}$$

This is the fundamental relation between risk and return.

Our basic argument can be extended to more than just two assets. In fact, no matter how many assets we had, we would always reach the same conclusion:

The reward-to-risk ratio must be the same for all assets in a competitive financial market.

This result is really not too surprising. What it says is that, for example, if one asset has twice as much systematic risk as another asset, its risk premium will simply be twice as large.

Because all assets in the market must have the same reward-to-risk ratio, they all must plot on the same line. This argument is illustrated in Figure 12.2, where the subscript i on the return R_i and beta β_i indexes Assets A, B, C, and D. As shown, Assets A and B plot directly on the line and thus have the same reward-to-risk ratio. If an asset plotted above the line, such as C in Figure 12.2, its price would rise and its expected return would fall until it plotted exactly on the line. Similarly, if an asset plotted below the line, such as D in Figure 12.2, its price would fall, and its expected return would rise until it too plotted directly on the line.

The arguments we have presented apply to active, competitive, well-functioning markets. Active financial markets, such as the NYSE, best meet these criteria. Other markets, such as real asset markets, may or may not. For this reason, these concepts are most useful in examining active financial markets.

FIGURE 12.2

Expected Returns and Systematic Risk

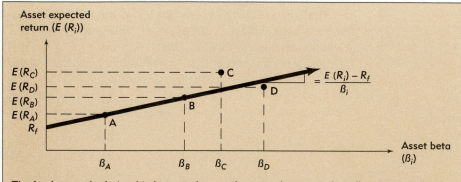

The fundamental relationship between beta and expected return is that all assets must have the same reward-to-risk ratio, $[E(R_i) - R_f]/\beta_i$. This means that they would all plot on the same straight line. Assets A and B are examples of this behavior. Asset C's expected return is too high; Asset D's is too low.

BUY LOW, SELL HIGH

EXAMPLE 12.5

A security is said to be *overvalued* relative to another security if its price is too high given its expected return and risk. Suppose you observe the following situation:

Security	Beta	Expected Return
Melan Co.	1.3	14%
Choly Co.	.8	10

The risk-free rate is currently 6 percent. Is one of the two securities overvalued relative to the other?

To answer, we compute the reward-to-risk ratio for both. For Melan, this ratio is (14% − 6%)/1.3 = 6.15%. For Choly, this ratio is 5 percent. What we conclude is that Choly offers an insufficient expected return for its level of risk, at least relative to Melan. Because its expected return is too low, its price is too high. In other words, Choly is overvalued relative to Melan, and we would expect to see its price fall relative to Melan. Notice that we could also say Melan is *undervalued* relative to Choly.

The Security Market Line

The line that results when we plot expected returns and beta coefficients is obviously of some importance, so it's time we gave it a name. This line, which we use to describe the relationship between systematic risk and expected return in financial markets, is usually called the **security market line (SML)**, and it is one of the most important concepts in modern finance.

security market line (SML) Graphical representation of the linear relationship between systematic risk and expected return in financial markets.

Market Portfolios   We will find it very useful to know the equation of the SML. Although there are many different ways we could write it, we will discuss the most frequently seen version. Suppose we consider a portfolio made up of all of the assets in the market. Such a portfolio is called a *market portfolio*, and we will express the expected return on this market portfolio as $E(R_M)$.

Because all the assets in the market must plot on the SML, so must a market portfolio made up of those assets. To determine where it plots on the SML, we need to know the beta of the market portfolio, β_M. Because this portfolio is representative of all of the assets in the market, it must have average systematic risk. In other words, it has a beta of 1. We could therefore express the slope of the SML as

$$\text{SML slope} = \frac{E(R_M) - R_f}{\beta_M} = \frac{E(R_M) - R_f}{1} = E(R_M) - R_f$$

market risk premium The risk premium on a market portfolio, i.e., a portfolio made of all assets in the market.

The term $E(R_M) - R_f$ is often called the **market risk premium** because it is the risk premium on a market portfolio.

The Capital Asset Pricing Model   To finish up, if we let $E(R_i)$ and β_i stand for the expected return and beta, respectively, on any asset in the market, then we know that asset must plot on the SML. As a result, we know that its reward-to-risk ratio is the same as that of the overall market:

$$\frac{E(R_i) - R_f}{\beta_i} = E(R_M) - R_f$$

If we rearrange this, then we can write the equation for the SML as

$$E(R_i) = R_f + [E(R_M) - R_f] \times \beta_i \qquad (12.7)$$

This result is the famous **capital asset pricing model (CAPM)**.[2]

What the CAPM shows is that the expected return for an asset depends on three things:

capital asset pricing model (CAPM) A theory of risk and return for securities in a competitive capital market.

1. *The pure time value of money.* As measured by the risk-free rate, R_f, this is the reward for merely waiting for your money, without taking any risk.

2. *The reward for bearing systematic risk.* As measured by the market risk premium, $E(R_M) - R_f$, this component is the reward the market offers for bearing an average amount of systematic risk.

3. *The amount of systematic risk.* As measured by β_i, this is the amount of systematic risk present in a particular asset relative to that in an average asset.

By the way, the CAPM works for portfolios of assets just as it does for individual assets. In an earlier section, we saw how to calculate a portfolio's beta in the CAPM equation.

Figure 12.3 summarizes our discussion of the SML and the CAPM. As before, we plot expected return against beta. Now we recognize that, based on the CAPM, the slope of the SML is equal to the market risk premium, $E(R_M) - R_f$.

This concludes our presentation of concepts related to the risk-return trade-off. Table 12.2 summarizes the various concepts in the order in which we discussed

There's a CAPM calculator (if you really need it!) at www.moneychimp.com

---

FIGURE 12.3

Security Market Line (SML)

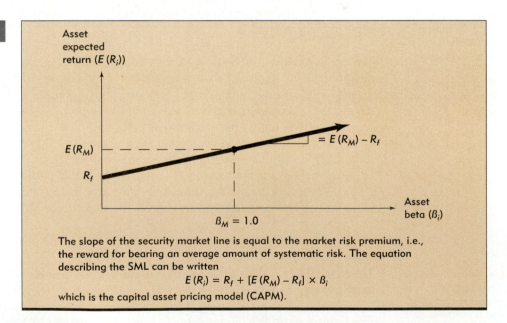

The slope of the security market line is equal to the market risk premium, i.e., the reward for bearing an average amount of systematic risk. The equation describing the SML can be written

$$E(R_i) = R_f + [E(R_M) - R_f] \times \beta_i$$

which is the capital asset pricing model (CAPM).

---

[2]Our discussion of the CAPM is actually closely related to the more recent development, arbitrage pricing theory (APT). The theory underlying the CAPM is more complex than we have indicated here, and it has implications beyond the scope of this discussion. As we present it here, the CAPM has essentially identical implications to those of the APT, so we don't distinguish between them.

TABLE 12.2	Risk and Return Summary

1. **Total risk.** The *total risk* of an investment is measured by the variance or, more commonly, the standard deviation of its return.

2. **Total return.** The *total return* on an investment has two components: the expected return and the unexpected return. The unexpected return comes about because of unanticipated events. The risk from investing stems from the possibility of an unanticipated event.

3. **Systematic and unsystematic risks.** *Systematic risks* (also called *market risks*) are unanticipated events that affect almost all assets to some degree because the effects are economywide. *Unsystematic risks* are unanticipated events that affect single assets or small groups of assets. Unsystematic risks are also called *unique* or *asset-specific risks*.

4. **The effect of diversification.** Some, but not all, of the risk associated with a risky investment can be eliminated by diversification. The reason is that unsystematic risks, which are unique to individual assets, tend to wash out in a large portfolio, but systematic risks, which affect all of the assets in a portfolio to some extent, do not.

5. **The systematic risk principle and beta.** Because unsystematic risk can be freely eliminated by diversification, the *systematic risk principle* states that the reward for bearing risk depends only on the level of systematic risk. The level of systematic risk in a particular asset, relative to the average, is given by the *beta* of that asset.

6. **The reward-to-risk ratio and the security market line.** The *reward-to-risk ratio* for Asset i is the ratio of its risk premium, $E(R_i) - R_f$, to its beta, β_i.

$$\frac{E(R_i) - R_f}{\beta_i}$$

In a well-functioning market, this ratio is the same for every asset. As a result, when asset expected returns are plotted against asset betas, all assets plot on the same straight line, called the *security market line* (SML).

7. **The capital asset pricing model.** From the SML, the expected return on Asset i can be written

$$E(R_i) = R_f + [E(R_M) - R_f] \times \beta_i$$

This is the *capital asset pricing model* (CAPM). The expected return on a risky asset thus has three components. The first is the pure time value of money (R_f), the second is the market risk premium, $E(R_M) - R_f$, and the third is the beta for that asset (β_i).

them. You may also wish to read the article on risk in the nearby *Investment Updates* box.

RISK AND RETURN

EXAMPLE 12.6

Suppose the risk-free rate is 4 percent, the market risk premium is 8.6 percent, and a particular stock has a beta of 1.3. Based on the CAPM, what is the expected return on this stock? What would the expected return be if the beta were to double?

With a beta of 1.3, the risk premium for the stock is $1.3 \times 8.6\%$, or 11.18 percent. The risk-free rate is 4 percent, so the expected return is 15.18 percent. If the beta were to double to 2.6, the risk premium would double to 22.36 percent, so the expected return would be 26.36 percent.

Fixating on Risk Can Sink Your Investment Portfolio

As you decide how much to invest in stocks, a lot supposedly rides on whether you have knees of jelly or nerves of steel. But this notion of risk tolerance is a dangerous idea. For proof, look no further than our reaction to recent market movements. Last year, risky technology stocks were all the rage. This year, we are ready to throw in our lot with cowardly money-market fund holders. Our tolerance for risk, it seems, has plunged along with the market. But clearly, that doesn't mean we should cut back on stocks. If we slashed our stock-market exposure every time we felt queasy, we would buy high, sell low and garner disastrous investment results.

"After the stock market has gone up, people think that the probability of the market continuing to go up is high," says Meir Statman, a finance professor at Santa Clara University in Santa Clara, Calif. "When the market goes down, people think it will continue to go down." What to do? As we settle on our portfolio's stock allocation, maybe we should forget about risk tolerance and instead focus on four other factors.

Taking Aim: "This fixation on risk isn't getting us anyplace," Mr. Statman argues. "Instead, people should think about the goals they have." You might want a cash reserve to cover emergencies and help you sleep better at night. But you also want to amass enough for retirement, which means buying stocks in the hope of notching high returns. "One goal is to avoid being poor," Mr. Statman says. "The other goal is having a shot at being rich. Each goal is desirable. The question is, how do we allocate our portfolio between these two goals?"

Hitting the Target: Unlike many financial planners, San Francisco investment adviser Tim Kochis doesn't start by asking new clients about their risk tolerance. "You're not going to get a useful answer," he contends. "People don't understand risk very well. Most people will underestimate the risk of bond investments, because they don't understand interest-rate risk. And even after the great performance of the past few years, they'll overestimate the risk of a diversified stock portfolio over the long term."

Instead, Mr. Kochis begins by both educating clients about risk and figuring out what sort of investment returns they need to meet their goals. He then presents them with a mix of stocks and conservative investments that he thinks will generate the returns they need. "At that point, clients typically change their professed tolerance for risk, rather than changing their goals," Mr. Kochis says. "Clients can see the tie-in between the portfolio's risk and the accomplishment of their goals. It provides the motivation to take risk and stay invested when things look grim." Still, there is a downside to this approach. "Once you've shown people that the portfolio that is most likely to meet their future needs is an aggressive portfolio, they tend to ignore short-term risks," argues Jeff Schwartz, a vice president at mPower, a San Francisco online-investment adviser. "But the problem is, it's these short-term events that we react to."

Biding Time: As you decide how to divvy up your money between stocks and more-conservative investments, time is a critical factor. Even if you are an aggressive investor and you need high returns to meet your goals, stocks may not be a wise choice if you have a short time horizon. "We think that any money needed in three years or less should be saved rather than invested, and that means Treasury bills, money-market funds and certificates of deposit," says Minneapolis financial planner Ross Levin. "But most people's time horizon is longer than they think. Your kid may be three years from college. But you won't pay the last bill for seven years."

Pick a Reasonable Range: For all the talk about risk tolerance, it doesn't appear to make much difference to the portfolios that financial advisers recommend. Experts aren't likely to suggest an all-bond portfolio. After all, a mix of 80% bonds and 20% stocks will have comparable portfolio gyrations, but with a significantly higher expected return. At the other extreme, advisers probably won't recommend an all-stock portfolio. They will plunk at least some money in conservative investments, to temper the stock portfolio's price swings and provide money in an emergency.

In practice, the range gets narrower still. No matter what the client's age or professed risk tolerance, experts typically recommend that long-term investors have 50% to 90% in stocks, Mr. Levin says. Sound like a lot in equities? Initially, you may not be comfortable with such hefty stock exposure. But with time, you should get used to the market swings. And the fact is, without the stocks, you may not amass enough to reach your goals. "Clients may indicate that they're very risk averse," says Eleanor Blayney, a financial planner in McLean, Va. "But they may not be able to afford to be that conservative."

Source: Jonathan Clements, *The Wall Street Journal*, June 6, 2000.

12.5a   What is the fundamental relationship between risk and return in active markets?

12.5b   What is the security market line (SML)? Why must all assets plot directly on it in a well-functioning market?

12.5c   What is the capital asset pricing model (CAPM)? What does it tell us about the required return on a risky investment?

12.6 More on Beta

In our last several sections, we discussed the basic economic principles of risk and return. We found that the expected return on a security depends on its systematic risk, which is measured using the security's beta coefficient, β. In this final section, we examine beta in more detail. We first illustrate more closely what it is that beta measures. We then show how betas can be estimated for individual securities, and we discuss why it is that different sources report different betas for the same security.

A Closer Look at Beta

Going back to the beginning of the chapter, we discussed how the actual return on a security, R, could be written as follows:

$$R - E(R) = m + \epsilon \tag{12.8}$$

Recall that in Equation 12.8, m stands for the systematic or marketwide portion of the unexpected return. Based on our discussion of the CAPM, we can now be a little more precise about this component.

Specifically, the systematic portion of an unexpected return depends on two things. First, it depends on the size of the systematic effect. We will measure this as $R_M - E(R_M)$, which is simply the difference between the actual return on the overall market and the expected return. Second, as we have discussed, some securities have greater systematic risk than others, and we measure this risk using beta. Putting it together, we have

$$m = [R_M - E(R_M)] \times \beta \tag{12.9}$$

In other words, the marketwide, or systematic, portion of the return on a security depends on both the size of the marketwide surprise, $R_M - E(R_M)$, and the sensitivity of the security to such surprises, β.

Now, if we combine Equations 12.8 and 12.9, we have

$$R - E(R) = m + \epsilon$$
$$= [R_M - E(R_M)] \times \beta + \epsilon \tag{12.10}$$

Equation 12.10 gives us some additional insight into beta by telling us why some securities have higher betas than others. A high-beta security is simply one that is relatively sensitive to overall market movements, whereas a low-beta security is one that is relatively insensitive. In other words, the systematic risk of a security is just a reflection of its sensitivity to overall market movements.

A hypothetical example is useful for illustrating the main point of Equation 12.10. Suppose a particular security has a beta of 1.2, the risk-free rate is 5 percent, and the expected return on the market is 12 percent. From the CAPM, we know that the expected return on the security is

$$E(R) = R_f + [E(R_M) - R_f] \times \beta$$
$$= .05 + (.12 - .05) \times 1.2$$
$$= .134$$

Thus, the expected return on this security is 13.4 percent. However, we know that in any year the actual return on this security will be more or less than 13.4 percent because of unanticipated systematic and unsystematic events.

Columns 1 and 2 of Table 12.3 list the actual returns on our security, R, for a five-year period along with the actual returns for the market as a whole, R_M, for the same period. Given these actual returns and the expected returns on the security (13.4 percent) and the market as a whole (12 percent), we can calculate the unexpected returns on the security, $R - E(R)$, along with the unexpected return on the market as a whole, $R_M - E(R_M)$. The results are shown in columns 3 and 4 of Table 12.3.

Next we decompose the unexpected returns on the security—that is, we break them down into their systematic and unsystematic components in columns 5 and 6. From Equation 12.9, we calculate the systematic portion of the unexpected return by taking the security's beta, 1.2, and multiplying it by the market's unexpected return:

$$\text{Systematic portion} = m = [R_M - E(R_M)] \times \beta$$

Finally, we calculate the unsystematic portion by subtracting the systematic portion from the total unexpected return:

$$\text{Unsystematic portion} = \epsilon = [R - E(R)] - [R_M - E(R_M)] \times \beta$$

Notice that the unsystematic portion is essentially whatever is left over after we account for the systematic portion. For this reason, it is sometimes called the "residual" portion of the unexpected return.

Figure 12.4 illustrates the main points of this discussion by plotting the unexpected returns on the security in Table 12.3 against the unexpected return on the market as a whole. These are the individual points in the graph, each labeled with its year. We also plot the systematic portions of the unexpected returns in Table 12.3 and connect them with a straight line. Notice that the slope of the straight line is equal to 1.2, the beta of the security. As indicated, the distance from the straight line to an individual point is the unsystematic portion of the return, ϵ, for a particular year.

TABLE 12.3						
		**Decomposition of Total Returns into Systematic and Unsystematic Portions**				
	Actual Returns		**Unexpected Returns**		**Systematic Portion**	**Unsystematic Portion (ϵ)**
Year	R	R_M	$R - E(R)$	$R_M - E(R_M)$	$[R_M - E(R_M)] \times \beta$	$[R - E(R)] - [R_M - E(R_M)] \times \beta$
1999	20%	15%	6.6%	3%	3.6%	3%
2000	−24.6	−3	−38	−15	−18	−20
2001	23	10	9.6	−2	−2.4	12
2002	36.8	24	23.4	12	14.4	9
2003	3.4	7	−10	−5	−6	−4

FIGURE 12.4

Unexpected Returns and Beta

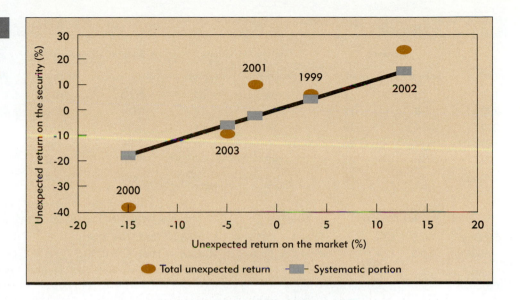

Where Do Betas Come From?

As our discussion to this point shows, beta is a useful concept. It allows us to estimate the expected return on a security, it tells how sensitive a security's return is to unexpected market events, and it lets us separate out the systematic and unsystematic portions of a security's return. In our example just above, we were given that the beta was 1.2, so the required calculations were all pretty straightforward. Suppose, however, that we didn't have the beta ahead of time. In this case, we would have to estimate it.

A security's beta is a measure of how sensitive the security's return is to overall market movements. That sensitivity depends on two things: (1) how closely correlated the security's return is with the overall market's return and (2) how volatile the security is relative to the market. Specifically, going back to our previous chapter, let $Corr(R_i, R_M)$ stand for the correlation between the return on a particular security i and the overall market. As before, let σ_i and σ_M be the standard deviations on the security and the market, respectively. Given these numbers, the beta for the security, β_i, is simply

$$\beta_i = Corr(R_i, R_M) \times \sigma_i / \sigma_M \qquad (12.11)$$

In other words, the beta is equal to the correlation multiplied by the ratio of the standard deviations.

From previous chapters, we know how to calculate the standard deviations in Equation 12.11. However, we have not yet discussed how to calculate correlations. This is our final task for this chapter. The simplest way to proceed is to construct a worksheet like Table 12.4.

The first six columns of Table 12.4 are familiar from Chapter 1. The first two contain five years of returns on a particular security and the overall market. We add these up and divide by 5 to get the average returns of 10 percent and 12 percent for the security and the market, respectively, as shown in the table. In the third and fourth columns we calculate the return deviations by taking each individual return and subtracting out the average return. In columns 5 and 6 we square these return deviations. To calculate the variances, we total these squared deviations and divide by $5 - 1 = 4$. We calculate the standard deviations by taking the square roots of the variances, and

TABLE 12.4			Calculating Beta					
	Returns		Return Deviations		Squared Deviations			
Year	Security	Market	Security	Market	Security	Market	Product of Deviations
1999	10%	8%	.00	−.04	.0000	.0016	.0000
2000	−8	−12	−.18	−.24	.0324	.0576	.0432
2001	−4	16	−.14	.04	.0196	.0016	−.0056
2002	40	26	.30	.14	.0900	.0196	.0420
2003	12	22	.02	.10	.0004	.0100	.0020
Totals	50	60	0	0	.1424	.0904	.0816

	Average Returns	Variances	Standard Deviations
Security	50/5 = 10%	.1424/4 = .0356	$\sqrt{.0356}$ = .1887 = 18.87%
Market	60/5 = 12%	.0904/4 = .0226	$\sqrt{.0226}$ = .1503 = 15.03%

Covariance = $Cov(R_i, R_M)$ = .0816/4 = .0204
Correlation = $Corr(R_i, R_M)$ = .0204 / (.1887 × .1503) = .72
Beta = β = .72 × (.1887 / .1503) = .9031 ≈ .9

we find that the standard deviations for the security and the market are 18.87 percent and 15.03 percent, respectively.

Now we come to the part that's new. In the last column of Table 12.4, we have calculated the *product* of the return deviations by simply multiplying columns 3 and 4. When we total these products and divide by $5 - 1 = 4$, the result is called the **covariance**.

covariance A measure of the tendency of two things to move or vary together.

Covariance, as the name suggests, is a measure of the tendency of two things to vary together. If the covariance is positive, then the tendency is to move in the same direction, and vice versa for a negative covariance. A zero covariance means there is no particular relation. For our security in Table 12.4, the covariance is +.0204, so the security tends to move in the same direction as the market.

A problem with covariances is that, like variances, the actual numbers are hard to interpret (the sign, of course, is not). For example, our covariance is .0204, but, just from this number, we can't really say if the security has a strong tendency to move with the market or only a weak one. To fix this problem, we divide the covariance by the product of the two standard deviations. The result is the correlation coefficient, introduced in the previous chapter.

From Table 12.4, the correlation between our security and the overall market is .72. Recalling that correlations range from −1 to +1, this .72 tells us that the security has a fairly strong tendency to move with the overall market, but that tendency is not perfect.

Now, we have reached our goal of calculating the beta coefficient. As shown in the last row of Table 12.4, from Equation 12.11, we have

$$\beta_i = Corr(R_i, R_M) \times \sigma_i / \sigma_M$$
$$= .72 \times (.1887 / .1503)$$
$$= .90$$

SPREADSHEET ANALYSIS

	A	B	C	D	E	F	G	H
1								
2			**Using a spreadsheet to calculate correlations**					
3								
4		To illustrate how to calculate correlations using a spreadsheet, we						
5		have repeated the information from Table 12.4 just below. Here we						
6		use Excel functions to do all the calculations.						
7								
8			Returns					
9			Security	Market				
10		1999	10%	8%				
11		2000	−8%	−12%				
12		2001	−4%	16%				
13		2002	40%	26%				
14		2003	12%	22%				
15								
16		Average:	10%	12%	(Using the =AVERAGE function)			
17		Std dev:	18.87%	15.03%	(Using the =STDEV function)			
18								
19		Correlation:	0.72	= CORREL(C10:C14,D10:D14)				
20								
21		Excel also has a covariance function, =COVAR, but we don't use						
22		it because it divides by n instead of n − 1.						
23								

We find that this security has a beta of .9, so it has slightly less than average systematic risk. As our nearby *Spreadsheet Analysis* box shows, these calculations can be done easily with a spreadsheet.

Why Do Betas Differ?

Finally, we consider why different sources report different betas. The important thing to remember is that betas are estimated from actual data. Different sources estimate differently, possibly using different data. We discuss some of the key differences next.

First, there are two issues concerning data. Betas can be calculated using daily, weekly, monthly, quarterly, or annual returns. In principle, it does not matter which is chosen, but with real data, different estimates will result. Second, betas can be estimated over relatively short periods such as a few weeks or over long periods of 5 to 10 years or even more.

The trade-off here is not hard to understand. Betas obtained from high-frequency returns, such as daily returns, are less reliable than those obtained from less frequent returns, such as monthly returns. This argues for using monthly or longer returns. On the other hand, any time we estimate something, we would like to have a large number of recent observations. This argues for using weekly or daily returns. There is no ideal balance; the most common choices are three to five years of monthly data or a single year of weekly data. The betas we get from a year of weekly data are more current in the sense that they reflect only the previous year, but they tend to be less stable than those obtained from longer periods.

Another issue has to do with choice of a market index. All along, we have discussed the return on the "overall market," but we have not been very precise about how to measure this. By far the most common choice is to use the S&P 500 stock market index to measure the overall market, but this is not the only alternative. Different sources use different indexes to capture the overall market, and different indexes will lead to different beta estimates.

You might wonder whether some index is the "correct" one. The answer is yes, but a problem comes up. In principle, in the CAPM, when we speak of the overall market, what we really mean is the market for *every* risky asset of every type. In other words, what we would need is an index that included all the stocks, bonds, real estate, precious metals, and everything else in the entire world (not just the United States). Obviously, no such index exists, so instead we must choose some smaller index to proxy for this much larger one.

Last, a few sources (including *Value Line*, the source for Table 12.1) calculate betas the way we described in Table 12.4, but then they go on to adjust them for statistical reasons. The nature of the adjustment goes beyond our discussion, but such adjustments are another reason why betas differ across sources.

12.7 Summary and Conclusions

This chapter has covered the essentials of risk and return. Along the way, we have introduced a number of definitions and concepts. The most important of these is the security market line, or SML. The SML is important because it tells us the reward offered in financial markets for bearing risk.

Because we have covered quite a bit of ground, it's useful to summarize the basic economic logic underlying the SML as follows:

1. Based on capital market history, there is a reward for bearing risk. This reward is the risk premium on an asset.

2. The total risk associated with an asset has two parts: systematic risk and unsystematic risk. Unsystematic risk can be freely eliminated by diversification (this is the principle of diversification), so only systematic risk is rewarded. As a result, the risk premium on an asset is determined by its systematic risk. This is the systematic risk principle.

3. An asset's systematic risk, relative to the average, can be measured by its beta coefficient, β_i. The risk premium on an asset is then given by the market risk premium multiplied by the asset's beta coefficient, $[E(R_M) - R_f] \times \beta_i$.

4. The expected return on an asset, $E(R_i)$, is equal to the risk-free rate, R_f, plus the asset's risk premium:

$$E(R_i) = R_f + [E(R_M) - R_f] \times \beta_i$$

This is the equation of the SML, and it is often called the capital asset pricing model (CAPM).

Finally, to close out the chapter we showed how betas are calculated, and we discussed some of the main reasons different sources report different beta coefficients.

Get Real

This chapter introduced you to the famous capital asset pricing model, or CAPM for short. For investors, the CAPM has a stunning implication: What you earn, through time, on your portfolio depends only on the level of systematic risk you bear. The corollary is equally striking: As a diversified investor, you don't need to be concerned with the total risk or volatility of any individual asset in your portfolio—it is simply irrelevant.

An immediate implication of the CAPM is that you, as an investor, need to be aware of the level of systematic risk you are carrying. Look up the betas of the stocks you hold in your simulated brokerage account and compute your portfolio's systematic risk. Is it bigger or smaller than 1.0? More important, is the portfolio's beta consistent with your desired level of portfolio risk?

Betas are particularly useful for understanding mutual fund risk and return. Since most mutual funds are at least somewhat diversified (the exceptions being sector funds and other specialized funds), they have relatively little unsystematic risk, and their betas can be measured with some precision. Look at the funds you own and learn their betas (www.morningstar.com is a good source). Are the risk levels what you intended? As you study mutual fund risk, you will find some other measures exist, most of which are closely related to the measures discussed in this chapter. Take a few minutes to understand these as well.

Of course, we should note that the CAPM is a theory, and, as with any theory, whether it is correct or not is a question for the data. So does the CAPM work or not? Put more directly, does expected return depend on beta, and beta alone, or do other factors come into play? There is no more hotly debated question in all of finance, and the research that exists to date is inconclusive. (Some researchers would dispute this!) At a minimum, it appears that beta is a useful measure of market-related volatility, but whether it is a useful measure of expected return (much less a comprehensive one) awaits more research. Lots more research.

Key Terms

systematic risk 398
unsystematic risk 398
systematic risk principle 401
beta coefficient (β) 401

security market line (SML) 409
market risk premium 409
capital asset pricing model (CAPM) 410
covariance 416

Chapter Review Problems and Self-Test

1. **Risk and Return**   Suppose you observe the following situation:

Security	Beta	Expected Return
Sanders	1.8	22.00%
Janicek	1.6	20.44

If the risk-free rate is 7 percent, are these two stocks correctly priced relative to each other? What must the risk-free rate be if they are correctly priced?

2. **CAPM**   Suppose the risk-free rate is 8 percent. The expected return on the market is 16 percent. If a particular stock has a beta of .7, what is its expected return based on the CAPM? If another stock has an expected return of 24 percent, what must its beta be?

Answers to Self-Test Problems

1. If we compute the reward-to-risk ratios, we get $(22\% - 7\%)/1.8 = 8.33\%$ for Sanders versus 8.4% for Janicek. Relative to Sanders, Janicek's expected return is too high, so its price is too low.

    If they are correctly priced, then they must offer the same reward-to-risk ratio. The risk-free rate would have to be such that

    $$\frac{22\% - R_f}{1.8} = \frac{20.44\% - R_f}{1.6}$$

    With a little algebra, we find that the risk-free rate must be 8 percent:

    $$22\% - R_f = (20.44\% - R_f)(1.8/1.6)$$
    $$22\% - 20.44\% \times 1.125 = R_f - R_f \times 1.125$$
    $$R_f = 8\%$$

2. Because the expected return on the market is 16 percent, the market risk premium is $16\% - 8\% = 8\%$ (the risk-free rate is also 8 percent). The first stock has a beta of .7, so its expected return is $8\% + 8\% \times .7 = 13.6\%$.

    For the second stock, notice that the risk premium is $24\% - 8\% = 16\%$. Because this is twice as large as the market risk premium, the beta must be exactly equal to 2. We can verify this using the CAPM:

    $$E(R_i) = R_f + [E(R_M) - R_f] \times \beta_i$$
    $$24\% = 8\% + (16\% - 8\%) \times \beta_i$$
    $$\beta_i = 16\%/8\% = 2.0$$

Test Your Investment Quotient

1. **Portfolio Return**   According to the CAPM, what is the rate of return of a portfolio with a beta of 1?
    a. Between R_M and R_f
    b. The risk-free rate, R_f
    c. Beta $\times (R_M - R_f)$
    d. The return on the market, R_M

2. **Stock Return**   The return on a stock is said to have which two of the following basic parts?
    a. An expected return and an unexpected return.
    b. A measurable return and an unmeasurable return.
    c. A predicted return and a forecast return.
    d. A total return and a partial return.

3. **News Components**   A news announcement about a stock is said to have which two of the following parts?
    a. An expected part and a surprise.
    b. Public information and private information.

   c. Financial information and product information.
   d. A good part and a bad part.

4. **News Effects**   A company announces that its earnings have increased 50 percent over the previous year, which matches analysts' expectations. What is the likely effect on the stock price?

   a. The stock price will increase.
   b. The stock price will decrease.
   c. The stock price will rise and then fall after an overreaction.
   d. The stock price will not be affected.

5. **News Effects**   A company announces that its earnings have decreased 25 percent from the previous year, but analysts expected a small increase. What is the likely effect on the stock price?

   a. The stock price will increase.
   b. The stock price will decrease.
   c. The stock price will rise and then fall after an overreaction.
   d. The stock price will not be affected.

6. **News Effects**   A company announces that its earnings have increased 25 percent from the previous year, but analysts actually expected a 50 percent increase. What is the likely effect on the stock price?

   a. The stock price will increase.
   b. The stock price will decrease.
   c. The stock price will rise and then fall after an overreaction.
   d. The stock price will not be affected.

7. **News Effects**   A company announces that its earnings have decreased 50 percent from the previous year, but analysts only expected a 25 percent decrease. What is the likely effect on the stock price?

   a. The stock price will increase.
   b. The stock price will decrease.
   c. The stock price will rise and then fall after an overreaction.
   d. The stock price will not be affected.

8. **Security Risk**   The systematic risk of a security is also called its

   a. Perceived risk.
   b. Unique or asset-specific risk.
   c. Market risk.
   d. Fundamental risk.

9. **Security Risk**   Which type of risk is essentially eliminated by diversification?

   a. Perceived risk
   b. Market risk
   c. Systematic risk
   d. Unsystematic risk

10. **Security Risk**   The systematic risk principle states that

   a. Systematic risk doesn't matter to investors.
   b. Systematic risk can be essentially eliminated by diversification.
   c. The reward for bearing risk is independent of the systematic risk of an investment.
   d. The reward for bearing risk depends only on the systematic risk of an investment.

11. **Security Risk**   The systematic risk principle has an important implication, which is that

   a. Systematic risk is preferred to unsystematic risk.
   b. Systematic risk is the only risk that can be reduced by diversification.
   c. The expected return on an asset is independent of its systematic risk.
   d. The expected return on an asset depends only on its systematic risk.

12. **CAPM**   A financial market's security market line (SML) describes

    a. The relationship between systematic risk and expected returns.
    b. The relationship between unsystematic risk and expected returns.
    c. The relationship between systematic risk and unexpected returns.
    d. The relationship between unsystematic risk and unexpected returns.

13. **Risk Aversion**   Which of the following is not an implication of risk aversion for the investment process?

    a. The security market line is upward sloping.
    b. The promised yield on AAA-rated bonds is higher than on A-rated bonds.
    c. Investors expect a positive relationship between expected return and risk.
    d. Investors prefer portfolios that lie on the efficient frontier to other portfolios with equal rates of return.

14. **Unsystematic Risk**   In the context of capital market theory, unsystematic risk

    a. Is described as unique risk.
    b. Refers to nondiversifiable risk.
    c. Remains in the market portfolio.
    d. Refers to the variability in all risk assets caused by macroeconomic factors and other aggregate market-related variables.

15. **Security Market Line**   Which of the following statements about the security market line (SML) is false?

    a. Properly valued assets plot exactly on the SML.
    b. The SML leads all investors to invest in the same portfolio of risky assets.
    c. The SML provides a benchmark for evaluating expected investment performance.
    d. The SML is a graphic representation of the relationship between expected return and beta.

Concept Questions

1. **Diversifiable Risk**   In broad terms, why is some risk diversifiable? Why are some risks nondiversifiable? Does it follow that an investor can control the level of unsystematic risk in a portfolio, but not the level of systematic risk?

2. **Announcements and Prices**   Suppose the government announces that, based on a just-completed survey, the growth rate in the economy is likely to be 2 percent in the coming year, compared to 5 percent for the year just completed. Will security prices increase, decrease, or stay the same following this announcement? Does it make any difference whether the 2 percent figure was anticipated by the market? Explain.

3. **Announcements and Risk**   Classify the following events as mostly systematic or mostly unsystematic. Is the distinction clear in every case?

    a. Short-term interest rates increase unexpectedly.
    b. The interest rate a company pays on its short-term debt borrowing is increased by its bank.
    c. Oil prices unexpectedly decline.
    d. An oil tanker ruptures, creating a large oil spill.
    e. A manufacturer loses a multimillion-dollar product liability suit.
    f. A Supreme Court decision substantially broadens producer liability for injuries suffered by product users.

4. **Announcements and Risk**   Indicate whether the following events might cause stocks in general to change price, and whether they might cause Big Widget Corp.'s stock to change price.

    a. The government announces that inflation unexpectedly jumped by 2 percent last month.

    b. Big Widget's quarterly earnings report, just issued, generally fell in line with analysts' expectations.

    c. The government reports that economic growth last year was at 3 percent, which generally agreed with most economists' forecasts.

    d. The directors of Big Widget die in a plane crash.

    e. Congress approves changes to the tax code that will increase the top marginal corporate tax rate. The legislation had been debated for the previous six months.

5. Diversification and Risk True or false: The most important characteristic in determining the expected return of a well-diversified portfolio is the variances of the individual assets in the portfolio. Explain.

6. Announcements As indicated by examples in this chapter, earnings announcements by companies are closely followed by, and frequently result in, share price revisions. Two issues should come to mind. First, earnings announcements concern past periods. If the market values stocks based on expectations of the future, why are numbers summarizing past performance relevant? Second, these announcements concern accounting earnings. Such earnings may have little to do with cash flow, so, again, why are they relevant?

7. Beta Is it possible that a risky asset could have a beta of zero? Explain. Based on the CAPM, what is the expected return on such an asset? Is it possible that a risky asset could have a negative beta? What does the CAPM predict about the expected return on such an asset? Can you give an explanation for your answer?

8. Relative Valuation Suppose you identify a situation in which one security is overvalued relative to another. How would you go about exploiting this opportunity? Does it matter if the two securities are both overvalued relative to some third security? Are your profits certain in this case?

9. Reward-to-Risk Ratio Explain what it means for all assets to have the same reward-to-risk ratio. How can you increase your return if this holds true? Why would we expect that all assets have the same reward-to-risk ratio in liquid, well-functioning markets?

10. Systematic versus Firm-Specific Risk Dudley Trudy, CFA, recently met with one of his clients. Trudy typically invests in a master list of 30 securities drawn from several industries. After the meeting concluded, the client made the following statement: "I trust your stock-picking ability and believe that you should invest my funds in your five best ideas. Why invest in 30 companies when you obviously have stronger opinions on a few of them?" Trudy plans to respond to his client within the context of Modern Portfolio Theory.

    a. Contrast the concept of systematic and firm-specific risk and give one example of each.

    b. Critique the client's suggestion. Discuss the impact of the systematic risk and firm-specific risk on portfolio risk as the number of securities in a portfolio is increased.

Questions and Problems

Core Questions

1. Stock Betas A stock has an expected return of 12.5 percent, the risk-free rate is 5 percent, and the market risk premium is 6 percent. What must the beta of this stock be?

2. Market Returns A stock has an expected return of 11 percent, its beta is .9, and the risk-free rate is 5 percent. What must the expected return on the market be?

3. Risk-Free Rates A stock has an expected return of 13 percent and a beta of 1.3, and the expected return on the market is 11 percent. What must the risk-free rate be?

4. **Market Risk Premium**   A stock has a beta of 1.3 and an expected return of 17 percent. If the risk-free rate is 6 percent, what is the market risk premium?

5. **Portfolio Betas**   You own a stock portfolio invested 30 percent in Stock Q, 25 percent in Stock R, 20 percent in Stock S, and 25 percent in Stock T. The betas for these four stocks are 1.2, .6, 1.5, and .8, respectively. What is the portfolio beta?

6. **Portfolio Betas**   You own 300 shares of Stock A at a price of $50 per share, 400 shares of Stock B at $70 per share, and 200 shares of Stock C at $25 per share. The betas for the stocks are 1.2, .9, and 1.6, respectively. What is the beta of your portfolio?

7. **Stock Betas**   You own a portfolio equally invested in a risk-free asset and two stocks. If one of the stocks has a beta of 1.4, and the total portfolio is exactly as risky as the market, what must the beta be for the other stock in your portfolio?

8. **Expected Returns**   A stock has a beta of .7, the expected return on the market is 15 percent, and the risk-free rate is 6.5 percent. What must the expected return on this stock be?

9. **CAPM and Stock Price**   A share of stock sells for $60 today. The beta of the stock is 1.2, and the expected return on the market is 12 percent. The stock is expected to pay a dividend of $3 in one year. If the risk-free rate is 5 percent, what will the share price be in one year?

10. **Portfolio Weights**   A stock has a beta of .9 and an expected return of 12 percent. A risk-free asset currently earns 6 percent.

   a. What is the expected return on a portfolio that is equally invested in the two assets?
   b. If a portfolio of the two assets has a beta of .5, what are the portfolio weights?
   c. If a portfolio of the two assets has an expected return of 11 percent, what is its beta?
   d. If a portfolio of the two assets has a beta of 1.80, what are the portfolio weights? How do you interpret the weights for the two assets in this case? Explain.

Intermediate Questions

11. **Portfolio Risk and Return**   Asset W has an expected return of 14 percent and a beta of 1.4. If the risk-free rate is 7 percent, complete the following table for portfolios of Asset W and a risk-free asset. Illustrate the relationship between portfolio expected return and portfolio beta by plotting the expected returns against the betas. What is the slope of the line that results?

Percentage of Portfolio in Asset W	Portfolio Expected Return	Portfolio Beta
0%		
25		
50		
75		
100		
125		
150		

12. **Relative Valuation**   Stock Y has a beta of 1.45 and an expected return of 17 percent. Stock Z has a beta of .85 and an expected return of 12 percent. If the risk-free rate is 6 percent and the market risk premium is 7.5 percent, are these stocks correctly priced?

13. **Relative Valuation**   In the previous problem, what would the risk-free rate have to be for the two stocks to be correctly priced relative to each other?

14. **CAPM**   Using the CAPM, show that the ratio of the risk premiums on two assets is equal to the ratio of their betas.

15. **Relative Valuation**   Suppose you observe the following situation:

Security	Beta	Expected Return
Oxy Co.	1.20	18%
More-On Co.	.85	14

Assume these securities are correctly priced. Based on the CAPM, what is the expected return on the market? What is the risk-free rate?

16. **Calculating Beta**   Show that another way to calculate beta is to take the covariance between the security and the market and divide by the variance of the market's return.

17. **Calculating Beta**   Fill in the following table, supplying all the missing information. Use this information to calculate the security's beta.

	Returns		Return Deviations		Squared Deviations		Product of Deviations
Year	Security	Market	Security	Market	Security	Market	
1995	12%	6%					
1996	−9	−12					
1997	−6	0					
1998	30	−4					
1999	18	30					
Totals	45	20					

18. **Analyzing a Portfolio**   You have $100,000 to invest in a portfolio containing Stock X, Stock Y, and a risk-free asset. You must invest all of your money. Your goal is to create a portfolio that has an expected return of 16.5 percent and that has only 70 percent of the risk of the overall market. If X has an expected return of 28 percent and a beta of 1.7, Y has an expected return of 14 percent and a beta of 1.1, and the risk-free rate is 7 percent, how much money will you invest in Stock Y? How do you interpret your answer?

19. **Systematic versus Unsystematic Risk**   Consider the following information on Stocks I and II:

State of Economy	Probability of State of Economy	Rate of Return if State Occurs	
		Stock I	Stock II
Recession	.25	.09	−.30
Normal	.50	.42	.12
Irrational exuberance	.25	.26	.44

The market risk premium is 8 percent, and the risk-free rate is 5 percent. Which stock has the most systematic risk? Which one has the most unsystematic risk? Which stock is "riskier?" Explain.

20. **Systematic and Unsystematic Risk**   The beta for a certain stock is 1.15, the risk-free rate is 6 percent, and the expected return on the market is 13 percent. Complete the following table to decompose the stock's return into the systematic return and the unsystematic return.

	Actual Returns		Unexpected Returns		Systematic Portion	Unsystematic Portion (ϵ)
Year	R	R_M	$R - E(R)$	$R_M - E(R_M)$	$[R_M - E(R_M)] \times \beta$	$[R - E(R)] - [R_M - E(R_M)] \times \beta$
1999	34%	28%				
2000	18	15				
2001	−13	−8				
2002	−8	−17				
2003	21	9				

21. **CAPM** John Wilson, a portfolio manager, is evaluating the expected performance of two common stocks, Furhman Labs, Inc., and Garten Testing, Inc. The risk-free rate is 5 percent, the expected return on the market is 11.5 percent, and the betas of the two stocks are 1.5 and .8, respectively. Wilson's own forecasts of the returns on the two stocks are 13.25 percent for Furhman Labs and 11.25 percent for Garten. Calculate the required return for each stock. Is each stock undervalued, fairly valued, or overvalued?

Use the following information for the next four questions: Abigail Grace has a $900,000 fully diversified portfolio. She subsequently inherits ABC Company common stock worth $100,000. Her financial adviser provided her with the forecasted information below:

	Monthly Expected Returns	Expected Standard Deviation of Monthly Returns
Original portfolio	.67%	2.37%
ABC Company	1.25	2.95

The expected correlation coefficient of ABC stock returns and the original portfolio is .40. The inheritance changes her overall portfolio and she is deciding whether to keep the ABC stock.

22. **Portfolio Return and Standard Deviation** Assuming Grace keeps the ABC stock, calculate the expected return of the new portfolio, the covariance of ABC stock with the original portfolio, and the expected standard deviation of the new portfolio.

23. **Portfolio Return and Standard Deviation** If Grace sells the ABC stock, she will invest the proceeds in risk-free government securities yielding .42 percent monthly. Calculate the expected return of the new portfolio, the covariance of the government security returns with the original portfolio, and the expected standard deviation of the new portfolio.

24. **Beta** Determine whether the beta of Grace's new portfolio, which includes the government securities, will be higher or lower than the beta of her original portfolio. Justify your response with one reason. No calculations are necessary.

25. **Diversification** Based on a conversation with her husband, Grace is considering selling the $100,000 of ABC stock and acquiring $100,000 of XYZ Company common stock instead. XYZ stock has the same expected return and standard deviation as ABC stock. Her husband comments, "It doesn't matter whether you keep all of the ABC stock or replace it with $100,000 of the XYZ stock." Are her husband's comments correct or incorrect? Justify your response.

Spreadsheet Problem

26. Calculating Correlation You are given the following information concerning a stock and the market:

	Returns	
Year	Market	Stock
1998	34%	49%
1999	27	24
2000	11	6
2001	19	10
2002	−12	−25
2003	8	3

Calculate the average return and standard deviation for the market and the stock. Next, calculate the correlation between the stock and the market. Use a spreadsheet to calculate your answers.

STANDARD &POOR'S

S&P Problems

www.mhhe.com/edumarketinsight

Note: These problems can be calculated manually, but a spreadsheet program such as Excel is recommended for use in calculations.

1. **Return Correlations** Go to the "Excel Analytics" link for Kellogg (K) and Delta Airlines (DAL) and download the monthly adjusted stock prices. Copy the monthly returns for each stock into a new spreadsheet. Calculate the correlation between the two stock returns. Would you expect a higher or lower correlation if you had chosen American Airlines instead of Kellogg? What is the standard deviation of a portfolio 75 percent invested in K and 25 percent in DAL? What about a portfolio equally invested in the two stocks? What about a portfolio 25 percent in K and 75 percent in DAL?

2. **Beta** Go to the "Excel Analytics" link for Harley-Davidson (HD) and download the monthly adjusted stock prices. Copy the monthly returns for Harley-Davidson and the monthly S&P 500 returns into a new spreadsheet. Calculate the beta of Harley-Davidson for the entire period of data available. Now download the monthly stock prices for Emerson Electric (EMR) and calculate the beta for this company. Are the betas similar? Would you have expected the beta of Harley-Davidson to be higher or lower than the beta for Emerson Electric? Why?

What's on the Web?

1. **Expected Return** You want to find the expected return for Home Depot using the CAPM. First you need the market risk premium. Go to money.cnn.com, follow the "Bonds & Rates" link and the "Latest Rates" link. Find the current interest rate for three-month Treasury bills. Use the average large-company stock return in Chapter 1 to calculate the market risk premium. Next, go to finance.yahoo.com, enter the ticker symbol HD for Home Depot, and follow the "Profile" link. In the Statistics at a Glance section you will find the beta for Home Depot. What is the expected return for Home Depot using the CAPM? What assumptions have you made to arrive at this number?

www.mhhe.com/cj3e

2. **Portfolio Beta**   You have decided to invest in an equally-weighted portfolio consisting of American Express, Procter & Gamble, Johnson and Johnson, and United Technologies, and you need to find the beta of your portfolio. Go to finance.yahoo.com and follow the "Global Symbol Lookup" link to find the ticker symbols for each of these companies. Next, go back to finance.yahoo.com, enter one of the ticker symbols, and get a stock quote. Follow the "Profile" link to find the beta for this company. You will then need to find the beta for each of the companies. What is the beta for your portfolio?

3. **Beta**   Which stock has the highest and lowest beta? Go to www.hoovers.com and follow the "StockScreener" link. Enter 0 as the maximum beta and enter search. How many stocks currently have a beta less than 0? Which stock has the lowest beta? Go back to the stock screener and enter 3 as the minimum value. How many stocks have a beta greater than 3? What about 4? Which stock has the highest beta?

4. **Security Market Line**   Go to finance.yahoo.com and enter the ticker symbol GE for General Electric. Follow the "Profile" link to get the beta for the company. Next, follow the "Research" link to find the estimated price in 12 months according to market analysts. Using the current share price and the mean target price, compute the expected return for this stock. Don't forget to include the expected dividend payments over the next year. Now go to money.cnn.com, follow the "Bonds & Rates" link, then the "Latest Rates" link, and find the current interest rate for three-month Treasury bills. Using this information, calculate the expected return on the market using the reward-to-risk ratio. Does this number make sense? Why or why not?

Chapter 13

Performance Evaluation and Risk Management

"It is not the return on my investment that I am concerned about; it is the return of my investment!"

–Will Rogers

"The stock market will fluctuate!"

–J. P. Morgan

Humorist Will Rogers expressed concern about "the return of [his] investment." Famed financier J. P. Morgan, when asked by a reporter what he thought the stock market would do, replied, "The stock market will fluctuate!" Both Will Rogers and J. P. Morgan understood a basic fact of investing—investors holding risky assets worry: How well are my investments doing? How much money am I making (or losing)? and What are my chances of incurring a significant loss? ∎

This chapter examines methods to deal with two related problems faced by investors in risky assets. These are (1) evaluating risk-adjusted investment performance and (2) assessing and managing the risks involved with specific investment strategies. Both subjects have come up previously in our text, but we have deferred a detailed discussion of them until now.

We first consider the problem of performance evaluation. Specifically, suppose we have investment returns data for several portfolios covering a recent period, and we wish to evaluate how well these portfolios have performed relative to other portfolios or some investment benchmark. The need for this form of scrutiny arises in a number of situations, including:

- An investor wishing to choose a mutual fund wants to first compare the investment performance of several dozen candidate funds.
- A pension fund administrator wants to select a money manager and thus needs to compare the investment performance of a group of money managers.
- An employer wants to compare the performance of several investment companies before selecting one for inclusion in her company-sponsored 401(k) retirement plan.

In the first section of this chapter, we examine several useful evaluation measures of portfolio performance and discuss how they might be applied to these and similar situations.

In the second part of the chapter, we discuss the important problem of risk management from the perspective of an investor or money manager concerned with the possibility of a large loss. Specifically, we examine methods to assess the probabilities and magnitudes of losses we might expect to experience during a set future time period. These risk assessment techniques are commonly employed in a number of situations, including:

- A New York Stock Exchange specialist wants to know how much of a loss is possible with a 5 percent probability during the coming day's trading from the specialist firm's inventory.
- The foreign currency manager of a commercial bank wants to know how much of a loss is possible with a 2 percent probability on the bank's foreign currency portfolio during the coming week.
- A futures exchange clearinghouse wants to know how much margin funds should be deposited by exchange members to cover extreme losses that might occur with a "once in a century" probability.

Methods used to assess risk in these and similar scenarios fall into the category commonly referred to as "Value-at-Risk." Value-at-Risk techniques are widely applied by commercial banks, securities firms, and other financial institutions to assess and understand the risk exposure of portfolios under their management.

13.1 Performance Evaluation

Investors have a natural (and very rational) interest in how well particular investments have done. This is true whether the investor manages his or her own portfolio or has money managed by a professional. Concern with investment performance motivates the topic of **performance evaluation**. In general terms, performance evaluation focuses on assessing how well a money manager achieves high returns balanced with acceptable risks.

Going back to our discussion of efficient markets in Chapter 8, we raised the question of risk-adjusted performance and whether anyone can consistently earn an "excess" return, thereby "beating the market." The standard example is an evaluation of investment performance achieved by the manager of a mutual fund. Such a performance evaluation is more than an academic exercise, since its purpose is to help

performance evaluation The assessment of how well a money manager achieves a balance between high returns and acceptable risks.

investors decide whether they would entrust investment funds with this fund manager. Our goal here is to introduce you to the primary tools used to make this assessment.

Performance Evaluation Measures

A variety of measures are used to evaluate investment performance. Here, we examine three of the best-known and most popular measures: the Sharpe ratio, the Treynor ratio, and Jensen's alpha. But before we do so, let us first briefly discuss a naive measure of performance evaluation—the **raw return** on a portfolio.

raw return States the total percentage return on an investment with no adjustment for risk or comparison to any benchmark.

The raw return on an investment portfolio, here denoted by R_p, is simply the total percentage return on the portfolio with no adjustment for risk or comparison to any benchmark. Calculating percentage returns was discussed in Chapter 1. The fact that a raw portfolio return does not reflect any consideration of risk suggests that its usefulness is limited when making investment decisions. After all, risk is important to almost every investor.

The Sharpe Ratio

A basic measure of investment performance that includes an adjustment for risk is the Sharpe ratio, originally proposed by Nobel laureate William F. Sharpe. The **Sharpe ratio** is computed as a portfolio's risk premium divided by the standard deviation of the portfolio's return:

Sharpe ratio Measures investment performance as the ratio of portfolio risk premium over portfolio return standard deviation.

$$\text{Sharpe ratio} = \frac{R_p - R_f}{\sigma_p} \qquad (13.1)$$

In this case, the portfolio risk premium is the raw portfolio return less a risk-free return, that is, $R_p - R_f$, which we know is the basic reward for bearing risk. The return standard deviation, σ_p, is a measure of risk, which we discussed in Chapter 1 and again in Chapter 11.

Visit Professor Sharpe at www.stanford.edu/~wfsharpe

More precisely, return standard deviation is a measure of the *total* risk (as opposed to systematic risk) for a security or a portfolio. Thus, the Sharpe ratio is a reward-to-risk ratio that focuses on total risk. Because total risk is used to make the adjustment, the Sharpe ratio is probably most appropriate for evaluating relatively diversified portfolios.

LOOK SHARPE

EXAMPLE 13.1

Over a recent three-year period, the average annual return on a portfolio was 20 percent, and the annual return standard deviation for the portfolio was 25 percent. During the same period, the average return on 90-day Treasury bills was 5 percent. What is the Sharpe ratio for this portfolio during this three-year period?

Referring to the equation above, we calculate

$$\text{Sharpe ratio} = \frac{.20 - .05}{.25} = .6$$

This indicates that the Sharpe ratio of portfolio excess return to total risk is .6.

The Treynor Ratio

Another standard measure of investment performance that includes an adjustment for systematic risk is the Treynor ratio (or index), originally suggested by Jack L. Treynor.

Treynor ratio
Measures investment performance as the ratio of portfolio risk premium over portfolio beta.

The **Treynor ratio** is computed as a portfolio's risk premium divided by the portfolio's beta coefficient:

$$\text{Treynor ratio} = \frac{R_p - R_f}{\beta_p} \qquad (13.2)$$

As with the Sharpe ratio, the Treynor ratio is a reward-to-risk ratio. The key difference is that the Treynor ratio looks at systematic risk only, not total risk.

THE TREYNOR RATIO

EXAMPLE 13.2

Over a three-year period, the average return on a portfolio was 20 percent, and the beta for the portfolio was 1.25. During the same period, the average return on 90-day Treasury bills was 5 percent. What is the Treynor ratio for this portfolio during this period?

Referring to the Treynor ratio equation above, we calculate

$$\text{Treynor ratio} = \frac{.20 - .05}{1.25} = .12$$

This reveals that the Treynor ratio of portfolio excess return to portfolio beta is .12.

You may recall that we saw the Treynor ratio in our previous chapter. There we said that in an active, competitive market, a strong argument can be made that all assets (and portfolios of those assets) should have the same Treynor ratio, that is, the same reward-to-risk ratio, where "risk" refers to systematic risk. To the extent that they don't, then there is evidence that at least some portfolios have earned excess returns.

Jensen's Alpha

Jensen's alpha
Measures investment performance as the raw portfolio return less the return predicted by the Capital Asset Pricing Model.

A third common measure of investment performance that draws on capital asset pricing theory for its formulation is Jensen's alpha, proposed by Michael C. Jensen. **Jensen's alpha** is computed as the raw portfolio return less the expected portfolio return predicted by the Capital Asset Pricing Model (CAPM).

Recall from our previous chapter that, according to the CAPM, the expected return on a portfolio, $E(R_p)$, can be written as:

$$E(R_p) = R_f + [E(R_M) - R_f] \times \beta_p \qquad (13.3)$$

To compute Jensen's alpha, we compare the actual return, R_p, to the predicted return. The difference is the alpha, denoted α_p:

$$\alpha_p = R_p - E(R_p)$$

$$= R_p - \{R_f + [E(R_M) - R_f] \times \beta_p\} \qquad (13.4)$$

Jensen's alpha is easy to understand. It is simply the excess return above or below the security market line, and, in this sense, it can be interpreted as a measure of how much the portfolio "beat the market." This interpretation is illustrated in Figure 13.1, which shows a portfolio with a positive (A), zero (B), and negative (C) alpha, respectively. As shown, a positive alpha is a good thing because the portfolio has a relatively high return given its level of systematic risk.

FIGURE 13.1

Jensen's Alpha

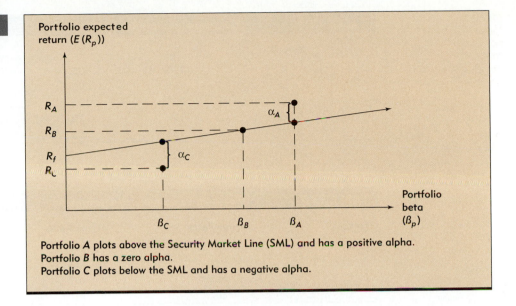

Portfolio A plots above the Security Market Line (SML) and has a positive alpha.
Portfolio B has a zero alpha.
Portfolio C plots below the SML and has a negative alpha.

JENSEN'S ALPHA

EXAMPLE 13.3

Over a three-year period, the average annual return on a portfolio was 20 percent, and the beta for the portfolio was 1.25. During the same period, the average annual return on 90-day Treasury bills was 5 percent, and the average return on the market portfolio was 15 percent. What is Jensen's alpha for this portfolio during this period?

Referring to the Jensen-alpha equation above, we calculate

$$.20 - [.05 + (.15 - .05)1.25] = .025$$

This shows that the portfolio had an alpha measure of portfolio excess return of 2.5 percent.

Check This

13.1a What is the Sharpe ratio of portfolio performance?

13.1b What is the Treynor ratio of portfolio performance?

13.1c What is Jensen's alpha?

13.1d Why can Jensen's alpha be interpreted as measuring by how much an investment portfolio beat the market?

13.2 Comparing Performance Measures

Table 13.1 presents investment performance data for three risky portfolios, A, B, and C, along with return data for the market portfolio and a risk-free portfolio, denoted by M and F, respectively. Based on the performance data in Table 13.1, Table 13.2

TABLE 13.1	Investment Performance Data		
Portfolio	R_p	σ_p	β_p
A	12%	40%	.5
B	15%	30%	.75
C	20%	22%	1.4
M	15%	15%	1
F	5%	0%	0

TABLE 13.2	Portfolio Performance Measurement		
Portfolio	Sharpe Ratio	Treynor Ratio	Jensen Alpha
A	.175	.14	2%
B	.333	.133	2.5%
C	.682	.107	1%
M	.667	.10	0%

provides computed performance measures for portfolios A, B, and C, along with a market portfolio, M. The market portfolio is a benchmark of investment performance. Often the familiar S&P 500 index is the adopted proxy for the market portfolio.

As shown in Table 13.2, the Sharpe ratio ranks the three risky portfolios in the ascending order of performance A, B, and C. By contrast, the Treynor ratio ranks these three risky portfolios in the reversed order of performance C, B, and A. Jensen's alpha yields another portfolio ranking altogether, with the ascending order of performance C, A, and B.

The example above illustrates that the three performance measures can yield substantially different performance rankings. The fact that each of the three performance measures can produce such different results leaves us with the burning question: "Which performance measure should we use to evaluate portfolio performance?"

Well, the simple answer is: "it depends." If you wish to select a performance measure to evaluate an entire portfolio held by an investor, then the Sharpe ratio is appropriate. But if you wish to choose a performance measure to individually evaluate securities or portfolios for possible inclusion in a broader (or "master") portfolio, then either the Treynor ratio or Jensen's alpha is appropriate.

In broader terms, all three measures have strengths and weaknesses. Jensen's alpha is, as we have seen, easy to interpret. Comparing Jensen's alpha and the Treynor ratio, they are really very similar. The only difference is that the Treynor ratio standardizes everything, including any excess return, relative to beta. If you were to take Jensen's alpha and divide it by beta, then you would have a Jensen-Treynor alpha, which measures excess return relative to beta.

A common weakness of the Jensen and Treynor measures is that both require a beta estimate. As we discussed in our last chapter, betas from different sources can differ a lot, and, as a result, what appears to be a positive alpha might just be due to a mismeasured beta.

The Sharpe ratio has the advantage that no beta is necessary, and standard deviations can be calculated unambiguously. The drawback is that total risk is frequently not

WORK THE WEB

The various performance measures we've discussed are commonly used to evaluate mutual funds or, more accurately, mutual fund managers. For example, the information below concerns the Fidelity Low-Priced Stock Fund, which is a small-cap value fund. We obtained the numbers from www.morningstar.com by entering the fund's ticker symbol (FLPSX) and selecting "Morningstar Ratings" under the "Ratings" drop-down menu. By the way, you'll see the abbreviation "MPT" in this context quite a bit. MPT is an acronym for "Modern Portfolio Theory," which is the general label for measures related to Markowitz-type portfolio analysis and the CAPM.

For this fund, the beta is .65, so the degree of market risk is relatively low. The fund's alpha is 19.78 percent, an extremely high number. The fund's standard deviation is 15.57 percent. The mean reported, 8.31 percent, is actually the geometric average return for the fund over the past three years. The Sharpe ratio for the fund is .32. Of course, we can't judge this value in isolation, but at least we know it is positive. Other measures of risk are reported here, but they are specific to Morningstar. To learn more, visit the website.

Morningstar Rating (Relative to Category)　　　　　03-31-03

	Morningstar Return	Morningstar Risk	Morningstar Rating™
3-Year	High	Low	★★★★★
5-Year	Above Average	Low	★★★★★
10-Year	High	Low	★★★★★
Overall	High	Low	★★★★★

Morningstar Category: Small Blend 　　　　　Click here to see our Methodology

Volatility Measurements　　　Trailing 3-Yr through 03-31-03 | *Trailing 5-Yr through 03-31-03

Standard Deviation	15.57	Sharpe Ratio	0.32
Mean	8.31	Bear Market Decile Rank*	2

Modern Portfolio Theory Statistics　　　　　Trailing 3-Yr through 03-31-03

	Standard Index	Best Fit Index
	S&P 500	Russell 2000 Value
R-Squared	64	85
Beta	0.65	0.76
Alpha	19.78	3.92

what really matters. However, for a relatively well-diversified portfolio, most of the risk is systematic, so there's not much difference between total risk and systematic risk. For this reason, for doing things like evaluating mutual funds, the Sharpe ratio is probably the most commonly used. Furthermore, if a mutual fund is not very diversified, then its standard deviation would be larger, resulting in a smaller Sharpe ratio. Thus, the Sharpe ratio, in effect, penalizes a portfolio for being undiversified.

To see how these performance measures are used in practice, have a look at our nearby *Work the Web* box, which shows some actual numbers for a mutual fund.

PICKING PORTFOLIOS

EXAMPLE 13.4

Suppose you are restricted to investing all of your money in only a single portfolio from among the choices A, B, and C presented in Table 13.1. Which portfolio should you choose?

Since you can only select a single portfolio, the Sharpe-ratio measure of portfolio performance should be used. Referring to Table 13.2, we see that portfolio C has the highest Sharpe ratio of excess return per unit of total risk. Therefore, portfolio C should be chosen.

PICKING PORTFOLIOS AGAIN

EXAMPLE 13.5

Suppose you are considering whether portfolios A, B, and C presented in Table 13.1 should be included in a master portfolio. Should you select one, two, or all three portfolios for inclusion in your master portfolio?

Since you are selecting portfolios for inclusion in a master portfolio, either the Treynor ratio or Jensen's alpha should be used. Suppose you decide to consider any portfolio that outperforms the market portfolio M, based on either the Treynor ratio or Jensen's alpha. Referring to Table 13.2, we see that all three portfolios have Treynor ratios and Jensen alphas greater than the market portfolio. Therefore, you decide to include all three portfolios in your master portfolio.

Check This

13.2a   Explain the difference between systematic risk measured by beta and total risk measured by standard deviation. When are they essentially the same?

13.2b   Alter the returns data in Table 13.1 so that portfolios A, B, and C all have a raw return of 15 percent. Which among these three portfolios then have a Treynor ratio or Jensen alpha greater than that of the market portfolio M?

Sharpe-Optimal Portfolios

In this section, we show how to obtain a funds allocation with the highest possible Sharpe ratio. Such a portfolio is said to be "Sharpe optimal." The method is closely related to the procedure of obtaining a Markowitz efficient frontier discussed in Chapter 11. This is no surprise, as both methods are used to achieve an optimal balance of risk and return for investment portfolios.

To illustrate the connection, have a look at Figure 13.2. This figure actually reproduces Figure 11.4, which shows the investment opportunity set of risk-return possibilities for a portfolio of two assets, a stock fund and a bond fund. Now the question is: "Of all of these possible portfolios, which one is Sharpe optimal?" To find out, consider the portfolio labeled A in the figure. Notice that we have drawn a straight line from the risk-free rate running through this point.

FIGURE 13.2

**The Sharpe-
Optimal Portfolio**

Portfolio *T* has the
highest Sharpe ratio of
any possible combination
of these two assets, so it
is Sharpe optimal.

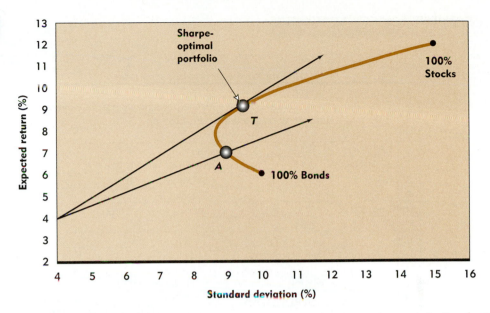

What is the slope of this straight line? As always, the slope of a straight line is the "rise over the run." In this case, the return rises from the risk-free rate, R_f, to the expected return on portfolio A, so the rise is $E(R_A) - R_f$. At the same time, risk moves from zero for a risk-free asset up to the standard deviation on portfolio A, so the run is $\sigma_A - 0 = \sigma_A$. Thus, the slope is $[E(R_A) - R_f]/\sigma_A$, which is just the Sharpe ratio for portfolio A.

So, the slope of a straight line drawn from the risk-free rate to a portfolio in Figure 13.2 tells us the Sharpe ratio for that portfolio. This is always the case, even if there are many assets, not just two. The problem of finding the Sharpe-optimal portfolio thus boils down to finding the line with the steepest slope. Looking again at Figure 13.2, we quickly figure out that the line with the steepest slope is always going to be the one that just touches (i.e., is tangent to) the investment opportunity set. We have labeled this portfolio *T* (for tangent).

We now have an interesting and important result. The Markowitz efficient frontier tells us which portfolios are efficient, but it does not tell us which of the efficient portfolios is the best. What Figure 13.2 shows is that, of those efficient portfolios, one is the very best, at least in the sense of being Sharpe optimal.

To illustrate actually finding the Sharpe optimal portfolio, recall from Chapter 11 that the returns of the stock and bond funds are 12 percent and 6 percent. The standard deviations are 15 percent and 10 percent, respectively, and the correlation is .10. From our discussion in Chapter 11, we know that the expected return on a portfolio of two assets is given by:

$$E(R_P) = x_S E(R_S) + x_B E(R_B)$$

where x_S and x_B are the percentages invested in the stock and bond fund, respectively. Also from Chapter 11, the variance on a portfolio of these two assets is:

$$\sigma_P^2 = x_S^2 \sigma_S^2 + x_B^2 \sigma_B^2 + 2x_S x_B \sigma_S \sigma_B \text{Corr}(R_S, R_B)$$

Putting it all together, the Sharpe ratio for our two-asset portfolio looks like this:

$$\frac{E(R_P) - R_f}{\sigma_P} = \frac{x_S E(R_S) + x_B E(R_B) - R_f}{\sqrt{x_S^2 \sigma_S^2 + x_B^2 \sigma_B^2 + 2x_S x_B \sigma_S \sigma_B \text{Corr}(R_S, R_B)}} \qquad (13.5)$$

SPREADSHEET ANALYSIS

	A	B	C	D	E	F	G	H
1			**Solving for the optimal Sharpe ratio**					
2								
3	Given the data inputs below, solve for the portfolio weight Xs yielding the optimal							
4	(maximum) Sharpe ratio. Use the Solver function.							
5								
6	ER(S) =	0.12		Xs =	0.700			
7	STD(S) =	0.15		ER(P) =	0.102			
8	ER(B) =	0.06		STD(P) =	0.112			
9	STD(B) =	0.1		Sharpe				
10	Corr(S,B) =	0.1		ratio =	0.553			
11	Rf =	0.04						
12								
13								
14								
15		ER(P)	= \$E\$6*\$B\$6+(1−\$E\$6)*\$B\$8					
16		STD(P)	= SQRT((\$E\$6*\$B\$7)^2+((1−\$E\$6)*\$B\$9)^2					
17			+2*\$E\$6*(1−\$E\$6)*\$B\$7*\$B\$9*\$B\$10)					
18		Sharpe	= (\$E\$7−\$B\$11)/\$E\$8					

Our job is to find the values of x_S and x_B that make this ratio as large as possible. This looks like a tough job, but, as our nearby *Spreadsheet Analysis* box shows, it can be done relatively easily. As shown there, assuming a risk-free interest rate of 4 percent, the highest possible Sharpe ratio is .553 based on a 70–30 mix between stocks and bonds.

Check This

13.2c What is a Sharpe-optimal portfolio?

13.2d Among the many Markowitz efficient portfolios, which one is Sharpe optimal?

13.3 Investment Risk Management

investment risk management
Concerns a money manager's control over investment risks, usually with respect to potential short-run losses.

In the first part of this chapter, we discussed performance evaluation within a framework of optimizing the trade-off between risk and return for an investment portfolio. In the remainder of this chapter, we examine **investment risk management** within the framework of a money manager's concern over potential losses for an investment portfolio within a specific time horizon. We focus on what is known as the Value-at-Risk approach. However, risk can be viewed in many different ways, and, for some alternative viewpoints, we suggest reading the nearby *Investment Updates* box.

Value-at-Risk (VaR)
Assesses risk by stating the probability of a loss a portfolio might experience within a fixed time horizon with a specified probability.

Value-at-Risk

An important goal of this chapter is to learn how to assess portfolio risk using **Value-at-Risk**. In essence, the Value-at-Risk (usually abbreviated VaR) method involves evaluating the probability of a significant loss. The basic approach we describe here is widely used by many different financial institutions.

VᴀR RISK STATISTIC

EXAMPLE 13.6

You agree with J. P. Morgan that the stock market will fluctuate and have become concerned with how these fluctuations might affect your stock portfolio. Having read about the VaR method for measuring investment risk, you decide to apply it to your portfolio.

Suppose you believe that there is a 5 percent chance of a return of −18 percent or worse in the coming week. Mathematically, this risk assessment can be stated as:

$$Prob(R_p \leq -18\%) = 5\%$$

Taken together, this −18 percent or worse expected loss and 5 percent probability form a VaR "statistic" for your stock portfolio.

The VaR measure of investment risk is closely related to something we discussed way back in Chapter 1. There we said that if the returns on an investment follow a **normal distribution**, then we can state the probability that a portfolio's return will be within a certain range. Since a normal distribution is completely specified by its mean and standard deviation, these are all that we need to state this probability.

For example, suppose you own an S&P 500 index fund. What is the probability of a return of −7 percent or worse in a particular year? As we saw in Chapter 1, since 1925, the return on the S&P 500 index has averaged 13 percent per year with a standard deviation of about 20 percent per year. A return of −7 percent is exactly one standard deviation below the average (.13 − .20 = −.07). We know from Chapter 1 (and basic statistics) that the odds of being within one standard deviation are about 2/3 or .67. Being *within* one standard deviation of the mean of .13 means being *between* .13 plus .20 and .13 minus .20, i.e., between −.07 and +.33.

If the odds of being within this range are 2/3, then the odds of being *outside* this range are about 1/3. Finally, if we are outside this range, then half of the time we'll be above and half of the time we'll be below. Half of 1/3 is 1/6, so we'll experience a return of −.07 or worse 1/6, or about 17 percent, of the time.

Putting it together, if you own an S&P 500 index fund, this risk assessment can be stated:

$$Prob(R_p \leq -.07) = 17\%$$

Your VaR statistic is thus a return of −.07 or worse with a probability of 17 percent. By the way, here is an important note: When we say a loss of −.07 or worse, we mean that, *one year from now*, your portfolio value is down by 7 percent or more.

normal distribution A statistical model for assessing probabilities related to many phenomena, including security returns.

Learn all about VaR at www.gloriamundi.org

Check This

13.3a   What is the probability of realizing a portfolio return one or more standard deviations below the expected mean return?

13.3b   What is the probability of realizing a portfolio return two or more standard deviations below the expected mean return?

13.3c   Your portfolio has a mean return of 15 percent and a return standard deviation of 25 percent. What portfolio return is two standard deviations below the mean?

How to Play the Game of Risk When Investing Your Money

If we want our portfolios to go up, we need to spend a little time looking down. Take too much risk with our investments, and we could end up selling in a panic at the worst possible time. Take too little risk, and we will likely clock unnecessarily low returns. So how do we settle on the right amount of risk? Here are some thoughts on this messy notion:

Looking for Danger

High risk is meant to lead to high returns. But what do we mean by "high risk"? If we bet all our money on a couple of hot stocks, we are undoubtedly taking a ton of risk. But there is every chance we will lose our shirts. Instead, when academics talk about risk getting rewarded, they are referring to market risk. When investing in stocks, we can eliminate the risk of owning any one stock by spreading our money across a fistful of different companies. But even if we do that, we will still take a hit if the broad market declines. This market risk, which we can't diversify away, is the risk we get rewarded for taking.

What does this mean for our portfolios? If we want higher long-run returns, we need to take more market risk, by keeping less in conservative investments and more in stocks. But to be confident of getting our reward, we need to ensure that our stock portfolios are well diversified. This diversification has the added advantage of bolstering our tenacity. Have shares just tumbled 20%? If all we own are a couple of stocks, we

will no doubt fret over whether our shares will ever bounce back. But if we own a broadly diversified portfolio, we will have greater confidence that our stocks should eventually generate decent gains.

Looking Up

To gauge risk, investment experts have traditionally looked at an investment's volatility, as reflected in statistical measures such as standard deviation and beta. Standard deviation is a gauge of how far an investment's results have strayed from its average performance, while beta measures an investment's price gyrations relative to a broad market index.

But investors often dismiss such statistical measures, complaining that they aren't bothered when volatility works to their advantage and generates big gains. Instead, what they care about is losses, and it is these losses that risk measures should seek to capture. But in fact, upside volatility is a great measure of downside risk. Consider technology stocks. Their dismal performance in the recent bear market was foretold by their equally astonishing rise during the late 1990s bull market.

Looking Out

When measuring risk, some experts don't just look at volatility. They also consider longer-run performance. For

(continued)

13.4 More on Computing Value-at-Risk

In this section we extend our discussion of computing VaR. Our goal is mainly to examine how to evaluate horizons that are shorter or longer than one year. The easiest way to do this is to take our earlier example concerning the S&P 500 and extend it a bit.

Once again, suppose you own an S&P 500 index fund. What is the probability of a loss of 30 percent or more over the next *two* years? To answer, we need to know the average two-year return and the average two-year return standard deviation. Getting the average two-year return is easy enough; we just have to double the one-year average. So, the two-year average return is $2 \times .13 = .26$, or 26 percent.

The two-year standard deviation is a little trickier. The two-year *variance* is just double the one-year variance. In our case, the one-year variance is $.20^2 = .04$, and the two-year variance is thus .08. As always, to get the two-year standard deviation, we take the square root of this, which is .28, or 28 percent. The main thing to notice is that the two-year standard deviation is not just double the one-year number. In fact, if you look at it, the two-year number is equal to the one-year number multiplied by the square root of 2, or 1.414.

instance, if we hold stocks for 20 years, we are unlikely to lose money and we will almost certainly outpace bonds. That has led some commentators to argue that stocks are less risky than bonds. But this is nonsense. If we look out far enough, the highest-returning investments will always appear to be the least risky. Indeed, I fear such foolishness could lead folks to bet far too much on stocks.

"Over a long enough period, risk and return become the same thing," says William Bernstein, author of "The Intelligent Asset Allocator" and an investment adviser in North Bend, Ore. "The reason stocks have seemed so low risk is because the returns have been so high. But the high returns may not be true going forward." Moreover, not everybody has a 20-year time horizon, and not many investors can ignore short-term market turmoil. "People feel risk in their gut in the short term and in their brain in the long term," Mr. Bernstein says. "Unfortunately, they react to their gut."

Looking Pale

How much risk can each of us stomach? Mutual-fund companies and investment advisers have questionnaires that try to help folks figure out whether they are aggressive or conservative investors. But often, people later discover that their risk tolerance is far higher or lower. What to do? Eleanor Blayney, a financial planner in McLean, Va., says investors should spend time studying their own investment history. "The best indicator of risk tolerance is past behavior," she argues. In particular, Ms. Blayney

likes to ask clients what they believe their best and worst investment decisions were. She says aggressive investors tend to fret about missing out on gains, while conservative investors tend to dwell on their losses.

Looking for Safety

Even if we set out to take a lot of risk, we often gravitate toward investments we perceive to be safe. For instance, we may choose to invest a hefty amount in the stock market. But when it comes to picking individual stocks, we often select companies we view as safe. Indeed, if we didn't think a stock was a pretty safe bet, we probably wouldn't have the courage to buy.

Result? We tend to invest in widely admired corporations or those shares that have lately performed well. Meanwhile, we shy away from companies that have had financial problems or have suffered steep share-price declines, even though studies suggest that these tarnished companies often generate market-beating gains. "People will accept that risk gets rewarded if they are forced to listen to the finance-professor spiel," says Hersh Shefrin, a finance professor at Santa Clara University in California. "They will accept the notion intellectually. But emotionally, they associate good stocks with safe stocks."

Source: Jonathan Clements, *The Wall Streeet Journal*, February 2, 2002. © 2002 Dow Jones & Company, Inc. All Rights Reserved Worldwide.

Now we can answer our question. A two-year loss of 30 percent is equal to the two-year average return of 26 percent less two standard deviations: $.26 - 2 \times .28 = -.30$. From Chapter 1, we know that the odds of being within two standard deviations are 95 percent, so the odds of being outside this range are 5 percent. The odds of being on the bad side (the loss side) are half that, namely, 2.5 percent.

VAR RISK STATISTIC

EXAMPLE 13.7

The Ned Kelley Hedge Fund focuses on investing in bank and transportation companies in Australia with above-average risk. The average annual return is 15 percent with an annual return standard deviation of 50 percent. What loss level can we expect over a two-year investment horizon with a probability of .17?

We assume a two-year expected return of 30 percent. The one-year variance is $.50^2 = .25$, so the two-year variance is .50. Taking the square root, we get a two-year standard deviation of .7071, or

(continued)

70.71 percent. A loss probability of .17 corresponds to one standard deviation below the mean, so the answer to our question is .30 − .7071 = −.4071, a substantial loss. We can write this succinctly as

$$Prob(R_P \leq -40.71\%) = 17\%$$

Notice that there is a 17 percent chance of a 40.71 percent loss or worse over the next two years.

VaR RISK STATISTIC

EXAMPLE 13.8

Going back to the Ned Kelley Hedge Fund in our previous example, what loss level might we expect over six months with a probability of .17?

The six-month expected return is half of 15 percent, or 7.5 percent. The six-month standard deviation is $.5 \times \sqrt{1/2} = .3536$. So the answer to our question is $.075 - .3536 = -.2786$. Again, we can write this succinctly as

$$Prob(R_P \leq -27.86\%) = 17\%$$

Thus there is a 17 percent chance of a 27.86 percent loss or worse over the next six months.

A ONE-IN-TWENTY LOSS

EXAMPLE 13.9

For the Ned Kelley Hedge Fund specified in our previous examples, what is the expected loss for the coming year with a probability of 5 percent?

In this case, with an annual return mean of 15 percent and an annual return standard deviation of 50 percent, set $T = 1$ for a one-year time horizon and calculate this VaR statistic:

$$Prob[R_{P1} \leq E(R_P) \times 1 - 1.645\sigma_P \times \sqrt{1}] = Prob(R_{P,1} \leq 15\% - 1.645 \times 50\%)$$
$$= Prob(R_{P,1} \leq -67.25\%) = 5\%$$

Thus we can expect a loss of −67.25 percent or worse over the next year with a 5 percent probability.

A ONE-IN-A-HUNDRED LOSS

EXAMPLE 13.10

For the Ned Kelley Hedge Fund specified in our previous examples, what is the expected loss for the coming month with a 1 percent probability?

Setting $T = 1/12$ for a one-month time horizon, we calculate this VaR statistic:

$$Prob[R_{PT} \leq E(R_P) \times 1/12 - 2.326\sigma_P \times \sqrt{1/12}] = Prob(R_{PT} \leq 1.25\% - 2.326 \times 50\% \times .2887)$$
$$= Prob(R_{PT} \leq -32.32\%) = 1\%$$

Thus we can expect a loss of −32.32 percent or more with a 1 percent probability over the next month.

In general, if we let T stand for the number of years, then the expected return on a portfolio over T years, $E(R_{p,T})$ can be written as:

$$E(R_{p,T}) = E(R_p) \times T \tag{13.6}$$

Similarly, the standard deviation can be written as:

$$\sigma_{p,T} = \sigma_p \times \sqrt{T} \tag{13.7}$$

If the time period is less than a year, the T is just a fraction of a year.

When you do a VaR analysis, you have to pick the time horizon and loss level probability. You can pick any probability you want, of course, but the most common are 1, 2.5, and 5 percent. We know that 2.5 percent, which is half of 5 percent, corresponds to two standard deviations (actually 1.96 to be more precise) below the expected return. To get the 1 percent and 5 percent numbers, you would need to find an ordinary "z" table to tell you the number of standard deviations. We'll save you the trouble. The 1 percent level is 2.326 standard deviations below the average, and the 5 percent level is 1.645 "sigmas" below.

Check out risk grades at www.riskmetrics.com

Wrapping up our discussion, the VaR statistics for these three levels can be summarized as follows:

$$Prob(R_{p,T} \leq E(R_p) \times T - 2.326 \times \sigma_p \sqrt{T}) = 1\% \tag{13.8}$$

$$Prob(R_{p,T} \leq E(R_p) \times T - 1.96 \times \sigma_p \sqrt{T}) = 2.5\%$$

$$Prob(R_{p,T} \leq E(R_p) \times T - 1.645 \times \sigma_p \sqrt{T}) = 5\%$$

Notice that if T, the number of years, is equal to 1, the 1 percent level corresponds to once in a century. Similarly, 5 percent is once every 20 years, and 2.5 percent is once every 40 years.

As an application of Value-at-Risk, consider the problem of determining VaR statistics for a Sharpe-optimal stock and bond portfolio. As with any VaR problem for a portfolio, remember that the key to the problem is to first determine the expected return and standard deviation for the portfolio. From our discussion in Chapter 11 and earlier in this chapter, we know that the expected return and standard deviation of a stock and bond portfolio are specified by these two equations:

$$E(R_P) = x_S E(R_S) + x_B E(R_B)$$

$$\sigma_P = \sqrt{x_S^2 \sigma_S^2 + x_B^2 \sigma_B^2 + 2 x_S x_B \sigma_S \sigma_B \text{Corr}(R_S, R_B)}$$

Thus the problem of calculating VaR statistics for a Sharpe-optimal portfolio is the same for any portfolio once the appropriate portfolio weights are determined.

VAR FOR A SHARPE-OPTIMAL PORTFOLIO

EXAMPLE 13.11

Suppose you have the following expected return and risk information for stocks and bonds that will be used to form a Sharpe-optimal portfolio. Calculate VaR risk statistics for a one-year investment horizon.

$E(R_S) = .12$ $\sigma_S = .25$ $E(R_B) = .06$ $\sigma_B = .10$ $Corr(R_S, R_B) = .10$

(continued)

In the case of just two assets, stocks and bonds, the formulas for the portfolio weights for the optimal Sharpe portfolio are known to be these:

$$x_S = \frac{\sigma_B^2 \times E(R_S) - Corr(R_S R_B) \times \sigma_S \times \sigma_B \times E(R_B)}{\sigma_S^2 \times E(R_B) + \sigma_B^2 \times E(R_S) - [(E(R_S) + E(R_B)] \times Corr(R_S,R_B) \times \sigma_S \times \sigma_B \times E(R_B)}$$

$$x_B = 1 - x_S$$

$$x_S = \frac{.10^2 \times .12 - .10 \times .25 \times .10 \times .06}{.25^2 \times .06 + .10^2 \times .12 - (.12 + .06) \times .10 \times .25 \times .10 \times .06} = .2333$$

$$x_B = 1 - .2333 = .7667$$

Inserting the parameter values into the preceding formulas yields these optimal Sharpe portfolio weights for stocks and bonds:

$$E(R_P) = x_S E(R_S) + x_B E(R_B)$$

$$= .2333 \times .12 + .7667 \times .06 = .074$$

$$\sigma_P = \sqrt{x_S^2 \sigma_S^2 + x_B^2 \sigma_B^2 + 2x_S x_B \sigma_S \sigma_B Corr(R_S,R_B)}$$

$$= \sqrt{.2333^2 \times .25^2 + .7667^2 \times .10^2 + 2 \times .2333 \times .7667 \times .25 \times .10 \times .10} = .1009$$

With these results, we now have all the information needed to calculate the expected return and standard deviation for the Sharpe portfolio. Thus, with a one-year investment horizon, you obtain the following VaR risk statistics for 5 percent and 1 percent probabilities:

$$Prob[R_P \leq E(R_P) - 1.645\sigma_P] = Prob(R_P \leq 7.4\% - 1.645 \times 10.09\%)$$

$$= Prob(R_P \leq -9.198\%) = 5\%$$

$$Prob[R_P \leq E(R_P) - 2.326\sigma_P] = Prob(R_P \leq 7.4\% - 2.326 \times 10.09\%)$$

$$= Prob(R_P \leq -16.069\%) = 1\%$$

These indicate that we can expect a loss of -9.198 percent or more with a 5 percent probability and a loss of -16.069 percent with a 1 percent probability over the next year.

Check This

13.4a Your portfolio allocates 40 percent of funds to ABC stock and 60 percent to XYZ stock. ABC has a return mean and standard deviation of 15 percent and 20 percent, respectively. XYZ stock has a return mean and standard deviation of 25 percent and 30 percent, respectively. What is the portfolio return standard deviation if the return correlation between ABC and XYZ stocks is zero?

13.4b Based on your answer to the previous question, what is the smallest expected loss for your portfolio in the coming year with a probability of 1 percent? What is the smallest expected loss for your portfolio in the coming month with a probability of 5 percent?

13.5 Summary and Conclusions

In this chapter, we covered the related topics of performance measurement and risk management. Our goal with performance measurement is essentially to rank investments based on their risk-adjusted returns. We introduced and discussed the three most common tools used to do this: the Sharpe ratio, the Treynor ratio, and Jensen's alpha. As we saw, each has a somewhat different interpretation and which one is the most suitable depends on the specific question.

We then moved over to the issue of risk management by introducing you to the popular and widely used "Value-at-Risk," or VaR, approach. Here the goal is usually to assess the probability of a large loss within a fixed time frame. Investors use this tool both to better understand the risks of their existing portfolios and to assess the risks of potential investments.

Get Real

This chapter covered the essentials of performance evaluation and investment risk management. With thousands of mutual funds and investment companies competing for performance while trying to control risk, these topics are especially important. If you wish to learn more about these subjects, a good place to start is the Internet.

Some useful and informative websites on investment performance analysis are: Performance Analysis (www.andreassteiner.net/performanceanalysis), an informative website on investment performance analysis; Professor William F. Sharpe (www.stanford.edu/~wfsharpe), website of the Nobel laureate who created the Sharpe ratio; and FinPlan (www.finplan.com), a financial planning website with a useful section on investment performance analysis. You can also consult www.garp.com, which is the website of the Global Association of Risk Professionals (GARP), an independent organization of financial risk management practitioners and researchers.

Since financial institutions generally prefer that their risk profiles be kept private, a large part of the world of financial risk management is hidden from public view. Nevertheless, the field of risk management is large and growing. If you want to know more about this fascinating subject, some interesting websites that provide a wealth of information are: Gloria Mundi (www.gloriamundi.org), a site that tells you all about Value-at-Risk; Risk Metrics (www.riskmetrics.com), a leading risk management consultancy group; Margrabe (www.margrabe.com), the website of a professional risk management consultant; and E-Risks (www.erisks.com), a general resource site for risk management.

Key Terms

performance evaluation 430
raw return 431
Sharpe ratio 431
Treynor ratio 432

Jensen's alpha 432
investment risk management 438
Value-at-Risk (VaR) 438
normal distribution 439

Chapter Review Problems and Self-Test

1. **Performance Measures**   Compute Sharpe ratios, Treynor ratios, and Jensen alphas for portfolios A, B, and C based on the following returns data, where M and F stand for the market portfolio and risk-free rate, respectively:

Portfolio	R_P	σ_P	β_P
A	10%	30%	0.75
B	15%	25%	1.00
C	20%	40%	1.50
M	15%	15%	1.00
F	5%	0%	0.00

2. **Value-at-Risk (VaR)**   A portfolio manager believes her $100 million stock portfolio will have a 10 percent return standard deviation during the coming week and that her portfolio's returns are normally distributed. What is the probability of her losing $10 million or more? What is the dollar loss expected with a 5 percent probability? What is the dollar loss expected with a 1 percent probability?

Answers to Self-Test Problems

1. Using Equations 13.1, 13.2, 13.3 yields these performance measurement values:

Portfolio	Sharpe Ratio	Treynor Ratio	Jensen Alpha
A	.167	.0667	−2.5%
B	.400	.10	0%
C	.375	.10	0%
M	.667	.10	0%

2. Since a mean is not given but the time horizon is only one week, we can simply assume a mean of zero. Thus the probability of a $10 million or greater loss is the probability of a loss of one or more return standard deviations, which for a normal distribution is 15.87 percent. For a normal distribution, a realization 1.645 or more standard deviations below the mean occurs with a 5 percent probability, yielding a potential loss of at least 1.645 × $10 million = $16.45 million. For a normal distribution, a realization 2.326 or more standard deviations below the mean occurs with a 1 percent probability, yielding a potential loss of at least 2.326 × $10 million = $23.26 million.

Test Your Investment Quotient

1. **Beta and Standard Deviation**   Beta and standard deviation differ as risk measures in that beta measures
   a. Only unsystematic risk, whereas standard deviation measures total risk.
   b. Only systematic risk, whereas standard deviation measures total risk.
   c. Both systematic and unsystematic risk, whereas standard deviation measures only unsystematic risk.
   d. Both systematic and unsystematic risk, whereas standard deviation measures only systematic risk.

Answer Questions 2 through 8 based on the following information.

	Risk and Return Data		
Portfolio	Average Return	Standard Deviation	Beta
P	17%	20%	1.1
Q	24%	18%	2.1
R	11%	10%	0.5
S	16%	14%	1.5
S&P 500	14%	12%	1.0

A pension fund administrator wants to evaluate the performance of four portfolio managers. Each manager invests only in U.S. common stocks. During the most recent five-year period, the average annual total return on the S&P 500 was 14 percent, and the average annual rate on Treasury bills was 8 percent. The table above shows risk and return measures for each portfolio.

2. **Treynor Ratio**   The Treynor portfolio performance measure for Portfolio P is
   a. 8.18
   b. 7.62
   c. 6.00
   d. 5.33

3. **Sharpe Ratio**   The Sharpe portfolio performance measure for Portfolio Q is
   a. .45
   b. .89
   c. .30
   d. .57

4. **Jensen Alpha**   The Jensen alpha portfolio performance measure for Portfolio R is
   a. 2.4 percent
   b. 3.4 percent
   c. 0 percent
   d. −1 percent

5. **Treynor Ratio**   Which portfolio has the highest Treynor ratio?
   a. P
   b. Q
   c. R
   d. S

6. **Sharpe Ratio**   Which portfolio has the highest Sharpe ratio?
   a. P
   b. Q
   c. R
   d. S

7. **Jensen Alpha**   Which portfolio has the highest Jensen alpha?
   a. P
   b. Q
   c. R
   d. S

8. **Sharpe Ratio**   Assuming uncorrelated returns, the Sharpe ratio for a master portfolio with equal allocations to Portfolio S and Portfolio Q is
   a. .71

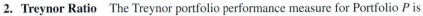

www.mhhe.com/cj3e

   b. 1.4
   c. .95
   d. 1.05

9. **Normal Distribution**   Given a data series that is normally distributed with a mean of 100 and a standard deviation of 10, about 95 percent of the numbers in the series will fall within

   a. 60 to 140
   b. 70 to 130
   c. 80 to 120
   d. 90 to 110

10. **Normal Distribution**   Given a data series that is normally distributed with a mean of 100 and a standard deviation of 10, about 99 percent of the numbers in the series will fall within

   a. 60 to 140
   b. 80 to 120
   c. 70 to 130
   d. 90 to 110

11. **Normal Distribution**   A normal distribution is completely specified by its

   a. Mean and correlation
   b. Variance and correlation
   c. Variance and standard deviation
   d. Mean and standard deviation

12. **Standard Normal Distribution**   A normal random variable is transformed into a standard normal random variable by

   a. Subtracting its mean and dividing by its standard deviation.
   b. Adding its mean and dividing by its standard deviation.
   c. Subtracting its mean and dividing by its variance.
   d. Adding its mean and multiplying by its standard deviation.

13. **Standard Normal Distribution**   The probability that a standard normal random variable is either less than -1 or greater than $+1$ is

   a. 2 percent
   b. 5 percent
   c. 10 percent
   d. 31.74 percent

14. **Standard Normal Distribution**   The probability that a standard normal random variable is either less than -1.96 or greater than $+1.96$ is approximately

   a. 2 percent
   b. 5 percent
   c. 10 percent
   d. 31.74 percent

15. **Value-at-Risk (VaR)**   The Value-at-Risk statistic for an investment portfolio states

   a. The probability of an investment loss.
   b. The value of the risky portion of an investment portfolio.
   c. The smallest investment loss expected with a specified probability.
   d. The largest investment loss expected with a specified probability.

Concept Questions

1. **Performance Evaluation Ratios**   Explain the difference between the Sharpe ratio and the Treynor ratio.

2. **Performance Evaluation Measures** What is a common weakness of Jensen's alpha and the Treynor ratio?

3. **Jensen's Alpha** Explain the relationship between Jensen's alpha and the Security Market Line (SML) of the Capital Asset Pricing Model (CAPM).

4. **Sharpe Ratio** What are an advantage and a disadvantage of the Sharpe ratio?

5. **Normal Distribution** Which two parameters completely specify a normal distribution?

6. **Optimal Sharpe Ratio** What is meant by a Sharpe-optimal portfolio?

7. **Optimal Sharpe Ratio** What is the relationship between the Markowitz efficient frontier and the optimal Sharpe ratio?

8. **Value-at-Risk (VaR) Statistic** Explain the meaning of a Value-at-Risk statistic in terms of a smallest expected loss and the probability of such a loss.

9. **Value-at-Risk (VaR) Statistic** The largest expected loss for a portfolio is -20 percent with a probability of 95 percent. Relate this statement to the Value-at-Risk statistic.

10. **Normal Probabilities** The probability that a normal random variable X is less than x is equal to 50 percent, i.e., $Pr(X < x)$. What is this value of x?

Questions and Problems

Core Questions

1. **Standard Deviation** You find a particular stock has an annual standard deviation of 48 percent. What is the standard deviation for a three-month period?

2. **Standard Deviation** A portfolio has an annual variance of .0420. What is the standard deviation over a two-month period?

3. **Standard Deviation** You find the monthly standard deviation of a stock is 14.10 percent. What is the annual standard deviation of the stock?

4. **Standard Deviation** The weekly standard deviation of a stock is 8.16 percent. What is the monthly standard deviation? The annual standard deviation?

5. **Performance Evaluation** You are given the following information concerning three portfolios, the market portfolio, and the risk-free asset:

Portfolio	R_P	σ_P	β_P
X	17%	50%	1.3
Y	15	56	1.2
Z	9	33	.8
Market	12	22	1.0
Risk-free	4	0	.0

What is the Sharpe ratio, Treynor ratio, and Jensen's alpha for each portfolio?

6. **Normal Probabilities** What is the probability that a normal random variable is less than one standard deviation below its mean?

7. **Normal Probabilities** What are the probabilities that a normal random variable is less than n standard deviations below its mean for values of n equal to 1.645, 1.96, 2.326?

8. **Normal Probabilities** The probabilities that a normal random variable X is less than various values of x are 5 percent, 2.5 percent, and 1 percent. What are these values of x?

9. **Value-at-Risk (VaR) Statistic** Raybrooks Co. stock has an annual return mean and standard deviation of 14 percent and 28 percent, respectively. What is the smallest expected loss in the coming year with a probability of 5 percent?

www.mhhe.com/cj3e

10. **Value-at-Risk (VaR) Statistic**   Greta, Inc., stock has an annual return mean and standard deviation of 18 percent and 45 percent, respectively. What is the smallest expected loss in the coming month with a probability of 2.5 percent?

11. **Value-at-Risk (VaR) Statistic**   Your portfolio allocates equal funds to the Raybrooks Co. and Greta, Inc., stocks referred to in the previous two questions. The return correlation between Raybrooks Co. and Greta, Inc., is zero. What is the smallest expected loss for your portfolio in the coming month with a probability of 2.5 percent?

12. **Value-at-Risk (VaR) Statistic**   The stock of Metallica Bearings has an average annual return of 13 percent and a standard deviation of 32 percent. What is the smallest expected loss in the next year with a probability of 1 percent?

13. **Value-at-Risk (VaR) Statistic**   Osbourne, Inc., stock has an annual mean return of 16 percent and a standard deviation of 42 percent. What is the smallest expected loss in the next week with a probability of 2.5 percent?

14. **Value-at-Risk (VaR) Statistic**   Your portfolio is equally weighted between Metallica Bearings and Osbourne, Inc., stocks in the previous two questions. The return correlation between the two stocks is zero. What is the smallest expected loss on your portfolio in the next month with a probability of 5 percent?

15. **Sharpe Ratio**   What is the formula for the Sharpe ratio for a stock and bond portfolio with a zero correlation between stock and bond returns?

16. **Sharpe Ratio**   What is the formula for the Sharpe ratio for an equally-weighted portfolio of stocks and bonds?

17. **Sharpe Ratio**   What is the formula for the Sharpe ratio for a portfolio of stocks and bonds with equal expected returns, i.e., $E(R_S) = E(R_B)$, and a zero return correlation?

18. **Value-at-Risk (VaR) Statistic**   A stock has an annual return of 13 percent and a standard deviation of 65 percent. What is the smallest expected loss over the next year with a probability of 1 percent? Does this number make sense?

19. **Value-at-Risk (VaR) Statistic**   For the stock in the previous problem, what is the smallest expected gain over the next year with a probability of 1 percent? Does this number make sense? What does this tell you about stock return distributions?

20. **Value-at-Risk (VaR) Statistic**   Tyler Trucks stock has an annual return mean and standard deviation of 14 percent and 31 percent, respectively. Michael Moped Manufacturing stock has an annual return mean and standard deviation of 22 percent and 56 percent, respectively. Your portfolio allocates equal funds to Tyler Trucks stock and Michael Moped Manufacturing stock. The return correlation between Tyler Trucks and Michael Moped Manufacturing is .5. What is the smallest expected loss for your portfolio in the coming month with a probability of 5 percent?

21. **Value-at-Risk (VaR) Statistic**   Using the same return means and standard deviations as in the previous question for Tyler Trucks and Michael Moped Manufacturing stocks, but assuming a return correlation of $-.5$, what is the smallest expected loss for your portfolio in the coming month with a probability of 5 percent?

22. **Value-at-Risk (VaR) Statistic**   Your portfolio allocates equal amounts to three stocks. All three stocks have the same mean annual return of 18 percent. Annual return standard deviations for these three stocks are 35 percent, 45 percent, and 55 percent. The return correlations among all three stocks are zero. What is the smallest expected loss for your portfolio in the coming year with a probability of 1 percent?

23. **Value-at-Risk (VaR) Statistic**   Using the same return means and standard deviations as in the previous question for the three stocks, but assuming a correlation of .2 among returns for all three stocks, what is the smallest expected loss for your portfolio in the coming year with a probability of 1 percent?

24. **Value-at-Risk (VaR) Statistic**   Your portfolio allocates equal amounts to four stocks. All four stocks have the same mean annual return of 16 percent and annual return standard deviation of 48 percent. The return correlations among all four stocks are zero. What is the smallest expected loss for your portfolio in the coming quarter with a probability of 5 percent?

Spreadsheet Problem

25. **Optimal Sharpe Ratio**   You are constructing a portfolio of two assets. Asset A has an expected return of 14 percent and a standard deviation of 65 percent. Asset B has an expected return of 11 percent and a standard deviation of 43 percent. The correlation between the two assets is .25 and the risk-free rate is 4 percent. What is the weight of each asset in the portfolio of the two assets that has the largest possible Sharpe ratio?

STANDARD &POOR'S

S&P Problem

www.mhhe.com/edumarketinsight

Note: This problem can be done manually, but a spreadsheet program such as Excel is recommended for use in calculations.

1. **Performance Evaluation**   Go to the "Excel Analytics" link for Pepsico (PEP) and download the monthly adjusted stock prices. Copy the monthly returns for Pepsico and the monthly S&P 500 returns into a new spreadsheet. Calculate the Sharpe ratio, Jensen's alpha, and the Treynor ratio for this company. Assume a risk-free rate of 5 percent.

What's on the Web?

1. **Morningstar Ratings**   Go to www.morningstar.com and find out how to interpret the "Bear Market Decile Rank." While you are at the website, also learn more about the best fit index numbers. What do the best fit index numbers mean?

2. **Morningstar Risk**   Go to www.morningstar.com and find out how Morningstar calculates the "Morningstar Risk" category. What percentage of funds are rated as Below Average by Morningstar? What percentage are rated Average?

3. **Sharpe Ratio**   Go to www.cpadvantage.com and look for the Sharpe ratio calculator under "Financial Calculators." Use the Sharpe ratio calculator to find the Sharpe ratio for a portfolio with an average return of 13 percent and a standard deviation of 32 percent if the risk-free rate is 4.5 percent. Verify the number the website calculates.

4. **Modified VaR**   Go to www.alternativesoft.com and learn about modified VaR proposed at the website. Why would you want to use a modified VaR?

www.mhhe.com/cj3e

Part 5
Options and
Futures

Chapter 14

Stock Options

"Derivatives, like NFL quarterbacks, probably get more credit and more blame than they deserve."

–Gerald Corrigan of Goldman Sachs

Options have fascinated investors for centuries. The option concept is simple. Instead of buying stock shares today, you buy an option to buy the stock at a later date at a price specified in the option contract. You are not obligated to exercise the option, but if doing so benefits you, of course you will. Moreover, the most you can lose is the original price of the option, which is normally only a fraction of the stock price. Sounds good, doesn't it? ■

Options on common stocks have traded in financial markets for about as long as common stocks have. However, it was not until 1973, when the Chicago Board Options Exchange was established, that options trading became a large and important part of the financial landscape. Since then, the success of options trading has been phenomenal.

Much of the success of options trading is attributable to the tremendous flexibility that options offer investors in designing investment strategies. For example, options can be used to reduce risk through hedging strategies or to increase risk through speculative strategies. As a result, when properly understood and applied, options are appealing both to conservative investors and to aggressive speculators.

In this chapter, we discuss options generally, but our primary focus is on options on individual common stocks. However, later in the chapter we also discuss options on stock market indexes, which are options on portfolios of common stocks. We begin by reviewing some of the ideas we touched on in Chapter 3, where we very briefly discussed options.

14.1 Options on Common Stocks

Option Basics

derivative security Security whose value is derived from the value of another security. Options are a type of derivative security.

As we have discussed, options on common stock are a type of **derivative security** because the value of a stock option is "derived" from the value of the underlying common stock. For example, the value of an option to buy or sell IBM stock is derived from the value of IBM stock. However, the relationship between the value of a particular stock option and the value of the underlying stock depends on the specific type of option.

Recall that there are two basic option types: **call options** and **put options**. Call options are options to buy, and put options are options to sell. Thus, a call option on IBM stock is an option to buy IBM shares, and a put option on IBM stock is an option to sell IBM shares. More specifically, a call option on common stock grants the holder the right, but not the obligation, to buy the underlying stock at a given **strike price** before the option expiration date. Similarly, a put option on common stock grants the holder the right, but not the obligation, to sell the underlying stock at a given strike price before the option expiration date. The strike price, also called the *exercise price*, is the price at which stock shares are bought or sold to fulfill the obligations of the option contract.

call option On common stock, grants the holder the right, but not the obligation, to buy the underlying stock at a given strike price.

put option On common stock, grants the holder the right, but not the obligation, to sell the underlying stock at a given strike price.

Options are contracts, and, in practice, option contracts are standardized to facilitate convenience in trading and price reporting. Standardized stock options have a contract size of 100 shares of common stock per option contract. This means that a single call option contract involves an option to buy 100 shares of stock. Likewise, a single put option contract involves an option to sell 100 shares of stock.

strike price Price specified in an option contract that the holder pays to buy shares (in the case of call options) or receives to sell shares (in the case of put options) if the option is exercised. Also called the *exercise price*.

Because options are contracts, an understanding of stock options requires that we know the specific contract terms. In general, options on common stock must stipulate at least the following six contract terms:

1. The identity of the underlying stock.
2. The strike price, also called the striking or exercise price.
3. The option contract size.
4. The option expiration date, also called the option maturity.
5. The option exercise style.
6. The delivery or settlement procedure.

First, a stock option contract requires that the specific stock issue be clearly identified. While this may seem to be stating the obvious, in financial transactions it is important that the "obvious" is in fact clearly and unambiguously understood by all concerned parties.

Second, the strike price, also called the exercise price, must be stipulated. The strike price is quite important, since the strike price is the price that an option holder will pay (in the case of a call option) or receive (in the case of a put option) if the option is exercised.

Third, the size of the contract must be specified. As stated earlier, the standard contract size for stock options is 100 stock shares per option.

The fourth contract term that must be stated is the option expiration date. An option cannot be exercised after its expiration date. If an option is unexercised and its expiration date has passed, the option becomes worthless.

Fifth, the option's exercise style determines when the option can be exercised. There are two basic exercise styles: American and European. **American options** can be exercised any time before option expiration, but **European options** can be exercised only on the last day before expiration. Options on individual stocks are normally American style, and stock index options are usually European style.

Finally, in the event that a stock option is exercised, the settlement process must be stipulated. For stock options, standard settlement requires delivery of the underlying stock shares several business days after a notice of exercise is made by the option holder.

Stock options are traded in financial markets in a manner similar to the way that common stocks are traded. For example, there are organized options exchanges, and there are over-the-counter (OTC) options markets. The largest volume of stock options trading in the United States takes place at the Chicago Board Options Exchange (CBOE). However, stock options are also actively traded at the Philadelphia Stock Exchange (PHLX), the New York Stock Exchange (NYSE), the American Stock Exchange (AMEX), and the Pacific Stock Exchange (PSE). Like a stock exchange, or, for that matter, any securities exchange, an options exchange is a marketplace where customer buy orders and sell orders are matched up with each other.

Option Price Quotes

Current prices for a relatively small number of stock options traded at the major options exchanges are reported each day in *The Wall Street Journal*. Only the most heavily traded stock options are included. Figure 14.1 reproduces the "Listed Options Quotations" section from *The Wall Street Journal*.

In Figure 14.1, the table entitled "Most Active Contracts" reports data on selected option contracts with the highest trading volumes in the previous day's options trading. Reference information immediately above this table is useful for interpreting data in the options listings. In the table itself, the first three columns report the name of the option's underlying stock, the expiration month, and the strike price for the option. A "p" following the strike price indicates a put option; otherwise, it is a call option. The next two columns report volume, measured as the number of contracts traded on the previous day, and the exchange where that particular option contract is traded. ("Composite" means more than one exchange.)

The column labeled "Last" reports the contract price for the last trade of the previous day, and the column labeled "Net Chg" reports the price change from the last price recorded a day earlier. The next column contains the late afternoon closing price on the underlying asset. The final column reports open interest, which is the total number of contracts outstanding. Notice that all option contracts listed in this table are sorted by trading volume.

The rest of the "Listed Options Quotations" page reports options trading data grouped by the underlying stock. For each underlying stock with options listed in Figure 14.1, the first column under a stock name is simply a repeated statement of the stock's closing price. The second column states strike prices of the various options

American option An option that can be exercised any time before expiration.

European option An option that can be exercised only on the last day before expiration.

Visit these option exchanges:
www.cboe.com
www.amex.com
www.phlx.com
www.nyse.com
www.pacificex.com

For information on options ticker symbols, see
www.cboe.com
www.optionsites.com

FIGURE 14.1

Listed Options Quotations

Source: Reprinted by permission of *The Wall Street Journal,* July 2, 2003, via Copyright Clearance Center, Inc. © 2003 Dow Jones & Company, Inc. All Rights Reserved Worldwide.

LISTED OPTIONS QUOTATIONS

Wednesday, July 2, 2003

Composite volume and close for actively traded equity and LEAPS, or long-term options, with results for the corresponding put or call contract. Volume figures are unofficial. Open interest is total outstanding for all exchanges and reflects previous trading day. Close when possible is shown for the underlying stock or primary market. **XC**-Composite. **p**-Put. **o**-Strike price adjusted for split.

Most Active Contracts

OPTION/STRIKE			VOL	EXCH	LAST	NET CHG	CLOSE	OPEN INT	OPTION/STRIKE			VOL	EXCH	LAST	NET CHG	CLOSE	OPEN INT
Nasd100Tr	Aug	30 p	110,184	XC	0.85	-0.20	30.97	73,410	Nasd100Tr	Dec	29 p	14,865	XC	1.00	-0.20	30.97	14,933
Nasd100Tr	Jan 05	27 p	48,778	XC	2.25	-0.15	30.97	29,117	MicronT	Aug	15	14,646	XC	0.35	0.15	12.94	655
Nasd100Tr	Jul	30 p	47,299	XC	0.35	-0.20	30.97	233,553	SemiHTr	Jul	30	13,372	XC	0.70	0.25	29.64	32,472
Nasd100Tr	Jul	29	46,088	XC	2.10	0.55	30.97	107,895	Nasd100Tr	Sep	30	13,207	XC	2.25	0.45	30.97	60,212
Nasd100Tr	Jul	31	41,634	XC	0.70	0.30	30.97	158,858	Cisco	Jul	17.50	13,059	XC	0.65	0.30	17.86	122,627
Nasd100Tr	Jul	30	39,375	XC	1.30	0.45	30.97	178,726	Oracle	Jul	12.50	12,915	XC	0.35	0.10	12.45	29,646
Intel	Jul	22.50	36,674	XC	0.55	0.25	22.21	82,004	I B M	Aug	85	12,419	XC	2.90	0.65	84.74	2,765
Nasd100Tr	Jul	28 p	35,404	XC	0.05	-0.05	30.97	198,622	Cisco	Jan	17.50 p	12,201	XC	1.65	-0.25	17.86	16,590
Microsft	Jul	27.50	32,350	XC	0.45	0.25	26.88	196,438	Microsft	Jul	25	12,169	XC	1.95	0.50	26.88	122,483
Nasd100Tr	Jul	29 p	25,285	XC	0.15	-0.10	30.97	229,647	Nasd100Tr	Aug	31	11,167	XC	1.20	0.35	30.97	46,120
Microsft	Aug	27.50	19,923	XC	0.80	0.25	26.88	22,605	Kroger	Jul	17.50	11,008	XC	0.20	0.05	16.97	17,747
Oracle	Sep	15	18,754	XC	0.20	0.05	12.45	27,908	Nasd100Tr	Aug	27 p	10,122	XC	0.20	-0.10	30.97	99,050
Vodfne	Jul	20	18,043	XC	0.60	0.20	20.41	32,077	Dynegy	Jan 04	5	10,064	XC	0.65	0.10	4.31	30,055
Nasd100Tr	Jul	31 p	17,077	XC	0.75	-0.35	30.97	70,841	Nasd100Tr	Sep	28 p	9,724	XC	0.65	-0.10	30.97	217,682
Vodfne	Oct	20	16,903	XC	1.70	0.55	20.41	1,403	Intel	Jul	22.50 p	9,620	XC	0.85	-0.55	22.21	25,452
Nasd100Tr	Jul	32	16,637	XC	0.25	0.10	30.97	74,452	Microsft	Jul	25 p	9,357	XC	0.15	-0.10	26.88	91,800
EMC	Jul	10	16,547	XC	1		0.30	10.89	46,521	Anadrk	Jul	45 p	8,692	XC	1.50	...	44.09	4,728
EMC	Jul	11	15,857	XC	0.40	0.20	10.89	740	EKodak	Jan	30	8,629	XC	1.20	0.05	27.25	11,943
Nasd100Tr	Aug	32	15,350	XC	0.80	0.35	30.97	21,322	EKodak	Oct	30	8,604	XC	0.80		27.25	17,736
									AppldMat	Aug	15 p	8,299	XC	0.60	-0.05	16.27	3,228

OPTION/STRIKE	EXP	CALL VOL	CALL LAST	PUT VOL	PUT LAST	OPTION/STRIKE	EXP	CALL VOL	CALL LAST	PUT VOL	PUT LAST	OPTION/STRIKE	EXP	CALL VOL	CALL LAST	PUT VOL	PUT LAST
AOL TW	15 Jul	3812	1.40	273	0.10	84.74	85 Aug	12419	2.90	735	3.20	17.98	17.50 Aug	4226	1.20	3551	0.85
16.40	16 Jul	3585	0.65	214	0.35	84.74	90 Jul	6219	0.35	297	5.70	Qualcom	37.50 Oct	479	2.90	5061	2.85
Abgenix	12.50 Jul	4182	0.75	153	2.10	JnprNtw	12.50 Jul	1750	1.15	6554	0.40	Sears	7.50 Oct	3574	1.30	...	...
ATower	10 Oct	6109	1.25	...	...	Kroger	17.50 Jul	11008	0.20	30	0.75	32.91	27.50 Oct	20	6.70	4200	1.40
Amgen	70 Jul	3746	0.40	185	3.30	Level3	5 Aug	315	1.15	5200	0.20	SemiHTr	30 Jul	13372	0.70	756	1.10
Anadrk	45 Jul	573	0.65	8692	1.50	MerrLyn	50 Oct	4790	2.35	3	4	Seprcr	20	6034	2.95	157	3.50
AppldMat	15 Aug	292	1.75	8299	0.60	MicronT	12.50 Jul	3446	0.75	5691	0.40	SiebelSys	10 Jul	4263	0.30	1587	0.85
Brocade	10 Oct	...	...	5000	3.90	12.94	15 Aug	14646	0.35	192	2.40	9.46	10 Aug	6474	0.60	135	1.10
CapOne	55 Aug	4282	1.25	10	6.70	Microsft	22.50 Aug	115	4.50	4652	0.15	Sony	35 Jan	3648	1.65	15	5.30
Cerner	20 Jul	112	1.55	4096	1.35	26.88	25 Jul	12169	1.95	9357	0.15	Starbcks	30 Jan	6601	1.15	60	4.20
ChkPoint	20 Jul	4275	0.80	354	0.85	26.88	25 Aug	5978	2.35	1516	0.45	TelMexL	32.50 Jul	4725	0.55	2141	0.75
Cisco	15 Jul	959	2.90	7485	0.05	26.88	25 Oct	2390	2.80	4017	0.95	TexasInst	15 Jan	21	4.20	7691	0.95
17.86	17.50 Jul	13059	0.65	6682	0.30	26.88	27.50 Jul	32350	0.45	2833	1	18.22	17.50 Jul	3800	1	1875	0.25
17.86	17.50 Aug	4183	1.05	6389	0.65	26.88	27.50 Aug	19923	0.80	885	1.40	TycoIntl	20 Jan	3673	1.45	12	2.40
17.86	17.50 Jan	7360	2	12201	1.65	26.88	30 Jul	3631	0.05	411	3.20	USG	20	3449	2.15	1	3
Citigrp	45 Jul	4311	0.65	1015	1.20	26.88	30 Aug	3678	0.15	159	3.40	Vodfne	20 Jul	18043	0.60	8	0.30
44.40	50 Aug	4085	0.15	...	...	26.88	30 Jan	3402	1.25	152	4.40	20.41	20 Oct	16903	1.70	...	...
Comcast	30 Jul	5814	1.30	322	0.60	Mirant	2.50 Aug	265	0.95	4972	0.50	WDigit	12.50 Jul	1684	0.80	4148	0.45
DellCptr	32.50 Jul	6444	0.65	1286	0.75	MorgStan	45 Jul	5164	1	132	1.25						
eBay	105 Jul	3955	5.20	6926	1.05	Nasd100Tr	27 Jul	1294	3.90	4371	0.05						
109.26	110 Jul	4129	2.20	2899	2.90	30.97	27 Aug	84	4.10	10122	0.20						
EMC	10 Jul	16547	1	944	0.15	30.97	28 Jul	2646	3	35404	0.05	**Volume & Open Interest Summaries**					
10.89	11 Jul	15857	0.40	901	0.50	30.97	28 Aug	104	3.30	6640	0.35	**AMERICAN**					
EKodak	30 Oct	8604	0.80	95	3.70	30.97	28 Sep	2773	3.60	9724	0.65	Call Vol: 440,825		Open Int: 46,117,222			
27.25	30 Jan	8629	1.20	13	4.50	30.97	29 Jul	46088	2.10	25285	0.15	Put Vol: 325,062		Open Int: 34,783,457			
EricsnTl	10 Aug	...	...	5005	0.60	30.97	29 Aug	885	2.50	33068	0.55	**CHICAGO BOARD**					
FHLB	55 Jul	3380	0.85	463	1.95	30.97	29 Dec	13	3.50	14865	1.60	Call Vol: 643,998		Open Int: 60,884,512			
54.00	60 Oct	3475	1.35	1055	7.90	30.97	30 Jul	39375	1.30	47299	0.35	Put Vol: 496,199		Open Int: 46,810,737			
54.00	65 Oct	6035	0.55	...	...	30.97	30 Aug	7180	1.80	110184	0.85	**INTL SECURITIES**					
GoldmnS	90 Jul	4948	0.40	10	4.80	30.97	30 Sep	13207	2.25	3683	0.15	Call Vol: 485,678		Open Int: 52,734,469			
Halbtn	25 Oct	5323	1.15	...	...	30.97	31 Jul	41634	0.70	17077	0.75	Put Vol: 263,501		Open Int: 40,012,142			
HarleyDav	40 Jul	438	1.05	3909	1.35	30.97	31 Aug	11167	1.20	7364	1.25	**PHILADELPHIA**					
HewlettPk	22.50 Jul	3509	0.65	56	1.60	30.97	32 Jul	16637	0.25	7354	1.35	Call Vol: 161,204		Open Int: 43,242,963			
Intel	20 Jul	5129	2.30	3445	0.15	30.97	32 Aug	15350	0.80	1012	1.80	Put Vol: 138,868		Open Int: 29,738,539			
22.21	20 Aug	2487	2.60	3826	0.45	30.97	33 Dec	4372	1.55	1012	3.40	**PACIFIC**					
22.21	22.50 Jul	36674	0.55	9620	0.85	NokiaCp	12.50 Oct	4062	4.30	...	...	Call Vol: 211,305		Open Int: 54,476,412			
22.21	22.50 Aug	4154	0.95	926	1.35	Oracle	12.50 Jul	12915	0.35	659	0.40	Put Vol: 118,907		Open Int: 41,443,859			
22.21	25 Jul	4167	0.05	368	2.95	12.45	12.50 Sep	847	0.95	3617	0.95	**TOTAL**					
I B M	75 Jul	15	10	3777	0.15	12.45	15 Sep	18754	0.20	3	2.55	Call Vol: 1,943,010					
84.74	80 Jul	847	5.30	3938	0.60	PG&E Cp	20 Dec	3815	2.95	250	1.15	Put Vol: 1,342,537					
84.74	85 Jul	4542	1.80	1341	2.05	Peoplesoft	17.50 Jul	5838	0.70	4082	0.40						

available for each stock. Notice that the range of available strike prices for stock options typically brackets a current stock price.

The third column states the expiration months of each available option contract. By convention, standardized stock options expire on the Saturday following the third Friday of their expiration month. Because of this convention, the exact date that an option

Here is an option chain for Walt Disney Co. (DIS) from Yahoo! Finance (finance.yahoo.com):

Symbol	Last Trade	Change		Volume
DIS	3:14pm 20.69	+0.62	+3.09%	4,916,000

Chart, Financials, Historical Prices, Industry, Insider, Messages, News
Options, Profile, Reports, Research, SEC Filings, more...

Get a snapshot of today's market action in Market Overview

Expires After: Fri 18-Jul-03

Options: Jul-03 | Aug-03 | Oct-03 | Jan-04 | Jan-05 | Jan-06

Options Center | Analyzer NEW! | Most Actives | Symbology | Calendar

Highlighted options are in-the-money

	Calls						Strike Price		Puts					
Symbol	Last Trade	Chg	Bid	Ask	Vol	Open Int		Symbol	Last Trade	Chg	Bid	Ask	Vol	Open Int
DISGT.X	8.30	0.00	8.10	8.30	0	92	12.50	DISST.X	0.05	0.00	0.00	0.05	0	1,808
DISGC.X	5.40	+0.30	5.60	5.80	7	1,197	15.00	DISSC.X	0.10	0.00	0.00	0.05	0	6,390
DISGW.X	2.95	+0.25	3.10	3.30	1	18,168	17.50	DISSW.X	0.10	0.00	0.00	0.05	0	14,413
DISGD.X	0.85	+0.35	0.80	0.85	147	27,376	20.00	DISSD.X	0.25	-0.15	0.15	0.25	26	7,681
DISGX.X	0.05	0.00	0.00	0.10	0	6,711	22.50	DISSX.X	2.00	0.00	1.70	1.95	0	794
DISGE.X	0.05	0.00	0.00	0.05	0	808	25.00	DISSE.X	4.30	0.00	4.20	4.40	0	17

expires can be known exactly by referring to a calendar to identify the third Friday of its expiration month.

These first three contract terms—the identity of the underlying stock, the strike price, and the expiration month—will not change during the life of the option. However, since the price of a stock option depends on the price of the underlying stock, the price of an option changes as the stock price changes.

Option prices are reported in columns 5 and 7 in the stock options listing displayed in Figure 14.1. Column 5 gives call option prices, and column 7 gives put option prices. Option prices are stated on a per-share basis, but the actual price of an option contract is 100 times the per-share price. This is because each option contract represents an option on 100 shares of stock. Fractional contracts for, say, 50 shares, are not normally available.

In Figure 14.1, trading volume for each contract is reported in columns 4 and 6. Column 4 states the number of call option contracts traded for each available strike-maturity combination, while column 6 states the number of put option contracts traded for each strike-maturity combination.

Useful online sources for option prices include the Chicago Board Options Exchange (quote.cboe.com) and Yahoo! Finance (finance.yahoo.com). The nearby *Work the Web* exhibit contains an **option chain** for Walt Disney Co. (DIS) stock options. The small box reports the time and price for the last trade in Disney stock, along with the change in price from the previous day and the trading volume for the current day. The large box contains the Disney option chain, with separate sections for call options and put options and with a strike price column dividing the two sections.

The first column of each section (labeled "Symbol") lists ticker symbols for specific option contracts. The tickers for Disney options have five letters identifying the contract. The sixth letter (X) is just used by Yahoo! to indicate an option ticker. The first

option chain A list of available option contracts and their prices for a particular security arrayed by strike price and maturity.

three letters are DIS, which is the ticker symbol for Disney stock. For the next two letters, the first letter specifies the expiration month and whether the option is a call or a put, while the second letter identifies the strike price. Option tickers are discussed in more detail in the *Stock-Trak* section at the end of this chapter.

The second column ("Last Trade") reports the option price for the last trade. The third column ("Chg") states the change in price from the previous day's last trade, where a zero indicates either no change in price or no trade that day. The next two columns ("Bid" and "Ask") contain representative bid and ask price quotes from dealers. Finally, the sixth column ("Vol") reports trading volume as the number of contracts traded that day, and the seventh column ("Open Int") states open interest as the total number of contracts outstanding.

Check This

14.1a	What is a call option? What is a put option?
14.1b	What are the six basic contract terms that an options contract must specify?
14.1c	What is an option chain?

14.2 Why Options?

As a stock market investor, a basic question you might ask is: "Why buy stock options instead of shares of stock directly?" Good question! To answer it properly, we need to compare the possible outcomes from two investment strategies. The first investment strategy entails simply buying stock. The second strategy involves buying a call option that allows the holder to buy stock any time before option expiration.

For example, suppose you buy 100 shares of IBM stock at a price of $90 per share, representing an investment of $9,000. Afterwards, three things could happen: the stock price could go up, go down, or remain the same. If the stock price goes up, you make money; if it goes down, you lose money. Of course, if the stock price remains the same, you break even.

Now, consider the alternative strategy of buying a call option with a strike price of $90 expiring in three months at a per-share price of $5. This corresponds to a contract price of $500 since the standard option contract size is 100 shares. The first thing to notice about this strategy is that you have invested only $500, and therefore the most that you can lose is only $500.

To compare the two investment strategies just described, let's examine three possible cases for IBM's stock price at the close of trading on the third Friday of the option's expiration month. In case 1, the stock price goes up to $100. In case 2, the stock price goes down to $80. In case 3, the stock price remains the same at $90.

Case 1: If the stock price goes up to $100, and you originally bought 100 shares at $90 dollars per share, then your profit is $100 \times (\$100 - \$90) = \$1,000$. As a percentage of your original investment amount of $9,000, this represents a return on investment of $1,000 / $9,000 = 11.11\%.

Alternatively, if you originally bought the call option, you can exercise the option and buy 100 shares at the strike price of $90 and sell the stock at the $100

For more information on options education, see www.optionscentral.com

market price. After accounting for the original cost of the option contract, your profit is 100 × ($100 − $90) − $500 = $500. As a percentage of your original investment of $500, this represents a return on investment of $500 / $500 = 100%.

Case 2: If the stock price goes down to $80, and you originally bought 100 shares at $90 dollars per share, then your loss is 100 × ($80 − $90) = −$1,000. As a percentage of your original investment, this represents a return of −$1,000 / $9,000 = −11.11%.

If instead you originally bought the call option, it would not pay to exercise the option, and it would expire worthless. You would then realize a total loss of your $500 investment, and your return is −100 percent.

Case 3: If the stock price remains the same at $90, and you bought 100 shares, you break even, and your return is zero percent.

However, if you bought the call option, it would not pay to exercise the option, and it would expire worthless. Once again, you would lose your entire $500 investment.

As these three cases illustrate, the outcomes of the two investment strategies differ significantly, depending on subsequent stock price changes. Whether one strategy is preferred over another is a matter for each individual investor to decide. What is important is the fact that options offer an alternative means of formulating investment strategies.

STOCK RETURNS

EXAMPLE 14.1

Suppose you bought 100 shares of stock at $50 per share. If the stock price goes up to $60 per share, what is the percentage return on your investment? If, instead, the stock price falls to $40 per share, what is the percentage return on your investment?

If the stock goes to $60 per share, you make $10/$50 = 20%. If it falls to $40, you lose $10/$50 = 20%.

CALL OPTION RETURNS

EXAMPLE 14.2

In Example 14.1 just above, suppose that you bought one call option contract for $200. The strike price is $50. If the stock price is $60 just before the option expires, should you exercise the option? If you exercise the option, what is the percentage return on your investment? If you don't exercise the option, what is the percentage return on your investment?

If the stock price is $60, you should definitely exercise. If you do, you will make $10 per share, or $1,000, from exercising. Once we deduct the $200 original cost of the option, your net profit is $800. Your percentage return is $800/$200 = 400%. If you don't exercise, you lose your entire $200 investment, so your loss is 100 percent.

MORE CALL OPTION RETURNS

EXAMPLE 14.3

In Example 14.2, if the stock price is $40 just before the option expires, should you exercise the option? If you exercise the option, what is the percentage return on your investment? If you don't exercise the option, what is the percentage return on your investment?

  If the stock price is $40, you shouldn't exercise since, by exercising, you will be paying $50 per share. If you did exercise, you would lose $10 per share, or $1,000, plus the $200 cost of the option, or $1,200 total. This would amount to a $1,200/$200 = 600% loss! If you don't exercise, you lose the $200 you invested, for a loss of 100 percent.

Of course, we can also calculate percentage gains and losses from a put option purchase. Here we make money if the stock price declines. So, suppose you buy a put option with a strike price of $20 for $.50. If you exercise your put when the stock price is $18, what is your percentage gain?

You make $2 per share since you are selling at $20 when the stock is worth $18. Your put contract cost $50, so your net profit is $200 − $50 = $150. As a percentage of your original $50 investment, you made $150 / $50 = 300%.

Check This

14.2a   If you buy 100 shares of stock at $10 and sell out at $12, what is your percentage return?

14.2b   If you buy one call contract with a strike of $10 for $100 and exercise it when the stock is selling for $12, what is your percentage return?

14.3 Option Payoffs and Profits

Options are appealing because they offer investors a wide variety of investment strategies. In fact, there is essentially no limit to the number of different investment strategies available using options. However, fortunately for us, only a small number of basic strategies are available, and more complicated strategies are built from these. We discuss the payoffs from basic strategies in this section and the following section.

option writing Taking the seller's side of an option contract.

call writer One who has the obligation to sell stock at the option's strike price if the option is exercised.

put writer One who has the obligation to buy stock at the option's strike price if the option is exercised.

Option Writing

Thus far, we have discussed options from the standpoint of the buyer only. However, options are contracts, and every contract must link at least two parties. The two parties to an option contract are the buyer and the seller. The seller of an option is called the "writer," and the act of selling an option is referred to as **option writing**.

  By buying an option you buy the right, but not the obligation, to exercise the option before the option's expiration date. By selling or writing an option, you take the seller's side of the option contract. As a result, option writing involves receiving the option price and, in exchange, assuming the obligation to satisfy the buyer's exercise rights if the option is exercised.

  For example, a **call writer** is obligated to sell stock at the option's strike price if the buyer decides to exercise the call option. Similarly, a **put writer** is obligated to buy stock at the option's strike price if the buyer decides to exercise the put option.

Option Payoffs

It is useful to think about option investment strategies in terms of their initial cash flows and terminal cash flows. The initial cash flow of an option is the price of the option, also called the option *premium*. To the option buyer, the option price (or premium) is a cash outflow. To the option writer, the option price (or premium) is a cash inflow. The terminal cash flow of an option is the option's payoff that could be realized from the exercise privilege. To the option buyer, a payoff entails a cash inflow. To the writer, a payoff entails a cash outflow.

For example, suppose the current price of IBM stock is $80 per share. You buy a call option on IBM with a strike price of $80. The premium is $4 per share. Thus, the initial cash flow is −$400 for you and +$400 for the option writer. What are the terminal cash flows for you and the option writer if IBM has a price of $90 when the option expires? What are the terminal cash flows if IBM has a price of $70 when the option expires?

If IBM is at $90, then you experience a cash inflow of $10 per share, whereas the writer experiences an outflow of $10 per share. If IBM is at $70, you both have a zero cash flow when the option expires because it is worthless. Notice that in both cases the buyer and the seller have the same cash flows, just with opposite signs. This shows that options are a "zero-sum game," meaning that any gains to the buyer must come at the expense of the seller and vice versa.

Payoff Diagrams

When investors buy options, the price that they are willing to pay depends on their assessment of the likely payoffs (cash inflows) from the exercise privilege. Likewise, when investors write options, an acceptable selling price depends on their assessment of the likely payoffs (cash outflows) resulting from the buyers' exercise privilege. Given this, a general understanding of option payoffs is critical for understanding how option prices are determined.

A payoff diagram is a very useful graphical device for understanding option payoffs. The payoffs from buying a call option and the payoffs from writing a call option are seen in the payoff diagram in Figure 14.2. The vertical axis of Figure 14.2 measures option payoffs, and the horizontal axis measures the possible stock prices on the option expiration date. These examples assume that the call option has a strike price of $50 and that the option will be exercised only on its expiration date.

In Figure 14.2, notice that the call option payoffs are zero for all stock prices below the $50 strike price. This is because the call option holder will not exercise the option to buy stock at the $50 strike price when the stock is available in the stock market at a lower price. In this case, the option expires worthless.

In contrast, if the stock price is higher than the $50 strike price, the call option payoff is equal to the difference between the market price of the stock and the strike price of the option. For example, if the stock price is $60, the call option payoff is equal to $10, which is the difference between the $60 stock price and the $50 strike price. This payoff is a cash inflow to the buyer, because the option buyer can buy the stock at the $50 strike price and sell the stock at the $60 market price. However, this payoff is a cash outflow to the writer, because the option writer must sell the stock at the $50 strike price when the stock's market price is $60.

Putting it all together, the distinctive "hockey-stick" shape of the call option payoffs shows that the payoff is zero if the stock price is below the strike price. Above the

To learn more on options, see www.e-analytics.com www.tradingmarkets.com

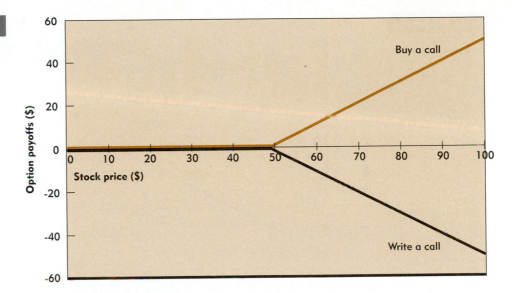

FIGURE 14.2

Call Option Payoffs

strike price, however, the buyer of the call option gains $1 for every $1 increase in the stock price. Of course, as shown, the call option writer loses $1 for every $1 increase in the stock price above the strike price.

Figure 14.3 is an example of a payoff diagram illustrating the payoffs from buying a put option and from writing a put option. As with our call option payoffs, the vertical axis measures option payoffs, and the horizontal axis measures the possible stock prices on the option expiration date. Once again, these examples assume that the put has a strike price of $50, and that the option will be exercised only on its expiration date.

In Figure 14.3, the put option payoffs are zero for all stock prices above the $50 strike price. This is because a put option holder will not exercise the option to sell stock at the $50 strike price when the stock can be sold in the stock market at a higher price. In this case, the option expires worthless.

In contrast, if the stock price is lower than the $50 strike price, the put option payoff is equal to the difference between the market price of the stock and the strike price of the option. For example, if the stock price is $40, the put option payoff is equal to $10, which is the difference between the $40 stock price and the $50 strike price. This payoff is a cash inflow to the buyer, because the option buyer can buy the stock at the $40 market price and sell the stock at the $50 strike price. However, this payoff is a cash outflow to the writer, because the option writer must buy the stock at the $50 strike price when the stock's market price is $40.

Our payoff diagrams illustrate an important difference between the maximum possible gains and losses for puts and calls. Notice that if you buy a call option, there is no upper limit to your potential profit because there is no upper limit to the stock price. However, with a put option, the most you can make is the strike price. In other words, the best thing that can happen to you if you buy a put is for the stock price to go to zero. Of course, whether you buy a put or a call, your potential loss is limited to the option premium you pay.

Similarly, as shown in Figure 14.2, if you write a call, there is no limit to your possible loss, but your potential gain is limited to the option premium you receive. As shown in Figure 14.3, if you write a put, both your gain and loss are limited, although the potential loss could be substantial.

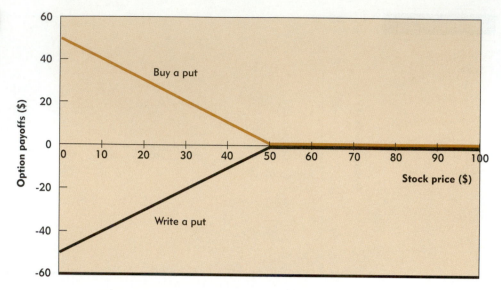

FIGURE 14.3

Put Option Payoffs

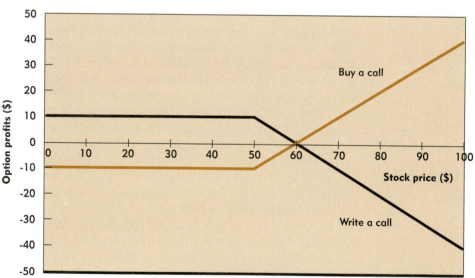

FIGURE 14.4

Call Option Profits

Option Profits

For even more on options, see www.investorlinks. com

Between them, Figures 14.2 and 14.3 tell us essentially everything we need to know about the payoffs from the four basic strategies involving options, buying and writing puts and calls. However, these figures give the payoffs at expiration only and so do not consider the original cash inflow or outflow. Option profit diagrams are an extension of payoff diagrams that do take into account the initial cash flow.

As we have seen, the profit from an option strategy is the difference between the option's terminal cash flow (the option payoff) and the option's initial cash flow (the option price, or premium). An option profit diagram simply adjusts option payoffs for the original price of the option. This means that the option premium is subtracted from the payoffs from buying options and added to payoffs from writing options.

To illustrate, Figures 14.4 and 14.5 are profit diagrams corresponding to the four basic investment strategies for options. In each diagram, the vertical axis measures option

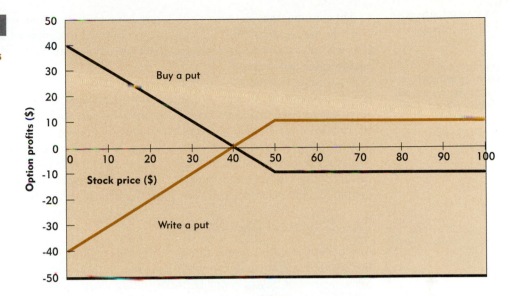

FIGURE 14.5

Put Option Profits

profits, and the horizontal axis measures possible stock prices. Each profit diagram assumes that the option's strike price is $50 and that the put and call option prices are both $10. Notice that in each case the characteristic hockey-stick shape is maintained; the "stick" is just shifted up or down.

Check This

14.3a What is option writing?

14.3b What are the payoffs from writing call options?

14.3c What are the payoffs from writing put options?

14.4 Option Strategies

Thus far, we have considered the payoffs and profits from buying and writing individual calls and puts. In this section, we consider what happens when we start to combine puts, calls, and shares of stock. There are numerous combinations that we could examine, but we will stick to just a few of the most basic and most important strategies.

The Protective Put Strategy

Suppose you own a share of TelMex (Teléfonos de México) stock, currently worth $50. Suppose you additionally purchase a put option with a strike price of $50 for $2. What is the net effect of this purchase?

To answer, we can compare what happens if TelMex stock stays at or above $50 to what happens if it drops below $50. If TelMex stays at or above $50, your put will expire worthless since you would choose not to exercise it. You would be out the $2. However, if TelMex falls below $50, you would exercise your put, and the put writer would pay you $50 for your stock. No matter how far below $50 the price falls, you have guaranteed that you will receive $50 for your stock.

For ideas on option trading strategies, see www.commodityworld. com

Thus, by purchasing a put option, you have protected yourself against a price decline. In the jargon of Wall Street, you have paid $2 to eliminate the "downside risk." For this reason, a strategy of buying a put option on a stock you already own is called a **protective put** strategy.

protective put
Strategy of buying a put option on a stock already owned. This protects against a decline in value.

Notice that this use of a put option *reduces* the overall risk faced by an investor, so it is a conservative strategy. This is a good example of how options, or any derivative asset, can be used to decrease risk rather than increase it. Stated differently, options can be used to hedge as well as speculate, so they do not inherently increase risk.

Buying a put option on an asset you own is just like buying term insurance. When you buy car insurance, for example, you are effectively buying a put option on your car. If, because of an accident or theft, your car's value declines, you "exercise" your option, and the insurance company essentially pays for the decline in value.

The Covered Call Strategy

For more on covered calls, see www.writecall.com www.giscor.com

Another conservative option strategy is to write call options on stock you already own. For example, again suppose you own some TelMex stock currently selling at $50. Now, instead of buying a put, consider selling a call option for, say, $2, with an exercise price of $55. What is the effect of this transaction?

To answer, we can compare what happens if TelMex stays below $55 (the exercise price on the option you sold) to what happens if it rises above $55. If TelMex stays below $55, the option will expire worthless, and you pocket the $2 premium you received. If the stock rises above $55, the option will be exercised against you, and you will deliver the stock in exchange for $55.

Thus, when you sell a call option on stock you already own, you keep the option premium no matter what. The worst thing that can happen to you is that you will have to sell your stock at the exercise price. Since you already own the stock, you are said to be "covered," and this strategy is known as a **covered call** strategy.

covered call Strategy of selling a call option on stock already owned.

With our covered call strategy, the stock is currently selling for $50. Since the strike price on the option is $55, the net effect of the strategy is to give up the possibility of a profit greater than $5 on the stock in exchange for the certain option premium of $2. This decreases the uncertainty surrounding the return on the investment and therefore decreases its risk.

In the jargon of Wall Street, a covered call exchanges "upside" potential for current income. In contrast, a strategy of selling call options on stock you do not own is a "naked" call strategy and, as we saw earlier, has unlimited potential losses. Thus, selling call options is either quite risky or else acts to reduce risk, depending on whether you are covered or naked. This is important to understand.

Straddles

straddle Buying or selling a call and a put with the same exercise price. Buying is a *long straddle*; selling is a *short straddle*.

Suppose a share of stock is currently selling at $50. You think the price is going to make a major move, but you are uncertain about the direction. What could you do? One answer is buy a call *and* buy a put, both with a $50 exercise price. That way, if the stock goes up sharply, your call will pay off; if it goes down sharply, your put will pay off. This is an example of a long **straddle**.

This is called a "straddle" because you have, in effect, straddled the current $50 stock price. It is a long straddle because you bought both options. If you thought the stock price was *not* going to move in either direction, you might sell a put and a call, thereby generating some income. As long as the stock price stays at $50, both options would expire worthless. This is an example of a short straddle.

There are many other strategies, with colorful names such as strips, strangles, collars, and spreads, but we need to move on. In our next section, we discuss some upper and lower bounds on option values. For some interesting discussions of option strategies, see our nearby *Investment Updates* box.

OPTION STRATEGIES

EXAMPLE 14.4

You own a share of stock worth $80. Suppose you sell a call option with a strike price of $80 and also buy a put with a strike of $80. What is the net effect of these transactions on the risk of owning the stock?

Notice that what you have done is combine a protective put and a covered call strategy. To see the effect of doing this, suppose that, at option expiration, the stock is selling for more than $80. In this case, the put is worthless. The call will be exercised against you, and you will receive $80 for your stock. If the stock is selling for less than $80, the call is worthless. You would exercise your put and sell the stock for $80. In other words, the net effect is that you have guaranteed that you will exchange the stock for $80 no matter what happens, so you have created a riskless asset!

Check This

14.4a What is a protective put strategy? A covered call strategy?

14.4b What is a short straddle? When might it be appropriate?

14.5 Option Prices, Intrinsic Values, and Arbitrage

There are strict limits to the range of values that an option price can attain in competitive options markets. We will have much to say about the determinants of an option's value in the next chapter. Here we touch on the subject by discussing some basic boundaries for the price of an option.

The Upper Bound for a Call Option Price

What is the most a call option could sell for? To answer, suppose we have a call option on a share of stock. The current stock price is $60. Without more information, we can't say a lot about the price of the call option, but we do know one thing: The price of the option must be less than $60!

If you think about it, the right to buy a share of stock cannot be worth more than the share itself. To illustrate, suppose the call option was actually selling for $65 when the stock was selling at $60. What would you do?

What you would do is get very rich, very fast. You would sell call options at $65 and buy stock at $60. You pocket the $5 difference. The worst thing that can happen to you is the options are exercised and you receive the exercise price. In this case, you make an unlimited amount of money at no risk.

This is an example of a true *arbitrage* opportunity. An arbitrage is an opportunity that (1) requires no net investment on your part, (2) has no possibility of loss, and

Some Stock-Option Strategies Win a Guarded Endorsement

Let's start with a concession: Maybe options aren't totally devoid of merit.

I don't like exchange-traded stock options. They are complicated. They are often used for mindless speculation. And the odds are unattractive. For every winner, there is a loser. In fact, after trading costs, investors collectively end up out of pocket. Still, I did manage to find two options strategies that almost pass muster. Options come in two flavors: puts and calls. By buying a put, you acquire the right to sell stock at a fixed price. Similarly, by purchasing a call, you acquire the right to buy stock at a set price.

But these rights don't come cheap. You have to pay a premium to the sellers of these options. Indeed, many folks sell puts and calls as a way of generating extra investment income. But that strategy can backfire if the stock involved has a big move. Sellers of call options may miss out on big gains by the underlying shares, while sellers of puts can be forced to pay a lofty price for a now-battered stock.

Sound confusing? To get a better handle on what is involved, consider these two strategies that may appeal to certain investors.

Easing Out

Suppose you have 1,000 shares of Microsoft that you bought for a pittance. You know you ought to diversify, but you are reluctant to sell because of the resulting tax bill. Options could ease the pain of selling. The idea is to write call options against your Microsoft position. Let's say you sold July calls, with a $75 strike price, somewhat above the current $68.47 share price. By writing the calls, you agree to sell your Microsoft shares for $75 any time between now and the options' expiration date. In return, you will receive $4,200 in option premiums, which will help to offset the tax bill, should your stock get called away.

"The problem is the downside," says Eric Seff, a financial planner in Mamaroneck, N.Y. What if your Microsoft shares plunge? Mr. Seff says the option premiums you collected probably wouldn't compensate for your losses. To guard against a big decline in Microsoft's shares, you could combine the sale of call options with the purchase of Microsoft puts. That would give you downside protection. But the premium you pay for the puts will likely wipe out the income you earned by selling the calls.

What to do? Maybe you should forget the puts and instead sell calls with a strike price very close to today's share price. For instance, you could sell Microsoft calls with a strike price of $70, just above the current stock price. That way, you will earn some extra income, while being almost certain that the options you sold will be exercised and thus your Microsoft stock will get called away. Or maybe you should just dump the shares. "If you know you should get out of the stock, then get out of the stock and forget the options," advises Minneapolis financial planner Ross Levin. "The taxes may hurt. But that's the price of good investment choices you made in the past."

Looking Down

What if a bear market hits when you are retired? If you are already a few years into retirement, you are probably in fine shape, thanks to the cushion created by earlier investment gains. But if you have just retired, you could find yourself in deep trouble, as your portfolio is rapidly depleted through a combination of tumbling stock prices and your own withdrawals.

To protect yourself during the critical first few years of retirement, you might buy put options, says Moshe Milevsky, a finance professor at York University in Toronto and author of "The Probability of Fortune." Suppose you bought puts on the Standard & Poor's 500-stock index that expire in December and that will limit your losses during the next year to 8%. This insurance will currently cost you about 5% of your stock portfolio's value. Sound like a heap of change? To pay for this downside protection, you could sell call options. But those calls will limit your potential gain. To earn enough to pay for the puts, you would probably have to write calls that cap your stock-market earnings during the next year at 8%.

That would be a big mistake if your first year of retirement turns out to be a gangbuster year for stocks. "If you are worried about the upside, sell a call at a higher strike price and finance part of the put out of your own pocket," Prof. Milevsky suggests. Because these calls with a higher strike price won't generate as big a premium, protecting against a one-year market decline of greater than 8% might cost you 3% or 4% of your stock portfolio's value. For antsy investors, that might be money well spent. But I would rather keep the cash and take my chances.

Source: Jonathan Clements, *The Wall Street Journal*, January 15, 2002.

(3) has at least the potential for a gain. The case of a call option selling for more than its underlying asset is a particularly juicy arbitrage because it puts money in your pocket today, and later either leaves you with stock you acquired at no cost or else leaves you with the exercise price on the option. Very nice, indeed! But too good to be true.

The Upper Bound for a Put Option Price

We've seen that a call option cannot sell for more than the underlying stock. How about a put option? To answer, suppose again that the stock price is $60. If a put sells for $65, is there an arbitrage opportunity?

It may look a little odd, but, without more information, we can't tell if there is an arbitrage or not. To see this, suppose the exercise price on the put option is $1,000. The right to sell a share of stock for $1,000 when its current worth is only $60 is obviously valuable, and it is obviously worth more than $65.

As this example suggests, the upper bound on a put option's price depends on the strike price. To illustrate, suppose we have a put option with an exercise price of $50 and a price of $60. What would you do?

This situation is an arbitrage opportunity. You would simply sell puts at $60 and put the money in the bank. The worst thing that could happen to you is that you would have to buy the stock for $50 a share, leaving you with stock and $10 per share in cash (the difference between the $60 you received and the $50 you paid for the stock). So you would either end up with stock that cost you nothing to acquire plus some cash or, if the option expires worthless, you would keep the entire $60. We therefore conclude that a put option must sell for less than its strike price.

The Lower Bounds on Option Prices

Having established the most a call or put could sell for, we now want to know what is the least they could sell for. We observe that an option cannot have a negative value, since, by definition, an option can simply be discarded.

intrinsic value The payoff that an option holder receives assuming the underlying stock price remains unchanged from its current value.

To further address this question, it is useful to define what is known as the **intrinsic value** of an option. The intrinsic value of an option is the payoff that an option holder receives if the underlying stock price does not change from its current value. Equivalently, it is what the option would be worth if it were expiring immediately.

For example, suppose a certain call option contract specifies a strike price of $50, and the underlying stock price for the option is currently $45. Suppose the option was about to expire. With the stock price at $45 and the strike at $50, this option would have no value. Thus, this call option's intrinsic value is zero.

Alternatively, suppose the underlying stock price is currently $55. If the option was about to expire, it would be exercised, yielding a payoff of $5. This $5, which is simply the difference between the $55 stock price and the $50 strike price, is the call option's intrinsic value.

As another example of intrinsic value, suppose a put option has a strike price of $50, and the current stock price is $55. If the put were about to expire, it would be worthless. In this case, the put option's intrinsic value is zero.

Alternatively, suppose the underlying stock price was $45. The put option would be exercised, yielding a payoff of $5, which is the difference between the $50 strike price and the $45 stock price. In this case, the put option's intrinsic value is $5.

Based on our examples, the intrinsic value of a call option and a put option can be written as follows, where S is the current stock price and K is the option's strike price. The term "*max*" is a shorthand notation for maximum.

$$\text{Call option intrinsic value} = max \ [0, S - K] \qquad (14.1)$$
$$\text{Put option intrinsic value} = max \ [0, K - S]$$

This notation simply means that the intrinsic value of a call option is equal to $S - K$ or zero, whichever is bigger. Similarly, the intrinsic value of a put option is equal to $K - S$ or zero, whichever is bigger.

An option with a positive intrinsic value is said to be "in the money," and an option with a zero intrinsic value is said to be "out of the money" or "out the money." If the stock price and the strike price are essentially equal, the option is said to be "at the money." Thus, a call option is in the money when the stock price is greater than the strike price, and a put option is in the money when the stock price is less than the strike price.

Having defined an option's intrinsic value, we now ask: Is it possible for an option to sell for less than its intrinsic value? The answer is no. To see this, suppose a current stock price is $S = \$60$, and a call option with a strike price of $K = \$50$ has a price of $C = \$5$. Clearly, this call option is in the money, and the $5 call price is less than the option's intrinsic value of $S - K = \$10$.

If you are actually presented with these stock and option prices, you have an arbitrage opportunity to obtain a riskless arbitrage profit by following a simple three-step strategy. First, buy the call option at its price of $C = \$5$. Second, immediately exercise the call option and buy the stock from the call writer at the strike price of $K = \$50$. At this point, you have acquired the stock for $55, which is the sum of the call price plus the strike price.

As a third and final step, simply sell the stock at the current market price of $S = \$60$. Since you acquired the stock for $55 and sold the stock for $60, you have earned an arbitrage profit of $5. Clearly, if such an opportunity continued to exist, you would repeat these three steps over and over until you became bored with making easy money (as if that could ever happen!). But realistically, such easy arbitrage opportunities do not exist, and it therefore follows that a call option price is never less than its intrinsic value.

A similar arbitrage argument applies to put options. For example, suppose a current stock price is $S = \$40$, and a put option with a strike price of $K = \$50$ has a price of $P = \$5$. This $5 put price is less than the option's intrinsic value of $K - S = \$10$. To exploit this opportunity, you first buy the put option at its price of $P = \$5$, and then buy the stock at its current price of $S = \$40$. At this point, you have acquired the stock for $45, which is the sum of the put price plus the stock price. Now you immediately exercise the put option, thereby selling the stock to the option writer at the strike price of $S = \$50$. Since you acquired the stock for $45 and sold the stock for $50, you have earned an arbitrage profit of $5. Again, you would not realistically expect such an easy arbitrage opportunity to actually exist, and therefore we conclude that a put option's price is never less than its intrinsic value.

Our conclusion that call option and put option prices are never less than their intrinsic values can be stated as follows, where the mathematical symbol "$\geq$" means "greater than or equal to:"

$$\text{Call option price} \geq max \ [0, S - K] \qquad (14.2)$$
$$\text{Put option price} \geq max \ [0, K - S]$$

In plain English, these equations simply state that an option's price is never less than the intrinsic value of the option.

There is an important caveat concerning our lower bounds on option values. If you pick up *The Wall Street Journal*, it is relatively easy to find cases in which it appears an option is selling for less than its intrinsic value, at least by a small amount. However, if you tried to actually exploit the apparent arbitrage, you would find that the prices in the *Journal* are not the ones you could actually trade at! There are a variety of reasons for this, but, at a minimum, keep in mind that the prices you see for the stock and the option are probably not synchronous, so the two prices may never have existed at the same point in time.

Check This

14.5a What is the most a call option could be worth? The least?

14.5b What is the most a put option could be worth? The least?

14.5c What is an out-of-the-money put option?

14.6 Employee Stock Options

employee stock option (ESO) An option granted to an employee by a company giving the employee the right to buy shares of stock in the company at a fixed price for a fixed time.

In this section, we take a brief look at **employee stock options**, or **ESOs**. An ESO is, in essence, a call option that a firm gives to employees giving them the right to buy shares of stock in the company. The practice of granting options to employees has become widespread. It is almost universal for upper management, but some companies, like The Gap and Starbucks, have granted options to almost every employee. Thus, an understanding of ESOs is important. Why? Because you may very soon be an ESO holder!

ESO Features

Since ESOs are basically call options, we have already covered most of the important aspects. However, ESOs have a few features that make them different from regular stock options. The details differ from company to company, but a typical ESO has a 10-year life, which is much longer than most ordinary options. Unlike traded options, ESOs cannot be sold. They also have what is known as a "vesting" period. Often, for up to three years or so, an ESO cannot be exercised and also must be forfeited if an employee leaves the company. After this period, the options "vest," which means they can be exercised. Sometimes employees who resign with vested options are given a limited time to exercise their options.

Why are ESOs granted? There are basically two reasons. First, the owners of a corporation (the shareholders) face the basic problem of aligning shareholder and management interests and also of providing incentives for employees to focus on corporate goals. ESOs are a powerful motivator because, as we have seen, the payoffs on options can be very large. High-level executives in particular stand to gain enormous wealth if they are successful in creating value for stockholders.

The second reason some companies rely heavily on ESOs is that an ESO has no immediate, upfront, out-of-pocket cost to the corporation. In smaller, possibly cash-strapped, companies, ESOs are simply a substitute for ordinary wages. Employees are willing to accept them instead of cash, hoping for big payoffs in the future. In fact, ESOs are a major recruiting tool, allowing businesses to attract talent that they otherwise could not afford.

ESO Repricing

ESOs are almost always "at the money" when they are issued, meaning that the stock price is equal to the strike price. Notice that, in this case, the intrinsic value is zero, so there is no value from immediate exercise. Of course, even though the intrinsic value is zero, an ESO is still quite valuable because of, among other things, its very long life.

If the stock falls significantly after an ESO is granted, then the option is said to be "underwater." On occasion, a company will decide to lower the strike price on underwater options. Such options are said to be "restruck" or "repriced."

The practice of repricing ESOs is very controversial. Companies that do it argue that once an ESO becomes deeply out of the money, it loses its incentive value because employees recognize there is only a small chance that the option will finish in the money. In fact, employees may leave and join other companies where they receive a fresh options grant.

Critics of repricing point out that a lowered strike price is, in essence, a reward for failing. They also point out that if employees know that options will be repriced, then much of the incentive effect is lost. Today, many companies award options on a regular basis, perhaps annually or even quarterly. That way, an employee will always have at least some options that are near the money even if others are underwater. Also, regular grants ensure that employees always have unvested options, which gives them an added incentive to stay with their current employer rather than forfeit the potentially valuable options.

14.6a	What are the key differences between a traded stock option and an ESO?
14.6b	What is ESO repricing? Why is it controversial?

Check This

14.7 Put-Call Parity

put-call parity
Theorem asserting a certain parity relationship between call and put prices for European-style options with the same strike price and expiration date.

Put-call parity is perhaps the most fundamental parity relationship among option prices. **Put-call parity** states that the difference between a call option price and a put option price for European-style options with the same strike price and expiration date is equal to the difference between the underlying stock price and the discounted strike price. The put-call parity relationship is algebraically represented as

$$C - P = S - Ke^{-rT} \qquad (14.3)$$

where the variables are defined as follows:

C = Call option price	P = Put option price
S = Current stock price	K = Option strike price
r = Risk-free interest rate	T = Time remaining until option expiration

The logic behind put-call parity is based on the fundamental principle of finance stating that two securities with the same riskless payoff on the same future date must have the same price. To illustrate how this principle is applied to demonstrate put-call parity, suppose we form a portfolio of risky securities by following these three steps:

For information on trading options, see www.ino.com

1. Buy 100 shares of Microsoft stock (MSFT).

2. Write one Microsoft call option contract.

3. Buy one Microsoft put option contract.

Both Microsoft options have the same strike price and expiration date. We assume that these options are European style and, therefore, cannot be exercised before the last day prior to their expiration date.

Table 14.1 states the payoffs to each of these three securities based on the expiration date stock price, denoted by S_T. For example, if the expiration date stock price is greater than the strike price, that is, $S_T > K$, then the put option expires worthless and the call option requires a payment from writer to buyer of $(S_T - K)$. Alternatively, if the stock price is less than the strike price, that is, $S_T < K$, the call option expires worthless and the put option yields a payment from writer to buyer of $(K - S_T)$.

In Table 14.1, notice that no matter whether the expiration date stock price is greater or less than the strike price, the payoff to the portfolio is always equal to the strike price. This means that the portfolio has a risk-free payoff at option expiration equal to the strike price. Since the portfolio is risk-free, the cost of acquiring this portfolio today should be no different from the cost of acquiring any other risk-free investment with the same payoff on the same date. One such riskless investment is a U.S. Treasury bill.

To learn more about trading options, see www.optionetics.com

The cost of a U.S. Treasury bill paying K dollars at option expiration is the discounted strike price Ke^{-rT}, where r is the risk-free interest rate and T is the time remaining until option expiration, which together form the discount factor e^{-rT}. By the fundamental principle of finance stating that two riskless investments with the same payoff on the same date must have the same price, it follows that this cost is also equal to the cost of acquiring the stock and options portfolio. Since this portfolio is formed by (1) buying the stock, (2) writing a call option, and (3) buying a put option, its cost is the sum of the stock price, plus the put price, less the call price. Setting this portfolio cost equal to the discounted strike price yields this equation:

$$S + P - C = Ke^{-rT}$$

By a simple rearrangement of terms we obtain the originally stated put-call parity equation, thereby validating our put-call parity argument:

$$C - P = S - Ke^{-rT}$$

The put-call parity argument stated above assumes that the underlying stock paid no dividends before option expiration. If the stock does pay a dividend before option

TABLE 14.1	Put-Call Parity		
		Expiration Date Payoffs	
Expiration Date Stock Price		$S_T > K$	$S_T < K$
Buy stock		S_T	S_T
Write one call option		$-(S_T - K)$	0
Buy one put option		0	$(K - S_T)$
Total portfolio expiration date payoff		K	K

expiration, then the put-call parity equation is adjusted as follows, where *y* represents the dividend yield:

$$C - P = Se^{-yT} - Ke^{-rT} \qquad (14.4)$$

The logic behind this adjustment is the fact that a dividend payment reduces the value of the stock, since company assets are reduced by the amount of the dividend payment. When the dividend payment occurs before option expiration, investors adjust the effective stock price determining option payoffs to be made after the dividend payment. This adjustment reduces the value of the call option and increases the value of the put option.

IMPLIED PUT OPTION PRICES

EXAMPLE 14.5

A current stock price is $50, and a call option with a strike price of $55 maturing in two months has a price of $8. The stock has a 4 percent dividend yield. If the interest rate is 6 percent, what is the price implied by put-call parity for a put option with the same strike price and maturity?

Rearranging the put-call parity equations yields the following price for a put option:

$$P = C + Ke^{-rT} - Se^{-yT}$$

Substituting numerical values yields this price for the put option:

$$\$12.78 = \$8 + \$55e^{-.06 \times (2/12)} - \$50e^{-.04 \times (2/12)}$$

Check This

14.7a The argument supporting put-call parity is based on the fundamental principle of finance that two securities with the same riskless payoff on the same future date must have the same price. Restate the demonstration of put-call parity based on this fundamental principle. (*Hint*: Start by recalling and explaining the contents of Table 14.1.)

14.7b Exchange-traded options on individual stock issues are American style, and, therefore, put-call parity does not hold exactly for these options. In the "Listed Options Quotations" page of *The Wall Street Journal*, compare the differences between selected call and put option prices with the differences between stock prices and discounted strike prices. How closely does put-call parity appear to hold for these American-style options?

14.8 Stock Index Options

Following the tremendous success of stock options trading on the Chicago Board Options Exchange, the exchange looked for other new financial products to offer to investors and portfolio managers. In 1982, the CBOE created stock index options, which, at the time, represented a new type of option contract.

Index Options: Features and Settlement

stock index option An option on a stock market index. The most popular stock index options are options on the S&P 100 index, S&P 500 index, and Dow Jones Industrials index.

A **stock index option** is an option on a stock market index. The first stock index options were contracts on the Standard & Poor's index of 100 large companies representative of American industry. This index is often simply called the "S&P 100." S&P 100 index options trade under the ticker symbol OEX, and S&P 100 index options are referred to as "OEX options." The second stock index options introduced by the CBOE were contracts on the Standard & Poor's index of 500 companies, the "S&P 500." S&P 500 index options trade under the ticker symbol SPX and are referred to as "SPX options." In 1997, the CBOE introduced options on the Dow Jones Industrial Average (DJIA), which trade under the ticker symbol DJX.

Besides the different underlying indexes, the major difference between SPX, DJX, and OEX contracts are that OEX options are American style, whereas SPX and DJX options are European style. As we noted earlier, American-style options can be exercised any time before expiration, whereas European-style options can be exercised only on the last day before option expiration.

Before stock index options could be introduced, one very important detail that had to be worked out was what to do when an option is exercised. It was obvious to exchange officials that actual delivery of all stocks comprising a stock index was impractical. Instead, a cash settlement procedure was adopted for stock index options. With cash settlement, when a stock index option is exercised, the option writer pays a cash amount to the option buyer based on the difference between the exercise date index level and the option's strike price. For example, suppose you had purchased an SPX call option with a strike price of $1,520, and the S&P 500 index was $1,540 on the day before option expiration. The difference between the index level and the strike price is $1,540 − $1,520 = $20. Since the contract size for SPX options is 100 times the S&P 500 index, the option writer must pay $100 \times $20 = $2,000, which you receive as the option holder.

In the example above, the contract size for SPX options was stated to be 100 times the S&P 500 index. In fact, the contract size for almost all standardized stock index options is 100 times the underlying index. Thus, the actual price of a stock index option is 100 times the price stated on an index level basis. There are only a few exceptions to this rule. For example, the CBOE offers so-called Reduced Value index options with a contract size that is one-tenth the size of standard index options. Reduced Value index options are appealing to some individual investors, but they represent only a minuscule share of all index options trading.

Visit exchanges trading index options at
www.cboe.com
www.cbot.com
www.cme.com

Index Option Price Quotes

There now exists a wide variety of stock market indexes for which options are available. Each business day, *The Wall Street Journal* provides a summary of the previous day's activity in stock index options. Figure 14.6, "Index Options Trading," excerpts this column.

The most prominent component of this column is the box entitled "Underlying Indexes," which contains information on the more than 35 major stock market indexes for which index options are now available. In the first column of this box, the name of each index and (in parentheses) its ticker symbol are listed. Columns 2, 3, 4, and 5 report the corresponding high, low, close, and net change values, respectively, for each stock market index from the previous day's trading. For each stock index, the columns labeled "From 12/31" and "% Chg" report the dollar value change and percentage value change, respectively, since the beginning of the current year.

FIGURE 14.6

Index Options Trading

Source: Reprinted by permission of *The Wall Street Journal*, July 1, 2003, via Copyright Clearance Center, Inc. © 2003, Dow Jones & Company, Inc. All Rights Reserved Worldwide.

INDEX OPTIONS TRADING

Monday, June 30, 2003

Volume, last, net change and open interest for all contracts. Volume figures are unofficial. Open interest reflects previous trading day. p-Put c-Call. The totals for call and put volume are midday figures

Underlying Indexes

	HIGH	LOW	CLOSE	NET CHG	FROM 12/31	% CHG
DJ Indus (DJX)	90.68	89.70	89.85	-0.04	6.43	7.7
DJ Trans (DTX)	243.26	239.90	241.29	-0.41	10.29	4.5
DJ Util (DUX)	251.48	249.53	250.99	1.47	35.81	16.6
S&P 100 (OEX)	495.58	490.18	490.39	-1.22	45.64	10.3
S&P 500 (SPX)	983.63	973.65	974.50	-1.72	94.68	10.8
CB-Tech (TXX)	428.20	420.81	421.30	-0.80	78.11	22.8
CB-Mexico (MEX)	65.73	64.65	64.79	-0.67	5.57	9.4
CB-Lps Mex (VEX)	6.57	6.47	6.48	-0.07	0.56	9.5
M5 Multintl (NFT)	569.51	562.40	562.84	-1.83	48.47	9.4
GSTI Comp (GTC)	148.79	146.33	146.53	-0.16	26.05	21.6
Nasdaq 100 (NDX)	1218.80	1199.83	1201.69	-3.56	217.33	22.1
NYSE (NYZ)	525.15	520.41	521.10	-0.75	48.23	10.2
Russell 2000 (RUT)	452.64	446.20	448.35	-0.40	65.26	17.0
Lps S&P 100 (OEX)	99.12	98.04	98.08	-0.24	9.13	10.3
Lps S&P 500 (SPX)	98.36	97.36	97.45	-0.17	9.47	10.8
Volatility (VIX)	22.04	20.98	21.62	-0.09	-10.41	-32.5
S&P Midcap (MID)	485.18	480.18	480.22	-2.03	50.43	11.7
Major Mkt (XMI)	931.10	922.50	923.42	-2.25	44.52	5.1
Eurotop 100 (AEUR)	192.76	189.45	190.00	-2.23	-0.94	-0.5
HK Fltg (HKO)	187.10	187.10	187.10	-1.71	4.42	2.4
IW Internet (IIX)	113.30	111.46	111.66	0.10	28.67	34.5
AM-Mexico (MXY)	86.49	85.64	85.66	-0.68	9.03	11.8
Institut'l-A.M. (XII)	517.81	512.57	512.64	-1.04	43.43	9.3
Japan (JPN)			96.00	-0.20	4.37	4.8
MS Cyclical (CYC)	498.94	493.34	495.46	0.35	45.83	10.2
MS Consumr (CMR)	514.06	508.98	510.40	0.20	16.99	3.4
MS Hi Tech (MSH)	371.69	365.79	366.70	-0.14	79.01	27.5
MS Internet (MOX)	11.11	10.89	10.95	-0.03	3.03	38.3
Pharmaceutical (DRG)	333.04	327.86	328.75	-1.86	30.22	10.1
Biotech (BTK)	441.20	429.86	431.72	-6.78	93.50	27.6
Gold/Silver (XAU)	78.81	77.16	78.65	1.11	1.89	2.5
Utility Index (UTY)	292.88	291.09	291.99	0.87	34.32	13.3
Value Line (VAY)	1232.22	1220.25	1222.44	-0.98	188.69	18.3
Bank (BKX)	867.34	857.50	857.56	-3.17	109.59	14.7
Semicond (SOXX)	366.46	358.18	359.69	0.23	70.45	24.4
Street.com (DOT)	124.33	121.37	121.90	-0.59	36.24	42.3
Oil Service (OSX)	93.57	91.46	91.59	-1.04	4.89	5.6
PSE Tech (PSE)	570.58	561.24	562.33	-3.06	104.00	22.7

CHICAGO

DJ INDUS AVG(DJX)

STRIKE		VOL	LAST	NET CHG	OPEN INT
Sep	72 p	10	0.35	0.10	6,005
Sep	76 p	67	0.40	...	11,330
Aug	78 p	4	0.20	-0.05	4,328
Sep	78 p	30	0.40	-0.15	4,068
Aug	80 c	5	10.50	0.20	1,010
Sep	80 p	8	0.75	...	12,408
Jul	82 c	100	8	-0.10	1,062
Jul	82 p	30	0.05	-0.05	6,294
Sep	82 p	140	1	0.10	12,780
Jul	84 p	64	0.20	...	22,168
Aug	84 p	61	0.70	-0.05	3,217
Sep	84 p	4,606	1.30	-0.15	20,425
Jul	85 c	150	5.40	-0.60	1,234
Jul	85 p	160	0.25	-0.05	5,796
Jul	86 p	100	0.35	-0.05	8,858
Aug	86 p	4,782	1.05	-0.15	5,277
Jul	87 c	15	3.60	0.20	12,493
Jul	87 p	37	0.50	-0.10	3,127
Jul	88 c	19	3	0.30	7,960
Jul	88 p	220	0.75	-0.10	5,730
Aug	88 c	134	3.50	...	1,573
Aug	88 p	181	1.65	-0.10	5,784
Sep	88 p	47	2.35	-0.15	6,929
Aug	89 p	38	1.90	0.10	553
Jul	90 c	1,380	1.40	0.10	14,238
Jul	90 p	427	1.50	-0.10	6,867
Aug	90 c	24	2.20	-0.10	7,408
Aug	90 p	67	2.45	-0.15	993
Sep	91 p	25	3.90	0.10	14,241
Jul	92 c	367	0.55	-0.05	16,199
Jul	92 p	171	2.80	-0.05	6,645
Aug	92 c	14	1.25	-0.25	14,259
Aug	92 p	514	3.60	...	2,517
Sep	92 c	45	2	-0.10	23,878
Sep	92 p	1,137	4.10	-0.30	13,867
Aug	93 c	100	1	-0.30	1,739
Aug	93 p	30	4	-0.30	691
Aug	94 c	4,475	0.75	...	6,728
Sep	94 c	60	1.35	-0.05	4,535
Sep	94 p	2	5.60	0.60	446
Jul	96 c	10	0.05	-0.05	3,999
Aug	96 c	1	0.40	-0.05	2,551
Sep	96 c	4,595	0.80	...	10,698
Aug	100 c	500	0.05	-0.10	1,789
Sep	100 c	700	0.25	-0.10	3,518

Call Vol...... 17,143 Open Int. 377,534
Put Vol...... 15,631 Open Int. 547,327

S & P 100(OEX)

STRIKE		VOL	LAST	NET CHG	OPEN INT
Sep	380 p	1	1.20	0.30	858
Oct	380 p	10	1.80	0.10	26
Aug	400 p	18	0.65	-0.10	1,029
Sep	400 p	150	1.45	-0.40	1,395
Aug	410 p	10	0.50	-0.20	108
Jul	420 p	255	0.05	-0.05	3,955
Sep	420 p	3	3	0.20	1,959
Oct	420 p	20	4.40	0.40	45
Jul	430 p	210	0.15	...	2,325
Sep	430 p	28	3.70	0.10	10
Jul	440 p	15	0.20	-0.30	3,016
Aug	440 p	129	2.10	-0.20	3,269
Sep	440 p	6	4.70	-0.40	2,947
Jul	445 p	49	0.40	-0.05	789
Jul	450 c	7	46	2.00	650
Jul	450 p	206	0.45	-0.35	5,783
Aug	450 p	5	2.80	-0.30	622
Jul	455 p	252	0.80	-0.20	2,741
Aug	455 p	10	3.70	-0.10	32
Jul	460 c	1	35.50	1.50	984
Jul	460 p	918	1.25	-0.05	4,287
Aug	460 p	18	4.20	-0.40	906
Sep	460 p	12	9.20	0.30	1,242
Jul	465 c	1	29.70	-1.30	294
Jul	465 p	385	1.75	-0.20	2,449
Jul	470 c	702	23	-1.40	1,004
Jul	470 p	1,131	2.30	-0.20	4,291
Aug	470 c	10	29	-11.50	763
Aug	470 p	23	5.80	0.60	608
Sep	470 p	102	10.50	0.20	8
Jul	475 c	2	18.60	-2.90	774
Jul	475 p	375	3.20	-0.30	2,368
Aug	475 p	12	6.60	-1.10	177
Jul	480 c	59	14.80	-1.20	2,743
Jul	480 p	2,010	4.50	-0.10	8,476
Aug	480 c	17	20.90	-0.30	1,592
Aug	480 p	101	9.70	0.70	581
Sep	480 p	3	13	-1.00	1,493
Oct	480 p	2	16.70	...	6
Jul	485 c	40	11.20	-0.80	370
Jul	485 p	1,260	6.10	-0.20	3,681

STRIKE		VOL	LAST	NET CHG	OPEN INT
Jul	485 p	1,260	6.10	-0.20	3,681
Aug	485 p	52	10	-2.00	149
Jul	490 c	2,051	8.60	-0.50	4,221
Jul	490 p	1,659	8.30	-0.10	6,701
Aug	490 c	72	13.50	-1.10	1,681
Aug	490 p	987	12.30	-1.60	3,541
Sep	490 c	2	20	0.60	3
Sep	490 p	2	17	1.20	256
Aug	495 c	2	11.70	-2.70	90
Aug	495 p	68	16	-0.20	104
Jul	500 c	2,896	4.20	-0.30	5,736
Jul	500 p	678	14.80	0.10	4,193
Aug	500 c	4,686	8.60	-1.70	5,419
Aug	500 p	132	17	-1.90	3,088
Sep	500 c	4,599	13.20	-0.60	1,071
Sep	500 p	21	21.40	-2.40	775
Oct	500 p	1	25.80	0.80	1
Jul	505 c	724	2.60	-0.50	3,378
Jul	505 p	24	16.20	-1.20	822
Aug	505 c	11	7.60	0.50	11
Jul	510 c	2,065	1.70	-0.40	6,595
Jul	510 p	61	22	1.00	617
Aug	510 c	38	5	-0.70	1,157
Aug	510 p	6	22.40	-3.60	154
Sep	510 p	6	29.40	0.40	9
Jul	515 c	2,694	1.10	-0.20	4,501
Jul	515 p	4	27.50	4.00	94
Aug	515 c	22	4.80	0.50	198
Jul	520 c	2,251	0.65	-0.20	5,275
Jul	520 p	7	32	4.00	99
Aug	520 c	68	2.80	-0.50	1,497
Aug	520 p	6	34	...	39
Sep	520 c	175	6	-0.60	1,593
Sep	520 p	10	33.50	...	17
Aug	530 c	325	1.65	-0.10	245
Jul	535 c	62	0.35	0.10	9,501
Aug	535 c	20	1.20	-0.50	605
Jul	540 c	322	0.15	-0.05	5,584
Aug	540 c	34	0.90	-0.30	1,471
Aug	550 c	34	0.50	-0.05	487
Jul	560 c	15	0.05	...	1,599
Sep	560 c	30	1.10	-0.05	1,664

Call Vol...... 26,345 Open Int. 104,455
Put Vol...... 13,472 Open Int. 124,790

S & P 500(SPX)

STRIKE		VOL	LAST	NET CHG	OPEN INT
Sep	500 c	100	475.90	-9.10	21,342
Sep	500 p	237	0.10	...	22,578
Aug	700 p	1,560	0.25	-0.05	3,614
Sep	700 p	4	0.90	0.20	25,595

STRIKE		VOL	LAST	NET CHG	OPEN INT
Sep	700 p	4	0.90	0.20	25,595
Aug	725 p	200	0.30	-0.20	186
Sep	725 p	4	1.20	0.10	7,178
Aug	750 p	1,740	0.50	...	3,618
Sep	750 p	182	1.95	0.20	44,974
Jul	775 p	13	0.10	0.05	3,368
Aug	775 p	411	0.65	-0.10	378
Sep	775 p	1,000	2	-0.25	7,364
Jul	800 p	10	0.20	0.05	11,411
Aug	800 c	2	175.50	-5.20	65
Aug	800 p	221	1	-0.20	3,583
Sep	800 p	864	3	-0.80	19,191
Jul	825 p	15	0.20	-0.05	13,395
Aug	825 p	10	1.30	-0.70	6,068
Sep	825 c	7	150	-5.00	2,378
Sep	825 p	915	4.60	0.30	27,065
Jul	835 p	24	0.20	-0.15	9,866
Jul	850 c	8	129	...	491
Jul	850 p	529	0.40	-0.05	10,885
Aug	850 c	47	129	-3.20	60
Aug	850 p	670	2.60	-0.10	6,658
Sep	850 c	5	134	-4.60	11,159
Sep	850 p	46	6.80	0.70	33,353
Jul	875 c	142	103.50	0.50	6,794
Jul	875 p	968	0.65	-0.15	40,364
Aug	875 c	4	100	-15.00	26
Aug	875 p	1,011	4	0.30	15,994
Sep	875 c	1	108	-9.00	16,134
Sep	875 p	11	9.30	0.10	28,672
Jul	890 p	35	1	-0.20	1,767
Jul	900 c	449	76	-2.00	5,546
Jul	900 p	971	1.40	-0.05	37,000
Aug	900 c	86	78	-10.50	2,057
Aug	900 p	1,239	6.10	-0.40	11,804
Sep	900 c	9	84.50	-2.50	12,368
Sep	900 p	97	12.50	-0.50	28,365
Jul	905 p	7	1.60	0.10	16
Jul	910 p	18	1.80	-0.20	579
Jul	920 p	844	2.40	-0.50	6,373
Jul	925 c	11	52	-11.50	19,436
Jul	925 p	1,954	3	-0.50	26,574
Aug	925 c	11	57.50	-11.00	455
Aug	925 p	516	9.80	-0.50	4,779
Sep	925 c	331	66	-3.00	12,426
Sep	925 p	368	17.20	-0.80	13,889
Jul	940 c	6	43.50	-5.00	961
Jul	940 p	2,102	4.90	0.20	5,253
Jul	945 p	31	4.70	-1.40	3,409
Jul	950 c	571	31	-3.50	11,312
Jul	950 p	4,224	7.50	-0.30	24,163

STRIKE		VOL	LAST	NET CHG	OPEN INT
Jul	950 p	4,224	7.50	-0.30	24,163
Aug	950 c	38	38.50	-2.10	3,466
Aug	950 p	2,726	16.60	-0.80	12,713
Sep	950 c	6	47.50	-3.50	13,751
Sep	950 p	1,500	26.20	0.20	15,046
Jul	965 c	53	22	...	905
Jul	965 p	992	12	0.70	4,881
Jul	975 c	495	14.50	-1.20	24,412
Jul	975 p	3,501	16	-0.40	17,614
Aug	975 c	118	24.50	-1.50	8,245
Aug	975 p	234	22.80	-2.10	6,600
Sep	975 c	2,734	32	-3.00	31,064
Sep	975 p	2,898	35	...	21,242
Jul	990 c	1,716	9	...	4,180
Jul	990 p	754	25.50	0.50	3,604
Aug	995 c	40	15	-1.50	5,603
Aug	995 p	46	32.70	-3.80	2,469
Sep	995 c	1,216	25	...	27,767
Sep	995 p	174	41	-3.00	21,908
Jul	1005 c	2,473	4.20	-0.40	12,430
Jul	1005 p	359	35	1.00	8,174
Aug	1005 c	106	10.20	-1.60	2,058
Aug	1005 p	947	43.50	2.50	1,052
Jul	1010 c	766	3.50	-0.50	6,547
Jul	1010 p	164	42.20	3.70	2,506
Jul	1025 c	10,186	1.75	-0.10	24,028
Jul	1025 p	257	54	3.50	3,121
Aug	1025 c	723	6.40	-0.60	6,186
Aug	1025 p	2	52	-3.00	602
Sep	1025 c	53	15	1.60	20,189
Jul	1040 c	96	0.80	-0.20	2,105
Jul	1050 c	1,619	0.50	-0.10	15,695
Jul	1050 p	45	70	6.40	1,684
Aug	1050 c	2,166	2.50	-0.50	9,097
Sep	1050 c	951	7	-1.80	24,778
Sep	1050 p	2	85	9.50	2,114
Jul	1075 c	110	0.10	-0.20	14,327
Aug	1075 c	20	1.60	-0.15	5,546
Aug	1075 p	40	97	-4.90	350
Sep	1075 c	622	2.80	-1.20	5,459
Sep	1075 p	7	100	-2.50	833
Aug	1100 c	6	0.55	-0.10	2,844
Aug	1100 p	10	119	-8.10	34
Sep	1100 c	64	1.70	-0.30	12,932
Sep	1100 p	1	124	6.00	542
Sep	1125 c	3	0.95	-0.25	3,371
Sep	1300 c	237	0.10	-0.05	18,057

Call Vol........33,156 Open Int..982,601
Put Vol........ 48,844 Open Int.1,302,755

Outside the indexes box, index options trading data are reported separately for each options exchange and index. Figure 14.6 contains information for options on several indexes. The first column of data for each index reports contract expiration months, and the second column reports strike prices. The letters next to each strike price denote whether the option is a call or a put. The third column reports trading volume measured as the number of contracts traded during the previous day's trading. The fourth column, labeled "Last," reports the contract price for the last trade of the previous day, and the fifth column, labeled "Net Chg," reports the price change from the last price on the previous day. Finally, the sixth column, labeled "Open Int," lists the total number of contracts outstanding.

At the bottom of each index options listing, total call volume and open interest are reported, followed by put volume and open interest. Trading volume is measured by the number of contracts traded on a given day. Open interest is measured by the total number of contracts outstanding on a given day.

The majority of trading in stock index options is conducted on the Chicago Board Options Exchange. Figure 14.6 provides OEX and SPX information. Notice the large number of strike prices available for these contracts. Also notice the large open interest on the SPX.

INDEX OPTIONS

EXAMPLE 14.6

Suppose you bought 10 July 990 SPX call contracts at a quoted price of $5. How much did you pay in total? At option expiration, suppose the S&P 500 is at 1000. What would you receive?

The price per SPX contract is 100 times the quoted price. Since you bought 10 contracts, you paid a total of $5 \times 100 \times 10 = $5,000. If, at expiration, the S&P 500 is at 1000, you would receive $100 \times (1000 - 990) = $1,000 per contract, or $10,000 in all. This $10,000 would be paid to you in cash, since index options feature cash settlement.

Check This

14.8a In addition to the underlying asset, what is the major difference between any ordinary stock option and a stock index option?

14.8b In addition to the underlying index, what is the major difference between the OEX and SPX option contracts?

14.9 The Options Clearing Corporation

Suppose that you ordered a new car through a local dealer and paid a $2,000 deposit. Further suppose that two weeks later you receive a letter informing you that your dealer had entered bankruptcy. No doubt, you would be quite upset at the prospect of losing your $2,000 deposit.

Now consider a similar situation where you pay $2,000 for several call options through a broker. On the day before expiration you tell your broker to exercise the options, since they would produce, say, a $5,000 payoff. Then, a few days later, your broker tells you that the call writer entered bankruptcy proceedings and that your

$2,000 call premium and $5,000 payoff were lost. No doubt, this would also be quite upsetting. However, if your options were traded through a registered options exchange, the integrity of your options investment would be guaranteed by the **Options Clearing Corporation (OCC)**.

Options Clearing Corporation (OCC)
Private agency that guarantees that the terms of an option contract will be fulfilled if the option is exercised; issues and clears all option contracts trading on U.S. exchanges.

The Options Clearing Corporation is the clearing agency for all options exchanges in the United States. Both the exchanges and the clearing agency are subject to regulation by the Securities and Exchange Commission (SEC). Most options investors are unaware of the OCC because only member firms of an options exchange deal directly with it. However, in fact, all option contracts traded on U.S. options exchanges are originally issued, guaranteed, and cleared by the OCC. Brokerage firms merely act as intermediaries between investors and the OCC.

To better understand the function of the OCC, let us examine a hypothetical order to buy options. In this example, assume that you instruct your broker to buy, say, 10 August 100 put options on IBM. For simplicity, let us also assume that your broker works for a member firm of the CBOE and therefore can relay your order directly to the CBOE.

When the order arrives at the CBOE, it is directed to one of several dealers for IBM options. The CBOE dealer accepts the order by taking the position of a writer for the 10 put contracts. The order is then transferred to the OCC. Once the OCC verifies that there are matching orders from a buyer and a writer, for a small fee it takes over the dealer's position as the writer for your 10 August 100 puts.

By assuming the writer's obligation, the clearing corporation guarantees that the terms of your put contracts will be fulfilled if you later decide to exercise the options. From the CBOE dealer's perspective, the clearing corporation becomes the buyer of the 10 August 100 puts. As such, the CBOE dealer becomes obligated to the clearing corporation as the writer of 10 August 100 put options.

Visit the OCC at www.optionsclearing.com

In this way, all dealer default risk is transferred to the clearing corporation. Ultimately, the OCC ensures the performance of all options traded on all registered options exchanges in the United States. Without the OCC, these options exchanges could not function nearly as efficiently as they do in practice.

14.10 Summary and Conclusions

In 1973, organized stock options trading began when the Chicago Board Options Exchange (CBOE) was established. Since then, options trading has grown enormously. In this chapter, we examined a number of concepts and issues surrounding stock options. We saw that:

1. Options on common stock are derivative securities because the value of a stock option is derived from the value of the underlying common stock. There are two basic types of options: call options and put options. Call options are options to buy, and put options are options to sell.

2. Options are contracts. Standardized stock options represent a contract size of 100 shares of common stock per option contract. We saw how standardized option prices are quoted in the financial press.

3. Various strategies exist with options, ranging from buying and selling individual puts and calls to combination strategies involving calls, puts, and the underlying stock. There are many common strategies, including protective puts and covered calls.

4. Option prices have boundaries enforced by arbitrage. A call option cannot sell for more than the underlying asset, and a put option cannot sell for more than the strike price on the option.

5. An option's intrinsic value is a lower bound for an option's price. The intrinsic value of an option is the payoff that an option holder receives if the underlying stock price does not change from its current value.

6. An employee stock option (ESO) is an option granted by a firm to an employee. Such options provide an incentive for employees to work to increase the firm's stock price.

7. Put-call parity states that the difference between a call price and a put price for European-style options with the same strike price and expiration date is equal to the difference between the dividend-adjusted stock price and the discounted strike price.

8. A stock index option is an option on a stock market index such as the S&P 500. All stock index options use a cash settlement procedure when they are exercised. With a cash settlement procedure, when a stock index option is exercised, the option writer pays a cash amount to the option buyer.

9. The Options Clearing Corporation (OCC) is the clearing agency for all options exchanges in the United States. It guarantees that the terms of an option contract are fulfilled if the option is exercised.

Get Real

This chapter added to your understanding of put and call options by covering the rights, obligations, and potential gains and losses involved in trading options. How should you put this information to work? You need to buy and sell options to experience the gains and losses that options can provide. So, with a simulated brokerage account (such as *Stock-Trak*), you should first execute each of the basic option transactions: buy a call, sell a call, buy a put, and sell a put.

For help getting started, you can find an enormous amount of information about options on the Internet. Useful places to start are the options exchanges: Chicago Board Options Exchange (www.cboe.com), American Stock Exchange (www.amex.com), Pacific Stock Exchange (www.pacificex.com), and Philadelphia Stock Exchange (www.phlx.com). Excellent websites devoted to options education are the Options Industry Council (www.optionscentral.com) and the Options Clearing Corporation (www.optionsclearing.com). You might also look at the options section of E-Analytics (www.e-analytics.com), Trading Markets (www.tradingmarkets.com), or Investor Links (www.investorlinks.com).

For information on option trading strategies, try entering the strategy name into an Internet search engine. For example, enter the search phrases "covered calls" or "protective puts" for online information about those strategies. For more general information, try the search phrase "options trading strategies" to find sites like Commodity World (www.commodityworld.com). For a sales pitch on writing covered calls, check out Write Call (www.writecall.com) or Global Investor Solutions (www.giscor.com).

(continued)

If you're having trouble understanding options ticker symbols, don't feel alone as most everyone has trouble at first. For help on the net, try the search phrases "option symbols" or "options symbols" to find sites like Option Sites (www.optionsites.com). Of course, the options exchanges listed above also provide complete information on the option ticker symbols they use.

Key Terms

derivative security 453
call option 453
put option 453
strike price 453
American option 454
European option 454
option chain 456
option writing 459
call writer 459

put writer 459
protective put 464
covered call 464
straddle 464
intrinsic value 467
employee stock option (ESO) 469
put-call parity 470
stock index option 473
Options Clearing Corporation (OCC) 476

Chapter Review Problems and Self-Test

1. **Call Option Payoffs**   You purchase 25 call contracts on Blue Ox stock. The strike price is $22, and the premium is $1. If the stock is selling for $24 per share at expiration, what are your call options worth? What is your net profit? What if the stock were selling for $23? $22?

2. **Stock versus Options**   Stock in Bunyan Brewery is currently priced at $20 per share. A call option with a $20 strike and 60 days to maturity is quoted at $2. Compare the percentage gains and losses from a $2,000 investment in the stock versus the option in 60 days for stock prices of $26, $20, and $18.

3. **Put-Call Parity**   A call option sells for $8. It has a strike price of $80 and six months until expiration. If the underlying stock sells for $60 per share, what is the price of a put option with an $80 strike price and six months until expiration? The risk-free interest rate is 6 percent.

Answers to Self-Test Problems

1. Blue Ox stock is selling for $24. You own 25 contracts, each of which gives you the right to buy 100 shares at $22. Your options are thus worth $2 per share on 2,500 shares, or $5,000. The option premium was $1, so you paid $100 per contract, or $2,500 total. Your net profit is $2,500. If the stock is selling for $23, your options are worth $2,500, so your net profit is exactly zero. If the stock is selling for $22, your options are worthless, and you lose the entire $2,500 you paid.

2. Bunyan stock costs $20 per share, so if you invest $2,000, you'll get 100 shares. The option premium is $2, so an option contract costs $200. If you invest $2,000, you'll get $2,000/$200 = 10 contracts. If the stock is selling for $26 in 60 days, your profit on the stock is $6 per share, or $600 total. The percentage gain is $600/$2,000 = 30%.

    In this case, your options are worth $6 per share, or $600 per contract. You have 10 contracts, so your options are worth $6,000 in all. Since you paid $2,000 for the 10 contracts, your profit is $4,000. Your percentage gain is a whopping $4,000/$2,000 = 200%.

If the stock is selling for $20, your profit is $0 on the stock, so your percentage return is 0 percent. Your options are worthless (why?), so the percentage loss is -100 percent. If the stock is selling for $18, verify that your percentage loss on the stock is -10 percent and your loss on the options is again -100 percent.

3. Using the put-call parity formula, we have

$$C - P = S - Ke^{-rT}$$

Rearranging to solve for P, the put price, and plugging in the other numbers gets us

$$P = C - S + Ke^{-rT}$$
$$= \$8 - \$60 + \$80e^{-.06(.5)}$$
$$= \$25.64$$

Test Your Investment Quotient

1. **Option Contracts**   Which of the following is not specified by a stock option contract?
   a. The underlying stock's price.
   b. The size of the contract.
   c. Exercise style—European or American.
   d. Contract settlement procedure—cash or delivery.

2. **Option Contracts**   A July 50 call option contract for SOS stock is identified by which ticker symbol? (*Hint*: See the *Stock-Trak* section at the end of this chapter.)
   a. SOS-JG
   b. SOS-JS
   c. SOS-GJ
   d. SOS-SJ

3. **Option Contracts**   An April 40 put option contract for SOS stock is identified by which ticker symbol? (*Hint*: See the *Stock-Trak* section at the end of this chapter.)
   a. SOS-HD
   b. SOS-HP
   c. SOS-DH
   d. SOS-PH

4. **Option Payoffs**   All of the following statements about the value of a call option at expiration are true, except the:
   a. Short position in the same call option can result in a loss if the stock price exceeds the exercise price.
   b. Value of the long position equals zero or the stock price minus the exercise price, whichever is higher.
   c. Value of the long position equals zero or the exercise price minus the stock price, whichever is higher.
   d. Short position in the same call option has a zero value for all stock prices equal to or less than the exercise price.

5. **Option Strategies**   Which of the following stock option strategies has the greatest potential for large losses?
   a. Writing a covered call
   b. Writing a covered put
   c. Writing a naked call
   d. Writing a naked put

6. **Option Strategies**   Which statement does not describe an at-the-money protective put position (comprised of owning the stock and the put)?
   a. Protects against loss at any stock price below the strike price of the put.
   b. Has limited profit potential when the stock price rises.

c. Returns any increase in the stock's value, dollar for dollar, less the cost of the put.
d. Provides a pattern of returns similar to a stop-loss order at the current stock price.

7. **Put-Call Parity**   Which of the following is not included in the put-call parity condition?

   a. Price of the underlying stock.
   b. Strike price of the underlying call and put option contracts.
   c. Expiration dates of the underlying call and put option contracts.
   d. Volatility of the underlying stock.

8. **Put-Call Parity**   According to the put-call parity condition, a risk-free portfolio can be created by buying 100 shares of stock and

   a. Writing one call option contract and buying one put option contract.
   b. Buying one call option contract and writing one put option contract.
   c. Buying one call option contract and buying one put option contract.
   d. Writing one call option contract and writing one put option contract.

9. **Option Strategies**   Investor A uses options for defensive and income reasons. Investor B uses options as an aggressive investment strategy. What is an appropriate use of options for Investors A and B, respectively?

   a. Writing covered calls / buying puts on stock not owned.
   b. Buying out-of-the-money calls / buying puts on stock owned.
   c. Writing naked calls / buying in-the-money calls.
   d. Selling puts on stock owned / buying puts on stock not owned.

10. **Option Strategies**   Which one of the following option combinations best describes a straddle? Buy both a call and a put on the same stock with

   a. Different exercise prices and the same expiration date.
   b. The same exercise price and different expiration dates.
   c. The same exercise price and the same expiration date.
   d. Different exercise prices and different expiration dates.

11. **Option Strategies**   Which of the following strategies is the riskiest options transaction if the underlying stock price is expected to increase substantially?

   a. Writing a naked call option.
   b. Writing a naked put option.
   c. Buying a call option.
   d. Buying a put option.

12. **Option Gains and Losses**   You create a "strap" by buying two calls and one put on ABC stock, all with a strike price of $45. The calls cost $5 each, and the put costs $4. If you close your position when ABC stock is priced at $55, what is your per-share gain or loss?

   a. $4 loss
   b. $6 gain
   c. $10 gain
   d. $20 gain

13. **Option Gains and Losses**   A put on XYZ stock with a strike price of $40 is priced at $2.00 per share, while a call with a strike price of $40 is priced at $3.50. What is the maximum per-share loss to the writer of the uncovered put and the maximum per-share gain to the writer of the uncovered call?

	Maximum Loss to Put Writer	Maximum Gain to Call Writer
a.	$38.00	$ 3.50
b.	$38.00	$36.50
c.	$40.00	$ 3.50
d.	$40.00	$40.00

14. **Option Pricing**   If a stock is selling for $25, the exercise price of a put option on that stock is $20, and the time to expiration of the option is 90 days, what are the minimum and maximum prices for the put today?
    a. $0 and $5
    b. $0 and $20
    c. $5 and $20
    d. $5 and $25

15. **Option Strategies**   Which of the following strategies is most suitable for an investor wishing to eliminate "downside" risk from a long position in stock?
    a. A long straddle position.
    b. A short straddle position.
    c. Writing a covered call option.
    d. Buying a protective put option.

16. **Covered Calls**   The current price of an asset is $75. A three-month, at-the-money American call option on the asset has a current value of $5. At what value of the asset will a covered call writer break even at expiration?
    a. $70
    b. $75
    c. $80
    d. $85

17. **Option Strategies**   The current price of an asset is $100. An out-of-the-money American put option with an exercise price of $90 is purchased along with the asset. If the breakeven point for this hedge is at an asset price of $114 at expiration, then the value of the American put at the time of purchase must have been
    a. $0
    b. $4
    c. $10
    d. $14

18. **Option Strategies**   The following diagram shows the value of a put option at expiration:

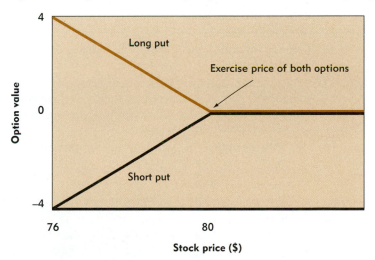

Ignoring transaction costs, which of the following statements about the value of the put option at expiration is true?
    a. The value of the short position in the put is $4 if the stock price is $76.
    b. The value of the long position in the put is −$4 if the stock price is $76.
    c. The long put has value when the stock price is below the $80 exercise price.
    d. The value of the short position in the put is zero for stock prices equaling or exceeding $76.

www.mhhe.com/cj3e

19. **Options Tickers** A letter indicating an exchange is sometimes added to an options ticker. Which of the following correctly matches these letters with their exchanges?
    a. X–PSX, A–AMEX, C–CBOE, P–PHLX
    b. X–NYSE, A–AMEX, C–CBOT, P–PSE
    c. X–PSX, A–AMEX, C–CBOT, P–PHLX
    d. X–PHLX, A–AMEX, C–CBOE, P–PSE

20. **Options Tickers** Which of the following is not a legitimate option ticker?
    a. DIS-JF
    b. DIS-VL
    c. DIS-ZG
    d. DIS-PH

Concept Questions

1. **Basic Properties of Options** What is a call option? A put option? Under what circumstances might you want to buy each? Which one has greater potential profit? Why?

2. **Calls versus Puts** Complete the following sentence for each of these investors:
   a. A buyer of call options
   b. A buyer of put options
   c. A seller (writer) of call options
   d. A seller (writer) of put options

   The (buyer/seller) of a (put/call) option (pays/receives) money for the (right/obligation) to (buy/sell) a specified asset at a fixed price for a fixed length of time.

3. **Option Breakeven** In general, if you buy a call option, what stock price is needed for you to break even on the transaction ignoring taxes and commissions? If you buy a put option?

4. **Protective Puts** Buying a put option on a stock you own is sometimes called "stock price insurance." Why?

5. **Defining Intrinsic Value** What is the intrinsic value of a call option? How do we interpret this value?

6. **Defining Intrinsic Value** What is the intrinsic value of a put option? How do we interpret this value?

7. **Arbitrage and Options** You notice that shares of stock in the Patel Corporation are going for $50 per share. Call options with an exercise price of $35 per share are selling for $10. What's wrong here? Describe how you could take advantage of this mispricing if the option expires today.

Use the following options quotations to answer questions 8 through 11:

Option & N.Y. Close	Strike Price	Expiration	Calls Vol.	Calls Last	Puts Vol.	Puts Last
Milson						
59	55	Mar	98	3.5	66	1.06
59	55	Apr	54	6.25	40	1.94
59	55	Jul	25	8.63	17	3.63
59	55	Oct	10	10.25	5	3.25

8. **Interpreting Options Quotes** How many options contracts on Milson stock were traded with an expiration date of July? How many underlying shares of stock do these options contracts represent?

9. **Interpreting Options Quotes**   Are the call options in the money? What is the intrinsic value of a Milson Corp. call option?

10. **Interpreting Options Quotes**   Are the put options in the money? What is the intrinsic value of a Milson Corp. put option?

11. **Interpreting Options Quotes**   Two of the options are clearly mispriced. Which ones? At a minimum, what should the mispriced options sell for? Explain how you could profit from the mispricing in each case.

12. **Option Strategies**   Recall the options strategies of a protective put and covered call discussed in the text. Suppose you have sold short some shares of stock. Discuss analogous option strategies and how you would implement them. (*Hint*: They're called protective calls and covered puts.)

13. **Put-Call Parity**   A put and a call option have the same maturity and strike price. If both are at the money, which is worth more? Prove your answer and then provide an intuitive explanation.

14. **Put-Call Parity**   A put and a call option have the same maturity and strike price. If they also have the same price, which one is in the money?

15. **Put-Call Parity**   One thing the put-call parity equation tells us is that given any three of a stock, a call, a put, and a T-bill, the fourth can be synthesized or replicated using the other three. For example, how can we replicate a share of stock using a put, a call, and a T-bill?

Questions and Problems

Core Questions

1. **Call Option Payoffs**   Suppose you purchase five call contracts on Macron Technology stock. The strike price is $60, and the premium is $2. If, at expiration, the stock is selling for $67 per share, what are your call options worth? What is your net profit?

2. **Put Option Payoffs**   Suppose you purchase eight put contracts on Testaburger Co. The strike price is $30, and the premium is $4. If, at expiration, the stock is selling for $21 per share, what are your put options worth? What is your net profit?

3. **Stock versus Options**   Stock in Cheezy-Poofs Manufacturing is currently priced at $90 per share. A call option with a $90 strike and 90 days to maturity is quoted at $4. Compare the percentage gains and losses from an $18,000 investment in the stock versus the option in 90 days for stock prices of $70, $90, and $110.

Use the following options quotations to answer questions 4 through 7:

Option & N.Y. Close	Strike Price	Expiration	Calls Vol.	Calls Last	Puts Vol.	Puts Last
Hendreeks						
86	80	July	72	6.60	50	.45
86	80	Aug	41	7.30	29	1.10
86	80	Oct	16	8.60	10	2.50
86	80	Jan	8	10.20	2	4.10

4. **Calculating Option Payoffs**   Suppose you buy 50 August 80 call option contracts. How much will you pay, ignoring commissions?

5. **Calculating Option Payoffs**   In Problem 4, suppose that Hendreeks stock is selling for $95 per share on the expiration date. How much is your options investment worth? What if the terminal stock price is $86?

www.mhhe.com/cj3e

6. **Calculating Option Payoffs**   Suppose you buy 30 January 80 put option contracts. What is your maximum gain? On the expiration date, Hendreeks is selling for $55 per share. How much is your options investment worth? What is your net gain?

7. **Calculating Option Payoffs**   In Problem 6, suppose you write 30 of the January 80 put contracts. What is your net gain or loss if Hendreeks is selling for $55 at expiration? For $100? What is the break-even price, that is, the terminal stock price that results in a zero profit?

8. **Put-Call Parity**   A call option is currently selling for $7. It has a strike price of $60 and six months to maturity. What is the price of a put option with a $60 strike price and six months to maturity? The current stock price is $61, and the risk-free interest rate is 5 percent.

9. **Put-Call Parity**   A call option currently sells for $9. It has a strike price of $75 and six months to maturity. A put with the same strike and expiration date sells for $3. If the risk-free interest rate is 4 percent, what is the current stock price?

10. **Put-Call Parity**   A put option with a strike price of $75 sells for $4.50. The option expires in four months, and the current stock price is $72. If the risk-free interest rate is 5 percent, what is the price of a call option with the same strike price?

Intermediate Questions

11. **Put-Call Parity**   A call option is currently selling for $8.75. It has a strike price of $65 and five months to maturity. The current stock price is $67, and the risk-free rate is 5 percent. The stock has a dividend yield of 3 percent. What is the price of a put option with the same exercise price?

12. **Put-Call Parity**   A call option is currently selling for $5.50. It has a strike price of $70 and three months to maturity. A put option with the same strike price sells for $7.10. The risk-free rate is 6 percent, and the stock has a dividend yield of 4 percent. What is the current stock price?

13. **Put-Call Parity**   A put option is currently selling for $8.50. It has a strike price of $90 and seven months to maturity. The current stock price is $95. The risk-free rate is 5 percent, and the stock has a dividend yield of 2 percent. What is the price of a call option with the same strike price?

14. **Call Option Writing**   Suppose you write 20 call option contracts with a $40 strike. The premium is $2.50. Evaluate your potential gains and losses at option expiration for stock prices of $30, $40, and $50.

15. **Put Option Writing**   Suppose you write 15 put option contracts with a $20 strike. The premium is $1.15. Evaluate your potential gains and losses at option expiration for stock prices of $10, $20, and $30.

16. **Index Options**   Suppose you buy one SPX call option contract with a strike of 1100. At maturity, the S&P 500 index is at 1180. What is your net gain or loss if the premium you paid was $28?

17. **Option Strategies**   You write a put with a strike price of $70 on stock that you have shorted at $70 (this is a "covered put"). What are the expiration date profits to this position for stock prices of $60, $65, $70, $75, and $80 if the put premium is $3?

18. **Option Strategies**   You buy a call with a strike price of $70 on stock that you have shorted at $70 (this is a "protective call"). What are the expiration date profits to this position for stock prices of $60, $65, $70, $75, and $80 if the call premium is $4?

19. **Option Strategies**   You simultaneously write a covered put and buy a protective call, both with strike prices of $70, on stock that you have shorted at $70. What are the expiration date payoffs to this position for stock prices of $60, $65, $70, $75, and $80?

20. **Option Strategies**   You simultaneously write a put and buy a call, both with strike prices of $70, naked, i.e., without any position in the underlying stock. What are the expiration date payoffs to this position for stock prices of $60, $65, $70, $75, and $80?

21. **Option Strategies** You buy a straddle, which means you purchase a put and a call with the same strike price. The put price is $2 and the call price is $4. Assume the strike price is $75. What are the expiration date profits to this position for stock prices of $65, $70, $75, $80, and $85? What are the expiration date profits for these same stock prices? What are the break-even stock prices?

22. **Index Option Positions** Suppose you buy one SPX call option with a strike of 1200 and write one SPX call option with a strike of 1250. What are the payoffs at maturity to this position for S&P 500 index levels of 1150, 1200, 1250, 1300, and 1350?

23. **Index Option Positions** Suppose you buy one SPX put option with a strike of 1200 and write one SPX put option with a strike of 1250. What are the payoffs at maturity to this position for S&P 500 index levels of 1100, 1150, 1200, 1250, and 1300?

24. **Index Option Positions** Suppose you buy one SPX call option with a strike of 1200 and write one SPX put option with a strike of 1200. What are the payoffs at maturity to this position for S&P 500 index levels of 1100, 1150, 1200, 1250, and 1300?

25. **Index Option Positions** Suppose you buy one each SPX call options with strikes of 1100 and 1300 and write two SPX call options with a strike of 1200. What are the payoffs at maturity to this position for S&P 500 index levels of 1100, 1150, 1200, 1250, 1300, 1350, and 1400?

What's on the Web?

1. **Option Prices** You want to find option prices for Intel (INTC). Go to finance.yahoo.com, get a stock quote, and follow the "Options" link. What is the option premium and strike price for the highest and lowest strike price options that are nearest to expiring? What are the option premium and strike price for the highest and lowest strike price options expiring next month?

2. **Option Symbol Construction** What is the option symbol for a call option on Cisco Systems (CSCO) with a strike price of $25 that expires in July? Go to www.cboe.com, follow the "Trading Tools" link, then the "Symbol Lookup" link. Find the basic ticker symbol for Cisco Systems options. Next, follow the "Strike Price Code" link. Find the codes for the expiration month and strike price and construct the ticker symbol. Now construct the ticker symbol for a put option with the same strike price and expiration.

3. **Option Expiration** Go to www.cboe.com, highlight the "Trading Tools" tab, then follow the "Expiration Calendar" link. What day do equity options expire in the current month? What day do they expire next month?

4. **LEAPS** Go to www.cboe.com, highlight the "Products" tab, then follow the "LEAPS" link. What are LEAPS? What are the two types of LEAPS? What are the benefits of equity LEAPS? What are the benefits of index LEAPS?

5. **FLEX Options** Go to www.cboe.com, highlight the "Institutional" tab, then follow the "FLEX Options" link. What is a FLEX option? When do FLEX options expire? What is the minimum size of a FLEX option?

www.mhhe.com/cj3e

Stock-Trak®
Portfolio Simulations

Trading Stock Options with Stock-Trak

Once you know how to trade common stocks and understand the basics of stock options, you should try your hand at trading stock options. You can buy, sell, and write stock options with your Stock-Trak account. There are some limitations, however, since options are not available for all stocks, and Stock-Trak restricts stock options trading to short-term options with maturities of less than one year. But these restrictions are quite minor.

There are four basic types of stock option trades:

1. Buy an option to open or increase a long position.
2. Sell an option to close or reduce a long position.
3. Write an option to open or increase a short position.
4. Buy an option to cover or reduce a short position.

We will discuss by example the first two types of option trades: "buying" an option to take a long position and "selling" an option to close all or part of a long position. Until you have acquired extensive experience with these trade types, you should avoid options writing.

To trade a particular stock option, you must first know the stock ticker symbol for the underlying stock. Then you must also know the ticker extension representing the strike price and maturity month of the specific contract you wish to trade. The process of obtaining this information is described next.

Suppose you want to buy five call option contracts for Coca-Cola (KO) and four put option contracts for Disney (DIS). Further suppose that both options have a $50 strike price and a March expiration month. Your orders might look like this:

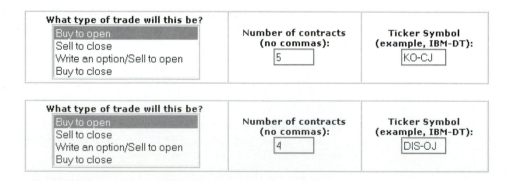

Notice that in addition to the stock ticker symbols, these option tickers have a two-letter extension denoting the option type—call or put—and the expiration month and strike price. The first letter represents the option type and expiration month. The second letter represents the strike price.

Converting option type, expiration month, and strike price to the correct two-letter ticker extension is easily done using Table ST.1. When the strike price is greater than 100, simply subtract 100 and use the result to specify a strike code; for example, a strike of 135 has the strike code G, the same as for a strike of 35.

TABLE ST.1			Stock Option Ticker Symbol Codes			
Expiration Month	Calls	Puts	Strike		Strike	
January	A	M	5	A	70	N
February	B	N	10	B	75	O
March	C	O	15	C	80	P
April	D	P	20	D	85	Q
May	E	Q	25	E	90	R
June	F	R	30	F	95	S
July	G	S	35	G	100	T
August	H	T	40	H	7.5	U
September	I	U	45	I	12.5	V
October	J	V	50	J	17.5	W
November	K	W	55	K	22.5	X
December	L	X	60	L	27.5	Y
			65	M	32.5	Z

TABLE ST.2	Exchange and Stock-Trak Tickers for July 40 Call (GH) Options	
Nasdaq Company (Ticker)	Exchange Ticker	Stock-Trak Ticker
Microsoft (MSFT)	MSQ-GH	MSFT-GH
Novell (NOVL)	NKQ-GH	NOVL-GH
Sun Microsystems (SUNW)	SUQ-GH	SUNW-GH

Notice in Table ST.1 that the 12 letters A–L denote the 12 expiration months January through December for call options. Similarly, the 12 letters M–X denote the 12 expiration months for put options. The 20 letters A–T represent the strike prices 5 through 100 in five-dollar increments. The six letters U–Z are reserved for the six strikes 7.5, 12.5, 17.5, 22.5, 27.5, and 32.5, respectively.

Options exchanges use special option tickers for Nasdaq stocks, which have four or more letters in their ticker symbols. Stock-Trak insulates its customers from this inconvenience and accepts the full Nasdaq stock ticker for option orders. This is also standard practice among brokerage firms accepting customer orders. Table ST.2 provides several examples of Stock-Trak option tickers and their corresponding options exchange versions. If you are interested in seeing more options exchange tickers, a complete list can be found at the CBOE website (www.cboe.com).

Stock-Trak Exercises

1. What are the option types, expiration months, and strike prices for the following Micron Technology (MU) options: MU-FF, MU-RF, MU-HK, and MU-TL?

2. What are the two-letter ticker extensions for the following options: January 80 calls, July 25 puts, April 12.5 calls, and October 27.5 puts?

Trading Dow Jones Index Options with Stock-Trak

In addition to trading stock options with your Stock-Trak account, you can also trade options on many stock market indexes. To trade stock index options, you must first decide which particular stock index you want to use for options trading and find the ticker symbol for that index. You

www.mhhe.com/cj3e

must also know the ticker extension for the strike price and maturity month. Also, be aware that the ticker extensions for stock index options may not be the same as for stock options.

To find the complete index option ticker symbol, look under the "Ticker Look-Up" link on the Stock-Trak options trading pit. For this, you just need the ticker symbol for the index. Here is a list of the more popular index options: Dow Jones Industrial Average (DJX), Dow Jones Transportation Average (DJT), Dow Jones Utility Average (DJU), S&P 100 (OEX), and the S&P 500 (SPX). For more information on these options consult the Chicago Board Options Exchange (www.cboe.com) website.

For a wealth of online information about index options, try the search phrases "index options," "Dow options," or "OEX options" for sites like Derivatives Strategy (www. derivativesstrategy.com), OEX Street (www.oexstreet.com), OEX Trader (www.oextrader. com), Schaeffers Research (www.schaeffersresearch.com), or Day Trader Toad (www. daytradertoad.com).

Stock-Trak Exercises

1. Pick a stock (or index) you feel will increase in value and buy a call option on the stock. Pick a stock (or index) you feel will decline in value and buy a put option on the stock. Create a graph showing the potential payoffs and profits for each option.

2. Using a stock you already own, write a covered call on the stock. Graph the payoffs from this strategy.

3. Short a stock and write a protective put on the stock at the closest strike price. Graph the payoffs and profits for your position.

4. Find a stock (or index) that you feel will move dramatically in the next month and do a long straddle on the stock. Graph the payoffs and profits for your strategy.

5. Find a stock (or index) that you feel will not move dramatically in the next month and do a short straddle on the stock. Graph the payoffs and profits for your strategy.

www.mhhe.com/cj3e

Chapter 15

Option Valuation

"I have compared the results of observation with those of theory…to show that the market, unwittingly, obeys a law which governs it, the law of probability."
—Louis Bachelier

Just what is an option worth? Actually, this is one of the more difficult questions in finance. Option valuation is an esoteric area of finance since it often involves complex mathematics. Fortunately, just like most options professionals, you can learn quite a bit about option valuation with only modest mathematical tools. But no matter how far you might wish to delve into this topic, you must begin with the Black-Scholes-Merton option pricing model. This model is the core from which all other option pricing models trace their ancestry. ■

The previous chapter introduced the basics of stock options. From an economic standpoint, perhaps the most important subject was the expiration date payoffs of stock options. Bear in mind that when investors buy options today, they are buying risky future payoffs. Likewise, when investors write options today, they become obligated to make risky future payments. In a competitive financial marketplace, option prices observed each day are collectively agreed on by buyers and writers assessing the likelihood of all possible future payoffs and payments and setting option prices accordingly.

In this chapter, we discuss stock option prices. This discussion begins with the Black-Scholes-Merton option pricing model, which is widely regarded by finance professionals as the premier model of stock option valuation.

15.1 The Black-Scholes-Merton Option Pricing Model

Option pricing theory made a great leap forward in the early 1970s with the development of the Black-Scholes option pricing model by Fischer Black and Myron Scholes. Recognizing the important theoretical contributions by Robert Merton, many finance professionals knowledgeable in the history of option pricing theory refer to an extended version of the model as the Black-Scholes-Merton option pricing model. In 1997, Myron Scholes and Robert Merton were awarded the Nobel Prize in Economics for their pioneering work in option pricing theory. Unfortunately, Fischer Black had died two years earlier and so did not share the Nobel Prize, which cannot be awarded posthumously. The nearby *Investment Updates* box presents *The Wall Street Journal* story of the Nobel Prize award.

The Black-Scholes-Merton option pricing model states the value of a stock option as a function of these six input factors:

1. The current price of the underlying stock.
2. The dividend yield of the underlying stock.
3. The strike price specified in the option contract.
4. The risk-free interest rate over the life of the option contract.
5. The time remaining until the option contract expires.
6. The price volatility of the underlying stock.

To learn more about the Black-Scholes-Merton formula, see www.jeresearch.com

The six inputs are algebraically defined as follows:

S = Current stock price

y = Stock dividend yield

K = Option strike price

r = Risk-free interest rate

T = Time remaining until option expiration

σ = Sigma, representing stock price volatility

In terms of these six inputs, the Black-Scholes-Merton formula for the price of a call option on a single share of common stock is

$$C = Se^{-yT}N(d_1) - Ke^{-rT}N(d_2) \qquad (15.1)$$

The Black-Scholes-Merton formula for the price of a put option on a share of common stock is

$$P = Ke^{-rT}N(-d_2) - Se^{-yT}N(-d_1) \qquad (15.2)$$

The CBOE has a free options calculator that will do most of the calculations in this chapter at www.cboe.com

In these call and put option formulas, the numbers d_1 and d_2 are calculated as

$$d_1 = \frac{\ln (S/K) + (r - y + \sigma^2/2)T}{\sigma\sqrt{T}} \quad \text{and} \quad d_2 = d_1 - \sigma\sqrt{T}$$

In the formulas above, call and put option prices are algebraically represented by C and P, respectively. In addition to the six input factors S, K, r, y, T, and σ, the following three mathematical functions are used in the call and put option pricing formulas:

1. e^x, or $exp(x)$, denoting the natural exponent of the value of x.
2. $ln(x)$, denoting the natural logarithm of the value of x.
3. $N(x)$, denoting the standard normal probability of the value of x.

Two economists with close ties to Wall Street, Robert C. Merton and Myron S. Scholes, won the Nobel Memorial Prize in Economic Science for path-breaking work that helped spawn the $148 billion stock-options industry.

The Nobel economics prize is given to innovators whose work breaks new ground and sires whole bodies of economic research. But this year, the prize committee chose laureates not only with distinguished academic records, but also with especially pragmatic bents, to split the $1 million award. Prof. Merton, 53 years old, teaches at Harvard Business School, while Prof. Scholes, 56, has emeritus status from the Stanford Graduate School of Business.

In the early 1970s, Prof. Scholes, with the late mathematician Fischer Black, invented an insightful method of pricing options and warrants at a time when most investors and traders still relied on educated guesses to determine the value of various stock-market products. Prof. Merton later demonstrated the broad applicability of the Black-Scholes options-pricing formula, paving the way for the incredible growth of markets in options and other derivatives.

"Thousands of traders and investors now use this formula every day to value stock options in markets throughout the world," the Royal Swedish Academy of Sciences said yesterday.

The Black-Scholes Formula

In their paper, Black and Scholes obtained exact formulas for pricing options.

$$C = SN(d) - Ke^{-rT}N(d - \sigma \sqrt{T})$$

According to the formula, the value of the call option C is given by the difference between the expected share value (the first term on the right-hand-side of the equation) and the expected cost (the second term) if the option is exercised at maturity.

The Black-Scholes option-pricing model "is really the classic example of an academic innovation that has been adopted widely in practice," said Gregg Jarrell, professor of economics at the University of Rochester's William E. Simon Business School and former chief economist at the Securities and Exchange Commission. "It is one of the most elegant and precise models that any of us has ever seen."

Options allow investors to trade the future rights to buy or sell assets—such as stocks—at a set price. An investor who holds 100 shares of International Business Machines Corp. stock today, for example, might buy an option giving them the right to sell 100 IBM shares at a fixed price in three months' time. The investor is therefore partially protected against a fall in the stock price during the life of the option.

Until the Black-Scholes model gained acceptance, the great minds of economics and finance were unable to develop a method of putting an accurate price on those options. The problem was how to evaluate the risk associated with options, when the underlying stock price changes from moment to moment. The risk of an option depends on the price of the stock underlying the option.

That breakthrough allowed the economists to create a pricing formula that included the stock price, the agreed sale or "strike" price of the option, the stock's volatility, the risk-free interest rate offered with a secure bond, and the time until the option's expiration. They published their work in 1973, the same year the Chicago Board Options Exchange turned the scattered world of options trading into a more formal market.

Prof. Merton himself forged a formal theoretical framework for the Black-Scholes formula, and extended the analysis to other derivative products—financial instruments in which the value of the security depends on the value of another indicator, such as mortgage, interest or exchange rates. More broadly, his work allowed economists and financial professionals to view a wide variety of commonly traded financial instruments—such as corporate bonds—as derivatives and to price them using the ideas first expounded by Dr. Black and Prof. Scholes. "For the most part, the thing was conceived entirely in theory," said Prof. Merton.

The practical implications soon became apparent, however, as market participants flocked to the Black-Scholes-Merton approach to determine how much options are worth. "It's just a terrific yardstick for investors to help make that judgment," said Bill Kehoe, vice president and manager of the options marketing group at Merrill Lynch & Co., and an options trader since 1961.

Options markets have grown astronomically in the quarter century since the formula reached trading floors around the country. The value of U.S. exchange-traded options in 1995 was $118 billion. Last year, it surged to $148 billion, and in the first nine months of 1997, the figure hit $155 billion. More than 100,000 options series are now available. "Even now, we calculate the value of options world-wide using the Black-Scholes formula," said Yair Orgler, chairman of the Tel Aviv Stock Exchange.

COMPUTING BLACK-SCHOLES-MERTON OPTION PRICES

EXAMPLE 15.1

Calculate call and put option prices, given the following inputs to the Black-Scholes-Merton option pricing formula.

Stock price	$S = \$50$
Dividend yield	$y = 2\%$
Strike price	$K = \$45$
Time to maturity	$T = 3$ months
Stock volatility	$\sigma = 25\%$
Interest rate	$r = 6\%$

Referring to equations 15.1 and 15.2, first we compute values for d_1 and d_2:

$$d_1 = \frac{\ln(50/45) + (.06 - .02 + .25^2/2).25}{.25\sqrt{.25}}$$

$$= \frac{.10536 + .07125 \times .25}{.125}$$

$$= .98538$$

$$d_2 = d_1 - .25\sqrt{.25}$$

$$= .86038$$

The following standard normal probabilities are provided (see next example):

$N(d_1) = N(.98538) = .83778$ $N(-d_1) = 1 - N(d_1) = .16222$

$N(d_2) = N(.86038) = .80521$ $N(-d_2) = 1 - N(d_2) = .19479$

We can now calculate the price of the call option as

$$C = \$50 \times e^{-.02 \times .25} \times .83778 - \$45 \times e^{-.06 \times .25} \times .80521$$

$$= \$50 \times .99501 \times .83778 - \$45 \times .98511 \times .80521$$

$$= \$5.985$$

and the price of the put option as

$$P = \$45 \times e^{-.06 \times .25} \times .19479 - \$50 \times e^{-.02 \times .25} \times .16222$$

$$= \$45 \times .98511 \times .19479 - \$50 \times .99501 \times .16222$$

$$= \$.565$$

OBTAINING STANDARD NORMAL PROBABILITIES WITH EXCEL

EXAMPLE 15.2

Exact standard normal probabilities provided in the previous example are obtained from Excel using the function NORMSDIST(x). A detailed example of how to use an Excel spreadsheet to calculate Black-Scholes-Merton option prices is shown in the nearby *Spreadsheet Analysis* box.

Standard normal probabilities may also be obtained from a table of standard normal probabilities such as Table 15.1. This table was created using the Excel function NORMSDIST(x). However, since any table has a limited number of values, a slight inaccuracy may be introduced. Consider the value for d_1 in the example above:

$$d_1 = .98538$$

(continued)

TABLE 15.1 — Standard Normal Probability Values

Z-value	P-value	Z-value	P-value	Z-value	P-value	Z-value	P-value	Z-value	P-value	Z-value	P-value
−3	0.0013	−2	0.0228	−1	0.1587	0	0.5000	1	0.8413	2	0.9772
−2.95	0.0016	−1.95	0.0256	−0.95	0.1711	0.05	0.5199	1.05	0.8531	2.05	0.9798
−2.9	0.0019	−1.9	0.0287	−0.9	0.1841	0.1	0.5398	1.1	0.8643	2.1	0.9821
−2.85	0.0022	−1.85	0.0322	−0.85	0.1977	0.15	0.5596	1.15	0.8749	2.15	0.9842
−2.8	0.0026	−1.8	0.0359	−0.8	0.2119	0.2	0.5793	1.2	0.8849	2.2	0.9861
−2.75	0.0030	−1.75	0.0401	−0.75	0.2266	0.25	0.5987	1.25	0.8944	2.25	0.9878
−2.7	0.0035	−1.7	0.0446	−0.7	0.2420	0.3	0.6179	1.3	0.9032	2.3	0.9893
−2.65	0.0040	−1.65	0.0495	−0.65	0.2578	0.35	0.6368	1.35	0.9115	2.35	0.9906
−2.6	0.0047	−1.6	0.0548	−0.6	0.2743	0.4	0.6554	1.4	0.9192	2.4	0.9918
−2.55	0.0054	−1.55	0.0606	−0.55	0.2912	0.45	0.6736	1.45	0.9265	2.45	0.9929
−2.5	0.0062	−1.5	0.0668	−0.5	0.3085	0.5	0.6915	1.5	0.9332	2.5	0.9938
−2.45	0.0071	−1.45	0.0735	−0.45	0.3264	0.55	0.7088	1.55	0.9394	2.55	0.9946
−2.4	0.0082	−1.4	0.0808	−0.4	0.3446	0.6	0.7257	1.6	0.9452	2.6	0.9953
−2.35	0.0094	−1.35	0.0885	−0.35	0.3632	0.65	0.7422	1.65	0.9505	2.65	0.9960
−2.3	0.0107	−1.3	0.0968	−0.3	0.3821	0.7	0.7580	1.7	0.9554	2.7	0.9965
−2.25	0.0122	−1.25	0.1056	−0.25	0.4013	0.75	0.7734	1.75	0.9599	2.75	0.9970
−2.2	0.0139	−1.2	0.1151	−0.2	0.4207	0.8	0.7881	1.8	0.9641	2.8	0.9974
−2.15	0.0158	−1.15	0.1251	−0.15	0.4404	0.85	0.8023	1.85	0.9678	2.85	0.9978
−2.1	0.0179	−1.1	0.1357	−0.1	0.4602	0.9	0.8159	1.9	0.9713	2.9	0.9981
−2.05	0.0202	−1.05	0.1469	−0.05	0.4801	0.95	0.8289	1.95	0.9744	2.95	0.9984

The closest bracketing probabilities from the standard normal table are

$$N(.95) = .8289 \qquad N(1) = .8413$$

Similarly, the value for d_2 from the example above is

$$d_2 = .86038$$

Its closest bracketing probabilities from the table are

$$N(.85) = .8023 \qquad N(.9) = .8159$$

Fairly good accuracy can be achieved with only these bracketing probabilities by a linear interpolation scheme. A linear interpolation of bracketing probabilities for d_1 and d_2 yields these approximations:

$$N(d_1) \approx .8289 \times \frac{1 - .98538}{1 - .95} + .8413 \times \frac{.98538 - .95}{1 - .95} = .83767$$

$$N(d_2) \approx .8023 \times \frac{.9 - .86038}{.9 - .85} + .8159 \times \frac{.86038 - .85}{.9 - .85} = .80512$$

Using these approximate probabilities to compute the call option price yields

$$C = \$50 \times e^{-.02 \times .25} \times .83767 - \$45 \times e^{-.06 \times .25} \times .80512$$
$$= \$50 \times .99501 \times .83767 - \$45 \times .98511 \times .80512$$
$$= \$5.984$$

In this example, the error introduced by interpolating probabilities from a table is trivial. However, errors of 5 to 10 cents are possible. In practice, options professionals will use special computer programs.

SPREADSHEET ANALYSIS

	A	B	C	D	E	F	G	H	I	J	K
1											
2			**Calculating Black-Scholes-Merton Option Prices**								
3											
4	XYZ stock has a price of $65 and an annual return volatility of 50%. The riskless										
5	interest rate is 5 percent, and the stock pays a 1 percent dividend yield. Calculate										
6	call and put option prices with a strike of $60 and a 3-month time to expiration.										
7											
8	Stock =	65		d1 =	0.4852		N(d1) =	0.6862		N(−d1) =	0.3138
9	Strike =	60									
10	Sigma =	0.5		d2 =	0.2352		N(d2) =	0.5930		N(−d2) =	0.4070
11	Yield =	0.01									
12	Time =	0.25			exp(− Yield x Time) =			0.9975			
13	Rate =	0.05			exp(− Rate x Time) =			0.9876			
14											
15	Call =	Stock x exp(− Yield x Time) x N(d1)									
16											
17					−Strike x exp(− Rate x Time) x N(d2) =						$9.36
18											
19	Put =	Strike x exp(− Rate x Time) x N(−d2)									
20											
21					−Stock x exp(− Yield x Time) x N(−d1) =						$3.77
22											
23	Formula entered in E8 is =(LN(B8/B9) + (B13 − B11 + 0.5*B10^2)*B12)/(B10*SQRT(B12))										
24	Formula entered in E10 is =E8 − B10*SQRT(B12)										
25	Formula entered in H8 is =NORMSDIST(E8)										
26	Formula entered in K8 is =NORMSDIST(−E8)										
27	Formula entered in K17 is =B8*H8*H12 − B9*H10*H13										
28	Formula entered in K21 is =B9*K10*H13 − B8*K8*H12										
29											

Check This

15.1a   Consider the following inputs to the Black-Scholes-Merton option pricing model.

$$S = \$50 \qquad y = 0\%$$
$$K = \$50 \qquad r = 5\%$$
$$T = 60 \text{ days} \qquad \sigma = 25\%$$

These input values yield a call option price of $2.22 and a put option price of $1.81.

Verify these prices from your own calculations.

15.2 Valuing Employee Stock Options

An interesting application of the Black-Scholes-Merton option pricing formula is the valuation of employee stock options, which we discussed in our previous chapter.

TABLE 15.2	Coca-Cola Employee Stock Options	
Inputs	**Input Value Assumptions**	
Stock price	$44.55	$44.55
Exercise price	$44.655	$44.655
Time horizon	15 years	6 years
Volatility	25.53%	30.20%
Risk-free interest rate	5.65%	3.40%
Dividend yield	1.59%	1.70%
Black-Scholes-Merton option value	$19.92	$13.06

Companies issuing stock options to employees must report estimates of their value in financial statements. The Black-Scholes-Merton formula is widely used for this purpose. For example, in December 2002, the Coca-Cola Company granted employee stock options to several executives representing over a half million shares of Coke stock. The options had a stated term of 15 years, but, to allow for the fact that employee stock options are often exercised before maturity, Coca-Cola used two time horizon assumptions to value the options: the longest possible term of 15 years and an expected term of 6 years. The company then adjusted their interest rate, dividend yield, and volatility assumptions to each of these terms.

The different input values assumed and the resulting Black-Scholes option values are summarized in Table 15.2. Notice that Coca-Cola assumed a higher volatility and dividend yield, but a lower riskless interest rate for the six-year time horizon assumption. This seems reasonable given that stock market volatility was high and interest rates were low in 2002 compared to recent historical experience. A *Wall Street Journal* article discussing the valuation of these Coke options is contained in the nearby *Investment Updates* box.

Visit the Coca-Cola website at www.coca-cola.com for more investor information

Check This

15.2a Go to finance.yahoo.com, check the current price of Coca-Cola stock under the ticker symbol KO, and compare it to the stock price on the employee stock option grant data given in Table 15.2.

15.2b Recalculate the Black-Scholes option value for the Coca-Cola employee stock options based on the current stock price for Coke shares.

15.3 Varying the Option Price Input Values

An important goal of this chapter is to provide an understanding of how option prices change as a result of varying each of the six input values. Table 15.3 summarizes the sign effects of the six inputs on call and put option prices. A plus sign indicates a positive effect, and a minus sign indicates a negative effect. Where the magnitude of the input impact has a commonly used name, this is stated in the rightmost column.

The two most important inputs determining stock option prices are the stock price and the strike price. However, the other input factors are also important determinants of option value. We next discuss each input factor separately.

Coke Plan for Option Valuing Fizzles Out after Few Months: News Dashes Hopes for Alternative to Black-Scholes Expensing Models

Coca-Cola Co.'s novel plan for valuing its employee stock-option compensation has fizzled out.

The world's biggest soft-drink company made a splash in July by announcing it would begin recognizing stock-option compensation as an expense on its financial statements. But it wasn't just Coke's decision to expense that piqued market interest. Even more noteworthy was the unique valuation method it planned to use, at Coke director Warren Buffett's urging. Instead of using Wall Street's much maligned, but widely used, Black-Scholes mathematical models, Coke said it would solicit quotations from two independent financial institutions to buy and sell Coke shares under the identical terms of the options to be expensed. Coke then would average the quotations to determine the value of the options.

So much for that plan.

Coke now concedes it won't work and that it will use Black-Scholes after all, notwithstanding the method's drawbacks. The disclosure almost certainly will disappoint investors who favor mandatory expensing of option-based compensation, but had been hoping for a feasible alternative to the subjective results often produced by Black-Scholes models.

It also signals that Black-Scholes, like it or not, may remain the norm even should the Financial Accounting Standards Board follow through with its plans to unveil a proposal this year mandating that public companies treat stock-option compensation as an expense.

Coke executives Thursday said they had no choice but to abandon the Buffet-backed plan. They said the company eventually concluded that current accounting standards wouldn't allow the new approach and instead require companies to perform their own value calculations.

In any event, the disclosure in Coke's proxy shows that dealer quotes wouldn't have yielded any different results than a Black-Scholes calculation. Coke says it determined the value of the options through Black-Scholes calculations—and only then obtained independent market quotes from two dealers "to ensure the best market-based assumptions were used." And, as it turned out, "our Black-Scholes value was not materially different from the independent quotes," Coke's proxy says. Coke declined to name the two financial institutions.

(continued)

Input	Sign of Input Effect		Common Name
	Call	Put	
Underlying stock price (S)	+	−	Delta
Strike price of the option contract (K)	−	+	
Time remaining until option expiration (T)	+	+	Theta
Volatility of the underlying stock price (σ)	+	+	Vega
Risk-free interest rate (r)	+	−	Rho
Dividend yield of the underlying stock (y)	−	+	

TABLE 15.3   Six Inputs Affecting Option Prices

For option trading strategies and more, see
www.numa.com

Varying the Underlying Stock Price

Certainly, the price of the underlying stock is one of the most important determinants of the price of a stock option. As the stock price increases, the call option price increases and the put option price decreases. This is not surprising, since a call option grants the right to buy stock shares and a put option grants the right to sell stock shares

Because the dealer quotes were so similar, "you can assume they use Black-Scholes too," says Gary Fayard, Coke's chief financial officer. Asked if an alternative to Black-Scholes is needed, Mr. Fayard says, "I think it's something that business and the accounting profession need to work on and evaluate."

Given the lack of any meaningful difference, some accounting specialists say future efforts to seek market quotations for employee options likely will be pointless. "All they did was go to the expense of getting quotes from two independent parties who may have used the Black-Scholes model themselves," says Jack Ciesielski, publisher of the Analyst's Accounting Observer newsletter in Baltimore. "The whole affair winds up being an exercise in circularity."

While expensing options remains voluntary, all public companies are required to disclose what the effect on their earnings would be if they did expense options. Most such disclosures rely on variants of the model published in the 1970s by economists Fischer Black and Myron Scholes.

Like almost all valuation models, Black-Scholes hinges on lots of assumptions. For instance, option-pricing models typically require projections of the underlying security's future volatility, as well as the option's expected life. Those aren't easy to project with any precision. Even small changes in assumptions can make crucial differences in results and, consequently, a company's reported expenses. What's more, the Black-Scholes model wasn't designed to value options that, like the kind companies grant to employees, aren't freely transferable.

For example, SEC proxy rules required Coke to assume the options' time horizon would be the full life of the options' terms, or 15 years. That drove Coke to assume relatively lower volatility, given the lengthy time horizon. Using those assumptions, Coke calculated that the value of its options was $19.92 a share. However, accounting rules required Coke to use the options' "expected life" when calculating the time horizon. Coke assumed six years. That reduced the options' value, though the effect was partly offset by Coke's assumptions that volatility would be higher, given the shorter time span. The result: Under that Black-Scholes calculation, the value was $13.06 a share.

Source: Jonathan Weil and Betsy McKay, *The Wall Street Journal*, March 7, 2003. © 2003 Dow Jones & Company, Inc. All Rights Reserved Worldwide.

at a fixed strike price. Consequently, a higher stock price at option expiration increases the payoff of a call option. Likewise, a lower stock price at option expiration increases the payoff of a put option.

For a given set of input values, the relationship between call and put option prices and an underlying stock price is illustrated in Figure 15.1. In Figure 15.1, stock prices are measured on the horizontal axis and option prices are measured on the vertical axis. Notice that the graph lines describing relationships between call and put option prices and the underlying stock price have a convex (bowed) shape. Convexity is a fundamental characteristic of the relationship between option prices and stock prices.

Varying the Option's Strike Price

As the strike price increases, the call price decreases and the put price increases. This is reasonable, since a higher strike price means that we must pay a higher price when we exercise a call option to buy the underlying stock, thereby reducing the call option's value. Similarly, a higher strike price means that we will receive a higher price when we exercise a put option to sell the underlying stock, thereby increasing the put option's value. Of course, this logic works in reverse also; as the strike price decreases, the call price increases and the put price decreases.

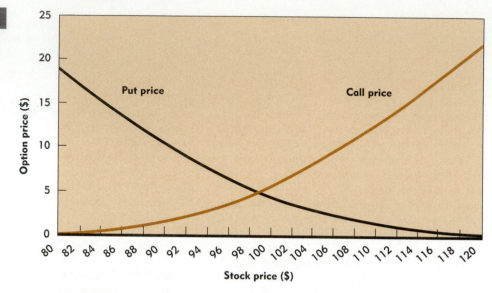

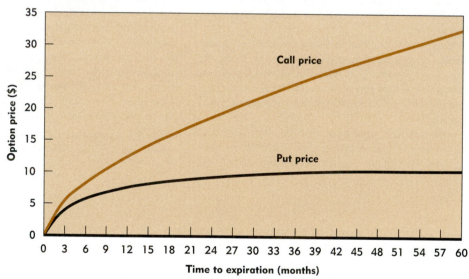

Varying the Time Remaining until Option Expiration

Time remaining until option expiration is an important determinant of option value. As time remaining until option expiration lengthens, both call and put option prices normally increase. This is expected, since a longer time remaining until option expiration allows more time for the stock price to move away from a strike price and increase the option's payoff, thereby making the option more valuable. The relationship between call and put option prices and time remaining until option expiration is illustrated in Figure 15.2, where time remaining until option expiration is measured on the horizontal axis and option prices are measured on the vertical axis.

Varying the Volatility of the Stock Price

Stock price volatility (sigma, σ) plays an important role in determining option value. As stock price volatility increases, both call and put option prices increase. This is as

FIGURE 15.3

Option Prices and Sigma

Input values:
S = $100
K = $100
T = ¼ year
r = 5%
y = 0%

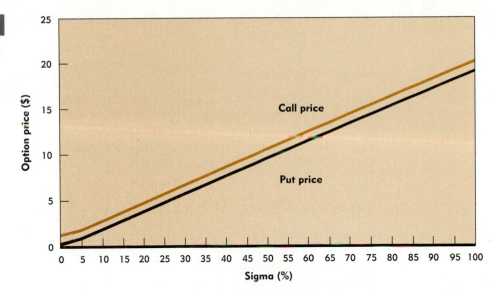

FIGURE 15.4

Option Prices and Interest Rates

Input values:
S = $100
K = $100
T = ¼ year
σ = 25%
y = 0%

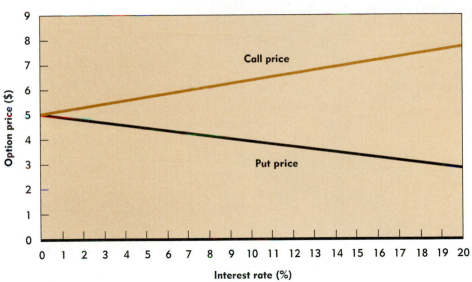

expected, since the more volatile the stock price, the greater is the likelihood that the stock price will move farther away from a strike price and increase the option's payoff, thereby making the option more valuable. The relationship between call and put option prices and stock price volatility is graphed in Figure 15.3, where volatility is measured on the horizontal axis and option prices are measured on the vertical axis.

Varying the Interest Rate

Although seemingly not as important as the other inputs, the interest rate still noticeably affects option values. As the interest rate increases, the call price increases and the put price decreases. This is explained by the time value of money. A higher interest rate implies a greater discount, which lowers the present value of the strike price that we pay when we exercise a call option or receive when we exercise a put option. Figure 15.4 graphs the relationship between call and put option prices and interest rates, where the interest rate is measured on the horizontal axis and option prices are measured on the vertical axis.

Varying the Dividend Yield

A stock's dividend yield has an important effect on option values. As the dividend yield increases, the call price decreases and the put price increases. This follows from the fact that when a company pays a dividend, its assets are reduced by the amount of the dividend, causing a like decrease in the price of the stock. Then, as the stock price decreases, the call price decreases and the put price increases.

15.4 Measuring the Impact of Input Changes on Option Prices

delta Measure of the dollar impact of a change in the underlying stock price on the value of a stock option. Delta is positive for a call option and negative for a put option.

Investment professionals using options in their investment strategies have standard methods to state the impact of changes in input values on option prices. The two inputs that most affect stock option prices over a short period, say, a few days, are the stock price and the stock price volatility. The approximate impact of a stock price change on an option price is stated by the option's **delta**. In the Black-Scholes-Merton option pricing model, expressions for call and put option deltas are stated as follows, where the mathematical functions e^x and $N(x)$ were previously defined:

$$Call\ option\ delta = e^{-yT}N(d_1) \quad >0$$
$$Put\ option\ delta\ =\ -\,e^{-yT}N(-d_1) \quad <0$$

As shown above, a call option delta is always positive and a put option delta is always negative. This corresponds to Table 15.3, where + indicates a positive effect for a call option and − indicates a negative effect for a put option resulting from an increase in the underlying stock price.

COMPUTING CALL AND PUT OPTION DELTAS

EXAMPLE 15.3

Given the inputs to the Black-Scholes-Merton option pricing formula provided in Example 15.1, calculate call and put option deltas.

The necessary probabilities for d_1 and $-d_1$ were provided in Example 15.1.

$N(d_1) = N(.98538) = .83778$ $N(-d_1) = 1 - N(d_1) = .16222$

Deltas are then calculated as

Call option delta = .99501 × .83778 = .83360

Put option delta = −.99501 × .16222 = −.16141

eta Measure of the percentage impact of a change in the underlying stock price on the value of a stock option. Eta is positive for a call option and negative for a put option.

The approximate percentage impact of a stock price change on an option price is stated by the option's **eta**. In the Black-Scholes-Merton option pricing model, expressions for call and put option etas are stated as follows, where the mathematical functions e^x and $N(x)$ were previously defined:

$$Call\ option\ eta = e^{-yT}N(d_1)S/C \quad >1$$
$$Put\ option\ eta\ =\ -\,e^{-yT}N(-d_1)S/P < -1$$

In the Black-Scholes-Merton option pricing model, a call option eta is greater than $+1$ and a put option eta is less than -1.

COMPUTING CALL AND PUT OPTION ETAS

EXAMPLE 15.4

Given the inputs to the Black-Scholes-Merton option pricing formula provided in Example 15.1, calculate call and put option etas.

As shown above, option etas are simply option deltas multiplied by the stock price and divided by the option price. Thus, in this example, they are calculated from values provided above as follows:

Call option eta = .83360 × 50/5.985 = 6.964

Put option eta = −.16141 × 50/.565 = −14.284

vega Measure of the impact of a change in stock price volatility on the value of a stock option. Vega is positive for both a call option and a put option.

The approximate impact of a volatility change on an option's price is measured by the option's **vega**.[1] In the Black-Scholes-Merton option pricing model, vega is the same for call and put options and is stated as follows, where the mathematical function $n(x)$ represents a standard normal density.

$$Vega = Se^{-yT}n(d_1)\sqrt{T} > 0$$

As shown above, vega is always positive. Again this corresponds with Table 15.3, where $+$ indicates a positive effect for both a call option and a put option from a volatility increase.

COMPUTING CALL AND PUT OPTION VEGAS

EXAMPLE 15.5

Given the inputs to the Black-Scholes-Merton option pricing formula provided in Example 15.1, calculate call and put option vegas.

The vega for a call option is the same as the vega for a put option. Computing vega requires calculation of the standard normal density value for d_1. This is calculated as shown here.

$$n(d_1) = \frac{e^{-d_1^2/2}}{\sqrt{2\pi}} = \frac{e^{-.98538^2/2}}{\sqrt{6.28318}} = .245508$$

Substituting appropriate values into the vega formula above yields this vega value:

$$Vega = 50 \times .99501 \times .245508 \times \sqrt{.25} = 6.107$$

Refer to the *Spreadsheet Analysis* box on the next page for examples of calculating deltas, etas, and vega using a spreadsheet. Note that this spreadsheet is a continuation of the one we developed earlier in the chapter for calculating Black-Scholes-Merton option prices.

---

[1]Those of you who are scholars of the Greek language recognize that "vega" is not a Greek letter like the other option sensitivity measures. (It is a star in the constellation Lyra.) Alas, the term vega has entered the options professionals' vocabulary and is in widespread use.

SPREADSHEET ANALYSIS

	A	B	C	D	E	F	G	H	I	J	K
30					Calculating the Greeks						
31											
32	Calculate call and put option deltas and etas, and the vega for the above options.										
33											
34	Call Delta =	exp(–Yield x Time) x N(d1)=						0.685			
35											
36	Put Delta =	–exp(–Yield x Time) x N(–d1)=						–0.313			
37											
38	Call Eta =	Call Delta x Stock / Call =						4.755			
39											
40	Put Eta =	Put Delta x Stock / Put =						–5.390			
41											
42	Vega =	exp(–D1 x D1/2) x exp(–Yield x Time)									
43		x Stock x sqrt(Time)/sqrt(2 x Pi)=						11.497			
44											
45	Formula entered in H34 is = H12*H8										
46	Formula entered in H36 is = –H12*K8										
47	Formula entered in H38 is = H34*B8/K17										
48	Formula entered in H40 is = H36*B8/K21										
49	Formula entered in H43 is = B8*H12*EXP(–E8*E8/2)*SQRT(B12)/SQRT(2*PI())										

Interpreting Option Deltas

Interpreting the meaning of an option delta is relatively straightforward. Delta measures the impact of a change in the stock price on an option price, where a $1 change in the stock price causes an option price to change by approximately delta dollars. For example, using the input values stated immediately below, we obtain a call option price of $5.99 and a put option price of $.56. These yield a call option delta of $+.83$ and a put option delta of $-.16$.

$$S = \$50 \qquad y = 2\%$$
$$K = 45 \qquad r = 6\%$$
$$T = .25 \qquad \sigma = 25\%$$

Now if we change the stock price from $50 to $51, we get a call option price of $6.84 and a put option price of $.42. Thus, a $+\$1$ stock price change increased the call option price by $.85 and decreased the put option price by $.14. These price changes are close to, but not exactly equal to, the call option delta value of $+.83$ and put option delta value of $-.16$.

Interpreting Option Etas

Eta measures the percentage impact of a change in the stock price on an option price, where a 1 percent change in the stock price causes an option price to change by approximately eta percent. For example, the input values stated above yield a call option price of $5.99, and a put option price of $.56, a call option eta of 6.96, and a put option eta of -14.28. If the stock price changes by 1 percent from $50 to $50.50, we get a call option price of $6.41 and a put option price of $.49. Thus, a 1 percent stock price change increased the call option price by 7.01 percent and decreased the put option price by 12.50 percent. These percentage price changes are close to the call option eta value of $+6.96$ and put option eta value of -14.28.

Interpreting Option Vegas

Interpreting the meaning of an option vega is also straightforward. Vega measures the impact of a change in stock price volatility on an option price, where a 1 percent change in sigma changes an option price by approximately the amount .01 times vega. For example, using the same input values stated earlier we obtain call and put option prices of $5.99 and $.56, respectively. We also get an option vega of $+6.1$. If we change the stock price volatility to $\sigma = 26\%$, we then get call and put option prices of $6.05 and $.63. This $+1$ percent stock price volatility change increased call and put option prices by $.06 and $.07, respectively, as predicted by vega.

Interpreting an Option's Gamma, Theta, and Rho

gamma Measure of delta sensitivity to a stock price change.

theta Measure of the impact on an option price from a change in time remaining until option expiration.

rho Measure of option price sensitivity to a change in the interest rate.

In addition to delta, eta, and vega, options professionals commonly use three other measures of option price sensitivity to input changes: gamma, theta, and rho.

Gamma measures delta sensitivity to a stock price change, where a one-dollar stock price change causes delta to change by approximately the amount gamma. In the Black-Scholes-Merton option pricing model, gammas are the same for call and put options.

Theta measures option price sensitivity to a change in time remaining until option expiration, where a given change in option maturity causes the option price to change by approximately the amount theta. A common convention is to calibrate theta so that it measures an option price change due to a one-week change in option maturity.

Rho measures option price sensitivity to a change in the interest rate, where a 1 percent interest rate change causes the option price to change by approximately the amount rho. Rho is positive for a call option and negative for a put option.

15.5 Implied Standard Deviations

The Black-Scholes-Merton stock option pricing model is based on six inputs: a stock price, a strike price, an interest rate, a dividend yield, the time remaining until option expiration, and the stock price volatility. Of these six factors, only the stock price volatility is not directly observable and must be estimated somehow. A popular method to estimate stock price volatility is to use an implied value from an option price. A stock price volatility estimated from an option price is called an **implied standard deviation** or **implied volatility**, often abbreviated as **ISD** or **IVOL**, respectively. Implied volatility and implied standard deviation are two terms for the same thing.

implied standard deviation (ISD) An estimate of stock price volatility obtained from an option price.

implied volatility (IVOL) Another term for implied standard deviation.

Calculating an implied volatility requires that all input factors have known values, except sigma, and that a call or put option price be known. For example, consider the following option price input values, absent a value for sigma.

$$S = \$50 \qquad y = 2\%$$
$$K = \$45 \qquad r = 6\%$$
$$T = .25$$

Suppose we also have a call price of $C = \$5.99$. Based on this call price, what is the implied volatility? In other words, in combination with the input values stated above, what sigma value yields a call price of $C = \$5.99$? The answer comes from Example

15.1, which shows that a sigma value of .25, or 25 percent, yields a call option price of $5.99.

Now suppose we wish to know what volatility value is implied by a call price of $C = \$7$. To obtain this implied volatility value, we must find the value for sigma that yields this call price. By trial and error, you can try various sigma values until a call option price of $7 is obtained. This occurs with a sigma value of 39.22 percent, which is the implied standard deviation (ISD) corresponding to a call option price of $7.

COMPUTING IMPLIED VOLATILITY

EXAMPLE 15.6

Options professionals compute implied volatilities using special computer programs. The formula immediately below provides a useful alternative to compute implied volatility when you do not have a special computer program. This formula yields accurate implied volatility values as long as the stock price is not too far from the strike price of the option contract.

$$\sigma \approx \frac{\sqrt{2\pi/T}}{Y+X}\left[C - \frac{Y-X}{2} + \sqrt{\left(C - \frac{Y-X}{2}\right)^2 - \frac{(Y-X)^2}{\pi}}\right]$$

$$Y = Se^{-yT} \qquad X = Ke^{-rT}$$

As an example calculation, substitute the following input values into the above formula:

$S = \$50 \qquad y = 2\%$

$K = \$45 \qquad r = 6\%$

$T = .25 \qquad C = \$7$

The result yields this implied standard deviation value:

$$\frac{\sqrt{6.2832/.25}}{49.75 + 44.33}\left[7 - \frac{49.75 - 44.33}{2} + \sqrt{\left(7 - \frac{49.75 - 44.33}{2}\right)^2 - \frac{(49.75 - 44.33)^2}{3.1416}}\right]$$

$$= .3889 = 38.89\%$$

This is quite close to the exact implied standard deviation of 39.22 percent obtained using a special computer program.

You can easily obtain an estimate of stock price volatility for almost any stock with option prices reported in *The Wall Street Journal*. For example, suppose you wish to obtain an estimate of stock price volatility for Microsoft common stock. Since Microsoft stock trades on Nasdaq under the ticker MSFT, stock price and dividend yield information are obtained from the "Nasdaq National Market Issues" pages. Microsoft options information is obtained from the "Listed Options Quotations" page. Interest rate information is obtained from the "Treasury Bonds, Notes and Bills" column.

The following information was obtained for Microsoft common stock and Microsoft options from *The Wall Street Journal*.

For applications of implied volatility, see www.ivolatility.com

Stock price = $89 \qquad Dividend yield = 0%

Strike price = $90 \qquad Interest rate = 5.5%

Time until contract expiration = 73 days

Call price = $8.25

From our discussion of implied standard deviations (ISDs), you know that solving for an ISD when you know the option price can be tedious. Fortunately, most option calculators will do the work for you. Suppose you have a call option with a strike price of $95 that matures in 75 days. The stock currently sells for $98.12, the option sells for $10.25, and the interest rate is 4.5 percent per year, compounded continuously. What is the ISD? To find out, we went to the options calculator at www.numa.com. After entering all this information, here is what we got:

implied volatility for european call option

INPUT DATA	Share Price:	98.120	Strike Price:	95.000	Maturity(yrs):	0.205
	Dividend Yld:	0	Interest Rate:	4.5	Option Price:	10.250

Implied Volatility = 46.73

Intrinsic Value:	3.120	Time Value:	7.130

Notice the calculator changes the days to maturity to .205, which is 75/365 of a year. So, the underlying stock has an ISD of 46.73 percent per year.

Substituting these input values into the formula from Example 15.6 yields this implied volatility for Microsoft:

$$\frac{\sqrt{6.2832/.2}}{89 + 89.0154}\left[8.25 - \frac{89 - 89.0154}{2} + \sqrt{\left(8.25 - \frac{89 - 89.0154}{2}\right)^2 - \frac{(89 - 89.0154)^2}{3.1416}}\right]$$

$$= .52 = 52\%$$

This is quite close to the exact implied standard deviation of 52.12 percent obtained using a special computer program. Our nearby *Work the Web* box shows how to get ISDs the easy way.

CBOE Implied Volatilities for Stock Indexes

VIX, VXN Volatility indexes for the S&P 100 and Nasdaq 100 stock indexes, respectively, based on options for the corresponding stock indexes.

The Chicago Board Options Exchange (CBOE) publishes two implied volatility series, the CBOE Volatility Index (VIX) and the CBOE Nasdaq Volatility Index (VXN). These are two of the world's most popular measures of investor expectations about future stock market volatility. They are based on options traded on two popular stock indexes, the S&P 100 and the Nasdaq 100. In particular, **VIX** is an average implied standard deviation based on the prices of eight S&P 100 index options, four puts and four calls. **VXN** is also an average based on the prices of eight index options, four puts and four calls for the Nasdaq 100. The ticker symbols for these volatility indexes and the underlying stock indexes are summarized as follows:

Volatility Index Ticker	Stock Index	Stock Index Ticker
VIX	S&P 100	OEX
VXN	Nasdaq 100	NDX

For more information on VIX and VXN volatility indexes, visit the CBOE website at www.cboe.com

Current levels of these volatility indexes and the underlying stock indexes are available at the CBOE website (www.cboe.com). You can also check them at Yahoo! Finance (finance.yahoo.com), but note that the ticker symbols VIX, VXN, OEX, and NDX do not correspond to traded securities, and they must therefore be prefixed with a carat sign, that is, ^VIX, ^VXN, ^OEX, and ^NDX.

VIX and VXN implied volatilities are reported as annualized standard deviations. The VIX and VXN volatility indexes provide investors with current market estimates of expected volatility in the month ahead. Figures 15.5A and 15.5B plot VIX and VXN

FIGURE 15.5A

VIX versus S&P 100 Index Realized Volatility

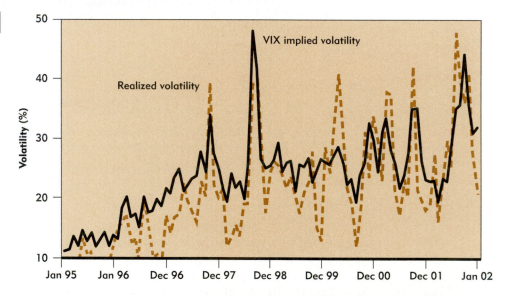

FIGURE 15.5B

VXN versus Nasdaq 100 Index Realized Volatility

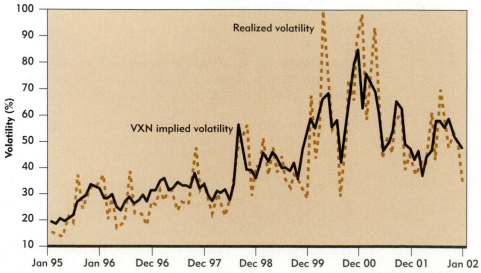

volatility index levels along with corresponding historical volatilities for the S&P 100 and Nasdaq 100 indexes over the period 1995 through 2002. Notice that volatility levels can vary significantly from month to month and that typical volatility levels have approximately doubled over this period.

Check This

15.5a　In a recent issue of *The Wall Street Journal*, look up the stock price, dividend yield, strike price, interest rate, and time to expiration for an option on Microsoft common stock. Note the call price corresponding to the selected strike and time values. From these values, use the formula in Example 15.6 to obtain an implied standard deviation estimate for Microsoft stock price volatility. (*Hint*: When determining time until option expiration, remember that options expire on the Saturday following the third Friday of their expiration month.)

15.5b　Check the current levels of the volatility and stock indexes VIX, VXN, OEX, and NDX at finance.yahoo.com. Don't forget to prefix each ticker with a carat.

15.6 Hedging a Stock Portfolio with Stock Index Options

Hedging is a common use of stock options among portfolio managers. In particular, many institutional money managers make some use of stock index options to hedge the equity portfolios they manage. In this section, we examine how an equity portfolio manager might hedge a diversified stock portfolio using stock index options.

To begin, suppose that you manage a $10 million diversified portfolio of large-company stocks and that you maintain a portfolio beta of 1 for this portfolio. With a beta of 1, changes in the value of your portfolio closely follow changes in the Standard & Poor's 500 index. Therefore, you decide to use options on the S&P 500 index as a hedging vehicle. S&P 500 index options trade on the Chicago Board Options Exchange (CBOE) under the ticker symbol SPX. SPX option prices are reported daily in the "Index Options Trading" column of *The Wall Street Journal*. Each SPX option has a contract value of 100 times the current level of the S&P 500 index.

For stock option reports, see www.aantix.com

SPX options are a convenient hedging vehicle for an equity portfolio manager because they are European style and because they settle in cash at expiration. For example, suppose you hold one SPX call option with a strike price of 1500 and at option expiration, the S&P 500 index stands at 1507. In this case, your cash payoff is 100 times the difference between the index level and the strike price, or $100 \times (1507 - 1500) = \$700$. Of course, if the expiration date index level falls below the strike price, your SPX call option expires worthless.

Hedging a stock portfolio with index options requires first calculating the number of option contracts needed to form an effective hedge. While you can use either put options or call options to construct an effective hedge, we assume that you decide to use call options to hedge your $10 million equity portfolio. Using stock index call options to hedge an equity portfolio involves writing a certain number of option contracts. In general, the number of stock index option contracts needed to hedge an equity portfolio is stated by the equation

$$\text{Number of option contracts} = \frac{\text{Portfolio beta} \times \text{Portfolio value}}{\text{Option delta} \times \text{Option contract value}} \quad (15.3)$$

Money Managers Use Options to Hedge Portfolios

Traders and money managers began using options to hedge their portfolios yesterday after spending the past week ignoring defensive strategies to speculate on earnings and stock price movements.

The turning point came late in the morning when the Standard & Poor's 500 index slid below 1140. This wiped out many S&P 500 index futures positions and market professionals responded by buying S&P 500 index options to protect their portfolios from the market's volatility.

This hedging activity marked a change in the approach they have taken to the market. Many professionals recently stopped hedging their portfolios because the stock market has quickly corrected in the past. They spent money for hedges they ultimately didn't need.

"A lot of people were completely unhedged when the decline began," said Leon Gross, Salomon Smith Barney's options strategist. He noted that the S&P 500 index's rise to 1186 from 1086 took six weeks, while it dropped 50 points in only four days.

The fear in the options market spiked higher as the S&P index fell along with the Dow Jones Industrial Average.

The option market's fear gauge, the Chicago Board Options Exchange Volatility Index, rose 1.72, or 7.5%, to 24.66. "This is an indication that people are getting nervous and paying for puts," Mr. Gross said.

Options prices reflected this discomfort, which made hedging portfolios even more expensive than normal. For more aggressive traders, such as hedge funds, high options prices created opportunities to short sell puts and sectors.

The Nasdaq index of the 100 largest nonfinancial stocks was a popular way to short the technology sector. Other traders sold put options because they think the fear is overdone and they'll be able to buy the contracts back for less money.

Source: Steven M. Sears, *The Wall Street Journal*, July 29, 1998. Reprinted by permission of Dow Jones & Company, Inc., via Copyright Clearance Center, Inc. © 1998 Dow Jones & Company, Inc. All Rights Reserved Worldwide.

In your particular case, you have a portfolio beta of 1 and a portfolio value of $10 million. You now need to calculate an option delta and option contract value.

The option contract value for an SPX option is simply 100 times the current level of the S&P 500 index. Checking the "Index Options Trading" column in *The Wall Street Journal* you see that the S&P 500 index has a value of 1508, which means that each SPX option has a current contract value of $150,800.

To calculate an option delta, you must decide which particular contract to use. You decide to use options with an October expiration and a strike price of 1500, that is, the October 1500 SPX contract. From the "Index Options Trading" column, you find the price for these options is 64⅝, or 64.625. Options expire on the Saturday following the third Friday of their expiration month. Counting days on your calendar yields a time remaining until option expiration of 73 days. The interest rate on Treasury bills maturing closest to option expiration is 6 percent. The dividend yield on the S&P 500 index is not normally reported in *The Wall Street Journal*. Fortunately, the S&P 500 trades in the form of depository shares on the American Stock Exchange (AMEX) under the ticker SPY. SPY shares represent a claim on a portfolio designed to match the S&P 500 as closely as possible. By looking up information on SPY shares on the Internet, you find that the dividend yield is 1.5 percent.

With the information now collected, you use the input values $S = 1508.80$, $K = 1500$, $T = .2$, $r = 6\%$, and $y = 1.5\%$ and option price $C = 64.625$ to get an implied volatility of 20 percent. This represents a current estimate of S&P 500 index volatility. Using this sigma value of 20 percent then yields a call option delta of .579. You now have sufficient information to calculate the number of option contracts needed to effectively hedge your equity portfolio. By using equation 15-3, we can calculate the number of October 1500 SPX options that you should write to form an effective hedge.

$$\frac{1.0 \times \$10,000,000}{.579 \times \$150,800} \approx 115 \text{ contracts}$$

Furthermore, by writing 115 October 1500 call options, you receive $115 \times 100 \times 64.625 = \$743,187.50$.

To assess the effectiveness of this hedge, suppose the S&P 500 index and your stock portfolio both immediately fall in value by 1 percent. This is a loss of $100,000 on your stock portfolio. After the S&P 500 index falls by 1 percent, its level is 1493.71, which then yields a call option price of $C = 56.21$. Now, if you were to buy back the 115 contracts, you would pay $115 \times 100 \times 56.21 = \$646,415$. Since you originally received $743,187.50 for the options, this represents a gain of $743,187.50 - \$646,415 = \$96,772.50$, which cancels most of the $100,000 loss on your equity portfolio. In fact, your final net loss is only $3,227.50, which is a small fraction of the loss that would have been realized with an unhedged portfolio.

To maintain an effective hedge over time, you will need to rebalance your options hedge on, say, a weekly basis. Rebalancing simply requires calculating anew the number of option contracts needed to hedge your equity portfolio, and then buying or selling options in the amount necessary to maintain an effective hedge. The nearby *Investment Updates* box contains a brief *Wall Street Journal* report on hedging strategies using stock index options.

THE OPTION HEDGE RATIO FOR A STOCK PORTFOLIO

EXAMPLE 15.7

You are managing a $15 million stock portfolio with a beta of 1.1 which you decide to hedge by buying index put options with a contract value of $125,000 per contract and a delta of .4. How many option contracts are required?

Plugging our information into equation 15.3 yields this calculation:

$$\frac{1.1 \times \$15,000,000}{.4 \times \$125,000} = 330 \text{ contracts}$$

Thus, you would need to buy 330 put option contracts.

Check This

15.6a In the hedging example above, suppose instead that your equity portfolio had a beta of 1.5. What number of SPX call options would be required to form an effective hedge?

15.6b Alternatively, suppose that your equity portfolio had a beta of .5. What number of SPX call options would then be required to form an effective hedge?

15.7 Implied Volatility Skews

volatility skew
Description of the relationship between implied volatilities and strike prices for options. Also called *volatility smiles*.

We earlier defined implied volatility (IVOL) and implied standard deviation (ISD) as the volatility value implied by an option price and stated that implied volatility represents an estimate of the price volatility (sigma, σ) of the underlying stock. We further noted that implied volatility is often used to estimate a stock's price volatility over the period remaining until option expiration. In this section, we examine the phenomenon of implied **volatility skews**—the relationship between implied volatilities and strike prices for options.

To illustrate the phenomenon of implied volatility skews, Table 15.4 presents option information for MSFT stock options observed in June 2003 for options expiring 49 days later in July 2003. This information includes strike prices, call option prices, put option prices, and call and put implied volatilities calculated separately for each option. Notice how the individual implied volatilities differ across different strike prices. Figure 15.6 provides a visual display of the relationship between implied volatilities and strike prices for these MSFT options. The negative slopes for call and put implied volatilities might be called volatility skews.

Logically, there can be only one stock price volatility since price volatility is a property of the underlying stock, and each option's implied volatility should be an estimate

TABLE 15.4	Volatility Skews for MSFT Options			
Strikes	**Calls**	**Call ISD (%)**	**Puts**	**Put ISD (%)**
21.25	3.6	34.56	.225	37.84
22.5	2.6	35.06	.4	34.50
23.75	1.725	33.94	.775	33.57
25	1.025	32.39	1.325	32.12
27.5	.275	31.18	3.1	32.01
30	.075	33.07	5.4	35.22
32.5	.025	35.96	7.85	40.90
Other information: $S = 24.64$, $y = 0\%$, $T = 37$ days, $r = 5.9\%$				

FIGURE 15.6

Volatility Skews for MSFT Options

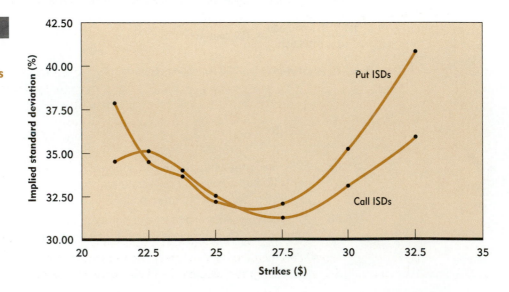

of a single underlying stock price volatility. That this is not the case is well known to options professionals, who commonly use the terms "volatility smile" and "volatility skew" to describe the anomaly. Why do volatility skews exist? Many suggestions have been proposed regarding possible causes. However, there is widespread agreement that the major factor causing volatility skews is **stochastic volatility**. Stochastic volatility is the phenomenon of stock price volatility changing over time, where the price volatility changes are largely random.

stochastic volatility
The phenomenon of stock price volatility changing randomly over time.

The Black-Scholes-Merton option pricing model assumes that stock price volatility is constant over the life of the option. Therefore, when stock price volatility is stochastic, the Black-Scholes-Merton option pricing model yields option prices that may differ from observed market prices. Nevertheless, the simplicity of the Black-Scholes-Merton model makes it an excellent tool, and many options professionals consider it an invaluable tool for analysis and decision making. Its simplicity is an advantage especially because option pricing models that account for stochastic volatility can be quite complex, and therefore difficult to work with. Furthermore, even when volatility is stochastic, the Black-Scholes-Merton option pricing model yields accurate option prices for options with strike prices close to a current stock price. For this reason, when using implied volatility to estimate an underlying stock price volatility it is best to use at-the-money options—that is, options with a strike price close to the current stock price.

For volatility summaries, see www.pmpublishing.com

Check This

15.7a   Using information from a recent *Wall Street Journal*, calculate IBM implied volatilities for options with at least one month until expiration.

15.8 Summary and Conclusions

In this chapter, we examined stock option prices. Many important aspects of option pricing were covered, including the following:

1. The Black-Scholes-Merton option pricing formula states that the value of a stock option is a function of the current stock price, the stock dividend yield, option strike price, risk-free interest rate, time remaining until option expiration, and the stock price volatility.

2. The two most important determinants of the price of a stock option are the price of the underlying stock and the strike price of the option. As the stock price increases, call prices increase and put prices decrease. Conversely, as the strike price increases, call prices decrease and put prices increase.

3. Time remaining until option expiration is an important determinant of option value. As time remaining until option expiration lengthens, both call and put option prices normally increase. Stock price volatility also plays an important role in determining option value. As stock price volatility increases, both call and put option prices increase.

4. Although less important, the interest rate can noticeably affect option values. As the interest rate increases, call prices increase and put prices decrease. A stock's dividend yield also affects option values. As the dividend yield increases, call prices decrease and put prices increase.

5. The two input factors that most affect stock option prices over a short period, say, a few days, are the stock price and the stock price volatility. The impact of a stock price change on an option price is measured by the option's delta. The impact of a volatility change on an option's price is measured by the option's vega.

6. A call option delta is always positive, and a put option delta is always negative. Delta measures the impact of a stock price change on an option price, where a one-dollar change in the stock price causes an option price to change by approximately delta dollars.

7. Vega measures the impact of a change in stock price volatility (sigma, σ) on an option price, where a 1 percent change in volatility changes an option price by approximately the amount vega.

8. Of the six input factors to the Black-Scholes-Merton option pricing model, only the stock price volatility is not directly observable and must be estimated somehow. A stock price volatility estimated from an option price is called an implied volatility or an implied standard deviation, which are two terms for the same thing.

9. Options on the S&P 500 index are a convenient hedging vehicle for an equity portfolio because they are European style and because they settle for cash at option expiration. Hedging a stock portfolio with index options requires calculating the number of option contracts needed to form an effective hedge.

10. To maintain an effective hedge over time, you should rebalance the options hedge on a regular basis. Rebalancing requires recalculating the number of option contracts needed to hedge an equity portfolio and then buying or selling options in the amount necessary to maintain an effective hedge.

11. Volatility skews, or volatility smiles, occur when individual implied volatilities differ across call and put options with different strike prices. Volatility skews commonly appear in implied volatilities for stock index options and also appear in implied volatilities for options on individual stocks. The most important factor causing volatility skews is stochastic volatility, the phenomenon of stock price volatility changing over time in a largely random fashion.

12. The Black-Scholes-Merton option pricing model assumes a constant stock price volatility and yields option prices that may differ from stochastic volatility option prices. Nevertheless, even when volatility is stochastic, the Black-Scholes-Merton option pricing model yields accurate option prices for options with strike prices close to a current stock price. Therefore, when using implied volatility to estimate an underlying stock price volatility, it is best to use at-the-money options.

Get Real

This chapter began by introducing you to the Nobel-Prize-winning Black-Scholes-Merton option pricing formula. We saw that the formula and its associated concepts are fairly complex, but, despite that complexity, the formula is very widely used by traders and

(continued)

money managers. You can find out more about the Black-Scholes-Merton option pricing model on the Internet. Enter "Black-Scholes-Merton" into an Internet search engine for links to hundreds of websites, like J&E Research (www.jeresearch.com).

To put into practice some real-world uses for the concepts we discussed, you should gather options trading information off the Web and then use the information to trade options through Stock-Trak. Some suggested websites are the Web Center for Futures and Options (www.ino.com), NUMA Derivatives (www.numa.com), Optionetics (www.optionetics.com), PM Publishing (www.pmpublishing.com), and Antix Stock Option Report (www.aantix.com). Of course, don't forget the most extensive website for options at the Chicago Board Options Exchange (www.cboe.com).

Another important use for option pricing theory is to gain some insight into stock market volatility. Recall that in Chapter 1 we discussed the probabilities associated with returns equal to the average plus or minus a particular number of standard deviations. Implied standard deviations (ISDs) provide a means of broadening this analysis to anything with traded options. Try calculating a few ISDs for both stock index options and some high-flying technology stocks. You can learn a lot about implied volatilities and how they are used by options professionals on the Internet. Enter the search phrases "implied volatility" or "implied standard deviation" into your favorite Internet search engine for links to dozens of websites, like IVolatility (www.ivolatility.com).

Key Terms

delta 500
eta 500
vega 501
gamma 503
theta 503
rho 503

implied standard deviation (ISD) 503
implied volatility (IVOL) 503
VIX, VXN 505
volatility skew 510
stochastic volatility 511

Chapter Review Problems and Self-Test

1. **Black-Scholes Formula**   What is the value of a call option if the underlying stock price is $100, the strike price is $90, the underlying stock volatility is 40 percent, and the risk-free rate is 4 percent? Assume the option has 60 days to expiration.

2. **Black-Scholes Formula**   What is the value of a put option using the assumptions from the previous problem?

Answers to Self-Test Problems

1. We will use these input values to calculate the price of the call option.

   S = current stock price = $100

   K = option strike price = $90

   r = risk-free interest rate = .04

   σ = stock volatility = .40

   T = time to expiration = 60 days

We first compute values for d_1 and d_2.

$$d_1 = \frac{\ln(100/90) + (.04 + .4^2/2) \times 60/365}{.4\sqrt{60/365}}$$

$$= \frac{.10536 + .12 \times .16438}{.16218}$$

$$= .77130$$

$$d_2 = d_1 - .16218$$

$$= .60912$$

The following standard normal probabilities are given:

$$N(d_1) = N(.7713) = .77973 \qquad N(d_2) = N(.60912) = .72878$$

We can now calculate the price of the call option as

$$C = \$100 \times .77973 - \$90 \times e^{-.04 \times 60/365} \times .72878$$

$$= \$100 \times .77973 - \$90 \times .99345 \times .72878$$

$$= \$12.81$$

2. Since we already know the values for d_1 and d_2, we can solve for $N(-d_1)$ and $N(-d_2)$ as follows:

$$N(-d_1) = 1 - N(d_1) = 1 - .77973 = .22027$$
$$N(-d_2) = 1 - N(d_2) = 1 - .72878 = .27122$$

We can now calculate the price of the put option as

$$P = \$90 \times e^{-.04 \times 60/365} \times .27122 - \$100 \times .22027$$

$$= \$90 \times .99345 \times .27122 - \$100 \times .22027$$

$$= \$2.22$$

Alternatively, using put-call parity from the previous chapter:

$$P = C + Ke^{-rT} - S$$

$$= \$12.81 + \$90 \times e^{-.05 \times 90/365} - \$100$$

$$= \$12.81 + \$90 \times .99345 - \$100$$

$$= \$2.22$$

 ## Test Your Investment Quotient

1. **Black-Scholes-Merton Model**   The only variable in the Black-Scholes-Merton option pricing model that cannot be directly observed is the

    a. Stock price volatility
    b. Dividend yield
    c. Stock price
    d. Risk-free rate

2. **Delta**   You purchase a call option with a delta of .34. If the stock price decreases by $2.00, the price of the option will

    a. Increase by $.34
    b. Decrease by $.34
    c. Increase by $.68
    d. Decrease by $.68

3. **Black-Scholes-Merton Model**   In the Black-Scholes-Merton option pricing model, the value of an option contract is a function of six inputs. Which of the following is not one of these inputs?

a. The price of the underlying stock.
b. The strike price of the option contract.
c. The expected return on the underlying stock.
d. The time remaining until option expiration.

4. **Black-Scholes Formula**   In the Black-Scholes option valuation formula, an increase in a stock's volatility

a. Increases the associated call option value.
b. Decreases the associated put option value.
c. Increases or decreases the option value, depending on the level of interest rates.
d. Does not change either the put or call option value because put-call parity holds.

5. **Option Prices**   Which of the following variables influence the value of options?

   I. Level of interest rates
  II. Time to expiration of the option
 III. Dividend yield of underlying stock
 IV. Stock price volatility

a. I and IV only
b. II and III only
c. I, III, and IV only
d. I, II, III, and IV

6. **Option Prices**   Which of the following factors does not influence the market price of options on a common stock?

a. Expected return on the underlying stock.
b. Volatility of the underlying stock.
c. Relationship between the strike price of the options and the market price of the underlying stock.
d. Option's expiration date.

7. **Option Prices**   Which one of the following will increase the value of a call option?

a. An increase in interest rates.
b. A decrease in time to expiration of the call.
c. A decrease in the volatility of the underlying stock.
d. An increase in the dividend rate of the underlying stock.

8. **Option Prices**   Which one of the following would tend to result in a high value of a call option?

a. Interest rates are low.
b. The variability of the underlying stock is high.
c. There is little time remaining until the option expires.
d. The exercise price is high relative to the stock price.

9. **Option Price Factors**   Which of the following incorrectly states the signs of the impact of an increase in the indicated input factor on call and put option prices?

	Call	Put
a. Risk-free interest rate	+	−
b. Underlying stock price	+	−
c. Dividend yield of the underlying stock	−	+
d. Volatility of the underlying stock price	+	−

10. **Option Price Factors**   Which of the following incorrectly states the signs of the impact of an increase in the indicated input factor on call and put option prices?

	Call	Put
a. Strike price of the option contract	+	−
b. Time remaining until option expiration	+	+
c. Underlying stock price	+	−
d. Volatility of the underlying stock price	+	+

11. **Option Price Sensitivities**   Which of the following measures the impact of a change in the underlying stock price on the option price?

    a. Vega
    b. Rho
    c. Delta
    d. Theta

12. **Option Price Sensitivities**   Which of the following measures the impact of a change in the time remaining until option contract expiration on the option price?

    a. Vega
    b. Rho
    c. Delta
    d. Theta

13. **Option Price Sensitivities**   Which of the following measures the impact of a change in the underlying stock's price volatility on the option price?

    a. Vega
    b. Rho
    c. Delta
    d. Theta

14. **Option Price Sensitivities**   Which of the following measures the impact of a change in the risk-free interest rate on the option price?

    a. Vega
    b. Rho
    c. Delta
    d. Theta

15. **Hedging with Options**   You wish to hedge a $5 million stock portfolio with a portfolio beta equal to 1. The hedging index call option has a delta equal to .5 and a contract value equal to $100,000. Which of the following hedging transactions is required to hedge the stock portfolio?

    a. Write 200 index call option contracts.
    b. Write 100 index call option contracts.
    c. Buy 200 index call option contracts.
    d. Buy 100 index call option contracts.

16. **Hedging with Options**   You wish to hedge a $10 million stock portfolio with a portfolio beta equal to 1. The hedging index put option has a delta equal to .5 and a contract value of $200,000. Which of the following hedging transactions is required to hedge the stock portfolio?

    a. Write 200 put option contracts.
    b. Write 100 put option contracts.
    c. Buy 200 put option contracts.
    d. Buy 100 put option contracts.

17. **Implied Volatility**   Which of the following provides the best economic interpretation of implied volatility for an underlying stock?

    a. Implied volatility predicts the stock's future volatility.
    b. Implied volatility states the stock's historical volatility.
    c. Implied volatility is unrelated to the underlying stock.
    d. Implied volatility is an accurate measure of interest rate risk.

18. **Implied Volatility**   Two call options on the same underlying stock with the same expiration dates have strike prices of $40 and $60 and yield implied volatilities of 45 percent and 35 percent, respectively. The stock price is $50. This means that

    a. The underlying stock has two different volatilities.
    b. Both options are incorrectly priced.

  c. The volatility skew has a negative slope.
  d. The underlying stock will soon pay a dividend.

19. **Implied Volatility** With respect to call options with three months to expiration on a particular underlying stock, in-the-money implied volatilities are higher than out-of-the-money implied volatilities. This means that

  a. The volatility skew is shifting.
  b. The volatility skew is flat.
  c. The volatility skew has a negative slope.
  d. The volatility skew has a positive slope.

20. **Implied Volatility** The implied volatility for an at-the-money call option suddenly jumps from 25 percent to 50 percent. This most likely means that

  a. The underlying stock has just paid a dividend.
  b. The volatility jump is temporary.
  c. The option has a short time to expiration.
  d. An unforeseen event has increased the risk of the underlying stock.

Concept Questions

1. **Option Prices** What are the six factors that determine an option's price?

2. **Options and Expiration Dates** What is the impact of lengthening the time to expiration on an option's value? Explain.

3. **Options and Stock Price Volatility** What is the impact of an increase in the volatility of the underlying stock on an option's value? Explain.

4. **Options and Dividend Yields** How do dividend yields affect option prices? Explain.

5. **Options and Interest Rates** How do interest rates affect option prices? Explain.

6. **Time Value** What is the time value of a call option? Of a put option? What happens to the time value of a call option as the maturity increases? What about a put option?

7. **Delta** What does an option's delta tell us? Suppose a call option with a delta of .60 sells for $5.00. If the stock price rises by $1, what will happen to the call's value?

8. **Eta** What is the difference between an option's delta and its eta? Suppose a call option has an eta of 10. If the underlying stock rises from $100 to $104, what will be the impact on the option's price?

9. **Vega** What does an option's vega tell us? Suppose a put option with a vega of .80 sells for $15.00. If the underlying volatility rises from 40 to 41 percent, what will happen to the put's value?

10. **Rho** What does an option's rho measure? Suppose a call option with a rho of .14 sells for $10.00. If the interest rate rises from 4 to 5 percent, what will happen to the call value?

Questions and Problems

Core Questions

1. **Call Option Prices** What is the value of a call option if the underlying stock price is $98, the strike price is $105, the underlying stock volatility is 62 percent, and the risk-free rate is 4 percent? Assume the option has 270 days to expiration.

2. **Call Option Prices** What is the value of a call option if the underlying stock price is $23, the strike price is $25, the underlying stock volatility is 50 percent, and the risk-free rate is 4 percent? Assume the option has 60 days to expiration and the underlying stock has a dividend yield of 2 percent.

3. **Call Option Prices** What is the value of a call option if the underlying stock price is $81, the strike price is $75, the underlying stock volatility is 60 percent, and the risk-free rate is 5 percent? Assume the option has 180 days to expiration.

4. **Call Option Prices**   A stock is currently priced at $87 and has an annual standard deviation of 55 percent. The dividend yield of the stock is 2 percent, and the risk-free rate is 6 percent. What is the value of a call option on the stock with a strike price of $95 and 45 days to expiration?

5. **Call Option Prices**   The stock of Nugents Nougats currently sells for $53 and has an annual standard deviation of 45 percent. The stock has a dividend yield of 1.5 percent, and the risk-free rate is 7 percent. What is the value of a call option on the stock with a strike price of $50 and 65 days to expiration?

6. **Put Option Prices**   The stock of Lead Zeppelin, a metal manufacturer, currently sells for $86 and has an annual standard deviation of 67 percent. The risk-free rate is 6 percent. What is the value of a put option with a strike price of $85 and 48 days to expiration?

7. **Put Option Prices**   What is the value of a put option if the underlying stock price is $75, the strike price is $80, the underlying stock volatility is 62 percent, the dividend yield of the stock is 2 percent, and the risk-free rate is 5 percent? Assume the option has 120 days to expiration.

8. **Put Option Prices**   A stock with an annual standard deviation of 75 percent currently sells for $104. The dividend yield of the stock is 3 percent, and the risk-free rate is 6 percent. What is the value of a put option with a strike price of $115 and 150 days to expiration?

9. **Hedging with Options**   You are managing a pension fund with a value of $400 million and a beta of 1.2. You are concerned about a market decline and wish to hedge the portfolio. You have decided to use SPX calls. How many contracts do you need if the delta of the call option is .60 and the S&P index is currently at 1050?

10. **Hedging with Options**   Suppose you have a stock market portfolio with a beta of 1.4 that is currently worth $200 million. You wish to hedge against a decline using index options. Describe how you might do so with puts and calls. Suppose you decide to use SPX calls. Calculate the number of contracts needed if the contract you pick has a delta of .50, and the S&P 500 index is at 1100.

Intermediate Questions

11. **Black-Scholes-Merton Model**   A call option matures in six months. The underlying stock price is $85, and the stock's return has a standard deviation of 20 percent per year. The risk-free rate is 4 percent per year, compounded continuously. If the exercise price is $0, what is the price of the call option?

12. **Black-Scholes-Merton Model**   A call option has an exercise price of $75 and matures in six months. The current stock price is $80, and the risk-free rate is 5 percent per year, compounded continuously. What is the price of the call if the standard deviation of the stock is 0 percent per year?

13. **Black-Scholes-Merton Model**   A stock is currently priced at $35. A call option with an expiration of one year has an exercise price of $50. The risk-free rate is 12 percent per year, compounded continuously, and the standard deviation of the stock's return is infinitely large. What is the price of the call option?

14. **ISDs**   A call option has a price of $8.25. The underlying stock price, strike price, and dividend yield are $105, $120, and 3 percent, respectively. The option has 100 days to expiration, and the risk-free interest rate is 6 percent. What is the implied volatility?

15. **ISDs**   A put option has a price of $19.15. The underlying stock price, strike price, and dividend yield are $110, $120, and 3 percent, respectively. The option has 100 days to expiration, and the risk-free interest rate is 6 percent. What is the implied volatility?

16. **Calculating the Greeks**   Calculate the price and the following "greeks" for a call and a put option with 180 days to expiration: delta, eta, and vega. The stock price is $93, the strike price is $90, the volatility is 50 percent, the dividend yield is 3 percent, and the risk-free interest rate is 5 percent.

17. **Employee Stock Options**   At year-end 1999, Adolph Coors' Company had outstanding employee stock options (ESOs) representing over 2.64 million shares of its stock. Coors

accountants estimated the value of these options using the Black-Scholes-Merton formula and the following assumptions:

S = current stock price = \$47.61
K = option strike price = \$36.05
r = risk-free interest rate = .0503
y = dividend yield = .0109
σ = stock volatility = .3066
T = time to expiration = 7.8 years

What was the estimated value of these employee stock options per share of stock?

18. **Employee Stock Options** Suppose you hold Coors employee stock options (ESOs) representing options to buy 10,000 shares of Coors stock. You wish to hedge your position by buying put options with three-month expirations and a \$50 strike price. How many put option contracts are required? (Use the same assumptions specified in the previous problem.)

19. **Employee Stock Options** Immediately after establishing your put options hedge, volatility for Coors stock suddenly jumps to 40 percent. This changes the number of put options required to hedge your Coors employee stock options (ESOs). How many put option contracts are now required? (Except for the new volatility, use the same assumptions specified in the previous problem.)

20. **Employee Stock Options** Suppose the put option in the previous problem has a price of \$6. What is the implied volatility? (Use the same assumptions specified in the previous problems.)

Use the following information for the next three problems: Donna Donie, CFA, has a client who believes the common stock price of TRT Materials (currently \$58 per share) could move substantially in either direction in reaction to an expected court decision involving the company. The client currently owns no TRT shares, but asks Donie for advice about implementing a strangle strategy to capitalize on the possible stock price movement. Donie gathers the TRT option pricing data shown below. *Note:* A long strangle is similar to a long straddle, but involves purchasing a put option at K_1 and purchasing a call option at K_2 where $K_1 < K_2$.

	Call Option	Put Option
Price	\$ 5	\$ 4
Strike price	\$60	\$55
Time to expiration	90 days	90 days

21. **Strangles** Should Donie choose a long strangle strategy or a short strangle strategy to achieve the client's objective? Justify your recommendation with one reason.

22. **Strangle Payoff** For the appropriate strategy in the previous problem, calculate at expiration the maximum possible loss per share, the maximum possible gain per share, and the break-even stock price(s).

23. **Delta** The delta of the call option in the previous problems is .625, and TRT stock does not pay any dividends. Calculate the approximate change in price for the call option if TRT's stock price immediately increases to \$59.

24. **Black-Scholes-Merton Model** A stock has a price of \$83 and an annual return volatility of 60 percent. The risk-free rate is 4 percent, and the stock pays a 2 percent dividend yield. Using a computer spreadsheet program, calculate the call and put option prices with a strike price of \$80 and a 180-day expiration.

25. **Greeks** Using the information in the previous problem, construct a second spreadsheet that calculates the delta for the put and call, the eta for the put and call, and the vega.

What's on the Web?

WWW

1. **Black-Scholes**   Go to www.cfo.com. Under "Tools," follow the "Stock Options Calculator." There is a call and a put option on a stock that expire in 30 days. The strike price is $55, and the current stock price is $58.70. The standard deviation of the stock is 45 percent per year, and the risk-free rate is 4.8 percent per year, compounded continuously. What is the price of the call and the put? What are the delta, gamma, theta, and vega of the call and the put?

2. **Black-Scholes**   Go to www.cboe.com, click on the "Trading Tools" tab, then the "Option Calculator" link. A stock is currently priced at $98 per share and has a standard deviation of 58 percent per year. Options are available with an exercise price of $95, and the risk-free rate of interest is 5.2 percent per year, compounded continuously. What is the price of the call and the put that expire next month? What are the delta, gamma, seven-day theta, vega, and rho of the call and the put? How do you interpret these numbers? How do your answers change for an exercise price of $100?

3. **Implied Standard Deviation**   Go to www.numa.com, look under the section titled "Options," and follow the calculator link. You purchased a call option for $11.50 that matures in 55 days. The strike price is $95, and the underlying stock has a price of $99.50. If the risk-free rate is 5.4 percent, compounded continuously, what is the implied standard deviation of the stock? Using this implied standard deviation, what is the price of a put option with the same characteristics?

4. **Black-Scholes with Dividends**   Recalculate the first two problems assuming a dividend yield of 2 percent per year. How does this change your answers?

Chapter 16

Futures Contracts

"There are two times in a man's life when he should not speculate: when he can't afford it and when he can."

–Mark Twain

"When you bet on a sure thing—hedge!"

–Robert Half

Futures contracts can be used for speculation or for risk management. For would-be speculators, Mark Twain's advice is well worth considering. In addition to their risk dimension, trading in futures contracts adds a time dimension to commodity markets. A futures contract separates the date of the agreement—when a delivery price is specified—from the date when delivery and payment actually occur. By separating these dates, buyers and sellers achieve an important and flexible tool for risk management. So fundamental is this underlying principle that it has been practiced for several millennia and is likely to be around for many more. ■

This chapter covers modern-day futures contracts. The first sections discuss the basics of futures contracts and how their prices are quoted in the financial press. From there, we move into a general discussion of how futures contracts are used and the relationship between current cash prices and futures prices.

16.1 Futures Contracts Basics

forward contract
Agreement between a buyer and a seller, who both commit to a transaction at a future date at a price set by negotiation today.

futures contract
Contract between a seller and a buyer specifying a commodity or financial instrument to be delivered and paid at contract maturity. Futures contracts are managed through an organized futures exchange.

futures price Price negotiated by buyer and seller at which the underlying commodity or financial instrument will be delivered and paid for to fulfill the obligations of a futures contract.

By definition, a **forward contract** is a formal agreement between a buyer and a seller who both commit to a commodity transaction at a future date at a price set by negotiation today. The genius of forward contracting is that it allows a producer to sell a product to a willing buyer before it is actually produced. By setting a price today, both buyer and seller remove price uncertainty as a source of risk. With less risk, buyers and sellers mutually benefit and commerce is stimulated. This principle has been understood and practiced for centuries.

Futures contracts represent a step beyond forward contracts. Futures contracts and forward contracts accomplish the same economic task, which is to specify a price today for future delivery. This specified price is called the **futures price**. However, while a forward contract can be struck between any two parties, futures contracts are managed through an organized futures exchange. Sponsorship through a futures exchange is a major distinction between a futures contract and a forward contract.

Modern History of Futures Trading

The oldest organized futures exchange in the United States is the Chicago Board of Trade (CBOT). The CBOT was established in 1848 and grew with the westward expansion of American ranching and agriculture. Today, the CBOT is the largest, most active futures exchange in the world. Other early American futures exchanges still with us today include the MidAmerica Commodity Exchange (founded in 1868), New York Cotton Exchange (1870), New York Mercantile Exchange (1872), Chicago Mercantile Exchange (1874), New York Coffee Exchange (1882), and the Kansas City Board of Trade (1882).

For more than 100 years, American futures exchanges devoted their activities exclusively to commodity futures. However, a revolution began in the 1970s with the introduction of financial futures. Unlike commodity futures, which call for delivery of a physical commodity, financial futures require delivery of a financial instrument. The first financial futures were foreign currency contracts introduced in 1972 at the International Monetary Market (IMM), a division of the Chicago Mercantile Exchange (CME).

Next came interest rate futures, introduced at the Chicago Board of Trade in 1975. An interest rate futures contract specifies delivery of a fixed-income security. For example, an interest rate futures contract may specify a U.S. Treasury bill, note, or bond as the underlying instrument. Finally, stock index futures were introduced in 1982 at the Kansas City Board of Trade (KBT), the Chicago Mercantile Exchange, and the New York Futures Exchange (NYFE). A stock index futures contract specifies a particular stock market index as its underlying instrument.

Financial futures have been so successful that they now constitute the bulk of all futures trading. This success is largely attributed to the fact that financial futures have become an indispensable tool for financial risk management by corporations and portfolio managers. As we will see, futures contracts can be used to reduce risk through hedging strategies or to increase risk through speculative strategies. In this chapter, we discuss futures contracts generally, but, since this text deals with financial markets, we will ultimately focus on financial futures.

Visit these futures exchange websites:
www.cbot.com
www.nymex.com
www.cme.com
www.kcbt.com
www.nybot.com

Futures Contract Features

Futures contracts are a type of derivative security because the value of the contract is derived from the value of an underlying instrument. For example, the value of a futures contract to buy or sell gold is derived from the market price of gold. However, because a futures contract represents a zero-sum game between a buyer and a seller, the net value of a futures contract is always zero. That is, any gain realized by the buyer is exactly equal to a loss realized by the seller, and vice versa.

Futures are contracts, and, in practice, exchange-traded futures contracts are standardized to facilitate convenience in trading and price reporting. Standardized futures contracts have a set contract size specified according to the particular underlying instrument. For example, a standard gold futures contract specifies a contract size of 100 troy ounces. This means that a single gold futures contract obligates the seller to deliver 100 troy ounces of gold to the buyer at contract maturity. In turn, the contract also obligates the buyer to accept the gold delivery and pay the negotiated futures price for the delivered gold.

To properly understand a futures contract, we must know the specific terms of the contract. In general, futures contracts must stipulate at least the following five contract terms:

1. The identity of the underlying commodity or financial instrument.
2. The futures contract size.
3. The futures maturity date, also called the expiration date.
4. The delivery or settlement procedure.
5. The futures price.

First, a futures contract requires that the underlying commodity or financial instrument be clearly identified. This is stating the obvious, but it is important that the obvious is clearly understood in financial transactions.

Second, the size of the contract must be specified. As stated earlier, the standard contract size for gold futures is 100 troy ounces. For U.S. Treasury note and bond futures, the standard contract size is $100,000 in par value notes or bonds, respectively.

The third contract term that must be stated is the maturity date. Contract maturity is the date on which the seller is obligated to make delivery and the buyer is obligated to make payment.

Fourth, the delivery process must be specified. For commodity futures, delivery normally entails sending a warehouse receipt for the appropriate quantity of the underlying commodity. After delivery, the buyer pays warehouse storage costs until the commodity is sold or otherwise disposed.

Finally, the futures price must be mutually agreed on by the buyer and seller. The futures price is quite important, since it is the price that the buyer will pay and the seller will receive for delivery at contract maturity.

For financial futures, delivery is often accomplished by a transfer of registered ownership. For example, ownership of U.S. Treasury bill, note, and bond issues is registered at the Federal Reserve in computerized book-entry form. Futures delivery is accomplished by a notification to the Fed to make a change of registered ownership.

Other financial futures feature cash settlement, which means that the buyer and seller simply settle up in cash with no actual delivery. We discuss cash settlement in more detail when we discuss stock index futures. The important thing to remember for now is

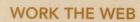

WORK THE WEB

One problem with futures quotes from newspapers is that the prices are from the previous trading day. If you need quotes from today, one of the best places to find current quotes is the exchange website. We wanted to find current prices for the Dow Jones Industrial Average (DJIA) futures, so we went to www.cbot.com, the Chicago Board of Trade, where DJIA futures are traded. Here is what we found:

May 13, 2003 04:00 PM CST - Open Outcry   a/c/e

Dow Jones Industrial Average (DJ)

	Settle	Net Chg	Opening	High	Low	Close	Prev Srtl	High Limits	Low Limits
03Jun	8667	-28	8660 8670 7:21 am	8705 12:03 pm	8625 1:27 pm	8670 8663 3:15 pm	8695	9667	7667
03Sep	8647	-28	8645 8:08 am	8680 12:04 pm	8615 9:42 am	8645 8647 3:16 pm	8675	9647	7647
03Dec	8617	-28	8660 11:45 am	8660 11:45 am	8600 1:38 pm	8617 3:16 pm	8645	9617	7617
04Mar	8597	Unch	8600 8601 11:30 am	8630 12:05 pm	8580 1:07 pm	8597 3:17 pm			
04Dec	8567	-33				8567 3:17 pm	8600	9567	7567

As you can see, most of the information is self-explanatory. There were five futures contracts on the Dow Jones Industrial Average, three that expire in 2003 and two that expire in 2004. In an unfortunate sign for the market, the contracts mostly traded down on this day.

that delivery procedures are selected for convenience and low cost. Specific delivery procedures are set by the futures exchange and may change slightly from time to time.

Futures Prices

The largest volume of futures trading in the United States takes place at the Chicago Board of Trade, which accounts for about half of all domestic futures trading. However, futures trading is also quite active at other futures exchanges. Current futures prices for contracts traded at the major futures exchanges are reported each day in *The Wall Street Journal*. Our nearby *Work the Web* box shows how to get prices online, and Figure 16.1 reproduces a portion of the daily "Futures Prices" report of *The Wall Street Journal*.

FIGURE 16.1 Futures Prices

Wednesday, May 7, 2003

Grain and Oilseed Futures

Corn (CBT)-5,000 bu.; cents per bu.

	OPEN	HIGH	LOW	SETTLE	CHG	LIFETIME HIGH	LIFETIME LOW	OPEN INT
May	241.00	246.00	241.00	245.75	5.25	301.00	227.25	10,642
July	237.50	243.00	237.50	242.50	5.00	297.25	227.25	222,432
Sept	238.75	241.00	238.00	240.75	3.75	276.00	229.00	46,784
Dec	239.00	242.50	239.00	242.00	3.00	269.00	230.50	99,813
Mr04	246.00	248.75	246.00	248.50	2.50	264.00	236.75	11,268
May	250.50	252.00	250.00	252.00	3.00	255.50	241.00	1,418
July	253.00	254.50	252.50	254.50	3.00	264.50	241.75	3,469
Dec	242.00	244.50	242.00	244.25	1.50	260.00	232.50	2,874

Est vol 99,985; Tue 55,520; open int 399,096, –1,003.

Oats (CBT)-5,000 bu.; cents per bu.

May	175.00	175.00	174.00	174.00	4.00	221.00	132.00	56
July	148.75	154.75	148.25	153.50	3.75	197.00	146.50	3,819
Sept	143.00	143.00	141.50	143.00	3.00	175.00	138.50	241
Dec	140.50	143.50	140.50	143.00	2.75	163.50	140.00	1,617

Est vol 1,150; Tue 848; open int 5,869, +77.

Soybeans (CBT)-5,000 bu.; cents per bu.

May	627.00	628.50	621.00	623.00	–2.00	631.50	460.00	4,898
July	630.50	633.50	625.25	627.00	–2.50	637.00	450.00	135,694
Aug	624.75	625.50	618.50	619.25	–1.75	630.00	510.00	12,670
Sept	590.00	591.50	585.50	586.00	–2.00	596.50	466.00	11,096
Nov	557.25	560.00	553.00	555.50	–2.00	565.00	484.00	57,517
Ja04	561.00	562.50	556.00	557.50	–2.00	567.00	507.00	2,994
Mar	563.00	565.00	559.50	560.00	–2.00	569.50	508.00	1,529
Nov	531.00	531.00	528.00	527.25	...	531.00	483.00	528

Est vol 53,680; Tue 61,650; open int 227,968, –2,770.

Soybean Meal (CBT)-100 tons; $ per ton.

May	196.30	196.30	192.50	193.20	–2.60	198.50	146.00	5,991
July	195.70	196.70	191.80	192.40	–2.70	198.50	147.00	73,415
Aug	191.00	191.20	187.20	187.50	–2.80	194.50	148.00	18,350
Sept	183.00	183.00	179.20	179.50	–2.70	185.70	148.00	12,384
Oct	166.50	171.50	166.50	168.00	–2.20	173.50	148.10	10,836
Dec	169.30	169.30	166.20	166.80	–1.70	172.20	148.00	34,033
Ja04	169.00	169.00	166.50	166.60	–1.70	172.50	151.00	6,272
Mar	170.40	170.40	168.00	168.30	–1.50	173.50	152.50	2,708
May	170.50	170.50	169.00	169.50	–1.50	173.50	153.00	1,529
July	172.50	172.50	170.50	170.50	–1.50	175.00	152.50	914

Est vol 28,908; Tue 24,094; open int 167,324, –3,512.

Soybean Oil (CBT)-60,000 lbs.; cents per lb.

May	21.83	22.15	21.72	22.15	.40	22.57	16.80	4,806
July	21.77	22.20	21.77	22.12	.36	22.64	16.95	71,725
Aug	21.85	22.19	21.81	22.10	.32	22.52	19.32	19,162
Sept	21.74	22.00	21.67	21.96	.29	22.15	19.20	7,671
Oct	21.40	21.63	21.33	21.63	.30	21.70	18.95	6,841
Dec	21.08	21.38	21.04	21.34	.32	21.50	18.90	18,515
Jl04	20.60	20.60	20.60	20.65	.30	20.75	19.20	671

Est vol 22,052; Tue 26,530; open int 135,101, –4,090.

Wheat (CBT)-5,000 bu.; cents per bu.

May	290.00	297.00	288.00	296.00	9.00	422.00	273.00	324
July	293.75	302.50	293.00	301.75	8.75	380.00	279.00	71,558
Sept	298.75	306.00	298.00	305.25	6.75	382.00	285.00	10,753
Dec	308.25	316.00	307.25	315.50	8.25	385.00	291.00	12,934
Mr04	314.00	322.00	314.00	322.50	7.50	346.00	301.50	1,624
July	309.50	315.00	309.50	317.00	8.00	333.00	298.00	136

Est vol 37,508; Tue 22,546; open int 97,476, –2,639.

Wheat (KC)-5,000 bu.; cents per bu.

May	337.00	344.00	337.00	341.00	5.00	458.25	299.50	655
July	308.50	318.00	307.00	317.00	9.25	408.00	294.00	34,160
Sept	310.00	318.50	310.00	318.50	8.50	405.00	300.75	9,625
Dec	319.00	326.50	318.50	326.50	7.50	408.00	309.00	5,776
Mr04	325.00	332.00	325.00	332.00	7.00	408.00	314.00	1,263
May	333.00	333.00	333.00	333.00	8.00	333.00	315.00	36
July	326.00	333.00	326.00	333.00	12.00	333.00	313.00	32

Est vol 12,268; Tue 5,795; open int 51,547, –924.

Wheat (MPLS)-5,000 bu.; cents per bu.

May	347.00	351.50	347.00	350.50	6.50	492.00	313.00	60
July	346.00	351.00	345.25	350.75	6.75	460.00	314.50	10,595
Sept	342.50	347.00	342.50	346.25	5.00	422.00	318.00	4,552
Dec	346.00	348.75	345.25	348.25	4.25	425.00	325.50	3,440
Mr04	352.50	354.50	352.00	353.50	3.00	419.00	344.00	663

Est vol 3,764; vol Tue 1,538; open int 19,315, +47.

Metal Futures

Copper-High (CMX)-25,000 lbs.; cents per lb.

May	72.80	73.05	72.70	73.05	1.15	81.05	65.80	919
June	73.05	73.45	73.05	73.30	1.10	80.50	68.00	3,901
July	72.40	73.70	71.80	73.50	1.10	80.80	66.80	44,379
Aug	73.50	73.75	73.50	73.70	1.10	80.30	67.40	1,280
Sept	73.45	73.90	73.45	73.85	1.10	81.00	66.00	15,354
Dec	73.80	74.40	73.80	74.35	1.10	81.60	68.90	6,741
Jl04	75.30	75.30	75.30	75.25	1.10	79.90	70.90	1,287
Dec	75.80	75.80	75.80	75.75	1.10	81.80	74.20	745

Est vol 13,000; vol Tue 6,615; open int 81,212, +1,992.

Gold (CMX)-100 troy oz.; $ per troy oz.

May	...	...	...	341.90	–0.60	353.50	320.00	1
June	344.80	345.20	339.60	342.20	–0.60	391.70	280.00	102,634
Aug	345.50	346.00	340.20	343.00	–0.60	390.00	303.50	14,20[illegible]
Oct	344.20	344.40	341.30	343.60	–0.70	386.60	310.00	4,83[illegible]
Dec	347.10	347.10	341.80	344.20	–0.70	391.00	280.00	19,60[illegible]
Fb04	345.50	345.50	343.10	344.80	–0.70	390.60	322.00	8,97[illegible]
Apr	347.70	347.70	347.70	345.30	–0.80	386.20	320.00	2,71[illegible]
Dec	350.00	350.00	347.60	347.70	–1.20	396.30	290.00	11,12[illegible]

Est vol 45,000; vol Tue 28,020; open int 178,933, +238.

Platinum (NYM)-50 troy oz.; $ per troy oz.

July	616.50	629.80	615.00	626.80	9.60	694.00	552.50	6,23[illegible]

Est vol 1,709; vol Tue 941; open int 6,275, +90.

Silver (CMX)-5,000 troy oz.; cnts per troy oz.

May	476.0	476.5	473.5	472.9	–5.8	523.0	432.0	75
July	480.0	481.5	471.5	474.2	–5.8	551.0	421.0	63,1[illegible]
Sept	481.0	481.5	473.5	475.4	–5.9	520.0	437.0	4,0[illegible]
Dec	483.5	484.0	474.0	476.9	–6.0	565.0	419.0	11,2[illegible]
Dc04	483.0	484.0	482.0	482.9	–6.3	560.0	440.0	1,5[illegible]

Est vol 12,000; vol Tue 11,880; open int 84,773, +2,066.

Petroleum Futures

Crude Oil, Light Sweet (NYM)-1,000 bbls.; $ per bbl.

June	25.70	26.35	25.50	26.23	0.51	34.90	19.82	119,552
July	25.59	26.20	25.40	26.12	0.50	33.39	20.76	89,667
Aug	25.39	25.95	25.25	25.91	0.44	32.35	21.16	39,614
Sept	25.32	25.70	25.21	25.72	0.40	31.53	21.05	29,826
Oct	25.14	25.45	25.10	25.56	0.39	30.93	20.55	21,399
Nov	25.00	25.35	25.00	25.43	0.37	30.40	20.70	13,516
Dec	24.90	25.30	24.82	25.33	0.36	29.96	15.92	38,409
Ja04	24.72	25.00	24.72	25.22	0.35	29.40	20.35	14,306
Feb	24.97	24.97	24.97	25.11	0.34	28.70	20.35	7,821
June	24.42	24.60	24.35	24.71	0.30	26.63	20.53	16,931
Aug	24.50	24.50	24.50	24.60	0.28	25.90	20.84	2,834
Dec	24.30	24.30	24.30	24.40	0.24	25.00	16.35	16,477
Ju05	24.00	24.00	23.99	24.15	0.23	24.10	22.40	4,350

Est vol 154,544; vol Tue 163,802; open int 487,632, –9,656.

Heating Oil No. 2 (NYM)-42,000 gal.; $ per gal.

June	.6780	.6950	.6750	.6893	.0115	.9240	.5550	32,108
July	.6790	.6940	.6750	.6920	.0143	.8875	.5625	17,703
Aug	.6835	.6980	.6830	.6965	.0138	.8680	.5705	9,650
Sept	.6890	.7040	.6890	.7020	.0138	.8620	.6215	8,696
Oct	.6980	.7070	.6950	.7085	.0138	.8500	.6290	4,361
Nov	.7040	.7160	.7020	.7145	.0138	.8550	.6450	6,378
Dec	.7080	.7220	.7080	.7205	.0138	.8610	.6500	15,691
Ja04	.7110	.7260	.7105	.7235	.0138	.8530	.6540	4,775
Feb	.7090	.7230	.7075	.7200	.0138	.8350	.6500	3,490
Mar	.6910	.7050	.6900	.7025	.0138	.7980	.6370	4,996
Apr	.6740	.6865	.6740	.6840	.0138	.7590	.6275	2,900
May	.6680	.6680	.6625	.6655	.0138	.7200	.6140	532
June	.6570	.6570	.6570	.6590	.0138	.7055	.6354	2,996

Est vol 3,833; vol Tue 46,094; open int 114,869, +1,434.

Gasoline-NY Unleaded (NYM)-42,000 gal.; $ per gal.

June	.7710	.7850	.7640	.7796	.0111	1.1070	.7425	47,003
July	.7639	.7730	.7579	.7721	.0101	1.0500	.7250	25,188
Aug	.7476	.7625	.7473	.7616	.0121	.9900	.7200	9,068
Sept	.7280	.7380	.7280	.7446	.0146	.9180	.6900	8,668

Est vol 48,098; vol Tue 42,946; open int 94,587, +326.

Natural Gas (NYM)-10,000 MMBtu.; $ per MMBtu

June	5.571	5.680	5.460	5.660	.092	6.600	2.610	46,956
July	5.645	5.750	5.535	5.735	.102	6.460	2.550	27,191
Aug	5.670	5.760	5.560	5.750	.092	6.300	2.890	22,688
Sept	5.656	5.730	5.570	5.730	.087	6.229	2.880	24,820
Oct	5.660	5.730	5.575	5.735	.082	6.220	2.910	24,324
Nov	5.713	5.800	5.660	5.808	.073	6.259	3.050	20,104
Dec	5.810	5.890	5.760	5.898	.069	6.270	3.250	24,259
Ja04	5.880	5.950	5.850	5.968	.057	6.350	3.300	18,174
Feb	5.759	5.820	5.740	5.843	.054	6.188	3.260	11,008
Mar	5.570	5.600	5.550	5.628	.039	5.825	3.150	14,177
Apr	4.970	4.990	4.960	5.006	.017	5.100	2.970	11,640
May	4.870	4.880	4.840	4.866	–.011	4.900	3.030	8,413
June	4.830	4.850	4.800	4.828	–.011	4.850	3.010	8,389
July	4.800	4.825	4.800	4.816	–.013	4.850	3.040	6,041
Aug	4.835	4.835	4.835	4.828	–.006	4.050	3.120	7,132
Sept	4.820	4.820	4.820	4.808	–.011	5.640	3.100	6,408
Oct	4.790	4.825	4.790	4.808	–.011	4.830	3.100	6,866
Dec	5.130	5.130	5.095	5.108	–.006	5.130	3.460	7,800
Ja05	5.200	5.220	5.190	5.200	–.004	5.220	3.520	5,279
Feb	5.124	5.124	5.124	5.123	–.001	5.125	3.400	3,207
July	4.590	4.590	4.590	4.587	.053	4.590	3.560	2,708
Dec	4.830	4.830	4.830	4.892	.078	4.830	3.960	2,988
Ja06	4.905	4.949	4.905	4.967	.078	4.949	4.020	1,981
Feb	4.790	4.790	4.790	4.853	.080	4.800	3.850	954

Est vol 62,296; vol Tue 62,296; open int 356,633, +2,705.

Brent Crude (IPE)-1,000 net bbls.; $ per bbl.

June	23.67	24.17	23.37	24.11	0.54	32.45	19.45	62,600
July	23.83	24.20	23.47	24.14	0.43	31.51	22.50	69,794
Aug	23.94	24.22	23.61	24.22	0.42	30.75	22.32	27,387
Sept	23.96	24.15	23.70	24.23	0.41	30.00	20.21	12,352
Oct	23.73	24.14	23.73	24.22	0.41	29.38	22.65	5,238
Nov	23.62	24.00	23.62	24.19	0.42	29.00	22.30	7,866
Dec	23.86	24.06	23.58	24.12	0.41	28.79	18.65	33,191
Mr04	23.40	23.40	23.40	23.82	0.40	26.83	21.97	5,970
June	23.10	23.11	23.10	23.52	0.37	25.50	20.90	4,630
Dec	23.15	23.27	22.95	23.31	0.35	24.10	19.85	11,791
Dc05	22.74	22.74	22.74	23.06	0.35	23.40	22.00	6,470

Est vol 121,000; vol Tue 95,937; open int 266,173, +7,407.

Currency Futures

Japanese Yen (CME)-¥12,500,000; $ per ¥ (.00)

June	.8517	.8629	.8499	.8613	.0105	.8800	.7769	98,625
Sept	.8616	.8642	.8616	.8638	.0105	.8815	.8220	1,005
Dec	.8645	.8645	.8645	.8665	.0105	.8915	.8350	270

Est vol 27,375; vol Tue 32,982; open int 99,924, +5,676.

Canadian Dollar (CME)-CAD 100,000; $ per CAD

June	.7166	.7219	.7107	.7141	–.0002	.7219	.6197	89,367
Sept	.7125	.7140	.7065	.7103	–.0002	.7140	.6185	4,152
Dec	.7078	.7106	.7030	.7067	–.0002	.7106	.6160	2,404
Mr04	.7012	.7030	.7010	.7030	–.0002	.7030	.6150	885
June	.7005	.7005	.6965	.6993	–.0002	.7005	.6201	699
Sept	.6930	.6945	.6930	.6956	–.0002	.6960	.6505	295

Est vol 19,488; vol Tue 14,916; open int 97,802, –957.

British Pound (CME)-£62,500; $ per £

June	1.6112	1.6120	1.5864	1.5934	–.0188	1.6416	1.5000	30,333
Sept	1.5992	1.5992	1.5760	1.5832	–.0188	1.6256	1.5100	679

Est vol 10,234; vol Tue 10,130; open int 31,088, +855.

Swiss Franc (CME)-CHF 125,000; $ per CHF

June	.7561	.7618	.7519	.7577	.0018	.7618	.5940	48,024
Sept	.7572	.7597	.7548	.7593	.0018	.7597	.6270	698

Est vol 9,667; vol Tue 19,285; open int 48,748, +2,676.

Australian Dollar (CME)-AUD 100,000; $ per AUD

June	.6397	.6415	.6321	.6359	–.0028	.6415	.5050	40,878
Sept	.6331	.6336	.6275	.6307	–.0028	.6360	.5075	555
Dec	.6276	.6280	.6238	.6255	–.0028	.6280	.5025	234

Est vol 4,314; vol Tue 4,238; open int 41,820, –644.

Mexican Peso (CME)-MXN 500,000; $ per MXN

June	.09725	.09760	.09682	.09735	00040	.09820	.08650	42,163
July	...	...	...	.09690	00040	.09740	.08800	250

Est vol 7,599; vol Tue 7,685; open int 44,029, –313.

Euro/US Dollar (CME)-€125,000; $ per €

June	1.1416	1.1428	1.1313	1.1358	–.0046	1.1440	.8615	112,105
Sept	1.1380	1.1390	1.1285	1.1326	–.0046	1.1408	.8780	2,351
Dec	1.1260	1.1318	1.1260	1.1297	–.0046	1.1355	.9551	524

Est vol 46,049; vol Tue 42,858; open int 115,082, +550.

Euro/US Dollar (FINEX)-€200,000; $ per €

June	...	...	...	1.1357	–.0041	1.1305	1.0709	1,410

Est vol 187; vol Tue 267; open int 1,414, –9.

Interest Rate Futures

Treasury Bonds (CBT)-$100,000; pts 32nds of 100%

June	114-26	116-02	114-25	115-28	38	116-02	105-00	465,492
Sept	113-20	114-23	113-19	114-18	38	114-23	106-02	41,595
Dec	113-02	113-09	112-19	113-08	39	113-09	106-04	542

Est vol 269,921; vol Tue 185,308; open int 507,652, +2,874.

Treasury Notes (CBT)-$100,000; pts 32nds of 100%

June	15-265	16-205	15-245	16-145	23.5	16-205	109-10	865,290
Sept	115-01	115-22	115-01	115-21	25.5	115-22	10-055	58,956

Est vol 650,930; vol Tue 475,890; open int 924,260, +4,239.

10 Yr. Agency Notes (CBT)-$100,000; pts 32nds of 100%

June	13-315	114-18	13-315	114-18	32.5	114-18	109-10	5,609

Est vol 6; vol Tue 4; open int 5,609, unch.

5 Yr. Treasury Notes (CBT)-$100,000; pts 32nds of 100%

June	114-11	114-28	114-08	14-245	15.5	114-28	10-125	801,839

Est vol 366,549; vol Tue 271,786; open int 850,697, –10,710.

2 Yr. Treasury Notes (CBT)-$200,000; pts 32nds of 100%

June	08-037	08-042	07-317	08-032	.2	08-042	07-015	111,599

Est vol 15,219; vol Tue 8,375; open int 111,599, +1,564.

30 Day Federal Funds (CBT)-$5,000,000; 100 - daily avg.

May	98.760	98.760	98.750	98.755	–.005	99.870	98.420	95,008
June	98.81	98.81	98.79	98.79	–.02	99.01	98.48	72,219
July	98.93	98.93	98.89	98.90	–.03	99.06	98.48	36,872
Aug	98.95	98.96	98.92	98.93	–.05	99.10	98.44	13,350
Sept	98.96	98.96	98.93	98.95	–.03	99.10	98.21	8,907

Est vol 55,288; vol Tue 93,078; open int 257,085, –3,878.

1 Month Libor (CME)-$3,000,000; pts of 100%

	OPEN	HIGH	LOW	SETTLE	CHG	YIELD	CHG	OPEN INT
May	98.69	98.70	98.69	98.69	–.01	1.31	.01	25,533
June	98.77	98.77	98.75	98.76	–.03	1.24	.03	12,298
July	98.81	98.81	98.80	98.81	–.03	1.19	.03	8,059

Est vol 3,706; vol Tue 5,847; open int 52,763, unch.

Index Futures

DJ Industrial Average (CBT)-$10 x index

June	8550	8615	8500	8548	–22	9452	7380	32,479
Sept	8535	8590	8490	8529	–21	8700	7460	770
Dec	8503	8555	8460	8501	–21	11490	7675	184

Est vol 17,811; vol Tue 23,805; open int 33,433, –643.
Idx prl: Hi 8635.06; Lo 8529.04; Close 8560.63, –27.73.

Mini DJ Industrial Average (CBT)-$5 x index

June	8556	8612	8501	8548	–22	8835	7395	29,039

Vol Wed 50,673; open int 30,683, –1,095.

S&P 500 Index (CME)-$250 x index

June	93460	93700	92520	92950	–520	133280	77050	609,384
Sept	92880	93450	92500	92830	–520	121490	77200	20,994

Est vol 63,181; vol Tue 65,514; open int 633,857, +2,376.
Idx prl: Hi 937.22; Lo 926.41; Close 929.62, –4.77.

Mini S&P 500 (CME)-$50 x index

June	93450	93700	92525	92950	–525	93950	78725	685,863

Vol Wed 716,989; open int 690,439, +21,911.

S&P Midcap 400 (CME)-$500 x index

June	448.00	450.25	445.50	447.75	–1.25	497.25	374.75	12,942

Est vol 890; vol Tue 666; open int 12,942, –143.
Idx prl: Hi 450.05; Lo 445.75; Close 447.85, –1.63.

Nasdaq 100 (CME)-$100 x index

June	115350	115900	113200	113950	–1300	116400	81850	79,151
Sept	113800	114400	113800	114250	–1300	115650	95250	1,643

Est vol 14,797; vol Tue 18,001; open int 80,796, +74.
Idx prl: Hi 1152.68; Lo 1131.37; Close 1135.85, –16.93.

Mini Nasdaq 100 (CME)-$20 x index

June	1153.5	1159.5	1132.5	1139.5	–13.0	1163.5	941.5	240,125

Vol Wed 247,291; open int 240,541, +11,157.

Most Active Single-Stock Futures

Mini iShares Russell 2000 (NQLX)

	OPEN	HIGH	LOW	SETTLE	CHG	VOL	OPEN INT
May	82.20	82.34	81.80	81.92	–0.43	1,869	370
June	82.06	82.06	81.70	81.77	–0.42	130	203

Halliburton (ONE)

June	23.41	23.67	23.30	23.30	0.76	1,503	1,273

DIAMONDS Trust (ONE)

May	85.53	86.15	85.26	85.83	...	990	2,766
June	85.35	85.74	85.15	85.69	...	395	5,493

Amazon.com (ONE)

June	30.64	30.83	30.30	30.71	–0.27	553	1,969

Microsoft (NQLX)

May	26.21	26.23	26.15	26.00	–0.36	142	60
June(ONE)	26.23	26.26	25.95	26.01	–0.41	369	2,062
June	26.18	26.26	26.04	26.03	–0.36	131	495
July(ONE)	26.19	26.25	25.99	26.06	–0.39	300	424
July	26.25	26.30	26.09	26.06	–0.42	143	463
Sept(ONE)	26.24	26.26	26.18	26.14	–0.31	140	397

Exchange Abbreviations

For commodity futures and futures options

CBT-Chicago Board of Trade;
CME-Chicago Mercantile Exchange;
CSCE-Coffee, Sugar & Cocoa Exchange, New York;
CMX-COMEX (Div. of New York Mercantile Exchange);
EUREX-European Exchange;
FINEX-Financial Exchange (Div. of New York Cotton Exchange);
IPE-International Petroleum Exchange;
KC-Kansas City Board of Trade;
LIFFE-London International Financial Futures Exchange;
MATIF-Marche a Terme International de France;
ME-Montreal Exchange;
MPLS-Minneapolis Grain Exchange;
NQLX-Nasdaq Liffe
NYCE-New York Cotton Exchange;
NYFE-New York Futures Exchange (Sub. of New York Cotton Exchange);
NYM-New York Mercantile Exchange;
ONE-OneChicago
SFE-Sydney Futures Exchange;
SGX-Singapore Exchange Ltd.;

Futures prices reflect day and overnight trading
Open interest reflects previous day's trading

Source: Reprinted from *The Wall Street Journal*, May 8, 2003, via Copyright Clearance Center, Inc. © 2003 Dow Jones & Company, Inc. All Rights Reserved Worldwide.

This section of the *Journal* contains a box labeled "Exchange Abbreviations," which lists the major world futures exchanges and their exchange abbreviation codes. Elsewhere, the information is divided into sections according to categories of the underlying commodities or financial instruments. For example, the section "Grain and Oilseed Futures" lists futures price information for wheat, oats, soybeans, and similar crops. The sections "Metal Futures" and "Petroleum Futures" report price information for copper, gold, and petroleum products. There are separate sections for financial futures, which include "Currency," "Interest Rate," and "Index" categories.

Each section states the contract name, futures exchange, and contract size, along with price information for various contract maturities. For example, under "Metal Futures" we find the Copper contract traded at the Commodities Exchange (CMX), the COMEX (Division of the New York Mercantile Exchange). The standard contract size for copper is 25,000 pounds per contract. The futures price is quoted in cents per pound.

FUTURES QUOTES

EXAMPLE 16.1

In Figure 16.1, locate the gold and wheat contracts. Where are they traded? What are the contract sizes for the gold and wheat contracts and how are their futures prices specified?

The gold contract trades on the CMX, the COMEX Division of the New York Mercantile Exchange. One gold contract calls for delivery of 100 troy ounces. The gold futures price is quoted in dollars per ounce.

Wheat contracts are traded on the Chicago Board of Trade (CBT), the Kansas City Board of Trade (KC), and the Minneapolis Grain Exchange (MPLS). One wheat contract calls for delivery of 5,000 bushels of wheat, and wheat futures prices are quoted in cents per bushel.

For futures prices and price charts, visit these websites:
www.futuresworld.com
futures.pcquote.com

The reporting format for each futures contract is similar. For example, the first column of a price listing gives the contract delivery/maturity month. For each maturity month, the next five columns report futures prices observed during the previous day at the opening of trading ("Open"), the highest intraday price ("High"), the lowest intraday price ("Low"), the price at close of trading ("Settle"), and the change in the settle price from the previous day ("Chg").

The next two columns ("Lifetime," "High" and "Low") report the highest and lowest prices for each maturity observed over the previous year. Finally, the last column reports open interest for each contract maturity, which is the number of contracts outstanding at the end of that day's trading. The last row below these eight columns summarizes trading activity for all maturities by reporting aggregate trading volume and open interest for all contract maturities.

By now, we see that four of the contract terms for futures contracts are stated in the futures prices listing. These are:

1. The identity of the underlying commodity or financial instrument.
2. The futures contract size.
3. The futures maturity date.
4. The futures price.

Exact contract terms for the delivery process are available from the appropriate futures exchange on request.

FUTURES PRICES

EXAMPLE 16.2

In Figure 16.1, locate the soybean contract with the greatest open interest. Explain the information provided.

The soybean (or just "bean") contract with the greatest open interest is specified by the contract maturity with the greatest number of contracts outstanding, so the July 2003 contract is the one we seek. One contract calls for delivery of 5,000 bushels of beans (a bushel, of course, is four pecks). The closing price for delivery at that maturity is stated as a quote in cents per bushel. Since there are 5,000 bushels in a single contract, the total contract value is the quoted price per bushel times 5,000, or $31,350 for the July contract.

To get an idea of the magnitude of financial futures trading, take a look at the first entry under "Interest Rate Futures" in Figure 16.1, the CBT Treasury bond contract. One contract calls for the delivery of $100,000 in par value bonds. The total open interest in this one contract is often close to half a million contracts. Thus, the total face value represented by these contracts is close to half a *trillion* dollars.

Who does all this trading? The orders originate from money managers around the world and are sent to the various exchanges' trading floors for execution. On the floor, the orders are executed by professional traders who are quite aggressive at getting the best prices. On the floor and off, futures traders can be recognized by their colorful jackets. As *The Wall Street Journal* article in the nearby *Investment Updates* box reports, these garish jackets add a touch of clamor to the trading pits. In the next section we will discuss how and why futures contracts are used for speculation and hedging.

Check This

16.1a What is a forward contract?

16.1b What is a futures contract, and why is it different from a forward contract?

16.1c What is a futures price?

16.2 Why Futures?

Futures contracts can be used for speculation or for hedging. Certainly, hedging is the major economic purpose for the existence of futures markets. However, a viable futures market cannot exist without participation by both hedgers and speculators. Hedgers transfer price risk to speculators, and speculators absorb price risk. Hedging and speculating are complementary activities. We next discuss speculating with futures; then we discuss hedging with futures.

Speculating with Futures

To learn more about futures, visit
www.usafutures.com

Suppose you are thinking about speculating on commodity prices because you believe you can accurately forecast future prices most of the time. The most convenient way to speculate is with futures contracts. If you believe that the price of gold will go up, then

Garish Jackets Add to Clamor of Chicago Pits

For the inhabitants of Chicago's futures and options trading pits, dressing for success means throwing good taste to the wind.

Take James Oliff, a trader in the Chicago Mercantile Exchange's newly opened Mexican peso futures pit. Daily, he dons a multicolored jacket bedecked with cacti and sombreros, in keeping, he says, with the "theme" of the product he trades.

Twisting and turning to display his gaudy garb, the veteran currency options trader explains: "I wanted a jacket that would be easy to pick out in the crowd. Runners get orders to me more quickly, and clerks find me faster when I'm trying to do trades."

It's important to have what veterans of the mayhem describe as "pit presence" to make money in the crowded and noisy trading pits of the Merc and the Chicago Board of Trade. That elusive quality, they say, involves such stratagems as finding the best spot in the pit from which to communicate with clerks and other traders, maintaining good posture and using a loud, well-projected voice and forceful hand signals to attract attention.

Increasingly, in places such as the CBOT's bond pit, where hundreds of people cram into a space only slightly larger than a tennis court, garb is being used to grab attention. Hence the insatiable demand for magenta, lime-green, and silver-lamé jackets, featuring designs that run the gamut from the Mighty Morphin Power Rangers to bucolic farmhouses and sunflowers.

"I'd come in buck naked if I could," says Thomas Burke, a trader in the CBOT's overpopulated bond-futures pit. "As it is, the more obnoxious the jacket, the better. The louder it is, the more I can rest my voice and let my jacket draw the attention."

Chicago's exchanges quietly tolerate the proliferation of the garish trading jackets. Dress codes ban jeans and still require members to wear shirts with collars and don ties (although some of these may be little more than strings, having been worn daily for more than a decade). The rules also say that trading jackets must have sleeves that come below the elbow and contain pockets into which the traders stuff their trading cards and other documents. But during the past decade, traders say, exchange efforts to regulate the color and design of the jackets, or gently encourage their wearers to opt for something in quiet good taste, have been dropped as an exercise in futility.

Robert Pierce, who trades corn options at the CBOT, says the old brown jackets made him look like a UPS delivery man. "When someone gave me a UPS cap on the floor one day as a joke, I decided it was time for a change of style," he says. The switch, to a comparatively tasteful multicolored geometric pattern, has the added advantage of disguising pen and pencil marks, adds his wife, Cathy.

Dawn Guera, a former clerk at the CBOT, has spun the traders' need to stand out in the crowd into a four-year-old business designing and manufacturing custom trading jackets. Traders wander into her storefront operation next door to the CBOT to choose from dozens of fabrics with designs ranging from a subdued Harvard University crest on a crimson background to a slinky leopard skin pattern or turquoise frogs cavorting on a neon-pink background.

"Everyone has their own hobbies and interests and wants the jackets to reflect that," she explains, pointing to fabrics with designs of dice and cards aimed at traders willing to acknowledge their addiction to gambling in the markets. "It's like a vanity license plate."

And, at $50 a pop, traders are willing, even eager, to order multiple jackets, Ms. Guera says, especially since many believe that washing or dry cleaning a "lucky" jacket will launder out the luck in it. Some, like the CBOT's Gilbert Leistner, take a seasonal approach to jackets: in summer and fall he wears a brightly colored turquoise and aquamarine jacket decorated with tropical fish, but switches to a Southwestern theme come Thanksgiving.

"It's my version of going south for the winter," he says, adding he's contemplating donning something in gold lamé for New Year's celebrations.

Ms. Guera, a former sportswear designer in New York, says traders have a long way to go before they'll pull themselves off the worst-dressed lists. To be sure, some of the early emphasis on flashiness is easing a bit, she says, and demands for fluorescent geometric patterns are giving way to a new trend favoring subtler paisley-type patterns with lapels, cuffs, and pockets in a contrasting, solid color.

"I think it would be great if we could really push the fashion envelope here and remove the collar and cuffs from the jackets, or even persuade the exchanges to let traders wear vests instead," she says. "I'm looking for a way of making this whole trading process more artistic and creative."

Source: Suzanne McGee, *The Wall Street Journal*, July 31, 1995. Reprinted by permission of Dow Jones & Company, Inc., via Copyright Clearance Center, Inc. © 1995 Dow Jones & Company, Inc. All Rights Reserved Worldwide.

you can speculate on this belief by buying gold futures. Alternatively, if you think gold will fall in price, you can speculate by selling gold futures. To be more precise, you think that the current futures price is either too high or too low relative to what gold prices will be in the future.

long position In futures jargon, refers to the contract buyer. A long position profits from a futures price increase.

Buying futures is often referred to as "going long," or establishing a **long position**. Selling futures is often called "going short," or establishing a **short position**. A **speculator** accepts price risk in order to bet on the direction of prices by going long or short.

To illustrate the basics of speculating, suppose you believe the price of gold will go up. In particular, the current futures price for delivery in three months is $400 per ounce. You think that gold will be selling for more than that three months from now, so you go long 100 three-month gold contracts. Each gold contract represents 100 troy ounces, so 100 contracts represents 10,000 ounces of gold with a total contract value of $10,000 \times \$400 = \$4,000,000$. In futures jargon, this is a $4 million long gold position.

short position In futures jargon, refers to the seller. A short position profits from a futures price decrease.

Now, suppose your belief turns out to be correct, and, at contract maturity, the market price of gold is $420 per ounce. From your long futures position, you accept delivery of 10,000 troy ounces of gold at $400 per ounce and immediately sell the gold at the market price of $420 per ounce. Your profit is $20 per ounce, or $10,000 \times \$20 = \$200,000$, less applicable commissions.

speculator Trader who accepts price risk by going long or short to bet on the future direction of prices.

Of course, if your belief turned out wrong and gold fell in price, you would lose money since you must still buy the 10,000 troy ounces at $400 per ounce to fulfill your futures contract obligation. Thus, if gold fell to, say, $390 per ounce, you would lose $10 per ounce, or $10,000 \times \$10 = \$100,000$. As this example suggests, futures speculation is risky, but it is potentially rewarding if you can accurately forecast the direction of future commodity price movements.

As another example of commodity speculation, suppose an analysis of weather patterns has convinced you that the coming winter months will be warmer than usual, and that this will cause heating oil prices to fall as unsold inventories accumulate. You can speculate on this belief by selling heating oil futures.

The standard contract size for heating oil is 42,000 gallons. Suppose you go short 10 contracts at a futures price of 55 cents per gallon. This represents a short position with a total contract value of $10 \times 42,000 \times \$.55 = \$231,000$.

If, at contract maturity, the price of heating oil is, say, 50 cents per gallon, you could buy 420,000 gallons for delivery to fulfill your futures commitment. Your profit would be 5 cents per gallon, or $10 \times 42,000 \times \$.05 = \$21,000$, less applicable commissions. Of course, if heating oil prices rise by 5 cents per gallon, you would lose $21,000 instead. Again, speculation is risky but rewarding if you can accurately forecast the weather.

WHAT WOULD JUAN VALDEZ DO?

EXAMPLE 16.3

After an analysis of political currents in Central and South America, you conclude that future coffee prices will be lower than currently indicated by futures prices. Would you go long or short? Analyze the impact of a swing in coffee prices of 10 cents per pound in either direction if you have a 10-contract position, where each contract calls for delivery of 37,500 pounds of coffee.

You would go short since you expect prices to decline. You're short 10 contracts, so you must deliver $10 \times 37,500 = 375,000$ pounds of coffee. If coffee prices fall to 10 cents below your originally

(continued)

contracted futures price, then you make 10 cents per pound, or $37,500. Of course, if you're wrong and prices are 10 cents higher, you lose $37,500.

Hedging with Futures

Many businesses face price risk when their activities require them to hold a working inventory. For example, suppose you own a regional gasoline distributorship and must keep a large operating inventory of gas on hand, say, 5 million gallons. In futures jargon, this gasoline inventory represents a long position in the underlying commodity.

If gas prices go up, your inventory goes up in value; but if gas prices fall, your inventory value goes down. Your risk is not trivial, since even a 5-cent fluctuation in the gallon price of gas will cause your inventory to change in value by $250,000. Because you are in the business of distributing gas, and not speculating on gas prices, you would like to remove this price risk from your business operations. Acting as a **hedger**, you seek to transfer price risk by taking a futures position opposite to an existing position in the underlying commodity or financial instrument. In this case, the value of your gasoline inventory can be protected by selling gasoline futures contracts.

Gasoline futures are traded on the New York Mercantile Exchange (NYM), and the standard contract size for gasoline futures is 42,000 gallons per contract. Since you wish to hedge 5 million gallons, you need to sell 5,000,000 / 42,000 = 119 gasoline contracts. With this hedge in place, any change in the value of your long inventory position is canceled by an approximately equal but opposite change in value of your short futures position. Because you are using this short position for hedging purposes, it is called a **short hedge**.

By hedging, you have greatly reduced or even eliminated the possibility of a loss from a decline in the price of gasoline. However, you have also eliminated the possibility of a gain from a price increase. This is an important point. If gas prices rise, you would have a substantial loss on your futures position, offsetting the gain on your inventory. Overall, you are long the underlying commodity because you own it; you offset the risk in your long position with a short position in futures.

Of course, your business activities may also include distributing other petroleum products like heating oil and natural gas. Futures contracts are available for these petroleum products also, and therefore they may be used for inventory hedging purposes.

hedger Trader who seeks to transfer price risk by taking a futures position opposite to an existing position in the underlying commodity or financial instrument.

short hedge Sale of futures to offset potential losses from falling prices.

SHORT HEDGING

EXAMPLE 16.4

Suppose you have an inventory of 1.2 million pounds of soybean oil. Describe how you would hedge this position.

Since you are long in the commodity, bean oil, you need to go short in (sell) futures. A single bean oil contract calls for delivery of 60,000 pounds of oil. To hedge your position, you need to sell 1.2 million / 60,000 = 20 futures contracts.

long hedge Purchase of futures to offset potential losses from rising prices.

The opposite of a short hedge is a **long hedge**. In this case, you do not own the underlying commodity, but you need to acquire it in the future. You can lock in the price you will pay in the future by buying, or going long in, futures contracts. In effect, you are short the underlying commodity because you must buy it in the future. You offset your short position with a long position in futures.

MORE HEDGING

EXAMPLE 16.5

You need to buy 600,000 pounds of orange juice in three months. How can you hedge the price risk associated with this future purchase? What price will you effectively lock in? One orange juice contract calls for delivery of 15,000 pounds of juice concentrate.

You are effectively short orange juice since you don't currently own it but plan to buy it. To offset the risk in this short position, you need to go long in futures. You should buy 600,000/15,000 = 40 contracts. The price you lock in is the original futures price.

EVEN MORE HEDGING

EXAMPLE 16.6

Suppose your company will receive payment of £10 million in six months, which will then be converted to U.S. dollars. What is the standard futures contract size for British pounds? Describe how you could use futures contracts to lock in an exchange rate from British pounds to U.S. dollars for your planned receipt of £10 million, including how many contracts are required.

Your company will be receiving £10 million, so you are effectively long pounds. To hedge, you need to short (sell) futures contracts. Put differently, you will want to exchange pounds for dollars. By selling a futures contract, you obligate yourself to deliver the underlying commodity, in this case currency, in exchange for payment in dollars. One British pound contract calls for delivery of £62,500. You will therefore sell £10 million / £62,500 = 160 contracts.

Check This

16.2a What is a long position in futures? A short position?

16.2b For a speculator, when is a long position appropriate and when is a short position appropriate?

16.2c What is a long hedge? A short hedge?

16.2d For a hedger, when is a long hedge appropriate and when is a short hedge appropriate?

16.3 Futures Trading Accounts

A futures exchange, like a stock exchange, allows only exchange members to trade on the exchange. Exchange members may be firms or individuals trading for their own accounts, or they may be brokerage firms handling trades for customers. Some firms conduct both trading and brokerage operations on the exchange. In this section, we discuss the mechanics of a futures trading account as it pertains to a customer with a trading account at a brokerage firm.

For a list of online futures brokers visit the Commodities & Futures section of Investor Links at www.investorlinks.com

The biggest customer trading accounts are those of corporations that use futures to manage their business risks and money managers who hedge or speculate with clients' funds. Many individual investors also have futures trading accounts of their own, although speculation by individual investors is not recommended without a full understanding of all risks involved. Whether a futures trading account is large or small, the mechanics of account trading are essentially the same.

There are several essential things to know about futures trading accounts. The first thing is that margin is required. In this way, futures accounts resemble the stock margin accounts we discussed in Chapter 2; however, the specifics are quite different. **Futures margin** is a deposit of funds in a futures trading account dedicated to covering potential losses from an outstanding futures position. An **initial margin** is required when a futures position is first established. The amount varies according to contract type and size, but margin requirements for futures contracts usually range between 2 percent and 5 percent of total contract value. Initial margin is the same for both long and short futures positions.

The second thing to know about a futures trading account is that contract values in outstanding futures positions are marked to market on a daily basis. **Marking-to-market** is a process whereby gains and losses on outstanding futures positions are recognized at the end of each day's trading.

For example, suppose one morning you call your broker and instruct her to go long five U.S. Treasury bond contracts for your account. A few minutes later, she calls back to confirm order execution at a futures price of 110. Since the Treasury bond contract size is \$100,000 par value, contract value is 110% × \$100,000 = \$110,000 per contract. Thus, the total position value for your order is \$550,000, for which your broker requires \$25,000 initial margin. In addition, your broker requires that at least \$20,000 in **maintenance margin** be present at all times. The necessary margin funds are immediately wired from a bank account to your futures account.

Now, at the end of trading that day Treasury bond futures close at a price of 108. Overnight, all accounts are marked to market. Your Treasury bond futures position is marked to \$108,000 per contract, or \$540,000 total position value, representing a loss of \$10,000. This loss is deducted from your initial margin to leave only \$15,000 of margin funds in your account.

Since the maintenance margin level on your account is \$20,000, your broker will issue a **margin call** on your account. Essentially, your broker will notify you that you must immediately restore your margin level to the initial margin level of \$25,000, or else she will close out your Treasury bond futures position at whatever trading price is available at the exchange.

This example illustrates what happens when a futures trading account is marked to market and the resulting margin funds fall below the maintenance margin level. The alternative, and more pleasant, experience occurs when a futures price moves in your favor, and the marking-to-market process adds funds to your account. In this case, marking-to-market gains can be withdrawn from your account so long as remaining margin funds are not less than the initial margin level.

The third thing to know about a futures trading account is that a futures position can be closed out at any time; you do not have to hold a contract until maturity. A futures position is closed out by simply instructing your broker to close out your position. To actually close out a position, your broker will enter a **reverse trade** for your account.

A reverse trade works like this: Suppose you are currently short five Treasury bond contracts, and you instruct your broker to close out the position. Your broker responds by going long five Treasury bond contracts for your account. In this case, going long

futures margin Deposit of funds in a futures trading account dedicated to covering potential losses from an outstanding futures position.

initial margin Amount required when a futures contract is first bought or sold. Initial margin varies with the type and size of a contract, but it is the same for long and short futures positions.

marking-to-market In futures trading accounts, the process whereby gains and losses on outstanding futures positions are recognized on a daily basis.

maintenance margin The minimum margin level required in a futures trading account at all times.

margin call Notification to increase the margin level in a trading account.

reverse trade A trade that closes out a previously established futures position by taking the opposite position.

five contracts is a reverse trade because it cancels exactly your previous five-contract short position. At the end of the day in which you make your reverse trade, your account will be marked to market at the futures price realized by the reverse trade. From then on, your position is closed out, and no more gains or losses will be realized.

This example illustrates that closing out a futures position is no more difficult than initially entering into a position. There are two basic reasons to close out a futures position before contract maturity. The first is to capture a current gain or loss, without realizing further price risk. The second is to avoid the delivery requirement that comes from holding a futures contract until it matures. In fact, over 98 percent of all futures contracts are closed out before contract maturity, which indicates that less than 2 percent of all futures contracts result in delivery of the underlying commodity or financial instrument.

Before closing this section, let's briefly list the three essential things to know about a futures trading account as discussed above:

1. Margin is required.

2. Futures accounts are marked to market daily.

3. A futures position can be closed out any time by a reverse trade.

Understanding the items in this list is important to anyone planning to use a futures trading account.

Check This

16.3a What are the three essential things you should know about a futures trading account?

16.3b What is meant by initial margin for a futures position? What is meant by maintenance margin for a futures position?

16.3c Explain the process of marking-to-market a futures trading account. What is a margin call, and when is one issued?

16.3d How is a futures position closed out by a reverse trade? What proportion of all futures positions are closed out by reverse trades rather than by delivery at contract maturity?

16.4 Cash Prices versus Futures Prices

cash price Price of a commodity or financial instrument for current delivery. Also called the *spot price*.

cash market Market in which commodities or financial instruments are traded for essentially immediate delivery. Also called the *spot market*.

We now turn to the relationship between today's price of some commodity or financial instrument and its futures price. We begin by examining current cash prices.

Cash Prices

The **cash price** of a commodity or financial instrument is the price quoted for current delivery. The cash price is also called the *spot price*, as in "on the spot." In futures jargon, terms like "spot gold" or "cash wheat" are used to refer to commodities being sold for current delivery in what is called the **cash market** or the *spot market*.

Figure 16.2 reproduces the "Cash Prices" column of *The Wall Street Journal*, published the same day as the "Futures Prices" column seen in Figure 16.1. The column is divided into sections according to commodity categories. For example, the first section, "Grains and Feeds," lists spot price information for wheat, corn, soybeans, and

Cash Prices
May 7, 2003

	LO/HI RANGE WED	WED	TUE	YEAR AGO
Grains and Feeds				
Barley, top-quality Mpls., bu	u3.85	sp	3.85	2.45
Bran, wheat middlings, KC ton	u44	47	45.5	39.5
Corn, No. 2 yel. Cent. Ill. bu	bpu2.415	sp	2.365	1.92
Corn Gluten Feed, Midwest, ton	60	65	62.5	55.5
Cottonseed Meal, Clksdle, Miss. ton	142.5	sp	142.5	117.5
Hominy Feed, Cent. Ill. ton	51	96	73.5	c35
Meat-Bonemeal, 50% pro Ill. ton	180	182.5	181.25	172.5
Oats, No. 2 milling, Mpls., bu	u1.735	1.755	1.7075	1.935
Sorghum, (Milo) No. 2 Gulf cwt	u4.87	4.88	4.785	4
Soybean Meal, Cent. Ill., rail, ton 48%	u193	196	197	162.75
Soybeans, No. 1 yel Cent. Ill., bu	bpu6.185	sp	6.205	4.605
Wheat, Spring 14%-pro Mpls. bu	u4.2075	sp	n4.04	3.5775
Wheat, No. 2 sft red, St.Lou. bu	bpu3.195	sp	3.135	2.795
Wheat, hard, KC, bu	3.775	sp	3.7125	3.1525
Wheat, No. 1 sft wht, del Port Ore	u3.38	sp	332	3.33
Foods				
Beef, Carcass Equiv. Index Value, choice 1-3,600-750 lbs.	u124.88	sp	124.26	c102.96
Beef, Carcass Equiv. Index Value, select 1-3,600-750 lbs.	u108.48	sp	108.23	c95.16
Broilers, Dressed "A" lb.	ux.5527	sp	.5595	.5346
Broilers, 12-Cty Comp Wtd Av	u.5789	sp	.5789	.5583
Butter, AA, Chgo., lb.	u1.09	sp	1.09	1.03
Cheddar Cheese, barrels, Chgo lb.	n113	sp	113	118
Cheddar Cheese, blocks, Chgo lb.	n115.75	sp	115.75	121
Milk, Non-fat Dry, Chgo	84	sp	84	94
Cocoa, Ivory Coast, $metric ton	2,086	sp	2,139	1,750
Coffee, Brazilian, Comp.	n.5475	sp	.535	.455
Coffee, Colombian, NY lb.	n.71	sp	.6925	.6375
Eggs, Lge white, Chgo doz.	u.53	.59	.56	.41
Flour, hard winter KC cwt	10.5	sp	10.35	9.15
Hams, 17-20 lbs, Mid-US lb fob	u.44	sp	.44	z
Hogs, Iowa-S.Minn. avg. cwt	u54.06	sp	53.59	44.81
Hogs, Sioux Falls, SD avg cwt	u43	sp	42	31.25
Pork Bellies, 12-14 lbs Mid-US lb	u.93	sp	.93	z
Pork Loins, 13-19 lbs, Mid-US lb	u1	1.06	1.015	z
Steers, Tex.-Okla. ch avg cwt	u78	sp	z	z
Steers, Feeder, Okl Cty, av cwt	u95.38	sp	95.37	90.63
Sugar, cane, raw, world, lb. fob	7.37	sp	7.41	7.22
Fats and Oils				
Corn Oil, crd wet/dry mill	u-s28	29	28.5	17
Grease, choice white, Chgo lb.	.1425	sp	n.1425	n.085
Lard, Chgo lb.	.165	sp	.165	z
Soybean Oil, crd, Central Ill. Lb.	u.2245	.229	.22275	.15065
Tallow, bleachable, Chgo lb.	.1525	sp	.155	.1075
Tallow, edible, Chgo lb.	.165	sp	.165	z

	WED	TUE	YEAR AGO
Fibers and Textiles			
Burlap, 10 oz 40-in NY yd	n.325	.325	.355
Cotton, 1 1/16 str lw-md Mphs lb	.4586	.4701	.2895
Wool, 64s Staple, Terr. Del. Lb.	u2.15	2.15	1.8
Miscellaneous			
Rubber, smoked sheets, NY lb.	z	z	.36
Hides, hvy native steers lb., fob	u79.25-83.5	79.25-83.5	z
Precious Metals			
Gold, troy oz.			
Engelhard indus bullion	343.08	344.08	311.68
Engelhard fabric prods	360.23	361.28	327.26
Handy & Harman base price	341.85	342.85	310.50
Handy & Harman fabric price	369.20	370.28	335.34
London fixing AM 343.00 PM	341.85	342.85	310.50
Krugerrand, whol	ae346.35	347.00	311.00
Maple Leaf, troy oz.	ae355.19	355.86	319.00
American Eagle, troy oz.	ae355.19	355.86	319.00
Platinum, (Free Mkt.)	636.00	625.00	531.00
Platinum, indust (Engelhard)	638.00	628.00	534.00
Platinum, fabrc prd (Engelhard)	738.00	728.00	634.00
Palladium, indust (Engelhard)	165.00	160.00	360.00
Palladium, fabrc prd (Engelhard)	265.00	260.00	460.00
Silver, troy oz.			
Engelhard indust bullion	4.760	4.815	4.580
Engelhard fabric prods	5.522	5.585	5.313
Handy & Harman base price	4.745	4.815	4.575
Handy & Harman fabric price	5.504	5.585	5.307
London Fixing (in pounds)			
Spot (U.S. equiv. $4.7600)	2.9620	2.9783	3.1601
Coins, whol $1,000 face val	a3,625	3,668	3,564
Metals			
Aluminum Comex lb.	0.6485	0.64	0.6505
Antimony, RN Spot, $/lb.	d1.18-20	1.18-20	0.60
Copper, high gr lb., Cmx sp price	0.7305	0.719	0.7275
Lead, RN NA Solder, cts./lb.	d39.711	39.416	40.03
St. Steel Scrap, US, $/gross ton	d900	900	755
Tin, RN NA Solder, cts./lb.	d320419	320.271	290.449
Zinc, RN NA Dealer, cts./lb.	d37.132	36.680	39.674

a-Asked. b-Bid. bp-Country elevator bids to producers. c-Corrected. d-Ryan's Notes h-Reuters. e-Manfra, Tordella & Brookes, Inc. n-Nominal. na-Not available. r-Rail bids. s-high price—asked, low price—bid. u-U.S. Dept. of Agriculture. x-Less than truckloads. z-Not quoted. xx-f.o.b tankcars. sp-Single price.

Oil Prices
CRUDE GRADES
May 7, 2003

	WED	TUE YR AGO	
Offshore-d			
European "spot" or free market prices			
Arab lt.	na	na	22.80
Arab hvy.	na	na	22.05
Forties	23.92	23.61	25.86
Brent	23.82	23.53	26.21
Bonny lt.	23.92	23.58	26.31
Urals-Medit.	21.97	21.68	24.56
Domestic-f			
Spot market			
W. Tex. Int Cush (2200-2673) (Jun)	26.23	25.73	27.85
W. Tex.sour, Midl (1750-2372)	24.65	24.25	26.80
LA sweet St.James (2150-2525)	26.05	25.63	27.38
Al. No. Slope Pacific Del.	24.26	23.75	26.95

Open-Market crude oil values in Northwest Europe around 17:50 GMT in dlrs per barrel. for main loading ports in country of origin for prompt loading, except as indicated.

Refined Products			
Fuel Oil, No. 2 NY gal.	.7143	.7253	.6683
Diesel Fuel, 0.05 S. NY harbor low sulfur	.7243	.7403	.6803
Gasoline, unlded, premium NY gal. non-oxygenated	.7821	.7713	.8140
Gasoline, unlded, premium NY gal. Oxygenated	.8471	.8310	.8427
Gasoline, unlded, reg. NY gal. non-oxygenated	.7021	.6873	.6990
Gasoline, unlded, reg. NY gal. Oxygenated	.8134	.7960	.7777
Propane, non-tet, Mont Belvieu, Texas, gal.	.5137	.5069	.4225
Propane, wet-tet, Mont Belvieu, Texas, gal.	.5150	.5057	.4225
Butane, normal, Mont Belvieu, Texas, gal.	.5494	.5432	.4975

Raw Products			
Natural gas Henry Hub, $ per mmbtu	5.515	5.615	3.780

a-Asked. b-Bid. c-Corrected. d-As of 11 a.m. ET in Northwest Europe. f-As of 4 p.m. ET. Refiners' posted buying prices are in parentheses. na-Not available. z-Not quoted. n-Nominal. r-Revised.
Source: Dow Jones Energy Service

similar crops. Other commodity sections include "Foods," "Fats and Oils," "Metals," and "Precious Metals." Each section gives commodity names along with cash market prices for the last two days of trading and one year earlier.

Cash-Futures Arbitrage

Intuitively, you might think that there is a close relationship between the cash price of a commodity and its futures price. If you do, then your intuition is quite correct. In fact, your intuition is backed up by strong economic argument and more than a century of experience observing the simultaneous operation of cash and futures markets.

As a routine matter, cash and futures prices are closely watched by market professionals. To understand why, suppose you notice that spot gold is trading for $400 per ounce while the two-month futures price is $450 per ounce. Do you see a profit opportunity?

You should, because buying spot gold today at $400 per ounce while simultaneously selling gold futures at $450 per ounce locks in a $50 per ounce profit. True, gold has storage costs (you have to put it somewhere), and a spot gold purchase ties up capital that could be earning interest. However, these costs are small relative to the $50 per ounce gross profit, which works out to be $50 / $400 = 12.5% per two months, or about 100 percent per year (with compounding). Furthermore, this profit is risk-free! Alas, in reality, such easy profit opportunities are the stuff of dreams.

Earning risk-free profits from an unusual difference between cash and futures prices is called **cash-futures arbitrage**. In a competitive market, cash-futures arbitrage has very slim profit margins. In fact, the profit margins are almost imperceptible when they exist at all.

Comparing cash prices for commodities in Figure 16.2 with their corresponding futures prices reported in Figure 16.1, you will find that cash prices and futures prices are seldom equal. In futures jargon, the difference between a cash price and a futures price is called **basis**.[1]

For commodities with storage costs, the cash price is usually less than the futures price. This is referred to as a **carrying-charge market**. Sometimes, however, the cash price is greater than the futures price, and this is referred to as an **inverted market**. We can summarize this discussion of carrying-charge markets, inverted markets, and basis as follows:

Carrying-charge market: Basis = Cash price − Futures price < 0 (16.1)
Inverted market: Basis = Cash price − Futures price > 0

A variety of factors can lead to an economically justifiable difference between a commodity's cash price and its futures price, including availability of storage facilities, transportation costs, and seasonal price fluctuations. However, the primary determinants of cash-futures bases are storage costs and interest costs. Storage cost is the cost of holding the commodity in a storage facility, and interest cost refers to interest income forgone because funds are being used to buy and hold the commodity.

If a futures price rises far enough above a cash price to more than cover storage costs and interest expense, commodity traders will undertake cash-futures arbitrage by

cash-futures arbitrage Strategy for earning risk-free profits from an unusual difference between cash and futures prices.

basis The difference between the cash price and the futures price for a commodity, i.e., basis = cash price − futures price.

carrying-charge market The case where the futures price is greater than the cash price; i.e., the basis is negative.

inverted market The case where the futures price is less than the cash price; i.e., the basis is positive.

[1]Confusingly, basis is sometimes presented as the futures price less the cash price. The official Commodity Trading Manual of the Chicago Board of Trade defines basis as the difference between the cash and the futures price, i.e., basis = cash price − futures price. We will be consistent with the CBOT definition.

buying in the cash market and selling in the futures market. This drives down the futures price and drives up the cash price until the basis is restored to an economically justifiable level.

Similarly, if a futures price falls far enough relative to a cash price, traders will undertake cash-futures arbitrage by short selling in the cash market and buying in the futures market. This drives down the cash price and drives up the futures price until an economically justifiable basis is restored. In both cases, arbitrage ensures that the basis is kept at an economically appropriate level.

Spot-Futures Parity

For more information on single-stock futures trading visit www.nqlx.com www.onechicago.com and the Futures Source website at www.futuresource.com

We can be slightly more precise in illustrating the relationship between spot and futures prices for financial futures. Consider the example of futures contracts for shares of stock in a single company. One place such futures contracts are traded in the United States is the wholly electronic futures exchange, the Nasdaq-Liffe Markets (NQLX). Another is OneChicago, a joint venture of the major Chicago exchanges. Single-stock futures contracts traded on NQLX have a standard contract size of 100 shares of the underlying stock, but futures prices are quoted on a per-share basis.

Suppose we are examining a particular single-stock futures contract that calls for delivery of 100 shares of stock in one year. The current (i.e., cash or spot) stock price is $50 per share, and the stock does not pay dividends. Also, 12-month T-bills are yielding 6 percent. What should the futures price be? To answer, notice that you can buy 100 shares of stock for $50 per share, or $5,000 total. You can eliminate all of the risk associated with this purchase by selling one futures contract. The net effect of this transaction is that you have created a risk-free asset. Since the risk-free rate is 6 percent, your investment must have a future value of $5,000 × 1.06 = $5,300. In other words, the futures price should be $53 per share.

Suppose the futures price is, in fact, $52 per share. What would you do? To make money, you would short 100 shares of stock at $50 per share and invest the $5,000 proceeds at 6 percent.[2] Simultaneously, you would buy one futures contract.

At the end of the year, you would have $5,300. You would use $5,200 to buy the stock to fulfill your obligation on the futures contract and then return the stock to close out the short position. You pocket $100. This is just another example of cash-futures arbitrage.

More generally, if we let F be the futures price, S be the spot price, and r be the risk-free rate, then our example illustrates that

$$F = S(1 + r) \qquad (16.2)$$

spot-futures parity
The relationship between spot prices and futures prices that holds in the absence of arbitrage opportunities.

In other words, the futures price is simply the future value of the spot price, calculated at the risk-free rate. This is the famous **spot-futures parity** condition. This condition must hold in the absence of cash-futures arbitrage opportunities.

More generally, if r is the risk-free rate per period, and the futures contract matures in T periods, then the spot-futures parity condition is

$$F_T = S(1 + r)^T \qquad (16.3)$$

Notice that T could be a fraction of one period. For example, if we have the risk-free rate per year, but the futures contract matures in six months, T would be 1/2.

[2]For the sake of simplicity, we ignore the fact that individual investors don't earn interest on the proceeds from a short sale.

PARITY CHECK

EXAMPLE 16.7

A non–dividend-paying stock has a current price of $12 per share. The risk-free rate is 4 percent per year. If a futures contract on the stock matures in three months, what should the futures price be?

From our spot-futures parity condition, we have

$$F_T = S(1 + r)^T$$
$$= \$12(1.04)^{1/4}$$
$$= \$12.12$$

The futures price should be $12.12. Notice that T, the number of periods, is 1/4 because the contract matures in one quarter.

More on Spot-Futures Parity

In our spot-futures parity example just above, we assumed that the underlying financial instrument (the stock) had no cash flows (no dividends). If there are dividends (for a stock future) or coupon payments (for a bond future), then we need to modify our spot-futures parity condition.

For a stock, we let D stand for the dividend, and we assume that the dividend is paid in one period, at or near the end of the futures contract's life. In this case, the spot-futures parity condition becomes

$$F = S(1 + r) - D \qquad (16.4)$$

Notice that we have simply subtracted the amount of the dividend from the future value of the stock price. The reason is that if you buy the futures contract, you will not receive the dividend, but the dividend payment will reduce the stock price.

An alternative, and very useful, way of writing the dividend-adjusted spot-futures parity result in Equation 16.4 is to define d as the dividend yield on the stock. Recall that the dividend yield is just the upcoming dividend divided by the current price. In our current notation, this is just $d = D/S$. With this in mind, we can write the dividend-adjusted parity result as

$$F = S(1 + r) - D\,(S/S) \qquad (16.5)$$
$$= S(1 + r) - S\,(D/S)$$
$$= S(1 + r) - Sd$$
$$= S(1 + r - d)$$

Finally, as above, if there is something other than a single period involved, we would write

$$F_T = S(1 + r - d)^T \qquad (16.6)$$

where T is the number of periods (or fraction of a period).

For example, suppose there is a futures contract on a stock with a current price of $80. The futures contract matures in six months. The risk-free rate is 7 percent per year, and the stock has an annual dividend yield of 3 percent. What should the futures price be?

Plugging in the values to our dividend-adjusted parity equation, we have

$$F_T = S(1 + r - d)^T$$
$$= \$80(1 + .07 - .03)^{1/2}$$
$$= \$81.58$$

Notice that we set T equal to 1/2 since the contract matures in six months.

Check This

16.4a	What is the spot price for a commodity?
16.4b	With regard to futures contracts, what is the basis?
16.4c	What is an inverted market?
16.4d	What is the spot-futures parity condition?

16.5 Stock Index Futures

There are a number of futures contracts on stock market indexes. Because these contracts are particularly important, we devote this entire section to them. We first describe the contracts and then discuss some trading and hedging strategies involving their use.

Basics of Stock Index Futures

For information on stock index futures visit the CBOT website at www.cbot.com

Locate the section labeled "Index Futures" in Figure 16.1. Here we see various stock index futures contracts. The third contract listed, on the S&P 500 index, is the most important. With this contract, actual delivery would be very difficult or impossible because the seller of the contract would have to buy all 500 stocks in exactly the right proportions to deliver. Clearly, this is not practical, so this contract features cash settlement.

To understand how stock index futures work, suppose you bought one S&P 500 contract at a futures price of 1,500. The contract size is $250 times the level of the index. What this means is that, at maturity, the buyer of the contract will pay the seller $250 times the difference between the futures price of 1,500 and the level of the S&P 500 index at contract maturity.

For example, suppose that at maturity the S&P had actually fallen to 1,470. In this case, the buyer of the contract must pay $250 \times (1,500 - 1,470) = \$7,500$ to the seller of the contract. In effect, the buyer of the contract has agreed to purchase 250 "units" of the index at a price of $1,500 per unit. If the index is below 1,500, the buyer will lose money. If the index is above that, then the seller will lose money.

INDEX FUTURES

EXAMPLE 16.8

Suppose you are convinced that Midcap stocks are going to skyrocket in value. Consequently, you buy 20 S&P Midcap 400 contracts maturing in six months at a price of 395. Suppose that the S&P Midcap 400 index is at 410 when the contracts mature. How much will you make or lose?

(continued)

> The futures price is 395, and the contract size is $500 times the level of the index. If the index is actually at 410, you make $500 × (410 − 395) = $7,500 per contract. With 20 contracts, your total profit is $150,000.

Index Arbitrage

index arbitrage
Strategy of monitoring the futures price on a stock index and the level of the underlying index to exploit deviations from parity.

The spot-futures parity relation we developed above is the basis for a common trading strategy known as **index arbitrage**. Index arbitrage refers to monitoring the futures price on a stock index along with the level of the underlying index. The trader looks for violations of parity and trades as appropriate.

For example, suppose the S&P 500 futures price for delivery in one year is 1,540. The current level is 1,500. The dividend yield on the S&P is projected to be 3 percent per year, and the risk-free rate is 5 percent. Is there a trading opportunity here?

From our dividend-adjusted parity equation (16.6), the futures price should be

$$
\begin{aligned}
F_T &= S(1 + r - d)^T \\
&= 1,500(1 + .05 - .03)^1 \\
&= 1,530
\end{aligned}
$$

Thus, based on our parity calculation, the futures price is too high. We want to buy low, sell high, so we buy the index and simultaneously sell the futures contract.

program trading
Computer-assisted monitoring of relative prices of financial assets; it sometimes includes computer submission of buy and sell orders to exploit perceived arbitrage opportunities.

Index arbitrage is often implemented as a **program trading** strategy. While this term covers a lot of ground, it generally refers to the monitoring of relative prices by computer to more quickly spot opportunities. In some cases it includes submitting the needed buy and sell orders using a computer to speed up the process.

Whether a computer is used in program trading is not really the issue; instead, a program trading strategy is any coordinated, systematic procedure for exploiting (or trying to exploit) violations of parity or other arbitrage opportunities. Such a procedure is a trading "program" in the sense that whenever certain conditions exist, certain trades are made. Thus, the process is sufficiently mechanical that it can be automated, at least in principle.

Technically, the NYSE defines program trading as the simultaneous purchase or sale of at least 15 different stocks with a total value of $1 million or more. Program trading accounts for about 15 percent of total trading volume on the NYSE, and about 20 percent of all program trading involves stock-index arbitrage.

There is another phenomenon often associated with index arbitrage and, more generally, futures and options trading. S&P 500 futures contracts have four expiration months per year, and they expire on the third Friday of those months. On these same four Fridays, options on the S&P index and various individual stock options also expire. These Fridays have been dubbed the "triple witching hour" because all three types of contracts expire, sometimes leading to unusual price behavior.

For information on program trading, visit www.programtrading.com

In particular, on triple witching hour Fridays, all positions must be liquidated, or "unwound." To the extent that large-scale index arbitrage and other program trading has taken place, enormous buying or selling sometimes occurs late in the day on such Fridays, as positions are closed out. Large price swings and, more generally, increased volatility are often seen. To curtail this problem to a certain extent, the exchanges have adopted rules regarding the size of a position that can be carried to expiration, and other rules have been adopted as well.

Hedging Stock Market Risk with Futures

We earlier discussed hedging using futures contracts in the context of a business protecting the value of its inventory. We now discuss some hedging strategies available to portfolio managers based on financial futures. Essentially, an investment portfolio is an inventory of securities, and financial futures can be used to reduce the risk of holding a securities portfolio.

We consider the specific problem of an equity portfolio manager wishing to protect the value of a stock portfolio from the risk of an adverse movement of the overall stock market. Here, the portfolio manager wishes to establish a short hedge position to reduce risk and must determine the number of futures contracts required to properly hedge a portfolio.

In this hedging example, you are responsible for managing a broadly diversified stock portfolio with a current value of $100 million. Analysis of market conditions leads you to believe that the stock market is unusually susceptible to a price decline during the next few months. Of course, nothing is certain regarding stock market fluctuations, but still you are sufficiently concerned to believe that action is required.

A fundamental problem exists for you, however, in that there is no futures contract that exactly matches your particular portfolio. As a result, you decide to protect your stock portfolio from a fall in value caused by a falling stock market using stock index futures. This is an example of a **cross-hedge**, where a futures contract on a related, but not identical, commodity or financial instrument is used to hedge a particular spot position.

cross-hedge Hedging a particular spot position with futures contracts on a related, but not identical, commodity or financial instrument.

Thus, to hedge your portfolio, you wish to establish a short hedge using stock index futures. To do this, you need to know how many index futures contracts are required to form an effective hedge. There are three basic inputs needed to calculate the number of stock index futures contracts required to hedge a stock portfolio:

1. The current value of your stock portfolio.
2. The beta of your stock portfolio.
3. The contract value of the index futures contract used for hedging.

Based on previous chapters, you are familiar with the concept of beta as a measure of market risk for a stock portfolio. Essentially, beta measures portfolio risk relative to the overall stock market. We will assume that you have maintained a beta of 1.25 for your $100 million stock portfolio.

You decide to establish a short hedge using futures contracts on the Standard & Poor's index of 500 stocks (S&P 500), since this is the index you used to calculate the beta for your portfolio. From *The Wall Street Journal*, you find that the S&P 500 futures price for three-month maturity contracts is currently, say, 1,500. Since the contract size for S&P 500 futures is 250 times the index, the current value of a single index futures contract is $250 \times 1,500 = \$375,000$.

You now have all inputs required to calculate the number of contracts needed to hedge your stock portfolio. The number of stock index futures contracts needed to hedge a stock portfolio is determined as follows:

$$\text{Number of contracts} = \frac{\beta_P \times V_P}{V_F} \tag{16.7}$$

where: β_P = Beta of the stock portfolio
V_P = Value of the stock portfolio
V_F = Value of a single futures contract

For your particular hedging problem, $\beta_P = 1.25$, $V_P = \$100$ million, and $V_F = \$375{,}000$, thereby yielding this calculation:

$$\text{Number of contracts} = \frac{1.25 \times \$100{,}000{,}000}{\$375{,}000} \approx 333$$

Thus, you can establish an effective short hedge by going short 333 S&P 500 index futures contracts. This short hedge will protect your stock portfolio against the risk of a general fall in stock prices during the life of the futures contracts.

HEDGING WITH STOCK INDEX FUTURES

EXAMPLE 16.9

How many futures contracts are required to hedge a $250 million stock portfolio with a portfolio beta of .75 using S&P 500 futures with a futures price of 1,500?

Using the formula for the number of contracts, we have

$$\text{Number of contracts} = \frac{.75 \times \$250{,}000{,}000}{\$375{,}000} = 500$$

You therefore need to sell 500 contracts to hedge this $250 million portfolio.

Hedging Interest Rate Risk with Futures

Having discussed hedging a stock portfolio, we now turn to hedging a bond portfolio. As we will see, the bond portfolio hedging problem is similar to the stock portfolio hedging problem. Once again, we will be cross-hedging, but this time using futures contracts on U.S. Treasury notes. Here, our goal is to protect the bond portfolio against changing interest rates.

In this example, you are responsible for managing a bond portfolio with a current value of $100 million. Recently, rising interest rates have caused your portfolio to fall in value slightly, and you are concerned that interest rates may continue to trend upward for the next several months. You decide to establish a short hedge based on 10-year Treasury note futures.

The formula for the number of U.S. Treasury note futures contracts needed to hedge a bond portfolio is

$$\text{Number of contracts} = \frac{D_P \times V_P}{D_F \times V_F} \tag{16.8}$$

where: D_P = Duration of the bond portfolio
V_P = Value of the bond portfolio
D_F = Duration of the futures contract
V_F = Value of a single futures contract

We already know the value of the bond portfolio, which is $100 million. Also, suppose that the duration of the portfolio is given as eight years. Next, we must calculate the duration of the futures contract and the value of the futures contract.

As a useful rule of thumb, the duration of an interest rate futures contract is equal to the duration of the underlying instrument plus the time remaining until contract maturity:

$$D_F = D_U + M_F \qquad (16.9)$$

where: D_F = Duration of the futures contract
D_U = Duration of the underlying instrument
M_F = Time remaining until contract maturity

For simplicity, let us suppose that the duration of the underlying U.S. Treasury note is 6 1/2 years and the futures contract has a maturity of 1/2 year, yielding a futures contract duration of 7 years.

The value of a single futures contract is the current futures price times the futures contract size. The standard contract size for U.S. Treasury note futures contracts is $100,000 par value. Now suppose that the futures price is 98, or 98 percent of par value. This yields a futures contract value of $100,000 × .98 = $98,000.

You now have all inputs required to calculate the number of futures contracts needed to hedge your bond portfolio. The number of U.S. Treasury note futures contracts needed to hedge the bond portfolio is calculated as follows:

$$\text{Number of contracts} = \frac{8 \times \$100,000,000}{7 \times \$98,000} = 1,166$$

Thus, you can establish an effective short hedge by going short 1,166 futures contracts for 10-year U.S. Treasury notes. This short hedge will protect your bond portfolio against the risk of a general rise in interest rates during the life of the futures contracts.

HEDGING WITH U.S. TREASURY NOTE FUTURES

EXAMPLE 16.10

How many futures contracts are required to hedge a $250 million bond portfolio with a portfolio duration of 5 years using 10-year U.S. Treasury note futures with a duration of 7.5 years and a futures price of 105?

Using the formula for the number of contracts, we have

$$\text{Number of contracts} = \frac{5 \times \$250,000,000}{7.5 \times \$105,000} = 1,587$$

You therefore need to sell 1,587 contracts to hedge this $250 million portfolio.

cheapest-to-deliver option Seller's option to deliver the cheapest instrument when a futures contract allows several instruments for delivery. For example, U.S. Treasury note futures allow delivery of any Treasury note with a maturity between 6 1/2 and 10 years.

Futures Contract Delivery Options

Many futures contracts have a delivery option, whereby the seller can choose among several different "grades" of the underlying commodity or instrument when fulfilling delivery requirements. Naturally, we expect the seller to deliver the cheapest among available options. In futures jargon, this is called the **cheapest-to-deliver option**. The cheapest-to-deliver option is an example of a broader feature of many futures contracts, known as a "quality" option. Of course, futures buyers know about the delivery option, and therefore the futures prices reflect the value of the cheapest-to-deliver instrument.

As a specific example of a cheapest-to-deliver option, the 10-year Treasury note contract allows delivery of *any* Treasury note with a maturity between 6 1/2 and 10 years. This complicates the bond portfolio hedging problem. For the portfolio manager trying to hedge a bond portfolio with U.S. Treasury note futures, the cheapest-to-deliver feature means that a note can be hedged only based on an assumption about which note will actually be delivered. Furthermore, through time the cheapest-to-deliver note may vary, and, consequently, the hedge will have to be monitored regularly to make sure that it correctly reflects the note issue that is most likely to be delivered. Fortunately, because this is a common problem, many commercial advisory services provide this information to portfolio managers and other investors.

Check This

16.5a What is a cross-hedge?

16.5b What are the three basic inputs required to calculate the number of stock index futures contracts needed to hedge an equity portfolio?

16.5c What are the basic inputs required to calculate the number of U.S. Treasury note futures contracts needed to hedge a bond portfolio?

16.5d What is the cheapest-to-deliver option?

16.6 Summary and Conclusions

This chapter surveyed the basics of futures contracts. In it, we saw that:

1. A forward contract is an agreement between a buyer and a seller for a future commodity transaction at a price set today. Futures contracts are a step beyond forward contracts. Futures contracts and forward contracts accomplish the same task, but a forward contract can be struck between any two parties, while standardized futures contracts are managed through organized futures exchanges.

2. Commodity futures call for delivery of a physical commodity. Financial futures require delivery of a financial instrument or, in some cases, cash. Futures contracts are a type of derivative security, because the value of the contract is derived from the value of an underlying instrument.

3. Hedging is the major economic reason for the existence of futures markets. However, a viable futures market requires participation by both hedgers and speculators. Hedgers transfer price risk to speculators, and speculators absorb price risk. Hedging and speculating are thus complementary activities.

4. Futures trading accounts have three essential features: margin is required, futures accounts are marked to market daily, and a futures position can be closed out any time by a reverse trade.

5. The cash price of a commodity or financial instrument is the price quoted for current delivery. The cash price is also called the spot price.

6. The difference between a cash price and a futures price is called basis. For commodities with storage costs, the cash price is usually less than the futures price. This is referred to as a carrying-charge market. Sometimes the cash price is greater than the futures price, and this case is referred to as an inverted market.

7. There is a simple relationship between cash and futures prices known as spot-futures parity. Violations of parity give rise to arbitrage opportunities, including index arbitrage, which involves stock index futures.

8. Cross-hedging refers to using futures contracts on a related commodity or instrument to hedge a particular spot position. Stock index futures, for example, can be used to hedge an equities portfolio against general declines in stock prices, and U.S. Treasury note futures can be used to hedge a bond portfolio.

Get Real

This chapter covered the essentials of what many consider to be a complex subject, futures contracts. As we hope you realize, futures contracts per se are not complicated at all; in fact, they are, for the most part, quite simple. This doesn't mean that they're for everybody, of course. Because of the tremendous leverage possible, very large gains and losses can (and do) occur with great speed.

To experience some of the gains and losses from outright speculation, you should buy and sell a variety of contracts in a simulated brokerage account such as Stock-Trak. Be sure to go both long and short and pick a few of each major type of contract.

The Internet offers a rich source for more information on trading futures. Probably the best place to begin is by visiting the websites of the major futures exchanges: the Chicago Board of Trade (www.cbot.com), the Chicago Mercantile Exchange (www.cme.com), the New York Mercantile Exchange (www.nymex.com), and the Kansas City Board of Trade (www.kcbt.com). You might also visit the websites of some major international futures exchanges: the London International Financial Futures Exchange (www.liffe.com), Sydney Futures Exchange (www.sfe.com.au), Tokyo International Financial Futures Exchange (www.tiffe.or.jp), and the Singapore Exchange (www.ses.com.sg). The reference section of Numa Web (www.numa.com) maintains an extensive list of the world's futures exchanges.

For information on futures markets regulation, the federal agency charged with regulating U.S. futures markets is the Commodities Futures Trading Commission (www.cftc.gov). The professional organization charged with self-regulation is the National Futures Association (www.nfa.futures.org). General information on futures markets and trading can be found at the Futures Industry Association (www.fiafii.org).

Useful websites on trading futures are Futures Trading (www.futures-trading.org), Commodity Traders Club (www.ctcn.com), Daily Futures (www.dailyfutures.com), and Trading Markets (www.tradingmarkets.com). For a very large list of links to anything and everything related to futures, visit the commodities and futures section of Investor Links (www.investorlinks.com).

Key Terms

forward contract 522	speculator 529
futures contract 522	hedger 530
futures price 522	short hedge 530
long position 529	long hedge 530
short position 529	futures margin 532

Chapter Review Problems and Self-Test

1. **Futures Gains and Losses** Suppose you purchase 10 orange juice contracts today at the settle price of $1 per pound. How much do these 10 contracts cost you? If the settle price is lower tomorrow by 2 cents per pound, how much do you make or lose? The contract size is 15,000 pounds.

2. **Spot-Futures Parity** There is a futures contract on a stock, which is currently selling at $200 per share. The contract matures in two months; the risk-free rate is 5 percent annually. The current dividend yield on the stock is 0 percent. What does the parity relationship imply the futures price should be?

Answers to Self-Test Problems

1. If you go long (purchase) 10 contracts, you pay nothing today (you will be required to post margin, but a futures contract is an agreement to exchange cash for goods later, not today). If the settle price drops by 2 cents per pound, you lose 15,000 pounds (the contract size) × $.02 = $300 per contract. With 10 contracts, you lose $3,000.

2. The spot-futures parity condition is

$$F_T = S(1 + r - d)^T$$

where S is the spot price, r is the risk-free rate, d is the dividend yield, F is the futures price, and T is the time to expiration measured in years.

   Plugging in the numbers we have, with zero for the dividend yield and 1/6 for the number of years (2 months out of 12), gets us

$$F_{1/6} = \$200(1 + .05)^{1/6} = \$201.63$$

Test Your Investment Quotient

1. **Futures Exchanges** Which of the following is the oldest and currently the most active futures exchange in the United States?

   a. Kansas City Board of Trade (KBOT)
   b. Chicago Mercantile Exchange (CME)
   c. New York Mercantile Exchange (NYMX)
   d. Chicago Board of Trade (CBOT)

2. **Futures Exchanges** The first financial futures contracts, introduced in 1972, were

   a. Currency futures at the CME.
   b. Interest rate futures at the CBOT.
   c. Stock index futures at the KBOT.
   d. Wheat futures at the CBOT.

3. **Futures Exchanges**   Which of the following futures exchanges trades futures contracts on common stocks?

   a. OneBoston
   b. OneChicago
   c. FutureRama
   d. Niffe-Quorum

4. **Futures versus Forward Contracts**   Which of the following statements is true regarding the distinction between futures contracts and forward contracts?

   a. Futures contracts are exchange-traded, whereas forward contracts are OTC-traded.
   b. All else equal, forward prices are higher than futures prices.
   c. Forward contracts are created from baskets of futures contracts.
   d. Futures contracts are cash-settled at maturity, whereas forward contracts result in delivery.

5. **Futures versus Forward Contracts**   In which of the following ways do futures contracts differ from forward contracts?

   I. Futures contracts are standardized.
   II. For futures, performance of each party is guaranteed by a clearinghouse.
   III. Futures contracts require a daily settling of any gains or losses.

   a. I and II only
   b. I and III only
   c. II and III only
   d. I, II, and III

6. **Futures Contracts**   The open interest on a futures contract at any given time is the total number of outstanding

   a. Contracts
   b. Unhedged positions
   c. Clearinghouse positions
   d. Long and short positions

7. **Futures Margin**   Initial margin for a futures contract is usually

   a. Regulated by the Federal Reserve.
   b. Less than 2 percent of contract value.
   c. In the range between 2 percent to 5 percent of contract value.
   d. In the range between 5 percent to 15 percent of contract value.

8. **Futures Margin**   In futures trading, the minimum level to which an equity position may fall before requiring additional margin is *most accurately* termed the

   a. Initial margin
   b. Variation margin
   c. Cash flow margin
   d. Maintenance margin

9. **Futures Margin**   A silver futures contract requires the seller to deliver 5,000 troy ounces of silver. An investor sells one July silver futures contract at a price of $8 per ounce, posting a $2,025 initial margin. If the required maintenance margin is $1,500, the price per ounce at which the investor would first receive a maintenance margin call is closest to

   a. $5.92
   b. $7.89
   c. $8.11
   d. $10.80

10. **Futures Margin**   Which of the following statements is false about futures account margin?

   a. Initial margin is higher than maintenance margin.

   b. A margin call results when account margin falls below maintenance margin.

   c. Marking-to-market of account margin occurs daily.

   d. A margin call results when account margin falls below initial margin.

11. Futures Contracts   Which of the following contract terms changes daily during the life of a futures contract?

   a. Futures price

   b. Futures contract size

   c. Futures maturity date

   d. Underlying commodity

12. Futures Trading Accounts   Which of the following is perhaps the least essential thing to know about a futures trading account?

   a. Margin is required.

   b. Futures accounts are marked-to-market daily.

   c. A futures position can be closed by a reverse trade.

   d. A commission is charged for each trade.

13. Futures Delivery   On the maturity date, stock index futures contracts require delivery of

   a. Common stock.

   b. Common stock plus accrued dividends.

   c. Treasury bills.

   d. Cash.

14. Futures Delivery   On the maturity date, Treasury note futures contracts require delivery of

   a. Treasury notes plus accrued coupons over the life of the futures contract.

   b. Treasury notes.

   c. Treasury bills.

   d. Cash.

15. Spot-Futures Parity   A Treasury bond futures contract has a quoted price of 100. The underlying bond has a coupon rate of 7 percent, and the current market interest rate is 7 percent. Spot-futures parity then implies a cash bond price of

   a. 93

   b. 100

   c. 107

   d. 114

16. Spot-Futures Parity   A stock index futures contract maturing in one year has a currently traded price of $1,000. The cash index has a dividend yield of 2 percent, and the interest rate is 5 percent. Spot-futures parity then implies a cash index level of

   a. $933.33

   b. $970.87

   c. $1,071

   d. $1,029

17. Spot-Futures Parity   A stock index futures contract matures in one year. The cash index currently has a level of $1,000 with a dividend yield of 2 percent. If the interest rate is 5 percent, then spot-futures parity implies a futures price of

   a. $943.40

   b. $970.87

   c. $1,060

   d. $1,030

18. Futures Hedging   You manage a $100 million stock portfolio with a beta of .8. Given a contract size of $100,000 for a stock index futures contract, how many contracts are needed to hedge your portfolio?

a. 8
b. 80
c. 800
d. 8,000

19. **Futures Hedging**   You manage a $100 million bond portfolio with a duration of 9 years. You wish to hedge this portfolio against interest rate risk using T-bond futures with a contract size of $100,000 and a duration of 12 years. How many contracts are required?

   a. 750
   b. 1,000
   c. 133
   d. 1,333

20. **Futures Hedging**   Which of the following is not an input needed to calculate the number of stock index futures contracts required to hedge a stock portfolio?

   a. The value of the stock portfolio.
   b. The beta of the stock portfolio.
   c. The contract value of the index futures contract.
   d. The initial margin required for each futures contract.

Concept Questions

1. **Understanding Futures Quotations**   Using Figure 16.1, answer the following questions:
   a. How many exchanges trade wheat futures contracts?
   b. If you have a position in 10 gold futures, what quantity of gold underlies your position?
   c. If you are short 20 oat futures contracts and you opt to make delivery, what quantity of oats must you supply?
   d. Which maturity of the unleaded gasoline contract has the largest open interest? Which one has the smallest open interest?

2. **Hedging with Futures**   Kellogg's uses large quantities of corn in its breakfast cereal operations. Suppose the near-term weather forecast for the corn-producing states is droughtlike conditions, so corn prices are expected to rise. To hedge its costs, Kellogg's decides to use the Chicago Board of Trade corn futures contracts. Should the company be a short hedger or a long hedger in corn futures?

3. **Hedging with Futures**   Suppose one of Fidelity's mutual funds closely mimics the S&P 500 index. The fund has done very well during the year, and, in November, the fund manager wants to lock in the gains he has made using stock index futures. Should he take a long or short position in S&P 500 index futures?

4. **Hedging with Futures**   A mutual fund that predominantly holds long-term Treasury bonds plans on liquidating the portfolio in three months. However, the fund manager is concerned that interest rates may rise from current levels and wants to hedge the price risk of the portfolio. Should she buy or sell Treasury bond futures contracts?

5. **Hedging with Futures**   An American electronics firm imports its completed circuit boards from Japan. The company signed a contract today to pay for the boards in Japanese yen upon delivery in four months; the price per board in yen was fixed in the contract. Should the importer buy or sell Japanese yen futures contracts?

6. **Hedging with Futures**   Jed Clampett just dug another oil well, and, as usual, it's a gusher. Jed estimates that, in 2 months, he'll have 2 million barrels of crude oil to bring to market. However, Jed would like to lock in the value of this oil at today's prices, since the oil market has been skyrocketing recently. Should Jed buy or sell crude oil futures contracts?

www.mhhe.com/cj3e

7. **Hedging with Futures** The town of South Park is planning a bond issue in six months and Kenny, the town treasurer, is worried that interest rates may rise, thereby reducing the value of the bond issue. Should Kenny buy or sell Treasury bond futures contracts to hedge the impending bond issue?

8. **Futures Markets** Is it true that a futures contract represents a zero-sum game, meaning that the only way for a buyer to win is for a seller to lose, and vice versa?

9. **Program Trading** Program traders closely monitor relative futures and cash market prices, but program trades are not actually made on a fully mechanical basis. What are some of the complications that might make program trading using, for example, the S&P 500 contract more difficult than the spot-futures parity formula indicates?

10. **Short Selling** What are the similarities and differences in short selling a futures contract and short selling a stock? How do the cash flows differ?

Questions and Problems

Core Questions

1. **Understanding Futures Quotations** Using Figure 16.1, answer the following questions:
   a. What was the settle price for September 2003 corn futures on this date? What is the total dollar value of this contract at the close of trading for the day?
   b. What was the settle price for CBT December 2003 Treasury bond futures on this date? If you held 10 contracts, what is the total dollar value of your futures position?
   c. Suppose you held an open position of 25 S&P Midcap 400 index futures on this day. What is the change in the total dollar value of your position for this day's trading? If you held a long position, would this represent a profit or a loss to you?
   d. Suppose you are short 10 July 2003 soybean oil futures contracts. Would you have made a profit or a loss on this day?

2. **Futures Profits and Losses** You are long 20 May 2003 oats futures contracts. Calculate your dollar profit or loss from this trading day using Figure 16.1.

3. **Futures Profits and Losses** You are short 15 September 2003 corn futures contracts. Calculate your dollar profit or loss from this trading day using Figure 16.1.

4. **Futures Profits and Losses** You are short 30 June 2003 five-year Treasury note futures contracts. Calculate your profit or loss from this trading day using Figure 16.1.

5. **Open Interest** Referring to Figure 16.1, what is the total open interest on the Japanese yen contract? Does it represent long positions, short positions, or both? Based on the settle price on the June contract, what is the dollar value of the open interest?

6. **Spot-Futures Parity** A non-dividend-paying stock is currently priced at $52.30. The risk-free rate is 5 percent, and a futures contract on the stock matures in five months. What price should the futures be?

7. **Spot-Futures Parity** A non-dividend-paying stock has a futures contract with a price of $93.25 and a maturity of three months. If the risk-free rate is 4.5 percent, what is the price of the stock?

8. **Spot-Futures Parity** A non-dividend-paying stock has a current share price of $48.73 and a futures price of $50.29. If the maturity of the futures contract is eight months, what is the risk-free rate?

9. **Spot-Futures Parity** A stock has a current share price of $98.25 and a dividend yield of 2.5 percent. If the risk-free rate is 5.4 percent, what is the futures price if the maturity is four months?

10. **Spot-Futures Parity** A stock futures contract is priced at $84.21. The stock has a dividend yield of 2 percent, and the risk-free rate is 6.1 percent. If the futures contract matures in six months, what is the current stock price?

Intermediate Questions

11. **Margin Call**   Suppose the initial margin on heating oil futures is $1,500, the maintenance margin is $1,250 per contract, and you establish a long position of 10 contracts today, where each contract represents 42,000 gallons. Tomorrow, the contract settles down .01 from the previous day's price. Are you subject to a margin call? What is the maximum price decline on the contract that you can sustain without getting a margin call?

12. **Marking-to-Market**   You are long 10 gold futures contracts, established at an initial settle price of $355 per ounce, where each contract represents 100 ounces. Your initial margin to establish the position is $1,000 per contract, and the maintenance margin is $750 per contract. Over the subsequent four trading days, gold settles at $351, $354, $358, and $360, respectively. Compute the balance in your margin account at the end of each of the four trading days, and compute your total profit or loss at the end of the trading period.

13. **Marking-to-Market**   You are short 25 gasoline futures contracts, established at an initial settle price of .712 per gallon, where each contract represents 42,000 gallons. Your initial margin to establish the position is $1,600 per contract, and the maintenance margin is $1,200 per contract. Over the subsequent four trading days, oil settles at .734, .719, .709, and .710, respectively. Compute the balance in your margin account at the end of each of the four trading days, and compute your total profit or loss at the end of the trading period.

14. **Futures Profits**   You went long on 20 March 2004 Brent Crude oil futures contracts at a price of 25.10. Looking back at Figure 16.1, if you closed your position at the settle price on this day, what was your profit?

15. **Futures Profits**   You shorted 15 June 2003 British pound futures contracts at the lifetime high of the contract. Looking back at Figure 16.1, if you closed your position at the settle price on this day, what was your profit?

16. **Index Arbitrage**   Suppose the CAC-40 index (a widely followed index of French stock prices) is currently at 1,800, the expected dividend yield on the index is 2 percent per year, and the risk-free rate in France is 7 percent annually. If CAC-40 futures contracts that expire in six months are currently trading at 1,860, what program trading strategy would you recommend?

17. **Cross-Hedging**   You have been assigned to implement a three-month hedge for a stock mutual fund portfolio that primarily invests in medium-sized companies. The mutual fund has a beta of 1.2 measured relative to the S&P Midcap 400, and the net asset value of the fund is $300 million. Should you be long or short in the Midcap 400 futures contracts? Assuming the Midcap 400 index is at 445 and its futures contract size is 500 times the index, determine the appropriate number of contracts to use in designing your cross-hedge strategy.

18. **Spot-Futures Parity**   Suppose the 180-day S&P 500 futures price is 1,046.70, while the cash price is 1,030.22. What is the *implied difference* between the risk-free interest rate and the dividend yield on the S&P 500?

19. **Spot-Futures Parity**   Suppose the 180-day S&P 500 futures price is 1,041.25, while the cash price is 1,020.50. What is the *implied dividend yield* on the S&P 500 if the risk-free interest rate is 7 percent?

20. **Hedging Interest Rate Risk**   Suppose you want to hedge a $900 million bond portfolio with a duration of 6.5 years using 10-year Treasury note futures with a duration of 9 years, a futures price of 102, and 3 months to expiration. The multiplier on Treasury note futures is $100,000. How many contracts do you buy or sell?

21. **Hedging Interest Rate Risk**   Suppose you want to hedge a $400 million bond portfolio with a duration of 14.5 years using 10-year Treasury note futures with a duration of 8 years, a futures price of 98, and 70 days to expiration. The multiplier on Treasury note futures is $100,000. How many contracts do you buy or sell?

22. **Futures Arbitrage** A non-dividend-paying stock is currently priced at $64.26 per share. A futures contract maturing in five months has a price of $66.02 and the risk-free rate is 4 percent. Describe how you could make an arbitrage profit from this situation. How much could you make on a per-share basis?

23. **Futures Arbitrage** A stock is currently priced at $80.34 and the futures on the stock that expire in six months have a price of $82.76. The risk-free rate is 7 percent, and the stock is not expected to pay a dividend. Is there an arbitrage opportunity here? How would you exploit it? What is the arbitrage opportunity per share of stock?

24. **Futures Arbitrage** Joan Tam, CFA, believes she has identified an arbitrage opportunity as indicated by the information given below:

Spot price for commodity:	$120
Futures price for commodity expiring in one year:	$125
Interest rate for one year:	8%

    a. Describe the transactions necessary to take advantage of this specific arbitrage opportunity.
    b. Calculate the arbitrage profit.
    c. Describe two market imperfections that could limit Tam's ability to implement this arbitrage strategy.

25. **Futures Arbitrage** Donna Doni, CFA, wants to explore inefficiencies in the futures market. The TOBEC stock index has a spot value of 185 now. TOBEC futures are settled in cash and underlying contract values are determined by multiplying $100 times the index value. The current annual risk-free interest rate is 6 percent.

    a. Calculate the theoretical price of the futures contract expiring six months from now, using the cost-of-carry model.
    b. The total (round-trip) transaction cost for trading a futures contract is $15. Calculate the lower bound for the price of the futures contract expiring six months from now.

What's on the Web?

1. **OneChicago** Go to www.onechicago.com. How many single stock futures and narrow-based indexes are traded at OneChicago? What is the contract size of a single stock future? What is the minimum tick size, contract month, and contract expiration? What is the margin requirement?

2. **Spot-Futures Parity** Go to www.onechicago.com and find the futures quotes for Halliburton Co. Now go to finance.yahoo.com and find the current stock price for Halliburton. What is the implied risk-free rate using these prices? Does each different maturity give you the same interest rate? Why or why not?

3. **Contract Specifications** You want to find the contract specifications for futures contracts. Go to the Chicago Board of Trade at www.cbot.com, and, under the "Market Info" pull-down menu, follow the "Contract Specs" link. Now follow the "Agricultural Contracts" link and find the contract specifications for corn and rough rice. What are the contract sizes? Now follow the "MidAm Livestock" link and find the contract size for cattle and lean hogs.

4. **New York Board of Trade** Go to the New York Board of Trade website at www.nybot.com and follow the "Market Information" link and the "Contract Specs" link. What contracts are traded on the New York Board of Trade? What does FCOJ stand for? What are the trading months for FCOJ futures contracts? What are the position limits for FCOJ futures contracts? What is the last trading day of the expiration month for FCOJ futures? What are the trading months and last trading day for FCOJ options contracts? What is the FCOJ Differential contract?

5. **Hedging with Futures**   You are working for a company that processes beef and will take delivery of 200,000 pounds of cattle in August. You would like to lock in your costs today because you are concerned about an increase in cattle prices. Go to the Chicago Mercantile Exchange (CME) at www.cme.com, follow the "Products" link, the "Agricultural Commodities" link, and the "Contract Specs" link. How many futures contracts will you need to hedge your exposure? How will you use these contracts? Go back to the CME home page, follow the "Prices" link, the "10-Minute Futures Updates" link, the "Agricultural Commodity Futures" link, and the "Live Cattle Futures" link. What price are you effectively locking in if you traded at the last price? Suppose cattle prices increase 5 percent before the expiration. What is your profit or loss on the futures position? What if the price decreases by 5 percent? Explain how your futures position has eliminated your exposure to price risk in the live cattle market.

Stock-Trak®
Portfolio Simulations

Trading Commodity Futures with Stock-Trak

Commodity futures trading is popular among many individual investors. Stock-Trak allows its customers to trade a large number of different commodity futures: corn, wheat, gold, silver, oil, and many others. If you are interested in trying your hand at commodities trading with Stock-Trak, simply select the commodities you wish to trade from *The Wall Street Journal* "Futures" column, and then note the contract size for those commodities before deciding how many contracts you wish to trade. Table ST.1 lists contract sizes and ticker symbols for some popular commodities futures contracts.

Suppose you wish to take a long position in 100,000 pounds of copper in the hope that copper prices will go up, and, at the same time, take a short position in 300,000 pounds of coffee in the belief that coffee prices are about to fall. You would then buy four copper contracts and sell eight coffee contracts. But before submitting these orders, you must decide on a contract maturity month. For Stock-Trak trading, it is convenient to pick a month at or after the end of the semester, say, December or June.

Commodity futures tickers have two-character extensions denoting the contract expiration date. The first character is a letter representing the expiration month, and the second character is a number representing the expiration year. Futures ticker extensions for contracts expiring in 2004 are specified in Table ST.2.

TABLE ST.1	Commodity Futures Contract Size and Tickers		
Instrument	**Ticker**	**Instrument**	**Ticker**
Corn (5,000 bushels)	C	Copper (25,000 lb)	HG
Soybeans (5,000 bushels)	S	Gold (100 oz)	GC
Wheat (5,000 bushels)	W	Platinum (50 oz)	PL
Coffee (37,500 lb)	KC	Crude oil (1,000 bbl)	CL
Sugar (112,000 lb)	SB	Heating oil (42,000 gal)	HO
Orange juice (15,000 lb)	JO	Unleaded gas (42,000 gal)	HU

TABLE ST.2	Futures Ticker Extension Codes (2004 Expirations)		
Expiration Month	Code	Expiration Month	Code
January	F4	July	N4
February	G4	August	Q4
March	H4	September	U4
April	J4	October	V4
May	K4	November	X4
June	M4	December	Z4

There are four basic types of futures trades:

1. Buy to open or increase a long position.

2. Sell to open or increase a short position.

3. Sell to close or decrease a long position.

4. Buy to close or decrease a short position.

Examples of the first two types of trades are orders to go long 4 June 2004 copper contracts and go short 8 December 2005 coffee contracts. Using standard futures ticker symbols, these orders are stated as:

Buy 4 HG-M4 contracts

Sell 8 KC-Z5 contracts

Examples of the next two trade types are orders that close out these positions:

Sell 4 HG-M4 contracts

Buy 8 KC-Z5 contracts

Stock-Trak Exercises

1. What are the complete tickers for the following commodity futures contracts: September 2005 orange juice, March 2004 unleaded gas, June 2005 gold?

2. Using your Stock-Trak account, take positions in orange juice futures, unleaded gas futures, and gold futures. First decide whether you think each futures price will go up or down in the near future. If up, take a long position and, if down, take a short position.

Trading Stock Index Futures with Stock-Trak

Once you have mastered the basics of trading commodity futures, you may wish to begin trading stock index futures. Your Stock-Trak account allows you to trade futures on a number of different stock market indexes. To trade stock index futures, you first choose the stock index you want to use and find the ticker symbol for that index. You must also know the ticker extension for the maturity month of the futures contract.

The most popular stock market indexes are the Dow Jones Industrial Average (DJIA) and the Standard & Poor's 500 (S&P 500). Futures contracts for the DJIA trade under the futures ticker symbol DJ. Futures contracts for the S&P 500 trade under the futures ticker symbol SP.

At the time this was written, the contract value for a single DJ futures contract was 10 times the underlying index level, and the contract value for the SP futures contract was 250 times the underlying index level. However, these contract values may change, and you should consult the Stock-Trak website for the latest contract specifications. If you wish to know more

TABLE ST.3	Futures Ticker Extension Codes (2005 Expirations)		
Expiration Month	**Code**	**Expiration Month**	**Code**
January	F5	July	N5
February	G5	August	Q5
March	H5	September	U5
April	J5	October	V5
May	K5	November	X5
June	M5	December	Z5

TABLE ST.4	Interest Rate Futures Contract Size and Tickers		
Instrument	**Ticker**	**Instrument**	**Ticker**
5-year T-note ($100,000)	FV	13-week T-bills ($1 million)	TB
10-year T-note ($100,000)	TY	Eurodollar ($1 million)	ED
30-year T-bond ($100,000)	US	LIBOR ($3 million)	EM

detail about contract specifications, you should consult the Chicago Board of Trade website (www.cbot.com).

For example, suppose you go short a single DJ futures contract when the futures price is 10,150, and then at contract maturity the underlying index has a value of 10,025. Your dollar gain is then $10 \times (10{,}150 - 10{,}025) = \$1{,}250$. Alternatively, suppose you go long a single SP futures contract when the futures price is 1,510, and then at contract maturity the S&P 500 index is at 1,502. Your dollar loss is then $250 \times (1{,}510 - 1{,}502) = \$2{,}000$.

Futures tickers for stock indexes have a two-character extension denoting the contract expiration date. Just like commodity futures, the first character is a letter representing the expiration month, and the second character is an integer representing the expiration year. Futures ticker extensions for contracts expiring in 2005 are listed in Table ST.3.

For example, orders to go long 2 DJ June 2004 futures contracts and go short 4 SP December 2005 futures contracts are abbreviated as:

Buy 2 DJ-M4 contracts

Sell 4 SP-Z5 contracts

Stock-Trak Exercises

3. What are the complete tickers for the following stock index futures contracts: DJIA March 2004, S&P 500 September 2005?

4. Decide whether you think the stock market will go up or down in the near future, then using your Stock-Trak account take an appropriate position in a stock index futures contract.

Trading Interest Rate Futures with Stock-Trak

You can trade on interest rate changes using interest rate futures with your Stock-Trak account. The most widely used interest rate futures contracts are based on Eurodollar rates and rates on U.S. Treasury bills, notes, and bonds. To trade interest rate futures with Stock-Trak, you first select the desired instrument and the number of futures contracts. Table ST.4 lists futures contract sizes and ticker symbols for several interest rate contracts.

For example, orders to go long 3 Treasury bill June 2004 futures contracts and go short 2 Eurodollar December 2005 futures contracts are abbreviated as:

Buy 3 TB-M4 contracts

Sell 2 ED-Z5 contracts

Going long implies buying the underlying instrument, and going short implies selling the underlying instrument. The futures price specifies the price paid upon delivery at contract expiration. Detailed contract specifications for interest rate futures are available at the Chicago Board of Trade website (www.cbot.com) and the Chicago Mercantile Exchange website (www.cme.com).

Stock-Trak Exercises

5. What are the complete tickers for the following interest rate futures contracts: 5-year Treasury note September 2005, LIBOR March 2004, 30-year Treasury bond June 2005?

6. Decide whether you think interest rates will rise or fall in the near future. If you think rates will rise, then use your Stock-Trak account to take a short position in an interest rate futures contract. If you think interest rates will fall, then take a long position.

7. Through the website for this textbook (www.mhhe.com/cj3e), go to the Stock-Trak website and review the latest information about trading futures contracts through Stock-Trak.

www.mhhe.com/cj3e

Chapter 17

Corporate Bonds

"If you'd know the value of money, go and borrow some."

–Benjamin Franklin

A corporation issues bonds intending to meet all obligations of interest and repayment of principal. Investors buy bonds believing the corporation intends to fulfill its debt obligation in a timely manner. Although defaults can and do occur, the market for corporate bonds exists only because corporations are able to convince investors of their original intent to avoid default. Reaching this state of trust is not a trivial process, and it normally requires elaborate contractual arrangements. ■

Almost all corporations issue notes and bonds to raise money to finance investment projects. Indeed, for many corporations, the value of notes and bonds outstanding can exceed the value of common stock shares outstanding. Nevertheless, most investors do not think of corporate bonds when they think about investing. This is because corporate bonds represent specialized investment instruments that are usually bought by financial institutions like insurance companies and pension funds. For professional money managers at these institutions, a knowledge of corporate bonds is absolutely essential. This chapter introduces you to the specialized knowledge that these money managers possess.

17.1 Corporate Bond Basics

Corporate bonds represent the debt of a corporation owed to its bondholders. More specifically, a corporate bond is a security issued by a corporation that represents a promise to pay to its bondholders a fixed sum of money at a future maturity date, along with periodic payments of interest. The fixed sum paid at maturity is the bond's *principal*, also called its par or face value. The periodic interest payments are called *coupons*.

From an investor's point of view, corporate bonds represent an investment distinct from common stock. The three most fundamental differences are these:

1. Common stock represents an ownership claim on the corporation, whereas bonds represent a creditor's claim on the corporation.

2. Promised cash flows—that is, coupons and principal—to be paid to bondholders are stated in advance when the bond is issued. By contrast, the amount and timing of dividends paid to common stockholders may change at any time.

3. Most corporate bonds are issued as callable bonds, which means that the bond issuer has the right to buy back outstanding bonds before the maturity date of the bond issue. When a bond issue is called, coupon payments stop and the bondholders are forced to surrender their bonds to the issuer in exchange for the cash payment of a specified call price. By contrast, common stock is almost never callable.

For more information on corporate bonds visit www.investinginbonds.com

The corporate bond market is large, with several trillion dollars of corporate bonds outstanding in the United States. The sheer size of the corporate bond market prompts an important inquiry: Who owns corporate bonds and why? The answer is that most corporate bond investors belong to only a few distinct categories. The single largest group of corporate bond investors is life insurance companies, which hold about a third of all outstanding corporate bonds. Remaining ownership shares are roughly equally balanced among individual investors, pension funds, banks, and foreign investors.

The pattern of corporate bond ownership is largely explained by the fact that corporate bonds provide a source of predictable cash flows. While individual bonds occasionally default on their promised cash payments, large institutional investors can diversify away most default risk by including a large number of different bond issues in their portfolios. For this reason, life insurance companies and pension funds find that corporate bonds are a natural investment vehicle to provide for future payments of retirement and death benefits, since both the timing and amount of these benefit payments can be matched with bond cash flows. These institutions can eliminate much of their financial risk by matching the timing of cash flows received from a bond portfolio to the timing of cash flows needed to make benefit payments—a strategy called cash flow matching. For this reason, life insurance companies and pension funds together own more than half of all outstanding corporate bonds. For similar reasons, individual investors might own corporate bonds as a source of steady cash income. However, since individual investors cannot easily diversify default risk, they should normally invest only in bonds with higher credit quality.

Every corporate bond issue has a specific set of issue terms associated with it. The issue terms associated with any particular bond can range from a relatively simple arrangement, where the bond is little more than an IOU of the corporation, to a complex contract specifying in great detail what the issuer can and cannot do with respect

TABLE 17.1		Software Iz Us Five-Year Note Issue
Issue amount	$20 million	Note issue total face value is $20 million
Issue date	12/15/2003	Notes offered to the public in December 2003
Maturity date	12/31/2008	Remaining principal due December 31, 2008
Face value	$1,000	Face value denomination is $1,000 per note
Coupon interest	$100 per annum	Annual coupons are $100 per note
Coupon dates	6/30, 12/31	Coupons are paid semiannually
Offering price	100	Offer price is 100 percent of face value
Yield to maturity	10%	Based on stated offer price
Call provision	Not callable	Notes may not be paid off before maturity
Security	None	Notes are unsecured
Rating	Not rated	Privately placed note issue

plain vanilla bonds
Bonds issued with a relatively standard set of features. Also known as *bullet bonds*.

to its obligations to bondholders. Bonds issued with a standard, relatively simple set of features are popularly called **plain vanilla bonds** or "bullet" bonds.

As an illustration of a plain vanilla corporate debt issue, Table 17.1 summarizes the issue terms for a note issue by Software Iz Us. Referring to Table 17.1, we see that the Software Iz Us notes were issued in December 2003 and mature five years later in December 2008. Each individual note has a face value denomination of $1,000. Since the total issue amount is $20 million, the entire issue contains 20,000 notes. Each note pays a $100 annual coupon, which is equal to 10 percent of its face value. The annual coupon is split between two semiannual $50 payments made each June and December. Based on the original offer price of 100, which means 100 percent of the $1,000 face value, the notes have a yield to maturity of 10 percent. The notes are not callable, which means that the debt may not be paid off before maturity.

unsecured debt
Bonds, notes, or other debt issued with no specific collateral pledged as security for the bond issue.

The Software Iz Us notes are **unsecured debt**, which means that no specific collateral has been pledged as security for the notes. In the event that the issuer defaults on its promised payments, the noteholders may take legal action to acquire sufficient assets of the company to settle their claims as creditors.

When issued, the Software Iz Us notes were not reviewed by a rating agency like Moody's or Standard & Poor's. Thus, the notes are unrated. If the notes were to be assigned a credit rating, they would probably be rated as "junk grade." The term "junk," commonly used for high-risk debt issues, is unduly pejorative. After all, your company must repay the debt. However, the high-risk character of the software industry portends an above-average probability that your company may have difficulty paying off the debt in a timely manner.

Reflecting their below-average credit quality, the Software Iz Us notes were not issued to the general public. Instead, the notes were privately placed with two insurance companies. Such private placements are common among relatively small debt issues. Private placements will be discussed in greater detail later in this chapter.

17.2 Types of Corporate Bonds

debentures
Unsecured bonds issued by a corporation.

Debentures are the most frequently issued type of corporate bond. Debenture bonds represent an unsecured debt of a corporation. Debenture bondholders have a legal claim as general creditors of the corporation. In the event of a default by the issuing corporation, the bondholders' claim extends to all corporate assets. However, they may have to share this claim with other creditors who have an equal legal claim or yield to creditors with a higher legal claim.

In addition to debentures, there are three other basic types of corporate bonds: mortgage bonds, collateral trust bonds, and equipment trust certificates. **Mortgage bonds** represent debt issued with a lien on specific property, usually real estate, pledged as security for the bonds. A mortgage lien gives bondholders the legal right to foreclose on property pledged by the issuer to satisfy an unpaid debt obligation. However, in actual practice, foreclosure and sale of mortgaged property following a default may not be the most desirable strategy for bondholders. Instead, it is common for a corporation in financial distress to reorganize itself and negotiate a new debt contract with bondholders. In these negotiations, a mortgage lien can be an important bargaining tool for the trustee representing the bondholders.

Collateral trust bonds are characterized by a pledge of financial assets as security for the bond issue. Collateral trust bonds are commonly issued by holding companies, which may pledge the stocks, bonds, or other securities issued by their subsidiaries as collateral for their own bond issue. The legal arrangement for pledging collateral securities is similar to that for a mortgage lien. In the event of an issuer's default on contractual obligations to bondholders, the bondholders have a legal right to foreclose on collateralized securities in the amount necessary to settle an outstanding debt obligation.

Equipment trust certificates represent debt issued by a trustee to purchase heavy industrial equipment that is leased and used by railroads, airlines, and other companies with a demand for heavy equipment. Under this financial arrangement, investors purchase equipment trust certificates, and the proceeds from this sale are used to purchase equipment. Formal ownership of the equipment remains with a trustee appointed to represent the certificate holders. The trustee then leases the equipment to a company. In return, the company promises to make a series of scheduled lease payments over a specified leasing period. The trustee collects the lease payments and distributes all revenues, less expenses, as dividends to the certificate holders. These distributions are conventionally called dividends because they are generated as income from a trust. The lease arrangement usually ends after a specified number of years when the leasing company makes a final lease payment and may take possession of the used equipment. From the certificate holders' point of view, this financial arrangement is superior to a mortgage lien since they actually own the equipment during the leasing period. Thus, if the leasing corporation defaults, the equipment can be sold without the effort and expense of a formal foreclosure process. Since the underlying equipment for this type of financing is typically built according to an industry standard, the equipment can usually be quickly sold or leased to another company in the same line of business.

Figure 17.1 is a *Wall Street Journal* bond announcement for an aircraft equipment trust for Northwest Airlines. Notice that the $243 million issue is split into two parts: $177 million of senior notes paying 8.26 percent interest and $66 million of subordinated notes paying 9.36 percent interest. The senior notes have a first claim on the aircraft in the event of a default by the airline, while the subordinated notes have a secondary claim. In the event of a default, investment losses for the trust will primarily be absorbed by the subordinated noteholders. For this reason the subordinated notes are riskier and, therefore, pay a higher interest rate. Of course, if no default actually occurs, it would turn out that the subordinated notes were actually a better investment. However, there is no way of knowing this in advance.

---

mortgage bond Debt secured with a property lien.

collateral trust bond Debt secured with financial collateral.

equipment trust certificate Shares in a trust with income from a lease contract.

Visit the Northwest Airlines website at www.nwa.com

FIGURE 17.1   Equipment Trust Notes Issue

These securities have not been registered under the Securities Act of 1933 and may not be offered or sold in the United States or to U.S. persons except in accordance with the resale restrictions applicable thereto. These securities having been previously sold, this announcement appears as a matter of record only.

$243,000,000

NWA Trust No. 1

$177,000,000 8.26% Class A Senior Aircraft Notes
$66,000,000 9.36% Class B Subordinated Aircraft Notes

The 8.26% Class A Senior Aircraft Notes and the 9.36% Class B Subordinated Aircraft Notes are secured by, among other things, a security interest in certain aircraft sold by Northwest Airlines, Inc. ("Northwest") to an owner trust for a purchase price of $443 million and the lease relating to such Aircraft, including the right to receive amounts payable by Northwest under such lease. The Noteholders also have the benefit of a liquidity facility, initially provided by General Electric Capital Corporation, to support certain payments of interest on the Notes.

Lehman Brothers   BT Securities Corporation

Source: Reprinted by permission of Dow Jones & Company, Inc., via Copyright Clearance Center, Inc., © 1994 Dow Jones & Company, Inc. All Rights Reserved Worldwide.

Check This

17.2a	Given that a bond issue is one of the four basic types discussed in this section, how would the specific bond type affect the credit quality of the bond?
17.2b	Why might some bond types be more or less risky with respect to the risk of default?
17.2c	Given that a default has occurred, why might the trustee's job of representing the financial interests of the bondholders be easier for some bond types than for others?

17.3 Bond Indentures

indenture summary
Description of the contractual terms of a new bond issue included in a bond's prospectus.

prospectus Document prepared as part of a security offering detailing information about a company's financial position, its operations, and investment plans.

A bond indenture is a formal written agreement between the corporation and the bond-holders. It is an important legal document that spells out in detail the mutual rights and obligations of the corporation and the bondholders with respect to the bond issue. Indenture contracts are often quite long, sometimes several hundred pages, and make for very tedious reading. In fact, very few bond investors ever read the original indenture, but instead might refer to an **indenture summary** provided in the **prospectus** that was circulated when the bond issue was originally sold to the public. Alternatively, a summary of the most important features of an indenture is published by debt rating agencies.

The Trust Indenture Act of 1939 requires that any bond issue subject to regulation by the Securities and Exchange Commission (SEC), which includes most corporate bond and note issues sold to the general public, must have a trustee appointed to represent the interests of the bondholders. Also, all responsibilities of a duly appointed trustee must be specified in detail in the indenture. Some corporations maintain a blanket or open-ended indenture that applies to all currently outstanding bonds and any new bonds that are issued, while other corporations write a new indenture contract for each new bond issue sold to the public.

Descriptions of the most important provisions frequently specified in a bond indenture agreement are presented next.

Bond Seniority Provisions

The Trust Indenture Act of 1939 is available at the SEC website www.sec.gov

A corporation may have several different bond issues outstanding; these issues normally can be differentiated according to the seniority of their claims on the firm's assets. Seniority usually is specified in the indenture contract.

Consider a corporation with two outstanding bond issues: (1) a mortgage bond issue with certain real estate assets pledged as security and (2) a debenture bond issue with no specific assets pledged as security. In this case, the mortgage bond issue has a senior claim on the pledged assets but no specific claim on other corporate assets. The debenture bond has a claim on all corporate assets not specifically pledged as security for the mortgage bond, but it would have only a residual claim on assets pledged as security for the mortgage bond issue. This residual claim would apply only after all obligations to the mortgage bondholders have been satisfied.

As another example, suppose a corporation has two outstanding debenture issues. In this case, seniority is normally assigned to the bonds first issued by the corporation.

senior debentures
Bonds that have a higher claim on the firm's assets than other bonds.

subordinated debentures Bonds that have a claim on the firm's assets after those with a higher claim have been satisfied.

negative pledge clause Bond indenture provision that prohibits new debt from being issued with seniority over an existing issue.

bond refunding Process of calling an outstanding bond issue and refinancing it with a new bond issue.

The bonds issued earliest have a senior claim on the pledged assets and are called **senior debentures**. The bonds issued later have a junior or subordinate claim and are called **subordinated debentures**.

The seniority of an existing debt issue is usually protected by a **negative pledge clause** in the bond indenture. A negative pledge clause prohibits a new issue of debt with seniority over a currently outstanding issue. However, it may allow a new debt issue to share equally in the seniority of an existing issue. A negative pledge clause is part of the indenture agreement of most senior debenture bonds.

Call Provisions

Most corporate bond issues have a call provision allowing the issuer to buy back all or part of its outstanding bonds at a specified call price sometime before the bonds mature. The most frequent motive for a corporation to call outstanding bonds is to take advantage of a general fall in market interest rates. Lower interest rates allow the corporation to replace currently outstanding high-coupon bonds with a new issue of bonds paying lower coupons. Replacing existing bonds with new bonds is called **bond refunding**.

From an investor's point of view, a call provision has a distinct disadvantage. For example, suppose an investor is currently holding bonds paying 10 percent coupons. Further suppose that, after a fall in market interest rates, the corporation is able to issue new bonds that only pay 8 percent coupons. By calling existing 10 percent coupon bonds, the issuer forces bondholders to surrender their bonds in exchange for the call price. But this happens at a time when the bondholders can reinvest funds only at lower interest rates. If instead the bonds were noncallable, the bondholders would continue to receive the original 10 percent coupons. For this reason, callable bonds are less attractive to investors than noncallable bonds. Consequently, a callable bond will sell at a lower price than a comparable noncallable bond.

Despite their lower prices, corporations generally prefer to issue callable bonds. However, to reduce the price gap between callable and noncallable bonds, issuers typically allow the indenture contract to specify certain restrictions on their ability to call an outstanding bond issue. Three features are commonly used to restrict an issuer's call privilege:

1. Callable bonds usually have a *deferred call provision* which provides a *call protection period* during which a bond issue cannot be called. For example, a bond may be call-protected for a period of five years after its issue date.

2. A call price often includes a *call premium* over par value. A standard arrangement stipulates a call premium equal to one-year's coupon payments for a call occurring at the earliest possible call date. Over time, the call premium is gradually reduced until it is eliminated entirely. After some future date, the bonds become callable at par value.

3. Some indentures specifically prohibit an issuer from calling outstanding bonds for the purpose of refunding at a lower coupon rate but still allow a call for other reasons. This *refunding provision* prevents the corporation from calling an outstanding bond issue solely as a response to falling market interest rates. However, the corporation can still pay off its bond debt ahead of schedule by using funds acquired from, say, earnings, or funds obtained from the sale of newly issued common stock.

FIGURE 17.2   **Callable and Noncallable Bonds**

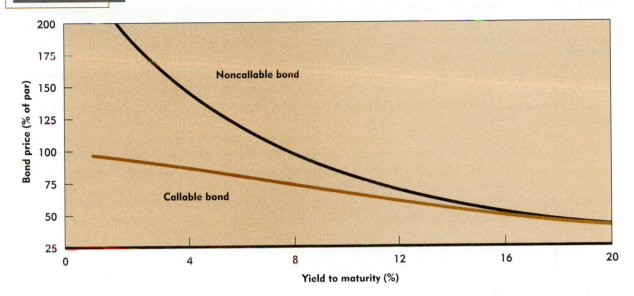

Graphical Analysis of Callable Bond Prices

After a bond's call protection period has elapsed, a rational investor would be unwilling to pay much more than the call price for the bond since the issuer might call the bond at any time and pay only the call price for the bond. Consequently, a bond's call price serves as an effective ceiling on its market price. It is important for bond investors to understand how the existence of a price ceiling for callable bonds alters the standard price-yield relationship for bonds.

The relationship between interest rates and prices for comparable callable and noncallable bonds is illustrated in Figure 17.2. In this example, the vertical axis measures bond prices, and the horizontal axis measures bond yields. In this two-bond example, both bonds pay an 8 percent coupon and are alike in all respects except that one of the bonds is callable any time at par value.

As shown, the noncallable bond has the standard *convex price-yield relationship*, where the price-yield curve is bowed toward the origin. When the price-yield curve is bowed to the origin this is called *positive convexity*. In contrast, the callable bond has a convex or bowed price-yield relationship in the region of high yields, but is bowed away from the origin in the region of low yields. This is called *negative convexity*. The important lesson here is that no matter how low market interest rates might fall, the maximum price of an unprotected callable bond is generally bounded above by its call price.

Check This

17.3a   After a call protection period has elapsed, why is the call price an effective ceiling on the market price of a callable bond?

Put Provisions

put bonds Bonds that can be sold back to the issuer at a prespecified price on any of a sequence of prespecified dates. Also called *extendible bonds*.

A bond issue with a put provision grants bondholders the right to sell their bonds back to the issuer at a special *put price*, normally set at par value. These so-called **put bonds** are "putable" on each of a series of designated *put dates*. These are often scheduled to occur annually but sometimes occur at more frequent intervals. At each put date, the bondholder decides whether to sell the bond back to the issuer or continue to hold the bond until the next put date. For this reason, put bonds are often called *extendible bonds* because the bondholder has the option of extending the maturity of the bond at each put date.

Notice that by granting bondholders an option to sell their bonds back to the corporation at par value, the put feature provides an effective floor on the market price of the bond. Thus, the put feature offers protection to bondholders from rising interest rates and the associated fall in bond prices.

A put feature also helps protect bondholders from acts of the corporation that might cause a deterioration of the bond's credit quality. However, this protection is not granted without a cost to bond investors, since a putable bond will command a higher market price than a comparable nonputable bond.

Check This

17.3b   Using Figure 17.2 as a guide, what would the price-yield relationship look like for a noncallable bond putable at par value?

17.3c   Under what conditions would a put feature not yield an effective floor for the market price of a put bond? (*Hint*: Think about default risk.)

Bond-to-Stock Conversion Provisions

convertible bonds Bonds that holders can exchange for common stock according to a prespecified conversion ratio.

Some bonds have a valuable bond-to-stock conversion feature. These bonds are called convertible bonds. **Convertible bonds** grant bondholders the right to exchange each bond for a designated number of common stock shares of the issuing firm. To avoid confusion in a discussion of convertible bonds, it is important to understand some basic terminology.

1. The number of common stock shares acquired in exchange for each converted bond is called the *conversion ratio*:

   Conversion ratio = Number of stock shares acquired by conversion

2. The par value of a convertible bond divided by its conversion ratio is called the bond's *conversion price*:

$$\text{Conversion price} = \frac{\text{Bond par value}}{\text{Conversion ratio}}$$

3. The market price per share of common stock acquired by conversion times the bond's conversion ratio is called the bond's *conversion value*:

   Conversion value = Price per share of stock × Conversion ratio

For example, suppose a convertible bond with a par value of $1,000 can be converted into 20 shares of the issuing firm's common stock. In this case, the conversion price is $1,000 / 20 = $50. Continuing this example, suppose the firm's common stock has a market price of $40 per share, then the conversion value of a single bond is 20 × $40 = $800.

Figure 17.3 is *The Wall Street Journal* announcement of an issue of convertible subordinated notes by Advanced Micro Devices (AMD). The notes pay a 6 percent coupon rate and mature in 2005. The conversion price for this note issue is $37 per share, which implies a conversion ratio of 27.027 shares of common stock for each $1,000 face value note.

From an investor's perspective, the conversion privilege of convertible bonds has the distinct advantage that bondholders can receive a share of any increase in common stock value. However, the conversion option has a price. A corporation can sell convertible bonds at par value with a coupon rate substantially less than the coupon rate of comparable nonconvertible bonds. This forgone coupon interest represents the price of the bond's conversion option.

When convertible bonds are originally issued, their conversion ratio is customarily set to yield a conversion value 10 percent to 20 percent less than par value. For example, suppose the common stock of a company has a price of $30 per share and the company issues convertible bonds with a par value of $1,000 per bond. To set the original conversion value at $900 per bond, the company would set a conversion ratio of 30 stock shares per bond. Thereafter, the conversion ratio is fixed, but each bond's conversion value becomes linked to the firm's stock price, which may rise or fall in value. The price of a convertible bond reflects the conversion value of the bond. In general, the higher the conversion value the higher is the bond price, and vice versa.

Investing in convertible bonds is more complicated than owning nonconvertible bonds, because the conversion privilege presents convertible bondholders with an important timing decision. When is the best time to exercise a bond's conversion option and exchange the bond for shares of common stock? The answer is that investors should normally postpone conversion as long as possible, because while they hold the bonds they continue to receive coupon payments. After converting to common stock, they lose all subsequent coupons. In general, unless the total dividend payments on stock acquired by conversion are somewhat greater than the forgone bond coupon payments, investors should hold on to their convertible bonds to continue to receive coupon payments.

The rational decision of convertible bondholders to postpone conversion as long as possible is limited, however, since convertible bonds are almost always callable. Firms customarily call outstanding convertible bonds when their conversion value has risen by 10 percent to 15 percent above bond par value, although there are many exceptions to this rule. When a convertible bond issue is called by the issuer, bondholders are forced to make an immediate decision whether to convert to common stock shares or accept a cash payment of the call price. Fortunately, the decision is simple—convertible bondholders should choose whichever is more valuable, the call price or the conversion value.

Check This

17.3d Describe the conversion decision that convertible bondholders must make when the bonds mature.

FIGURE 17.3 Convertible Notes Issue

This announcement is neither an offer to sell, nor a solicitation of an offer to buy, any of these securities. The offer is made only by the Prospectus and related Prospectus Supplement.

$517,500,000

AMD

Advanced Micro Devices, Inc.

6% Convertible Subordinated Notes due 2005

The 6% Convertible Subordinated Notes due 2005 (the "Notes") will be convertible at the option of the holder into shares of common stock, par value $.01 per share (the "Common Stock"), of Advanced Micro Devices, Inc. (the "Company") at any time at or prior to maturity, unless previously redeemed or repurchased, at a conversion price of $37.00 per share (equivalent to a conversion rate of 27.027 shares per $1,000 principal amount of Notes), subject to adjustment in certain events.

Price 100%

Copies of the Prospectus and related Prospectus Supplement may be obtained in any State from such of the undersigned as may legally offer these securities in compliance with the securities laws of such State.

Donaldson, Lufkin & Jenrette
Securities Corporation

Salomon Smith Barney

Source: Reprinted with permission from Dow Jones & Company, Inc., via Copyright Clearance Center, Inc.,

Graphical Analysis of Convertible Bond Prices

The price of a convertible bond is closely linked to the value of the underlying common stock shares that can be acquired by conversion. A higher stock price implies a higher bond price, and, conversely, a lower stock price yields a lower bond price.

The relationship between the price of a convertible bond and the price of the firm's common stock is depicted in Figure 17.4. In this example, the convertible bond's price is measured on the vertical axis, and the stock price is measured along the horizontal axis. The straight, upward-sloping line is the bond's conversion value; the slope of the line is the conversion ratio. The horizontal line represents the price of a comparable nonconvertible bond with the same coupon rate, maturity, and credit quality.

in-the-money bond A convertible bond whose conversion value is greater than its call price.

A convertible bond is said to be an **in-the-money bond** when its conversion value is greater than its call price. If an in-the-money convertible bond is called, rational bondholders will convert their bonds into common stock. When the conversion value is less than the call price, a convertible bond is said to be *out of the money*. If an out-of-the-money bond is called, rational bondholders will accept the call price and forgo the conversion option. In practice, however, convertible bonds are seldom called when they are out of the money.

intrinsic bond value The price below which a convertible bond cannot fall, equal to the value of a comparable nonconvertible bond. Also called *investment value*.

The curved line in Figure 17.4 shows the relationship between a convertible bond's price and the underlying stock price. As shown, there are two lower bounds on the value of a convertible bond. First, a convertible bond's price can never fall below its **intrinsic bond value**, also commonly called its *investment value* or *straight bond value*. This value is what the bond would be worth if it were not convertible, but otherwise identical in terms of coupon, maturity, and credit quality. Second, a convertible bond can never sell for less than its *conversion value* because, if it did, investors could simply buy the bond and convert, thereby realizing an immediate, riskless profit.

Thus, the *floor value* of a convertible bond is its intrinsic bond value or its conversion value, whichever is larger. As shown in Figure 17.4, however, a convertible bond will generally sell for more than this floor value. This extra is the amount that investors

FIGURE 17.4   **Convertible Bond Prices**

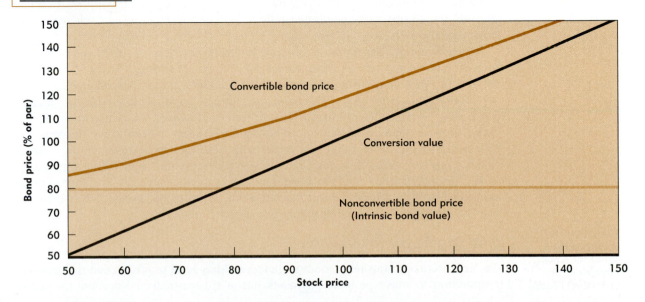

are willing to pay for the right, but not the obligation, to convert the bond at a future date at a potentially much higher stock price.

An interesting variation of a bond-to-stock conversion feature occurs when the company issuing the bonds is different from the company whose stock is acquired by the conversion. In this case, the bonds are called **exchangeable bonds**. Figure 17.5 presents a *Wall Street Journal* announcement of an issue of exchangeable subordinated debentures by the McKesson Corporation. These debentures are exchangeable for common stock shares of Armor All Products Corporation. McKesson is a retail distributor, and Armor All markets consumer chemical products. Exchangeable bonds, while not unusual, are less common than convertible bonds.

exchangeable bonds
Bonds that can be converted into common stock shares of a company other than the issuer's.

Check This

> **17.3e**   For nonconvertible bonds, the call price is a ceiling on the market price of the bond. Why might the call price not be an effective ceiling on the price of a convertible bond?

Bond Maturity and Principal Payment Provisions

term bonds Bonds issued with a single maturity date.

Term bonds represent the most common corporate bond maturity structure. A term bond issue has a single maturity date. On this date, all outstanding bond principal must be paid off. The indenture contract for a term bond issue normally stipulates the creation of a *sinking fund,* that is, an account established to repay bondholders through a series of fractional redemptions before the bond reaches maturity. Thus, at maturity, only a fraction of the original bond issue will still be outstanding. Sinking fund provisions are discussed in more detail later.

serial bonds Bonds issued with a regular sequence of maturity dates.

An alternative maturity structure is provided by **serial bonds**, where a fraction of an entire bond issue is scheduled to mature in each year over a specified period. Essentially, a serial bond issue represents a collection of subissues with sequential maturities. As an example, a serial bond issue may stipulate that one-tenth of an entire bond issue must be redeemed in each year over a 10-year period, with the last fraction redeemed at maturity. Serial bonds generally do not have a call provision, whereas term bonds usually do have a call provision.

When originally issued, most corporate bonds have maturities of 30 years or less. However, in recent years some companies have issued bonds with 40- and 50-year maturities. In 1993, Walt Disney Company made headlines in the financial press when it sold 100-year maturity bonds. This bond issue became popularly known as the "Sleeping Beauty" bonds, after the classic Disney movie. However, the prince might arrive early for these bonds since they are callable after 30 years. Nevertheless, this was the first time since 1954 that 100-year bonds were sold by any borrower in the United States. Only days later, however, Coca-Cola issued $150 million of 100-year maturity bonds. Both the Disney and Coke bond issues locked in the unusually low interest rates prevailing in 1993. *The Wall Street Journal* article covering the Disney century bond issue is reproduced in the accompanying *Investment Updates* box.

Sinking Fund Provisions

sinking fund An account used to provide for scheduled redemptions of outstanding bonds.

The indentures of most term bonds include a **sinking fund** provision that requires the corporation to make periodic payments into a trustee-managed account. Account

FIGURE 17.5 Exchangeable Debentures Issue

This announcement is neither an offer to sell nor a solicitation of an offer to buy any of these Securities.
The offer is made only by the Prospectus.

$180,000,000

McKesson Corporation

4½% Exchangeable Subordinated Debentures Due 2004

Exchangeable for Shares of Common Stock of
Armor All Products Corporation

Interest Payable March 1 and September 1

Price 100% and Accrued Interest, if any

Copies of the Prospectus may be obtained in any State from only such
of the undersigned as may legally offer these Securities in
compliance with the securities laws of such State.

MORGAN STANLEY & CO.
Incorporated

MONTGOMERY SECURITIES

MONNESS, CRESPI, HARDT & CO. INC.   **WHEAT FIRST BUTCHER & SINGER**
Capital Markets

Disney Amazes Investors with Sale of 100-Year Bonds

The corporate race to lock in low credit costs hit a fever pitch as Walt Disney Co. began marketing the first 100-year bonds to be sold by any borrower since 1954.

Bond traders were stunned to hear that the entertainment concern is expecting to sell $150 million of 100-year bonds at a yield of only about 7.5%, barely 0.95 percentage points above 30-year U.S. Treasury bonds.

"It's crazy," said William Gross, head of fixed-income investments at Pacific Investment Management Co. Noting the ups and downs of the entertainment industry, he said: "Look at the path of Coney Island over the last 50 years and see what happens to amusement parks."

"Obviously we're going through a phase in the market where everyone is pushing the envelope where they can," said Glenn Murphy, chief investment officer of Travelers Asset Management, Inc. The Disney issue will turn out to be a "historic artifact, a curiosity," he said.

Disney's bond issue may not really be around for a century. It can be called away from investors by the company after 30 years. But demand for the issue is said to be brisk and there is even some talk that the offering size might be increased.

The 100-year buyers are expected to be the usual flock of pension funds, insurers, and financial advisers, according to Mark Seigel, head of corporate underwriting at Morgan Stanley & Co., which will lead the underwriting. Merrill Lynch & Co. will co-manage the deal.

While 100-year bonds are rare, they seem a fitting climax to a recent flurry of very long-dated corporate bonds. So far this year, five companies have sold 50-year bonds for a total of $1.13 billion. Last year one company sold 50-year bonds, and before that, none had sold such long-dated securities in decades.

Demand for such long-dated bond issues has grown in recent months because investors, sick of measly returns, are becoming more willing to shoulder greater risks in return for higher yields, even marginally higher ones as in the case of the Disney bonds.

reserves are then used to provide for scheduled redemptions of outstanding bonds. The existence of a sinking fund is an important consideration for bond investors mainly for two reasons:

1. A sinking fund provides a degree of security to bondholders, since payments into the sinking fund can be used only to pay outstanding obligations to bondholders.

2. A sinking fund provision requires fractional bond issue redemptions according to a preset schedule. Therefore, some bondholders will be repaid their invested principal before the stated maturity for their bonds whether they want repayment or not.

As part of a *scheduled sinking fund redemption*, some bondholders may be forced to surrender their bonds in exchange for cash payment of a special *sinking fund call price*. For this reason, not all bondholders may be able to hold their bonds until maturity, even though the entire bond issue has not been called according to a general call provision. For example, the indenture for a 25-year maturity bond issue may require that one-twentieth of the bond issue be retired annually, beginning immediately after an initial 5-year call protection period.

Typically, when a redemption is due, the sinking fund trustee will select bonds by lottery. Selected bonds are then called, and the affected bondholders receive the call price, which for sinking fund redemptions is usually par value. However, the issuer normally has a valuable option to buy back the required number of bonds in the open market and deliver them to the sinking fund trustee instead of delivering the cash required for a par value redemption. Issuers naturally prefer to exercise this option when bonds can be repurchased in the open market at less than par value.

Check This

17.3f   For bond investors, what are some of the advantages and disadvantages of a sinking fund provision?

Coupon Payment Provisions

Coupon rates are stated on an annual basis. For example, an 8 percent coupon rate indicates that the issuer promises to pay 8 percent of a bond's face value to the bondholder each year. However, splitting an annual coupon into two semiannual payments is an almost universal practice in the United States. An exact schedule of coupon payment dates is specified in the bond indenture when the bonds are originally issued.

If a company suspends payment of coupon interest, it is said to be in default. Default is a serious matter. In general, bondholders have an unconditional right to the timely payment of interest and principal. They also have a right to bring legal action to enforce such payments. Upon suspension of coupon payments, the bondholders could, for example, demand an acceleration of principal repayment along with all past-due interest. However, a corporation in financial distress has a right to seek protection in bankruptcy court from inflexible demands by bondholders. As a practical matter, it is often in the best interests of both the bondholders and the corporation to negotiate a new debt contract. Indeed, bankruptcy courts normally encourage a settlement that minimizes any intervention on their part.

17.4 Protective Covenants

protective covenants
Restrictions in a bond indenture designed to protect bondholders.

In addition to the provisions already discussed, a bond indenture is likely to contain a number of **protective covenants**. These agreements are designed to protect bondholders by restricting the actions of a corporation that might cause a deterioration in the credit quality of a bond issue. Protective covenants can be classified into two types: negative covenants and positive, or affirmative, covenants.

A *negative covenant* is a "thou shalt not" for the corporation. Here are some examples of negative covenants that might be found in an indenture agreement:

1. The firm cannot pay dividends to stockholders in excess of what is allowed by a formula based on the firm's earnings.

2. The firm cannot issue new bonds that are senior to currently outstanding bonds. Also, the amount of a new bond issue cannot exceed an amount specified by a formula based on the firm's net worth.

3. The firm cannot refund an existing bond issue with new bonds paying a lower coupon rate than the currently outstanding bond issue it would replace.

4. The firm cannot buy bonds issued by other companies, nor can it guarantee the debt of any other company.

A *positive covenant* is a "thou shalt." It specifies things that a corporation must do, or conditions that it must abide by. Here are some common examples of positive covenants:

1. Proceeds from the sale of assets must be used either to acquire other assets of equal value or to redeem outstanding bonds.

2. In the event of a merger, acquisition, or spinoff, the firm must give bondholders the right to redeem their bonds at par value.

3. The firm must maintain the good condition of all assets pledged as security for an outstanding bond issue.

4. The firm must periodically supply audited financial information to bondholders.

Check This

17.4a   Why would a corporation voluntarily include protective covenants in its bond indenture contract?

17.5 Event Risk

event risk The possibility that the issuing corporation will experience a significant change in its bond credit quality.

Protective covenants in a bond indenture help shield bondholders from event risk. **Event risk** is broadly defined as the possibility that some structural or financial change to the corporation will cause a significant deterioration in the credit quality of a bond issue, thereby causing the affected bonds to lose substantial market value.

A classic example of event risk, and what could happen to bondholders without adequate covenant protection, is provided by an incident involving Marriott Corporation, best known for its chain of hotels and resorts. In October 1992, Marriott announced its intention to spin off part of the company. The spinoff, called Host Marriott, would acquire most of the parent company's debt and its poorly performing real estate holdings. The parent, Marriott International, would be left relatively debt-free with possession of most of the better performing properties, including its hotel management division.

On the announcement date, the affected Marriott bonds fell in value by about 30 percent, reflecting severe concern about the impact of the spinoff on the credit quality of the bonds. On the same day, Marriott stock rose in value by about 30 percent, reflecting a large wealth transfer from bondholders to stockholders. A subsequent bondholder legal challenge was unsuccessful. Standard & Poor's later announced that it was formally revising its credit ratings on Marriott bonds to recognize the impact of the spinoff. (Credit ratings are discussed in detail in a later section.) Debt remaining with Marriott International would have an investment-grade rating, while bonds assigned to Host Marriott would have junk bond status. *The Wall Street Journal* report covering the story is reproduced in the nearby *Investment Updates* box.

Visit Marriott and Host Marriott websites at www.marriott.com and www.hostmarriott.com

Check This

17.5a   What are some possible protective covenants that would have protected Marriott bondholders from the adverse impact of the spinoff described here?

Marriott Corp. shareholders approved a plan to split the company into a real-estate concern, with most of Marriott's debt, and a high-growth hotel-management company.

The split, approved by 85% of the shares voted, was the main issue at Marriott's annual meeting Friday. Under the plan, which is expected to take effect in September, stockholders will receive a share of Marriott International, Inc., the hotel-management operation, for each Marriott share they own. Then Marriott Corp. will be renamed Host Marriott Corp., an entity that will operate the real-estate side of the business.

The plan stunned bondholders when it was announced in October. They argued that the financial support of their debt was being undermined, and a suit by some of the bondholders is still pending.

Marriott shares have risen 60% since the plan's announcement. In New York Stock Exchange trading Friday, Marriott closed at $27.785, up 12.5 cents. The stock has traded as low as $15.50 in the past year.

The Marriott family controls more than 25% of the 100.8 million shares outstanding as of Jan. 1.

Marriott's directors set a distribution date for the split dividend of Sept. 10 for shares of record Sept. 1.

J. W. Marriott, 61 years old and currently chairman and president of the company, will be chairman, president and chief executive officer of Marriott International, while his brother, Richard E. Marriott, 54, will be chairman of Host Marriott. Richard Marriott is currently vice chairman and executive vice president of the company.

In addition to the bondholders' lawsuit seeking to block the reorganization, Marriott had faced a suit by holders of preferred stock. Marriott said that the holders have agreed to dismiss their case and convert their preferred shares into common stock.

The suit by the group of bondholders, representing about a dozen institutional investors, is still pending, however. Under the reorganization plan, holders of about $1.5 billion in Marriott bonds would have the option to swap their notes for new notes of a unit of the new real-estate entity. The company will retain $2.1 billion of Marriott's $3 billion long-term debt and will own 139 hotels and other real-estate assets.

Larry Kill, attorney for the bondholders, said the suit would proceed despite the shareholder vote. "This was a very unfair transaction," he said.

As a separate company, Host Marriott would have had about $1.2 billion in sales in 1992, according to the company's estimates. Marriott International, Inc., the new hotel concern, will operate more than 760 hotels through Marriott's four hotel-management units and related management services. Marriott International would have had $7.8 billion in sales last year, the company estimates.

In 1992, Marriott had net income of $85 million, or 64 cents a share, on sales of $8.72 billion. It had about $3 billion in long-term debt as of Jan. 1.

Moody's Investors Service, Inc., downgraded its ratings on the senior unsecured debt of Marriott Corp., affecting about $2.3 billion in debt, to Ba-2 from single-B-2. Moody's said the bond-exchange plan will leave a Host Marriott unit highly leveraged "with modest debt protection." Moody's said it expects only gradual improvement in operating earnings, given the sluggish economy and glut of hotel rooms. Moody's said, however, that the Host Marriott unit will be well-positioned for increased earnings when the recovery hits full speed.

Source: Jyoti Thottam, *The Wall Street Journal*, July 26, 1993. Reprinted by permission of Dow Jones & Company, Inc., via Copyright Clearance Center, Inc. © 1993 Dow Jones & Company, Inc. All Rights Reserved Worldwide.

17.6 Bonds without Indentures

private placement A new bond issue sold to one or more parties in private transactions not available to the public.

The Trust Indenture Act of 1939 does not require an indenture when a bond issue is not sold to the general public. For example, the bonds may be sold only to one or more financial institutions in what is called a **private placement**. Private placements are exempt from registration requirements with the SEC. Nevertheless, even privately placed debt issues often have a formal indenture contract.

When a corporation issues debt without an indenture, it makes an unconditional promise to pay interest and principal according to a simple debt contract. Debt issued without an indenture is basically a simple IOU of the corporation. Bond analysts sometimes reserve the designation "bonds" to mean corporate debt subject to an indenture and refer to corporate debt not subject to an indenture as "notes." However, it is more common to distinguish between bonds and notes on the basis of maturity, where bonds designate relatively long maturities, say, 10 years or longer, and notes designate maturities less than 10 years. Both definitions overlap since most long-term debt is issued subject to an indenture, and most privately placed short-term debt is issued as a simple IOU. In between, however, privately placed intermediate-maturity debt may or may not be issued subject to an indenture and therefore might be referred to as either a bond or a note regardless of the existence of an indenture. As in any profession, the jargon of investments is sometimes ambiguous.

17.7 Preferred Stock

preferred stock A security with a claim to dividend payments that is senior to common stock.

Preferred stock has some of the features of both bonds and common stock. Preferred stockholders have a claim to dividend payments that is senior to the claim of common stockholders—hence the term "preferred stock." However, their claim is subordinate to the claims of bondholders and other creditors. A typical preferred stock issue has the following basic characteristics:

1. Preferred stockholders do not normally participate with common stockholders in the election of a board of directors. However, a few preferred stock issues do grant voting rights to their holders.

2. Preferred stockholders are promised a stream of fixed dividend payments. Thus, preferred dividends resemble bond coupons.

3. Preferred stock normally has no specified maturity, but it is often callable by the issuer.

4. Management can suspend payment of preferred dividends without setting off a bankruptcy process, but only after suspending payment of all common stock dividends.

5. If preferred dividends have been suspended, all unpaid preferred dividends normally become a cumulative debt that must be paid in full before the corporation can resume any payment of common stock dividends. Preferred stock with this feature is termed *cumulative preferred*.

6. Some preferred stock issues have a conversion feature similar to convertible bonds. These are called *convertible preferred stock*.

All else equal, preferred stock normally pays a lower interest rate to investors than do corporate bonds. This is because, when most investors buy preferred stock, the dividends received are taxed at the same rate as bond interest payments. However, if a business corporation buys preferred stock, it can usually exclude at least 70 percent of the preferred dividends from income taxation. As a result, most preferred stock is owned by corporations that can take advantage of the preferential tax treatment of preferred dividends. However, companies that issue ordinary preferred stock must treat preferred dividends the same as common stock dividends for tax purposes and, therefore, cannot deduct preferred dividends from their taxable income.

17.7a From the perspective of common stockholders and management, what are some of the advantages of issuing preferred stock instead of bonds or new shares of common stock?

17.8 Adjustable-Rate Bonds and Adjustable-Rate Preferred Stock

adjustable-rate bonds Securities that pay coupons that change according to a prespecified rule. Also called *floating-rate bonds* or simply *floaters*.

Many bond, note, and preferred stock issues allow the issuer to adjust the annual coupon according to a rule or formula based on current market interest rates. These securities are called **adjustable-rate bonds**; they are also sometimes called *floating-rate bonds* or *floaters*.

For example, a typical adjustment rule might specify that the coupon rate be reset annually to be equal to the current rate on 180-day maturity U.S. Treasury bills plus 2 percent. Alternatively, a more flexible rule might specify that the coupon rate on a bond issue cannot be set below 105 percent of the yield to maturity of newly issued five-year Treasury notes. Thus, if five-year Treasury notes have recently been sold to yield 6 percent, the minimum allowable coupon rate is $1.05 \times 6\% = 6.3\%$.

Adjustable-rate bonds and notes are often putable at par value. For this reason, an issuer may set a coupon rate above an allowable minimum to discourage bondholders from selling their bonds back to the corporation.

17.8a How does an adjustable coupon rate feature affect the interest rate risk of a bond?

17.8b How might bondholders respond if the coupon rate on an adjustable-rate putable bond was set below market interest rates?

17.9 Corporate Bond Credit Ratings

credit rating An assessment of the credit quality of a bond issue based on the issuer's financial condition.

When a corporation sells a new bond issue to investors, it usually subscribes to several bond rating agencies for a credit evaluation of the bond issue. Each contracted rating agency then provides a **credit rating**—an assessment of the credit quality of the bond issue based on the issuer's financial condition. Rating agencies charge a fee for this service. As part of the contractual arrangement between the bond issuer and the rating agency, the issuer agrees to allow a continuing review of its credit rating even if the rating deteriorates. Without a credit rating a new bond issue would be very difficult to sell to the public, which is why almost all bond issues originally sold to the general public have a credit rating assigned at the time of issuance. Also, most public bond issues have ratings assigned by several rating agencies.

Visit these rating
agency websites:
Duff & Phelps at
www.duffllc.com
Fitch at
www.fitchibca.com
Moody's at
www.moodys.com
S&P at
www.standardandpoors.
com
MCM at
www.mcmwatch.com

Established rating agencies in the United States include Duff and Phelps, Inc. (D&P); Fitch Investors Service (Fitch); McCarthy, Crisanti and Maffei (MCM); Moody's Investors Service (Moody's); and Standard & Poor's Corporation (S&P). Of these, the two best known rating agencies are Moody's and Standard & Poor's. These companies publish regularly updated credit ratings for thousands of domestic and international bond issues.

It is important to realize that corporate bond ratings are assigned to particular bond issues and not to the issuer of those bonds. For example, a senior bond issue is likely to have a higher credit rating than a subordinated issue even if both are issued by the same corporation. Similarly, a corporation with two bond issues outstanding may have a higher credit rating assigned to one issue because that issue has stronger covenant protection specified in the bond's indenture contract.

Seniority and covenant protection are not the only things affecting bond ratings. Bond rating agencies consider a number of factors before assigning a credit rating, including an appraisal of the financial strength of the issuer, the caliber of the issuer's management, and the issuer's position in an industry as well as the industry's position in the economy. In general, a bond rating is intended to be a comparative indicator of overall credit quality for a particular bond issue. However, the rating in itself is not a recommendation to buy or sell a bond.

Table 17.2 summarizes corporate bond rating symbols and definitions used by Moody's (first column), Duff and Phelps (second column), and Standard & Poor's (third column). As shown, bond credit ratings fall into three broad categories: investment grade, speculative grade, and extremely speculative grade.

Why Bond Ratings Are Important

Bond credit ratings assigned by independent rating agencies are quite important to bond market participants. Only a few institutional investors have the resources and expertise necessary to properly evaluate a bond's credit quality on their own. Bond ratings provide investors with reliable, professional evaluations of bond issues at a reasonable cost. This information is indispensable for assessing the economic value of a bond.

prudent investment guidelines
Restrictions on investment portfolios stipulating that securities purchased must meet a certain level of safety.

Furthermore, many financial institutions have **prudent investment guidelines** stipulating that only securities with a certain level of investment safety may be included in their portfolios. For example, bond investments for many pension funds are limited to investment-grade bonds rated at least Baa by Moody's or at least BBB by Standard & Poor's. Bond ratings provide a convenient measure to monitor implementation of these guidelines.

Individual investors investing in bonds also find published bond ratings useful. Individual investors generally do not have the ability to diversify as extensively as do large institutions. With limited diversification opportunities, an individual should invest only in bonds with higher credit ratings.

✔

Check This

17.9a   Does a low credit rating necessarily imply that a bond is a bad investment?

17.9b   What factors besides the credit rating might be important in deciding whether a particular bond is a worthwhile investment?

TABLE 17.2			Corporate Bond Credit Rating Symbols
Rating Agency			
Moody's	Duff and Phelps	Standard & Poor's	Credit Rating Description
Investment-Grade Bond Ratings			
Aaa	1	AAA	Highest credit rating, maximum safety
Aa1	2	AA+	
Aa2	3	AA	High credit quality, investment-grade bonds
Aa3	4	AA−	
A1	5	A+	
A2	6	A	Upper-medium quality, investment-grade bonds
A3	7	A−	
Baa1	8	BBB+	
Baa2	9	BBB	Lower-medium quality, investment-grade bonds
Baa3	10	BBB−	
Speculative-Grade Bond Ratings			
Ba1	11	BB+	Low credit quality, speculative-grade bonds
Ba2	12	BB	
Ba3	13	BB−	
B1	14	B+	Very low credit quality, speculative-grade bonds
B2	15	B	
B3	16	B−	
Extremely Speculative-Grade Bond Ratings			
Caa	17	CCC+	Extremely low credit standing, high-risk bonds
		CCC	
		CCC−	
Ca		CC	Extremely speculative
C		C	
		D	Bonds in default

17.10 Junk Bonds

high-yield bonds
Bonds with a speculative credit rating that is offset by a yield premium offered to compensate for higher credit risk. Also called *junk bonds*.

Bonds with a speculative or low grade rating—that is, those rated Ba or lower by Moody's or BB or lower by Standard & Poor's—are commonly called **high-yield bonds**, or, more colorfully, *junk bonds*. The designation "junk" is somewhat misleading and often unduly pejorative, since junk bonds *have* economic value. Junk bonds simply represent debt with a higher than average credit risk. To put the term in perspective, one should realize that most consumer debt and small business debt represents higher than average credit risk. Yet it is generally considered desirable from an economic and social perspective that credit be available to consumers and small businesses.

Junk bonds that were originally issued with an investment-grade credit rating that subsequently fell to speculative grade because of unforeseen economic events are called *fallen angels*. Another type, *original-issue junk*, is defined as bonds originally issued with a speculative-grade rating.

Junk bonds are attractive investments for many institutional investors with well-diversified portfolios. The logic of junk bond investing revolves around the possibility that the *yield premium* for junk bonds might be high enough to justify accepting the higher default rates of junk bonds. As an example of this logic, consider the following back-of-the-envelope calculations.

Suppose that the average yield on junk bonds is 10 percent when U.S. Treasury bonds yield 7 percent. In this case, the yield premium of junk bonds over default-free Treasury bonds is 3 percent. Further suppose that an investor expects about 4 percent of all outstanding junk bonds to default each year, and experience suggests that when junk bonds default bondholders on average receive 50 cents for each dollar of bond face value. Based on these rough assumptions, diversified junk bond investors expect to lose 2 percent (.04 × .50) of their portfolio value each year through defaults. But with a junk bond yield premium of 3 percent, the junk bond portfolio is expected to outperform U.S. Treasury bonds by 1 percent per year. It is true that a junk bond portfolio is much more expensive to manage than a Treasury bond portfolio. However, for a $1 billion bond portfolio, a junk bond yield premium of 1 percent represents $10 million of additional interest income per year. Our nearby *Work the Web* box has more on credit ratings and yield spreads.

Of course, actual default rates could turn out to be much different than expected. History suggests that the major determinant of aggregate bond default rates is the state of economic activity. During an expansionary economic period, bond default rates are usually low. But in a recession, default rates can rise dramatically. For this reason, the investment performance of a junk bond portfolio largely depends on the health of the economy.

Prices and yields of selected junk bonds are published regularly in *The Wall Street Journal* in its "High-Yield Bonds" report. A sample report is displayed in Figure 17.6. We discuss the data in Figure 17.6 in more detail in our next section. For an interesting discussion on investing in junk bonds, see the nearby *Investment Updates* box.

Check This

17.10a Can junk bond default risk be completely diversified away by large institutional bond investors?

17.10b From an investor's perspective, is there any importance in distinguishing between fallen angels and original-issue junk?

FIGURE 17.6

Junk Bond Trading

High-Yield Bonds

Monday, July 7, 2003

Ten most active fixed-coupon high-yield, or "junk", corporate bonds

COMPANY (TICKER)	COUPON	MATURITY	LAST PRICE	LAST YIELD	*EST SPREAD	UST†	EST VOL (000's)
Charter Communications Holdings (CHTR)	8.625	Apr 01, 2009	71.250	16.581	1400	5	44,079
Allied Waste North America (AW)	10.000	Aug 01, 2009	106.875	7.734	516	5	19,280
Huntsman International LLC (HUNTSM)	10.125	Jul 01, 2009	97.063	10.803	824	5	7,800
HMH Properties (HMT)	7.875	Aug 01, 2008	101.000	7.504	493	5	7,220
Nextel Communications (NXTL)	9.375	Nov 15, 2009	107.875	6.546	399	5	6,365
Fleming Companies (FLMIQ)	10.125	Apr 01, 2008	14.033	88.291	8573	5	5,580
Yum! Brands (YUM)	8.875	Apr 15, 2011	117.688	5.990	226	10	5,532
Lucent Technologies (LU)	6.450	Mar 15, 2029	69.500	9.688	495	30	4,985
Tenneco Automotive (TEN)	11.625	Oct 15, 2009	86.375	15.046	1249	5	4,050
Finova Group (FNVG)	7.500	Nov 15, 2009	43.750	26.074	2351	5	3,530

Volume represents total volume for each issue; price/yield data are for trades of $250,000 and greater. * Estimated spreads, in basis points (100 basis points is one percentage point), over the 2, 3, 5, 10 or 30-year hot run Treasury note/bond. 2-year: 1.125 06/05; 3-year: 2.000 05/06; 5-year: 2.625 05/08; 10-year: 3.625 05/13; 30-year: 5.375 02/31. †Comparable U.S. Treasury issue.

Source: MarketAxess Corporate BondTicker

WORK THE WEB

One important reason you need the credit rating for a bond is the yield spread. The yield spread is the extra return, in the form of an increased yield to maturity, that investors receive for buying a bond with a lower credit rating. Because of the credit risk, investors demand a risk premium for investing in lower rated bonds. You can create a yield curve for bonds with different credit ratings. We went to www.bondsonline.com and followed the "Corporate Bond Spreads" link. Here is what we got:

Reuters Corporate Spreads for Banks

Spreads compiled using : Reuters Evaluators ▾   Refresh   Download spread file

Rating	1 yr	2 yr	3 yr	5 yr	7 yr	10 yr	30 yr
Aaa/AAA	27	36	47	59	77	90	110
Aa1/AA+	33	49	53	68	87	101	121
Aa2/AA	35	54	56	72	90	103	124
Aa3/AA-	37	57	58	77	94	107	133
A1/A+	61	73	77	92	110	125	148
A2/A	64	76	79	94	111	127	151
A3/A-	68	79	82	98	115	130	153
Baa1/BBB+	81	98	104	123	158	184	207
Baa2/BBB	84	106	112	130	163	187	212
Baa3/BBB-	91	111	117	134	168	194	217
Ba1/BB+	605	615	625	635	655	675	695
Ba2/BB	615	625	635	645	665	685	705
Ba3/BB-	625	635	645	655	675	695	715
B1/B+	775	785	795	825	865	905	955
B2/B	785	795	805	835	875	915	965
B3/B-	795	805	815	845	885	925	975
Caa/CCC	1195	1205	1215	1240	1270	1330	1280

Note: Reuters Evaluator spreads for bullet bonds.

Here is how you interpret the table. If you look at the three-year Aaa/AAA-rated bonds, you will find the number 47. This means the yield spread is 47 basis points, or .47 percent greater than the yield to maturity for a three-year Treasury note. If you think credit rating is unimportant, look at the 30-year Caa/CCC bonds, where the spread above a comparable maturity Treasury bond is 12.80 percent!

17.11 Bond Market Trading

Consistent with the need to hold bonds for predictable cash flows, most corporate bond investors buy and hold bonds until they mature. However, many investors need

Stock Investors Could Stand a Little "Junk" in Their Diets

Hungry for healthy stock-market returns? Here's an intriguing suggestion: Buy junk bonds. Like stocks, junk (or "high yield") bonds have had a rough time lately. Mutual funds that invest in junk bonds tumbled an average 8.1% last year and shed an additional 1.8% in this year's first 10 months, according to Chicago researcher Morningstar Inc.

Stocks, of course, have suffered even more. Still, I believe there is a decent chance that high-yield bonds, those risky securities issued by heavily indebted companies, could outpace stocks in the years ahead. As I have argued in many columns this year, expected stock-market returns remain modest, despite the 30% decline in share prices. The outlook seems especially grim for blue-chip U.S. shares, which continue to sport nosebleed share-price-to-earnings multiples and skimpy dividend yields.

By contrast, junk bonds today offer lush 13% yields. Don't believe junk-bond prices will rebound soon? As they say on Wall Street, you are getting paid to wait. "One of the reasons investors may gravitate in this direction is, in part, because they don't see a lot of upside in stocks," says Martin Fridson, chief high-yield strategist at Merrill Lynch & Co. "They might say, 'Ordinarily, I'm not that excited about bonds, but that 12% or 13% looks pretty attractive right now.'"

Today's 13% yield is some nine percentage points higher than the yield on 10-year Treasury notes. How unusual is that? Put it this way: The spread between junk and Treasury yields was only slightly wider during the economic turmoil of 1990–91. That was the last time that junk bonds got really pummeled, and many investors still remember the pain. In the late 1980s, unscrupulous securities salesmen hawked junk-bond funds as higher-yielding certificates of deposit.

That fantasy was shredded in late 1989 and 1990, as junk-bond issuers struggled with an overdose of debt and a slowing economy. Junk-bond funds proved anything but safe, as their rich yields failed to compensate for shrinking fund-share prices. But for those who hung tough, the story had a happy ending. After getting hammered in 1990, both junk bonds and stocks came roaring back in 1991. In fact, in 1991, junk-bond funds soared an average 37.1%, rivaling the performance of diversified U.S.-stock funds. Naysayers might dismiss the parallels, noting that the economy is likely to deteriorate further in 2002, triggering a rash of defaults among junk-bond issuers. But that won't necessarily mean lousy junk-bond returns, says Ken Gregory, president of Litman/Gregory, a money manager in Orinda, Calif.

For instance, 1991 was a terrible year for junk-bond defaults, and yet the bonds posted fabulous gains. "Like every other financial asset, high-yield bonds discount the future," Mr. Gregory notes. "There are a lot of defaults forecasted for next year, but that's not inconsistent with high returns." In 1990–91, junk bonds and stocks seemed to move in lockstep, first losing money together and then rebounding together. But junk bonds could do well in the next few years, even if stocks don't. Mr. Gregory reckons that the worst-case scenario for junk bonds is "a zero return over the next 12 months," as slumping junk-bond prices and defaults wipe out the entire gain from the 13% yield. "I think the downside in stocks is a lot greater than that," Mr. Gregory says. "It's hard to argue that the stock market is at bargain levels. Over the next five years, I see annual returns of maybe 3% on the low side and 9% on the high side."

By contrast, junk bonds seem to offer far higher potential gains. Historically, junk-bond investors have lost 2% a year to defaults. Even if you subtract two percentage points from today's 13% yield, that still leaves investors collecting 11%. And returns could be much higher, if junk-bond prices bounce back. If you are intrigued by junk bonds, consider no-load funds such as Fidelity Capital & Income, Northeast Investors Trust, T. Rowe Price High-Yield, Strong High-Yield Bond and Vanguard High-Yield Corporate. According to Morningstar, all have expenses below 1%, managers with better-than-average five-year records, and investment minimums of $3,000 and below. Because junk funds are so tax inefficient, they are best held in a retirement account, unless you plan to spend the income.

Here's an added consideration: Don't buy a fund that has done too well this year. Again, cast your mind back to 1990–91. The 50% of funds that held up best in 1990 went on to gain an average 32.8% in 1991. But the funds that got hit hardest in 1990 did even better in 1991, climbing 42.1%. That suggests the best funds to own may be those that have made little or no money this year. "If you look just at the funds that have done best this year, you're limiting yourself to the higher-quality high-yield funds," Mr. Gregory says. "We would rather look at funds that we consider pure plays."

Source: Jonathan Clements, *The Wall Street Journal*, November 13, 2001. © 2001 Dow Jones & Company, Inc. All Rights Reserved Worldwide.

to liquidate some bonds before they mature, and others wish to purchase outstanding bonds originally issued by a particular corporation several years earlier. For these and many other reasons, the existence of an active secondary market for corporate bonds is important for most bond investors. Fortunately, an active secondary market with a substantial volume of bond trading does exist to satisfy most of the liquidity needs of investors.

Almost as many different bond issues are listed on the New York Stock Exchange (NYSE) as there are different common stock issues. These NYSE-traded bond issues represent the most actively traded bonds of large corporations. However, there are many more thousands of different corporate debt issues outstanding. Most of these debt issues trade in the over-the-counter (OTC) market. In fact, it is estimated that less than 1 percent of all corporate bond trading actually takes place on the New York Stock Exchange. While some bond trading activity occurs on the American Stock Exchange and other regional exchanges, corporate bond trading is characteristically an OTC activity.

Before mid-2002, the OTC corporate bond market had limited transparency, meaning that, unlike stocks, relatively little information was available on trading. This lack of transparency made it difficult for bond investors to get accurate, up-to-date prices. However, at the request of the Securities and Exchange Commission (SEC), recently adopted rules require reporting of corporate bond trades through what is known as the Trade Reporting and Compliance Engine (TRACE), and transparency has dramatically improved. As this is written, transaction prices are now reported on more than 4,000 bonds, amounting to approximately 75 percent of investment-grade market volume. More bonds will be added over time.

As shown in Figure 17.7, *The Wall Street Journal* now provides a daily snapshot of the data from TRACE by reporting on the 40 most active issues. The information reported is largely self-explanatory. The "Est Spread" is the estimated yield spread, in basis points, over a particular Treasury issue (the Treasury issue's maturity is supplied under "UST"). A "hot run" Treasury is the most recently issued of a particular maturity, better known as an "on-the-run" issue. Finally, the reported volume is the face value of bonds traded.

Learn more about TRACE at www.nasd.com/mkt sys/trace_info.asp See TRACE data at www.nasdbondinfo. com

Check This

17.11a All else equal, is an actively traded bond more or less risky as an investment than a thinly traded bond? (*Hint*: Is liquidity a good or a bad thing for a bond?)

17.11b Why might a current yield for a convertible bond be uninformative for the purpose of making a comparison between two or more bonds?

17.12 Summary and Conclusions

This chapter covers the important topic of corporate bonds, a major source of capital used by corporations. In this chapter we saw that:

1. A corporate bond represents a corporation's promise to pay bondholders a fixed sum of money at maturity, along with periodic payments of interest. The sum

FIGURE 17.7

Corporate Bond Trading

Corporate Bonds

Wednesday, June 25, 2003

Forty most active fixed-coupon corporate bonds

COMPANY (TICKER)	COUPON	MATURITY	LAST PRICE	LAST YIELD	*EST SPREAD	UST†	EST VOL (000's)
General Motors Acceptance (GMAC)	6.875	Aug 28, 2012	100.743	6.763	336	10	204,160
Ford Motor Credit (F)	7.250	Oct 25, 2011	104.129	6.595	319	10	185,587
General Motors Acceptance (GMAC)	8.000	Nov 01, 2031	100.106	7.989	352	30	180,144
Ford Motor Credit (F)	6.875	Feb 01, 2006	105.750	4.492	294	3	150,733
Tenet Healthcare (THC)	7.375	Feb 01, 2013	98.250	7.634	423	10	141,748
Tenet Healthcare (THC)	6.375	Dec 01, 2011	94.250	7.300	389	10	112,466
General Motors (GM)	7.200	Jan 15, 2011	101.726	6.902	350	10	92,063
Ford Motor Credit (F)	7.875	Jun 15, 2010	108.501	6.344	294	10	89,159
Walt Disney (DIS)-c	2.125	Apr 15, 2023	104.435	1.239	n.a.	n.a.	86,995
Ford Motor (F)	7.450	Jul 16, 2031	94.635	7.929	347	30	83,118
Medtronic (MDT)-c	1.250	Sep 15, 2021	105.097	0.139	n.a.	n.a.	82,112
DaimlerChrysler North America Holding (DCX)	4.050	Jun 04, 2008	99.680	4.122	184	5	75,056
General Motors Acceptance (GMAC)	6.750	Jan 15, 2006	106.220	4.145	259	3	62,824
AOL Time Warner (AOL)	5.625	May 01, 2005	106.472	2.015	74	2	61,459
Household Finance (HSBC)	6.500	Jan 24, 2006	111.175	2.023	47	3	61,008
AT&T Broadband (CMCSA)	8.375	Mar 15, 2013	126.182	4.945	154	10	60,811
General Motors Acceptance (GMAC)	7.750	Jan 19, 2010	108.042	6.235	288	10	59,233
General Electric Capital (GE)	5.375	Mar 15, 2007	111.023	2.259	9	5	55,399
General Motors Acceptance (GMAC)	5.125	May 09, 2008	99.840	5.161	290	5	54,758
Weyerhaeuser (WY)	6.750	Mar 15, 2012	114.619	4.685	128	10	54,084
Bear Stearns Companies (BSC)	4.650	Jul 02, 2018	99.018	4.742	134	10	52,630
General Motors Acceptance (GMAC)	7.500	Jul 15, 2005	107.695	3.558	227	2	52,496
Verizon Global Funding (VZ)	4.375	Jun 01, 2013	101.243	4.220	84	10	52,140
Ford Motor Credit (F)	7.600	Aug 01, 2005	107.750	3.703	243	2	51,665
Eop Operating Limited Partnership (EOP)	7.000	Jul 15, 2011	117.011	4.459	106	10	51,490
CIT Group (CIT)	7.625	Aug 16, 2005	110.790	2.410	113	2	50,274
General Dynamics (GD)	4.250	May 15, 2013	102.611	3.928	65	10	48,524
General Electric Capital (GE)	6.800	Nov 01, 2005	111.768	1.643	43	2	46,570
Ford Motor Credit (F)	7.375	Oct 28, 2009	106.050	6.202	404	5	45,512
Citigroup (C)	4.875	May 07, 2015	104.628	4.370	102	10	44,807
Devon Financing (DVN)	6.875	Sep 30, 2011	119.188	4.108	72	10	42,969
Liberty Media (L)	5.700	May 15, 2013	103.244	5.273	188	10	41,725
Ford Motor (F)	6.625	Oct 01, 2028	86.970	7.813	344	30	41,393
Wyeth (WYE)	5.250	Mar 15, 2013	106.965	4.361	95	10	41,289
Boeing Capital (BA)	5.125	Feb 15, 2013	107.404	4.182	78	10	40,200
Tribune (TRB)	6.610	Sep 15, 2027	120.155	5.144	84	30	40,000
Ford Motor Credit (F)	6.500	Jan 25, 2007	105.750	4.729	245	5	38,879
General Motors Acceptance (GMAC)	7.250	Mar 02, 2011	103.814	6.606	320	10	38,446
General Electric Capital (GE)	5.350	Mar 30, 2006	108.965	1.983	44	3	36,400
Metlife (MET)	6.125	Dec 01, 2011	116.380	3.830	55	10	36,331
Wal-Mart Stores (WMT)	4.550	May 01, 2013	105.120	3.917	51	10	36,192

Volume represents total volume for each issue; price/yield data are for trades of $1 million and greater. ☆ Estimated spreads, in basis points (100 basis points is one percentage point), over the 2, 3, 5, 10 or 30-year hot run Treasury note/bond. 2-year: 1.250 05/05; 3-year: 2.000 05/06; 5-year: 2.625 05/08; 10-year: 3.625 05/13; 30-year: 5.375 02/31. †Comparable U.S. Treasury issue. c - Convertible Bond

Source: MarketAxess Corporate BondTicker

---

paid at maturity is the bond's principal, and the periodic interest payments are coupons. Most bonds pay fixed coupons, but some pay floating coupon rates adjusted regularly according to prevailing market interest rates.

2. Corporate bonds are usually callable, which means that the issuer has the right to buy back outstanding bonds before maturity. When a bond issue is called, bondholders surrender their bonds in exchange for a prespecified call price.

3. The largest category of corporate bond investors is life insurance companies, which own about a third of all outstanding corporate bonds. Remaining ownership shares are roughly equally distributed among individual investors, pension funds, banks, and foreign investors.

4. Debentures are the most common type of corporate bond. Debenture bonds represent the unsecured debt of a corporation. Mortgage bonds represent debt issued with a lien on specific property pledged as security for the bonds. Collateral trust bonds are characterized by a pledge of financial assets as

security for a bond issue. Equipment trust certificates are issued according to a lease form of financing, where investors purchase equipment trust certificates and the proceeds from this sale are used to purchase equipment that is leased to a corporation.

5. A bond indenture is a formal agreement between the corporation and bondholders that spells out the legal rights and obligations of both parties with respect to a bond issue. An indenture typically specifies the seniority of a bond issue, along with any call provisions, put provisions, bond-to-stock conversion provisions, and sinking fund provisions.

6. When a corporation sells a new bond issue to the public, it usually has a credit rating assigned by several independent bond rating agencies. Without a credit rating, a new bond issue would be difficult to sell, which is why almost all bond issues sold to the public have credit ratings assigned.

7. Bonds with a speculative or lower grade rating, commonly called high-yield bonds, or junk bonds, represent corporate debt with higher than average credit risk. Credit ratings for junk bonds are frequently revised to reflect changing financial conditions.

8. The existence of an active secondary market for corporate bonds is important to most bond investors. The greatest total volume of bond trading occurs in the OTC market.

Get Real

This chapter explored the world of corporate bonds, an important category of investments for institutions, such as pension funds and life insurance companies, and also for individuals. This category also includes convertible bonds and preferred stock. How should you put this information to work?

Now that you understand the most important features of corporate bonds, you need to buy several different issues to experience the real-world gains and losses that come with managing a bond portfolio. So, with a simulated brokerage account (such as Stock-Trak), try putting roughly equal dollar amounts into three or four different corporate bond issues. Be sure to include some junk bonds in your selections. Check the credit ratings of the bond issues you have selected at a site such as Bonds Online (www.bondsonline.com).

You can find out more information about corporate bonds at the many websites now specializing in bonds, including Investing In Bonds (www.investinginbonds.com), Bond Markets (www.bondmarkets.com), and Convertible Bonds (www.convertbond.com). The websites of bond rating agencies such as Moody's (www.moodys.com), Standard & Poor's (www.standardandpoors.com), Duff & Phelps (www.duffllc.com), and Fitch (www.fitchibca.com) are also quite informative.

As you monitor the prices of your bonds, notice how interest rates influence their prices. You may also notice that for bonds with lower credit ratings, the stock price of the issuing company is an important influence. Why do you think this is so?

Of course, with the convertible issues the bond price will definitely be influenced by the underlying stock value, but the impact depends on the specific conversion features of the bond, including whether the bond is in the money or not.

Key Terms

plain vanilla bonds 558	in-the-money bond 567
unsecured debt 558	intrinsic bond value 567
debentures 558	exchangeable bonds 568
mortgage bond 559	term bonds 568
collateral trust bond 559	serial bonds 568
equipment trust certificate 559	sinking fund 568
indenture summary 561	protective covenants 571
prospectus 561	event risk 572
senior debentures 562	private placement 573
subordinated debentures 562	preferred stock 574
negative pledge clause 562	adjustable-rate bonds 575
bond refunding 562	credit ratings 575
put bonds 564	prudent investment guidelines 576
convertible bonds 564	high-yield bonds 577

Chapter Review Problems and Self-Test

1. **Callable Bonds** A particular bond matures in 30 years. It is callable in 10 years at 110. The call price is then cut by 1 percent of par each year until the call price reaches par. If the bond is called in 12 years, how much will you receive? Assume a $1,000 face value.

2. **Convertible Bonds** A convertible bond features a conversion ratio of 50. What is the conversion price? If the stock sells for $30 per share, what is the conversion value?

3. **Convertible Bonds** A convertible bond has an 8 percent coupon, paid semiannually, and will mature in 15 years. If the bond were not convertible, it would be priced to yield 9 percent. The conversion ratio on the bond is 40, and the stock is currently selling for $24 per share. What is the minimum value of this bond?

Answers to Self-Test Problems

1. The call price will be 110% − 2 × 1% = 108% of face value, or $1,080.

2. The conversion price is face value divided by the conversion ratio, $1,000/50 = $20. The conversion value is what the bond is worth on a converted basis, 50 × $30 = $1,500.

3. The minimum value is the larger of the conversion value and the intrinsic bond value. The conversion value is 40 × $24 = $960. To calculate the intrinsic bond value, note that we have a face value of $1,000 (by assumption), a semiannual coupon of $40, an annual yield of 9 percent (4.5 percent per half-year), and 15 years to maturity (30 half-years). Using the standard bond pricing formula from Chapter 10, the bond's price (be sure to verify this) if it were not convertible is $918.56. This convertible bond thus will sell for more than $960.

Test Your Investment Quotient

1. **Trust Certificates** An airline elects to finance the purchase of some new airplanes using equipment trust certificates. Under the legal arrangement associated with such certificates, the airplanes are pledged as collateral, but which other factor applies?

   a. The airline still has legal title to the planes.
   b. Legal title to the planes resides with the manufacturer.
   c. The airline does not get legal title to the planes until the manufacturer is paid off.
   d. Legal title to the planes resides with a third party who then leases the planes to the airline.

2. **Callable Bonds**   What does the call feature of a bond mean?

   a. Investor can call for payment on demand.
   b. Investor can only call if the firm defaults on an interest payment.
   c. Issuer can call the bond issue prior to the maturity date.
   d. Issuer can call the issue during the first three years.

3. **Callable Bonds**   Who benefits from a call provision on a corporate bond?

   a. The issuer
   b. The bondholders
   c. The trustee
   d. The government regulators

4. **Callable Bonds**   Which of the following describes a bond with a call feature?

   a. It is attractive, because the immediate receipt of principal plus premium produces a high return.
   b. It is more likely to be called when interest rates are high, because the interest savings will be greater.
   c. It would usually have a higher yield than a similar noncallable bond.
   d. It generally has a higher credit rating than a similar noncallable bond.

5. **Callable Bonds**   Which of the following is not a component of call risk for a bond investor?

   a. The cash flow pattern for the bond is not known with certainty.
   b. When the issuer calls a bond, the investor is exposed to reinvestment risk.
   c. The value of a callable bond drops when expected interest rate volatility decreases.
   d. The capital appreciation potential of a callable bond is lower than a noncallable bond.

6. **Callable Bonds**   Two bonds are identical, except one is callable and the other is noncallable. Compared to the noncallable bond, the callable bond has

   a. Negative convexity and a lower price.
   b. Negative convexity and a higher price.
   c. Positive convexity and a lower price.
   d. Positive convexity and a higher price.

7. **Convexity**   What does positive convexity on a bond imply?

   a. The direction of change in yield is directly related to the change in price.
   b. Prices increase at a faster rate as yields drop than they decrease as yields rise.
   c. Price changes are the same for both increases and decreases in yields.
   d. Prices increase and decrease at a faster rate than the change in yield.

8. **Convexity**   A bond with negative convexity is best described as having a price-yield relationship displaying

   a. Positive convexity at high yields and negative convexity at low yields.
   b. Negative convexity at high yields and positive convexity at low yields.
   c. Negative convexity at low and high yields and positive at medium yields.
   d. Positive convexity at low and high yields and negativity at medium yields.

9. **Convexity and Duration**   Which of the following *most accurately* measures interest rate sensitivity for bonds with embedded options?

   a. Convexity
   b. Effective duration
   c. Modified duration
   d. Macaulay duration

10. **Convexity and Duration**   Which of the following most accurately measures interest rate sensitivity for bonds *without* embedded options?

   a. Convexity
   b. Effective duration

    c. Modified duration
    d. Macaulay duration

11. **Indentures**   Which of the following is not a responsibility of a corporate trustee with regard to a bond's trust indenture?

    a. Checking compliance
    b. Authenticating the bonds issued
    c. Negotiating the terms
    d. Declaring defaults

12. **Refundings**   The refunding provision of an indenture allows bonds to be retired unless

    a. They are replaced with a new issue having a lower interest cost.
    b. The remaining time to maturity is less than five years.
    c. The stated time period in the indenture has not passed.
    d. The stated time period in the indenture has passed.

13. **Debentures**   Holders of unsecured debentures with a negative pledge clause can claim which of the following assurances?

    a. No additional secured debt will be issued in the future.
    b. If any secured debt is issued in the future, the unsecured debentures must be redeemed at par.
    c. The debentures will be secured, but to a lesser degree than any secured debt issued in the future.
    d. The debentures will be secured at least equally with any secured debt issued in the future.

14. **Credit Risk**   An "original issue junk" bond is *best* described as a bond issued

    a. Below investment grade.
    b. At an original issue discount.
    c. As investment grade, but declined to speculative grade.
    d. As below investment grade, but upgraded to speculative grade.

15. **Credit Risk**   A "fallen angel" bond is *best* described as a bond issued

    a. Below investment grade.
    b. At an original issue discount.
    c. As investment grade, but declined to speculative grade.
    d. As a secured bond, but the collateral value declined below par value.

16. **Preferred Stock**   Nonconvertible preferred stock has which of the following in comparison to common stock?

    a. Preferential claim on a company's earnings.
    b. A predetermined dividend rate.
    c. Preferential voting rights.
    d. All of the above.

17. **Preferred Stock**   A preferred stock that is entitled to dividends in arrears is known as

    a. Convertible
    b. Cumulative
    c. Extendible
    d. Participating

18. **Preferred Stock**   Why does a firm's preferred stock often sell at yields below its bonds?

    a. Preferred stock generally carries a higher agency rating.
    b. Owners of preferred stock have a prior claim on the firm's earnings.
    c. Owners of preferred stock have a prior claim on the firm's assets in a liquidation.
    d. Corporations owning stock may exclude from income taxes most of the dividend income they receive.

19. **Convertible Bonds** Which one of the following statements about convertible bonds is true?

    a. The longer the call protection on a convertible, the less the security is worth.
    b. The more volatile the underlying stock, the greater the value of the conversion feature.
    c. The smaller the spread between the dividend yield on the stock and the yield to maturity on the bond, the more the convertible is worth.
    d. The collateral that is used to secure a convertible bond is one reason convertibles are more attractive than the underlying common stocks.

20. **Convertible Bonds** Which one of the following statements about convertible bonds is false?

    a. The yield on the convertible will typically be higher than the yield on the underlying common stock.
    b. The convertible bond will likely participate in a major upward movement in the price of the underlying common stock.
    c. Convertible bonds are typically secured by specific assets of the issuing company.
    d. A convertible bond can be valued as a straight bond with an attached option.

21. **Convertible Bonds** Consider the possible advantages of convertible bonds for investors:

    I. The conversion feature enables the convertible to participate in major upward moves in the price of the underlying common stock.
    II. The bonds are typically secured by specific assets of the issuing company.
    III. Investors may redeem their bonds at the stated conversion price any time during the life of the issue.
    IV. The yield on the convertible will almost always be higher than the yield on the underlying common stock.

    Which are true?

    a. I and II only.
    b. II and III only.
    c. I and III only.
    d. I and IV only.

22. **Convertible Bonds** A convertible bond sells at $1,000 par with a conversion ratio of 40 and an accompanying stock price of $20 per share. The conversion price and conversion value are, respectively,

    a. $20 and $1,000
    b. $20 and $800
    c. $25 and $1,000
    d. $25 and $800

23. **Convertible Bonds** A convertible bond sells at $1,000 par with a conversion ratio of 25 and conversion value of $800. What is the price of the underlying stock?

    a. $12
    b. $48
    c. $40
    d. $32

24. **Convertible Bonds** A convertible bond has a par value of $1,000 and a conversion ratio of 20. The price of the underlying stock is $40. What is the conversion value?

    a. $20
    b. $800
    c. $1,000
    d. $25

25. International Bonds   A U.S. investor who buys Japanese bonds will most likely maximize his return if interest rates

   a. Fall and the dollar weakens relative to the yen.
   b. Fall and the dollar strengthens relative to the yen.
   c. Rise and the dollar weakens relative to the yen.
   d. Rise and the dollar strengthens relative to the yen.

Concept Questions

   1. Bond Types   What are the four main types of corporate bonds?

   2. Bond Features   What is a bond refunding? Is it the same thing as a call?

   3. Callable Bonds   With regard to the call feature, what are call protection and the call premium? What typically happens to the call premium through time?

   4. Put Bonds   What is a put bond? Is the put feature desirable from the investor's perspective? The issuer's?

   5. Bond Yields   What is the impact on a bond's coupon rate from

     a. A call feature?
     b. A put feature?

   6. Exchangeable Bonds   What is the difference between an exchangeable bond and a convertible bond?

   7. Event Risk   What is event risk? In addition to protective covenants, what bond feature do you think best reduces or eliminates such risk?

   8. Floaters   From the bondholder's perspective, what are the potential advantages and disadvantages of floating coupons?

   9. Effective Duration   Why is effective duration a more accurate measure of interest rate risk for bonds with embedded options?

  10. Embedded Options   What are some examples of embedded options in bonds? How do they affect the price of a bond?

  11. Junk Bonds   Explain the difference between an original issue junk bond and a fallen angel bond.

  12. Put Bonds   What is the difference between put bonds and extendible bonds?

  13. Callable Bonds   All else the same, callable bonds have less interest rate sensitivity than noncallable bonds. Why? Is this a good thing?

  14. Callable Bonds   Two callable bonds are essentially identical, except that one has a refunding provision while the other has no refunding provision. Which bond is more likely to be called by the issuer? Why?

  15. Inverse Floaters   An "inverse floater" is a bond with a coupon that is adjusted down when interest rates rise and up when rates fall. What is the impact of the floating coupon on the bond's price volatility?

Questions and Problems

Core Questions

   1. Conversion Price   A convertible bond has a $1,000 face value and a conversion ratio of 40. What is the conversion price?

   2. Conversion Price   A convertible bond has a conversion ratio of 34 and a par value of $1,000. What is the conversion price?

3. **Conversion Ratio** A company just sold a convertible bond at par value of $1,000. If the conversion price is $55, what is the conversion ratio?

4. **Conversion Value** A convertible bond has a $1,000 face value and a conversion ratio of 60. If the stock price is $18, what is the conversion value?

5. **Conversion Value** A convertible bond has a conversion ratio of 15 and a par value of $1,000. If the stock is currently priced at $82, what is the conversion value?

6. **Conversion Ratio** You find a convertible bond outstanding with a conversion value of $832. The stock is currently priced at $62. What is the conversion ratio of the bond?

7. **Callable Bonds** A bond matures in 25 years, but is callable in 10 years at 110. The call premium decreases by 2 percent of par per year. If the bond is called in 13 years, how much will you receive?

8. **Call Premium** You own a bond with a 7 percent coupon rate and a yield to call of 7.45 percent. The bond currently sells for $1,030.06. If the bond is callable in five years, what is the call premium of the bond?

9. **Convertible Bonds** A convertible bond has a 7 percent coupon, paid semiannually, and will mature in 10 years. If the bond were not convertible, it would be priced to yield 9 percent. The conversion ratio on the bond is 20, and the stock is currently selling for $46 per share. What is the minimum value of this bond?

10. **Convertible Bonds** You own a convertible bond with a conversion ratio of 35. The stock is currently selling for $40 per share. The issuer of the bond has announced a call; the call price is 110. What are your options here? What should you do?

Intermediate Questions

11. **Convertible Bonds** There is a 30-year bond with an 8 percent coupon and a 6 percent yield to maturity. The bond is callable in five years at par value. What is the Macaulay duration of the bond assuming it is not called? What is the Macaulay duration if the bond is called? Which number is more relevant?

Use the following information to answer the next two questions: Rajiv Singh, a bond analyst, is analyzing a convertible bond. The characteristics of the bond are given below.

Convertible Bond Characteristics	
Par value	$1,000
Annual coupon rate (annual pay)	6.5%
Conversion ratio	22
Market price	105% of par
Straight value	99% of par
Underlying Stock Characteristics	
Current market price	$40 per share
Annual cash dividend	$1.20 per share

12. **Convertible Bonds** Compute the bond's conversion value and market conversion price.

13. **Convertible Bonds** Determine whether the value of a callable convertible bond will increase, decrease, or remain unchanged if there is an increase in stock price volatility. What if there is an increase in interest rate volatility? Justify each of your responses.

Use the following information to answer the next two questions: Rich McDonald, CFA, is evaluating his investment alternatives in Ytel Incorporated by analyzing a Ytel convertible bond and Ytel common equity. Characteristics of the two securities are as follows:

Characteristic	Convertible Bond	Common Equity
Par value	$1,000	
Coupon (annual payment)	4%	
Current market price	$980	$35 per share
Straight bond value	$925	
Conversion ratio	25	
Conversion option	At any time	
Dividend		$0
Expected market price in one year	$1,125	$45 per share

14. **Convertible Bonds**   Calculate the following:
   a. The current market conversion price for the Ytel convertible bond.
   b. The expected one-year rate of return for the Ytel convertible bond.
   c. The expected one-year rate of return for the Ytel common equity.

15. **Convertible Bonds**   One year has passed and Ytel's common equity price has increased to $51 per share. Also, over the year, the interest rate on Ytel's nonconvertible bonds of the same maturity has increased, while credit spreads remained unchanged. Name the two components of the convertible bond's value. Indicate whether the value of each component should increase, stay the same, or decrease in response to the increase on Ytel's common equity and the increase in interest rates.

What's on the Web?

1. **Bond Quotes**   Go to www.bondsonline.com and find the corporate bond search. Enter "Ford" for Ford Motor Company in the Issue box and search for Ford bonds. How many bonds are listed for sale? What are the different credit ratings for these bonds? What is the yield to maturity for the longest maturity bond? What is its price?

2. **Credit Spreads**   What are the current credit spreads? Go to www.bondsonline.com and look for corporate yield spreads. Are the yield spreads linear? In other words, does the yield spread increase by the same number of basis points for each decline in credit rating? Why or why not? Why are the yield spreads higher for longer term bonds?

3. **Historical Credit Spreads**   The St. Louis Federal Reserve Board has files with historical interest rates on its website at www.stls.frb.org. Go to the site and find the monthly Moody's Seasoned Aaa Corporate Bond Yield and the monthly Moody's Seasoned Baa Corporate Bond Yield. You can calculate a credit spread as the difference between these two returns. When was the largest credit spread? The smallest? What factors do you think led to the large credit spreads and the small credit spreads?

4. **Bond Terminology**   Go to www.investinginbonds.com and find the definitions for the following terms: bond resolution, cap, collar, defeasance, extraordinary redemption, overcollateralization, and refunding.

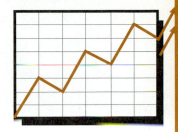

Stock-Trak®
Portfolio Simulations

Trading Corporate Bonds with Stock-Trak

Stock-Trak supports trading in a select number of corporate bond issues. These bonds trade in sufficient volume for Stock-Trak to obtain timely price quotes. The list of available bonds changes from time to time, so you should consult the Stock-Trak website (www.stocktrak.com/cj) for the most recent list. Ticker symbols for these bonds are not necessary, because Stock-Trak lists the bonds by issuer name, coupon, and maturity. These three bonds are shown as they were listed by Stock-Trak:

    AT&T 8.125 2022
    Dow Chemical 6.85 2013
    IBM 7 2025

Following standard practice, corporate bonds available for Stock-Trak trading have a face value denomination of $1,000 per bond. To purchase 25 of the AT&T 8.125 2022 bonds, you would enter the following:

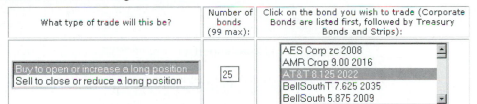

Stock-Trak will take you to the trade confirmation screen, where you will confirm the amount of your trade and submit it.

Stock-Trak Exercises

1. Buy two different corporate bonds with maturities of at least 10 years. One bond should have a low coupon rate (but not a zero coupon) and the other should have a high coupon rate. Compare the two bonds by keeping a record of their weekly price changes.

2. Stock-Trak corporate bonds typically include several zero coupon issues. Two such bonds issued by IBM and Motorola were listed by Stock-Trak as

    IBM zc 2009
    Motorola zc 2013

    Buy two zero-coupon bonds and compare their performance by keeping a record of their weekly price changes.

3. Stock-Trak follows the bond market convention of quoting clean bond prices. When you submit the bond trade it will be based on yesterday's closing price, but Stock-Trak will charge you today's closing price, plus accrued interest. Buy at least 10 of one corporate bond available on Stock-Trak. The next day, look at your account detail. What was the price per bond? How much did you pay in accrued interest per bond? Be careful on your calculation—Stock-Trak includes the commission in this amount. Mark down your accrued interest on bonds in the bottom of the account detail. One week later check the accrued interest again. How much interest did you receive per day?

www.mhhe.com/cj3e

Chapter 18

Government Bonds

"Blessed are the young, for they shall inherit the national debt."

–Herbert Hoover

U.S. Treasury bonds are among the safest investments available because they are secured by the considerable resources of the federal government. Many bonds issued by federal government agencies, and by state and local municipal governments, are also nearly free of default risk. Consequently, government bonds are generally excellent vehicles for conservative investment strategies seeking predictable investment results. ■

The largest and most important debt market is that for debt issued by the U.S. government. This market is truly global in character since a large share of federal debt is sold to foreign investors, and it thereby sets the tone for debt markets around the world. In contrast, the market for debt issued by states and municipalities is almost exclusively a domestic market since almost all U.S. municipal securities are owned by U.S. investors. These two broad categories make up the government bond market. In this chapter, we examine securities issued by federal, state, and local governments, which combined represent well over $10 trillion of outstanding securities.

18.1 Government Bond Basics

The U.S. federal government is the largest single borrower in the world. In 2003, the public debt of the U.S. government was about $4 trillion. Responsibility for managing outstanding government debt belongs to the U.S. Treasury, which acts as the financial agent of the federal government.

The U.S. Treasury finances government debt by issuing marketable securities and nonmarketable securities. Most of the gross public debt is financed by the sale of marketable securities at regularly scheduled Treasury auctions. Marketable securities include Treasury bills, Treasury notes, and Treasury bonds, often simply called T-bills, T-notes, and T-bonds, respectively. Outstanding marketable securities trade among investors in a large, active financial market called the Treasury market. Nonmarketable securities include U.S. Savings Bonds, Government Account Series, and State and Local Government Series. Many individuals are familiar with U.S. Savings Bonds since they are sold only to individual investors. Government Account Series are issued to federal government agencies and trust funds, in particular, the Social Security Administration trust fund. State and Local Government Series are purchased by municipal governments.

Treasury security ownership is registered with the U.S. Treasury. When an investor sells a U.S. Treasury security to another investor, registered ownership is officially transferred by notifying the U.S. Treasury of the transaction. However, only marketable securities allow registered ownership to be transferred. Nonmarketable securities do not allow a change of registered ownership and therefore cannot trade among investors. For example, a U.S. Savings Bond is a nonmarketable security. If an investor wishes to sell a U.S. Savings Bond, it must be redeemed by the U.S. Treasury. This is normally a simple procedure. For example, most banks handle the purchase and sale of U.S. Savings Bonds for their customers.

Another large market for government debt is the market for municipal government debt. There are more than 80,000 state and local governments in the United States, almost all of which have some form of outstanding debt. In a typical year, well over 10,000 new municipal debt issues are brought to market. Total municipal debt outstanding in the United States is over $2 trillion. Of this total, individual investors hold about half, either through direct purchase or indirectly through mutual funds. The remainder is split about equally between holdings of property and casualty insurance companies and commercial banks.

Visit
www.investinginbonds.com
for more information
on U.S. Treasury
securities

18.2 U.S. Treasury Bills, Notes, Bonds, and STRIPS

face value The value of a bill, note, or bond at its maturity when a payment of principal is made. Also called *redemption value*.

discount basis Method of selling a Treasury bill at a discount from face value.

Treasury bills are short-term obligations that mature in six months or less. They are originally issued with maturities of 4, 13, or 26 weeks. A T-bill entitles its owner to receive a single payment at the bill's maturity, called the bill's **face value** or *redemption value*. The smallest denomination T-bill has a face value of $1,000. T-bills are sold on a **discount basis**, where a price is set at a discount from face value. For example, if a $10,000 bill is sold for $9,500, then it is sold at a discount of $500, or 5 percent. The discount represents the **imputed interest** on the bill.

Treasury notes are medium-term obligations with original maturities of 10 years or less, but more than 1 year. They are normally issued with original maturities of 2, 5, or 10 years, and they have face value denominations as small as $1,000. Besides a payment of face value at maturity, T-notes also pay semiannual coupons.

imputed interest The interest paid on a Treasury bill determined by the size of its discount from face value.

Treasury bonds are long-term obligations with much longer original-issue maturities. Since 1985, the Treasury has only issued T-bonds with a maturity of 30 years in its regular bond offerings. Like T-notes, T-bonds pay their face value at maturity, pay semiannual coupons, and have face value denominations as small as $1,000.

The coupon rate for T-notes and T-bonds is set according to interest rates prevailing at the time of issuance. For example, if the prevailing interest rate for a Treasury note of a certain maturity is 5 percent, then the coupon rate—that is, the annual coupon as a percentage of par value—for a new issue with that maturity is set at or near 5 percent. Thus, a $10,000 par value T-note paying a 5 percent coupon would pay two $250 coupons each year. Coupon payments normally begin six months after issuance and continue to be paid every six months until the last coupon is paid along with the face value at maturity. Once set, the coupon rate remains constant throughout the life of a U.S. Treasury note or bond.

Treasury STRIPS are derived from Treasury notes originally issued with maturities of 10 years and from Treasury bonds issued with 30-year maturities. Since 1985, the U.S. Treasury has sponsored the **STRIPS** program, an acronym for *Separate Trading of Registered Interest and Principal of Securities*. This program allows brokers to divide Treasury bonds and notes into *coupon strips* and *principal strips*, thereby allowing investors to buy and sell the strips of their choice. Principal strips represent face-value payments, and coupon strips represent coupon payments. For example, a 30-year maturity T-bond can be separated into 61 strips, representing 60 semiannual coupon payments and a single face value payment. Under the Treasury STRIPS program, each of these strips can be separately registered to different owners.

STRIPS Treasury program allowing investors to buy individual coupon and principal payments from a whole Treasury note or bond. Acronym for *Separate Trading of Registered Interest and Principal of Securities*.

zero coupon bond A note or bond paying a single cash flow at maturity. Also called *zeroes*.

The terms "STRIPS" and "strips" can sometimes cause confusion. The acronym STRIPS is used when speaking specifically about the Treasury STRIPS program. However, the term *strips* now popularly refers to any separate part of a note or bond issue broken down into its component parts. In this generic form, the term strips is acceptable.

Since each strip created under the STRIPS program represents a single future payment, STRIPS securities effectively become **zero coupon bonds** and are commonly called *zeroes*. The unique characteristics of Treasury zeroes make them an interesting investment choice.

The yield to maturity of a zero coupon bond is the interest rate that an investor will receive if the bond is held until it matures. Table 18.1 lists bond prices for zero coupon bonds with a face value of $10,000, maturities of 5, 10, 20, and 30 years, and yields from 3 percent to 15 percent. As shown, a $10,000 face-value zero coupon bond with a term to maturity of 20 years and an 8 percent yield has a price of $2,082.89.

Visit the U.S. Treasury at www.ustreas.gov

CALCULATING A STRIPS PRICE

EXAMPLE 18.1

What is the price of a STRIPS maturing in 20 years with a face value of $10,000 and a yield to maturity of 7 percent?

The STRIPS price is calculated as the present value of a single cash flow as follows:

$$\text{STRIPS price} = \frac{\$10,000}{(1 + 0.07/2)^{40}}$$
$$= \$2,525.72$$

(continued)

You can also calculate a STRIPS price using a built-in spreadsheet function. For example, the nearby *Spreadsheet Analysis* box contains this STRIPS price calculation using an Excel spreadsheet.

CALCULATING A STRIPS YIELD

EXAMPLE 18.2

What is the yield to maturity of a STRIPS maturing in 10 years with a face value of $10,000 and a price of $5,500?

The STRIPS yield is calculated as a yield to maturity of a single cash flow as follows:

$$\text{STRIPS yield} = 2 \times \left[\left(\frac{\$10,000}{\$5,500}\right)^{1/20} - 1\right]$$

$$= 6.07\%$$

The nearby *Spreadsheet Analysis* box contains an example of this STRIPS yield calculation using an Excel spreadsheet.

TABLE 18.1	Zero Coupon Bond Prices, $10,000 Face Value			
Yield to Maturity	Bond Maturity			
	5 Years	10 Years	20 Years	30 Years
3.0%	$8,616.67	$7,424.70	$5,512.62	$4,092.96
3.5	8,407.29	7,068.25	4,996.01	3,531.30
4.0	8,203.48	6,729.71	4,528.90	3,047.82
4.5	8,005.10	6,408.16	4,106.46	2,631.49
5.0	7,811.98	6,102.71	3,724.31	2,272.84
5.5	7,623.98	5,812.51	3,378.52	1,963.77
6.0	7,440.94	5,536.76	3,065.57	1,697.33
6.5	7,262.72	5,274.71	2,782.26	1,467.56
7.0	7,089.19	5,025.66	2,525.72	1,269.34
7.5	6,920.20	4,788.92	2,293.38	1,098.28
8.0	6,755.64	4,563.87	2,082.89	950.60
8.5	6,595.37	4,349.89	1,892.16	823.07
9.0	6,439.28	4,146.43	1,719.29	712.89
9.5	6,287.23	3,952.93	1,562.57	617.67
10.0	6,139.13	3,768.89	1,420.46	535.36
10.5	5,994.86	3,593.83	1,291.56	464.17
11.0	5,854.31	3,427.29	1,174.63	402.58
11.5	5,717.37	3,268.83	1,068.53	349.28
12.0	5,583.95	3,118.05	972.22	303.14
12.5	5,453.94	2,974.55	884.79	263.19
13.0	5,327.26	2,837.97	805.41	228.57
13.5	5,203.81	2,707.96	733.31	198.58
14.0	5,083.49	2,584.19	667.80	172.57
14.5	4,966.23	2,466.35	608.29	150.02
15.0	4,851.94	2,354.13	554.19	130.46

SPREADSHEET ANALYSIS

	A	B	C	D	E	F	G	H
1								
2				Calculating the Price of a Zero-Coupon STRIPS				
3								
4	A STRIPS traded on March 30, 2002, matures in 20 years on March 30, 2022.							
5	Assuming a 7 percent yield to maturity, what is the STRIPS price?							
6	Hint: Use the Excel function PRICE with the coupon rate set to zero.							
7								
8		$25.2572	=PRICE("3/30/2002","3/30/2022",0,0.07,100,2,3)					
9								
10	For a bond with a $10,000 face value, multiply the price by 100 to get $2,525.72.							
11								
12				Calculating the Yield to Maturity of a STRIPS				
13								
14	A STRIPS traded on March 30, 2002, matures in 10 years on March 30, 2012.							
15	The STRIPS price is $55, what is its yield to maturity?							
16	Hint: Use the Excel function YIELD with the coupon rate set to zero.							
17								
18		6.07%	=YIELD("3/30/2002","3/30/2012",0,55,100,2,3)					
19								
20								

Figure 18.1 graphs prices of zero coupon bonds with a face value of $10,000. The vertical axis measures bond prices, and the horizontal axis measures bond maturities. Bond prices for yields of 4, 8, and 12 percent are illustrated.

Check This

18.2a	What are some possible reasons why individual investors might prefer to buy Treasury STRIPS rather than common stocks?
18.2b	What are some possible reasons why individual investors might prefer to buy individual Treasury STRIPS rather than whole T-notes or T-bonds?
18.2c	For zero coupon bonds with the same face value and yield to maturity, is the price of a zero with a 15-year maturity larger or smaller than the average price of two zeroes with maturities of 10 years and 20 years? Why?

Treasury Bond and Note Prices

Figure 18.2 displays a partial *Wall Street Journal* listing of prices and other relevant information for Treasury securities. Notice that Treasury notes and bonds are listed

FIGURE 18.1   **Zero Coupon Bond Prices ($10,000 Face Value)**

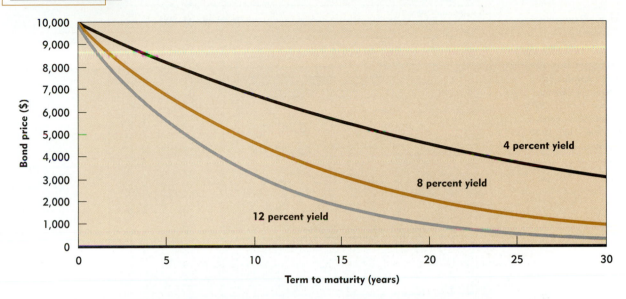

together, but there are separate sections for Treasury bills and Treasury STRIPS. The sections for Treasury bills and STRIPS were discussed in detail in Chapter 9. We discuss the section for Treasury notes and bonds next.

Treasury bond and note price quotes are stated on a percentage of par basis where, for example, a price of 102 equals par value plus 2 percent. Fractions of a percent are stated in thirty-seconds. Thus a price stated as 102:28 is actually equal to $102 + 28/32$, or 102.875. To illustrate, the first column in the section for notes and bonds in Figure 18.2 states the annual coupon rate. The next two columns report maturity in month–year format. Dealer bid and asked price quotes come next, followed by changes in ask quotes from the previous day. The last column gives the yield to maturity implied by an asked price quote. The letter *n* next to various maturity dates indicates a T-note. The absence of the letter *n* indicates a T-bond.

About a dozen of the T-bonds in Figure 18.2 are callable. If a particular issue is callable, the Treasury has the right to buy it back at face value, but only during the last five years of its life. For example, locate the bond maturing in November 2009. Although it is not indicated, this issue becomes callable in 2004. Because the Nov 09 bond pays a 10.375 percent coupon, but has a much lower yield to maturity, this bond has a price well above par value. It is likely that this bond will be called at its earliest possible call date in November 2004. Therefore, the reported asked yield is actually a yield to call. A **yield to call** (**YTC**) is the interest rate for a bond assuming the bond will be called at its earliest possible call date and the bondholder will hold the bond until it is called. When a callable T-bond has a price above par, the reported yield is a yield to call.

You can find out which T-bonds are callable by going to the Bureau of Public Debt (www.publicdebt.treas.gov) and looking at the monthly statement of the public debt. You'll see that the callable issues have maturity dates clustered in the 2009–2015 range. Since 1985, the Treasury has issued only noncallable bonds. Thus, all listed bonds with a maturity of 2015 or later are noncallable.

yield to call (YTC)
The interest rate on a bond that assumes the bond will be called at its earliest possible call date.

FIGURE 18.2

U.S. Treasury Securities

Source: Reprinted with permission from *The Wall Street Journal*, via Copyright Clearance Center, May 21, 2003. © 2003 Dow Jones & Company, Inc. All Rights Reserved Worldwide.

Treasury Bonds, Notes and Bills

May 20, 2003

Explanatory Notes

Representative Over-the-Counter quotation based on transactions of $1 million or more. Treasury bond, note and bill quotes are as of mid-afternoon. Colons in bid-and-asked quotes represent 32nds; 101:01 means 101 1/32. Net changes in 32nds. n-Treasury note. i-Inflation-Indexed issue. Treasury bill quotes in hundredths, quoted on terms of a rate of discount. Days to maturity calculated from settlement date. All yields are to maturity and based on the asked quote. Latest 13-week and 26-week bills are boldfaced. For bonds callable prior to maturity, yields are computed to the earliest call date for issues quoted above par and to the maturity date for issues below par. *When issued.

Source: eSpeed/Cantor Fitzgerald

U.S. Treasury strips as of 3 p.m. Eastern time, also based on transactions of $1 million or more. Colons in bid and asked quotes represent 32nds; 99:01 means 99 1/32. Net changes in 32nds. Yields calculated on the asked quotation. ci-stripped coupon interest. bp-Treasury bond, stripped principal. np-Treasury note, stripped principal. For bonds callable prior to maturity, yields are computed to the earliest call date for issues quoted above par and to the maturity date for issues below par.

Source: Bear, Stearns & Co. via Street Software Technology Inc.

Government Bonds & Notes

RATE	MATURITY MO/YR	BID	ASKED	CHG	ASK YLD
4.250	May 03n	100:03	100:04	1	0.26
5.500	May 03n	100:04	100:05	1	0.37
3.875	Jun 03n	100:10	100:11	...	0.61
5.375	Jun 03n	100:19	100:20	4	0.69
3.875	Jul 03n	100:17	100:18	-1	0.91
5.250	Aug 03n	101:00	101:00	...	0.95
5.750	Aug 03n	101:03	101:04	...	0.92
11.125	Aug 03	102:15	102:16	2	0.57
3.625	Aug 03n	101:00	101:00	9	0.96
2.750	Sep 03n	101:00	101:00	12	0.96
2.750	Oct 03n	100:24	100:25	1	0.98
4.250	Nov 03n	101:17	101:18	...	1.00
11.875	Nov 03	105:06	105:07	-1	1.03
3.000	Nov 03n	101:00	101:01	...	1.03
3.250	Dec 03n	101:10	101:11	...	1.01
3.000	Jan 04n	101:11	101:12	1	1.01
4.750	Feb 04n	102:22	102:23	1	1.02
5.875	Feb 04n	103:16	103:17	...	1.03
3.000	Feb 04n	101:16	101:17	1	1.02
3.625	Mar 04n	102:06	102:07	1	1.01
3.375	Apr 04n	102:05	102:06	1	1.02
5.250	May 04n	104:02	104:03	1	1.04
7.250	May 04n	106:01	106:02	1	1.04
12.375	May 04	111:00	111:01	...	1.07
3.250	May 04n	102:06	102:07	1	1.06
2.875	Jun 04n	102:00	102:00	1	1.04
2.250	Jul 04n	101:12	101:13	2	1.05
2.125	Aug 04n	101:10	101:11	2	1.06
6.000	Aug 04n	106:01	106:02	1	1.04
7.250	Aug 04n	107:19	107:20	1	1.03
13.750	Aug 04	115:18	115:19	1	1.03
1.875	Sep 04n	101:01	101:02	2	1.07
2.125	Oct 04n	101:14	101:15	2	1.10
5.875	Nov 04n	106:30	106:31	2	1.12
7.875	Nov 04n	109:28	109:29	2	1.12
11.625	Nov 04	115:13	115:14	2	1.11
2.000	Nov 04n	101:09	101:10	3	1.12
1.750	Dec 04n	100:30	100:31	3	1.14
1.625	Jan 05n	100:23	100:24	3	1.17
7.500	Feb 05n	110:26	110:27	2	1.17
1.500	Feb 05n	100:16	100:17	3	1.19
1.625	Mar 05n	100:22	100;23	3	1.22
1.625	**Apr 05n**	**100:20**	**100:21**	**3**	**1.27**
6.500	May 05n	110:07	110:08	3	1.24
6.750	May 05n	110:23	110:24	3	1.25
12.000	May 05	121:02	121:03	4	1.21
6.500	Aug 05n	111:12	111:13	3	1.30
10.750	Aug 05	120:22	120:23	4	1.31
5.750	Nov 05n	110:16	110:17	4	1.41
5.875	Nov 05n	110:25	110:26	4	1.42
5.625	Feb 06n	111:02	111:03	4	1.47
9.375	Feb 06	121:01	121:02	4	1.49
2.000	May 06n	101:04	101:05	5	1.60
4.625	May 06n	108:24	108:25	4	1.59
6.875	May 06n	115:08	115:09	5	1.61
7.000	Jul 06n	116:08	116:09	6	1.67
6.500	Oct 06n	115:17	115:18	8	1.77
3.500	Nov 06n	105:23	105:24	8	1.79
3.375	Jan 07i	109:30	109:31	8	0.61
6.250	Feb 07n	115:23	115:24	8	1.87
6.625	May 07n	117:24	117:25	9	1.96
4.375	May 07n	109:03	109:04	10	1.98
3.250	Aug 07n	104:24	104:25	11	2.07
6.125	Aug 07n	116:12	116:13	10	2.06
3.000	Nov 07n	103:18	103:19	11	2.15
3.625	Jan 08i	112:14	112:15	15	0.88
3.000	Feb 08n	103:13	103:14	10	2.23
5.500	Feb 08n	114:22	114:23	11	2.21
2.625	**May 08n**	**101:12**	**101:13**	**11**	**2.32**
5.625	May 08n	115:14	115:15	11	2.32
8.375	Aug 08	101:23	101:24	-2	0.91
4.750	Nov 08n	111:16	111:17	11	2.48
8.750	Nov 08	103:23	103:24	...	0.93
3.875	Jan 09i	114:26	114:27	14	1.15
5.500	May 09n	116:00	116:01	12	2.59
9.125	May 09	107:24	107:25	1	1.15
6.000	Aug 09n	118:27	118:28	13	2.69
10.375	Nov 09	113:17	113:18	2	1.13
4.250	Jan 10i	118:08	118:09	26	1.36
6.500	Feb 10n	122:14	122:15	17	2.81
11.750	Feb 10	117:28	117:29	3	1.29
10.000	May 10	116:24	116:25	4	1.39
5.750	Aug 10n	118:06	118:07	18	2.93
12.750	Nov 10	127:07	127:08	6	1.52
3.500	Jan 11i	114:03	114:04	28	1.54
5.000	Feb 11n	113:12	113:13	18	3.04
13.875	May 11	135:15	135:16	7	1.63
5.000	Aug 11n	113:12	113:13	18	3.14
14.000	Nov 11	141:01	141:02	9	1.79
3.375	Jan 12i	114:07	114:08	34	1.60
4.875	Feb 12n	112:13	112:14	20	3.23
3.000	Jul 12i	111:11	111:12	35	1.66
4.375	Aug 12n	108:16	108:17	20	3.30
4.000	Nov 12n	105:10	105:11	19	3.34
10.375	Nov 12	134:24	134:25	12	2.19
3.875	Feb 13n	104:07	104:08	19	3.36
3.625	**May 13n**	**102:02**	**102:03**	**19**	**3.38**
12.000	Aug 13	146:30	146:31	14	2.40
13.250	May 14	158:09	158:10	10	2.65
12.500	Aug 14	155:17	155:18	16	2.75
11.750	Nov 14	152:20	152:21	13	2.81
11.250	Feb 15	173:00	173:01	34	3.57
10.625	Aug 15	168:12	168:13	34	3.64
9.875	Nov 15	161:14	161:15	34	3.69
9.250	Feb 16	155:15	155:16	35	3.73
7.250	May 16	134:29	134:30	31	3.81
7.500	Nov 16	137:30	137:31	31	3.86
8.750	May 17	152:04	152:05	36	3.88
8.875	Aug 17	153:26	153:27	38	3.91
9.125	May 18	157:27	157:28	42	3.96
9.000	Nov 18	157:09	157:10	46	4.00
8.875	Feb 19	155:25	155:26	44	4.05
8.125	Aug 19	147:08	147:09	43	4.11
8.500	Feb 20	152:16	152:17	45	4.12
8.750	May 20	155:27	155:28	45	4.14
8.750	Aug 20	156:02	156:03	48	4.16
7.875	Feb 21	145:13	145:14	45	4.21
8.125	May 21	148:25	148:26	45	4.22
8.125	Aug 21	149:00	149:01	43	4.24
8.000	Nov 21	147:19	147:20	46	4.25
7.250	Aug 22	138:05	138:06	43	4.31
7.625	Nov 22	143:13	143:14	45	4.31
7.125	Feb 23	136:25	136:26	43	4.33
6.250	Aug 23	125:03	125:04	41	4.37
7.500	Nov 24	143:14	143:15	46	4.36
7.625	Feb 25	145:13	145:14	47	4.37
6.875	Aug 25	134:28	134:29	44	4.40
6.000	Feb 26	122:16	122:17	43	4.42
6.750	Aug 26	133:18	133:19	47	4.42
6.500	Nov 26	130:00	130:01	45	4.43
6.625	Feb 27	132:00	132:01	48	4.43
6.375	Aug 27	128:15	128:16	47	4.44
6.125	Nov 27	124:29	124:30	45	4.44
3.625	Apr 28i	125:15	125:16	59	2.28
5.500	Aug 28	115:19	115:20	45	4.46
5.250	Nov 28	111:28	111:29	43	4.46
5.250	Feb 29	112:00	112:01	43	4.46
3.875	Apr 29i	131:12	131:13	63	2.26
6.125	Aug 29	125:17	125:18	48	4.46
6.250	May 30	128:00	128:00	51	4.46
5.375	**Feb 31**	**115:29**	**115:30**	**48**	**4.38**
3.375	Apr 32i	125:19	125:20	67	2.18

U.S. Treasury Strips

MATURITY		TYPE	BID	ASKED	CHG	ASK YLD
Jul	03	ci	99:27	99:27	...	1.03
Aug	03	ci	99:25	99:25	...	0.97
Aug	03	np	99:25	99:25	...	0.97
Nov	03	ci	99:18	99:18	...	0.91
Nov	03	np	99:16	99:16	...	1.03
Jan	04	ci	99:11	99:11	1	1.00
Feb	04	ci	99:07	99:08	1	1.04
Feb	04	np	99:07	99:08	1	1.04
May	04	ci	98:27	98:28	1	1.17
May	04	np	98:31	98:31	1	1.05
Jul	04	ci	98:31	98:31	2	0.89
Aug	04	ci	98:27	98:28	2	0.93
Aug	04	np	98:24	98:24	2	1.01
Nov	04	ci	98:12	98:13	2	1.09
Nov	04	bp	98:12	98:13	2	1.09
Nov	04	np	98:12	98:13	2	1.10
Jan	05	ci	98:21	98:22	3	0.80
Feb	05	ci	98:01	98:02	3	1.13
Feb	05	np	97:31	98:00	2	1.17
May	05	ci	97:14	97:15	3	1.29
May	05	bp	97:18	97:19	3	1.23
May	05	np	97:17	97:18	3	1.25
May	05	np	97:16	97:17	3	1.27
Jul	05	ci	97:25	97:27	3	1.02
Aug	05	ci	96:31	97:01	3	1.36
Aug	05	bp	96:31	97:01	3	1.36
Aug	05	np	97:02	97:03	3	1.32
Nov	05	ci	96:19	96:21	4	1.38
Nov	05	np	96:15	96:17	4	1.43
Nov	05	np	96:17	96:18	4	1.41
Jan	06	ci	96:27	96:29	3	1.20
Feb	06	ci	95:29	95:30	4	1.52
Feb	06	bp	95:31	96:00	4	1.50
Feb	06	np	96:00	96:02	4	1.48
May	06	ci	95:08	95:10	4	1.62
May	06	np	95:06	95:08	4	1.64
Jul	06	ci	95:26	95:28	3	1.35
Jul	06	np	94:23	94:25	4	1.71
Aug	06	ci	94:22	94:24	4	1.67
Nov	06	ci	93:26	93:28	5	1.82
Nov	06	np	93:26	93:28	5	1.82
Feb	07	ci	93:00	93:02	8	1.93
Feb	07	np	93:04	93:07	8	1.89
May	07	ci	92:04	92:07	9	2.05
May	07	np	92:10	92:12	9	2.00
Aug	07	np	91:17	91:19	9	2.08
Aug	07	ci	91:18	91:20	9	2.08
Aug	07	np	91:14	91:16	9	2.11
Nov	07	ci	91:12	91:15	10	2.00
Nov	07	np	90:22	90:25	10	2.17
Feb	08	ci	89:27	89:30	10	2.26
Feb	08	np	89:27	89:29	10	2.26
May	08	ci	88:25	88:28	10	2.38
May	08	np	88:25	88:28	10	2.38
Aug	08	ci	88:12	88:15	11	2.36
Nov	08	ci	87:11	87:14	11	2.46
Nov	08	np	86:30	87:01	11	2.55
Feb	09	ci	86:00	86:03	17	2.63
May	09	ci	84:29	85:00	17	2.74
May	09	np	85:13	85:16	17	2.64
Aug	09	ci	84:09	84:12	18	2.74
Aug	09	np	84:04	84:08	18	2.77
Nov	09	ci	83:28	83:31	18	2.71
Nov	09	bp	81:26	81:29	18	3.10
Feb	10	ci	81:18	81:22	19	3.03
Feb	10	np	82:01	82:05	19	2.94
May	10	ci	80:19	80:23	19	3.09
Aug	10	ci	79:29	80:01	20	3.10
Aug	10	np	80:06	80:10	20	3.05
Nov	10	ci	79:09	79:13	20	3.11
Feb	11	ci	77:16	77:20	17	3.30
Feb	11	np	78:11	78:15	17	3.16
May	11	ci	76:16	76:20	17	3.36
Aug	11	ci	75:25	75:29	17	3.38
Aug	11	np	76:13	76:17	17	3.28
Nov	11	ci	74:29	75:01	18	3.42
Feb	12	ci	73:27	73:31	17	3.48
Feb	12	np	74:19	74:23	17	3.36
May	12	ci	72:24	72:28	17	3.55
Aug	12	ci	72:00	72:04	17	3.57
Aug	12	np	73:00	73:04	18	3.42
Nov	12	ci	71:04	71:08	18	3.61
Nov	12	np	72:05	72:09	18	3.45
Feb	13	ci	70:05	70:09	18	3.65
May	13	ci	69:05	69:10	18	3.71
Aug	13	ci	68:07	68:11	19	3.75
Nov	13	ci	67:10	67:14	19	3.79

Treasury Bills

MATURITY	DAYS TO MAT	BID	ASKED	CHG	ASK YLD
May 22 03	1	1.06	1.05	-0.04	1.06
May 29 03	8	1.03	1.02	0.02	1.03
Jun 05 03	15	0.98	0.97	...	0.98
Jun 12 03	22	1.00	0.99	0.01	1.00
Jun 19 03	29	1.03	1.02	-0.01	1.04
Jun 26 03	36	0.99	0.98	-0.01	0.99
Jul 03 03	43	1.00	0.99	-0.01	1.00
Jul 10 03	50	1.00	0.99	-0.01	1.01
Jul 17 03	57	0.99	0.98	-0.02	1.00
Jul 24 03	64	1.00	0.99	-0.01	1.01
Jul 31 03	71	0.99	0.98	-0.02	1.00
Aug 07 03	78	1.00	0.99	...	1.01
Aug 14 03	**85**	**1.01**	**1.00**	**-0.02**	**1.02**
Aug 21 03	92	1.02	1.01	-0.01	1.03
Aug 28 03	99	1.01	1.00	-0.02	1.02
Sep 04 03	106	1.01	1.00	-0.02	1.02
Sep 11 03	113	1.01	1.00	-0.02	1.02
Sep 18 03	120	1.01	1.00	-0.03	1.02
Sep 25 03	127	1.02	1.01	-0.02	1.03
Oct 02 03	134	1.01	1.00	-0.03	1.02
Oct 09 03	141	1.01	1.00	-0.03	1.02
Oct 16 03	148	1.03	1.02	...	1.04
Oct 23 03	155	1.03	1.02	...	1.04
Oct 30 03	162	1.03	1.02	-0.01	1.04
Nov 06 03	169	1.02	1.01	-0.02	1.03
Nov 13 03	**176**	**1.02**	**1.01**	**-0.02**	**1.03**

Inflation-Indexed Treasury Securities

RATE	MAT	BID/ASKED	CHG	*YLD	ACCR PRIN
3.375	01/07	109-30/31	8	0.612	1160
3.625	01/08	112-14/15	15	0.885	1138
3.875	01/09	114-26/27	14	1.155	1121
4.250	01/10	118-08/09	26	1.366	1092
3.500	01/11	114-03/04	28	1.537	1056
3.375	01/12	114-07/08	34	1.605	1035
3.000	07/12	111-11/12	35	1.656	1024
3.625	04/28	125-15/16	59	2.278	1136
3.875	04/29	131-12/13	63	2.265	1118
3.375	04/32	125-19/20	67	2.176	1035

*Yield to maturity on accrued principal.

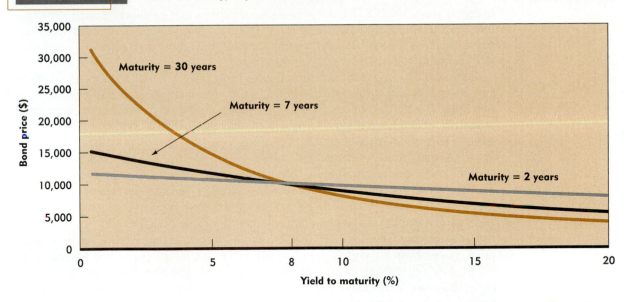

FIGURE 18.3 Bond Prices ($10,000 Face Value)

Since Treasury bonds and notes pay semiannual coupons, bond yields are stated on a semiannual basis. The relationship between the price of a note or bond and its yield to maturity was discussed in Chapter 10. For convenience, the bond price formula from that chapter is restated here:

$$\text{Bond price} = \frac{\text{Annual coupon}}{YTM} \times \left[1 - \frac{1}{(1 + YTM/2)^{2M}}\right] + \frac{\text{Face value}}{(1 + YTM/2)^{2M}}$$

Figure 18.3 illustrates the relationship between the price of a bond and its yield to maturity for 2-year, 7-year, and 30-year terms to maturity. Notice that each bond has a price of 100 when its yield is 8 percent. This indicates that each bond has an 8 percent coupon rate, because when a bond's coupon rate is equal to its yield to maturity, its price is equal to its par value.

bid-ask spread The difference between a dealer's ask price and bid price.

The difference between a dealer's asked and bid prices is called the **bid-ask spread**. The bid-ask spread measures the dealer's gross profit from a single round-trip transaction of buying a security at the bid price and then selling it at the asked price.

Check This

18.2d   What would Figure 18.3 look like if the three bonds all had coupon rates of 6 percent? What about 10 percent?

18.2e   In Figure 18.2, which Treasury issues have the narrowest spreads? Why do you think this is so?

18.2f   Examine the spreads between bid and asked prices for Treasury notes and bonds listed in a recent *Wall Street Journal*.

Inflation-Indexed Treasury Securities

In recent years, the U.S. Treasury has issued securities that guarantee a fixed rate of return in excess of realized inflation rates. These inflation-indexed Treasury securities pay a fixed coupon rate on their current principal and adjust their principal semiannually according to the most recent inflation rate.

For example, suppose an inflation-indexed note is issued with a coupon rate of 3.5 percent and an initial principal of $1,000. Six months later, the note will pay a coupon of $1,000 \times 3.5\%/2 = 17.50. Assuming 2 percent inflation over the six months since issuance, the note's principal is then increased to $1,000 \times 102\% = $1,020$. Six months later, the note pays $1,020 \times 3.5\%/2 = 17.85, and its principal is again adjusted to compensate for recent inflation.

Price and yield information for inflation-indexed Treasury securities is reported in *The Wall Street Journal* in the same section with other Treasury securities, as shown in Figure 18.2. Locating the listing for inflation-indexed Treasury securities in Figure 18.2, we see that the first and second columns report the fixed coupon rate and maturity, respectively. The third and fourth columns report current bid/ask prices and the price change from the previous trading day. Prices for inflation-indexed securities are reported as a percentage of current accrued principal. The fifth and sixth columns list an inflation-adjusted yield to maturity and current accrued principal reflecting all cumulative inflation adjustments.

For investors wanting long-term protection against inflation along with the safety of U.S. Treasury bonds, inflation-indexed Treasury securities are perhaps the perfect investment. The nearby *Investment Updates* box further discusses the attractive features of inflation-indexed Treasury securities.

18.3 U.S. Treasury Auctions

For recent information on Treasury auctions visit
www.publicdebt.
treas.gov

The Federal Reserve Bank conducts regularly scheduled auctions for Treasury securities. At each Treasury auction, the Federal Reserve accepts sealed bids of two types: competitive bids and noncompetitive bids. Competitive bids for T-bills specify a bid price and a bid quantity. The bid price is what the bidder is willing to pay, and the bid quantity is the face value amount that the bidder will purchase if the bid is accepted. Noncompetitive bids specify only a bid quantity since the price charged to noncompetitive bidders will be determined by the results of the competitive auction process. Individual investors can submit noncompetitive bids, but only Treasury securities dealers can submit competitive bids.

At the close of bidding, all sealed bids are forwarded to the U.S. Treasury for processing. As a first step, all noncompetitive bids are accepted automatically and are subtracted from the total issue amount. Then a **stop-out bid** is determined; this is the price at which all competitive bids are sufficient to finance the remaining issue amount. Competitive bids at or above the stop-out bid are accepted, and bids below the stop-out bid are rejected.

Since 1998, all U.S. Treasury auctions have been single-price auctions in which all accepted competitive bids pay the stop-out bid. The stop-out bid is also the price paid by noncompetitive bidders. For example, suppose an auction for T-bills with $20 billion of face value receives $28 billion of competitive bids and $4 billion of noncompetitive bids. Noncompetitive bids are automatically accepted, leaving $16 billion for competitive bidders. Now suppose the stop-out bid for this $16 billion amount is

stop-out bid The lowest competitive bid in a U.S. Treasury auction that is accepted.

"Inflation-Linked Treasurys Hold Surprising Appeal"

Inflation-indexed treasury bonds don't quite rival the Swiss Army Knife. But It's amazing what you can do with them. Need income? Worried about stocks? Want a place to park some cash? Inflation bonds can come in handy. Here's how:

RISING INCOME: Each year, the value of inflation bonds is stepped up along with consumer prices. Investors also collect interest based on this ever-rising principal value. Those twin attributes make the bonds an intriguing investment for retirees.

Suppose you invested $1,000 in inflation bonds at the current yield of 3.8%. If consumer prices rose 2.5% over the next year, your principal would climb to $1,025 and you would earn interest equal to 3.8% of this growing sum. Thus, if you spent the interest but didn't cash in any bonds, you would enjoy a rising stream of income, while keeping your principal's spending power intact.

Retirees should still keep some money in stocks, so they have a shot at even higher returns. After all, many folks won't have a big enough portfolio to live off inflation bonds' 3.8% yield. Still, inflation bonds are a good choice for at least part of your portfolio. "The long-run total return may not be as high as it is from stocks," says Ken Volpert, co-manager of Vanguard Inflation Protected Securities Fund, a no-load fund with $120 million in assets. "But you have greater certainty that the rise in your income and your principal will be in line with inflation."

INFLATION INSURANCE: Need protection against rising consumer prices? Inflation bonds may be just the ticket. "Say you were going to retire next year, and you plan to buy an annuity at that point," Mr. Hammond says. "With inflation bonds, you've protected yourself against a short-term spike in inflation."

Alternatively, suppose you sold your house and won't buy another for a few years. Maybe you are taking a job overseas or planning to rent while you look for the perfect spot to retire. If you plunked your home equity into inflation bonds and earned 3.8 percentage points a year more than inflation, you should have a good shot at keeping pace with real-estate prices.

PORTFOLIO PROTECTION: If inflation takes off or the economy tumbles into recession, stocks will get whacked. Want to cushion that blow? Traditionally, stock investors have added a dollop of regular bonds to their portfolios. That works well in a recession, when interest rates tend to fall, driving up the price of regular bonds, whose fixed-interest payouts now seem more attractive. But when inflation takes off, interest rates climb. Result: Both stocks and regular bonds get crushed.

That is where inflation bonds come in. They won't do as well as regular bonds in a recession. But during periods of rising consumer prices, inflation bonds will sparkle, thus helping to offset your stock-market losses.

PARKING PLACE: Because inflation bonds don't perform as erratically as regular bonds, they can be a good place to stash your emergency money. You never know when you will need this emergency money. Maybe you will have to call on your reserve next month—or maybe the money will sit untouched for the next decade. Because your time horizon is uncertain, you want the money to be readily available, but you also want it to earn healthy returns. Inflation bonds look good on both counts. Mr. Volpert figures your chances of losing money in any given year are slim. "You might even have better downside protection than you would with a short-term bond fund," he says.

$9,700 for a $10,000 face-value T-bill. Accepted competitive bidders and all noncompetitive bidders pay this price of $9,700.

The process is similar for T-bond and T-note issues, except that bids are made on a yield basis, where competitive bids state yields instead of prices. A coupon rate for the entire issue is then set according to the average competitive-bid yield.

Check This

18.3a The Federal Reserve announces an offering of Treasury bills with a face value amount of $25 billion. The response is $5 billion of noncompetitive bids, along with the following competitive bids:

(continued)

Bidder	Price Bid	Quantity Bid
A	$9,500	$5 billion
B	9,550	5 billion
C	9,600	5 billion
D	9,650	5 billion
E	9,700	5 billion

In a single-price auction, which bids are accepted and what prices are paid by each bidder? How much money is raised by the entire offering?

18.4 U.S. Savings Bonds

The U.S. Treasury offers an interesting investment opportunity for individual investors in the form of savings bonds. Two types of savings bonds are currently available, Series EE and Series I. Other types exist, but they are either no longer available or can be obtained only by converting one type to another.

Series EE Savings Bonds

For the latest on Savings Bonds visit www.savingsbonds. com

Series EE bonds are available in face value denominations ranging from $50 to $10,000, but the original price of a Series EE bond is always set at exactly half its face value. Thus, Series EE bonds are sold to resemble zero coupon securities. However, individuals purchasing Series EE bonds receive semiannual interest accruals. Each May 1 and November 1, the Treasury sets the interest rate on EE bonds at 90 percent of the yield on newly issued five-year maturity T-notes. For example, suppose the yield on newly issued five-year maturity T-notes is 5.56 percent. In this case, the Treasury will set an interest rate of $.90 \times 5.56\% = 5.0\%$ on savings bonds for the next six months. This interest is paid as an accrual to the redemption value of the bond, where the current redemption value is the original price of the bond plus all prior accrued interest.

Series I Savings Bonds

Series I bonds are also available in face value denominations ranging from $50 to $10,000, but they are originally sold at face value. Each May 1 and November 1, the Treasury sets the interest rate on Series I bonds at a fixed rate plus the recent inflation rate. In this way, Series I bonds are indexed to inflation. For example, suppose the fixed rate is 3 percent, and the recent inflation rate is 2 percent. In this case, the Treasury will set an interest rate of $3\% + 2\% = 5\%$ for the next six months. This interest is paid as an accrual to the redemption value of the bond.

Savings bonds offer several tax advantages to individual investors. First, as with all U.S. Treasury securities, savings bonds are not subject to state or local taxes. Also, federal income tax payment on U.S. Savings Bond interest is deferred until the bonds are redeemed. With all factors considered, their overall attractiveness has led individual investors to hold almost $200 billion of U.S. Savings Bonds.

18.4a   Compare the methods by which interest is paid for Series EE savings bonds and Series I inflation-indexed Treasury securities.

18.5 Federal Government Agency Securities

Most U.S. government agencies consolidate their borrowing through the Federal Financing Bank, which obtains funds directly from the U.S. Treasury. However, several federal agencies are authorized to issue securities directly to the public. For example, the Resolution Trust Funding Corporation, the World Bank, and the Tennessee Valley Authority issue notes and bonds directly to investors. Bonds issued by U.S. government agencies share an almost equal credit quality with U.S. Treasury issues. Although most agency debt does not carry an explicit guarantee of the U.S. government, a federal agency on the verge of default would probably receive government support to ensure timely payment of interest and principal on outstanding debt. This perception is supported by historical experience and the political reality that Congress would likely feel compelled to rescue an agency that it created if it became financially distressed.

    What makes government agency notes and bonds attractive to many investors is that they offer higher yields than comparable U.S. Treasury securities. However, the market for agency debt is less active than the market for U.S. Treasury debt, and therefore the spread between dealers' bid and asked prices is greater for agency issues than for Treasury issues. For example, Figure 18.4 presents dealer price quotes for agency issues as reported in *The Wall Street Journal*. The listing format is the same as for Treasury notes and bonds described previously, except that callable bonds are indicated by an asterisk with only the maturity date shown.

    If you compare bid and asked dealer price quotes for agency bonds listed in Figure 18.4 with similar Treasury bonds listed in Figure 18.2, you will find that agency bonds have a higher bid-ask spread than Treasury bonds. The reason for the higher bid-ask spread is that agency bond trading volume is much lower than Treasury bond trading volume. To compensate for the lower volume, dealers charge higher spreads. Thus, trading agency bonds is more costly than trading Treasury bonds. Consequently, agency bonds are usually purchased by institutional investors planning to hold the bonds until they mature. Another reason for the higher yields on agency bonds compared to Treasury bonds is that interest income from agency bonds is subject to state and local taxation, whereas Treasury interest payments are subject only to federal taxation.

Visit
www.investinginbonds.
com
for more information
on agency securities

18.5a   In Figure 18.4, what does the asterisk indicate?

18.5b   Examine spreads between bid and asked prices for government agency notes and bonds listed in a recent *Wall Street Journal*. What is the typical bid-ask spread?

FIGURE 18.4

Agency Securities

Source: Reprinted with permission from *The Wall Street Journal*, July 8, 2003, via Copyright Clearance Center, Inc. © 2003 Dow Jones & Company, Inc. All Rights Reserved Worldwide.

Government Agency & Similar Issues

Over-the-Counter mid-afternoon quotations based on large transactions, usually $1 million or more. Colons in bid and asked quotes represent 32nds; 101:01 means 101 1/32.

All yields are calculated to maturity, and based on the asked quote.

*Callable issue, maturity date shown. For issues callable prior to maturity, yields are computed to the earliest call date for issues quoted above par, or 100, and to the maturity date for issues below par.

Source: Bear, Stearns & Co. via Street Software Technology Inc.

Fannie Mae Issues

RATE	MAT	BID	ASKED	YLD
3.63	4-04	101:31	102:01	0.95
5.63	5-04	103:29	103:31	0.92
3.00	6-04	101:25	101:27	1.01
6.50	8-04	105:25	105:27	1.13
3.50	9-04	102:24	102:26	1.10
1.88	12-04	100:29	100:31	1.20
7.13	2-05	109:05	109:07	1.27
3.88	3-05	104:07	104:09	1.29
5.75	6-05	108:07	108:09	1.39
7.00	7-05	110:29	110:31	1.46
3.13	8-05*	100:06	100:08	0.47
2.88	10-05	102:27	102:29	1.57
2.75	11-05*	100:14	100:16	1.25
6.00	12-05	110:11	110:13	1.62
2.75	12-05*	100:18	100:20	1.31
5.50	2-06	109:12	109:14	1.77
2.13	4-06	100:23	100:25	1.83
5.50	5-06	109:10	109:12	2.05
2.25	5-06	101:02	101:04	1.84
5.25	6-06	109:15	109:17	1.90
5.50	7-06*	100:03	100:05	0.00
5.25	8-06*	100:13	100:15	0.55
4.38	10-06	107:11	107:13	2.02
4.50	10-06*	100:28	100:30	1.01
4.00	11-06*	100:30	101:00	1.21
4.75	12-06*	101:17	101:19	1.24
5.00	1-07*	109:15	109:17	2.17
5.00	1-07*	102:01	102:03	1.03
7.13	3-07	117:07	117:09	2.21
5.25	3-07*	102:17	102:19	1.51
5.25	4-07	110:20	110:22	2.28
5.00	5-07*	102:31	103:01	1.37
4.25	7-07	107:02	107:04	2.38
6.63	10-07	116:14	116:16	2.52
3.50	10-07*	101:24	101:26	2.05
3.25	11-07	102:29	102:31	2.53

RATE	MAT	BID	ASKED	YLD
3.25	1-08	102:21	102:23	2.61
3.50	1-08*	101:28	101:30	2.22
5.75	2-08	113:08	113:10	2.66
6.00	5-08	114:19	114:21	2.75
5.25	1-09	111:10	111:12	2.99
6.38	6-09	117:10	117:12	3.14
6.63	9-09	118:28	118:30	0.65
7.25	1-10	122:22	122:24	3.34
7.13	6-10	122:14	122:16	3.45
6.63	11-10	119:21	119:23	3.55
6.25	2-11	114:06	114:08	4.05
5.50	3-11	112:07	112:09	3.65
6.00	5-11	115:15	115:17	3.70
6.25	7-11*	104:17	104:19	1.70
5.50	10-11*	104:05	104:07	2.11
5.38	11-11	111:01	111:03	3.81
5.00	11-11*	102:25	102:27	2.84
6.00	12-11*	105:21	105:23	1.98
6.00	1-12*	105:27	105:29	2.05
6.13	3-12	116:12	116:14	3.88
6.25	3-12*	107:06	107:08	1.90
5.50	7-12*	104:29	104:31	2.96
5.25	8-12	106:14	106:16	4.37
4.38	9-12	103:00	103:02	3.97
4.75	2-13*	101:20	101:22	4.06
4.63	5-13	101:07	101:09	4.46
6.25	5-29	113:31	114:03	5.25
7.13	1-30	126:18	126:22	5.25
7.25	5-30	128:16	128:20	5.25
6.63	11-30	119:24	119:28	5.25

Freddie Mac

RATE	MAT	BID	ASKED	YLD
3.75	4-04	102:02	102:04	0.94
5.00	5-04	103:12	103:14	0.93
6.25	7-04	105:05	105:07	1.08
3.00	7-04	102:00	102:02	0.96
4.50	8-04	103:20	103:22	1.26
3.25	11-04	102:22	102:24	1.20
6.88	1-05	108:11	108:13	1.26

RATE	MAT	BID	ASKED	YLD
1.88	1-05	100:27	100:29	1.27
3.88	2-05	104:00	104:02	1.30
1.75	5-05	100:20	100:22	1.37
4.25	6-05	105:10	105:12	1.42
7.00	7-05	110:29	110:31	1.47
2.88	9-05*	102:25	102:27	1.55
2.88	9-05*	100:11	100:13	0.93
5.25	1-06	108:21	108:23	1.70
2.38	4-06	101:11	101:13	1.86
5.50	7-06*	110:09	110:11	1.95
4.88	3-07	109:05	109:07	2.26
4.50	7-07*	102:28	102:30	1.63
3.50	9-07	104:01	104:03	2.47
3.25	2-08*	101:01	101:03	2.55
2.75	3-08	100:10	100:12	2.66
3.50	4-08*	101:21	101:23	2.47
5.75	4-08	113:14	113:16	2.71
5.13	10-08	110:28	110:30	2.87
5.75	3-09	113:28	113:30	3.06
5.75	4-09*	103:15	103:17	1.32
4.75	8-09*	103:01	103:03	1.88
6.63	9-09	118:26	118:28	3.23
7.00	3-10	121:13	121:15	3.38
6.88	9-10	121:03	121:05	3.52
5.63	3-11	113:00	113:02	3.66
5.88	3-11	111:20	111:22	4.09
6.00	6-11	115:13	115:15	3.73
6.38	8-11*	107:22	107:24	3.67
5.50	9-11	111:29	111:31	3.79
5.75	1-12	113:18	113:20	3.86
6.25	3-12*	108:30	109:00	3.60
6.00	5-12*	103:27	103:29	1.49
5.13	7-12	108:21	108:23	3.97
5.13	8-12*	101:24	101:26	3.45
4.75	10-12*	101:23	101:25	3.91
5.25	11-12*	103:04	103:06	4.43
4.50	1-13	103:13	103:15	4.06
4.38	3-13	102:13	102:15	4.06
4.75	5-13*	99:11	99:13	4.83
6.75	9-29	120:23	120:27	5.27
6.75	3-31	121:18	121:22	5.25
6.25	7-32	114:20	114:24	5.25

Federal Farm Credit Bank

RATE	MAT	BID	ASKED	YLD
2.38	10-04	101:18	101:20	1.02
3.88	12-04	103:20	103:22	1.26
3.88	2-05	103:29	103:31	1.29
4.38	4-05	105:08	105:10	1.33

RATE	MAT	BID	ASKED	YLD
2.13	8-05	101:07	101:09	1.50
2.50	11-05	101:27	101:29	1.67
2.63	12-05	102:04	102:06	1.70
2.50	3-06	101:23	101:25	1.82
2.25	9-06	100:21	100:23	2.01
4.08	4-08*	101:06	101:08	2.72

Federal Home Loan Bank

RATE	MAT	BID	ASKED	YLD
4.88	4-04	103:00	103:02	0.87
3.63	10-04	103:03	103:05	1.09
4.13	11-04	103:27	103:29	1.20
4.00	2-05	104:06	104:08	1.32
4.38	2-05	104:26	104:28	1.28
6.88	8-05	110:30	111:00	1.19
2.50	12-05	101:31	102:01	1.65
5.13	3-06	108:17	108:19	1.80
2.50	3-06	101:17	101:19	1.89
5.38	5-06	109:17	109:19	1.90
2.25	5-06	101:01	101:03	1.86
4.88	11-06	108:25	108:27	2.12
4.88	2-07	108:31	109:01	2.25
5.38	2-07	110:08	110:10	2.37
2.75	3-08	100:11	100:13	2.66
5.80	9-08	114:01	114:03	2.84
6.00	5-11	110:29	110:31	4.33
5.63	11-11	112:13	112:15	3.86
5.75	5-12	113:29	113:31	3.87
4.50	11-12	104:05	104:07	3.96

GNMA Mtge. Issues

RATE	MAT	BID	ASKED	YLD
4.00	30Yr	96:06	96:08	4.57
4.50	30Yr	99:01	99:03	4.68
5.00	30Yr	101:23	101:25	4.66
5.50	30Yr	103:22	103:24	4.41
6.00	30Yr	104:24	104:26	3.49
6.50	30Yr	105:00	105:02	2.55
7.00	30Yr	105:19	105:21	2.61
7.50	30Yr	106:10	106:12	3.24
8.00	30Yr	107:21	107:23	3.53
8.50	30Yr	107:23	107:25	4.26

Tennessee Valley Authority

RATE	MAT	BID	ASKED	YLD
4.75	7-04	103:19	103:21	1.11
6.38	6-05	109:13	109:15	1.38
5.38	11-08	111:30	112:00	2.93
5.63	1-11	112:15	112:17	3.70
6.75	11-25	120:17	120:20	5.18
7.13	5-30	126:31	127:03	5.23

18.6 Municipal Bonds

Visit www.investinginbonds.com for more about municipal bonds

Municipal notes and bonds are intermediate- to long-term interest-bearing obligations of state and local governments or agencies of those governments. The defining characteristic of municipal notes and bonds, often called "munis," is that coupon interest is usually exempt from federal income tax. Consequently, the market for municipal debt is commonly called the *tax-exempt market*. Most of the 50 states also have an income tax, but their tax treatment of municipal debt interest varies. Only a few states exempt coupon interest on out-of-state municipal bonds from in-state income tax, but most states do allow in-state municipal debt interest an exemption from in-state income tax. In any case, state income tax rates are normally much lower than federal income tax rates, and state taxes can be used as an itemized deduction from federal taxable income. Consequently, state taxes are usually a secondary consideration for municipal bond investors.

The federal income tax exemption makes municipal bonds attractive to investors in the highest income tax brackets. This includes many individual investors, commercial banks, and property and casualty insurance companies—precisely those investors who actually hold almost all municipal debt. However, yields on municipal debt are less than on corporate debt with similar features and credit quality. This eliminates much, but not all, of the advantage of the tax exemption. Therefore, tax-exempt investors, including pension funds and retirement accounts of individuals, nonprofit institutions, and some life insurance companies, normally do not invest in municipal bonds. Instead, they prefer to invest in higher-yielding corporate bonds. For some more interesting details on the tax status of various municipal bonds, see the nearby *Investment Updates* box.

Municipal bonds are typically less complicated investments than corporate bonds. However, while municipal debt often carries a high credit rating, **default risk** does exist. Thus, investing in municipal debt requires more care than investing in U.S. Treasury securities.

To illustrate some standard features of a municipal bond issue, Table 18.2 summarizes the issue terms for a hypothetical bond issued by the city of Bedford Falls. We see that the bonds were issued in December 1999 and mature 30 years later in December 2029. Each bond has a face value denomination of $5,000 and pays an annual coupon equal to 6 percent of face value. The annual coupon is split between two semiannual payments each June and December. Based on the original offer price of 100, or 100 percent of par value, the bonds have a yield to maturity of 6 percent. The Bedford Falls bonds are call-protected for 10 years, until January 2009. Thereafter, the bonds are callable any time at par value.

The Bedford Falls bonds are **general obligation bonds** (**GOs**), which means that the bonds are secured by the full faith and credit of the city of Bedford Falls. "Full faith and credit" means the power of the municipality to collect taxes. The trustee for the bond issue is the Potters Bank of Bedford Falls. A trustee is appointed to represent the financial interests of bondholders and administer the sinking fund for the bond issue. A sinking fund requires a bond issuer to redeem for cash a fraction of an outstanding bond issue on a periodic basis. The sinking fund in this example requires that, beginning 10 years after issuance, the city must redeem at par value $2.5 million of the bond issue each year. At each annual redemption, a fraction of the bond issue is called and the affected bondholders receive the par value call price.

default risk The risk that a bond issuer will cease making scheduled payments of coupons or principal or both.

general obligation bonds (GOs) Bonds issued by a municipality that are secured by the full faith and credit of the issuer.

TABLE 18.2	City of Bedford Falls General Obligation Bonds	
Issue amount	$50 million	Bond issue represents a total face value amount of $50 million
Issue date	12/15/99	Bonds were offered to the public on December 15, 1999
Maturity date	12/31/29	All remaining principal must be paid at maturity on December 31, 2029
Par value	$5,000	Each bond has a face value of $5,000
Coupon rate	6%	Annual coupons of $300 per bond
Coupon dates	12/31, 6/30	Semiannual coupons of $150
Offering price	100	Offer price is 100% of par value
Yield to maturity	6%	Based on stated offer price
Call provision	Callable after 12/31/09	Bonds are call-protected for 10 years
Call price	100	Bonds are callable at par value
Trustee	Potters Bank of Bedford Falls	The trustee is appointed to represent the bondholders and administer the sinking fund
Sinking fund	$2.5 million annual par redemptions after 12/31/09	City must redeem at par value $2.5 million of the bond issue each year beginning in 2010

Not All Tax-Free Muni Bonds Are Really Exempt from Tax

For safety-conscious investors looking for tax-free income, this is a good time to consider municipal bonds. Just be careful: Not all tax-free bonds are really tax-free. Even tax experts agree the $1.7 trillion market for state and local government bonds can be surprisingly tricky. Municipal bonds come in many different shades and flavors. The Bond Market Association, a trade group that represents securities firms and banks that buy, sell and trade bonds (www.bondmarkets.com), estimates there are more than 50,000 state and local entities that issue "munis," and there are more than two million separate bond issues outstanding. So never purchase a muni without carefully investigating the bond's tax status with your broker or financial advisor. This subject can get so tricky that I recommend you ask the same question of more than one expert. I speak from experience here: I covered the credit markets for *The Wall Street Journal* for nearly a decade and found many myths and misconceptions about this area. Here are just a few tax considerations to keep in mind when you're shopping for munis:

State and Local Taxes. Muni-bond income isn't always exempt from state and local taxes. The general rule of thumb is that bonds issued by the state you live in, or municipalities of that state, pay tax-free interest. But if you live in a state with an income tax and you buy out-of-state bonds, the interest typically would be taxable in your home state.

For example, I live in New York City. If I buy a New York City or New York State bond, I typically wouldn't owe any federal, state or local taxes on the interest. Those bonds are, as bond peddlers like to call them, "triple tax-free." But if I buy an out-of-state bond, such as one issued by California, the interest income would be fully taxable in New York. That's why many investors in high-tax areas such as New York City favor bonds issued within their home state. Or they may buy shares of mutual funds that specialize in bonds only from a single state. Just don't be a slave to this strategy. Sometimes, investors can do better by buying out-of-state bonds, even though it means having to pay their home state's tax.

Unfortunately, you also can't assume that all in-state bonds will be free from your state tax. That can depend on what state you call home, says Alexandra Lebenthal, president of Lebenthal & Co., a New York-based firm specializing in municipal bonds. Check this not only with your broker but also with your state tax department. The Federation of Tax Administrators in Washington, D.C., has a Web site that includes links to state tax departments.

Intangible Property. Naturally, you don't have to worry about such state income-tax considerations if you're from a state with no income tax, such as Florida or Texas. But Floridians have another taxing issue to

(continued)

Municipal Bond Features

Municipal bonds are typically callable, pay semiannual coupons, and often have a par value denomination of $5,000. Municipal bond prices are stated as a percentage of par value. Thus, a price of 102 indicates that a bond with a par value of $5,000 has a price of $5,100. By convention, however, municipal bond dealers commonly use yield quotes rather than price quotes in their trading procedures. For example, a dealer might quote a bid-yield of 6.25 percent for a 5 percent coupon bond with seven years to maturity, indicating a willingness to buy at a price determined by that yield. The actual dollar bid price in this example is $4,649.99, as shown in the following bond price calculation:

Check out municipal bonds at www.municipalbonds.com

$$\frac{\$250}{.0625} \times \left[1 - \frac{1}{(1.03125)^{14}} \right] + \frac{\$5,000}{(1.03125)^{14}} = \$4,649.99$$

Because there are many thousands of different municipal bond issues outstanding, only a few large issues trade with sufficient frequency to justify having their prices reported in the financial press. A *Wall Street Journal* listing of some actively traded municipal bonds is seen in Figure 18.5. The listing reports the name of the issuer, the coupon rate and maturity of the issue, the most recent bid price quote and the consider: The state has an "intangible personal property" tax, an annual tax based on the market value of stock holdings and other "intangible" personal property. Some types of investments, such as bonds issued by the state of Florida, aren't subject to this tax. To find out what other investments are exempt from this tax, see the Web site of the Florida Department of Revenue.

Alternative Minimum Tax. Lawmakers created the AMT decades ago to prevent high-income people from escaping all federal income taxes through a combination of tax credits, deductions and other items. But since the tax wasn't adjusted for inflation, it's now hitting rapidly growing numbers of Americans. Unfortunately, some types of bonds pay interest that is considered income when you're calculating the AMT.

Investinginbonds.com, another Web site run by the Bond Market Association, offers a helpful primer on muni-bond income and the AMT. (Click on "Taxation of Municipals" in the left-hand navigation bar and then scroll way down to the "Alternative Minimum Tax" section.) If you're subject to this tax and you're on the phone with an eager bond salesman, be sure to ask if a bond you're considering is an "AMT bond."

Social Security. One of the biggest surprises for many elderly investors is that buying munis can affect how much, if any, of their Social Security benefits are taxable. The law says that you have to include tax-exempt bond income when you're doing the number-crunching. The *Investinginbonds.com* Web site also has more information on this subject—in fact, you'll find it right below the section mentioned above on the AMT. So if you're receiving Social Security income, be sure to have a tax professional evaluate your situation before purchasing muni bonds.

Taxable Munis. A taxable muni is just what it sounds like: It's a muni bond where the interest "is not excluded from the gross income of its owners for federal income tax purposes," says Lynnette K. Hotchkiss, senior vice president and associate general counsel of the Bond Market Association. She says some munis are taxable because they were issued "for purposes that the federal government deems not to provide a significant benefit to the public at large," such as certain types of economic-development projects that solely benefit a corporation.

Capital Gains and Losses. There also may be capital-gains tax considerations. If you sell a muni bond—or a muni-bond fund—for more than you paid for it, capital gains taxes may have to be considered.

While this isn't a comprehensive list, it's a reminder that buying munis can be much trickier than it may seem at first glance.

Source: Tom Herman, *The Wall Street Journal*, May 21, 2002.

change from an earlier price quote, and a yield to maturity based on a dealer's bid yield. Our nearby *Work the Web* box provides more information on municipal bond prices and liquidity.

A **call provision** is a standard feature of most municipal bond issues. A call provision allows an issuer to retire outstanding bonds before they mature, usually to refund with new bonds after a fall in market interest rates. When the bond is called, each bondholder receives the bond's call price in exchange for the bond. However, two bond features often limit an issuer's call privilege. First, callable municipal bonds usually offer a period of call protection following their original issue date. Since a bond issue is not callable during this period, the earliest possible call date is the end of the call protection period. Second, a call price is often specified with a call premium. A call premium is the difference between a bond's call price and its par value. A common arrangement is to specify a call premium equal to one year's coupons for a call occurring at the earliest possible call date. This is then followed by a schedule of call premium reductions, until about 5 to 10 years before maturity, when the call premium is eliminated entirely. Thereafter, the bond issue is callable any time at par value.

Municipal bonds are commonly issued with a serial maturity structure, hence the term **serial bonds**. In a serial bond issue, a fraction of the total issue amount is scheduled

call provision Feature of a municipal bond issue that specifies when the bonds may be called by the issuer and the call price that must be paid.

serial bonds Bonds issued with maturity dates scheduled at intervals, so that a fraction of the bond issue matures in each year of a multiple-year period.

607

WORK THE WEB

As we mentioned in this chapter, municipal bonds are less liquid than Treasury securities and often have higher bid-ask spreads. So how high can the spreads go? We went to www.municipalbonds.com to find out. Below you see part of what we found for the fourth quarter of 2002.

4Q/2002 Worst Bid/Offer Spreads

Here is the 2002 Q4 list of the one hundred worst "actively traded" Municipal Bond market spreads between the lowest bid and the highest offer. To be labeled as actively traded on a specific day, a Municipal Bond must have traded at least four, three or two times.

Date	CUSIP	Municipal Bond Name / Description	Coupon	Maturity	Bid Side Customer Sold to Dealer (Lowest / Highest)	Offer Side Customer Purchase from Dealer (Lowest / Highest)	Spread	# of Trades	Volume (000)
12/04/2002	585650-GJ-7	MELROSE PARK ILL TAX INCREMENT-SER A	4.900	12/15/2021	33.386 / 99.386	99.386 / 99.386	66.000	5	835
11/21/2002	130684-BX-0	CALIFORNIA ST PUB WKS BRD LEASE REV DEPT GEN SVCS-CAP EAST END-A	5.250	12/01/2014	61.256 / 61.256	109.176 / 109.777	48.521	7	13390
12/04/2002	35823H-AC-7	FRESNO CALIF REV VAR-TRINITY HEALTH CREDIT-C		12/01/2030	63.500 / 63.500	100.000 / 100.000	36.500	2	1050
11/14/2002	544628-GA-2	LOS ANGELES CALIF REGL ARPTS IMPT CORP LEASE REV FACS-SUBLEASE-CONTINENTAL	9.250	08/01/2024	70.250 / 99.000	99.250 / 99.250	29.000	5	2045
12/30/2002	123593-BS-3	BUTLER CNTY PA INDL DEV AUTH COML DEV FIRST MTG REV REF-KMART CORP-SER A	6.875	06/15/2006	73.000 / 73.450	100.250 / 100.250	27.250	4	60

This table shows the top five bid-side spreads. As you can see, the biggest spread for a bond on a single day was the Melrose Park, Illinois, municipal bond with a spread of 66.000. The lowest price paid for the bond by an investor on this day was 33.386 and the highest price paid was 99.386. Assuming a $5,000 par value, this means one investor purchased the bond for about $1,669 and another investor purchased the same bond for about $4,969. That's what you call a spread! The website also has the worst offer-side spreads, which is the price at which investors sold bonds to a dealer. Almost unbelievably, the worst offer-side spread for the same period was 70.125.

FIGURE 18.5

Municipal Securities

Source: Reprinted with permission from *The Wall Street Journal*, July 8, 2003, via Copyright Clearance Center, Inc. © 2003 Dow Jones & Company, Inc. All Rights Reserved Worldwide.

Tax-Exempt Bonds

Representative prices for several active tax-exempt revenue and refunding bonds, based on institutional trades. Yield is to maturity. n-new.
Source: The Bond Buyer/Standard & Poor's Securities Evaluations.

ISSUE	COUPON	MAT	PRICE	CHG	BID YLD	ISSUE	COUPON	MAT	PRICE	CHG	BID YLD
Calif St Var purpose gen	5.000	02-01-33	103.272	-.248	4.59	MichiganStHospFinRfRv	5.375	12-01-30	102.931	-.231	4.98
Calif StvarPrpGOSrs2003	5.000	02-01-33	97.731	-.297	5.15	Minn MN Hlth Care Sys	5.750	11-15-32	104.630	-.232	5.13
Calif StvarPrpGOSrs2003	5.250	02-01-28	101.638	-.080	5.04	N.TexasTwyAthDallasN.Twy	5.000	01-01-38	102.968	-.236	4.61
CaliforniaHlthFacsFngAth	5.000	03-01-33	96.987	-.441	5.20	NYC MuniWtrFinAthWtr&Swr	5.000	06-15-34	103.175	-.246	4.60
DallasFtWorthTX JointRv0	5.000	11-01-32	98.062	-.448	5.13	NYC MuniWtrFinAthWtr&Swr	5.000	06-15-38	102.757	-.244	4.65
DallasFtWorthTX JointRv0	5.500	11-01-33	105.054	-.254	4.88	NYC NY gen oblig bond	5.250	06-01-28	102.423	-.239	4.94
Denver ConvHotelAthCoSnr	5.000	12-01-33	102.358	-.251	4.71	NYSDormAthHspRv2003Srs I	5.000	07-01-34	102.697	-.245	4.66
DenverCity&CntyCOAirport	5.000	11-15-33	102.349	-.250	4.71	Orlando Orange Co Exprwy	5.000	07-01-35	103.797	-.249	4.53
Detroit MI SewageDispSys	5.000	07-01-32	104.066	-.250	4.49	PrtoRico(Cmwlth)pubimprv	5.000	07-01-32	104.563	-.233	4.39
Forsyth Mont Poll Cntrl	5.000	03-01-31	103.930	-.261	4.53	PtAuthorityNYNJCnslRvSr1	4.750	06-15-33	95.912	-.450	5.01
JeffersonCoALSwr imprv	5.000	02-01-42	102.480	-.226	4.66	PtAuthorityNYNJCnslRvSr1	4.625	12-15-29	95.248	-.426	4.95
LAX Dep Wtr & Pwr CA	5.000	07-01-43	102.449	-.225	4.67	PuertoRicoHwyTransAthSnr	5.000	07-01-42	101.001	-.239	4.87
LAX Unif Sch Dist Ca	5.000	01-01-28	104.230	-.086	4.48	PuertoRicoHwyTransAthSnr	5.000	07-01-33	101.491	-.241	4.81
MaricopaCoPollutionAZ	5.050	05-01-29	104.242	-.237	4.49	S.CarolinaPubSvcAuthRev	4.750	01-01-32	101.029	-.242	4.62
MetropolitanPierExpoIL	5.000	12-15-28	103.652	-.247	4.54	S.MiamiHlthFacsAuthFL	5.250	11-15-33	100.819	-.227	5.14
MetropolitanTransAthNY	5.000	11-15-31	103.786	-.236	4.50	SaltRiver Prj Agri Imprv	4.750	01-01-32	100.912	-.231	4.63
MetropolitanTransAuthNY	5.000	11-15-32	104.097	-.257	4.51	SaltRiver Prj Agri Imprv	5.000	01-01-34	104.295	-.241	4.45
Miami-Dade Co FL Aviat	5.000	10-01-33	100.728	-.223	4.90	SCarolina JobsEconDev	5.625	11-15-30	103.334	-.229	5.18
Miami-DadeCoFLAviationRv	5.000	10-01-33	100.790	-.241	4.90	TexasTpkeAuthRvBds	5.000	08-15-42	102.629	-.227	4.65
Miami-DadeCoFLAviationRv	4.750	10-01-35	96.445	-.468	4.97	Triborough Bdg & Tunl NY	5.000	11-15-32	103.778	-.237	4.50

to mature in each year over a multiple-year period. As an example, a serial bond issue may contain bonds that mature in each year over a 5-year period, with the first group maturing 11 years after the original issue date and the last group maturing 15 years after issuance. The purpose of a serial maturity structure is to spread out the principal repayment, thereby avoiding a lump-sum repayment at a single maturity date.

term bonds Bonds from an issue with a single maturity date.

When an entire bond issue matures on a single date, the bonds are called **term bonds**. Term bonds normally have a sinking fund provision. A sinking fund is a trustee-managed account to which the issuer makes regular payments. Account reserves are dedicated to redeeming a fraction of the bond issue on each of a series of scheduled redemption dates. Each redemption usually proceeds by lottery, where randomly selected bonds are called and the affected bondholders receive the sinking fund call price. Alternatively, scheduled redemptions can be implemented by purchasing bonds from investors at current market prices. This latter option is usually selected by the issuer when the bonds are selling at a discount from par value. The motive for a sinking fund provision is similar to that for a serial maturity structure; it provides a means for the issuer to avoid a lump-sum principal repayment at a single maturity date.

put bonds Bonds that can be sold back to the issuer.

Some municipal bonds are putable, and these are called **put bonds**. The holder of a put bond, also called a *tender offer bond*, has the option of selling the bond back to the issuer, normally at par value. Some put bonds can be tendered any time, whereas others can be tendered only on regularly scheduled dates. Weekly, monthly, quarterly, semiannual, and annual put date schedules are all used. Notice that with a put bond, maturity is effectively the choice of the bondholder. This feature protects bondholders from rising interest rates and the associated fall in bond prices. However, a putable bond will have a higher price than a comparable nonputable bond. The price differential simply reflects the value of the put option to sell back the bonds.

variable-rate notes Securities that pay an interest rate that changes according to market conditions. Also called *floaters*.

While most municipal bonds maintain a constant coupon rate (hence the term fixed-rate bonds), interest rate risk has induced many municipalities to issue **variable-rate notes**, often called *floaters*. For these debt issues, the coupon rate is adjusted periodically according to an index-based rule. For example, at each adjustment the coupon rate may be set at 60 percent of the prevailing rate on 91-day maturity U.S. Treasury bills. A variable-rate note may also be putable, in which case it is called a *variable-rate demand obligation*, often abbreviated to VRDO. A stipulation attached to most VRDOs allows the issuer to convert an entire variable-rate issue to a fixed-rate issue following a specified conversion procedure. Essentially, the issuer notifies each VRDO holder of the intent to convert the outstanding VRDO issue to a fixed-rate issue on a specific future date. In response, VRDO holders have the option of tendering their VRDOs for cash, or they can accept conversion of their VRDOs into fixed-rate bonds.

Types of Municipal Bonds

There are two basic types of municipal bonds: revenue bonds and general obligation bonds, often referred to as GOs. General obligation bonds are issued by all levels of municipal governments, including states, counties, cities, towns, school districts, and water districts. They are secured by the general taxing powers of the municipalities issuing the bonds. For state governments and large city governments, tax revenue is collected from a diverse base of income taxes on corporations and individuals, sales taxes, and property taxes. In contrast, tax revenues for smaller municipalities are largely derived from property taxes, although sales taxes have become increasingly important. Because of their large, diverse tax bases, general obligation bonds issued by states and large cities are often called *unlimited tax bonds* or *full faith and credit bonds*.

However, some general obligation bonds are called *limited tax bonds*. The distinction between limited and unlimited tax bonds arises when a constitutional limit or other statutory limit is placed on the power of a municipality to assess taxes. For example, an amendment to the California state constitution, popularly known as Proposition 13 when it was enacted, placed rigid limits on the ability of California municipalities to assess taxes on real estate.

revenue bonds
Municipal bonds secured by revenues collected from a specific project or projects.

Revenue bonds constitute the bulk of all outstanding municipal bonds. **Revenue bonds** are bonds secured by proceeds collected from the projects they finance. Thus, the credit quality of a revenue bond issue is largely determined by the ability of a project to generate revenue. A few examples of the many different kinds of projects financed by revenue bonds are listed below.

Airport and seaport bonds: Used to finance development of airport and seaport facilities. Secured by user fees and lease revenues.

College dormitory bonds: Used to finance construction and renovation of dormitory facilities. Secured by rental fees.

Industrial development bonds: Used to finance development of projects ranging from factories to shopping centers. Secured by rental and leasing fees.

Multifamily housing bonds: Used to finance construction of housing projects for senior citizens or low-income families. Secured by rental fees.

Highway and road gas tax bonds: Used to finance highway construction. May be secured by specific toll revenues or general gas tax revenues.

Student loan bonds: Used to purchase higher education guaranteed student loans. Secured by loan repayments and federal guarantees.

hybrid bonds
Municipal bonds secured by project revenues with some form of general obligation credit guarantees.

Many municipal bonds possess aspects of both general obligation and revenue bonds; these are called **hybrid bonds**. Typically, a hybrid is a revenue bond secured by project-specific cash flows, but with additional credit guarantees. A common form of hybrid is the *moral obligation bond*. This is a state-issued revenue bond with provisions for obtaining general revenues when project-specific resources are inadequate. Usually, extra funds can be obtained only with approval of a state legislature, which is said to be "morally obligated" to assist a financially distressed state-sponsored project. However, a moral obligation is not a guarantee, and the likelihood of state assistance varies. Municipal bond credit analysts consider each state's history of assistance, as well as current state financial conditions, when evaluating the credit-quality enhancement of the moral obligation. In general, experienced municipal bond investors agree that a state will first service its own general obligation debt before providing service assistance to moral obligation debt. This is typically evidenced by the higher yields on moral obligation debt compared to general obligation debt.

Since 1983, all newly issued municipal bonds have had to be registered—that is, with the identity of all bondholders registered with the issuer. With registered bonds, the issuer sends coupon interest and principal payments only to the registered owner of a bond. Additionally, it is now standard practice for registered bonds to be issued in book entry form; bondholders are not issued printed bond certificates, but instead receive notification that their ownership is officially registered. The actual registration record is maintained by the issuer in computer files. This contrasts with the now defunct practice (in the U.S.) of issuing bearer bonds, where coupon interest and principal were paid to anyone presenting the bond certificates.

Municipal Bond Credit Ratings

Check out these rating
agency websites:
Moody's at
www.moodys.com
Fitch at
www.fitchibca.com
S&P at
www.
standardandpoors.com

Municipal bond credit rating agencies provide investors with an assessment of the credit quality of individual bond issues. As part of the issuance and credit rating process, the rating agency is paid a fee to assign a credit rating to a new bond issue, to periodically reevaluate the issue, and to make these ratings available to the public. The three largest municipal bond credit rating agencies are Moody's Investors Service, Standard & Poor's Corporation, and Fitch Investors Service. Among them, they rate thousands of new issues each year. Table 18.3 compares and briefly describes the credit rating codes assigned by these three agencies.

The highest credit rating that can be awarded is "triple-A," which indicates that interest and principal are exceptionally secure because of the financial strength of the issuer. Notice that "triple-A" and "double-A" ratings are denoted as AAA and AA, respectively, by Standard & Poor's and Fitch, but as Aaa and Aa, respectively, by Moody's. Also notice that "triple-B" and "double-B" ratings—that is, BBB and BB, respectively—by Standard & Poor's and Fitch correspond to "B-double-a" and "B-single-a" ratings—Baa and Ba, respectively—by Moody's. The same pattern holds for C ratings.

The highest four credit ratings, BBB or Baa and above, designate investment-grade bonds. As a matter of policy, many financial institutions will invest only in investment-grade bonds. Lower rankings indicate successively diminishing levels of credit quality. Ratings of BB or Ba and below designate speculative-grade bonds. Individual investors should probably avoid speculative-grade bonds. A rating of C or below indicates that actual or probable default makes the bond issue unsuitable for most investors.

Visit websites of these
municipal bond
insurers:
www.mbia.com
www.ambac.com

It is not unusual for the ratings assigned to a particular bond issue to differ slightly across credit rating agencies. For example, a bond issue may be rated AA by Standard

TABLE 18.3		**Municipal Bond Credit Ratings**	
	Rating Agency		
Standard & Poor's	**Moody's**	**Fitch**	**Credit Rating Description**
Investment-Grade Bond Ratings			
AAA	Aaa	AAA	Highest credit quality
AA	Aa	AA	High credit quality
A	A	A	Good credit quality
BBB	Baa	BBB	Satisfactory credit quality
Speculative-Grade Bond Ratings			
BB	Ba	BB	Speculative credit quality
B	B	B	Highly speculative quality
CCC	Caa	CCC	Poor credit quality
CC	Ca	CC	Probable default
Extremely Speculative-Grade Bond Ratings			
C	C	C	Imminent default
D		DDD	In default
		DD, D	

& Poor's, Aa by Moody's, but only A by Fitch. When this occurs, it usually reflects a difference in credit rating methods rather than a disagreement regarding basic facts. For example, Moody's may focus on the budgetary status of the issuer when assigning a credit rating, while Standard & Poor's may emphasize the economic environment of the issuer. Remember that Standard & Poor's, Moody's, and Fitch are competitors in the bond rating business, and, like competitors in any industry, they try to differentiate their products.

Municipal Bond Insurance

insured municipal bonds Bonds secured by an insurance policy that guarantees bond interest and principal payments should the issuer default.

In the last two decades, it has become increasingly common for municipalities to obtain bond insurance for new bond issues. **Insured municipal bonds**, besides being secured by the issuer's resources, are also backed by an insurance policy written by a commercial insurance company. The policy provides for prompt payment of coupon interest and principal to municipal bondholders in the event of a default by the issuer. The cost of the insurance policy is paid by the issuer at the time of issuance. The policy cannot be canceled while any bonds are outstanding. With bond insurance, the credit quality of the bond issue is determined by the financial strength of the insurance company, not the municipality alone. Credit rating agencies are certainly aware of this fact. Consequently, a bond issue with insurance can obtain a higher credit rating than would be possible without insurance, and therefore sell at a higher price.

Municipal bond insurance companies manage default risk in three ways. First, they insure bond issues only from municipalities that have a good credit rating on their own. Second, municipal bond insurers diversify default risk by writing insurance policies for municipalities spread across a wide geographic area. Third, and perhaps most important, to compete in the municipal bond insurance business, insurers must maintain substantial investment portfolios as a source of financial reserves. Without sizable reserves, a company's insurance policies are not credible and municipalities will avoid purchasing insurance from them.

18.7 Equivalent Taxable Yield

Consider an individual investor who must decide whether to invest in a corporate bond paying annual coupon interest of 8 percent or a municipal bond paying annual coupon interest of 5 percent. Both bonds are new issues with a triple-A credit rating, both bonds sell at par value, and the investor plans to hold the bonds until they mature. Since both bonds are purchased at par value, their coupon rates are equal to their originally stated yields to maturity. For the municipal bond this is a tax-exempt yield, and for the corporate bond this is a taxable yield.

Clearly, if the investment was for a tax-exempt retirement account, corporate debt is preferred since the coupon interest is higher and tax effects are not a consideration. But if the investment is not tax-exempt, the decision should be made on an aftertax basis. Essentially, the investor must decide which investment provides the highest return after accounting for income tax on corporate debt interest. This is done by comparing the tax-exempt yield of 5 percent on municipal bonds with an equivalent taxable yield. An equivalent taxable yield depends on the investor's marginal tax rate and is computed as follows:

$$\text{Equivalent taxable yield} = \frac{\text{Tax-exempt yield}}{1 - \text{Marginal tax rate}}$$

For example, suppose the investor is in a 35 percent marginal tax bracket. Then a tax-exempt yield of 5 percent is shown to correspond to an equivalent taxable yield of 7.69 percent as follows:

$$\text{Equivalent taxable yield} = \frac{5\%}{1 - .35} = 7.69\%$$

In this case, the investor would prefer the taxable yield of 8 percent on the corporate bond rather than the equivalent taxable yield of 7.69 percent on the municipal bond.

Alternatively, the investor could compare the aftertax yield on the corporate bond with the tax-exempt yield on the municipal bond. An aftertax yield is computed as follows:

$$\text{Aftertax yield} = \text{Taxable yield} \times (1 - \text{Marginal tax rate})$$

To change the example, suppose that the investor is in a 40 percent marginal tax bracket. This results in an aftertax yield of 4.8 percent, as shown below.

$$\text{Aftertax yield} = 8\% \times (1 - .40) = 4.8\%$$

In this case, the tax-exempt yield of 5 percent on the municipal bond is preferred to the aftertax yield of 4.8 percent on the corporate bond.

Another approach is to compute the critical marginal tax rate that would leave an investor indifferent between a given tax-exempt yield on a municipal bond and a given taxable yield on a corporate bond. A critical marginal tax rate is found as follows:

$$\text{Critical marginal tax rate} = 1 - \frac{\text{Tax-exempt yield}}{\text{Taxable yield}}$$

For the example considered here, the critical marginal tax rate is 37.5 percent, determined as follows:

$$\text{Critical marginal tax rate} = 1 - \frac{5\%}{8\%} = 37.5\%$$

Investors with a marginal tax rate higher than the critical marginal rate would prefer the municipal bond, whereas investors in a lower tax bracket would prefer the corporate bond.

Check This

18.7a   An investor with a marginal tax rate of 30 percent is interested in a tax-exempt bond with a yield of 6 percent. What is the equivalent taxable yield of this bond?

18.7b   A taxable bond has a yield of 10 percent, and a tax-exempt bond has a yield of 7 percent. What is the critical marginal tax rate for these two bonds?

18.8 Taxable Municipal Bonds

The Tax Reform Act of 1986 imposed notable restrictions on the types of municipal bonds that qualify for federal tax exemption of interest payments. In particular, the

private activity bonds
Taxable municipal bonds used to finance facilities used by private businesses.

1986 act expanded the definition of **private activity bonds**. Private activity bonds include any municipal security where 10 percent or more of the issue finances facilities used by private entities and is secured by payments from private entities.

Interest on private activity bonds is tax-exempt only if the bond issue falls into a so-called qualified category. Qualified private activity bonds that still enjoy a tax-exempt interest privilege include public airport bonds, multifamily housing bonds, nonvehicular mass commuting bonds, and various other project bonds. The major types of private activity bonds that do not qualify for tax-exempt interest are those used to finance sports stadiums, convention facilities, parking facilities, and industrial parks. However, these taxable private activity bonds may still enjoy exemption from state and local income tax. In any case, as a result of the 1986 act and the continuing need to finance private activity projects, new issues of taxable municipal revenue bonds are frequently sold with yields similar to corporate bond yields.

18.9 Summary and Conclusions

This chapter covers the topic of government bonds, including U.S. Treasury bonds, notes, and bills, and state, city, county, and local municipal bonds. In the chapter, we saw that:

1. The U.S. federal government is the largest single borrower in the world, with about $4 trillion of publicly held debt. Responsibility for managing this debt belongs to the U.S. Treasury, which issues Treasury bills, notes, and bonds at regular auctions to finance government debt.

2. Treasury bills are short-term obligations that are sold on a discount basis. Treasury notes are medium-term obligations that pay fixed semiannual coupons as well as payment of face value at maturity. Treasury bonds are long-term obligations that pay their face value at maturity and pay fixed semiannual coupons.

3. The U.S. Treasury sponsors the STRIPS program, where Treasury bonds and notes are broken down into principal strips, which represent face value payments, and coupon strips, which represent individual coupon payments. Since each strip created under the STRIPS program represents a single future payment, strips effectively become zero coupon bonds.

4. Several federal agencies are authorized to issue securities directly to the public. Bonds issued by U.S. government agencies have a credit quality almost identical to U.S. Treasury issues, but agency notes and bonds are attractive to many investors because they offer higher yields than comparable U.S. Treasury securities. However, the market for agency debt is less active than the market for U.S. Treasury debt and investors are potentially subject to state income taxes on agency debt interest, while U.S. Treasury debt interest is not subject to state taxes.

5. Another large market for government debt is the market for municipal government debt. Total municipal debt outstanding currently exceeds $2 trillion, divided among almost all of the more than 80,000 state and local governments in the United States. Individual investors hold about half this debt, while the remainder is roughly split equally between holdings of property and casualty insurance companies and commercial banks.

6. Municipal notes and bonds are intermediate- to long-term interest-bearing obligations of state and local governments or agencies of those governments. Municipal debt is commonly called the tax-exempt market because the coupon interest is usually exempt from federal income tax, which makes municipal bonds attractive to investors in the highest income tax brackets. However, yields on municipal debt are less than yields on corporate debt with similar features and credit quality, thus eliminating much of the advantage of the tax exemption.

7. Most municipal bonds pay a constant coupon rate, but some municipal notes pay variable coupon rates that change according to prevailing market interest rates. Also, a call provision is a standard feature of most municipal bond issues. A call provision allows an issuer to retire outstanding bonds before they mature. When the bond is called, each bondholder receives the bond's call price in exchange for returning the bond to the issuer.

8. There are two basic types of municipal bonds: revenue bonds and general obligation bonds. Revenue bonds, which constitute the bulk of all outstanding municipal bonds, are secured by proceeds collected from the projects they finance. General obligation bonds, which are issued by all levels of municipal governments, are secured by the general taxing powers of the municipalities issuing the bonds.

9. As part of the process for issuing municipal bonds to the public, a rating agency is paid a fee to assign a credit rating to a new bond issue. In the last two decades, it has become increasingly common for municipalities to obtain bond insurance for new bond issues through an insurance policy written by a commercial insurance company. With bond insurance, the credit quality of the bond issue is determined by the financial strength of the insurance company, not the municipality alone.

Get Real

This chapter covered government bonds, a large and important securities market. How should you put your knowledge to work? Begin by purchasing (in a simulated brokerage account like Stock-Trak) the various types of government securities that are available for trading out there. Observe how their prices and yields change over time.

You should also learn more about buying Treasury securities. A great place to start is the Bureau of Public Debt website (www.publicdebt.treas.gov). There you can examine and download the forms needed to bid in the regular auctions. You can also obtain current Treasury auction information, including forthcoming auctions and the results of previous auctions. You can also read about the *Treasury Direct* program, which is probably the best way of purchasing Treasury issues for individual investors. But if you prefer U.S. Savings Bonds, then check out the website that tells you all you need to know about them (www.savingsbonds.gov).

You will probably find that you cannot trade municipal bonds through a simulated brokerage account. The reason is that the market for municipals is so thin that getting timely price information for a particular issue isn't possible. In practice, municipal bonds are best suited for buy-and-hold investors who buy the bonds when originally issued and

(continued)

> hold them until maturity. You can now buy municipal bonds online through a number of brokers. Try, for example, First Miami (www.firstmiami.com) or Lebenthal Investments (www.lebenthal.com). Also take a look at Muni Auction (www.muniauction.com).

Key Terms

face value 593
discount basis 593
imputed interest 594
STRIPS 594
zero coupon bonds 594
yield to call (YTC) 597
bid-ask spread 599
stop-out bid 600
default risk 605
general obligation bonds (GOs) 605

call provision 607
serial bonds 607
term bonds 609
put bonds 609
variable-rate notes 609
revenue bonds 610
hybrid bonds 610
insured municipal bond 612
private activity bond 614

Chapter Review Problems and Self-Test

1. **Treasury Yields**   A callable Treasury bond's price is 140:25. It has a coupon rate of 10 percent, makes semiannual payments, and matures in 21 years. What yield would be reported in the financial press?

2. **Equivalent Yields**   A particular investor faces a 40 percent tax rate. If a AA-rated municipal bond yields 4 percent, what must a similar taxable issue yield for the investor to be impartial to them?

Answers to Self-Test Problems

1. First, note that this is a callable issue selling above par, so the yield to call will be reported. All callable Treasury bonds are callable at face value five years before they mature. Thus, to calculate the yield to call, all we have to do is pretend that the bond has 16 years to maturity instead of 21. We therefore have a bond with a price of 140.78125 (after converting from thirty-seconds), a coupon of 10 percent paid semiannually, and a maturity of 16 years (or 32 periods). Verify, using the standard bond formula from Chapter 10, that the semiannual yield to call is 3 percent, so the reported yield would be 6 percent.

2. The equivalent taxable yield is the municipal yield "grossed up" by one minus the tax rate:

$$\frac{4\%}{1 - .40} = 6.67\%$$

Test Your Investment Quotient

1. **Zero Coupon Bonds**   What is the yield to maturity (YTM) on a zero coupon bond?

   a. The interest rate realized if the bond is held to maturity.

    b. The interest rate realized when the bond is sold.

    c. The coupon yield for an equivalent coupon bond.

    d. A fixed rate when the bond is issued.

2. **Treasury Notes**   The coupon rate for a Treasury note is set

    a. The same for all Treasury note issues.

    b. By a formula based on the size of the Treasury note issue.

    c. According to prevailing interest rates at time of issuance.

    d. According to the supply and demand for money.

3. **Treasury Notes and Bonds**   U.S. Treasury notes and bonds have face value denominations as small as

    a. $1,000

    b. $5,000

    c. $10,000

    d. $25,000

4. **Treasury Bonds**   What is the dollar value of a U.S. Treasury bond quoted at 92:24?

    a. $922.75

    b. $922.40

    c. $927.50

    d. Indeterminable

5. **Treasury Bonds**   The following are quotes for a U.S. Treasury bond:

Bid	Asked
102:02	102:05

If the face value of the bond is $1,000, the price an investor should pay for the bond is *closest* to

    a. $1,020.63

    b. $1,021.56

    c. $1,025.00

    d. $1,026.25

6. **Treasury Bonds**   A trader purchases $5 million face value of Treasury bonds at 95:16 and then later sells the bonds at 95:24. What is the round-trip gain on these transactions?

    a. $1,250

    b. $12,500

    c. $4,000

    d. $40,000

7. **Treasury STRIPS**   When originally issued, a 10-year maturity Treasury note can be stripped into how many separate components?

    a. 10

    b. 11

    c. 20

    d. 21

8. **Treasury Bills**   Treasury bills are sold on a discount basis, meaning that the difference between their issued price and their redemption value is

    a. The same for all T-bill issues.

    b. The imputed interest on the T-bill.

    c. Never less than the issued price.

    d. The bond equivalent yield for the T-bill.

9. **Treasury Auctions**   Which of the following statements about single-price Treasury auctions is false?

   a. Competitive bidders pay the stop-out bid.
   b. Noncompetitive bidders pay the stop-out bid plus a small premium.
   c. Noncompetitive bidders pay the stop-out bid.
   d. All of the above are true.

10. **Treasury Dealers**   When trading U.S. Treasury securities, Treasury dealers

   a. Buy at the bid price and sell at the asked price.
   b. Sell at the bid price and buy at the asked price.
   c. Buy at the stop-out bid price and sell at the market price.
   d. Sell at the stop-out bid price and buy at the market price.

11. **Savings Bonds**   A Series EE Savings Bond with a face value of $1,000 is originally sold for

   a. $1,000.
   b. $500.
   c. A price based on the recent inflation rate.
   d. 90 percent of the price of a recently issued five-year T-note.

12. **Savings Bonds**   The interest rate on Series EE Savings Bonds is reset every six months as

   a. 90 percent of the rate on newly issued five-year T-notes.
   b. 90 percent of the rate on newly issued five-year T-notes plus the recent inflation rate.
   c. A fixed rate plus the recent inflation rate.
   d. An adjustable rate plus the recent inflation rate.

13. **Savings Bonds**   A Series I Savings Bond with a face value of $1,000 is originally sold at a price of

   a. $1,000.
   b. $500.
   c. A price based on the recent inflation rate.
   d. 90 percent of the price of a recently issued five-year T-note.

14. **Savings Bonds**   The interest rate on Series I Savings Bonds is reset every six months as

   a. 90 percent of the rate on newly issued five-year T-notes.
   b. 90 percent of the rate on newly issued five-year T-notes plus the recent inflation rate.
   c. A fixed rate plus the recent inflation rate.
   d. An adjustable rate plus the recent inflation rate.

15. **Agency Bonds**   Which statement applies to a bond issued by an agency of the U.S. government?

   a. It is exempt from the federal income tax on interest.
   b. It becomes a direct obligation of the U.S. Treasury in case of default.
   c. It is secured by assets held by the agency.
   d. None of the above.

16. **Agency Bonds**   Which is true for bonds issued by all agencies of the U.S. government?

   a. They become direct obligations of the U.S. Treasury.
   b. They are secured bonds backed by government holdings.
   c. They are exempt from federal income tax.
   d. None of the above.

17. **Agency Bonds**   Which of the following investors is most likely to invest in agency bonds?

   a. High-income individual with a need for liquidity.
   b. High-income individual living in a triple income tax municipality.

c. Commercial bank.
d. Life insurance company.

18. **Municipal Bonds** Which of the following constitutes the bulk of all outstanding municipal bonds?

a. Revenue bonds
b. General obligation bonds
c. Moral obligation bonds
d. Private activity bonds

19. **Municipal Bonds** Which of the following investors is most likely to invest in locally issued municipal bonds?

a. High-income individual with a need for liquidity.
b. High-income individual living in a triple income tax municipality.
c. Commercial bank.
d. Life insurance company.

20. **Revenue Bonds** A revenue bond is distinguished from a general obligation bond in that revenue bonds have which of the following characteristics?

a. They are issued by counties, special districts, cities, towns, and state-controlled authorities, whereas general obligation bonds are issued only by the states themselves.
b. They are typically secured by limited taxing power, whereas general obligation bonds are secured by unlimited taxing power.
c. They are issued to finance specific projects and are secured by the revenues of the project being financed.
d. They have first claim to any revenue increase of the issuing tax authority.

21. **Insured Municipal Bonds** Which of the following is not a method used by municipal bond insurers to manage default risk?

a. Only insure bonds from municipalities with a good credit rating.
b. Diversify default risk by writing insurance policies for municipalities spread across a wide geographic area.
c. Maintain substantial investment portfolios as a source of financial reserves.
d. All of the above are used to manage default risk.

22. **Insured Municipal Bonds** Which one of the following generally is not true of an insured municipal bond?

a. The price on an insured bond is higher than that on an otherwise identical uninsured bond.
b. The insurance can be canceled in the event the issuer fails to maintain predetermined quality standards.
c. The insurance premium is a one-time payment made at the time of issuance.
d. The insurance company is obligated to make all defaulted principal and/or interest payments in a prompt and timely fashion.

23. **Taxable Equivalent Yield** A municipal bond carries a coupon of 6 3/4 percent and is trading at par. To a taxpayer in the 34 percent tax bracket, what would the taxable equivalent yield of this bond be?

a. 4.5 percent
b. 10.2 percent
c. 13.4 percent
d. 19.9 percent

24. **Taxable Equivalent Yield** A 20-year municipal bond is currently priced at par to yield 5.53 percent. For a taxpayer in the 33 percent tax bracket, what equivalent taxable yield would this bond offer?

a. 8.25 percent
b. 10.75 percent

   c. 11.40 percent
   d. None of the above

CFA® PROBLEMS

25. **Taxable Equivalent Yield**   The coupon rate on a tax-exempt bond is 5.6 percent, and the coupon rate on a taxable bond is 8 percent. Both bonds sell at par. At what tax bracket (marginal tax rate) would an investor show no preference between the two bonds?

   a. 30.0 percent
   b. 39.6 percent
   c. 41.7 percent
   d. 42.9 percent

Concept Questions

1. **Bills versus Bonds**   What are the key differences between T-bills and T-bonds?

2. **Notes versus Bonds**   What are the key differences between T-notes and T-bonds?

3. **Zeroes**   What two Treasury securities are zeroes?

4. **Spreads**   What are typical spreads for T-notes and T-bonds? Why do you think they differ from issue to issue?

5. **Agencies versus Treasuries**   From an investor's standpoint, what are the key differences between Treasury and agency issues?

6. **Municipals versus Treasuries**   From an investor's standpoint, what are the main differences between Treasury and municipal issues?

7. **Serial Bonds**   What are serial bonds? What purpose does this structure serve?

8. **VRNs**   In the context of the muni market, what are variable-rate notes? What is likely true about their risks compared to those of ordinary issues?

9. **Revenues versus General Obligation Munis**   What is the difference between a revenue bond and a general obligation bond?

10. **Private Activity Munis**   What is a private activity muni? What type of investor would be interested?

11. **Treasury versus Municipal Bonds**   Treasury and municipal yields are often compared to calculate critical tax rates. What concerns might you have about such a comparison? What do you think is true about the calculated tax rate?

12. **Callable Treasury Bonds**   For a callable Treasury bond selling above par, is it necessarily true that the yield to call will be less than the yield to maturity? Why or why not?

13. **Callable Agency Issues**   For a callable agency bond selling above par, is it necessarily true that the yield to call will be less than the yield to maturity? Why or why not?

14. **Treasury versus Municipal Bonds**   Why might the yield to maturity on, say, a BBB-rated municipal bond with moderate default risk actually be less than that of a U.S. Treasury bond with no default risk?

15. **Treasury versus Municipal Bonds**   In a recent issue of *The Wall Street Journal*, compare the yields on U.S. Treasury bonds with the yields on municipal bonds. Why might these yield spreads depend on the state of the economy?

Questions and Problems

Core Questions

1. **STRIPS Price**   What is the price of a STRIPS with a maturity of 15 years, a face value of $10,000, and a yield to maturity of 8 percent?

2. **STRIPS YTM**   A STRIPS with 18 years until maturity and a face value of $10,000 is trading for $3,225. What is the yield to maturity?

3. **Treasury Auctions**   The Federal Reserve announces an offering of Treasury bills with a face value of $30 billion. Noncompetitive bids are made for $7 billion, along with the following competitive bids:

Bidder	Price Bid	Quantity Bid
A	$9,250	$10 billion
B	9,300	8 billion
C	9,320	7 billion
D	9,350	6 billion
E	9,400	5 billion
F	9,410	5 billion

In a single-price auction, which bids are accepted and what prices are paid by each bidder? How much money is raised by the entire offering?

4. **Municipal Bonds**   A municipal bond with a coupon rate of 4.5 percent has a yield to maturity of 3.8 percent. If the bond has 10 years to maturity, what is the price of the bond?

5. **Yield to Maturity**   A municipal bond with a coupon rate of 5.4 percent sells for $5,604 and has eight years until maturity. What is the yield to maturity of the bond?

6. **Yield to Maturity**   A municipal bond has 23 years until maturity and sells for $6,120. If the coupon rate on the bond is 6.20 percent, what is the yield to maturity?

7. **Yield to Call**   Assume the bond in the previous problem can be called in eight years. What is the yield to call if the call price is 103 percent of par?

8. **Aftertax Yield**   A municipal bond has a yield to maturity of 5.4 percent. What corporate bond yield would make an investor in the 38 percent tax bracket indifferent between the two bonds, all else the same?

9. **Tax Equivalent Yields**   A taxable corporate issue yields 9 percent. For an investor in a 31 percent tax bracket, what is the equivalent aftertax yield?

10. **Tax Rates**   A taxable issue yields 8.4 percent, and a similar municipal issue yields 5.5 percent. What is the critical marginal tax rate?

Intermediate Questions

11. **Treasury Prices**   A Treasury bill has a bid yield of 5.34 and an asked yield of 5.31. The bill matures in 160 days. What is the least you could pay to acquire a bill? (Note: You may need to review Chapter 9 for the relevant formula.)

12. **Treasury Prices**   At what price could you sell the Treasury bill referred to in the previous question? What is the dollar spread for this bill? (Note: You may need to review Chapter 9 for the relevant formula.)

13. **Treasury Prices**   A Treasury issue is quoted at 125:13 bid and 125:17 ask. What is the least you could pay to acquire a bond?

14. **Treasury Prices**   A noncallable Treasury bond has a quoted yield of 5.62 percent. It has a 6 percent coupon and 16 years to maturity. What is its dollar price assuming a $1,000 par value? What is its quoted price?

15. **Treasury Yields**   A Treasury bond with the longest maturity (30 years) has an asked price quoted at 99:13. The coupon rate is 5.25 percent, paid semiannually. What is the yield to maturity of this bond?

16. **Treasury Yields**   In a recent *Wall Street Journal*, locate the Treasury bond with the longest maturity (the so-called bellwether bond). Verify that, given the ask price, the reported yield is correct.

17. **Yield to Call**   A Treasury bond maturing in November 2014 and callable in November 2009 has a quoted price of 121:19 and a coupon rate of 11.75 percent. Assuming the bond matures in exactly 9 years, what is the yield to call?

18. **Callable Treasury Bonds**   In a recent *Wall Street Journal*, examine the yields on Treasury bonds maturing in 2014 and 2015. Why do you think the yields for the issues maturing in 2014 are so different?

Spreadsheet Problems

19. **Zero Price**   A STRIPS traded on May 1, 2004, matures in 25 years on May 1, 2029. Assuming a 6 percent yield to maturity, what is the STRIPS price?

20. **Zero YTM**   A STRIPS traded on July 1, 2004, matures in 15 years on July 1, 2019. The STRIPS price is $45. What is its yield to maturity?

What's on the Web?

1. **Treasury Auctions**   Go to www.publicdebt.treas.gov and find the next Treasury auctions scheduled. When are the auctions scheduled? What instruments will be offered at these auctions?

2. **Treasury Auctions**   Go to www.publicdebt.treas.gov and find the recently completed Treasury auctions for bills and notes. When did the auctions occur? What were the yields for each bill and note sold at these auctions?

3. **Municipal Bond Spreads**   Go to www.municipalbonds.com. What was the highest bid-side spread for the most recent quarter? What was the highest offer-side spread over this same period? What were the dollar amounts of these spreads?

4. **Municipal Bond Prices**   Go to www.municipalbonds.com and find the municipal bonds traded yesterday for your state. What was the most active bond in terms of the number of trades? Which bond traded the highest dollar amount? How many bonds had a spread of more than one point in trading yesterday?

5. **Savings Bonds**   In this chapter, we discussed U.S. Series EE Savings bonds. There are also Series HH savings bonds. These two bonds are different in several respects. Go to www.publicdebt.treas.gov and find out how the Series HH bonds work. What are the differences in these two types of savings bonds?

Stock-Trak®
Portfolio Simulations

Trading Government Bonds with Stock-Trak

U.S. Treasury bonds are available for trading through your Stock-Trak account. The list of available bonds changes from time to time, and you should consult the Stock-Trak website (www.stocktrak.com/cj) for the most recent list. Ticker symbols for Treasury bonds are not necessary to submit buy and sell orders. However, special ticker symbols are used by Stock-Trak to identify Treasury bonds in your account statements. The following is a sample of some U.S. Treasury bonds and their Stock-Trak ticker symbols:

www.mhhe.com/cj3e

Ticker	Description	Explanation
B-T106	US Feb 2010 6.50	6.50 percent coupon, Feb 2010 maturity
B-T315	US Feb 2031 5.375	5.375 percent coupon, Feb 2031 maturity

Stock-Trak also has a limited number of U.S. Treasury STRIPS. The ticker symbol is used to identify the STRIPS in your account. One of the STRIPS listed and its Stock-Trak ticker symbol is:

Ticker	Description	Explanation
B-ST18	May 2018 STRIP	Treasury STRIPS maturing in 2018

Since all Treasury bonds are free of default risk, the only factors that affect their prices are related to the structure of interest rates in the economy. If you expect interest rates to increase, then you can benefit from the resulting fall in bond prices by short selling bonds. On the other hand, if you expect interest rates to decrease, you should buy bonds and wait for the resulting increase in bond prices.

Stock-Trak Exercises

1. Buy the longest- and shortest-maturity Treasury issues in equal dollar amounts. Observe which yields the greatest return over your investment period.

2. Invest equal amounts in similar-maturity Treasury bonds and corporate bonds. What is their yield spread? Observe which provides the highest return over your investment period.

3. Buy the longest- and shortest-maturity STRIPS in equal dollar amounts. Observe which yields the greatest return over your investment period.

www.mhhe.com/cj3e

Chapter 19

Mortgage-Backed Securities

"I had been putting what little money I had in Ocean Frontage, for the sole reason that there was only so much of it and no more, and that they wasn't making any more."

–Will Rogers

Will Rogers wryly advised buying real estate because "they wasn't making any more." Almost all real estate purchases are financed by mortgages. Indeed, most of us become familiar with mortgages by financing the purchase of a home. But did you ever stop to think about what happens to a mortgage after it is originated? Today, they are usually pooled to create mortgage-backed securities. The basic concept is simple. Collect a portfolio of mortgages into a mortgage pool. Then issue securities with pro rata claims on mortgage pool cash flows. These mortgage-backed securities are attractive to investors because they represent a claim on a diversified portfolio of mortgages and, therefore, are considerably less risky than individual mortgage contracts. ■

Mortgage financing makes home ownership possible for almost everyone. With mortgage financing, a home buyer makes only a down payment and borrows the remaining cost of a home with a mortgage loan. The mortgage loan is obtained from a mortgage originator, usually a local bank or other mortgage broker. Describing this financial transaction, we can say that a home buyer *issues* a mortgage and an originator *writes* a mortgage. A mortgage loan distinguishes itself from other loan contracts by a pledge of real estate as collateral for the loan. In this chapter, we carefully examine the investment characteristics of mortgage pools.

19.1 A Brief History of Mortgage-Backed Securities

Visit
www.investinginbonds.
com
for more information
on mortgage-backed
securities

Traditionally, savings banks and savings and loans (S&Ls) wrote most home mortgages and then held the mortgages in their portfolios of interest-earning assets. This changed radically during the 1970s and 1980s when market interest rates ascended to their highest levels in American history. Entering this financially turbulent period, savings banks and S&Ls held large portfolios of mortgages written at low pre-1970s interest rates. These portfolios were financed from customers' savings deposits. When market interest rates climbed to near 20 percent levels in the early 1980s, customers flocked to withdraw funds from their savings deposits to invest in money market funds that paid higher interest rates. As a result, savings institutions were often forced to sell mortgages at depressed prices to satisfy the onslaught of deposit withdrawals. For this, and other reasons, the ultimate result was the collapse of many savings institutions.

mortgage passthroughs Bonds representing a claim on the cash flows of an underlying mortgage pool passed through to bondholders.

mortgage-backed securities (MBSs) Securities whose investment returns are based on a pool of mortgages.

Today, home buyers still commonly turn to local banks for mortgage financing, but few mortgages are actually held by the banks that originate them. After writing a mortgage, an originator usually sells the mortgage to a mortgage repackager who accumulates them into mortgage pools. To finance the creation of a mortgage pool, the mortgage repackager issues mortgage-backed bonds, where each bond claims a pro rata share of all cash flows derived from mortgages in the pool. A pro rata share allocation pays cash flows in proportion to a bond's face value. Essentially, each mortgage pool is set up as a trust fund, and a servicing agent for the pool collects all mortgage payments. The servicing agent then passes these cash flows through to bondholders. For this reason, mortgage-backed bonds are often called **mortgage passthroughs**, or simply *pass-throughs*. However, all securities representing claims on mortgage pools are generically called **mortgage-backed securities** (**MBSs**). The primary collateral for all mortgage-backed securities is the underlying pool of mortgages.

mortgage securitization The creation of mortgage-backed securities from a pool of mortgages.

The transformation from mortgages to mortgage-backed securities is called **mortgage securitization**. More than $3 trillion of mortgages have been securitized in mortgage pools. This represents tremendous growth in the mortgage securitization business, since in the early 1980s less than $1 billion of home mortgages were securitized in pools. Yet despite the multi-trillion-dollar size of the mortgage-backed securities market, the risks involved with these investments are often misunderstood even by experienced investors.

19.2 Fixed-Rate Mortgages

fixed-rate mortgage Loan that specifies constant monthly payments at a fixed interest rate over the life of the mortgage.

Understanding mortgage-backed securities begins with an understanding of the mortgages from which they are created. Most home mortgages are 15-year or 30-year maturity **fixed-rate mortgages** requiring constant monthly payments. As an example of a fixed-rate mortgage, consider a 30-year mortgage representing a loan of $100,000 financed at an annual interest rate of 8 percent. This translates into a monthly interest rate of 8 percent / 12 months = .67%, and it requires a series of 360 monthly payments. The size of the monthly payment is determined by the requirement that the present value of all monthly payments, based on the financing rate specified in the mortgage contract, be equal to the original loan amount of $100,000. Mathematically, the constant monthly payment for a $100,000 mortgage is calculated using the following formula:

$$\text{Monthly payment} = \frac{\text{Mortgage amount} \times r/12}{1 - \dfrac{1}{(1 + r/12)^{T \times 12}}} \tag{19.1}$$

where: r = Annual mortgage financing rate
$r/12$ = Monthly mortgage financing rate
T = Mortgage term in years
$T \times 12$ = Mortgage term in months

In the example of a $100,000, thirty-year mortgage financed at 8 percent, the monthly payment is $733.76. This amount is calculated as follows:

$$\text{Monthly payment} = \frac{\$100{,}000 \times .08/12}{1 - \dfrac{1}{(1 + .08/12)^{360}}}$$

$$= \$733.76$$

CALCULATING MONTHLY MORTGAGE PAYMENTS

EXAMPLE 19.1

What is the monthly payment for a 15-year, $100,000 mortgage loan financed at 8 percent interest?

A 15-year mortgage specifies 180 monthly payments. Using the monthly payment formula we get a monthly payment of $955.65 as follows:

$$\text{Monthly payment} = \frac{\$100{,}000 \times 0.08/12}{1 - \dfrac{1}{(1 + 0.08/12)^{180}}}$$

$$= \$955.65$$

If you wish to calculate mortgage payments for other interest rates, maturities, and loan amounts, we suggest using a built-in spreadsheet function. For example, the nearby *Spreadsheet Analysis* box contains an example mortgage payment calculation using an Excel spreadsheet.

Check This

19.2a   The most popular fixed-rate mortgages among home buyers are those with 15-year and 30-year maturities. What might be some of the comparative advantages and disadvantages of these two mortgage maturities?

19.2b   Suppose you were to finance a home purchase using a fixed-rate mortgage. Would you prefer a 15-year or 30-year maturity mortgage? Why?

Monthly mortgage payments are sensitive to the interest rate stipulated in the mortgage contract. Table 19.1 provides a schedule of monthly payments required for 5-year, 10-year, 15-year, 20-year, and 30-year mortgages based on annual interest rates ranging from 5 percent to 15 percent in increments of .5 percent. Notice that monthly payments required for a $100,000 thirty-year mortgage financed at 5 percent are only $536.82, while monthly payments for the same mortgage financed at 15 percent are $1,264.44.

SPREADSHEET ANALYSIS

	A	B	C	D	E	F	G
1							
2			**Monthly Payments for a 30-year Mortgage**				
3							
4	A 30-year mortgage specifies an annual interest rate of 8 percent and a						
5	loan amount of $100,000. What are the monthly payments?						
6	Hint: Use the Excel function PMT.						
7							
8		−$733.76	=PMT(0.08/12,360,100000,0,0)				
9							
10	Monthly interest is 8% / 12 = .667%.						
11	Number of monthly payments is 12 x 30 = 360.						
12	Initial principal is $100,000.						
13	First zero indicates complete repayment after last monthly payment.						
14	Second zero indicates end-of-month payments.						
15							
16	For a 15-year mortgage we get a bigger monthly payment.						
17							
18		−$955.65	=PMT(0.08/12,180,100000,0,0)				
19							
20							

TABLE 19.1	$100,000 Mortgage Loan Monthly Payments				
Interest Rate	Mortgage Maturity				
	30-Year	20-Year	15-Year	10-Year	5-Year
5.0%	$ 536.82	$ 659.96	$ 790.79	$1,060.66	$1,887.12
5.5	567.79	687.89	817.08	1,085.26	1,910.12
6.0	599.55	716.43	843.86	1,110.21	1,933.28
6.5	632.07	745.57	871.11	1,135.48	1,956.61
7.0	665.30	775.30	898.83	1,161.08	1,980.12
7.5	699.21	805.59	927.01	1,187.02	2,003.79
8.0	733.76	836.44	955.65	1,213.28	2,027.64
8.5	768.91	867.82	984.74	1,239.86	2,051.65
9.0	804.62	899.73	1,014.27	1,266.76	2,075.84
9.5	840.85	932.13	1,044.22	1,293.98	2,100.19
10.0	877.57	965.02	1,074.61	1,321.51	2,124.70
10.5	914.74	998.38	1,105.40	1,349.35	2,149.39
11.0	952.32	1,032.19	1,136.60	1,377.50	2,174.24
11.5	990.29	1,066.43	1,168.19	1,405.95	2,199.26
12.0	1,028.61	1,101.09	1,200.17	1,434.71	2,224.44
12.5	1,067.26	1,136.14	1,232.52	1,463.76	2,249.79
13.0	1,106.20	1,171.58	1,265.24	1,493.11	2,275.31
13.5	1,145.41	1,207.37	1,298.32	1,522.74	2,300.98
14.0	1,184.87	1,243.52	1,331.74	1,552.66	2,326.83
14.5	1,224.56	1,280.00	1,365.50	1,582.87	2,352.83
15.0	1,264.44	1,316.79	1,399.59	1,613.35	2,378.99

Fixed-Rate Mortgage Amortization

mortgage principal
The amount of a mortgage loan outstanding, which is the amount required to pay off the mortgage.

Each monthly mortgage payment has two separate components. The first component represents payment of interest on outstanding **mortgage principal**. Outstanding mortgage principal is also called a mortgage's *remaining balance* or *remaining principal*. It is the amount required to pay off a mortgage before it matures. The second component represents a pay-down, or *amortization*, of mortgage principal. The relative amounts of each component change throughout the life of a mortgage. For example, a 30-year $100,000 mortgage financed at 8 percent requires 360 monthly payments of $733.76. The first monthly payment consists of a $666.67 payment of interest and a $67.10 pay-down of principal. The first month's interest payment, representing one month's interest on a mortgage balance of $100,000, is calculated as

$$\$100,000 \times .08/12 = \$666.67$$

After this payment of interest, the remainder of the first monthly payment, that is, $733.76 − $666.67 = $67.10 (there's a small rounding error), is used to amortize outstanding mortgage principal. Thus, after the first monthly payment, outstanding principal is reduced to $100,000 − $67.10 = $99,932.90.

The second monthly payment includes a $666.22 payment of interest calculated as

$$\$99,932.90 \times .08/12 = \$666.22$$

The remainder of the second monthly payment, that is, $733.76 − $666.22 = $67.54, is used to reduce mortgage principal to $99,932.91 − $67.54 = $99,865.37.

This process continues throughout the life of the mortgage. The interest payment component gradually declines, and the payment of principal component gradually increases. Finally, the last monthly payment is divided into a $4.86 payment of interest and a final $728.91 pay-down of mortgage principal. The process of paying down mortgage principal over the life of a mortgage is called **mortgage amortization**.

mortgage amortization The process of paying down mortgage principal over the life of the mortgage.

Mortgage amortization is described by an amortization schedule. An amortization schedule states the remaining principal owed on a mortgage at any point in time and also states the scheduled principal payment and interest payment in any month. Amortization schedules for 15-year and 30-year $100,000 mortgages financed at a fixed rate of 8 percent are listed in Table 19.2. The payment month is given in the left-hand column. Then, for each maturity, the first column reports remaining mortgage principal immediately after a monthly payment is made. Columns 2 and 3 for each maturity list the principal payment and the interest payment scheduled for each monthly payment. Notice that immediately after the 180th monthly payment for a 30-year $100,000 mortgage, $76,781.56 of mortgage principal is still outstanding. Notice also that as late as the 252nd monthly payment, the interest payment component of $378.12 still exceeds the principal payment component of $355.65.

MORTGAGE AMORTIZATION

EXAMPLE 19.2

After five years of payments on a mortgage loan financed at 8 percent, what are the remaining balance and interest and principal reduction components of the monthly payment?

For the 30-year mortgage, referring to Table 19.1 we see that the monthly payment is $733.76. Referring to the 60th monthly payment in Table 19.2, we find that the remaining balance on the mortgage is $95,069.86. Principal reduction for this payment is $99.30, and the interest payment is $634.46.

(continued)

| TABLE 19.2 | $100,000 Mortgage Loan Amortization Schedules for 15-year and 30-year Mortgages |

30-Year Mortgage $733.76 Monthly Payment				15-Year Mortgage $955.65 Monthly Payment			
Payment Month	Remaining Principal	Principal Reduction	Interest Payment	Payment Month	Remaining Principal	Principal Reduction	Interest Payment
1	$99,932.90	$ 67.10	$666.67	1	$99,711.01	$288.99	$666.67
12	99,164.64	72.19	661.58	12	96,402.15	310.90	644.75
24	98,259.94	78.18	655.59	24	92,505.69	336.70	618.95
36	97,280.15	84.67	649.10	36	88,285.81	364.65	591.00
48	96,219.04	91.69	642.07	48	83,715.70	394.91	560.74
60	95,069.86	99.30	634.46	60	78,766.26	427.69	527.96
72	93,825.29	107.55	626.22	72	73,406.02	463.19	492.46
84	92,477.43	116.47	617.29	84	67,600.89	501.64	454.02
96	91,017.70	126.14	607.63	96	61,313.93	543.27	412.38
108	89,436.81	136.61	597.16	108	54,505.16	588.36	367.29
120	87,724.70	147.95	585.82	120	47,131.26	637.20	318.46
132	85,870.50	160.23	573.54	132	39,145.34	690.08	265.57
144	83,862.39	173.53	560.24	144	30,496.58	747.36	208.29
156	81,687.61	187.93	545.84	156	21,129.99	809.39	146.26
168	79,332.33	203.53	530.24	168	10,985.97	876.57	79.08
180	76,781.56	220.42	513.35	180	0.00	949.32	6.33
192	74,019.08	238.71	495.05				
204	71,027.31	258.53	475.24				
216	67,787.23	279.98	453.78				
228	64,278.22	303.22	430.54				
240	60,477.96	328.39	405.38				
252	56,362.29	355.65	378.12				
264	51,905.02	385.16	348.60				
276	47,077.79	417.13	316.63				
288	41,849.91	451.75	282.01				
300	36,188.12	489.25	244.52				
312	30,056.40	529.86	203.91				
324	23,415.75	573.83	159.93				
336	16,223.93	621.46	112.30				
348	8,435.20	673.04	60.72				
360	0.00	728.91	4.86				

For the 15-year mortgage, the monthly payment is $955.65 and, after the 60th monthly payment, the remaining balance is $78,766.26, principal reduction is $427.69, and the interest payment is $527.96.

If you wish to calculate interest and principal reduction components for other interest rates, maturities, and loan amounts, we suggest using built-in spreadsheet functions. A nearby *Spreadsheet Analysis* box contains an example calculation of interest and principal reduction components for a mortgage using an Excel spreadsheet. Another *Spreadsheet Analysis* box contains an example calculation of the remaining balance on a mortgage.

FIGURE 19.1

Mortgage
Principal and
Payments for a
$100,000 30-Year
Mortgage with
an 8 Percent
Interest Rate

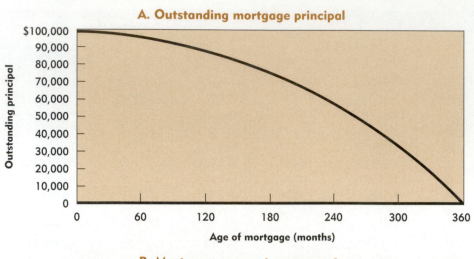

A. Outstanding mortgage principal

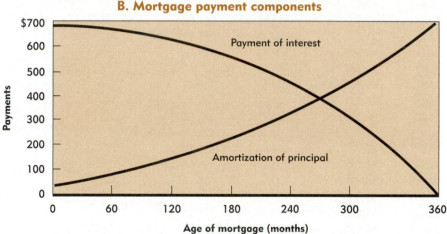

B. Mortgage payment components

The amortization process for a 30-year $100,000 mortgage financed at 8 percent interest is illustrated graphically in Figure 19.1. Figure 19.1A graphs the outstanding mortgage principal over the life of the mortgage. Figure 19.1B graphs the rising principal payment component and the falling interest payment component of the mortgage.

Fixed-Rate Mortgage Prepayment and Refinancing

A mortgage borrower has the right to pay off an outstanding mortgage at any time. This right is similar to the call feature on corporate bonds, whereby the issuer can buy back outstanding bonds at a prespecified call price. Paying off a mortgage ahead of its amortization schedule is called **mortgage prepayment**.

mortgage prepayment Paying off all or part of outstanding mortgage principal ahead of its amortization schedule.

Prepayment can be motivated by a variety of factors. A homeowner may pay off a mortgage in order to sell the property when a family moves because of, say, new employment or retirement. After the death of a spouse, a surviving family member may pay off a mortgage with an insurance benefit. These are examples of mortgage prepayment for personal reasons. However, mortgage prepayments often occur for a purely financial reason: an existing mortgage loan may be refinanced at a lower interest rate when a lower rate becomes available.

SPREADSHEET ANALYSIS

	A	B	C	D	E	F	G
1							
2			**Amortization Schedule for a 30-year Mortgage**				
3							
4	A 30-year mortgage specifies an annual interest rate of 8 percent and a						
5	loan amount of $100,000. What are the interest and principal payments?						
6	Hint: Use the Excel function IPMT and PPMT.						
7							
8	For the 120th payment after 10 years, interest and principal payments are						
9							
10		−$585.82	=IPMT(0.08/12,120,360,100000,0)				
11							
12		−$147.95	=PPMT(0.08/12,120,360,100000,0)				
13							
14	For the 240th payment after 20 years, interest and principal payments are						
15							
16		−$405.38	=IPMT(0.08/12,240,360,100000,0)				
17							
18		−$328.39	=PPMT(0.08/12,240,360,100000,0)				
19							
20							

	A	B	C	D	E	F	G
1							
2			**Remaining Balance for a 30-year Mortgage**				
3							
4	A 30-year mortgage specifies an annual interest rate of 8 percent and a						
5	loan amount of $100,000. What is the remaining balance?						
6	Hint: Use the Excel function CUMPRINC.						
7							
8	Remaining balance at the 100th payment after 8 years and 4 months is						
9	the present value of payments 101 through 360.						
10							
11		−$90,504.68	=CUMPRINC(0.08/12,360,100000,101,360,0)				
12							
13	Remaining balance at the 200th payment after 16 years and 8 months is						
14	the present value of payments 201 through 360.						
15							
16		−$72,051.18	=CUMPRINC(0.08/12,360,100000,201,360,0)				
17							
18							
19							
20							

Consider a 30-year $100,000 fixed-rate 8 percent mortgage with a monthly payment of $733.76. Suppose that, 10 years into the mortgage, market interest rates have fallen, and the financing rate on new 20-year mortgages is 6.5 percent. After 10 years (120 months), the remaining balance for the original $100,000 mortgage is $87,724.70. The monthly payment on a new 20-year $90,000 fixed-rate 6.5 percent mortgage is $671.02, which is $62.74 less than the $733.76 monthly payment on the old 8 percent

Manage Your Home Like an Investment

Smart investing begins at home. Many folks diligently nurture their portfolios of stocks, bonds and mutual funds. Got a mortgage on your house? You should manage your home loan with the same sort of investment savvy. Planning to refinance? Considering extra principal payments? Here's how to make smarter decisions when handling your mortgage:

Reducing Your Rate

Imagine you bought your house seven years ago. At the time, you borrowed $200,000 through a 30-year mortgage with a fixed 7% rate, resulting in a monthly mortgage payment of $1,331. Now, a loan officer at the local bank says that, for $2,500 in fees, you could refinance and get a new 30-year loan at 6%.

At first blush, that might seem appealing. Your seven years of mortgage payments has left you with a loan balance of $182,295. If you refinanced that sum at 6% over 30 years, your monthly payment would drop to $1,093.

A sweet deal? It isn't quite as sweet as it seems. Think about it: You are replacing what's now a 23-year loan with a 30-year loan. Even if your mortgage rate stayed the same, your monthly payment would still drop, because you are now paying back the sum borrowed over an additional seven years.

Instead, to make a fair comparison, you have to compare your current 23-year 7% loan with a new 23-year 6% loan. To that end, try playing with mortgage calculators at sites like www.bankrate.com, www.hsh.com, www.mortgage-x.com and www.realestateabc.com.

If you compare the two 23-year loans, you'll find you could save $111 a month by refinancing. Divide that $111 into the $2,500 in fees. Result: Refinancing makes sense, provided you stay in your current house for just over 22 months. Your local bank won't actually offer you a 23-year loan. Instead, you might opt for, say, a 20-year loan. But taking that shorter loan could be a smart move, says Michael Maloon, a financial planner in San Ramon, Calif.

"If people are refinancing and going back to a 30-year mortgage, they're crazy," he contends. "If you do that and you end up with an extra couple of hundred dollars a month in discretionary income, you will get used to spending that amount. Now, you need even more to retire," because you are accustomed to a higher standard of living. Instead, Mr. Maloon argues that folks who refinance should look to shorten the length of their loans, with a view to getting their mortgages paid off before they retire. "To win in the refi game, you want to lower the rate, lower your payments and pay off your mortgage sooner," he says. "I don't know how you retire if you still have a mortgage."

Paying Down Principal

To get your mortgage paid off by the time you retire, you might also want to make extra principal payments. By

(continued)

mortgage with 20 years of payments remaining. Thus, a homeowner could profit by prepaying the original 8 percent mortgage and refinancing with a new 20-year 6.5 percent mortgage. Monthly payments would be lower by $62.75, and the $2,275.30 difference between the new $90,000 mortgage balance and the old $87,724.70 mortgage balance would defray any refinancing costs.

As this example suggests, during periods of falling interest rates, mortgage refinancings are an important reason for mortgage prepayments. The nearby *Investment Updates* box presents a *Wall Street Journal* article discussing the merits of mortgage refinancing.

The possibility of prepayment and refinancing is an advantage to mortgage borrowers but a disadvantage to mortgage investors. For example, consider investors who supply funds to write mortgages at a financing rate of 8 percent. Suppose that mortgage interest rates later fall to 6.5 percent, and, consequently, homeowners rush to prepay their 8 percent mortgages so as to refinance at 6.5 percent. Mortgage investors recover their outstanding investment principal from the prepayments, but the rate of

adding $100 or $200 to each monthly mortgage check, you could save yourself thousands of dollars in interest and pay off your loan years earlier.

Sound attractive? To figure out whether this is the right strategy for you, consider not only the interest rate on your mortgage, but also your tax situation and what else you might do with the money. Let's say you have a mortgage with a 6.5% interest rate. That 6.5% is the interest expense you avoid by making extra principal payments and thus that is the effective pretax rate of return you earn. You should be able to do better than that 6.5% by buying stocks or bonds within a retirement account or by purchasing stocks in a taxable account.

But what if you have maxed out on your retirement accounts and you already own plenty of stocks? What if the alternative is to buy bonds or certificates of deposit within your taxable account? In that case, making extra principal payments could be a smart strategy. Suppose you are choosing between paying down your 6.5% mortgage and buying a corporate bond for your taxable account that yields 5.5%. If your mortgage interest is tax-deductible and you are in the 27% federal income-tax bracket, the after-tax return from paying down your mortgage is 4.75%. But the after-tax return on the corporate bond would be even lower. After paying federal income taxes on the bond's 5.5% yield, you would be left with just 4.02%.

In fact, paying down your mortgage may garner you an even higher return. Imagine you are married and you file a joint tax return. In 2003, you and your spouse are entitled to a standard deduction of $7,950. But let's assume you don't take the standard deduction. Instead, you itemize your deductions by filing Schedule A along with your federal tax return. This year, you expect to have itemized deductions of $10,000, consisting of $5,000 in mortgage interest and another $5,000 in property taxes, charitable gifts and state income taxes. Because your total of $10,000 in itemized deductions is greater than your $7,950 standard deduction, you save taxes by itemizing.

Even so, the tax benefit you get from your mortgage interest is still fairly modest. Indeed, I would argue that just $2,050 of your mortgage interest is truly tax-deductible. The reason: If you had $2,050 less in annual mortgage interest, you would take the standard deduction instead and thus you wouldn't get any tax benefit from your mortgage. Nonetheless, the after-tax return from adding an extra $100 to your mortgage check would still be 4.75%. How come? The interest you avoid by making extra principal payments is interest you could have deducted. Eventually, however, as you pay down your mortgage and thereby reduce the amount of interest you incur each year, your itemized deductions will fall below $7,950 and you will take the standard deduction instead. At that point, the after-tax return from making extra principal payments jumps to the full 6.5%.

Source: Jonathan Clements, *The Wall Street Journal*, April 27, 2003.
© 2003 Dow Jones & Company, Inc. All Rights Reserved Worldwide.

return that they can realize on a new investment is reduced because mortgages can now be written only at the new 6.5 percent financing rate. The possibility that falling interest rates will set off a wave of mortgage refinancings is an ever-present risk that mortgage investors must face.

19.3 Government National Mortgage Association

Government National Mortgage Association (GNMA) Government agency charged with promoting liquidity in the home mortgage market.

In 1968, Congress established the **Government National Mortgage Association** (**GNMA**), colloquially called "Ginnie Mae," as a government agency within the Department of Housing and Urban Development (HUD). GNMA was charged with the mission of promoting liquidity in the secondary market for home mortgages. Liquidity is the ability of investors to buy and sell securities quickly at competitive market prices. Essentially, mortgages repackaged into mortgage pools are a more liquid investment product than the original unpooled mortgages. GNMA has successfully

633

sponsored the re-packaging of several trillion dollars of mortgages into hundreds of thousands of mortgage-backed securities pools.

GNMA mortgage pools are based on mortgages issued under programs administered by the Federal Housing Administration (FHA), the Veteran's Administration (VA), and the Farmer's Home Administration (FmHA). Mortgages in GNMA pools are said to be **fully modified** because GNMA guarantees bondholders full and timely payment of both principal and interest even in the event of default of the underlying mortgages. The GNMA guarantee augments guarantees already provided by the FHA, VA, and FmHA. Since GNMA, FHA, VA, and FmHA are all agencies of the federal government, GNMA mortgage passthroughs are free of default risk. But while investors in GNMA passthroughs do not face default risk, they still face **prepayment risk**.

GNMA operates in cooperation with private underwriters certified by GNMA to create mortgage pools. The underwriters originate or otherwise acquire the mortgages to form a pool. After verifying that the mortgages comply with GNMA requirements, GNMA authorizes the underwriter to issue mortgage-backed securities with a GNMA guarantee.

As a simplified example of how a GNMA pool operates, consider a hypothetical GNMA fully modified mortgage pool containing only a single mortgage. After obtaining approval from GNMA, the pool has a GNMA guarantee and is called a *GNMA bond*. The underwriter then sells the bond, and the buyer is entitled to receive all mortgage payments, less servicing and guarantee fees. If a mortgage payment occurs ahead of schedule, the early payment is passed through to the GNMA bondholder. If a payment is late, GNMA makes a timely payment to the bondholder. If any mortgage principal is prepaid, the early payment is passed through to the bondholder. If a default occurs, GNMA settles with the bondholder by making full payment of remaining mortgage principal. In effect, to a GNMA bondholder, mortgage default is the same thing as a prepayment.

When originally issued, the minimum denomination of a GNMA mortgage-backed bond is $25,000 with subsequent increments of $5,000. The minimum size for a GNMA mortgage pool is $1 million, although it could be much larger. Thus, for example, a GNMA mortgage pool might conceivably represent only 40 bonds with an initial bond principal of $25,000 par value per bond. However, initial bond principal only specifies a bond's share of mortgage pool principal. Over time, mortgage-backed bond principal declines because of scheduled mortgage amortization and mortgage prepayments.

GNMA Clones

While GNMA is perhaps the best-known guarantor of mortgage-backed securities, two government-sponsored enterprises (GSEs) are also significant mortgage repackaging sponsors. These are the **Federal Home Loan Mortgage Corporation** (**FHLMC**), colloquially called "Freddie Mac," and the **Federal National Mortgage Association** (**FNMA**), called "Fannie Mae." FHLMC was chartered by Congress in 1970 to increase mortgage credit availability for residential housing. It was originally owned by the Federal Home Loan Banks operated under direction of the U.S. Treasury. But in 1989, FHLMC was allowed to become a private corporation with an issue of common stock. Freddie Mac stock trades on the New York Stock Exchange under the ticker symbol FRE.

The Federal National Mortgage Association was originally created in 1938 as a government-owned corporation of the United States. Thirty years later FNMA was

---

fully modified mortgage pool
Mortgage pool that guarantees timely payment of interest and principal.

prepayment risk
Uncertainty faced by mortgage investors regarding early payment of mortgage principal and interest.

Visit the GNMA and HUD websites at
www.ginniemae.gov
www.hud.gov

Federal Home Loan Mortgage Corporation (FHLMC) and Federal National Mortgage Association (FNMA) Government-sponsored enterprises charged with promoting liquidity in the home mortgage market.

split into two government corporations: GNMA and FNMA. Soon after, in 1970, FNMA was allowed to become a private corporation and has since grown to become one of the major financial corporations in the United States. Fannie Mae stock trades on the New York Stock Exchange under the ticker symbol FNM.

Like GNMA, both FHLMC and FNMA operate with qualified underwriters who accumulate mortgages into pools financed by an issue of bonds that entitle bondholders to cash flows generated by mortgages in the pools, less the standard servicing and guarantee fees. However, the guarantees on FHLMC and FNMA passthroughs are not exactly the same as for GNMA passthroughs. Essentially, FHLMC and FNMA are only government-sponsored enterprises, whereas GNMA is a government agency. Congress may be less willing to rescue a financially strapped GSE.

Before June 1990, FHLMC guaranteed timely payment of interest but only *eventual* payment of principal on its mortgage-backed bonds. However, beginning in June 1990, FHLMC began its Gold program whereby it guaranteed timely payment of both interest and principal. Therefore, FHLMC Gold mortgage-backed bonds are fully modified passthrough securities. FNMA guarantees timely payment of both interest and principal on its mortgage-backed bonds, and, therefore, these are also fully modified passthrough securities. But since FHLMC and FNMA are only GSEs, their fully modified passthroughs do not carry the same default protection as GNMA fully modified passthroughs.

Check This

19.3a	Look up prices for Freddie Mac (FHLMC) and Fannie Mae (FNMA) common stock under their ticker symbols FRE and FNM in *The Wall Street Journal*.

19.4 Public Securities Association Mortgage Prepayment Model

prepayment rate The probability that a mortgage will be prepaid during a given year.

Mortgage prepayments are typically described by stating a **prepayment rate**, which is the probability that a mortgage will be prepaid in a given year. The greater the prepayment rate for a mortgage pool, the faster the mortgage pool principal is paid off, and the more rapid is the decline of bond principal for bonds supported by the underlying mortgage pool. Historical experience shows that prepayment rates can vary substantially from year to year depending on mortgage type and various economic and demographic factors.

Conventional industry practice states prepayment rates using a prepayment model specified by the Public Securities Association (PSA). According to this model, prepayment rates are stated as a percentage of a PSA benchmark. The PSA benchmark specifies an annual prepayment rate of .2 percent in month 1 of a mortgage, .4 percent in month 2, then .6 percent in month 3, and so on. The annual prepayment rate continues to rise by .2 percent per month until reaching an annual prepayment rate of 6 percent in month 30 of a mortgage. Thereafter, the benchmark prepayment rate remains constant at 6 percent per year. This PSA benchmark represents a mortgage prepayment schedule called 100 PSA, which means 100 percent of the PSA benchmark. Deviations from the 100 PSA benchmark are stated as a percentage of the benchmark. For example, 200 PSA means 200 percent of the 100 PSA benchmark, and it doubles all

FIGURE 19.2

PSA Prepayment Model Showing Conditional Prepayment Rates (CPR)

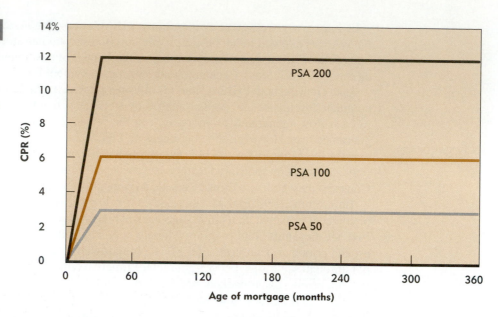

prepayment rates relative to the benchmark. Similarly, 50 PSA means 50 percent of the 100 PSA benchmark, halving all prepayment rates relative to the benchmark. Prepayment rate schedules illustrating 50 PSA, 100 PSA, and 200 PSA are graphically presented in Figure 19.2.

Based on historical experience, the PSA prepayment model makes an important distinction between **seasoned mortgages** and **unseasoned mortgages**. In the PSA model, unseasoned mortgages are those less than 30 months old with rising prepayment rates. Seasoned mortgages are those over 30 months old with constant prepayment rates.

seasoned mortgages Mortgages over 30 months old.

unseasoned mortgages Mortgages less than 30 months old.

conditional prepayment rate (CPR) The prepayment rate for a mortgage pool conditional on the age of the mortgages in the pool.

Prepayment rates in the PSA model are stated as **conditional prepayment rates** (**CPRs**), since they are conditional on the age of mortgages in a pool. For example, the CPR for a seasoned 100 PSA mortgage is 6 percent, which represents a 6 percent probability of mortgage prepayment in a given year. By convention, the probability of prepayment in a given month is stated as a *single monthly mortality (SMM)*. SMM is calculated using a CPR as follows:

$$SMM = 1 - (1 - CPR)^{1/12} \qquad (19.2)$$

For example, the SMM corresponding to a seasoned 100 PSA mortgage with a 6 percent CPR is .5143 percent, which is calculated as

$$SMM = 1 - (1 - .06)^{1/12}$$
$$= .5143\%$$

As another example, the SMM corresponding to an unseasoned 100 PSA mortgage in month 20 of the mortgage with a 4 percent CPR is .3396 percent, which is calculated as

$$SMM = 1 - (1 - .04)^{1/12} = .3396\%$$

average life Average time for a mortgage in a pool to be paid off.

Some mortgages in a pool are prepaid earlier than average, some are prepaid later than average, and some are not prepaid at all. The **average life** of a mortgage in a pool is the average time for a single mortgage in a pool to be paid off, either by prepayment or by making scheduled payments until maturity. Because prepayment shortens the life of a mortgage, the average life of a mortgage is usually much less than a mortgage's stated maturity. We can calculate a mortgage's projected average life by assuming a particular prepayment schedule. For example, the average life of a mortgage in a pool of 30-year mortgages, assuming several PSA prepayment schedules, is stated immediately below.

Prepayment Schedule	Average Mortgage Life (years)
50 PSA	20.40
100 PSA	14.68
200 PSA	8.87
400 PSA	4.88

Notice that an average life ranges from slightly less than 5 years for 400 PSA prepayments to slightly more than 20 years for 50 PSA prepayments.[1]

Bear in mind that these are expected averages given a particular prepayment schedule. Since prepayments are somewhat unpredictable, the average life of mortgages in any specific pool are likely to deviate somewhat from an expected average.

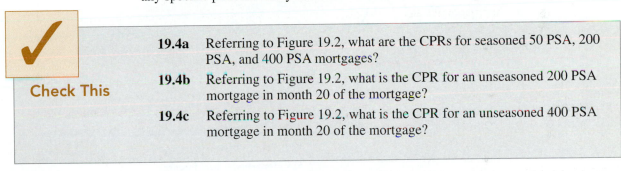

Check This

19.4a   Referring to Figure 19.2, what are the CPRs for seasoned 50 PSA, 200 PSA, and 400 PSA mortgages?

19.4b   Referring to Figure 19.2, what is the CPR for an unseasoned 200 PSA mortgage in month 20 of the mortgage?

19.4c   Referring to Figure 19.2, what is the CPR for an unseasoned 400 PSA mortgage in month 20 of the mortgage?

19.5 Cash Flow Analysis of GNMA Fully Modified Mortgage Pools

Each month, GNMA mortgage-backed bond investors receive pro rata shares of cash flows derived from fully modified mortgage pools. Each monthly cash flow has three distinct components:

1. Payment of interest on outstanding mortgage principal.

2. Scheduled amortization of mortgage principal.

3. Mortgage principal prepayments.

As a sample GNMA mortgage pool, consider a $10 million pool of 30-year 8 percent mortgages financed by the sale of 100 bonds at a par value price of $100,000 per bond. For simplicity, we ignore servicing and guarantee fees. The decline in bond principal for these GNMA bonds is graphed in Figure 19.3A for the cases of prepayment rates

---

[1]Formulas used to calculate average mortgage life are complicated and depend on the assumed prepayment model. For this reason, average life formulas are omitted here.

FIGURE 19.3

Principal and Cash Flows for $100,000 Par Value 30-Year 8 Percent GNMA Bonds

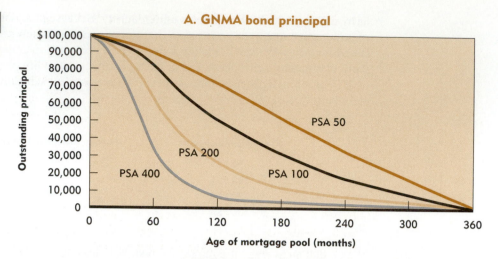

A. GNMA bond principal

B. GNMA bond cash flow

following 50 PSA, 100 PSA, 200 PSA, and 400 PSA schedules. In Figure 19.3A, notice that 50 PSA prepayments yield a nearly straight-line amortization of bond principal. Also notice that for the extreme case of 400 PSA prepayments, over 90 percent of bond principal is amortized within 10 years of mortgage pool origination.

Monthly cash flows for these GNMA bonds are graphed in Figure 19.3B for the cases of 50 PSA, 100 PSA, 200 PSA, and 400 PSA prepayment schedules. In Figure 19.3B, notice the sharp spike in monthly cash flows associated with 400 PSA prepayments at about month 30. Lesser PSA prepayment rates blunt the spike and level the cash flows.

As shown in Figures 19.3A and 19.3B, prepayments significantly affect the cash flow characteristics of GNMA bonds. However, these illustrations assume that prepayment schedules remain unchanged over the life of a mortgage pool. This can be unrealistic, since prepayment rates often change from those originally forecast. For example, sharply falling interest rates could easily cause a jump in prepayment rates from 100 PSA to 400 PSA. Since large interest rate movements are unpredictable, future prepayment rates can also be unpredictable. Consequently, GNMA mortgage-backed bond investors face substantial cash flow uncertainty. This makes GNMA bonds an unsuitable investment for many investors, especially relatively unsophisticated investors unaware of the risks involved. Nevertheless, GNMA bonds offer higher yields than U.S. Treasury bonds, which makes them attractive to professional fixed-income portfolio managers.

Check This

19.5a	GNMA bond investors face significant cash flow uncertainty. Why might cash flow uncertainty be a problem for many portfolio managers?
19.5b	Why might cash flow uncertainty be less of a problem for investors with a very long-term investment horizon?

Macaulay Durations for GNMA Mortgage-Backed Bonds

Macaulay duration A measure of interest rate risk for fixed-income securities.

For mortgage pool investors, prepayment risk is important because it complicates the effects of interest rate risk. With falling interest rates, prepayments speed up and the average life of mortgages in a pool shortens. Similarly, with rising interest rates, prepayments slow down and average mortgage life lengthens. Recall from a previous chapter that interest rate risk for a bond is often measured by **Macaulay duration**. However, Macaulay duration assumes a fixed schedule of cash flow payments. But the schedule of cash flow payments for mortgage-backed bonds is not fixed because it is affected by mortgage prepayments, which in turn are affected by interest rates. For this reason, Macaulay duration is a deficient measure of interest rate risk for mortgage-backed bonds. The following examples illustrate the deficiency of Macaulay duration when it is unrealistically assumed that interest rates do not affect mortgage prepayment rates.[2]

1. *Macaulay duration for a GNMA bond with zero prepayments.* Suppose a GNMA bond is based on a pool of 30-year, 8 percent fixed-rate mortgages. Assuming an 8 percent interest rate, their price is equal to their initial par value of $100,000. The Macaulay duration for these bonds is 9.56 years.

2. *Macaulay duration for a GNMA bond with a constant 100 PSA prepayment schedule.* Suppose a GNMA bond based on a pool of 30-year 8 percent fixed-rate mortgages follows a constant 100 PSA prepayment schedule. Accounting for this prepayment schedule when calculating Macaulay duration, we obtain a Macaulay duration of 6.77 years.

Examples 1 and 2 illustrate how Macaulay duration can be affected by mortgage prepayments. Essentially, faster prepayments cause earlier cash flows and shorten Macaulay durations.

However, Macaulay durations are still misleading because they assume that prepayment schedules are unaffected by changes in interest rates. When falling interest rates speed up prepayments, or rising interest rates slow down prepayments, Macaulay durations yield inaccurate price-change predictions for mortgage-backed securities. The following examples illustrate the inaccuracy.

3. *Macaulay duration for a GNMA bond with changing PSA prepayment schedules.* Suppose a GNMA bond based on a pool of 30-year 8 percent fixed-rate mortgages has a par value price of $100,000 and that, with no change in

---

[2]The Macaulay duration formula for a mortgage is not presented here since, as our discussion suggests, its usage is not recommended.

interest rates, the pool follows a 100 PSA prepayment schedule. Further suppose that when the market interest rate for these bonds rises to 9 percent, prepayments fall to a 50 PSA schedule. In this case, the price of the bond falls to $92,644, representing a 7.36 percent price drop, which is more than .5 percent larger than the drop predicted by the bond's Macaulay duration of 6.77.

4. *Macaulay duration for a GNMA bond with changing PSA prepayment schedules.* Suppose a GNMA bond based on a pool of 30-year 8 percent fixed-rate mortgages has a par value price of $100,000 and that, with no change in interest rates, the pool follows a 100 PSA prepayment schedule. Further suppose that when the market interest rate for these bonds falls to 7 percent, prepayments rise to a 200 PSA schedule. In this case, the bond price rises to $105,486, which is over 1.2 percent less than the price increase predicted by the bond's Macaulay duration of 6.77.

Examples 3 and 4 illustrate that simple Macaulay durations overpredict price increases and underpredict price decreases for changes in mortgage-backed bond prices caused by changing interest rates. These errors are caused by the fact that Macaulay duration does not account for prepayment rates changing in response to interest rate changes. The severity of these errors depends on how strongly interest rates affect prepayment rates. Historical experience indicates that interest rates significantly affect prepayment rates and that Macaulay duration is a very conservative measure of interest rate risk for mortgage-backed securities.

To correct the deficiencies of Macaulay duration, a method often used in practice to assess interest rate risk for mortgage-backed securities is to first develop projections regarding mortgage prepayments. Projecting prepayments for mortgages requires analyzing both economic and demographic variables. In particular, it is necessary to estimate how prepayment rates will respond to changes in interest rates. A duration model that accounts for these factors is called **effective duration**. In practice, effective duration is used to calculate predicted prices for mortgage-backed securities based on hypothetical interest rate and prepayment scenarios.

effective duration for MBS Duration measure that accounts for how mortgage prepayments are affected by changes in interest rates.

Check This

19.5c Why is it important for portfolio managers to know by how much a change in interest rates will affect mortgage prepayments?

19.5d Why is it important for portfolio managers to know by how much a change in interest rates will affect mortgage-backed bond prices?

19.6 Collateralized Mortgage Obligations

collateralized mortgage obligations (CMOs) Securities created by splitting mortgage pool cash flows according to specific allocation rules.

When a mortgage pool is created, cash flows from the pool are often carved up and distributed according to various allocation rules. Mortgage-backed securities representing specific rules for allocating mortgage cash flows are called **collateralized mortgage obligations** (**CMOs**). Indeed, a CMO is defined by the rule that created it. Like all mortgage passthroughs, primary collateral for CMOs are the mortgages in the underlying pool. This is true no matter how the rules for cash flow distribution are actually specified.

The three best-known types of CMO structures using specific rules to carve up mortgage pool cash flows are (1) interest-only strips (IOs) and principal-only strips (POs), (2) sequential CMOs, and (3) protected amortization class securities (PACs). Each of these CMO structures is discussed immediately below. Before beginning, however, we retell an old Wall Street joke that pertains to CMOs: Question: "How many investment bankers does it take to *sell* a lightbulb?" Answer: "401; one to hit it with a hammer, and 400 to sell off the pieces."

The moral of the story is that mortgage-backed securities can be repackaged in many ways, and the resulting products are often quite complex. Even the basic types we consider here are significantly more complicated than the basic fixed-income instruments we considered in earlier chapters. Consequently, we do not go into great detail regarding the underlying calculations for CMOs. Instead, we examine only the basic properties of the most commonly encountered CMOs.

Interest-Only and Principal-Only Mortgage Strips

interest-only strips (IOs) Securities that pay only the interest cash flows to investors.

principal-only strips (POs) Securities that pay only the principal cash flows to investors.

Perhaps the simplest rule for carving up mortgage pool cash flows is to separate payments of principal from payments of interest. Mortgage-backed securities paying only the interest component of mortgage pool cash flows are called **interest-only strips**, or simply **IOs**. Mortgage-backed securities paying only the principal component of mortgage pool cash flows are called **principal-only strips**, or simply **POs**. Mortgage strips are more complicated than straight mortgage passthroughs. In particular, IO strips and PO strips behave quite differently in response to changes in prepayment rates and interest rates.

Let us begin an examination of mortgage strips by considering a $100,000 par value GNMA bond that has been stripped into a separate IO bond and a PO bond. The whole GNMA bond receives a pro rata share of all cash flows from a pool of 30-year 8 percent mortgages. From the whole bond cash flow, the IO bond receives the interest component, and the PO bond receives the principal component. The sum of IO and PO cash flows reproduces the whole bond cash flow.

Assuming various PSA prepayment schedules, cash flows to IO strips are illustrated in Figure 19.4A, and cash flows to PO strips are illustrated in Figure 19.4B. Holding the interest rate constant at 8 percent, IO and PO strip values for various PSA prepayment schedules are listed immediately below:

Prepayment Schedule	IO Strip Value	PO Strip Value
50 PSA	$63,102.80	$36,897.20
100 PSA	53,726.50	46,273.50
200 PSA	41,366.24	58,633.76
400 PSA	28,764.16	71,235.84

Notice that total bond value is $100,000 for all prepayment schedules because the interest rate is unchanged from its original 8 percent value. Nevertheless, even with no change in interest rates, faster prepayments imply *lower* IO strip values and *higher* PO strip values, and vice versa.

There is a simple reason why PO strip value rises with faster prepayment rates. Essentially, the only cash flow uncertainty facing PO strip holders is the timing of PO

FIGURE 19.4

Cash Flows for
$100,000 Par
Value 30-Year 8
Percent Bonds

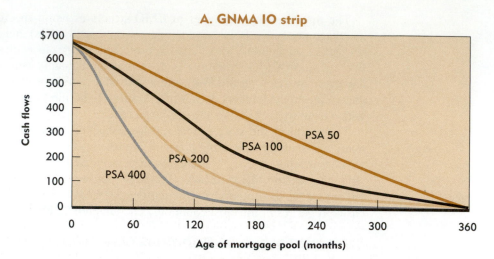

A. GNMA IO strip

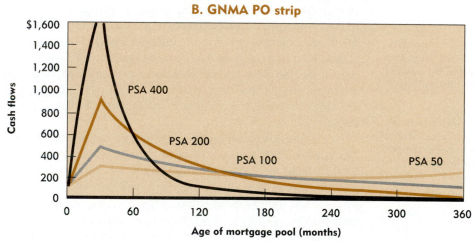

B. GNMA PO strip

cash flows, not the total amount of cash flows. No matter what prepayment schedule applies, total cash flows paid to PO strip holders over the life of the pool will be equal to the initial principal of $100,000. Therefore, PO strip value increases as principal is paid earlier to PO strip holders because of the time value of money.

In contrast, IO strip holders face considerable uncertainty regarding the total amount of IO cash flows that they will receive. Faster prepayments reduce principal more rapidly, thereby reducing interest payments since interest is paid only on outstanding principal. The best that IO strip holders could hope for is that no mortgages are prepaid, which would maximize total interest payments. Prepayments reduce total interest payments. Indeed, in the extreme case, where all mortgages in a pool are prepaid, IO cash flows stop completely.

The effects of changing interest rates compounded by changing prepayment rates are illustrated by considering IO and PO strips from a $100,000 par value GNMA bond based on a pool of 30-year 8 percent mortgages. First, suppose that an interest rate of 8 percent yields a 100 PSA prepayment schedule. Also suppose that a lower interest rate of 7 percent yields 200 PSA prepayments, and a higher interest rate of 9 percent yields 50 PSA prepayments. The resulting whole bond values and separate IO and PO strip values for these combinations of interest rates and prepayment rates are listed immediately below:

Interest Rate	Prepayments	IO Strip Value	PO Strip Value	Whole Bond Value
9%	50 PSA	$59,124.79	$35,519.47	$ 94,644.26
8	100 PSA	53,726.50	46,273.50	100,000.00
7	200 PSA	43,319.62	62,166.78	105,486.40

When the interest rate increases from 8 percent to 9 percent, total bond value falls by $5,355.74. This results from the PO strip price *falling* by $10,754.03 and the IO strip price *increasing* by $5,398.29. When the interest rate decreases from 8 percent to 7 percent, total bond value rises by $5,486.40. This results from the PO strip price *increasing* by $15,893.28 and the IO strip price *falling* by $10,406.88. Thus, PO strip values change in the same direction as the whole bond value, but the PO price change is larger. Notice that the IO strip price changes in the opposite direction of the whole bond and PO strip price change.

Check This

19.6a Suppose a $100,000 mortgage financed at 8 percent (.75 percent monthly) is paid off in the first month after issuance. In this case, what are the cash flows to an IO strip and a PO strip from this mortgage?

Sequential Collateralized Mortgage Obligations

sequential CMOs
Securities created by splitting a mortgage pool into a number of slices, called tranches.

One problem with investing in mortgage-backed bonds is the limited range of maturities available. An early method developed to deal with this problem is the creation of **sequential CMOs**. Sequential CMOs carve a mortgage pool into a number of tranches. *Tranche*, the French word for slice, is a commonly used financial term to describe the division of a whole into various parts. Sequential CMOs are defined by rules that distribute mortgage pool cash flows to sequential tranches. While almost any number of tranches are possible, a basic sequential CMO structure might have four tranches: A-tranche, B-tranche, C-tranche, and Z-tranche. Each tranche is entitled to a share of mortgage pool principal and interest on that share of principal.

As a hypothetical sequential CMO structure, suppose a 30-year, 8 percent GNMA bond initially represents $100,000 of mortgage principal. Cash flows to this whole bond are then carved up according to a sequential CMO structure with A-, B-, C-, and Z-tranches. The A-, B-, and C-tranches initially represent $30,000 each of mortgage principal each. The Z-tranche initially represents $10,000 of principal. The sum of all four tranches reproduces the original whole bond principal of $100,000. The cash flows from the whole bond are passed through to each tranche according to the following rules:

Rule 1: Mortgage principal payments. All payments of mortgage principal, including scheduled amortization and prepayments, are first paid to the A-tranche. When all A-tranche principal is paid off, subsequent payments of mortgage principal are then paid to the B-tranche. After all B-tranche principal is paid off, all principal payments are then paid to the C-tranche. Finally, when all C-tranche principal is paid off, all principal payments go to the Z-tranche.

Rule 2: Interest payments. All tranches receive interest payments in proportion to the amount of outstanding principal in each tranche. Interest on A-, B-, and C-tranche principal is passed through immediately to A-, B-, and C-tranches. Interest on Z-tranche principal is paid to the A-tranche as cash in exchange for the transfer of an equal amount of principal from the A-tranche to the Z-tranche. After A-tranche principal is fully paid, interest on Z-tranche principal is paid to the B-tranche in exchange for an equal amount of principal from the B-tranche to the Z-tranche. This process continues sequentially through each tranche.

For example, the first month's cash flows from a single whole bond are allocated as follows. Scheduled mortgage payments yield a whole bond cash flow of $733.76, which is divided between $67.10 principal amortization and $666.67 payment of interest. All scheduled principal amortization is paid to the A-tranche, and A-tranche principal is reduced by a like amount. Since outstanding principal was *initially* equal to $30,000 for the A-, B-, and C-tranche bonds, each of these tranches receives an interest payment of $30,000 $\times$ .08 / 12 = $200. In addition, the Z-tranche interest payment of $10,000 $\times$ .08/12 = $66.67 is paid to the A-tranche in cash in exchange for transferring $66.67 of principal to the Z-tranche. In summary, A-tranche principal is reduced by $67.10 + $66.67 = $133.77 plus any prepayments, and Z-tranche principal is increased by $66.67.

Remaining principal amounts for A-, B-, C-, and Z-tranches, assuming 100 PSA prepayments, are graphed in Figure 19.5A. Corresponding cash flows for the A-, B-, C-, and Z-tranches, assuming 100 PSA prepayments, are graphed in Figure 19.5B.

Check This

> **19.6b** Figures 19.5A and 19.5B assume a 100 PSA prepayment schedule. How would these figures change for a 200 PSA prepayment schedule or a 50 PSA prepayment schedule?
>
> **19.6c** While A-, B-, and C-tranche principal is being paid down, Z-tranche interest is used to acquire principal for the Z-tranche. What is the growth rate of Z-tranche principal during this period?

Protected Amortization Class Bonds

protected amortization class bond (PAC)
Mortgage-backed security that takes priority for scheduled payments of principal.

Another popular security used to alleviate the problem of cash flow uncertainty when investing in mortgage-backed bonds is a **protected amortization class (PAC) bond**, or simply **PAC**. Like all CMOs, PAC bonds are defined by specific rules that carve up cash flows from a mortgage pool. Essentially, a PAC bond carves out a slice of a mortgage pool's cash flows according to a rule that gives PAC bondholders first priority entitlement to promised PAC cash flows. Consequently, PAC cash flows are predictable so long as mortgage pool prepayments remain within a predetermined band. PAC bonds are attractive to investors who require a high degree of cash flow certainty from their investments.

FIGURE 19.5

Sequential CMO Principal and Cash Flows for a $100,000 Par Value GNMA Bond

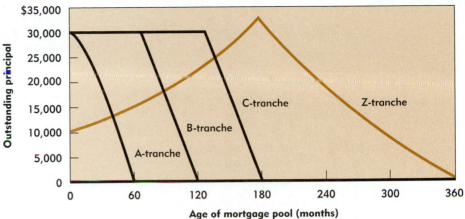

A. Sequential CMO principal

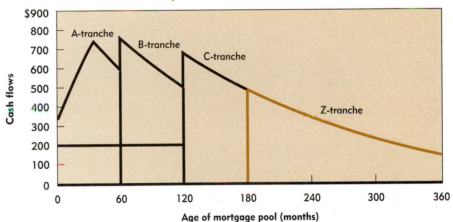

B. Sequential CMO cash flows

PAC support bond Mortgage-backed security that has subordinate priority for scheduled payments of principal. Also called *PAC companion bond*.

PAC collar Range defined by upper and lower prepayment schedules of a PAC bond.

After PAC bondholders receive their promised cash flows, residual cash flows from the mortgage pool are paid to non-PAC bonds, often referred to as **PAC support bonds** or *PAC companion bonds*. In effect, almost all cash flow uncertainty is concentrated in the non-PAC bonds. The non-PAC bond supports the PAC bond and serves the same purpose as a Z-tranche bond in a sequential CMO structure. For this reason, a non-PAC bond is sometimes called a PAC Z-tranche.

Creation of a PAC bond entails three steps. First, we must specify two PSA prepayment schedules that form the upper and lower prepayment bounds of a PAC bond. These bounds define a **PAC collar**. For example, suppose we create a single PAC bond from a new $100,000 par value GNMA bond based on a pool of 30-year fixed rate mortgages. The PAC collar specifies a 100 PSA prepayment schedule as a lower bound and a 300 PSA prepayment schedule as an upper bound. Cash flows to the PAC bond are said to enjoy protected amortization so long as mortgage pool prepayments remain within this 100–300 PSA collar.

Our second step in creating a PAC bond is to calculate principal-only (PO) cash flows from our 30-year, $100,000 par value GNMA bond, assuming 100 PSA and 300 PSA prepayment schedules. These PO cash flows, which include both scheduled

FIGURE 19.6

GNMA PAC
100/300 Cash
Flows for
$100,000 Par
Value 30-Year 8
Percent Bond

A. PAC cash flows

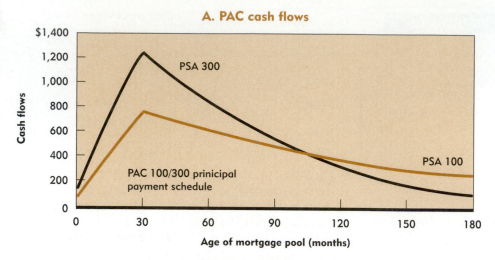

B. Total cash flows

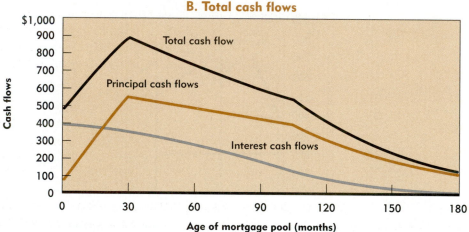

amortization and prepayments, are plotted in Figure 19.6A. In Figure 19.6A, notice that principal-only cash flows for 100 PSA and 300 PSA prepayment schedules intersect in month 103. Before the 103rd month, 300 PSA PO cash flows are greater. After that month, 100 PSA PO cash flows are greater. PAC bond cash flows are specified by the 100 PSA schedule before month 103 and the 300 PSA schedule after month 103. Because the PAC bond is specified by 100 PSA and 300 PSA prepayment schedules, it is called a PAC 100/300 bond.

Our third step is to specify the cash flows to be paid to PAC bondholders on a priority basis. PAC bondholders receive payments of principal according to the PAC collar's lower PSA prepayment schedule. For the PAC 100/300 bond in this example, principal payments are made according to the 100 PSA prepayment schedule until month 103, when the schedule switches to the 300 PSA prepayment schedule. The sum of all scheduled principal to be paid to PAC 100/300 bondholders represents total initial PAC bond principal. In addition to payment of principal, a PAC bondholder also receives payment of interest on outstanding PAC principal. For example, if the mortgage pool financing rate is 9 percent, the PAC bondholder receives an interest payment of .75 percent per month of outstanding PAC principal.

Total monthly cash flows paid to the PAC bond, including payments of principal and interest, are graphed in Figure 19.6B. As shown, total cash flow reaches a maximum in month 30, thereafter gradually declining. So long as mortgage pool prepayments remain within the 100/300 PSA prepayment collar, PAC bondholders will receive these cash flows exactly as originally specified.

PAC collars are usually sufficiently wide so that actual prepayments move outside the collar only infrequently. In the event that prepayments move outside a collar far enough to interfere with promised PAC cash flows, PAC bonds normally specify the following two contingency rules:

PAC contingency rule 1. When actual prepayments fall below a PAC collar's lower bound, there could be insufficient cash flow to satisfy a PAC bond's promised cash flow schedule. In this case, the PAC bond receives all available cash flow, and any shortfall is carried forward and paid on a first-priority basis from future cash flows. Non-PAC bonds receive no cash flows until all cumulative shortfalls to PAC bonds are paid off.

PAC contingency rule 2. When actual prepayments rise above a PAC collar's upper bound, it is possible that all outstanding principal for the non-PAC support bonds is paid off before the PAC bond. When all non-PAC principal is paid off, the PAC cash flow schedule is abandoned and all mortgage pool cash flows are paid to PAC bondholders.

Check This

19.6d	A PAC 100/300 bond based on a pool of fully modified 30-year fixed-rate mortgages switches payment schedules after 103 months. Would switching occur earlier or later for a PAC 50/300 bond? For a PAC 100/500 bond?
19.6e	Figures 19.6a and 19.6b assume a PAC 100/300 bond based on a pool of fully modified 30-year fixed-rate mortgages. What would these figures look like for a PAC 50/300 and a PAC 100/500 bond?
19.6f	How might a large change in market interest rates cause mortgage pool prepayments to move outside a PAC collar far enough and long enough to interfere with an originally stated PAC bond cash flow schedule?

19.7 Yields for Mortgage-Backed Securities and Collateralized Mortgage Obligations

Yields for mortgage-backed securities (MBSs) and collateralized mortgage obligations (CMOs) for representative GNMA, FHLMC, and FNMA mortgage pools are published daily in *The Wall Street Journal*. Figure 19.7 is a sample listing. The first column lists the type of mortgage pool. For example, the first mortgage pool type is 30-year FMAC (i.e., Freddie Mac) Gold paying 5.5 percent interest on outstanding principal. The second mortgage pool type is 30-year FMAC Gold paying 6.0 percent interest on outstanding principal. Column 2 reports the price (in 32nds of a point) for the MBS. The third column is the change in the price from the previous day. The fourth column shows the estimated average life of the mortgages in the underlying pool. The fifth column

FIGURE 19.7

MBS Yields

Source: *The Wall Street Journal*, May 21, 2003. Reprinted by permission of Dow Jones & Company, Inc., via Copyright Clearance Center, Inc. © 2003 Dow Jones & Company. All Rights Reserved Worldwide.

Mortgage-Backed Securities

Indicative, not guaranteed; from Bear Stearns Cos./Street Pricing Service

RATE		PRICE (JUN) (PTS-32DS)	PRICE CHANGE (32DS)	AVG LIFE (YEARS)	SPRD TO AVG LIFE (YEARS)	SPREAD CHANGE (BPS)	PSA (PREPAY SPEED)	YIELD TO MAT*
30-year								
FMAC GOLD	5.5%	103-19	+02	1.8	205	+2	1063	3.30
FMAC GOLD	6.0%	103-24	+01	1.0	87	+2	1738	1.99
FMAC GOLD	6.5%	104-04	−01	0.8	-9	+7	1320	0.99
FNMA	5.5%	103-23	+02	1.8	187	+2	1095	3.11
FNMA	6.0%	103-31	+01	0.9	24	+2	1910	1.34
FNMA	6.5%	104-08	−01	0.8	-51	+6	1353	0.58
GNMA **	5.5%	104-12	+05	2.2	195	-2	770	3.30
GNMA **	6.0%	104-23	+01	1.2	75	+7	1053	1.91
GNMA **	6.5%	104-29	−01	1.0	16	+18	1120	1.27
15-year								
FMAC GOLD	5.0%	103-10	+02	2.0	189	+5	902	3.18
FNMA	5.0%	103-16	+02	1.9	167	+6	962	2.94
GNMA **	5.0%	104-22	+06	2.6	156	...	633	3.04

*Extrapolated from benchmarks based on projections from Bear Stearns prepayment model, assuming interest rates remain unchanged. ** Government guaranteed.

Collateralized Mortgage Obligations

Spread of CMO yields above U.S. Treasury securities of comparable maturity, in basis points (100 basis points = 1 percentage point of interest)

MAT	SPREAD	CHG FROM PREV DAY
Sequentials		
2-year	230	...
5-year	220	...
7-year	200	...
10-year	172	...
20-year	100	...
PACS		
2-year	135	...
5-year	150	...
7-year	149	...
10-year	142	...
20-year	77	...

gives the spread (in basis points) between the yield to maturity on the MBS and the yield on a U.S. Treasury note or bond with a maturity similar to the average life of the MBS. Column 6 shows the change in this spread from the previous day.

Finally, column 7 shows the assumed PSA prepayment rate and the last column shows the yield to maturity on the MBS calculated using the assumed prepayment rate. This yield to maturity is also known as the **cash flow yield**. Essentially, cash flow yield is the interest rate that equates the present value of all future cash flows on the mortgage pool to the current price of the pool, assuming a particular prepayment rate. Spread information on CMOs is also reported.

cash flow yield Yield to maturity for a mortgage-backed security conditional on an assumed prepayment pattern.

19.8 Summary and Conclusions

This chapter discusses the large and growing market for mortgage-backed securities. Many aspects of this market were covered, including the following items.

1. Most Americans finance their homes with mortgages. The buyer makes a down payment and borrows the remaining cost with a mortgage loan. Mortgages are often repackaged into mortgage-backed securities through a process called mortgage securitization. Currently, about half of all mortgages in the United States have been securitized, yet the risks involved in these investments are often misunderstood.

2. Most home mortgages are 15- or 30-year fixed-rate mortgages requiring constant monthly payments. The present value of all monthly payments is equal to the original amount of the mortgage loan. Each monthly payment has two components: payment of interest on outstanding mortgage principal and a scheduled pay-down of mortgage principal. The relative amounts of each component change throughout the life of a mortgage. The interest payment component gradually declines, and the pay-down of principal component gradually increases.

3. A mortgage borrower has the right to pay off a mortgage early, which is called mortgage prepayment. Borrowers frequently prepay to refinance an existing mortgage at a lower interest rate. Prepayment and refinancing, advantages to mortgage borrowers, are disadvantages to mortgage investors. Thus, mortgage investors face prepayment risk.

4. In 1968, Congress established the Government National Mortgage Association (GNMA) as a government agency charged with promoting liquidity in the secondary market for home mortgages. GNMA is the largest single guarantor of mortgage-backed securities. Two government-sponsored enterprises (GSEs) are also significant mortgage repackaging sponsors: the Federal Home Loan Mortgage Corporation (FHLMC) and the Federal National Mortgage Association (FNMA).

5. Each month, GNMA, FHLMC, and FNMA mortgage-backed bond investors receive cash flows derived from fully modified mortgage pools. Each monthly cash flow has three distinct components: payment of interest on outstanding mortgage principal, scheduled amortization of mortgage principal, and mortgage principal prepayments.

6. Mortgage prepayments are stated as a prepayment rate. The greater the prepayment rate, the faster mortgage pool principal is paid off. Prepayment rates can vary substantially from year to year, depending on mortgage type and various economic and demographic factors. Conventional industry practice states prepayment rates using a prepayment model specified by the Public Securities Association (PSA). This model states prepayment rates as a percentage of a PSA benchmark, which represents an annual prepayment rate of 6 percent for seasoned mortgages, and is called 100 PSA. Deviations from the 100 PSA benchmark are stated as a percentage of the benchmark.

7. Prepayment risk complicates the effects of interest rate risk. Interest rate risk for a bond is related to its effective maturity as measured by Macaulay duration. However, Macaulay duration assumes a fixed schedule of cash flow payments. But the schedule of cash flow payments for mortgage-backed bonds is not fixed because it is affected by mortgage prepayments, which in turn are affected by interest rates. For this reason, Macaulay duration is a deficient measure of interest rate risk for mortgage-backed bonds.

8. Cash flows from mortgage pools are often carved up and distributed according to various rules. Mortgage-backed securities representing specific rules for allocating mortgage cash flows are called collateralized mortgage obligations (CMOs). The three best known types of CMO structures using specific rules to carve up mortgage pool cash flows are interest-only (IO) and principal-only (PO) strips, sequential CMOs, and protected amortization class securities (PACs).

9. Cash flow yields for mortgage-backed securities (MBSs) and collateralized mortgage obligations (CMOs) for GNMA, FHLMC, and FNMA mortgage pools are published daily in *The Wall Street Journal*. Cash flow yield for a mortgage-backed security corresponds to the yield to maturity for an ordinary bond. Essentially, cash flow yield is the interest rate that discounts all future expected cash flows from a mortgage pool to be equal to the price of the mortgage pool.

Get Real

This chapter covered one of the more complex investments available, mortgage-backed securities (MBSs). Ironically, these investments are fairly complicated, but unlike most exotic instruments, the basic types of MBSs are very suitable for ordinary individual investors. In fact, GNMAs and similar investments are frequently recommended, and rightly so, for even very conservative investors.

However, as a practical matter, directly buying into mortgage pools is not practical for most individual investors. It is also probably unwise, because not all pools are equally risky in terms of prepayments, and analysis of individual pools is best left to experts. Instead, most investors in MBSs end up in mutual funds specializing in these instruments, and most of the major mutual fund families have such funds.

If you are interested in learning more about these investments, the Internet contains a large amount of information. The first places to visit are the websites for GNMA (www.ginniemae.gov), FNMA (www.fanniemae.com), and FHLMC (www.freddiemac.com). For much information on the home mortgage business, along with current mortgage rates across the country, try Mortgage Mag (www.mortgagemag.com). Some informative sites with good-to-excellent sections on mortgage-backed securities include Investing in Bonds (www.investinginbonds.com) and Bond Markets (www.bondmarkets.com). If you are thinking about a research project and need some data on mortgage-backed securities, look at what's available at Financial Data Services (www.dataonfindata.com).

Key Terms

mortgage passthroughs 625
mortgage-backed securities (MBSs) 625
mortgage securitization 625
fixed-rate mortgage 625
mortgage principal 628
mortgage amortization 628
mortgage prepayment 630
Government National Mortgage Association (GNMA) 633
fully modified mortgage pool 634
prepayment risk 634
Federal Home Loan Mortgage Corporation (FHLMC) 634
Federal National Mortgage Association (FNMA) 634
prepayment rate 635

seasoned mortgages 636
unseasoned mortgages 636
conditional prepayment rate (CPR) 636
average life 636
Macaulay duration 639
effective duration 640
collateralized mortgage obligations (CMOs) 640
interest-only strips (IOs) 641
principal-only strips (POs) 641
sequential CMOs 643
protected amortization class bond (PAC) 644
PAC support bond 645
PAC collar 645
cash flow yield 648

Chapter Review Problems and Self-Test

1. **Mortgage Payments**   What are the monthly payments on a 30-year $150,000 mortgage if the mortgage rate is 6 percent? What portion of the first payment is interest? Principal?

2. **Mortgage Prepayments**   Consider a 15-year $210,000 mortgage with a 7 percent interest rate. After 10 years, the borrower (the mortgage issuer) pays it off. How much will the lender receive?

Answers to Self-Test Problems

1. This is a standard time value of money calculation in which we need to find an annuity-type payment. The present value is $150,000. The interest rate is .06/12 = .005, or .5 percent, per month. There is a total of 360 payments. Using the formula from the text, we have

    $$\text{Monthly payment} = \frac{\text{Mortgage amount} \times r/12}{1 - \dfrac{1}{(1 + r/12)^{T \times 12}}}$$

    Plugging in $r = .06$ and $T = 30$, we get a payment of $899.33. The interest portion for a month is equal to the mortgage balance at the beginning of the month ($150,000 in this case) multiplied by the interest rate per month (.5 percent), or $150,000 × .005 = $750. The remaining portion of the payment, $899.33 − $750 = $149.33, goes to reduce the principal balance.

2. We first need to know the monthly payment. Here, the original balance is $210,000, the rate is 7 percent, and the original life is 15 years. Plugging in the numbers using the formula just above, check that we get a monthly payment of $1,887.54. From here, there are two ways to go. One is relatively easy, the other is relatively tedious. The tedious way would be to construct an amortization table for the mortgage and then locate the balance in the table. However, we need only a single balance, so there is a much faster way. After 10 years, we can treat this mortgage as though it were a five-year mortgage with payments of $1,887.54 and an interest rate of 7 percent. We can then solve for the mortgage balance using the same formula:

    $$\text{Monthly payment} = \frac{\text{Mortgage balance} \times .07/12}{1 - \dfrac{1}{(1 + .07/12)^{5 \times 12}}} = \$1,887.54$$

    Solving for the mortgage balance gets us $95,324.50.

Test Your Investments Quotient

1. **Fixed-Rate Mortgages** Which of the following statements about fixed rate mortgages is false?
    a. 15-year mortgages have higher monthly payments than 30-year mortgages.
    b. Scheduled monthly payments are constant over the life of the mortgage.
    c. Actual monthly payments may vary over the life of the mortgage.
    d. Actual monthly payments are never more than scheduled monthly payments.

2. **Fixed-Rate Mortgages** The interest component of a monthly payment for a fixed-rate mortgage is
    a. Highest during the first year of the mortgage.
    b. Highest during the middle year of the mortgage.
    c. Highest during the last year of the mortgage.
    d. Constant throughout the life of the mortgage.

3. **Fixed-Rate Mortgages** The principal reduction component of a monthly payment for a fixed-rate mortgage is
    a. Highest during the first year of the mortgage.
    b. Highest during the middle year of the mortgage.
    c. Highest during the last year of the mortgage.
    d. Constant throughout the life of the mortgage.

4. **Fixed-Rate Mortgages**   The remaining balance on a 30-year $100,000 mortgage loan financed at 8 percent after the 180th payment is (no calculation necessary)

   a. $100,000
   b. $50,000
   c. $76,782
   d. $23,219

5. **Fixed-Rate Mortgages**   Which of the following mortgages has the lowest monthly payment (no calculation necessary)?

   a. 30-year, 8 percent
   b. 30-year, 10 percent
   c. 15-year, 8 percent
   d. 15-year, 10 percent

6. **Fixed-Rate Mortgages**   Which of the following mortgages will pay the smallest total interest over the life of the mortgage (no calculation necessary)?

   a. 30-year, 8 percent
   b. 30-year, 10 percent
   c. 15-year, 8 percent
   d. 15-year, 10 percent

7. **Fixed-Rate Mortgages**   Which of the following mortgages will have the largest remaining balance after 180 monthly payments (no calculation necessary)?

   a. 30-year, 8 percent
   b. 30-year, 10 percent
   c. 15-year, 8 percent
   d. 15-year, 10 percent

8. **GNMA Bonds**   Mortgages in GNMA pools are said to be fully modified because GNMA guarantees bondholders which of the following?

   a. A minimum rate of return on their investment.
   b. A modified schedule of cash flows over the life of the pool.
   c. Full and timely payment of both principal and interest in the event of default.
   d. Eventual payment of both principal and interest in the event of default.

9. **GNMA Bonds**   Which of the following is not a source of risk for GNMA mortgage pool investors?

   a. Prepayment risk
   b. Default risk
   c. Interest rate risk
   d. Reinvestment risk

CFA®
PROBLEMS

10. **GNMA Bonds**   Which one of the following sets of features most accurately describes a GNMA mortgage passthrough security?

	Average Life	Payment Frequency	Credit Risk
a.	Predictable	Monthly	High
b.	Predictable	Semiannual	Low
c.	Unpredictable	Monthly	Low
d.	Unpredictable	Semiannual	Low

CFA®
PROBLEMS

11. **GNMA Bonds**   In contrast to original-issue U.S. Treasury securities, original-issue GNMA passthrough securities

   a. Provide quarterly payments to the investor.
   b. Have a limited availability of maturities.

c. Are often issued in zero coupon form.

d. Have interest payments.

12. **GNMA Bonds**   Which of the following should a bond portfolio manager who is looking for mortgage-backed securities that would perform best during a period of rising interest rates purchase?

a. A 12 percent GNMA with an average life of 5.6 years.

b. An 8 percent GNMA with an average life of 6.0 years.

c. A 10 percent GNMA with an average life of 8.5 years.

d. A 6 percent GNMA with an average life of 9.0 years.

13. **GNMA Bonds**   Why will the effective yield on a GNMA bond be higher than that of a U.S. Treasury bond with the same quoted yield to maturity? Because

a. GNMA yields are figured on a 360-day basis.

b. GNMAs carry higher coupons.

c. GNMAs have longer compounding periods.

d. GNMA interest is paid monthly.

14. **Mortgage-Backed Bonds**   If a mortgage-backed bond is issued as a fully modified passthrough security, it means that

a. Bondholders will receive full and timely payment of principal and interest even if underlying mortgage payments are not made.

b. The bond has been structured to include both conforming and nonconforming loans.

c. The interest rates on the underlying mortgages have been altered so that they equal the weighted-average coupon on the bond.

d. The security carries a balloon payment to ensure that the bond is fully amortized in a set time frame (12 to 15 years).

15. **Prepayments**   Projecting prepayments for mortgage passthrough securities

a. Requires only a projection of changes in the level of interest rates.

b. Requires analyzing both economic and demographic variables.

c. Is not necessary to determine a cash flow yield.

d. Is not necessary to determine duration.

16. **Prepayments**   A bond analyst at Omnipotent Bank (OB) notices that the prepayment experience on his holdings of high-coupon GNMA issues has been moving sharply higher. What does this indicate?

a. Interest rates are falling.

b. The loans comprising OB's pools have been experiencing lower default rates.

c. The pools held by OB are older issues.

d. All of the above.

17. **Mortgage-Backed Bonds**   Which of the following statements about mortgage passthrough securities is (are) correct?

   I. Passthroughs offer better call protection than most corporates and Treasuries.

  II. Interest and principal payments are made on a monthly basis.

 III. It is common practice to use the weighted-average maturity on a passthrough in place of its duration.

  IV. Passthroughs are relatively immune from reinvestment risk.

a. I and III only

b. II and III only

c. II only

d. IV only

18. **Mortgage-Backed Bonds**   Which of the following are advantages of mortgage-backed securities (MBSs)?

   I. MBS yields are above those of similarly rated corporate and U.S. Treasury bonds.

  II. MBSs have high-quality ratings, usually AAA, with some backed by the full faith and credit of the U.S. government.

III. MBSs have no call provision, thus protecting the investor from having to make a reinvestment decision before maturity.

   a. I and II only
   b. II and III only
   c. I and III only
   d. I, II, and III

19. **Mortgage-Backed Bonds**   Which of the following are characteristics that would make mortgage-backed securities (MBSs) inappropriate for less sophisticated, conservative investors?

   I. The maturity of MBSs is quite variable and difficult to determine.
   II. Due to their convexity, the realized total return on MBSs is often more dependent on interest rate levels than other bonds of similar maturity.
   III. Due to a possible unfamiliarity with prepayment concepts, investors may not be able to evaluate the true yield on MBS issues.
   IV. Many MBS issues are not quoted widely and are difficult to monitor.

   a. I, II, and III only
   b. I, III, and IV only
   c. II and IV only
   d. I, II, III, and IV

20. **Collateralized Mortgage Obligations**   For a given mortgage pool, which of the following CMOs based on that pool is the riskiest investment?

   a. 100/300 PAC bond
   b. A-tranche sequential CMO
   c. Interest-only (IO) strip
   d. Principal-only (PO) strip

21. **Collateralized Mortgage Obligations**   For a given mortgage pool, which of the following CMOs based on that pool is most likely to increase in price when market interest rates increase?

   a. 100/300 PAC bond
   b. A-tranche sequential CMO
   c. Interest-only (IO) strip
   d. Principal-only (PO) strip

22. **MBS Duration**   Higher prepayments has what impact on the effective duration of a mortgage passthrough security?

   a. Decreases effective duration for all maturity mortgages.
   b. Increases effective duration for all maturity mortgages.
   c. Increases (decreases) effective duration for short (long) maturity mortgages.
   d. Increases (decreases) effective duration for long (short) maturity mortgages.

23. **MBS Duration** Which of the following *most accurately* measures interest rate sensitivity for mortgage passthrough securities with prepayment risk?

   a. Static duration
   b. Effective duration
   c. Modified duration
   d. Macaulay duration

24. **CMO Duration**   Which of the following *most accurately* measures interest rate sensitivity for collateralized mortgage obligations?

   a. Static duration
   b. Effective duration
   c. Modified duration
   d. Macaulay duration

25. **MBS Duration** The most important difference between effective duration and Macaulay duration for a mortgage passthrough security is that

   a. Macaulay duration is easier to calculate.
   b. Effective duration is easier to calculate.
   c. Macaulay duration accounts for prepayment sensitivity.
   d. Effective duration accounts for prepayment sensitivity.

Concept Questions

1. **Mortgage Securitization** How does mortgage securitization benefit borrowers?

2. **Mortgage Securitization** How does mortgage securitization benefit mortgage originators?

3. **Mortgage Payments** All else the same, will the payments be higher on a 15-year mortgage or a 30-year mortgage? Why?

4. **Ginnie, Freddie, and Fannie** From an investor's point of view, what is the difference between mortgage pools backed by GNMA, FNMA, and FHLMC?

5. **Mortgage Pools** What does it mean for a mortgage pool to be fully modified?

6. **Prepayments** What are some of the reasons that mortgages are paid off early? Under what circumstances are mortgage prepayments likely to rise sharply? Explain.

7. **Prepayments** Explain why the right to prepay a mortgage is similar to the call feature contained in most corporate bonds.

8. **Prepayments** Evaluate the following argument: "Prepayment is not a risk to mortgage investors because prepayment actually means that the investor is paid both in full and ahead of schedule." Is the statement always true or false?

9. **Prepayments** Mortgage pools also suffer from defaults. Explain how defaults are handled in a fully modified mortgage pool. In the case of a fully modified mortgage pool, explain why defaults appear as prepayments to the mortgage pool investor.

10. **CMOs** What is a collateralized mortgage obligation? Why do they exist? What are three popular types?

11. **IO and PO Strips** What are IO and PO strips? Assuming interest rates never change, which is riskier?

12. **IO and PO Strips** Which has greater interest rate risk, an IO or a PO strip?

13. **Sequential CMOs** Consider a single whole bond sequential CMO. It has two tranches, an A-tranche and a Z-tranche. Explain how the payments are allocated to the two tranches. Which tranche is riskier?

14. **PACs** Explain in general terms how a protected amortization class CMO works.

15. **Duration and MBSs** Why is Macaulay duration an inadequate measure of interest rate risk for an MBS? Why is effective duration a better measure of interest rate risk for an MBS?

Questions and Problems

Core Questions

1. **Mortgage Payments** What is the monthly payment on a 30-year fixed rate mortgage if the original balance is $175,000 and the rate is 7 percent?

2. **Mortgage Balances** If a mortgage has monthly payments of $1,100, a life of 30 years, and a rate of 5.5 percent per year, what is the mortgage amount?

3. **Mortgage Payments** A homeowner takes out a $210,000, 30-year fixed-rate mortgage at a rate of 6.4 percent. What are the monthly mortgage payments?

4. **Mortgage Balance**   You have decided to buy a house. You can get a mortgage rate of 6.8 percent, and you want your payments to be $1,200 or less. How much can you borrow on a 30-year fixed-rate mortgage?

5. **SMM**   What is the single monthly mortality assuming the conditional prepayment rate is 5 percent?

6. **CPR**   What is the conditional prepayment rate if the single monthly mortality is .625 percent?

7. **IO and PO Values**   A $100,000 GNMA passthrough bond issue has a value of $108,320. The value of the interest-only payments is $41,564. What is the value of the principal-only payment?

8. **Mortgage Interest**   A 30-year $200,000 mortgage has a rate of 6.5 percent. What are the interest and principal portions in the first payment? In the second?

9. **Mortgage Balances**   A homeowner takes a 25-year fixed-rate mortgage for $250,000 at 7.8 percent. After seven years, the homeowner sells the house and pays off the remaining principal. How much is the principal payment?

10. **Mortgage Balances**   Consider a 30-year $300,000 mortgage with a 6.9 percent interest rate. After 10 years, the borrower (the mortgage issuer) pays it off. How much will the lender receive?

www.mhhe.com/cj3e

Intermediate Questions

11. **Prepayments**   Consider a 30-year $160,000 mortgage with a rate of 8 percent. Ten years into the mortgage, rates have fallen to 6 percent. What would be the monthly saving to a homeowner from refinancing the outstanding mortgage balance at the lower rate?

12. **Prepayments**   Consider a 15-year $110,000 mortgage with a rate of 9 percent. Eight years into the mortgage, rates have fallen to 6 percent. What would be the monthly saving to a homeowner from refinancing the outstanding mortgage balance at the lower rate?

13. **Prepayments**   Consider a 30-year $150,000 mortgage with a rate of 6.375 percent. Five years into the mortgage, rates have fallen to 6 percent. Suppose the transaction cost of obtaining a new mortgage is $1,500. Should the homeowner refinance at the lower rate?

14. **Mortgage Prepayments**   A homeowner took out a 30-year fixed-rate mortgage of $175,000. The mortgage was taken out six years ago at a rate of 7.4 percent. If the homeowner refinances, the charges will be $4,000. What is the highest interest rate at which it would be beneficial to refinance the mortgage?

15. **Mortgage Prepayments**   A homeowner took out a 30-year fixed rate mortgage of $205,000. The mortgage was taken out 22 years ago at a rate of 8.15 percent. If the homeowner refinances, the charges will be $3,000. What is the highest interest rate at which it would be beneficial to refinance the mortgage?

16. **CPRs**   What are the conditional prepayment rates for seasoned 50 PSA, 200 PSA, and 400 PSA mortgages? How do you interpret these numbers?

17. **SMMs**   What is the single monthly mortality for seasoned 50 PSA, 200 PSA, and 400 PSA mortgages? How do you interpret these numbers?

Spreadsheet Problems

18. **Mortgage Payments**   A 30-year mortgage has an annual interest rate of 6.25 percent and a loan amount of $180,000. What are the monthly mortgage payments?

19. **Mortgage Amortization**   A 30-year mortgage has an annual interest rate of 6.48 percent and a loan amount of $250,000. What are the interest and principal for the 130th payment?

20. **Mortgage Balance**   A 30-year mortgage has an annual interest rate of 6.80 percent and a loan amount of $200,000. What is the remaining balance at the 140th payment?

What's on the Web?

1. **FICC** Go to www.ficc.com. What is the role of the FICC? What par value of mortgage-backed securities was cleared in each of the last three months?

2. **Fannie Mae** Go to the mortgage-backed security section at www.fanniemae.com. What were the longest term bonds recently issued by Fannie Mae? What are the coupon rates? What are the coupon rates on the shortest term bonds issued?

3. **SMBS** Go to the mortgage-backed security section at www.fanniemae.com. Find the SMBS section. What is an SMBS? How do they work? Is an SMBS a suitable investment for most investors?

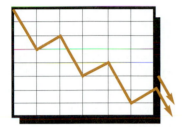
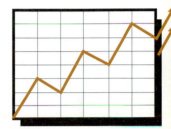

Stock-Trak®
Portfolio Simulations

Stock-Trak supports trading in a select number of mortgage issuer bonds. These bonds trade in sufficient volume for Stock-Trak to obtain timely quotes. The list of bonds changes from time to time, so you should consult the Stock-Trak website (www.stocktrak.com/cj) for the most recent list. You do not need the ticker symbol to trade these bonds, but Stock-Trak assigns a ticker symbol to the bonds for your account summary. When you trade the bonds, they are listed by issuer, maturity, coupon rate, and month of maturity. You will see two bonds below as they are listed by Stock-Trak.

Bond	Ticker	Explanation
GNMA 30 yr 7% Jul	B-GN07	30-year maturity Ginnie Mae bond with a 7% coupon
FNMA 30 yr 6% May	B-FN06	30-year maturity Fannie Mae bond with a 6% coupon

The bonds available for trading on Stock-Trak have a face value of $1,000.

Stock-Trak Exercise

1. Invest equal amounts in GNMA bonds, FNMA bonds, corporate bonds, and government bonds. Try to buy bonds with coupons and maturities that are the same. Each week, calculate the return on each of the bonds.

www.mhhe.com/cj3e

Answers to Test Your Investment Quotient Questions

Chapter 1

1-1 b (*Source:* 1994 Level I CFA Study Guide © 1994)
1-2 b (*Source:* 2001 Level I CFA Practice Exam © 2001)
1-3 c (*Source:* 2001 Level I CFA Practice Exam © 2001)
1-4 b (*Source:* 2001 Level I CFA Practice Exam © 2001)
1-5 b (*Source:* 2003 Level I CFA Practice Exam © 2003)
1-6 c (*Source:* 1994 Level I CFA Study Guide © 1994)
1-7 d
1-8 a
1-9 a
1-10 d
1-11 d
1-12 d
1-13 d
1-14 a (*Source:* 2003 Level I CFA Practice Exam © 2003)
1-15 b (*Source:* 2001 Level I CFA Practice Exam © 2001)

Chapter 2

2-1 a (*Source:* 2003 Level I CFA Practice Exam © 2003)
2-2 c (*Source:* 2003 Level I CFA Practice Exam © 2003)
2-3 c
2-4 c
2-5 b
2-6 b
2-7 b
2-8 a
2-9 c
2-10 b
2-11 a
2-12 a
2-13 c
2-14 c
2-15 d

Chapter 3

3-1 d
3-2 a
3-3 c
3-4 a
3-5 c
3-6 b
3-7 c
3-8 c
3-9 c
3-10 c (*Source:* 2003 Level I CFA Practice Exam © 2003)

Chapter 4

4-1 c (*Source:* 2001 Level I CFA Practice Exam © 2001)
4-2 b
4-3 d
4-4 d
4-5 d
4-6 d
4-7 a
4-8 b
4-9 a
4-10 c
4-11 b
4-12 d
4-13 a
4-14 a
4-15 d

Chapter 5

5-1 a (*Source:* 1986 Level I CFA Study Guide © 1986)
5-2 b (*Source:* 1986 Level I CFA Study Guide © 1986)
5-3 c
5-4 c (*Source:* 2003 Level I CFA Practice Exam © 2003)
5-5 a (*Source:* 2003 Level I CFA Practice Exam © 2003)
5-6 b (*Source:* 1991 Level I CFA Study Guide © 1991)
5-7 c (*Source:* 1991 Level I CFA Study Guide © 1991)
5-8 a (*Source:* 1991 Level I CFA Study Guide © 1991)
5-9 a (*Source:* 1991 Level I CFA Study Guide © 1991)
5-10 b (*Source:* 1990 Level I CFA Study Guide © 1990)
5-11 c (*Source:* 1990 Level I CFA Study Guide © 1990)
5-12 b
5-13 c
5-14 d
5-15 c

Chapter 6

6-1 c
6-2 a (*Source:* 1994 Level I CFA Study Guide © 1994)
6-3 a (*Source:* 1998 Level I CFA Practice Exam © 1998)
6-4 a (*Source:* 1994 Level I CFA Study Guide © 1994)
6-5 b (*Source:* 1994 Level I CFA Study Guide © 1994)
6-6 b (*Source:* 1994 Level I CFA Study Guide © 1994)
6-7 c (*Source:* 1994 Level I CFA Study Guide © 1994)
6-8 d (*Source:* 1994 Level I CFA Study Guide © 1994)
6-9 c (*Source:* 1998 Level I CFA Practice Exam © 1998)
6-10 d
6-11 c

6-12 c (*Source:* 1994 Level I CFA Study Guide © 1994)
6-13 a (*Source:* 1991 Level I CFA Study Guide © 1991)
6-14 a (*Source:* 1994 Level I CFA Study Guide © 1994)
6-15 d
6-16 d
6-17 c
6-18 c (*Source:* 1998 Level I CFA Study Guide © 1998)
6-19 c (*Source:* 2001 Level I CFA Practice Exam © 2001)
6-20 c (*Source:* 2001 Level I CFA Practice Exam © 2001)

Chapter 7

7-1 b (*Source:* 1999 Level I CFA Practice Exam © 1999)
7-2 b
7-3 d
7-4 c
7-5 a
7-6 a
7-7 c
7-8 b
7-9 a
7-10 a
7-11 b
7-12 c
7-13 c
7-14 b (*Source:* 1994 Level I CFA Study Guide © 1994)
7-15 c (*Source:* 1994 Level I CFA Study Guide © 1994)
7-16 b (*Source:* 1994 Level I CFA Study Guide © 1994)
7-17 a (*Source:* 1994 Level I CFA Study Guide © 1994)
7-18 b (*Source:* 1994 Level I CFA Study Guide © 1994)
7-19 c
7-20 d

Chapter 8

8-1 d (*Source:* 1994 Level I CFA Study Guide © 1994)
8-2 d (*Source:* 2003 Level I CFA Practice Exam © 2003)
8-3 c (*Source:* 2001 Level I CFA Practice Exam © 2001)
8-4 c
8-5 d
8-6 b
8-7 a
8-8 b
8-9 d
8-10 a
8-11 d
8-12 d
8-13 c
8-14 a
8-15 a

Chapter 9

9-1 b
9-2 a
9-3 a
9-4 d
9-5 d (*Source:* 1988 Level I CFA Study Guide © 1988)
9-6 b
9-7 a

9-8 c
9-9 c (*Source:* 1991 Level I CFA Study Guide © 1991)
9-10 b (*Source:* 2001 Level I CFA Practice Exam © 2001)
9-11 a (*Source:* 2001 Level I CFA Practice Exam © 2001)
9-12 a
9-13 d (*Source:* 1993 Level I CFA Study Guide © 1993)
9-14 a (*Source:* 1988 Level I CFA Study Guide © 1988)
9-15 b (*Source:* 1989 Level I CFA Study Guide © 1989)
9-16 a (*Source:* 1992 Level I CFA Study Guide © 1992)
9-17 b
9-18 c
9-19 d (*Source:* 1994 Level I CFA Study Guide © 1994)
9-20 d (*Source:* 1998 Level I CFA Practice Exam © 1998)

Chapter 10

10-1 b (*Source:* 1993 Level I CFA Study Guide © 1993)
10-2 c (*Source:* 1989 Level I CFA Study Guide © 1989)
10-3 d (*Source:* 1992 Level I CFA Study Guide © 1992)
10-4 a
10-5 a
10-6 b (*Source:* 1991 Level I CFA Study Guide © 1991)
10-7 a (*Source:* 1991 Level I CFA Study Guide © 1991)
10-8 a (*Source:* 1998 Level I CFA Practice Exam © 1998)
10-9 b (*Source:* 1992 Level I CFA Study Guide © 1992)
10-10 c (*Source:* 1992 Level I CFA Study Guide © 1992)
10-11 a (*Source:* 1994 Level I CFA Study Guide © 1994)
10-12 a
10-13 c (*Source:* 1988 Level I CFA Study Guide © 1988)
10-14 c (*Source:* 1990 Level I CFA Study Guide © 1990)
10-15 c (*Source:* 1992 Level I CFA Study Guide © 1992)
10-16 a (*Source:* 1991 Level I CFA Study Guide © 1991)
10-17 a (*Source:* 1992 Level I CFA Study Guide © 1992)
10-18 b (*Source:* 1992 Level I CFA Study Guide © 1992)
10-19 a (*Source:* 1992 Level I CFA Study Guide © 1992)
10-20 d (*Source:* 2003 Level I CFA Practice Exam © 2003)
10-21 b
10-22 a
10-23 c
10-24 c (*Source:* 2003 Level I CFA Practice Exam © 2003)
10-25 c (*Source:* 2003 Level I CFA Practice Exam © 2003)

Chapter 11

11-1 d
11-2 c
11-3 c
11-4 b (*Source:* 1994 Level I CFA Study Guide © 1994)
11-5 c (*Source:* 2003 Level I CFA Practice Exam © 2003)
11-6 a (*Source:* 2003 Level I CFA Practice Exam © 2003)
11-7 a (*Source:* 2003 Level I CFA Practice Exam © 2003)
11-8 b
11-9 b
11-10 a
11-11 d
11-12 b
11-13 d
11-14 c (*Source:* 1994 Level I CFA Study Guide © 1994)
11-15 a (*Source:* 1994 Level I CFA Study Guide © 1994)

Chapter 12

12-1 d (*Source:* 1994 Level I CFA Study Guide © 1994)
12-2 a
12-3 a
12-4 d
12-5 b
12-6 b
12-7 b
12-8 c
12-9 d
12-10 d
12-11 d
12-12 a
12-13 b (*Source:* 2003 Level I CFA Practice Exam © 2003)
12-14 a (*Source:* 2003 Level I CFA Practice Exam © 2003)
12-15 b (*Source:* 2003 Level I CFA Practice Exam © 2003)

Chapter 13

13-1 b (*Source:* 1994 Level I CFA Study Guide © 1994)
13-2 a (*Source:* 1994 Level I CFA Study Guide © 1994)
13-3 b (*Source:* 1994 Level I CFA Study Guide © 1994)
13-4 c
13-5 a
13-6 b
13-7 b
13-8 d
13-9 c (*Source:* 1994 Level I CFA Study Guide © 1994)
13-10 c
13-11 d
13-12 a
13-13 d
13-14 b
13-15 c

Chapter 14

14-1 a
14-2 c
14-3 d
14-4 c (*Source:* 2003 Level I CFA Practice Exam © 2003)
14-5 c
14-6 b (*Source:* 1992 Level I CFA Study Guide © 1992)
14-7 d
14-8 a
14-9 a (*Source:* 1990 Level I CFA Study Guide © 1990)
14-10 c (*Source:* 1994 Level I CFA Study Guide © 1994)
14-11 a
14-12 b (*Source:* 1993 Level I CFA Study Guide © 1993)
14-13 a (*Source:* 1993 Level I CFA Study Guide © 1993)
14-14 b (*Source:* 1991 Level I CFA Study Guide © 1991)
14-15 d
14-16 a (*Source:* 2003 Level I CFA Practice Exam © 2003)
14-17 d (*Source:* 2003 Level I CFA Practice Exam © 2003)
14-18 c (*Source:* 2003 Level I CFA Practice Exam © 2003)
14-19 d
14-20 c

Chapter 15

15-1 a
15-2 d
15-3 c
15-4 a (*Source:* 1992 Level I CFA Study Guide © 1992)
15-5 d (*Source:* 1990 Level I CFA Study Guide © 1990)
15-6 a (*Source:* 1989 Level I CFA Study Guide © 1989)
15-7 a (*Source:* 1993 Level I CFA Study Guide © 1993)
15-8 b (*Source:* 1998 Level I CFA Study Guide © 1998)
15-9 d
15-10 a
15-11 c
15-12 d
15-13 a
15-14 b
15-15 b

Chapter 16

16-1 d
16-2 a
16-3 b
16-4 a
16-5 d (*Source:* 1993 Level I CFA Study Guide © 1993)
16-6 a (*Source:* 1999 Level I CFA Practice Exam © 1999)
16-7 c
16-8 d (*Source:* 2003 Level I CFA Practice Exam © 2003)
16-9 c (*Source:* 2003 Level I CFA Practice Exam © 2003)
16-10 d
16-11 a
16-12 d
16-13 d (*Source:* 1993 Level I CFA Study Guide © 1993)
16-14 b
16-15 b
16-16 b
16-17 d
16-18 c
16-19 a
16-20 d

Chapter 17

17-1 d (*Source:* 1990 Level I CFA Study Guide © 1990)
17-2 c (*Source:* 1988 Level I CFA Study Guide © 1988)
17-3 a (*Source:* 1989 Level I CFA Study Guide © 1989)
17-4 c (*Source:* 1990 Level I CFA Study Guide © 1990)
17-5 c (*Source:* 1998 Level I CFA Practice Exam © 1998)
17-6 a
17-7 b (*Source:* 1991 Level I CFA Study Guide © 1991)
17-8 a
17-9 b (*Source:* 2003 Level I CFA Practice Exam © 2003)
17-10 b
17-11 c (*Source:* 1992 Level I CFA Study Guide © 1992)
17-12 a (*Source:* 1989 Level I CFA Study Guide © 1989)
17-13 d (*Source:* 1990 Level I CFA Study Guide © 1990)
17-14 a
17-15 c (*Source:* 1998 Level I CFA Practice Exam © 1998)
17-16 b (*Source:* 1990 Level I CFA Study Guide © 1990)

17-17 b (*Source:* 1988 Level I CFA Study Guide © 1988)
17-18 d (*Source:* 1994 Level I CFA Study Guide © 1994)
17-19 b (*Source:* 1991 Level I CFA Study Guide © 1991)
17-20 c (*Source:* 1993 Level I CFA Study Guide © 1993)
17-21 c (*Source:* 1991 Level I CFA Study Guide © 1991)
17-22 d (*Source:* 1994 Level I CFA Study Guide © 1994)
17-23 d
17-24 b
17-25 a (*Source:* 2003 Level I CFA Practice Exam © 2003)

Chapter 18

18-1 a
18-2 c
18-3 a
18-4 c (*Source:* 1990 Level I CFA Study Guide © 1990)
18-5 b (*Source:* 1998 Level I CFA Practice Exam © 1998)
18-6 b
18-7 d
18-8 b
18-9 b
18-10 a
18-11 b
18-12 a
18-13 a
18-14 c
18-15 d (*Source:* 1992 Level I CFA Study Guide © 1992)
18-16 d (*Source:* 1989 Level I CFA Study Guide © 1989)
18-17 d
18-18 a
18-19 b
18-20 c (*Source:* 1990 Level I CFA Study Guide © 1990)
18-21 d

18-22 b (*Source:* 1991 Level I CFA Study Guide © 1991)
18-23 b (*Source:* 1992 Level I CFA Study Guide © 1992)
18-24 a (*Source:* 1991 Level I CFA Study Guide © 1991)
18-25 a (*Source:* 1994 Level I CFA Study Guide © 1994)

Chapter 19

19-1 d
19-2 a
19-3 c
19-4 c
19-5 a
19-6 c
19-7 b
19-8 c
19-9 b
19-10 c (*Source:* 1988 Level I CFA Study Guide © 1988)
19-11 b (*Source:* 1988 Level I CFA Study Guide © 1988)
19-12 a (*Source:* 1989 Level I CFA Study Guide © 1989)
19-13 d (*Source:* 1991 Level I CFA Study Guide © 1991)
19-14 a (*Source:* 1991 Level I CFA Study Guide © 1991)
19-15 b (*Source:* 1990 Level I CFA Study Guide © 1990)
19-16 a (*Source:* 1989 Level I CFA Study Guide © 1989)
19-17 c (*Source:* 1991 Level I CFA Study Guide © 1991)
19-18 a (*Source:* 1991 Level I CFA Study Guide © 1991)
19-19 d (*Source:* 1989 Level I CFA Study Guide © 1989)
19-20 c
19-21 c
19-22 a
19-23 b
19-24 b
19-25 d

Answers to Selected Questions and Problems

Chapter 1

1-1 $970

1-3 Dollar return = −$5,287.50
Capital gains yield = −13.46%
Dividend yield = 2.62%
Total return = −10.85%

1-5 Jurassic average return = 7.80%
Stonehenge average return = 5.00%

1-7 Capital gains yield = −11.67%
Total return = −8.47%

1-9 Arithmetic average return = 8.17%
Geometric average return = 6.38%

1-11 2.28%

1-13 Probability of doubling = .62%
Probability of tripling = .0000017%

1-15 13.38%

1-17 Small-company stocks = 12.15%
Long-term government bonds = 5.45%
Treasury bills = 3.79%
Inflation = 3.05%

1-19 Arithmetic average return = 12.65%
Geometric average return = 12.02%

Chapter 2

2-1 320 shares

2-3 Stock price = $70
Return with margin = 27.78%
Return without margin = 16.67%
Stock price = $50
Return with margin = −27.78%
Return without margin = −16.67%

2-5 $16,667

2-7 −33.33%

2-9 Critical stock price = $51.43
Account equity = $20,570

2-11 58.3%; 42.3%

2-13 $42.86

2-15 75.00%

2-17 $5,283.68

2-19 19.09%

2-21 Holding-period return = −13.20%
EAR = −34.60%

2-25 52.80%

Chapter 3

3-1 Closing price = $32.90
Round lots traded = 8,153

3-3 $.81

3-5 Next payment = $18,750
Payment at maturity = $518,750

3-7 $4,210; −$3,000

3-9 $90.90

3-11 Open interest = 45,070
Contracts to sell = 8
Amount received = $194,880

3-13 $66,075

3-15 Cheapest: December 40 put
Most expensive: February 60 put

3-20 206.25%

Chapter 4

4-1 $31.82

4-3 $39.49; $493,625,000

4-5 $17.46

4-7 $16.80

4-9 $14.93; −16.19%

4-11 $768,000,000

4-13 .89%

4-18 $7,380

4-19 1 year: 5.45%
2 years: 8.19%
5 years: 9.87%
10 years: 10.43%
20 years: 10.72%
30 years: 10.89%

4-21 7.48%

4-23 Municipal fund = 2.40%
Taxable fund = 2.93%
New Jersey municipal fund = 2.80%

4-25 $80,950

Chapter 5

5-1 2.10121

5-3 Buy order: $84.04
Sell order: $81.01

5-5 12.14%

5-7 475.72

5-9 3.42915

5-11 If MMM increases 5%:   7971.51
If DIS increases 5%:   7935.12

5-13 .682128

5-15 −12.52%

Chapter 6

6-1 $38.76
6-3 $12.75
6-5 $281.02
6-7   10.13%
6-9 $3.20; $3.53
6-11 $67.52
6-13 $73.37
6-15 $2.79
6-17 $63.21
6-19 $23.00
6-21 $159.82
6-23 13.94
6-25 $g = 2.40\%$
          $k = 8.26\%$
          $P = \$14.68$
6-29 ROE = 11.87%
          $g = 8.31\%$
6-31 $44.04

Chapter 7

7-1 $15,695
7-3   Gross margin = 39.49%
          Operating margin = 18.46%
          ROA = 8.35%
          ROE = 17.28%
7-5   P/B = 5.05
          P/E = 29.25
          P/CF = 17.62
7-7   7.70
7-9 $72,500
7-11 Gross margin = 21.67%
          Operating margin = 11.25%
7-13 P/B = 5.63
          P/E = 17.78
          P/CF = 11.80
7-15 P/B = $23.21
          P/E = $21.80
          P/CF = $20.53

Chapter 8

8-3   1.00; .806; .826; .808; .752; .791
8-13 Feb 18: $23.61
          Feb 19: $24.34
          Feb 20: $24.91
          Feb 21: $25.54

Chapter 9

9-1   73.49; 73:16
9-3   3.98%
9-5   9.50%; 9.14%
9-7 $985,333.33
9-9 $997,551.39
9-11 Discount yield = 3.516%
          BEY = 3.593%
          EAR = 3.643%
9-13 BEY = 6.085%
          Discount yield = 5.865%

9-15 4.275%
9-17 5-year STRIPS = 73:03
          $f_{1,5} = 6.470\%$
          2-year STRIPS = 86:24
          $f_{3,2} = 7.365\%$
9-21 $f_{1,1} = 6.31\%$
          $f_{1,2} = 4.95\%$
          $f_{1,3} = 6.37\%$
9-24 $98,683.33; 6.164%
9-25 8.08%

Chapter 10

10-1 $1,071.06
10-3 $1,186.62
10-5   7.46%
10-7   5.90%
10-9   12.41%
10-11 8.60%
10-13 8.85%
10-15 9.00%
10-19 17
10-21 YTM = 9.72%
           Realized yield = 8.10%
10-23 Macaulay duration = 6.541
           Modified duration = 6.390
10-25 Macaulay duration = 8.541
           Modified duration = 8.212
10-27 Macaulay duration = 11.232
           Modified duration = 10.905
10-29 Strategy I: -4.14%
           Strategy II: -3.59%
10-31 7.20%

Chapter 11

11-1   14.00%
11-3   17.00%
11-7   16.17%
11-9 $E(R) = 8.41\%$
           $\sigma^2 = .03029$
           $\sigma = 17.41\%$
11-11 $E(R) = 12.39\%$
           $\sigma = 8.11\%$
11-14 $E(R) = 13.27\%$
           $\sigma = 40.21\%$
11-17 $E(R) = 16.26\%$
           $\sigma = 34.71\%$
11-19 $E(R) = 16.73\%$
           $\sigma = 40.06\%$
11-20 $E(R) = 14.80\%$
           $\sigma = 43.36\%$

Chapter 12

12-1   1.25
12-3   4.33%
12-5   1.01
12-7   1.60
12-9 $65.04
12-13 4.92%

12-15 $R_F = 4.29\%$
$E(R_M) = 15.71\%$
12-17 $\beta = 0.69$
12-19 Stock I: $\sigma = 13.65\%$
$\beta = 3.09$
Stock II: $\sigma = 26.28\%$
$\beta = 0.56$
12-23 $E(R) = 0.645\%$
$\sigma = 2.13\%$

Chapter 13

13-3 8.37%
13-5 Monthly standard deviation = 16.32%
Annual standard deviation = 58.84%
13-7 15.87%
13-10 −32.06%
13-11 −23.96%
13-13 −61.44%
13-15 −11.33%
13-19 164.21%
13-21 −10.04%
13-23 −44.55%

Chapter 14

14-1 $2,500.00
14-3 Stock price = $70
Stock return = −22.22%
Option return = −100.00%
Stock price = $90
Stock return = .00%
Option return = −100.00%
Stock price = $110
Stock return = 22.22%
Option return = 400.00%
14-9 $75.91
14-11 $6.24
14-13 $14.99
14-15 Stock price = $10:   −$13,275.00
Stock price = $20: $1,725.00
Stock price = $30: $1,725.00
14-16 $5,200.00

Chapter 15

15-1 $19.10
15-3 $17.14
15-5 $5.85
15-7 $13.03
15-9 7,619
15-11 $85.00
15-13 $35.00
15-15 60.01%
15-17 $23.28
15-19 147
15-25 Call delta = 0.6143
Put delta = −0.3758
Call eta = 4.6494
Put eta = −4.3212
Vega = 21.9674

Chapter 16

16-1 *a.* $12,037.50
b. $1,132,500.00
c. −$15,625.00
d. −$216,000.00
16-3 −$2,812.50
16-5 $10,758,067,550
16-7 $92.23
16-9 $99.19
16-11 $.00595
16-13 Day 1: $40,000
Day 2: $55,750
Day 3: $66,250
Day 4: $65,200
Profit = $2,100
16-15 $45,187.50
16-17 1,618
16-19 2.89%
16-21 7,225
16-23 $.34
16-25 *a.* 190.55
b. 190.40

Chapter 17

17-1 $40
17-3 18.18
17-5 $1,230
17-7 104%
17-9 At least $920
17-11 Duration to maturity = 13.555 years
Duration to call = 4.254 years
17-14 Conversion price = $39.20
One-year bond return = 18.88%
One-year stock return = 28.57%

Chapter 18

18-1 $3,083.19
18-3 Accepted bid = $9,230
Total raised = $27.96 billion
18-5 3.65%
18-7 3.32%
18-9 6.21%
18-11 $976.40
18-13 $1,255.3125
18-15 5.29%
18-17 5.64%
18-19 22.81

Chapter 19

19-1 $1,164.28
19-3 $1,313.56
19-5 .4265%
19-7 $66,756.00
19-9 $219,784.89
19-11 $168.44
19-13 $22.75
19-15 7.39%
19-17 PSA 50:   .2535%
PSA 200: 1.0596%
PSA 400: 2.2610%

Name Index

A

Ambachtsheer, Keith, 67
Arms, Richard, 254

B

Bachelier, Louis, 489
Baruch, Bernard, 250
Bernstein, William, 371, 441
Bhirud, Suresh, 131
Bickel, Joanna, 60–61
Black, Fischer, 490–491, 497
Blayney, Eleanor, 412, 441
Blume, Marshal, 27n
Bogle, John, 121
Bohr, Niels, 176
Booth, David, 194–195
Brennan, Jack, 121
Buffett, Warren, 176, 266–267, 496
Burke, Thomas, 528

C

Calvetti, Paul, 300
Ciesielski, Jack, 497
Clements, Jonathan, 17n, 67n, 121n,
        195n, 199n, 339n, 371n,
        412n, 441n, 466n, 580n,
        601n, 633n
Cordaro, Chris, 338
Corrigan, Gerald, 452
Corter, James, 60
Crowley, Kathleen, 199

D

Damato, Karen, 131n
Deitrich, Paul, 131
DeSanctis, Steven, 195
Devoe, Raymond, 323
Dorfman, John R., 267n
Dow, Charles, 251

E

Edison, Thomas, 88
Einstein, Albert, 181, 223
Elton, E. J., 372n
Engel, Andrew, 194

Evans, Frazier, 199

F

Fay, James, 131
Fayard, Gary, 497
Feather, William, 144
Fisher, Irving, 307
Ford, Henry, 2
Franklin, Benjamin, 286, 556
Fridson, Martin, 580

G

Goldsmith, James, 250
Graham, Benjamin, 79, 267
Greenspan, Alan, 300
Gregory, Ken, 580
Gross, Leon, 508
Gross, William, 570
Gruber, M. J., 372n
Guera, Dawn, 528

H

Half, Robert, 521
Herman, Tom, 607n
Hoover, Herbert, 592
Hotchkiss, Lynnette K., 607

I

Ibbotson, Roger G., 15n, 18–19n, 21n

J

Jarrell, Gregg, 491
Jensen, Michael C., 432
Johnson, Darrell R., 257n
Jong, Erica, 107

K

Kaufman, Arnold, 199
Kehoe, Bill, 491
Keillor, Garrison, 126n
Kelly, Kate, 57n
Kennedy, Joseph, 1
Keynes, John Maynard, 267

Kill, Larry, 573
Kinney, Jerome, 131
Kochis, Tim, 412

L

Laporte, John, 194
Lebenthal, Alexandra, 606
Lebor, Todd, 87
Leistner, Gilbert, 528
Levin, Ross, 412, 466
Lynch, Peter, 116, 267

M

Macaulay, Frederick, 340
McGee, Suzanne, 528
Macheski, Edward, 267
McKay, Betsy, 497n
MacKenzie, Michael, 301n
MacMillan, Harold, 394
Malkiel, Burton G., 274n, 337, 337n
Maloon, Michael, 632
Markowitz, Harry, 361
Marriott, J. W., 573
Marriott, Richard E., 573
Matus, Drew, 300
Mendelson, Alan, 262
Merton, Robert C., 490–491
Milevsky, Moshe, 466
Miller, Bruce, 86–87
Morgan, J. P., 429
Moss, Jim, 86
Murphy, Glenn, 570

N

Norwitz, Steven, 17, 338

O

Oliff, James, 528
Opdyke, Jeff D., 62n, 87
Orgler, Yair, 491

P

Perritt, Gerald, 16
Phillips, Michael M., 491n
Pierce, Robert, 528

Equation Index

Subject Index

N